Well-Being and Fair Distribution

Well-Being and Fair Distribution

Beyond Cost-Benefit Analysis

Matthew D. Adler

OXFORD
UNIVERSITY PRESS

OXFORD
UNIVERSITY PRESS

Oxford University Press, Inc., publishes works that further Oxford University's objective of excellence in research, scholarship, and education.

Oxford New York
Auckland Cape Town Dar es Salaam Hong Kong Karachi Kuala Lumpur Madrid Melbourne
Mexico City Nairobi New Delhi Shanghai Taipei Toronto

With offices in
Argentina Austria Brazil Chile Czech Republic France Greece Guatemala Hungary Italy
Japan Poland Portugal Singapore South Korea Switzerland Thailand Turkey Ukraine
Vietnam

Published by Oxford University Press, Inc.
198 Madison Avenue, New York, New York 10016

Oxford is a registered trademark of Oxford University Press
Oxford University Press is a registered trademark of Oxford University Press, Inc.

Library of Congress Cataloging-in-Publication Data

Adler, Matthew D.
 Well-being and fair distribution : beyond cost-benefit analysis / Matthew D. Adler.
  p. cm.
 Includes bibliographical references and index.
 ISBN 978-0-19-538499-4 (hbk. : alk. paper)
1. Welfare economics. 2. Public welfare. 3. Well-being.
4. Distributive justice. I. Title.
 HB846.A35 2011
 174—dc22   2011017012

3 4 5 6 7 8 9

Printed in the United States of America on acid-free paper

Note to Readers
This publication is designed to provide accurate and authoritative information in regard to the subject
matter covered. It is based upon sources believed to be accurate and reliable and is intended to be current
as of the time it was written. It is sold with the understanding that the publisher is not engaged in rendering
legal, accounting, or other professional services. If legal advice or other expert assistance is required, the
services of a competent professional person should be sought. Also, to confirm that the information has
not been affected or changed by recent developments, traditional legal research techniques should be used,
including checking primary sources where appropriate.

(Based on the Declaration of Principles jointly adopted by a Committee of the
American Bar Association and a Committee of Publishers and Associations.)

You may order this or any other Oxford University Press publication by
visiting the Oxford University Press website at www.oup.com

For Julia, Jonathan, and Spencer

ACKNOWLEDGMENTS

I am indebted to the many people who helped me write this book. For their comments and criticisms, or for imparting their expertise, I would like to thank: David Abrams, Chrisolua Andreou, Richard Arneson, Gustaf Arrhenius, Aditi Bagchi, Jonathan Baron, Seth Baum, Charles Blackorby, Robin Boadway, David Brink, John Broome, Satya Chakravarty, Bruce Chapman, Cary Coglianese, Daniel Cole, Bob Cooter, Angus Corbett, Adam Cox, Tony Cox, Steve Croley, Paul Dolan, David Donaldson, Elizabeth Emens, David Enoch, Dan Farber, Scott Farrow, Lee Fennell, John Ferejohn, Adam Finkel, Claire Finkelstein, Marc Fleurbaey, Charles Fried, Jerry Gaus, Axel Gosseries, John Graham, Kent Greenawalt, Gillian Hadfield, Bob Hahn, Jim Hammitt, Kevin Haninger, Alon Harel, Iwao Hirose, Bob Hockett, Nils Holtug, Adam Hosein, Olof Johansson–Stenman, Jason Johnston, Louis Kaplow, Avery Katz, Leo Katz, Jonathan Klick, Lewis Kornhauser, Jody Kraus, Prasad Krishnamurthy, Howard Kunreuther, Brian Leiter, Michael Livermore, Yoram Margalioth, Dan Markovits, Jonathan Masur, Richard McAdams, Jeff McMahan, Cherie Metcalf, Talya Miron–Shatz, Martha Nussbaum, Jacob Nussim, Efe Ok, Michael Otsuka, Gideon Parchomovsky, Mitch Polinsky, Ariel Porat, Eric Posner, Katie Pratt, Wlodek Rabinowicz, Dan Raff, Lisa Robinson, Ed Rock, Connie Rosati, Arden Rowell, Chris Sanchirico, Ted Seto, Stuart Shapiro, Seana Shiffrin, Matt Spitzer, Lior Strahilevitz, David Strauss, Cass Sunstein, Nicolas Treich, Bertil Tungodden, Peter Vallentyne, David Weisbach, Robin West, John Weymark, Jonathan Wiener, Chris Wonnell, David Zaring, and Larry Zelenak. I am especially grateful to David Brink, Marc Fleurbaey, and Wlodek Rabinowicz, who each patiently fielded what must have seemed like an unending stream of questions from me about, respectively, well-being, social choice, and intertemporal choice; and to Eric Posner and Chris Sanchirico, close collaborators on books or articles from which this project grew. Of course, the normal disclaimer applies: the only person who can be presumed to concur in what follows is me.

I presented chapters from the book, or precursor papers, in law, philosophy, public policy, or economics workshops at Arizona State University, Bar-Ilan University, Catholic University Louvain-la-Neuve, Columbia University, Copenhagen University, Duke University, Georgetown University, George Washington University, Harvard University, Hebrew University, Illinois Institute of Technology, NYU, Queen's University, Stanford University, the Toulouse School of Economics, UCLA, University of California-Berkeley, the University of Chicago, University College London, the University of Illinois, the University of Michigan, the University Paris-Descartes, the

University of Pennsylvania, the University of Southern California, the University of Tel Aviv, the University of Toronto, and the University of Virginia; and to conferences organized by the American Law and Economics Association, the Society for Environmental Law and Economics, the Society for Risk Analysis, and the U.S. Environmental Protection Agency. Thanks very much to the workshop and conference organizers for the opportunity to present this material, and to participants for their questions.

I have been aided by truly excellent research assistants, librarians, and secretarial staff. Every author should be so blessed. Larbi Alaoui and Navin Pal worked closely with me on all the mathematical aspects of the book, checking my proofs, formulas, and calculations; answering technical questions; and preparing the tables and charts. Matthew Bush and Drew Frederick spent hundreds of hours polishing the substance and style of the manuscript and helping me prepare the notes and bibliography— here, drawing on a large database of sources which Eric Diallogue had inputted, and which Isabel Bello, Jason Parris, Rachel Roof, Chris Smith, and Laura Smith had reviewed for accuracy. My library liaison, Bill Draper, has been exceptionally resourceful and indefatigable. Bill dealt with my daily onslaught of queries and requests, and Tom Laws, Joe Parsio, and Merle Slyhoff made sure that books and articles were found and delivered.

I am grateful to Mike Fitts, Dean of the University of Pennsylvania Law School, for generous financial support.

Many thanks to the editorial, production, and marketing staff at Oxford University Press for their excellent work on this project, in particular: Maureen Cirnitski, Chris Collins, James Geronimo, Michelle Lipinski, Emily Perry, Jessica Picone, Aravind Raveendran, Ninell Silberberg, and Enid Zafran.

Finally, to my wife Julia, and my sons Jonathan and Spencer: thanks for your love, support, and understanding as I struggled with this project; for listening when I talked out loud about it; and for tolerating my silences when, preoccupied, I didn't.

CONTENTS

INTRODUCTION

Well-Being and Fair Distribution: Beyond Cost-Benefit Analysis provides a comprehensive, philosophically grounded defense of the use of social welfare functions as a framework for evaluating governmental policies and other large-scale choices.

The "social welfare function" (SWF) is a concept that originates in theoretical welfare economics. It is employed as a policy-analysis methodology in a number of economic literatures, such as "optimal tax" scholarship, growth theory, and environmental economics. But other methodologies—in particular, cost-benefit analysis (CBA)—are currently dominant. While CBA is defensible as a rough proxy for overall well-being, it is insensitive to the distribution of well-being. By contrast, the SWF approach can incorporate distributive considerations into policy analysis in a systematic fashion.

Although I see SWFs as practical policy-evaluation tools, the tenor of this book is theoretical. Just as the now-massive body of CBA scholarship is grounded in a theoretical literature regarding CBA, so, too, the proper design of the SWF framework raises many questions of normative theory—questions that this book will engage. In doing so, I draw upon welfare economics, social choice theory, and related formal literatures (such as utility theory and decision theory), and upon philosophical scholarship concerning a variety of topics, in particular, well-being, equality, and personal identity.

Chapter 1 sets the stage. I see the SWF framework as a *moral* choice-evaluation framework. "Moral" reasoning is the species of normative reasoning characterized by a concern for human interests; by impartiality between different persons; and by a willingness to transcend and criticize existing social norms. The SWF approach provides a systematic methodology for *morally* evaluating governmental policies and other large-scale choices. Chapter 1 explores the difference between moral evaluation and other kinds of normative evaluation, and briefly reviews questions of metaethics and normative epistemology that no work of normative theory can ignore. It also sets forth the basic argumentative strategy of this book: to take as given that a moral choice-evaluation framework should be *person-centered, consequentialist,* and *welfarist* (for short, "welfarist") and to argue that the SWF approach is the most attractive framework of this sort.

In other words, this book works *within* welfarism, rather than engaging ongoing debates between welfarists and non-welfarists. Chapter 1 explains why this is a plausible strategy. However, it also takes some pains to explain why non-welfarists, too, should find the book of interest.

Chapter 1 concludes by offering a formal, generic architecture for welfarism. The generic welfarist architecture derives a ranking of choices from a ranking of outcomes. The ranking of outcomes, in turn, depends upon individual well-being. The connection between the ranking of outcomes and individual well-being is formalized via the concept of a "life-history": a pairing of a person and an outcome. Life-history $(x; i)$ means being individual i in outcome x. A welfarist choice-evaluation framework includes an account of well-being, which at a minimum makes *intrapersonal* comparisons, ranking life-histories belonging to the same person. The Pareto principles constrain the ranking of outcomes—requiring it to be consistent with the intrapersonal ranking of life-histories in certain basic ways.

The SWF approach is one *specification* of this generic welfarist architecture; CBA is a competing specification.

Chapter 2 introduces the SWF framework. This approach has the distinctive feature of making *interpersonal* comparisons between life-histories—not just intrapersonal comparisons. Furthermore, it employs a utility function (or a set of such functions) to map each outcome onto a "vector" or list of numbers, representing the well-being of each individual in the population in that outcome. Outcome x is mapped by utility function $u(.)$ onto $(u_1(x), u_2(x), . . ., u_N(x))$, where $u_i(x)$ is a numerical measure of the well-being of individual i in outcome x. An SWF, in turn, is a mathematical rule for ranking outcomes as a function of their corresponding utility vectors. One simple possibility is to add up utilities: this is the utilitarian SWF. Another possibility is to employ an outcome-ranking rule that is sensitive to the distribution of utilities. There turn out to be a multiplicity of such distribution-sensitive SWFs.

Chapter 2 explains these ideas, and also reviews the intellectual history of the SWF approach (which originates in work by Abram Bergson and Paul Samuelson some 70 years ago, and, as mentioned, is well-accepted within certain subfields of economics). The bulk of the chapter, however, focuses on criticizing the competing policy-analytic frameworks that are currently dominant. These competitors include not only CBA, but also inequality metrics (such as the well-known Gini coefficient or Atkinson index); various other types of metrics for quantifying inequity, such as poverty metrics, "social gradient" metrics, and tax incidence metrics; and cost-effectiveness analysis (CEA). Each of these approaches is widely employed in academic work, and CBA now also has a firm legal status in governmental practice. However, each of these approaches is problematic—at least from the perspective of welfarism.[1] As Chapter 2 will show, these approaches may fail to rank outcomes in a well-behaved

---

[1] Alternatively, certain ways of employing currently dominant frameworks turn out to be variations on the SWF approach. This is true, in particular, of the use of CBA with so-called "distributive weights." See Chapter 2.

manner,[2] or may be vulnerable to violations of the Pareto principles. And even if non-SWF methodologies *are* structured so as to yield a well-behaved, Pareto-respecting ranking of outcomes, they turn out to be problematic in other ways.

The analysis in Chapter 2 is meant to *motivate* the defense and elaboration of the SWF approach which occurs in Chapters 3 through 7. In these five chapters, I address the central questions that must be confronted by any proponent of this approach.

Chapter 3 focuses on well-being. One philosophically contested issue, here, concerns the choice between preferentialist, hedonic, and objective-good accounts of human welfare. Insofar as utility numbers are meant to quantify individual well-being in outcomes, what exactly should these numbers be measuring? A cross-cutting issue concerns interpersonal comparability. How are we to make sense of the statement that life-history $(x; i)$ is better for well-being than life-history $(y; j)$: that individual i in outcome x is better off than individual j in outcome y? Why believe that this statement is meaningful? What are the criteria for ranking life-histories involving different persons? Economists outside the SWF tradition are usually skeptical about the possibility of interpersonal comparisons. Many SWFs involve, not merely interpersonal comparisons of well-being levels, but also interpersonal comparisons of well-being *differences*—to the effect that the difference in well-being between life-histories $(x; i)$ and $(y; j)$ is greater than the difference in well-being between life-histories $(z; k)$ and $(w; l)$. But what are the criteria that would enable us to make sense of *these* sorts of comparisons?

Chapter 3 tackles these problems, proposing to analyze well-being in terms of fully informed, fully rational, convergent extended preferences. While an ordinary preference is simply a ranking of outcomes and choices, an *extended preference* is a ranking of life-histories. To say that individual k has an extended preference for $(x; i)$ over $(y; j)$ means that k prefers the life-history of i in x to the life-history of j in y. The idea of an extended preference originates with John Harsanyi. More specifically, Harsanyi proposes that an interpersonally comparable metric of individual well-being be constructed by appealing to individuals' extended preferences over life-history *lotteries*—on the premise that these extended lottery preferences comply with expected utility theory. Chapter 3 will develop Harsanyi's fruitful ideas. To be sure, many challenges arise in doing so; and the account of well-being presented in Chapter 3, in a number of important respects, diverges from Harsanyi's views. In particular, my definition of extended preferences builds in a self-interest component, designed to screen out preferences for features of outcomes that have no impact on well-being; and I allow for heterogeneity in extended preferences.

The thrust of Chapter 3 is to defend the following approach for making intra- and interpersonal comparisons, and for measuring well-being via utility numbers. There

---

[2] By "well-behaved," I mean that the ranking of outcomes possesses the reflexivity and transitivity properties constitutive of a quasiordering. See Chapter 1.

is a set **U** of utility functions, pooling the fully informed, fully rational, extended preferences of everyone in the population. Life-history $(x; i)$ is at least as good for well-being as life-history $(y; j)$ just in case $u(x; i) \geq u(y; j)$ for all $u(.)$ in **U**. A similar rule is proposed for well-being differences.[3]

Chapter 4 discusses how to implement the account of well-being and well-being measurement proposed in Chapter 3. How, in practice, should a decisionmaker construct a set **U** of utility functions representing the fully informed, fully rational, extended preferences of everyone in the population?

To begin, Chapter 4 addresses the problem of outcome simplification. The outcomes which are ranked by a choice-evaluation framework (be it the SWF framework or a competing framework, such as CBA) are *simplified* descriptions of reality. Simplification is necessary for the framework to be cognitively tractable. (If an outcome were a fully precise specification of a possible reality, i.e., a complete "possible world," a *human* decisionmaker would be unable to use the framework.) But what does it mean for individuals to have extended preferences regarding life-histories involving simplified outcomes—outcomes that are missing some characteristics? For example, much SWF scholarship in the "optimal tax" tradition employs outcomes that describe each individual's consumption and leisure, but fail to describe other individual attributes (health, happiness, social life, etc.). How should individual k think about her preference regarding $(x; i)$ and $(y; j)$, where she is told only that individual i consumes a certain amount and has a certain amount of leisure time in outcome x, and that individual j consumes a certain amount and has a certain amount of leisure time in outcome y?

Chapter 4 proposes an answer to this important problem. With that answer in hand, it discusses how we can use information about an individual's ordinary preferences in order to make inferences about her extended preferences. And it reviews, in detail, the wealth of existing data concerning individuals' ordinary preferences that enable a policy analyst to construct a set **U**: data regarding individuals' preferences for consumption lotteries; evidence concerning intertemporal substitution; "ordinal" preference data, such as the data supplied by economic research concerning labor supply and consumer demand; so-called "QALY" surveys, which reveal how individuals rank health states and lotteries over health states; and happiness surveys. This chapter also proposes a novel preference-elicitation format—what I term a "life-history" survey.

Chapter 5 addresses the functional form of the SWF. An SWF is some rule for *using* the well-being information captured in the set **U** of utility functions in order to rank outcomes. Chapter 5 argues that the most attractive such rule is a "prioritarian" SWF (more precisely, a "continuous prioritarian" SWF). In defending this view, Chapter 5 draws heavily on the contemporary philosophical literature concerning

---

[3] The well-being difference between life-history $(x; i)$ and $(y; j)$ is at least as great as the well-being difference between life-history $(z; k)$ and life-history $(w; l)$ iff, for all $u(.)$ in **U**, $u(x; i) - u(y; j) \geq u(z; k) - u(w; l)$.

equality. One major theme in this literature is the debate between those who hold a prioritarian conception of fair distribution, and those who reject this view. Prioritarianism corresponds to an SWF which satisfies two key axioms, explained in Chapter 5: the "Pigou–Dalton" axiom and an axiom of separability. If we add a continuity requirement, the upshot is an SWF which sums up individual utilities that have been "transformed" by a transformation function, rather than simply summing utilities in utilitarian fashion.

Formally, a continuous prioritarian SWF says: outcome x is morally at least as good as outcome y iff[4], for all $u(.)$ belonging to $\mathbf{U}$, $\sum_{i=1}^{N} g(u_i(x)) \geq \sum_{i=1}^{N} g(u_i(y))$, where the $g(.)$ function is strictly increasing and strictly concave. Chapter 5 argues that this SWF represents the most attractive specification of welfarism.[5] A central idea in Chapter 5, and indeed throughout the book, is that welfarism and a concern for *fairness* are fully compatible. A moral view is sensitive to fairness insofar as it "respects the separateness of persons." A concern for the "separateness of persons" is best meshed with welfarism by seeing each individual as the holder of a separate moral claim, where such claims have an "across-outcome" structure and are valenced in terms of individual well-being. (In other words, if individual i is better off in outcome x than outcome y, i has a claim in favor of x over y.) Chapter 5 begins by elaborating and defending this "claim-across-outcome" conception of fairness. I then seek to show that this conception argues in favor of the two key axioms that define prioritarian SWFs. Whether a prioritarian SWF should, in addition, satisfy the continuity requirement—and I believe it should—implicates questions regarding tradeoffs that are also reviewed in Chapter 5.

Chapter 6 addresses the temporal dimension. The SWF framework, as presented in Chapter 2 and elaborated in subsequent chapters, makes the ranking of outcomes depend upon utility numbers representing individuals' lifetime well-being. A whole-lifetime view is, indeed, adopted by the theoretical literature on SWFs; by most extant scholarship that uses SWFs to evaluate governmental policies; and by the philosophical literature on equality, which generally argues that moral norms concerning fair distribution are properly focused on the distribution of lifetime well-being. But is the whole-lifetime approach really defensible? Why not represent an outcome as a list of "sublifetime" utilities, each representing the well-being of some individual during some portion of her life (for example, her annual or momentary well-being), and then apply a continuous prioritarian SWF to these sublifetime utilities? Chapter 6 will describe and seek to respond to two arguments that challenge whole-lifetime prioritarianism and that seem to cut in favor of sublifetime prioritarianism or some other approach.[6] One argument, tendered by Derek Parfit,

---

[4] Throughout the book, I use "iff" to mean "if and only if."

[5] More precisely, Chapter 5 argues for the "Atkinson" SWF, which is a particular type of continuous prioritarian SWF—and one that, in fact, is fairly widely used within existing SWF scholarship.

[6] A third approach would be "attribute based," whereby an SWF is applied directly to individual attributes, rather than to lifetime or sublifetime utilities representing individuals' lifetime or sublifetime well-being.

suggests that a proper understanding of personal identity undercuts a concern for the distribution of lifetime well-being. A different argument, advanced by Dennis McKerlie and other philosophers, suggests that various kinds of intuitions about equality—for example, intuitions about the moral significance of short-term hardship and suffering—are inconsistent with a whole-lifetime view.

Chapters 3 through 6 all focus on the ranking of outcomes. Is the well-being of a given individual in a given outcome determined by her preference-satisfaction, her mental states, or her realization of objective goods? How should her well-being be measured by utility functions? What sorts of data enable us to estimate these functions? What is the appropriate SWF for ranking outcomes in light of individual utilities? Is it a utilitarian SWF, a prioritarian SWF, or some other form?

Chapter 7 turns from these questions, to the problem of generating a ranking of choices from the ranking of outcomes. A choice-evaluation framework functions to provide guidance to a decisionmaker. In particular, the SWF framework—as I conceptualize it—is a systematic methodology that yields guidance to governmental policymakers or others confronted with large-scale choices.[7] But a human decisionmaker operates under conditions of uncertainty. She is not sure which particular outcome would result from any given choice available to her. How to implement a continuous prioritarian SWF under conditions of uncertainty raises thorny problems. It turns out that no methodology for doing so can simultaneously respect, on the one hand, certain axioms which seem to capture the essence of consequentialism; and, on the other hand, the ex ante versions of the Pareto and Pigou–Dalton principles.

Expected utility theory, if refined along certain lines, provides an attractive generic structure for choice under uncertainty.[8] Chapter 7 argues that a continuous prioritarian SWF should be merged with a (refined version of) expected utility theory so as to generate a ranking of choices—notwithstanding violations of the ex ante Pareto and Pigou–Dalton principles. While the SWF framework defended here satisfies the Pareto and Pigou–Dalton principles in terms of the ranking of outcomes, the ex ante versions of these principles constitute an *additional* requirement which, on balance, should be rejected. The dilemmas that arise in specifying norms of fair distribution under conditions of uncertainty have been discussed by philosophers and social choice theorists; Chapter 7 builds upon this scholarship.

---

[7] Policy-evaluation frameworks such as the SWF approach, CBA, or the other frameworks reviewed in Chapter 2 are appropriate for governmental policies or other large-scale choices, but not for smaller choices where the expected benefits of using a systematic framework are too small to justify the decision costs of doing so. Identifying the boundary between small and large choices is very difficult. See Chapter 1.

[8] To be clear, expected utility theory surfaces at two different junctures in this book: in Chapter 3, regarding the measurement of well-being; and in Chapter 7, regarding the moral ranking of choices under conditions of uncertainty.

Chapters 3 through 7 are the analytic core of the book. There are two key claims that I aim to defend: first, that well-being should be understood in terms of extended preferences; and, second, that the most attractive functional form for an SWF is the continuous prioritarian form. The first claim lies at the core of chapters 3 and 4; the second claim, at the core of chapters 5, 6, and 7. I hope that the reader is persuaded by both claims, but it is worth noting that the claims are entirely separable. The extended-preference account of well-being developed in Chapters 3 and 4 yields a set **U** of utility functions that can be meshed with *any* arbitrary SWF (any rule for ranking utility vectors), be it a utilitarian SWF, a continuous prioritarian SWF, or any other rule.

Reciprocally, the continuous prioritarian SWF says: outcome *x* is morally at least as good as outcome *y* iff, for all $u(.)$ belonging to **U**, $\sum_{i=1}^{N} g(u_i(x)) \geq \sum_{i=1}^{N} g(u_i(y))$, where the $g(.)$ function is strictly increasing and strictly concave. This formula can be meshed with any arbitrary methodology for constructing the set **U**—be it a methodology that analyzes well-being in terms of extended preferences, or some other.

In short, the analysis in chapters 3 and 4, and the analysis in chapters 5 through 7, are two separate "modules" neither of which presupposes the other.

Chapter 8, the concluding chapter, outlines three large, difficult, and important problems, connected to the SWF framework. Analyzing these three problems and proposing solutions would make an already overly long book much, much longer, and so Chapter 8 does no more than to describe the problems.

One problem concerns the optimal design of legal institutions. To say that the SWF approach is an attractive framework for morally evaluating governmental policies and other large-scale choices is not necessarily to say that it is optimal to structure legal institutions so that policymakers are legally instructed to employ this framework. Policy analysis tools may be distorted by political forces. (In particular, research examining the effects of laws requiring regulatory agencies to employ CBA has reached mixed conclusions concerning whether such laws have actually produced more efficient regulations.) A cross-cutting idea is that it may be optimal to channel distribution through the tax system, and thus to instruct non-tax bodies to evaluate their decisions using CBA rather than using some SWF which is sensitive to distributive considerations.

A second problem concerns future generations. My analysis throughout the book assumes a fixed and finite population. The same *N* individuals exist in each of the possible outcomes of the policy choices at hand. Scholarship on future generations relaxes this assumption, by allowing for the possibility that choices might affect the size or identity of the population, or for an infinite future and thus infinite population. How to structure policy choice under such conditions raises new and difficult questions: the so-called "repugnant conclusion," "non-identity" problems, and the incompatibility between the Pareto principles and an axiom of impartiality in the case of an infinite future.

A third problem concerns individual responsibility. A key deficit of welfarism is that it fails to differentiate between bad luck and irresponsibility—between a case in which someone is badly off through no fault of her own, and a case in which someone is (wholly or partly) responsible for her well-being shortfall. Over the last several decades, the philosophical literature on equality has intensively investigated problems of responsibility; and a growing body of work in welfare economics and social choice theory is now also engaging such problems. How exactly should the utility numbers that function as inputs into the SWF (the set **U**, in my account) be adjusted so as to reflect individual responsibility? This is a critically important question for the SWF framework—but, given space limitations, not one that I can attempt to tackle in this book.

This book is, evidently, interdisciplinary. It is aimed at welfare economists who are receptive to philosophical argumentation; at philosophers who are receptive to the mathematical tools of welfare economics; and at law and policy scholars who find value in both fields. It builds upon, and draws inspiration from, the tradition of scholarly work at the intersection of philosophy and economics, exemplified by journals such as *Economics and Philosophy* and *Social Choice and Welfare*. The methodology of welfare economics is axiomatic and deductive. The focus is on clarifying the logical implications of various axioms for ranking outcomes and choices which we might be inclined to endorse. The methodology of moral philosophy is coherentist. Given a plurality of logically possible approaches to ranking outcomes and choices, which ones are most attractive in the "reflective equilibrium" sense? Which approaches fit best with our intuitive judgments about concrete cases and with general normative principles, regarding well-being, equality, and so forth?

It would be arrogant and wrongheaded to suggest that normative understanding can only be advanced by interdisciplinary work. Clearly, that is not true; there are large epistemic gains to be had from specialization. However, it seems to this author equally wrongheaded to insist that specialization is the only viable path. This book is animated by the belief that scholars can make real progress in specifying normative tools and frameworks by marrying the methodologies of economics and philosophy. I will leave it to the reader to judge whether they are, in fact, fruitfully married here.

1

PRELIMINARIES
MORALITY, CONSEQUENTIALISM, WELFARISM

This book defends the use of social welfare functions (SWFs) as an attractive framework for morally evaluating governmental policies and other large-scale choices—a framework for ranking the governmental policies (or other large-scale actions) in a given choice situation as morally better or worse and thereby determining which policies are morally choice-*worthy*.

A comprehensive defense of the SWF approach would begin at the very beginning. It would consider, first, whether moral choice-evaluation frameworks should focus exclusively on the interests of persons, or should balance those interests against competing values, such as animal well-being or intrinsic environmental goods. Having presented a full argument for the proposition that animal well-being, intrinsic environmental goods, and other possible extra-personal values have no *moral* weight, the defense of the SWF framework would then engage the large debate between consequentialists and nonconsequentialists. The SWF approach is a kind of *consequentialism*: its structure for evaluating choices revolves around an impartial ranking of the *outcomes* that the choices would produce. Nonconsequentialists assert that moral views with this structure are problematic in many ways. Finally—because the SWF framework is not merely consequentialist, but uses individuals' well-being as the basis for ranking outcomes, rather than individuals' resources, capabilities, or some other non-well-being basis—the analysis would seek to establish that the most attractive moral criterion is indeed well-being oriented.

This book, although ambitious, is not *that* ambitious. It takes as given the premises that morality is person-focused, consequentialist, and well-being oriented, and asks: What is the best specification of morality thus conceived? Answering *that* question will be labor enough. I will need many long chapters to elaborate the workings of the SWF framework and to show that this particular set of choice-evaluation tools is, indeed, the most attractive variant of person-centered consequentialist welfarism (for short, "welfarism").

It is also worth noting, here, that the attractiveness of welfarism has been quite fully mooted in the philosophical literature, while the question of specification has been given relatively less attention by philosophers—particularly with respect to the many different questions regarding formal structure and measurement that I will address at length. So this book makes a larger contribution to knowledge (I hope) by working within the confines of welfarism, rather than by pursuing familiar debates pitting welfarism against its competitors.

Still, something preliminary can be said to explain why welfarism is worth elaborating. That is one task of this chapter. I will explain, if only relatively briefly, why a person-centered view of morality and consequentialism are both plausible premises, and why even the reader who rejects them might find this book of interest. And what of the fact that welfarism ranks outcomes in light of human well-being, rather than resources, capabilities, etc.? Here, I suggest that welfarism should be seen as an approximation to a truly plausible moral view, namely *responsibility-sensitive welfarism*; and that the elaboration of the SWF framework undertaken in this book should be understood as a large step toward elaborating a decision procedure that would implement responsibility-sensitive welfarism.

This chapter also seeks to accomplish two other vital preliminary tasks. The first is to distinguish between moral evaluation and other types of normative evaluation. The SWF framework, clearly, is a normative tool: a tool for guiding choice. I claim, more specifically, that it can be used as a tool for *moral* decisionmaking. What exactly do I mean by *that*? The second task is briefly to review questions of metaethics and epistemology that no work of normative theory can wholly ignore. I will be arguing that the SWF approach is the most "attractive" choice-evaluation framework, that it helps us determine which governmental policies (or other large-scale choices) are "better" or "worse." How do these assertions relate to deeply contested questions regarding normative truth and evidence?

Having addressed these preliminary questions, the chapter concludes by providing a formal, generic structure for a welfarist choice-evaluation procedure. This structure will be the foundation for my discussion of the SWF approach and competing welfarist approaches throughout the remainder of the book.

I. WHAT IS A MORAL DECISION PROCEDURE?

Subsequent chapters will defend the SWF approach as a particular kind of normative tool: namely, a framework for *morally* evaluating governmental policies or other large-scale choices. This section clarifies the distinction between morality and normative evaluation more generally; discusses, in particular, the distinction between morality and *law*; and emphasizes that the aim of this book is to elaborate a moral *decision procedure*, which can be used to provide guidance to actual decisionmakers, operating under cognitive constraints, conditions of uncertainty, and non-zero decision costs.

A. Normative Evaluation, Moral Evaluation, and Persons

Normativity is the realm of the "ought." To normatively evaluate a choice situation faced by some decisionmaker—an array of options that she can choose among—is to take a stance regarding which option "should" be performed, which choice is "appropriate."

Moral evaluation is a particular kind of normative evaluation. What distinguishes it? I believe the following characterization is reasonably uncontroversial. Moral evaluation gives a central role (if not necessarily an exclusive role) to the interests of *persons* and, more specifically, human persons. Moral evaluation tries to achieve some kind of *impartiality* between persons. And moral evaluation has a critical aspect—by which I mean that the morally appropriate choice, for some decisionmaker in some society, is not reducible to the social norms or conventions in her society.[1]

In these regards, moral evaluation is different from aesthetic evaluation, "prudential" evaluation, and legal evaluation. *Aesthetic* evaluation means assessing objects as more or less beautiful. It is at least plausible to say that the question whether some painting, sculpture, or landscape is more or less beautiful has nothing to do with human well-being. By contrast, the view that one can morally evaluate choices without any reference to human interests is wildly implausible. *Prudential* evaluation focuses on the interests of one particular person (either the decisionmaker or some other particular person), rather than being impartial between that person's interests and others'. Finally, as shall be elaborated in a moment, *legal* evaluation is more tightly tied to social norms than moral evaluation.

The term "moral" is widely used by philosophers to refer to the particular species of normative reasoning I have just described. It is also thus employed in other scholarly fields, although less pervasively. Economists sometimes *do* refer to normative frameworks that are impartially concerned with human persons' interests and potentially critical of existing social norms as "moral" frameworks.[2] But they often use other language to mean more or less the same thing—referring to the problem of structuring moral evaluation as an "ethical" problem, the problem of "social choice," or simply the problem of "normative economics" or "welfare economics."[3]

---

[1] To characterize morality as "impartial" is relatively uncontroversial *if* that characterization is understood to allow for first-order moral norms that are agent-relative. See Jollimore (2006). Indeed, although I argue below for consequentialism, I do not suggest that this is a mere entailment of moral impartiality. The proposition that morality does not reduce to social norms is consistent with any moral view that creates some "space" between social practices and morality—both views that make moral norms largely or wholly independent of social practice, and weaker versions of moral relativism, e.g., Wong (2006).

[2] See, e.g., Harsanyi (1986, pp. 48–51).

[3] See, e.g., Boadway and Bruce (1984, pp. 1–8); Just, Hueth, and Schmitz (2004, pp. 3–5); Samuelson (1947, p. 221). Welfare economists typically embrace impartiality or "anonymity" as a basic axiom.

The device of the "social welfare function," which I conceptualize as a very useful tool for moral decisionmaking, has been developed by economists in a field called "social choice theory"—not "moral choice theory." However, I think the term "moral choice" is preferable to "social choice," which is beset by certain ambiguities, as is the term "ethical."[4] And "normative" is too general—since, as I just explained, moral reasoning is a subcategory of normative reasoning more generally.

While it is reasonably uncontroversial that moral reasoning is concerned, at least in part, with the interests of persons, impartially considered, this book will adopt a more contestable premise: namely, that morality is *exclusively* focused on persons' interests, as opposed to the well-being of non-human animals that are not persons, intrinsic environmental goods, or other considerations that potentially figure in normative reasoning independent of the interests of persons.[5]

A full defense of this premise would take its own treatise. Here, I will briefly explain why the premise has plausibility, and why those who dispute it might still have reason to continue reading this book. Moreover, although some adopt the view that a human being is a person in virtue of possessing a soul, I will here survey the case for an exclusively person-centered account of morality on the assumption that humans are persons because of certain psychological properties or the potential to acquire such properties: not merely having beliefs and desires, but also properties such as language use, the capacity for deliberation and planning, and self-awareness.[6]

See below, p. 52. By contrast, consistency with existing social norms is certainly *not* thus embraced.

[4] The literature on "social choice" addresses the problem of ranking outcomes and choices in light of the preferences (and utility functions measuring those preferences) of some population of persons. Scholars in the field have held different views about what motivates this inquiry. See Sen (1987b, pp. 382–383). One motivation is to adopt a preference-satisfaction view of well-being. Then the problem of "social choice" *is* equivalent to the problem of "moral choice" as I construe it, combined with a particular view of well-being. However, a different motivation is to view each individual's preferences as her own moral ranking of outcomes. On this view, the problem of social choice is a special second-order problem, namely, moving from a plurality of moral rankings to a consensus ranking.

As for "ethical" versus "moral": the latter term has a more strongly interpersonal flavor that makes it the better term for my purposes.

[5] I describe environmental goods that might have moral relevance independent of human or animal well-being as "intrinsic" so as to emphasize that independence.

[6] On different accounts of personhood, see Chapter 6. Many religious traditions favor the soul view, but the dominant (if not exclusive) approach in contemporary philosophical scholarship is to analyze personhood in terms of psychological properties, and I will follow the lead of this literature.

As I explain immediately below, I focus in this book on how morality should be structured in light of *human* persons' interests—bracketing the question of the moral status of non-human beings who are full persons. It should be noted, however, that a psychological account of personhood permits a straightforward resolution of the moral status of such beings, while the soul account does not. The straightforward resolution is just that non-human beings who are full persons have equal moral status with human persons. But on the soul view of personhood, this approach may face serious obstacles— if some non-human beings who possess souls lack the rationality properties of human persons.

An interesting question is how an exclusively person-centered account should handle (1) beings that are not humans but are fully persons (super-intelligent computers, aliens); (2) human beings who, by virtue of impaired psychological capacities, are at the margins of personhood or even determinately not persons; and (3) non-human animals, such as certain primates, that have some of the psychological attributes constitutive of personhood in a rudimentary way and are also, arguably, at the margins of personhood.

I will not address these questions in this book. On any plausible account of the psychology of persons, the vast majority of human beings are persons, while the vast majority of non-human animals (let alone non-living entities) are not persons. What is characteristic of the person-centered approach to moral reasoning (however it treats the boundary questions just raised) is that human beings who are determinately persons have their interests considered, while non-human animals and other non-human entities that are determinately not persons have their interests ignored. What justifies that? To make the discussion that follows less cumbersome (and indeed throughout the book, unless otherwise noted), I henceforth use the term "person" and "human" as synonyms, to mean a full, human person, and "animal" to mean a non-human being that lacks even the rudiments of the attributes constitutive of personhood.

Economists, at least, will not dispute the proposition that persons' interests are normatively distinctive, and that we should craft our normative theories and concepts so as to provide for a distinctive realm of normative reasoning that revolves solely around persons. All of welfare economics is person-centered. The Pareto principles are the cornerstone of welfare economics—and what they say, in effect, is that outcomes should be ranked solely in light of persons' preference-satisfaction or (more generically) their well-being.[7] The Pareto-indifference principle says: If each person is just as well off in outcome x as in outcome y, then the two outcomes are equally good. The possibility that one of the two outcomes might be better, independent of human well-being—because some animal is better off, or because of an intrinsically valuable improvement in the quality of some ecosystem—is ignored. The Pareto-superiority principle says: If each person is at least as well off in outcome x as in outcome y, and at least one person is strictly better off in x, x is a better outcome. The possibility that y might be the better outcome because the persons

First, how will we develop an account of well-being that allows us to compare the welfare of ensouled but non-rational entities with the welfare of human persons? (The account of well-being developed in Chapter 3 ascribes well-being to the members of a population of beings by assuming that they all have extended preferences. What if these ensouled but non-rational beings who are persons cannot formulate extended preferences?). Second, morality—insofar as human persons are concerned—is very plausibly oriented around considerations of fairness. But how can humans be unfair to ensouled but non-rational beings? (See below, generally discussing why the fact that animals lack reasoning abilities plausibly means that fairness considerations do not govern the treatment of animals.)

[7] See below, pp. 52–55.

who gain from x are only slightly better off there, and the extent of animal suffering or ecosystem damage is much greater, is ignored.

Cost-benefit analysis (CBA) is the leading policy-analysis tool employed by economists. Like the Pareto principles, CBA is unabashedly person-centered. CBA ranks outcomes by choosing some baseline outcome x; for every other outcome z, determining the amount of money that each person is willing to pay (WTP) for the occurrence of z rather than x (if she is better off in z) or willing to accept (WTA) for its occurrence (if she is worse off); assigning each outcome an aggregate amount equaling the sum of WTP amounts minus the sum of WTA amounts; and ranking outcomes in the order of these aggregate WTP/WTA amounts.[8] Animal welfare, ecological improvement, and all other such extra-personal facts about the world that have arguable normative relevance have no role in CBA, except insofar as they affect some person's well-being and thus change his WTP/WTA amount. The SWF framework—a policy-analysis tool that also grows out of welfare economics, although is used less pervasively than CBA—is person-centered in virtue of being structured around persons' *utilities*. As we shall see, the framework works as follows: each outcome is mapped by a "utility function" onto a vector (list) of N utilities, each representing the well-being of the N persons who exist in the outcome; and a "social welfare function" then ranks outcomes based on their corresponding utility vectors, *not* as a function of their corresponding utility vectors and additional information (about animals, the environment, etc.).[9]

The fact that welfare economics is person-centered may do little to persuade the dubious reader that moral reasoning is *properly* seen to have this feature. "This is just more evidence that welfare economics embodies a flawed moral view," this reader might say. "At a minimum, non-human animals that are *sentient* possess a well-being. These animals can be caused to suffer, and the suffering of a sentient non-human animal makes it worse off. So even if one accepts the (itself contestable) premise that morality is oriented around well-being, rather than non-well-being values, shouldn't it encompass animal well-being and not just persons' well-being?"

Although sentient non-human animals can indeed be made better or worse off, human well-being is qualitatively different from animal well-being.[10] Pain and

---

[8] This is a slight simplification, since CBA might instead rank outcomes by aggregating WTP/WTA amounts in x rather than z. For a detailed discussion of CBA, see Chapter 2. (Moreover, in that discussion, I will not distinguish between WTP and WTA and will instead assign each individual a single "WTP/WTA" amount that can be either positive or negative in sign. See Chapter 2, n. 66). In any event, CBA is unabashedly person-centered.

[9] See Chapter 2.

[10] There is a vast literature on animals' moral status. For an overview, see DeGrazia (1996, ch. 3). Scholarship specifically discussing animals' status for purposes of Kantianism and contractualism is cited in the footnotes below. DeGrazia's book is a good discussion of animals' psychological capacities. Although DeGrazia argues *for* animals' moral status, and emphasizes the range of psychological capacities which many animal species *do* possess, his discussion is consistent with my claim that there are a variety of important capacities which are uniquely human—more precisely, which characterize

suffering is one aspect of human well-being—but only one. There are other dimensions of human welfare which are uniquely human—uniquely, because they presuppose the cognitive and deliberational abilities that only humans possess. For example, only humans can pursue knowledge; engage in meaningful work or accomplish other sorts of long-range goals; have the kinds of friendships, family lives, and social interactions that are massively enriched by the tool of language; and experience mental states that combine a sophisticated cognitive component with positive or negative affects (for example, fearing death, or feeling a sense of satisfaction with one's life).

Thus person-centered welfarism is a plausible moral view even if takes the form of utilitarianism: even if it focuses solely on total well-being, rather than attending to the fair distribution of well-being. The person-centered *utilitarian* might plausibly take the position that human well-being is qualitatively more important than animal well-being; that interspecies comparisons of well-being are also qualitatively more difficult than interpersonal comparisons of well-being; and that it therefore makes sense to delineate a separate realm of normative reasoning (call it "moral" reasoning) that concerns what maximizes total human well-being, recognizing that animal well-being has normative (but not "moral") weight.

The case for person-centered welfarism becomes yet stronger if one adopts the position (a position I *will* adopt) that impartial normative reasoning involving persons should be centered on questions of *fairness*. Intuitively, it is not possible to be *unfair* to animals (let alone the environment). It is implausible that harming animals or damaging the environment, if wrong, is wrong in virtue of violating distributive justice—norms of fair distribution.

Why is *fairness* so clearly person-focused? I think the answer is this. Identifying norms of fair conduct means doing the following: identifying some community of individuals and determining the norms that everyone in the group has reason to follow, in virtue of the fact that the norms impartially balance the interests of all the group's members. Norms of fairness are always recommended as norms *for* an entire group—as norms which everyone in the group is advised to comply with, because the norms are suitably impartial between group members. But animals (let alone the environment or other non-living entities) are incapable of normative reasoning. Whatever guidance we might formulate, these beings will not follow it. Our criteria for determining which choices are *fair* thus reflect only the interests of those beings—persons—who can be guided by these very criteria.

A closely related thought is that a norm for determining what conduct would be fair to some individual should be such that the individual, under suitably idealized conditions, would judge the norm to be fair to her. (Parenthetically, it is this thought, I think, which helps explain the link between the concepts of fairness and the

---

few if any animal species, and if so at most in a rudimentary fashion. Among other things, I argue that animals are not the subject of fairness, because they cannot engage in moral deliberation; and, indeed, DeGrazia agrees that very few, if any, animals are moral agents. See ibid., pp. 207–210.

separateness of persons.[11] Norm n is fair to individual i only if i would judge n to be fair to her, and thus would act in compliance with n; but i would judge n to be fair to her only if n takes account of her separateness, her distinct perspective.) But an animal, lacking normative concepts, cannot judge whether a norm would be fair to her.

This basic idea—that the unique deliberational capacities of persons warrants some normative realm in which persons, alone, have standing—is characteristic of much non-utilitarian moral philosophy. Kant took the position that we lack moral duties to animals; at most we have moral duties to persons regarding the treatment of animals. This is clear, both from his explicit discussion of animals, and from one standard framing of Kant's categorical imperative: "Act in such a way that you treat humanity, whether in your own person or in the person of another, always at the same time as an end and never simply as a means."[12] Only rational beings, not animals, have moral worth because only rational beings can identify, and freely choose to follow, the moral laws that universally bind rational beings as such.

Rawls suggests that morality may subsume the treatment of animals, but that distributive justice does not. Animals are not participants in the hypothetical contracting scenario, behind the "veil of ignorance," that identifies the principles for a just society, and are not among the beneficiaries of these principles.

> While I have not maintained that the capacity for a sense of justice is necessary in order to be owed the duties of justice, it does seem that we are not required to give strict justice anyway to creatures lacking this capacity. . . . Certainly it is wrong to be cruel to animals and the destruction of a whole species can be a great evil. The capacity for feelings of pleasure and pain and for the forms of life of which animals are capable clearly imposes duties of compassion and humanity in their case. I shall not attempt to explain these considered beliefs. They are outside the scope of the theory of justice, and it does not seem possible to extend the contract doctrine so as to include them in a natural way.[13]

Principles of justice, for Rawls, are norms to regulate a scheme of cooperation; but beings without a "capacity for a sense of justice" lack the ability to cooperate, because they are unable to be motivated to comply with some proposed scheme of cooperation in virtue of recognizing that the scheme is just.[14]

Thomas Scanlon, a leading contemporary moral theorist, also uses the device of a hypothetical contract to identify moral rules. Moral rules, in the broad sense, are

---

[11] See Chapter 5, pp. 314–317.

[12] See Denis (2000, p. 406); Skidmore (2001, p. 542). See also Broadie and Pybus (1974).

[13] Rawls (1999b, p. 448). See also ibid., pp. 15, 441.

[14] Rawls does not state this explicitly, but there are good reasons to think this line of thought helps motivate his exclusion of animals from the domain of justice. See Bernstein (1997, p. 58). For other discussions of Rawls' views concerning animals or, more generally, their status within contractualist moral views, see Abbey (2007); Carruthers (1992); A. Cohen (2009); Rowlands (1997).

heterogeneous; but there is a "narrower domain" of moral rules that concern "what we owe to each other"—what a community of persons, seeking to identify rules that no person could reasonably reject, would agree to. And Scanlon suggests that animals lack standing within this "narrower domain." "[A]lthough it is morally objectionable, in the broad sense, to fail to take account of the pain and distress of nonrational creatures, we do not have the reason that we have in the case of rational creatures to accept the general requirement that our conduct be justifiable to them."[15] We cannot engage in the exercise of justifying a rule to an animal: of seeking to persuade her that she has no reason to reject the rule, given her interests and views.

I agree with Scanlon that there is a distinct domain of normative thought that involves persons; and I agree with him about how reasoning within this domain should be structured, namely in terms of what persons "owe to each other" (in other words, fairness). But I believe it is simpler and more perspicuous to use the term "morality," full stop, to refer to rules grounded in the interests of persons, rather than to differentiate between morality in narrower and broader senses.[16]

The argument I have been advancing for why morality should be person-focused—flowing from the idea that only persons can engage in normative reasoning—has been quite abstract. A more concrete but perhaps more compelling rationale is this. Prioritarianism is the most attractive account of how we should balance persons' interests, or so I will argue at length in a later chapter of the book.[17] But extending prioritarianism to encompass all beings that can possess well-being (animals, and not just persons) would be massively counterintuitive. Person-centered prioritarianism says: give greater weight to well-being changes affecting worse-off persons. More specifically, a prioritarian SWF with a fairly modest degree of inequality aversion would say that we should be indifferent between increasing the well-being of an individual at level U by small amount $\Delta u/K$, and increasing the well-being of an individual at level KU by amount Δu.[18] Consider, now, *inclusive* prioritarianism, which says: give greater weight to well-being changes affecting worse-off *beings* (be they animals or persons). Since the well-being level of most animals is presumably a modest fraction of an average human's (isn't it many times better to be a human than a cow or a gerbil?), this would mean choosing to produce small benefits for animals at the expense of substantially larger benefits for humans—and even when using an SWF with only a modest degree of inequality aversion.

---

[15] Scanlon (1998, p. 184). See generally ibid., pp. 171–187.

[16] This is more perspicuous because it underscores the qualitative difference between the kind of normative reasoning that is internal to the community of persons, and the kind required to balance persons' interests against those of non-persons.

[17] See Chapter 5.

[18] This would be the upshot of an Atkinson SWF with $\gamma = 1$. Strictly, "U" should be "rU," and so forth, because well-being is not measurable exactly, only at best up to a positive ratio transformation. See Chapters 3 and 5.

Even the most stalwart defender of animal rights will find it uncomfortable to take this position.[19] And, of course, because the ecosystem or other entities that are neither persons nor sentient animals do not possess a well-being at all, extending prioritarianism to them is just impossible.

To be clear, my position is *not* that animal well-being lacks any normative relevance. That is also deeply counterintuitive. We have *reason* not to impose gratuitous suffering on animals. Furthermore, at least arguably, we have reasons that transcend human or animal well-being. Rather, the structure of reasoning by which we appropriately balance interests within the community of persons is qualitatively different from the structure of reasoning by which we balance human interests against the values associated with non-persons. And thus, for purposes of facilitating good normative reasoning, it is useful to differentiate these two realms.[20] My argument for this position is, to some extent, separable from the case for prioritarianism that I will present later in the book; but if I am correct that person-centered morality is best specified via the concept of fairness and, more specifically, a prioritarian approach, the case for the distinctive structure of normative reasoning concerning the interests of persons is substantially bolstered.

So much for the plausibility of a person-centered view of morality. So why should the reader who rejects this view keep reading? Such a reader might (1) agree with me that normative reasoning internal to the community of persons is qualitatively different from normative reasoning once non-persons are introduced, but prefer to use the term "moral" to encompass (at least some) reasons associated with non-persons; (2) disagree with me that reasoning involving persons' interests is distinctive, but believe (or at least be persuadable that) the most attractive moral view is a kind of inclusive prioritarianism, encompassing animal well-being as well as the well-being of persons; or (3) disagree with me that reasoning involving persons' interests is distinctive, and be firmly committed to a non-prioritarian moral approach (e.g., an inclusive utilitarianism that encompasses both human and animal interests, or an inclusive perfectionism that advances the good of humans, animals, and some

---

[19] See Vallentyne (2005b, p. 404). Might it be possible to include animals within the ambit of prioritarianism, but modify its structure (in effect, discounting animal well-being), so as to avoid the proposition that small changes to animal well-being morally trump large changes to human well-being? Holtug (2007a) reviews and rejects a variety of proposals for doing so—and concludes that the proposition, albeit counterintuitive, is true. I would instead conclude that prioritarianism is not the proper structure for balancing animal and human interests.

[20] I take no position here about how to commensurate humans' interests with animal well-being, or more generally how to commensurate moral and non-moral considerations—or even about the possibility of commensuration. Some moral philosophers take the position that moral reasons always override non-moral reasons. Given a person-centered account of morality, that seems implausible. Imagine purchasing a small improvement in well-being for a few persons, at the expense of massive suffering for many animals. But the problem of explicating all-things-considered normative reasoning, encompassing both moral and non-moral reasons, is beyond what I can hope to engage in this book.

non-sentient entities that lack a well-being). My difference with the first reader, as with Scanlon, is small.[21] My disagreement with the second reader is more substantial: but even this reader may find valuable my discussion of the formal structure of a prioritarian SWF, which may well be transposable to an inclusive prioritarianism. My disagreement with the third reader is yet more substantial. But even this reader should keep going. This book presents (what I take to be) the strongest case for prioritarianism, resting upon a particular understanding of fairness. She can see the book as a contribution to a larger debate about the appropriate structure of normative thought, a debate between utilitarianism, prioritarianism, and other approaches; and, if she likes, she can use its analysis as a foil to strengthen her counterarguments.

B. Morality, Social Norms, and Law

Moral evaluation is centered on the interests of persons (indeed, exclusively person-focused, for reasons I have just reviewed); it is impartial between the interests of persons; and, finally, it is not reducible to social norms. To ask what a decisionmaker ought to do, morally speaking, is not the same as asking what the social norms or conventions of her society require of her.

Perhaps it would be useful to distinguish between "critical morality" and "social morality." "Social morality" is just another term for the extant social conventions within a given society. It certainly *is* possible to evaluate choices in light of such conventions. I do not mean to deny that this is one kind of normative assessment. But there is also a species of normative assessment that looks beyond social conventions. The term "critical morality" is sometimes used to denote normative principles that are not seen as reducible to social practices, and that may be brought to bear to criticize such practices. (For example, slavery was socially approved in the antebellum South, but as a matter of critical morality, if not social morality in the South at the time, slavery was wrong.) For short, I drop the adjective "critical" and use the term "moral" reasoning to involve just this: normative reasoning regarding some choice that, inter alia, is not reducible to the social norms applicable to that choice.

Of course, what moral reasoning *does* depend upon—if not social norms—is an open question. That raises controversial issues of metaethics, to be reviewed a little later in this chapter. But virtually all contemporary metaethicists, whatever their particular views, agree that it is coherent to say that (1) some choice is permitted or required by social norms, but (2) the choice is morally wrong.

This brings us to the topic of law versus morality. The most important work of jurisprudence in the last century, H.L.A. Hart's book *The Concept of Law*, does reduce *law* to social norms. Hart argues that all law, within a given society, is

---

[21] One might think the difference is purely semantic. That's not quite right, since the theorist who characterizes non-persons' interests as "moral" is surely committed to believing that these are commensurable, to some extent, with persons' interests; while, on the person-centered view of morality, the question of the methodology and extent of commensurability is left open.

ultimately derivable from a "rule of recognition": a *social norm* among governmental officials, identifying fundamental legal criteria.[22] Hart's view, although hugely influential, is controversial. The precise connection between law, morality, and social practice is a matter of continuing debate among jurisprudents. However, all serious contemporary jurisprudents would agree that law is more tightly bound up with social practices than is morality,[23] and that law and morality are therefore distinct. In order to *legally* evaluate some choice—to determine whether the choice is legally permitted, required, or prohibited—one starts with authoritative legal texts, such as a written Constitution, statutes, regulations, or case law. These texts are authoritative as a matter of social practice: they are seen as legally authoritative by the community of judges, officials, and lawyers. Bringing authoritative legal texts to bear on a given choice situation is a complex process, involving interpretation, gaps in the law, conflict between different texts, and so forth—but in any event this is a different process from morally evaluating the choice, and may reach a different conclusion about which choice "ought" to be performed.

The example of CBA helps to illustrate the difference between legal evaluation and moral evaluation. As I have already implied—and surprising as this may sound to some readers—CBA is a kind of moral decision procedure. I will argue, in Chapter 2, that it is ultimately less attractive than the SWF approach. Still, CBA has the basic characteristics of *moral* assessment described in this section. It is focused on human interests: A given individual's WTP/WTA amount for some outcome z, relative to baseline x, is a monetary measure of her well-being change between z and x. CBA preserves a kind of impartiality between persons: It ranks outcomes by summing WTP/WTA amounts of everyone within a population of interest—not just one particular "dictator."

Finally—and this is the critical point, here—CBA is not a reliable formula for determining the *legal* status of some choice.[24] This point is obvious, but it bears reflection, because it illuminates the law/morality divide. Law can *incorporate* a moral decision procedure: some statutes require or permit regulatory agencies to use CBA in determining which regulations to adopt. However, legal requirements and the deliverances of the decision procedure are certainly not necessarily coextensive: some statutes preclude regulatory agencies from using CBA as a decisional standard. It would be malpractice for the office of legal counsel in a regulatory agency to advise the agency administrator about her legal obligations by using CBA as the starting point—by following a nutty approach to "legal research" which says that a

---

[22] Hart (1994).

[23] See Chapter 8 for further discussion of the connection between law, morality, and social norms, and for citations to the scholarly literature on this topic.

[24] Nor, more generally, is CBA reducible to social conventions. Its evaluation of outcomes is a function of individuals' preferences. Such preferences (as aggregated, per CBA, via the device of summing individual WTP/WTA amounts, measuring the strength of the preferences on a monetary scale) can readily conflict with social conventions. Indeed, this helps explain why CBA can be so controversial.

regulation is legally required just in case CBA approves it. Rather, the policymaker's counsel, if he is competent as a lawyer, will provide guidance concerning the policy-maker's legal obligation by starting with the various statutes, executive orders, and judicial cases on point, and will advise the policymaker to employ CBA only insofar as these texts permit or require.

The CBA example also illustrates, pretty dramatically, that individuals can be motivated to engage in *moral* rather than legal evaluation of governmental policy choices. There is a large community of academic scholars and other researchers who engage in cost-benefit analysis of governmental policies. Sometimes these scholars are helping to flesh out existing legal requirements, but often the upshot of the CBA is to criticize these requirements—so as to persuade lawmakers to repeal or amend them. The same could be said of the other policy-evaluation tools discussed in Chapter 2, as well as the SWF framework itself: all of these have the basic character-istics of moral evaluation frameworks that I have outlined here, and are already in reasonably widespread use by various academic communities to assess governmen-tal policies, often in the service of arguments for law reform.

The reader might wonder why I purport to defend the SWF approach as a frame-work for morally evaluating *governmental* policies. Why think that governmental policies are the principal objects of moral assessment—given that legal and moral assessment can diverge? Here, I should stress that the SWF approach, as I conceive it, is meant to facilitate the moral evaluation of *any* large-scale choice situation—including *but not limited to* the choice of governmental policies. Because the frame-work itself requires substantial analytic effort, it would be silly to employ it indiscriminately, for each and every choice regardless of a threshold prediction about the magnitude of the choice's impact on well-being. (More on this in the next subsection.) A governmental choice regarding some nationwide regulation, large infrastructure project, amendment to the tax laws, spending program, or other such high-impact decision is the paradigmatic "large-scale" choice where the effort to analyze this choice using a tool such as CBA or the SWF approach seems sensible. But one can certainly imagine choices by private institutions or even private individuals (for example, philanthropists) that are also sufficiently "large-scale" to warrant the kind of systematic evaluation that the SWF approach permits.

Finally, the reader might wonder about the appropriate legal role of the SWF framework. Granted, the framework may be of interest to scholars, researchers, and others whether or not its verdicts dovetail with legal requirements. But assume I make my case that the framework *is* an excellent device for morally evaluating gov-ernmental policies (and other large-scale choices). Wouldn't that, in turn, suggest that our legal institutions should be restructured so that governmental officials are encouraged or required to employ SWFs as a general policy-evaluation tool (at least for large-scale choices)? To put the idea here more precisely: If M is an attractive moral decision procedure, then doesn't it follow that legal regime L, which imposes a legal requirement that officials employ M, is morally better than legal regime L^*, which fails to include such a legal requirement?

Actually, that does not follow. The question of morally optimal legal institutions raises a host of complicated empirical and theoretical issues. These issues are described (although hardly resolved) in Chapter 8. Until that point, the book focuses on the simpler (although hardly simple!) enterprise of elaborating and defending the SWF approach as a tool for moral evaluation. Only after that defense has been mounted can we begin to engage the yet trickier question of what the morally optimal legal role of the SWF framework is.

C. Moral Decision Procedures

It has become standard, within moral philosophy, to distinguish between a "decision procedure" and a "criterion of rightness." As David Brink explains:

> A standard or criterion of rightness explains what makes an action or motive right or justified; a decision procedure provides a method of deliberation. [Consequentialist theories such as utilitarianism] do provide criteria of rightness, but need not provide decision procedures. Just as an agent may best secure her own happiness not by always seeking her own happiness but by pursing certain activities for their own sake (the so-called paradox of egoism), so, too, an agent may act best not as the result of deliberating about how to do so or acting out of [a desire to maximize good consequences], but by reasoning in 'nonutilitarian' ways or acting on 'nonutilitarian' . . . motives.[25]

It is undoubtedly true that a given principle can play some role within a moral theory without the theory advising decisionmakers to advert to that principle in deciding what to do. That is the sense in which a given principle can be merely a "criterion of rightness." *On the other hand*: If a moral theory is meant to be a *normative* theory, then it will be incomplete unless it contains *some* decision procedure. A normative theory functions to provide guidance to actors. A body of moral theory that merely describes the conditions under which actions are good and bad, without more—neither instructing decisionmakers to think consciously about those conditions, nor providing other advice about how to choose—does not fulfill this function. It is incomplete as a normative framework. An actor, furnished with this body of theory, will ask (if she is intelligent and morally motivated): "OK, but how *should* I think about what to *do*?"

In particular, the SWF framework is defended, in this book, as a methodology that policymakers, researchers, and analysts can actually use to evaluate governmental policies and other large-scale choices. So it better contain a decision procedure. And indeed it does. The continuous prioritarian SWF formula I elaborate— outcome x is morally at least as good as outcome y iff, for all utility functions $u(.)$

---

[25] Brink (1989, pp. 216–217). On the decision procedure/criterion-of-rightness distinction, see also Bales (1971); Hudson (1989); Jackson (1991, pp. 465–467); Parfit (1987, ch. 1); M. Zimmerman (2006).

belonging to **U**, $\sum_{i=1}^{N} g(u_i(x)) \geq \sum_{i=1}^{N} g(u_i(y))$, with $g(.)$ strictly increasing and strictly concave—is meant to be a formula that is usable by real-world decisionmakers in assessing their large-scale choices. Chapter 4 discusses how, in practice, decisionmakers should go about constructing the set **U**, using the extended-preference account of well-being set forth in Chapter 3. Chapter 5 addresses how decisionmakers should identify a particular functional form for the $g(.)$ function. Chapter 7 discusses how the decisionmaker can move from the ranking of the outcome set **O** generated by this formula to a ranking of her choice set, when she is operating under conditions of uncertainty. The "outcomes" in the outcome set **O** need to be items that decisionmakers can actually think about, given their limited cognitive abilities. Chapter 4 engages this issue.

The ambition to defend a consequentialist moral framework, where outcomes function as a central part of the decision procedure, is not quixotic. This is exactly how CBA works.[26] CBA texts do not tell analysts that the cost-benefit test—the sum of WTP/WTA amounts—is merely a criterion of rightness, and that they should actually decide which policies are better or worse via nonconsequentialist reasoning. Rather, this formula is meant to be *used* (and is!). Policies are meant to be characterized in terms of outcomes; the net benefits and costs of outcomes are meant to be actually calculated; and a vast body of empirical work and theory exists to assist analysts in estimating WTP/WTA amounts.

An important objection to a moral framework that employs consequentialism in its decision procedure—as the SWF framework does—is that reasoning this way can be time consuming and expensive. In other words, an explicitly consequentialist framework has relatively high "decision costs." One response, as we will see in Chapter 4, is that the outcomes in **O** can be quite simplified (which lowers the decision costs of gathering and analyzing information to determine how the outcome set should be ranked). A complementary point is that I intend to defend the SWF framework only as a decision procedure for large-scale choices, where it seems at the threshold that the stakes (the variation in expected social welfare between choices) are sufficiently large to justify the relatively high decision costs of this framework. Here again CBA furnishes a precedent: the current Presidential cost-benefit order in the U.S., which requires administrative agencies to undertake full CBA analysis, does so *only* for sufficiently large decisions—specifically, regulations that (prior to full-blown analysis) can be anticipated to have annual monetized costs or benefits exceeding $100 million.[27]

Admittedly, the criterion of "large-scale" is vague. I will not try to flesh out the component of the SWF decision procedure that enables decisionmakers to decide whether they are above the threshold mentioned in the previous paragraph. This is a

---

[26] This is also how the SWF framework itself already functions in scholarly work.

[27] Executive Order 12866 (1993, secs. 6(a), 3(f)).

very hard problem that I will not attempt to address. (The literature on CBA doesn't tackle it well either.) Nor do I take a position about what procedure is morally advisable for below-threshold decisions. Still, this book, if its arguments are persuasive, will have helped us make substantial progress in crafting tools that real decisionmakers—decisionmakers whose cognitive abilities are bounded, whose information is limited, and who face non-zero decision costs—can employ in deciding what they morally ought to do.

II. MORAL FACTS AND MORAL EPISTEMOLOGY

A. Metaethics

What is the factual grounding, if any, for moral claims? If I assert that some decisionmaker morally "ought" to choose some particular course of action, or that she morally "ought" to use some particular tools in thinking about her choice, what exactly am I saying? Am I asserting the existence of moral facts? Am I saying that a particular choice or decision procedure has the "attribute" of moral goodness, the way that I might assert that a physical object has some physical property (weight), or that an organism has some biological property (being a mammal), or that a person has some psychological property (feeling pain)? If so, what could moral facts and attributes possibly consist in?

These matters are debated in the field of metaethics.[28] Some scholars of metaethics, so-called "noncognitivists," deny that moral statements assert the existence of moral facts. Instead, according to noncognitivists, moral statements express some non-belief ("non-cognitive") state on the part of the speaker. Consider the statement "killing is wrong." The syntax of that statement appears to be factual. It appears to mean something like: "the act of killing has the property of wrongness"; "it is a fact that killing is wrong"; "killing is truly wrong." But what this statement really means—say noncognitivists—is something like this: "Down with killing"; "don't kill"; "I (the speaker) commit myself not to kill." On this view, a moral statement is an expression of a preference, a commitment, a plan, a prescription, an emotion, or something like that, not the assertion of a moral fact.[29]

Economists tend to be deeply skeptical about the existence of moral facts and truths and are thus, typically, noncognitivists.[30] When economists say that

---

[28] For overviews, see Darwall, Gibbard, and Railton (1992); Miller (2003); Railton (1996); Smith (1994; 2004, ch. 10). Sayre-McCord (1988) and Shafer-Landau and Cuneo (2007) are useful anthologies.

[29] Simon Blackburn and Alan Gibbard are the leading contemporary non-cognitivists. See, e.g., Blackburn (1998); Gibbard (1990).

[30] Strictly, noncognitivism is a view about the semantic content of moral statements, namely that such statements do not assert facts. One could take the hybrid position that moral statements do assert facts, but there really are no moral facts (this is the "error theory" famously adopted by

normative questions are just "value choices," or words to that effect, what they seem to be doing (with less fancy terminology) is adopting a particular metaethical view, namely noncognitivism. Indeed, this is a perfectly respectable position, and at one point was the dominant view in academic metaethics. However, it should be noted that *cognitivism* is now equally if not more widespread within metaethics.

But what could moral facts possibly be? Contemporary cognitivists typically do *not* adopt the counterintuitive position that moral facts "float free" from the natural facts. They typically adopt the "naturalist" position that moral facts and properties are ultimately anchored in "natural" facts—where "natural," here, means the physical, biological, psychological, and other such facts that scientists in various fields uncontroversially rely upon to predict and explain occurrences in the world. There turn out to be a number of variants of cognitivism that are consistent with naturalism, including the following sort of views.

(1) *Ideal-Approval Views.* Perhaps the moral status of a choice depends on whether it would be approved by some idealized individual or group of individuals. For example, Roderick Firth analyzes "*a* is right" in terms of the reactions of an "ideal observer," namely an observer who is fully informed about the non-moral facts, can vividly imagine those facts, and is disinterested, dispassionate, and consistent.[31] More recently, Peter Railton has argued for a position he calls idealized subjectivism: "'X is wrong' means 'We the people (i.e., people in general, including the speaker) would disapprove of allowing X as part of our basic scheme of social cooperation were we to consider the question with full information from a standpoint that considers the well-being of all affected without partiality.'"[32] Along similar lines, Michael Smith analyzes normative facts in terms of convergent fully rational preferences:

> I have been arguing that the truth of a normative reason claim requires a convergence in the desires of fully rational agents. However note that the convergence required is not at the level of desires about how each such agent is to organize her own life in her own world. In their own worlds fully rational agents will find themselves in quite different circumstances from each other, circumstances that are conditioned by their different embodiments, talents, environments and attachments in their respective worlds. Their desires about how to organize their own lives in their own worlds will therefore reflect these differences in their circumstances. The convergence required is rather at the level of their hypothetical desires about what is to be done in the various circumstances in which they might find themselves.

John Mackie [1977]), or the position that moral statements do not assert facts, but there are moral facts. So as not to overcomplexify matters, I'm using "noncognitivism" to mean the joint claim that (1) moral statements do not assert facts and (2) there are no moral facts; and "cognitivism" to mean the contradictory position on both issues.

[31] Firth (1952).
[32] Railton (1996, p. 69).

The mere fact that a convergence in the hypothetical desires of fully rational creatures is required for the truth of normative reasons claims does nothing to guarantee that such a convergence is forthcoming. . . . [I]n order to discover whether there are any normative reasons, and if so what they are, we have no alternative but to give the arguments and see where they lead.[33]

A different kind of ideal-approval view is outlined by Ronald Milo, who suggests that moral truths might be reducible to the choices that would be made in a hypothetical social contract.

What the moral facts are . . . is determined by which principles would be chosen by the hypothetical agents of construction [i.e., contractors]. . . . The agents of construction are not to be conceived of as trying to reach an agreement on which moral principles are true, since apart from their agreement there are no antecedently given moral truths for them to discover. Rather, they determine through their choices which moral principles are true. . . .[34]

Understand that an ideal-approval view *is* cognitivist. It takes the statement "action *a* is wrong," not to have non-factual content along the lines of "down with *a*" or "I (the speaker) commit not to *a*," but rather as having factual content, namely: a group of individuals with certain psychological properties would disapprove of *a*. Understand, too, that an ideal-approval view is consistent with naturalism: whether *a* is truly right or wrong is determined by the psychology of the idealized individuals plus the natural properties of *a*—by whether individuals with that kind of information, in that kind of emotional state, with those cognitive abilities, and with those preferences and attitudes, would approve or disapprove *a*, given the causal impacts on the physical and social world that *a* has.

(2) *Ideal-Approval Views: Secondary Quality Variant.* Some contemporary metaethicists argue that moral properties are like colors.[35] A color is what Locke called a "secondary quality." It is the property, in an object, of producing a matching perception in an observer. "*X* is red" means "*X* is such as to look red to normal observers." Similarly, "*a* is good" might mean "*a* is such as to be judged good by normal observers." A secondary quality account is best seen as a kind of ideal-approval view—one in which the reasoning process that leads to an ideal observer's approval of some item as morally good is value-laden rather than value-free. Is this viciously circular? Perhaps not. The distinction between value-laden and value-free versions of ideal-approval cognitivism will be further explored in Chapter 3, since disagreement between these two subschools is one theme in philosophical debate

---

[33] Smith (1994, p. 173).

[34] Milo (1995, p. 186).

[35] Leading examples are John McDowell and David Wiggins. For a discussion, with citations to their work, see Darwall, Gibbard, and Railton (1992, pp. 152–165).

about the nature of well-being. Suffice it to say that this approach, too, amounts to a kind of naturalistic cognitivism.

(3) *Moral Properties as Explanatory Properties*. Some cognitivists argue that moral facts are akin to biological or psychological facts.[36] Biological and psychological facts are ultimately determined by bedrock physical facts: the body of each organism or person is an arrangement of subatomic particles, and everything that occurs in that body, including the brain, ultimately depends on this subatomic composition plus the basic physical laws governing subatomic particles. Still, it is very useful to have a separate science (biology or psychology) that explains occurrences in terms of biological or psychological properties, not bedrock physical properties; and we may not be able to simply analyze biological or psychological properties in terms of bedrock physical properties. (Try to analyze the property of being alive, or of being in pain, in terms of quarks or atoms.) Similarly, it is suggested, moral properties have explanatory utility. A standard example: the immorality of slavery helps to explain why it was abolished. And it may be difficult to draw any kind of simple one-to-one correspondence between moral properties and natural properties.

My own sympathies are with cognitivism; more specifically with an ideal-approval approach; more specifically yet with the kind of ideal-approval approach outlined by Michael Smith, which analyzes moral facts in terms of convergent idealized preferences. *However*: the defense of the SWF approach presented in his book does not presuppose an ideal-preference view of moral facts, or cognitivism more generally. In particular, the account of well-being presented in Chapter 3, which analyzes well-being in terms of fully informed, fully rational, extended preferences, meshes neatly with a convergent-ideal-preference view of moral facts—but (as we shall see) does not presuppose such a view.

Metaethics is treacherous ground. If I can successfully argue for the use of SWFs as a moral choice-evaluation framework without committing myself to any particular metaethical position—and I believe I can—then it seems sensible to bracket questions of metaethics. The book will therefore adopt a posture of agnosticism regarding debates between cognitivists and noncognitivists, and within cognitivism.

Of course it can now be asked: If this book is really agnostic on metaethical issues, then how can it present an *argument* for the SWF approach? When I say that the SWF framework is more "attractive" than competitors, or argue that the SWF framework is "best" specified in one manner rather than another, what do these statements mean?

The answer is that such statements can be interpreted in different ways, depending on whether the reader's sympathies are noncognitivist or cognitivist. If the reader is inclined toward noncognitivism, then she can read my "argument" for the SWF approach as an expression of my approval of that approach and an attempt to

---

[36] See, for example, the work of David Brink, Richard Boyd, and Nicholas Sturgeon, reviewed by Darwall, Gibbard, and Railton (1992, pp. 169–174) and by Miller (2003, ch. 8). See also Railton (1986b).

illustrate various considerations that, I hope, will cause her to approve it. On the noncognitivist reading, when I say that the SWF approach is an "attractive" framework for moral decisionmaking, or "better" than competitors, what I really mean is something like: I hereby endorse the use of SWFs as a decision procedure for policy choices or other large-scale decisions, and express my desire that the reader also endorse that procedure. Alternatively, if the reader is inclined toward cognitivism, then she can read my "argument" for the SWF approach as an attempt to demonstrate what the moral facts are. For example, if the reader is inclined toward convergent-ideal-preference cognitivism, then she can read this argument as an attempt to demonstrate that an idealized group of individuals would converge in preferring that governmental decisionmakers, or other actors faced with large-scale choices, employ the SWF approach as their decision procedure.

B. Moral Epistemology

The discussion of metaethics brings us immediately to the topic of moral epistemology.[37] Most academic moral philosophy employs the method of "reflective equilibrium" famously described by John Rawls. This method starts with our provisional moral judgments about both particular cases and general principles. It seeks to make these different kinds of judgments coherent with each other, and with background non-moral facts. It takes any given moral judgment, whether about a particular case or about a general principle, to be both (1) a potential stepping-stone for an argument concerning what our moral judgment regarding some other case or principle should be, and yet (2) potentially revisable if shown to be in tension with other judgments, or with non-moral facts. There is a "back-and-forth" quality to moral argument in the reflective-equilibrium mode. The speaker sometimes appeals to her interlocutor's intuitions about particular cases, sometimes to her intuitions about general principles, and sometimes tries to undermine the interlocutor's intuitions about particular cases or general principles by showing these to be inconsistent with something else.

> The key idea underlying the method of reflective equilibrium is that we 'test' various parts of our system of moral beliefs against other beliefs we hold, seeking coherence among the widest set of moral and non-moral beliefs by revising and refining them at all levels. For example, we might test the appropriateness of a purported principle of justice by seeing whether we can accept its implications in a broad range of cases and whether it accounts for those cases better than alternatives. . . .

---

[37] On moral epistemology, see generally Brink (1989, ch. 5); Sinnott-Armstrong (2006); Sinnott-Armstrong and Timmons (1996). Rawls' concept of reflective equilibrium, which originates in his early work on "a decision procedure for ethics" (1999a), figures centrally in *A Theory of Justice*. See in particular Rawls (1999b, pp. 15–19, 40–46, 507–508.). For commentary, see Daniels (1996); S. Freeman (2007, pp. 29–42); Scanlon (2003).

Our moral beliefs about particular cases count in the process. They have justificatory weight. Yet they are not decisive. Even firmly held beliefs about particular cases may be revised. For example, if a principle incompatible with such a firmly held belief about a particular case accounts better than alternatives for an appropriate range of cases we seem equally confident about, and if the principle also has theoretical support from other parts of our belief system, we may revise our particular belief and save the principle.[38]

It should be stressed that the appeal of the reflective-equilibrium approach outstrips the substantive views defended by Rawls in *A Theory of Justice*. The vast majority of contemporary moral philosophers, consequentialists and nonconsequentialists alike, rely on reflective-equilibrium reasoning. And this book will be no exception.

What explains the widespread appeal of reflective-equilibrium reasoning in moral philosophy? Not just Rawls' personal prestige! The answer, I think, is that the approach is *modular*: It meshes neatly with a range of metaethical views, and with the full panoply of substantive moral positions.

Metaethical modularity is the point I wish to stress here. This book, again, is meant to be agnostic with regard to metaethical disputes. Therefore, the basic methodology I employ—reflective equilibrium—had better be consistent with such agnosticism. And I believe it is. First, reflective-equilibrium reasoning meshes neatly with noncognitivism. If the "argumentation" in this book is a matter of getting you to endorse the SWF framework—the noncognitivist reading—then I can get you to do that by showing you how the framework coheres with other views that you endorse, or that I can get you to endorse.

Second, reflective-equilibrium reasoning also meshes neatly with ideal-approval variants of cognitivism. Reflective-equilibrium reasoning, here, can be understood as an attempt to *simulate* the process that individuals in the idealized setting would go through. I acquire evidence of the moral facts—facts about what the idealized individuals would approve—by putting myself under the very pressure for coherence that they would presumably face, and reflecting on what I approve under such pressure. As Michael Smith explains: "[B]y far the most important way in which we create new and destroy old underived desires when we deliberate is by trying to find out whether our desires are *systematically justifiable*. . . . And we do this in a certain characteristic way: namely, by trying to integrate the object of [those] desire[s] into a more coherent and unified desiderative profile and evaluative outlook."[39]

The link between reflective-equilibrium reasoning and other variants of cognitivism may be less apparent. One point (stressed in the literature on moral epistemology) is that sound empirical reasoning *generally* takes a coherentist form. Each belief depends, for its justification, on other beliefs. My belief that I am picking up traces of a particular kind of particle in the electron microscope is justified by my belief

---

[38] Daniels (1996, pp. 2–3).
[39] Smith (1994, pp. 158–159).

that the microscope is working in a particular manner, in turn justified by my belief in various basic laws that allow me to predict how the microscope will function, in turn justified by a wide variety of observations, each of which has generated observational beliefs that are seen as justified by virtue of beliefs about the technology used to produce those observations, in turn justified. . . . So there is a back-and-forth flavor to scientific reasoning that is paralleled in the reflective-equilibrium approach, and that plausibly would be attractive to the moral cognitivist whatever exactly she believes moral facts to consist in.

While reflective-equilibrium reasoning is pervasive in moral philosophy, it rarely figures in welfare economics, at least not in any explicit or self-conscious manner. The basic methodology of welfare economics and social choice is deductive logic, embodied in mathematical proofs. The focus is on demonstrating which combinations of premises (about the measurability of well-being, the connection between well-being and the ranking of outcomes, the functional form of an SWF, and so forth) are logically possible. Unfortunately, there are a multiplicity of logically possible choice-evaluation frameworks which can be constructed (even if one assumes that the structure of such a framework should be person-centered, consequentialist, and oriented around human well-being). In choosing *between* these frameworks, coherentist reasoning (albeit fuzzier and more contestable than formal deduction) becomes essential. There is really no other game in town.

III. CONSEQUENTIALISM

A choice-evaluation framework is *consequentialist* if it revolves around a ranking of outcomes. Because moral decision procedures have the special feature of being person-centered (or so I presuppose) and being *impartial* between persons' interests, we can say that a *moral* choice-evaluation framework is consequentialist if it revolves around an *impartial* ranking of outcomes.

What does it mean for a choice-evaluation framework to "revolve around a ranking of outcomes"? I will give a more formal characterization later in this chapter. The basic idea is that the framework takes some set of outcomes (simplified possible worlds); generates a ranking of the outcomes, whereby each outcome is ranked as better than, worse than, equally good as, or incomparable with every other outcome; and ranks the available choices in light of the outcome ranking.

In the case where the decisionmaker is choosing under conditions of uncertainty, the choice-evaluation framework will see each choice as a probability distribution over outcomes (or set of such distributions) and will instruct the decisionmaker how to integrate the outcome ranking with this probability information to rank choices. The best developed theory for doing so is expected utility (EU) theory.

The applicability of EU theory to *moral* decision procedures is controversial—a topic covered in Chapter 7. In that chapter, I will argue that (some refinement of) EU theory is indeed the most attractive way to generate a moral ranking of choices from a moral ranking of outcomes. However, this position is in no way essential to my espousal of consequentialism. Consequentialism is a more generic idea than EU theory. The idea, again, is that the outcome ranking be combined with probability information *in some way* (via the route of EU theory or in some other way) to yield a ranking of choices.

In the (highly simplified) case where the decisionmaker is choosing under conditions of certainty—she knows for certain which outcome each choice available to her would yield—the debate about EU theory drops aside. A consequentialist decision procedure, in that case, says: choose the action with the best outcome (or, if no such action exists, any action yielding an undominated outcome[40]).

In particular, a moral decision procedure, if consequentialist, says in the case of choice under certainty: choose the action with the *morally* best outcome. And the ranking of outcomes, in this case, must at least satisfy a condition of "impartiality" (the essence of moral reasoning.). What exactly does it mean for a ranking of outcomes to be "impartial"? A full answer is controversial; it will depend on whether the moral view is welfarist, if so whether well-being is interpersonally comparable, and other complications. At a minimum, however, we can say this: the criterion for ranking outcomes as morally better or worse must not refer to particular individuals, using their proper names or other expressions that refer to particular individuals.[41] For example, a criterion which says that outcome x is better than outcome y iff x is better for the well-being of Jim would hardly be suitable as the outcome-ranking component of a *moral* decision procedure. Nor would a criterion which says that outcome x is better than outcome y iff x is better for the well-being of the decision-maker. *That* criterion would work well in specifying a kind of "prudential" consequentialist decision procedure, but not in specifying a consequentialist decision procedure which is meant to provide moral guidance.

Who could object to the consequentialist position that the morally appropriate choice (under conditions of certainty) is the choice with the best outcome, as ranked using some impartial criterion for assessing the goodness of outcomes; and that (under conditions of uncertainty) the morally appropriate choice should be identified by integrating the impartial outcome ranking with probability information? How on earth should one make a *moral* decision, except by striving to make the consequences the best they can be, as seen from an impartial viewpoint?

In fact, there are very serious objections to this position, mooted at great length in the philosophical literature. They fall under two main headings: objections to

---

[40] This qualification is needed to deal with the possibilities of ties and incomparability. Under conditions of certainty, with action a yielding outcome x for sure, this action yields an undominated outcome if no outcome yielded by any other action in the choice set is better than x. See below, p. 42.

[41] In other words, consequentialism employs an *agent-neutral* ranking of outcomes. The distinction between agent-neutral and -relative considerations, and the relevance of that distinction to understanding consequentialism, has been much discussed in the philosophical literature. See, e.g., Brown (2010); Louise (2004); McNaughton and Rawling (1991); Nagel (1970); Pettit (1997); Portmore (2007); Rønnow-Rasmussen (2009); Scheffler (1994, ch. 1); Schroeder (2007); Skorupski (1995).

consequentialism based on agent-relative constraints, and objections based on agent-relative permissions.

A. Agent-Relative Constraints

One major objection to consequentialism is based on the putative moral force of traditional, deontological moral norms prohibiting acts such as killing, injuring, lying, breaking promises, or coercion.[42] A crucial feature of these norms, as explored in the literature, is that they are "agent-relative." The norms do *not* have the structure of describing some type of act in generic terms and then instructing decisionmakers to make choices which minimize the number of acts of that type. For example, the deontological norm against killing does not instruct agents to act so as to minimize the number of killings. If it did, such a norm (at least under conditions of certainty) would be isomorphic to a consequentialist view that ranks outcomes in terms of the number of killings. But the deontological moral norm against killing (as understood by those who espouse this norm) tells the decisionmaker that she is prohibited from performing a single killing, even if that act prevents K killings (where K may not be infinite, but is greater than one).

More generally, an agent-relative constraint first identifies some type of act in generic terms (killing, injuring, lying), and then in guiding the agent's choices gives priority to the nonoccurrence of this type of act when performed by the agent, as opposed to its nonoccurrence when performed by others. It says to each decision-maker: as between your performing an act of that type, and some other choice whose upshot is that K other actors (with K greater than one) perform an act of that type, make the latter choice.

A moral framework incorporating such a norm is not isomorphic to *any* consequentialist moral framework (where a consequentialist moral framework, again, revolves around an *impartial* ranking of an outcome set). In order to express the agent-relative constraint in the form of a choice procedure that revolves around a ranking of an outcome set—even for the highly simplified case of choice under certainty—we would need to rank outcomes so that the occurrence of a certain type of action when performed by the decisionmaker is given more negative weight than the occurrence of the very same type of action when performed by someone else. But this would be a stark violation of impartiality. We would have ranked outcomes using a criterion that refers to a particular person—not by using a proper name, but by using an indexical, "you."

At first blush, agent-relative constraints are puzzling. Morality, again, is impartial. Everyone—consequentialists and nonconsequentialist alike—agrees to that. Nonconsequentialists do not suggest that a normative framework telling each actor

---

[42] The philosophical literature on agent-relative constraints is vast. See, e.g., Brand-Ballard (2004); Darwall (1986); Hurley (1997); Kagan (1989); Kamm (1992); Korsgaard (1993); Kumar (1999); Lippert-Rasmussen (1996, 1999); Nagel (1986, ch. 9); Nozick (1974, ch. 3); Scheffler (1994).

to maximize her own interests is a plausible *moral* view. So why is it morally plausible that each actor should give priority to her nonperformance of some problematic act, as opposed to the nonoccurrence of such actions when performed by others? Various philosophers have emphasized this puzzling feature of agent-relative constraints. As Thomas Nagel puts the puzzle: "How can there be a reason not to twist someone's arm which is not equally a reason to prevent his arm from being twisted by someone else?"[43]

But nonconsequentialists have proposed a variety of defenses of agent-relative constraints. One defense appeals to intuitive judgments about particular cases. For example, it seems intuitively quite wrong for a doctor to kill her patient and harvest the patient's organs in order to save five other persons who will die without the organs. It seems wrong for officials to execute a prisoner they know to be innocent, even if that is the only way to stop an angry mob that demands the execution (a mob which, if not appeased, will kill the prisoner and many others). Hypothetical cases such as these are standard in the literature.

A second defense appeals to more general principles. In particular, various authors have suggested that agent-relative constraints flow from morality's focus on *persons*. For example, Frances Kamm argues that agent-relative constraints express the "inviolability" of persons.[44] Stephen Darwall argues that agent-relativity arises from a dyadic, "person-to-person" structure that, he suggests, is the foundation of moral obligations: each person is a separate source of moral considerations that she can rightly demand each actor recognize, and each actor is accountable to each such person.[45]

A third defense relies on rule-consequentialism. "Consequentialism," as I have defined it here—and as I will elaborate it via the SWF approach—is an *act*-consequentialist approach to moral evaluation. Its decision procedure derives a ranking of each choice situation, directly, from an impartial ranking of outcomes.[46] By contrast, a rule-consequentialist moral theory has a two-tier structure: it uses an impartial ranking of outcomes to rank moral rules, and then instructs agents to follow those rules in making their choices. Rule consequentialism has been defended by various scholars, most recently and quite comprehensively by Brad Hooker, who advocates the following general approach.

> An act is wrong if and only if it is forbidden by the code of rules whose internalization
> by the overwhelming majority of everyone everywhere in each new generation has

---

[43] Nagel (1986, p. 178). For others who have emphasized this puzzling feature of constraints, see sources discussed in Lippert-Rasmussen (1999).

[44] See Kamm (1992).

[45] See Darwall (2006, pp. 35–38).

[46] "Directly" meaning that, in the case of choice under certainty, actions are ranked in accordance with the outcomes they would produce; and, in the case of uncertainty, in virtue of the probability distributions over outcomes (or sets of such distributions, to allow for imprecise probabilities) that each action corresponds to.

maximum expected value in terms of well-being (with some priority for the worst off). The calculation of a code's expected value includes all costs of getting the code internalized.[47]

As is evident in this quotation, Hooker's criterion for good and bad outcomes—like the approach I will defend in this book—is not merely welfarist, but in fact prioritarian. Critically, however, in Hooker's view, the prioritarian ranking of outcomes should not be directly translated into recommendations for any given choice situation, but instead should generate such recommendations in a rule-consequentialist manner. And a key element of Hooker's defense of his variant of rule-consequentialism is that the moral rules it generates (he claims) will track ordinary morality, including the inclusion of agent-relative constraints.

> We believe that, at least generally, physical attack, torture, theft, promise-breaking, lying, and the like are morally wrong. Rule-consequentialism agrees. On the whole, the consequences will be far better if there are generally accepted rules forbidding physical attack, torture, theft, promise-breaking, lying, and the like.[48]

I believe that there are convincing responses to each of these lines of defense of agent-relative constraints. First, our intuitive judgments about particular hypothetical cases may rest upon implicit empirical assumptions that are both hard to dislodge and different from the hypothetical facts needed to make the intuitions truly deontological. In the doctor case, for example, our resistance to killing the one patient for the sake of saving five is a genuinely deontological intuition *if* we believe the five are sure to die absent the killing of the one and *if* the only harms that flow from the killing are the death of this one person. But we may find these factual suppositions too implausible to credit, and actually have different beliefs in thinking about the case. We may believe that there must be some chance of saving the five even if the organs aren't harvested; we may be thinking, not simply about the harm to the patient, but about the incentive effects on future patients who will decline to seek care from the doctor (at a cost to their health) if they anticipate a harvesting risk; and we may be plausibly assuming that the doctor is acting illegally, thus bringing into play the murky question of the moral authority of legal requirements.

Note also that the standard deontological hypotheticals may involve cases in which a putatively agent-relative constraint is breached in order to prevent some other type of act or event, not the very type covered by the constraint. The doctor *kills* a patient to prevent *deaths* (not killings); the authorities bring to bear the legal apparatus of the state to *execute* the innocent prisoner in order to stop the mob from *killing* many people (not to stop the mob from *executing* anyone). Intuitions of this

---

[47] Hooker (2000, p. 32).

[48] Ibid., p. 126.

sort are logically consistent, in the first instance, with a consequentialism that distinguishes between killings and deaths in an impartial ranking of outcomes; and, in the second, one that distinguishes between executions and killings.

Second, arguments to the effect that the person-centered aspect of morality produces agent-relative constraints are, in my view, highly dubious. Consider a case in which I kill one victim with the intention of preventing multiple killings. Why not view this act as more fully expressing my equal respect for all the persons involved—my victim and those whose victimization I prevent—than a decision not to perform the killing?[49] Nor is it clear why a dyadic structure of moral reasons yields agent-relative constraints. Each person may well be a separate source of moral reasons, for each actor; but the totality of each actor's reasons is generated by the whole community of persons, not any person individually. So how do we end up with *agent-relative* constraints that give priority, for each actor, to those persons she directly harms, as opposed to those persons whose harms she prevents? Imagine that some physical action on my part would kill one person but would prevent two other persons from being killed. I am morally accountable to the first person for performing the action, but no less accountable to the two others for not performing it.

Indeed, a central thrust of my defense and elaboration of prioritarianism, in subsequent chapters of this book, will be to merge the person-centered aspect of morality with *consequentialism*: to argue that the most attractive variant of welfare consequentialism is person-centered in the robust sense that it is animated by considerations of fairness (namely, a respect for the separateness of persons), and thus incorporates a prioritarian rather than utilitarian SWF. Far from being inconsistent with consequentialism, the recognition that each person is a distinct source of moral concerns is the key justification—in my view—for a prioritarian ranking of outcomes, sensitive to the fair distribution of well-being.[50]

What about the rule-consequentialist defense of agent-relative constraints?[51] To begin, even assuming that rule-consequentialism is a more attractive moral framework than act-consequentialism, it is at best an empirical conjecture that the optimal rules would incorporate agent-relative constraints, for the kinds of decisions that are

---

[49] See Brand-Ballard (2004, pp. 288–289); Kagan (1991, pp. 919–920); Lippert-Rasmussen (1996, pp. 333–343); Norcross (2009, pp. 94–95).

[50] See in particular Chapter 5. See also Chapters 6 and 7, which rely upon the claim-across-outcome conception of fairness developed in Chapter 5.

In their well-known book, *Fairness versus Welfare*, Kaplow and Shavell (2002) use "fairness" to mean non-welfarism, and argue against "fairness" thus understood. By contrast, I see "fairness" as a way to structure moral argument which is perfectly consistent with welfarism. Thus the account advanced here differs *semantically* from theirs—they use "fairness" and "non-welfarism" as synonyms, I do not—but this semantic difference, without more, has no substantive implications. Both my account, and theirs, is welfarist. Moreover, I argue for a distribution-sensitive SWF, while they stress that welfarism is potentially sensitive to distribution.

[51] For critiques of rule-consequentialism, see Arneson (2005); Kagan (1998, pp. 223–239); and the critical essays in Hooker, Mason, and Miller (2000).

the focus of this book, namely governmental policy choices and other large-scale choices. Hovering over the rule-consequentialism debate is the possibility that rule- and act-consequentialism might converge, either in general or at least in a large subset of cases.[52] Why exactly is there nonconvergence in this kind of case? Wouldn't the expected benefit of explicitly consequential evaluation of large-scale choices swamp decision costs and other rationales for rule-based thinking that might apply to less impactful actions? To investigate that conjecture systematically would require the very sorts of tools elaborated in this book. Extant philosophical discussion about whether the optimal rules would incorporate deontological limitations (even in the case of large-scale choices) has been informal and, frankly, somewhat speculative.

A more fundamental point, which directly challenges rule-consequentialism, is that the framework handles noncompliance in a counterintuitive manner. Hooker's approach, for example, says to abide by the rule r^* that would have best consequences if internalized by the vast majority. But what if I'm acting under conditions where, in fact, the vast majority have not internalized r^*? In that case, wouldn't it be rational to take account of how they're actually behaving? It might be responded that rule-consequentialism needs to be structured in the manner Hooker proposes so as to be consistent with our deontological intuitions about particular cases. But structuring it in his preferred manner produces counterintuitive results in other cases, namely intuitions about correct behavior in second-best situations. Imagine that it would be best for the work day to start at 7 a.m. In my society, everyone starts work at 8 a.m. Should I show up at 7 a.m. nonetheless?

These brief responses to major elements of the case for agent-relative constraints can at most show that the debate about such constraints is a genuine debate. Act-consequentialism is not the non-starter that many nonconsequentialists suggest. Still, nothing I have said in this quick discussion will convince the reader who firmly believes in agent-relative constraints or even the reader who is uncertain but still skeptical about consequentialism. What can *you* get out of this book?

First, some nonconsequentialists adopt a *hybrid* view. They believe that it is morally best or morally encouraged to maximize good consequences, within the limits of agent-relative constraints.[53] On this sort of view, the exercise undertaken in the remainder of this book can be seen as an attempt to specify one *part* of morality, namely the identification of good consequences.

Second, as already suggested, the SWF framework has much relevance to rule-consequentialists. Assume (which I dispute) that rule-consequentialism, as developed by Hooker or in some other manner, is the most attractive moral theory. If so, we need an account of what good consequences are, and a decision procedure that scholars (if not actors) can use to compare *rules* in light of those. The bulk of the book engages the core question, relevant to rule- and act-consequentialists alike, of

[52] See Lyons (1965).
[53] See Kagan (1998, pp. 78–84).

how to rank an outcome set. And the method the book defends in Chapter 7 for deriving a ranking of an action set from the outcome ranking can readily be transposed to the case of deriving a ranking of rules. Simply substitute **R**, a set of possible rules, for **A**, a set of possible actions.

Third, and most generally, this book can be seen as a contribution to the debate between consequentialists and nonconsequentialists. To reach a fully considered judgment about whether consequentialism can indeed respect the moral status of persons, we should have on the table a well-specified version of consequentialism that attempts to do just that, and compare it with moral views that incorporate agent-relative constraints. This book helps (I hope) to improve our understanding of the structure of a moral choice-evaluation framework which, on the one hand, is consequentialist because it revolves around an impartial ranking of outcomes, but on the other hand seeks to make this ranking fair to each person—doing so by seeing each person as a distinct locus of a moral claim in favor of an outcome in which she is better off, with worse-off individuals having stronger such claims.

B. Agent-Relative Options

An important worry about utilitarianism and, more generally, consequentialism is that it undermines the natural partiality that a decisionmaker has for her own concerns. Bernard Williams famously attacked utilitarianism along these lines, arguing that it undermines individual "integrity."[54] The worry is that the particular kind of impartiality required by utilitarianism and, more generally, consequentialism, would function to *alienate* individuals from their friends, families, and projects. As Samuel Scheffler elaborates:

> [Utilitarianism] requires the agent to pursue his projects, commitments, and personal relationships whenever and to the extent that doing so would have the best overall outcome impersonally judged, and to neglect or abandon them whenever and to the extent that *that* would have the best overall outcome impersonally judged. Utilitarianism thus requires the agent to allocate energy and attention to the projects and people he cares most about *in strict proportion* to the value from an impersonal standpoint of his doing so, even though people typically acquire and care about their commitments quite independently of, and out of proportion to, the value that their having and caring about them is assigned in an impersonal ranking of overall states of affairs.[55]

For short, let us call this the "alienation" critique of consequentialism.

It is important to distinguish the alienation critique from worries about decision costs in the sense of time and resources. The latter concern is that the expenditure of

---

[54] See Smart and Williams (1973, especially pp. 108–118).
[55] Scheffler (1994, p. 9). See also, e.g., Card (2004); Jackson (1991); Kagan (1989); Railton (1984).

a quantum of time implementing a consequentialist decision procedure, or the expenditure of resources to do so (computers, overhead for facilities to house analysts, etc.), prevents the use of that time and those resources in other valuable ways. I have tried to respond to the time/resource worry, admittedly in a somewhat vague fashion, by limiting the applicability of the consequentialist decision procedure defended here to "large-scale" projects.

By contrast, the alienation critique is that the impartial perspective demanded of the evaluator by a consequentialist decision procedure is such as to undercut the kind of attachment to friends, family, and particular projects that is a precondition of the welfare value of those relationships and projects. Relationships with friends and family are a major source of well-being; but to be a real friend or a good parent is to be partial toward the friend or child. An individual's well-being can be advanced, too, by her pursuit of personal projects (for example, working for some cause, writing a book, building a house, etc.); but such pursuit advances well-being only if the individual is committed to the project, if it is hers. By stepping back from the posture of attachment to the projects and relationships to which the evaluator is normally partial, in order to engage in consequentialist deliberation, the evaluator undermines the welfare-value of those projects and relationships (for herself and in the case of relationships, for the others involved)—and not only during the time spent deliberating, but also perhaps at other times by virtue of her *disposition* to adopt this alienated perspective. That, in a nutshell, is the alienation critique of consequentialist decision procedures.

To begin, the alienation critique seems at first blush inapplicable to paradigmatic large-scale decisions, namely governmental policy choices. Who worries that governmental officials might be alienated from their relationships or personal projects? We already expect officials to be impartial. Ronald Dworkin has expressed this idea eloquently:

> We each claim a personal point of view, ambitions and attachments of our own we are at liberty to pursue, free from the claims of others to equal attention, concern, and resource. We insist on an area of personal moral sovereignty within which each of us may prefer the interests of family and friends and devote himself to projects that are selfish. . . .
>
> We allow officials acting in their official capacity no such area at all. They must, we say, treat all members of their community as equals, and the individual's normal latitude for self-preference is called corruption in their case.[56]

Because governmental officials are in any event held to strict standards of impartiality, it is hard to see how the employment by officials (or the researchers advising them) of a consequentialist rather than nonconsequentialist choice-evaluation procedure would, as such, undermine anyone's well-being.

---

[56] Dworkin (1986, p. 174).

Generalizing this point, we might say that a decisionmaker making the kind of large-scale decisions where policy-analytic frameworks typically come into play (and where this book recommends the use of the SWF framework) is doing so in virtue of social practices that (1) confer upon her some powerful social role, e.g., the role of government official, that allows her to have a large impact on the world; and that (2) in virtue of this powerful role *already* include a social norm that obligates the decisionmaker not to take account of her special attachments—so that it is hard to see how it would reduce well-being for *her* to engage in consequentialist reasoning.

This response may not fully rebut the alienation critique.[57] But I believe that a more fundamental response to that critique is available. It is simply not clear why a moral decision procedure is *especially* alienating in virtue of having a consequentialist structure. The moral perspective is an impartial one. It means adopting a point of view in which the agent's interests are not given priority, just because they are hers, over others'. Impartial decisionmaking might be specified, in consequentialist fashion, as a mandate to think about how outcomes are impartially ranked; or it might be specified, in nonconsequentialist fashion, as a mandate to think about which agent-relative constraints emerge from the equal status of persons. But in either event a willingness to consider choice from a broader perspective that encompasses other persons' interests, relationships, projects and attachments, not just the agent's own, is the hallmark of any variant of moral thinking. So it is very hard to see how the alienation critique undercuts consequentialism in particular.

Clearly, there are delicate questions here—about squaring the attitudinal preconditions of various welfare goods with the kind of thinking required by consequentialist or nonconsequentialist moral deliberation—that bear fuller discussion. For the reader who remains worried that explicitly consequentialist deliberation can be alienating, this book still has much to offer. One standard solution to the alienation critique, advanced by Scheffler, is to argue that morality contains "agent-relative" *permissions*.

> Such a prerogative would . . . make it permissible for agents to devote time and energy to their projects, commitments, and personal relationships out of proportion to the weight

---

[57] As already mentioned, one can imagine private individuals (e.g., philanthropists) making large-scale choices. Furthermore, it is important to distinguish between the kind of impartiality that is socially required of government decisionmakers and other impactful actors, and the kind of impartiality that is required by consequentialism. Consequentialism, plausibly, requires decisionmakers to employ a ranking of outcomes that is impartial as between all members of the world's population—indeed, impartial between all members of all generations, past, present, and future. By contrast, governmental officials are required to be impartial between citizens, but not between citizens and non-citizens. And it might be argued that this kind of *limited* impartiality quite typically demanded of an individual who acts in her capacity as a member of some social group—impartiality as between group members, but a general partiality for group members as opposed to outsiders—allows the existence of such groups to be a source of well-being. Cf. Dworkin (1986, ch. 6), arguing that genuine associative obligations can arise in groups in which members have a sense of special responsibility to each other.

from an impersonal standpoint of their doing so. . . . At the same time, however, such a prerogative would not permit one to pursue one's own projects at all costs. Thus such a prerogative would enable a normative view to accommodate personal integrity without collapsing into egoism.[58]

If a consequentialist moral framework includes agent-relative permissions, the morally *best* choice can be different from the choice that the framework tells the agent she morally *ought* to take. If choice *a* maximizes good consequences, but choice *b* advances the agent's projects and commitments in such a manner as to be subsumed by an agent-relative permission, then the agent is not told that she morally "ought" to choose *a*. Instead, she is permitted to make either choice. Choice *a*, the better choice, is "supererogatory"—which is just another way of saying that this choice is morally best, but not a choice that morality instructs the agent to perform.[59]

To be clear, this book will *not* defend a moral framework that has this structure of agent-relative permissions, supererogation, and an ought/best disjunction. Instead, I defend the use of the SWF framework as a tool for ranking choices as better or worse, and thereby directly determining which choice the agent morally ought to undertake. However, the reader worried about the alienation critique can see the framework as a tool for ranking choices as morally better or worse, which is then employed *along with* some criterion for identifying agent-relative permissions, in order to arrive at a conclusion concerning what the decisionmaker ought to do.[60]

IV. WELFARISM

Welfarism is a particular species of consequentialism. I have assumed that any moral choice-evaluation framework is person-centered. Such a framework is, in addition, consequentialist if it revolves around an impartial ranking of outcomes. It is not only consequentialist, but *welfarist* if it tells the decisionmaker to characterize outcomes, as far as possible, in terms of the various sources of human well-being; and to rank outcomes as a sole function of human well-being (more precisely, so that the

---

[58] Scheffler (1994, p. 21). See also Kagan (1998, pp. 153–170), on the structure of such permissions.

[59] Even without agent-relative permissions, the choice singled out by a moral choice-evaluation framework as the one which the agent morally ought to perform need not be the choice which, all-things-considered, she ought to perform. Whether moral reasons always override other considerations is an open question. See above, n. 20. The thrust of agent-relative permissions is to incorporate the overriding significance of the decisionmaker's personal projects *within* morality, by giving her a *moral* permission to pursue them.

[60] And if the reader both is worried about the alienation critique, and is a hybrid deontologist who believes good consequences should be pursued within agent-relative constraints, she can see the SWF framework as a tool that can be integrated with two other elements—agent-relative constraints and agent-relative permissions—in order to arrive at a conclusion regarding which choice the decisionmaker morally ought to perform.

Pareto-indifference and Pareto-superiority principles are satisfied—see the last section of this chapter for a more formal characterization of welfarism.)

Utilitarianism, in turn, is simply one variant of welfarism. In many discussions it is assumed that the welfarist necessarily ranks outcomes in utilitarian fashion, by calculating the simple, unweighted sum of individual utilities. That is just false. An important theme in the social choice literature is that the SWF framework (which is welfarist) can employ an SWF whose functional form is *not* the straight summation of utilities, but instead is sensitive to the distribution of well-being.

But this observation immediately raises a question. If one is attempting to structure a person-centered, consequentialist decision procedure so as to be sensitive to fair distribution, why make that procedure *welfarist*? Such a procedure, because person-centered, must attend to persons' interests. But the concept of an "interest" is meant to be vague, here. There are a variety of ways to specify this concept; "well-being" is only one among several.

Indeed, a large scholarly literature addresses precisely this problem: identifying the appropriate "currency" for distributive justice. Insofar as morality requires the fair interpersonal distribution of some item, what exactly is that item? Is distributive justice concerned with the distribution of resources, as Ronald Dworkin suggests? With the distribution of what Amartya Sen terms "functionings" and "capabilities" (which are opportunities to function)? Or with the distribution of well-being?[61]

I believe that a strong prima facie case can be made for ranking outcomes in terms of well-being, as opposed to resources, "functionings" and "capabilities" (insofar as these are distinct from well-being), or any other currency. To adopt a resourcist currency for distributive justice seems to fetishize material resources, as Amartya Sen argues. Imagine that I'm better than you in converting resources into well-being. Why, then, think that we're treated fairly if you and I receive the same amount of material resources? But an exactly parallel critique can be leveled against using any other currency (insofar as it can diverge from well-being). Sen is vague in what he means by "functioning," and the term may well be just a synonym for well-being, properly understood, but let us imagine that it is not. Imagine that "functioning" does not include the quality of someone's social and professional life. You and I are equally well fed, housed, and educated, but you have a rich and rewarding social and professional life, while I'm lonely and unsuccessful, through no fault of my own. You've been lucky in your achieved well-being; I've been unlucky. Why think that

---

[61] The seminal contributions to this literature are: Arneson (1989, 1990); G. Cohen (1989, 1993); Dworkin (1981a, 1981b); and Sen (1982, ch. 16; 1985b). Sen has elaborated his theory of "functionings" and "capabilities" in many other publications. See, e.g., Sen (1985a, 1987a, 1993, 1995). For discussions of Sen's ideas, see, e.g., Alkire (2002); Moore and Crisp (1996, pp. 604–608); Sumner (1996, pp. 60–68). For general discussions of welfarism or the "equality of what?" debate, see, e.g., Arneson (2000b); Clayton and Williams (1999); Daniels (1990); Moore and Crisp (1996); Scanlon (1998, ch. 3); Sumner (1996, ch. 7); Vallentyne (2005a). The cross-cutting literature on individual responsibility is cited in Barry (2008).

this outcome is no worse, qua fair distribution, than one in which we both end up at the same level of well-being?

However, the literature just referenced suggests a variety of potential objections to using well-being as the currency for distributive justice. This literature is particularly complicated and nuanced. All I can hope to do, here, is to summarize what I take to be the major objections to welfarism.[62]

One worry is that interpersonal comparisons of well-being are impossible, and so we are forced to adopt some non-well-being currency for measuring distributive justice as a fallback. Chapter 3 will argue at length that we can make interpersonal comparisons, building on seminal ideas developed by John Harsanyi.

A second worry is that a welfarist currency for distributive justice disadvantages individuals who are happy or whose preferences are easily satisfied. This concern is suggested by Sen's well-known discussion of persons whose lives seem quite unfortunate but have adapted to their fates.

> [One difficulty] with welfarism arises from the particular interpretation of well-being that utility provides. To judge the well-being of a person exclusively in the metric of happiness or desire-fulfillment has some obvious limitations. These limitations are particularly damaging in the context of interpersonal comparisons of well-being, since the extent of happiness reflects what one can expect and how the social "deal" seems in comparison with that. A person who has had a life of misfortune, with very little opportunities, and rather little hope, may be more easily reconciled to deprivations than others reared in more fortunate and affluent circumstances. The metric of happiness may, therefore, distort the extent of deprivation, in a specific and biased way. The hopeless beggar, the precarious landless labourer, the dominated housewife, the hardened unemployed or the over-exhausted coolie may all take pleasures in small mercies, and manage to suppress intense suffering for the necessity of continuing survival, but it would be ethically deeply mistaken to attach a correspondingly small value to the loss of their well-being because of this survival strategy. The same problem arises with the other interpretation of utility, namely, desire-fulfillment, since the hopelessly deprived lack the courage to desire much, and their deprivations are muted and deadened in the scale of desire-fulfillment.[63]

But well-being need not be reduced to happiness (good mental states), nor need it be reduced to the satisfaction of individuals' actual preferences. We can say that the persons Sen describes have a low level of well-being because they fail to realize a range of objective welfare goods. Chapter 3 will pursue an approach which is closely related to this—analyzing well-being in terms of individuals' convergent, fully informed, fully rational extended preferences (preferences over life-histories). Imagine, very plausibly, that individuals under conditions of full information and

---

[62] My analysis, here, is indebted to Arneson (2000b).

[63] Sen (1987a, pp. 45–46).

rationality would strongly disprefer to live the life-histories of the persons Sen describes—strongly disprefer in virtue of the fact that these persons have an abased social status, are unable to pursue intellectual and professional pursuits, lack leisure time, and so forth, and despite the fact that these persons have reasonably positive mental states and easily satisfied desires. Then the ideal-preferentialist account of well-being defended in Chapter 3 will reach the verdict that the persons are quite badly off indeed.

A third worry is that well-being understood as preference satisfaction is too idiosyncratic to be the currency for distributive justice. However, if we understand well-being in terms of *convergent* fully informed, fully rational extended preferences, then idiosyncratic benefits do not influence the ranking of outcomes.

A fourth and reciprocal worry is that any objective index of well-being will be "illiberal." Individuals have a diversity of conceptions of the good life. To say that one life is better than another, in terms of objective goods, fails to respect this diversity. But if we rank outcomes based on individuals' *convergent* fully informed, fully rational, extended preferences—so that well-being is generated from a kind of overlapping consensus of individuals' conceptions of the good life—the illiberalism worry can be parried.

With respect to all four of these worries about using well-being as the currency for distributive justice, my response has not been to reject the worry out of hand. Instead, I have suggested that the worry raises a real concern, but can be accommodated by a suitable version of welfarism. Of course, this suggestion is just a promissory note. The reader is invited to read the rest of the book and see whether the note is redeemed.

A fifth worry *is* one that I reject out of hand. One aspect of Sen's multifaceted discussion of functionings and capabilities is the suggestion that we might care about advancing individuals' "agency goals," even where doing so does not advance individuals' well-being.

> A person's agency achievement refers to the realization of goals and values she has reasons to pursue, whether or not they are connected with her own well-being. A person as an agent need not be guided only by her own well-being, and agency achievement refers to the person's success in the pursuit of the totality of her considered goals and objectives. If a person aims at, say, the independence of her country, or the prosperity of her community, or some such general goal, her agency achievement would involve evaluation of states of affairs in light of those objects, and not merely in the light of the extent to which those achievements would contribute to her own well-being.[64]

Sen is quite right to distinguish between a person's "agency goals" and her well-being. Indeed, the distinction between all-things-considered preferences and

---

[64] Sen (1995, p. 56). See Sobel (1998).

self-interested preferences will be a major element of Chapter 3. We might say that an individual's "agency goals" are considerations that can prompt the individual to have an all-things-considered preference in favor of one rather than a second outcome even though, as a matter of self-interest, she is indifferent between the two outcomes.

However, I believe it is problematic to think that distributive justice is concerned with the satisfaction of individuals' all-things-considered preferences, as opposed to the advancement of individual well-being. Part of the difficulty in thinking clearly about this problem is that many different features of outcomes can contribute to someone's well-being—not just the quality of the individual's physical or mental states—and thus she can quite rationally have a self-interested preference for these features. So let us carefully construct a case in which the preferences involved are pretty clearly disinterested. The members of a prosperous community, let us imagine, are all more or less equally well off. The community has a budget surplus. The community has agreed that the surplus should be used to help the impoverished. Some of the members prefer that it be sent to one far-off country (whose plight they have learned about through the internet), others that the surplus be sent to a different far-off country. None of the members have any particular involvement with either country. The matter is resolved by a vote, and one country is chosen. Sending the funds to that country rather than the alternative advances the winners' disinterested preferences, and frustrates the losers', without affecting anyone's well-being within the prosperous community. Do we think that the losers now have a claim in distributive justice against the winners? That seems counterintuitive.

A sixth and very important worry involves opportunity. Shouldn't the ranking of outcomes be sensitive to individuals' *opportunity* for well-being, rather than well-being per se?

There are actually several distinct ideas subsumed under the rubric of "opportunity." One is that having options, itself, is or can be a source of well-being. If there are more options open to Jim in outcome x than outcome y, then (ceteris paribus) outcome x is better for Jim than outcome y.

This insight does not press *against* welfarism, but toward a suitably nuanced, non-hedonic conception of well-being (one that recognizes that freedom is itself a determinant of individual welfare) and toward a relatively rich description of outcomes (so as to characterize the options that are open to individuals at various points in their lives, and not just the end-states they realize).

A different construal of the "opportunity" worry presents what I take to be the most powerful challenge to welfarism: namely, that the ranking of outcomes should be sensitive to individual *responsibility* for well-being shortfalls. As Richard Arneson observes:

> Suppose that two individuals have identical welfare at present and that the social planner can choose between two policies, policy A, which confers a one unit welfare gain on the first individual, Smith, and policy B, which confers a one unit welfare gain on the second individual, Jones. On a welfarist view, it seems there is nothing to choose between Smith

and Jones. . . . But suppose we add to the story the detail that whereas both Smith and Jones have low welfare at present, Smith has been prudent and responsible in the conduct of his life but suffered an accident through no fault of his own, whereas Jones, born to every advantage, has behaved in a thoroughly irresponsible fashion and culpably mismanaged his life in all respects. We may then feel that justice should favor aid to Smith over aid to Jones, and thus policy A over policy B, but this thought seem not to be available to any variety of welfarist.[65]

For the consequentialist who seeks to structure a ranking of outcomes that will be sensitive to what individuals can claim, as a matter of fairness, this objection to welfarism is quite devastating. To put Arneson's story in outcome form: Consider outcomes x, y, and z. For each person i, with the exception of Smith and Jones, it is the case that i's well-being level in the three outcomes is the same. Smith's welfare level in x is the same as Jones' in x (denote this level as u). In outcome y, Jones' welfare level has been raised to $u + \Delta u$, while Smith remains at u. In outcome z, Smith has been raised to $u + \Delta u$, while Jones now remains at u.[66] If the fact that Jones is at level u in x is Jones' fault, while the fact that Smith is at level u in x is not Smith's fault, might it not be *fairer* that z rather than y occur? And yet because the welfarist orders outcomes solely as a function of individual well-being, she is committed to counting y and z as equally good outcomes.

I therefore see the SWF framework as a first step toward a choice-evaluation framework that would implement a *refinement* of welfarism: a choice-evaluation framework such that the "currency" for ranking outcomes is not well-being, but responsibility-adjusted well-being. How the adjustment process should work raises large questions about the best analysis of "responsibility." It is beyond the scope of this book to address such questions. To even begin doing so, with any thoroughness, would take many more pages than I have available. The problem of responsibility is, intrinsically, deeply difficult, tied up with the philosophically vexed problem of free will. And the philosophical literature on responsibility is arguably more contested (and certainly no less contested) than the literatures I do engage in this book, regarding well-being, prioritarianism and competing conceptions of equality, and personal identity.

For these reasons, problems of responsibility are placed to one side. I adopt the premise of welfarism as a kind of *approximation*: a premise which is valid in ranking outcome sets where individual responsibility is not at issue (where everyone's well-being in every outcome is a matter of "brute luck"[67]), but which otherwise needs to be modified. This book focuses on the task of specifying welfarism, hopeful that the

---

[65] Arneson (2000b, p. 504).

[66] Strictly, because the utilities measuring well-being are at most unique up to a positive ratio transformation, these should be "ru" and "$r\Delta u$." See Chapter 3.

[67] Meaning that, for any outcome x and any individual i, any shortfall between i's well-being in x and a higher level would not be i's responsibility, were x to occur. See Chapter 5, pp. 319–320; Chapter 8, pp. 579–584.

tools thereby developed can ultimately be modified in light of the thorny problem of responsibility. What the modification might look like is discussed, briefly, in Chapter 8.

V. WELFARISM: A FORMAL CHARACTERIZATION

Prior sections have reviewed the case for why a moral decision procedure should be "welfarist"—that is, exclusively person-centered, consequentialist, and oriented around human well-being rather than other possible currencies for ranking outcomes. Here, I provide a more rigorous characterization of the structure of a welfarist decision procedure. This formal structure will be the basis for discussions throughout the rest of the book.

There is some decisionmaker, who at some moment in time t^* is trying to decide what she morally ought to do at t^*. A moral decision procedure or evaluation framework consists in methodologies, formulas, principles, etc., that the decisionmaker can actually use in arriving at a conclusion about what she should do.[68]

A welfarist decision procedure, because it is consequentialist, helps the decisionmaker answer this question via the following structure. It tells the decisionmaker to construct a choice set $A = \{a, b, c, \ldots\}$, comprising some of the actions that the decisionmaker might take; it tells the decisionmaker to construct an outcome set $O = \{x, y, z, \ldots\}$, comprising some of the possible outcomes of the choices; it furnishes principles for morally ranking the outcomes in O; and it furnishes principles for deriving a moral ranking of the choices in A from the ranking of the outcome set O. These sets can be finite, countably infinite, or uncountably infinite.

More precisely, the decision procedure tells the decisionmaker to reason in this explicitly consequentialist fashion for sufficiently "large-scale" choices. I will not discuss what the form of normative guidance for small-scale choices is, nor do I have any insight into the threshold procedure that the decisionmaker should use in deciding whether the choice at hand is "large-scale."

An important debate in decision theory concerns whether the elements of a choice set A should be thought of as immediate actions (physical actions or speech acts that the decisionmaker can perform at t^*) or intertemporal plans (plans which the decisionmaker can adopt at t^*, whereby she formulates an intention to perform various physical actions or speech acts at some points in time after t^*, typically contingent on what occurs after t^*). In the case of a policymaker, an immediate action

---

[68] In addition, a researcher or adviser can presumably use it to evaluate what the decisionmaker morally should do; and these third parties, or the decisionmaker herself, can presumably use the procedure at some time before t^* or after t^* in order to decide what the decisionmaker morally should do or should have done at t^*. A welfarist choice-evaluation procedure will have the very same structure in these cases of third-party or noncontemporaneous assessment as in the paradigm case of first party, contemporaneous assessment, although the particular probabilities assigned to outcomes (in moving from the outcome to the action ranking) will be different.

might be making a legal utterance (enacting a regulation or statute) at t^*, while a temporally extended plan might be formulating an intention to make a series of legal utterances over time. This question is discussed in Chapter 7. The question is, obviously, a very important one—but it can be detached from questions concerning the construction and ranking of the outcome set **O**, which will be the focus of Chapters 2 through 6. The analysis and argumentation in those chapters is fully consistent both with the view that the elements of the choice set are immediate actions, and with the view that they are intertemporal plans.

The decisionmaker is a human decisionmaker, and thus her cognitive abilities are limited. She is "boundedly rational." An attractive moral decision procedure must be one that *she* can use. This means, to begin, that the choice set **A** cannot consist of every possible immediate action that the decisionmaker can perform at t^*, or every possible plan she can formulate at t^*. It is not within the cognitive capacities of a human decisionmaker (even aided by computers) to think about the totality of her possible choices. So **A** must consist in some subset of the immediate actions/plans available to the decisionmaker at t^*. She consciously considers some alternatives, and just ignores others. How to identify that subset is a huge problem in decision theory—not just for welfare consequentialists, but for anyone who purports to give normative guidance—and little intellectual progress has been made in solving it.[69] I will not try to tackle the problem in this book, but will rather assume that the decisionmaker has somehow constructed a cognitively tractable set of alternatives **A**, and is now trying to rank its elements as morally better or worse.

The bounded rationality of the decisionmaker means, too, that the outcomes in **O** cannot be complete "possible worlds." A possible world is a full description of a possible history of the universe, from start to finish. It is beyond the cognitive abilities of a human decisionmaker (even aided by computers) to contemplate or mentally process a single possible world, let alone a set of them. Thus each outcome in **O** will be a limited, incomplete description of a possible world.[70]

---

[69] See Adler (2009a).

[70] It is sometimes argued that the "outcomes" which figure in consequentialist analysis should not be whole possible worlds (or simplified descriptions thereof), but *future* outcomes (descriptions of possible future histories of the world), or only those states of affairs that would be *caused* by the choice at hand. See generally Carlson (1995).

As for the first possibility: to the extent that the moral ranking of future outcomes is not separable from what has occurred in the past, why shouldn't the outcomes that figure in moral decisionmaking potentially describe the past as well as the future? (The moral ranking of future outcomes is separable from the past if that ranking is the same regardless of what has occurred in the past. Whether the SWF framework yields such separability depends both on the functional form of the SWF and on the separability properties of the utility functions in **U**. I will not attempt to discuss this topic in detail here, but will note this: the utilitarian SWF yields moral separability of the future from the past if the utility functions in **U** have the temporally additive form, but the continuous prioritarian SWF does not do so even if the utility functions are temporally additive, let alone if they are not. On the temporally additive form, see Chapter 6.)

More specifically, each outcome will have a single period or multiple periods. A period is some length of time: a day, year, decade, etc. The generic characterization of each period in a given outcome is $(\mathbf{a}_{1,t}, \mathbf{a}_{2,t}, \ldots, \mathbf{a}_{N,t}, \mathbf{a}_{imp,t})$, where $\mathbf{a}_{i,t}$ is a vector of attributes of individual i during period t; and $\mathbf{a}_{imp,t}$ are background facts about the world ("imp" is an abbreviation for "impersonal"), such as the price vector, environmental quality, causal laws, or any other facts that are not attributes of individual persons. ("N" appears in the subscript for the final vector of individual attributes because—as discussed below—I assume that there are N individuals who exist in all of the outcomes.) The individual attributes included in $\mathbf{a}_{i,t}$ will be a subset of the totality of types of attributes that characterize persons in a full possible world; similarly, background facts will be an incomplete description of the background facts that obtain in any possible world.

For example, an outcome might simply describe each individual's period-specific consumption of M marketed goods, so that $\mathbf{a}_{i,t}$ takes the form $(q_{i,t}^1, q_{i,t}^2, \ldots, q_{i,t}^M)$, where $q_{i,t}^m$ is the quantity of good m that individual i consumes during period t. Or it might simply describe the total money value of each individual's consumption during the period, so that $\mathbf{a}_{i,t}$ takes the very simple form $c_{i,t}$. In these cases, all of an individual's non-consumption attributes are left undescribed. A different possibility is that an outcome describes an individual's total consumption, leisure, and level of some public good during the period, so that $\mathbf{a}_{i,t}$ takes the form $(c_{i,t}, l_{i,t}, z_{i,t})$. Alternatively, it might characterize an individual's health state (alone, or in conjunction with other attributes).

(A notational aside: It will sometimes aid clarity to denote some individual's attributes in some outcome using functional notation, i.e., a symbol such as "$\mathbf{a}_{i,t}(x)$," which means the attributes of individual i in outcome x during period t. Often, however, it will be clear from context which outcome is involved, and so this functional notation will be unnecessary; in such cases, I will employ a simpler notation and refer to some individual's attributes in some outcome using a symbol such as "$\mathbf{a}_{i,t}$".)

That the elements of $\mathbf{O}$ consist of partially described possible worlds should be unsurprising to anyone familiar with policy analysis or, more generally, economic modeling. The outcomes that are ranked using CBA or other standard policy-analytic

---

As for the second possibility: The moral value of those states of affairs that would be caused by the choice at hand may not be separable from states of affairs which obtain independently. Thus ignoring the latter may skew choice. The best rationale for "causal consequentialism" has to do with a worry concerning choice under uncertainty—namely, that the increase in probability of some outcome x which is associated with performing action a rather than b should reflect the fact that a is likelier to cause x, and not merely the fact that a's performance is stronger evidence that x will obtain. But this important worry is handled by the apparatus of causal decision theory (for example, via the Savage set-up, which assigns probabilities to outcomes by assigning them to "states" which are causally independent of the choices at hand). See Chapter 7. If this apparatus is employed, outcomes should include everything that matters to the decisionmaker (modulo the need to simplify outcomes so as to make them cognitively tractable), not merely causal consequences.

frameworks, or that figure in economic models, are always the kinds of limited descriptions of reality discussed two paragraphs above. (The types of individual attributes included in these simplified outcomes are very often some subset of the types mentioned in that paragraph: an individual's consumption, leisure, health, and enjoyment of different public goods.) The simplified character of the elements of **O** is discussed at great length in Chapter 4.

The decision procedure derives a ranking of the choice set **A** from a ranking of the outcome set **O**. More precisely, each ranking is a quasiordering, possibly incomplete. Throughout the book, when I use terms such as "ranking," "ordering," and so forth, I mean a possibly incomplete quasiordering, unless I specify otherwise.

What is a "quasiordering"? This is a very general idea, which can be used in talking about any set of objects $S = \{q, r, s \ldots\}$. A quasiordering is a *reflexive* and *transitive* binary relation on the set. It is typically denoted by the symbol "$\succeq$" or the phrase "at least as good as." The relation is *reflexive*: Each object is at least as good as itself. The relation is *transitive*: If q is at least as good as r, and r is at least as good as s, then q is at least as good as s.[71]

A quasiordering can, but need not, be complete. A *complete* quasiordering has the following property: For every possible pair of items in **S**, either the first is at least as good as the second, or the second is at least as good as the first, or both. An incomplete quasiordering lacks this completeness property. That means that there is at least one pair of items, call them s and t, such that s is not at least as good as t, nor t at least as good as s. In this case, it is typical to say that s and t are *incomparable* or *noncomparable*.

Given some set **S** and some reflexive and transitive binary relation on that set (the "at least as good as" relation, $\succeq$), we can define two other relations: a *transitive, irreflexive,* and *asymmetric* relation denoted "$>$" or "better than"; and a *transitive, reflexive,* and *symmetric* relation denoted "$\sim$" or "equally good as."[72] Given two items in **S**, the first is better than the second iff (1) the first is at least as good as the second and (2) the second is not at least as good as the first. Given two items in **S**, the first is equally good as the second iff (1) the first is at least as good as the second and (2) the second is at least as good as the first. It is easy to see that the binary relations of "better than" and "equally good as," defined in this way from the basic relation of "at least as good as," are indeed transitive, irreflexive, and asymmetric (in the case of "better than") and transitive, reflexive, and symmetric (in the case of "equally good as").

---

[71] "Quasiorderings" are sometimes referred to as "quasiorders" or as "preorders." On their properties, see, e.g., Ok (2007, pp. 9–20); Sen (1979a, ch. 1*).

[72] To say that a binary relation is "asymmetric" means: for any two items, if the first bears the relation to the second, then the second does not bear the relation to the first. To say that a binary relation is "symmetric" means: for any two items, if the first bears the relation to the second, then the second bears the relation to the first. Finally, a binary relation is "irreflexive" if no item bears the relation to itself.

Strictly speaking, a quasiordering is any reflexive, transitive binary relation $\geqslant$ on a set S, and the relations $>$ and $\sim$ are just the relations generated from $\geqslant$ in the manner just described. But it is extremely natural to use the natural-language term "at least as good as" to refer to $\geqslant$, and the terms "better than" and "equally good as" to refer to $>$ and $\sim$, respectively. It is a platitude about the ordinary concept of "better than" that it is transitive, irreflexive, and asymmetric; it is a platitude about the ordinary concept of "equally good as" that it is transitive, reflexive, and symmetric. Intuitively (at least if one is a consequentialist) it seems that our decisions should reflect the comparative "goodness" of outcomes and actions, in the ordinary sense of "good," and it is a natural thought to formalize this concept via the relations $\geqslant$, $>$ and $\sim$.

As I have said, a quasiordering is a very general notion. In the case of a welfarist decision procedure, as I conceptualize it, there are three kinds of sets that are associated with quasiorderings: the outcome set O, the action set A, and a set H of life-histories (an idea I'll get to in a moment).

The decision procedure will provide tools for arriving at a quasiordering of the outcome set O. In other words, it will provide tools for associating a reflexive, transitive, possibly incomplete binary relation with O, the binary relation "morally at least as good as," which I will abbreviate $\geqslant^M$. Each outcome will be morally at least as good as itself. If x is morally at least as good as y, and y is morally at least as good as z, then x is morally at least as good as z. The relation may, but need not, be complete. (If incomplete, there will be at least one pair of outcomes, x and y, such that x is not morally at least as good as y nor y morally at least as good as x.) Once the decision maker has employed the furnished tools to arrive at the $\geqslant^M$ relation, she can immediately construct two other relations, "morally better than" and "morally equally good as," which we can denote as $>^M$ and $\sim^M$, respectively.[73]

The decision procedure will also provide tools for using the quasiordering of the outcome set O to arrive at a quasiordering of the action set A. This will be a reflexive, transitive, possibly incomplete binary relation of the *actions* in that choice set, ranking some as "morally at least as good as" others. Denote this quasiordering as "$\geqslant^{MA}$." With the moral quasiordering of the action set in hand, at least if that set is finite, it is straightforward for the decisionmaker to determine what she morally should do: She should perform some "undominated" action (one which is not morally worse than any other), and if there are multiple undominated actions is permitted to perform any one.[74]

What about the derivation of the moral quasiordering of the action set, $\geqslant^{MA}$, from the moral ordering of the outcome set, $\geqslant^M$? In the case of choice under certainty—where the decisionmaker knows which outcome any given action would

---

[73] That is: $x >^M y$ iff (1) $x \geqslant^M y$ and (2) not $y \geqslant^M x$. And $x \sim^M y$ iff (1) $x \geqslant^M y$ and (2) $y \geqslant^M x$.

[74] See Sen (1997a, pp. 763–769; 2000, pp. 486–487). If the action set is infinite, there may not be any such undominated action—raising complications I will not pursue. See Ruggeri, Ríos Insua, and Martín (2005, sec. 3). These complications are not a consequence of incompleteness. A complete ranking of an infinite set may be such that, for each item, there is some other item which is better.

produce—this derivation is trivial. The decision procedure simply says this: if action a yields outcome x and action b yields outcome y, then $a \succeq^{MA} b$ just in case $x \succeq^M y$. In the more realistic case of choice under uncertainty, the process of deriving the moral quasiordering of the action set from the moral quasiordering of the outcome set is much more complicated and contestable—involving the assignment of probabilities to outcomes and the different possible ways to integrate this probability information with $\succeq^M$ to derive $\succeq^{MA}$. This topic is the focus of Chapter 7.

In particular, Chapter 7 will discuss the use of expected utility (EU) theory—the best developed tool for moving from a ranking of outcomes to a ranking of choices. The applicability of EU theory to the particular case of *moral* choice is controversial. I argue in Chapter 7 that (a refined version of) EU theory *is* applicable in the moral case, as in other cases of deriving an action ranking from a choice ranking; but, as we shall see, rejecting EU theory for the moral case is a position that some prominent social choice theorists have advocated.

Another complication, discussed in Chapter 7, is that the decision procedure may furnish the decisionmaker with principles for constructing a quasiordering of the outcome set O, but the decisionmaker may be uncertain how to implement those principles. For example, the decision procedure may tell the decisionmaker that whether x is at least as good as y depends on individuals' fully informed, fully rational extended preferences—but the decisionmaker may not know what individuals' fully informed, fully rational extended preferences are. In this event, the decision procedure—in order to function as a genuine guide to choice—will need to contain methodologies that allow the decisionmaker to integrate the basic principles about how to quasiorder O, together with her imperfect information about how to implement those principles, and her imperfect information about which outcomes a given action yields, to arrive at a quasiordering of A.

For most of this book, until Chapter 7, the complications posed by decisionmaker uncertainty about the connection between actions and outcomes, and about the implementation of principles for quasiordering outcomes, will be ignored. The focus, instead, will be on developing attractive principles for quasiordering a given outcome set O. Such principles are the absolute core (although certainly not the totality) of a consequentialist decision procedure.

The reader may well raise a number of different objections to a decisionmaking structure that allows for a quasiordering (possibly incomplete) on an outcome set and a quasiordering (possibly incomplete) on an action set.

First, the reader may object that the ordering of outcomes and actions should be complete. Each outcome should be morally better, worse, or equally good as every other; similarly, each pair of actions should be thus ranked. Indeed, welfare economists and social choice theorists usually assume completeness in the "social" (what I am calling "moral") ordering of outcomes and policies; economists typically assume that an individual's preference ordering of outcomes and choices is complete; and the generic structure for rational choice provide by EU theory also assumes completeness. So allowing for incompleteness *is* a deviation from—I view it as a refinement of—EU theory.

However, Amartya Sen has powerfully argued that we should allow for incompleteness in various domains, and other prominent scholars have concurred with Sen.[75] It is especially natural for the welfarist to allow for an incomplete moral ordering of outcomes and actions, because a strong case can be made that well-being is incomplete. Those who deny the possibility of interpersonal welfare comparisons espouse a wide-ranging kind of incompleteness: on this view, it is never possible to compare one person's well-being in some outcome to another person's well-being in some outcome. This is (I will ultimately argue) too extreme; but the insistence that each person's well-being in each outcome is *comparable* with every other person's well-being in each outcome goes too far in the other direction. The most plausible ranking of individual lives in terms of well-being is incomplete, or at least may well be.[76] In turn, therefore, to require completeness of the moral ordering of outcomes—an ordering which, for the welfarist, is a function of the pattern of individual well-being—seems dogmatic. If we cannot always make comparisons of individual well-being, why assume, as welfarists, that we can always make moral comparisons of outcomes?

Another part of the welfarist case for incompleteness involves the Pareto principles. The Pareto principles, themselves, only generate an incomplete quasiordering of outcomes—the Pareto quasiordering (see below). The project of welfarism, in effect, is to "extend" the Pareto quasiordering; but, once more, to insist that it be "extended" all the way to a complete ordering seems too restrictive.

The strongest case for completeness involves the worry that incompleteness may generate "value pumps." This *is* a serious worry; but "value pumps" are best handled by structuring rules for dynamic choice that avoid or mitigate them, rather than by stipulating that the action and outcome rankings must be complete. See Chapter 7.[77]

---

[75] For Sen's views, see, e.g., Sen (1979a, chs. 7–7*; 1982, ch. 9; 1995, pp. 46–49; 2004). For philosophical discussion of incomparability, see Broome (1995, pp. 92–93; 1997; 2004, ch. 12); Chang (1997, 2002a, 2002b); Levi (1986); Raz (1986, ch. 13).

[76] The account of well-being presented in Chapter 3 derives a well-being ranking of life-histories from a set **U**, which is the union of sets of the form $\mathbf{U}^{k,t,x}$, representing the extended preferences of spectator k at time t in outcome x. One life-history is at least as good as another if its utility is at least as great for all utility functions in **U**. Because individuals' extended preferences may be heterogeneous (formally, the extended preferences of spectator k at time t in outcome x are heterogeneous with the extended preferences of spectator j at time t^* in outcome y iff $\mathbf{U}^{k,t,x} \neq \mathbf{U}^{j,t^*,y}$), this approach naturally yields some incompleteness in the well-being ranking of life-histories even if each $\mathbf{U}^{k,t,x}$ is itself unique up to a positive ratio transformation.

[77] Admittedly, one rule for structuring dynamic choice so as to avoid value pumps, which I term "partly resolute choice," *does* require a complete ordering of outcomes. (In effect, the "partly resolute" decisionmaker selects one complete ordering of outcomes prior to engaging in an intertemporal series of choices, and sticks with that ordering as she makes choices over time.) However, other plausible rules for avoiding value pumps do not require a complete ordering of outcomes. See Chapter 7.

A second objection comes from the reader who accepts that outcomes and actions may be morally incomparable, but objects to the use of the quasiordering as the formal device for capturing such incomparability. There is a substantial literature regarding quasiorderings, in mathematical logic, and also in economics, where this has become the dominant approach to handling incomparability insofar as that is discussed.[78] Other approaches are not equally well developed.[79] Furthermore, the quasiordering has an elegant "intersectional" structure: if there is a set of complete orderings on S, then the relation R^+ constructed by saying, $s\ R^+\ t$ iff s is at least as good as t according to each of the complete orderings, is a quasiordering; and it turns out that the converse is true, namely that every quasiordering can be represented as the intersection of some set of complete orderings.[80] The "intersectional"

Moreover, even the proponent of "partly resolute" choice need not insist that a moral theory, itself, must yield a complete ordering of outcomes in every outcome set. A fundamental result in the theory of quasiorderings is that, for every quasiordering, there is a complete ordering which "extends" it. See Ok (2007, p. 17). In particular, if $\geqslant^M$ is an incomplete moral quasiordering of some outcome set, there is a complete ordering $\geqslant^{M+}$ such that: if $x \geqslant^M y$, then $x \geqslant^{M+} y$; and if $x \succ^M y$, then $x \succ^{M+} y$.

Thus, the proponent of partly resolute choice can *agree* that the most attractive principles for morally ordering outcomes will sometimes yield an incomplete ordering, for the reasons I have outlined. Her choice-evaluation framework can include an $\geqslant^M$ which is incomplete in some outcome sets; if so, the framework will instruct the decisionmaker to "extend" $\geqslant^M$ in some arbitrary manner and then use the extension, $\geqslant^{M+}$, as the basis for making choices over time.

[78] Quasiorderings figure in mathematical logic as part of "poset" theory. See, e.g., Kaye (2007, ch. 2). They figure in welfare economics in the analysis of EU theory without the completeness axiom, see Dubra, Maccheroni, and Ok (2004); Evren (2008); Ok (2002; 2007, pp. 499–521); in the Lorenz quasiordering, which is central to the literature on inequality measurement (see sources cited in Chapter 2, n. 101); and in the Pareto quasiordering, see Sen (1979a, chs. 2–2*).

[79] Ruth Chang (1997, Introduction; 2002a; 2002b) has argued that two items might be "on a par" rather than incomparable. However, the existence of this fourth relation is controversial. See, e.g., Boot (2009); Gert (2004). Moreover, the formal apparatus for handling the "on a par" relation is underdeveloped (and indeed may end up being very close to the intersectional apparatus employed here; see Rabinowicz [2008]).

Another possibility, argued for by John Broome (1997; 2004, ch. 12), is that apparent incomparability is really a form of vagueness. Broome's account, too, has not been widely adopted. One count against it is that vagueness, standardly, is a feature of language, not properties. It might be countered that normative properties, such as moral goodness or well-being, are especially language dependent and thus infectable by vagueness. However, the Pareto quasiordering involves a kind of incomparability that has nothing to do with language. For any arbitrary account of well-being (language dependent or not), the Pareto quasiordering says that outcome x is equally morally good as outcome y if each individual in x is just as well off as she is in y (on that account); that outcome x is morally better than outcome y if at least one person is better off in x than y and everyone else is at least as well off; and that, otherwise, the two outcomes are morally incomparable. The formalization of incomparability, for purposes of welfarism, should be able to capture this kind of non-language-dependent incomparability—because the whole project of welfarism is to start with the Pareto quasiordering and then extend it.

[80] See Donaldson and Weymark (1998).

structure of quasiorderings also means that the standard mathematical apparatus of functions used by economists to represent complete orderings smoothly generalizes to the quasiordering case: if there is a set of complete orderings on **S**, each represented by a function, then the intersection of these functions generates a quasiordering.[81] Finally, it means that the quasiordering is a natural way to represent the kind of incompleteness that results when a variety of perspectives are relevant to ordering some set, and we require convergence among the perspectives in order to conclude that one item is better.[82]

A third objection is more radical. Note that a quasiordering drops the requirement of completeness but retains the standard transitivity properties associated with "at least as good as," "better than," and "equally good as." The more radical suggestion is that we drop transitivity.[83] Imagine that an outcome set **O** is ordered by a relation $\succcurlyeq^{M^*}$ which is reflexive but not transitive, and that we define $\succ^{M^*}$ (intransitive betterness) and $\sim^{M^*}$ (intransitive equal goodness) in terms of $\succcurlyeq^{M^*}$. Then, at least in the case of choice under certainty, the following would seem to be a possible rule for choice: choose any action a such that its corresponding outcome x is not worse than any other action's outcome, i.e., there is no action yielding a y such that $y \succ^{M^*} x$.

However, I do not pursue the approach of dropping transitivity here, for a variety of reasons: (1) This rule may fail to yield a choice even if the action set is finite.[84] (2) As a matter of reflective equilibrium, the formal devices used to rank outcomes should track our intuitive concept of "goodness." I suggest that our deepest intuitions about "goodness" involve reflexivity (that each item is equally good as itself, and that no item is better than itself). Denying transitivity may be less counterintuitive than denying reflexivity, but it is certainly more counterintuitive than denying completeness. (3) Although individuals, in their actual choices, may fail transitivity, such examples do not make a normative case for dropping transitivity. Such a case would be made if there were strong examples where we intuitively judge that x better than y better than z, but not x better than z, but the existence of such examples is quite contestable. (4) Dropping transitivity means a large restriction of the inferential properties of goodness, which ceteris paribus is undesirable. Without transitivity, if x is better than y, we can still infer that y is not better than x; but information

---

[81] Indeed, it can be shown that *every* quasiordering can be represented as the intersection of a set of functions. See Evren and Ok (2010).

[82] See Chapter 3.

[83] See Temkin (1987, 1996a), and also Fishburn (1991); Sen (1986, pp. 1084–1090). But see Binmore and Voorhoeve (2003); Norcross (1999).

[84] This can occur because of a "cycle" in the intransitive betterness relation, e.g., a case of three actions producing three outcomes, where the first is better than the second, in turn better than the third, in turn better than the first. By contrast, the rule suggested earlier for choice under conditions of certainty with a quasiordering of outcomes will always yield a permissible choice unless the action and outcome sets are infinite. See above, p. 42. Admittedly, this difficulty with an intransitive ordering of outcomes can be addressed by requiring that the ordering be acyclic (which is weaker than transitivity).

about the comparative goodness of x and y, and of y and z, now does not warrant inferences about the comparative goodness of x and z. (5) Our formal techniques for handling intransitivity are not nearly as well developed as those for handling complete orderings or incomplete quasiorderings, and presumably would be much more complicated than those. This is a real strike against intransitivity, insofar as tractability is one desideratum in a decision procedure. (6) Extending this approach to choice under uncertainty creates serious difficulties, because denying transitivity means denying a very attractive dominance axiom for choice under uncertainty.[85]

A final objection is that it is unnecessary to construct a full quasiordering. Why not just partition the set of outcomes into two subsets—a subset consisting of optimal outcomes and a subset consisting of suboptimal outcomes—without any further ranking of the outcomes within these two subsets? This is the approach taken, for example, in the literature on "fair" allocations.[86] However, in the case of choice under uncertainty, a partition of the outcome set into suboptimal and optimal outcomes may yield insufficient guidance for choice. What if each choice, with nonzero probability, yields some optimal outcomes but also some suboptimal outcomes? If the outcome set is merely partitioned into optimal and suboptimal outcomes, how do we move from the outcome set to a partition of the choice set into optimal and suboptimal actions?

In any event, if the reader prefers to characterize the outcome set in this more minimal way, the tools presented here certainly allow her to do so. Given a quasiordering $\succcurlyeq^M$ of an outcome set, the set of optimal outcomes consists of all outcomes each of which is not worse than any other outcomes in the set; suboptimal outcomes are all others.

In short, I believe a strong case can be made for structuring a welfare consequentialist decision procedure around a possibly incomplete quasiordering of actions and outcomes, rather than insisting on completeness; modeling incomparability via different formal devices than the quasiordering; allowing intransitivity; or simply characterizing outcomes and actions as optimal versus suboptimal.[87]

*****

---

[85] See Fishburn (1991, p. 116).

[86] See Fleurbaey, Suzumura, and Tadenuma (2005).

[87] I have not mentioned the idea of "feasibility," which figures in much economic analysis. In my setup, feasibility considerations most naturally come into play in constructing the choice set or in determining outcome probabilities. (For example, some hypothetical course of action may be impossible, given technological factors; and what would happen, if some course of action were pursued, will depend on technology.) Feasibility may also be used to prune down the outcome set. If every action which would yield outcome x with nonzero probability is infeasible, outcome x might be dropped from the outcome set.

Thus far, I have focused on the outcome and action sets and their quasiordering features, but have said nothing systematic about persons or well-being. How, more precisely, do these figure into the decision procedure?

I assume that there is a population of N persons; the decision is supposed to be an impartial function of their well-being. Because *moral* decisionmaking, arguably, should be unconcerned with national or temporal differences, it is natural to think that the N individuals are the entire population of the world, past, present, and future. However, the SWF framework and the others discussed in this book can also be applied to some subset of the world's intertemporal population—for example, a British decisionmaker might apply it to all British citizens.

Each of the N persons is a human being who is determinately a person.[88] Furthermore, I assume throughout the book that N is a finite number and that each member of the N individuals exists in each and every outcome in O. (In other words, the person comes into existence in either the first period or a subsequent period, in every outcome, and lives for at least one period.) Relaxing these assumptions generates a number of very difficult problems in welfarist theory—nonidentity problems, the "repugnant conclusion," infinite populations—that are briefly reviewed in the final chapter, but that this book does not attempt to resolve. It will be enough work to craft a decision procedure for the core case of a fixed, finite population.

The welfarist decision procedure will include some account of individual well-being. What is human well-being? That question is hotly debated by philosophers, economists, and psychologists and will be discussed at length in Chapter 3. Does well-being consist in actual or idealized preference-satisfaction? In the occurrence of positive mental states, e.g., pleasant sensations? In various objective goods? The generic structure I set up here is meant to accommodate all these possibilities. The decision procedure includes *some* account of well-being, which may revolve around mental states, objective goods, preference satisfaction, or some combination.

This account of well-being has two critical functions. First, it helps generate the initial construction of the outcome set O, in any given choice situation. Remember that outcomes are incomplete characterizations of the different possible worlds that might result from choice. How to construct such characterizations—whether to describe outcomes in terms of consumption, health, public goods, leisure, happiness, or something else—is a matter of balancing the decision costs of reasoning with more finely specified outcomes, against the benefits of taking account of additional well-being relevant characteristics. What types of attributes of possible worlds are well-being relevant is, of course, not uncontroversial, but rather one of the critical questions that an account of well-being helps us to answer.

---

[88] Again, I do not discuss the treatment of non-humans who are determinate persons, nor humans who are indeterminate persons or determinately non-persons, nor non-humans who are indeterminate persons. I assume that human persons have this status in virtue of their psychological properties, not in virtue of being ensouled. Finally (see Chapter 6) I assume that each of the N persons has a normal psychological and physical history.

The second critical function of an account of well-being—and one that will be a central focus of the book—is to help the decisionmaker arrive at a moral quasiordering of a given outcome set, **O**, once the outcome set has been specified. How does the account of well-being do this? It does so by taking the set **H** of life-histories; constructing various rankings on that set; and using this well-being information regarding the life-history set to help determine the moral quasiordering of the outcome set **O**.

A life-history simply means being some individual in some outcome. Formally, a life-history is a pairing of some individual in the set of N individuals, and some outcome in the outcome set **O**. The pairing $(x; i)$ is one life-history—meaning being individual i in outcome x. The pairing $(y; j)$ is another life-history—meaning being individual j in outcome y. I will often refer to the individual "in" the life-history (for example, individual i in life-history $(x; i)$) as the "subject" of the life-history.

The life-history set **H** is the set of all life-histories, consisting of all such possible pairings. If **O** is finite (which it need not be), with O members, then the life-history set has $N \times O$ elements; otherwise it is infinite.

The account of well-being furnishes principles whereby the decisionmaker can construct a quasiordering of the life-history set (call it "$\succcurlyeq^{\text{WB}}$"). The account of well-being may also furnish principles whereby the decisionmaker can construct other types of rankings associated with the life-history set, to be mentioned below. The idea of rankings of a life-history set may sound weird, but in fact it is very general and (I think) elegant. It accommodates the full range of accounts of well-being; crisply engages the topic of interpersonal comparisons; allows but does not require completeness; and leads to a generalized definition of the Pareto principles and a generalized characterization of welfarism.

The quasiordering of the life-history set **H** is a reflexive, transitive, possibly incomplete binary relation on **H**. $(x; i) \succcurlyeq^{\text{WB}} (y; j)$ means: life-history $(x; i)$ is at least as good for well-being as life-history $(y; j)$ or, to say the same thing more colloquially, individual i's well-being in outcome x is at least as great as individual j's well-being in outcome y. The well-being quasiordering makes an *intrapersonal* comparison when it takes two life-histories involving the same subject, $(x; i)$ and $(y; i)$, and says $(x; i) \succcurlyeq^{\text{WB}} (y; i)$. The well-being quasiordering makes an *interpersonal* comparison when it takes two life-histories involving different subjects, $(x; i)$ and $(y; j)$, i and j distinct, and says: $(x; i) \succcurlyeq^{\text{WB}} (y; j)$. We can now straightforwardly say what it means for an account of well-being to involve or allow for interpersonal comparisons (more precisely, interpersonal comparisons of well-being levels). That is just to say that there is *some* pair of life-histories involving distinct subjects $(x; i)$ and $(y; j)$—at least one such pair, perhaps many more—such that $(x; i) \succcurlyeq^{\text{WB}} (y; j)$ according to the well-being quasiordering generated by that account.

Note that the definition of interpersonal comparability just offered is relative to a given outcome set. It is quite possible that a given account W of well-being allows for interpersonal comparisons of well-being levels in one outcome set **O**, constructed for one choice situation (W ranks the life-history set associated with **O** so as to compare at least one pair of life-histories involving different subjects), but not in some other outcome set O^*, constructed for some other choice situation. One might also say that a given well-being account allows for interpersonal comparisons of well-being levels, simpliciter, if there is some outcome set in which two life-histories involving different subjects are ranked.

Throughout this book, I will sometimes be discussing interpersonal comparability in the first sense, sometimes in the second. Context will make clear which sense is being employed.

It is of course a hotly disputed question whether the most attractive account of well-being allows for interpersonal comparisons in any outcome set. The notion of a well-being quasiordering over life-histories provides a formal structure for representing views on both sides of this dispute.

Consider the traditional, economic account of well-being, which reduces well-being to preference satisfaction. This account of course allows for *intra*personal comparisons of well-being levels, saying specifically that $(x; i) \succcurlyeq^{WB} (y; i)$ iff individual i either prefers outcome x to outcome y or is indifferent. However, the traditional preference-satisfaction account does not allow for interpersonal comparisons: it never compares the well-being of one person in some outcome to the well-being of a different person in some outcome. By contrast, a mental-state account would make the comparison of life-histories a function of individuals' mental states in the outcomes, and might make some comparisons of the form $(x; i) \succcurlyeq^{WB} (y; j)$, where i and j are distinct individuals. For example, it might say that i's well-being in x is greater than j's well-being in y because i in outcome x experiences more pleasure and less pain than does j in outcome y.

Although the notion of a quasiordering of life-histories is very general with respect to both the range of accounts of well-being, and the question of interpersonal comparisons, it might be argued that my set-up is not general enough because it assumes that the kind of well-being which will be morally relevant is *lifetime* well-being. A life-history is an entire lifetime of an individual in an outcome. To say that $(x; i) \succcurlyeq^{WB} (y; j)$ is to say that i's lifetime well-being in x is at least as great as j's lifetime well-being in y. What if the welfarist believes that the moral quasiordering of outcomes should be a function of "sublifetime" well-being: individual well-being during some "time slice," such as annual or momentary well-being?

Because each human person (with a normal physical and psychological history) remains the very same particular person from birth until death, the sublifetime view is problematic—a point more fully argued in Chapter 6. I could set up the welfarist structure in a yet more generic fashion, allowing for both a lifetime approach and a sublifetime approach. But that would yet further complexify an already complicated structure. Thus, anticipating the discussion in Chapter 6, my presentation here of a general format for welfarist decisionmaking builds in a whole-lifetime approach.[89]

---

[89] We could also see each pairing of an individual and an attribute as a separate "history," and specify welfarism in these terms. This possibility, like the sublifetime approach, is discussed and rejected in Chapter 6.

I have mentioned that an account of well-being may be used to construct various rankings associated with the life-history set. I have described one: the quasiordering of **H** ($\succeq^{WB}$). At a minimum, any account of well-being will generate such a ranking (with some degree of intra- and perhaps also interpersonal comparability of well-being levels). However, an account of well-being may also generate a quasiordering of *differences* between life-histories (call it "$\succeq^D$"), with some degree of intra- and perhaps interpersonal comparability of well-being differences.[90] A further possibility: an account of well-being might determine whether a given life-history is better, worse, equally good as, or incomparable with nonexistence. (As it turns out, the account of well-being I argue for in Chapter 3 will generate all three of these types of rankings.)[91]

In turn, all the information about well-being contained in the various well-being rankings associated with **H** determines the moral quasiordering of the outcome

---

The argument in Chapter 6 for a whole-lifetime approach focuses on the case of a continuous prioritarian SWF. But (as I note there) the argument is really more general. It flows from the claim-across-outcome conception of fairness, suggesting that any SWF (or for that matter any non-SWF approach) grounded in this conception of fairness warrants a whole-lifetime approach. Moreover, the welfarist has good grounds to care about fairness—both as an intuitive matter, and because of the person-centered cast of welfarism (see Chapter 5). Finally (as suggested in Chapter 5), the claim-across-outcome conception of fairness fits snugly with the Pareto principles.

Although the veil-of-ignorance conception of fairness, yielding utilitarianism (see Chapter 5), also fits with the Pareto principles, it seems plausible that this conception—too—is best specified in a whole-lifetime way.

All these considerations suggest that Paretian welfarism in general (not merely the continuous prioritarian SWF) is best understood in whole-lifetime terms.

[90] Let us say that a difference quasiordering of life-histories, $\succeq^D$, ranks *pairs* of life-histories. It takes the form $[(x; i), (y; j)] \succeq^D [(z; k), (w; l)]$, meaning that the difference between the pair of life-histories $(x; i)$ and $(y; j)$ is at least as great as the difference between the pair of life-histories $(z; k)$ and $(w; l)$. This idea is based on the literature on difference measurement. Formally, $\succeq^D$ is a binary relation on the product set $\mathbf{H} \times \mathbf{H}$, with the following features: (1) This relation is transitive and reflexive. (2) If $[(x; i), (y; j)] \succeq^D [(z; k), (w; l)]$, then $[(w; l), (z; k)] \succeq^D [(y; j), (x; i)]$. (3) If $[(x; i), (y; j)] \succeq^D [(x'; i'), (y'; j')]$ and $[(y; j), (z; k)] \succeq^D [(y'; j'), (z'; k')]$, then $[(x; i), (z; k)] \succeq^D [(x'; i'), (z'; k')]$.

We can say that a difference quasiordering of life-histories *allows for interpersonal comparisons of well-being differences* iff there is at least one pair of pairs such that $[(x; i), (y; j)] \succeq^D [(z; k), (w; l)]$, where it is not the case that $i = j = k = l$. Here, as with interpersonal level comparability, we might distinguish between the relative-to-an-outcome-set definition just offered, and saying that a given account of well-being allows for interpersonal difference comparability in the sense that there is *some* outcome set in which the account make an interpersonal difference comparison.

This concept of a difference quasiordering draws upon existing scholarship regarding difference measurement (in particular, so-called "algebraic-difference" structures), relaxing the requirement of a complete ordering of differences and omitting the technical axioms that permit the representation of a complete such ordering by a single utility function. See Krantz et al. (2007, pp. 150–152).

[91] I use comparisons of life-histories to nonexistence to arrive at ratios between life-histories. Such comparisons are not necessary for setting ratios, if some other life-history is used as the zero point. See Chapter 5, pp. 379–382.

set **O**. How exactly? That is one of the chief topics of controversy among welfarists: between welfarists who reject interpersonal comparisons and welfarists who allow such comparisons; and, within the latter camp, between welfarists with different views about how interpersonally comparable utilities should drive the ranking of outcomes (in particular, between utilitarians who believe that utilities should be summed and non-utilitarians who believe that the ranking should be sensitive to the distribution of utility).

At a minimum, however, all welfarists—because welfarism is a moral view— agree that the ranking of outcomes should be *impartial*. What exactly this means in the case of an account of well-being that does not allow for interpersonal comparisons is not obvious. Of course, the ranking should not depend on individuals' proper names, but what more to say is not clear. In the case of an account of well-being that *does* allow for interpersonal comparisons, impartiality is more straightforwardly characterizable. It can be expressed, in this case, as an "anonymity" (or "permutation") axiom: Given some outcome x, if the arrangement of well-being levels in y is simply a permutation of the well-being levels in x, then y and x are equally morally good. For a given pattern of well-being, it should not matter which particular person is at which level.[92]

Just as fundamentally, all welfarists agree that the ranking of outcomes should satisfy the Pareto-indifference principle. And virtually all agree that this ranking should satisfy the principle of Pareto-superiority (strong Pareto).

What are these principles? Standardly, within economics, the Pareto principle is formulated in terms of preferences. The Pareto-indifference principle (in terms of

---

[92] Formally, a permutation is a mapping from some set, to itself, which is a bijection (one-to-one and onto). Assume that $\sigma(.)$ is a permutation on the set of N individuals. Then anonymity says: if there is some $\sigma(.)$ such that it is the case that $(x; i) \sim^{WB} (y; \sigma(i))$ for all i, then $x \sim^M y$. Cf. Bossert and Weymark (2004, p. 1108). Difficulties arise in using the notion of a permutation to express an impartiality requirement where N is infinite (see Chapter 8), but not in the case under discussion in this book, with N finite.

The definition of anonymity that I employ here is analogous to what social choice theorists term a "single profile" definition, because the definition holds fixed the well-being associated with different life-histories. A different approach (analogous to what social choice theorists term a "multiprofile" approach) would be to impose consistency conditions on the ranking of outcomes, allowing the well-being associated with the life-histories in the outcomes to vary. For example, it might say: if there is a permutation $\sigma(.)$ on the set of N individuals, such that for each subject i the ranking (intra- and interpersonal) of i's life-histories furnished by account W of well-being is the same as the ranking of $\sigma(i)$'s histories furnished by account W^*, then the ranking of outcomes using W and W^* must be the same. See Mongin and d'Aspremont (1998, in particular pp. 414, 422–424).

However, it might be protested that the true account of well-being (be it W, W^*, or some other account) is fixed and that anonymity should not be defined on the supposition that this account might itself change. Cf. Blackorby, Bossert, and Donaldson (2006, p. 281). Alternatively, it might be protested that, if the nature of well-being were to change, the moral criteria for ranking outcomes might change as well. The "single profile" definition of anonymity that I offer does not face these objections.

preferences) says: if each individual is indifferent between outcome x and outcome y, then the two outcomes are equally good. The strong Pareto principle (in terms of preferences) says: if there is at least one individual who prefers outcome x to outcome y, and everyone else either prefers x to y or is indifferent, then x is better than y. The weak Pareto principle (in terms of preferences) says: if everyone prefers outcome x to outcome y, then x is better than y. Note that the strong Pareto principle implies the weak principle, but not vice versa.[93]

Because my account of welfarist decisionmaking is meant to allow for both preference-based and competing accounts of well-being, it needs to formulate the Pareto principles in a more general manner. This more general formulation is what John Broome calls "the principle of personal good."[94] The Pareto-indifference principle (general version) says: if there are two outcomes x and y, such that each person is just as well off in both outcomes, then x and y are equally morally good. Formally: if $(x; i) \sim^{WB} (y; i)$ for each individual i, then $x \sim^M y$. The strong Pareto principle (general version) says: if there are two outcomes x and y, such that at least one person is better off in x than y, and everyone is at least as well off in x, then x is morally better than y. Formally: if $(x; i) \geqslant^{WB} (y; i)$ for each individual i, and there is at least one individual j such that $(x; j) >^{WB} (y; j)$, then $x >^M y$. The weak Pareto principle (general version) says: if everyone is better off in x than y, then x is morally better than y. Formally: if $(x; i) >^{WB} (y; i)$ for each individual i, then $x >^M y$. Note that the strong Pareto principle (general version) implies the weak Pareto principle (general version), but not vice versa.

Henceforth, I refer to these principles as the Pareto principles—emphasizing, again, that they are meant to reflect *whatever* account of well-being the welfarist uses (preferentialist or not) and whatever particular quasiordering over life-histories this account generates. I realize that there is some risk of terminological confusion, but the careful reader will not, I hope, be confused, and this terminology underscores the way in which my principles are faithful to, but generalize, the traditional economic formulation.

I assume that any welfarist principle for quasiordering an outcome set, whatever it may be, will satisfy the principle of Pareto-indifference and the strong Pareto principle. Why assume this? The principle of Pareto-indifference captures the essence of welfarism. Welfarism says, informally, that the ranking of outcomes is solely a function of individual well-being. Moral goodness *supervenes* on well-being. Unless there is a well-being difference between two outcomes, they must be equally morally good. But this is exactly what Pareto-indifference stipulates. If x and y are not ranked

---

[93] On these different versions of the Pareto principle, see Bossert and Weymark (2004, pp. 1105–1108).

[94] See Broome (1995, p. 162). However, unlike Broome, I see these generalized Pareto principles as a constraint on the ranking of outcomes, *not* actions. See Chapter 7, rejecting the ex ante Pareto principles.

as equally morally good, and yet each individual is just as well off in x as in y, then some fact other than a fact about well-being must be driving the ranking.[95]

Weak Pareto and strong Pareto do not logically follow from the notion that moral goodness supervenes on well-being. It is logically possible to accept that notion, and Pareto-indifference, but give a higher moral ranking to outcomes in which everyone is worse off. For example, it is possible and not morally unthinkable to say that some outcome y in which well-being is unequally distributed is worse than some outcome x in which there has been "leveling down," with the upshot that everyone's welfare is lower but there is perfect equality of welfare.[96]

Still, the vast majority of welfarists accept not merely weak Pareto, but strong Pareto. This is true, certainly, of economists (strong Pareto is one of the most basic building blocks of welfare economics) but it also seems to be true of most moral philosophers who are sympathetic to welfarism.[97] These principles are intuitively powerful. If everyone is strictly better off, then—regardless of the pattern of their

---

[95] Social choice theorists typically offer a different definition of "welfarism"—one that assumes well-being is measurable by utilities, and that the ranking of outcomes satisfies not merely a Pareto-indifference condition but a condition of "binary independence of irrelevant alternatives." See Bossert and Weymark (2004, pp. 1102–1111). While I believe that the most *attractive* version of welfarism (namely, an SWF using the simple R-based form, see Chapter 2) does satisfy these conditions, the conditions are overly restrictive as a definition of welfarism. For example, imagine that there is some U representing the well-being quasiordering of life-histories and the difference quasiordering. The rule for morally ranking outcomes is: outcome x is morally at least as good as outcome y iff, for all u(.) in U, R* ranks x at least as good as y—where R* ranks x and y, given each u(.), by taking account not merely of u(x) and u(y) but also the utility vectors assigned by u(.) to other outcomes. This approach violates "binary independence of irrelevant alternatives"—and may well be substantively unattractive—but shouldn't it count as "welfarist," since the ranking of outcomes depends solely on utility information? Similarly, imagine that, in some outcome set, well-being turns out not to be measurable by utilities. Does that mean that the moral ranking of this set is necessarily not welfarist?

A worry about my definition of welfarism (Pareto-indifference, supplemented by Pareto-superiority and by impartiality) is that this counts as welfarist an approach which uses non-well-being information to influence the ranking of Pareto-noncomparable outcomes. We might try to avoid this problem by imposing consistency conditions on the moral ranking of outcomes as the nature of well-being changes. But that itself may be problematic, see above, n. 92; and so I will stick with the inclusive definition of welfarism as Pareto-indifference, supplemented by Pareto-superiority and impartiality.

[96] See Broome (1995, chs. 8–9); Holtug (2003).

[97] On the centrality of the strong Pareto principle to economics, see, e.g., Boadway and Bruce (1984, pp. 2–3); Just, Hueth, and Schmitz (2004, p. 3); Kaplow and Shavell (2002, pp. 24–26); Mas-Colell, Whinston, and Green (1995, pp. 307–313). The strong Pareto principle has no such bedrock status within philosophy. Even philosophers sympathetic to welfarism have entertained the possibility that it might be rejected, as in the works cited in the previous footnote. However, there seem to be few, if any, philosophers in this camp who actually conclude that it should be rejected. Larry Temkin, a prominent recent example of a philosopher who leans toward rejecting the strong Pareto principle (Temkin 1996b, pp. 139–140; 2003b), is not a counterexample. Although Temkin focuses on

gains—how could the outcome, too, not be a better one, all things considered? And (since we are willing to embrace this principle regardless of the pattern of individual gains) why wouldn't it extend to the case in which everyone is at least as well off and some are strictly better off? Moreover, as Chapter 5 explores, there is a strong conceptual link between the strong and weak Pareto principles and at least one conception of fairness.

This book will therefore take the strong Pareto principle (which I will henceforth refer to as the principle of "Pareto-superiority") and Pareto-indifference as basic axioms, along with impartiality. A key question for subsequent chapters will be: Can we develop an impartial principle for quasiordering outcome sets that conforms to the axioms of Pareto-indifference and Pareto-superiority, but also goes beyond these axioms? Such a principle takes some pairs of outcomes that are *Pareto-noncomparable*—pairs such that the Pareto principles themselves do not require that one member be ranked better than the other or that the two be ranked equally good—and ranks one outcome in the pair as better than the other, or ranks the two as equally good. A key argument in subsequent chapters will be that the SWF approach is the most attractive way to do this.

Formally, we are looking for a principle for generating a moral quasiordering of a given outcome set that can *extend* the Pareto quasiordering.[98] Let us say that $x \succ^{\text{Pareto}} y$ iff $(x; i) \succ^{\text{WB}} (y; i)$ for at least one subject i and $(x; j) \succcurlyeq^{\text{WB}} (y; j)$ for every subject j. And let us say that $x \sim^{\text{Pareto}} y$ iff $(x; i) \sim^{\text{WB}} (y; i)$ for every subject i. (In other words, $x \succ^{\text{Pareto}} y$ means that x is ranked morally better than y by virtue of the principle of Pareto-superiority. And $x \sim^{\text{Pareto}} y$ means that x and y are ranked as equally morally good by virtue of Pareto-indifference.) Then we can use these relations to define the Pareto quasiordering: $x \succcurlyeq^{\text{Pareto}} y$ iff $x \succ^{\text{Pareto}} y$ or $x \sim^{\text{Pareto}} y$. x and y are Pareto-noncomparable if it is neither the case that $x \succcurlyeq^{\text{Pareto}} y$ nor the case that $y \succcurlyeq^{\text{Pareto}} x$. Pareto-noncomparability will occur, for example, if some individuals are better off in x, but others are better off in y; and it can occur in other ways as well.

We want our principle $\succcurlyeq^{\text{M}}$ to be consistent with the Pareto quasiordering, meaning more precisely that (1) if $x \succ^{\text{Pareto}} y$, then $x \succ^{\text{M}} y$, and (2) if $x \sim^{\text{Pareto}} y$, then $x \sim^{\text{M}} y$. But, intuitively, an attractive principle for quasiordering an outcome set should go beyond the Pareto quasiordering (at least in some outcome sets). It will at least sometimes be the case that neither $x \succcurlyeq^{\text{Pareto}} y$ nor $y \succcurlyeq^{\text{Pareto}} x$, and yet $x \succcurlyeq^{\text{M}} y$.

What is wrong with just using $\succcurlyeq^{\text{Pareto}}$ as $\succcurlyeq^{\text{M}}$? Why not say that the moral quasiordering of outcomes just is the Pareto quasiordering? The problem is not that the Pareto quasiordering is incomplete. After all, the most attractive $\succcurlyeq^{\text{M}}$ may be incomplete as well. Rather, it is that the Pareto quasiordering is *too* incomplete. Intuitively, there are surely *some* outcome sets, with *some* pairs of outcomes that are Pareto-noncomparable—and that are therefore ranked by the Pareto quasiordering as

---

inequality of well-being in his influential book, *Inequality* (Temkin 1996b, p. 10), his all-things-considered views are nonwelfarist. See Temkin (2003b).

[98] See Sen (1979a, chs. 2–2*).

noncomparable—and yet one of the outcomes is morally better than, worse than, or equally good as the other, *not* morally incomparable.[99]

This intuition is certainly shared by welfarists who believe in interpersonal comparisons. Imagine that a few very well off individuals are slightly better off in x than y, and many badly off individuals are substantially worse off in x than y. Surely we can say that x, on balance, is a morally worse outcome than y.

But even welfarists who reject interpersonal comparisons intuit that some Pareto-noncomparable outcomes can be morally ranked.[100] For example, the Kaldor–Hicks principle was spearheaded by economists who eschewed interpersonal comparisons but felt that the Pareto principle was too limited. The egalitarian-equivalent ordering, too, which we will discuss in the next chapter, is an attempt to move beyond the Pareto quasiordering without making interpersonal comparisons.

In short: how shall we preserve Pareto-indifference and Pareto-superiority, but also rank at least some Pareto-noncomparable outcomes in an attractive way? This is the question to which we now turn.

---

[99] My claim, here, is not that an attractive principle for ordering outcomes will extend the Pareto quasiordering in every outcome set. There might well be outcome sets in which, intuitively, all Pareto-noncomparable outcomes are indeed morally incomparable. The claim, rather, is that the Pareto quasiordering as a principle for ranking all outcome sets is too abstemious—and that an attractive ranking principle will extend it in at least some.

[100] I will use the phrase to "rank Pareto-noncomparable outcomes" as a shorthand for taking a pair of Pareto-noncomparable outcomes and determining that one of the two is morally better than the other, or that the two are equally good, *rather than* their being morally incomparable.

2

THE SWF APPROACH AND
ITS COMPETITORS

Chapter 1 outlined the agenda for the book: to elaborate a *welfarist* framework for morally evaluating governmental policies and other large-scale choices, one that has the basic welfarist features of being exclusively person-centered, consequentialist, and focused on well-being.

Chapter 1 also set forth the formal architecture of a welfarist choice-evaluation framework. It derives a moral ranking of an action set from a moral ranking of an outcome set. The ranking of the outcome set, in turn, is derived from information about individual well-being, encapsulated in a ranking of individual life-histories and other rankings associated with the life-history set. All these rankings are "quasi-orderings," possibly incomplete.

The moral ranking of the outcome set must satisfy some basic criteria. First, it must satisfy the basic reflexivity and transitivity properties of any quasiordering: each outcome must be morally at least as good as itself, and if one outcome is mor-ally at least as good as a second, in turn morally at least as good as a third, then the first must be morally at least as good as the third. Second, it must be "Pareto-respecting," i.e., satisfy the two Pareto principles: Pareto-indifference (if each indi-vidual is just as well off in outcome x as outcome y, then x and y are equally morally good); and Pareto-superiority[1] (if one or more individuals are better off in x than y, and everyone is at least as well off in x as in y, then x is morally better than y). Finally, the ranking must be impartial.[2]

---

[1] The reader is reminded that the Pareto-indifference and Pareto-superiority principles, as discussed throughout this book, are *generic* principles, formulated in terms of an individual's well-being rather than her preference satisfaction, so as to encompass the full range of theories of well-being.
[2] An impartial criterion for ordering outcomes, at a minimum, does not yet use individuals' proper names or other expressions that refer to particular individuals ("you," "I"), in ranking outcomes.

However, an attractive welfarist decision procedure will do more than satisfy the minimal criteria just articulated: producing an impartial quasiordering that conforms to the two Pareto principles. The Pareto quasiordering does all this, and yet is commonly seen to be too incomplete. There are surely some pairs of Pareto-noncomparable outcomes such that one can be ranked as morally better than, worse than, or equally good as the other. Thus, we are looking here for a welfarist decision procedure that *extends* the Pareto quasiordering: that not only satisfies the minimal criteria just stated, but also ranks at least some Pareto-noncomparable outcomes, in some outcome sets[3]—and does so in an "attractive" manner, one that we can accept in reflective equilibrium.

One way to structure a decision procedure in light of these aims is the SWF approach. This approach, originating in scholarship by Abram Bergson and Paul Samuelson in the 1930s, and developed most fully by welfare economists beginning in the 1970s, has the following general features: it allows for interpersonal as well as intrapersonal welfare comparisons; uses utility functions to represent the ranking of life-histories, and to transform each outcome into a vector of utilities (or a set of such vectors); and ranks outcomes as a function of their corresponding utility vectors.

The chapter begins by introducing the SWF approach. This section is certainly *not* meant as a full elaboration or defense of the approach. That will occur in subsequent chapters. In particular, it will be the burden of Chapter 3 to develop an account of well-being that meets the needs of the SWF framework: an account that indeed allows for interpersonal comparisons and for the measurement of well-being via utility functions. Chapters 4 through 7 will grapple with a variety of other important questions that arise concerning the elaboration and practical implementation of the approach. Rather, this section of the chapter is meant to provide the reader an initial sense of how the framework works, and of why it holds promise as a way to structure a welfarist decision procedure in a manner that not only meets the minimal criteria but also extends the Pareto quasiordering in an attractive way.

The bulk of the chapter will be devoted, not to discussing the SWF framework, but to criticizing the competing approaches to policy analysis that are currently dominant. Although SWFs are in fact used by some scholars for purposes of evaluating actual government policies—particularly within the scholarly field of optimal tax policy—other approaches are currently much more widespread, both among scholars and in governmental practice. The dominant such frameworks are: cost-benefit

---

Given interpersonal comparability of well-being levels, a stronger impartiality criterion can be formulated, namely anonymity. See Chapter 1.

[3] Two outcomes are "Pareto-noncomparable" if ranked as noncomparable by the Pareto quasiordering. To say that a decision procedure "ranks Pareto-noncomparable outcomes" is shorthand for saying that it takes at least one such pair of outcomes and reaches the conclusion that one of the two outcomes is morally better than or equally good as the other, *rather* than their being morally incomparable. See Chapter 1.

analysis (CBA); inequality metrics, such as the well-known "Gini coefficient"; other equity metrics, in particular poverty metrics, social-gradient metrics, and tax incidence metrics; and QALY-based cost-effectiveness analysis (CEA).[4]

This chapter will critically examine these various frameworks, familiar to anyone who works on policy analysis. It will do so from the perspective of welfarism. The main thrust of this chapter will be to argue the following: each framework either fails to furnish an attractive basis for constructing an impartial, Pareto-respecting, quasi-ordering of an outcome set, or achieves this goal only by functioning as a variation on the SWF approach.

The reader might wonder why I have chosen to organize the book by focusing first on the competitors to the SWF approach, in this chapter, and only then undertaking an extended discussion of the approach. Isn't this backwards?

I believe that a critical discussion of existing policy-analysis frameworks is helpful in *motivating* a full-blown analysis of the SWF approach. By seeing the inadequacies in currently dominant frameworks, we can see why it makes sense to devote the considerable intellectual effort required to work through the variety of technical, philosophical, and empirical challenges that arise in elaborating the SWF approach—the challenges that I discuss in subsequent chapters and that other scholars in the SWF tradition have also spent much effort engaging. However, the reader who prefers to read Chapters 3 through 7 first and then return to this chapter can certainly do so.

It is also important to emphasize that the criticisms of CBA, inequality metrics, other equity metrics, and CEA presented in this chapter do not generally presuppose the possibility of interpersonal comparisons. In particular, I will show that certain ways of using these frameworks to order outcome sets fail to meet basic welfarist criteria. These particular approaches fail to yield a quasiordering of outcome sets, or

---

[4] Why aren't "happiness" metrics on the list of current policy-evaluation frameworks? Quantifying individuals' happiness or "subjective well-being," via surveys, and studying the correlates of happiness, has become a huge topic in economics and psychology. See, e.g., Diener et al. (1999); Frey (2008); Kahnemann, Diener, and Schwarz (1999); Van Praag and Ferrer-i-Carbonell (2004). A number of prominent scholars in the field have suggested that governmental policy should be focused on, or at least give greater weight to, the promotion of happiness. See Diener and Seligman (2004); Dolan and Peasgood (2010); Kahneman and Sugden (2005); Layard (2005). However, this suggestion has not—as yet—given rise to a well-developed policy-evaluation framework distinct from those already mentioned. Rather, insofar as they have attempted to quantify policy impacts, happiness scholars have mainly worked within existing frameworks. For example, some happiness scholars have calculated willingness-to-pay/accept values, for purposes of CBA, by using happiness surveys rather than the preference data traditionally employed by CBA researchers. See Welsch (2009). Work has also been done using inequality metrics to study the distribution of happiness, and using poverty metrics to determine the extent to which individuals are below a subjective-well-being threshold. See Kingdon and Knight (2006); Stevenson and Wolfers (2010). Happiness research, thus, is not given its own rubric in this chapter, but is discussed in connection with the various policy frameworks addressed here. It is also discussed at various junctures in subsequent chapters.

they run afoul of Pareto-indifference and Pareto-superiority. What is critical to understand is that even the skeptic about interpersonal comparisons—if she is a welfarist—should not embrace a choice-evaluation framework that violates the basic Pareto criteria, or that doesn't serve to produce a well-behaved ranking of outcomes (a ranking that respects the basic reflexivity, symmetry, and transitivity properties of "better than" and "equally good as"). Moreover, even the skeptic about interpersonal comparisons may recognize that a proposed choice-evaluation framework, albeit consistent with minimal welfarist criteria, is substantively unattractive.

In a few instances, however, I will concede that certain ways of using current policy-evaluation frameworks to rank outcome sets do meet minimal welfarist criteria and, further, are *conditionally* attractive—conditional on the premise that well-being is not interpersonally comparable and measurable by utilities.[5] These approaches are plausible "fallbacks," in the event that the argument for interpersonal comparability and the SWF approach that I attempt to mount in subsequent chapters is unpersuasive. But there are various other ways of using current frameworks to order outcome sets that should be seen as problematic independent of the success of my eventual argument for the SWF approach.

One objection to the strategy followed in this chapter—examining currently dominant policy-evaluation frameworks from a welfarist perspective—is that some of these frameworks, in particular QALY-based CEA and social-gradient metrics, are not intended as welfarist methodologies. It is certainly true that these two approaches are often defended in non-welfarist terms; whether they actually succeed in providing an appealing non-welfarist framework for policy choice is a different question, one that I will not attempt to engage. This book works *within* welfarism, for reasons belabored in Chapter 1—and it is important (if only for the sake of completeness) to see why the whole gamut of prevalent non-SWF frameworks for policy evaluation are problematic from the perspective of welfarism.

Another objection is that existing frameworks have some useful role other than as the outcome-ranking component of a moral decision procedure. In particular, it is often suggested that CBA has an important *legal* role: for example, that non-tax bodies should employ CBA, with redistribution handled through the tax system; or that the use of a cost-benefit test by governmental bodies will benefit everyone in the long run.

The difficult problem of optimal legal structures is discussed in Chapter 8. The main focus of this book, however, is designing a welfarist framework for engaging in the distinctive species of normative evaluation that I have referred to as "moral"—the species of normative evaluation that is characterized by a focus on persons, by impartiality between persons, and by a willingness to transcend existing social

---

[5] I argue that the income-evaluation-function approach and the egalitarian-equivalent approach, both discussed below under the heading of inequality metrics, are conditionally attractive in this way.

norms. Existing frameworks (to the extent they are not merely variations on the SWF approach) fail to meet the needs of *this* sort of normative deliberation. Whether the frameworks fulfill some other function is not a question I address in this chapter.

I. THE SWF APPROACH: AN INTRODUCTION

This section begins by characterizing the SWF framework and discussing why it seems a promising blueprint for a welfarist choice-evaluation procedure. This section then reviews the existing literature on SWFs, surveying the history, theory, and current scholarly uses of the "social welfare function."

A. What Is an SWF?

What is the SWF framework for policy choice? I offer the following account. As I shall explain in the next subsection, this is not precisely what is meant by a "social welfare function" in existing scholarship, but rather a generalization of the current definition—one that accommodates the possibility of an incomplete ranking of life-histories and outcomes.

Remember that *any* welfarist procedure will contain an account of well-being that furnishes a quasiordering of the life-history set **H** (and perhaps other rankings associated with the life-history set), in a given choice situation, and will use this information to generate a moral ranking of the outcome set **O**. The SWF framework, as I conceptualize it, accomplishes these tasks in a distinctive way. First, it represents the rankings of the life-history set using *utility numbers*. Second, it produces a moral ranking of the outcome set as a function of the utility numbers associated with life-histories. Third, it assumes some degree of interpersonal comparability of well-being.

I will discuss these features of the SWF approach in turn. At the same time, my discussion will show how the SWF format can easily satisfy the minimal criteria that any welfarist decision procedure should meet: producing a ranking of any given outcome set which is a quasiordering, which satisfies the Pareto principles, and which is impartial. And it will show how the approach promises to extend the Pareto quasi-ordering in an attractive manner (assuming interpersonal comparisons are indeed possible).

(1) The first characteristic feature of the SWF framework is that it uses utility functions to *represent* individual well-being. In general, a welfarist choice-evaluation procedure provides guidance for a given choice situation by constructing a choice set **A**, an outcome set **O**, and an associated life-history set **H**. The SWF framework does all this *and* constructs a set **U** of utility functions for the particular choice situation. Each utility function $u(.)$ belonging to **U** maps a life-history onto a real number. So $u(.)$ takes the form $u(x; i)$. And **U** then represents the various rankings associated with the life-history set. Those rankings are *reflected* by the numerical information contained in **U**.

How can utility numbers mirror well-being rankings? Consider first the well-being quasiordering of life-histories. This is what I referred to, in the last chapter, as "$\succcurlyeq^{\text{WB}}$." Remember that, in general, a quasiordering is a reflexive, transitive, binary relation on some set. This particular quasiordering, $\succcurlyeq^{\text{WB}}$, is a reflexive, transitive, binary relation on the set $\mathbf{H}$ of life-histories. It has the form: $(x; i) \succcurlyeq^{\text{WB}} (y; j)$. What this says, in English, is that life-history $(x; i)$ is at least as good for well-being as life-history $(y; j)$ or, equivalently, that subject i in outcome x is at least as well off as subject j in outcome y. The relation $\succcurlyeq^{\text{WB}}$ is *reflexive*: each life-history is at least as good as itself. It is *transitive*: If one life-history is at least as good for well-being as a second, and the second is at least as good for well-being as a third, then the first life-history is at least as good as the third. Furthermore (because this relation is a quasi-ordering), it can—but need not—be complete. To say that relation $\succcurlyeq^{\text{WB}}$ is *complete* means that, for every pair of life-histories, either the first is at least as good for well-being as the second, or the second is at least as good for well-being as the first, or both. If the relation $\succcurlyeq^{\text{WB}}$ is incomplete, then there is a pair or multiple pairs of life-histories such that the first life-history is not at least as good as the second, and the second is not at least as good as the first. These pairs are *incomparable*.

Remember, also, that the relation "at least as good as" can be used to define the relations of "better than" and "equally good as."

Consider, first, the case in which the well-being quasiordering of life-histories is complete. In that case (bracketing technical complications) it will be possible to use a *single* utility function to represent the ranking of life-histories. In particular, a single utility function could mirror the ranking of life-histories via a very natural "representational rule," which makes the "at least as good as" relation between life-histories isomorphic to the "greater than or equal to" relation between real numbers. In other words, in the case of a complete quasiordering of life-histories, we could (bracketing technical complications) identify some $v(.)$ such that $v(x; i) \geq v(y; j)$ iff $(x; i)$ is at least as good for well-being as $(y; j)$.[6]

---

[6] There are actually a variety of "representational rules" that allow utility numbers to represent well-being. In the case of a complete ordering of life-histories, we could assign life-histories utility numbers such that the better life-history is assigned a higher number; or, we could use the less natural rule which assigns the better life-history a *lower* number. In the case of a complete ordering of differences between life-histories, we could identify a utility function $u(.)$ which represents that difference ordering via the following natural rule: The difference between life-histories $(x; i)$ and $(y; j)$ is at least as great as the difference between life-histories $(z; k)$ and $(w; l)$ iff $u(x; i) - u(y; j) \geq u(z; k) - u(w; l)$. But consider that if we define $v(.)=e^{u(.)}$, then $v(.)$ represents the very same difference ordering via this less natural rule: the difference between life-histories $(x; i)$ and $(y; j)$ is at least as great as the difference between life-histories $(z; k)$ and $(w; l)$ iff $v(x; i)/v(y; j) \geq v(z; k)/v(w; l)$. (On the plurality of numerical rules for representing a given relation, see Weymark [2005, pp. 540–544].) However, it is almost invariably assumed in the literature on SWFs that utility numbers represent well-being levels and differences via the natural rules, and that will be my assumption throughout the book as well.

What are the "technical complications" alluded to in the text? A complete ordering of a finite or countably infinite set of items *can* always be represented by a single utility function. A complete

For example, imagine that the outcome set contains three outcomes, x, y, z, and the population contains two individuals, i and j, yielding a life-history set with six elements. And imagine that they are completely ordered, as shown in Table 2.1. In this particular case, we can *represent* $\succcurlyeq^{WB}$ via the following assignment of numbers: $v(x; i) = 20$; $v(y; i) = 12$; $v(y; j) = 12$; $v(z; i) = 9$; $v(z; j) = 7$; $v(x; j) = 7$.

Table 2.1 A Complete Well-Being Quasiordering

	$(x; i)$	$(x; j)$	$(y; i)$	$(y; j)$	$(z; i)$	$(z; j)$
$(x; i)$	Yes	Yes	Yes	Yes	Yes	Yes
$(x; j)$	No	Yes	**No**	No	No	Yes
$(y; i)$	No	Yes	Yes	Yes	Yes	Yes
$(y; j)$	No	Yes	Yes	Yes	Yes	Yes
$(z; i)$	No	Yes	No	No	Yes	Yes
$(z; j)$	No	Yes	No	No	No	Yes

In this table, "Yes" means that the life-history in the row stands in relation $\succcurlyeq^{WB}$ to the life-history in the column, i.e., is "at least as good as" the life-history in the column. For example, the bold **No** means that the life-history $(x; j)$ is not at least as good as the life-history $(y; i)$, i.e., that not $(x; j) \succcurlyeq^{WB} (y; i)$.

Inspection will show that the relation set forth by this table is indeed a complete quasiordering. It is reflexive, meaning that each life-history is at least as good as itself (this can be seen by seeing that the diagonal entries are all "Yes"). It is transitive, meaning that if one life-history is at least as good as a second, and the second at least as good as a third, then the first life-history is at least as good as the third. Finally, it is complete, meaning that for each pair of life-histories, either the first is at least as good as the second, or the second is at least as good as the first, or both.

The complete quasiordering in this table gives rise to various "betterness" and "equally good as" relations between the life-histories, which can be compactly summarized as follows: Life-history $(x; i)$ is better than life-history $(y; i)$, which in turn is equally good as life-history $(y; j)$, which in turn is better than life-history $(z; i)$, which in turn is better than life-history $(z; j)$, which is equally good as life-history $(x; j)$. If we assign $(x; i)$ the largest number, $(y; i)$ the second largest, $(y; j)$ the same number as $(y; i)$, $(z; i)$ a lower number, $(z; j)$ a yet lower number, and $(x; j)$ the same number as $(z; j)$, then these numbers will represent the quasiordering. For example, as stated in the text, we can say that $v(x; i) = 20$; $v(y; i) = 12$; $v(y; j) = 12$; $v(z; i) = 9$; $v(z; j) = 7$; $v(x; j) = 7$.

By assigning numbers this way, we ensure that one life-history will be better than another iff it is assigned a higher number, and that one life-history will be equally

ordering of an uncountably infinite set *may*, but need not, be thus representable. See Kreps (1988, ch. 3).

good as a second iff it is assigned the same number. That in turn implies that one life-history will be at least as good as a second iff the number assigned the first is at least as large as the number assigned the second. Inspecting Table 2.1 will show that the numbers assigned by $v(.)$ here do indeed represent the quasiordering. Take any pair of a row life-history and a column life-history. Whenever the entry in the table is "Yes," the row life-history is assigned a $v(.)$ value which is greater than or equal to the column life-history's value. Whenever it is "No," the row-life-history is assigned a smaller $v(.)$ value.

Of course, this is *not* the only $v(.)$ that represents this quasiordering. Any assignment of numbers which gives the largest number to $(x; i)$, the second largest to $(y; i)$, and so forth, will work equally well. For example, consider $v^*(.)$ such that $v^*(x; i)$ = 1900; $v^*(y; i)$ =555; $v^*(y; j)$ = 555; $v^*(z; i)$ = 3; $v^*(z; j)$ = 2.75; $v^*(x; j)$ = 2.75.

Again, however, the well-being quasiordering of life-histories need not be complete. And if $\succeq^{WB}$ turns out to be incomplete, it will *not* be possible to represent this quasiordering via a single utility function.[7]

However, it *will* be possible to represent $\succeq^{WB}$ via a whole *set* of utility functions. We can construct a set of utility functions and use the "zone of agreement" between them to mirror the ranking of life-histories. In other words, whenever one life-history is at least as good as a second, each and every utility function in U will assign the first life-history a number which is at least as large as the number it assigns to the second. Whenever one life-history is equally good as a second, each utility function in U will assign the two the very same number. And whenever one life-history is incomparable with a second, the utility functions will "disagree" about their ranking: some will assign the first life-history a larger number, but others will assign the first life-history a smaller number.

In short, it *will* be possible to represent the well-being quasiordering of life-histories via the following set-valued rule: Life-history $(x; i)$ is at least as good for well-being as life-history $(y; j)$ iff, for all $u(.)$ belonging to **U**, $u(x; i) \geq u(y; j)$.

---

[7] Any real number is equal to, greater than, or less than any other. But in the case of a quasiordering, there are four possibilities regarding any two life-histories: namely that the first is equally good as the second, better than the second, worse than the second, or incomparable with the second. Incomparability is symmetric: If one life-history is incomparable with a second, then the second will be incomparable with the first. So we cannot represent this relation by assigning the first life-history a larger number than the second, since the relation of "greater than" between numbers is asymmetric. Nor, in general, can we represent it by assigning the two life-histories the same number, since incomparability doesn't have the transitivity properties of "equal to." If one life-history is incomparable with a second, and the second with a third, the first need not be incomparable with the third. If one life-history is incomparable with a second, and the second is better than a third, the first need not be better than the third. Figure 2.1 provides a simple example which shows why an incomplete quasiordering can't be represented by a single utility function.

This set-valued rule will serve to represent $\succcurlyeq^{\text{WB}}$, not only in the case where $\succcurlyeq^{\text{WB}}$ is complete, but also in the case where it is incomplete.[8]

To see how the set-valued rule can function to mirror an incomplete quasiordering of life-histories, consider the following example.

Imagine that outcomes characterize individuals as having two attributes a and b (health, leisure, consumption, happiness, etc.). Assume, further, that attributes have different numerical levels, and that life-histories are ordered using the following "attribute dominance" relation: One life-history is at least as good as a second iff the a level of the first life-history is at least as large as the a level of the second *and* the b level of the first life-history is at least as large as the b level of the second. This in turn means that two life-histories are equally good just in case they have the same a and b levels; and that one life-history is better than a second just in case both of its attribute levels are at least as large, and one is larger. For example, the life-history with attributes $(4, 8)$ is better than the life-history with attributes $(3, 6)$. It is also better than the life-history with attributes $(3, 8)$. It is incomparable with the life-history with attributes $(3, 9)$.

This relation between life-histories is an incomplete quasiordering. It *cannot* be represented by a single utility function. It can, however, be represented by the following set-valued rule. Let one utility function $v^a(.)$ be such that it assigns life-histories a number which depends solely on the a attribute, increasing as that attribute does; and a second utility function, $v^b(.)$, be such that it assigns life-histories a number which depends solely on the b attribute, increasing as that attribute does. Most simply, we can say that $v^a(a, b)$ = a, and that $v^b(a, b) = b$. Then if $\mathbf{U}$ consists of $v^a(.)$ and $v^b(.)$, it will be the case that (a, b) $\succcurlyeq^{\text{WB}}$ (a^*, b^*) according to the attribute-dominance relation iff $u(a, b) \geq u(a^*, b^*)$ for all $u(.)$ belonging to $\mathbf{U}$, i.e., just in case $v^a(a; b) \geq v^a(a^*, b^*)$ *and* $v^b(a; b) \geq v^b(a^*, b^*)$.

For example, imagine that each attribute can have levels 1, 2, or 3. This yields 9 possible combinations of attributes that a life-history might possess; the quasiordering of these attribute bundles is represented by Figure 2.1. A given bundle (a, b) is better than all bundles in the quadrant "southwest" of it (in other words, bundles lying on the

---

[8] It bears emphasis that the set-valued rule covers *both* the case where $\succcurlyeq^{\text{WB}}$ is complete *and* the case where $\succcurlyeq^{\text{WB}}$ is incomplete. A paper by Evren and Ok (2010), also discussed below, n. 11, shows that *every* quasiordering, complete or not, can be represented by a set of utility functions. For example, as they point out, a lexicographic ordering of N-dimensional Euclidean space, which is complete but not representable by a single utility function, *is* representable by a set of utility functions.

To further understand why the set-valued rule covers *both* the case where $\succcurlyeq^{\text{WB}}$ is complete *and* the case where $\succcurlyeq^{\text{WB}}$ is incomplete, consider the "constructive" case (see text immediately below) where we start with a set $\mathbf{U}$ of utility functions, and use the set-valued rule to define $\succcurlyeq^{\text{WB}}$. We say that $(x; i)$ $\succcurlyeq^{\text{WB}} (y; j)$ iff for all $u(.)$ belonging to $\mathbf{U}$, $u(x; i) \geq u(y; j)$. If the utility functions in $\mathbf{U}$ bear an appropriate relation to each other, $\succcurlyeq^{\text{WB}}$ will be complete. Trivially, this is true if $\mathbf{U}$ is a singleton. $\succcurlyeq^{\text{WB}}$ thus constructed will also be complete in other sorts of cases. For example, the account of well-being advanced in Chapter 3 yields a $\mathbf{U}$ which is unique up to a positive ratio transformation if individuals have identical extended preferences. It is not hard to see that, if $\mathbf{U}$ is unique up to a positive ratio transformation, the relation $\succcurlyeq^{\text{WB}}$ defined via the set-valued rule will be complete.

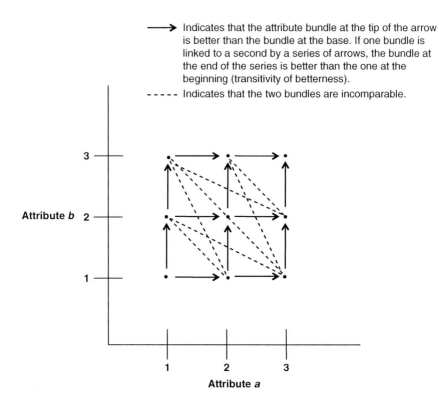

Figure 2.1 An Incomplete Well-Being Quasiordering.

horizontal line segment to the left of (a, b), bundles lying on the vertical line segment below (a, b), or bundles in the quadrant between these two line segments). It is worse than all bundles in the quadrant "northeast" of it. And it is incomparable with all other bundles.

Note that no single $v(.)$ can represent these relations. We clearly can't represent incomparability by saying that one life-history is incomparable with a second if it is assigned a larger number. The relation of incomparability is *symmetric*. As can be seen by the figure, if one life-history is incomparable with a second, the second is incomparable with the first. Nor can we represent incomparability by assigning two life-histories the very same number. That would imply that, if one life-history is incomparable with a second, and the second with a third, then the first is incomparable with the third. But incomparability is *intransitive*. For example, the life-history with attributes $(1, 2)$ is incomparable with the life-history with attributes $(3, 1)$; that latter life-history, in turn, is incomparable with the life-history with attributes $(2, 2)$; but the life-history with attributes $(1, 2)$ is worse than the life-history with attributes $(2, 2)$, not incomparable with it.

However, the relations of the life-histories can be represented via a **U** which includes both $v^a(.)$ which assigns each life-history the level of the a attribute, i.e., $v^a(1, 1) = 1$, v^a

$(1, 2) = 1$, $v^a(1, 3) = 1$, $v^a(2, 1) = 2$, $v^a(2, 2) = 2$, etc.; and a $v^b(.)$ which assigns each life-history the level of the $b(.)$ attribute. It can be seen that one life-history is at least as good as a second iff $v^a(.)$ and $v^b(.)$ assign the first life-history a number at least as large as the second. In other words, it can be seen that (1) two life-histories are equally good iff both $v^a(.)$ and $v^b(.)$ assign them the same number; that (2) one life-history is better than a second iff $v^a(.)$ and $v^b(.)$ assign the first life-history a number at least as large as the second, and one or both utility functions assign it a strictly greater number; and that otherwise (3) the life-histories are incomparable.

The reader may wonder about the typicality of the example. Why think that the set-valued rule is *generally* a good recipe for representing a quasiordering of life-histories?

Imagine, first, that we *start* with a set **U** of utility functions, which have been identified in some manner, and we then *construct* a relation $\succcurlyeq^{WB}$. We use the set-valued rule to *define* $\succcurlyeq^{WB}$. We say that $(x; i) \succcurlyeq^{WB} (y; j)$ iff for all $u(.)$ belonging to **U**, $u(x; i) \geq u(y; j)$, and that $(x; i)$ and $(y; j)$ are incomparable iff this is not the case. The reader can readily ascertain that a relation $\succcurlyeq^{WB}$ constructed in this manner will be a quasiordering: it will be reflexive and transitive.[9]

Indeed, this constructive strategy is more or less the strategy that I will pursue in Chapter 3. Very roughly, the idea will be this: I will start with each individual's idealized extended preferences over life-histories, which I will assume to be complete; identify a utility function that represents these preferences; pool these utility functions to create **U**; and then define $\succcurlyeq^{WB}$ by saying that life-history $(x; i)$ is at least as good for well-being as life-history $(y; j)$ iff, for all $u(.)$ belonging to **U**, $u(x; i) \geq u(y; j)$.[10]

But what if a decision procedure *starts* with a well-being quasiordering of life-histories as a primitive? Why think, in that case, that the quasiordering can necessarily be represented via the set-valued rule? A beautiful and surprising result in the

---

[9] To see why a $\succcurlyeq^{WB}$ relation thus constructed is *reflexive*, take any $(x; i)$. Consider that, for all $u(.)$ belonging to **U**, $u(x; i) = u(x; i)$. Therefore, for all $u(.)$ belonging to **U**, $u(x; i) \geq u(x; i)$. Because $\succcurlyeq^{WB}$ has been defined such that one life-history $\succcurlyeq^{WB}$ a second if and only if its $u(.)$ value is at least as large for all $u(.)$ in **U**, it follows that $(x; i) \succcurlyeq^{WB} (x; i)$.

To see why a $\succcurlyeq^{WB}$ thus constructed is *transitive*, consider any triple of life-histories such that $(x; i) \succcurlyeq^{WB} (y; j)$ and $(y; j) \succcurlyeq^{WB} (z; k)$. Because $\succcurlyeq^{WB}$ has been defined such that one life-history $\succcurlyeq^{WB}$ a second if and only if its $u(.)$ value is at least as large for all $u(.)$ in **U**, it follows that $u(x; i) \geq u(y; j)$ for all $u(.)$ belonging to **U**; and that $u(y; j) \geq u(z; k)$ for all $u(.)$ belonging to **U**. It thus follows, mathematically, that $u(x; i) \geq u(z; k)$ for all $u(.)$ belonging to **U**. Because $\succcurlyeq^{WB}$ has been defined such that one life-history $\succcurlyeq^{WB}$ a second if and only if its $u(.)$ value is at least as large for all $u(.)$ in **U**, it follows—in turn—that $(x; i) \succcurlyeq^{WB} (z; k)$.

[10] This is only a rough statement of the approach in Chapter 3, because I actually employ utility functions that represent each individual's extended preferences over life-history lotteries and comparisons to nonexistence. Furthermore, each individual's extended preferences are actually represented by an entire individual set of utility functions; these are then pooled to form **U**.

theory of quasiorderings shows that a quasiordering of any arbitrary set (be it **H** or any other set) can indeed be represented via the set-valued rule.[11]

What about the other rankings that may be associated with **H**? I assume that any welfarist decision procedure at least includes the relation $\succcurlyeq^{\text{WB}}$. But it may also include other rankings associated with the life-history set. A welfarist decision procedure that does include these additional rankings, and employs the SWF format, will also represent *these* rankings using utility numbers.

One such ranking is the quasiordering of *differences* between life-histories. The natural representational idea, here, is that numerical differences between utility numbers can be employed to mirror well-being differences between lives. That idea—generalized to allow for incomparability—yields the following rule for representing the difference quasiordering: The difference between $(x; i)$ and $(y; j)$ is at least as great as the difference between $(z; k)$ and $(w; l)$ iff, for all $u(.)$ belonging to **U**, $u(x; i) - u(y; j) \geq u(z; k) - u(w; l)$.[12]

Another such ranking is the comparison of life-histories to nonexistence, naturally represented as follows: life-history $(x; i)$ is at least as good as nonexistence iff, for all $u(.)$ belonging to **U**, $u(x; i) \geq 0$.[13]

(2) A second characteristic feature of the SWF format is that it ranks outcomes as a function of their associated utility numbers. The SWF format *uses* **U** to generate the moral quasiordering of the outcome set **O**.

How does this occur? Each utility function $u(.)$ has a dual aspect. To begin, each $u(.)$ is a "scalar-valued" function from the elements of **H** onto the real numbers. In other words, a given $u(.)$ maps each life-history onto a single, real number. For example, $u(x; i) = 5$, or $u(y; j) = 6$.

But note that each outcome in **O** corresponds to a whole package of life-histories, with N elements (N being the population size). For example, outcome x corresponds to the package of life-histories $(x; 1), (x; 2), ..., (x; N)$, where $(x; 1)$ means being individual 1 in outcome x, $(x; 2)$ means being individual 2 in outcome x, and

---

[11] See Evren and Ok (2010, p. 5). It had previously been established that every quasiordering can be represented by a set of complete orderings. See Donaldson and Weymark (1998). Because a complete ordering of an uncountable set need not be representable by a single utility function, the Evren and Ok result is powerful and surprising. For examples of economic scholarship using a set-valued approach to represent quasiorderings, see sources discussed in their paper; Evren (2008); Ok (2007, pp. 499–501).

[12] Under what conditions can a difference quasiordering be represented by this representational rule? That is an interesting question (note that the Evren and Ok [2010] result doesn't guarantee the existence of a set of utility functions representing a difference quasiordering via this particular rule). However, it is not a question I need to address, because my difference quasiordering is *constructed* from preexisting utility functions that represent individuals' extended preferences over life-history lotteries. See Chapter 3.

[13] See Chapter 3 and 5, discussing the use of a zero point to set well-being ratios and the possibility that this zero point might be nonexistence.

so forth. So each $u(.)$ can also be understood as a "vector-valued" function, mapping the elements of **O** (outcomes) onto N-entry lists or "vectors" of utility numbers.

In general, a function that maps outcomes onto N-entry vectors has the form, $v(x) = (v_1(x), v_2(x),\ldots, v_N(x))$, where $v_1(x)$ is the first component of this N-entry vector, $v_2(x)$ the second component,$\ldots$, $v_i(x)$ the ith component,$\ldots$, $v_N(x)$ the last component. So let us start with the utility functions in **U**, understood as scalar-valued functions from life-histories to real numbers. For each such scalar-valued $u(.)$, we can define its vector-valued counterpart as follows: $u(x) = (u(x; 1), u(x, 2),\ldots, u(x; i),\ldots, u(x; N))$. In other words, the first component of $u(x)$ is the utility assigned by scalar-valued $u(.)$ to the life-history of individual 1 in x; the second component of $u(x)$ is the utility assigned by scalar-valued $u(.)$ to the life-history of individual 2 in x; $\ldots$; the ith component of $u(x)$ is the utility assigned by scalar-valued $u(.)$ to the life-history of individual i in outcome x; and so forth.

For example, imagine that $N = 3$, and that a utility function $u(.)$ in **U** assigns the following numbers to life-histories: $u(x; 1) = 10$, $u(x; 2) = 7$, $u(x; 3) = 8$. Then the vector-valued counterpart of $u(.)$ maps x onto the following three-entry vector: $(10, 7, 8)$.

Henceforth, I will use the single symbol "$u(.)$" to mean both a scalar-valued function from life-histories to single real numbers, and its vector-valued counterpart. The context will make clear which I am referring to. Where "$u(.)$" is being used to mean a vector-valued function from outcomes to N-entry vectors, I will often use the following symbolism: $u(x) = (u_1(x), u_2(x),\ldots, u_N(x))$. The number $u_i(x)$ is the ith component of this vector; it is the utility number assigned to individual i in outcome x, and is just equal to $u(x; i)$, the utility of having the life-history that consists in being individual i in outcome x.

So now we have the materials for moving *from* the set **U**, which numerically represents our account of well-being, *to* a moral quasiordering of the outcome set. How exactly shall we do so?

The most straightforward way to do so is as follows. There is some single rule R for ranking the set of all possible N-entry utility vectors.[14] R provides a complete quasiordering of these vectors. With R in hand, along with **U**, a ranking of the set **O** of outcomes is produced as follows: outcome x is morally at least as good as outcome y iff, for all $u(.)$ in **U**, $u(x)$ is ranked by R as being at least as good as $u(y)$. For short, call this the "simple R-based form for an SWF."

The simple R-based form for an SWF corresponds to the dominant tradition in existing social-welfare-function scholarship.[15] There are also more complex possibilities, for example the following. (1) Outcomes might be ranked using the above

---

[14] Or at least all N-entry vectors in some orthant of N-dimensional space, e.g., all N-entry vectors with positive elements. This qualification is needed because some important rules for ranking utility vectors, such as the rule used by the Atkinson SWF, do not handle negative utilities well. See Chapter 5.

[15] See Bossert and Weymark (2004).

formula, but with a single rule R^* that provides only an incomplete quasiordering of all utility vectors, rather than a complete ordering. (2) The SWF might say: outcome x is morally at least as good as outcome y iff x is ranked at least as good as y by rule R^*, for each $u(.)$ in $\mathbf{U}$, where the ranking of x and y by R^* for a given $u(.)$ may depend *not merely* on $u(x)$ and $u(y)$ but also on the utility vectors that $u(.)$ assigns to other outcomes in $\mathbf{O}$. (3) R might vary, depending upon which utility function in $\mathbf{U}$ is being used. Rather than there being a single rule R, each $u(.)$ would have its own rule for ranking utility vectors, $R^{u(.)}$, and the rule for ranking outcomes would be: outcome x is morally at least as good as outcome y iff, for all $u(.)$ in $\mathbf{U}$, $u(x)$ is ranked by $R^{u(.)}$ as being at least as good as $u(y)$.

In this book, I often ignore these more complex possibilities and assume that the SWF assumes the simple R-based form—both for the sake of simplicity and because (at least to some extent) the more complex possibilities are substantively problematic. See the margin for details.[16] In general, unless otherwise noted, I henceforth use the term "SWF" to mean the simple R-based form.

It is easy to see that the simple R-based form for an SWF effortlessly satisfies minimal welfarist criteria. Imagine that some rule R provides a complete quasiordering of all N-entry utility vectors and, further, has the following features: (a) R is

[16] To begin, it should be noted that there are methodologies for using the information in $\mathbf{U}$ to rank outcomes that do not meet minimal welfarist criteria (i.e., do not reliably yield a quasiordering of the outcome set that respects the principles of Pareto-indifference and -superiority and impartiality). For example, imagine that $\mathbf{U}$ can be partitioned into N subsets $\mathbf{U}^1, \ldots, \mathbf{U}^N$, each corresponding to one of the N individuals in the population. (This will be true, in particular, if $\mathbf{U}$ is constructed along the lines recommended in Chapter 3, and each spectator's extended preferences do not vary over time or across outcomes; each spectator k will thus have her own set $\mathbf{U}^k$, and these will be merged to form $\mathbf{U}$.) And imagine that we rank outcomes by picking some percentage F which is less than 100%, and some single rule R that completely ranks all utility vectors, and say: x is at least as good as y iff $u(x)$ is ranked by R at least as good as $u(y)$ for all $u(.)$ within $\mathbf{U}^k$, $k = 1, 2, \ldots, N$, for at least F percent of the N sets $\mathbf{U}^1, \ldots, \mathbf{U}^N$. (Note the contrast with the simple R-based approach, as stated in the text, which requires that $u(x)$ be ranked at least as good as $u(y)$ for *all* $u(.)$ in $\mathbf{U}$.) It is not too hard to see that, for any F less than 100%, this approach can yield an intransitive ranking of outcomes, hence does not satisfy minimal welfarist criteria.

The three alternatives to the simple R-based approach described in the text *can* (if appropriately specified) satisfy minimal welfarist criteria. However, the second possibility violates the axiom of "binary independence of irrelevant alternatives." See Bossert and Weymark (2004, pp. 1102–1111). In other words, whether x is morally better than y can depend, not merely upon individuals' well-being in x and y (as measured by the set $\mathbf{U}$), but upon what their well-being would be in other outcomes. But, if the question at hand is determining how one outcome morally compares to a second, why should facts about well-being in further outcomes be relevant?

The third possibility (at least given certain approaches for associating a rule $R^{u(.)}$ with a utility function $u(.)$) seems inconsistent with the spirit of welfarism. See Chapter 5, n. 155.

The first possibility is harder to rule out, other than on the grounds of additional complexity. Indeed, on certain metaethical views, it may be quite plausible that there is a rule R^* which generates an incomplete quasiordering of utility vectors. See Chapter 5, pp. 399–404.

anonymous, meaning that if one utility vector is just a reordering or "permutation" of a second, it ranks them as equally good; and (b) R is "Paretian," meaning that if every utility number in $u(x)$ is at least as large as the corresponding entry in $u(y)$, with at least one strictly larger, R ranks $u(x)$ as better than $u(y)$. If so, an SWF that takes the simple form, using R as its rule, will necessarily satisfy the minimal welfarist criteria. This SWF will produce a quasiordering of the outcome set **O**; this quasiordering will respect the principles of Pareto-indifference and Pareto-superiority; and it will be impartial.[17]

Unless otherwise noted, for the remainder of this book, I will assume that the SWFs being discussed indeed satisfy the Pareto principles and the principle of anonymity—rather than explicitly describing the SWF as "Paretian" and "anonymous."

A further note about the R-based form for an SWF is important. While R itself (a rule for ranking all possible utility vectors) is, for simplicity, assumed to provide a complete quasiordering of these vectors, the simple R-based form for an SWF may well yield an incomplete quasiordering of the *outcomes* in **O**. This is because R is merged with an entire set **U** of utility functions, not necessarily a singleton. Again, outcomes are ranked by saying: x is morally at least as good as y iff, *for all u(.)* in **U**, $u(x)$ is ranked by R at least as good as $u(y)$. The quasiordering of outcomes produced by this rule may be complete, or incomplete, depending on the content of **U** and the form of R.

There are many different rules R that have the basic welfarist properties of being Paretian and anonymous. One standard such R is the utilitarian rule, which ranks vectors by summing unweighted utilities. A different standard rule R is the continuous prioritarian rule, which ranks vectors by summing utilities "transformed" by a strictly increasing, strictly concave function. Yet a different standard possibility is that R is a "rank-weighted" rule—summing utilities multiplied by fixed weights, with larger utilities receiving smaller weights.[18] A final, oft-discussed possibility is that R is the so-called "leximin" rule for ranking utility vectors.[19]

---

[17] Because R is anonymous, the SWF is clearly impartial in the basic sense of not using proper names or other expressions that refer to particular individuals. If **U** is such as to allow for interpersonal level comparability—which means that impartiality can be formulated in the stronger sense of giving an equal moral ranking to x and y if the well-being levels in y are a permutation of the levels in x—the SWF will be impartial in this stronger sense.

[18] Formally, the rank-weighted rule R uses N numbers $a_1, \ldots, a_N$, where each is larger than the next. For a given utility vector $u(x)$, produce a corresponding rank-ordered vector $u^*(x)$ by ordering the elements of $u(x)$ from smallest to largest. Assign $u(x)$ a number $w(u(x))$ equaling a_1 times the first element of $u^*(x)$ plus a_2 times the second element of $u^*(x)$ plus ... plus a_N times the last element. Then the rank-weighted rule says that $u(x)$ is at least as good as $u(y)$ iff $w(u(x)) \geq w(u(y))$. See Chapter 5.

[19] The leximin rule compares $u(x)$ and $u(y)$ according to the utility of the worst-off individuals; if these are equal, according to the utility of the second-worst off individuals; if these are equal,

Coupling each of these rules with a set $\mathbf{U}$ of utility functions, we arrive at a variety of possible SWFs—a variety of possible approaches to ranking outcomes. The utilitarian SWF says: outcome x is morally at least as good as outcome y iff, for all $u(.)$ in $\mathbf{U}$, $\sum_{i=1}^{N} u_i(x) \geq \sum_{i=1}^{N} u_i(y)$. The continuous prioritarian SWF says: outcome x is morally at least as good as outcome y iff, for all $u(.)$ in $\mathbf{U}$, $\sum_{i=1}^{N} g(u_i(x)) \geq \sum_{i=1}^{N} g(u_i(y))$, with $g(.)$ strictly increasing and strictly concave. (See Figure 2.2 for a visual illustration of a strictly increasing, strictly concave function.) An important subfamily of continuous prioritarian SWFs is the Atkinson subfamily, which says: outcome x is morally at least as good as outcome y iff, for all $u(.)$ in $\mathbf{U}$, $(1-\gamma)^{-1} \sum_{i=1}^{N} u_i(x)^{1-\gamma} \geq (1-\gamma)^{-1} \sum_{i=1}^{N} u_i(y)^{1-\gamma}$. The parameter γ, here, is an inequality-aversion parameter that takes some value greater than zero.[20] The rank-weighted SWF has the form: outcome x is morally at least as good as outcome y iff, for all $u(.)$ belonging to $\mathbf{U}$, the sum of rank-weighted utilities in $u(x)$ is at least as large as the sum of rank-weighted utilities in $u(y)$. The leximin SWF has the form: outcome x is morally at least as good as outcome y iff, for all $u(.)$ belonging to $\mathbf{U}$, $u(x)$ is ranked at least as good as $u(y)$ using the leximin rule. There are yet further, plausible kinds of Paretian anonymous SWFs, which along with these standard possibilities will be reviewed in Chapter 5.

The leximin SWF illustrates the important point that the rule R for ranking utility vectors may not assume the form of a real-valued function.[21] R is *some* procedure for ranking all possible utility vectors which achieves a complete ordering of these vectors—be it by using a mathematical formula that assigns each such vector a single real value, or in some other way. The term SWF ("social welfare function") is therefore a bit misleading. A more precise term might be "social welfare ordering"—but because the term "social welfare function" is more familiar and less awkward, I will use it to cover both the case in which R assumes the form of a real-valued function and the case in which it does not.

(3) A third characteristic of the SWF format is that it assumes some degree of interpersonal comparability of well-being.

The reader will be reminded what this means. To begin, the literature on interpersonal comparisons emphasizes that we should differentiate between two different

---

according to the utility of the third-worst-off individuals; and so forth. *See* Chapter 5 for a more precise statement.

[20] In the special case where $\gamma = 1$, the Atkinson SWF takes a different form. It says: outcome x is morally at least as good as outcome y iff, for all $u(.)$ in $\mathbf{U}$, $\sum_{i=1}^{N} \ln u_i(x) \geq \sum_{i=1}^{N} \ln u_i(y)$. I use the term "Atkinson," because this family of SWFs derives from Anthony Atkinson's (1970) pioneering work on the measurement of inequality.

[21] R assumes the form of a real-valued function if it uses some $w(.)$ which maps utility vectors onto real numbers and says: $u(x)$ is at least as good as $u(y)$ iff $w(u(x)) \geq w(u(y))$. Note that the utilitarian, continuous prioritarian, and rank-weighted SWFs employ an R of this sort—but not the leximin SWF. Two other SWFs discussed in Chapter 5, namely the sufficientist SWF and the prioritarian SWF with a lexical threshold, also do not rank utility vectors using a real-valued function.

kinds of comparability: interpersonal comparability of well-being *levels* and inter-personal comparability of well-being *differences*. Using the generic formal architecture of a welfarist decision procedure employed in this book, I have expressed interpersonal level comparability, for a given outcome set and associated life-history set, as follows: there is at least one pair of life-histories involving different subjects, such that the two are not incomparable according to the quasiordering of **H**. In other words, there exist $(x; i)$ and $(y; j)$, i and j distinct, such that $(x; i) \succcurlyeq^{WB} (y; j)$. And I have expressed interpersonal difference comparability, for a given outcome and life-history set, in terms of the quasiordering of differences between life-histories (assuming there is one): there exists at least one group of four life-histories, $(x; i)$, $(y; j)$, $(z; k)$, and $(w; l)$, such that the four subjects are not all identical, and such that the difference between the first two is at least as large as the difference between the second two.

Where the welfarist choice-evaluation procedure uses the SWF format—so that the rankings associated with **H** are represented by a set **U** of utilities—these two kinds of interpersonal comparability can be translated into conditions on **U**. Interpersonal level comparability means: there exists at least one pair of life-histories $(x; i)$ and $(y; j)$, i and j distinct, such that $u(x; i) \geq u(y; j)$ for all $u(.)$ belonging to **U**. Interpersonal difference comparability means: there exists at least one group of four life-histories, $(x; i)$, $(y; j)$, $(z; k)$, and $(w; l)$, such that the four subjects are not all identical, and such that $u(x; i) - u(y; j) \geq u(z; k) - u(w; l)$ for all $u(.)$ belonging to **U**.

The existing literature on social welfare functions assumes that the utility numbers which function as inputs to the social welfare function are indeed interpersonally comparable to some extent—either in terms of levels, or in terms of differences, or both. And my conceptualization of the SWF framework will incorporate this critical requirement. Strictly, I will be assuming that the SWF framework has the *resources* to make interpersonal comparisons—in other words, that there are *some* outcome sets and associated life-history sets in which it makes interpersonal level comparisons, difference comparisons, or both.[22]

The reader might wonder why the SWF framework needs interpersonal comparability. Imagine that the account of well-being is such that neither well-being levels, nor well-being differences, are interpersonally comparable *at all*, in any outcome sets. However, the account makes *intra*personal level comparisons, and also perhaps *intra*personal difference comparisons, and in any outcome set these are faithfully represented by a set **U**. What would be wrong with taking some rule R, such as the utilitarian, continuous prioritarian, rank-weighted, or leximin rule, and saying: x is at least as good as y iff, for all $u(.)$ belonging to **U**, $u(x)$ is at least as good as $u(y)$ according to R?

---

[22] There may be some outcome sets in which the SWF framework functions perfectly well without making any interpersonal comparisons—namely outcome sets in which the Pareto quasiordering itself furnishes a complete ordering of the outcomes, or in which Pareto-noncomparable outcomes are, intuitively, morally noncomparable.

A full rigorous answer to this question is beyond the scope of this book. But for reasons discussed in the margin, there is a real worry that many plausible SWFs will "collapse" to the Pareto quasiordering absent some degree of interpersonal comparability. Remember that a key ambition of a welfarist decision procedure is to *extend* the Pareto quasiordering: to produce a ranking of outcomes that is consistent with Pareto-indifference and Pareto-superiority, but also ranks at least some pairs of Pareto-noncomparable outcomes, in some outcome sets, in an attractive manner. Without some degree of interpersonal comparability, this ambition may well be unrealized.[23]

---

[23] The following analysis will suggest why plausible SWFs *which assume the simple R-based form* may well collapse to the Pareto quasiordering absent some degree of interpersonal comparability. Whether SWFs that do not assume this form can avoid collapse to the Pareto quasiordering is a complicated issue that I will not attempt to discuss here.

Imagine that $u^+(.)$ is in **U**. This function will make intrapersonal level and difference comparisons in a particular manner, and will assign intrapersonal ratios (ratios between two life-histories belonging to the same subject) in a particular manner. Consider, now, some $u^*(.)$ which is constructed from $u^+(.)$ via individual-specific ratio transformations. (This is *different* from the kind of ratio transformation of utility functions generally discussed in this book. What it means is this: There are N positive constants, $r_1, r_2, \ldots, r_N$, such that, for any $(x; i)$ in the life-history set **H**, $u^*(x; i) = r_i u^+(x; i)$.) Note that a $u^*(.)$ constructed in this manner makes the very same intrapersonal level and difference comparisons as $u^+(.)$ and assigns intrapersonal ratios in the very same manner as $u^+(.)$.

Thus, if the account of well-being at hand allows for no *interpersonal* comparisons, it would be arbitrary not to add $u^*(.)$ to **U**. (After all, it contains the very same intrapersonal information as $u^+(.)$.) But the worry now is that if we have an SWF which ranks Pareto-noncomparable outcomes in a particular manner, we can eviscerate that ranking by adding $u^*(.)$ to **U**.

To see how this works for the utilitarian SWF, imagine that x and y are Pareto-noncomparable but the utilitarian SWF says that x is at least as good as y (rather than incomparable). In other words, for all $u(.)$ in **U**, $\sum_{i=1}^{N} u_i(x) \geq \sum_{i=1}^{N} u_i(y)$. Because x and y are Pareto-noncomparable, there must be some individual k and at least one $u^+(.)$ in **U** such that $u^+(y; k) > u^+(x; k)$. The idea, now, is that if we choose $u^*(.)$ appropriately, we can "blow up" the difference between $(x; k)$ and $(y; k)$, as calculated by $u^*(.)$, so that the utilitarian SWF no longer favors x. More precisely, set $K = \sum_{j \neq k} [u_j^+(x) - u_j^+(y)]$. Note that $K > 0$, because $\sum_{i=1}^{N} u_i^+(x) \geq \sum_{i=1}^{N} u_i^+(y)$ and $u^+(y; k) > u^+(x; k)$. Now define $u^*(.)$ as follows. For all j distinct from k, set $r_j = 1$. In other words, $u^*(z; j) = u^+(z; j)$ for all outcomes z. In the case of k, pick r_k so that $r_k > K/[u^+(y; k) - u^+(x; k)]$. Set $u^*(z; k) = r_k u^+(z; k)$ for all outcomes z.

With $u^*(.)$ included in **U**, it is no longer the case that, for all $u(.)$ in **U**, $\sum_{i=1}^{N} u_i(x) \geq \sum_{i=1}^{N} u_i(y)$. Note that $\sum_{i=1}^{N} [u_i^*(y) - u_i^*(x)] = (u_k^*(y) - u_k^*(x)) + \sum_{j \neq k} [u_j^*(y) - u_j^*(x)]$. The second term is $-K$. The first term is $r_k[u^+(y; k) - u^+(x; k)]$ which, by construction, is a positive number greater than K.

A similar strategy can, I believe, be used for many other plausible SWFs—in particular, the SWFs mentioned in this section, i.e., the leximin, rank-weighted, and continuous prioritarian SWFs—to show that, without interpersonal comparability, these SWFs collapse to the Pareto quasiordering. One important caveat is that this strategy may not succeed in demonstrating collapse, for certain SWFs, if some utility functions in **U** assign *negative* as well as positive utilities to some life-histories. To see why, consider again the case in which outcomes x and y are Pareto-noncomparable; x is ranked at least as good as y by some SWF; and $u^+(.)$ is such that $u^+(y; k) > u^+(x; k)$ for some k. Assume that $u^+(x; k)$ and $u^+(y; k)$ are positive numbers; and, further, that there is some j such that $u^+(x; j)$ and

And what if we *can* make interpersonal comparisons? Given sufficient interpersonal comparability, we will be able to extend the Pareto quasiordering. Consider first the simple, limiting case of the well-being account presented in Chapter 3: where **U** is unique up to a positive ratio transformation.[24] In that case, there is full interpersonal and intrapersonal comparability of well-being levels and differences. If so, it is easy to see, all the standard SWFs mentioned here—the utilitarian SWF, leximin SWF, rank-weighted SWF, and continuous prioritarian SWF (in the Atkinson form)—will produce a complete ordering of outcomes.[25]

$u^+(y; j)$ are negative, with $u^+(y; j) < u^+(x; j)$. Then if we construct $u^*(.)$ using individual-specific ratio transformations, because the scaling coefficients $r_1, r_2, \ldots, r_N$ must be *positive* (to preserve intrapersonal level and difference comparisons), it must be the case that $u^*(y; j) < u^*(x; j) < u^*(x; k) < u^*(y; k)$ regardless of how $r_1, r_2, \ldots, r_N$ are chosen. For *certain* SWFs (not the utilitarian), this may mean that the SWF using $u^*(.)$ will continue to rank x over y. Consider, in particular, the leximin SWF. By way of illustration, assume that j and k are the only individuals and that $u^+(x; k) = 5, u^+(y; k) = 10, u^+(x; j) = -3, u^+(y; j) = -6$. Then, regardless of how $r_1, r_2, \ldots, r_N$ are chosen, it will be the case that $u^*(y; j) < u^*(x; j) < u^*(x; k) < u^*(y; k)$. Thus the leximin SWF, applied to $u^*(.)$, will continue to rank x over y.

However, it might be observed that the case of leximin and negative utilities is not really a counterexample to the claim that, without interpersonal comparability, SWFs collapse to the Pareto quasiordering. Consider that, if $u^+(.)$ assigns a negative utility to some life-history of one individual, $(y; j)$ and a positive utility to some life-history of a different individual, $(x; k)$, then any $u^*(.)$ which is produced by positive individual-specific ratio transformations (so as to preserve intrapersonal level and difference information) *also* preserves an interpersonal level comparison, namely that $(y; j)$ is worse than $(x; k)$. So we actually have a kind of interpersonal comparability here.

[24] In other words, **U** consists of some $u(.)$ and all positive ratio transformations of $u(.)$. A function $v(.)$ that assigns numbers to life-histories in some set **H** of life-histories is a positive ratio transformation of some other such function, $u(.)$, if there exists some single positive constant r such that, for every life-history $(x; i)$ in **H**, $v(x; i) = ru(x; i)$. See Chapter 3. I will sometimes indicate that $v(.)$ is a positive ratio transformation of $u(.)$ by writing "$v(.) = ru(.)$." I also frequently use simple examples where particular life-histories are assigned specific numbers followed by the letter "r," e.g., 15r, 8r, 30r, and 12r. Unless I say otherwise, this is shorthand for the proposition that **U** in the example is unique up to a positive ratio transformation, and that each utility function in **U** assigns the array of life-histories either those specific numbers, or numbers that are a common multiple r of the specific numbers indicated.

[25] In the case of the utilitarian SWF, this is very easy. Assume that **U** consists of some $u(.)$ and all utility functions that are positive ratio transformations thereof. Take some $u^*(.)$ belonging to **U**, where $u^*(.) = r^*u(.)$ and r^* is positive. Consider any two outcomes x and y. Using the utilitarian SWF, the ranking of x and y according to $u^*(.)$ depends on summing their utilities. In other words, x is morally at least as good as y according to $u^*(.)$ just in case $u^*(x; 1) + u^*(x; 2) + \ldots + u^*(x; N) \geq u^*(y; 1) + u^*(y; 2) + \ldots + u^*(y; N)$. That relation is complete: for any two outcomes, x and y, and any given $u^*(.)$, either the first outcome's sum of utilities is greater than or equal to the second outcome's sum of utilities, or vice versa, or both (in the case of equality). But note that, for any two utility functions in **U**, $u^*(.)$ and $u^{**}(.)$, the two will rank x and y the very same way using the utilitarian SWF, since $u^*(.) = r^*u(.)$ and $u^{**}(.) = r^{**}u(.)$, with both r^* and r^{**} positive. Therefore the ranking achieved by the utilitarian SWF—using the formula x is at least as good as y iff $u(x; 1) + u(x; 2) + \ldots + u(x; N) \geq u(y; 1) + u(y; 2) + \ldots + u(y; N)$ for all $u(.)$ belonging to **U**—is complete too.

However, it is also not hard to show that—even if **U** is not so well-behaved, and there is some incomparability in the ranking of life-histories or differences—these SWFs may well be able to extend the Pareto quasiordering.

Consider the case in which life-histories have two attributes, which have a numerical level greater than zero. **U** is based upon two different utility functions. One utility function, $u(.)$, values life-histories by summing the attributes. That is, $u(a, b) = a + b$. A second utility function, $v(.)$, values them by multiplying the attributes. That is, $v(a, b) = ab$. **U** consists of $u(.)$ and all positive ratio transformations of $u(.)$, plus $v(.)$ and all positive ratio transformations of $v(.)$. For short, I will indicate that **U** has this structure by assigning a given life-history two different utility numbers: a number such as "15r" meaning that $u(.)$ assigns the life-history the number 15, and each positive ratio transformation of $u(.)$ assigns it 15 multiplied by some positive number r; *and* a number such as "20s" meaning that $v(.)$ assigns the life-history the number 20, and each positive ratio transformation of $v(.)$ assigns it the number 20 multiplied by some positive number s.[26]

Given $x = ((a_1, b_1), (a_2, b_2),\ldots, (a_N, b_N))$ and $y = ((a_1{}^*, b_1{}^*), (a_2{}^*, b_2{}^*),\ldots, (a_N{}^*, b_N{}^*))$, the Pareto quasiordering says that x is equally morally good as y iff life-history (a_1, b_1) is equally good as life-history $(a_1{}^*, b_1{}^*)$ and life-history (a_2, b_2) is equally good as life-history $(a_2{}^*, b_2{}^*)$ and ... and life-history (a_N, b_N) is equally good as life-history $(a_N{}^*, b_N{}^*)$. It says that x is morally better than y iff life-history (a_1, b_1) is at least as good as life-history $(a_1{}^*, b_1{}^*)$, life-history (a_2, b_2) is at least as good as life-history $(a_2{}^*, b_2{}^*)$, and so forth, with at least one case in which (a_i, b_i) is strictly better than $(a_i{}^*, b_i{}^*)$. Otherwise x and y are morally incomparable.

To see how various SWFs can extend the Pareto quasiordering, without necessarily producing a complete ordering, consider a case in which there are two individuals.

Similar reasoning shows that the ranking of life-histories by the leximin and rank-weighted SWFs are complete. In the case of the continuous prioritarian SWF, with **U** unique up to a positive ratio transformation, the ranking will *not* necessarily be complete. This is because, in general, with $g(.)$ a strictly increasing and strictly concave function and r positive, it is *not* necessarily the case that $\sum_{i=1}^{N} g(u_i(x)) \geq \sum_{i=1}^{N} g(u_i(y))$ iff $\sum_{i=1}^{N} g(ru_i(x)) \geq \sum_{i=1}^{N} g(ru_i(y))$. However, this *is* true in the case of the Atkinson SWF, where $g(u(x;i)) = (1-\gamma)^{-1} u(x;i)^{1-\gamma}$. With **U** unique up to a positive ratio transformation, pick some $u^*(.) = r^*u(.)$, with r^* positive. With $u^*(.)$ in hand, the Atkinson SWF says that x is morally at least as good as y iff $(1-\gamma)^{-1} \sum_{i=1}^{N} (r^* u_i(x))^{1-\gamma} \geq (1-\gamma)^{-1} \sum_{i=1}^{N} (r^* u_i(y))^{1-\gamma}$. But that is true just in case $(1-\gamma)^{-1}(r^*)^{1-\gamma} \sum_{i=1}^{N} (u_i(x))^{1-\gamma} \geq (1-\gamma)^{-1}(r^*)^{1-\gamma} \sum_{i=1}^{N} (u_i(y))^{1-\gamma}$. And that in turn will be true if r^* is replaced by any r^{**}, with r^{**} also positive, and thus for $u^{**}(.)$ in **U** equaling $r^{**}u(.)$.

[26] See above, n. 24 for an explanation of what it means for one utility function to be a positive ratio transformation of another. The example at hand could arise, in accordance with the account of well-being presented in Chapter 3, if some spectators have extended preferences over life-history lotteries and comparisons to nonexistence represented by $u(.)$ and positive multiples, while others have preferences represented by $v(.)$ and positive multiples.

Imagine, first, that $x = ((3, 3), (3, 3))$ while $y = ((4, 4), (3, 2))$. Then, according to $u(.)$ and all positive ratio transformations, the utility vector corresponding to x is $(6r, 6r)$ and the utility vector corresponding to y is $(8r, 5r)$. According to $v(.)$ and all positive ratio transformations, the utility vector corresponding to x is $(9s, 9s)$ while the utility vector corresponding to y is $(16s, 6s)$. Note that, in this case, the outcomes are Pareto-noncomparable. (According to $u(.)$ and all positive ratio transformations, the first individual is better off in y, while the second is better off in x. And that is also true for $v(.)$ and all positive ratio transformations.) However the utilitarian SWF, both using $u(.)$ and all positive ratio transformations, *and* using $v(.)$ and all positive transformations, says that y is a better outcome. $(8r + 5r > 6r + 6r$ *and* $16s + 6s > 9s + 9s.)$

On the other hand, if $x = ((3, 3), (3, 3))$ and $y = ((9, 2), (1/3, 1/3))$, then the outcomes are both Pareto-noncomparable and noncomparable according to the utilitarian SWF. Note that, according to $u(.)$ and all positive ratio transformations, the utility vector corresponding to $x = (6r, 6r)$ while the utility vector corresponding to $y = (11r, 2/3r)$. According to $v(.)$ and all positive ratio transformations, the utility vector corresponding to $x = (9s, 9s)$ while the utility vector corresponding to $y = (18s, 1/9s)$. Thus the utilitarian SWF, using $u(.)$ and all positive ratio transformations, says that x is a better outcome (because $6r + 6r > 11r + 2/3r$). However, using $v(.)$ and all positive ratio transformations, it says that y is a better outcome (because $9s + 9s < 18s + 1/9s.)$

Similar examples can be constructed for the other SWFs mentioned here (leximin, continuous prioritarian, rank-weighted).

Let me underscore that my discussion here is *not* meant to persuade the reader that well-being is indeed interpersonally comparable. All that I have done, in this chapter and the preceding one, is to explicate the concept of interpersonal comparability, and to explain why some degree of interpersonal comparability is critical for the SWF approach. The burden of presenting and defending an account of well-being that allows for interpersonal comparability (and also for the representing of well-being via utility functions, in a set **U**) will be taken up in the following chapter, Chapter 3. Even apart from the question of interpersonal comparisons, Chapter 3 will need to take on a large philosophical task: what *is* the most attractive account of well-being? Why believe (as I will ultimately argue) that well-being is a matter of idealized preferences?

Chapter 5 will take on a different task: the burden of sorting *between* different Paretian anonymous SWFs. In particular, Chapter 5 will argue in favor of the continuous prioritarian SWF—yet more specifically, in favor of a continuous prioritarian SWF which assumes the Atkinson form.

Unlike the utilitarian SWF, the continuous prioritarian SWF is *sensitive to the distribution of well-being.* What exactly this means is a subtle matter, explored in Chapter 5.[27] The most straightforward definition of what it means for an SWF, or some other

---

[27] See Chapter 5, n. 6.

policy-evaluation framework, to be "sensitive to distribution" appeals to the so-called "Pigou–Dalton principle." The "Pigou–Dalton" principle can be given different framings: in terms of income, attributes, or well-being.[28] The relevant framing, for purposes of characterizing SWFs, is in terms of well-being. An SWF satisfies the Pigou–Dalton principle in terms of well-being if it gives greater weight to well-being changes affecting worse-off individuals. Formally, the SWF must incorporate a rule R which has the following feature.[29]

The Pigou–Dalton Principle (for Ranking Utility Vectors)

Take any utility vector $(u_1, \ldots, u_i, \ldots, u_j, \ldots, u_N)$, and alter it to $(u_1, \ldots, u_i + \Delta u, \ldots, u_j - \Delta u, \ldots, u_N)$, where $\Delta u > 0$, $u_j > u_i$, and $u_j - \Delta u \geq u_i + \Delta u$. Then R satisfies the Pigou–Dalton principle for ranking utility vectors if it always ranks the second vector as being better than the first.

The utilitarian SWF fails the Pigou–Dalton principle in terms of well-being. By contrast, because the continuous prioritarian SWF sums utilities transformed by a strictly concave $g(.)$ function (see Figure 2.2), it satisfies the Pigou–Dalton principle in terms of well-being.[30]

As we shall see in Chapter 5, the two other SWFs I have mentioned—the rank-weighted SWF and the leximin SWF—also satisfy the Pigou–Dalton principle in terms of well-being. These SWFs, too, are sensitive to the distribution of well-being. However, the rank-weighted SWF fails to satisfy a *separability* property which is satisfied by the continuous prioritarian SWF. The leximin SWF possesses this separability property but fails to possess a *continuity* property which is satisfied by the continuous prioritarian SWF (hence its name).

Sorting between these various SWFs, and further possibilities, will require much intellectual labor. All I have tried to do here is introduce the framework, so as to see its promise and so as to better understand the features of competing approaches.

---

[28] See below, pp. 114–115.

[29] Chapter 5 provides a more general definition of the Pigou–Dalton principle in terms of well-being, applicable both to SWFs that assume the simple R-based form and to more complicated types of SWFs.

[30] The continuous prioritarian SWF uses a $g(.)$ function which is not only strictly concave but also strictly increasing. An SWF using a $g(.)$ function without the latter feature would still satisfy the Pigou–Dalton principle in terms of well-being, but would violate the axiom of Pareto-superiority in some outcome sets.

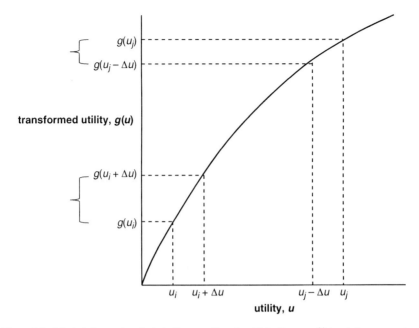

Figure 2.2 A Strictly Increasing, Strictly Concave Function. *Note:* Because $g(.)$ is strictly concave, the difference between $g(u_i + \Delta u)$ and $g(u_i)$ is greater than the difference between $g(u_j)$ and $g(u_j - \Delta u)$, as indicated by the brackets on the y-axis. Thus $g(u_i) + g(u_j)$ is less than $g(u_i + \Delta u) + g(u_j - \Delta u)$; and therefore the continuous prioritarian SWF satisfies the Pigou–Dalton principle.

B. The Social Welfare Function in Welfare Economics and Contemporary Policy Analysis

I have provided a definition of "the SWF framework," which sees it as one particular specification of the more generic architecture of a welfarist choice-evaluation procedure. Again, this definition is my own; the existing literature does not conceptualize the social welfare function in precisely this way, and, to keep things clear, I will use the abbreviation "SWF" only to refer to my particular definition. Still, my definition has many connections to the literature.

The notion of a social welfare function was introduced into economics by Abram Bergson in a 1938 article and was adopted by Paul Samuelson in Chapter 8 of his influential work, *Foundations of Economic Analysis*, published in 1947.[31] My understanding of the SWF framework as a way to outfit a *moral* decision procedure is in accordance with Bergson's and Samuelson's views. Although these authors do not use the term "moral," they clearly do see the social welfare function as a way to

---

[31] See Bergson (1938); Samuelson (1947). See also Bergson (1948, 1954).

encapsulate a set of normative judgments—and not just any old normative judgments, but the particular species of normative judgment I am referring to with the term "moral." Bergson writes that the social welfare function is a "scale of values for the evaluation of alternative uses of resources," and also describes it as resting on "ethical" premises;[32] I take "ethical," here, to be a synonym for "moral." Samuelson writes: "[W]e take as a starting point for our discussion a function [the social welfare function] of all the economic magnitudes of a system which is supposed to characterize some ethical belief—that of a benevolent despot, or a complete egotist, or 'all men of good will,' a misanthrope, the state, race, or group mind, God, etc."[33]

Bergson is particularly clear in emphasizing that specifying the form of the social welfare function involves normative reasoning, and therefore has the characteristic features of such reasoning. He writes: "A notable feature in welfare economics is the attempt to formulate a criterion of social welfare without recourse to controversial ethical premises. . . . [T]his goal for the criterion is an illusion."[34] Or to put the point in terms of contemporary moral epistemology: there are a wide variety of logically possible SWFs, and choosing between them cannot be a matter of formal deduction, but should involve seeking a reflective equilibrium.

Bergson also states quite explicitly that the social welfare function is a tool that can be used to provide ethical advice to *anyone*, regarding "large" decisions, not merely to governmental decisionmakers.

> [I conceive] the problem of the [social welfare] criterion as having two aspects. First, it is necessary to determine the ethical values which one would take as data in counseling one or another citizen in any particular community on decisions involving alternative social states. Reference is not to decisions of the restricted sort taken in the market, but to decisions of the large sort usually implemented by actions of government, e.g., a tax reform. . . .
>
> I have been assuming that the concern of welfare economics is to counsel individual citizens generally. If a public official is counseled, it is on the same basis as any other citizen. In every instance reference is made to some ethical values which are appropriate for the counseling of the individual in question.[35]

There are certainly subsequent authors who have adopted a different view of the social welfare function—for example, as providing a special kind of second-order normative advice that pertains only to governmental choice; or even as a descriptive

---

[32] Bergson (1948, p. 417). The characterization of the social welfare function as connected to "ethics" or "ethical" judgments occurs repeatedly in this work and in Bergson (1954).

[33] Samuelson (1947, p. 221).

[34] Bergson (1954, p. 249).

[35] Ibid., pp. 240, 242.

rather than a normative tool.[36] Here, I should stress that the concept of the social welfare function can be employed to serve the particular aims of this book—helping to structure a decision procedure that can be used to *morally* evaluate anyone's large-scale choice—even if others in the social-welfare-function tradition have understood it as serving a different role. But it *is* heartening to note that my understanding seems close to that of the first movers in this tradition, Bergson and Samuelson.

Bergson and Samuelson stress that the social welfare function, in its most generic form, is defined directly on (roughly) what I term an "outcome," namely a description of reality incorporating whatever features are taken to be of moral relevance.

> [T]he present writer has found it useful to introduce into the analysis a welfare function, W, the value of which is understood to depend on all the variables that might be considered as affecting [the community's] welfare: the amounts of each and every kind of good consumed by and service performed by each and every household, the amount of each and every kind of capital investment undertaken, and so on. The welfare function is understood initially to be entirely general in character; its shape is determined by the specific decisions on ends that are introduced into the analysis. Given the decisions on ends, the welfare function is transformed into a scale of values for the evaluation of alternative uses of resources.[37]

Admittedly, Bergson and Samuelson, as well as subsequent scholars, have given too little attention to the point that a social welfare function meant to be used as a decision-making tool must be cognitively tractable, and thus that its arguments cannot be anything like *complete* descriptions of possible realities. Thus I have stressed that an "outcome" is a *simplified* possible world.

In any event, modulo this point about simplification, the Bergson–Samuelson social welfare function in its most generic form is defined directly on outcomes. It takes the form $w(x)$; the numerical fact $w(x) > w(y)$ embodies the moral ("ethical") judgment that x is a morally ("ethically") better outcome than y. Furthermore, it provides a *complete* quasiordering, i.e., a complete, reflexive, and transitive ordering of the outcomes. As Samuelson explains, the "ethical" belief which the social welfare function reflects must be "such as to admit of an unequivocal answer as to whether one configuration of the economic system is 'better' or 'worse' than any other or 'indifferent,' and . . . these relationships [must be] transitive; i.e., A better than B, B better than C, implies A better than C, etc."[38] I too will see the SWF as furnishing a quasiordering of outcomes—but not necessarily a complete one.

Bergson and Samuelson then explain that this generic form $w(x)$, coupled with the further "ethical" judgment that the goodness of outcomes depends on individuals'

---

[36] On these possibilities, see Arrow (1963, pp. 17–19, 107–108); Sen (1987b, pp. 382–383); Stern (1987, pp. 46–47).
[37] Bergson (1948, p. 417). See Samuelson (1947, p. 221).
[38] Samuelson (1947, p. 221).

preferences, yields a social welfare function whose arguments are individual *utilities* representing each individual's preference satisfaction. It becomes $w(u_1(x), u_2(x), \ldots, u_N(x))$.[39]

Bergson and Samuelson believed that ranking outcomes using a social welfare function with individual utilities as its arguments did not presuppose the possibility of interpersonal comparisons. Indeed, they believed that a social welfare function not only could "extend" the Pareto quasiordering, but could indeed yield a complete ordering of outcomes, even if well-being was not interpersonally comparable.[40]

However, this view was seriously called into question by Kenneth Arrow's earth-shattering work, *Social Choice and Individual Values*. Arrow addressed himself directly to the problem of formulating a social welfare function. For Arrow, as for Bergson and Samuelson, this device will produce a complete quasiordering of what he calls "states," i.e., "outcomes" (modulo simplification):

> The most precise definition of a social state would be a complete description of the amount of each type of commodity in the hands of each individual, the amount of labor to be supplied by each individual, the amount of each productive resource invested in each type of productive activity, and the amounts of various types of collective activity, such as municipal services, diplomacy and its continuation by other means, and the erection of statues to famous men.[41]

But, importantly, Arrow formulates the problem differently than Bergson and Samuelson. What Arrow calls a "social welfare function" is not a mathematical function of the form $w(u_1(x), u_2(x), \ldots, u_N(x))$. It takes as its input, not individual utility numbers, but rather each individual's preference ranking. The Arrow set-up is this: Each individual's preferences take the form of a complete quasiordering of the set of outcomes; and the "social welfare function" is a rule that maps this profile of individual orderings (one for each of the N individuals in the population) onto a social ordering.

> By a social welfare function will be meant a process or rule which, for each set of individual orderings $R_1, \ldots, R_n$ for alternative social states (one ordering for each individual), states a corresponding social ordering of alternative social states, R.[42]

Arrow proved that it was impossible to produce such a "process or rule" that satisfied several seemingly innocuous axioms, namely nondictatorship, universal domain, a Pareto condition, and the "independence of irrelevant alternatives."[43]

---

[39] See Bergson (1948, pp. 417–418); Samuelson (1947, pp. 228–229).

[40] See Fleurbaey and Mongin (2005).

[41] Arrow (1963, p. 17).

[42] Ibid., p. 23 (italics omitted).

[43] See Sen (1986, pp. 1074–1078).

Since Arrow's book, theoretical work regarding social welfare functions has proceeded in two directions. One body of scholarship retains the basic Arrow set-up. It seeks to produce a social ranking of outcomes as a function of the profile of individual preference rankings—investigating the possibility of doing so if one or more of the Arrow conditions are relaxed, in particular universal domain and the independence of irrelevant alternatives.[44] In substantial part, the conclusions of this literature have been to confirm Arrow's impossibility result even with such relaxation. However, the literature is not completely negative. One positive result is the so-called "egalitarian equivalent" ordering. This rule for ordering outcomes assumes no interpersonal comparability, is sensitive to distribution, and gets around the Arrow result by relaxing the independence-of-irrelevant-alternatives condition. It will be discussed later in the chapter, in connection with inequality metrics.

A second body of theoretical scholarship commenced in the early 1970s, triggered by Amartya Sen's 1970 work *Collective Choice and Social Welfare*. This literature returns to the original Bergson/Samuelson idea of making the social ordering of outcomes a function of individual *utilities*. Unlike Bergson and Samuelson, however, this literature is not resistant to the notion of interpersonal welfare comparisons.[45]

More precisely, the set-up in this second body of post-Arrovian work is as follows. There is a set of social states (what I am calling an outcome set **O**) and a set of N individuals. Each individual i has a *utility function* $u_i(.)$, where each such $u_i(.)$ maps the various states onto real numbers. Given the N individuals, there is a profile of individual utility functions $[u_1(.), \ldots, u_N(.)]$. The central problem that this literature focuses upon is arriving at a complete quasiordering of the social states as a function of this profile of individual utility functions.

By moving from the Arrow set-up (a profile of individual preference orderings) to the newer set-up (a profile of individual utility functions), this literature accommodates the possibility of interpersonal comparisons.[46]

> Central to Arrow's impossibility theorem is the inability of a social welfare function to use any information beyond that given by the individual preference orderings on the set

---

[44] See generally Campbell and Kelly (2002); Sen (1986).

[45] For overviews of this body of scholarship, see Blackorby, Bossert, and Donaldson (2005, chs. 3–4); Boadway and Bruce (1984, ch. 5); Bossert and Weymark (2004); d'Aspremont and Gevers (2002); Mongin and d'Aspremont (1998); Sen (1986). *Collective Choice and Social Welfare* has been reprinted as Sen (1979a).

[46] It might be asked whether scholars working in this particular literature see individual utilities as representing individual preference satisfaction and, thus, individual well-being (on the assumption that well-being reduces to preference satisfaction), or as representing preference satisfaction independent of well-being (e.g., the satisfaction of moral preferences). See Chapter 1, n. 4. It seems that many in this literature take the first view (as suggested by the quotation in the text immediately below). In any event, whatever the interpretation of the social welfare function that some in the literature may adopt, it provides a formal structure that I can use for my welfarist purposes.

of possible alternatives. In particular, the very formulation of the problem rules out the use of *interpersonal comparisons* of well-being or utility. Classical social decision rules such as utilitarianism, or any other rule which allows for trade-offs between the utilities experienced by different individuals, simply cannot be expressed in terms of an Arrovian social welfare function. ...

In order for the social choice procedure to incorporate information about interpersonal comparisons of utility, the notion of a social welfare function has to be generalized. Instead of determining the social preference on the basis of a profile of individual preference orderings, a *social welfare functional* assigns a social preference to each admissible profile of individual *utility functions*. Different assumptions concerning the measurability and interpersonal comparability of utility can be formalized by partitioning the set of admissible profiles of utility functions into sets of informationally equivalent profiles and requiring the social welfare functional to be constant on a cell of the partition.[47]

The SWF framework, as I have defined it, is very closely related to this literature. My framework yields a quasiordering of outcomes by using a set $\mathbf{U}$ of utility functions and a rule R for ranking utility vectors, applied as follows: x is at least as good as y iff $u(x)$ is ranked at least as good as $u(y)$ by R, for all $u(.)$ belonging to $\mathbf{U}$. Each $u(.)$, in my framework, is a vector-valued function that maps a given outcome onto an N-entry list of numbers. The literature now under discussion uses the idea of a *profile* of individual utility functions $[u_1(.), \ldots, u_N(.)]$, each of which maps a given outcome onto a single real number. So a particular utility function, in my set-up, is just the same thing as what this literature sees as a particular profile of individual utility functions.[48]

Moreover, as the last sentence of the immediately quoted paragraph suggests, a central focus of this literature is the problem of *invariance*. An invariance requirement says that, if combining a social welfare function with a given profile of individual utility functions $[u_1(.), u_2(.), \ldots, u_N(.)]$ produces a particular ordering of outcomes, then the ordering produced by combining that function with a stipulated kind of transformation of that profile, $[\varphi_1(u_1(.)), \varphi_2(u_2(.)), \ldots, \varphi_N(u_N(.))]$, must be the same. To give one example, we might say that the ordering of outcomes must not change if a given profile is transformed by a "common positive affine transformation" (i.e., choosing a positive number a and a number b, and defining $\varphi_i(u_i(.)) = au_i(.) + b$). Or, we might say that the ordering of outcomes must not change if a given profile is transformed by applying a so-called "common increasing transformation" to each function in the profile.

---

[47] Bossert and Weymark (2004, p. 1100).

[48] Indeed, there is a small subliterature, discussing so-called "generalized," "extensive," or "extended" social welfare functions, that involves utility functions identical in structure to the $u(.)$ functions in my set-up—utility functions that assign numbers to the totality of life-histories. See sources cited ibid., p. 1119, and also Arrow (1977); Ooghe and Lauwers (2005); Roberts (1980b, 1995, 1997); Suzumura (1996).

In effect, then, this literature thinks of the ordering of outcomes as being produced by the combination of a social welfare function and a *set* of profiles: a given profile plus all the profiles that are equivalent given some invariance requirement. My approach, too, sees the ordering of outcomes as being generated by a combination of a rule R and a *set* of vector-valued utility functions, i.e., a set of profiles.

There *are* some differences between my approach and this literature's. In particular, the literature focuses on the possibility of deriving a *complete* ranking of outcomes from a set of profiles of individual utility functions. In other words, this literature might be understood as adopting the SWF framework as I have defined it, with the additional stipulation that: R and U must be such that the rule, x is at least as good as y iff $u(x)$ is ranked at least as good as $u(y)$ by R, for all $u(.)$ belonging to U, yields a complete quasiordering of the outcome set O. For reasons I have elaborated, I see no reason to insist on completeness.[49]

Furthermore, the literature sees the utility functions as representing preferences—the number $u_i(x)$ represents something about individual i's preference satisfaction in outcome x—while I see the utility functions in U as more generic. They represent *some* account of well-being, be it preferentialist, mental state, or objective.

My account of interpersonal comparisons is closely related to the literature's, but also more general. Within my framework, whether an account of well-being allows for interpersonal comparisons will "show up" in U. And that is, roughly, what the literature says as well.[50] But I allow for different *degrees* of interpersonal comparability

---

[49] Sen himself in *Collective Choice and Social Welfare* (1979a, ch. 7*) suggested the possibility of a possibly incomplete quasiordering of outcomes, generated by applying a rule R to a set of utility functions. (Sen focuses on the utilitarian R, and uses the term "W" instead of my "$u(.)$" to refer to these utility functions.) To date, little work has been done pursuing Sen's suggestion or the possibility of an incomplete ordering. For one exception, see Ooghe and Lauwers (2005).

[50] Strictly speaking, the literature associates different kinds of inter- and intrapersonal comparability with different invariance requirements, while I see the extent of inter- and intrapersonal comparability as being features of the quasiordering of life-histories and differences achieved by a particular set U in a particular choice situation (for short, "comparability in the U-based sense"). However, each invariance requirement can be seen as corresponding to a particular kind of set U, and thus to a particular kind of inter- and intrapersonal comparability in the U-based sense. For example, the invariance requirement that goes under the heading of "ordinal measurability and full comparability" stipulates that if a profile of individual utility functions is subject to a common, increasing transformation, the SWF's ordering of outcomes should not change. A common increasing transformation of a profile of individual utility functions $[u_1(.), u_2(.),\ldots, u_N(.)]$ is the same as an increasing transformation of the kind of utility function $u(.)$ that I have been discussing, i.e., a utility function that assigns values to all life-histories in some life-history set H. If $u(.)$ is such a utility function, then to say that $v(.)$ is an increasing transformation of $u(.)$ means: for all pairs of life-histories $(x; i)$ and $(y; j)$ in H, $u(x: i) \geq u(y; j)$ iff $v(x; i) \geq v(y; j)$.

Thus the invariance requirement "ordinal measurability and full comparability" corresponds to a set U which consists of some $u(.)$ and all increasing transformations thereof. Note, now, that for any such set U, there will be complete inter- and intrapersonal comparability of well-being levels in the

of well-being levels or differences. Some pairs of life-histories belonging to different subjects might be comparable, while other pairs might not be (and similarly for difference comparisons). By contrast, the literature tends to assume that interpersonal level or difference comparability is "all or nothing."[51]

Finally, the literature does not really grapple with the problem of how to make interpersonal comparisons. Rather, it focuses on the important mathematical problem of identifying the possible forms of the rule R that will yield a complete ranking of outcomes (and perhaps have other properties, such as continuity and separability), given a set U consisting of some $u(.)$ and stipulated transformations thereof. The more philosophical question concerning how we arrive at that particular set U, from an underlying account of well-being (preference-based or otherwise), is not confronted.

Still, the SWF framework as I present it is a really just an incremental extension of what this literature understands as a social welfare function. Moreover, the

U-based sense. For any two life-histories, $(x; i)$ and $(y; j)$, with i and j the same or different subjects, it will be the case that $u(x; i) \geq u(y; j)$ for all $u(.)$ in U; or $u(y; j) \geq u(x; i)$ for all $u(.)$ in U; or both. No pair of life-histories will be incomparable in the U-based sense.

Along similar lines, the invariance requirement under the heading "cardinal measurability and full comparability" corresponds to a set U consisting of a $u(.)$ and all positive affine transformations thereof. Given such a U, there will be complete inter- and intrapersonal comparability of well-being levels and differences in the U-based sense. No pair of life-histories will be incomparable, nor will any pair of differences.

[51] The prior footnote discussed how each kind of invariance requirement corresponds to a particular kind of set U, and thus to a particular kind of comparability in the U-based sense. However, many of the standard invariance requirements correspond to sets U with the feature that inter- or intrapersonal comparability of levels and differences is either complete or completely absent. (By "complete" or "completely absent" I mean, in the case of interpersonal level comparability, that either all pairs of life-histories with different subjects are comparable, or none are—with parallel definitions for interpersonal difference comparability, and intrapersonal level and different comparability).

However, there are sets U that do not correspond to any of the standard invariance requirements discussed in the literature, and where inter- or intrapersonal comparability is neither complete nor completely absent. For example, imagine that H has four life-histories $(x; 1), (x; 2), (y; 1), (y; 2)$. U consists of $u(.)$ and all positive ratio transformations thereof, plus $v(.)$ and all positive ratio transformations thereof. Assume that $u(.)$ assigns the four histories, respectively, the numbers 1, 3, 6, 9, while $v(.)$ assigns them the numbers 2, 4, 7, 1. Then it can be seen that $(x; 2)$ is comparable with $(y; 1)$—all utility functions in U assign the first history a lower number. Moreover, the difference between $(x; 2)$ and $(x; 1)$ is comparable with the difference between $(y; 1)$ and $(x; 2)$—all utility functions in U say that the first difference is less than the second difference. However, $(x; 1)$ and $(y; 2)$ are *not* comparable, nor is the difference between $(x; 2)$ and $(x; 1)$ comparable with the difference between $(y; 2)$ and $(y; 1)$.

On this score, it should be noted that my U-based definition of comparability is related to an idea discussed in some of the extant literature: that comparability should be understood in terms of "meaningful statements" rather than invariance requirements. See Bossert and Weymark (2004, pp. 1126–1129). Sen, too, suggests the possibility of different degrees of interpersonal comparability. See Sen (1979a, chs. 7–7*); see also Khmelnitskaya and Weymark (2000).

literature's axiomatic results about the possible forms of R will come into play at many junctures in my analysis.

The body of scholarship that I have been discussing is purely theoretical. But the concept of a social welfare function also plays a role in a number of other literatures, which use that concept—at least in part—to formulate policy guidance. Perhaps the most important example is the field of "optimal tax theory," spurred by James Mirrlees' 1971 article, "An Exploration in the Theory of Optimum Income Taxation,"[52] for which he ultimately won the Nobel Prize. In this article, Mirrlees addressed the very difficult problem of optimizing an income tax schedule, given the heterogeneity of individuals' abilities, the incomplete observability of individual abilities to the tax authorities, and the disincentive effects of income taxes on labor. He did so in a much more rigorous fashion than had previously been accomplished by seeking to identify the tax schedule that maximized a social welfare function, taking as its arguments the array of individual utilities associated with each outcome; each individual's utility, in turn, was a function of that individual's consumption and labor.

"Optimal tax" scholars pursue the approach that Mirrlees pioneered. In this field, now quite substantial, economists investigate a particular policy domain (taxes), via social welfare functions defined on individual utilities; and they do so on the assumption that individual well-being is interpersonally comparable. Mirrlees characterizes the social welfare function as "embodying interpersonal comparisons of welfare."[53] Matti Tuomala, surveying the field of optimal-tax theory, observes that it is "firmly based on explicit interpersonal comparisons."[54] It also bears noting that the main functional form for analyzing tax policies, employed in the optimal-tax literature, is either a utilitarian social welfare function or a continuous prioritarian social welfare function—and, if the latter, the Atkinson form I will argue for in detail in Chapter 5.[55]

Social welfare functions have also been used or at least discussed as a policy-analysis tool in a number of other scholarly literatures, including: optimal-growth theory; environmental economics (including several major recent studies on climate change); agricultural economics; the estimation of cost-of-living indices; health economics (a number of scholars have proposed using social welfare functions to evaluate health policy, with utility numbers representing individuals' health states); and legal scholarship (Kaplow and Shavell argue in a prominent book, *Fairness versus Welfare*, that legal scholars should use social welfare functions to evaluate legal doctrines).[56] Furthermore, an important strand of the inequality measurement

---

[52] Reprinted as Mirrlees (2006a). See Tuomala (1990, chs. 1, 6), discussing the Mirrlees model.

[53] Mirrlees (2006b, p. 260).

[54] Tuomala (1990, p. 24).

[55] See Creedy (2007, p. 5); Heady (1996, p. 29); Salanié (2003, p. 80); Tuomala (1990, p. 28).

[56] For reviews of the optimal-tax literature, see sources cited in Chapter 4, n. 9. On the use of the social welfare function in studying environmental economics, climate change, and optimal growth,

literature sees a close link between social welfare functions and inequality measures. As we'll see, the Atkinson *inequality metric* is related to the Atkinson *SWF*. Similarly, there turns out to be a connection between the Gini coefficient (another standard inequality metric) and the rank-weighted SWF.

Finally, although social welfare functions are not (as far as I'm aware) currently employed by governmental bodies, the U.K. government has endorsed the use of cost-benefit analysis with *distributive weights*—an approach which is a variation on the social-welfare-function approach.[57]

In short, the idea of a social welfare function has a rich background in economic theory, and also has gone well beyond the stage of theoretical elaboration. Still, the approach is not nearly as widely used in contemporary policy analysis as a number of competing approaches, to which we now turn.

II. COST-BENEFIT ANALYSIS

Cost-benefit analysis (CBA) has come to dominate policy analysis within the U.S. federal government. Since 1981, federal administrative agencies subject to Presidential control have been required to prepare a full CBA whenever a sufficiently large-scale regulation is issued. These documents—which are typically voluminous, and can cost millions of dollars to prepare—are reviewed by a powerful oversight body within the Office of Management and Budget. Similar systems of "regulatory review" have existed for some time in Australia and Canada and, more recently, have been put in place in Britain, the European Union, and other jurisdictions. CBA also has an important role outside the regulatory-review context. For many years, dating from the mid-1930s, CBA has been the key methodology employed by the U.S. Army Corps of Engineers in designing levees and other measures to control flooding or enhance waterborne navigation. And it is used by European governments to evaluate large infrastructure projects.[58]

Within the scholarly field of economics, CBA has an odd status. On the one hand, it is often viewed critically by theoretical welfare economists, who are keenly aware of the various difficulties with the approach and the closely related Kaldor–Hicks tests—difficulties that I shall discuss below. Yet CBA is the foundation for modern

---

see sources cited in Chapter 4, nn. 11–12. On its use in agricultural economics and the construction of cost-of-living indices, see, respectively, Bullock and Salhofer (2003), and Crossley and Pendakur (2010). On the idea of using social welfare functions applied to health utilities, see Bleichrodt, Diecidue, and Quiggin (2004); Bleichrodt, Doctor, and Stolk (2005); Dolan (1998); Lindholm and Rosen (1998); Østerdal (2005); Rodríguez-Miguez and Pinto-Prades (2002); Wagstaff (1991); Williams (1997). *Fairness versus Welfare* is Kaplow and Shavell (2002).

[57] See HM Treasury (2003, pp. 24–25, 91–96).

[58] On governmental use of CBA, see Adler and Posner (2006); Florio (2007); Kirkpatrick and Parker (2007); Morgenstern (1997); National Research Council (2004); Sunstein (2002); Wiener (2007). See also Executive Order 13563 (2011), reaffirming CBA.

applied welfare economics. Most contemporary economists who actually evaluate governmental policies, or undertake related empirical work, do so using CBA as the basic evaluation tool. For example, vast bodies of scholarship by applied economists are devoted to estimating willingness-to-pay/accept (WTP/WTA) amounts, the inputs for CBA, either by inferring WTP/WTA amounts from market prices and other "revealed preference" data, or by conducting survey research. Within the broader policy-analysis community—including not only academic economists, but also researchers at "think tanks" and the like—CBA is similarly widespread.[59]

What explains the dominance of CBA within applied economics, despite the widespread view among theoretical welfare economists that it lacks convincing foundations? This is an interesting sociological and historical question. It seems that the answer has much to do with the unease that many economists feel about making interpersonal welfare comparisons. Kaldor–Hicks tests were constructed at a time (the 1930s and 1940s) when such comparisons were universally disfavored within economics. It soon became clear that those tests were problematic, and a sublitera-ture within theoretical economics eventually emerged, a generation later, in which interpersonal comparisons were accepted and interpersonally comparable utilities used as inputs to social welfare functions. Around the same time, "optimal tax" scholars began to utilize social welfare functions in their work; and social welfare functions are now also used in certain other areas of economics. There *are* therefore a number of contemporary economic literatures where interpersonal comparability is embraced. But the suspicion of interpersonal comparisons has remained wide-spread in the profession at large—so much so that many economists view welfare economics as being a "dead" field.[60] In point of fact, welfare economics is not "dead" at all; interesting and important theorizing continues apace. What the characteriza-tion indicates, instead, is that many economists outside the fields where social welfare functions are accepted—many applied welfare economists, and many econ-omists whose work is positive rather than normative—disagree with the proponents of that approach on the very basic question of interpersonal welfare comparability.

So much for background. Let us now focus on CBA itself. As already stated, the key building block for CBA is the construct of a WTP/WTA amount.[61] This con-struct presupposes that outcomes are characterized, at least, in terms of individuals' consumption. More specifically, let us imagine that outcomes are described as having a single period, characterized in terms of each individual's consumption plus

---

[59] For skepticism about CBA from the perspective of theoretical welfare economics, see, e.g., Blackorby and Donaldson (1990); Boadway and Bruce (1984, ch. 9). On CBA as a central tool of applied welfare economics, see, e.g., Bateman and Willis (2001); A. Freeman (2003); Harberger and Jenkins (2002); Just, Hueth, and Schmitz (2004); Mishan (1988). For a crisp description of the flourishing of CBA despite theoretical critiques, see Just, Hueth, and Schmitz (2004, p. 7).

[60] Fleurbaey and Mongin (2005, pp. 381–382).

[61] See, e.g., Boadway and Bruce (1984, chs. 2, 7); A. Freeman (2003, ch. 3); Just, Hueth, and Schmitz (2004, chs. 5–6).

perhaps other individual attributes and background facts. For short, each outcome has the form $(c_1, \ldots, c_N, \mathbf{b})$.[62] The $\mathbf{b}$ term here encompasses all individual nonconsumption attributes and background facts that are included in the description of the outcome (such as individuals' health states, the levels of public goods, environmental quality, individuals' happiness states, and/or the price vector). Taking outcome x as baseline, individual i's WTP/WTA for y is the change in his consumption in y which would make him indifferent between x and y. In other words, if $x = (c_1, \ldots, c_N, \mathbf{b})$ and $y = (c_1^*, \ldots, c_N^*, \mathbf{b}^*)$, then individual i's WTP/WTA for outcome y, taking x as baseline, is the amount Δc_i such that i is indifferent between $(c_1^*, \ldots, c_i^* - \Delta c_i, \ldots, c_N^*, \mathbf{b}^*)$ and $(c_1, \ldots, c_i, \ldots, c_N, \mathbf{b})$.

Welfarist decisionmaking can also, of course, employ outcomes that have multiple periods. CBA readily generalizes to the multiperiod set-up—as do the criticisms I will present—but to simplify the presentation I will focus on the one-period case. I similarly simplify the presentation, later in the chapter, in discussing other policy-analysis approaches. Thus, throughout the chapter, I will talk about an individual having a single level of some attribute (a single consumption amount, health amount, leisure level, etc.) in an outcome, or background facts being set at a particular level. This is meaningful in the case of a single-period outcome but not in the case of a multi-period outcome—where we would need to distinguish between the individual's consumption during one period and her consumption during another period, and so forth for other attributes or background facts.

Back to the one-period set-up and the definition of CBA in that set-up. Here, an individual's consumption in some outcome means the total value, in terms of market prices in that outcome, of the array of marketed goods and services that she uses up. If the physical quantities of goods or services consumed by individual i in outcome x are $q_i^1, \ldots, q_i^M$, and the prices of those goods or services are $p^1, \ldots, p^M$, then individual i's consumption in x is $p^1 q_i^1 + \ldots + p^M q_i^M$. (In the highly simplified case where individuals are modeled as consuming but a single good, q^1, individual i's consumption is simply q_i^1.) Another term that economists often use for consumption is "expenditure." An individual's consumption can, of course, deviate from his income (even in the one-period set-up, e.g., by virtue of bequests), but often economists simplify matters by ignoring such divergence. (In this chapter, I will generally do the same. Whenever I discuss different possibilities for ranking outcomes as a function of individual incomes, I will be assuming—unless otherwise noted—that each individual's income is equal to his consumption.)[63]

---

[62] As already explained, the generic form of the characterization of some period in an outcome is $(\mathbf{a}_{1,t}, \mathbf{a}_{2,t}, \ldots, \mathbf{a}_{N,t}, \mathbf{a}_{imp,t})$, where $\mathbf{a}_{i,t}$ is a vector of attributes of individual i during period t, and $\mathbf{a}_{imp,t}$ are background facts about the world during period t.

[63] The reader might wonder how WTP/WTA amounts can be well-defined, once we move away from the super-simple context of a single consumption good. Imagine that $x = (c_1, \ldots, c_N, \mathbf{p}, \mathbf{b})$ and that $y = (c_1^*, \ldots, c_N^*, \mathbf{p}^*, \mathbf{b}^*)$. There are M different marketed goods. In outcome x, the vector of prices of those M goods is $\mathbf{p}$; in outcome y, the vector of prices of those M goods is $\mathbf{p}^*$. In this case, c_i is the

WTP/WTA amounts are defined—it bears emphasis—in terms of individual's preferences, which are assumed to be complete. For each pair of outcomes, it is assumed, each individual either weakly prefers the first to the second, or weakly prefers the second to the first, or both; this relation of "weak preference" is complete, reflexive, and transitive, and gives rise to relations of indifference and strict preference that are, respectively, reflexive, symmetric, and transitive and irreflexive, asymmetric, and transitive. It also bears emphasis that WTP/WTA amounts are traditionally understood in terms of individuals' actual (non-ideal) preferences. Although individuals *are* assumed to satisfy basic rationality properties, there is no assumption that the preferences used to determine WTP/WTA amounts are idealized in any strong sense.[64]

We have discussed how to calculate WTP/WTA amounts for each individual. The basic CBA test is then simply to add these. Given two outcomes, x and y, pick one as baseline (x); and say outcome y is better than x if the sum of WTP/WTA amounts is positive, worse if the sum is negative, and equally good if the sum is zero.

total value of the goods that i consumes in x, as calculated using the vector of prices $\mathbf{p}$; c_i^* is the total value of the marketed goods that i consumes in y, as calculated using the vector of prices $\mathbf{p}^*$. How can we determine that individual i's WTP/WTA amount is a particular amount Δc_i? To know whether i is indifferent between $(c_1, \ldots, c_i \ldots, c_N, \mathbf{p}, \mathbf{b})$ and $(c_1^*, \ldots, c_i^* - \Delta c_i \ldots, c_N^*, \mathbf{p}^*, \mathbf{b}^*)$, don't we need to know what particular array of goods i *purchases* in the two outcomes?

The answer is that CBA builds in a particular behavioral assumption. The assumption is that, in all outcomes, individuals are preference-maximizers. For a given price vector, and a given amount of consumption—i.e., total expenditure on marketed goods—CBA assumes that this expenditure is allocated between the goods so as to maximize the individual's preference satisfaction. Formally, this is handled by assigning each individual a "direct" intrapersonal utility function defined on vectors of consumption goods; by deriving from that an "indirect" utility function with consumption and the price vector as its arguments, i.e., the maximum achievable direct utility for a given consumption and price vector; and calculating WTP/WTA amounts using indirect utility.

However, the specific behavioral assumption here—that individuals act in each outcome to maximize their preferences—is actually not essential to CBA. All that is needed is *some* set of behavioral regularities that determine, in each outcome, which array of marketed goods and services individual i will purchase—as a function of the individual's consumption c_i, the price vector $\mathbf{p}$, and perhaps other characteristics of the individual or outcome. With those behavioral regularities in hand, we can map variations in individual i's consumption in a given outcome y onto variations in the array of marketed goods and services that he purchases, and thus determine individual i's WTP/WTA for y relative to baseline x (that is, Δc_i).

[64] "Idealized" preferences are preferences that satisfy strong informational and rationality conditions: being fully informed, fully deliberative, and so forth. Throughout this chapter, and typically throughout the book, I use the term "actual" to mean "non-ideal," i.e., preferences that may fall short of such strong conditions.

Occasionally, I use "actual" in a different sense: to denote preferences (idealized or not) in the actual world, rather than preferences in some non-actual, possible world. Whenever I use "actual" in *this* sense, I specifically state that I am doing so.

CBA has wide potential applicability—as evidenced by the very wide array of policy areas where it is employed, by analysts inside and outside government. CBA *measures* each individual's well-being change in terms of a consumption change, but the technique in no way requires that outcomes be characterized solely in terms of consumption. CBA can, in principle, be used to rank outcomes that include many different sorts of non-market characteristics. Or, at least, CBA can be so used if preferences are "well-behaved"—a point to be discussed in a moment. CBA also, clearly, does not presuppose the possibility of interpersonal welfare comparisons. A given individual's WTP/WTA amounts for various outcomes, relative to some baseline outcome, are a function of her preferences over outcomes—in other words, of her ranking of her own life-histories. We can determine such amounts regardless of whether life-histories involving different subjects can be ranked in terms of well-being.

However, I shall argue that CBA is not an attractive welfarist procedure for morally evaluating governmental policies and other large-scale choices—except in the case of distributively weighted CBA, which adjusts WTP/WTA amounts using weighting factors and is just a variation on the SWF approach. I will ignore distributively weighted CBA for the moment, and focus on the standard approach to CBA, which aggregates WTP/WTA amounts without distributive weights. My discussion (as throughout this chapter) concerns difficulties in producing an acceptable moral ranking of an outcome set. I discuss, first, the difficulties in using CBA to construct an outcome ranking that satisfies the minimal welfarist criteria of being a quasiordering that respects Pareto-indifference and Pareto-superiority. I then argue that the standard Kaldor–Hicks defense of CBA is very unpersuasive. I next discuss a possible revisionary defense of CBA that accepts the possibility of interpersonal comparisons and sees CBA as a proxy for overall well-being. Finally, I describe some plausible roles that CBA might play, other than as a criterion of the moral goodness of outcomes, and clarify that nothing in the discussion here is meant to undercut those possible roles.

A. Minimal Welfarist Criteria

As explained, traditional CBA defines WTP/WTA amounts in terms of actual preferences, and estimates policy impacts by estimating the sum of WTP/WTA amounts, thus defined. But what if our welfarist decisional framework is built around some alternative account of well-being W, which we take to be more attractive than an actual-preference-based theory? If so, CBA can clearly violate the principles of Pareto-indifference or Pareto-superiority, understood in terms of W.

For example, imagine that W analyzes individual well-being in terms of idealized (fully informed, fully rational) extended preferences, along the lines I will defend in the next chapter. In that case, two outcomes x and y are Pareto-indifferent (in terms of W) if, for every individual k, and every pair of life-histories $(x; i)$ and $(y; i)$, individual k under idealized conditions would be indifferent between the two life-histories.[65] But it is quite possible for *x* and *y* to be Pareto-indifferent in this sense and yet for some individuals to actually prefer *y* over *x*, or vice versa—in which case those individuals will have positive or negative WTP/WTA amounts for *y*, and thus the sum of WTP/WTA amounts for *y* could be nonzero, producing a ranking of *x* and *y* that violates Pareto-indifference. Individual *i*'s *actual* preferences, regarding *x* and *y*, can readily deviate from her *idealized, self-interested* preferences regarding those outcomes. Individual *i* might be poorly informed, less than fully rational, or non-self-interested.

Similarly, imagine that *W* analyzes individual well-being in terms of some list of objective goods. In that case, two outcomes *x* and *y* are Pareto-indifferent (in terms of *W*) if each individual is just as well off in the two outcomes, in terms of the goods. But even if *x* and *y* are Pareto-indifferent in this sense, an individual's actual preferences can deviate from the list of goods, and individuals can have positive or negative WTP/WTA amounts for *y*. Finally, imagine that *W* analyzes individual well-being in terms of good or bad mental states. In that case, *however* exactly the goodness and badness of mental states is specified, outcomes *x* and *y* must be Pareto-indifferent, in terms of *W*, if each person's mental states in *x* are the same as her mental states in *y*. But individuals can actually prefer features of outcomes other than their own mental states, and thus the sum of WTP/WTA amounts for *y* can be nonzero.

I have been discussing how the sum of WTP/WTA amounts can yield violations of *Pareto-indifference* understood in terms of accounts of well-being other than an actual-preference account. A parallel analysis will show how the sum of WTP/WTA amounts can yield violations of *Pareto-superiority* understood in terms of accounts of well-being other than actual-preference accounts.

Of course, the proponent of CBA might respond that an actual-preference-based account of well-being simply *is* the best account of well-being. But there is very good reason to reject this response: strong critical arguments can be mounted (and will be mounted in Chapter 3) against an actual-preference-based theory of well-being. Even if the reader rejects my affirmative claim that the most attractive *W* is an ideal-preference account, there remains very good reason for concluding that the most attractive *W* is not an actual-preference account; and thus that the sum of WTP/WTA amounts can run afoul of Pareto-indifference and -superiority in terms of *W*, whatever exactly it may be.

A solution, here, is to construct a more generic version of CBA. For any given outcome set **O**, and any account of well-being *W*, we can define WTP/WTA amounts in terms of *W*. Let us say that individual *i*'s WTP/WTA amount for

---

[65] More precisely, as explained in the next chapter, this means that *i* herself, if fully rational, fully informed, and self-interested, must be indifferent between outcomes *x* and *y*; and that other individuals, if fully rational, fully informed, and focused on *i*'s well-being, must be indifferent between the outcomes.

outcome y, relative to outcome x, is the change in individual i's consumption in y that makes him equally well off as in x, as judged by W. Formally, if $x = (c_1, \ldots, c_N, \mathbf{b})$, and $y = (c_1^*, \ldots, c_N^*, \mathbf{b}^*)$, then individual i's WTP/WTA amount for y, relative to x, is the amount Δc_i such that life-history $(c_1, \ldots, c_i, \ldots, c_N, \mathbf{b}; i)$ is ranked by W as equally good as life-history $(c_1^*, \ldots, c_i^* - \Delta c_i, \ldots, c_N^*, \mathbf{b}^*; i)$.[66]

This more generic definition of WTP/WTA amounts will at least give us a shot at using CBA as a basis for producing a Pareto-respecting quasiordering of outcome sets—regardless of what theory of well-being the welfarist takes to be most attractive. Generic CBA is *modular*: if we are using an actual-preference-based account of well-being, it reduces to traditional CBA, but in other cases it generates WTP/WTA amounts so as to track the theory of well-being on hand.

I should note that the idea of redefining WTP/WTA amounts in terms of an account of well-being other than an actual-preference-based theory is not merely a theoretical proposal. Within the burgeoning field of "happiness" studies, a number of researchers have defined WTP/WTA amounts in terms of *happiness* rather than preference satisfaction, and have employed happiness surveys to estimate WTP/WTA amounts thus defined.[67]

However, even the generic version of CBA encounters some challenges in meshing with a given theory of well-being W and an outcome set to produce a Pareto-respecting quasiordering of that outcome set. One issue concerns the completeness of the ordering of individual life-histories. Traditional CBA is built on the premise that each individual has a complete preference ranking of her own life-histories; but the most attractive W may well *not* provide a complete well-being ranking of each individual's life-histories. There may be pairs of life-histories, $(x; i)$ and $(y; i)$, both involving a given individual i, such that two are incomparable according to W. If so, defining a single WTP/WTA amount for y relative to x poses a technical challenge (although one that may be overcome along lines elaborated in the margin).[68]

A second issue concerns lexical orderings of non-market goods relative to consumption. This is distinct from the problem of completeness just mentioned. Imagine that W does generate a complete ranking of each individual's life-histories. However, this ranking is such that there are certain reductions in the level of some

---

[66] Referring to Δc_i as a "WTP/WTA" amount is a shorthand. Strictly, we should say that individual i's willingness-to-pay (WTP) for y, relative to x, is Δc_i if Δc_i is positive; and that his willingness-to-accept (WTA) for y, relative to x, is $-\Delta c_i$ if Δc_i is negative. The issue, here, is purely semantic. My shorthand is a compact name for the quantity Δc_i, but does not change the mathematics of CBA in any way.

[67] See Welsch (2009).

[68] If W's ranking of life-histories is representable by a set of utility functions $\mathbf{U}$, then we can define a WTP/WTA amount, for a pair $(x; i)$ and $(y; i)$, for each utility function in the set $\mathbf{U}$; we can assign each outcome the sum of WTP/WTA amounts for each such utility function; and we can use some version of a CBA test that ranks outcomes depending on the whole set of aggregate WTP/WTA amounts thus assigned to outcomes.

non-market attribute that cannot be compensated for by increased consumption. If so, there will be cases in which individual i has no finite WTP/WTA amount for outcome y relative to x.[69]

Let us now bracket these issues and assume, instead, that the nexus between well-being and consumption is "well-behaved." By "well-behaved," I mean something like the following: (1) *Complete intrapersonal comparisons.* Our theory of well-being W is such that any life-history involving a given individual is ranked as better than, equally good as, or worse than any other life-history involving the same individual. (2) *Determinate WTP/WTA amounts that point in the same direction as well-being.* For any two outcomes x and y, if i is better off in y than x, then i's WTP/WTA amount for y relative to x is a single, finite, positive amount. And if we substitute "worse off" or "equally well off" for "better off" in the preceding sentence, "positive" becomes "negative" or "zero." (3) *Well-being is strictly increasing in consumption.* For any triple of outcomes x, y, z, if i is better off in z than y, the WTP/WTA amount for x relative to y is greater than the WTP/WTA amount for x relative to z.[70]

Even with a well-behaved nexus between well-being and consumption, WTP/WTA amounts may well be subject to what might be termed "baseline dependence." By this I mean that i's WTP/WTA for outcome y, relative to outcome x, may not be the same magnitude (i.e., absolute value) as i's WTP/WTA for outcome x, relative to outcome y. This can readily arise in the case of an actual-preference-based theory of well-being; has been much discussed by the CBA literature; and would presumably generalize to alternative theories of well-being. WTP/WTA baseline-dependence can occur because the prices of marketed goods are different in y than x; or it can occur, even without price change, if individuals have different levels of non-market goods in the two outcomes.[71]

Because of WTP/WTA baseline-dependence, it is possible that the *sum* of WTP/WTA values for outcome y, relative to outcome x, will have the *same* sign (positive

---

[69] These two issues are not just theoretical niceties. CBA researchers have encountered many difficulties estimating WTP/WTA values for non-market goods, which may in part be a result of incomparabilities and lexical orderings in individuals' ranking of life-histories. See sources cited in Adler (2006b, pp. 1906–07, nn. 106–110; p. 1917, n. 143). Admittedly, with respect to lexicality, it is quite possible that this is being driven by individuals' moral preferences, and that a theory of well-being which washes out such preferences (as does the theory I will argue for in the next chapter) would not see non-market attributes as lexically ordered vis a vis consumption.

[70] That well-being is strictly increasing in consumption is, actually, entailed by the first two conditions, but for convenience this third condition is stated separately here, in a form suitable for the "money metric" style CBA test discussed below.

[71] See, e.g., A. Freeman (2003, ch. 3); Sugden (2001, pp. 155–159). Once again, the issue identified here is quite a real one for CBA practice. The literature has extensively discussed the substantial differences that are sometimes observed between the amounts that individuals are willing to pay in return for the provision of some good, and the amount they are willing to accept in return for the deprivation of that good; and the difficulties that these "offer/ask" disparities pose for policy analysis. See Adler and Posner (2006, pp. 166–173).

or negative) as the sum of WTP/WTA values for outcome x, relative to outcome y.[72] Thus, clearly, we cannot produce a quasiordering of an outcome set by a naive use of the WTP/WTA criterion: by saying that y is morally better than x iff the sum of WTP/WTA amounts for y, relative to x, is positive. A "morally better than" relation, generated in this manner, will not necessarily be asymmetric. There will be cases in which y is morally better than x, but x is morally better than y. Yet, at a minimum, the "morally better than relation" should be asymmetric.

---

[72] See Blackorby and Donaldson (1990, pp. 486–489). For a very simple example, consider a two-person case. Outcomes are characterized in terms of the individuals' consumption, plus some non-consumption attribute. The intrapersonal ranking of life-histories, for each individual, is captured by an intrapersonal utility function with the additive form $u_i(x) = v(c_i) + b_i$ with c_i individual i's consumption in x and b_i his level of the non-consumption attribute in x, and $v(.)$ a "subutility" function which takes consumption as its argument.

Imagine, now, a pair of outcomes, x, y, in which individual 1's level of the non-consumption attribute is greater in outcome y than outcome x; his level of consumption is the same in both outcomes; and the benefit is "paid for" by individual 2, i.e., individual 2 has the same level of the non-consumption attribute in both outcomes, but his consumption level is lower in y than x. (For example, think of a case in which someone is taxed to pay for a health improvement or improvement in environmental quality realized by someone else.)

In this set-up, if we assume that the $v(.)$ function is *convex*, it is very easy to generate examples where both the sum of WTP/WTA amounts for y, relative to x, *and* the sum of WTP/WTA amounts for x, relative to y, are positive. For example, assume that the $v(.)$ function is consumption squared. Imagine, now, that in both outcomes individual 1 has consumption level 10; in outcome x, his level of the b attribute is 70; in outcome y, his level of the b attribute is 90. For purposes of this discussion, denote individual 1's WTP/WTA for y, relative to x, as Δc^y; and denote his WTP/WTA for x, relative to y, as Δc^x. Then Δc^y equals $10 - \sqrt{80} \approx 1.06$ while $\Delta c^x = 10 - \sqrt{120} \approx (-.95)$. (To see why, note that Δc^y must be such that $10^2 + 70 = (10 - \Delta c^y)^2 + 90$, while Δc^x must be such that $(10 - \Delta c^x)^2 + 70 = 10^2 + 90$.) Thus, if the "cost" of the improvement in the level of the b attribute (the loss of consumption that individual 2 suffers, moving from x to y) has a value in between .95 and 1.06, we will have a case in which the sum of WTP/WTA amounts for y, relative to x, is positive, and yet the sum of WTP/WTA amounts for x, relative to y, is also positive.

It might be protested that this example is contrived, because it is typically assumed that a "subutility" function of consumption would be concave, not convex. However, the definition of moral betterness should be such that it is *impossible* to have a "reversal" case where outcome x is better than y, and at the same time y is better than x. The example shows in a simple way that, if we analyze "x is morally better than y" as "the sum of WTP/WTA amounts for x, relative to y, is positive," such a reversal is possible.

In any event, if we are inclined to analyze the relation of "morally better than" in terms of a positive sum of WTP/WTA amounts, then we will also presumably be inclined to analyze the relation of "morally worse than" in terms of a negative sum of WTP/WTA amounts. Using the above set-up and a *concave* $v(.)$ function (for example, assuming that $v(.)$ is the square root of consumption), it is very easy to generate examples where both the sum of WTP/WTA amounts for y relative to x, *and* the sum of WTP/WTA amounts for x relative to y, are *negative*. In turn, because x is morally worse than y iff y is morally better than x, these are also "reversal" cases, in which x is better than y, and yet y is better than x.

A more sophisticated application of the WTP/WTA test ranks a given outcome set by arbitrarily picking some baseline x; calculating the sum of WTP/WTA amounts relative to that baseline; and ranking the outcomes in the order of these total amounts. But this approach is not yet sophisticated enough. It has been shown that this approach can violate Pareto-superiority, at least if WTP/WTA amounts are defined in the traditional way, in terms of actual preference satisfaction; and the problem would presumably generalize to various other accounts of well-being. It is possible that every individual has complete, well-behaved preferences; that z is Pareto-superior to y; and yet that the sum of WTP/WTA amounts for z, taking x as baseline, is actually less than the sum of WTP/WTA amounts for y, taking x as baseline.[73]

It might be argued that the problems with the WTP/WTA tests described in the previous three paragraphs may not arise in many outcome sets. These problems are theoretical possibilities, but in practice (given a well-behaved consumption/well-being nexus and generically defined WTP/WTA amounts in terms of whatever theory of well-being W is at hand) the WTP/WTA tests just described will typically suffice to yield a Pareto-respecting quasiordering of an outcome set. Or so the argument might go.

The pervasiveness of the problems is a matter of some dispute. In any event, they can be circumvented by a yet more sophisticated application of the WTP/WTA test than the possibilities yet described. (The idea here is based on the notion of "money metric" utility, which some researchers have identified as a way to solve some of the ordering anomalies associated with CBA.[74]) For a given outcome set and a given theory of well-being W, arbitrarily choose some outcome x. Then, for every other outcome y, determine each individual's WTP/WTA for x, relative to y. If the nexus between well-being and consumption is well-behaved, given W, this amount will exist. Sum these amounts, across individuals, and assign y a net benefit value equaling the negative of the sum. Call this the "monetized aggregate benefit" of y. Order the outcomes in the order of their monetized aggregate benefits, with x itself assigned a monetized aggregate benefit of zero. It is not too hard to show that this ordering will be a complete ordering; that it will assign the same monetized aggregate benefit number to Pareto-indifferent outcomes (so that it respects the principle of Pareto-indifference); and that it will assign a larger monetized aggregate benefit number to z rather than y if z is Pareto-superior to y (so that it respects the principle of Pareto-superiority).

To sum up: substantial challenges do arise in using CBA to construct a Pareto-respecting quasiordering of any given outcome set, given some theory of well-being W. But, with WTP/WTA defined in terms of W, there does seem to be a reliable way to meet this goal, via a sufficiently sophisticated application of the sum-of-WTP/WTA

[73] See Pauwels (1978).

[74] See, e.g., Donaldson (1992, pp. 91–92).

test—at least if the nexus between well-being and consumption is well-behaved.

B. Using CBA to Rank Outcomes: The Kaldor–Hicks Defense

Granted that we can use CBA to rank an outcome set in a manner that satisfies minimal welfarist criteria, what would *justify* this ranking? CBA will end up ranking the Pareto-noncomparable outcomes in an outcome set one way; a different welfarist approach will rank them a different way. Why believe that the ranking generated by CBA is the morally attractive ranking?

The traditional justification for CBA appeals to the construct of a *potential Pareto-improvement*. This construct was developed during the 1930s and 1940s, by leading figures in economics (in particular Kaldor and Hicks), at a point when these scholars were attempting to rebuild the field of welfare economics without using interpersonal welfare comparisons—a notion that had become strongly disfavored.[75] The basic idea was to appeal to the possibility of transforming y into an outcome Pareto-superior to x, as a basis for judging y to be a better outcome than x, even where y and x themselves are Pareto-noncomparable.

The term "Kaldor–Hicks efficiency" is often used as a synonym for a potential Pareto-improvement test, and that shall be my usage here. Although Kaldor and Hicks actually proposed different versions of such a test, I shall ignore this historical nicety and use the term "Kaldor–Hicks efficiency" to mean the entire genus of potential-Pareto-improvement tests—whatever the precise details.

Kaldor–Hicks tests, whatever their details, focus on the possibility of producing a Pareto-improvement via costless, lump-sum redistribution of the total stock of marketed goods associated with a given outcome.[76] Consider two outcomes $x = (c_1,\ldots,c_N, \mathbf{q}, \mathbf{p}, \mathbf{t}, \mathbf{b})$ and $y = (c_1{}^*,\ldots,c_N{}^*, \mathbf{q}^*, \mathbf{p}^*, \mathbf{t}^*, \mathbf{b}^*)$. Vector $\mathbf{q}$ is the grand vector of marketed goods in x: the items that individuals actually consume and directly benefit from. If there are M of these, $\mathbf{q}$ has the form $(q_1^1,\ldots,q_1^M, q_2^1,\ldots,q_2^M,\ldots,q_N^1,\ldots,q_N^M)$. In other words, $\mathbf{q}$ is a particular allocation of each of the M goods among the N individuals. Vector $\mathbf{p}$ is the price vector, listing the prices of the M goods. Vector $\mathbf{t}$ is the technology and stock of inputs in x: a description of the factors of production possessed by each producer, as well as the technological processes she employs in transforming those inputs into marketed goods. Vector $\mathbf{b}$ denotes other individual

---

[75] See Hicks (1939); Kaldor (1939); Hotelling (1938); Scitovszky (1941). For analysis of the various Kaldor–Hicks tests, discussion of their historical development, and analysis of their relation to CBA, see Arrow (1963, ch. 4); Blackorby and Donaldson (1990); Boadway and Bruce (1984, chs. 3, 9); Chipman (2008); Chipman and Moore (1978); Gorman (1955); Gravel (2001); Keenan and Snow (1999); Little (1957); Ruiz-Castillo (1987).

[76] Theoretical treatments of Kaldor–Hicks tests focus on redistribution of goods rather than services, although presumably this could be generalized.

attributes or background facts.[77] Individual i's consumption c_i is simply the market value of i's allotment of the M goods as per $\mathbf{q}$, given the prices in $\mathbf{p}$.

One version of the Kaldor–Hicks test looks at possible redistributions of the actual stock of goods in a given outcome. It says: y is a potential Pareto-improvement over x iff there is some eligible reallocation of $\mathbf{q}^*$ (call it $\mathbf{q}^+$), such that some individuals strictly prefer $(\mathbf{q}^+, \mathbf{b}^*)$ to $(\mathbf{q}, \mathbf{b})$, and everyone is at least indifferent.[78] An eligible reallocation is *any* reassignment of the particular allocation of goods to individuals specified by $\mathbf{q}^*$—as long as the total amount of each good is no more than the total amount of each good in $\mathbf{q}^*$. Thus a reallocation is eligible, for purposes of the Kaldor–Hicks test, even if the actual redistributive mechanism that government would use to try get from $\mathbf{q}^*$ to $\mathbf{q}^+$ would be costly, and would actually produce an allocation with a smaller total stock of goods than $\mathbf{q}^+$.

This test—like CBA and everything else in welfare economics—is standardly framed in terms of preferences, but we can make the test more generic by framing it in terms of well-being. Thus framed, the test says: given some account of well-being W, y is a potential Pareto-improvement over x iff $\mathbf{q}^+$ is some eligible reallocation of $\mathbf{q}^*$ and $(\mathbf{q}^+, \mathbf{b}^*)$ is Pareto-superior to $(\mathbf{q}, \mathbf{b})$ in terms of W.

A variation on this test looks at eligible reallocations in both outcomes, saying: y is a potential Pareto-improvement over x iff (1) $\mathbf{q}^+$ is some eligible reallocation of $\mathbf{q}^*$ and $(\mathbf{q}^+, \mathbf{b}^*)$ is Pareto-superior to $(\mathbf{q}, \mathbf{b})$, and (2) there is *no* $\mathbf{q}'$ which is an eligible reallocation of $\mathbf{q}$, such that $(\mathbf{q}', \mathbf{b})$ is Pareto-superior to $(\mathbf{q}^*, \mathbf{b}^*)$.

A different version of the Kaldor–Hicks test looks at possible redistributions of the total stock of marketed goods that can be produced in a given outcome, given the productive technology and stock of inputs associated with that outcome. This version of the test (framed generically in terms of well-being) says: given some account of well-being W, y is a potential Pareto-improvement over x iff there is some eligible reallocation of the inputs to producers specified by $\mathbf{t}^*$, some production plan which is feasible given the technology specified by $\mathbf{t}^*$, and some eligible reallocation, $\mathbf{q}^{++}$, of the vector of goods thus produced, such that $(\mathbf{q}^{++}, \mathbf{b}^*)$ is Pareto-superior to $(\mathbf{q}, \mathbf{b})$ in light of W.

Here, too, a variation on this test applies it in both outcomes.

---

[77] Although theoretical work on Kaldor–Hicks tests rarely discusses nonmarket characteristics, the literature on CBA certainly does, and so if we're looking to Kaldor–Hicks tests as a potential justification for CBA, we should allow for $\mathbf{b}$ to include non-market characteristics.

[78] Here and for the next few paragraphs, I drop the price vector, technology and stock of inputs, and vector of individual monetary consumption amounts, $c_1, \ldots, c_N$, from the description of the outcomes. This is just to simplify the presentation, and does not at all bear upon my critique of the Kaldor–Hicks tests. As we reallocate goods from $\mathbf{q}^*$ to $\mathbf{q}^+$, prices will change too; but prices, technology, and inputs are not seen by the proponents of the Kaldor–Hicks tests as direct determinants of individuals' well-being. Note also that, with outcomes characterized so as to explicitly describe what specific goods individuals consume, consumption, i.e., total expenditure, will not be a separate determinant of well-being (or at least economists typically assume it will not).

Note that the Kaldor–Hicks tests described thus far compare the entire set of eligible reallocations corresponding to one outcome, to the actual allocation achieved in another. A different version compares sets to sets. In other words, it says: y is Kaldor–Hicks superior to x if, for every eligible reallocation of the marketed goods in x, there is some eligible reallocation of the marketed goods in y which is Pareto-superior. Or it says: for every eligible reallocation of the marketed goods producible in x given the technology and stock of productive factors in x, there is some eligible reallocation of the marketed goods producible in y given the technology and stock of productive factors in y which is Pareto-superior.

In turn, CBA is very often seen as way to implement one of these Kaldor–Hicks tests. However, Robin Boadway discovered in 1974 that the apparent correspondence between a given version of CBA and a seemingly equivalent Kaldor–Hicks test may be illusory.[79] Specifically, Boadway showed the following. Imagine that we are dealing with what economists call an "exchange economy." There is a single, fixed, total stock of marketed goods in all possible outcomes, and non-market characteristics are ignored. So x has the form $(c_1, \ldots, c_N, \mathbf{q}, \mathbf{p})$, where c_i is simply the total market value of the marketed goods and services that i uses (as described by $\mathbf{q}$), calculated using the extant prices $\mathbf{p}$. Outcome y has the form $(c_1^*, \ldots, c_N^*, \mathbf{q}^*, \mathbf{p}^*)$. Finally, let us imagine a case in which x and y are on the so-called "Pareto frontier" for the exchange economy (the set of allocations of the total fixed stock of goods that are not Pareto-inferior to any allocation)—so that there is no eligible reallocation of the goods in y which is Pareto-superior to x, and no eligible reallocation of the goods in x which is Pareto-superior to y.

Nonetheless—Boadway showed—it is quite possible, indeed to be expected, that the sum of WTP/WTA amounts for y relative to x will be positive, and that the sum of WTP/WTA amounts for x relative to y will be positive. This result is not particularly intuitive, and I will not discuss it in detail here, but the basic point is that the difference between the price vector in y and x drives a wedge between the CBA test and the Kaldor–Hicks tests. Subsequent theoretical scholarship has further elaborated the ways in which various versions of CBA can deviate from various versions of the Kaldor–Hicks test. Boadway and Bruce, surveying this scholarship, observe: "The use of the unweighted sum of household compensating or equivalent variations [i.e., WTP/WTA amounts] as a necessary and sufficient indicator of potential Pareto improvements is rife with difficulties."[80]

---

[79] See Boadway (1974).

[80] Boadway and Bruce (1984, p. 271). See also Blackorby and Donaldson (1990). It might be argued that, to cure the possible deviation between CBA and whatever version of the Kaldor–Hicks test we might prefer, we should simply use the test directly as a basis for ranking outcome sets. There are computational difficulties in doing so, and Kaldor–Hicks tests seem rarely to be used directly by policy analysts. See Keenan and Snow (1999, p. 218). Rather, they tend to use CBA and to justify CBA with reference to Kaldor-Hicks.

However, the most telling objection to the Kaldor–Hicks defense of CBA is different. Even where CBA *does* track the Kaldor–Hicks criterion, it is very hard to see why this feature of CBA provides a *justification* for it.

Imagine that we have used CBA to produce a Pareto-respecting quasiordering of some outcome set. Like all the other frameworks considered in this chapter, the justifiability of CBA in this outcome-ranking role will hinge on how it ranks Pareto-noncomparable outcomes. If the reader is content to take the position that all Pareto-noncomparable outcomes are morally incomparable, she does not need CBA as a criterion for ordering outcomes. She can simply use the Pareto quasiordering to do so. Reciprocally, if the reader shares the intuition of this author and many others that the Pareto quasiordering seems too abstemious—surely there are *some* cases in which x and y are Pareto-noncomparable and yet x is morally better than, equal to, or worse than y, not morally incomparable—she will entertain criteria that extend the Pareto quasiordering (CBA and the others considered in this chapter) and evaluate those criteria by how they rank pairs of outcomes that are Pareto-noncomparable.

Consider, then, a case in which x and y are Pareto-noncomparable; some version of CBA (some kind of sum-of-WTP/WTA-amounts test) ranks y as *better* than x; and it turns out that CBA, here, tracks some version of a Kaldor–Hicks test. Outcome y is also better than x in terms of this Kaldor–Hicks test. There is an eligible reallocation of the stock of marketed goods in y which is Pareto-superior to x; or there is an eligible such reallocation, plus no eligible reallocation of the stock of marketed goods in x which is Pareto-superior to y; or an eligible reallocation of the total stock of marketed goods producible in y given local technology and productive factors which is Pareto-superior to x; or such an eligible reallocation, plus no eligible reallocation of the total stock of marketed goods producible in x which is Pareto-superior to y; or some such similar fact comparing the entire sets of eligible reallocations

Furthermore, there turn out to be serious difficulties in using Kaldor–Hicks tests to produce a Pareto-respecting quasiordering of an outcome set. This is the nub of the literature on "Scitovsky reversals." See Scitovszky (1941); Gorman (1955); and other sources cited above, n. 75. If we use a "single" test which ranks y over x by considering whether there is some eligible reallocation of the goods in y (or goods producible given the technology and stock of productive factors in y) which is Pareto-superior to x, then it is possible that y is better than x by this single test, and yet x is better than y by the single test. In short, the single test is not asymmetric, and thus can't possibly be the test of moral betterness (which is asymmetric). Scitovsky proposed to cure this through the sort of "double test" mentioned in the text, which says: y is better than x if there is some eligible reallocation of the goods in y (or goods producible given the technology and stock of productive factors in y) which is Pareto-superior to x, and no such reallocation in x that makes x Pareto-superior to y. However, Gorman showed that this double test can be intransitive.

How to specify a version of the Kaldor–Hicks test that yields a Pareto-respecting quasiordering is still unclear. See in particular Gravel (2001). More fundamentally, even if a version of the Kaldor–Hicks test that reliably produced a Pareto- respecting quasiordering were engineered, the problem of *justification* stressed below would remain.

corresponding to x and y. In general, what these tests do is to map y onto a set including y plus *stipulated transformations* of y, to map x onto a set including x plus *stipulated transformations* of x, and to rank the two outcomes, y and x, depending on relations of Pareto-superiority between one or more members of the y set and one or more members of the x set.

Why should such a Kaldor–Hicks test convince us that y itself is morally better than x? How can we leap from a relation of *potential* Pareto-superiority to the relation of actual moral betterness? The following line of argument is a complete non sequitur: (1) Outcomes y and x are Pareto-noncomparable; (2) if outcome w is Pareto-superior to outcome z, then w is morally better than z; (3) y and/or some of its stipulated transformations are Pareto-superior to x and/or some of its stipulated transformations; therefore (4) outcome y is morally better than outcome x. This is Amartya Sen's objection to the Kaldor–Hicks test:

> In what sense is a rise of "potential welfare" of interest to *actual* welfare comparisons? Even if gainers *could* overcompensate the losers, why is that an improvement? It might be thought that the answer depends on whether compensations are *actually* paid or not. But there is a problem in *either* case.
>
> . . . The particular example, *viz.*, the repeal of the Corn Laws in Britain that motivated the formulation of compensation tests [i.e., Kaldor–Hicks tests], involved losses for land-lords but gains for the rest. The fact that landlords don't typically receive much sympathy may have played a psychological part in making unpaid compensation more acceptable. But the losers can just as easily be the poorest of the poor. Or, the most deserving according to any criterion of desert that we might wish to specify. A change that leaves them losers, though potentially compensatable, may not be an improvement in any obvious sense.
>
> If, on the other hand, compensation *is* actually paid, then *after* the act of compensa-tion, everyone is at least as well off as before and someone is strictly better off. That being the case, the situation is a welfare improvement on straightforward Paretian grounds. But then no compensation tests are needed, since the Pareto criterion itself is sufficient! Thus it would seem that compensation tests are either unconvincing (when compensations are not actually made) or redundant (when they are).[81]

In general, the fact that an outcome, action, individual, or other item is *transformable* into an item with some attribute does not mean that the original item is normatively equivalent to one that already has the attribute. For example, it would be absurd to say that an outcome x in which individual i has a life full of unhappiness and pain yields the same well-being level for him as an outcome y in which i's life is happier and more pleasurable—and that x and y should therefore be treated as morally equivalent—merely because we could transform the first outcome into the second via a change in i's psychological dispositions. And it would be absurd to say that the

---

[81] Sen (1979b, pp. 24–25).

appropriate choice by two different actors facing the same, physical choice situation, but with different beliefs, is the same—merely because we could change one actor's belief state into the other by adding some information. There *is* a special kind of case in which we *do* plausibly judge a certain kind of transformability of one item into a second to produce a kind of normative equivalence—namely, where considerations of responsibility are involved. For example, responsibility-sensitive welfarists *might* well plausibly say that an outcome x in which i's life is unhappy and painful should be treated as morally equivalent to an outcome y in which his life is happier and less painful, if the occurrence of x rather than y would be i's responsibility. But the potential Pareto test (in all of its various formulations) builds in no connection to responsibility, as Sen points out: "But the losers can just as easily be . . . the most deserving according to any criterion of desert that we might wish to specify."

Note that the objection to the Kaldor–Hicks defense of CBA that I have pressed here does not trade on the possibility of interpersonal comparisons. Assume that such comparisons are impossible. Even so, it is very difficult to see how the transformability of y into an outcome Pareto-superior to x means that y itself is better than x, given that y and x are themselves Pareto-noncomparable. Nor does the objection trade on exactly how the stipulated variations from y and x are defined, for purposes of the Kaldor–Hicks test. Imagine that we focus on allocations which are feasible given the administrative costs of reallocation (rather than ignoring such costs, as in the standard versions of the Kaldor–Hicks test). There is a set of vectors of marketed goods including the vector in y itself plus vectors which are achievable from y, given administrative costs; and a set of vectors of marketed goods including the vector in x itself plus vectors which are achievable from x, given administrative costs. Some of the elements in the first set bear a relation of Pareto-superiority to some of the elements in the second set. So what? Why does this mean that y is better than x, since y itself is Pareto-noncomparable with x?

Finally, the objection pressed here does not trade on the well-known fact that CBA and the Kaldor–Hicks tests are insensitive to the distribution of consumption or other well-being relevant attributes. Many readers, like the author, will indeed firmly believe that an attractive welfarist choice-evaluation procedure should rank Pareto-noncomparable outcomes in a manner that is sensitive to fair distribution. But even if the reader does not share this belief, she should still see the Kaldor–Hicks justification of CBA as unpersuasive for the reasons I have tried to outline.

Parenthetically, one might wonder whether the scholars associated with the Kaldor–Hicks test really saw it as a fundamental principle for ranking outcomes, on a par with other fundamental principles (in particular the Pareto principles). At certain points, at least, some of them suggested a different sort of role for the test—namely as a criterion whose use by government would produce long-run improvements.[82] However, there is certainly a substantial literature in economics

---

[82] See Hicks (1941, pp. 111–112); Hotelling (1938, pp. 257–260); Chapter 8.

that analyzes the Kaldor–Hicks test as a fundamental principle for ranking outcomes.[83] I have argued that it fails in that role. CBA may or may not yield a ranking of an outcome set that corresponds to a Kaldor–Hicks test (given Boadway-type divergences); but even where there *is* such correspondence, that fact does nothing to establish that the ranking achieved by CBA is morally attractive.

C. CBA, Overall Well-Being, and the Ranking of Outcomes

In prior work, Eric Posner and I presented a revisionary defense of CBA. We rejected the standard justification for CBA that links it to Kaldor–Hicks efficiency, and we also rejected the view among many economists that interpersonal welfare comparisons are impossible. Instead, we argued for the possibility of such comparisons, and therefore for the intelligibility of the concept of *overall well-being*. And we suggested that CBA was a rough proxy for overall well-being.

Critically, Posner and I did *not* claim that CBA furnished a principle for morally ranking outcomes. We wrote:

> Cost-benefit analysis is not a moral criterion. The fact that the sum-of-[WTP/WTA amounts] is greater in outcome O than in O^* does not mean that O is *in any way* morally better or more attractive than O^*.[84]

Rather, we suggested that CBA was a decision procedure that governmental officials ought to be legally required to employ. In other words, we suggested that a legal structure L in which administrative agencies employ CBA as a policy-analysis tool is morally preferable to a legal structure L^* in which they employ some other tool. In general, to endorse a procedure as a component of a morally attractive set of legal institutions is not the same as endorsing the procedure *as a moral decision procedure*. It is not the same as claiming that the procedure works well to furnish guidance concerning which choices, in any given choice situation, are morally better and which are morally worse. (For more on this distinction, see Chapter 8.)

Furthermore, we stressed that CBA was at best a *rough* proxy for overall well-being, and that governmental officials should consider using CBA with distributive weights attached, or using a different procedure in policy choice situations characterized by large wealth skews and, thus, large skews in the marginal utility of income.

To see why interpersonal comparability does not strengthen the case for using CBA as a principle for generating a moral ranking of outcomes, let us assume now that the most attractive welfarist decision-evaluation framework includes a theory of well-being, W, that generates an interpersonal as well as intrapersonal ranking of

---

[83] See sources cited above, n. 75.

[84] Adler and Posner (2006, p. 62).

life-histories and differences between them, represented by a set **U**. For simplicity, assume that this ranking is represented by a single utility function $u(.)$, unique up to a positive ratio transformation. We can therefore refer to the utility assigned to a given life-history $(x; i)$ as "$ru(x; i)$," indicating that $(x; i)$ is assigned the value $u(x; i)$ by $u(.)$, and that some other utility function is in **U** iff there is some positive number r such that this function assigns $(x; i)$ the number $ru(x; i)$.[85]

In line with the discussion earlier, we are assuming that outcomes have been specified at least in terms of individual consumption and also, perhaps, other characteristics; that WTP/WTA amounts have been given a generic definition in term of W, not in terms of actual preference satisfaction; that the connection between well-being and consumption is well-behaved; and that we are ranking outcomes using a "money metric" style sum-of-WTP/WTA-amounts test, which avoids the problems in producing a Pareto-respecting quasiordering associated with other versions of CBA. The test says: Pick one baseline outcome x; for each individual i, determine her WTP/WTA amount for x, relative to outcome y; add these up across individuals; and assign the negative of the sum to y. This number is the "monetized aggregate benefit" of y. Then one outcome is at least as good as a second iff its monetized aggregate benefit is at least as large.

Formally, if $x = (c_1, \ldots, c_N, \mathbf{b})$, and $y = (c_1{}^*, \ldots, c_N{}^*, \mathbf{b}^*)$, then individual i's WTP/WTA amount for x, relative to y, is the amount Δc_i^y such that life-history $(c_1, \ldots, c_i - \Delta c_i^y, \ldots, c_N, \mathbf{b}; i)$ is ranked by W as equally good as life-history $(c_1{}^*, \ldots, c_i{}^*, \ldots, c_N{}^*, \mathbf{b}^*; i)$. Because the well-being assigned to life-histories is now representable by a utility function, we can express WTP/WTA amounts in terms of the utility function. Δc_i^y is such that $ru_i(c_1, \ldots, c_i - \Delta c_i^y, \ldots, c_N, \mathbf{b}) = ru_i(c_1{}^*, \ldots, c_i{}^*, \ldots, c_N{}^*, \mathbf{b}^*)$. And the monetized aggregate benefits rule for ranking outcomes is: outcome y is at least as good as outcome z iff $\sum_{i=1}^{N}(-\Delta c_i^y) \geq \sum_{i=1}^{N}(-\Delta c_i^z)$.

It is clear that the ranking of outcomes in terms of their monetized aggregate benefits need not match their ranking in terms of overall well-being. (This is why Posner and I argued that CBA is at most a *rough* proxy for overall welfare.) The ranking of outcomes in terms of overall well-being is given by a *utilitarian* SWF. On the assumption that utility is unique up to a positive ratio transformation, the utilitarian SWF says: outcome y is at least as good as outcome z iff $\sum_{i=1}^{N}ru_i(y) \geq \sum_{i=1}^{N}ru_i(z)$.

To see why the CBA test and the utilitarian test can deviate, consider first the simplest case, where outcomes are specified solely in terms of consumption and

[85] Again, the case where **U** is unique up to a positive ratio transformation is the limiting case of the account of well-being presented in Chapter 3.

My critique of CBA does not in any way hinge upon the assumption that **U** is unique up to a positive ratio transformation, which is adopted merely to ease the presentation. The analysis that I present in the next several paragraphs, showing a deviation between CBA and various SWFs, readily extends to the more general case where there is some interpersonal comparability and the ranking of life-histories is represented by a set **U** of utility functions whose elements are not all related by a positive ratio transformation.

each individual's utility is just a function of his own consumption.[86] Consider, now, a graph relating an individual's consumption level in some outcome to his utility. There is no particular reason to assume that this graph will be linear. Indeed, economists and others who accept the possibility of interpersonal welfare comparisons typically assume that money has "declining marginal utility." In other words, they assume, very plausibly, that this sort of graph will be strictly *concave* (as illustrated by Figure 2.3).[87]

But, given a strictly concave graph, or indeed any non-linear form, the monetized aggregate benefits test can deviate from the utilitarian SWF.[88]

The point readily generalizes to more complicated cases. Imagine now that outcomes are characterized both in terms of individual consumption and in terms of certain other individual attributes and/or background facts, summarized in the term **b**. An individual's utility is now a function both of her consumption and of these other attributes and/or facts. If this utility function can, in turn, be additively decomposed into the "subutility" of individual consumption plus a "subutility" value assigned to the **b** term, and *if* the subutility of consumption is linear rather than concave (or nonlinear in some other way),[89] then the monetized aggregate benefits test and the utilitarian SWF will necessarily coincide. But these are very restrictive conditions on the utility function. It is implausible to think that a utility function tracking individual well-being will necessarily satisfy these conditions. Once they are relaxed, the monetized aggregate benefits test and the utilitarian SWF can deviate.[90]

---

[86] In other words, $u(x; i) = v(c_i)$, where c_i is individual i's consumption in x and $v(.)$ is some function.

[87] A point of caution: the concavity here is concavity *within* the utility function mapping consumption onto utility, which is to be distinguished from concavity within the rule R that the SWF uses to rank utility vectors. The continuous prioritarian SWF is characterized by the latter sort of concavity, while the utilitarian SWF is not.

[88] This is very easy to see, but in any event an example will illustrate. Imagine that the $v(.)$ function is the logarithm function to a base greater than 1 (e.g., to the base 10), a standard concave function. In other words, $u(x; i) = \log_{10}(c_i)$, and **U** is in turn all positive ratio transformations of $u(.)$. Assume that there are two individuals. Take x as the baseline outcome in which each has a consumption level of 1. In outcome y, the first individual has a consumption level of 900, while the second individual has a consumption level of 10. In outcome z, the first individual has a consumption level of 1000, while the second has a consumption level of 8. Note that the utilitarian SWF ranks z as worse than y. $\log_{10}(900) + \log_{10}(10) > \log_{10}(1000) + \log_{10}(8)$. The monetized aggregate benefits rule assigns y the number 908, i.e., $900 - 1 + 10 - 1$. And it assigns z a larger number, 1006, i.e., $1000 - 1 + 8 - 1$.

[89] In other words, $u(x; i) = v(c_i) + h(\mathbf{b})$, where c_i is i's consumption in x; and **b** are other attributes and/or background facts in x; and where $v(.)$ is linear, i.e., $v(c_i) = ac_i + b$, with a a positive constant and b a constant.

[90] On such divergence, see also Medin, Nyborg, and Bateman (2001).

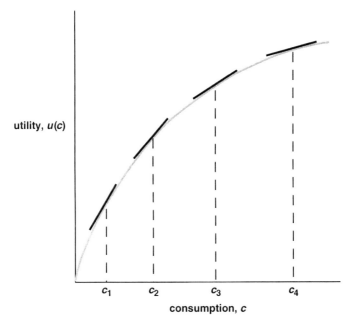

Figure 2.3 The Declining Marginal Utility of Consumption. *Note:* Utility, $u(c)$, is a strictly concave (and strictly increasing) function of consumption. Marginal utility at any consumption level c, such as c_1, c_2, c_3, or c_4, is the slope of the tangent line to $u(c)$. Note that marginal utility decreases as consumption increases.

Moreover, even if CBA *were* a perfect proxy for overall well-being, non-utilitarian welfarists who believe that the most attractive moral ranking of outcomes can *deviate* from overall well-being would still properly reject CBA as an outcome-ranking principle. Consider, in particular, the continuous prioritarian SWF: the SWF that I will defend in Chapter 5 against the utilitarian SWF (and also against other distribution-sensitive SWFs). In the case where utility is unique up to a positive ratio transformation, and the continuous prioritarian SWF is the Atkinson variety,[91] the criterion for ranking outcomes is: outcome y is at least as good as outcome z iff $(1-\gamma)^{-1}\sum_{i=1}^{N}r^{1-\gamma}u_i(y)^{1-\gamma}\geq(1-\gamma)^{-1}\sum_{i=1}^{N}r^{1-\gamma}u_i(z)^{1-\gamma}$, where γ is an inequality aversion parameter, a positive number that encapsulates the degree of priority given to well-being changes affecting worse-off individuals. Assume, now, that individual utility has the special additive form described in the preceding paragraph, so that the monetized aggregate benefits test and the utilitarian SWF coincide. Because the

[91] I argue for the Atkinson SWF because it is the only continuous prioritarian SWF which is invariant to a ratio transformation—and this feature is indeed useful for purposes of the discussion, addressing distributively weighted CBA in the simple case where **U** has the form $ru(.)$.

continuous prioritarian SWF is distribution-sensitive and can deviate from the utilitarian SWF, it can also—therefore—deviate from the monetized aggregate benefits test.

Table 2.2 The Deviation between a Continuous Prioritarian SWF and CBA

	Outcome x			Outcome y			
	Consumption	Labor	Utility	Consumption	Labor	Utility	$-\Delta c_i^y$
Individual A	80	40	91.31r	130	65	140.15r	48.84
Individual B	400	80	409.38r	300	60	310.39r	−98.99
Utilitarian SWF			500.69r			450.54r	
Atkinson SWF, $\gamma = 2$			−.013/r			−.010/r	

The table shows each individual's consumption (specifically, annual consumption divided by 1000) and labor (specifically, hours worked each week). Note that individual B has a higher wage rate than individual A. Leisure is total hours in the week (168) minus labor. Assume that $u(.)$ equals consumption plus the square root of leisure—thus has the special additive form. **U**, in turn, consists of all positive ratio transformations of $u(.)$

Individual A works more in outcome y, and is better off there, while individual B works less in outcome y, and is worse off there. Summing utilities, the utilitarian SWF says outcome x is better. Note that this coincides with the monetized aggregate benefits test. $(-\Delta c_i^y)$ amounts for each individual are shown in the last column, with Δc_i^y the reduction in the individual's consumption in outcome x required to make him equally well off in both outcomes, given the formula for $u(.)$. However, utilities are distributed more equally in outcome y, and the Atkinson SWF with a sufficiently large γ parameter will say that y is better. For example, the Atkinson SWF with $\gamma = 2$ assigns outcome x a value of $-.013/r$, but it assigns y a larger value, $-.010/r$.

So let us now turn to the possibility of CBA with distributive weights. There is actually a substantial academic literature on this topic.[92] The literature typically draws a close connection between distributively weighted CBA and social welfare functions, suggesting that distributive weights be specified using some social welfare function. Although CBA, in governmental practice, is typically undertaken without distributive weights—certainly that is true in the United States, which has spearheaded the use of CBA as a governmental decision procedure—there are some exceptions. Distributive weights have been employed at the World Bank (although apparently not in recent years), and the current guidance document for CBA in the U.K. encourages their use.[93]

---

[92] See, e.g., Boadway and Bruce (1984, pp. 271–281); Cowell and Gardiner (1999); Drèze and Stern (1987); Johansson-Stenman (2005); Ray (1984). For a famously skeptical view, see Harberger (1978).
[93] HM Treasury (2003, pp. 24–25, 91–96); Little and Mirrlees (1994); Johansson-Stenman (2005, p. 337).

Distributively weighted CBA takes the form of summing individual WTP/WTA amounts multiplied by individual weights. Rather than assigning each outcome y a monetized aggregate benefits value equaling $\sum_{i=1}^{N}(-\Delta c_i^y)$, and ranking outcomes in the order of these values, distributively weighted CBA assigns each outcome a monetized *weighted* aggregate benefits value equaling $\sum_{i=1}^{N} w_i^y (-\Delta c_i^y)$, where w_i^y is the weight for individual i in outcome y, and ranks outcomes corresponding to *these* values.

It is easy to see that, in principle, distributive weights *can* cure the deviation between CBA and various SWFs. I am assuming here that the weighting scheme has a fair degree of flexibility: the weighting factor for an individual can vary from outcome to outcome, and can be a function of a variety of well-being relevant characteristics, not just consumption.[94]

Using a flexible weighting scheme of this sort, it is trivial to specify weights so as to cure any deviation between CBA and the utilitarian SWF. Simply calculate the weighting factor w_i^y for individual i in outcome y by taking the difference between i's utility in the baseline outcome x and y, and dividing by the WTP/WTA amount Δc_i^y.[95] Then it is absolutely straightforward to see that the ordering of outcomes using the values assigned them by the formula $\sum_{i=1}^{N} w_i^y (-\Delta c_i^y)$ is exactly the same as the ordering using the values assigned by the utilitarian SWF, i.e., $\sum_{i=1}^{N} ru_i(y)$. Similarly, using a flexible weighting scheme, it is trivial to specify a different set of weights so as to cure any deviation between CBA and the prioritarian SWF of the Atkinson variety. Now, calculate the weighting factor w_i^y for individual i in outcome y by taking the difference between i's *transformed* utility in the baseline outcome x and her *transformed* utility in outcome y, and dividing this difference by the

---

[94] Proponents of distributive weights often discuss a simpler approach, where an individual is assigned a single weight as a function of his attributes just in the baseline outcome (perhaps just his consumption). Even where outcomes are just specified in terms of consumption, distributively weighted CBA using a single individual weight (rather than an outcome-specific individual weight) will not reliably mirror an SWF when there is one or more individuals whose consumption levels vary substantially (rather than "marginally") between outcomes. See Ray (1984, ch. 6). And where utility is a function of consumption as well as other attributes, distributive weights will not reliably cure the deviation between CBA and an SWF if weights are solely a function of individual consumption. Another possible way to specify distributive weights in this last case is to *normalize* consumption to reflect non-consumption attributes, and make distributive weights a function of normalized consumption plus the reference level of the non-consumption attributes. On normalization, see below, pp. 125–130.

[95] More precisely pick any $u(.)$ arbitrarily, and set $w_i^y = (u_i(x) - u_i(y))/\Delta c_i^y$, or any positive number if Δc_i^y is zero. Let us denote $\sum_{i=1}^{N} u_i(x)$ as K. Then $\sum_{i=1}^{N} w_i^y(-\Delta c_i^y) = \sum_{i=1}^{N}(u_i(y) - u_i(x)) = \sum_{i=1}^{N} u_i(y) - K$. Thus the ordering of outcomes achieved by ranking outcomes according to their monetized weighted aggregate benefits is exactly the same as ordering them by summing utilities using $u(.)$. And this is, in turn, the same for all $u(.)$ in $\mathbf{U}$ if that set is unique up to a positive ratio transformation.

In fact, we could even more simply define weights for each individual equaling $-u_i(y)/\Delta c_i^y$, but weights thus defined might be negative.

WTP/WTA amount Δc_i^y.[96] With the individual weights calculated in this manner, it is straightforward to see that the ordering of outcomes using the values assigned them by the formula $\sum_{i=1}^{N} w_i^y (-\Delta c_i^y)$ is exactly the same as the ordering using the values assigned to outcomes by the Atkinson SWF, i.e., $(1-\gamma)^{-1} \sum_{i=1}^{N} r^{1-\gamma} u_i (y)^{1-\gamma}$.

Moreover, this procedure for curing the deviation between CBA and utilitarian or Atkinson SWFs generalizes to the case in which utility is not necessarily unique up to a positive ratio transformation.[97] It generalizes beyond the Atkinson SWF to any continuous prioritarian SWF. Indeed, it can be shown that appropriately chosen weights will produce convergence between CBA and *any* SWF that can be encapsulated in a mathematical function, i.e., any SWF that takes the form: outcome x is at least as good as outcome y iff, for all $u(.)$ belonging to U, $s(u(x)) \geq s(u(y))$.[98]

However, it is unclear why the welfarist who accepts the possibility of interpersonal comparisons and the representability of well-being via utility numbers should advocate using distributively weighted CBA as the outcome-ranking component of her choice-evaluation procedure. Why not rank outcomes directly, using whatever SWF the welfarist takes to be attractive, rather than via this more roundabout technique? Distributively weighted CBA, like the direct application of an SWF, requires the estimation of a utility function—which is critical in specifying weights. And in the case of a non-utilitarian SWF, it also requires specifying the parameters of the $s(.)$ function—for example, the inequality aversion parameter γ for the Atkinson SWF. But, in addition, it requires the extra step of converting well-being impacts into WTP/WTA amounts. Why take this extra step? Why not more directly rank outcomes using the formula: outcome x is at least as good as outcome y iff, for all $u(.)$ belonging to U, $s(u(x)) \geq s(u(y))$?

---

[96] More precisely, pick one $u(.)$ arbitrarily and set $w_i^y = [(1-\gamma)^{-1} u_i (x)^{1-\gamma} - (1-\gamma)^{-1} u_i (y)^{1-\gamma}]/\Delta c_i^y$, or any positive number if Δc_i^y is zero.

[97] In that case, we calculate WTP/WTA amounts and weights for each $u(.)$ belonging to U; assign each outcome a monetized weighted aggregate benefit for each $u(.)$; and order outcomes depending on the entire set of monetized weighted aggregate benefit amounts assigned each outcome.

[98] As in the previous footnote, we will generally need to calculate WTP/WTA amounts and weights for each $u(.)$. To do so for a given $u(.)$—and in a manner that avoids negative weights—proceed as follows. For a given outcome y (with x the baseline outcome used to calculate WTP/WTA amounts), arbitrarily identify a positive number B and negative number C such that $s(u(y)) - s(u(x)) = B + C$. Take the group of individuals whose $(-\Delta c_i^y)$ amounts are positive, and arbitrarily assign positive weights w_i^y to each individual i in this group so that the sum of weighted $(-\Delta c_i^y)$ amounts in this group is equal to B. Now take the group of individuals whose $(-\Delta c_i^y)$ amounts are negative, and arbitrarily assign positive weights to each individual in this group so that the sum of weighted $(-\Delta c_i^y)$ amounts is equal to C. Finally, for any individual with a $(-\Delta c_i^y)$ amount equal to zero, assign her any positive weight.

In the case where some individuals have positive $(-\Delta c_i^y)$ amounts and none have negative amounts, modify this methodology, by simply setting $B = s(u(y)) - s(u(x))$ and $C = 0$. And in the case where some individuals have negative such amounts and none positive, set $C = s(u(y)) - s(u(x))$ and $B = 0$.

One possible answer has to do with optimal legal structures. Assume it is indeed morally attractive to establish legal institutions whereby some range of decision-makers, within some given society's government, are legally required to employ an SWF of some kind in evaluating their decisions. If CBA is currently widely used within the government or society, then—as a kind of transitional measure—it may be perhaps appropriate to instruct those decisionmakers to build upon their expertise with CBA and attach distributive weights to WTP/WTA amounts, rather than shifting to direct implementation of an SWF. But this line of argument, which concerns the content of certain legal requirements, does not address the distinct (and logically prior) question now on the table: What is the most attractive way to outfit a moral decision procedure? Why does the welfarist have good reason to favor the blueprint of distributively weighted CBA, rather than the SWF blueprint, as the general format for ranking outcomes as morally better or worse?

In any event, even if it *is* the case that distributively weighted CBA is an attractive format for a moral choice-evaluation procedure, this proposition does not undermine the basic claim of this chapter. I claim that existing policy-evaluation approaches either are less attractive than the SWF approach, as a basis for morally ranking outcomes, or alternatively are variations on the SWF approach. By a variation on the SWF approach, I mean an approach to ranking outcomes that accepts that well-being is interpersonally comparable to some extent; accepts that well-being is measurable by utilities; and uses these utilities to generate a ranking of outcomes which is identical to the ranking generated by some Paretian, anonymous SWF. And this is precisely what distributively weighted CBA is.[99]

D. Other Roles for CBA?

This section has thus far focused on whether CBA provides an attractive welfarist criterion for morally ordering outcomes. Without distributive weights attached, CBA fails in this role, or so I have argued. Distributively weighted CBA, too, seems less attractive than ranking outcomes via direct application of an SWF, and in any event is simply a variation on the SWF approach.

However, nothing in the analysis up to this point precludes CBA from playing a function other than as a criterion of the moral goodness of outcomes. I will now revert to using "CBA" to mean some version of a sum-of-WTP/WTA test without distributive weights.

Assume that the most attractive welfarist decision procedure uses a SWF of some kind (*not* CBA) as the criterion for morally ranking outcomes. This SWF will say: x is at least as good as y iff R ranks $u(x)$ as being at least as good as $u(y)$, for all $u(.)$

---

[99] Nor is seeing distributively weighted CBA this way artificial, since as already mentioned those who favor it *do* generally take the position that weights should be set with reference to a social welfare function.

belonging to **U**, where R is a Paretian and anonymous rule for ranking utility vectors.

This decision procedure, besides telling us how to construct an outcome set and rank outcomes, will also provide some principles (whatever they might be) for constructing a choice set **A**, and for ranking choices in light of the probability distribution over outcomes each choice yields. Because the decisionmaker is bounded in her cognitive abilities, **A** too will be bounded. It will not include *every* action that the decisionmaker is able to perform; thinking about such a choice set would be cognitively impossible.[100]

CBA might function here as a *choice-set-expansion heuristic*. To see how this might work, let us imagine (to start) that the decisionmaker is operating under conditions of certainty. Each choice in **A** yields one outcome for sure. Let us designate by a^x the action that yields outcome x with certainty, and so forth for other outcomes. Imagine now that the decisionmaker has used the SWF formula to rank the outcomes corresponding to the choices in **A**, and that she has determined that y is the best outcome produced by some choice in **A** and that a^y is therefore the best action. She is about to select a^y—until someone points out that a^z, which is also in **A**, is preferred to a^y by CBA, and that CBA here tracks a simple kind of Kaldor–Hicks test. In other words, there is some outcome z^*, which is reached via a reallocation of the consumption goods in z (the outcome produced by a^z), such that z^* is Pareto-superior to y.

This observation should prompt the decisionmaker to consider expanding her choice set. Might there be some new choice b, which is not in the initial choice set, but which the decisionmaker is physically capable of performing, and that yields either z^* or at least some other outcome which is Pareto-superior to y? There need not be such a choice b, given the administrative costs of the tax system, the distortionary effects of the income tax, the limited ability of the tax authorities to detect individuals' abilities, and so forth. The extant technology of taxation might not make it possible for the decisionmaker to "vary" a^z, so that consumption is shifted, without too much loss in well-being, and an outcome Pareto-superior to y is produced. Furthermore, whatever the technology of taxation, the decisionmaker may not be able to use the tax system to redistribute consumption—either because she is not a governmental decisionmaker, or because she is an official within some non-tax governmental body.

Still, if a feasible choice b did exist, the SWF formula—x at least as good as y iff R ranks $u(x)$ as being at least as good as $u(y)$, for all $u(.)$ belonging to **U**—would *favor* b over the initially chosen action a^y. This is because the SWF is Paretian: it always prefers a Pareto-superior to a Pareto-inferior outcome.

It is critical to be clear about the role that CBA is playing here. If decisionmakers were unboundedly rational, a moral decision procedure would not need choice-set-expansion heuristics: the decisionmaker would simply be instructed, at the outset,

---

[100] See Adler (2009a).

to consider all possible alternatives. However, given bounded rationality, an attractive moral decision procedure might plausibly take the form of coupling guidance for the construction of an initial choice set with guidance to "search" for additional choices under certain conditions. Furthermore, because the SWF's ranking of outcomes is *Paretian*, the fact that the outcome *z* yielded by a choice within the initial choice set, a^z, is *potentially Pareto-superior* to the outcome *y* yielded by the favored choice a^y, is plausibly an attractive *trigger* for a search for an additional option *b* that will yield an outcome Pareto-superior to *y*. Crucially, however, the *ranking* of outcomes, for purposes of choice from whatever choice set is at hand (the initial choice set, or the choice set expanded after search), is performed by the SWF, not by CBA.

I am not actually arguing for the use of CBA as a choice-set-expansion heuristic. Note that the construction of a CBA test that will usefully function as such a heuristic becomes more complicated in the (realistic) case of choice under uncertainty. Rather, I am trying to clarify that this sort of role for CBA is *distinct* from its use as the criterion for morally ranking outcomes; that nothing in my argument against CBA as a criterion for morally ranking outcomes precludes this alternative role; and that, indeed, if we use a Paretian SWF as the outcome-ranking principle, there is some substantial plausibility in thinking that CBA should play this role as a choice-set-expansion heuristic.

Actually, there is already a scholarly literature that uses CBA as something like a choice-set-expansion heuristic. This literature, which will be discussed in Chapter 8, works *within* the optimal-tax tradition. It uses a Paretian, anonymous SWF, *not* CBA or a Kaldor–Hicks standard, as the fundamental criterion for evaluating different tax and non-tax policies. But it suggests that, at least under certain assumptions concerning the structure and heterogeneity of individual preferences and concerning government's information and administrative costs, a governmental regulation or other non-tax policy that fails a cost-benefit test can always be improved upon (in light of the SWF) by choosing a different policy and coupling that with some change to the schedule of income taxes.

A second possible role for CBA, also suggested by this literature and discussed in Chapter 8, has to do with morally optimal legal structures. As between a legal structure *L* that instructs non-tax decisionmakers to use CBA as their policy-analysis tool, and a legal structure L^* that instructs non-tax decisionmakers to use a different tool, it *might* be the case that a Paretian SWF would favor *L* over L^*. Perhaps legal structures that channel redistribution through the tax system, and tell non-tax decisionmakers to use CBA, would make everyone better off. A different sort of argument for *L* rather than L^*, also mentioned in Chapter 8, is that the benefits of the various governmental policies passing the CBA test would be "spread around," so that everyone would benefit from *L* rather than L^* in the long run (and thus that a Paretian SWF would favor *L* over L^* even without a tax system that converts potential into actual Pareto-improvements).

These claims about the role of CBA in optimal legal structures, whatever their ultimate persuasiveness, are again conceptually distinct from the claim criticized in this chapter—that CBA is a principle for morally ranking outcomes. Unfortunately, much of the discussion of CBA and the Kaldor–Hicks principle has been marred by a failure to clearly delineate what particular function is being mooted.

III. INEQUALITY METRICS

There is a large empirical literature in economics that employs inequality metrics to quantify the degree of inequality in the distribution of income. Standard metrics include the Gini coefficient, the coefficient of variation, the generalized entropy family of metrics, and the Atkinson index.[101]

Although inequality metrics are often employed simply to quantify the status quo distribution of income, or changes over time in that distribution, they can also be used to measure policy impacts: namely by estimating the change in the degree of income inequality that would be produced by some policy, or that has been caused by some past policy. Furthermore, although inequality metrics are typically applied to incomes, they are equally applicable to the distribution of any personal good— anything which takes the form of being possessed by one particular person—and indeed have been used by some scholars to quantify the inequality of various non-income items, such as health, longevity, or happiness.[102]

What, mathematically, characterizes the standard inequality metrics? First, all of them satisfy an anonymity principle: if two distributions of an item are identical, except for the proper names of the individuals who receive particular amounts of the item, they are assigned the same inequality number.

Second, all of them satisfy the *Pigou–Dalton* principle, as applied to whatever item is being distributed.[103] The Pigou–Dalton principle was already mentioned earlier in the chapter. An important feature of this principle, which must be kept in mind throughout the book, is that it can be applied to a variety of different items. We can talk about the Pigou–Dalton principle in terms of *income*, the Pigou–Dalton principle in terms of *health*, the Pigou–Dalton principle in terms of *well-being*, and so forth. Consider some item *s*: this could be some attribute that an outcome might characterize individuals as having, such as income, health, etc., or it could be a utility number measuring an individual's well-being.[104] Let $[s_1, \ldots, s_N]$ represent some distribution of *s* among *N* individuals. Consider a new distribution which is identical to the first, except that some amount of *s* has been transferred (without losing any) from one person to someone else at a lower level of *s*, without their switching ranks.

[101] On inequality metrics, see Blackorby, Bossert, and Donaldson (2005, ch. 4); Bojer (2003); Chakravarty (2009); Cowell (1995, 2000); Dutta (2002); Lambert (2001); Sen (1997b); Silber (1999).

[102] See, e.g., Le Grand (1987); Stevenson and Wolfers (2010).

[103] This is sometimes called the "principle of transfers."

[104] In my set-up, individual well-being is not itself an attribute that outcomes describe, but a further property attached to outcomes by a theory of well-being and represented by utility functions.

That is, the new distribution is $[s_1, . . ., s_i + \Delta s, . . ., s_j - \Delta s, . . ., s_N]$, where $\Delta s > 0$ and $s_j - \Delta s \geq s_i + \Delta s$. Then the Pigou–Dalton principle, as applied to s, counts the second distribution as better than the first; and indeed all standard inequality metrics will assign the second distribution a lower degree of inequality than the first.

A crucial mathematical proposition undergirding the literature on inequality measurement is this: if $[s_1, . . ., s_N]$ is an unequal distribution of some item s, while $[s_1^*, . . ., s_N^*]$ is a perfectly equal distribution, and the total amount of s is the same in the two distributions, then the latter distribution can be reached from the former by a series of Pigou–Dalton transfers.

Finally, inequality metrics satisfy what might be termed the "equality-as-a-lower-bound" axiom.[105] They give a smaller number (a smaller degree of inequality) to a perfectly equal distribution of some item, as opposed to any unequal distribution $[s_1, . . ., s_N]$, whether the total amounts of s are the same in both distributions or different.

Henceforth, I will use "inequality metric" as a synonym for a measure of the distribution of some item that satisfies the axioms of anonymity, Pigou–Dalton, and equality-as-a-lower-bound. Again, all the standard measures characterized as inequality metrics satisfy at least these properties—whatever their differences in other regards.

Is it plausible to employ an inequality metric as a tool for morally ranking outcome sets? Here, as elsewhere, we want to construct a Pareto-respecting quasi-ordering that also ranks Pareto-noncomparable outcomes in an attractive manner. Non-utilitarian welfarists, at least, will find plausible the thought that inequality metrics might be used so as to help rank Pareto-noncomparable outcomes in a manner that is sensitive to fairness considerations.

However, difficulties arise in satisfying even minimal welfarist criteria.[106] Consider, first, outcomes that are "unidimensional"—characterized with respect to

---

[105] Standard inequality metrics, such as those mentioned in the text, satisfy a "zero-normalization" axiom. They assign the number zero to a perfectly equal distribution of some item. See Blackorby, Bossert, and Donaldson (2005, p. 101); Chakravarty (2009, p. 22). Equality-as-a-lower bound follows immediately from the zero normalization axiom, plus the Pigou–Dalton principle. The Pigou–Dalton principle entails that any unequal distribution of s is given a higher number than an equal distribution of the same total amount of s. Zero normalization entails that this latter distribution is assigned zero. So any unequal distribution is assigned a positive number, while equal distributions are assigned zero.

[106] Throughout this discussion, I assume that the Pareto principle is itself defined in life-history terms, *not* in attribute-based terms. It is possible to divide up a life-history into attribute slices; ascribe an attribute-slice well-being to each such slice; and then define relations of Pareto-indifference and -superiority between outcomes in terms of comparisons of individual attribute-slices. However, this attribute-based construal of the Pareto principles has no justification. See Chapter 6.

On the tension between the Pareto principle and the Pigou–Dalton principle, see Bosmans, Lauwers, and Ooghe (2009); Fleurbaey (2006); Fleurbaey and Trannoy (2003). Cf. Shorrocks (2004).

a single individual attribute, such as individual consumption, or individual health, or individual happiness.[107] Even in this basic case, a simple-minded use of inequality metrics runs headlong into the principle of Pareto-superiority. Imagine that we say, simple-mindedly, that an outcome is better if it has a lower degree of inequality. Imagine, now, that the attribute is distributed perfectly equally in x; that some but not all individuals have more of the attribute in y than x; and that the attribute, therefore, is distributed unequally in y. Then (given the equality-as-a-lower-bound axiom) the simple-minded ranking says that x is better than y. But imagine that individual well-being is (at least sometimes) strictly increasing in the attribute.[108] Then Pareto-superiority will require (at least sometimes) that y be ranked as a better outcome than x.

We can avoid this problem by limiting the use of inequality metrics to comparing pairs of unidimensional outcomes in which the sum total of the attribute is the same. Doing so (at least if well-being is always strictly increasing in the attribute) will never violate Pareto-indifference or Pareto-superiority. However, a quasiordering of a unidimensional outcome set that never ranks Pareto-noncomparable outcomes in which the sum total of the attribute is different is counterintuitive. Consider so-called cases of "Suppes" dominance[109]—where the two outcomes are Pareto-noncomparable, but a permutation of the attributes in one outcome yields an outcome that is Pareto-superior to the other outcome. For example, x has attribute levels (10, 20, 30, 40), and y has attribute levels (60, 50, 20, 10). Surely y is a better outcome than x (assuming well-being is strictly increasing in the attribute).

Moreover, conflicts with Pareto-indifference and Pareto-superiority are not so easily avoided, even if inequality metrics *are* merely used to rank outcomes with the same total amount of an attribute, once we move to "multidimensional" outcomes— outcomes characterized in terms of multiple individual attributes.

Assume that we are comparing multidimensional outcomes and limiting the use of inequality metrics to comparisons where the sum total of each attribute does not change. I will illustrate the difficulties by focusing on two-attribute outcomes, with each individual having attribute a and attribute b (the discussion generalizes). So we are comparing $x = (a_1, \ldots, a_N, b_1, \ldots, b_N)$ to $y = (a_1{}^*, \ldots, a_N{}^*, b_1{}^*, \ldots, b_N{}^*)$, such that the total amount of a is the same in both outcomes, and the total amount of b is the same in both outcomes. How shall we apply an inequality metric to rank such pairs of outcomes? One possibility is to apply the metric simply to one of the attributes. But this can yield a violation of Pareto-indifference or -superiority. Imagine that the inequality metric is applied to attribute a. Imagine that some individuals have

---

[107] Moreover, for purposes of the discussion in this subsection, assume that outcomes are not characterized with respect to background facts or that such facts are identical in all outcomes.

[108] When I say that "well-being is sometimes strictly increasing in the attribute," I mean that—in some outcome sets—increasing an individual's attribute level always makes him better off. Well-being is "always strictly increasing in the attribute" if this is true in every outcome set.

[109] See, e.g., Fleurbaey and Trannoy (2003, p. 247).

different amounts of *a* in the two outcomes, and that the degree of *a*-inequality in the two outcomes is different. However, in each individual's case the *a*-difference is counterbalanced by the *b*-difference. Our theory of well-being says that, for each individual *i*, her life-history with (a_i, b_i) is just as good as her life-history with (a_i^*, b_i^*). So the inequality metric ranks one outcome over the other, but Pareto-indifference requires that they be ranked as equally morally good. A variation on this story yields a violation of Pareto-superiority.[110]

A different, more sophisticated possibility is to apply the inequality metric to each of the multiple attributes. But here, too, problems with Pareto-indifference and -superiority can arise. Consider the following proposal, which employs a seemingly very plausible process of "dominance" reasoning to compare outcomes in light of the distribution of multiple attributes: In comparing $x = (a_1, \ldots, a_N, b_1, \ldots, b_N)$ to $y = (a_1^*, \ldots, a_N^*, b_1^*, \ldots, b_N^*)$, if some stipulated inequality metric says that both the *a* distribution *and* the *b* distribution are more equal in *x* than *y*, then *x* is better. However, as the following example illustrates, a package of Pigou–Dalton transfers in each of a plurality of attributes (which the dominance reasoning just described would necessarily approve) can yield a violation of Pareto-superiority.

Imagine that there are two individuals. Outcome *x* is $((10, 20), (20, 10))$ meaning that individual one is at level 10 of the *a* attribute and level 20 of the *b* attribute, while for individual two those levels are switched. Five units of each attribute are transferred from the individual at the higher attribute level to the individual at the lower attribute level. This yields outcome *y*, $((15, 15), (15, 15))$. Any inequality metric will say that the perfectly equal distribution of the *a* attribute is better in *y* than its unequal distribution in *x*, and ditto for the *b* attribute. So dominance reasoning says that *y* is better. But imagine that the intrapersonal ranking of life-histories is such that $(15, 15)$ is just as good as $(20, 10)$, in turn just as good as $(10, 20)$. (Most simply, well-being is linear in each attribute and they are perfect substitutes.) If so, the two outcomes are Pareto-indifferent. Imagine, instead, that some degree of "spread" in the attributes is desirable, given two life-histories with the same total sum, so that $(10, 20)$ and $(20, 10)$ are better than $(15, 15)$. A life at a

---

[110] For the simplest violation of Pareto-indifference, imagine that there are 3 individuals, 6 total units of the *a* attribute, 6 of the *b* attribute, and that each individual has an intrapersonal utility function that sums the attributes. So if $x = ((1, 3), (2, 2), (3, 1))$, meaning that individual 1 has the *a* attribute at level 1 and the *b* attribute at level 3, etc., while $y = ((2, 2), (2, 2), (2, 2))$, then any inequality metric applied to the *a* attribute will rank *y* as better than *x* (because the *a* attribute is perfectly equal in *y* but not *x*). Yet note that each individual is just as well off in *y* as *x*.

To tweak this story and produce a violation of Pareto-superiority, imagine that each individual has an intrapersonal utility function that multiplies the attributes. So if $x = ((3, 3), (2, 2), (1, 1))$ and $y = ((2, 4), (2, 2), (2, 0))$, then any inequality metric applied to the *a* attribute says that *y* is better, and yet both the first individual and the third individual are worse off in *y* while the second is equally well off in the two outcomes.

high level of at least one attribute, with the other not too low, is better than being at an average level of both. Then Pareto-superiority says that y is worse than x.

It might appear, from this last example, that the conflict between the Pareto principle and the Pigou–Dalton principle in the multiattribute context can be cured by limiting the scope of the Pigou–Dalton principle to attribute transfers between a person who is at a higher level *in each attribute* to one who is at a lower level in each attribute. However, Fleurbaey and Trannoy have shown that there can be a conflict between the Pareto principles and the Pigou–Dalton principle even if the scope of the Pigou–Dalton principle is thus limited.[111]

Table 2.3 A Conflict between the Pareto and Pigou-Dalton Principles

	Outcome x		Outcome y		Outcome z		Outcome w	
	a	b	a	b	a	b	a	b
Individual 1	15	1	16	2	3	17	4	18
Individual 2	18	4	17	3	2	16	1	15

The "a" and "b" columns show the individuals' levels of each attribute in outcomes x, y, z, w. Note that, in outcome x, individual 2 is at a higher level in both attributes than individual 1, and y is reached by a Pigou–Dalton transfer in both attributes. Reciprocally, individual 1 is at a higher level in both attributes in outcome w, and z is reached by a Pigou–Dalton transfer in both attributes.

But imagine the following indifferences: Individual 1 is equally well off in x as in z, and in y as in w. Similarly, individual 2 is equally well off in x as in z, and in y as in w.

This yields a contradiction between Pareto-indifference and the Pigou–Dalton principle. Pareto-indifference says that x is equally good as z and y is equally good as w. The Pigou–Dalton principle says that y is better than x and that z is better than w. These can't both hold true.

Clearly, challenging issues arise in employing inequality metrics to rank outcomes in even a minimally welfarist manner. I will consider four possible solutions to the tensions with Pareto-indifference and Pareto-superiority just described, each deriving from some approach to using inequality metrics that is suggested by the extant scholarly literature. The first solution involves using inequality metrics to measure the distribution of *utility*. The second involves the conversion of each outcome into a distribution of "equivalent" incomes, and the use of some income evaluation function to rank the distribution of equivalent incomes. The third involves a Pigou–Dalton test that is applied to each of a plurality of attributes, together with a

---

[111] See Fleurbaey (2006, pp. 239–240).

limitation on the intrapersonal ranking of life-histories so as to avoid Pareto violations. Finally, the fourth employs the so-called "egalitarian equivalent" principle for ordering outcomes.

A. Applying Inequality Metrics to the Distribution of Utility

If one believes that well-being is interpersonally comparable, and that individual well-being can be represented by utility numbers, it is natural to think of using inequality metrics to measure the distribution of *utility*. Imagine that I is an inequality metric, and that $u(.)$ is a utility function which maps a given outcome x onto a vector of utilities $u(x) = (u_1(x), \ldots, u_N(x))$. We *could* quantify the degree of well-being inequality in x via the formula $I(u(x))$.

This thought can be given a rigorous basis in the following, important theorem, deriving from work by Atkinson, Kolm, and Sen.[112] Imagine that R is a rule for ranking utility vectors which produces a complete ordering and which is not only Paretian and anonymous, but also satisfies a continuity requirement and the Pigou–Dalton axiom in terms of well-being.[113] If so, it can be shown that we can use R to construct an inequality metric corresponding to R, call it "I^R"—one that has the standard three properties of such metrics that I mentioned previously (anonymity, Pigou–Dalton, equality-as-a-lower-bound).[114] And I^R will have the following very elegant property. The ranking of vectors achieved by taking the sum total of utility in each vector,

---

[112] See Atkinson (1970); Kolm (1969); Sen (1997b). Often, in the literature on inequality measurement, the Atkinson–Kolm–Sen approach is presented as a way to decompose an "income evaluation function" (a term I explain below) into total (or mean) income and an inequality metric applied to individual incomes. See, e.g., Dutta (2002, pp. 600–601); Blackorby, Bossert, and Donaldson (1999); Weymark (2006, pp. 303–310). However, the very same strategy can be used to decompose an SWF into total *utility* and an inequality metric applied to individual *utilities*. See Blackorby, Bossert, and Donaldson (2005, ch. 4).

[113] As mentioned previously in this chapter, to say that a rule R for ranking utility vectors satisfies the Pigou–Dalton principle in term of well-being means: if we take a utility vector $(u_1, \ldots, u_i, \ldots, u_j, \ldots, u_N)$, and alter it to $(u_1, \ldots, u_i + \Delta u, \ldots, u_j - \Delta u, \ldots, u_N)$, where $\Delta u > 0$, $u_j > u_i$, and $u_j - \Delta u \geq u_i + \Delta u$, then R ranks the second vector above the first.

A rule R that produces a complete ordering of all N-dimensional utility vectors (or all such vectors in some subset of N-dimensional space) is *continuous* if, for any given vector, the set of vectors that are ranked by R as better than the given vector, and the set of vectors that are ranked by R as worse, are open sets.

[114] The following demonstration assumes that all the utility vectors being discussed have only *positive* entries, i.e., lie in the positive orthant of N-dimensional space. I will use the abbreviation "Σ" to mean the total utility in a utility vector. And, to simplify presentation, I'll use letters such as "u," "v," and "z" to refer to utility vectors (omitting reference to the underlying outcomes that are mapped by utility functions onto one or another vector). I will use the shorthand "$u \, R \, v$" to mean that u is ranked by R as being at least as good as v; "$u \, P \, v$" to mean that u is ranked by R as being better than v, i.e., $u \, P \, v$ iff $u \, R \, v$ and not $v \, R \, u$; and "$u \, I \, v$" to mean that the two vectors are equally good, i.e., $u \, I \, v$ iff $u \, R \, v$ and $v \, R \, u$.

adjusted for the degree of inequality as measured using I^R, is exactly the same as the ranking of vectors produced by R. Formally, $u(x)$ is ranked by R as being at least as good as $u(y)$ iff $[1-I^R(u(x))]\sum_{i=1}^{N}u_i(x)\geq[1-I^R(u(y))]\sum_{i=1}^{N}u_i(y)$.[115]

In turn, therefore, any SWF which is built around such a continuous, Pigou–Dalton respecting R (for short, a "continuous, Pigou–Dalton SWF") produces an ordering of outcomes that can be *mirrored* by a formula that combines an inequality metric I^R with an overall well-being term. Any such SWF produces a quasiordering of outcomes using the basic SWF formula:

> (1) x is morally at least as good as y iff, for all $u(.)$ belonging to **U**, $u(x)$ is ranked by R as being at least as good as $u(y)$.

But the quasiordering produced by that formula turns out to be exactly the same as the quasiordering produced by the formula:

> (2) x is morally at least as good as y iff, for all $u(.)$ belonging to **U**, $[1-I^R(u(x))]\sum_{i=1}^{N}u_i(x)\geq[1-I^R(u(y))]\sum_{i=1}^{N}u_i(y)$.

Let us call this result the SWF decomposition theorem.[116]

To say that a vector is "on the line of perfect equality" means that each of its N entries is the same value. In the case of a Paretian, continuous R, for any vector u, there will be one and only one vector E^u on the line of perfect equality, such that E^u I u. Moreover, given two vectors on the line of perfect equality, r and s, r R s iff $\Sigma r \geq \Sigma s$. Therefore, for any two vectors u and v, u R v iff $\Sigma E^u \geq \Sigma E^v$. Finally, because R satisfies the Pigou–Dalton principle, it has a preference for perfect equality. In other words, if z is on the line of perfect equality, and v is not, and $\Sigma z = \Sigma v$, then z P v.

It therefore follows that $\Sigma E^u < \Sigma u$ if u is off the line of perfect equality. (To see this, consider z, such that $\Sigma z = \Sigma u$ and z is on the line of perfect equality. Because u is not on the line of perfect equality, z P u. Because E^u I u, it follows that z P E^u and thus that $\Sigma z > \Sigma E^u$. But $\Sigma z = \Sigma u$, and thus $\Sigma u > \Sigma E^u$.) Of course, if u is on the line of perfect equality, then $u = E^u$ and $\Sigma u = \Sigma E^u$.

Now we are ready to construct an inequality metric. Define $I^R(u)$ as $[1 - \Sigma E^u/\Sigma u]$. Note that $I^R(.)$ satisfies the three basic properties of inequality metrics. First, it is anonymous, because if u and v are permutations of each other, $E^u = E^v$ and $\Sigma u = \Sigma v$, thus $I^R(u) = I^R(v)$. Second, it satisfies the Pigou–Dalton principle. If u is reached via a Pigou–Dalton transfer from v, it will be the case that u P v, thus $\Sigma E^u > \Sigma E^v$, and also $\Sigma u = \Sigma v$, hence $I^R(u) < I^R(v)$. Finally, $I^R(.)$ satisfies equality-as-a-lower bound because it assigns the number zero to all vectors on the line of perfect equality, otherwise a positive number.

[115] Continuing the analysis of the previous footnote: Consider that $(\Sigma u)(1 - I^R(u)) = (\Sigma u)(1 - (1 - \Sigma E^u/\Sigma u)) = \Sigma E^u$. So $(\Sigma u)(1 - I^R(u)) \geq (\Sigma v)(1 - I^R(v))$ iff $E^u \geq E^v$. But we established earlier that, in turn, $E^u \geq E^v$ iff u R v.

[116] To be precise, my analysis above, n. 114, assumes that the utility vectors being ranked by R have only positive entries. Given this analysis, the SWF decomposition theorem can be straightforwardly demonstrated for the case where all individuals are assigned positive utilities for all outcomes, by all $u(.)$ in **U**. The extent to which the theorem can be extended to cover cases in which some utilities are negative is not a topic I will attempt to address.

What exactly is going on here? It is often suggested that non-utilitarian welfarists evaluate policy choices by "balancing" overall well-being against the degree of inequality of well-being. Non-utilitarian welfarism means amalgamating a concern for "efficiency" (overall well-being) with a concern for "equity" (equal distribution). The SWF decomposition theorem provides a rigorous basis for this informal suggestion. If the most attractive ordering of outcomes is provided by a Paretian, anonymous SWF which is also continuous and Pigou–Dalton respecting, as given by equation (1), then the very same ordering can be generated by taking each $u(.)$ belonging to **U**; multiplying total utility times the degree of equality of utility, as measured by an inequality metric I^R corresponding to the SWF (this is the "$[1 - I^R(u(.))]$" term in equation (2)); and doing this for all $u(.)$ belonging to **U**.

In general, the inequality metric I^R does not represent the moral ranking of outcomes on its own; rather, that ranking will be revealed by *combining* the inequality numbers assigned to outcomes by I^R with total well-being numbers (the "$\sum_{i=1}^{N} u_i(.)$" term in equation (2)). However, an ancillary result of the SWF decomposition theorem is this. Imagine that two outcomes, x and y, have the same total well-being. Then the ranking of the two outcomes by a continuous, Pigou–Dalton respecting SWF (as given by equation (1)) is exactly the same as using I^R alone to rank the outcomes.[117]

In short, the SWF decomposition theorem shows that the moral ordering of outcomes can indeed be separated into two aspects, overall well-being and equality of well-being, with the latter aspect measured by an inequality metric, one that satisfies the basic properties of such a metric (anonymity, equality-as-a-lower-bound, Pigou–Dalton). If two outcomes differ with respect to overall well-being, the ranking depends on both aspects; if two outcomes are the same with respect to overall well-being, the ranking depends solely on the equality-of-well-being aspect.

What is impressive about this theorem, in part, is its generality. It encompasses all Pigou–Dalton, continuous SWFs. This includes, in particular, the class of SWFs which I will defend in Chapter 5: continuous prioritarian SWFs. More specifically, it includes Atkinson SWFs, which are a subclass within this class, and which are my favored variant of continuous prioritarian SWFs. (The inequality metric corresponding to the Atkinson SWF is the Atkinson inequality metric.[118]) However, the SWF

---

[117] In other words, in the limiting case where $\sum_{i=1}^{N} u_i(x) = \sum_{i=1}^{N} u_i(y)$ for all $u(.)$ belonging to **U**, and these sums are positive (because all utilities are positive), equation (2) simplifies to: x is morally as least as good as y iff $[1 - I^R(u(x))] \geq [1 - I^R(u(y))]$ for all $u(.)$ belonging to **U**.

[118] The Atkinson inequality index is a mainstay of the literature on income inequality measurement. This index is parametrized by the parameter γ—so let us denote it as "I^γ." Applied to utility vectors, the Atkinson inequality index is defined as follows: $I^\gamma(u(x)) = 1 - \left[N / \sum_{i=1}^{N} u_i(x) \right] \left(N^{-1} \sum_{i=1}^{N} u_i(x)^{1-\gamma} \right)^{1/(1-\gamma)}$. The Atkinson SWF says: x is morally at least as good as y iff, for all $u(.)$ belonging to **U**, $(1-\gamma)^{-1} \sum_{i=1}^{N} u_i(x)^{1-\gamma} \geq (1-\gamma)^{-1} \sum_{i=1}^{N} u_i(y)^{1-\gamma}$. The SWF decomposition theorem shows that this yields the very same ordering of outcomes as the rule: x is morally at least as good as y iff, for all $u(.)$ belonging to **U**, $\left[\sum_{i=1}^{N} u_i(x) \right]\left[1 - I^\gamma(u(x))\right] \geq \left[\sum_{i=1}^{N} u_i(y) \right]\left[1 - I^\gamma(u(y))\right]$.

decomposition theorem also applies to certain *non-prioritarian* SWFs, namely those that satisfy the Pigou–Dalton condition and the continuity requirement. For example, it applies to rank-weighted SWFs. The inequality metric corresponding to one of the rank-weighted SWFs is the well-known Gini coefficient.[119]

Note, furthermore, that generating an inequality metric I^R from a Pigou–Dalton, continuous SWF, and applying it to vectors of utilities in accordance with equation (2), *handily* resolves all the tensions between such metrics and the Pareto principles discussed above. The ordering produced by the familiar formula (1) will necessarily satisfy Pareto-indifference and Pareto-superiority and therefore—because it is coextensive—so will the ordering produced by formula (2). In the case of multidimensional outcomes, interactions between individual attributes in producing each individual's well-being are taken account of by the utility functions in U; and by applying the inequality metric to the vectors of *utility* associated with each outcome, we avoid the dilemmas that arise in trying to apply it directly to attributes.[120] As for the tension between the equality-as-a-lower-bound axiom and Pareto-superiority, that is avoided by seeing the inequality metric as simply one component of the all-things-considered ranking of outcomes. In moving from an outcome in which well-being is distributed equally, to a Pareto-superior outcome in which well-being is distributed unequally, the degree of inequality of well-being (as measured by the inequality metric applied to utilities) will increase, but overall well-being will also increase, sufficiently so that overall well-being discounted by the inequality metric, as per formula (2), increases.

But some important caveats should be stressed about the approach to employing inequality metrics now under consideration. First, this approach is obviously just a variation on the SWF format. The approach assumes that well-being is interpersonally comparable and measurable by utilities; it is these utilities that are inputted into the inequality metric; and it is the particular functional form of the SWF (the rule R) which drives the choice of the inequality metric I^R.

Second, the SWF decomposition theorem does not furnish an indiscriminate justification for the use of inequality metrics. At most, it warrants the use of inequality metrics that correspond to the favored class of SWFs. For a given SWF, which incorporates some Pigou–Dalton respecting, continuous R, and orders outcomes in

---

[119] More specifically, the rank-weighted SWF with weights equaling the first N odd numbers (in reverse order) has the Gini coefficient as its corresponding inequality metric. See Blackorby, Bossert, and Donaldson (2005, pp. 99–100).

[120] It bears emphasis that a continuous Pigou–Dalton respecting SWF, because Paretian, will satisfy the Pareto principles judged in terms of any arbitrary set U. There is no restriction on the content of U. Therefore, the use of formula (2), because coextensive with the SWF, will also satisfy the Pareto principles in terms of any arbitrary set U. This is by contrast with the use of attribute evaluation functions, discussed below, which rank outcomes as a function of individual attributes, not utilities. This approach is consistent with the Pareto principles only if *certain* sets U are used to determine the ranking of life-histories.

accordance with equation (1), there exists *some* inequality metric I^R that yields the very same ordering of outcomes, if used in accordance with equation (2). This is of course *not* the same as the clearly false proposition that *any* inequality metric will yield the same ordering of outcomes as the given SWF, if used in accordance with equation (2). In particular, if the argument for an Atkinson SWF in Chapter 5 succeeds, then the SWF decomposition theorem will justify the application of an Atkinson inequality metric to vectors of utilities, in accordance with equation (2). It will *not* justify the use of ordinally distinct inequality metrics, such as the Gini coefficient. Such metrics rank utility vectors in a different manner than any Atkinson inequality metric, and employing them in accordance with equation (2) would rank outcome sets in a manner that does not correspond to any Atkinson SWF.[121]

Finally, the SWF decomposition theorem shows that the ordering of outcomes yielded by direct application of a Pigou–Dalton, continuous SWF, as per equation (1), *can be mirrored* by the use of an inequality metric in accordance with equation (2). It remains a further question whether the decisionmaker should in fact employ equation (2) in ranking outcomes. This is very much like the question raised earlier about distributively weighted CBA. It is true that distributively weighted CBA, with appropriate weights, can generate the very same ranking of outcomes as a given SWF, for a wide range of SWFs; but why should distributively weighted CBA be actually employed as a decisional tool? Why not just employ the SWF? Similarly, why is equation (2) a more attractive decisional tool than equation (1)?

Indeed, for reasons that will be explored in Chapter 5, which defends a continuous prioritarian SWF, I will argue that equation (2) is not a more attractive decisional tool than equation (1). The SWF decomposition theorem shows that it is *possible* to express a continuous prioritarian SWF as the result of "balancing" a concern for overall well-being with a concern for the equal distribution of well-being; but such a decomposition is not warranted by the (most persuasive) underlying *rationale* for a continuous prioritarian SWF. As we shall see in Chapter 5, this rationale is *not* that prioritarianism emerges from the process of balancing equality against overall welfare. It appeals, not to fairness understood as the distribution of well-being within outcomes, but rather to a *claim-across-outcome* conception of

---

[121] Again, a given selection of γ yields a particular Atkinson inequality metric I^r. Let us say that some inequality metric is ordinally equivalent to the Atkinson inequality metric if there is some value γ such that the metric yields the very same ranking of any set of distributions of some item s (in particular, any set of utility vectors) as I^r. A metric which is not ordinally equivalent to the Atkinson inequality metric might end up yielding the same ranking of utility vectors as I^r, for some value γ, in a *particular* outcome set—and thus, in accordance with equation (2), *might* rank some outcome set the same way as an Atkinson SWF with a particular γ—but it won't reliably do so in general.

There are also metrics which are ordinally but not cardinally equivalent to the Atkinson inequality metric, i.e., they are an increasing (but not affine) transformation of I^r for some γ. See Cowell (1995, pp. 151–152). If so, inserting such metrics into equation (2) will not reliably yield the same result as inserting I^r, because the inequality term is multiplied by an overall well-being term. On the relevance of the cardinal properties of inequality metrics, see generally Cowell (2000).

fairness. This understanding of fairness provides no warrant for expressing the ordering of outcomes along the lines of equation (2).

B. Income Evaluation Functions and Equivalent Incomes

Let us return to the case in which outcomes are specified solely with respect to each individual's income/consumption/expenditure.[122] Each outcome in the outcome set O takes the form $(c_1, \ldots, c_N)$. Our theory of well-being W may or may not allow for interpersonal comparisons. We are looking for a criterion for ranking an outcome set that meets minimal welfarist criteria and that also employs an inequality metric, or at least satisfies the Pigou–Dalton principle in some form.

The literature on inequality measurement suggests a variety of different approaches to ranking income distributions that can be adapted to suit our purposes here. One possibility is to employ so-called "generalized Lorenz" comparisons, a method that ranks distributions by comparing partial sums. Given $x = (c_1, \ldots, c_N)$ and $y = (c_1^*, \ldots, c_N^*)$, take the income amounts in each outcome and order them from smallest to largest. Compare the smallest income in x to the smallest income in y; the sum of the two smallest incomes in x to the sum of the two smallest incomes in y; and so forth. If the partial sums for x are always at least as large, then x "generalized Lorenz" dominates y.[123] It can be readily seen that the relation of "generalized Lorenz dominance" is a quasiordering; that it satisfies the Pigou–Dalton principle in terms of income; and that it satisfies Pareto-indifference and Pareto-superiority if each individual's well-being is strictly increasing in income.

Another possibility is to calculate total income in a given outcome; to discount that amount by the value of an inequality metric, applied to the distribution of incomes; and to rank outcomes using total income thus discounted. If an inequality metric is chosen appropriately, then this approach, too, will yield a quasiordering of the outcomes that is Pareto-respecting (assuming once more that well-being is

---

[122] The inequality measurement literature generally focuses on the inequality of income, not consumption. Thus, in this section, I discuss methodologies for ranking outcomes as a function of individual incomes, not individual consumption amounts. Doing so may be attractive where income and consumption converge, but becomes more problematic where they diverge. In that case, the "income evaluation functions" described here can, in principle, be reframed in terms of consumption. See above, p. 90; Chapter 4, p. 292.

[123] On generalized Lorenz dominance, see Chakravarty (2009, ch. 1); Lambert (2001, ch. 3); Shorrocks (1983). "Dominance" is a slight misnomer, since it is possible for x to generalized Lorenz (GL) dominate y in the sense just described, but at the same time for y to GL dominate x. We could define GL dominance in a different way—by requiring that the partial sums for x be always at least as large, and sometimes larger—but this relation would not be reflexive and hence would not be a quasiordering. Note, too, that we can use GL dominance, in the sense here, to define relations of equal goodness and betterness between outcomes (in the standard manner for quasiorderings). Outcome x is equally good as y if each GL dominates the other. Outcome x is better than y if x GL dominates y but y does not GL dominate x. See Shorrocks (1983, p. 16, n. 8).

strictly increasing in income) and that satisfies the Pigou–Dalton principle in terms of incomes.[124] Yet a third possibility is to use a leximin rule, applied to the distribution of incomes, to rank outcomes.

The three approaches just discussed are examples of a more general idea. Let us say that an "income evaluation function" applied to an outcome set characterized solely in terms of income is some kind of rule that generates a quasiordering, satisfies the Pigou–Dalton principle in terms of income, and satisfies a condition of monotonicity (namely, increasing one person's income without reducing anyone else's makes the outcome better). Then, on the assumption that well-being is strictly increasing in income, the income evaluation function meets minimal welfarist criteria; and to the extent that it ranks Pareto-noncomparable outcomes, it will do so in a manner that is sensitive to distribution (by virtue of satisfying the Pigou–Dalton principle in terms of income.)[125]

We have thus far focused on outcome sets characterized solely in terms of individual incomes. Can we employ generalized Lorenz comparisons, the technique of discounting total income by the degree of income inequality, a leximin rule applied to incomes, or some other income evaluation function to rank multidimensional outcomes? One approach that is widely used in the inequality-measurement literature, in handling income distributions among individuals who are heterogeneous in their non-income characteristics, is to "normalize" each individual's income to reflect her non-income characteristics. This is often referred to as an "equivalent income" approach.[126] For example, if $[(c_1, h_1), (c_2, h_2), \ldots, (c_N, h_N)]$ is a distribution that lists each individual's income and her health state, we might take perfect health (call it h^{ref}) as the reference state, and assign each individual an "equivalent income" c_i^{equiv} that (paired with perfect health) makes her just as well off as initially. This produces an "equivalent" distribution, in which individuals are *homogeneous* in their health characteristics—$[(c_1^{equiv}, h^{ref}), (c_2^{equiv}, h^{ref}), \ldots, (c_N^{equiv}, h^{ref})]$.

---

[124] As mentioned above, n. 112, and explained in the sources cited there, an income evaluation function is actually the typical setting for the results of Atkinson, Kolm, and Sen, which I relied upon as the basis for the "SWF decomposition theorem." Imagine an income evaluation function F, which ranks vectors of incomes, and satisfies a monotonicity requirement, a continuity requirement, and a Pigou–Dalton condition in terms of income. Then the ranking of income vectors achieved by F is identical to the ranking achieved by taking total income and discounting by the degree of income inequality as measured by an inequality metric corresponding to F (i.e., total income multiplied by a term equaling one minus the value of the inequality metric applied to incomes). If well-being is strictly increasing in income, then F will satisfy the Pareto principle; and so, too, will total income discounted by the matching inequality metric applied to incomes.

[125] On "income evaluation functions" (my terminology), see sources cited above, n. 112. The terminology is helpful in clarifying that such "functions" rank vectors of individual incomes, but the word "function" itself is a simplification, since what I mean is a rule for ordering income vectors that may or may not take the form of a mathematical function.

[126] See, e.g., Cowell and Mercader-Prats (1999); Ebert and Moyes (2003); Slesnick (1998, pp. 2145–2148).

The technique of income normalization, combined with an income evaluation function, provides a general recipe for ranking multidimensional outcomes in a manner that is minimally welfarist and also sensitive to distribution. Imagine that each outcome x in our outcome set takes the form $x = (c_1, \ldots, c_N, \mathbf{b})$, where $\mathbf{b}$ denotes all the non-income attributes of individuals and/or background facts. These may well vary between outcomes. So $x = (c_1, \ldots, c_N, \mathbf{b})$; $y = (c_1^*, \ldots, c_N^*, \mathbf{b}^*)$; $z = (c_1^{**}, \ldots, c_N^{**}, \mathbf{b}^{**})$, and so forth. Choose some reference level of non-income characteristics—call it $\mathbf{b}^{\text{ref}}$. Then, for each outcome $x = (c_1, \ldots, c_N, \mathbf{b})$, assign it an "equivalent outcome" $(c_1^{\text{equiv}}, \ldots, c_N^{\text{equiv}}, \mathbf{b}^{\text{ref}})$, as follows: for each individual i, c_i^{equiv} is such that the individual is equally well off with $(c_i^{\text{equiv}}, \mathbf{b}^{\text{ref}})$ as with $(c_i, \mathbf{b})$.[127] Rank outcomes by using some income evaluation function applied to the distribution of equivalent incomes corresponding to each outcome.[128]

For short, let us say that the "income evaluation function" approach ranks outcomes by applying an income evaluation function to incomes (in the case of unidimensional outcomes) or equivalent incomes (in the case of multidimensional outcomes).[129]

Is the income-evaluation-function approach an attractive technique for ranking outcome sets? Note, to begin, that there is an important connection between the income-normalization technique and CBA. CBA is centered around the construct of a WTP/WTA amount. Individual i's WTP/WTA for outcome y, relative to outcome x, is the change in i's consumption in y that makes him just as well off as in x.[130] Note, now, that an individual's *equivalent* income for a given outcome y is just his income in y minus his WTP/WTA relative to y for an outcome in which he has the same income as in y but non-income attributes are set to $\mathbf{b}^{\text{ref}}$. Moreover, just as

---

[127] My definition of $(c_i^{\text{equiv}}, \mathbf{b}^{\text{ref}})$ here assumes that there are no "consumption externalities"—that an individual's well-being is not affected by the income of other individuals. A more general definition of equivalent income could presumably be provided that allows for such externalities, but to keep things simple I ignore them here.

[128] It should be noted that some attribute other than income could be used as the "normalized" attribute. At least in principle, we could assign each individual an "equivalent happiness" by adjusting her *happiness* to reflect non-happiness characteristics; or we could assign each individual an "equivalent health" by adjusting her health to reflect non-health characteristics. However, the existing literature that handles multidimensional distributions via the normalization technique does so by adjusting income—and so that will be my focus here.

[129] A complicated set of issues for this approach arise when incomes are ascribed to households rather than individuals. I will not discuss those issues, but will assume that we have outcomes in which incomes are already ascribed to individuals. It should be noted that the household/individual distinction is no difficulty for the SWF approach. If outcomes are described in terms of certain household attributes, each $u(.)$ will assign individuals a utility level depending on those attributes plus a specification of which household each individual belongs to.

[130] See above, pp. 89–95.

CBA can be undermined if the connection between income/consumption and well-being is not well-behaved, so too can the income normalization technique.[131]

However, assuming that the connection between income/consumption and well-being *is* well-behaved, it is not too hard to show that the income-evaluation-function approach will generate a Pareto-respecting quasiordering of any outcome set. In the case of outcomes that are solely characterized in terms of income (so that normalization is not needed) this approach respects the Pigou–Dalton principle in terms of income. In the case of multidimensional outcomes, this approach respects the Pigou–Dalton principle in terms of *equivalent* income. We have seen that there are serious difficulties, in the multidimensional context, if the Pigou–Dalton principle is applied attribute by attribute. The income-evaluation-function approach does *not* require that the Pigou–Dalton principle be satisfied in this sense. Rather, it applies some income evaluation function to the vector of equivalent incomes corresponding to each outcome—and thus satisfies the Pigou–Dalton principle as applied to equivalent incomes.

I have mentioned that the approach may be undermined if the connection between income and well-being is not well-behaved. Another important worry is that the ranking of outcomes may be sensitive to the choice of reference characteristics. For example, if outcomes are specified in terms of individual health and income, we *might* choose perfect health as the reference health level; map the vector of incomes in each outcome onto the vector of equivalent incomes calculated using this reference health level; and apply some income evaluation function to incomes thus normalized. Or, we might choose a stipulated state of poor health as the reference health level; map the vector of incomes in each outcome onto a vector of equivalent incomes calculated using *this* reference health level; and apply the income evaluation function to incomes thus normalized. In general, for a given income evaluation function, there is no reason to expect that the ranking of outcomes will be invariant to the choice of reference non-income attributes used to normalize incomes. For short, call this the problem of "reference dependence."[132]

---

[131] Consider again the problem of identifying an equivalent income for a given individual i in outcome $x = (c_1, \ldots, c_N, \mathbf{b})$. With reference characteristics at $\mathbf{b}^{ref}$, that means identifying an amount c_i^{eqiuv} such that a life-history with $(c_i^{eqiuv}, \mathbf{b}^{ref})$ is equally good for i as one with characteristics $(c_i, \mathbf{b})$. But if the ordering of life-histories is incomplete, there may be no life-history with reference characteristics at $\mathbf{b}^{ref}$ that is equally good for i as $(c_i, \mathbf{b})$. Even if the ordering of life-histories is complete, the lexical ordering of non-market over market goods might undercut the existence of such an amount. And even without lexical orderings, non-increasingness in the connection between income and well-being might mean that there are multiple such c_i^{eqiuv} amounts.

[132] See, e.g., Blackorby, Laisney and Schmachtenberg (1993); Fleurbaey (2009, pp. 1052–1055); Roberts (1980c); Slesnick (1998, pp. 2147–2148).

How reference-dependence arises depends on the income evaluation function. By way of illustration, let us continue with the case where outcomes characterize health and income and consider, first, the generalized Lorenz approach. Assume that our theory W of well-being has the same intrapersonal ranking of health-income bundles for all individuals. There are two health states, Low and High, and

Before suggesting a verdict about the income-evaluation-function approach, let me note one critical fact about this approach. It has been shown that various income evaluation functions "correspond" to some SWF approach. For example, imagine that we rank outcomes specified solely in terms of income using the generalized Lorenz approach. The following can then be shown:

> Outcome $x = (c_1, \ldots, c_N)$ is at least as good as $y = (c_1^*, \ldots, c_N^*)$ according to the generalized Lorenz approach iff $\sum_{i=1}^{N} u_i(x) \geq \sum_{i=1}^{N} u_i(y)$ for all $u(.)$ belong to $\mathbf{U}^+$, where $\mathbf{U}^+$ consists of all utility functions that assign each individual a utility number based solely on his income, and that are increasing and concave in that income.[133]

This "correspondence" result can be readily extended to the case where the generalized Lorenz approach is used to rank distributions of equivalent income.[134] Other income evaluation functions may also "correspond" to some SWF approach: these functions, too, may produce the very same ranking of outcomes as would be generated via the application of some SWF to outcomes converted into utility vectors by sets of utility functions.[135]

a given income amount combined with health state Low is equally good for a given subject as the square root of that income amount combined with health state High. Imagine that there are 3 individuals. Outcome x is as follows (listing the income-health bundles for each individual): ((2, High), (9, Low), (5, High)), while outcome y is as follows: ((2, Low), ($\sqrt{12}$, High), (25, Low)). Then if we use Low health as the reference level, outcome x is mapped onto the equivalent incomes (4, 9, 25), and y onto (2, 12, 25), so that the two outcomes are incomparable (neither GL dominates the other). However, if we use High health as the reference level, then x is mapped onto equivalent incomes (2, 3, 5) and y onto ($\sqrt{2}$, $\sqrt{12}$, 5), so that x is ranked higher (it GL dominates y, but not vice versa).

Consider, now, a leximin rule applied to equivalent incomes. Assume that W makes the intrapersonal ranking of health-income bundles depend on each subject's preferences (or idealized preferences), and thus is not the same for all individuals. In particular, for individual 1, a given income level at Low health is the same as $1/3$ of that income at High health. For individual 2, a given income level at Low health is the same as $1/5$ of that income at High health. Assume, now, that these are the only two individuals in the population. Outcome x is ((7, Low), (2, High)), while outcome y is ((8/3, High), (9, Low)). If Low health is reference, x is mapped onto equivalent incomes (7, 10), and y to (8, 9). If High health is reference, x is mapped onto equivalent incomes (7/3, 2) and y to (8/3, 9/5). In the first case, the leximin rule prefers y, in the second case x.

[133] See Shorrocks (1983, p. 6 and n. 7).

[134] Just make $\mathbf{U}^+$ the set of utility functions that assign each individual a utility number based solely on his equivalent income, and that are increasing and concave in equivalent income.

[135] For example, in the case of the leximin income evaluation function, this is trivial: it corresponds to an SWF that uses the leximin rule R for ranking utility vectors and a singleton set $\mathbf{U}$ of utility functions consisting of a $u(.)$ that assigns a utility to a life-history just equaling each individual's income (or, if you like, a larger $\mathbf{U}$ comprising that $u(.)$ and all increasing transformations thereof). In the case of total income discounted by an inequality metric applied to incomes, if this metric is generated from an income evaluation function F (as per the discussion above, n. 124), then this approach

What shall we make of such correspondence results? Do they mean that the income-evaluation-function approach is just a variation on the SWF approach?

I don't think this is correct. The proponent of the income-evaluation-function approach *might* agree that well-being is interpersonally comparable and measurable by utilities. Indeed, proponents of the approach often *do* see it as a way to implement an SWF. However, the proponent of the approach is not conceptually *committed* to interpersonal comparisons or the existence of utility numbers representing those. She might, without logical error or any kind of incoherence, take the position that the most attractive welfarist decision procedure incorporates a theory of well-being that *rejects* interpersonal comparisons and employs the income-evaluation-function approach just because no such comparisons can be made.

It is critical, here, to note that the process of normalizing incomes and applying an evaluation function to the vector of normalized incomes (or just incomes, in the case of unidimensional outcomes) does not involve any explicit interpersonal comparisons or the explicit ascription of utilities to life-histories. Normalizing incomes to reflect a reference level of non-income characteristics requires only that there be an *intrapersonal* ranking of life-histories with a well-behaved connection between income and well-being. And the process of comparing distributions of income or equivalent incomes using generalized Lorenz comparisons, the technique of discounting total income by the degree of income inequality, a leximin rule applied to incomes, or some other income evaluation function does *not* require any conversion of those income amounts into utilities. The proponent of the income-evaluation-function approach, if she is skeptical about interpersonal comparisons or utility numbers, can react to a "correspondence" result by saying: "True, I rank outcomes as if I am using a set **U** of utility functions to assign utility numbers to life-histories. But these are just meaningless numbers, from my perspective. They do not represent *my* theory of well-being. I adopt a theory *W* of well-being that rejects interpersonal comparisons and/or the measurability of well-being via utilities."[136]

So here is my suggested bottom line. If one accepts the premise that the most attractive theory of well-being does indeed allow for interpersonal comparisons, representable by utilities, the income-evaluation-function approach should be seen

---

trivially corresponds to an SWF which has the same functional form as *F* and uses a singleton **U** which sets each individual's utility equal to his income.

[136] It should be noted that much of the extant scholarship on equivalent incomes does, in fact, embrace the possibility of interpersonal welfare comparisons. See sources cited above, n. 126, and the scholarship referenced in these sources. But, again, the methodology of normalizing a given individual's income to reflect the difference between his actual non-income characteristics and reference characteristics does not logically presuppose interpersonal well-being comparability. See Fleurbaey (2009, pp. 1046–1055); Fleurbaey, Luchini, Muller, and Schokkaert (2010). The disjunction between individual and household incomes raises further complications; but it should be noted that there *are* methods for normalizing household incomes that do not presuppose interpersonal comparability. See Browning, Chiappori, and Lewbel (2006).

as less attractive than direct application of an SWF. The former presupposes a well-behaved connection between income and well-being, while the SWF framework does not. There can exist a **U** representing the well-being associated with life-histories even absent such a connection; and outcomes can be ranked with **U** using the now-familiar SWF formula. More critically, in the case of multidimensional outcomes, the income-evaluation-function approach can make the ranking of outcomes dependent on the choice of reference characteristics. And it is hard to see how to justify this choice in a principled way. A well constructed **U** will not have this arbitrary feature.[137]

On the other hand, if it turns out that the most attractive theory of well-being does not allow for interpersonal comparability, or for the measurement of well-being with utilities, the income-evaluation-function approach may be the best we can do to produce a Pareto-respecting, distributionally sensitive, quasiordering of an outcome set.

C. Applying the Pigou–Dalton Principle to Attributes

A burgeoning subliterature regarding inequality measurement focuses on the problem of ranking multidimensional distributions in a different manner than that suggested in the prior two subsections: not by converting each distribution into a vector of utilities, and not by normalizing income to reflect non-income characteristics, but instead by ranking the distributions so as to satisfy various criteria applied to each attribute—in particular, a monotonicity criterion and some variant of the Pigou–Dalton principle.[138]

---

[137]   The extended-preference approach for constructing **U**, which I defend in Chapters 3 and 4, does not have this feature (with one exception, noted in a moment). **U** is produced by looking to spectators' rankings of life-history lotteries. Such rankings do not presuppose that some of the types of attributes included in the description of outcomes are set at a single level. Rather, each attribute can take a range of levels. Thus the construction of U^k, for each spectator k, and thus **U**, does not involve specifying a reference level for any of the attributes included in the description of outcomes.

The exception is that reference characteristics may come into play at the threshold stage of determining how to simplify outcomes—how to cope with the fact that some attributes are inevitably "missing" from outcomes. However, if this approach is used to deal with "missing" attributes, U^k can, in principle, take account of the level of reference characteristics. See Chapter 4, n. 29. Moreover, within the extended-preference methodology, the arbitrariness in constructing **U** that occurs by virtue of the simplified nature of outcomes can always be mitigated by using a more richly described outcome set. By contrast, the arbitrary reference-dependence of the income-evaluation-function approach now under discussion does not arise merely by virtue of the (inevitable) need to simplify outcomes; it can occur regardless of how fully outcomes are described.

[138]   Good reviews of this literature are Chakravarty (2009, ch. 5); Savaglio (2006); and Weymark (2006). Two recent contributions are Bosmans, Lauwers, and Ooghe (2009) and Lasso de la Vega, Urrutia, and de Sarachu (2010).

Adapting this approach to the problem of ranking outcomes, let us say that $x = (a_1, \ldots, a_N, b_1, \ldots, b_N, \ldots)$, $y = (a_1^*, \ldots, a_N^*, b_1^*, \ldots, b_N^*, \ldots)$. Attribute a is one type of individual attribute (income, health, happiness, etc.); b is another type of individual attribute; and each outcome is specified with respect to at least two such attributes, and perhaps more.[139] Monotonicity, here, says that if at least one individual in x is at a higher level with respect to one or more attributes than her level in y, and no individual in x is at a lower level with respect to any of the attributes than her level in y, then x is a better outcome than y. Various versions of an attribute-based Pigou–Dalton principle are possible (as discussed earlier). The simplest one says that shifting some amount of one attribute, from a person at a higher level of the attribute to a person at a lower level, without losing any and without the individuals switching ranks in the distribution of that attribute, yields a better outcome. A different version says that such a transfer yields a better outcome if the transferor starts out better in all the attributes. Another version says that if we make the same, proportional Pigou–Dalton transfer in all attributes between two persons, the outcome is better. There are yet further possibilities.[140]

For short, let us say that a rule F for ranking multiattribute outcomes which incorporates a monotonicity criterion[141] and some version of an attribute-based Pigou–Dalton principle is an "attribute evaluation function"—as distinct from an SWF or an income evaluation function.

The literature on attribute evaluation functions is quite technical and cannot be reviewed in detail here. What is worth noting, for our purposes, is that SWF "correspondence" results crop up in this literature, just as they do for income evaluation functions (and, as we'll see in a moment, for the "egalitarian equivalent" approach too). These results are varied, but their generic form is roughly the following: For a

---

[139] For simplicity, assume that background facts are omitted or held constant. It is not clear how the attribute-evaluation-function approach, about to be described, should be adapted to deal with facts about outcomes that are not any person's attributes.

[140] The "proportional" Pigou–Dalton principle says that if individual i has attribute levels $a_i, b_i, c_i, \ldots$ in outcome x, and individual k has attributes $a_k, b_k, c_k, \ldots$; and if in outcome y individual i has attribute levels $pa_i + (1-p)a_k, pb_i + (1-p)b_k, pc_i + (1-p)c_k, \ldots$, while individual k has attribute levels $(1-p)a_i + pa_k, (1-p)b_i + pb_k, (1-p)c_i + pc_k, \ldots$, with $0 < p < 1$ and everyone else unaffected, then y is a better outcome. In the case of the distribution of a single item, a Pigou–Dalton transfer in the item is achieved by multiplying the vector of individual holdings of the items by a special kind of matrix, a so-called "T-transform." Using this same kind of matrix in the multidimensional case produces the kind of proportional transfer just described. See Weymark (2006, p. 307).

Under the rubric of possible attribute-based Pigou–Dalton principles, I include principles such as "uniform majorization" or "correlation increasing majorization," which are not strictly speaking Pigou–Dalton principles, but which the literature sees as related principles and analyzes as possible elements of an attribute evaluation function. See ibid., pp. 307–308, 321–323.

[141] Note that if monotonicity is not incorporated in the attribute evaluation function, and individual well-being is strictly increasing in each attribute, there will be an immediate violation of Pareto-superiority.

given attribute evaluation function F, there is a "corresponding" Paretian, anonymous SWF (with set of utility functions $\mathbf{U}^F$ and rule for ranking utility vectors R^F), such that: $x = (a_1, \ldots, a_N, b_1, \ldots, b_N, \ldots)$ is at least as good as $y = (a_1^*, \ldots, a_N^*, b_1^*, \ldots, b_N^*, \ldots)$ according to F iff $u(x)$ is ranked at least as high as $u(y)$ by R^F for all $u(.)$ belonging to $\mathbf{U}^F$.[142]

On the face of it, this kind of result is quite puzzling. We saw earlier that the application of the Pigou–Dalton principle attribute-by-attribute risks a violation of the Pareto principles. And yet if F "corresponds" to a Paretian SWF in the manner set forth in the previous paragraph, there seemingly can't be a violation of Pareto-indifference or Pareto-superiority.

The key to resolving this puzzle is to see that the determination whether one outcome is Pareto-indifferent or -superior to another depends on a theory of well-being.[143] One theory of well-being W, with a quasiordering of life-histories represented by set $\mathbf{U}$, might say that x and y are Pareto-indifferent or that one is Pareto-superior to the other, while another theory of well-being W^*, with a quasiordering of life-histories represented by a set $\mathbf{U}^*$, might say that they are Pareto-noncomparable. If F corresponds to an SWF in the manner stated two paragraphs back, all that this means is that F is "consistent" with Pareto-indifference and -superiority *if* one takes the most attractive theory of well-being to be represented by $\mathbf{U}^F$.

[142] These correspondence results are scattered through the literature, but a number are presented in Weymark (2006, pp. 308, 314, 316, 322).

I say "roughly" because some of the results are one-way implications rather than equivalences between F and an SWF. I state the generic result as an equivalence because it shows most simply how F will be safeguarded against violations of Pareto-indifference and -superiority in terms of $\mathbf{U}^F$. Imagine that F and an SWF are equivalent as stated in the text. As a matter of logic, note that if x and y are Pareto-indifferent according to the utility functions in $\mathbf{U}^F$, then F must rank the two outcomes as equally good. (Since R^F is Paretian, x and y will be ranked as equally good by the SWF in the case where the outcomes are Pareto-indifferent according to $\mathbf{U}^F$, and thus F must also rank them as equally good.) Similarly, if x is Pareto-superior to y according to the utility functions in $\mathbf{U}^F$, it must be the case that F ranks x better than y.

Even with a one-way implication, however, F will be safeguarded against certain violations of Pareto-indifference or -superiority. For example, imagine that if x is at least as good as y according to F, then x is at least as good as y according to the SWF. F, then, *can* violate Pareto-indifference in terms of $\mathbf{U}^F$ (it is consistent with this one-way implication for the two outcomes to be Pareto-indifferent, and yet for F to rank one as better than the other, or to rank the two as incomparable). Moreover, it is possible for x to be Pareto-superior to y, and yet for F to rank the two outcomes as incomparable. However, it is *not* possible for x to be Pareto-superior to y, and yet for F to rank y better or to rank the outcomes as equally good.

Reciprocally, with a one-way implication in the other direction, F *cannot* violate Pareto-indifference in terms of $\mathbf{U}^F$. And if x is Pareto-superior to y then F must either rank x better than y or rank the two as equally good; it cannot rank y better or rank the outcomes as incomparable.

[143] This is just a consequence of the generic definition of Pareto-indifference and -superiority, in terms of W rather than preference satisfaction, used throughout the book.

Unfortunately, the types of sets $\mathbf{U}^F$ that have been identified in the literature on attribute evaluation functions are not particularly attractive. One kind of attribute evaluation function corresponds to a $\mathbf{U}^F$ consisting of utility functions which have an "averaging" property. This means that given a life-history with attributes $(a, b, c, \ldots)$ and a life-history with attributes $(a^*, b^*, c^*, \ldots)$, the weighted average of the utilities assigned to the two is less than the utility of a life-history with a weighted average of the attributes.[144] This in turn means that a life-history with a weighted average of the attributes is better than at least one (and maybe both) of the original life-histories. As a result, if a Paretian SWF employs a $\mathbf{U}$ each of whose members has the "averaging property," then a conflict with the Pareto principles cannot arise in the case of a proportional Pigou–Dalton transfer in each attribute.

> Return to the example given earlier of two individuals and attributes a and b. Outcome $x = ((10, 20), (20, 10))$ while outcome $y = ((15, 15), (15, 15))$. The latter outcome is reached by a Pigou–Dalton transfer in each attribute and yet, in principle, each individual might be just as well off as between x and y or even better off with x, so that a judgment that y is better than x could violate Pareto-indifference or Pareto-superiority. However, if the ranking of life-histories is given by a set $\mathbf{U}$ whose members have the "averaging" property, then $u(15, 15) > u(10, 20)$ or $u(15, 15) > u(20, 10)$ or both, for each $u(.)$ in $\mathbf{U}$. If so, it is impossible for x and y to be Pareto-indifferent or for x to be Pareto-superior to y.

However, the "averaging" property is quite a strong restriction on the structure of utility functions. Is it really true that, whatever the different kinds of attributes that outcomes might characterize individuals as having (be they health, consumption of different goods, happiness, leisure, social life, or anything else), the averaging of two different attribute packages, in any proportion, always yields a better package than at least one of the original packages? That seems a quite implausible general claim about well-being. An SWF framework which—faced with any arbitrary multiattribute outcome set—constructs a set $\mathbf{U}$ whose members satisfy the averaging property, seems quite unattractive. Nor do the other types of utility functions to which various attribute evaluation functions correspond seem much more plausible.[145]

This admittedly compressed discussion of a complicated area of research suggests that welfarists should see attribute evaluation functions as a problematic tool for

---

[144] The "averaging" property is just multiattribute concavity, but to avoid confusing the reader who is unfamiliar with the various senses of "concavity," I use this term instead. To express this formally: Let us denote by L a life-history with attributes $(a, b, c, \ldots)$, L^* a life-history with attributes $(a^*, b^*, c^*, \ldots)$, and $\lambda L + (1 - \lambda)L^*$ a life-history with attributes $(\lambda a + (1 - \lambda)a^*, \lambda b + (1 - \lambda)b^*, \lambda c + (1 - \lambda)c^*, \ldots)$, where $0 < \lambda < 1$. Then to say that $u(.)$ has the averaging property means that $\lambda u(L) + (1 - \lambda)u(L^*) < u(\lambda L + (1 - \lambda)L^*)$.

[145] Another correspondence result shows that certain attribute evaluation functions correspond to an SWF with a set $\mathbf{U}^F$ whose members satisfy a condition of "subadditivity." Yet another shows a correspondence with utility functions that are separable in attributes.

ranking an outcome set. If one accepts that well-being is interpersonally comparable and can be represented by utilities, then using an SWF without implausible restrictions on the content of $\mathbf{U}$ is a better course than ranking outcomes with an attribute evaluation function and, implicitly, using a less plausible set $\mathbf{U}$. But even absent interpersonal comparability, this approach is problematic, given the risk of violations of the Pareto principles[146]—a risk that can be avoided via the income-evaluation-function approach considered above, and the egalitarian-equivalent approach, to which we now turn.

D. Egalitarian Equivalence

As mentioned earlier, work in theoretical welfare economics since Arrow's theorem has branched in two different directions. One direction is the analysis of social welfare functions applied to interpersonally comparable utilities. A different branch continues to pursue the project of ranking outcomes as a function of individuals' preference rankings without allowing for interpersonally comparable utilities. Much of this latter branch, exemplified by the literature on "fair allocations," has focused on the problem of identifying the first-best subset of outcomes in a given outcome set—rather than trying to develop a quasiordering, complete or incomplete, of the outcome set. However, pioneering work by Marc Fleurbaey, Francois Maniquet, and Koichi Tadenuma, building on ideas developed in the "fair allocation" literature, has pursued the project of constructing quasiorderings of outcome sets that are Pareto-respecting, do not require interpersonal comparisons, and are sensitive to distribution.[147]

Much of this work has focused on outcomes characterized as bundles of consumption goods. In other words, there are M consumption goods $q^1,\ldots,q^M$, and a given outcome x has the form $(q_1^1,q_1^2,\ldots,q_1^M,\ldots,q_N^1,q_N^2,\ldots,q_N^M)$. More compactly, a given outcome x has the form $(\mathbf{q}_1,\mathbf{q}_2,\ldots,\mathbf{q}_N)$, where $\mathbf{q}_i$ is the bundle of the M goods held by individual i.

The linchpin of this scholarship has been the idea of "egalitarian equivalence." Let us say that an outcome z is "egalitarian" if everyone has the very same consumption bundle. In other words, $z = (\mathbf{q},\mathbf{q},\ldots,\mathbf{q})$.[148] And let us imagine that each individual is

---

[146] More precisely, the risk that arises if the intrapersonal ranking of life-histories is given by a theory of well-being that does not satisfy strong conditions such as the averaging property, subadditivity, or separability in attributes.

[147] On fair allocations, see generally Thomson (2011). The "egalitarian equivalent" conception of fair allocation was introduced by Pazner and Schmeidler (1978). Building on work by Pazner himself (1979), scholarship that uses the concept of egalitarian equivalence as the basis for a social ordering of outcomes includes: Fleurbaey (2005, 2007); Fleurbaey and Maniquet (2008); Tadenuma (2005).

[148] To be clear, this *doesn't* mean that each individual gets the same amount of each good, but that each individual receives the same amount of good q^1, the same amount of good q^2 and so forth for each of the M goods.

indifferent between a given outcome x and some "egalitarian" outcome. Then there is an intuitive sense in which x has egalitarian credentials. Although (as mentioned) the literature under discussion focuses on individual preferences, we can generalize the "egalitarian equivalent" idea to mesh with any account of well-being W. We can say that x is more equal than y if (1) there is some egalitarian outcome z such that each person is just as well off with x as with z, and (2) there is no egalitarian outcome z^+ such that each person is just as well off with y as with z^+.[149]

Moreover, the idea would seem to generalize beyond the consumption-bundle context, to allow the comparison of outcomes characterized as an array of any type of individual attribute for each individual. However, because the bulk of the literature on egalitarian equivalence focuses on consumption bundles, I will henceforth focus on that case. If the approach turns out to be problematic in that core case, as I believe it does (at least on the premise that well-being is interpersonally comparable), it is hard to see how it will be attractive when generalized.

One critical problem is that the idea floated two paragraphs back does not allow us to satisfy minimal welfarist criteria. Imagine that we try to produce a Pareto-respecting quasiordering of a given set of outcomes (characterized as consumption bundles) by saying: (1) if each person is equally well off in x as in y, the two outcomes are equally good; (2) if each person is at least as well off in x as in y, and at least one person is better off in x than y, x is better; and (3) if x and y are Pareto-noncomparable, and (a) there is some egalitarian outcome z such that each person is just as well off with x as with z, and (b) there is no egalitarian outcome z^+ such that each person is just as well off with y as with z^+, then x is better than y. It turns out that this approach can yield an intransitive ranking of outcomes, hence does not succeed in producing a quasiordering.

The literature has circumvented this difficulty by fixing some reference bundle of consumption goods, $\mathbf{q}^{ref}$, and defining egalitarian equivalence with respect to multiples of $\mathbf{q}^{ref}$. Let us say that x is egalitarian equivalent "in the direction of $\mathbf{q}^{ref}$" if there exists some single positive number λ, such that each individual is just as well off in x as with a bundle consisting of λ times the amount of each good in the reference bundle. Then if we change the third clause in the preceding paragraph to the following, we *do* succeed in producing a Pareto-respecting quasiordering: (3)* if x and y are Pareto-noncomparable, and x is egalitarian equivalent in the direction of $\mathbf{q}^{ref}$, while y is not egalitarian equivalent in the direction of $\mathbf{q}^{ref}$, then x is better than y.[150]

What exactly is the connection between the egalitarian-equivalent approach to ordering outcome sets, as just described, and inequality metrics—the general topic

---

[149] To be sure, the formal properties of the concept of egalitarian equivalence may well depend on certain assumptions about individual preferences over consumption bundles, for example that such preferences be continuous or monotonic. These assumptions would need to be carried over to the definition of egalitarian equivalence in terms of W if the formal results are supposed to carry over as well.

[150] For the claims in the last two paragraphs, see in particular Tadenuma (2005).

of this section of the chapter? The egalitarian-equivalent approach embodies a preference for a completely equal distribution of each of the M goods—and anyone who is attracted to the Pigou–Dalton principle will find such a preference plausible. More specifically, it can be shown that the egalitarian-equivalent approach will approve Pigou–Dalton transfers in one or more goods from an individual j to an individual i, if j has more of each of the M goods than i and if the intrapersonal ranking of i's life-histories (i's consumption of different possible bundles of goods) is the same as the intrapersonal ranking of j's life-histories (j's consumption of different possible bundles).[151]

As with the income-evaluation-function approach and the attribute-evaluation-function approach, an interesting "correspondence" result can be proven for the egalitarian-equivalent approach. It can be shown (roughly) that outcomes are ranked by the egalitarian-equivalent approach "as if" (1) each individual is assigned a utility number in a given outcome x equaling the multiple of the reference bundle that is equally good for her as her bundle in x; and (2) the vectors of these "utilities" corresponding to outcomes are ranked using a leximin rule.[152]

However, as with the income-evaluation-function approach and the attribute-evaluation-function approach, this correspondence result does not mean that the proponent of the egalitarian-equivalent approach is committed to interpersonal

---

[151] Strictly speaking, this is true *if* the egalitarian-equivalent approach is implemented via the leximin rule mentioned in the paragraph immediately below, where each individual's bundle in an outcome is assigned a number equaling the multiple of q^{ref} that is equally good for the individual as the bundle, and outcomes are then ranked by applying leximin to these numbers. If j has more of each good in some outcome than i, and if both have the same intrapersonal ranking of life-histories, then (on the assumption that well-being is strictly increasing in each of the M goods), j must be assigned a higher multiple of q^{ref} in that outcome than i, and the leximin rule just mentioned will approve a Pigou–Dalton transfer in any of the M goods from j to i. However, using the leximin rule, if j and i have different intrapersonal rankings (for example, if those rankings depend on their preferences, and their preferences differ), then it is quite possible that j has more of every good than i, yet would be indifferent to a smaller multiple of q^{ref} than i. Visually, this can be seen as occurring because j's indifference curves between consumption bundles cut across i's indifference curves. If so, the leximin approach would not favor a Pigou–Dalton transfer from j to i.

[152] In other words, if $x = (q_1, \ldots, q_N)$, and λ_i is such that individual i is equally well off as between q_i and a bundle consisting of λ_i times q^{ref}, then the vector assigned x is $(\lambda_1, \lambda_2, \ldots, \lambda_N)$. Strictly, formal analysis has shown the following: an ordering of outcomes which is consistent with the weak Pareto principle, plus ranks outcomes which are Pareto-noncomparable (in terms of the strong Pareto principle) so as to prefer an outcome which is egalitarian equivalent in the direction of q^{ref} to one which is not, corresponds to a maximin rule applied to outcomes represented as $(\lambda_1, \lambda_2, \ldots, \lambda_N)$ *or some refinement of maximin*. See Tadenuma (2005, p. 464). Leximin is a familiar refinement of maximin that (applied to outcomes represented as $(\lambda_1, \lambda_2, \ldots, \lambda_N)$) satisfies strong Pareto, not just weak Pareto, and ranks Pareto-noncomparable outcomes consistently with egalitarian equivalence in terms of q^{ref}; but there are other, less familiar refinements of maximin with these properties. For example, consider a rule that compares two vectors of λ_i values by first comparing the smallest λ_i values in each vector and, if these are equal, comparing the total sum of λ_i values for each vector.

comparisons. Instead, she might well deny such comparisons and still favor the approach—and indeed its actual proponents do seem to deny interpersonal comparability.

Whatever its plausibility as a "fallback" absent interpersonally comparable utilities, the egalitarian-equivalent approach is problematic if such utilities can indeed be constructed. First, its potential dependence on the choice of reference bundle is troubling. Again, the SWF approach I adopt is not thus dependent. Second, using a leximin rule for ranking utility vectors is problematic in giving absolute priority to worse-off individuals—a point elaborated at length in Chapter 5, where I argue against the leximin rule for ranking utility vectors and in favor of a prioritarian SWF.

IV. OTHER EQUITY METRICS

This section considers poverty metrics, social-gradient metrics, and tax incidence analysis. Some common themes will emerge in the analysis. First, if well-being is interpersonally comparable and measurable by utilities, these approaches would seem to be less attractive than the SWF framework. Second, even as "fallbacks"— absent interpersonally comparable utilities—the approaches are problematic. They do not (at least on their own) secure a Pareto-respecting quasiordering of outcomes. And they involve a problematic or overly limited conception of fair distribution.

A. Poverty Metrics

Poverty metrics are widely used by empirical economists in the field of development economics and also, to some extent, in other fields. It is instructive to compare their structure with that of inequality metrics. Like inequality metrics, poverty metrics were initially developed to rank income distributions. Let $[c_1, \ldots, c_N]$ be the distribution of income among N individuals. An inequality metric assigns an inequality number to each such distribution; thereby ranks the distributions, as having comparatively more or less inequality; and, in this ranking, satisfies the Pigou–Dalton principle as applied to incomes. A poverty metric assigns a poverty number to each distribution; thereby ranks the distributions, as having comparatively more or less poverty; but, in this ranking, does not satisfy the Pigou–Dalton principle as applied to incomes. Instead, a key structural feature of poverty metrics is the use of a threshold or "cutoff" level of income (individuals below the threshold are "poor," individuals above are not) and what is often called the "focus axiom": Two distributions with the same pattern of below-threshold incomes are ranked the same, regardless of any differences in their above-threshold incomes.[153]

Poverty metrics often do satisfy the Pigou–Dalton principle with respect to income transfers between below-threshold individuals; but the "focus" axiom has

---

[153] See Chakravarty (2009, ch. 2); Dutta (2002, pp. 619–627); Lambert (2001, ch. 6).

the obvious implication that poverty metrics do not satisfy it with respect to transfers between above-threshold individuals.

Just as the field of inequality measurement has moved beyond income—developing techniques for quantifying the degree of inequality associated with multidimensional distributions—so too with poverty measurement. Multidimensional poverty metrics are a burgeoning area of research.[154] Consider some multidimensional distribution $[a_1, \ldots, a_N, b_1, \ldots, b_N, \ldots]$, where a is some individual attribute, b is some other individual attribute, and so forth. (The attributes might be how much food the individual has, her health state, the state of her shelter, her income, her employment status, etc.) A poverty metric will start with a list of thresholds—one for each attribute. An individual is typically counted as "poor" if her attribute level is below the threshold for at least one of the attributes. (A different possibility is to count her as "poor" if her level is below the threshold for each attribute, or for more than a specified percentage of the attributes.) Multidimensional poverty metrics at least seek to conform to the "weak focus" axiom: if an individual is above the threshold for each attribute in some distribution, then her attribute levels should not affect the poverty value assigned by the metric to that distribution. And many in the literature take a yet stronger "focus" axiom to be plausible in this context, namely that if an individual is above the threshold for *any* attribute, then the poverty value assigned by the poverty metric to the distribution should not depend on her level of that attribute (as opposed to her attribute levels that lie below the thresholds for those attributes).

Although many in the poverty-measurement literature, particularly those working on multidimensional poverty, reject a preference-based account of well-being, it is less clear whether the views of these poverty researchers really fall within the category of nonwelfarism or rather represent a kind of non-actual-preference welfarism.[155] In any event, the question on the table, for our purposes, is the following: what is the value of poverty metrics within the framework of welfarism?

It is a truism that the moral impact of benefits and harms to some individual may depend upon whether the individual is above or below some threshold. For example, the moral importance of providing food to someone may depend on whether the individual is above or below the threshold of malnutrition. The moral importance of improving someone's housing may depend upon whether the individual is above or below the threshold of minimally adequate shelter. The moral importance of a psychological intervention, to improve the quality of someone's mental states, may depend on whether the person is in a state of psychological suffering, or merely non-suffering but ripe to be made even happier.

A welfarist choice-evaluation framework should certainly be structured so that it is sensitive to this truism. But it is far from clear whether poverty metrics are the most attractive means for doing so.

---

[154] See Alkire and Foster (2011); Bourguignon and Chakravarty (2003); Chakravarty (2009, ch. 6); Jenkins and Micklewright (2007, pt. 2); Kakwani and Silber (2007, 2008).

[155] There is a close connection between the literature on multidimensional poverty and Sen's scholarship on "functionings" and "capabilities."

Consider, first, the case in which well-being is interpersonally comparable and measurable by utilities, so that the SWF approach is viable. In this case, threshold effects can (in principle) be handled by incorporating thresholds *within* the utility functions in **U**. The value assigned by each $u(.)$ in **U**, to a given life-history $(x; i)$, might depend upon whether the subject's attributes in the life-history (either income, or other attributes) are above or below some threshold. Indeed, some scholarly work seeking to define utility functions with this threshold structure, and using them as inputs into a utilitarian or prioritarian social welfare function, has been undertaken.[156]

This sort of threshold is *different* from the structure of a poverty metric. A poverty metric (applied to rank outcomes) would take a given pair of outcomes, characterized in terms of individual incomes or other attributes, and directly rank those as a function of the income/attribute distributions plus the income/attribute threshold(s) incorporated in the metric. By contrast, what is being suggested here is a two-step approach: first, assign utilities to outcomes, recognizing that there may be threshold effects in the function from an individual's attributes to the utility number measuring her well-being; and second, use any arbitrary SWF (whichever is taken to be most attractive) to rank the utility vectors corresponding to outcomes.

The proponent of poverty metrics might respond that the SWF *itself* should incorporate a threshold. Consider, in particular, an SWF with a *lexical* threshold. Chapter 5 will describe two such SWFs.[157] An SWF with a lexical threshold says: x is morally at least as good as y iff, for all $u(.)$ belonging to **U**, $u(x)$ is ranked at least as high as $u(y)$ by rule R, where R is the following type of rule. A threshold level T is designated. R takes $u(x)$, the utility vector corresponding to x, and produces a *truncated utility vector* $u^T(x)$, namely, the elements of that vector "lopped off" at the level T. It does the same for $u(y)$. R then compares these *truncated* vectors using some primary rule R_1. This primary rule, because it is applied to the truncated vectors, ignores the pattern of utilities in $u(x)$ and $u(y)$ above the threshold level T. If $u^T(x)$ is ranked better than $u^T(y)$ by the primary rule, x is counted as a better outcome than y according to $u(.)$. Only if the truncated vectors are ranked as equally good by the primary rule does the SWF move on to apply some secondary rule R_2 which takes account of the pattern of above-threshold utilities in $u(x)$ and $u(y)$.

---

[156] See Creedy (1997); Lewis and Ulph (1988). It might be objected that the proposal here—to accommodate a concern for poverty by using an SWF with utility functions that incorporate thresholds—is not sufficient to accommodate certain moral intuitions concerning poverty, namely that we have a reason to alleviate short-term poverty and suffering, independent of the lifetime well-being of the individuals involved. I address this objection at the end of Chapter 6.

[157] Namely, the sufficientist SWF and the prioritarian SWF with a lexical threshold. SWFs that lack a threshold structure may also be decomposable into poverty and non-poverty components, given some exogenously given level of well-being or income poverty. See Lambert (2001, pp. 140–144). But in the case of such SWFs, it is especially hard to see why such a decomposition is illuminating. See Lewis and Ulph (1988, pp. 118–119).

If the most attractive SWF indeed takes this form, then poverty metrics applied to *utility vectors* (and not, as in current practice, distributions of individual incomes or other attributes) might function as one component of the outcome-ranking criterion. Imagine that the primary rule, whatever it may be, ranks $u^T(x)$ and $u^T(y)$ a certain way. Then we can engineer a poverty metric, with its threshold set at T, and which ranks $u(x)$ and $u(y)$ the very same way. Instead of seeing the SWF as the application of the primary rule to $u^T(x)$ and $u^T(y)$, followed by the application of the secondary rule to $u(x)$ and $u(y)$, we could—trivially—see it as the application of the poverty metric to $u(x)$ and $u(y)$, followed by the application of the secondary rule.

There is a nice parallel, here, to the discussion earlier of inequality metrics. Just as the application of inequality metrics to utility vectors might be one component of a formula that "mimics" a certain kind of SWF (a Pigou–Dalton, continuous SWF), so the use of poverty metrics, applied to utility vectors, might be one component of a formula that "mimics" a different kind of SWF (an SWF with a lexical threshold).

However, it remains an open question whether the most attractive SWF does indeed have the "lexical threshold" form. In Chapter 5, I argue against the two SWFs, there considered, which have this structure. One point, fleshed out in that chapter, is that SWFs with a lexical threshold give absolute priority to well-being changes affecting individuals who are below the threshold (however small the changes, and however small the number of individuals affected), as against well-being changes affecting above-threshold individuals (however large the changes and numerous the individuals). This is implausible.

The proponent of poverty metrics might try a different tack. She might say: "Although welfarism *can* be rendered sensitive to threshold effects in the manner you suggest, by incorporating thresholds within the utility functions in **U**, an alternative, non-SWF-based approach, remains possible—namely, to apply poverty metrics to rank outcomes as a function of individuals' incomes or other attributes in the outcomes. Why is the first approach preferable?"

But the use of a poverty metric to rank outcomes, using individuals' income amounts or other attributes as an input to the metric, is problematic. First, this approach is in obvious tension with the principle of Pareto-superiority. Imagine that x and y are identical in terms of below-threshold incomes or attributes. However, there are some individuals who are above the income threshold (in the case where the metric is a function of income) or all the attribute thresholds (in the case where the metric is a function of multiple attributes) in both outcomes; and these individuals are better off in x than y. Then poverty metrics will count x and y as equally good (whatever version of the "focus" axiom is being used), but the Pareto principle requires that x be ranked better than y.[158]

---

[158] A separate point, worth noting, is that researchers in the area of multidimensional poverty have adopted the very same attribute-based Pigou–Dalton principles (for below-threshold individuals) that have created tensions in the multiattribute context between inequality measures and the Pareto

The proponent of poverty metrics will presumably respond at this point that poverty metrics are *partial* tools for ranking outcomes. "These tools seek to measure how outcomes compare in terms of distribution. They must be combined with other tools to arrive at an all-things-considered outcome ranking that respects the Pareto principles." Yet (as far as I'm aware) the existing scholarly literature is silent as to what those supplementary tools would be.

Moreover, even understood as partial, distributive metrics rather than all-things-considered tools for ranking outcomes, poverty metrics are problematic—because they fail to attend to the pattern of income or attributes above the threshold(s). Why isn't the above-threshold pattern also a matter of distributive concern?[159]

The considerations described in the prior three paragraphs suggest, not only that poverty metrics are problematic as *competitors* to the SWF approach, but also that they are problematic even as "fallbacks" if the SWF project of developing an interpersonally comparable utility metric fails.

B. Social-Gradient Metrics

I use the term "social-gradient metrics" to mean the family of policy-evaluation measures that are sensitive to the correlation between some aspect of an individual's well-being, resources, or opportunities, and some measure of an individual's social status (such as her income; her occupation; or whether she has relatively low status by virtue of being a racial minority in a society with a history of race discrimination). Such tools are widely used in public health scholarship, which often seeks to quantify disparities in health between higher- and lower-social-status individuals. To quote Braveman and Gruskin, prominent researchers regarding health equity: "[E]quity in health can be defined as the absence of systematic disparities in health . . . between social groups who have different levels of underlying social advantage/disadvantage—that is, different positions in a social hierarchy."[160] As other scholars in the field explain:

> In much of the published literature, health inequalities are taken to be synonymous with social group differences in health. . . . [A] critical choice is that of the variable used to distribute the population into social groups. Analytical traditions vary: in the

---

principles. See, e.g., Chakravarty (2009, p. 142), mentioning "uniform majorization" and the "uniform Pigou–Dalton principle."

[159] See Chapter 5, discussing sufficientism, which emphasizes this point. Note that the alternative approach proposed here—ranking outcomes using an SWF, and incorporating thresholds within the utility functions in **U**—avoids both objections. First, as long as the SWF employs a rule *R* for ranking utility vectors which is Paretian, the SWF will automatically satisfy the Pareto principles. Second, because *R* can be any arbitrary form—for example, the continuous prioritarian form—it can be sensitive to the distribution of well-being throughout the population.

[160] Braveman and Gruskin (2003, p. 254).

United Kingdom, social groups have been defined using five categories of occupation-based social class; in some countries in continental Europe, educational attainment or occupational categories have been used; and in the USA, most research focuses on social categories defined in terms of racial groups.[161]

Various specific metrics are employed to quantify health gradients across social groups:

> [M]easurement almost always involves comparing an indicator of health or a health-related factor in one or more disadvantaged groups with the same indicator in a more advantaged group or groups. Most often, the reference group is the most advantaged group—e.g., the wealthiest/highest-income group for disparities by wealth/income, or the dominant racial/ethnic group for racial/ethnic disparities. . . .
>
> When only two groups are compared, the "rate ratio"—i.e., the rate of a given health indicator in one group divided by the rate in another group—is most commonly calculated to measure a particular disparity; for example, in the United States, the annual rate of infant mortality among African American babies . . . is more than two times the rate among European American babies. . . . Two groups can also be compared by calculating a "rate difference" or absolute difference in rates. . . .
>
> More complex methods, such as the population attributable risk, the slope and relative indices of inequality, and the concentration curve and index . . . also have been used.[162]

Recently, the "concentration curve" has become particularly popular in the health equity literature. Imagine that each individual is assigned both a measure of social status, and a cardinal measure of health (allowing us to calculate the total health of the entire population or of groups within it). Then we can order individuals from lowest to highest status; graph the number of individuals against the cumulative fraction of total population health; and calculate the deviation between this graph and the line of perfect equality.[163]

A "social gradient" approach to equity is also adopted in the literature on environmental justice, which looks at the extent to which racial minorities are disproportionately exposed to pollutants or other health and safety risks. Indeed, an Executive Order in the United States embodies this approach, instructing administrative agencies that:

---

[161] Murray, Gakidou, and Frenk (1999, pp. 537–538).

[162] Braveman (2006, p. 178).

[163] For a discussion of the concentration curve as well as other measures of social group differences in health, see Kakwani, Wagstaff, and van Doorslaer (1997); Mackenbach and Kunst (1997); Wagstaff, Paci, and van Doorslaer (1991). For a defense of the social-gradient approach to health inequality measurement, see Braveman (2006).

To the greatest extent practicable and permitted by law, . . . each Federal agency shall make achieving environmental justice part of its mission by identifying and addressing, as appropriate, disproportionately high and adverse human health or environmental effects of its programs, policies, and activities on minority populations and low-income populations. . . .[164]

There is an important parallel between poverty metrics and social-gradient metrics. It is a truism, I have suggested, that an individual's location relative to a threshold has moral relevance. But welfarists can recognize this truism *without* using poverty metrics. Instead, the utility functions in **U** might incorporate thresholds, and these utility functions might then be coupled with an SWF to rank outcomes.

Similarly, it is a truism that an individual's social status has moral relevance. (For example, a life-history in which an individual is socially stigmatized, as being a "lesser person," is surely much worse than one in which the subject is seen by others in her society as worthy of full concern and respect; and even less dramatic differences in social status can also presumably have a substantial effect on individual welfare.) But the SWF approach itself can reflect this insight about well-being via a sufficiently rich description of outcomes (to include various determinants of an individual's social status) and a sufficiently nuanced structure for the utility functions in **U**.[165]

Can the parallel between poverty metrics and social-gradient metrics be pushed further? I suggested above that a particular type of SWF (an SWF with a lexical threshold) might be decomposed into the application of a poverty metric to utility vectors, followed by the application of a secondary rule to utility vectors. Might the application of a social-gradient metric to *utility vectors* be seen as isomorphic to some SWF?

Without discussing this possibility at length, let me suggest the following: it is hard to see how the application of a social-gradient metric to utility vectors could be isomorphic to an SWF that satisfies the basic axiom of *anonymity*. To see the issue here, assume (for simplicity) that utility is unique up to a positive ratio transformation, so that the utility of individual i in outcome x is $ru_i(x)$ and so forth. In order to rank outcomes by applying a social-gradient metric to their corresponding utility vectors, we would need not merely information about individuals' utility in the two outcomes, but also information about their social status. Thus x is mapped onto $(ru_1(x), s_1(x), ru_2(x), s_2(x), \ldots, ru_N(x), s_N(x))$, where $s_i(x)$ is individual i's status in x.

[164] Executive Order 12898 (1994, sec. 1–101). For a discussion of the role of environmental justice in U.S. public law, and of the scholarly literature that seeks to measure disparate impact across racial lines, see Adler (2008, pp. 1–11).

[165] A utility function could take as one of its arguments an explicit measure of social status. Or, it could be "nonatomistic"—attending to the way in which an individual's location in the population distribution of an attribute that helps to determine status (such as income) can affect her well-being. See Chapter 6, pp. 463–466. On measures of social status, see, e.g., Bartley (2004, ch. 2).

Imagine that a social-gradient number $S(x)$ is then assigned to x as a function of the skew in individual utility across social-status lines (e.g., using a concentration curve), and that $S(x)$ together with other information (e.g., about the level of total well-being) is used to rank outcomes. It is easy to see how this approach might violate the anonymity axiom: namely, that if the pattern of well-being in one outcome is just a permutation of the pattern of well-being in another, the two should be ranked as equally good.[166]

Less formally, the difficulty with the approach on the table is that it sees equity as a matter of the distribution of well-being between social groups. Why should we "double count" social status, using it both as a potential determinant of the quality of each individual's life (i.e., an argument in the utility function) and then again as part of our moral assessment of the distribution of well-being between individuals? Why not determine the equity of an outcome by examining the distribution of well-being, simpliciter, ignoring proper names, social status, and all other characteristics except an individual's well-being?

An important line of response, pressed by Iris Young, is nonwelfarist. It sees attention to inequalities between social groups as flowing from a concern for individuals who are badly off through no fault of their own, rather than a concern for well-being per se.

> [I]f we simply identify some inequality of condition or situation between individuals at a particular time we have no account of the causes of this unequal condition. It is the causes and consequences of some pattern of inequality, rather than the pattern itself, that raises issues of justice. If the causes of an inequality lie in the uncoerced and considered decisions and preferences of the less well-off persons, for example, then the inequality is probably not unjust. . . .
>
> . . . [However], the causes of many inequalities of resources or opportunities among individuals lie in social institutions, their rules and relations, and the decisions others make within them that affect the lives of the individuals compared.[167]

Young concludes that an inequality must be a "structural inequality" to be a central concern of distributive justice: "Structural inequality . . . consists in the relative constraints some people encounter in their freedom and material well-being as the

---

[166] Imagine that the utility vector $u(x)$ is a permutation of the utility vector $u(y)$, and thus too for every other pair of vectors $ru(x)$ and $ru(y)$ corresponding to any $ru(.)$ in $\mathbf{U}$. In this case (at least if the additional information that $S(.)$ is combined with to rank outcomes is information about total well-being), the ranking of the outcomes is identical to their ranking in light of $S(.)$, since total well-being is the same for both outcomes. Assume, now, that $(ru_1(x), s_1(x), ru_2(x), s_2(x), \ldots, ru_N(x), s_N(x))$ is such that low utility levels are correlated with low status values, while this is not true for $(ru_1(y), s_1(y), ru_2(y), s_2(y), \ldots, ru_N(y), s_N(y))$. Then $S(.)$ will give a higher value to y than x, but the anonymity principle requires that they be ranked as equally good.

[167] Young (2001, p. 8).

cumulative effect of the possibilities of their social positions, as compared with others who in their social positions have more options or easier access to benefits."[168]

Although I have adopted the general strategy of working within welfarism, Young's particular non-welfarist defense of social-gradient metrics warrants a response here—because the SWF approach, I have suggested, is ultimately just a first step toward a policy-evaluation framework that will be sensitive to individual responsibility, the very concern that Young stresses. Where Young errs, I believe, is in conflating a *sufficient* condition for the absence of individual responsibility with a *necessary* condition. It is certainly very plausible that individuals who are badly off in virtue of their low social status lack responsibility for their well-being level, and that the inequality between their well-being and others' is therefore a moral concern. But individuals who have a high social status and end up badly off can also lack responsibility for their fate. For example, imagine two white males with good jobs and incomes, one of whom dies because he inhales a pollutant that a distant factory emitted. Or two wealthy white children, one of whom is secretly abused by a parent. Should decisionmakers who are trying to achieve a fair distribution of responsibility-adjusted well-being really ignore the skew in well-being between the luckier and less lucky individual in each of these pairs?

What about using social-gradient metrics as "fallbacks," absent interpersonal comparability? It is not difficult to see the tension with the Pareto principles. Imagine that x and y are identical, except that some high status individuals are better off in x than y. Then Pareto-superiority requires that x be ranked better than y, but a social-gradient metric may well say that x is worse. And, even taken as *partial*, distributive metrics, social-gradient metrics are problematic in focusing just on the distribution of attributes between groups of individuals with different social statuses, ignoring distribution among individuals with the same status.

C. Tax Incidence Analysis

Much empirical work in the area of tax policy takes the form of "incidence analysis." This line of scholarship estimates the burden of a tax on different groups of individuals, depending on their economic role. An incidence analysis then, often, repackages this information so that the population is divided into different income classes— typically, different ranges of annual income amounts[169]—and the average tax burden on each group is estimated. This allows the familiar characterization of a tax as "regressive," "progressive," or "proportional." A tax is *regressive* if its burden as a fraction of income decreases as income increases. It is progressive if its fractional burden

---

[168] Ibid., p. 15 (emphasis omitted).
[169] Some incidence analysis looks at lifetime income.

increases as income increases. Finally, a tax is proportional if its fractional burden stays constant as income increases.[170]

Although mainly employed to study various types of taxes, the incidence-analysis format has also been used as a framework to evaluate non-tax policies—for example to determine whether environmental regulatory policies have a progressive, regressive, or proportional impact.

There is an interesting conceptual link between incidence analysis and CBA. Why? Incidence analysis, again, hinges on the estimation of a tax's *burden* for different individuals. And the measure of burden adopted in the literature (at least as a theoretical standard) is the WTP/WTA amount.[171]

With that connection in mind, let us consider whether the incidence-analysis format provides an attractive tool for quasiordering an outcome set. Earlier in the chapter, we developed a version of CBA that is generic, meshing with non-preferentialist accounts of well-being, and that provides a Pareto-respecting quasiordering of an outcome set as long as the connection between consumption (or income) and well-being is well-behaved.[172] This version of CBA picks some outcome x as baseline; for every other outcome y, uses whatever theory of well-being W is at hand to determine each individual's WTP/WTA for x, relative to y; and orders outcomes according to the (negative) sum of WTP/WTA amounts.

Similarly, a generic kind of "incidence analysis" format that could be used to rank outcomes would be the following. An arbitrary outcome x is picked as baseline. For every other outcome y, we calculate each individual's WTP/WTA amount for x, relative to y, according to W. The distribution of these amounts, together with information about each individual's income in x, can then be used to assign an overall degree of progressivity/regressivity to each outcome; and outcomes can then be ordered according to their progressivity. We can think of this approach as mapping each outcome y onto a list of two numbers for each individual, showing each individual's income (in x) and his WTP/WTA for x relative to y. (In other words, y is mapped onto $[(c_1, \Delta c_1^y), (c_2, \Delta c_2^y), \ldots, (c_N, \Delta c_N^y)]$, where c_i is i's income in x and Δc_i^y is his WTP/WTA for x relative to y.) We can use some progressivity measure $PR(.)$ that assigns an overall number to the list of such pairs associated with each outcome.[173] If we like the idea that progressivity/regressivity is a matter of whether fractional burdens increase or decrease with income, we can repackage the information

---

[170] For reviews of the "incidence analysis" methodology and literature, see Fullerton and Metcalf (2002); Fullerton and Rogers (1993, ch. 1); Tresch (2002, chs. 16–17). As regards environmental policy, see Parry et al. (2006).

[171] See Fullerton and Metcalf (2002, pp. 1793–1794).

[172] Because the incidence-analysis literature tends to focus on income, not consumption, I frame the analysis in terms of income. See above, n. 122.

[173] Remember that i's WTP/WTA for x, relative to y, is the reduction in his income in x that makes him just as well off in x as in y. Thus, if i is worse off ("burdened by") y, as compared to x, the Δc_i^y value discussed here will be positive. If the $PR(.)$ measure requires that Δc_i^y be positive, for all individuals,

$[(c_1, \Delta c_1^y), (c_2, \Delta c_2^y), \ldots, (c_N, \Delta c_N^y)]$ by ordering the individuals from smallest to largest incomes and calculating $\Delta c_i^y/c_i$ for each individual.

Like CBA, this approach has the advantage (for skeptics about interpersonal comparisons) of not entailing interpersonal comparability. It is hard to see why incidence analysis would be attractive given interpersonal comparability and the possibility of using SWFs to rank outcomes—so I will focus here on its possible role as a "fallback."

First, like CBA (and other policy-analytic approaches that incorporate the construct of a WTP/WTA amount, such as the use of "income evaluation functions"), incidence analysis may well be undermined if the connection between income and well-being is not well-behaved.

What about the Pareto principles? Assuming the income/well-being connection *is* well-behaved, Pareto-indifference can readily be satisfied by stipulating that if each individual's WTP/WTA for x relative to y and to z are the same, then $PR(y) = PR(z)$.

Pareto-superiority is trickier. Note what happens if we make $PR(y)$ for a given outcome y a function of whether the fractional burden $\Delta c_i^y/c_i$ increases or decreases as income c_i increases. Assume that y is perfectly "proportional": each individual's $\Delta c_i^y/c_i$ value is the very same amount. Assume that each individual's WTP/WTA amount for x, relative to z (Δc_i^z) is half of this amount for y—so that each individual is better off in z than y, and z is also perfectly "proportional." Then $PR(y) = PR(z)$; and if we use these numbers as a measure of the all-things-considered goodness of the outcomes we have violated Pareto-superiority.[174]

The now-familiar response is that $PR(.)$ is not an all-things-considered measure of the goodness of outcomes. Rather, it is simply a measure of distribution. However, this response is speculative. Can a Pareto-respecting ranking of outcomes be decomposed into a PR-type metric combined with some other metric? The answer is not obvious. In general, the literature on incidence analysis ignores the problem of how to combine information about policy progressivity/regressivity into an all-things-considered ranking of outcomes.

Moreover, even taken as a measure of how outcomes compare with respect to fair distribution, rather than an all-things-considered measure, the $PR(.)$ measure is problematic. One problem involves "inframarginal" changes. We can characterize the pattern of fractional burdens associated with a given outcome y by looking at each individual's WTP/WTA amount, Δc_i^y, and dividing that by his income in the baseline outcome x; or by looking at each individual's WTP/WTA amount and dividing that by his income in y. If some individuals' incomes in x are substantially

---

we can choose as x some outcome such that each individual is better off in that outcome than in any other.

[174] Indeed, the so-called "Suits" index, a standard measure of progressivity/regressivity used in the incidence-analysis literature (see Anderson, Roy, and Shoemaker 2003) would say that $PR(y) = PR(z)$ in this case.

different than in y, these different choices of the "denominator" for the fractional burden calculation may yield quite different pictures of the pattern of fractional burdens associated with y. Perhaps the problem can be solved by making the $PR(y)$ value a function of the individual WTP/WTA amounts, incomes in x, *and* incomes in y.

A different point is that characterizing y as more or less fair than x as a function of the distribution of WTP/WTA amounts, plus total incomes in x (and perhaps y), does not take sufficient account of non-income attributes. Although *changes* in non-income attributes are captured in WTP/WTA amounts, the incidence-analysis approach then proceeds by examining how those WTP/WTA amounts correlate with individual *incomes*—ignoring how they are correlated with non-income characteristics. For a simple example of the issue, here, imagine that outcomes are characterized in terms of health and income. Imagine also that each individual's health state is the same in x as in y, but some individuals have different incomes in the two outcomes.[175] We associate y with a list of pairs of income amounts and WTP/WTA amounts, and assign it a $PR(.)$ value as a function of this information. $PR(y)$ will be invariant to the distribution of health states in the outcomes. But shouldn't that health distribution matter to our assessment of y as being more or less fair than x? If Δc_i^y amounts (either in absolute terms, or as a fraction of some measure of health) tend to increase as individuals become healthier, shouldn't that improve our assessment of how equitable y is? If those burdens tend to decrease as individuals become healthier, shouldn't that reduce the measure of equity that we assign to y?

Perhaps this problem can be solved by normalizing incomes in all outcomes, to reflect non-income characteristics, and then using incidence analysis to rank normalized outcomes. But then issues regarding the choice of reference characteristics for purposes of the normalization will arise.

V. QALY-BASED COST-EFFECTIVENESS ANALYSIS

QALY-based cost-effectiveness analysis (CEA) has become a standard policy-evaluation technique in the area of health policy. While CBA measures all impacts in WTP/WTA amounts—including not only changes in the consumption of marketed goods, but also changes in the level of health or other non-market goods—the hallmark of CEA is to resist the explicit commensuration of health effects with income/expenditure/consumption. Instead, health and longevity effects of a policy intervention are measured on some non-monetary scale.

The standard such scale is the so-called "quality adjusted life-year" (QALY) scale. Surveys are conducted to assign any given health state a value on a zero-one scale,

---

[175] In cases where health is different in the two outcomes, changes in health will be reflected in WTP/WTA amounts, so that health does show up in $PR(.)$. Even in those cases, though, WTP/WTA amounts are then correlated with incomes, not health. The case discussed in the text is a simple one designed to show the problem in its purest form.

with 0 representing a health state no better than death, and 1 representing perfect health. An individual's sequence of health states over a number of periods can then be assigned a QALY value equaling the sum or discounted sum of the value of her health state in each period. For example, if an individual lives for 60 years, for the first 30 years in perfect health, for the second 30 years in a health state with value 0.5, then (assuming a zero discount rate) the QALY value of the entire sequence is $30 \times 1 + 30 \times 0.5 = 45$. The QALY method allows us to be sensitive to the full range of policy impacts on individual health—both mortality impacts and the full range of morbidity impacts—and to measure these effects using a single, non-monetary scale. For example, if funding a new kind of scanner will allow us to quickly detect and cure a cases of nonfatal disease A, b cases of nonfatal disease B, and c cases of a fatal disease (otherwise expected to cause rapid death) among a given cohort of individuals who can be expected to live L more years in good health if the diseases are cured, we can express this effect as $a[1 - q(A)]L + b[1 - q(b)]L + cL$, where $q(A)$ and $q(B)$ are the values of these nonfatal diseases on the zero-one scale. Although other measures of non-monetary effectiveness are used in the health care cost-effectiveness literature, QALYs have become the gold standard.

Of course, a health care intervention will not merely have health impacts. Curing disease or reducing mortality is typically costly, in terms of income or other non-health effects. CEA evaluates a health policy by measuring its non-health impacts in dollars; by measuring its health impacts in QALYs; and by employing cost-effectiveness ratios to determine whether the policy is worthwhile. Where more than two policies are at issue, CEA typically uses *incremental* rather than absolute cost-effectiveness ratios to determine which policy is best. The technique of evaluating policies with cost-effectiveness ratios is employed by CEA practitioners both to select the policy which maximizes an exogenous, fixed budget, and to rank policies independent of any such budget. In the latter case (where there is no exogenous budget), a cutoff level specifying the maximum acceptable cost-effectiveness ratio must be selected; how policies are ranked will depend on which such cutoff level is specified.[176]

CEA, as mentioned, has become a very standard tool in the health policy area. It is used by a number of governments, including Australia, Britain, Canada, and New Zealand, to determine which pharmaceuticals or health technologies should receive public reimbursement. A large scholarly literature in health economics and public health has arisen to refine the theory of QALY measurement and to estimate QALY values from survey research. Furthermore, numerous cost-effectiveness studies of pharmaceuticals and health technologies are published in the academic literature every year.[177]

---

[176] On the measurement of health states using QALYs, and on CEA, see generally Adler (2006a) and the reviews of these approaches cited therein, particularly at p. 1, n. 1, and at pp. 8–9, nn. 25–26.
[177] See Adler (2006a, pp. 3–6).

CEA, in its standard form, is not sensitive to distribution. Assigning a health policy an absolute or incremental cost figure, and an absolute or incremental QALY figure, does not take account of the distribution of costs or health impacts across the population. However, substantial recent academic discussion has been given to the possibility of multiplying QALY changes by *weighting* factors, so as to give greater weight to health changes affecting individuals who are at a low level of health, and perhaps to give greater weight to health changes affecting individuals who are badly off in other ways.[178]

A full discussion of the measurement of health states with QALYs, the use of cost-effectiveness ratios to select policies, and equity weighting would consume much space, and is not necessary here. Even without such a discussion, it is not difficult to see why CEA (with or without equity weights) does not provide an attractive welfarist basis for ranking an outcome set.

This conclusion will probably surprise no one. There is a hot debate in health policy scholarship between those who favor CBA and those who favor CEA. Both the critics and defenders of CEA often see it as a kind of nonwelfarist technique—although as with poverty metrics it is not clear whether "nonwelfarism" in these debates really means some kind of non-preference-based account of well-being rather than "nonwelfarism" in the sense employed in this book.[179] In any event, it is useful for my purposes, in motivating the elaboration of the SWF framework, to show why CEA is not a viable candidate to help structure a welfarist choice-evaluation procedure.

The debate between the critics and proponents of QALYs has underscored, first, that CEA and CBA can deviate in their evaluation of health policies; and second, that the source of such deviation is heterogeneity in individual willingness-to-pay for a given QALY gain. However, the deviation between CEA and CBA is less important than the critics of CEA have tended to assume. The critics presuppose that CBA itself has impeccable welfarist credentials, and that demonstrating the deviation between CBA and CEA shows why CEA is an unacceptable technique for welfarists. Paul Dolan and Richard Edlin write:

> In showing that there is currently no meaningful link between CBA and CEA, we have also shown that CEA is not currently justifiable on strictly welfarist grounds. Instead, CEA would seem to be justifiable only on non-welfarist grounds where the output of health care is judged according to its contribution to health itself, rather than according to the extent to which it contributes to overall welfare. . . .[180]

---

[178] See, e.g., Cookson, Drummond, and Weatherly (2009); Haninger (2007); Nord (2005); Sassi, Archard, and Le Grand (2001, ch. 2); Wailoo, Tsuchiya, and McCabe (2009).

[179] See Adler (2006a, pp. 8–15); Brouwer et al. (2008).

[180] Dolan and Edlin (2002, p. 838).

Don Kenkel argues: "[W]hen we accept the methodology of welfare economics, we should use cost-benefit analysis, not cost-effectiveness analysis."[181]

But CBA *itself* is problematic from the perspective of welfarism, for reasons summarized earlier in the chapter, and CBA *itself* is often rejected by theoretical welfare economists. So showing that CEA deviates from CBA is hardly the stake through the heart that CEA's critics seem to think.

What has been overlooked by this debate is that a much more telling welfarist criticism of CEA is available. The heterogeneity of individual willingness-to-pay for a QALY not only causes CEA to deviate from CBA, but *also leads CEA to violate the Pareto principles*. The following insert provides a series of examples in which two outcomes, characterized in terms of consumption and health,[182] are compared by taking one as the baseline and calculating the total change in health and the total change in consumption yielded by the second. The examples are set up so that either the total change in health or the total change in consumption is zero—which means that one or the other outcome will be chosen, by anyone using cost-effectiveness ratios, regardless of which particular cutoff ratio is chosen. I do not assume interpersonal comparability; the failure of CEA to satisfy the Pareto principles means that even the skeptic about interpersonal comparability should reject CEA. However, I do assume that the *intrapersonal* ranking of life-histories is representable by a utility function with a very simple form that makes the example particularly easy to grasp: $u_i(c_i, h_i) = \log_{10}(c_i) + h_i$, where c_i is individual i's consumption in some outcome and h_i her health. This form means, inter alia, that incremental consumption has a diminishing effect in improving a given person's well-being as her consumption level increases; and that the amount of consumption she is willing to sacrifice for a health gain depends on her consumption level. With this utility function in hand, it is almost trivial to construct cases in which CEA violates Pareto-indifference or Pareto-superiority.

In all cases, there are two individuals, with a consumption amount and health amount. Outcome $x = (c_1, c_2, h_1, h_2)$, while $y = (c_1^*, c_2^*, h_1^*, h_2^*)$. "C/E" is the cost-effectiveness ratio, meaning the cost (loss of consumption) moving from x to y, divided by the health gain. In other words, C/E $= (c_1 + c_2 - c_1^* - c_2^*)/(h_1^* + h_2^* - h_1 - h_2)$. CEA says that y is better than x if C/E is below some stipulated cutoff level.

Violation of Pareto-superiority with zero aggregate health change and non-zero aggregate consumption change: Imagine that x is such that $c_1 = 5000$, $h_1 = 3$, $c_2 = 10$, $h_2 = 4$, while y is such that $c_1^* = 1000$, $h_1^* = 4$, $c_2^* = 200$, $h_2^* = 3$. Then using the intrapersonal utility

[181] Kenkel (1997, p. 755).
[182] The analysis generalizes. If outcomes have non-consumption, non-health attributes, those attributes will need to be translated into consumption in some way so that CEA can rank the outcomes (for example, by fixing the attributes at a reference level and normalizing consumption); and then the sort of problem with the Pareto principles noted here can arise.

function $u_i(c_i, h_i) = \log_{10}(c_i) + h_i$, each individual is better off in y than x. But C/E is infinite, so that x is chosen however high the cutoff level.

Violation of Pareto-indifference with zero aggregate health change and non-zero aggregate consumption change: Imagine that x is such that $c_1 = 10,000$, $h_1 = 3$, $c_2 = 10$ $h_2 = 4$; y is such that $c_1{}^* = 1000$, $h_1{}^* = 4$, $c_2{}^* = 100$, $h_2{}^* = 3$. Then each individual is just as well off in outcome y as x. But C/E is infinite, so that x is chosen however high the cutoff level.

Violation of Pareto-superiority with zero aggregate consumption change and non-zero aggregate health change: Imagine that x is such that $c_1 = 1000$, $h_1 = 3$, $c_2 = 10,000$, $h_2 = 4$; while y is such that $c_1{}^* = 1$, $h_1{}^* = 5$, $c_2{}^* = 10,999$, $h_2{}^* = 3$. Then C/E = 0, so that y is chosen regardless of how low the cut-off ratio is set. But both individuals are better off in x.

Violation of Pareto-indifference with zero aggregate consumption change and non-zero aggregate health change: Imagine that x is such that $c_1 = 1000$, $h_1 = 3$, $c_2 = 10,000$, $h_2 = 4$; while y is such that $c_1{}^* = 1$, $h_1{}^* = 6$, $c_2{}^* = 10,999$, $h_2{}^* = 3.958647$. Then each individual is just as well off in x as in y. But C/E = 0, so that y is chosen regardless of how low the cut-off ratio is set.

It might be objected that the intrapersonal utility function, $u_i(c_i, h_i) = \log_{10}(c_i) + h_i$, used to generate these examples does not capture how health and consumption interact, on the best account of well-being. But this function was chosen merely for its simplicity. Similar violations of Pareto-indifference and Pareto-superiority can be constructed using any utility function that allows for heterogeneity in the comparative impact of consumption changes and health changes on individual well-being.

A different objection is that these cases are nonrepresentative because the *direction* of policy impacts with respect to consumption and health is heterogeneous across consumers. In each case, moving from one outcome to a second increases one individual's consumption and reduces his health, while decreasing the other individual's consumption and improving his health. This "bidirectionality" allows us to push the cost-effectiveness ratio to zero or infinity (and thus to make the violations of Pareto-indifference and -superiority invariant to the choice of cutoff ratio.).

If CEA is to be a useful tool in ranking various sorts of outcome sets, it should be able to handle pairs of outcomes that have this "bidirectionality" feature. In any event, we can also produce violations of Pareto-indifference and -superiority in cases where both individuals have lower consumption and greater health in one outcome. Consider the following example:

The intrapersonal utility function is as before, $u_i(c_i, h_i) = \log_{10}(c_i) + h_i$. There are now more than two individuals, but the only individuals whose consumption and health levels vary between the outcomes are these two. (These two may have unusually high or low consumption or health levels compared to the rest of the population.)

Case One: Outcome x is such that $c_1 = 1000$, $h_1 = 3$, $c_2 = 10$, $h_2 = 3$, while y is such that $c_1{}^* = 100$, $h_1{}^* = 4$, $c_2{}^* = 1$, $h_2{}^* = 4$. Both individuals are just as well off in x as in y. The C/E ratio is $909/2$.

Case Two: Outcome x is such that $c_1 = c_2$, $h_1 = 3$, $h_2 = 3$, while y is such that $c_1{}^* = c_2{}^* = c_1/9$, $h_1{}^* = 4$, $h_2{}^* = 4$. Each individual is better off in y than x. The C/E ratio is $(8/9)c_1$.

Note that, in the first case, unless the cost-effectiveness ratio is set at the precise value of $909/2$, one outcome will be ranked as better than the other—in violation of Pareto-indifference. In the second case, unless the C/E cutoff is set above $(8/9)c_1$, outcome x will be selected—in violation of Pareto-superiority. Various proposals have been floated for how to set the cutoff cost-effectiveness ratio, such as looking at the implicit cutoffs in prior policies, or taking population average willingness-to-pay for a QALY. Clearly, neither approach would secure consistency with Pareto-indifference or -superiority in this sort of case. For an approach to do so, it must select a cutoff ratio that is sensitive to the comparative impact of consumption and health on the well-being of the particular individuals whose health and consumption are different in the two outcomes being compared; and while it might be possible to have highly context-dependent cutoff ratios that operate in this way, the literature has not pursued this approach. Moreover, even context-dependent cutoff ratios do not cure violations of Pareto-indifference and -superiority in the "bidirectionality" cases discussed above.

3

WELL-BEING AND
INTERPERSONAL COMPARISONS

A welfarist decision procedure requires an account of well-being. The SWF approach requires not just any such account, but one that allows for interpersonal comparisons of well-being, and that represents its well-being comparisons, in any choice situation, via a set U of utility functions constructed for that situation.

But what *is* the most attractive account of well-being? Why believe that it allows for interpersonal comparisons? What would such comparisons consist of? And even if interpersonal comparisons *are* possible, how do we construct numerical utilities that represent the well-being ranking of life-histories or the well-being differences between life-histories?

This chapter grapples with these issues. Drawing from the philosophical literature, I offer an analysis of well-being in terms of fully informed, fully rational, extended preferences. This account *is* preferentialist, for reasons I will elaborate, but it does not tie well-being to preferences in a crude or simplistic way. Instead, it is designed to be sensitive to important platitudes about well-being—that well-being has critical force, and that it cannot be too "remote" from the subject—which have been part of the motivation for philosophical views that draw a nexus between well-being and mental states or objective goods, rather than reducing an individual's well-being to the satisfaction of her actual preferences.

The idea of an *extended preference* derives from John Harsanyi. This idea fits hand-in-glove with the basic architecture of a welfarist decision procedure, built around a set of life-histories deriving from an outcome set and a group of N individuals. An individual's ordinary preferences take the form of ranking outcomes and choices. Individual k prefers outcome x to outcome y, or choice a to choice b. By contrast, an individual's *extended* preferences take the form of ranking *life-histories*. Individual k has an extended preference for life-history $(x; i)$ over $(y; j)$.

Of course, what it means to have an extended preference is a subtle question. But let us assume that individuals *can* have extended preferences—indeed, not just rankings of life-histories, but rankings of lotteries over life-histories. This is what Harsanyi assumes, and I believe the assumption can be defended. Harsanyi then proposes to use expected utility (EU) theory to construct utility functions that represent individuals' extended preferences, and this shall be my approach as well. Each individual k in the population, if fully informed and rational, would rank the set of lotteries over life-histories consistent with EU theory. This individual ranking can be represented by an individual set of utility functions, U^k. (More precisely, the set U^k represents individual k's ranking of lotteries over life-histories *and* is "zeroed out" so as to assign zero to nonexistence.[1]) Pooling these individual sets across all N individuals, we arrive at the set U. The set U, thus created, will not simply represent intra- and interpersonal comparisons of well-being levels. It will also represent intra- and interpersonal comparisons of well-being *differences*, and, finally, will allow us to make statements about the ratios between the well-being levels of different life-histories.

The chapter begins by surveying the philosophical literature on well-being. Some philosophers link well-being to preference satisfaction; some, to mental states; some, to "objective goods"; and some offer hybrid accounts which combine these elements. This diversity of philosophical approaches is mirrored in economics and in other literatures where the concept of well-being plays a role. A preference-satisfaction account of well-being has long been the dominant view within economics. However, much scholarship in economics now focuses on the determinants of "happiness" or "subjective well-being." Many economists in this area, as well as psychologists engaged in closely related work, stress the importance for human welfare of positive mental states and the avoidance of negative ones. Finally, Amartya Sen's scholarship on "capabilities" has triggered much recent work in development economics that is skeptical of both preferentialist and mental-state views of well-being, and that seems closer to an objective-good view. Various other bodies of work, for example the literature on "social indicators," also trend toward an objective-good approach.

What accounts for this diversity and controversy? The answer, I suggest, is both substantive and metaethical. As a substantive matter, an attractive account of well-being should be sensitive to various truisms about well-being, several of which I have already mentioned: that well-being has critical force; that it is not too "remote" from the individual involved; and finally that it has motivational force. Developing an account which is true to these platitudes and which is consistent with our intuitions about well-being in particular cases has proved difficult indeed. Adding further fuel to the dialectical fire is a dispute about whether the well-being associated with different lives is ultimately grounded in value-free preferences for such lives, or

---

[1] Furthermore, as I shall explain, each individual k ranks different subsets of life-history lotteries, subsets in which all the life-histories involved concern a single subject. Individual k doesn't directly rank all life-history lotteries, but rather constructs U^k via her rankings of these subsets plus certain other judgments.

Moreover, the account will be generalized, at the end of the chapter, to allow that k's extended preferences may vary over time or across outcomes.

whether instead well-formed preferences are always "value laden," the result of judgments or perceptions of well-being. The contending positions in this dispute flow naturally from competing metaethical views—in particular, from competing variants of an "ideal approval" account of moral facts.

The chapter next discusses the problem of interpersonal comparisons. While the nature of well-being is philosophically controversial, the possibility of interpersonal comparisons has not been much disputed by philosophers. Economics presents a mirror image. Economists (at least until the recent rise of "happiness" scholarship) have tended to concur in analyzing well-being in terms of preference satisfaction. But while some economists (particularly those who use social welfare functions) accept the possibility of interpersonal comparisons, many others do not. In this section of the chapter, I present a generic case for interpersonal comparisons, and then describe Harsanyi's use of extended preferences and EU theory to make sense of such comparisons.

Having reviewed both the philosophical literature and the question of interpersonal comparisons, the chapter presents my own account of well-being, which I have already adumbrated: one that derives interpersonal level and difference comparisons as well as ratio information from a set **U** of utility functions that represent the fully informed, fully rational, extended preferences of the various individuals in the population regarding life-histories, lotteries over life-histories, and comparisons to nonexistence.

Although my account of well-being is indebted to Harsanyi's work, it differs from his account in a number of critical respects. Harsanyi never offers a clear account of how an extended preference is possible. I grapple with that problem at length. Furthermore, unlike Harsanyi, I do not presuppose that individuals have identical extended preferences. While Harsanyi argues for utilitarianism, I will *reject* utilitarianism and instead will use the set **U** as the input to a prioritarian SWF. Unlike Harsanyi, I recognize the need to provide a substantive defense of the use of EU theory to measure well-being differences. Finally, although Harsanyi accepts that individuals' preferences may need to be laundered to some extent, he ignores the critical point that extended preferences need to be defined so as to "screen out" features of outcomes that are too remote from the subject's well-being.

One terminological point bears mention at the outset. A preference ranking of two items can be "strict" or "weak." To strictly prefer one item to another entails being in favor of the first—ranking it higher. To weakly prefer one item to another means strictly preferring the first or being indifferent between the two. Throughout the chapter, whenever I characterize someone as "preferring" one item to another (whether this is an ordinary preference regarding choices and outcomes, or an extended preference regarding life-histories), I mean a strict preference, except where I specifically characterize the preference as weak.[2]

---

[2] The concept of "weak preference" is particularly useful in articulating preference-based accounts of well-being in a compact yet rigorous fashion, and for this reason the concept appears most often at the end of the chapter, where I set forth my account.

I will also, frequently, refer to someone's "preferences," as opposed to his preference for one item over a second. By this, I mean his entire ranking structure, encompassing all his attitudes of strict preference, weak preference, and indifference between various pairs of items.

Finally, let me underscore that the analysis in this chapter is almost wholly independent of the argument, to be presented in Chapter 5, for a continuous prioritarian SWF. The aim, here, is to develop an account of well-being that, in any choice situation, will allow us to construct a set $\mathbf{U}$. The utility information in this set can then be coupled with any arbitrary SWF, be it continuous prioritarian, utilitarian, leximin, rank-weighted, or any other.[3]

I. WHAT IS WELL-BEING? PHILOSOPHICAL DEBATES

Well-being, at least for purposes of this book, is a *normative* concept. It figures, here, within a normative (in particular, a moral) theory, namely welfarism.

How is the normative concept of well-being best understood? This topic has been most rigorously addressed by philosophers. This section reviews the range of accounts of well-being proposed within the philosophical literature; shows how this diversity is mirrored in other scholarly fields where the normative concept of well-being plays a role; and suggests that diversity flows both from the first-order difficulty of reaching a point of reflective equilibrium regarding the nature of well-being, and from metaethical disputes.

In this section, I present and analyze philosophical disputes about the nature of well-being by focusing on what different philosophical schools say about the content of *intra*personal comparisons—namely, the conditions under which life-history $(x; i)$ is better for well-being than life-history $(y; i)$, i.e., the conditions under which one outcome, x, is better for the well-being of one particular subject, i, than another outcome, y. These differences, obviously, carry over to disagreements about the content of interpersonal comparisons. However, the very possibility of interpersonal

---

[3] My construction of $\mathbf{U}$ does implicitly presuppose that information about well-being differences is relevant to the SWF. This is true of many SWFs (including the utilitarian, rank-weighted, and continuous prioritarian SWFs), but not of the leximin SWF. If $\mathbf{U}$ were being constructed specifically for a leximin SWF, the aim would be to produce a $\mathbf{U}^k$ for each spectator k unique up to an increasing transformation, and across-person judgments (rather than self-interested and i-interested rankings of lotteries) might play a more substantial role. Still, $\mathbf{U}$ as constructed below can certainly be used by a leximin SWF.

What about the fact that I take each $\mathbf{U}^k$, constructed with reference to each spectator's self-interested preferences, i-interested preferences, and across-person judgments, and then "zero out" $\mathbf{U}^k$ so as to generate ratio information—even though ratio information is not relevant to various SWFs (in particular the leximin, rank-weighted, and utilitarian SWFs)? Here, it is not too hard to see that—if each $\mathbf{U}^k$ is unique up to a positive affine transformation—then such SWFs combined with a $\mathbf{U}^*$ created by merging non-zeroed-out sets $\mathbf{U}^k$ yield the very same ranking of outcomes as when merged with $\mathbf{U}$ as I construct it.

comparisons raises further and distinct difficulties, engaged in the next section. So as to avoid muddying the waters, this section generally focuses on the intrapersonal case.

A. Preferences, Mental States, and Objective Goods: Three Themes in the Philosophical Literature on Well-Being

Derek Parfit, in *Reasons and Persons,* writes that there are three plausible theories of well-being: a desire-fulfillment theory, a hedonistic theory, and an objective-list theory. Others have drawn similar taxonomies.[4] I suggest that it is most useful to think of desire (preferences), hedonic states (or, more generally, good and bad mental states), and objective goods as different possible *elements* of an account of well-being—rather than as the defining features of mutually exclusive accounts. A nuanced classification of theories of well-being should allow for hybrid accounts. For example, well-being might be analyzed in terms of preferences for mental states. Nor should we be too rigid in differentiating objective goods and preferences. For example, one plausible understanding of "objective goods" is that these are the items which individuals, under ideal conditions, converge in self-interestedly preferring.

Let us start with preferences. A preference is a *choice-relevant ranking*: a ranking of items of some sort, on the part of some person, that disposes her to make choices. A variety of kinds of items can be ranked by preferences. At a minimum, an individual can have preferences regarding *choices* (possible actions) and *outcomes.*

What it means to have a preference (a choice-relevant ranking) regarding choices is pretty straightforward: if I prefer action *a* to *b*, then I am disposed to choose *a* rather than *b* when both are on offer. In the case of preferences regarding outcomes, what this means is: I have an ordering of outcomes which, together with my beliefs about which outcomes the various actions available to me are more or less likely to yield, inclines me to select one of these actions.

That individuals can have preferences for both choices and outcomes is uncontroversial among philosophers and also among welfare economists.[5] These are what I shall term "ordinary" preferences. Later in this chapter, I will argue that an individual can have a preference regarding a third type of item—namely, a preference regarding a life-history. Preferences regarding life-histories—extended preferences—will be vital to explicating interpersonal comparisons. However, the concept of an extended

---

[4] For overviews of the philosophical literature on well-being, see Arneson (1999b, 2006); Griffin (1986, chs. 1–4); Parfit (1987, pp. 493–502); Scanlon (1998, pp. 108–143); Sumner (1996); Qizilbash (1998).

[5] Some welfare economists adopt the problematic view that an individual's choices perfectly reveal her preferences over outcomes—but it is certainly the standard position, at least within contemporary welfare economics, that an individual has preferences over outcomes (e.g., bundles of consumption goods) as well as choices. See Mas-Collel, Whinston, and Green (1995, chs. 1–3); Sen (1982, ch. 2).

preference does not figure much in the philosophical literature on well-being, and will not be discussed here. Insofar as this section discusses the various linkages that philosophers draw between preferences and well-being, I mean preferences for outcomes or preferences for choices.

It is standard in the literature to distinguish between an individual's actual preferences and her idealized preferences—between what the individual is in fact disposed to choose, and what she *would* be disposed to choose were she to have more information, be in a calm and deliberate state, and so forth. One subtlety, here, is that the very ascription of actual preferences to an individual entails her satisfying minimal rationality conditions. For example, imagine that Jim has an attitude of some sort regarding outcomes, connected to his choices, but this attitude fails a condition of asymmetry and fails a condition of transitivity. Jim has this attitude regarding the ordered pair of outcomes (x, y), but also regarding the ordered pair of outcomes (y, x); and although he has the attitude regarding the ordered pairs of outcomes (x, y) and (y, z), he lacks the attitude regarding the ordered pair of outcomes (x, z). Jim's attitude, presumably, is not a preference: because not asymmetric, it is not the attitude of strict preference; because intransitive, it is not the attitude of strict preference, weak preference, or indifference.

Notwithstanding this subtlety, the distinction between actual preferences and idealized preferences remains sensible. The minimal rationality conditions required even to have an actual preference are weak—so that it is perfectly intelligible to distinguish between an individual's actual preferences, and idealized, counterfactual preferences that meet stronger conditions of fuller information, fuller rationality, and so forth.

That the well-being realized by an individual in different outcomes depends on her preferences over those outcomes is a view adopted, not just by welfare economists, but also by a distinguished tradition within moral philosophy.[6] In his hugely influential early twentieth-century work, *The Method of Ethics*, Henry Sidgwick suggested that "a man's future good on the whole is what he would now desire and seek on the whole if all the consequences of all the different lines of conduct open to him were accurately foreseen and adequately realized in imagination at the present point of time."[7] Rawls' *Theory of Justice*, building upon Sidgwick's suggestion, provides a preference-based analysis of an individual's lifetime well-being. The best life-history for a person is the one that accords with a rational plan of life, namely "the plan that would be decided upon as the outcome of careful reflection in which the [individual]

---

[6] For reviews (as well as critical analysis) of this preferentialist tradition, see generally Brink (2008); Loeb (1995); Rosati (1995); Sobel (1994); D. Zimmerman (2003). On idealization, see also Enoch (2005).

[7] Sidgwick (1981, pp. 111–112). Sidgwick ultimately concludes that a rational individual's well-informed preferences focus on his own mental states—and thus analyzes well-being both in terms of preference satisfaction and in terms of mental states. See ibid., pp. 391–407; Sumner (1996, pp. 83–92).

reviewed, in the light of all the relevant facts, what it would be like to carry out [different possible plans] and thereby ascertained the course of action that would best realize his more fundamental desires."[8] Richard Brandt argues that it is rational for an individual to pursue the satisfaction of those of his desires that would survive a process which Brandt terms "cognitive psychotherapy."

> This whole process of confronting desires with relevant information, by repeatedly representing it, in an ideally vivid way, and at an appropriate time, I call *cognitive psychotherapy*. I call it so because the process relies simply upon reflection on available information, without influence by prestige of someone, use of evaluative language, extrinsic reward or punishment, or use of artificially induced feeling-states like relaxation. It is *value-free reflection*.

Brandt goes on to suggest that an individual's well-being might consist in what the individual self-interestedly prefers after "cognitive psychotherapy."[9]

One potential obstacle around which full-information preferentialist accounts of well-being need to navigate is this: what is good for someone who lacks knowledge of certain facts may be different from what would be good for him, were he to possess that knowledge. Drinking vintage wine rather than the ordinary stuff may only be better for me if I drink it with sufficient knowledge to be able to appreciate its quality. Peter Railton, sensitive to this point, suggests that the well-being of an individual (whatever his actual informational state) is determined by what his idealized, fully informed self (taking account of the individual's actual informational state) would want him to want.

> [An] individual's good consists in what he would want himself to want, or to pursue, were he to contemplate his present situation from a standpoint fully and vividly informed about himself and his circumstances, and entirely free of cognitive error or lapses of instrumental rationality.[10]

As these quotations suggest, philosophers who analyze well-being in terms of preference satisfaction tend to build in strong idealization conditions, requiring that the relevant preferences be very fully informed and meet high standards of rational deliberation. This is an important difference between welfare economics and the preferentialist strain within philosophical scholarship about well-being. Welfare

---

[8] Rawls (1999b, p. 366).

[9] Brandt (1998, pp. 113, 328–331). To be clear, Brandt does not in fact embrace this preference-based account of well-being, at least for moral purposes, given his concerns about changing preferences. See ibid., ch. 13. However his careful elaboration of a preference-based account of *rationality* is generally seen as a landmark in the rigorous development of preferentialism about well-being. See sources cited above, n. 6.

[10] Railton (1986a, p. 16). See also Railton (1986b).

economists require that preferences satisfy basic rationality conditions—the traditional such conditions within economics are that an individual's preferences regarding outcomes should be a complete quasiordering and that her preferences regarding choices should comply with EU theory—but economists typically do not assert that the preferences relevant to well-being are idealized in any more robust sense.[11]

A second theme that occurs repeatedly within the philosophical literature is the connection between well-being and good or bad mental states. Jeremy Bentham, famously, saw well-being as the occurrence of pleasurable mental states and the avoidance of painful mental states. A "pleasure," for Bentham, was a mental state with the property of feeling good; a "pain," a mental state with the property of feeling bad. Other philosophers have concurred with Bentham in linking well-being to mental states without sharing his view that the welfare-relevant attribute of a mental state consists in how it feels. John Stuart Mill, for example, analyzed well-being in terms of the occurrence of *desirable* mental states.[12] The contemporary philosopher Fred Feldman defends an account of well-being that he terms "attitudinal hedonism." He distinguishes between "sensory pleasures" and "attitudinal pleasures" and analyzes well-being in terms of the latter.

> A person takes attitudinal pleasure in some state of affairs if he enjoys it, is pleased about it, is glad that it is happening, is delighted by it. So, for example, suppose that you are a peace-loving person. Suppose you take note of the fact that there are no wars going on. The world is at peace. Suppose you are pleased about this. You are glad that the world is at peace. Then you have taken attitudinal pleasure in a certain fact—the fact that the world is at peace. Attitudinal pleasures are always directed onto objects, just as beliefs and hopes and fears are directed onto objects. This is one respect in which they are different from sensory pleasures. Another difference is that attitudinal pleasures need not have any 'feel.' We know we have them not by sensation, but in the same way (whatever it may be) that we know when we believe something, or hope for it, or fear that it might happen.[13]

Although Feldman does in fact describe his view of well-being as a "hedonistic" view, that term is potentially misleading because it suggests that mental states make a difference to well-being in virtue of how they feel—which clearly is *not* Feldman's view. A more helpful way of describing what Bentham and Mill have in common with each other, and with a number of contemporary philosophers of well-being (including not only Feldman, but also Wayne Sumner, Mark Bernstein, and

---

[11] For the standard economic account of rational preferences regarding outcomes, see, e.g., Mas-Colell, Whinston, and Green (1995, pp. 6–7, 41–45); and for EU theory, see ibid., ch. 6. Notably, Harsanyi—both economist and philosopher—does idealize preferences. See Harsanyi (1982, pp. 54–56).

[12] See Sumner (1996, pp. 83–92).

[13] Feldman (2006b, p. 56).

Roger Crisp[14]), is that the account of well-being proposed by each of these philosophers focuses on the occurrence or nonoccurrence of a certain kind or kinds of mental states as the basic source of well-being. This more generic characterization of such accounts encompasses the full range of plausible views about what the well-being relevant properties of mental states are.

The reader might, quite understandably, find it confusing that I distinguish between "preferences" and "mental states" as two distinct types of elements in accounts of well-being. Isn't a preference a mental state? For our purposes—namely, seeing what different philosophical views suggest about how to rank life-histories—the difference between a "preferentialist" and "mental state" approach can be framed as follows. What is it about life-history $(x; i)$ that makes it better or worse for well-being than life-history $(y; i)$? One type of answer, the preferentialist answer, points to i's preferences as between the outcomes that figure in these life-histories.[15] It says: $(x; i)$ is better than $(y; i)$ because i prefers outcome x to outcome y; or would prefer x after cognitive psychotherapy; or i's idealized counterpart would prefer outcome x; or something like that. A different type of answer, the mental-state answer, points to the mental states that i experiences in x and y. It says: $(x; i)$ is better than $(y; i)$ because, in some respect, individual i's mental states in x are different from his mental states in y.

A further subtlety, which the discussion has already illustrated, is that a given account of well-being can rely upon *both* these elements: it can make *both* preference satisfaction, *and* the occurrence of a certain type of mental state, a basis for the well-being ranking of $(x; i)$ as against $(y; i)$. Consider a view which says that $(x; i)$ is at least as good for well-being as $(y; i)$ iff i weakly prefers his mental states in x to his mental states in y in virtue of the intrinsic properties of his mental states in both outcomes.[16] Such an approach *does* make the difference between $(x; i)$ and $(y; i)$ depend on the mental states that i experiences in the two outcomes. Indeed, it draws

---

[14] See Bernstein (1998); Crisp (2006, ch. 4); Sumner (1996, ch. 6).

[15] Another kind of answer, also preferentialist, becomes possible once we have the idea of extended preferences in hand. It makes the ranking of $(x; i)$ and $(y; i)$ depend on everyone's extended preferences between the two life-histories. The account of well-being I defend later in the chapter adopts this answer.

[16] We can classify mental states in terms of their intrinsic properties or in terms of their relational properties. Intrinsically, a true belief and a false belief with the very same content are the same; relationally, they are not. The intrinsic properties of mental states are a matter of what is "in the head." (More precisely, the intrinsic property of a mental state is (1) an intrinsic property of the person who possesses the mental state which (2) is a mentalistic property. Arguably, it is not strictly correct to ascribe properties to a mental state, which is itself a property of a person rather than a separate entity.) A theory that makes the well-being ranking of $(x; i)$ and $(y; i)$ depend on i's mental states in outcomes x and y may classify mental states solely in terms of their intrinsic properties, or also in terms of their relational properties. Robert Nozick's famous "experience machine" hypothetical is meant to suggest that well-being is not solely a matter of the intrinsic properties of mental states. See Nozick (1974, pp. 42–45). Sumner, sensitive to this point, analyzes well-being in terms of "authentic happiness."

a very strong link between well-being and mental states. According to this theory, well-being *supervenes* on mental states.[17] On this theory, if i's mental states in x and y are intrinsically identical, then x and y are equally good for i's well-being. Yet the theory also makes the well-being ranking of $(x; i)$ and $(y; i)$ depend on i's preferences as between x and y.

On the other hand, these two potential determinants of well-being—preference satisfaction and mental states—are distinct. It is certainly possible for an account of well-being to make the ranking of $(x; i)$ and $(y; i)$ depend upon i's mental states in the two outcomes that figure in these life-histories, without appealing to i's preferences between the outcomes. Such would be a view that appeals to "pleasure" and "pain" understood in strictly sensationalist terms, rather than as preferred or dispreferred mental states.

It is also certainly possible for an account of well-being to ground the ranking of $(x; i)$ and $(y; i)$ in i's preferences between the outcomes, without drawing a strong link to i's mental states in the two outcomes. A critical point, here, is that a preference is simply a choice-relevant ranking. The content of a preference—what it is about outcomes that determine an individual's preference ranking—can be any feature of outcomes.[18] Individual i can prefer x to y in virtue of differences between the two outcomes other than differences between his own mental states. Therefore, an account that defines well-being in terms of preference satisfaction (be they actual or fully informed preferences) without restricting the content of the preferences will

See Sumner (1996, ch. 6). As between two happiness states that are intrinsically identical, one may be authentic, the other inauthentic.

[17] To say that well-being supervenes on certain properties is to say that, if individual i has the very same properties of that type in x and in y, then $(x; i)$ and $(y; i)$ are equally good for well-being. There must be some difference in the individual's properties, of the specified type, for there to be a well-being difference. In discussing *mental-state* supervenience, throughout this chapter, I mean supervenience on the intrinsic properties of mental states. An account of well-being incorporates a mental-state supervenience requirement if it says: If i's mental states in x and y are identical in their intrinsic properties, $(x; i)$ and $(y; i)$ are equally good. Whether well-being supervenes on mental states in this sense has been a salient issue in the philosophical literature, as crystallized by Nozick's experience machine.

[18] It might be argued that an individual cannot prefer x to y if the two outcomes are identical in terms of all features that the individual can causally influence—because, if so, there is no possible choice situation where the ranking would rationally motivate the individual to choose one action rather than another. I am inclined, not to accept this restriction on the content of preferences, but instead to allow an individual's preference ranking to include any arbitrary ranking of any arbitrary outcome set. Instead, it seems to me, causal decision theory—a set of principles for moving *from* an individual's ranking of an outcome set, *to* a ranking of the choices available to the individual—is the appropriate mechanism for taking account of what the individual can causally influence. See Chapter 7.

However, a full discussion of causal decision theory is well beyond the scope of this book. Here, I will simply note that, even if a "causal influence" restriction on the scope of preferences is accepted, individuals can causally influence—and thus prefer—many features of outcomes other than their own mental states.

not necessarily satisfy a mental-state supervenience requirement, and it may at the extreme reach the verdict that whether a given individual i is better or worse off with $(x; i)$ as compared to $(y; i)$ does not depend at all on his mental states.[19]

Just as the preferentialist theme within philosophical scholarship about well-being is echoed in economics, so too is the mentalistic theme. A burgeoning body of work within economics and psychology—the so-called literature on "happiness" or "subjective well-being"—employs survey data to measure individuals' mental states, and then correlates the answers with other individual characteristics. The typical surveys employed by scholars working in this area ask respondents to quantify their "happiness" or "life satisfaction" on a numerical scale. Although the normative commitments of those involved in this literature are diverse, a number of leading practitioners do seem to adopt a substantially or even exclusively mentalistic concept of individual well-being (for example, the view that well-being is a matter of experiencing positive affective states, avoiding negative affective states, and having a sense of satisfaction with life); and do seem to adopt the view that government should orient policy around producing individual well-being thus understood.[20]

A third philosophical approach about well-being, which Parfit refers to as the "objective list" approach, is to furnish some list of "goods" that are seen as intrinsic constituents of well-being. A leading modern example of this approach is John Finnis, who argues that life, knowledge, play, aesthetic experience, sociability, practical reasonableness, and religion are the basic forms of human good.[21] Finnis states

---

[19] Whether such an account satisfies a mental-state supervenience requirement, for a particular outcome set and population, will depend on the preferences of those individuals regarding that outcome set. But clearly a preference-based view that doesn't restrict the content of preferences will not *necessarily* satisfy a mental-state supervenience requirement. Imagine that individual i's actual preferences regarding outcomes, as well as his fully informed and rational preferences, are in part driven by features of outcomes other than the intrinsic properties of his own mental states. (For example, individual i might have a preference for being physically healthy, a preference which he retains under conditions of full information and rationality. Thus he prefers x to y because his physical body is healthier in outcome x, even though his mental states are intrinsically identical in the two outcomes. On an unrestricted preference-based view, $(x; i)$ is better than $(y; i)$.) At the extreme, individual i's actual and fully informed preferences may be largely or even exclusively driven by features of outcomes other than his own mental states. (For example, individual i is an artist who cares only about producing a work of beauty, regardless of the happiness, sadness, or other mental states that producing this work may cause him to feel.) Note that, even in this extreme case, it is an overstatement to say that individual i's well-being does not depend on his mental states. After all, a preference is a mental state. On the view under consideration, the basis for $(x; i)$ being better than $(y; i)$ is that individual i has a preference ranking and x is better than y in terms of that ranking. The point, rather, is that it is possible for an individual to have a preference ranking of outcomes such that what determines whether x is higher ranked than y has nothing to do with the individual's mental states in x and y.

[20] See generally Diener and Seligman (2004); Diener et al. (1999); Frey (2008); Kahneman, Diener, and Schwarz (1999); Kahneman and Sugden (2005); Layard (2005); Van Praag and Ferrer-i-Carbonell (2004).

[21] See Finnis (1988, ch. 4).

quite explicitly that how fully an individual realizes these goods is not merely a matter of what mental states that individual has.[22] Furthermore, whether an individual more or less fully attains these goods is not reducible to the satisfaction of his actual preferences. It is clearly *not* true that $(x; i)$ is better than $(y; i)$, in light of Finnis' list of goods, just in case i actually prefers outcome x to y. Finnis underscores the difference between realizing objective goods and preference-satisfaction in his discussion of the objective good of "knowledge."

> Nor can one validly infer the value of knowledge from the fact (if fact it be) that "all men desire to know." The *universality* of a desire is not a sufficient basis for inferring that the object of that desire is really desirable, objectively good. Nor is such a basis afforded by the fact that the desire or inclination manifests, or is part of, a *deep* structure shaping the human mind, or by the fact that the desire, or the structure, is *ineradicable*, or by the fact that in whole or part the desire is (or is not) *common* to all animals, or by the fact it is (or is not) *peculiar* to human beings. . . .
>
> It is obvious that a man who [possesses knowledge] *is* better off (other things being equal) than a man who [doesn't], not just in this particular case or that, but in all cases, as such, universally, and *whether I like it or not*. Knowledge is better than ignorance. Am I not compelled to admit it, willy nilly? It matters not that I may be feeling incurious myself. For the understanding affirmation [of the value of knowledge] is neither a reference to nor an expression of any desire or urge or inclination of mine. Nor is it merely a reference to (or implied presupposition of) any desires that my fellows happen to have. . . . It is a rational judgment about a general form of human well-being, about the fulfillment of a human potentiality. As such, it has, in its own way, the peremptoriness of all other rational judgments. It constitutes a critique of my passing likes and dislikes.[23]

Other contemporary philosophers who offer lists of well-being constituents that are "objective" in this sense—neither reducing to an individual's mental states, nor to the satisfaction of that individual's actual preferences—are Martha Nussbaum, George Sher, James Griffin, and Richard Kraut. Nussbaum argues that the central human capabilities are: life; bodily health; bodily integrity; the senses, imagination, and thought; emotions; practical reason; affiliation; other species; play; and control over one's environment. Sher endorses a list suggested by Parfit: moral goodness; rational activity; the development of one's abilities; having children and being a good parent; knowledge; and the awareness of true beauty. Griffin's is: accomplishment; "the components of human existence" (roughly, autonomy and physical integrity); understanding; enjoyment; deep personal relations. Kraut argues that

---

[22] See ibid., pp. 95–97.
[23] Ibid., pp. 66, 72.

the good for a human being consists of "the exercise of cognitive, social, affective, and physical skills."[24]

Although the philosophers I have just described *do* characterize an individual's well-being in terms that reduce it neither to the individual's mental states, nor to his actual preference satisfaction, it would be incorrect to say that mental states and preference satisfaction are wholly absent from these philosophers' accounts. First, although the accounts (as I read them) do not satisfy a mental-state supervenience requirement—each would endorse the proposition that $(x; i)$ can be better for well-being than $(y; i)$ even though the intrinsic properties of individual i's mental states are identical in the two outcomes—they all make the occurrence of different types of mental states *one* of the significant sources of well-being.

Second, objective-good accounts of well-being do not necessarily deny any link between well-being and preference satisfaction. Sher analyzes objective goods as those items that advance "near-universal, near-unavoidable goals."[25] A goal is a choice-connected attitude which is similar, if not identical, to a preference.[26] Griffin offers a different kind of nexus between objective goods and preferences, as we will discuss in greater detail below. On Griffin's view, a normal human being who recognizes that one of his life-histories is objectively better than another will come to prefer it.[27] Other objective-good theorists, too, might be happy to acknowledge this

---

[24] See Nussbaum (2000, pp. 78–80; 2006, pp. 76–78); Sher (1997, p. 201, quoting Parfit [1987, p. 499]); Griffin (1997, pp. 29–30); Kraut (2007, p. 145). Sher (1997, pp. 212–218) suggests that his list might be augmented, and in particular proposes adding "decency and good taste" as an additional item.

The reader should note that Nussbaum (2000, p. 77) sees her list as a "partial, not a comprehensive, conception of the good life"—a selected list of the elements of well-being supportable by an overlapping consensus, and providing the basis for constitutional guarantees, rather than a full, freestanding, theory of well-being. Still, for Nussbaum, the items on the list *are* constitutive of well-being: "The central capabilities are not just instrumental to further pursuits: they are held to have value in themselves, in making the life that includes them fully human." Ibid., p. 74. Moreover, these well-being components *are* "objective" in the sense I have described (not reducible to an individual's preference satisfaction, or to his mental states). Finally, although Nussbaum characterizes her list as "partial," it is longer and more detailed than Finnis', Sher's, Griffin's, or Kraut's lists. It is therefore plausible to include Nussbaum as an important example of a contemporary philosopher who defends an objective-list account of well-being.

[25] Sher (1997, p. 229 and generally ch. 9).

[26] I will not attempt to analyze the goal/preference distinction here, but it is clear that goals, like preferences, are conceptually connected to motivation and action. If an individual has a goal, then she is disposed to make choices that realize the goal. See, e.g., ibid., p. 236.

[27] Griffin in *Value Judgement* (1997) sees a strong link between *perceptions of well-being* and *motivation*. The items on his list of goods are those which individuals, under good informational conditions, and reasoning in a characteristically human way, perceive as valuable for humans. But such "perception" also brings in its train a preference or desire for the good. See below, pp. 183–184. Although desires figure less centrally in *Value Judgment* than in Griffin's earlier work, *Well-Being: Its Meaning,*

sort of motivational connection between recognizing an objective good and developing a preference for it.[28]

Pulling all this together, we might say that the philosophers who have presented objective-good accounts of well-being never reduce an individual's attainment of objective goods to his mental states, to his actual preference satisfaction, or even to the satisfaction of his idealized preferences, at least if the idealizing conditions are not designed to screen out idiosyncratic preferences. Even those objective-good philosophers who draw an explicit link between objective goods and preferences, such as Griffin and Sher, clearly deny that individual i's possession of a fully informed but idiosyncratic preference for x over y (a preference which is not widely shared) suffices to make $(x; i)$ objectively better than $(y; i)$.[29] On the other hand, the caveat that objective goods are not to be analyzed in terms of actual or idiosyncratic preferences allows for various *other* kinds of linkages between objective goods and preferences.

It is also worth clarifying the connection between objective goods and *human nature*. The idea of using human nature to specify a good human life goes back to Aristotle. The best developed contemporary account of this sort is Thomas Hurka's. Hurka identifies an individual's good with the development of those attributes which are "essential to humans and conditioned on their being living things": having a living body, and having "theoretical and practical rationality," i.e., the capacity for forming and acting on beliefs and intentions.[30]

This human-essence criterion yields an intuitively jarring account of objective goods. As Hurka freely admits, the theory "does not find intrinsic value in pleasure, not even pleasure in what is good, nor does it find intrinsic disvalue in pain."[31] Nor does it value happiness or enjoyment.[32] Finally, it values love and friendship, not as a source of emotional support, but because these are occasions for *teamwork*: for formulating and acting on goals with others.[33] But, intuitively, family relations and deep friendships that are not particularly collaborative are (or at least can be) much more important for well-being than relationships with mere collaborators.

Measurement and Moral Importance (Griffin 1986), his most recent account of well-being still retains a nexus to desire-satisfaction.

[28] See Finnis (1988, pp. 70–71). Cf. Nussbaum (2000, ch. 2), discussing the epistemic and (limited) justificatory connection between preference satisfaction and capabilities.

[29] Sher, again, says that the goals which objective goods realize must be "near-universal." Griffin stresses that the elements of well-being are those items which are seen as valuable by normal humans, reasoning in a characteristically human way. Reciprocally, he denies that something which some particular individual prefers under full information, and without logical error, is necessarily valuable for that person. See Griffin (1997, pp. 22–23).

[30] Hurka (1996, pp. 17, 37–40).

[31] Ibid, p. 190.

[32] See Sumner (1996, p. 195).

[33] See Hurka (1996, pp. 134–136). Hurka here characterizes the emotional support provided by friendship as merely "instrumentally" valuable.

However, it bears emphasis that the (implausible) strategy of analyzing well-being as the realization of those particular human capacities which are part of a human's essential nature is simply one *kind* of objective-good approach.[34] An account of well-being is characterizable as an objective-good account—I have suggested—if it does not reduce an individual's well-being to his mental states, or to the satisfaction of that particular individual's preferences (even idealized). An account might have these features *without* identifying objective goods as those goods that realize human nature. Indeed, the various prominent objective-good theorists I mentioned earlier—Finnis, Nussbaum, Sher, Griffin, Kraut—do *not* specify objective goods along the lines that Hurka pursues.[35] And the account of well-being that I will ultimately defend in this chapter—analyzing well-being in terms of individuals' fully informed, fully rational, convergent extended preferences—*is* indeed characterizable as an objective-good account, but it certainly does not use human nature to identify the sources of well-being.

So much for the philosophical literature on objective goods. The proposition that well-being is a matter of objective goods is also reflected in much scholarship outside philosophy. Amartya Sen's theoretical work on "capabilities" and "functionings" seems to involve an objective-good account of well-being, in the sense just characterized.[36] Sen's work, in turn, along with Martha Nussbaum's, has been the direct inspiration for a large body of recent empirical work in development economics and other areas, which seeks to measure how individuals are faring with respect to a range of capabilities/functionings—as opposed to focusing on individuals' happiness/life-satisfaction or income (income being the traditional measure used by economists who equate well-being and preference satisfaction, as in cost-benefit analysis, the measurement of income inequality, or the measurement of income poverty).[37] I think it fair to say that a kind of objective-good approach to well-being seems to be characteristic of much of this capabilities/functionings literature. So, too, is it characteristic of a different and somewhat older literature—the literature

---

[34] Actually, Hurka's theory is not intended as a theory of well-being. He is careful to distinguish between a good life and well-being, and claims to be analyzing only the former. See ibid., pp. 37–38. But the very fact that Hurka draws this distinction, and the particular list of goods he generates, suggests that using human nature to identify a list of the sources of human well-being is problematic.

[35] As already noted, Sher instead derives his list of objective goods from universal human goals, and Griffin from humans' normal judgments of well-being. Finnis (1988, chs. 3–4) frankly declines to offer a unifying rationale for his list, arguing that they are all self-evidently good. Nussbaum (2000, pp. 70–74; 2006, pp. 179–182) suggests that the various "capabilities" she describes all enable humans to lead a life of "dignity" and "worth." Finally, Kraut appeals to human development and "flourishing."

[36] See Chapter 1, n. 61.

[37] See, e.g., Alkire (2002); Canoy, Lerais, and Schokkaert (2010); Kakwani and Silber (2007); Kuklys (2005); and the symposium on capabilities in *Social Indicators Research* (2005, vol. 74, pp. 1–260).

regarding "social indicators," in which various indices of the "quality of life" are constructed and empirically deployed.[38]

B. Why the Debate?

For purposes of this book, an account of well-being is an element within a *moral* decisional framework. I have adopted a reflective-equilibrium methodology for constructing this framework. In particular, then, an attractive account of well-being—for purposes of this book—is one that readers can endorse in reflective equilibrium.

But reaching a point of reflective equilibrium with respect to the nature of well-being is *difficult*. It is difficult to construct an account of well-being which satisfies various basic principles that seem intuitively attractive, and which is also consistent with intuitions about concrete cases. This difficulty is *evidenced* by the philosophical debates about well-being and, indeed, helps *explain* these debates—since many of the participants, implicitly or explicitly, are trying themselves to reach a point of reflective equilibrium.

One very plausible basic principle about well-being is that it has *critical* force. In other words, an individual can be mistaken about his own well-being. Although many economists may reject the principle, it is one which most philosophers of well-being are prepared to endorse. This is true even of philosophers who make preference satisfaction a central element of their account. For example, Railton writes:

> [On one account, to] call something part of someone's intrinsic good [is] to say that he desires it for its own sake. This theory has many virtues: it is uncomplicated, nonpaternalistic, and epistemically as straightforward as the idea of desire. . . .
>
> Yet this theory is deeply unsatisfactory, since it seems incapable of capturing important elements of the critical and self-critical character of value judgments. On this theory one can, of course, criticize any particular current desire on the grounds that it ill fits with other, more numerous or more powerful current desires on one's part, or (if it is an instrumental desire) on the grounds that it is the result of a miscalculation with the information one has. But this hardly exhausts the range of assessment. Sometimes we wish to raise questions about the intrinsic desirability of the things that now are the main focus of our desires, even after any mistakes in calculation have been corrected. This appears to be a specific function of the vocabulary of goodness and badness, as distinct from the vocabulary of desire and aversion.[39]

Note, however, that the idealizing conditions offered by Railton—and by other leading examples of philosophical preferentialists about well-being, such as Sidgwick,

---

[38] See, e.g., Grasso and Canova (2008); Noll (2004).
[39] Railton (1986a, p. 11) (emphasis omitted). See also Brandt (1998, ch. 6).

Rawls, and Brandt—are *procedural*. By this term I mean conditions such as having good information; having preferences over outcomes which meet formal requirements such as being asymmetric or transitive; having coherence between first- and higher-order preferences; having preferences over choices which are linked to preferences over outcomes consistent with formal requirements, such as the requirements of EU theory; reasoning in a manner which is consistent with the norms of deductive logic; or having a certain kind of emotional state, e.g., a calm state suitable for deliberation.

Intuitively, there is a difference between such procedural conditions regarding idealized preferences and *historical* conditions (such as requiring that the holder of the preferences not have been the subject of certain kinds of parental or social influence); and both, in turn, are different from *substantive* conditions on preference formation, such as stipulating that a fully rational preference cannot be an intrinsic preference to eat a saucer of mud, to count blades of grass, or to be happy except on Tuesdays. Let us try to capture this difference by saying that: Procedural conditions for idealizing preferences depend on the occurrent mental state of the holder of the preference and are content-neutral (i.e., are logically consistent with every possible ranking of outcomes). Historical conditions depend on the past history of the holder of the preference and are content-neutral. Substantive conditions are not content-neutral.[40]

A substantial number of philosophers suggest that defining well-being in terms of procedurally idealized preferences is insufficient to capture the critical force of well-being. This is true, in particular, of leading philosophers within the objective-good camp. For example, Griffin writes:

> [A] particularly irrational desire—say, one planted deep when one was young—might well survive criticism by facts and logic, and its mere endurance is less than it takes for its fulfillment to make one better off. For instance, I might always wish to hog the limelight and have learned from long experience, perhaps even learned deeply from years of psychoanalysis, how this harms my life. But I might, none the less, still want to hog it. I might not react appropriately, or strongly enough, to what I have learned.[41]

---

[40] On the distinction between procedural and non-procedural accounts of rational preferences, see Hooker and Streumer (2004). See also Brink (2008, p. 27), discussing "purely formal" and "content-neutral" idealizations of preferences. The examples of a preference for mud or a preference that is sensitive to the day of the week are taken, respectively, from Anscombe and Parfit, as discussed in Hooker and Streumer (2004). The example of a preference for counting blades of grass is Rawls' (although Rawls himself does *not* use it to argue for a non-procedural account of rational preferences). See Rawls (1999b, pp. 379–380). Although Rawls does discuss the so-called "Aristotelian principle," he sees this principle as a feature of normal human motivation (see ibid., p. 375), not a substantive condition that a rational life-plan or a good life must satisfy. See ibid., p. 372 ("the definition of the good is purely formal").

[41] Griffin (1997, p. 22).

Richard Arneson argues that the following point is the "decisive objection" against informed-desire accounts of well-being.

> [T]he essence of the informed-desire view is that what the process of becoming fully informed and critically reflecting causes one to desire for its own sake is good for one. . . . But nothing bars this casual process from generating outcomes in a way that does not intuitively confer any desirability on the resultant basic desires. It might simply be a brute psychological fact about me that if I were to become fully informed about grapes, this process would set off a chemical process in my brain that would lead me to crave counting blades of grass on courthouse lawns as my primary life aim. This would seem to be an oddity of my brain, not an indicator of my true well-being. If this were true of everyone, not just me, the same point would still hold. The informed-desire theories purport to establish that a certain causal process confers desirability; but the characterization of the causal process does not secure this result, and it does not seem that it could be altered to guarantee the right result.[42]

Amartya Sen has famously argued that an account of well-being needs to be sensitive to the problem of adaptive preferences.

> A person who has had a life of misfortune, with very little opportunities, and rather little hope, may be more easily reconciled to deprivations than others reared in more fortunate and affluent circumstances. The metric of happiness may, therefore, distort the extent of deprivation, in a specific and biased way. The hopeless beggar, the precarious landless labourer, the dominated housewife, the hardened unemployed or the over-exhausted coolie may all take pleasures in small mercies, and manage to suppress intense suffering for the necessity of continuing survival, but it would be ethically deeply mistaken to attach a correspondingly small value to the loss of their well-being because of this survival strategy. The same problem arises with the other interpretation of utility, namely, desire-fulfillment, since the hopelessly deprived lack the courage to desire much, and their deprivations are muted and deadened in the scale of desire-fulfillment.[43]

This observation, too, provides a critique of procedural idealization. An individual's history and socialization might be such that she has adapted to a life which seems to furnish relatively little well-being, and yet which she prefers—even with good information, reasoning calmly, having formally coherent preferences, and so forth.[44]

In sum, the platitude that well-being has critical force pushes us away from an actual-preference account of well-being, and toward an account that adds procedural idealizing conditions or even stronger idealizing conditions.

---

[42] Arneson (1999b, p. 134).

[43] Sen (1987a, pp. 45–46).

[44] For other critiques of an analysis of well-being in terms of procedurally idealized preferences, see Nussbaum (2000, ch. 2); Sher (1997, ch. 8); sources cited above, n. 6.

Unfortunately, this platitude is in some tension with a second one: that well-being has *motivational* force. If individual *i* is not, at some level, disposed to choose outcome *x* over outcome *y*, then it is counterintuitive to say that individual *i* is better off with life-history (*x*; *i*) as opposed to (*y*; *i*). This principle should seem plausible, I suggest, independent of a more generic principle that moral considerations generally have motivational pull. Many metaethicists, so-called "internalists" about morality, adopt this more generic principle. But the platitude I am describing here involves "internalism" (of some sort) about *well-being*, which does not entail internalism about morality more generally—and indeed, I think, is intuitively more compelling than internalism about morality generally.[45] Imagine that I feel no inclination toward outcome *x* as opposed to *y*; it exerts no motivational pull on me, even when I am vividly informed about the two outcomes, think long and hard about them, and so forth. How, then, can *x* be better than *y for me*?

The following feature of well-being is worth noting at this point. Well-being entails goodness "for" the subject. Individual *i* realizes more well-being in outcome *x* than *y* iff outcome *x* is better *for individual i* than outcome *y*. Moreover, one outcome's being better *for* an individual than another outcome is not just a matter of the first outcome being better than the second in virtue of some attribute of that individual. For example, outcome *x* may be more beautiful than outcome *y*, in virtue of the fact that Jim is more beautiful in *x* than *y*, but this doesn't entail that *x* is better *for* Jim than *y*. (Jim's beauty may have no resonance for Jim: he may be indifferent to it, not have invested effort in producing it, etc.) Admittedly, what exactly it means for an outcome to be better for an individual is elusive. But one aspect of the "good-for" relation (at least in the case of persons, as opposed to other well-being subjects) is the tie to motivation. Some outcome is not better for a person unless she is disposed to choose it (at some level).[46]

An actual-preference account of well-being gives insufficient critical force to well-being, but it has the great virtue of according with the motivational platitude. Philosophers who link well-being to *idealized* preferences presumably hope to satisfy the motivational platitude while also bolstering well-being's critical force. Railton stresses the motivational force of well-being when he writes:

> Is it true that all normative judgments must find an internal resonance in those to whom they are applied? While I do not find this thesis convincing as a claim about all species of normative assessment, it does seem to me to capture an important feature of the concept

[45] This is not to say that internalism about morality lacks appeal. (Indeed, I reduce morality to fairness, and endorse internalism about fairness, see Chapter 1, pp. 7–8; Chapter 5, pp. 316–317.) However, internalism about well-being is, intuitively, even more compelling than internalism about morality.

[46] The propositions that well-being involves goodness *for* the subject and that well-being has motivational force are widely discussed in the literature. See, e.g., Brink (2008); Griffin (1997, pp. 32–36); Kagan (1992); Rosati (1996, 2006, 2008); Sumner (1996, ch. 2); as well as the quotation from Railton immediately below. Cf. Arneson (1999b), rejecting a motivational requirement.

of intrinsic value to say that what is intrinsically valuable for a person must have a connection with what he would find in some degree compelling or attractive, at least if he were rational and aware. It would be an intolerably alienated conception of someone's good to imagine that it might fail in any such way to engage him.[47]

It is trivially true that there is a link between *idealized* preferences and motivation under *idealized* conditions. A preference just *is* a choice disposition, and so the premise that I would prefer x to y under conditions C implies that, under conditions C, I would be disposed to choose x over y. Interestingly, however, an ideal-preference account may also have the upshot that well-being has wider motivational force— that it has force both under idealized conditions, and under less-ideal conditions that individuals in the actual world actually attain with some frequency. Railton suggests that individuals, under ordinary conditions, are normally motivated by knowledge of what they would want for themselves under the idealized conditions that he outlines: "[T]his notion of someone's good [which Railton has argued for] satisfies an appropriate internalist constraint: . . .[T]he views we would have were we to become free of present defects in knowledge or rationality would induce an internal resonance in us *as we now are*."[48] Brandt makes a similar claim: that for an individual under nonideal conditions to know that some of his desires would be lost under the ideal conditions of "cognitive psychotherapy" normally motivates the individual under nonideal conditions.

> By definition 'irrational' desires are one and all ones that the person would lose if he repeatedly reminded himself of known facts about himself or the world. . . .
>
> The proposal here is that awareness of the fact that one has irrational desires works in a way similar to awareness that one has incoherent beliefs or unjustified fears. One is made uncomfortable by the awareness, and is motivated to remove its source. I am not offering any reason why this should be the case. I am asserting that, as a fact, people. . . . do dislike having to think that their desires are irrational in my sense. . . .[49]

More generically, the claim that an individual, under ordinary conditions, is motivated by a belief about what he prefers under idealized conditions is a central aspect of Michael Smith's ideal-approval account of moral facts.[50]

A third basic principle which has intuitive force, and which anyone constructing an account of well-being should aim to satisfy, might be termed the principle of *non-remoteness*. An individual's well-being must not be too remote from him. Parfit stresses this point in a well-known example.

---

[47] Railton (1986a, p. 9).

[48] Ibid. p. 17 (emphasis added).

[49] Brandt (1998, pp. 156–157).

[50] See Smith (1994).

Suppose that I meet a stranger who has what is believed to be a fatal disease. My sympathy is aroused, and I strongly want this stranger to be cured. We never meet again. Later, unknown to me, this stranger is cured. On the [actual-preference theory of well-being], this event is good for me, and makes my life go better. This is not plausible. We should reject this theory.[51]

Many other contemporary philosophers of well-being concur with Parfit that a simple preference-based account of well-being—along the lines of $(x; i)$ is better for well-being than $(y; i)$ iff individual i prefers outcome x to outcome y—is problematic because such an account allows events that are too remote from the holder of the preference to benefit him. For example, Darwall writes:

> There are many things I rationally take an interest in, such as the survival of the planet and the happiness of my children long after I am dead, that will make no contribution to my welfare. A person may have rational *interests* that go well beyond what is for her good or *in her interest*. A person's good—what benefits her or advances her welfare—is different from what is good from her point of view or standpoint. The latter is the perspective of what she herself cares about, whereas her own good is what is desirable from the perspective of someone (perhaps she herself) who cares for her.[52]

Scanlon writes:

> [Desire theories of well-being are] open to serious objection. The most general view of this kind—it might be called the unrestricted actual-desire theory—holds that a person's well-being is measured by the degree to which all the person's actual desires are satisfied. Since one can have a desire about almost anything, this makes an implausibly broad range of considerations count as determinants of a person's well-being. Someone might have a desire about the chemical composition of some star, about whether blue was Napoleon's favorite color, or about whether Julius Caesar was an honest man. But it would be odd to suggest that the well-being of a person who has such desires is affected by these facts themselves (as opposed to the pleasure he or she derives from having certain beliefs about them). The fact that some distant star is made up of the elements I would like it to be does not seem to make my life better (assuming that I am not an astronomer whose life work has been devoted to a theory that would be confirmed or refuted by this fact).[53]

Arneson writes: "[N]ot all of an agent's desires plausibly bear on her well-being. I might listen to a televised plea for famine relief, and form the desire to aid distant starving strangers, without myself thinking (and without its being plausible for

---

[51] Parfit (1987, p. 494).
[52] Darwall (2002, p. 53).
[53] Scanlon (1998, pp. 113–114).

anyone else to think) that the fulfillment of this desire would in any way make my life go better."[54]

What exactly is the difficulty that "remoteness" poses for a simple actual-preference account of well-being? We return to the point that preferences, per se, are unrestricted in their content. The sheer fact that i prefers outcome x to outcome y imposes no constraint on the features that differentiate x and y.[55] Individual i might prefer x to y even though i's mental states, and the condition of his physical body, are identical in their intrinsic characteristics in the two outcomes, as are the mental states and physical bodies of his friends and family. This is Parfit's case of the diseased stranger.[56] A yet more powerful illustration of the remoteness objection involves preferences with posthumous content. Individual i can prefer x to y even though x and y differ only with respect to events that occur after his death.[57] (For example, i, who dies in the year 2000, prefers that the Grand Canyon never be despoiled; in outcome x, the Grand Canyon is never despoiled, in outcome y it is despoiled in the 24th century.)

A different aspect of the "remoteness" worry is that preferences can be grounded in a wide range of rationales. Individual i might prefer x to y for moral reasons, legal reasons, aesthetic reasons, because of social pressure, and so forth. Imagine that I am a member of a 5-member town council, trying to decide whether to spend funds to improve a school or a senior center. Neither I, nor anyone else on the council, have children in the school or relatives who use the center. I determine that, on balance, I have moral and legal reason to spend the funds on the school, because the state constitution requires an adequate public education, and because most children at the school are impoverished, while those who use the senior center are more affluent. Two other members of the council share my views, and the school funding is approved. My (morally and legally motivated) preference for the school has been satisfied. Am I better off than if the center had been funded?

---

[54] Arneson (1999b, p. 124). Other discussions of what I am terming the "remoteness" problem include: Bernstein (1998); Brandt (1998, ch. 17); Gibbard (1986); Griffin (1986, chs. 1–2); Hausman and McPherson (2009); Kagan (1992); Overvold (1980, 1982, 1984); Sumner (1996, ch. 5).

[55] Cf. above, n. 18. Even if this is denied, and we require that "preferred" features of outcomes be features that the holder of the preference can causally influence (call this the "causal restriction" view), the "remoteness" worry remains powerful. For example, future events, including events that occur after an individual's death, are often subject to an individual's causal influence. Thus, even on the "causal restriction" view of preferences, an individual can have a preference for various types of future events that, intuitively, are remote from his well-being.

[56] Parfit prefers (1) the stranger's being cured without Parfit learning of the stranger's fate, to (2) the stranger's dying of the disease without Parfit learning of his fate—even though Parfit's mind and body (and the minds and bodies of others who are not strangers to him) are intrinsically identical in both outcomes.

[57] See above, n. 55.

Note, too, that idealizing preferences by adding more information, or by requiring that preferences be highly rational in a variety of procedural senses, does not cure the "remoteness" worry.[58]

But why exactly should we endorse the principle that an individual's well-being must not be too "remote" from him, and thus reject an account that ties well-being to actual or ideal preferences without restricting the content of the preferences or their underlying rationales?

To begin, the "remoteness" principle is supported by our intuitions about particular cases (such as Parfit's stranger case and the others just described). Second, the principle is, intuitively, connected to the "good for" aspect of well-being.[59]

Finally, there is a serious tension between preference-based accounts of well-being which have not been structured to handle the remoteness objection and the possibility of non-self-interested reasoning and action. This is a point which Mark Overvold has stressed, using the example of self-sacrifice as a vivid illustration.[60] I will illustrate Overvold's point using a simple actual-preference account of well-being, which says that $(x; i)$ is better for well-being than $(y; i)$ just in case i prefers outcome x to y. The problems I am about to illustrate generalize to *ideal-preference* accounts that have not been structured to handle the remoteness problem.

Consider the case in which the heroic soldier i prefers an outcome x in which he dies and his comrade is saved, as opposed to an outcome y in which he survives and his comrade dies. He chooses an action a which he knows will lead to x, or believes will do so with a high probability, as opposed to an action b which he knows will lead to y, or believes will do so with a high probability. (Action a is, say, leaping on a grenade which threatens the comrade; action b is not doing so.) The hero chooses action a, and outcome x occurs. Yet on the simple actual-preference account of well-being, the hero is better off in x—because he prefers x to y—and thus is not a hero at all. In short, this account makes it impossible to be a hero—that is, to engage in self-sacrifice, deliberately choosing an action which yields an outcome that is dramatically worse for the actor than the outcome of some other choice.

The most striking examples of self-sacrifice involve an actor who is wholly partial to someone else's well-being, and ignores his own interests entirely. But there is a tension between preference-based accounts which have not been structured to handle the remoteness objection and *any* kind of non-self-interested reasoning and

---

[58] Some procedural restrictions—for example, requiring that the preference be the result of a certain kind of attitude, such as self-sympathy—may cure the remoteness problem. But many standard procedural restrictions will not do so. For example, an individual may have a calm and deliberate preference for remote features of outcomes; the reasoning giving rise to this preference may be consistent with norms of deductive logic; this preference may cohere with higher-order preferences; and so forth.

[59] Intuitively, the problem with remote features of outcomes that individuals may prefer is that they don't make the outcomes better *for* the persons involved.

[60] See Overvold (1980, 1982, 1984).

choice. Consider moral reasoning. Moral reasoning is supposed to be impartial. I am supposed to give no greater weight to anyone else's interests than my own. Presumably it is a constitutive condition of genuinely impartial reasoning that is *possible* (although not necessary) for me to end up making a choice which is worse for my own interests. Note, therefore, how a simple actual-preference account of well-being precludes an individual from engaging in genuinely impartial reasoning. I might try to adopt an impartial perspective, and rank the outcomes in a given outcome set in an impartial manner; but, on this account of well-being, whatever ranking I arrive at will correspond exactly to how the outcomes are ranked in light of my own well-being. And if, after this exercise in attempted impartiality, I choose action a in light of my outcome ranking—using the most attractive theory of how to rationally select choices in light of an outcome ranking, be it EU theory or some other theory—I will have chosen an action which is (ex ante) best for my well-being.

A major difference between philosophical writing about well-being, and welfare economics, is that philosophers have been much more sensitive to the remoteness worry than economists. Scholarship on social welfare functions, CBA, or other aspects of welfare economics rarely, if ever, builds in a condition on the content of preferences or their underlying rationale which is explicitly designed to distinguish between preferences that are welfare-enhancing and preferences that are not.[61]

How should the remoteness worry be handled, in constructing an account of well-being? One possibility is via a supervenience requirement, which says that $(x; i)$ and $(y; i)$ can differ for well-being only if the two outcomes that figure in these life-histories, x and y, differ with respect to certain sorts of facts. This observation helps shed light on why theories of well-being that draw a link to mental states have some real attractiveness. What could be more "proximate" to a person than his mental states? Consider a theory which says that $(x; i)$ is better than $(y; i)$ iff i's mental states in the two outcomes are different, in terms of their intrinsic properties, in some stipulated way—meaning for example that the mental states in x feel better to i, or that i prefers the mental states in x to those in y in virtue of the intrinsic differences

---

[61] The remoteness problem is sometimes finessed, sub rosa, in the literature by making each individual's preferences for outcomes depend solely on individual attributes that are clearly non-remote. For example, in the canonical set-up for the fundamental welfare theorems, each individual's preferences are a function solely of his consumption of different goods. See Mas-Colell, Whinston, and Green (1995, ch. 16). And, in much of the optimal-tax literature, an individual's utility function depends on his own consumption and leisure. See Chapter 4, pp. 241–245. However, there is rarely systematic discussion of the proposition that the content of preferences needs to be thus limited so as to deal with the remoteness problem. And there are certainly other contexts, in welfare economics, where the content of preferences is *not* thus limited. A very important example is "existence values" in cost-benefit analysis—where WTP/WTA values are elicited for environmental characteristics that may well be spatially or even temporally distant from the individuals whose WTP/WTA values are being elicited (for example, the preservation of a remote ecosystem or the saving of an endangered species with which the individual has never interacted). See Adler (2006b, pp. 1906–1911); Adler and Posner (2006, pp. 126–127).

between these mental states, or would have such a preference under ideal conditions. Seemingly, whatever other worries one might have about such an account, "remoteness" is not one of them.

But the theory now on the table goes too far. In its zeal to circumscribe the features of outcomes that can affect the ranking of an individual's life-histories, it leaves out those non-mentalistic features that, intuitively, are still welfare-relevant. This is the nub of Robert Nozick's famous "experience machine" objection to mental-state theories.

> Suppose there were an experience machine that would give you any experience you desired. Superduper neuropsychologists could stimulate your brain so that you would think and feel you were writing a great novel, or making a friend, or reading an interesting book. All the time you would be floating in a tank, with electrodes attached to your brain. Should you plug into this machine for life, preprogramming your life's experiences? If you are worried about missing out on desirable experiences, we can suppose that business enterprises have researched thoroughly the lives of many others. You can pick and choose from their large library or smorgasbord of such experiences. . . . Would you plug in?

Nozick concludes: "We learn that something matters to us in addition to experience [mental states] by imagining an experience machine and then realizing that we would not use it."[62]

Shelly Kagan and Mark Overvold have suggested other kinds of supervenience requirements to handle the remoteness objection. Kagan tentatively suggests that $(x; i)$ is better for well-being than $(y; i)$ only if the two outcomes differ either in terms of the intrinsic properties of i's mental states, or in terms of the intrinsic properties of his physical body.[63] Overvold argues that well-being consists in the satisfaction of "self-interested" preferences, defined as follow:

> [T]he only desires and aversions that are logically relevant to the determination of an individual's self-interest are those in which (1) it is logically necessary that the individual exist at t for the object of [his] desire or aversion to obtain at t, and (2) the reason for this desire is due to [his] essential involvement in the state of affairs.[64]

Translated into a condition on the ranking of outcome sets, Overvold's account says something like the following: Individual i's ranking of an outcome set is self-interested iff (1) for any pair of outcomes, x and y, such that i is not indifferent between the two, there is some difference between them that occurs when i is alive; and (2) if x^+ and y^+ are the "nearest possible" outcomes to x and y, respectively, in which i does not exist, then i is indifferent between x^+ and y^+.

---

[62] Nozick (1974, pp. 42–44).
[63] See Kagan (1992, p. 186).
[64] Overvold (1982, p. 190).

Both of these proposals, like the mental-state supervenience proposal, are counterintuitive in some cases. Kagan's proposal is counterintuitive because, seemingly, my well-being can be affected by events outside both my mind and my body. (A standard example is where someone's family, friends, or colleagues do or say things without her being aware of them. Imagine that Sheila is betrayed by her spouse, but believes that he is faithful, and never learns otherwise. Isn't the fact of the betrayal itself something that makes Sheila's life worse, independent of her learning of the betrayal?) Overvold's account is counterintuitive because, seemingly, I can have non-self-interested preferences regarding what happens to my mental states or physical body (despite the fact that occurrences in my mind or physical body entail my existence at the time of the occurrences). Imagine the penitent wrongdoer who develops a moral preference that he suffer pain and anguish as punishment for the wrongdoing. Surely *that* preference is not self-interested—but Overvold's account says otherwise.[65]

A different approach to handling the remoteness objection is to couple an idealized-preference account of well-being with some attitudinal restriction. In important recent work, Stephen Darwall draws a link between well-being and *sympathy*. He suggests (1) that sympathy is indeed a "natural" attitude, in the sense of not essentially involving beliefs about well-being or other normative beliefs; (2) that the sympathetic person can be partial in his sympathy and, at the extreme, exclusively sympathetic toward one particular person; and (3) that a person can be self-sympathetic. Building upon these ideas, we might say something like the following: $(x; i)$ is better for well-being than $(y; i)$ iff i prefers the first outcome under conditions of full information and full rationality, and under conditions where i is exclusively self-sympathetic.[66]

A final possibility is to handle the remoteness objection by coupling an ideal-preference account of well-being with a *value-laden* account of the formation of those preferences. We might say something like the following: $(x; i)$ is better for well-being than $(y; i)$ iff i, under conditions of full information and rationality, *judges x to be better for his well-being* and thereby comes to prefer x. Presumably i, in reaching

---

[65] This example, strictly, does not undermine a mental-state or physical-body restriction on preferences, if understood as merely necessary conditions for non-remoteness (by contrast with Overvold, who offers necessary and sufficient conditions). However, a proposal to the effect that i's preferences are non-remote if and only if they concern his mental states, or his physical body, *is* undermined by the example of the penitent who morally prefers to undergo physical suffering and mental anguish.

[66] For Darwall's account of sympathy, see Darwall (2002, especially ch. 3). Although Darwall *does* see the attitude of sympathy as a psychological primitive which does not essentially involve thinking about well-being, see, e.g., ibid., p. 12, he does not propose the account of well-being sketched in the final sentence of this paragraph. Rather, he makes a different suggestion: someone's well-being is what anyone caring for her has *reason* to want. See, e.g., ibid., p. 71. Thus Darwall presupposes a value-neutral account of the attitude of sympathy, but does not provide a value-neutral analysis of well-being. For critical discussion, see the symposium on Darwall in *Utilitas* (2006, vol. 18, pp. 400–444).

this idealized judgment about his own well-being, is insensitive to remote features of x and y (for example, features that occur after his death.) The viability of *this* strategy for handling remoteness hinges on the viability of a value-laden account of the preferences that undergird welfare—a topic to which we now turn.

C. Metaethical Disputes

The philosophical literature on well-being is not merely characterized by first-order disagreements about which account is most attractive. A further source of disagreement is metaethical.

In my brief overview of metaethics in Chapter 1, I discussed ideal-approval accounts of moral facts, and mentioned that so-called "secondary quality" accounts are a particular variant of ideal-approval accounts.

Remember that metaethical views can be cognitivist or noncognitivist. Cognitivists see moral "assertions" as genuine assertions of moral facts; believe that moral facts exist[67]; and therefore believe that moral assertions can be true or false, no less so than paradigmatic factual assertions, e.g., statements about the physical world. Ideal-approval accounts are one family of cognitivist accounts. Such accounts have the common feature that they analyze moral facts in terms of the approvals of some individual or group of individuals, reasoning under conditions that are idealized in some way. The statement "Item m is morally good," with m an action, an outcome, or some other item, means something like: "Individual(s) reasoning under conditions C would approve m."

An important distinction *within* the family of ideal-approval accounts is the distinction between "secondary quality" accounts (sometimes known as "sensibility" accounts) and other views. What is this distinction? It concerns whether the idealized reasoning specified by conditions C is supposed to be *value laden* or *value free*.[68]

Secondary-quality/sensibility accounts see these conditions as *value laden*. More precisely, such accounts argue that the idealized individuals whose approvals undergird moral facts are engaged in a reasoning process that involves moral judgments or perceptions. "Item m is morally good" means something like "Individuals under conditions C would perceive or judge m to be morally good, and thus would approve m." The proponents of secondary-quality accounts of moral facts often draw an analogy to facts about *colors*. Plausibly, the statement "Item m is red" means "Item m would look red to individuals under conditions C'. They would perceive m to be red."

---

[67] I am ignoring here the possibility of an "error theory" metaethics which sees moral "assertions" as genuine factual assertions but denies that such assertions are ever true. See Chapter 1.

[68] On sensibility accounts of moral facts, see generally Darwall, Gibbard, and Railton (1992, pp. 152–165); Miller (2003, chs. 7, 9–10); Sosa (2001). For discussion of the distinction between analyses of moral or well-being facts in terms of value-free approvals, and analyses in terms of value-laden approvals, see Brink (2008, pp. 19–21); Railton (1996, p. 80, n. 20).

Similarly, it is suggested, the moral rightness or goodness of some item means that individuals under suitable conditions would see or judge it to be morally right or good. For example, David Wiggins writes: "In so far as Hume ever came anywhere near to suggesting a semantical account of 'x is good/right/beautiful' ... it may seem that the best proposal implicit in his theory of valuation is that this sentence says that x is the kind of thing to arouse a certain sentiment of approbation." And Wiggins then explains:

> What after all is a sentiment of approbation? . . . Surely a sentiment of approbation cannot be identified except by its association with the thought or feeling that x is good (or right or beautiful) and with the various considerations in which that thought can be grounded. . . .
>
> In all these matters, an analogy with colour is suggestive. "x is red if and only if x is such as to give, under certain conditions specifiable as normal, a certain visual impression" naturally raises the question "which visual impression?" And that question attracts the answer "an impression as of seeing something red," which reintroduces red. But this finding of circularity scarcely amounts to proof that we can after all appeal to something beyond visual impressions to determine colour authoritatively.[69]

A different sort of ideal-approval view stipulates that the idealized reasoning giving rise to moral facts is *value free*—more precisely, that reasoning under conditions C does *not* involve moral judgments or perceptions. For example, Ronald Milo reduces moral facts to what would be chosen in an ideal contracting scenario and, in so doing, very clearly articulates a *value-free* variant of an ideal-approval construal of moral facts.

> What the moral facts are—for example, which acts are wrong—is determined by which principles would be chosen by the hypothetical agents. . . . It must be noted, however, that the moral principles chosen by the hypothetical contractors are viewed by them as *action guides*, not as *truth claims*. The agents of construction are not to be conceived of as trying to reach an agreement on which moral principles are true, since apart from their agreement there are no antecedently given moral truths for them to discover. Rather, they determine through their choices which moral principles are true. . . .
>
> . . . [The contractors' reasoning process] will include certain desires that all (normal) human beings can be presumed to share. . . . But it will not include any moral beliefs about what is right or wrong in our interactions with others or about which traits of character are other-regarding virtues. The hypothetical contractors are not presumed to have any such beliefs.[70]

---

[69] Wiggins (1998, pp. 187–189).
[70] Milo (1995, pp. 186, 189). See also Firth (1952, p. 326); Railton (1996, pp. 69–70).

Critics of a secondary-quality account of moral facts argue that such accounts are viciously circular or, at the very least, unilluminating. Proponents of such accounts argue that there is no vicious circularity; that it is impossible to provide an accurate characterization of good moral reasoning without allowing moral concepts, beliefs, etc., to figure in this reasoning; and that the hope to ground moral facts in idealized value-free reasoning is therefore chimerical.

How do these metaethical disputes relate to controversies about well-being? The value-free variant of an ideal-approval account of moral facts is naturally paired with an account of well-being in terms of idealized and *value-free* preferences—value free in the sense that the preferences are not themselves grounded in judgments or perceptions of well-being. If one worries that the secondary-quality analysis of moral facts is viciously circular or unilluminating, one should also worry that the following account of well-being is viciously circular or unilluminating: "One life-history is better for the subject's well-being than a second iff the subject, under stipulated conditions, would judge or perceive the first to be better for well-being."

Indeed, Richard Brandt—who suggests an analysis of well-being in terms of preferences that are fully informed and fully rational in the sense of surviving "cognitive psychotherapy"—characterizes that process as follows:

> This whole process of confronting desires with relevant information, by repeatedly representing it, in an ideally vivid way, and at an appropriate time, I call *cognitive psychotherapy*. I call it so because the process relies simply upon reflection on available information, without influence by prestige of someone, use of evaluative language, extrinsic reward or punishment, or use of artificially induced feeling-states like relaxation. It is *value-free reflection*.[71]

Conversely, if one is drawn to a secondary-quality view of moral facts, then an analysis of well-being in terms of idealized value-free preferences will also, naturally, be seen to be wrongheaded. If moral facts are not reducible to ideal reasoning shorn of moral concepts, then why would well-being facts be reducible to ideal reasoning shorn of well-being concepts? Indeed, the central thrust of James Griffin's critique of traditional preferentialist accounts of welfare is that the preferences giving rise to well-being are value laden. As Griffin argues (focusing on the good of accomplishment):

> [T]he taste model assumes that we can isolate valued objects in purely natural terms and then, independently, react to them with approval or disapproval. But can we? Prudential deliberation about accomplishment is not a case of first perceiving facts neutrally and then desire's entering and happening to fix on one object or other. The act of isolating the objects we value is far from neutral. We bring what I am calling "accomplishment" into focus only by resorting to such terms as "giving life weight or point," and such language

---

[71] Brandt (1998, p. 113).

already organizes our experience by selecting what we see favourably. Desire is not left free to happen to fix on one object or another; its direction is already fixed in, and manifested by, what we see favourably.

And he continues:

Desire . . . is not blind. . . . [D]esires are not independent of the recognition of the good. The very few desires of which this is not true —say, some baffling urge left by hypnotic suggestion—are only vestigial desires. . . . [I]f we were beset by mere urges, coming from we know not where and we know not why, inclining us this way and that, we should see them as something to resist, to rid ourselves of as much as we could.[72]

It should be stressed that Griffin's account of well-being retains a link to preferences. His assertion that "[d]esire is not blind," i.e., that well-formed preferences for different lives are the result of using normative concepts like "the good life" or "well-being," is coupled with an assertion that "reason is not inert," i.e., that seeing some life as good brings motivation in its train, at least for normal humans.

Values are . . . what one would want if one properly appreciated the object of desire. . . . [A]s we have seen, this account shifts importance away from the mere occurrence of desire on to the nature of its object. Desire is left playing very little role, even *many* people's desires. Still, desire reappears in another place. To recognize the nature of the relevant object is to see it under some desirability characterization, such as "accomplishment" or "enjoyment." These desirability characterizations give reasons for action, and those reasons in turn mesh with characteristic human motivation.[73]

Griffin's account of well-being is therefore a kind of full-information preferentialist account, with the critical proviso that the idealized conditions giving rise to preferences involve judgments or perceptions of well-being. Once more, there is an isomorphism to secondary-quality accounts of moral facts. The secondary-quality view, after all, is a kind of ideal-*approval* account. Seeing item m to be morally good produces an approval of m. Similarly, on Griffin's view of well-being, the fact that $(x; i)$ is better for well-being than $(y; i)$ can be more or less analyzed as: "If individual i were characterized by normal human desires and concepts and were to reason about outcomes x and y with good information, he would perceive or judge the first outcome to be better for his well-being and thus come to prefer it."[74]

[72] Griffin (1997, pp. 25, 32–33).

[73] Ibid., pp. 32, 35–36. See generally ibid., pp. 25, 32–36, 56–59.

[74] Griffin suggests at various junctures that the elements of well-being are those items normally or "characteristically" seen by humans as valuable. See, e.g., ibid., p. 56 ("Recognition [of prudential values] involves . . . a characteristic human sense of importance"); ibid., p. 25 ("There is no adequate

II. INTERPERSONAL COMPARISONS

The elements of well-being, and its metaethical basis, are topics of much philosophical debate, as we have just seen. By contrast, the possibility of interpersonal comparisons seems relatively uncontroversial among philosophers. The topic has received relatively little sustained philosophical attention, but it seems that most philosophers—even those who make preference satisfaction a central element of well-being—accept the possibility of comparing well-being levels and differences across persons.[75]

Indeed, as I shall review below, the prima facie case for interpersonal comparisons is a strong one. There are a variety of different considerations, both intuitive and more systematic, that count in favor of both level and difference comparability.

Philosophers are not alone in acknowledging interpersonal comparability. As discussed in Chapter 2, the possibility of interpersonal comparisons is also accepted by some economists—in particular, economists who work with social welfare functions. However, there is an older tradition in economics that is skeptical about interpersonal comparisons. The so-called "ordinalist revolution" of the 1930s and 1940s was an attempt to orient positive and normative economics around individual preferences, and without making interpersonal comparisons. The development of the Kaldor–Hicks criterion was one central element of this "ordinalist" school.[76]

The failures of the Kaldor–Hicks criterion soon came to light and indeed were a major impetus for the development, beginning in the 1970s, of the idea of a social welfare function using interpersonally comparable utilities as its inputs. But this approach is far from universally accepted by economists.[77]

Why were the "ordinalists" skeptical about interpersonal comparisons? And why does their skepticism continue to resonate among many contemporary economists?

One source of the ordinalists' aversion to interpersonal comparisons was their concern that such comparisons were "unscientific." In an influential 1932 book, Lionel Robbins argued that interpersonal comparisons were both unnecessary to explain market behavior and illegitimate as a component of *positive* economics,

---

explanation of [certain features] being *desirability* features without appeal to certain natural human motivations").

[75] On how interpersonal comparisons figure in the theoretical literature on social welfare functions, see Bossert and Weymark (2004). Other scholarly discussions include: Davidson (1986); Elster and Roemer (1991); Fleurbaey and Hammond (2004); Gibbard (1986); Griffin (1986, ch. 7); Hausman (1995); List (2003); Sen (1979a; 1982, pt. 3); Weintraub (1998); Weirich (1984). The scholarly literature addressed to Harsanyi's extended-preference account of interpersonal comparisons is cited below.

[76] On the "ordinalist" revolution and development of the Kaldor-Hicks criterion, see sources cited in Chapter 2, n. 75.

[77] See, e.g., Just, Hueth, and Schmitz (2004, pp. 41–45).

because they involved value judgments rather than observation. Kaldor and Hicks endorsed Robbins' argument—seeing it as a central justification for developing a new form of welfare economics that would abstain from interpersonal comparisons and instead be oriented around the Pareto(-superiority) principle and, by extension, the potential-Pareto (Kaldor–Hicks) tests.[78] But the lesson that Kaldor and Hicks drew from Robbins was, in fact, a non sequitur. Robbins' analysis may well show that interpersonal comparisons have no place in economics qua social science—the branch of the discipline concerned with predicting and explaining human action—but it can hardly show that interpersonal comparisons have no place in *welfare* economics. That branch of the discipline is *normative*. Like any conception of how to make interpersonal comparisons, the Pareto principle—the foundation of normative economics—involves a value judgment.[79] A methodological precept which enjoined welfare economists to proceed by means of observation and other purely "scientific" techniques, eschewing all value judgments, would be deeply misconceived.

But there is a different and more creditable basis for skepticism about interpersonal comparisons, even as a component of *normative* economics: namely, that individual *preferences* provide no evident basis for such comparisons. For anyone who adopts a view of well-being that makes preferences a central element, there is indeed a genuine intellectual puzzle about the possibility of interpersonal comparability.

Consider a person's ranking of outcomes. Such a ranking immediately allows us to make sense of *intrapersonal* comparisons. We can say something like the following: life-history $(x; i)$ is at least as good for well-being as life-history $(y; i)$ iff the subject of both life-histories, i, weakly prefers outcome x to outcome y under suitable conditions (for example, when i is well-informed, rational, and self-interested).[80]

---

[78] See Robbins (1935, ch. 6; 1938); Hicks (1939); Kaldor (1939).

[79] The Pareto(-superiority) principle involves the value judgment that an outcome or policy which increases at least one person's well-being, and makes no one worse off, is better. The question whether this particular value judgment is uncontroversial should be distinguished from its status as a value judgment. See Sen (1979a, pp. 56–58). Furthermore, although I concur with welfare economists in embracing the Pareto principle as foundational, this judgment is *not*, in fact, uncontroversial. Because the principle (arguably) conflicts with liberty, non-welfarists may reject it. See Sen (1982, ch. 13). And even those who see well-being as the currency for morality, but hold a certain sort of egalitarian view, might reject the Pareto principle. See Chapter 5.

The welfare economist might counter that her discipline is not genuinely normative. She is not endorsing the Pareto principle, simply positing that principle as a *possible* normative axiom, and examining its implications. But this line of defense, without more, fails to explain why welfare economists should eschew interpersonal comparisons. Why not also examine the implications of possible normative axioms (such as the Pigou–Dalton principle) that make interpersonal comparisons?

[80] To be clear, the account of well-being that I ultimately present does not say exactly this. Rather, it says that $(x; i)$ is at least as good as $(y; i)$ iff individual i, under conditions of full information and rationality and self-interest, weakly prefers outcome x to y; *and* every other individual, under conditions of full information and rationality and under a condition of being i-interested, weakly prefers outcome x to y.

But how on earth are we to make sense of an *inter*personal ranking of life-histories, within the confines of a preference-based view? The sheer fact of having a preference over outcomes seems to be the very same thing as—or at least closely connected to—a ranking of one's own life-histories; but no one, in ranking outcomes, produces a ranking of life-histories involving different individuals.

Harsanyi seeks to answer this challenge. In this section, I first review the prima facie case for interpersonal comparability, then discuss how Harsanyi employs the idea of an *extended preference* in his attempt to make sense of interpersonal comparisons. This discussion of Harsanyi's views, together with the review of the philosophical literature about well-being that has already been undertaken, will provide the underpinnings for the account of well-being that I shall present in the next section.

A. The Generic Case for Interpersonal Comparisons

In discussing interpersonal comparability, it is important to keep in mind the distinction—standard within the social choice literature—between interpersonal comparisons of well-being *levels* and interpersonal comparisons of well-being *differences*.[81] Within my framework, that distinction has been framed as follows. An outcome set O is constructed for a choice situation and, together with a population of interest of N individuals, gives rise to a set H of life-histories. An account of well-being produces a quasiordering of H, denoted $\succeq^{WB}$: a ranking of life-histories with respect to well-being. The account allows for *interpersonal comparisons of well-being levels*, with respect to this outcome and life-history set, iff there is at least one pair of life-histories involving different subjects, such that the first life-history is ranked at least as good for well-being as the second. The account of well-being may also produce a difference quasiordering, $\succeq^{D}$, which is a ranking of *pairs* of life-histories. The relation $[(x; i), (y; j)] \succeq^{D} [(z; k), (w; l)]$ means that the difference between the well-being of $(x; i)$ and $(y; j)$ is at least as large as the difference between the well-being of $(z; k)$ and $(w; l)$.[82] The account allows for interpersonal *comparisons of well-being differences*, with respect to this outcome and life-history set, iff it includes a difference quasiordering $\succeq^{D}$, and there is at least one such relation between pairs of life-histories where the four subjects are not identical.

Remember, too, my definition of the SWF approach to decisionmaking. Such an approach involves an account of well-being that allows for at least some interpersonal comparisons (of levels or differences), for some outcome and life-history sets. Moreover, it supplements the basic elements of the generic welfarist framework

---

[81] See, e.g., Bossert and Weymark (2004).

[82] Remember that a difference quasiordering of life-histories has the following features. (1) It is a transitive and reflexive relation, $\succeq^{D}$, on pairs of life-histories. (Formally, this is a binary relation on the product set $H \times H$). (2) If $[(x; i), (y; j)] \succeq^{D} [(z; k), (w; l)]$, then $[(w; l), (z; k)] \succeq^{D} [(y; j), (x; i)]$. (3) If $[(x; i), (y; j)] \succeq^{D} [(x'; i'), (y'; j')]$, and $[(y; j), (z; k)] \succeq^{D} [(y'; j'), (z'; k')]$, then $[(x; i), (z; k)] \succeq^{D} [(x'; i'), (z'; k')]$. See Chapter 1.

(outcome set, population, life-history set, and account of well-being) with a set **U** of utility functions. These utility functions assign numbers to the life-histories. **U** thereby represents $\geqslant^{WB}$ and, if it exists, $\geqslant^{D}$. At the same time, each member of **U** maps outcomes onto utility vectors. The SWF approach ranks outcomes as a function of these utility vectors.

The "ordinalist" tradition within economics is skeptical of both interpersonal level comparisons and interpersonal difference comparisons. However, an account of well-being that declines to make either sort of comparison is problematic in various ways.

To begin, such an account is counterintuitive. It is easy, indeed trivial, to describe specific cases in which, intuitively, one person is at a higher well-being level than another. (Imagine a case in which one individual has a low income, bad health, suffers terrible pain, is socially stigmatized, and has no friends, while another has a high income, excellent health, feels great, and has a high social status and lots of friends.) It is also easy, indeed trivial, to describe specific cases in which the change in someone's well-being is greater than the change in someone else's well-being—a kind of interpersonal difference comparison. (Imagine that individual i's attributes in x and y are identical, except that i has slightly more income in y. By contrast, j has much more income in x than y, is in much better health, feels happier, lives many more years, and so forth. Then, intuitively, the difference between $(x; j)$ and $(y; j)$ is greater than the difference between $(y; i)$ and $(x; i)$.)

More systematically, we saw in Chapter 2 that policy-evaluation frameworks which decline to make interpersonal comparisons are problematic. Either these frameworks fail to meet the minimal welfarist standard of producing a Pareto-respecting quasiordering of outcome sets; or they do so, but in a manner that is less attractive than the SWF approach.

Why does the SWF approach itself require interpersonal comparisons? Why not structure moral decisionmaking by employing an account of well-being that makes only *intrapersonal* comparisons; by representing *that* account via a set **U**; by using **U** to transform outcomes into utility vectors; and by ranking outcomes as a function of their corresponding vectors? Remember the answer I provided in Chapter 2: the SWF framework without any interpersonal comparisons (of levels or differences) threatens to collapse to the Pareto quasiordering.

Finally, it bears noting that rejecting interpersonal comparisons renders otiose many substantive debates within moral theory that philosophers have undertaken for many years. Much of moral philosophy since Bentham has involved a debate about utilitarianism, together with related debates to which this discussion has given rise (for example, the debate between welfarists and nonwelfarists, or consequentialists and deontologists).[83] But utilitarianism involves interpersonal comparisons, as do the non-utilitarian variants of welfarism that have been discussed by

---

[83] See Chapter 1.

philosophers and that correspond to a range of different SWFs reviewed in Chapter 5. Furthermore, and notably, the philosophical critics of these various welfarist views as well as their proponents have generally accepted the possibility of interpersonal level and difference comparisons. The criticism has been substantive: that utilitarianism doesn't take seriously the separateness of persons, that welfarist views ignore agent-relative constraints or the moral relevance of responsibility, and so forth. The critics have generally *not* claimed that utilitarianism and other welfarist views are just unintelligible, and can be rejected out of hand, because their presupposition of interpersonal comparability is false.

What about an account of well-being that allows for interpersonal level comparisons but not difference comparisons? Difference comparisons introduce an extra element of complexity into a decisionmaking framework. Moreover, as we'll see, how to construct utility functions that represent difference comparisons has been a particularly contentious issue among economists who accept interpersonal comparability. Why not avoid this controversy and employ an SWF paired with an account of well-being that makes interpersonal level comparisons but does not make difference comparisons (or at least does not make interpersonal difference comparison)?

Here, we need to introduce some additional terminology. Let us say that interpersonal difference comparisons are "required" for a particular SWF if the SWF always collapses to the Pareto quasiordering without difference comparisons.[84] A weaker idea is that interpersonal difference comparisons are "relevant" to an SWF. What "relevance" means is the following: If U contains some utility function $u(.)$, and we add a new function $u^*(.)$ to U which implies the very same ranking of well-being levels as $u(.)$ but a different ranking of well-being differences, then the SWF's ranking of outcomes may change once U is supplemented by adding $u^*(.)$.[85]

There certainly are SWFs that do not require interpersonal difference comparisons. The leximin SWF is the leading example. Indeed, information about well-being differences is not even *relevant* to the leximin SWF.

---

[84] If a moral decision procedure incorporates an account of well-being that makes interpersonal level but not difference comparisons, and represents the well-being quasiordering of a given set of life-histories H via some set U, then supplementing U with every increasing transformation of every member of U represents the ordering of life-histories equally well. (If $u(.)$ is a member of U, to say that $v(.)$ is an "increasing transformation" of $u(.)$ means: $v(x; i) \geq v(y; j)$ iff $u(x; i) \geq u(y; j)$ for all life-histories in H.) When I say that a given SWF always "collapses to the Pareto quasiordering without difference comparisons," what I mean is: given any outcome set and life-history set, it is the case that, for any U, if U is supplemented with every increasing transformation of every member, becoming U^*, the SWF's ranking of the outcome set using U^* is the Pareto quasiordering.

[85] More precisely, interpersonal difference comparisons are relevant to a given SWF if: (1) there exists some outcome and life-history set, and some U, such that if we supplement U with $v(.)$, where $v(.)$ is an increasing transformation of some member of U, the resulting set U^* implies a quasiordering of well-being differences which is not the same as that implied by U; and (2) the SWF, applied to U^*, yields a different quasiordering of the outcomes than when applied to U.

However, the leximin SWF has substantial difficulties (see Chapter 5), and inter-personal difference comparisons *are* relevant to all the plausible competitors to the leximin SWF discussed in Chapter 5—including standard functional forms such as the utilitarian SWF, a continuous prioritarian SWF, and the rank-weighted SWF. Why information about well-being differences is not relevant to the leximin SWF, but *is* relevant to these competing SWFs, is illustrated in Table 3.1.

Table 3.1 The Relevance of Well-Being Differences

	Utility function $u(.)$			Utility function $u^*(.)$		
	Outcome x	Outcome y	Difference	Outcome x	Outcome y	Difference
Individual 1	10	30	20	10	11	1
Individual 2	50	40	−10	50	40	−10
Utilitarian SWF	60	70		60	51	
Gini rank-weighted SWF	80	130		80	73	
Atkinson SWF, $\gamma = \frac{1}{2}$	20.47	23.60		20.47	19.28	

Utility function $u(.)$ maps outcome x onto utility vector $(10, 50)$ and y onto utility vector $(30, 40)$, while function $u^*(.)$ maps x onto utility vector $(10, 50)$ and y onto utility vector $(11, 40)$. Note that $u^*(.)$ is an increasing transformation of $u(.)$: both rank life-histories the same way. $u(x; 1) < u(y; 1) < u(y; 2) < u(x; 2)$ and $u^*(x; 1) < u^*(y; 1) < u^*(y; 2) < u^*(x; 2)$. However, $u(.)$ ranks the difference between $(y; 1)$ and $(x; 1)$ as being greater than the difference between $(x; 2)$ and $(y; 2)$, while $u^*(.)$ ranks the first difference as smaller than the second difference. (Note that $u(y; 1) - u(x; 1) = 20 > u(x; 2) - u(y; 2) = 10$, while $u^*(y; 1) - u^*(x; 1) = 1 < u^*(x; 2) - u^*(y; 2) = 10$.)

The table shows the values assigned to x and y by the utilitarian SWF, Gini rank-weighted SWF, and a continuous prioritarian SWF of the Atkinson family with $\gamma = 1/2$, depending upon whether $u(.)$ or $u^*(.)$ is used.[86] Note that all of these SWFs rank y over x using $u(.)$, but x over y using $u^*(.)$. By contrast, it can be observed that the leximin SWF ranks y as better than x regardless of whether $u(.)$ or $u^*(.)$ is used to map these outcomes onto utility vectors.

Can we make a stronger claim? Is it true that interpersonal difference compari-sons are *required* for plausible SWFs other than the leximin SWF—that these SWFs will always "collapse" to the Pareto quasiordering absent such information? This is

---

[86] The Atkinson SWF with $\gamma = 1/2$ is 2 times the sum of the square root of utilities. The Gini rank-weighted SWF uses the first N odd numbers (in reverse order) as the weights. With a 2-entry utility vector, that means assigning a value to a vector by multiplying the smaller utility times 3 and then adding the larger utility. On the Gini rank-weighted SWF, see Chapter 2, n. 119; and on rank-weighted SWFs in general, see Chapter 5.

not true, for reasons illustrated in the margin.[87] However, it is clearly true that information about interpersonal well-being differences is *relevant* to a wide range of SWFs other than the leximin SWF—and that is sufficient motivation to attempt to construct an account of well-being that allows for such comparisons as well as interpersonal comparisons of well-being levels.

Moreover, as already mentioned, it is easy to construct cases in which, intuitively, one person's well-being change is greater than another's. This also cuts against the plausibility of a well-being account that solely makes interpersonal level comparisons.

Finally, as we shall see in Chapter 5, a critical device for evaluating different kinds of SWFs is the *Pigou–Dalton principle* in terms of well-being. Whether an SWF satisfies this principle is a critical question in the "reflective equilibrium" process of sorting between different kinds of SWFs. However, the Pigou–Dalton principle in terms of well-being presupposes both interpersonal level and difference comparisons. What it says is: If individual i is worse off than individual j in outcome x, and there is a pure transfer of well-being from j to i—such that individual i's well-being is increased by a certain amount, with individual j's well-being reduced by the very

---

[87] Consider the set-up of Chapter 2, n. 23. **U** is such that x and y are Pareto-noncomparable, but the utilitarian SWF ranks x at least as good as y. Because the outcomes are Pareto-noncomparable, there is some $u^+(.)$ such that $u^+(y; k) > u^+(x; k)$ for some k. This SWF collapses to the Pareto quasiordering, without interpersonal difference comparisons, if there is at least one $u^*(.)$ which is an increasing transformation of $u^+(.)$, such that the utilitarian SWF applied to $u^*(.)$ ranks y over x. See above, n. 84.

In Chapter 2, n. 23, I showed why collapse will occur if $u^*(.)$ is any utility function which can be reached from $u^+(.)$ via individual-specific ratio transformations. (Such a $u^*(.)$ need not preserve the interpersonal level comparisons embodied in $u^+(.)$). By contrast, collapse need not occur if $u^*(.)$ is any utility function which can be reached from $u^+(.)$ via an increasing transformation (which does preserve interpersonal level comparisons). To see why not, imagine that there are two individuals, and $u^+(.)$ maps x onto $(10, 40)$ and y onto $(30, 5)$, thus ranks life-history $(y; 2)$ worse than $(x; 1)$ worse than $(y; 1)$ worse than $(x; 2)$. Because any $u^*(.)$ which is an increasing transformation of $u^+(.)$ must preserve this ranking, it can be seen that the utilitarian SWF applied to any such $u^*(.)$ will continue to rank x over y. For example, if $u^*(.)$ is such that x is mapped onto $(5, 101)$ and y onto $(100, 4)$—so that the utility difference between $(x; 2)$ and $(y; 2)$ is now 97 and only barely larger than the utility difference between $(y; 1)$ and $(x; 1)$, 95—it is *still* the case that the utilitarian SWF using $u^*(.)$ will rank x over y.

To be sure, there are other types of cases where x and y are Pareto-noncomparable according to **U**; the utilitarian SWF ranks x at least as good as y; $u^+(.)$ in **U** ranks $(y; k)$ over $(x; k)$; and adding a $u^*(.)$ to **U** *will* force a collapse to the Pareto quasiordering, where $u^*(.)$ is an increasing transformation of $u^+(.)$. (For example, imagine that **U** contains $u^+(.)$ which maps x onto $(10, 100)$ and y onto $(30, 40)$. Then $u^*(.)$ which maps x onto $(10, 32)$ and y onto $(30, 31)$ preserves all the level comparisons of $u^+(.)$, but alters utility differences in a fashion that means the utilitarian SWF using $u^*(.)$ ranks y over x.) Analyzing when collapse does and does not occur, with the utilitarian SWF and other non-leximin SWFs, absent interpersonal difference comparisons, is an interesting question—but not one I will attempt to address here. What the example of the previous paragraph shows is that interpersonal difference comparisons are not strictly required for the utilitarian SWF (and, presumably, for other plausible SWFs), because collapse does not always occur.

same amount, with no one else affected—and this transfer does not cause the individuals to "switch ranks," then the transfer is a moral improvement. Note that characterizing an outcome as one where some individual is better off than another involves an interpersonal level comparison. And characterizing the change in some individual's well-being as being the very same amount as the change in another individual's well-being involves an interpersonal difference comparison.

B. Harsanyi's "Extended Preference" Solution to the Puzzle of Interpersonal Comparisons

Thus the case for interpersonal comparisons, both level and difference comparisons, is strong. Harsanyi proposes to explicate comparisons of both kinds, and to represent such comparisons via utility numbers. The core of Harsanyi's proposal is the idea of an *extended preference*—a preference for life-histories or lotteries over life-histories—and the use of expected utility (EU) theory to represent individuals' extended preferences.[88]

This section presents these basic ideas, showing why they indeed hold promise as a basis for interpersonal comparisons. However, the section also outlines various problematic features of Harsanyi's views. Although Harsanyi is owed much credit for elaborating the idea of extended preferences and marrying it with EU theory, substantial work will be needed to incorporate these ideas into an attractive account of well-being—the account that I will present in the next section.

Harsanyi imagines that there is a population of N individuals. A given member of the population is morally ranking various outcomes.

> Society consists of n individuals. . . . Suppose that individual $[k]$ wants to make a *moral value judgment*. This will always involve comparing two or more social situations concerning their relative merits from a moral point of view. These social situations

---

[88] See Harsanyi (1953; 1955; 1982; 1986, ch. 4). The construct of extended preferences figures in what has come to be known as Harsanyi's "impartial observer" theorem. For a lucid presentation, see Weymark (1991). Other discussions of the impartial observer theorem or Harsanyi's analysis of extended preferences include: Binmore (1994, ch. 4; 2008); Broome (1998, 2008); Gajdos and Kandil (2008); Grant et al. (2010a, 2010b); Griffin (1991); Kaneko (1984); Karni (1998); Karni and Weymark (1998); MacKay (1986); Mongin (2001); Mongin and d'Aspremont (1998); Moreno-Ternero and Roemer (2008); Ng (1999); Pattanaik (1968); Roemer (2008); Safra and Weissengrin (2003); Sen (1986, pp. 1122–1123); Suzumura (1996); Weymark (2005).

Extended preferences do not figure in Harsanyi's so-called "aggregation theorem," and the account of well-being I develop in this chapter does not build from that theorem. It is discussed in Chapter 7 and the relevant literature cited in that chapter, n. 89.

Finally, although Harsanyi is by far the most influential proponent of the idea of extended preferences, other scholars have proposed the idea as well. See the literature on generalized/extended/extensive social welfare functions, Chapter 2, n. 48; and see also Serge Kolm's work on "fundamental" preferences, e.g., Kolm (1996, pp. 160–168).

may be alternative patterns of social behavior . . . , alternative institutional frameworks, alternative government policies, alternative patterns of income distributions, and so forth. Mathematically, any social situation can be regarded as a *vector* listing the economic, social, biological, and other variables that will affect the well-being of the individuals making up the society. Different social situations will be called *A, B. . . .*[89]

What Harsanyi calls a "social situation" is what I call an "outcome."

Harsanyi further supposes that individual *k* morally ranks outcomes by ranking life-histories and lotteries over life-histories—more specifically, by seeing each outcome as an equiprobability lottery over its component life-histories.

> Now if individual [*k*] wants to make a moral value judgment about the merits of alternative social situations *A, B,. . .* , he must make a serious attempt not to assess these social situations simply in terms of his own personal preferences and personal interests but rather in terms of some impartial and impersonal criteria. . . .
>
> Individual [*k*'s] choice among alternative social situations would certainly satisfy this requirement of impartiality and impersonality, if he simply *did not know in advance* what his own social position would be in each social situation – so that he would not know whether he himself would be a rich man or a poor man, a motorist or a pedestrian, a teacher or a student, a member of one social group or a member of another social group, and so forth. More specifically, this requirement would be satisfied if he thought that he would have an *equal probability* of being *put in the place* of any one among the *n* individual members of society. . . .
>
> . . . [Thus individual *k* will engage in] some process of *imaginative empathy*, i.e., by imagining himself to be *put in the place* of individual *j* in social situation *A*.
>
> This must obviously involve his imagining himself to be placed in individual *j*'s *objective position*, i.e., to be placed in the objective conditions (e.g., income, wealth, consumption level, state of health, social position) that *j* would face in social situation *A*. But it must also involve assessing these objective conditions in terms of *j*'s own *subjective attitudes* and *personal preferences. . . .*[90]

Harsanyi uses the symbol "A_i" to denote "individual *i*'s *personal position* in social situation *A* (i.e., the objective conditions that would face individual *i* in social situation *A*)."[91] This is what I term a life-history. A_i is a pairing of an individual with a "social situation" (outcome); and that is exactly how I have defined a life-history.

[89] Harsanyi (1986, p. 49). Harsanyi's account of extended preferences is most fully developed in this book, and in the next several paragraphs I describe the account as there stated. Harsanyi refers to the individual as "*i*," but I will generally refer to the spectator as "*k*," and so have changed his notation to be consistent with my own.

[90] Ibid., pp. 49–52.

[91] Ibid., p. 52.

And he refers to an individual's ranking of life-histories or lotteries over life-histories as her *extended-preference* ranking.[92]

Assume that this idea of an "extended preference" is a coherent one. If so, it will be useful to have a term to refer to the person who is ranking life-histories, and to distinguish that person from the individuals whose life-histories are being ranked. As previously, I will use the term "subject" to mean the latter individuals. I will use the term "spectator" to mean the former individual. These are my own terms, not Harsanyi's, but they help to explicate his ideas. If individual k possesses an extended-preference ranking of life-histories, such as $(x; i)$ and $(y; j)$, then individual k is a "spectator"; individual i is the subject of life-history $(x; i)$; individual j is the subject of life-history $(y; j)$. The term "spectator" does not denote some figure who is external to the population of N individuals, nor is there a single spectator. Rather (assuming the idea of an "extended preference" is coherent), *each* individual in the population of N possesses his own extended-preference ranking of the set of life-histories. Each individual in the population can function as a spectator. This is what Harsanyi supposes—and what my own account will suppose as well.

The final, critical, element of Harsanyi's analysis involves EU theory. EU theory, in the full form pioneered by Leonard Savage, provides a theory of rational choice under uncertainty, which has the following basic structure. Imagine that the decisionmaker is ranking a choice set (a set of possible actions she might undertake) in light of some outcome set. Imagine that the decisionmaker complies with certain axioms, which regiment the action and outcome rankings and how they intersect. Then these propositions will be true: (1) For each action a and each outcome x, there will exist a probability value $\pi_a(x)$, namely the probability that action a produces outcome x. (2) There will exist a utility function $v(.)$, which is unique up to a positive affine transformation, and which assigns a utility value $v(x)$ to any outcome x. (3) The decisionmaker will have a complete ranking of the action set, which corresponds to the expected utility of the actions. EU theory, in this full form, will be discussed at length in Chapter 7.

EU theory did not originate with Savage. In earlier, seminal work, von Neumann and Morgenstern had introduced a simpler version of the theory, which applies to

---

[92] Strictly, Harsanyi pairs each life-history with the subject's preferences. He terms this pairing an "extended alternative." An "extended preference," in turn, is a ranking of extended alternatives. See ibid., p. 53. My conception is more general: an extended preference ranks life-histories. The *description* of outcomes might include information about subjects' preferences. Or we might stipulate that everyone knows what everyone else's preferences are. But my conception of an extended preference also makes it possible that someone can possess an extended preference over other persons' life-histories without knowing what the subjects' preferences are. (Remember that an outcome, on my view, is a simplified possible world, which leaves out much information about subjects and background facts). On whether outcomes include a description of subjects' preferences, see Chapter 4, pp. 275–278.

lotteries over outcomes.[93] A lottery *l* over outcomes takes the form $[\pi_l(x), \pi_l(y), \ldots]$, where $\pi_l(x)$ denotes the probability that the lottery assigns to outcome *x*. Each such $\pi_l(x)$ value is between zero and one, inclusive, and the sum of their values is one. A "lottery" is not an action, but an abstract, mathematical item, with probability values already "built in." The von Neumann/Morgenstern version of EU theory does not explicate what these probabilities are. In particular, it does not demonstrate that each particular action in a choice set (if ranked by the decisionmaker in a rational manner) will correspond to a particular lottery across outcomes. Rather, what von Neumann/Morgenstern EU theory shows is this: If an individual is presented with a set of lotteries across outcomes, and ranks those lotteries consistently with a few simple axioms, then there will exist a utility function *v*(.), unique up to a positive affine transformation, such that the individual's ranking of the lottery set will correspond to the expected utility of the outcomes. The von Neumann/Morgenstern axioms are *completeness* (the ranking of lotteries and outcomes must be a complete quasiordering); an *independence* axiom; and an *Archimedean* axiom.[94]

---

[93] There are numerous presentations of EU theory, in both the von Neumann/Morgenstern version and other variants. A formal, but very clear, presentation is provided by Kreps (1988). Other formal treatments include Fishburn (1982); Gilboa (2009); Mas-Colell, Whinston, and Green (1995, ch. 6); and Ok (2007, pp. 395–409). A less formal discussion is Resnik (1987). An excellent philosophical treatment is Joyce (1999).

[94] Let **O** be a finite set of outcomes, and **L*** a set of all lotteries over the outcomes. (I denote this as **L*** to distinguish it from **L**, which is the set of all lotteries over *life-histories* that I discuss below.) The *completeness* axiom requires the decisionmaker to have a complete quasiordering of **L***. (Because an outcome is a "degenerate" lottery, assigning a probability 1 to the outcome, this means that the decisionmaker has a complete quasiordering of **O** as well.) The independence axiom involves the idea of "mixing" lotteries. A $(p, 1 - p)$ mixture of lottery *l* and lottery *l** assigns a given outcome a probability equaling *p* times the probability assigned it by *l* plus $(1 - p)$ times the probability assigned it by *l**. What the independence axiom requires is that, if the decisionmaker prefers *l* to *l**, then she must prefer a $(p, 1 - p)$ mixture of *l* with some lottery *l***, to a $(p, 1 - p)$ mixture of *l** with the same lottery *l***—for any *l*, *l**, and *l***. Finally, what the Archimedean axiom says is that, if the decisionmaker prefers lottery *l* to *l** to *l***, then there is some number *p* such that she prefers a $(p, 1 - p)$ mixture of *l* and *l*** to *l**; and some other number *q* such that she prefers *l** to a $(q, 1-q)$ mixture of *l* and *l***.

If the decisionmaker ranks **L*** consistently with these three axioms, then there exists a utility function *v*(.), such that the decisionmaker weakly prefers *l* to *l** iff $\sum_{x \in \mathbf{O}} \pi_l(x)v(x) \geq \sum_{x \in \mathbf{O}} \pi_{l*}(x)v(x)$. This utility function is "unique up to a positive affine transformation," meaning that *v**(.) also expectationally represents the decisionmaker's preferences over **L*** (the decisionmaker weakly prefers *l* to *l** iff $\sum_{x \in \mathbf{O}} \pi_l(x)v^+(x) \geq \sum_{x \in \mathbf{O}} \pi_{l*}(x)v^+(x)$), just in case $v^+(x) = av(x) + b$ for all *x*, with *a* positive. See Kreps (1988, ch. 5); Gilboa (2009, ch. 8).

This version of EU theory assumes that the outcome set is finite. More generally, where the "prizes" are not outcomes (for example, where the "prizes" are life-histories), this version of EU theory assumes a finite prize set. So as to simplify the analysis, that will generally be my assumption throughout the chapter: **O** and **H** will be finite. EU theory also extends to the case of an infinite prize set, but this requires additional axioms. See, e.g., Kreps (1988); Fishburn (1982). The construction of **U**, presented later in the chapter, using EU theory and extended preferences, may well be generalizable

Harsanyi employed the von Neumann/Morgenstern version of EU theory, with a twist. Instead of thinking of outcomes as the possible "prizes" in each lottery, he thought of *life-histories* as the possible "prizes" in each lottery. Specifically, given some set **O** of outcomes, and some population of *N* individuals, we can define not just a set **H** of life-histories, but a set **L** of all lotteries over the life-histories. Each element of this set **L** is a lottery *l* which has the following form: $[\pi_l(x; 1), \pi_l(x; 2),\ldots,$ $\pi_l(x; N), \pi_l(y; 1), \pi_l(y; 2),\ldots, \pi_l(y; N), \ldots]$. The symbol "$\pi_l(x; i)$" represents the probability assigned by lottery *l* to life-history $(x; i)$. A given lottery *l* will assign such a value to every life-history in **H**. The probability of any life-history must be a number between zero and one, inclusive. And the sum of the probabilities assigned by *l* to all the life-histories must be one. Set **L**, in turn, is the set of all possible such life-history lotteries.

Imagine, now, a given spectator *k*, who has extended preferences. Spectator *k* can rank the elements of the life-history set **H** and the elements of the life-history lottery set **L**. Furthermore, assume that spectator *k* complies with the von Neumann/Morgenstern axioms: she has a complete ranking of **H** and **L**, and this ranking satisfies the "independence" and "Archimedean" axioms.

If so, there will exist a utility function $u^k(x; i)$, such that the spectator's extended-preference ranking of the lotteries will correspond to their expected utility using this function. In other words, the spectator will weakly prefer lottery *l* to lottery *l** iff the sum of the utility values assigned to each life-history by $u^k(.)$, discounted by its probability according to *l*, is at least as large as the sum of the utility values assigned to each life-history by $u^k(.)$, discounted by its probability according to *l**. Formally, there will exist a utility function $u^k(.)$, such that the spectator weakly prefers *l* to *l** iff $\sum_{(x;i)\in H}\pi_l(x;i)u^k(x;i)\geq\sum_{(x;i)\in H}\pi_{l^*}(x;i)u^k(x;i)$. (The reader unaccustomed to this useful symbolism should consult the margin.)[95]

to the case of a countably infinite or uncountably infinite outcome and life-history set; but how to do so is not a question I will attempt to address.

Sometimes, EU theory substitutes one or another continuity axiom for the Archimedean axiom—showing that there exists a $v(.)$ which expectationally represents the decisionmaker's ranking of **L*** as long as this ranking is complete and satisfies the independence axiom and this continuity axiom. See, e.g., Mas-Colell, Whinston, and Green (1995, p. 171); Ok (2007, p. 398). In that case, the Archimedean requirement will be implied by the existence of $v(.)$, rather than used to prove its existence. However, because the continuity axioms employed in these versions of EU theory involve continuity in the ranking of lotteries, and thus are *different* from the continuity requirement generally discussed in this book (see Chapter 5)—continuity in the ranking of *N*-dimensional utility vectors—the reader may well find it easier to think of EU theory as starting with an Archimedean axiom.

[95] What the symbol "$\pi_l(x;i)u^k(x;i)$" means is the probability assigned to life-history $(x; i)$ by lottery *l*, multiplied by the utility assigned by $u^k(.)$ to that life-history. What the symbol "$\sum_{(x;i)\in H}$" means is that these values are calculated for each life-history belonging to **H** and summed. In other words, $\sum_{(x;i)\in H}\pi_l(x;i)u^k(x;i) = \pi_l(x; 1)u^k(x; 1) + \pi_l(x; 2)u^k(x; 2) + \ldots + \pi_l(x; N)u^k(x; N) + \pi_l(y; 1)u^k(y; 1) + \ldots + \pi_l(y; N)u^k(y; N) + \pi_l(z; 1)u^k(z; 1) + \ldots + \pi_l(z; N)u^k(z; N) + \ldots$.

For short, if spectator k's extended-preference ranking of **L** and **H** complies with the axioms of von Neumann/Morgenstern EU theory, there will exist a utility function which *expectationally represents* k's ranking of the lottery set **L**.[96] Moreover, because a life-history is simply a "degenerate" lottery—a lottery that assigns probability 1 to that life-history, and zero to all others—this utility function $u^k(.)$ will also represent the spectator's extended-preference ranking of **H**. It will be the case that the spectator weakly prefers $(x; i)$ to $(y; j)$ iff $u^k(x; i) \geq u^k(y; j)$. Finally, this utility function $u^k(.)$ will be unique up to a positive affine transformation. To say that $u^k(.)$ is "unique up to a positive affine transformation" means that some other utility function $v^k(.)$ will expectationally represent the spectator's preferences over **L** (as well as representing the spectator's preferences over **H**) iff there exists a positive number a and a number b such that $v^k(x; i) = au^k(x; i) + b$ for every life-history $(x; i)$ in **H**.

How does this construction relate to interpersonal comparisons? Harsanyi not only assumes that each spectator will have an extended-preference ranking of life-histories and lotteries, consistent with EU theory, but adopts the further premise that spectators' extended preferences are *identical*.[97] If so, there will be a single utility function $u(.)$, unique up to a positive affine transformation, which expectationally represents the preferences of all spectators. There will be no need to distinguish between a utility function $u^k(.)$ expectationally representing the preferences of spectator k and a function $u^j(.)$ expectationally representing the preferences of spectator j.

If Harsanyi is indeed correct in his package of assumptions (that spectators possess extended preferences, that these are identical, and that these conform to von Neumann/Morgenstern EU theory), then the utility function $u(.)$ that arises in virtue of these assumptions is—plausibly—a kind of metric of the well-being *levels* of the different life-histories. It is plausible to say that life-history $(x; i)$ is at least as good for well-being as life-history $(y; j)$ iff all the spectators weakly prefer the first to the second. Thus (granting Harsanyi his package of assumptions) it will be the case that life-history $(x; i)$ is at least as good for well-being as life-history $(y; j)$ iff $u(x; i) \geq u(y; j)$.

Of course, we don't really need the apparatus of EU theory to explicate comparisons of well-being levels. We could just say that life-history $(x; i)$ is at least as good for well-being as life-history $(y; j)$ iff all spectators weakly prefer the first to the second.

---

[96] By "expectationally represents," I mean that $u^k(.)$ represents the spectator's preferences over lotteries in the manner just described, via the probabilistic expectation of $u^k(.)$: The spectator weakly prefers l to l^* iff $\sum_{(x;i)\in\mathbf{H}} u^k(x;i)\pi_l(x;i) \geq \sum_{(x;i)\in\mathbf{H}} u^k(x;i)\pi_{l^*}(x;i)$. It is quite possible for some $w^k(.)$ to represent the spectator's preferences over lotteries, but not *expectationally* represent them. For example, if $u^k(.) = h(w^k(.))$, with $h(.)$ not a positive affine transformation, then $w^k(.)$ will *not* expectationally represent the spectator's preferences over lotteries, but it *will* represent them via the rule: the spectator prefers l to l^* iff $\sum_{(x;i)\in\mathbf{H}} h(w^k(x;i))\pi_l(x;i) \geq \sum_{(x;i)\in\mathbf{H}} h(w^k(x;i))\pi_{l^*}(x;i)$.

[97] See Harsanyi (1986, pp. 57–60). See also Harsanyi (1982, pp. 49–52).

The real contribution of the EU apparatus has to do with well-being *differences* between the life-histories. If spectators rank the lotteries over the life-histories in compliance with the axioms of von Neumann/Morgenstern EU theory and have identical rankings that can be expectationally represented by a single utility function $u(.)$, then we can employ $u(.)$ to construct a *difference* ordering of the life-histories.

This possibility emerges because $u(.)$ is unique up to a positive affine transformation. Note that, for any life-history set **H**, the family of utility functions consisting of $u(.)$ and all positive affine transformations of $u(.)$ generates a single, unique, difference ordering of the set. Let us construct a difference ordering from $u(.)$ by saying that the difference between one pair of life-histories $[(x; i), (y; j)]$ is at least as great as the difference between a second pair $[(z; k), (w; l)]$ iff $u(x; i) - u(y; j) \geq u(z; k) - u(w, l)$. This rule generates a complete difference ordering of the life-histories. Moreover—and this is the critical contribution of EU theory—the very same difference ordering of life-histories is generated by swapping $v(.)$ for $u(.)$, where $v(.)$ is a positive affine transformation of $u(.)$. Note that if $u(x; i) - u(y; j) \geq u(z; k) - u(w; l)$, it mathematically follows that $[au(x; i) + b] - [au(y; j) + b] \geq [au(z; k) + b] - [au(w, l) + b]$, for any numbers a and b, with a positive.

In short, Harsanyi has sketched a possible route to constructing exactly what the SWF framework needs: a quasiordering of life-histories and of differences between life-histories, which allows for inter- as well as intrapersonal comparisons, and which is representable by utility numbers. For this contribution he deserves much credit.

However, as mentioned, I believe there are a number of critical gaps or flaws in Harsanyi's analysis. Most fundamentally, he does not confront the philosophical problem of explaining how an extended preference is possible. A preference is a choice-connected ranking. An individual's ordinary preferences are rankings that are linked to her choices, actual or hypothetical. What, then, does it mean for a spectator to have an extended preference—in particular, an extended preference regarding life-histories where she is not the subject?

Harsanyi suggests that a spectator should evaluate life-histories by "imagining himself to be *put in the place*" of the subjects.[98] He suggests that spectator k's extended preference ranking of $(x; i)$ versus $(y; j)$ involves comparing the prospect of being individual i in outcome x, to the prospect of being individual j in outcome y. But there are deep philosophical mysteries here. If the spectator and a given subject are different people, it is *impossible* for the spectator to *be* the subject. More precisely, this is impossible in the "normal" case considered in this book: where there is a population of N, distinct, normal human beings, each of whom exists in all outcomes. In such a case, some spectator k is *necessarily* identical to herself, and *necessarily* distinct from every other person. For any other individual i, it is necessarily (in all outcomes) the case that k and i are distinct.[99]

---

[98] Harsanyi (1986, p. 51).

[99] On the proposition that identical individuals are identical in all possible worlds (and thus that distinct individuals are distinct in all possible worlds)—the so-called "necessity of identity"—see

Thus if spectator k is supposed to evaluate life-history $(x; i)$ by imagining a state of affairs whereby individual k is identical to subject i, and outcome x occurs, then this ranking exercise requires spectator k to imagine something which is impossible.[100]

The reader may protest that Harsanyi does not really intend that the spectator should imagine "assuming the identity" of the subject in any literal sense. Perhaps not. But then he owes us an explanation of what an extended-preference ranking *does* involve and how this ranking is consistent with the metaphysics of personal identity. Neither Harsanyi, nor the subsequent economists or social choice theorists who have employed the idea of an extended preference,[101] have provided such an explanation.

Assume that we can make sense of extended preferences in a manner which is consistent with the metaphysics of personal identity. (I will argue that we can.) If so, we must use extended preferences to construct interpersonal comparisons in a manner that is sensitive to the "remoteness" objection to preference-based accounts of well-being. What if spectator k prefers life-history $(x; i)$ to life-history $(y; j)$ by virtue of facts about outcomes x and y that occur after the deaths of both subjects, or in some other way are too "remote" from these individuals to affect their well-being? Harsanyi does not confront this problem.

Moreover, Harsanyi's premise that spectators will have identical extended preferences is highly problematic. He presents an argument to back up this premise, but the argument is flawed and has been powerfully criticized by John Broome.[102] The critical premise in Harsanyi's argument is that there is a single set of causal laws that explains the variation in individual preferences. These laws, together with specific facts about any given individual, determine what preferences that individual will have: what her preferences regarding various types of actions and outcomes will be;

Lowe (2002, ch. 5); P. Mackie (2006, p. 10). A Parfit-style account of personal identity, in which personal identity reduces to psychological and physical links, see Chapter 6, might call into question the "necessity of identity." This account, at first blush, allows for an esoteric case in which there are N persons in outcome x, with k and i having distinct bodies and brains in x; and k and i "merge" in outcome y to share a single body and brain and thus become the same person in y, leaving $N - 1$ persons there.

Whatever challenge this esoteric case might in fact pose to the "necessity of identity," it cannot arise when human beings have a normal psychological and physical history—the assumption throughout this book.

[100] Dilip Ninan (2009, pp. 445–450) suggests that the thought "I could have been someone else" is a natural one, and true if the relevant "centered worlds" are "accessible." However, this accessibility relation is left unanalyzed. Although "I could have been someone else" is perhaps a natural thought, it may just involve imagining a change in my contingent properties (having someone else's experiences, social status, etc.); or it might be imagining something impossible, like the thought that pi could have been a rational number.

[101] Here, I mean the entire scholarly literature on Harsanyi; the literature on generalized/extended/extensive social welfare functions; and Kolm's work. See above, n. 88.

[102] See Broome (1998). See also Suzumura (1996).

and what her extended preferences will be. But even if this causal premise is true, and even if spectators are aware of the causal laws that predict individual preferences, the purported conclusion that spectators will have the same extended preferences over histories and lotteries is a non sequitur.

For example, imagine that outcomes are specified to include information about individuals' health and consumption. Imagine, further, that in outcome x one individual (Jim) has good health but little consumption, while in outcome y another individual (June) has poorer health but more consumption. Moreover, some spectators rank their own life-histories and life-histories involving other subjects so as to give substantial weight to consumption, while other spectators rank their own life-histories and life-histories involving other subjects so as to give more weight to health. In particular, some spectators have extended preferences that favor $(y; \text{June})$ over $(x; \text{Jim})$, while other spectators have extended preferences that favor $(x; \text{Jim})$ over $(y; \text{June})$. Add, now, the further fact that (1) each spectator knows what Jim's and June's ordinary and extended preferences are; (2) each spectator knows what every other spectator's ordinary and extended preferences are; (3) each spectator knows the causal basis for everyone's ordinary and extended preferences. Does this further fact mean that, now, the spectators must converge in their ranking of $(y; \text{June})$ versus $(x; \text{Jim})$? Why would it? The fact that the members of a community possess common knowledge regarding the diversity of their tastes, and the causal basis for the diversity of their tastes, is, clearly, not the same thing as the members having uniform tastes.

Furthermore, even if spectators do have identical extended preferences over life-histories and lotteries, so that there exists a single $u(.)$ which expectationally represents these preferences, why assume that $u(.)$ is indeed the correct measure of well-being differences between the life-histories? Mightn't there be some other measure, which is a non-linear transformation of $u(.)$? One of the main themes in the critical literature regarding Harsanyi's scholarship is that he fails even to address this question.[103] Although my position will be that something like $u(.)$ is indeed the correct measure of well-being differences between life-histories, I agree with the critics that the position needs a fuller defense than Harsanyi provides. He leaps too quickly from the sheer existence of a utility function that expectationally represents extended preferences over life-histories, to the conclusion that this function measures well-being differences.

Finally, Harsanyi presents his ideas in the context of a defense of utilitarianism. As mentioned, Harsanyi assumes that each spectator develops a *moral* ranking of outcomes by construing each outcome as an equiprobability lottery over its component life-histories. This conception of what a moral ranking of outcomes involves

---

[103] See the discussion of "Bernoulli's hypothesis" in Broome (1995); and see Ng (1999); Risse (2002); Roemer (2008); Sen (1976; 1986, pp. 1122–1123); Weymark (1991, 2005).

leads to utilitarianism.[104] Harsanyi also presents a second, independent argument for utilitarianism, his so-called "aggregation theorem."

However, the concept of an extended preference regarding life-histories and lotteries is logically *separable* from utilitarianism. My account of well-being, below, will use that concept to build a set **U** of utility functions that represent the intra- and interpersonal ranking of life-histories and differences. It is a further and logically separate question, confronted in Chapter 5, whether **U** should be paired with a utilitarian SWF or some kind of non-utilitarian SWF. In Chapter 5, I argue for a *continuous prioritarian* SWF.

This point bears repetition, since Harsanyi is famously associated with utilitarianism, and the reader may thus assume that anyone who uses Harsanyi's ideas must end up with that position as well. This is simply not the case. This book claims that (1) the well-being ranking of life-histories reduces to spectators' convergent extended preferences, but it *rejects* the further claim that (2) outcome x is morally better than outcome y just in case spectators converge in preferring an equiprobability lottery over outcome x's life-histories, to an equiprobability lottery over outcome y's.

III. WELL-BEING: AN ACCOUNT

This section draws upon the discussion of interpersonal comparisons in the previous section, as well as the discussion earlier in the chapter of philosophical debates about well-being, to present an account of well-being. The basic structure of the account is this. Start with a choice situation, with an outcome set **O**, life-history set **H**, and population of N individuals. Using a set **L** of lotteries over the life-histories, each "spectator" k in the population of N individuals can be associated with a set U^k: the set of utility functions that expectationally represent her fully informed, fully rational, extended-preference ranking of **L** (more precisely, particular subsets of **L**) and that have nonexistence as the zero point. Pooling these individual sets across all spectators, we arrive at the set **U**.

In developing this account, I will of course need to provide an explanation of what an extended preference means—an explanation which is consistent with the metaphysics of personal identity. Again, this is a key issue which Harsanyi and other proponents of the idea of extended preferences have not confronted.

The account will be developed in a series of steps. First, I will begin the task of specifying a given spectator's extended preferences by specifying her "own-history" preferences: namely, extended preferences for life-histories in which she is the subject. Such preferences are metaphysically innocent. As we shall see, the idea of "self-interest" shall come into play in specifying a given spectator's "own-history" preferences. Next, I will discuss how the idea of own-history preferences can be

---

[104] See Chapter 5.

generalized to cover life-histories in which the spectator is not the subject. Third, I will discuss what it means for a spectator's extended preferences to be fully informed and fully rational. Fourth, I will discuss how the utility functions that expectationally represent a given spectator's preferences over **L** should be "zeroed out," so as to assign zero to nonexistence. Finally, I discuss the idea of pooling spectators' utility functions.

As we shall see, each spectator's extended-preference ranking of **L** involves certain *counterfactual* choice situations: how she *would* rank certain hypothetical choices, if she were fully informed and fully rational. I do not believe that this feature of my account of well-being is a deficit. Questions about counterfactual choices can have determinate answers[105]; and indeed the use of counterfactual choice situations to address questions about well-being or morality is widespread in philosophy. For example, full-information preferentialist views generally appeal to counterfactual rankings of outcomes and actions as the basis for well-being. The device of a hypothetical choice situation is a cornerstone of Rawls' approach to justice—principles for the basic structure of society are ascertained by asking which principles individuals would accept behind a hypothetical "veil of ignorance"—and of the "social contract" tradition in moral thought that Rawls built upon.

Furthermore, we should distinguish between the problem of *specifying* an account of well-being that invokes idealized extended preferences, and the problem of *estimating* well-being given that account. Tackling the first problem means identifying the particular hypothetical choice situations with reference to which the idea of an "extended preference" is to be understood, and making precise the concepts of "full information" and "rationality." A different question is how the nonomniscient moral deliberator (who will be using the account of well-being under construction here as a part of a moral decision procedure) should *estimate* a given spectator k's idealized extended preferences over **L**.

The problem of estimation is discussed at great length in Chapter 4. The focus, here, is the (logically prior) problem of specification.

A. Own-History Preferences

We can begin the task of specifying a spectator's extended preferences by identifying his own-history preferences. A given spectator's "own-history preferences," as I will define them, involve life-histories in which he is the subject. For a given spectator k, consider the subset of the life-history set **H** containing life-histories of the form $(x; k), (y; k), (z; k), \ldots$ And consider the subset of the set **L** of life-history lotteries, such that lottery l is within this subset iff it assigns probability zero to every life-history in which k is not the subject. Then spectator k's "own-history" preferences are limited in scope to this subset of **H** and this subset of **L**.

---

[105] See Railton (1986a, pp. 19–25).

But this specification of the scope of the spectator's own-history preferences does not, yet, provide a full definition of what they are. How do k's own-history preferences relate to his ordinary preferences for outcome and choices?

It is tempting to say that k's own-history preferences regarding life-histories are just *identical* to his preferences for outcomes: that k prefers $(x; k)$ to $(y; k)$ just in case k prefers outcome x to outcome y. But a spectator's preferences for outcomes may depend on features of outcomes that have nothing to do with his own well-being. If we define k's own-history preferences as his preferences for outcomes, simpliciter, and then make such preferences part of the basis for the well-being ranking of life-histories in which k is the subject, the resulting account of well-being will run afoul of the "remoteness" objection—even if the preferences are idealized to require full information and rationality.

I will therefore define a given spectator's own-history preferences as his *self-interested* preferences for the relevant outcomes. To be precise: Spectator k has a weak own-history preference for $(x; k)$ over $(y; k)$ just in case he *self-interestedly* weakly prefers outcome x to outcome y. Of course, we could achieve the same result by defining a spectator's own-history preferences as his preferences for outcomes, and then constructing an account of well-being that makes reference to spectators' "self-interested" own-history preferences. However, I think it is crisper to build the concept of self-interest into the very definition of an own-history preference.

What does it mean for spectator k to *self-interestedly* prefer outcome x to outcome y? As discussed earlier, I see two plausible approaches for defining "self-interest." One approach sees self-interested preferences as "value laden." It says: spectator k has a self-interested weak preference for outcome x over outcome y just in case k judges or perceives outcome x to be at least as good for his well-being as outcome y. Another approach defines self-interest in terms of *sympathy*—understood as a type of psychological state which is not essentially value-laden. For spectator k to be sympathetic to individual j is for spectator k to have an attitude of care and concern toward j. Sympathy can be self-directed, or directed at others. And it can be partial or unreserved. On this approach to defining "self-interest," spectator k has a "self-interested" weak preference for outcome x over outcome y iff the spectator, under conditions where he is unreservedly self-sympathetic, weakly prefers outcome x to outcome y.

My account will be agnostic between these two approaches to defining "self-interest."

I have discussed own-history preferences for life-histories, but what about own-history preferences for lotteries? A lottery, as mentioned, is a mathematical item, assigning probability numbers to "prizes." More specifically, spectator k's own-history lottery l is a lottery of the form $[\pi_l(x; 1), \ldots, \pi_l(x; k), \ldots, \pi_l(x; N), \pi_l(y; 1), \ldots, \pi_l(y; k), \ldots, \pi_l(y; N), \pi_l(z; 1), \ldots, \pi_l(z; k), \ldots, \pi_l(z; N), \ldots]$, with the special feature that $\pi_l(x; i)$ is given a non-zero value only if $i = k$. What the probability numbers in a lottery *mean* remains to be interpreted.

One standard interpretation sees a set of lotteries as a choice situation in which the decisionmaker's degrees of belief are fixed and exogenous. She enters the choice situation already possessing epistemic probabilities, measuring her degree of belief that any particular choice will yield a particular "prize." There has been some prior process (whatever it may be) yielding this assignment of epistemic probabilities to choices, and the decisionmaker now asks herself: Given that these are my degrees of belief, how do I rank the choices? On this interpretation, a particular lottery is just a numerical representation of a particular choice; and the probability numbers in the lottery are just the decisionmaker's exogenous degrees of belief that the choice will yield various prizes.[106]

Building on this approach, I will define a given spectator's ranking of the subset of L containing his own-history lotteries as follows. Each lottery l corresponds to a choice in a hypothetical choice situation in which the spectator has exogenous epistemic probabilities. The probability values in a given lottery are the epistemic probabilities of the relevant outcomes. Specifically, own-history lottery l represents a hypothetical choice such that k believes to degree $\pi_l(x; k)$ that outcome x will occur; k believes to degree $\pi_l(y; k)$ that outcome y will occur; k believes to degree $\pi_l(z; k)$ that outcome z will occur; and so forth.[107] A different own-history lottery, l^*, represents a different hypothetical choice: a choice such that k believes to degree $\pi_{l^*}(x; k)$ that outcome x will occur; k believes to degree $\pi_{l^*}(y; k)$ that outcome y will occur; k believes to degree $\pi_{l^*}(z; k)$ that outcome z will occur; and so forth.

Spectator k weakly prefers lottery l to lottery l^* just in case he *self-interestedly* weakly prefers the hypothetical choice corresponding to l, over the hypothetical choice corresponding to l^*. As before, I leave open whether "self-interest" should be defined in value-laden terms or in terms of a value-free attitude of unreserved self-sympathy.

B. Extended Preferences for Life-Histories in which the Spectator is not the Subject

I have specified a subset of a spectator's extended preferences, her own-history preferences, in a manner which uses the most familiar kinds of preferences, and which raises no difficulties concerning personal identity—by defining such preferences in

---

[106] A related view sees the probabilities in the von Neumann/Morgenstern set-up as relative frequencies. Each lottery is a hypothetical choice, with various probabilities—in the relative-frequency sense—of various outcomes. Note, however, that norms of rational choice do not, as such, constrain the ranking of choices in light of the relative frequencies associated with the choices. Rather, these norms take account of relative frequencies only insofar as rational beliefs are required to conform to those frequencies. Thus it is more straightforward, and generic, to see the von Neumann/Morgenstern set-up as mapping onto a choice situation with fixed epistemic probabilities (perhaps derived from relative frequencies, perhaps in some other manner).

[107] Because spectator k's own-history lotteries assign zero probability to life-histories in which k is not the subject, an own-history lottery *can* be construed as a choice with exogenous epistemic probabilities of *outcomes*. In other words, $\pi_l(x; i) = 0$ for every life-history $(x; i)$ where $i \neq k$, and thus $\sum_{x \in \mathbf{O}} \pi_l(x;k)=1$.

terms of the spectator's preferences for outcomes and lotteries over outcomes, together with a self-interest component.

How shall we generalize this definition so as to make sense of k's extended preferences regarding life-histories in which she is *not* the subject, and regarding lotteries in which the probability of life-histories in which she is not the subject is nonzero?

One possibility is to reduce a spectator's extended preferences to her own-history preferences, along the following lines. Imagine that life-history $(x; i)$ and life-history $(z; k)$ are related as follows: Subject i's attributes in outcome x are identical to subject k's attributes in outcome z. And imagine that life-history $(y; j)$ and life-history $(w; k)$ are related as follows. Subject j's attributes in outcome y are identical to subject k's attributes in outcome w. Then we might say that spectator k has a preference for life-history $(x; i)$ over $(y; j)$ just in case she has an own-history preference for $(z; k)$ over $(w; k)$.

This is a powerful idea. It will be the keystone of my *estimation* strategy, in Chapter 4: a strategy that uses existing data about an individual's preferences over outcomes and choices, to estimate her own-history preferences, and thereby to estimate her extended preferences more generally. Call this the "swapping attributes" approach to inferring a given spectator's extended preferences.

While the "swapping attributes" approach is a powerful inference tool, it is insufficiently general to serve as a *definition* of extended preferences. The key problem has to do with subjects' *essential properties*. A person's essential properties are properties that he cannot lose, without losing his identity; they are properties that he possesses in every possible world where he exists. What individual properties are essential and what are contingent (non-essential) is a matter of substantial debate. But, arguably, a person's essential properties might include her chromosomal makeup, the identity of her parents, or the date of her birth (if not the precise date, then the general time period). Arguably, it is impossible for Jim, who has chromosomes XY, and who was born in 2010, the child of Sam and Sheila, to have chromosomes XX, to be the child of other parents, or to be born in the year 500.[108]

Imagine that we pursue the "swapping attributes" approach to defining extended preferences. Remember that a given outcome x has the form $(a_1, a_2, \ldots, a_N, a_{imp})$,

---

[108] On essential properties, see Lowe (2002, ch. 6); P. Mackie (2006). One standard view of essential properties, "necessity of origin," would suggest that a person's parents and perhaps certain other circumstances of her coming into being (time of birth) are essential features of her; a second view, "necessity of constitution," would suggest that her DNA is an essential property. Both could be true.

An account of the essential properties of human persons will need to grapple with the general literature in metaphysics just referenced; and also with scholarship on personhood and personal identity, see Chapter 6, including a contested topic ("animalism") I do not discuss at length there, namely whether human persons are essentially human animals, essentially persons, or something else. See generally Olson (1997, 2007).

where a_i are individual i's attributes, and a_{imp} are background facts.[109] Imagine, now, that outcomes are specified so that each individual's attributes include not only her contingent attributes (her income, leisure, happiness, health), but also some of her essential attributes, whatever they may be. Imagine, further, that there are some subjects whose essential attributes are different from spectator k's. If so, the "swapping attribute" strategy collapses. That strategy says the following. If $x = (a_1, a_2, \ldots, a_N, a_{imp})$, then spectator k's extended preference for $(x; i)$ is defined by identifying a life-history $(z; k)$, where $z = (a_1^*, a_2^*, \ldots, a_N^*, a_{imp}^*)$, and where $a_k^* = a_i$. But if individual i's essential attributes are different from spectator k's, there will not exist any such outcome z.

The proponent of the "swapping attributes" strategy might try to get around this difficulty by saying that spectator k's extended preference for $(x; i)$ is defined by identifying some life-history $(z; k)$, where k's *contingent* attributes in z are identical to individual i's contingent attributes in x. But this "solution" would have a critical flaw: it would mean insisting, as a definitional matter, that a subject's essential properties cannot make any difference to his well-being.

I am not suggesting that subjects' essential properties do, in fact, have a substantial impact on their well-being. What I *am* suggesting is that this question should not be resolved as a conceptual or definitional matter. Seemingly, it is a conceptual *possibility* that individuals' essential properties do have some bearing on their well-being. And this seems to be a genuine possibility because of the room for debate about what, exactly, an individual's essential properties are. To pursue the "swapping attributes" approach to *defining* extended preferences would rule out the very possibility that subjects' essential properties—whatever they may turn out to be—can have any impact on well-being. That seems unattractive.

I will therefore pursue a different approach—one that does not stipulate, at the outset, which kinds of properties (contingent versus essential) can influence a spectator's ranking of life-histories and lotteries in which he is not the subject.[110]

---

[109] The symbol "a_i" here denotes a grand vector consisting of i's attributes during each of the T periods in the outcome, i.e., $(a_{i,1}, \ldots, a_{i,T})$, and similarly a_{imp} is a grand vector of the background facts in each period. See Chapter 1, p. 40.

[110] Two other possible approaches bear mention. One possibility, suggested by Zeno Vendler (1976), seems to be the following: when a particular person imagines being someone else, she imagines not that one natural person becomes identical to another, but that her occurrent consciousness is attached to the body and circumstances of that other person. However, it is not clear why I would care what happens to my occurrent consciousness (shorn of the rest of my other characteristics).

Another possibility is to analyze extended preferences for lotteries in terms of a veil of ignorance. There is no metaphysical difficulty in supposing an individual to be ignorant about what her characteristics are (including her essential characteristics). Thus a lottery over life-histories that gives probability $\pi(x;i)$ to life-history $(x; i)$ might be seen as a lottery over outcomes that accords outcome x a probability $p(x)$, undertaken by the spectator with a degree of belief $q(i \mid x)$, such that $p(x)q(i \mid x) = \pi(x;i)$. (The term "$q(i \mid x)$" is a conditional probability, and would be a numerical measure of the spectator's degree of belief that she is individual i, given that outcome x occurs.)

Note, to begin, that we can readily generalize our definition of a spectator's own-history preferences to certain special subsets of **H** and **L**. Consider the subset of **H** consisting of all life-histories in which some individual i is the subject, where i is distinct from k. And consider the subset of **L** consisting of all lotteries in which the only histories with a non-zero probability have i as the subject. Let us call spectator k's extended preferences for these particular subsets of **H** and **L** his "i-history" preferences. Then we can define these preferences the very same way as we defined the spectator's own-history preferences, with one twist. Instead of being "self-interested," the spectator is now "i-interested": interested in the subject i. While the spectator's own-history preferences have been defined as his *self-interested* preferences for outcomes and hypothetical choices, the spectator's *i-history* preferences can be defined as his *i-interested* preferences for outcomes and hypothetical choices.

In other words: spectator k has a weak extended preference for life-history $(x; i)$ over life-history $(y; i)$ just in case spectator k weakly prefers outcome x to outcome y when the spectator is i-interested. Spectator k has a weak extended preference for lottery l to lottery l^*, each according non-zero probability only to i's life-histories, just in case spectator k—when he is i-interested—weakly prefers a hypothetical choice in which the epistemic probabilities of outcomes correspond to the probabilities in l, to a hypothetical choice in which the epistemic probabilities of outcomes correspond to the probabilities in l^*.[111]

What does it mean for a spectator k to be "i-interested"? We can answer this question using the very kinds of answers we used to define "self-interest." One possibility, the value-laden possibility, says that spectator k has an i-interested weak preference for outcome x over outcome y just in case k sees outcome x to be at least as good for the well-being of i as outcome y. The other possibility invokes the value-free attitude of sympathy—but now directed by the spectator onto subject i, rather than onto the spectator himself. On this construal of "i-interest," spectator k has an i-interested weak preference for outcome x over outcome y just in case the spectator, under a condition of unreserved sympathy toward subject i, weakly prefers outcome x to y.

Just as I have been agnostic between the value-laden and sympathy-based construals of self-interest, so I will be agnostic between the parallel construals of "i-interest." And just as my definition of spectator k's own-history preferences builds in a

---

However, there is a very serious tension between requiring that the spectator's preferences be fully informed, as I *will* require, and construing her extended preferences as preferences behind a veil of ignorance about her own characteristics. In particular, the spectator should be fully informed about the origin of her own preferences (a point that Richard Brandt [1998] has pressed with his idea of "cognitive psychotherapy"). But a spectator cannot be both fully informed about the origin of his own preferences, and ignorant about which particular person he is.

[111] In other words, k sees l, a lottery in which only i's histories have non-zero probability, as a hypothetical choice over outcomes such that the probability of outcome x is $\pi_i(x; i)$, the probability of outcome y is $\pi_i(y; i)$, and so forth.

self-interest condition, so my definition of spectator k's i-history preferences builds in a condition of i-interest.

I have thus succeeded in explaining what it means for spectator k to have an extended preference regarding a life-history in which he is not the subject, *without* requiring k to engage in metaphysically impossible thought experiments (imagining that he assumes the identity of someone else), and without making the implausible *conceptual* stipulation that such extended preferences are just equivalent to his preferences for his own life-histories.

The strategy for specifying k's extended preferences over the entire set $\mathbf{H}$ and entire set $\mathbf{L}$ will be to identify the set $\mathbf{U}^k$ which is implied by his own-history and i-history preferences, and then "winnow down" that set using certain additional information. More precisely, imagine that a given spectator has own-history preferences, plus i-history preferences for each subject in the population other than himself. Furthermore, imagine that these preferences are complete. Finally, imagine that these preferences comply with EU theory. Then there will exist a set $\mathbf{U}^k$, consisting of all utility functions that expectationally represent the spectator's own-history and i-history preferences. In other words, if $u^k(.)$ belongs to $\mathbf{U}^k$, then spectator k has a weak extended preference for own-history lottery l over own-history lottery l^* just in case the expected value of $u^k(.)$ with lottery l is at least as large as the expected value of $u^k(.)$ with lottery l^*. Spectator k has a weak own-history preference for life-history $(x; k)$ over $(y; k)$ just in case $u^k(x; k) \geq u^k(y; k)$. Spectator k has a weak extended preference for i-history lottery l over i-history lottery l^*, just in case the expected value of $u^k(.)$ with lottery l is at least as large as the expected value of $u^k(.)$ with lottery l^*. Finally, spectator k has a weak extended preference for life-history $(x; i)$ over life-history $(y; i)$ just in case $u^k(x; i) \geq u^k(y; i)$.[112]

If a spectator has complete own-history and i-history preferences, compliant with EU theory, there will exist such a set $\mathbf{U}^k$. How to construct it from the spectator's own-history and i-history preferences is discussed in the margin.[113]

---

[112] That is: (1) spectator k weakly prefers l to l^* iff $\sum_{(x;i)\in\mathbf{H}} \pi_l(x;i)u^k(x;i) \geq \sum_{(x;i)\in\mathbf{H}} \pi_{l^*}(x;i)u^k(x;i)$, where l and l^* are own-history lotteries; and (2) the same is true where l and l^* are i-history lotteries. Note that, if this is true, $u^k(.)$ not merely represents k's ranking of own-history lotteries but it also, in particular, represents his ranking of any pair of his own life-histories, since each such life-history is a "degenerate" own-history lottery (a lottery assigning a probability 1 to that life-history). Similarly, $u^k(.)$ not merely represents k's ranking of any pair of i-history lotteries, but also any pair of life-histories belonging to some particular subject i.

[113] To create this set, consider the utility function $u_i^k(.)$, which is a utility function that expectationally represents spectator k's preferences over lotteries where i is the subject, and which assigns values *only* to life-histories where i is the subject. In the case where $i = k$, $u_i^k(.)$ becomes $u_k^k(.)$. This function expectationally represents k's own-history preferences, and assigns values *only* to life-histories where k is the subject. In the case where $i \neq k$, $u_i^k(.)$ expectationally represents what I have termed k's i-history preferences, that is, his ranking of life-histories belonging to some subject other than himself. This function, $u_i^k(.)$ assigns values only to the life-histories where the particular individual i (distinct from k) is the subject.

Each $u^k(.)$ in $\mathbf{U}^k$, as constructed thus far, not only represents the subject's own-history and i-history preferences. It also implies a complete ranking of the entire set $\mathbf{H}$ and entire set $\mathbf{L}$. It would be nice if every $u^k(.)$ in $\mathbf{U}^k$ implied the very same complete ranking of the entire set $\mathbf{H}$ and entire set $\mathbf{L}$. But this will *not* be the case.[114]

It might be observed that the grand set $\mathbf{U}$ which we are ultimately constructing in this chapter—the set which will represent the well-being ranking of life-histories and lotteries—can be constructed by pooling the various sets $\mathbf{U}^k$, without requiring

Why believe that such functions will exist? Consider k's own-history preferences. Consider a "prize" set consisting of all life-histories with k as subject, i.e., all life-histories $(x; j)$ which belong to $\mathbf{H}$, and which satisfy the further condition that $j = k$. Assume that k's own-history preferences—in other words, his ranking of this prize set and all lotteries over this prize set—satisfy the axioms of von Neumann/Morgenstern EU theory, i.e., completeness, the independence axiom, and the Archimedean axiom. Then there will exist a function $u_k^k(.)$ expectationally representing k's ranking of the lotteries. In other words, if l is an own-history lottery and l^* an own-history lottery, spectator k weakly prefers l to l^* iff $\sum_{(x;j)\in\mathbf{H},\,j=k} \pi_l(x;j)u_k^k(x;j) \geq \sum_{(x;j)\in\mathbf{H},\,j=k} \pi_{l^*}(x;j)u_k^k(x;j)$.

Similarly, consider k's i-history preferences, for a given particular subject i. Consider a "prize" set consisting of all life-histories with i as subject. If k's i-history preferences—in other words, his ranking of *this* prize set and all lotteries over it—satisfy the axioms of EU theory, then there will exist a function $u_i^k(.)$ expectationally representing k's ranking of the lotteries. In other words, if l is an i-history lottery and l^* a different i-history lottery, spectator k weakly prefers l to l^* iff $\sum_{(x;j)\in\mathbf{H},\,j=i} \pi_l(x;j)u_i^k(x;j) \geq \sum_{(x;j)\in\mathbf{H},\,j=i} \pi_{l^*}(x;j)u_i^k(x;j)$.

For each i in the population of N individuals, denote as $\mathbf{U}_i^k$ the set consisting of $u_i^k(.)$ and all positive affine transformations thereof. (The function $v_i^k(.)$ is a positive affine transformation of the function $u_i^k(.)$ iff there exists some positive number r and some number s such that, for all outcomes x in the outcome set, $v_i^k(x; i) = ru_i^k(x; i) + s$.)

Consider, now, the product set of these N sets. Each element of this product set is a vector of N utility functions, with the form $(u_1^k(.), u_2^k(.), \ldots, u_N^k(.))$. From each such vector of functions we can construct a grand function $u^k(.)$, by setting $u^k(x; i)$ equal to $u_i^k(x; i)$. Let $\mathbf{U}^k$ be the set of these. It is clear that $\mathbf{U}^k$ does expectationally represent the spectator's own-history and i-history preferences.

[114] Each $u^k(.)$ in $\mathbf{U}^k$, as constructed in the previous footnote, can be used to rank any arbitrary pair of lotteries in $\mathbf{L}$ (not merely pairs of own-history lotteries or i-history lotteries), by comparing the expected utilities of those lotteries according to $u^k(.)$. Because a life-history is merely a "degenerate" lottery assigning the value of 1 to that life-history, each $u^k(.)$ in $\mathbf{U}^k$ also can be used to rank any arbitrary pair of life-histories.

Furthermore, every $u^k(.)$ in $\mathbf{U}^k$ will imply the very same ranking of $\mathbf{L}$ and $\mathbf{H}$ iff $\mathbf{U}^k$ is unique up to a positive affine transformation. (Remember what this means: $v^k(.)$ is a positive affine transformation of $u^k(.)$ if there are numbers a, b, with a positive, such that $v^k(x; i) = au^k(x; i) + b$ for all $(x; i)$ in $\mathbf{H}$.)

However, $\mathbf{U}^k$ as constructed in the previous footnote is *not* unique up to a positive affine transformation. The reason is this. Take any $u^k(.)$ in $\mathbf{U}^k$. Consider, now, $v^k(.)$ such that: (1) there is some particular subject i, such that $v^k(z; i) = ru^k(z; i) + s$ for all life-histories $(z; i)$, with r positive, and either r not equal to 1 or s different than zero; and (2) for all other subjects j, $v^k(z; j) = u^k(z; j)$ for all life-histories $(z; j)$. This new function is not a positive affine transformation of $u^k(.)$ but it *does* expectationally represent the spectator's own-history and i-history preferences and *does* belong to $\mathbf{U}^k$, as it has been constructed.

that each U^k correspond to a single complete ranking of the entire sets H and L by a given spectator k.

This observation is absolutely correct. However, if U^k is defined along the lines thus far discussed in this section (consisting of all utility functions that expectationally represent the spectator's own-history and i-history preferences), it will be so "large" that the set U created by pooling these sets across spectators may involve massive incomparability in the ranking of life-histories and differences. Can't we further "winnow down" U^k?[115]

Indeed we can. In order to do so, we need to introduce a new kind of extended preference: an extended preference on the part of spectator k for life-history $(x; i)$ as opposed to life-history $(y; j)$, where i and j are different persons; or an extended preference on the part of spectator k for a lottery l in which all the life-histories with non-zero probability are life-histories of subject i, as against a lottery l^* in which all the life-histories with non-zero probability are life-histories of subject j, where i and j are different persons.

Unfortunately, I see no way to define this new kind of extended preference in wholly value-free terms. It is tempting to say that spectator k has an extended preference for $(x; i)$ over $(y; j)$ just in case the spectator, when unreservedly sympathetic toward the subject, prefers outcome x to outcome y. However, this seems meaningless when the subject is different in the two histories. It is meaningful to say that, when I am sympathetic toward myself, I prefer outcome x to outcome y. It is also meaningful to say that, when I am sympathetic toward Jim, I prefer outcome x to outcome y. But what does it mean to say that I prefer outcome x when I am sympathetic to Jim, to outcome y when I am sympathetic to Sheila? It is coherent to fix the spectator's valuational state (her information, rationality or, in this case, her attitudes of sympathy) and ask how she would rank outcomes with her valuational state thus fixed. What seems incoherent is to ask how she would rank outcomes given a valuational state which varies along with the outcomes being ranked.

Instead, I will define this type of extended preference as follows: spectator k has a weak extended preference for $(x; i)$ over $(y; j)$, with i and j not identical, if spectator k judges that individual i in outcome x is at least as well off as individual j in outcome y. Similarly, we can make sense of k's extended preferences as between a lottery l in which all the life-histories with non-zero probability belong to subject i, and a lottery l^* in which all the life-histories with non-zero probability belong to

---

[115] Indeed, the analysis of Chapter 2, n. 23, shows that, if U^k is not further "winnowed down," many plausible SWFs will collapse to the Pareto quasiordering when combined with U—even in the case where $U = U^k$, i.e., all spectators have the same extended preferences as k, and even if U^k has been "zeroed out" so that $u^k(.)$ is in U only if $u^k(x; i) = 0$ whenever spectator k regards $(x; i)$ as equally good for subject i as nonexistence.

subject j, by having k make judgments regarding the ex ante well-being level realized by the two different subjects with two different outcome lotteries.[116]

It should be stressed that these "value-laden" definitions of the kinds of extended preferences now under analysis are consistent with pursuing a "value-free" approach to defining own-history and i-history preferences. Furthermore, the relevant judgments of well-being need not be *thickly* value laden. In order to rank $(x; i)$ versus $(y; j)$, spectator k does not necessarily bring into play a wide range of value concepts. For example, he does not necessarily have in his head a whole list of objective goods. All that my definition requires is that spectator k, in some manner, reach the minimally value-laden conclusion that subject i is at least as well off in outcome x as subject j in outcome y, or that subject j's ex ante well-being with one choice is at least as large as subject i's with another.

Assume that the spectator has complete own-history and i-history preferences. By adding information about his rankings of pairs of life-histories in which the subjects are different, or pairs of lotteries in which all the life-histories of the first lottery belong to one subject and all the life-histories in the second belong to another, we can "winnow down" $\mathbf{U}^k$—by excluding utility functions which are inconsistent with this new information. And (as elaborated in the margin) we will often, thereby, be able to "winnow down" $\mathbf{U}^k$ to the point where $\mathbf{U}^k$ does correspond to a single, complete, ranking of the entire sets $\mathbf{H}$ and $\mathbf{L}$. In this case, we will have "winnowed down" $\mathbf{U}^k$ so that its elements are unique up to a positive affine transformation.[117] Remember that

---

[116] Just as k can make the judgment that individual i in outcome x is at least as well off as individual j in outcome y, so he can make judgments regarding the well-being upshots, for different individuals, of choices with *uncertain* outcomes—comparing the ex ante well-being level of one individual (were some hypothetical choice, with particular outcome probabilities, to be performed), to the ex ante well-being level of some other individual (were some hypothetical choice, with particular outcome probabilities, to be performed). We can therefore say that k has a weak extended preference for a lottery l in which all the life-histories with a non-zero probability belong to subject i, over a lottery l^* in which all the life-histories with non-zero probability belong to subject j, just in case k judges that the ex ante well-being level of individual i, given an outcome lottery with outcome probabilities corresponding to l, is at least as high as the ex ante well-being level of individual j, given an outcome lottery with outcome probabilities corresponding to l^*.

Note that, if the self-interest and i-interest conditions discussed earlier are construed in value-laden terms, the spectator must also make judgments of ex ante well-being in developing her own-history and i-history preferences. For example, the value-laden construal of a weak extended preference for own-history lottery l over own-history lottery l^* would be: the spectator judges that her own ex ante well-being level produced by a lottery over outcomes with the probabilities specified by l, is at least as high as her own ex ante well-being level produced by a lottery over outcomes with the probabilities specified by l^*.

[117] $\mathbf{U}^k$ can be thus "winnowed down" if there are at least two "points of contact" between the life-histories of individual i and individual $i +1$, for $i = 1$ to $N - 1$. (This is certainly *not* the only way to "winnow down" $\mathbf{U}^k$, but it is a sufficient condition for doing so.) To see how this works, consider a simple case of a population of 3 individuals (the idea generalizes to any finite population). Imagine that there are two outcomes, x and z, such that the spectator judges $(x; 1)$ to be as good as $(z; 2)$.

$v^k(.)$ is a positive affine transformation of $u^k(.)$ if there exists a positive number a and number b such that $v^k(x; i) = au^k(x; i) + b$ for every life-history $(x; i)$ in $\mathbf{H}$. When I say that the set $\mathbf{U}^k$ itself is "unique up to a positive affine transformation," what I mean is this: there exists some $u^k(.)$, such that $v^k(.)$ belongs to $\mathbf{U}^k$ if and only if $v^k(.)$ is a positive affine transformation of $u^k(.)$.

Note that we will have thereby arrived at a single, complete, ranking of $\mathbf{H}$ and $\mathbf{L}$ without ever inquiring into spectator k's preferences regarding lotteries that *mix*

Moreover, there are two other outcomes, y and w, such that: the spectator has an extended preference (a 1-history preference) for $(y; 1)$ over $(x; 1)$; she has an extended preference for $(w; 2)$ over $(z; 2)$; and she sees $(y; 1)$ as equally good as $(w; 2)$.

Choose some arbitrary $u^k(.)$ in $\mathbf{U}^k$. This function may already assign $u^k(x; 1) = u^k(z; 2)$ and $u^k(y; 1) = u^k(w; 2)$. If not, we can "rescale" it to do so as follows. Identify numbers a and b, a positive, such that $au^k(x; 1) + b = u^k(z; 2)$ and $au^k(y; 1) + b = u^k(w; 2)$. Then, specify a new function $v^k(.)$, such that $v^k(.)$ assigns numbers to any life-history $(m; i)$ as follows: $v^k(m; 1) = au^k(m; 1) + b$; $v^k(m; 2) = u^k(m; 2)$; $v^k(m; 3) = u^k(m; 3)$. Given how $\mathbf{U}^k$ has been constructed, $v^k(.)$ will be in $\mathbf{U}^k$.

Imagine, now, that there are also two "points of contact" between individuals 2 and 3. In other words, there are two outcomes, e and g, such that the spectator judges $(e; 2)$ to be as good as $(g; 3)$. Moreover, there are two other outcomes, f and h, such that: the spectator has an extended preference for $(f; 2)$ over $(e; 2)$; she has an extended preference for $(h; 3)$ over $(g; 3)$; and she sees $(f; 2)$ as equally good as $(h; 3)$. Identify numbers a^* and b^*, a^* positive, such that $a^*v^k(e; 2) + b^* = v^k(g; 3)$ and $a^*v^k(f; 2) + b^* = v^k(h; 3)$. Then specify a new function $w^k(.)$, such that $w^k(.)$ assigns numbers to any life-history $(m; i)$ as follows: $w^k(m; 1) = a^*v^k(m; 1) + b^*$; $w^k(m; 2) = a^*v^k(m; 2) + b^*$; $w^k(m; 3) = v^k(m; 3)$.

This function $w^k(.)$ will also be in $\mathbf{U}^k$. Thus it will expectationally represent the spectator's 1-history preferences, 2-history preferences, and 3-history preferences. Moreover, it will represent the spectator's across-person judgments. That is, $w^k(x; 1) = w^k(z; 2)$ and $w^k(y; 1) = w^k(w; 2)$; $w^k(e; 2) = w^k(g; 3)$ and $w^k(f; 2) = w^k(h; 3)$.

Finally, it is straightforward to see that any other function in $\mathbf{U}^k$ which *also* represents these across-person judgments must be a positive affine transformation of $w^k(.)$. Why? Consider any $z^k(.)$ in $\mathbf{U}^k$. Given how this set has been constructed, there must be subject-specific scaling factors that transform $w^k(.)$ into $z^k(.)$. In other words, there must exist $a_1, b_1, a_2, b_2, a_3, b_3$, such that, for any outcome m: $z^k(m; 1) = a_1w^k(m; 1) + b_1$; $z^k(m; 2) = a_2w^k(m; 2) + b_2$; $z^k(m; 3) = a_3w^k(m; 3) + b_3$.

If $z^k(.)$ represents the spectator's across-person judgments, it must be the case that $z^k(x; 1) = z^k(z; 2)$ and $z^k(y; 1) = z^k(w; 2)$. Thus $a_1w^k(x; 1) + b_1 = a_2w^k(z; 2) + b_2$. And $a_1w^k(y; 1) + b_1 = a_2w^k(w; 2) + b_2$. Subtracting one equation from the other, we arrive at the conclusion that $a_1 = a_2$, and thus $b_1 = b_2$. Similar reasoning leads to the conclusion that $a_2 = a_3$, and thus $b_2 = b_3$. Thus $z^k(.) = aw^k(.) + b$.

Although I have shown how to "winnow down" $\mathbf{U}^k$ using across-person "points of contact" that compare life-histories, the idea straightforwardly generalizes to the case where these consist in lotteries over life-histories. In other words, there is some lottery l over individual 1's life-histories which is as good as some lottery l^+ over individual 2's life-histories; and some *other* lottery l^* over individual 1's life-histories, which the spectator extendedly prefers to l, which is as good as some lottery l^{++} over individual 2's life-histories; and similarly for individuals 2 and 3, 3 and 4, and so on.

To be sure, if the spectator's various across-person judgments are to be used to "winnow down" $\mathbf{U}^k$, these judgments should be consistent with each other. "Consistency" can be most simply defined just by saying that there is at least one $u^k(.)$ in $\mathbf{U}^k$ that represents all these judgments. An inconsistent group of judgments will need to be revised.

life-histories. A mixed-history lottery l gives a non-zero probability to life-history $(x; i)$, and a non-zero probability to life-history $(y; j)$, where i and j are different individuals. It is not clear how to interpret a mixed-history lottery. What kind of hypothetical choice, and what kind of value-free or value-laden attitude on the spectator's part, does a mixed-history lottery correspond to? My account does not suppose that a mixed-history lottery *does* correspond to a hypothetical choice. Rather, a mixed-history lottery, like all the elements of **L**, is a mathematical construct. Other elements of **L** do correspond to hypothetical choices. The spectator's ranking of these choices is represented by some U^k, which in turn implies a ranking of all the elements of **L**, including mixed-history lotteries.

In some special cases, the spectator's complete own-history preferences and i-history preferences, together with the new information we have been discussing— his ranking of pairs of life-histories involving different subjects and his ranking of pairs of non-mixed lotteries with different subjects—will not suffice to produce a U^k so that it represents a single, complete ranking of **H** and **L**.[118] However, this possible eventuality is no insuperable obstacle to the account of well-being under development here. U^k will have been "windowed down" to some extent, at least. As in the case of a U^k that represents a complete ranking of **H** and **L**, it can be "zeroed out" (see below) and then pooled with other spectators' individual sets to create the grand set **U**.

C. Full Information and Rationality

The philosophical literature is persuasive on the point that well-being has *critical force*, and thus that an account of well-being which is centered around preferences but fails to idealize those preferences in some manner is problematic. In particular, it is implausible that life-history $(x; i)$ is better for well-being than life-history $(y; j)$ just because spectators, given their actual informational condition (perhaps quite imperfect) and state of rationality (perhaps quite poor), would have various self- and other-regarding preferences over outcomes and choices, and these would imply utility functions that converge in giving a higher ranking to $(x; i)$ than $(y; j)$.

I therefore stipulate that the various kinds of spectator preferences discussed in the previous subsection, used to construct U^k, should be "fully informed" and

---

[118] For example, imagine that there are two individuals and a set of outcomes, and the spectator judges that individual 1 is worse off in each of his life-histories than individual 2 is in any of his. Assume that $u^k(.)$ represents the spectator's own-history and i-history preferences, and is consistent with these across-person judgments. Consider $v^k(.)$ such that, for any outcome m, $v^k(m; 1) = a_1 u^k(m; 1) + b_1$, and $v^k(m; 2) = a_2 u^k(m; 2) + b_2$, with a_1 and a_2 positive. Then it is quite possible that $a_1 \neq a_2$ and $b_1 \neq b_2$ and yet $v^k(.)$ is also consistent with all the across-person judgments. This is also possible where there is only one "point of contact" between the individuals' life-histories, i.e., only one lottery (degenerate or non-degenerate) across individual 1's life-histories that the spectator judges to be equally good as one lottery (degenerate or non-degenerate) across individual 2's.

"fully rational." A spectator k has a fully informed and rational own-history preference for life-history $(x; k)$ over $(y; k)$ just in case the spectator, under conditions of
full information and rationality, would *self-interestedly* prefer outcome x to outcome
y. A spectator k has a fully informed and rational i-history preference for life-history
$(x; i)$ over $(y; i)$ just in case the spectator, under conditions of full information and
rationality, and under conditions where she is i-interested, would prefer outcome x
to outcome y. Full information and rationality conditions can be similarly appended
to the spectator's preferences for lotteries over his own life-histories, for lotteries
over someone else's life-histories, and for comparisons of life-histories or lotteries
involving different subjects.

What do I mean by "fully informed"? Philosophers who have included a "full
information" requirement in their favored account of well-being have specified this
condition in a variety of different ways. There is a need to balance the critical force
of additional information, with the fact that human beings do not have limitless
cognitive abilities.[119]

In my set-up, the spectators are either ranking outcomes or hypothetical choices
which correspond to lotteries—choices where the spectator's epistemic probabilities are fixed and exogenous. Thus we need not stipulate, and indeed should not
stipulate, that the spectator knows for sure which outcome would result from which
choice (for that would undercut the intendedly probabilistic nature of the choice-
outcome nexus). Further, outcomes are simplified descriptions of realities, not
complete possible worlds.

At one extreme, one might simply require that the spectators be fully informed
regarding the stated characteristics of the outcomes. For example, if $x = (c_1, c_2. . .,$
$c_N)$, then k should be aware that individual 1's consumption level in x is indeed c_1,
that individual 2's consumption level is c_2, and so forth. However, such information
is probably too minimal. As Richard Brandt has shown through his detailed discussion of "cognitive psychotherapy," an attractive specification of a full-information condition should include information about the origin of an individual's preferences—for
example, that he prefers outcome x because of social or parental pressure imposed
on him as a child, or because of the association between his attributes in x and
something pleasant.

I therefore tentatively propose the following specification of "full information":
each spectator is provided with (1) full information about the stated characteristics
of the outcomes in O; (2) full information regarding the origins of his own preferences; and (3) any other information which he thinks relevant given (1) and (2), if
fully rational and in a condition of self-interest, i-interest, or making an across-
person judgment. This third category might include information regarding the experiential quality of some feature of outcomes. For example, the description of some

---

[119] See above, pp. 160–162, discussing work by Brandt, Railton, Rawls, and Sidgwick on fully
informed preferences, and citing additional scholarship.

outcome, x, might describe individual i as having a particular health state in that outcome. Spectator k might never have experienced that health state himself and might want more information about what the health state feels like—information which k might find relevant in formulating his i-history preferences.

Let us turn, then, to "full rationality." I distinguished earlier between procedural, historical, and substantive specifications of "full rationality." At a minimum, "full rationality" on my account includes the following procedural requirements, very much in line with those suggested by other scholars who propose idealized-deliberation accounts of well-being or other normative constructs:[120] the spectator's various rankings used to construct U^k must comply with the axioms of EU theory;[121] the spectator should not make mistakes of deductive or inductive reasoning; her first-order and higher-order preferences should be coherent with each other; her attention should be focused on the ranking task at hand, rather than distracted by other issues; her emotional state should be calm.

Of course, as we've seen, various philosophers of well-being have objected that an ideal-preference account which merely incorporates a procedural conception of full rationality is inadequate to screen out certain kinds of distorted preferences. For example, individual i might with full procedural rationality self-interestedly prefer outcome x, in which he has a low status and hardship-filled life, as opposed to outcome y, in which he has a more comfortable and higher-status life, because he has been indoctrinated to believe that he is a low status person and deserves nothing better.

However, I am averse to specifying "full rationality" in partly non-procedural terms, for the following reasons. (1) On the account I am offering, the well-being ranking of life-histories depends on the preferences of all spectators. U is formed by pooling all the U^k sets. Individual i's distorted preference for x over y will not suffice to make $(x; i)$ better than $(y; i)$, if other spectators (lacking the historical or other attributes that have distorted i's preferences), have an i-interested preference for y over x and thus an extended preference for $(y; i)$ over $(x; i)$. (2) I have defined full information so that individuals are given full information about the causes of their preferences. In cases where the spectator's preferences are distorted in the historical sense, i.e., resulted from a process of indoctrination, undue social pressure, adaptation to terrible circumstances, and the like, the fully informed spectator will be made aware of the problematic origins of those preferences and may end up with different preferences after fully procedural rational deliberation. (3) There has been little headway in specifying plausible historical conditions for preference rationality.[122]

---

[120] See the work referenced in the immediately preceding footnote, and also Smith (1994, pp. 154–161).

[121] More specifically, she must comply with the von-Neumann/Morgenstern variant in choice situations where she has fixed, epistemic probabilities.

[122] Imagine that we stipulate that k's preferences at time t_2 are not fully rational if those preferences arose by a process of type D(istorted) at time t_1, even if k at t_2 is aware of what occurred at t_1 and fully

(4) There has also been little headway in specifying plausible substantive conditions for preference rationality. There *are* various specific things which, intuitively, it seems to be substantively irrational to prefer. For example, if k prefers counting blades of grass, eating a saucer of mud, or feeling happy except on Tuesday, this is (intuitively) irrational, even if k does so with full information, full procedural rationality, and a historically kosher process of preference formation. But little progress has been made providing a general rationale for the items that are substantively not preference-worthy.

D. Zeroing Out

Imagine that we have constructed a set $\mathbf{U}^k$ for some spectator k, in some choice situation, along the lines discussed thus far. As discussed, we may often be able to "winnow down" the elements of $\mathbf{U}^k$, so that it is unique up to a positive affine transformation. There is some utility function $u^k(.)$, such that $\mathbf{U}^k$ consists of $u^k(.)$ and all other utility functions $v^k(.)$ equaling $au^k(.) + b$, with a positive.[123] If so, $\mathbf{U}^k$ will correspond to a single, complete ranking of the entire set $\mathbf{H}$ of life-histories and the entire set $\mathbf{L}$ of lotteries over life-histories. And it will also generate a complete ranking of differences between life-histories.

Note, however, that even if $\mathbf{U}^k$ is unique up to a positive affine transformation, $\mathbf{U}^k$ will not imply a unique set of well-being ratios between life-histories (except in the trivial case where $\mathbf{U}^k$ ranks all life-histories as equally good). Imagine that $u^k(.)$ belongs to $\mathbf{U}^k$, and that $u^k(.)$ implies that the well-being ratio between life-history $(x; i)$ and life-history $(y; j)$ is $r \neq 1$. In other words, $u^k(x; i)/u^k(y; j) = r \neq 1$. Consider now any utility function $v^k(.) = u^k(.) + b$, where b is nonzero. Then $v^k(.)$ is a positive affine transformation of $u^k(.)$, hence also a member of $\mathbf{U}^k$. However, this utility function implies that the well-being ratio between the two life-histories is $v^k(x; i)/v^k(y; j)$, which is not equal to r because $[u^k(x; i) + b]/[u^k(y; j) + b] \neq u^k(x; i)/u^k(y; j)$. For example, if $u^k(.)$ assigns the first life-history a utility of 10, and the second a utility of 5, then it implies that the first life-history has twice the well-being of the first. However, if $b = 15$, so that $v^k(.) = u^k(.) + 15$, this new utility function assigns the first

---

procedurally rational. What makes a process of type D? A requirement that the preference-formation process not involve social pressure, or k's adaptation to his circumstances, or be the result of a deliberate attempt by someone else to inculcate preferences in k, is overbroad: such processes occur pervasively. A requirement that that process not involve "undue" social pressure or adaptation is vacuous. Perhaps one might say that the process must be autonomous—and define that non-vacuously by saying that the preferences k developed at t_2 must be preferences that k himself would endorse *at t_1*, if he were fully informed and fully procedurally rational at t_1. But this proposal for an historical condition on rationality seems to give undue weight to k's fully informed and fully procedurally rational views at t_1, as compared to his fully informed and fully procedurally rational views at t_2. On historical conditions, see Sumner (1996, pp. 169–171).

[123] The symbolism "$v^k(.) = au^k(.) + b$" just means that $v^k(x; i) = au^k(x; i) + b$ for all life-histories $(x; i)$ in $\mathbf{H}$.

life-history a utility of 25, and the second a utility of 20, implying a well-being ratio between the two life-histories of 5/4.

Why be concerned about well-being ratios? There are various kinds of quantitative information about well-being that might be represented by utility functions: information about the well-being *levels* of life-histories, information about the well-being *differences* between life-histories, and information about the well-being *ratios* between life-histories. Earlier in the chapter, I provided a formal definition of what it means for information about well-being differences to be relevant to an SWF. Such information is relevant to many SWFs, but not to all (for example, difference information is not relevant to the leximin SWF).

Along similar lines, we can analyze whether information about well-being *ratios* is relevant to an SWF.[124] Not surprisingly, such information is not relevant to the leximin SWF. Nor is it relevant to the utilitarian SWF. But it is relevant to various other SWFs—in particular, to a continuous prioritarian SWF, as Table 3.2 illustrates.

Table 3.2 The Relevance of Well-Being Ratios

	Utility function $u(.)$		Utility function $u^*(.)$	
	Outcome x	Outcome y	Outcome x	Outcome y
Individual 1	100	135	1100	1135
Individual 2	200	160	1200	1160
Utilitarian SWF	300	295	2300	2295
Gini rank-weighted SWF	500	565	4500	4565
Atkinson SWF, $\gamma = \frac{1}{2}$	48.28	48.54	135.61	135.50

Note that $u^*(.) = u(.) + 1000$, hence is a positive affine transformation, but since $b \neq 0$, the ratios between the life-histories according to $u^*(.)$ as opposed to $u(.)$ are different. (For example, the ratio between $(x; 2)$ and $(x; 1)$ according to $u(.)$ is 200/100, but according to $u^*(.)$ is 1200/1100.) The table shows the values assigned to each outcome by the utilitarian SWF, Gini rank-weighted SWF, and a continuous prioritarian SWF of the Atkinson variety with $\gamma = \frac{1}{2}$, according to $u(.)$ and to $u^*(.)$.[125] The utilitarian SWF says x is better in

[124] By "relevant," here, I mean relevant in addition to information about well-being levels and differences. We can say, then, that ratio information is relevant to a given SWF if there exists some choice situation, with some **O**, **H** and **U**, such that: (1) if we supplement **U** with $v(.)$, where $v(.)$ is a positive affine transformation of some member of **U**, thereby producing a new set **U***, the ratio facts regarding **H** according to **U*** are not the same as the ratio facts regarding **H** according to **U**; and (2) the SWF, applied to **U***, yields a different quasiordering of outcomes than when applied to **U**. On what I mean by "ratio facts," see Chapter 5, pp. 379–382. A positive affine transformation, of course, preserves level and difference information.

[125] On the Gini rank-weighted SWF, see Chapter 2, n. 119; and on rank-weighted SWFs in general, see Chapter 5.

either case; the Gini rank-weighted SWF says y is better in either case. (It is not hard to show that ratio information is not relevant to any rank-weighted SWF.) However, the Atkinson SWF using $u(.)$ says that y is better, but using $u^*(.)$ says that x is better.

Although this example involves one particular continuous prioritarian SWF, it can be shown that ratio information is relevant to every continuous prioritarian SWF.[126]

An intuitive argument for why ratio information is relevant to a continuous prioritarian SWF runs as follows. Any prioritarian SWF satisfies the Pigou–Dalton principle in terms of well-being. Decreasing a better-off person's well-being by some amount and improving a worse-off person's well-being by the very same amount, without affecting anyone else, is a moral improvement. But what if we arrange a "leaky" rather than perfect transfer of well-being between the two individuals? We decrease a better-off person's well-being by some amount, and increase the worse-off person's well-being by only a fraction of that amount, for example one-tenth. Nine-tenths of the amount "leaks away" in the transfer from the better to the worse-off person.[127] Intuitively, our judgment whether this "leaky" transfer is morally attractive will depend on the well-being ratio between the two individuals. We will find it relevant, in reaching that judgment, whether the better-off individual is 20 times better off (in which case the leaky transfer may well seem morally attractive) or only twice as well off (in which case it very well may not).

The topic of well-being ratios is discussed at substantial length in Chapter 5, in connection with the continuous prioritarian SWF. A central point emerging from that discussion is the following: assigning well-being ratios to life-histories depends on the specification of some life-history as the zero point. To say that the well-being of life-history $(x; i)$ is five times the well-being of life-history $(y; j)$ is just to say that

---

[126] A continuous prioritarian rule R for ranking utility vectors is anonymous and Paretian and also satisfies axioms of continuity and separability. See Chapter 5. If ratio information is not relevant to a continuous prioritarian SWF, then (as per the definition of "relevance" in the preceding footnote), it must be the case that the SWF produces the very same ranking of any outcome set using either $u(.)$ or any positive affine transformation of $u(.)$ to map outcomes onto utility vectors. But, by Theorem 13.6 in Bossert and Weymark (2004, p. 1160), this invariance feature together with separability, continuity, anonymity, and Paretianism implies that R is utilitarian, which is a contradiction.

[127] On leaky transfers, see Chapter 5. The reader might worry that this example is circular. Doesn't the assumption that a certain *fraction* of the transfer "leaks" *already* imply ratio information? Aren't we just starting with ratio information to argue for ratio information? In fact, no. Imagine that **U** is unique up to a positive affine transformation. Then **U**, it turns out, uniquely defines *ratios of differences*. If $v(.) = au(.) + b$, a positive, then $[u(x; i) - u(y; j)]/[u(z; k) - u(w; l)] = [v(x; i) - v(y; j)]/[v(z; k) - v(w; l)]$. But it is not true that $u(x; i)/u(y; j) = v(x; i)/v(y; j)$ unless b is zero or $u(x; i) = u(y; j)$. So we start with a **U** that gives complete information about well-being differences and levels and how "leaky" any transfer would be, and argue that it would be useful to "winnow down" this set so as to increase our information about well-being ratios.

the difference between the well-being of $(x; i)$ and a zero point, divided by the difference between the well-being of $(y; j)$ and a zero point, is five.

What then is the correct zero point for constructing well-being ratios? I suggest that the most attractive answer is *nonexistence*. There is no logical necessity in this answer. For a given life-history set, we could stipulate that some life-history $(x^*; i^*)$ is the zero point, where the well-being of $(x^*; i^*)$ might be better or worse than non-existence; and we could "winnow down" U^k by including only functions that assign the number 0 to $(x^*; i^*)$. But it is very hard to see what rationale we could provide for identifying $(x^*; i^*)$. By contrast, nonexistence quite naturally suggests itself as the zero point. Nonexistence constitutes a clear break point for life-histories. Life-histories above nonexistence are worth living; life-histories below nonexistence are not worth living; and this qualitative difference between the two is, intuitively, one that has much moral relevance. If some other life-history $(x^*; i^*)$ is supposed to be the zero point, one can ask: what are the special features of $(x^*; i^*)$ that give rise to a morally relevant distinction between life-histories better than $(x^*; i^*)$ and life-histories worse than it?

I therefore propose that we "winnow down" U^k by including only functions that assign the number zero to *nonexistence*.[128] More specifically, imagine that there is some life-history where the spectator is the subject, $(y^+; k)$, such that the spectator is indifferent between this life-history and nonexistence. In other words, the spectator under conditions of full information, full rationality, and self-interest, is indifferent between outcome y^+ (an outcome in which he exists) and a possible world in which he never comes into existence.[129] Some utility functions in U^k will assign zero to $(y^+; k)$, others will not. The latter should now be excluded from U^k.

Note that this procedure for "zeroing out" U^k requires the spectator to compare one of his own life-histories to nonexistence. So none of the subtleties involving a spectator's ranking of the life-histories of other subjects arise in this case. The spectator's own-history preferences, in general, are equivalent to his ranking of the corresponding outcomes under a condition of self-interest. The spectator's ranking of one of his own histories $(x; k)$, vis-à-vis nonexistence, is equivalent to his self-interested preference ranking as between the outcome in the life-history (x) and nonexistence.

It might be protested that this is impossible. It is impossible for the spectator to have a self-interested preference ranking of outcomes which includes not only various outcomes in which he exists (all the outcomes in O), but also nonexistence. But why *is* this impossible? One might argue that an individual's preference ranking is connected to her choices; and thus that an outcome can be included in the set of outcomes regarding which the individual has preferences only if she can causally

---

[128] As elaborated in Chapter 5, the use of the number zero to represent the zero point (as opposed to the designation of a life-history as the zero point) is merely a mathematical convenience.

[129] This construction plausibly assumes that, if the spectator is self-interested, then he is indifferent between all outcomes in which he does not exist.

influence whether the outcome occurs. And, of course, an individual who already exists cannot cause herself not to have existed. Although someone can cause herself to die (to "cease existing"), she cannot cause herself not to have come into existence.

It is far from clear whether the outcomes subsumed by a preference ranking must, indeed, be outcomes that the holder of the preference can causally influence.[130] In any event, there clearly are other types of pro-attitudes that are *not* choice connected and are not subject to a causal-control proviso. In particular, a "wish" is a pro-attitude which need not be choice connected. Although the past is outside my causal control, I can have *wishes* regarding the past. I can *wish* that I didn't make that embarrassing comment to Suzy Q in 10th grade, even though there is nothing that I can do now to cause the nonoccurrence of the comment.[131] Moreover, I can have an attitude of "wish indifference," akin to the attitude of indifference in a preference ranking. While I wish that I didn't make that comment to Suzy Q, I am indifferent to the fact that I ate Cheerios, not Wheaties, for breakfast when I was 5. For the reader who doubts that an individual can have preferences regarding outcomes outside his causal control, I suggest that the life-history $(y^+; k)$, used to "zero out" U^k, be such that the spectator, under conditions of full information, rationality, and self-interest, is wish-indifferent between y^+ and a possible world in which he does not exist.[132]

A different objection is that existence cannot be better or worse for a person than nonexistence—because if it were, nonexistence would be better or worse for the person than existence, which is nonsensical, since there would be no person to *be* better or worse off. But the difficult problem of whether existence can be a harm or benefit is beside the point, here.[133] Even if someone cannot be harmed or benefitted by nonexistence, it certainly remains possible for an existing person to prefer (or at least wish) not to have existed.

A final, more technical difficulty is this: In a given outcome set **O**, there may not exist a particular life-history $(y^+; k)$, such that the spectator is indifferent between that history and nonexistence. This difficulty can be readily circumvented, by using the spectator's preferences (or wishes) regarding lotteries that involve some probability of nonexistence.[134]

What results when U^k is "zeroed out", so that it includes only utility functions which assign zero to nonexistence? If U^k, to begin, was unique up to a positive affine transformation, it is now unique up to a positive ratio transformation. Utility function

[130] See above, n. 18.

[131] See Arneson (1999b, p. 128).

[132] To avoid terminological clutter, however, I will continue to use the term "preference" in discussing spectators' pro-attitudes regarding nonexistence—recognizing that they might be genuine preferences or just wishes.

[133] See Chapter 8 for a discussion of that problem and citations to the literature.

[134] See Chapter 4.

$v^k(.)$ is a positive ratio transformation of utility function $u^k(.)$ if there exists some positive number r, such that $v^k(x; i) = ru^k(x; i)$ for all life-histories $(x; i)$ in **H**. To say that $\mathbf{U}^k$ is "unique up to a positive ratio transformation" means that there is some $u^k(.)$ such that $v^k(.)$ belongs to $\mathbf{U}^k$ if and only if $v^k(.)$ is a positive ratio transformation of $u^k(.)$.

If $\mathbf{U}^k$ is unique up to a positive ratio transformation, it will not only imply a complete ranking of life-histories and a complete ranking of differences between life-histories. It will also assign unique ratios between life-histories. Note that if $u^k(x; i)/u^k(y; j)$ equals some value R, and if $v^k(.) = ru^k(.)$, with r positive, it follows that $v^k(x; i)/v^k(y; j) = R$. Moreover, even if $\mathbf{U}^k$, to begin, was *not* unique up to a positive affine transformation, the process of "zeroing out" may well mean that it assigns unique ratios to some pairs of life-histories, or places the ratios between others within reasonably circumscribed ranges.

E. Pooling Utility Functions

The prior sections specified a set $\mathbf{U}^k$ for each spectator. This set represents her fully informed, fully rational extended preferences regarding life-histories, life-history lotteries, and comparisons to nonexistence.

The set **U** is formed by pooling these sets, across all N spectators. **U** is the union of $\mathbf{U}^1$ and $\mathbf{U}^2$ and . . . and $\mathbf{U}^N$. Just as each $\mathbf{U}^k$ is a theoretical construct—representing how an individual under idealized conditions would rank certain counterfactual choices—so, too, is **U** a theoretical construct. How to estimate the various $\mathbf{U}^k$ and thus **U** is discussed in the next chapter.

If each $\mathbf{U}^k$ is unique up to a positive ratio transformation, *and* if spectators' fully informed, fully rational extended preferences are homogeneous—in other words, if $\mathbf{U}^1 = \mathbf{U}^2 = . . . = \mathbf{U}^N$—then **U** will be unique up to a positive ratio transformation too. It will consist of some $u(.)$, and all positive ratio transformations of $u(.)$. In this simple, limiting case, **U** will define a *complete* well-being quasiordering of life-histories, and a complete difference quasiordering of life-histories. Remember that the rule for generating a well-being quasiordering of life-histories from a set **U** is: life-history $(x; i)$ is at least as good as life-history $(y; j)$ iff, for all $u(.)$ belonging to **U**, $u(x; i) \geq u(y; j)$. And the rule for generating a difference quasiordering of life-histories from a set **U** is: the difference between $(x; i)$ and $(y; j)$ is at least as large as the difference between $(z; k)$ and $(w; l)$ iff, for all $u(.)$ belonging to **U**, $u(x; i) - (y; j) \geq u(z; k) - u(w; l)$. If **U** is unique up to a positive ratio transformation, both of these quasiorderings will be complete. Moreover, **U** will ascribe a unique ratio to any pair of life-histories; and will yield a definite verdict regarding whether any life-history is better or worse than nonexistence.

I suggested earlier that each spectator's $\mathbf{U}^k$ will normally, if not invariably, be unique up to a positive ratio transformation. Is there also reason to think that spectators will normally have homogeneous fully informed, fully rational extended preferences? I see no reason to assume, *a priori*, that they will. To begin, there is no reason to insist, *a priori*, that spectators' *non-ideal* extended preferences will be homogeneous.[135] Do we secure homogeneity in extended preferences by idealizing them? Since "full rationality" has been specified in procedural, rather than substantive terms, there is no reason to assume that every fully informed, fully rational spectator k will end up with the very same set $\mathbf{U}^k$.

A great virtue of the account presented here, I believe, is that it *allows* for spectators to have identical extended preferences, but does not insist on such homogeneity. Homogeneity might be the case as an empirical matter; or it might be adopted as a simplifying premise, for purposes of estimation or otherwise.[136] But where extended preferences *are* heterogeneous, the set $\mathbf{U}$ formed by pooling all the $\mathbf{U}^k$ will still be adequate as the basis for an SWF. It will still define an (incomplete) quasiordering of life-histories and differences, allowing for some interpersonal comparisons of levels and differences (at least absent radical heterogeneity). And it will define ranges of ratios between the levels of different life-histories, if not unique ratios.

One distinction between the quasiordering of life-histories, and the quasiordering of differences, is worth noting. In the former case, we can see $\mathbf{U}$ as numerically representing a quasiordering that can be defined independent of $\mathbf{U}$. We can say: life-history $(x; i)$ is at least as good as life-history $(y; j)$ iff all spectators, under conditions of full information and rationality, would weakly prefer $(x; i)$ to $(y; j)$. That, in turn, will be the case only if $u(x; i) \geq u(y; j)$ for all $u(.)$ belonging to $\mathbf{U}$. By contrast, the difference quasiordering that I am arguing for cannot be defined independent of $\mathbf{U}$. $\mathbf{U}$ is essentially involved in the very construction of that difference quasiordering. Of course, since $\mathbf{U}$ is essentially involved in the very construction of that difference quasiordering, $\mathbf{U}$—trivially—represents the difference quasiordering.

F. Why Is this an Attractive Account of Well-Being?

I have proposed to analyze well-being in terms of fully informed, fully rational extended preferences. But why is this account attractive? Why should it be endorsed? My answer returns to the earlier sections of this chapter, surveying the philosophical literature on well-being and the case for interpersonal comparisons. I believe that the account fulfills a variety of desiderata outlined in these sections. Let me briefly summarize how it does so.

---

[135] For example, spectator k and spectator l might have different i-interested preferences over outcomes and choices, regarding some third person i. Spectator k's i-interested preferences over outcomes and choices might differ from spectator i's self-interested preferences. Finally, spectators k and l might differ in their across-person judgments (that one individual in some outcome is at least as well off as another individual in some outcome, or that one lottery across outcomes is better for one individual than another lottery is for another).

[136] See Chapter 4.

There is a powerful case for interpersonal comparisons. And the account, indeed, makes well-being interpersonally comparable. The extent of comparability depends on the degree of heterogeneity in spectator preferences. At the limit, where these are homogeneous, and furthermore each $\mathbf{U}^k$ itself unique up to a positive ratio transformation, there will be full intra- *and* interpersonal comparability of life-histories and differences. Every life-history will be better, worse, or equally good as every other life-history (regardless of whether the subjects are the same or different); and the difference between any pair of life-histories will be larger, smaller, or equal to the difference between every other pair.

The philosophical literature on well-being suggested, furthermore, that an attractive account of well-being should have *critical* force; it should have *motivational* force; and it should not depend on features of outcomes too *"remote"* from the subject. My account is consistent with this trio of truisms. (1) *Critical force.* Because the preferences of a given individual k are *idealized* in the course of defining $\mathbf{U}^k$, and also because the well-being ranking of k's life-histories depends on the extended preferences of the entire population, an individual can be wrong about her own well-being. Individual k might incorrectly believe that $(y; k)$ is better for well-being than $(x; k)$ when, in fact, $u(x; k) > u(y; k)$ for all $u(.)$ in $\mathbf{U}$ and thus $(x; k)$ is better. (2) *Motivational force.* Well-being, thus defined, has motivating force under ideal conditions. If it is true that $(x; k)$ is better for well-being than $(y; k)$, then $u(x; k) \geq u(y; k)$ for all $u(.)$ in $\mathbf{U}$, with at least one inequality strict. Given how $\mathbf{U}$ has been constructed, this implies, in turn, that $u^k(x; k) \geq u^k(y; k)$ for all $u^k(.)$ belonging to $\mathbf{U}^k$, i.e., that the subject k, under conditions of full information and rationality, would self-interestedly weakly prefer x to y. The well-being ranking of the subject's life-histories is thus conceptually connected to her ideal *preferences*: to what she would be motivated to choose, if she had full information and rationality. Moreover, it is plausible that well-being has motivating force under some non-ideal conditions. Under some range of non-ideal conditions, individual k will be motivated by the knowledge that she would self-interestedly weakly prefer x to y under ideal conditions. (3) *Remoteness.* Because $\mathbf{U}^k$ is built up from the spectator's self-interested and *i*-interested preferences for outcomes, it screens out features of outcomes that are too remote from subjects.

What kind of account is this? Is it a mental-state account? A preference-based account? An objective-good account?

As I emphasized earlier, these are not mutually exclusive categories. My account makes reference, of course, to individual preferences. (Like other preferentialist accounts, such as the full-information preferentialist views defended by Brandt and Railton, it does so in order to preserve the motivational truism.) But the account can also be seen as a kind of objective-good account. A view of well-being is characterizable as an objective-good account if it filters out idiosyncratic preferences—if it does not reduce an individual's well-being to his own preferences, actual or idealized— and, further, does not make an individual's well-being solely a function of his mental states.

My account *is* an objective-good account in this sense. It analyzes the well-being ranking of life-histories, and differences between life-histories, in terms of individuals' *convergent* idealized preferences. One life-history is at least as good as a second iff *all* spectators, under conditions of full information and rationality, would weakly prefer the first to the second. This is true both when the subjects of the two histories are different, and when they are the same. For $(x; i)$ to be at least as good for well-being as $(y; i)$, it is a *necessary condition* that the subject under ideal conditions weakly prefer the first to the second; but this is not a sufficient condition.

Because the account appeals to *convergent* preferences, it has an appealing "liberal" flavor. Philosophical liberals insist that individuals may have a diversity of conceptions of the good life and that political theory and moral philosophy should respect such diversity. And indeed my account does respect such diversity. The well-being ranking of life-histories and differences represents the "zone of consensus" between individuals' rankings, which are permitted to be heterogeneous.

While the account is both a preference-based account and a kind of objective-good account, it cannot be characterized as a mental-state account. Nozick's experience machine provides a very strong case against insisting that well-being supervenes on mental states. To be sure, the account I propose is consistent with the proposition that mental states are an important source of well-being, perhaps the dominant source. (If spectators' extended preferences depend largely on subjects' mental states, that will be the case.) Indeed, the account is consistent with the proposition that mental states are, as a matter of contingent fact, the sole source of well-being. (If turns out to be the case that spectators' extended preferences solely depend on subjects' mental states, that will be true.) But the account does not *necessitate* that mental states are the sole source of well-being. It is possible that $(x; i)$ is better for well-being than $(y; j)$ even though individual i's mental states in x are identical to individual j's mental states in y. The well-being ranking of these two histories depends on the various kinds of preferences used to construct each U^k and, ultimately, U. These preferences are restricted in various ways (they must be self-interested, "i-interested," and so forth), but these restrictions have been carefully defined so as to permit them to be sensitive to feature of outcomes other than the subjects' mental states. The extent to which spectators' extended preferences are thus sensitive is an empirical question.

Finally, how does the account relate to various metaethical positions? It sits most comfortably with an ideal-approval metaethics. In particular, it sits very comfortably with an ideal-approval view which analyzes moral facts in terms of individuals' convergent idealized preferences. Such a view says that outcome x is morally at least as good as outcome y iff all individuals, with full information and rationality, and taking an impartial perspective, would converge in weakly preferring x to y. It is natural to combine this view with the further claim that the *well-being* ranking of life-histories is a matter of individual's idealized preferences (now, not impartial preferences, but self-interested, i-interested, etc.). However, the account here is at least logically consistent with a much broader range of metaethical positions: for example, a noncognitivist view, or a cognitivist view which is distinct from an ideal-approval view.[137]

IV. LINGERING OBJECTIONS

In the course of presenting the account, I have countered a number of potential objections; but there are several others, not yet discussed, which are worth addressing.

A. Intertemporal and Interworld Change in Preferences

In presenting the account, I assumed that each spectator k is associated with a single fully informed, fully rational, extended-preference ranking of various subsets of **H** and **L**, giving rise to a single set $\mathbf{U}^k$. But it might be objected that these rankings can vary from time to time. Just as there can be intertemporal variation in an individual's ordinary preferences, so, too, we should allow for intertemporal variation in a spectator's extended preferences. Indeed, because a spectator's extended preferences are defined, in various ways, in terms of his ordinary preferences, it would be incoherent to allow for intertemporal change in ordinary preferences but not extended preferences. For example, spectator k has a weak extended preference for $(x; k)$ over $(y; k)$ iff he has a self-interested weak preference for outcome x over outcome y, and a weak extended preference for $(x; i)$ over $(y; i)$ iff he has an i-interested weak preference for outcome x over y. But spectator k's preferences at one point in time regarding outcomes (be they self-interested preferences, i-interested preferences, or some other

---

[137] The noncognitivist sees a moral statement as the endorsement of a norm, expression of a preference, commitment to a plan, or something like that. Taking an impartial perspective, individual e might care about the distribution of an attribute which he calls "well-being," and might care about its distribution just because (in part) he sees well-being as something that motivates individuals. Thus: individual e might endorse a choice-evaluation procedure such that the ranking of outcomes depends, not merely on e's own preferences, but on other individuals' preferences as well, insofar as the satisfaction of those preferences is connected to the individuals' well-being.

To be sure, it might be wondered why e would endorse the construction of **U** that I have undertaken. Why pool everyone's extended preferences? Wouldn't e care only about the satisfaction of everyone else's ordinary self-interested preferences? Wouldn't e endorse a choice-evaluation procedure that sets **U** equal to $\mathbf{U}^e$ (the set that represents e's own extended preferences)—under a constraint that $\mathbf{U}^e$ be strongly sovereignty respecting (so as to take account of everyone else's ordinary self-interested preferences)? On strongly sovereignty-respecting extended preferences, see below.

However, there are a variety of difficulties with extended utilities that are strongly sovereignty respecting, discussed below, and to avoid them e might instead endorse the construction of **U** which I have recommended.

As for a cognitivist view which is distinct from ideal-approval view, and instead sees moral facts as having an explanatory role: it is quite possible that certain facts about convergent preferences have an explanatory role. See Railton (1986b).

kind of outcome-preference) need not be the same as his preferences regarding outcomes at some other time.

Moreover, if a spectator's extended preferences at different times are indeed different, it is hard to see what non-arbitrary basis we would have for using only the preferences at a subset of these times in constructing $\mathbf{U}$.

This objection is quite cogent. Of course, as an *estimation* matter, it may well be simplest to assume intertemporal homogeneity in extended preferences; but the account itself should not insist on this. For simplicity, my presentation of the account in the prior section ignored the possibility of preference change; but the account can and should be generalized to allow for that possibility. Assume there are T time periods (most straightforwardly, the T periods in an outcome set specified in terms of multiple periods). Then spectator k's fully informed and rational extended preferences at time t are captured in a set $\mathbf{U}^{k,t}$. With N spectators and T periods, there are NT such sets. Pooling all the sets, we arrive at $\mathbf{U}$.

Should we push the idea further? We can distinguish between an individual's extended preferences in the actual world,[138] and her extended preferences in some other possible world. Someone's ordinary preferences can vary across worlds (Eileen prefers to be a lawyer rather than a doctor, but had she been brought up differently would have preferred to be a doctor) and so, too, can someone's extended preferences. Why not construct a set $\mathbf{U}^{k,t,x}$ for each spectator k—representing his extended preferences in some outcome x in the outcome set $\mathbf{O}$, at time t—and then pool all these sets, across spectators, times, and outcomes in $\mathbf{O}$, to construct $\mathbf{U}$?

I am inclined to endorse this approach. Imagine, instead, an "actualist" approach which constructs $\mathbf{U}$ by pooling sets of the form $\mathbf{U}^{k,t,x^*}$, across times and spectators, where x^* is one particular outcome—the actual one. A key flaw of the "actualist" approach is that x^* is not predetermined. In a given choice situation, with a given outcome set, which outcome is actual depends upon which choice the decision-maker selects from the choice set $\mathbf{A}$. Thus the content of $\mathbf{U}$, constructed in "actualist" fashion, is sensitive to the decisionmaker's choice. But such choice-dependence eviscerates (or at least radically changes) the SWF approach. The ambition of that approach is to morally *guide* choice among possible options by drawing upon utility information ($\mathbf{U}$) and a rule R for ordering utility vectors that can be fixed independent of which option is selected.

A countervailing worry is that the construction of $\mathbf{U}$ by pooling extended preferences not only across spectators, but also times and possible outcomes, might make $\mathbf{U}$ so "large" as to inject massive incomparability into the ranking of outcomes. However, it must be remembered that the extended preferences of relevance, here, are *fully informed, fully rational* extended preferences. In many outcomes, a given individual's idealized extended preferences will not tend to vary much over time.

---

[138] Here, "actual" is meant to contrast with "merely possible," as opposed to the use of "actual" in distinguishing between actual (imperfectly informed, imperfectly rational) and idealized preferences. On preference change across times and outcomes, see, e.g., Bykvist (2006); Gibbard (1986).

And many of the policy choices that the SWF framework would be used to evaluate would not be so radical as to change an individual's idealized extended preferences (whatever effect the choices might have on his non-ideal preferences).[139]

For the remainder of this chapter and book, particularly where intertemporal or interworld variation in a spectator's extended preferences is not relevant to the discussion, I will often continue to use the symbol "U^k," which is less clumsy than "$U^{k,t,x}$." However, the reader should now see "U^k" as a shorthand. In discussing a spectator's extended preferences, and the set which represents these, I mean—strictly—his extended preferences at some time and in some outcome. U is the union of all such sets, across times, outcomes, and spectators.

B. Respecting Individual Sovereignty

An account of well-being might be described as "sovereignty respecting" insofar as it makes a given individual's own-history preferences, actual or idealized, determinative of the well-being ranking of those histories and differences between them. More precisely, an account might be termed "weakly" sovereignty respecting if it never *overrides* an individual's preferences regarding her own histories. And it might be termed "strongly" sovereignty respecting if it makes an individual's preferences regarding her own histories *decisive* in ranking the histories and differences between them.

The account I have proposed is weakly sovereignty respecting. If individual i, under conditions of full information and rationality, prefers life-history $(x; i)$ to life-history $(y; i)$, it will *not* be the case that the second life-history is ranked higher by U. This is because utility functions capturing individual i's own-history preferences, via the set U^i, are one component of U. Similarly, the account will never reach the conclusion that the difference between one pair of i's life-histories is greater than the difference between another pair if U^i itself implies that the first difference is smaller.

However, this account is *not* strongly sovereignty respecting. If individual i, under conditions of full information and rationality, prefers life-history $(x; i)$ to life-history $(y; i)$, but some other individuals prefer $(y; i)$ to $(x; i)$, the upshot will be that U counts the two life-histories as incomparable. A similar result holds for differences. Indeed, my observation that the account is characterizable not only as a preference-based

---

[139] This last observation assumes something like the following procedure for constructing O. For a given choice set A, and some initial O, we exclude from O all outcomes that have a zero (or very low) probability regardless of which choice is performed. O, thus winnowed down, includes only those outcomes such that, given at least one action in A, there is a non-zero (or non-trivial) probability of the outcome being actual.

If the policy choices at hand would not change a given individual's idealized extended preferences, then (if O is constructed along the lines just suggested), those preferences will be the same in all outcomes in O.

account, but also as a kind of objective-good account, would not be true if it were strongly sovereignty respecting.

By contrast, Harsanyi employs extended preferences to arrive at an account of well-being that *is* strongly sovereignty respecting (as captured in his so-called "principle of acceptance").[140] This is one of the important differences between his account and my own.

My approach *could* be revised to make it strongly sovereignty respecting. This is clearly possible if each individual's preferences over her own histories and lotteries over those histories are fixed (across time and worlds). Assume that everyone in the population is aware of everyone's own-history preferences. Then a given U^k could be constructed as follows. Spectator k should formulate her own-history preferences, as before, by looking to her self-interested preferences over outcomes and choices. But she should formulate her i-history preferences in a different way. Instead of defining those in terms of her i-interested preferences over outcomes and choices, spectator k's i-history preferences should just "piggy back" on individual i's own-history preferences. In other words, spectator k has a weak extended preference for $(x; i)$ over $(y; i)$ just in case individual i has a weak own-history preference for $(x; i)$ over $(y; i)$, i.e., just in case individual i would self-interestedly weakly prefer outcome x to outcome y. Spectator k has a weak extended preference for one lottery over i's histories, as opposed to another lottery over i's histories, just in case individual i would have a weak own-history preference for the first lottery rather than the second.

If each U^k is constructed in this manner, and these sets are then pooled to create U, the ranking of life-histories and differences with reference to U will be strongly sovereignty respecting.

However, I have not pursued this approach, for several reasons. First, the philosophical case for making U strongly sovereignty respecting is hardly overwhelming. Objective-good theories of well-being, which have substantial support in the literature, necessarily reject the proposition that well-being is strongly sovereignty respecting.

Second, it is far from clear how to develop a strongly sovereignty-respecting approach in the case where individuals' own-history preferences can vary across times and outcomes. Imagine that, at time t^*, individual i prefers $(x; i)$ to $(y; i)$; at time t^{**}, she prefers $(y; i)$ to $(x; i)$. Which of these contradictory preferences is spectator k supposed to respect? The same problem arises, of course, if, in outcome z, individual i prefers $(x; i)$ to $(y; i)$; but she has the opposite preference in outcome w.

Third, as a practical matter, a strongly sovereignty-respecting U is more difficult to *estimate* than a U constructed along the lines that I have advocated. Note that, on this approach, it is impossible for k to formulate her extended preferences without knowing what everyone's own-history preferences are. Thus, estimation would

---

[140] See Harsanyi (1986, p. 54); Weymark (1991, p. 290).

require a two-stage approach. To begin, the decisionmaker (or the analyst advising her) estimates the own-history preferences of everyone in the population (or at least of different categories of individuals). Then, the decisionmaker conducts special surveys, where respondents are advised of the information collected at the first stage, and asked about their extended preferences under the constraint that these respect each individual's ordering of her own life-histories and lotteries.

By contrast, as explored at length in the next chapter, the approach that I have recommended allows spectators to possess extended preferences without knowing what other individuals' preferences are;[141] and it allows for the estimation of extended preferences via standard sources of evidence about individual preferences, rather than requiring special life-history surveys.

C. The Limits of EU Theory (Herein of Incompleteness)

EU theory is an essential component of my account. The account assumes that each spectator's ranking of various hypothetical choices conforms to the simple von Neumann/Morgenstern variant of EU theory.

Is this problematic? It is now quite widely accepted that EU theory fails to *describe* how individuals in many contexts actually behave[142]; but I am employing EU theory here as a normative, not descriptive, theory. It is one aspect of the requirement that the spectator be "fully rational."

As we shall see in Chapter 7, there *are* a variety of possible challenges to the normative credentials of EU theory. One important challenge says that EU theory lacks normative status for purposes of moral decisionmaking. Here, however, I am using the theory to structure spectators' *self-interested* or *i-interested* ranking of various choices, not spectators' moral ranking of choices.

A different, normative objection to EU theory says that, in some choice situations, individuals may have *indeterminate* probabilities. Indeed, this is true. But to say that indeterminate probabilities may occur in some choice situations is not, of course, to say that determinate probabilities can never occur. In particular, it is *possible* for a decisionmaker to face a choice situation in which she takes as given exogenous and determinate epistemic probabilities and asks herself: given that these are my degrees of belief, how do I rank the choices at hand? By specifying spectators' hypothetical choices in this manner, we can bring von Neumann/Morgenstern EU theory into play and construct a set U^k which will represent difference as well as level comparisons. It is hard to see how the sheer fact that this construction employs a hypothetical choice situation with exogenous and determinate probabilities is a problematic feature of the construction—whatever its other flaws.

---

[141] As discussed in Chapter 4, my account is flexible: information about subjects' preferences might be included in the description of outcomes, but it might also (for simplicity) be treated as "missing."
[142] See, e.g., Hastie and Dawes (2001).

A third objection involves *incompleteness*. EU theory assumes that individuals have complete rankings of outcomes and lotteries, but it is far from clear why this is normatively compelling. In particular, my construction of each $\mathbf{U}^k$ assumes that spectator k's self-interested preferences concerning outcomes and choices are complete, yielding a complete ranking of his own life-histories, and a complete ranking of all lotteries over his own life-histories. It also assumes that spectator k's i-interested preferences concerning outcomes and choices are complete, yielding a complete ranking of i's life-histories and complete ranking of all lotteries over i's life-histories, for each subject i. Why believe that k, even if fully rational, would have complete rankings of this sort?

Indeed, a central thrust of this book has been to argue in favor of incomplete rankings of various kinds. I have claimed that the *moral* ranking of outcomes can be an incomplete quasiordering, and that the *well-being* rankings of life-histories and differences can also be incomplete quasiorderings. The assumption that each spectator's own-history and i-history preferences are complete helps to simplify the construction of $\mathbf{U}$, and to facilitate the implementation of the account presented here, but this assumption would be problematic—in serious tension with my eagerness to allow other kinds of incompleteness—if seen as a foundational feature of the account.

Fortunately, the assumption can be relaxed. Vitally important recent work in EU theory shows how it is possible to relax completeness but retain the other axioms of the theory. In particular, Juan Dubra, Fabio Maccheroni, and Efe Ok have demonstrated the following, in the von Neumann/Morgenstern set-up: if an individual has an incomplete preference ranking of outcomes and lotteries, but her ranking satisfies the independence axiom and a continuity axiom, that incomplete ranking can be expectationally represented by a set of utility functions.[143] This result means that it is possible to construct a $\mathbf{U}^k$ which represents the spectator's extended preferences even if his own-history or i-history preferences are incomplete. The details are discussed in the margin.[144]

---

[143] See Dubra, Maccheroni, and Ok (2004); Ok (2007, p. 499). See also Evren (2008).

[144] The Dubra, Maccheroni, and Ok result shows that spectator k's incomplete preferences regarding lotteries over subject i's histories, if consistent with the independence and continuity axioms, can be represented by $\mathbf{U}_i^k$. (This is true both in the case where $i \neq k$, and in the case where $i = k$, in which case $\mathbf{U}_i^k$ becomes $\mathbf{U}_k^k$ and represents k's own-history preferences.) Each $u_i^k(.)$ in the set $\mathbf{U}_i^k$ assigns a utility only to a life-history with subject i, one with the form $(x; i)$. The spectator will weakly prefer lottery l over i's histories to lottery l^* over i's histories iff, for all $u_i^k(.)$ in $\mathbf{U}_i^k$, $\sum_{(x;i)\in\mathbf{H}}\pi_l(x;i)u_i^k(x;i)\geq\sum_{(x;i)\in\mathbf{H}}\pi_{l^*}(x;i)u_i^k(x;i)$.

Consider, now, the product set of these N sets. Each element of the product set is a vector of N functions, $(u_1^k(.), u_2^k(.), \ldots, u_N^k(.))$. For each such vector, define a new function $u^k(.)$ as follows: $u^k(x; i) = u_i^k(x; i)$ for every life-history $(x; i)$. $\mathbf{U}^k$ is the set of all such functions. For any i, $\mathbf{U}^k$ thus constructed will represent the spectator's preferences regarding i-history lotteries, via the rule: l is at least as good as l^* iff, for all $u^k(.)$ in $\mathbf{U}^k$, $\sum_{(x;i)\in\mathbf{H}}\pi_l(x;i)u^k(x;i)\geq\sum_{(x;i)\in\mathbf{H}}\pi_{l^*}(x;i)u^k(x;i)$. However, by

D. Should We Use EU Theory to Construct a Difference Ordering?

An important theme in the critical literature regarding Harsanyi is that he provides no justification for using utilities that expectationally represent lotteries over life-histories to measure the well-being differences between those histories.[145] The objection, here, does not concern the general credentials of EU theory as an account of rational choice under uncertainty. Nor is the objection that well-being differences are not intra- or interpersonally comparable at all. (As we have seen, there is a strong case for difference comparability). The line of criticism I am referring to accepts the possibility of difference comparisons, and the generic credentials of EU theory, but challenges the use of EU theory to construct such comparisons.

Unlike certain other challenges to Harsanyi's views that have been frequently raised, this challenge can also be leveled at my account. The issue, here, is orthogonal to the question of homogeneous versus heterogeneous extended preferences, and to the possibility of spectators having extended preferences that vary over time or outcomes or yield an incomplete ordering of life-histories or differences. I will therefore simplify the discussion by assuming, first, that each spectator k has a single set $\mathbf{U}^k$ which is unique up to a positive affine transformation and which, zeroed out, is unique up to a positive ratio transformation; and, second, that these sets are identical across spectators. Thus $\mathbf{U}$ itself is unique up to a positive ratio transformation.

In general, of course, my approach *constructs* a difference ordering from $\mathbf{U}$. In the case where $\mathbf{U}$ is unique up to a positive ratio transformation, this difference ordering will be complete. It will be the case that the well-being difference between life-history $(x; i)$ and $(y; j)$ is at least as large as the well-being difference between life-history $(z; k)$ and life-history $(w; l)$ iff $u(x; i) - u(y; j) \geq u(z; k) - u(w; l)$, where $u(.)$ is any utility function in $\mathbf{U}$. (Given uniqueness up to a positive ratio transformation, every $u(.)$ in $\mathbf{U}$ will produce the same complete difference ordering.) In particular, it will be the case that the well-being difference between life-history $(x; i)$ and life-history $(y; i)$ is at least as large as the well-being difference between life-history $(z; i)$ and life-history $(w; i)$ iff $u(x; i) - u(y; i) \geq u(z; i) - u(w; i)$.

At the same time, $\mathbf{U}$ will expectationally represent spectators' preferences over life-history lotteries. Consider any lottery l over some subject i's histories, and any other lottery l^* over that subject's histories. Then, given how $\mathbf{U}$ has been "built up" from spectators' lottery preferences, it will be the case that spectators will prefer the first lottery to the second iff the expected utility from the first lottery, using $u(.)$, is greater than the expected utility from the second lottery, using $u(.)$. Of course, to say that $u(.)$ expectationally represents lotteries over i's life-histories is, in turn, equivalent

---

contrast with the case where the spectator's preferences are complete, this $\mathbf{U}^k$ cannot be "winnowed down." The preferences are represented by the entire set, not by each member taken alone.

[145] See sources cited above, n. 103.

to saying that $u(.)$ expectationally represents how spectators, concerned about i's well-being, would rank lotteries over outcomes.

But why think that there will necessarily exist a utility function which is able to play both these roles?[146] Why believe that we should be able to produce a $u(.)$ which can do two things at once: (1) represent whether the difference between an individual's well-being in two outcomes is larger or smaller than the difference between that individual's well-being in two other outcomes; and (2) expectationally represent how lotteries over outcomes should be ranked in light of that individual's well-being? Mightn't there be some measure $b(.)$, which is the true measure of well-being differences, and which need not equal $u(.)$ or a positive ratio or affine transformation thereof? If such a $b(.)$ existed, the relationship between $u(.)$ and $b(.)$ might be as shown in Figure 3.1.

If the relation between $b(.)$ and $u(.)$ were non-linear in this way, spectators, ranking lotteries over outcomes in light of individual i's well-being, would be risk-averse or risk-prone in $b(.)$. The expected value of $b(.)$ would *not* necessarily correspond to the spectators' ranking of the lotteries.

By contrast, if $u(.)$ is itself the measure of well-being differences, as my account supposes, the relation between $u(.)$ and $b(.)$ is necessarily linear. But to say that the relation between $u(.)$ and $b(.)$ is necessarily linear (as my account does) is to say that spectators, ranking lotteries over outcomes in light of individual i's well-being, must necessarily be risk-neutral in his well-being. Why believe that this is necessarily the case? It is a truism that the utilities provided by EU theory need not be linear in various sources of well-being. An individual can be risk-averse or risk-prone in terms of dollars, health, leisure, etc. Why shouldn't it also be possible for a self-interested individual, or a spectator concerned about that individual's well-being, to be risk-averse or risk-prone in well-being itself?

For this line of criticism of my account to be compelling, we would need to identify a competing method for arriving at a difference ordering of life-histories—one that does not construct a difference ordering via spectators' preferences over life-history lotteries—and that is attractive on its own terms. However, I suggest that competing methods for producing a difference ordering are beset by various difficulties that my account avoids.

One possibility assumes that spectators can directly compare differences between life-histories. In particular, assume that each $\mathbf{U}^k$ is constructed as follows. Spectator k starts with his own life-histories and, as before, compares pairs of life-histories such as $(x; k)$ and $(y; k)$ by asking whether he self-interestedly prefers x or y. However, spectator k does not then proceed to think about lotteries at all. Instead,

---

[146] Strictly, my account doesn't say that there will necessarily exist such a $u(.)$, just in the case where each spectator's $\mathbf{U}^k$ defines a complete ranking of the set of all life-history lotteries and the $\mathbf{U}^k$ are identical. But it is surprising that there should exist a $u(.)$ which can play both of these roles even under these circumstances—even if spectators have the same complete extended preferences over lotteries.

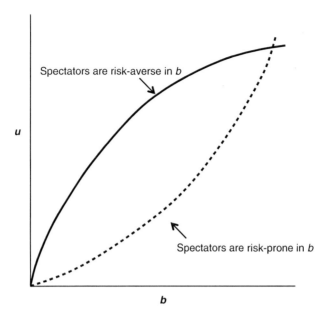

Figure 3.1 Possible Departures from Risk Neutrality with Respect to the Measure of Well-Being Differences. *Note:* The $b(.)$ function measures well-being differences between life-histories. In particular, $b(x; i) - b(y; i) \geq b(z; i) - b(w; i)$ whenever the well-being difference between $(x; i)$ and $(y; i)$ is at least as large as the well-being difference between $(z; i)$ and $(w; i)$. The $u(.)$ function expectationally represents spectators' preferences over life-history lotteries (for simplicity, spectators are assumed here to have identical such preferences). The solid and dotted lines illustrate two different ways in which the $u(.)$ value assigned a life-history might be a non-linear function of its $b(.)$ value.

he thinks about whether the difference between $(x; k)$ and $(y; k)$ is greater than the difference between $(z; k)$ and $(w; k)$, for various such pairings. He does this by asking: Is the difference in my well-being as between x and y greater than the difference in my well-being between z and w?

Spectator k then engages in a parallel exercise with respect to the life-histories of every other subject. Finally, k asks the sort of across-subject question suggested by my account. He ranks pairs of life-histories such as $(x; i)$ and $(y; j)$ by asking: Is i's well-being in x greater than j's well-being in y? If things go well, all of these level and difference comparisons on the part of k will be representable by a single utility function $u^k(.)$, unique up to a positive affine transformation.[147]

---

[147] The literature on difference measurement shows that a complete difference ordering can be represented by a utility function unique up to a positive affine transformation. See Krantz et al. (2007, pp. 151–152). See also Abdellaoui, Barrios, and Wakker (2007). Thus spectator k's ordering of the differences between individual i's histories can be represented by all the members of

This approach is, necessarily, much more thickly "value laden" than the approach I have argued for. As discussed, my approach allows for the possibility that the spectator arrives at most (if not all) of his various rankings of life-histories and lotteries via value-free comparisons—comparisons that do not themselves involve judgments or perceptions of well-being. (For example, his ranking of lotteries over his own life-histories might be specified as a "self-interested" ranking of lotteries over outcomes, with "self-interested" in turn understood in value-free terms, as a condition of unreserved self-sympathy.) The approach I defend *also* allows for the possibility that the spectator arrives at his rankings of life-histories via value-laden comparisons. (The spectator's "self-interested" ranking of lotteries over outcomes *might* be understood as a judgment that one lottery is better for his well-being than a second.) By contrast, comparing pairs of outcomes with respect to differences in someone's well-being is necessarily a value-laden exercise. The spectator necessarily does this by thinking *about* the subject's well-being.

My account thereby preserves a kind of agnosticism with respect to a controversial question, rooted in unresolved metaethical disputes: to what extent do facts about well-being reduce to idealized value-laden judgments? It has the virtue of being reasonably robust to these disputes, while the competing approach now under consideration does not.

Moreover even if one is comfortable making spectators' rankings pervasively value-laden, it is a further question whether spectators can make judgments about differences. Such judgments (on the view under consideration) would have to be "primitive" judgments, which (1) are distinct from judgments concerning well-being levels and (2) cannot be analyzed in terms of choices. As for (1): For spectator k to judge that individual i is at a higher level of well-being in x than y, and in z than w, leaves open whether the difference between i's well-being in the first two outcomes is larger or smaller than the difference between i's well-being in the second two outcomes. As for (2): If differences are not analyzable in terms of choices over lotteries, how does the spectator's judgment that the well-being difference between $(x; i)$ and $(y; i)$ is greater than the difference between $(z; i)$ and $(w; i)$ relate to any possible choice on her part? (Although one can choose an outcome, in the sense of selecting an action under a condition of certainty that the outcome would result from the action, it is not possible to choose an action yielding a difference between outcomes.). If the answer is negative, that direct difference comparisons have no connection to choices at all, one must then ask: are there really value judgments which are not choice connected?

Asking spectators to make direct difference comparisons is not the only competitor to the approach I have defended. There are a variety of other possible approaches, suggested by the literature. I cannot discuss these approaches at length.

---

some $\mathbf{U}_i^k$, unique up to a positive affine transformation. And we can generate $\mathbf{U}^k$ along the same lines as in nn. 113, 117 above.

However, for reasons very briefly reviewed in the margin, I suggest that these are even less attractive as a general methodology for constructing U^k than direct difference comparisons. (1) If a spectator's ranking of life-histories is assumed to be *temporally separable*, we might arrive at a U^k which is unique up to a positive ratio transformation, and which yields a complete difference ordering, without asking her to rank lotteries. (2) If a spectator's ranking of life-histories is assumed to be *separable across attributes*, we might again arrive at a U^k which is unique up to a positive ratio transformation, without asking the spectator to rank lotteries. (3) The "zero-one" approach first proposed by Isbell might be employed to construct U, namely by assigning utility to each spectator's own life-histories by taking a utility function that expectationally represents her own-history preferences and "scaling" this function so that 1 is assigned to the spectator's most preferred history and 0 to her least preferred.[148]

---

[148] Assume that life-histories have multiple "dimensions," e.g., each life-history has multiple periods, or there are multiple types of attributes that the subject is characterized as having. A standard result in utility theory shows that, if a ranking of items with multiple dimensions is appropriately separable across those dimensions, and also satisfies a continuity requirement, the ranking can be represented by an *additive* utility function $u(.)$. The utility assigned by $u(.)$ to a given item will be the sum of the values assigned to the item by M "subutility" functions, $v^1(.), v^2(.),\ldots, v^M(.)$, with M the number of dimensions. See Blackorby, Primont, and Russell (1998, pp. 70–73); von Winterfeldt and Edwards (1986, chs. 8–9, especially pp. 331–334). Moreover, it is easy to see why $u(.)$ might be unique up to a positive affine transformation. Note that if we subject the M subutility functions to a common positive affine transformation, i.e., produce a new subutility function $\varphi^m(.) = av^m(.) + b$, with a positive, for $m = 1$ to M, then ranking items by summing $\varphi^m(.)$ values will order the items exactly the same way as $u(.)$. This new array of subutility functions will correspond to a positive affine transformation of the original $u(.)$, namely $au(.) + Mb$. On the other hand, if we subject the M subutility functions to a common increasing transformation, and sum these new subutility values, the ranking will not generally be the same as that achieved by $u(.)$.

A $u(.)$ assigning values to life-histories that is unique up to a positive affine transformation will yield a complete difference ordering (even without being zeroed out); but, once zeroed out by assigning zero to nonexistence, becomes unique up to a positive ratio transformation.

There is indeed a literature that assumes attribute separability as a basis for constructing interpersonally comparable utilities. See Evans, Kula, and Sezer (2005), estimating the elasticity of marginal utility of income based on an assumption of "want independence" (additive separability) between groups of goods. Kahneman and co-authors have proposed an interpersonally comparable metric of experienced well-being. In moving from an ordinal measure of instantaneous experiential well-being to a cardinal measure of the experiential well-being of a temporally extended episode, they assume temporal separability. See Kahneman, Wakker, and Sarin (1997); Kahneman, Krueger, Schkade et al. (2004).

However, the temporal or attribute separability routes to the construction of U are problematic. The temporal separability approach is unavailing in the case of outcome sets with a single period. Moreover, while temporal and/or attribute separability are useful heuristics, well-informed preferences need not satisfy these conditions. See Chapter 6. Our methodology for ascribing utilities should be robust to the possibility that the conditions are not satisfied.

To be sure, the reader might concede that the various competitors to the account proposed here are problematic, but still argue that some such competitor is, on balance, more attractive. "It is deeply counterintuitive that the correct measure of well-being differences is necessarily a linear function of $u(.)$. It is deeply counterintuitive that spectators, ranking lotteries across outcomes in light of someone's well-being, should be risk-neutral in that person's well-being." But is this really deeply counterintuitive? I don't believe that our intuitions on this score are that strong or well-formed. As Mattias Risse points out: "[O]ur intuitions about risk-attitudes with regard to well-being are not as developed as our intuitions about risk-attitudes with regard to, say, money. . . ."[149] The fact that an account of well-being entails risk-neutrality in well-being itself (as mine does) is an acceptable price to pay if the account is, on other dimensions, sufficiently attractive.

The zero-one rule implies that everyone is equally productive of well-being: that moving one individual from his worst to best outcome yields the same well-being change as moving some other individual from his worst to best outcome. But why believe this? See Adler and Posner (2006, p. 47); on the zero-one rule, see also Fleurbaey and Hammond (2004, pp. 1227–1228); Hausman (1995).

[149] Risse (2002, p. 566).

4

ESTIMATING UTILITIES

Chapter 3 developed an account of well-being—involving individuals' extended preferences—and an associated methodology for assigning utilities to life-histories, captured in a set **U**. This chapter continues the work of Chapter 3. It addresses a wide variety of issues that the policy analyst would confront in using extended preferences to construct the set **U** in any given choice situation (given some outcome set, life-history set, and population). The analysis in this chapter, as in Chapter 3, is entirely independent of the functional form of the SWF. Subsequent chapters will argue for a continuous prioritarian SWF; but a **U** built up from extended preferences can, instead, be paired with a leximin SWF, a utilitarian SWF, a rank-weighted SWF, or any other.

The reader will be reminded of the central elements of the account of well-being developed in Chapter 3. Each individual in the population of N individuals possesses extended preferences. I describe each such individual as a "spectator"—a term which does *not* mean she is external to the population, but rather refers to some individual in the population in her capacity as a holder of extended preferences.

An extended preference, on the part of some spectator k, is her ranking of life-histories or life-history lotteries. Such a preference can be represented by an *extended* utility function (denote it as $u^k(.)$), which takes life-histories as its arguments. In other words, $u^k(.)$ takes the form $u^k(x; i)$, with $(x; i)$ a life-history. Extended preferences are to be distinguished from *ordinary* preferences. An *ordinary* preference, on the part of some spectator k, is her ranking of outcomes or outcome lotteries. Ordinary preferences are represented by an ordinary utility function (denote it as $\varphi^k(.)$), which takes outcomes as its arguments. In other words, $\varphi^k(.)$ takes the form $\varphi^k(x)$, with x an outcome.

While extended preferences and extended utility functions are formally distinct from ordinary preferences and ordinary utility functions—the two types of preferences differ in what they rank, the two types of utility functions in what they take as their arguments—there are critical, conceptual, connections between extended and ordinary preferences and utilities. Chapter 3 focused on three types of extended preferences: "own-history" preferences, "*i*-history" preferences, and "across-person judgments." Spectator k's own-history preferences are rankings of life-histories where *she* is the subject, or lotteries over such histories. Spectator k's *i*-history preferences are rankings of life-histories where some other person, i, is the subject, or lotteries over such histories. Spectator k's "across-person judgments" are rankings of pairs of life-histories, such as $(x; i)$ and $(y; j)$, where i and j are different subjects; or rankings of pairs of lotteries over life-histories, such that i is the subject of all the life-histories in one lottery, and j the subject of all the life-histories in the other.

Critically, "own-history" preferences were analyzed in terms of a certain kind of *ordinary* preference: namely, ordinary, self-interested preferences. Spectator k has a weak extended preference for life-history $(x; k)$ over life-history $(y; k)$ just in case, under conditions of self-interest, she has a weak preference for outcome x over outcome y.[1] A similar analysis was offered for extended preferences regarding own-history lotteries.[2]

Spectator k's *i*-history preferences were analyzed in terms of a *different* sort of ordinary preference, namely ordinary preferences under a condition of *i*-interest. Spectator k has a weak extended preference for life-history $(x; i)$ over life-history $(y; i)$, just in case, under conditions of *i*-interest, spectator k has a weak preference for outcome x over outcome y. A similar analysis was offered for spectator k's extended preferences regarding *i*-history lotteries.[3]

Finally, spectator k's across-person judgments were analyzed in terms of her judgments of well-being. She has a weak extended preference for $(x; i)$ over $(y; j)$ just in case she judges that individual i in x is at least as well off as individual j in y. A similar analysis was offered for across-person judgments involving lotteries.

Across-person judgments are necessarily value laden; they involve judgments of well-being. By contrast, the conditions of "self-interest" and "*i*-interest" used to define, respectively, own-history and *i*-history preferences might be understood in either value-laden or value-free terms. Chapter 3 was agnostic on that issue, and the analysis presented in this chapter also will be.

---

[1] Remember that preferences can be strict or weak, and that an individual weakly prefers one item to a second if she strictly prefers it or is indifferent. As throughout the book, the term "strict" will be implicit and "weak" explicit; when I say that an individual "prefers" one item to a second, simpliciter, I mean strict preference.

[2] An own-history lottery l, assigning probability $\pi_l(x; k)$ to life-history $(x; k)$, $\pi_l(y; k)$ to life-history $(y; k)$, and so forth, corresponds to a hypothetical choice where k believes to degree $\pi_l(x; k)$ that outcome x will occur, to degree $\pi_l(y; k)$ that outcome y will occur, and so on. Spectator k weakly prefers own-history lottery l to own-history lottery l^* just in case he weakly self-interestedly prefers the hypothetical choice corresponding to l over that corresponding to l^*. See Chapter 3.

[3] The analysis was exactly parallel to that summarized in the previous footnote. Each *i*-history lottery corresponds to a hypothetical choice with outcome probabilities, and we look to k's ranking of such choices, now under a condition of *i*-interest.

The three types of extended preferences can be represented by a set $\mathbf{U}^k$, which is (normally) unique up to a positive affine transformation.[4] Once $\mathbf{U}^k$ is "zeroed out," so as to assign the number zero to nonexistence, it will (normally) be unique up to a positive ratio transformation.

The account of well-being developed in Chapter 3 required each spectator's extended preferences to be fully rational and fully informed. In this chapter, too, whenever I discuss a spectator's extended preferences or the set $\mathbf{U}^k$ that represents these preferences, I mean her fully rational and informed preferences. In discussing a spectator's *ordinary* preferences, I usually mean her fully rational and informed preferences. Where I mean to discuss ordinary preferences that are irrational or less than fully informed, the context will make that clear or, if not, I will say so explicitly.

The set $\mathbf{U}$ is, in turn, formed by pooling the sets of individual extended utility functions. $\mathbf{U}$ is just the union of $\mathbf{U}^1, \mathbf{U}^2, \ldots, \mathbf{U}^k, \ldots, \mathbf{U}^N$, each representing the extended preferences of one individual in the population, functioning as a "spectator."[5]

Strictly, "$\mathbf{U}^k$" should be "$\mathbf{U}^{k,t,x}$." A given individual's extended preferences can vary across times and outcomes. In practice, policies may produce little variation in individuals' (fully informed and rational) extended preferences, so that $\mathbf{U}^{k,t,x}$ is in fact identical for all outcomes x. (And the same may be true of intertemporal variation.) Moreover, for purposes of *estimation*, it may be simplest to assume little inter-outcome or intertemporal variation. However, as a conceptual matter, extended preferences and the sets of utility functions which represent them are spectator-, time-, *and* outcome-relative. $\mathbf{U}$ is formed by pooling all these sets. Thus, throughout the chapter, "$\mathbf{U}^k$" should be read as a shorthand for "$\mathbf{U}^{k,t,x}$."

The material just summarized provides the backdrop for the problems addressed in this chapter. One such problem, a large and important one, concerns *simplified outcomes*. Outcomes are not complete possible worlds, but more limited descriptions of possible realities. This is a feature, not merely of the SWF approach, but of all policy frameworks. But the simplified nature of outcomes raises some distinct puzzles for the construction of the set $\mathbf{U}$. What exactly does it mean for an individual to have extended preferences with respect to life-histories that arise from simplified

---

[4] While Chapter 3 entertained the possibility that k might have incomplete ordinary preferences, this chapter will not address that complication.

[5] It is important for the reader to understand that the various elements of this construction of $\mathbf{U}$—the ordinary preferences of each "spectator" in the population; the extended preferences of each "spectator" in the population; the set $\mathbf{U}^k$; and $\mathbf{U}$ itself—are all defined in the context of a given outcome set $\mathbf{O}$ and life-history set $\mathbf{H}$. However, at certain junctures in the current chapter, I assume that the outcome set has been suitably expanded, and then discuss $\mathbf{U}^k$ and $\mathbf{U}$ for the expanded set. Certain important results concerning extended preferences will only be true if the outcome set is sufficiently "rich." See, e.g., below, n. 36. As long as the outcomes added to the original set are possible outcomes, this sort of expansion is not problematic.

outcomes: life-histories in which some of the subjects' attributes, and some background facts about the world, are missing?

The chapter proposes an answer to this crucial problem, and then confronts a second problem: What are the data sources that help us infer individuals' extended preferences? We *could*, in principle, estimate $\mathbf{U}^k$ for any given spectator by conducting "life-history" surveys. By a "life-history" survey, I mean a survey format which seeks to elicit the respondents' *i*-history preferences and/or her across-person judgments, not merely her own-history preferences. A life-history survey would ask the respondent to rank outcomes under a condition of interest in some other individual (thereby eliciting her *i*-history preferences) and/or would ask her to compare the well-being of some individual in some outcome with the well-being of some other individual in some outcome (thereby eliciting her across-person judgments).

However, there is a shortcut to the estimation of a spectator's extended utility functions. As this chapter will explain, if a spectator's extended preferences satisfy what I will term the *non-essentiality condition*, information about her own-history preferences (or equivalently, information about her ordinary, self-interested preferences) will suffice to estimate $\mathbf{U}^k$. We won't need to elicit her *i*-history preferences or across-person judgments.

This estimation shortcut is a vital tool in the construction of $\mathbf{U}^k$. Existing survey formats as well as behavioral evidence provide a wealth of information about individuals' ordinary self-interested preferences. Assuming (plausibly) that the "non-essentiality" condition holds true, we can use these standard data sources to estimate the various sets $\mathbf{U}^k$, for the different "spectators" in the population, and thereby to estimate $\mathbf{U}$.

This is not to say that SWF scholarship should wholly rely upon preference-elicitation formats focused on individuals' ordinary self-interested preferences. The chapter will discuss why life-history surveys could also be useful. Indeed, there is a small extant literature consisting of such surveys and related formats. But this body of scholarship is minuscule, compared with the vast body of existing work that provides information about ordinary self-interested preferences. It is critical to see that implementation of the SWF framework can largely rely upon existing preference data and existing empirical approaches for investigating preferences, rather than needing to start essentially from scratch.

Having discussed the two topics I have just described—simplified outcomes, and the use of existing preference data to estimate extended preferences—the chapter then addresses a range of further issues relating to the construction of $\mathbf{U}$. These include: the extent to which spectators' preferences are sensitive to subjects' preferences; how to model heterogeneity in extended preferences; using an assumption of temporal additivity to facilitate the estimation of extended preferences; the role of happiness surveys; and the use of surveys as opposed to behavioral data to estimate preferences.

The chapter closes by discussing the problem of "zeroing out" extended utility functions, so that they assign zero to nonexistence. Because outcomes are simplified (missing certain attributes), "zeroing out" raises special difficulties. These difficulties are postponed until the conclusion of the chapter. Until that point, the chapter focuses on the problem of estimating, for each spectator k, a non-zeroed-out set $\mathbf{U}^k$, normally unique up to a positive affine transformation, which reflects his own-history preferences, i-history preferences, and across-person judgments.

I. SIMPLIFIED OUTCOMES, MISSING ATTRIBUTES, AND EXTENDED PREFERENCES

Anyone who has waded into the "optimal tax" literature or other scholarship that employs social welfare functions[6] will be struck by the various simplifying devices that scholars employ to ease the analytic task. Consider the model of the economy that Mirrlees employed in his seminal work on optimal income taxation, which started the whole field of "optimal tax" and ultimately won him the Nobel Prize. As Matti Tuomala summarizes the Mirrlees model:

> Imagine an economy where individuals have the innate ability to transform working-time into a single consumption good, which is called income. Each individual's utility is a numerical function which depends only on his net income and the quantity of labour he supplies. . . . Individuals are regarded as identical except that they vary in their ability to supply labour. Thus they can be grouped by productivity types. For the same number of hours worked, a more able person naturally can produce more income. Each individual decides how much labour to supply, calculating what will maximize his utility. All these labour supply decisions taken together determine the output of the economy. A redistributive system is feasible if the output of the economy is sufficient to provide for public and private expenditures. Furthermore, it is supposed that the government or the tax authority does not know the productivity type of each individual. It cannot monitor the number of working hours a person chooses to work, but can only observe a person's income. For this reason the only policy the government can execute is to impose a tax schedule. The government chooses the income tax schedule which maximizes its social welfare function, knowing the manner in which individuals of any productivity type will respond.[7]

There are actually three different kinds of simplification here. The first concerns the enumeration of policy options open to government: in this case, only the choice of implementing different income tax schedules, nothing else. The second concerns the characterization of casual mechanisms. In the Mirrlees model, individuals are assumed to have a fixed productivity and to be perfect utility maximizers.

---

[6] Again, I use the abbreviation "SWF" to mean my specific account of how a social welfare function structures the ranking of outcomes; and "social welfare function" to refer to existing scholarship that uses some function, applied to interpersonally comparable utilities, to rank outcomes and policies, but does not necessarily follow the precise format defended here.

[7] Tuomala (1990, pp. 4–5). Mirrlees' seminal article is reprinted as Mirrlees (2006a).

The third kind of simplification, which shall be my focus in this chapter, involves the description of the possible *consequences* of government policy. Each outcome x in the outcome set for the Mirrlees analysis specifies some possible productivity level, wages received, hours worked, and consumption level, for each individual in the population. Contrast the sparse description of each possible outcome in the Mirrlees model with Martha Nussbaum's list of the elements of human well-being—the fullest list of "objective goods" that currently exists in the philosophical literature, and also quite plausibly a good first stab at identifying those things that individuals, with full information and rationality, would converge in self-interestedly preferring.[8]

Table 4.1 Nussbaum's List of Human Goods

—Life	—Bodily Health
—Bodily Integrity	—Senses, Imagination, and Thought
—Emotions	—Practical Reason
—Affiliation	—Other Species
—Play	—Control over the Environment

It is striking how many attributes on Nussbaum's list are omitted by the Mirrlees outcome set. A given outcome x in that set tells us that each worker has a particular productivity level, receives a particular hourly wage, works a certain number of hours, and consumes a particular amount; but x doesn't tell us how healthy the worker is, how many friends she has, what her mental states (pains, pleasures, emotional states, and so forth) are like, or what her status in the community is. Nor does x tell us anything about the temporal structure of a given individual's life. We are not told that she lives a certain number of years, and has various attributes in different periods. Rather, each outcome consists in a single period, with each worker realizing a given consumption level and leisure level in that period.

The utility function $u(.)$ that Mirrlees employs in his analysis is keyed to the sparse characterization of outcomes. In the Mirrlees analysis, the utility assigned to some individual j in some outcome x—what I represent as $u(x; j)$, the utility of life-history $(x; j)$—has the structure $u(x; j) = v(c_j, l_j)$, where c_j is individual j's consumption in x during the single period that x contains, and l_j is j's leisure during that single period.

---

[8] Nussbaum (2000, pp. 78–80; 2006, pp. 76–78). As discussed in Chapter 3, proponents of objective goods deny that these can be reduced to individuals' actual preferences or idealized idiosyncratic preferences. But one possible construal of objective goods is in terms of idealized preferences that individuals generally have. And existing lists of objective goods may be taken as initial evidence of idealized convergent preferences (at least if the list is not generated in a manner which is inconsistent with this construal, e.g., by deriving the goods from the human essence, as does Hurka).

(A notational aside: Throughout the chapter, as throughout the book, I use the symbol "$u(.)$" to mean an extended utility function, which takes life-histories as its arguments. In this particular chapter, ordinary utility functions, which take outcomes as their arguments, are frequently discussed; I use the symbol "$\varphi(.)$" to mean an ordinary utility function. Often, the values that these functions assign to life-histories or outcomes, respectively, will depend upon certain individual attributes in those histories or outcomes, and perhaps also upon background facts. I use the symbol "$v(.)$," in this particular chapter, to denote a function which takes some type of attribute or attribute cluster, plus perhaps background facts, as its arguments. Such $v(.)$ functions play a role in giving content to $u(.)$ and $\varphi(.)$ functions, and I will sometimes refer to them, too, as "utility functions"; but this nomenclature needs to be read with care, since the $v(.)$ functions do not take outcomes or life-histories as their arguments. Finally, where necessary for clarity, I will use functional notation to refer to attributes. For example, "$c_i(x)$" would mean the consumption of individual i in outcome x. Where an identification of the outcome giving rise to an attribute is clear from context, or unnecessary, I will simply use a letter to refer to an attribute, e.g., "c_i," to mean individual i's consumption.)

Mirrlees's decision to simplify the outcome set and utility function is perfectly understandable. His cognitive abilities, however impressive for a human, were still *human* abilities. As I have already suggested several times, the outcomes that figure in policy analysis as performed by humans cannot be complete possible worlds—a "possible world" being a maximally specific description of a possible history of the universe from start to finish. Even with the help of cognitive aids, such as computers, a human policy analyst can hardly hope to come close to producing a full description of a possible history of the universe, let alone a set of all such histories. And—if we are trying to calibrate utilities by eliciting individuals' preferences over life-histories—then the outcomes that comprise those life-histories, and are presented to individuals to think about, cannot be full possible worlds. It is beyond the cognitive powers of an actual human to hold in consciousness different possible worlds and think about which one she prefers.

Mirrlees's use of a simplified outcome set is, therefore, hardly idiosyncratic. The possible outcomes of tax policy or other governmental choices that policy-analysis scholars consider are invariably *simplified* possible worlds: highly *incomplete* characterizations of possible histories of the universe. Because these descriptions are incomplete, they omit much of relevance to human well-being. This can be seen by considering the standard utility functions that are employed in social-welfare-function scholarship. Much of the optimal-tax scholarship uses the one-period format, with the utility function taking one of the following forms.[9] For the sake of clarity,

---

[9] For reviews of the optimal-tax literature, describing inter alia the various functional forms used for the utility function, see Heady (1996); Kaplow (2008b); Myles (1995); Salanié (2003); Stern (1987); Tuomala (1990).

I have expressed the utility functions employed in this scholarship in the "life-history" form that this book develops.

$u(x; j) = v(c_j, l_j)$, with c_j individual j's total consumption or income in outcome x and l_j the amount of leisure time that j has[10]

$u(x; j) = v(\mathbf{p}_j, c_j)$ or $v(\mathbf{p}_j, c_j, l_j)$ with $\mathbf{p}_j$ the vector of prices of various marketed goods that j faces in outcome x, c_j her total consumption, and l_j her leisure time

$u(x; j) = v(\mathbf{q}_j)$ or $v(\mathbf{q}_j, l_j)$ with $\mathbf{q}_j$ a vector showing the quantity of various marketed goods that j consumes in outcome x, and l_j the amount of leisure time she has

Some scholarship on environmental economics makes externalities or public goods a separate determinant of utility, so that $u(.)$ has the form:

$u(x; j) = v(c_j, z_j)$, $v(c_j, l_j, z_j)$, $v(\mathbf{p}_j, c_j, z_j)$, etc., with z_j individual j's exposure to the externality or public good[11]

A substantial amount of scholarship on social welfare functions is yet more simplified, using a one-period format and a utility function of the form $u(x; j) = v(c_j)$, c_j an income or consumption amount. A very important recent example is work by Stern and Nordhaus on the economics of climate change. More generally, much social-welfare-function scholarship within the "optimal growth" literature employs a utility function with individual income or consumption as its sole argument.[12]

---

[10] Consumption is the total expenditure on marketed items, i.e., the vector product of $\mathbf{p}_j$ and $\mathbf{q}_j$, where $\mathbf{q}_j$ is the vector showing the quantity of each marketed item that j purchases. Often but not invariably, SWF scholarship assumes individuals face the same price vector, in which case $\mathbf{p}_j$ is the same for all j.

[11] See, e.g., Cremer, Gahvari, and Ladoux (2003); Eskeland (2000); Mayeres and Proost (2001); Micheletto (2008); Pirttilä and Tuomala (1997); Salanié (2003, ch. 10). A separate literature on optimal public goods provision also employs social welfare functions operating on utility as a function of consumption, leisure, and public goods. See, e.g., Johansson-Stenman (2005). Further citations to this literature are provided in Chapter 8, n. 14.

[12] A recent paper on climate change scholarship notes: "A large segment of the literature . . . postulates an individual or generational utility function with the consumption of a single, produced good as its only argument (sometimes augmented by leisure time)." Llavador, Roemer, and Silvestre (2009, p. 3). For the utility specifications used by Stern and Nordhaus (the most influential examples of economic studies of climate change), see Stern (2007, chs. 2–2A); Nordhaus (2008, p. 39). For other examples in the climate-change literature, see Anthoff, Hepburn, and Tol (2009, pp. 838–841); Fankhauser, Tol, and Pearce (1997, p. 256). On optimal-growth scholarship, see generally Acemoglu (2009). A "one-period" utility function, in the context of climate change or optimal-growth modeling, means that outcomes have multiple periods but each individual is part of a "generation" that exists for a single period. Some of this scholarship allows for individuals to exist for multiple periods, but once more with utility solely a function of consumption in each period.

Some scholarship on social welfare functions uses a multi-period format, typically with lifetime utility the sum of discounted sublifetime utility. In this set-up, $u(x; j) = \sum_{t=1}^{T} D(t)v(.)$, where $v(.)$ is a sublifetime utility function which takes as its arguments some characteristics of the world during each period (including some of individual j's attributes, and perhaps other characteristics as well); and $D(t)$ is a discount factor.[13] In scholarship that employs this multi-period set-up, the sublifetime utility function, $v(.)$, is often of the form $v(c_j)$, $v(c_j, l_j)$, $v(\mathbf{p}_j, c_j)$, $v(\mathbf{p}_j, c_j, l_j)$, $v(\mathbf{q}_j)$, $v(\mathbf{q}_j, l_j)$, or these forms with z_j added—where c_j, l_j, $\mathbf{p}_j$, $\mathbf{q}_j$ and z_j represent, respectively, individual j's income/consumption, leisure, the price vector she faces, the vector of goods she purchases, and externalities/public goods in outcome x during period t.

Health economists have proposed a different kind of simplification—namely, that social welfare functions be applied to individual lifetime utility, with lifetime utility in turn determined by the sequence of health states.[14] In other words, $u(x; j)$ $= \sum_{t=1}^{T} D(t)v(.)$, with $v(.)$ of the form $v(h_j)$, and h_j the subject j's health during a particular period.

Note that the majority of the determinants of well-being on Nussbaum's list are not explicit arguments in these standard utility functions. In some cases, some of these determinants may be implicit rather than explicit arguments in the utility functions—a possibility we will consider in a moment.[15] But I think it is fair to say that the outcome sets in even the fullest and most elaborate extant analyses in the social-welfare-function tradition[16] consist in highly incomplete descriptions of the possible consequences of policy choice, omitting much of relevance to individuals' well-being.

The use of simplified outcome sets for SWF analysis raises a number of questions. One question concerns *optimal* simplification. Given humans' cognitive limits, the appropriate outcome set that analysts should use in considering any given policy choice does *not* consist in the set of all possible worlds. So what *is* the appropriate outcome set?

---

[13] See, e.g., Acemoglu (2009, ch. 9); G. Anderson (2005); Córdoba and Verdier (2008); Diamond (2003); Erosa and Gervais (2002); Gaube (2007); Gervais (2009); Golosov, Tsyvinski, and Werning (2007); Heer (2001); Iqbal and Turnovsky (2008). Some authors apply a social welfare function to lifetime utilities that are simplified, e.g., a function of individual consumption and leisure during each period, but not necessarily temporally additive. See, e.g., Fenge, Uebelmesser, and Werding (2006); Kifmann (2008).

[14] See sources cited in Chapter 2, n. 56.

[15] This might occur if some welfare-relevant characteristic is fixed at some specific reference level in all outcomes, $\mathbf{m}^{ref}$, and the utility function over life-histories is sensitive to what level $\mathbf{m}^{ref}$ is, but does not take $\mathbf{m}^{ref}$ as an explicit argument, since it is the same in all outcomes. Another possibility is that the characteristics which do figure in the utility function have been normalized to reflect other characteristics. On these possibilities, see below.

[16] For example, Llavador, Roemer, and Silvestre (2009) work hard to recognize sources of well-being other than consumption and leisure, but still use a utility function with only four arguments, namely consumption, leisure, knowledge, and environmental quality.

The question of optimal simplification is not unique to the SWF approach. Any consequentialist approach to policy choice (for example, CBA) confronts the very same question. Unfortunately, the question has been generally ignored. Applied economists and other policy analysts tend to pick some stripped-down description of the possible consequences of the policy choice being analyzed, without attempting to justify their decision to omit various well-being-relevant attributes from the description. And the vast theoretical literature in welfare economics, while addressing in detail how society might value outcomes as a function of individuals' preferences, almost never discusses how outcomes are appropriately simplified so that individuals and social planners can actually *think* about them. A few philosophers have confronted this problem—in the course of considering consequentialism's viability as a decision procedure—but without making much progress.[17]

I won't hazard an answer to the question of optimal simplification here. The question is very important but, also, very hard. The answer cannot be that the consequentialist policy analyst should determine which outcome set to employ by engaging in a higher-level consequentialist analysis—because the problem of optimal simplification just reemerges at this higher level. So the appropriate procedure by which the analyst initially determines which outcome set to employ must be some non-consequentialist procedure. But what would *that* be?

A different and somewhat more tractable set of questions concerns the nature of simplified outcomes. If the possible outcomes being considered by SWF analysts are not whole possible worlds, what exactly *are* these outcomes?

One possibility is that simplified outcomes are *fictions*. On this view, a simplified outcome is not a stripped-down description of what might actually occur, but rather an abstraction that could never actually occur (at least not consistently with what we know about the laws of nature). For example, the Mirrlees model might be a representation of a fictional universe in which humans have no sense of the division of their lives into multiple periods, and consume a single homogeneous consumption good.

Fictions no doubt have a role in economics, as in other scholarly fields (consider the fiction of frictionless planes in physics). But it is deeply puzzling to think that the outcome sets which policy analysts appropriately use—in giving advice to *actual* governmental officials or other decisionmakers about *actual* choices—should consist in fictions. For one thing, the "fiction" view is very difficult to square with expected utility (EU) theory or any other probabilistic theory of rational choice under uncertainty. A probabilistic theory says that the rational social planner, like any rational actor, ranks choices in light of the probability distribution over

---

[17] See, e.g., Feldman (2006a); Lenman (2000). Economists *have* addressed the appropriateness of simplified explanatory models for purposes of positive economics. See, for example, the symposium on economic models in *Erkenntnis* (2009, vol. 70, pp. 1–131). However, I think it is fair to say that this literature does not arrive at much guidance for normative economists determining how radically to simplify outcomes for purposes of policy analysis.

outcomes that each choice produces. But if outcomes in an outcome set are fictions, which could never actually occur, then the probability of any one of them, given any actual choice, is *zero*. The probability that any actual income tax policy will yield a world in which individuals have no sense of temporal structure and consume but a single homogeneous consumption good is zero.

In this chapter, therefore, I will take a different approach to understanding the status of simplified outcomes. Insofar as SWF analysis is deployed to make actual policy recommendations, the appropriate outcomes to be considered are neither complete possible worlds (which are beyond the capacity of humans to think about), nor fictions, but *simplified descriptions of genuine possible realities.*

This leads to the next set of questions: the problem of *missing attributes*. Missing attributes are the well-being-relevant features of reality that a simplified outcome does not describe. A missing attribute may be something which is intrinsically valuable for well-being, but not described. (For example, each outcome in an outcome set may tell us about an individual's consumption and leisure, but not about the quality of her relationship with her friends and family.) Or, a missing attribute may be something which helps determine the impact of the listed attributes on well-being. This is particularly relevant insofar as outcomes in social-welfare-function analysis describe an individual's income or consumption (either in the form of a single total individual income or consumption number c_j, plus perhaps information about the price vector, or in the form of a consumption vector $\mathbf{q}_j$ describing how much an individual purchases of each of a plurality of marketed goods). As Amartya Sen has stressed, the sheer purchase of marketed goods is not, without more, a well-being benefit. (If I buy food but it rots in my fridge, I am not better off). Nor is the fact that an individual purchases and uses marketed goods sufficient to determine what the individual's well-being benefit from the goods is. (How much enjoyment and nourishment I reap from food will depend on my metabolism, what my taste buds are like, and other physiological attributes, as well as the quantity of food purchased and ingested. Therefore, an outcome that simply describes my total income, or my total expenditures on food, is missing an attribute that determines the impact of these characteristics on my well-being, namely my physiology.[18])

To put this abstractly, each outcome in a simplified outcome set will be characterized as having one or more periods, with each period describing certain individual attributes and background facts during that period: $(\mathbf{a}_{1,t}, \mathbf{a}_{2,t}, \ldots, \mathbf{a}_{N,t}, \mathbf{a}_{imp,t})$.[19] For short,

---

[18] See, e.g., Sen (1995, chs. 1–2).

[19] The symbol "$\mathbf{a}_{i,t}$" means the package of attributes that individual i is described as having during period t. This potentially includes both non-relational, i.e., monadic attributes, and relational, i.e., polyadic, attributes. Suzy's level of pain would be a monadic attribute of Suzy. The property of being Jose's aunt would be a polyadic attribute of Suzy. A person's polyadic attribute involves a relation between her and some other person or entity, and thus has entailments regarding the attributes of that other person. For example, that Suzy is Jose's aunt entails that Jose is Suzy's nephew. A person's monadic attributes are just "about him"; they do not entail that some other person or item has certain

let us use the symbol "**a**" to designate the totality of the features of an outcome that are explicitly described (all of individuals' stated attributes during all the periods, plus the stated background facts during all the periods). A complete description of a possible world would list not only the **a**-type characteristics, but would include a much longer list of **m**-type characteristics. The question then emerges: What does it mean to construct a set **U** of extended utility functions for this sort of outcome? How can a given spectator formulate her extended preferences where the outcomes that figure in life-histories are described only in terms of their **a**-type characteristics, and not also in terms of their **m**-type characteristics?

Consider own-history preferences. The spectator k weakly prefers $(x; k)$ to $(y; k)$ iff she has a self-interested weak preference for x over y; she weakly prefers own-history lottery l to own-history lottery l^* iff, under conditions of self-interest, she would weakly prefer a lottery over outcomes with the probabilities given by l to a lottery over outcomes with the probabilities given by l^*. But how can it be meaningful to ask whether the spectator self-interestedly prefers outcome x to outcome y, or self-interestedly prefers one outcome lottery to another, where outcomes are missing characteristics? The very same question can be asked about the content of the spectator's i-history preferences—her preferences regarding life-histories of some subject i. The spectator weakly prefers $(x; i)$ to $(y; i)$ iff she has an i-interested weak preference for x over y; she weakly prefers a lottery m over i's histories to a lottery m^* over i's histories iff, under conditions of i-interest, she would weakly prefer a lottery over outcomes with the probabilities given by m to a lottery over outcomes with the probabilities given by m^*. But how can it be meaningful to ask *these* questions

---

attributes. Jim's being in a certain mental state is logically compatible with an arbitrary assignment of attributes to all other entities in the world.

The symbol "$a_{imp,t}$" denotes background facts ("imp" is short for "impersonal"). These are all facts that the description of an outcome sets forth, other than the attributes of persons. These might be the attributes of non-human entities (for example, the attributes of animals or of various inanimate objects), or other facts (e.g., causal regularities).

Note that a person's standing in some relation to a non-human entity will "show up" both as one of the person's relational attributes, and as one of that entity's relational attributes. For example, if Robert adores a particular polar bear, then Robert has the relational attribute of adoring that bear, and the bear has the attribute of being adored by Robert. Thus "background facts" are not necessarily logically independent of the specification of persons' attributes. A particular specification of background facts, $a_{imp,t}$, may be logically incompatible with a given specification of persons' attributes, $a_{1,t}$, $a_{2,t}$..., $a_{N,t}$. This subtlety will not affect any of the arguments of this chapter.

Later in the chapter, in discussing how to infer a spectator's extended preferences from his ordinary self-interested preferences, I adopt the simplifying assumption that preferences are atomistic. For purposes of that discussion, I use the symbol "$a_{i,t}$" more restrictively—to denote monadic attributes or relational attributes which involve a relation only to entities that are not persons, and to exclude relational attributes which involve some other person. See below, n. 35. In general, however, "$a_{i,t}$" is more encompassing; it can denote *any* sort of attribute (property) of individual i during period t.

where outcomes are missing characteristics? Finally, consider the across-person rankings that Chapter 3 invited the spectator to make: ranking $(x; i)$ versus $(y; j)$ by comparing i's well-being in x to j's in y, or ranking a lottery l over i's histories to a lottery m over j's by comparing the ex ante well-being realized by i with the outcome lottery corresponding to l, to the ex ante well-being realized by j with the outcome lottery corresponding to m. Once more, how are such comparisons even possible where outcomes are simplified?

The answer to these questions, I suggest, involves the concept of conditional preferences and a conditional utility function—a concept that has been developed in the scholarly literature on multiattribute utility theory.[20] An ordinary conditional preference is a ranking of outcomes, or lotteries over outcomes, such that certain outcome characteristics are fixed in all outcomes. If an individual's conditional preferences are consistent with EU theory, they can be expectationally represented by a conditional utility function.

Imagine that outcomes vary with respect to **a**-type characteristics, but do not vary with respect to other characteristics, the **m**-type characteristics. Assume, for the moment, that these latter characteristics are not missing—they are specified in the description of outcomes—but instead of varying across outcomes, are held fixed in all outcomes at level $\mathbf{m^+}$. Thus the various outcomes are $(\mathbf{a}, \mathbf{m^+})$, $(\mathbf{a^*}, \mathbf{m^+})$, $(\mathbf{a^{**}}, \mathbf{m^+})$, etc.

Imagine that some spectator k's preferences regarding lotteries over these outcomes satisfy the axioms of von Neumann/Morgenstern EU theory. Then they can be expectationally represented by a utility function $v^k_{\mathbf{m^+}}(.)$, unique up to a positive affine transformation. For example, if k prefers a lottery that gives a q probability of outcome $(\mathbf{a}, \mathbf{m^+})$ and $(1 - q)$ probability of outcome $(\mathbf{a^*}, \mathbf{m^+})$ to a lottery that gives a p probability of outcome $(\mathbf{a^{**}}, \mathbf{m^+})$ and $(1 - p)$ probability of outcome $(\mathbf{a^{***}}, \mathbf{m^+})$, it will be the case that $qv^k_{\mathbf{m^+}}(\mathbf{a}) + (1 - q)v^k_{\mathbf{m^+}}(\mathbf{a^*}) > pv^k_{\mathbf{m^+}}(\mathbf{a^{**}}) + (1 - p)v^k_{\mathbf{m^+}}(\mathbf{a^{***}}).$[21]

---

[20] See Keeney and Raiffa (1993, chs. 5–6).

[21] Von Neumann/Morgenstern EU theory shows the following: Given a finite outcome set and a ranking of all lotteries over that set, if the ranking of lotteries is a complete ordering, and satisfies an independence axiom and an "Archimedean" axiom, then it can be expectationally represented by a utility function unique up to a positive affine transformation. See Chapter 3. Assume, now, that the outcome set is such that all outcomes have the **m**-type characteristics fixed at level $\mathbf{m^+}$; and that the spectator k's ranking of lotteries over that set is complete and satisfies these two axioms. Then if l and l^* are lotteries over outcomes, there will exist a utility function $\varphi^k(.)$ such that k weakly prefers l to l^* iff $\sum_{x \in O} \pi_l(x)\varphi^k(x) \geq \sum_{x \in O} \pi_{l^*}(x)\varphi^k(x)$, where $\pi_l(x)$ and $\pi_{l^*}(x)$ are the probabilities that lotteries l and l^*, respectively, assign to a given outcome x.

However, because **m**-type characteristics are fixed in all outcomes at level $\mathbf{m^+}$, the value assigned by $\varphi^k(.)$ to a given outcome is a function of the **a**-type characteristics in that outcome. In other words, $\varphi^k(x) = v^k_{\mathbf{m^+}}(\mathbf{a}(x))$, where "$\mathbf{a}(x)$" denotes the **a**-type characteristics in outcome x, and the "$\mathbf{m^+}$" subscript indicates that the **m**-type characteristics are fixed in all outcomes at $\mathbf{m^+}$. Thus we have that the spectator weakly prefers lottery l to lottery l^* iff $\sum_{x \in O} \pi_l(x)v^k_{\mathbf{m^+}}(\mathbf{a}(x)) \geq \sum_{x \in O} \pi_{l^*}(x)v^k_{\mathbf{m^+}}(\mathbf{a}(x)).$

Note that the utility function here, $v^k_{m+}(.)$, is a *conditional* utility function. Its inputs are a-type characteristics, not m-type characteristics. Because the m-type characteristics are fixed at level m^+ in all outcomes, they need not be expressed as inputs into the utility function. Rather, "m^+" is written as a subscript, to note that this function represents spectator k's ranking of the lotteries across a attributes *given* that the m attributes are fixed at m^+.

It is quite possible that the spectator's ranking of outcomes and lotteries, with m-type characteristics fixed at m^+, is different from her ranking of outcomes and lotteries with m-type characteristics fixed at m^{++}. In that case, the first ranking will be expectationally represented by $v^k_{m+}(.)$ and the second by $v^k_{m++}(.)$, and these two functions will not be positive affine transformations of each other.[22] On the other hand, it is also possible that the spectator's ranking of outcomes and lotteries, with a-type characteristics varying and m-type characteristics fixed, is invariant to the specific level at which the m-type characteristics are fixed. (In other words, it is possible that the spectator prefers a lottery with a q probability of a and a $(1 - q)$ probability of a^* to a lottery with a p probability of a^{**} and a $(1 - p)$ probability of a^{***} regardless of whether the m-type characteristics are set at m^+, m^{++}, m^{+++}, or any other level—and similarly for all other lotteries with respect to a attributes.) If the individual's conditional preferences are thus invariant to the specific level at which the m-type characteristics are fixed, they can be represented by a single $v^k(.)$, unique up to a positive affine transformation. In this case, the subscript for the particular level at which m characteristics are fixed can be dropped.

We can apply these ideas—regarding conditional preferences, conditional utility functions, and invariance—to *extended* preferences. Assume that outcomes and thus life-histories vary with respect to a-type characteristics, but that m-type characteristics are fixed at some level m^+. In other words, the various life-histories are $(a, m^+; i)$, $(a^*, m^+; j)$, $(a^{**}, m^+; l)$ and so forth. If so, we can straightforwardly use the approach described in Chapter 3 to formulate a set of *conditional* extended utility functions for spectator k that summarize her own-history, i-history, and across-person preferences, *given* that the m-type characteristics are fixed at level m^+. Call this set U^k_{m+}. Given that m-type characteristics are fixed at level m^+, the spectator will have certain own-history preferences (i.e., certain self-interested preferences over outcomes and outcome lotteries). Similarly, given that m-type characteristics are fixed at level m^+, the spectator will have certain i-history preferences (i.e., certain i-interested preferences over outcomes and outcome lotteries). The set U^k_{m+} will consist of all utility functions that expectationally represent these preferences.

---

[22] Implicitly, the discussion here is assuming that there is a single set Д of a-type characteristics. The outcome set with m-type characteristics at level m^+ is produced by pairing each element of Д with m^+; the outcome set with m-type characteristics at level m^{++} is produced by pairing each element of Д with m^{++}; and so forth. The functions $v^k_{m+}(.)$ and $v^k_{m++}(.)$ take as their arguments the elements of Д. The function $v^k_{m++}(.)$ is a positive affine transformation of $v^k_{m+}(.)$ if there exist numbers a and b, a positive, such that $v^k_{m++}(a) = av^k_{m+}(a) + b$ for every a in Д.

For example, imagine that spectator k's own-history preferences are such that she is indifferent between the life-history $(\mathbf{a}, \mathbf{m}^+; k)$ and a lottery that gives her a p probability of life-history $(\mathbf{a}^*, \mathbf{m}^+; k)$ and a $(1 - p)$ probability of life-history $(\mathbf{a}^{**}, \mathbf{m}^+; k)$. Then, for each $u^k(.)$ in $\mathbf{U}^k_{\mathbf{m}+}$, the utility it assigns to life-history $(\mathbf{a}, \mathbf{m}^+; k)$ will be equal to p times the utility it assigns to life-history $(\mathbf{a}^*, \mathbf{m}^+; k)$ plus $(1 - p)$ times the utility it assigns to life-history $(\mathbf{a}^{**}, \mathbf{m}^+; k)$. Similarly, imagine that the spectator's i-history preferences are such that she is indifferent between the life-history $(\mathbf{a}', \mathbf{m}^+; i)$ and a lottery that gives her a r probability of life-history $(\mathbf{a}'', \mathbf{m}^+; i)$ and a $(1 - r)$ probability of life-history $(\mathbf{a}''', \mathbf{m}^+; i)$. Then, for each $u^k(.)$ in $\mathbf{U}^k_{\mathbf{m}+}$, it will be the case that the utility it assigns to life-history $(\mathbf{a}', \mathbf{m}^+; i)$ is equal to r times the utility it assigns to life-history $(\mathbf{a}'', \mathbf{m}^+; i)$ plus $(1 - r)$ times the utility it assigns to life-history $(\mathbf{a}''', \mathbf{m}^+; i)$.

We can then "winnow down" $\mathbf{U}^k_{\mathbf{m}+}$ by using the spectator's across-person judgments, given that $\mathbf{m}$-type characteristics are fixed at $\mathbf{m}^+$. For example, the spectator may judge that individual j is equally well off in outcome $(\mathbf{a}, \mathbf{m}^+)$ as is individual i in outcome $(\mathbf{a}^*, \mathbf{m}^+)$. If so, a utility function $u^k(.)$ can be excluded from $\mathbf{U}^k_{\mathbf{m}+}$ unless it is consistent with this judgment, i.e., assigns the same utility to life-histories $(\mathbf{a}, \mathbf{m}^+; j)$ and $(\mathbf{a}^*, \mathbf{m}^+; i)$. Normally, a relatively small number of across-person judgments will enable us to "winnow down" $\mathbf{U}^k_{\mathbf{m}+}$ so that it is unique up to a positive affine transformation.[23]

---

[23] The discussion in the previous three paragraphs is a straightforward application of the discussion in Chapter 3, pp. 202–213. Imagine that there is a set Д of $\mathbf{a}$-type characteristics. Now imagine an outcome set $\mathbf{O}$, formed by combining each element of Д with $\mathbf{m}$-type characteristics set at level $\mathbf{m}^+$; and an associated life-history set H and lottery set L. Spectator k has extended preferences over L, analyzed exactly along the lines discussed in Chapter 3. (Her "own-history" lotteries assign probability zero to any life-history in which k is not the subject; for any such own-history lottery l, there is a corresponding hypothetical choice that assigns probability $\pi_i(x; k)$ to outcome x; and k has a weak extended preference for own-history lottery l over l^* just in case she has a self-interested weak preference for the hypothetical choice corresponding to l over the hypothetical choice corresponding to l^*. Spectator k's i-history lotteries assign probability zero to any life-history in which i is not the subject; for any i-history lottery l, there is a corresponding hypothetical choice that assigns probability $\pi_i(x; i)$ to outcome x; and k has a weak extended preference for i-history lottery l over l^* just in case, under conditions of interest in i, she weakly prefers the outcome lottery corresponding to l over the outcome lottery corresponding to l^*. Similarly, k's ranking of life-histories belonging to different subjects, and lotteries involving two different subjects, are analyzed exactly as in Chapter 3.) A set $\mathbf{U}^k_{\mathbf{m}+}$ representing these extended preferences can be constructed, again exactly along the lines discussed in Chapter 3. Moreover, because all outcomes in $\mathbf{O}$ have $\mathbf{m}$-type characteristics set at level $\mathbf{m}^+$, each $u^k(.)$ in $\mathbf{U}^k_{\mathbf{m}+}$ will take the form: $u^k(x; i) = v^k_{\mathbf{m}+}(\mathbf{a}(x), i)$. In other words, $u^k(.)$ assigns a utility to a given life-history as a function of the array of $\mathbf{a}$-type characteristics in that life-history, plus who the subject is. (These are the arguments for the $v^k_{\mathbf{m}+}(.)$ function.). What number that is may depend upon the particular level at which the $\mathbf{m}$-type characteristics are fixed. (This is why the $v^k_{\mathbf{m}+}(.)$ function has "$\mathbf{m}^+$" in the subscript.)

Each $u^k(.)$ in $\mathbf{U}^k_{\mathbf{m}+}$ will expectationally represent spectator k's own-history preferences. That is, she weakly prefers own-history lottery l to own-history lottery l^* iff

It is possible that this set $\mathbf{U}^k_{\mathbf{m}+}$—representing the spectator's own-history preferences, i-history preferences, and across-person judgments, with $\mathbf{m}$-type characteristics fixed at level $\mathbf{m}^+$—depends on that particular level. In other words, it is quite
possible that $\mathbf{U}^k_{\mathbf{m}+} \neq \mathbf{U}^k_{\mathbf{m}++}$, where $\mathbf{m}^+$ and $\mathbf{m}^{++}$ are different fixed levels of the $\mathbf{m}$-type
characteristics. On the other hand, it is at least *possible* that the spectator's own-
history preferences, i-history preferences, and across-person judgments are *invariant*
to the particular level at which $\mathbf{m}$ characteristics are fixed. In that case, $\mathbf{U}^k_{\mathbf{m}+} = \mathbf{U}^k_{\mathbf{m}++}$
$= \mathbf{U}^k_{\mathbf{m}+++} = \ldots$, and we can drop the "$\mathbf{m}$" subscript. We can then refer to $\mathbf{U}^k$, meaning
the set of utility functions that represent the spectator's various extended prefer-
ences, holding fixed $\mathbf{m}$-type characteristics, in the special case where these preferences are invariant to the particular level at which those characteristics are fixed.

The essential points, here, are twofold, and bear repetition. First, the spectator
will have *conditional* extended preferences (own-history, i-history, across-person), in
the case where $\mathbf{m}$-type characteristics are fixed at $\mathbf{m}^+$, and a corresponding set $\mathbf{U}^k_{\mathbf{m}+}$,
normally unique up to a positive affine transformation. This is just an application of
the analysis of extended preferences and utility functions provided in Chapter 3.
Second, and more interestingly, it is *possible* that these preferences and the representing set are invariant to the particular level at which those characteristics are
fixed.

It is this latter possibility—the invariance possibility—which in turn provides
the key for understanding how the SWF analyst should think about estimating a set
$\mathbf{U}$ for a simplified outcome set. Let us now return to the puzzling case that we're
trying to make sense of: the case in which $\mathbf{m}$-type characteristics are wholly missing
from an outcome set. The SWF analyst has (somehow) arrived at the position that
the optimal simplification of the outcome set will specify each outcome as a vector
of $\mathbf{a}$-type characteristics, but will not specify its $\mathbf{m}$-type characteristics at all. My
proposal for how to construct $\mathbf{U}$ in such a case is this: The analyst should construct
$\mathbf{U}$ by (1) assuming that $\mathbf{m}$-type attributes are set at some constant, unspecified level,
in all the outcomes; and by (2) presupposing that each spectator's conditional preferences regarding the life-histories, and regarding lotteries over the life-histories, are
invariant to whatever specific level the $\mathbf{m}$-type characteristics are set at. Given this

---

$\sum_{(x;k)\in\mathbf{H}} \pi_I(x;k)u^k(x;k) \geq \sum_{(x;k)\in\mathbf{H}} \pi_{I^*}(x;k)u^k(x;k)$ or, equivalently, $\sum_{(x;k)\in\mathbf{H}} \pi_I(x;k)v^k_{\mathbf{m}+}(\mathbf{a}(x),k)$
$\geq \sum_{(x;k)\in\mathbf{H}} \pi_{I^*}(x;k)v^k_{\mathbf{m}+}(\mathbf{a}(x),k)$. Each $u^k(.)$ in $\mathbf{U}^k_{\mathbf{m}+}$ will also expectationally represent the spectator's
i-history preferences and across-person judgments.

As per the discussion in Chapter 3, $\mathbf{U}^k_{\mathbf{m}+}$ will normally be unique up to a positive affine transformation. Extended utility function $w(.)$ is a positive affine transformation of function $u(.)$ if $w(x; i) =$
$au(x; i) + b$, a positive, for all life-histories in $\mathbf{H}$. Note that each $u^k(.)$ in $\mathbf{U}^k_{\mathbf{m}+}$ will correspond to its
own $v^k_{\mathbf{m}+}(.)$ function. And the set of these, too, will be unique up to a positive affine transformation.
(Function $v^{*}_{\mathbf{m}+}(.)$ is a positive affine transformation of function $v_{\mathbf{m}+}(.)$, both assigning numbers to
combinations of $\mathbf{a}$ characteristics and individuals, if there exist numbers a and b, a positive, such that
$v^{*}_{\mathbf{m}+}(\mathbf{a}, i) = av_{\mathbf{m}+}(\mathbf{a}, i) + b$, for every possible combination of some $\mathbf{a}$ in Д and some individual in the
population.)

invariance assumption, each spectator k's conditional preferences over the life-histories will be representable by the very same set $\mathbf{U}^k$, normally unique up to a positive affine transformation—regardless of what particular level $\mathbf{m}$ is. And it is the set of such $\mathbf{U}^k$ (across all spectators) that gives rise to the set $\mathbf{U}$ of utility functions (once we've taken the final step of "zeroing out" each $\mathbf{U}^k$, see below).

An example may help illustrate the invariance assumption which is critical to constructing $\mathbf{U}$ for a simplified outcome set. Imagine that each outcome has a single period and describes each individual in the population as consuming some amount of some good, but does not describe the individual's health. Each x takes the form $(c_1, c_2, \ldots, c_N)$, where c_j is the consumption of individual j. The analyst thinks of each individual as having some unspecified level of health h^+, be it good health, poor health, or perfect health, which is constant in all the outcomes and constant across individuals.[24] So each x is more accurately $((c_1, h^+), (c_2, h^+), \ldots, (c_N, h^+))$. And, although each life-history $(x; j)$ explicitly takes the form $(c_1, c_2, \ldots, c_N; j)$, its real form is more like $((c_1, h^+), (c_2, h^+), \ldots, (c_N, h^+); j)$.[25]

To simplify the example further, let us assume that each spectator's extended preferences are "atomistic."[26] With health taken to be fixed at unspecified level h^+, the real form of life-history $(c_1, c_2, \ldots, c_N; j)$ becomes more like $(c_j, h^+; j)$; the real form of life-history $(c_1, c_2, \ldots, c_N; k)$ becomes more like $(c_k, h^+; k)$ and so forth. Spectator k thinks of a lottery over his own life-histories as a self-interested lottery over his own consumption amounts, holding health fixed at some unspecified h^+; he thinks of a lottery over subject i's life-histories as an i-interested lottery over consumption amounts received by subject i, holding i's health fixed at some unspecified h^+. Finally, he thinks of an across-person judgment—between a life-history in which subject j gets a particular consumption amount c_j and a life-history in which subject i gets a particular consumption amount c_i—as a comparison between the well-being that subject j would reap from a package of c_j and some unspecified health state h^+, and the well-being that subject i would reap from a package of c_i and the very same unspecified health state h^+.

Let us now put in place the crucial invariance assumption. The SWF analyst assumes that these various extended preferences on the part of the spectator are

---

[24] For a discussion of why the unspecified level of health must be the same across all individuals, see below, n. 27.

[25] Of course the full possible world corresponding to $(c_1, c_2, \ldots, c_N)$ would be one in which individuals have consumption attributes *and* health attributes *and* yet further attributes. Thus $((c_1, h^+), (c_2, h^+), \ldots, (c_N, h^+))$ is a more accurate description of what the world would be like if x were to obtain, but hardly a complete description.

[26] On atomism, see below, n. 35. The proposal introduced in this section—to handle missing characteristics via an invariance assumption—in no way presupposes atomism. It is introduced, here, so as to produce an uncomplicated example. The example also meshes with the next section, which does rely on atomism as the simplest way to infer spectators' extended preferences from their ordinary, self-interested preferences.

invariant to the level at which health is fixed. The spectator's self-interested preferences over consumption lotteries for himself, his i-interested preferences regarding consumption lotteries for subject i, and his across-person comparisons of consumption amounts for different persons, do not depend upon whether all subjects' health is fixed at h^+, h^{++}, h^{+++}, or any other particular level. *With this invariance assumption in hand,* the analyst can elicit or estimate each spectator's set $\mathbf{U}^k$, representing these various extended preferences, *without needing to be specific about what the fixed health level is.*

Note that omitting the $\mathbf{m}$-type characteristics from the outcome set, and assuming each spectator's conditional utility function to be invariant to the specific level of the $\mathbf{m}$ attributes, eases the cognitive burdens in inferring utilities. If a spectator's conditional preferences over life-history lotteries (with $\mathbf{a}$-type characteristics varying and $\mathbf{m}$-type characteristics fixed) are invariant to the particular level of the $\mathbf{m}$ characteristics, we can coherently ask the spectator what those conditional preferences are, without telling her anything about the $\mathbf{m}$ characteristics—simply asking her to assume that those are fixed at some, unspecified, level. Furthermore, this approach eases the SWF analyst's task. Because all the outcomes in the outcome set are assumed to have a common, unspecified, level of the $\mathbf{m}$ attributes, the outcome set is smaller; and the task of ranking the outcome set, and characterizing policies as probability distributions across the outcome set, is easier.

Of course, omitting the $\mathbf{m}$ characteristics and valuing outcomes along the lines just described has various disadvantages as well. (1) The assumption that spectators' conditional preferences are invariant to the level of the $\mathbf{m}$ characteristics may be untrue. It may well be the case that some spectators rank life-histories or lotteries over life-histories varying with respect to the $\mathbf{a}$ characteristics differently when the $\mathbf{m}$ characteristics are held at one level (say, $\mathbf{m}^+$) than when they are held at some other level ($\mathbf{m}^{++}$). To continue with the example of health: the spectator's own-history preferences, i-history preferences, or across-person judgments regarding life-histories described in terms of the subject's consumption and the price vector may well depend on what the subject's health is (because certain goods become more important in poor health states).

(2) On the account tendered here, outcomes are meant to be simplified descriptions of genuine possible realities. So each outcome corresponds to a group of full possible worlds (all the possible worlds that have the particular $\mathbf{a}$ characteristics included in the description of the outcome). It is of course not the case that $\mathbf{m}$-type characteristics are fixed in all possible worlds. More plausibly, it might be the case that if we take the most probable possible world associated with each outcome, the $\mathbf{m}$ characteristics are fixed (or at least do not vary too much) across these. But even this assumption may well not hold true. The governmental policies or other choices being evaluated, using some outcome set with $\mathbf{m}$-type characteristics missing, may *change* those characteristics. (For example, policies may change individuals' health states, not just their consumption amounts.) In this kind of case, ranking the choices by using outcomes with $\mathbf{m}$-type characteristics missing—in effect, adopting the

simplifying but untrue assumption that the choices will not affect the **m**-type characteristics—will produce a distorted ranking of the choices.

(3) The omitted **m** characteristics can include various features of outcomes, including attributes of individuals, attributes of non-human entities, or other facts. For reasons further explored in the margin, the **m** characteristics which are attributes of humans will need to be assumed not merely constant across outcomes, but identical across the N individuals in the population, in each outcome—at least if these missing characteristics are not wholly irrelevant to how the spectator ranks life-histories.[27] For example, in the health-consumption example just discussed, it was assumed not only that the vector of individual health states $(h_1, h_2, . . ., h_N)$ was the same in all outcomes, but indeed that individuals had the very same health state, i.e., that $(h_1, h_2, . . ., h_N) = (h^+, h^+, . . ., h^+)$. However, even if it is true that the choices at hand will not substantially affect **m**-type characteristics, the assumption that individuals' **m**-type attributes are the same across individuals may be incorrect and may distort the ranking of outcomes. For example, it may be the case that (1) the policy choice at hand will not affect individual health, i.e., in all the possible worlds likely to result from that choice, the vector of individual health states is more or less the same; but (2) in those likely worlds, some individuals in the population will be in good health, while others will be in poor health. The former individuals should (ideally) receive higher utilities than the latter, for a given consumption level. But including only individual consumption, not health, in the description of outcomes and life-histories means that in any outcome where two individuals have the same consumption level, they are assigned the same utility.

How might we redress the possible distortions that flow from using outcomes that are described with respect to certain types of features that the world might have (the **a**-type characteristics), but are missing other features of the world (the **m** characteristics)? One possibility is to employ a richer outcome set and attendant set of life-histories, which are now described with respect to the **a** attributes and *some* of the **m** characteristics. Of course, we will never be able to do this with respect to *all* of

---

[27] The reason has to do with across-person judgments. Imagine that the spectator is meant to compare life-history $(x; i)$ with life-history $(y; j)$. Where characteristics of outcomes are missing, it is meaningful for the spectator to do this—I have suggested—if his across-subject comparisons are invariant to the specific level at which missing characteristics are set. But imagine that the missing characteristics include some individual attribute. It is absurd to think that the spectator's comparison of life-history $(a; j)$ and $(a^*; i)$ is invariant to the subjects' missing attributes, *even if these can be at unequal levels*—unless this is an attribute which the spectator does not see as relevant to well-being at all.

For example, imagine that outcomes specify individual consumption, but not health. Consider an across-person comparison between a life-history in which a subject gets consumption c, and a life-history in which a different subject gets consumption c^*. How can it possibly be the case that c, paired with any health attribute h, and c^*, paired with a (possibly different) health attribute h^*, are seen by the spectator as equally good regardless of what h and h^* are?

the $\mathbf{m}$ characteristics. To have an outcome set in which no characteristics are missing is just to have an outcome set in which each outcome is a complete possible world—which is cognitively infeasible, for analysts and spectators alike. But certainly it is possible to move from a simplified outcome set to a somewhat-less-simplified outcome set, which specifies a subset of the previously missing characteristics. For example, we can move from an outcome set which specifies each individual's consumption, to one that specifies each individual's consumption and health—recognizing that this latter set still fails to specify much of relevance to well-being, e.g., the individual's social life, happiness states, job status, and so forth.

Second, we might fix some of the $\mathbf{m}$ characteristics at a reference level. Call these the $\mathbf{m}^1$ characteristics. Outcomes in the outcome set vary with respect to $\mathbf{a}$ characteristics, and have the $\mathbf{m}^1$ characteristics fixed at a constant level $\mathbf{m}^{1\text{-ref}}$—where $\mathbf{m}^{1\text{-ref}}$ is presumably the most likely level of the $\mathbf{m}^1$ characteristics in the status quo. This spares the analytic expense of using a larger outcome set in which both $\mathbf{m}^1$ and $\mathbf{a}$ characteristics vary; but it allows the analysis to be sensitive to the fact that individuals' preferences over life-histories may not be invariant to the level of the $\mathbf{m}^1$ characteristics, and that interindividual variation in $\mathbf{m}^1$-type individual attributes can produce variation in utility levels.

To continue with the example of consumption and health: each outcome in the outcome set might have the form $x = ((c_1, h_1^{\text{ref}}), (c_2, h_2^{\text{ref}}), \ldots, (c_N, h_N^{\text{ref}}))$. The vector of individual health attributes $(h_1^{\text{ref}}, h_2^{\text{ref}}, \ldots, h_N^{\text{ref}})$ is now explicitly stated, and this reference vector is held constant across outcomes, but the reference health attributes may vary between individuals. It is *not* necessarily the case that $h_1^{\text{ref}} = h_2^{\text{ref}} = \ldots = h_N^{\text{ref}} = h^+$. The vector $(h_1^{\text{ref}}, h_2^{\text{ref}}, \ldots, h_N^{\text{ref}})$ is presumably the most likely status quo vector of individual health attributes.

Third, we might cure some of the distortions associated with missing characteristics by *normalizing the stated characteristics* to reflect the level of some of the missing attributes. This approach (for short, the "normalization approach") would work as follows. Outcomes are allowed to vary both with respect to $\mathbf{a}$-type characteristics and with respect to certain other characteristics, the $\mathbf{m}^1$ characteristics. Policies (actions) are mapped onto these outcomes (in the case of choice under certainty) or probability distributions over these outcomes. However, we assign a moral *value* to the outcomes, and thereby a moral value to policies, by valuing the outcomes' normalized counterparts. Outcome $x = (\mathbf{a}, \mathbf{m}^1)$ corresponds to the normalized outcome $(\mathbf{a}^{\text{norm}}, \mathbf{m}^{1\text{-ref}})$.[28] In particular, we develop a set of utility functions for the *normalized* outcomes by eliciting individuals' preferences over the *normalized* life-histories,

---

[28] $(\mathbf{a}, \mathbf{m}^1)$ and $(\mathbf{a}^{\text{norm}}, \mathbf{m}^{1\text{-ref}})$ should be such that each of the N individuals in the population is just as well off in both outcomes. A problem emerges here. The substitution of $(\mathbf{a}^{\text{norm}}, \mathbf{m}^{1\text{-ref}})$ for $(\mathbf{a}, \mathbf{m}^1)$ is meant to facilitate the construction of $\mathbf{U}$. Don't we need a preexisting set $\mathbf{U}$ to evaluate whether each individual is just as well off in both outcomes? To get around this problem, we might appeal to a given individual's preferences, or well informed preferences, to determine whether she is equally well off with $(\mathbf{a}, \mathbf{m}^1)$ and $(\mathbf{a}^{\text{norm}}, \mathbf{m}^{1\text{-ref}})$. This is admittedly an imperfect solution, from the perspective of the

which have the form $(\mathbf{a}^{norm}, \mathbf{m}^{1\text{-}ref}; j)$ or perhaps the form $(\mathbf{a}^{norm}; j)$. We then rank a given pair of outcomes in the original outcome set by taking the vector(s) of utility numbers for their normalized counterparts, and using these utility vectors as the input to the SWF.

What is the point of the normalization approach? By contrast with the approach that ignores the $\mathbf{m}^1$ characteristics entirely, or assumes them to be unaffected by policy choice, the normalization approach has the advantage of allowing the analyst to be sensitive to the impact of policies on the $\mathbf{m}^1$ characteristics as well as the $\mathbf{a}$ characteristics. Of course, this could also be accomplished without normalization— just by having an outcome set in which both types of characteristics vary, and in which the corresponding life-histories are directly ranked. However, the analyst may have better information about spectators' preferences regarding lotteries over normalized life-histories, as opposed to information about their preferences regarding lotteries over life-histories in which both $\mathbf{a}$ and $\mathbf{m}^1$ characteristics vary.

The reader may remember the discussion in Chapter 2, concerning a *competitor* to the SWF approach: namely, the use of *income evaluation functions* (not SWFs) to rank outcomes in light of the vector of individuals' incomes or normalized incomes in each outcome. The normalization approach, as I have just presented it, is a variant of the SWF methodology and should not be conflated with the normalization of incomes in the context of an income evaluation function. There are certain similarities between the two policy-analysis methodologies, but also important differences, as further explored in the margin.[29]

account of well-being presented in Chapter 3, since that generally appeals to *all* individuals' preferences to make well-being comparisons, even intrapersonal comparisons.

[29] The income-evaluation-function approach takes account of non-income attributes by setting these at a reference level, and then applying the evaluation function to the vector of normalized incomes. It runs afoul of the problem of "reference dependence": the vectors of normalized incomes corresponding to x and y, and thus the ranking of x and y by the income evaluation function, may depend on how the reference level is set; but the choice of any particular reference level seems arbitrary. By contrast, the normalization approach described here uses vectors of *utilities* as the inputs to the SWF. Those utilities can take account of the reference level. In other words, $\mathbf{U}$ can be constructed for life-histories with $(\mathbf{a}, \mathbf{m}^1)$ characteristics by eliciting extended preferences for matching life-histories with $(\mathbf{a}^{norm}, \mathbf{m}^{1\text{-}ref})$ characteristics. (Admittedly, if $\mathbf{U}$ is constructed for life-histories with $(\mathbf{a}, \mathbf{m}^1)$ characteristics by eliciting extended preferences for matching life-histories with $\mathbf{a}^{norm}$ characteristics, suppressing information about the reference level of the $\mathbf{m}^1$ characteristics, there *is* a reference-dependence problem. For a well-known empirical study, using a social welfare function applied to incomes normalized to take account of the vector of commodity prices—rather than to utility as a function of normalized incomes and the reference price vector—see King [1983].)

Moreover, normalization is simply *one* methodology available to the SWF approach in handling the multiplicity of attributes. By contrast, the income-evaluation-function approach (because it eschews utilities, and instead uses incomes as the currency for social evaluation) is committed to taking account of non-income attributes via normalization.

To sum up: we have discussed different ways in which characteristics of the world that are relevant to human welfare might be incorporated into the description of simplified outcomes, whose associated life-histories and life-history lotteries are to be ranked by spectators. Outcomes might be described with respect to a given type of characteristic, and allowed to vary with respect to that characteristic; the characteristic might be ignored entirely; it might be fixed at some reference level in all outcomes. Or, a somewhat more complicated normalization approach might be employed, where the characteristic is incorporated into the description of outcomes, which can vary with respect to it, but a utility function is developed for the outcomes by equating each with a corresponding normalized outcome in which the characteristic is held fixed at a reference level.

Choosing between these approaches brings us back to the thorny, and perhaps insoluble, topic of optimal simplification, which I will not attempt to address. Still, we have made some progress in understanding how the analyst might go about ranking a simplified outcome set. Note, in particular, that—regardless of the approach employed—the analyst will *always* be eliciting spectators' rankings of life-histories in which *some* characteristics are missing.[30] And the way to do *that*, I have argued, is to assume that the missing characteristics are fixed at some unspecified level in all the life-histories, and that spectators' preferences are invariant to the specific level of the missing characteristics. This assumption may not be fully accurate—which will press us to enrich the description of outcomes to reflect the missing characteristics. On the other hand, because this enrichment cannot be pursued indefinitely—lest we end up with outcomes that are whole possible worlds—the analyst will always need to accept that *some* characteristics are missing, and to presuppose the invariance of spectators' conditional utility functions with respect to *those*.

II. INFERRING EXTENDED PREFERENCES FROM ORDINARY PREFERENCES

A given spectator's extended utility functions (the content of his set U^k) reflect three different types of extended preferences: his own-history preferences, i-history preferences, and across-person judgments. However, if we assume that these extended preferences satisfy the *non-essentiality condition*, we can estimate U^k without specific information about the spectator's i-history preferences and across-person judgments. We can infer what the content of U^k must be, simply by knowing the specifics of the spectator's own-history preferences. In other words, if the *non-essentiality condition* is satisfied, we can infer what the content of U^k must be, simply by knowing the specifics of the spectator's ordinary, self-interested preferences. (Remember that

---

[30] Even if an outcome set is missing m-type characteristics and we more finely specify it to now include a subset of those (either by letting them vary, or by fixing them at a reference level), others will still be missing.

a spectator's own-history preferences are *defined* in terms of her ordinary, self-interested preferences.)

Why is this inferential step important? There currently exists a vast body of research concerning individuals' ordinary preferences: preferences for outcomes and outcome lotteries. To be sure, not all of this research provides evidence of individuals' *self-interested* preferences. Some of it, instead, focuses on moral preferences, or on preferences which are grounded in a mix of moral and self-interested considerations.[31] But much of this preference research *does* examine how individuals rank outcomes and outcome lotteries under conditions which would tend to induce a wholly or at least predominantly self-interested attitude in the individuals. This includes survey research where the respondent is asked questions regarding her own attributes or potential attributes: for example, to rank lotteries consisting of different income amounts which she might receive, or to rank different health states which she might experience, or to make tradeoffs between her own income and fatality risks to herself. It also includes research that infers ordinary preferences from behavior likely to be predominantly self-interested: for example, consumers' choices among different bundles of marketed goods, workers' labor supply choices, or investors' financial decisions.[32]

This body of research and methodologies will be helpful (at least quite often) in estimating spectators' ordinary self-interested preferences, for any given outcome set. The non-essentiality condition—in allowing us to move *from* this information, *to* an understanding of the content of U^k—thus constitutes a powerful inferential tool. Indeed, existing social-welfare-function scholarship often *does* employ ordinary preference data to estimate the utility functions that are used as inputs.[33] This section, in effect, offers a rigorous justification for this practice: namely, by showing that the practice is justified *if* the non-essentiality condition is satisfied.

Having clarified the conditions under which we can infer extended preferences from ordinary self-interested preferences, the section then discusses the role of life-history surveys. Such surveys can, in principle, be used to *test* the non-essentiality condition, and to elicit extended utility functions where that condition fails. Life-history surveys also have an important role quite apart from the non-essentiality condition: namely, in estimating extended preferences for life-histories which include certain attributes that are *not* essential attributes but, still, tend to be "cognitively immutable."

[31] For research concerning individuals' impartial preferences, see sources cited in Chapter 5, n. 164. For research concerning individual preferences that mix self-interest with a concern for fair treatment or other moral goals, see the literature on "social preferences," reviewed in Daruvala (2010).

[32] See sources cited below, nn. 75, 77, 81, 89, 92, 95.

[33] There are many examples. See, e.g., Banks, Blundell, and Lewbel (1996); Cremer, Gahvari, and Ladoux (2003); Diamond (1998); Ebrahimi and Heady (1988); Jorgenson and Slesnick (1984); Stern (1976, 1987); Tuomala (1990).

One reminder: the set $\mathbf{U}^k$ is, strictly, $\mathbf{U}^{k,t,x}$, namely the set of extended utility functions representing the extended preferences that k possesses at a particular time, in a particular outcome. What I will now discuss is why, under the right conditions, we can infer these extended utility functions from k's ordinary self-interested preferences *at the same time, and in the same outcome*, summarized in an ordinary utility function $\varphi^{k,t,x}(.)$. These ordinary and extended functions are person, time, and outcome relative. The time and outcome superscripts will be dropped in what follows, to avoid clutter; but the reader should remember their implicit presence. The $u^k(.)$ and $\varphi^k(.)$ functions need not be intertemporally or intermodally fixed. Moreover, there is no reason (or at least no logical reason) to think that we can infer someone's extended preferences at one time-outcome location from his ordinary preferences at a different time-outcome location.

A. The Non-Essentiality Condition

Start with some arbitrary outcome set. Outcomes take the generic form $(\mathbf{a}_1, \mathbf{a}_2, \ldots, \mathbf{a}_{imp})$.[34] Various individual attributes and background facts are missing. As discussed in the previous section, the theory for constructing $\mathbf{U}^k$ associated with a given spectator k handles missing attributes by assuming that they are fixed at some unspecified level and that the spectator's various extended preferences are invariant to the specific level at which the missing attributes are fixed.

Let us now make the assumption that the spectator's extended preferences are *atomistic* and, furthermore, satisfy a *non-essentiality* condition. In other words, these preferences depend only on the subject's contingent attributes and background facts, not the subject's essential attributes or the attributes of other individuals. (See the margin for a fully precise statement.[35]) More specifically: the spectator's

---

[34] Attribute $\mathbf{a}_i$, here, is a vector consisting of individual i's attributes in each of the periods; it includes $\mathbf{a}_{i,1}, \mathbf{a}_{i,2}, \ldots$, up to $\mathbf{a}_{i,T}$, with T periods in the outcomes. Similarly, $\mathbf{a}_{imp}$ includes background facts in each of the periods.

[35] The statement of atomism in the text is a little rough. More precisely, extended preferences are "atomistic" if they do not depend on the attributes of persons other than the subject, or on the subject's relational attributes that involve a relation to other persons. (On monadic versus relational attributes, see above, n. 19.) A different possible formulation would be: extended preferences are "atomistic" if they depend solely on the subject's monadic properties plus background facts. The difficulty with this latter formulation is that the typical individual attributes which are included in even the simplest utility functions may, technically, be relational rather than monadic—relational in the sense that they involve a relation between the subject and some other entity (if not another person). For example, Leo's property of consuming a particular consumption good is (arguably) relational rather than monadic, because it involves a relation between him and an entity (the particular good consumed).

A property is "essential" if the subject necessarily possesses it in every possible world (and, thus, every outcome—simplified possible world), otherwise it is contingent. Note that, because outcomes are simplified and outcome sets incomplete, it is possible for a subject to possess a contingent attribute in every outcome. But it is not possible for her to lack an essential property in any outcome.

self-interested ranking of outcomes and outcome lotteries depends only on his own contingent attributes in outcomes, plus background facts. The spectator's *i*-interested ranking of outcomes and outcome lotteries depends only on subject *i*'s contingent attributes in outcomes, plus background facts. Finally, whether the spectator judges $(x; i)$ to be as good as $(y; j)$ depends only on subject *i*'s contingent attributes in *x* and the background facts in *x*, and subject *j*'s contingent attributes in *y* and the background facts in *y*.

   If this is true, then we can show that $\mathbf{U}^k$ is unique up to a positive affine transformation. And the form of each $u^k(.)$ will be as follows: $u^k(x; j) = v^k(\mathbf{a}_j^{cont}(x), \mathbf{a}_{imp}(x))$, with $x = (\mathbf{a}_1, \mathbf{a}_2, \ldots, \mathbf{a}_{imp})$, and $\mathbf{a}_j^{cont}(x)$ the contingent attributes of individual *j* in outcome *x*. In other words, $u^k(.)$ will assign a number to a life-history as a function of the subject's contingent attributes in the outcome, plus background facts.[36]

Extended preferences satisfy non-essentiality if they do not depend on the subject's essential properties.

   Extended preferences that satisfy *both* the non-essentiality condition *and* the atomism condition, therefore, are such that they depend only on background facts, the subject's contingent monadic properties, or the subject's contingent relational properties which do not involve a relation to some person.

   In the text, I say that extended preferences which satisfy both conditions depend upon the subject's contingent attributes and background facts. The reader will understand that "attribute" here (and for the remainder of the chapter, whenever attributes are discussed with the atomism condition in play) is a shorthand which means "monadic attributes or relational attributes which do not involve a relation to some other person." Where the atomism condition is in play, I will use the symbol "$\mathbf{a}_i$" to denote individual *i*'s "attributes" in the restricted sense set forth in the previous sentence, and "$\mathbf{a}_i^{cont}$" to denote his contingent attributes of this sort. More generally, of course, the individual attributes included in the description of outcomes *can* include attributes which involve a relation to other persons. See above, n. 19.

[36] See Chapter 3, pp. 208–213, for the details of the construction of $\mathbf{U}^k$. What follows should be read together with that discussion.

   The spectator's own-history preferences, if consistent with EU theory, are expectationally represented by some utility function $u_k^k(.)$, which assigns values only to life-histories where *k* is the subject. We begin the construction of $\mathbf{U}^k$ by constructing the set $\mathbf{U}_k^k$ which consists of $u_k^k(.)$ and all positive affine transformations thereof. Note that, because *k*'s ranking of his own life-histories (i.e., his self-interested ranking of outcomes) depends only on his own contingent attributes and background facts, any $u_k^k(.)$ in $\mathbf{U}_k^k$ must satisfy a supervenience requirement—namely that if *x* and *y* are such that *k*'s contingent attributes and background facts are identical in the two outcomes, then $u_k^k(x; k) = u_k^k(y; k)$.

   Similarly, consider the extended utility function $u_i^k(.)$, which assigns values only to life-histories where *i* is the subject. For each *i*, we proceed with the construction of $\mathbf{U}^k$ by identifying some $u_i^k(.)$ which expectationally represents *k*'s *i*-history preferences. The set $\mathbf{U}_i^k$ consists of $u_i^k(.)$ and all positive affine transformations thereof. Note that, because *k*'s ranking of life-histories involving *i* (i.e., *k*'s *i*-interested ranking of outcomes) depends only on subject *i*'s contingent attributes and background facts, any $u_i^k(.)$ in $\mathbf{U}_i^k$ must also satisfy a supervenience requirement—namely that if *x* and *y* are such that *i*'s contingent attributes and background facts are identical in the two outcomes, then $u_i^k(x; i) = u_i^k(y; i)$.

(The reader will note that the utility functions typically used in SWF scholarship, which were presented earlier in the chapter, take this form.)

Moreover, in this case, we will be able to infer $u^k(.)$ from the spectator's self-interested preferences over outcomes. Imagine that we have in hand an ordinary utility function, $\varphi^k(.)$, which expectationally represents the spectator's self-interested preferences over outcomes and outcome lotteries. Because the spectator's own-history preferences are defined in terms of his self-interested outcome preferences, we can immediately conclude the following: there is some $u^k(.)$ in $\mathbf{U}^k$ such that the values assigned by $u^k(.)$ to k's own life-histories are given by $\varphi^k(.)$. In other words, for any outcome x, $u^k(x; k) = \varphi^k(x)$.[37] ($\mathbf{U}^k$, in turn, will consist of all positive affine transformations of $u^k(.)$). But—given atomism and nonessentiality—we can also infer, more generally, the values that $u^k(.)$ assigns to life-histories where k is not the subject. Take an arbitrary life-history $(x; j)$. Consider the "counterpart" life-history $(x^*; k)$, such that the contingent attributes of spectator k in x^* are the same

---

$\mathbf{U}^k$ is formed as the product set of the N sets $\mathbf{U}_1^k, \ldots, \mathbf{U}_N^k$. The set $\mathbf{U}^k$, thus constructed, is not yet unique up to a positive affine transformation. To achieve that, it suffices to have at least two "points of contact" between individual 1 and individual 2, individual 2 and 3, etc. But, because of the requirement that across-person judgments be sensitive only to the subject's contingent attributes and background facts, there will be at least two points of contact between any two individuals. Consider two outcomes, x and y, such that $u^k(x; j) \neq u^k(y; j)$. Consider any other individual i. Then if x^* is such that its background facts are the same as in x, and i's contingent attributes in x^* are the same as j's contingent attributes in x; and if y^* is such that its background facts are the same as in y, and i's contingent attributes in y^* are the same as j's contingent attributes in y; then there are two points of contact. (Strictly, for this argument to work, we may have to add an outcome x^* or y^* to the outcome set, if $\mathbf{O}$ doesn't already contain it. Because x^* and y^* are possible outcomes, there is no difficulty in doing so.)

Moreover, once we have "winnowed down" $\mathbf{U}^k$ to be consistent with these across-person judgments—so that $u^k(x; j) = u^k(x^*; i)$ whenever the two subjects have the same contingent attributes in both outcomes and background facts are the same—we can take any $u^k(.)$ in $\mathbf{U}^k$ and define a corresponding $v^k(.)$ function as follows. Where $(\mathbf{a}^{cont}, \mathbf{a}_{imp})$ is some package of contingent individual attributes and background facts, let $v^k(\mathbf{a}^{cont}, \mathbf{a}_{imp}) = u^k(x; i)$, where $(x; i)$ is *any* life-history such that individual i's attributes in x are $\mathbf{a}^{cont}$ and background facts are $\mathbf{a}_{imp}$. Because of the supervenience requirements mentioned above, and the across-subject consistency requirement just mentioned, $u^k(x; i)$ is the same value for all such life-histories, whatever outcome x is and whoever subject i is. Thus $v^k(.)$ is well-defined. And it is true that, for every life-history, $u^k(x; j) = v^k(\mathbf{a}^{cont}(x), \mathbf{a}_{imp}(x))$.

[37] Why exactly can we infer this? Because k's own-history preferences are defined in terms of his self-interested preferences for outcomes and outcome lotteries, each $u^k(.)$ in $\mathbf{U}^k$ expectationally represents these preferences. To be precise, let $\xi^k(x) = u^k(x; k)$ for every x. Then $\xi^k(.)$ is an ordinary utility function which expectationally represents k's self-interested preferences for outcomes and outcome lotteries. But so does $\varphi^k(.)$. By EU theory, these two functions must be positive affine transformations of each other; there must be numbers a and b, a positive, such that $\xi^k(x) = a\varphi^k(x) + b$ for every x. Thus there are numbers a, b, a positive, such that $u^k(x; k) = a\varphi^k(x) + b$ for every x.

But if $u^k(.)$ is in $\mathbf{U}^k$, then so is every positive affine transformation. Let $c = 1/a$ and $d = -b/a$. Consider extended utility function $w^k(.)$ such that $w^k(x; i) = cu^k(x; i) + d$ for every life-history $(x; i)$. This function is in $\mathbf{U}^k$ and $w^k(x; k) = \varphi^k(x)$ for every outcome x.

as the contingent attributes of subject j in x, and background facts are the same. Then it must be the case that $u^k(x; j) = u^k(x^*; k)$.

To express the same idea a different way: Imagine that we have in hand an ordinary utility function, $\varphi^k(.)$, which expectationally represents the spectator's self-interested preferences over outcomes and outcome lotteries. Because those preferences (as well as the spectator's extended preferences) are atomistic and satisfy the non-essentiality condition, this ordinary utility function will take the form $\varphi^k(x) = v^k(\mathbf{a}_k^{cont}(x), \mathbf{a}_{imp}(x))$. And because the spectator's own-history preferences are defined in terms of his self-interested outcome preferences, we can immediately conclude the following: there is some $u^k(.)$ in $\mathbf{U}^k$ such that, for any outcome x, $u^k(x; k) = v^k(\mathbf{a}_k^{cont}(x), \mathbf{a}_{imp}(x))$. ($\mathbf{U}^k$, in turn, will consist of all positive affine transformations of $u^k(.)$). But, in identifying $v^k(.)$, we have *also* more generally determined the values that this extended utility function $u^k(.)$ assigns to life-histories in which k is not the subject. For any arbitrary life-history $(x; j)$, its utility can be computed by plugging the subject's contingent attributes plus background facts into the $v^k(.)$ function. In other words, $u^k(x; j) = v^k(\mathbf{a}_j^{cont}(x), \mathbf{a}_{imp}(x))$.

An example may help. Imagine that the spectator's ranking of life-histories depends only on the subject's consumption, leisure, and health. That means, specifically, that the spectator's self-interested ranking of outcomes and outcome lotteries depends solely on his own consumption, leisure and health, and that his i-interested ranking of outcomes and outcome lotteries depends only on individual i's consumption, leisure and health. Furthermore, it means that the spectator's across-person judgments are regimented as follows: If $(x; j)$ and $(y; i)$ are such that subject j in outcome x has a given package of health, consumption, and leisure attributes, and subject i has the very same package in y, then the spectator judges the two subjects to be equally well off.

If all this is true, then each $u^k(.)$ in $\mathbf{U}^k$ assigns a utility to a life-history as a function of the subject's consumption, leisure, and health.

Imagine, now, that we know what the spectator's own-history preferences are. We know how he ranks his own consumption-health-leisure bundles and lotteries over these. If so, we have everything we need to estimate $\mathbf{U}^k$. Take an ordinary utility function $\varphi^k(.)$, expectationally representing k's self-interested preferences over outcomes and outcome lotteries. The values that this ordinary utility function assigns to outcomes will depend upon k's own consumption, leisure, and health. In other words, there will be some function $v^k(.)$, such that, for any outcome x, $\varphi^k(x) = v^k(c_k(x), l_k(x), h_k(x))$, with $c_k(x)$, $l_k(x)$, and $h_k(x)$ designating, respectively, k's consumption, leisure, and health in outcome x. Now, for any arbitrary $(x; j)$, define $u^k(x; j) = v^k(c_j(x), l_j(x), h_j(x))$. In other words, assign an arbitrary life-history the same utility that the spectator would assign his own life-history, were he to receive the amount of consumption, health, and leisure received by the subject. Then $\mathbf{U}^k$ is simply $u^k(.)$ and all positive affine transformations thereof.

What would interfere with our ability to infer $\mathbf{U}^k$ from the spectator's own-history preferences? The strategy for doing so that I have outlined assumed that $u^k(.)$ is atomistic: dependent only on the subject's attributes and background facts. This is a simplifying condition which is often adopted in social-welfare-function analysis,[38] but one which we may want to relax. For example, analysts sometimes entertain the possibility of "consumption externalities"—where someone's well-being depends both on her own consumption and on the consumption of other individuals.[39] However, even if the atomism assumption is dropped, it would seem possible to infer $\mathbf{U}^k$ from the spectator's own-history preferences—as long as $\mathbf{U}^k$ continues to satisfy a version of the non-essentiality condition, that spectators' preferences not be sensitive to subjects' essential properties. This point is elaborated in the margin.[40]

---

[38] As evidenced by the standard forms of utility functions considered at the beginning of this chapter.

[39] See, e.g., Aronsson and Johansson-Stenman (2008); Tuomala (1990, ch. 8).

[40] A rigorous discussion of how to infer extended preferences from ordinary self-interested preferences (own-history preferences) without atomism will not be undertaken here. What follows are some preliminary observations.

The easiest case for inferring spectator k's extended preferences from his own-history preferences, without atomism, is where $u^k(x; j)$ depends on background facts, the subject j's contingent monadic attributes, j's contingent relational attributes not involving a relation to persons, or the contingent attributes of other persons—without reference to the relation between those persons and the subject j.

In other words, the attributes of persons other than the subject should figure symmetrically in the extended utility function; permuting those attributes should not affect extended utility. (For example, $u^k(x; j)$ could be some function of j's consumption and the average consumption in the population; or some function of j's consumption and the distribution of consumption.) Indeed, to the extent that non-atomistic utility functions figure in social-welfare-function scholarship, this is typically the form they take. See Aronsson and Johansson-Stenman (2008, p. 988), noting that: "the dominating bulk of the literature [regarding preferences for relative consumption] . . . assume[s] that each individual compares his/her own consumption with a reference level determined by the average consumption in the economy."

In this case, we can infer $u^k(x; j)$ from k's own-history preferences, because $u^k(x; j) = u^k(x^*; k)$, where x^* is such that it has the same background facts as x; k's contingent attributes (monadic or relational-but-not-to-persons) in x^* are the same as j's in x; and the distribution of contingent attributes among non-subjects in x^* is the same as in x. (For example, if x is an outcome where j has a certain consumption and the average population consumption is at some level, then x^* would be an outcome where k has the same consumption as j in x and the average population consumption is the same as in x.)

A more complicated case is one where extended preferences depend on the attributes of certain persons other than the subject, namely those who stand in a certain relation to him. For example, Jim's well-being may depend, in part, on the happiness of those individuals who are his friends. Even in this case, I suggest, we can infer spectator k's extended preferences from his own-history preferences if the non-subjects whose attributes are relevant to $u^k(x; j)$ are individuals who stand in some *contingent* relation to j: a relation that a person can have or lack without losing his identity. For example, if $u^k(x; j)$ is determined by j's happiness and the happiness of j's best friend, if j has one, then $u^k(x; j) = u^k(x^*; k)$ where x^* is such that k is just as happy as j in x, and k has a best friend, and his best friend is just as happy as j's in x.

Indeed, we can push this further, to the case where $u^k(x; j)$ depends on the attributes of persons to whom j bears an essential relation (a relation that j cannot lack without losing his identity) if *everyone* bears that essential relation to someone. (For example, $u^k(x; j)$ might depend on j's happiness and the

The non-essentiality condition, by contrast, *is* absolutely vital to inferring $\mathbf{U}^k$ from the spectator's own-history preferences. For example, imagine that there is some binary property, P, which is an essential property. Each individual in the population either has P in all outcomes, or lacks P in all outcomes. Each individual is also characterized as having some level of attribute r and some level of attribute s. Imagine that the spectator himself lacks property P. We know how he self-interestedly ranks different possible packages of attributes r and s which he might receive. We also know how he self-interestedly ranks lotteries over his own r-s packages. All this information is summarized in an ordinary utility function $\varphi^k(.)$.

Assume, however, that utility functions in $\mathbf{U}^k$ are sensitive not only to the subject's levels of r and s, but also to whether the subject has or lacks property P. How could that happen? One possibility is that the spectator's i-interested preferences depend upon whether the subject, i, possesses or lacks P. If l is a lottery over r-s packages for some subject, and l^* a different lottery, then the spectator prefers l to l^* when he is i-interested and the subject has property P, but may prefer l^* to l when the spectator is i-interested and the subject lacks property P. Furthermore, even if the non-essentiality condition is not violated in this manner, it might be violated in another way: the spectator might make the across-person judgment that $(x; j)$ is better than $(y; i)$, even though the subjects have the same r and s levels in both histories, because one of them has P and the other lacks P.

If the non-essentiality condition *is* violated, it clearly is *not* possible to infer $\mathbf{U}^k$ from the spectator's self-interested preferences over outcomes.[41] Given spectator k's ordinary utility function, $\varphi^k(.)$, we can *still* immediately reach certain conclusions about $\mathbf{U}^k$: namely, that there is some $u^k(.)$ in $\mathbf{U}^k$ such that, for any one of k's life-histories $(x; k)$, $u^k(x; k) = \varphi^k(x)$. We can also infer the values that this $u^k(.)$ assigns to the life-histories of other subjects who, like spectator k, lack property P. But we

---

happiness of j's parents. The identity of someone's parents is arguably an essential feature of her—but the spectator also has the essential property of being the child of certain parents. Thus $u^k(x; j) = u^k(x^*; k)$ where x^* is such that k is just as happy as j in x, and k's parents in x^* are just as happy as j's in x.)

Difficulties in inferring extended preferences from own-history preferences will arise if $u^k(x; j)$ depends on the properties of non-subjects who stand in some essential relation to j, which the spectator doesn't bear to anyone. More simply, difficulties will arise if $u^k(x; j)$ depends on some essential monadic attributes of non-subjects. Imagine that the spectator essentially has property P, and everyone else essentially lacks P. Imagine that $u^k(x; j)$ takes a particular value because some person other than j has property P. We might try to infer $u^k(x; j)$ by setting $u^k(x; j) = u^k(x^*; k)$, where x^* is such that some person other than k has property P. But, necessarily, there will exist no such x^*.

[41] The problem, here, is akin to a problem described by Robert Pollak (1991)—namely, the difficulty in inferring an individual's "unconditional" preferences over combinations of consumption goods and non-consumption characteristics (e.g., demographic characteristics), from her "conditional" preferences for consumption goods holding fixed non-consumption characteristics. See also Kaneko (1984). Harsanyi himself addresses the difficulty of inferring extended preferences given fixed individual attributes—although conflates that with the problem of predicting the causal contribution that fixed properties make to individual satisfaction. See Harsanyi (1955, pp. 316–319).

cannot determine the values it assigns to the life-histories of subjects who possess P. Consider j, who possesses P. We *cannot* determine the value of $u^k(x; j)$ by identifying an outcome x^* such that k's contingent attributes in x^* are the same as j's in x, and say that $u^k(x; j) = u^k(x^*; k)$. We cannot do this because $u^k(.)$ is sensitive to whether the subject has P. Nor can we determine the value of $u^k(x; j)$ by identifying an outcome x^+ such that *all* of k's attributes in x^+ are the same as *all* of j's attributes in x, and setting $u^k(x; j) = u^k(x^+; k)$. We cannot do *this* because P is an essential property: j possesses the property P in x and there is no possible outcome in which k possesses it.

The following tables illustrate these points. In the first case, the spectator's i-history preferences depend upon whether the subject possesses or lacks P. In this case, we cannot make any inferences at all about $u^k(\_\_; j)$, where j possesses P. In the second case, the spectator's i-history preferences do not depend upon whether the subject possesses or lacks P, but his across-person comparisons are sensitive to P. In this case, we can make some inferences about the general structure of $u^k(\_\_; j)$, but we cannot nail down what this function must be. We still cannot say that, if j's contingent attributes in x are the same as the spectator's in x^*, and background facts are the same, then $u^k(x; j) = u^k(x^*; k)$.

Assume that there are three individuals. Individuals 1 and 2 lack essential property P; individual 3 has essential property P. Each life-history characterizes the subject as having or lacking P, plus having one of four possible r-s packages: rs, r^*s, rs^*, r^*s^*. We are trying to make inferences about the extended preferences of individual 1; for purposes of this example, he is the spectator. Assume, for simplicity, that his set $\mathbf{U}^1$ of extended utility functions consists of the function $u^1(.)$ plus all positive affine transformations thereof. The function $u^1(.)$ takes the form $u^1(x; i) = f^1(r_i(x), s_i(x), P_i)$, where $r_i(x)$ indicates the subject's level of the r attribute, $s_i(x)$ the subject's level of the s attribute, and P_i whether the subject has or lacks P.[42] The spectator's ordinary self-interested preferences are captured in an ordinary utility function $\varphi^1(.)$, which is a function of his own r and s attributes, i.e., takes the form $\varphi^1(x) = v^1(r_1(x), s_1(x))$.

Assume, further, that we are well informed about $\varphi^1(.)$. We know it assigns utilities to outcomes as follows: The outcome receives a utility of 10 if the spectator has the package rs, 20 if he has the package r^*s, 30 if rs^*, and 40 if r^*s^*. (In other words, $v^1(rs) = 10$, $v^1(r^*s) = 20$, and so forth.) What inferences can we make about $u^1(.)$? We can infer that $u^1(.)$ assigns exactly these values, or some positive affine transformation thereof, to the life-histories of individual 1. And we can infer that $u^1(.)$ assigns exactly these values, or some positive affine transformation thereof, to the life-histories of individual 2—since individual 2, like individual 1, lacks property P.[43] But we can make no inferences whatsoever

[42] Thus $w^1(.)$ is also in $\mathbf{U}^1$ iff there exist numbers c and d, c positive, such that—for every life-history $(x; i)$—$w^1(x; i) = cf^1(r_i(x), s_i(x), P_i) + d$.

[43] Whether or not the non-essentiality requirement is satisfied (here it is not), the logic of n. 37, above, allows us to infer that if $u^1(.)$ is in $\mathbf{U}^1$, there must be numbers a and b, a positive, such that $u^1(x; 1) = a\varphi^1(x) + b$ for all x. Moreover, because $u^1(x; i) = f^1(r_i(x), s_i(x), P_i)$, and individuals 1 and 2

about the values that $u^1(.)$ assigns to the life-histories of individual 3. It takes the form $u^1(x; i) = f^1(r_i(x), s_i(x), P_i)$, and there are no logical connections between the values that this $f^1(.)$ function assigns to individual 3's life-histories, and the spectator's ordinary utility function $\varphi^1(.)$.

Table 4.2 illustrates this case. It displays different possible life-histories—formed by pairing an individual with some package of r and s attributes plus property P, if the individual has that property, or the absence of P, if the individual lacks it. The numbers indicates what we can infer about the values that $u^1(.)$ assigns to each life-history, given our information about $\varphi^1(.)$. There must be numbers a and b, a positive, such that these values are as follows:

Table 4.2 A Violation of the Non-Essentiality Condition: First Example

	Package of r and s attributes				
	rs	r^*s	rs^*	r^*s^*	Property P
Individual 1	$a10 + b$	$a20 + b$	$a30 + b$	$a40 + b$	No
Individual 2	$a10 + b$	$a20 + b$	$a30 + b$	$a40 + b$	No
Individual 3	??	??	??	??	Yes

Because we can make no inferences concerning the values that $u^1(.)$ assigns to individual 3's histories, we cannot infer how it ranks those as compared to other subjects' histories. Nor can we infer how it ranks those histories as against each other, or how it ranks various lotteries over individual 3's histories.

Consider, now, a second case, illustrated by Table 4.3, where U^1 is still sensitive to whether the subject has or lacks P, but assumes a functional form which separates the influence of P and the r-s attributes. In particular, assume that $u^1(x; i) = f^1(r_i(x), s_i(x)) \times g^1(P_i)$, with $g^1(.)$ a positively valued function, and that U^1 consists of all positive affine transformations of $u^1(.).^{44}$ Now, given our information about $\varphi^1(.)$, we can infer that there

both lack property P, it follows that: if x is an outcome where individual 2 has a particular r-s package, and x^* an outcome where individual 1 has the very same r-s package, then $u^1(x; 2) = u^1(x^*; 1)$.

Table 4.2 shows the value that $u^1(.)$ assigns to r-s packages for individuals 1 or 2, namely $a10 + b$ for the package rs, $a20 + b$ for r^*s, etc. We therefore know how $u^1(.)$ orders these packages and lotteries over them, even without knowing the precise values of a and b—and thus how all utility functions in U^1 do, since U^1 consists of all positive affine transformations of $u^1(.)$. Further, by setting $c = 1/a$ and $d = -b/a$, we know that there is a $w^1(.)$ in $U^1(.)$ which is equal to $cu^1(.) + d$ and thus precisely equal to $\varphi^1(.)$, i.e., assigns the value 10 to an rs package for individuals 1 or 2, the value 20 to an r^*s package, and so forth.

[44] To be clear, this does not mean that all members of U^1 assume the multiplicative form of $u^1(.)$. Rather, it means that $w^1(.)$ is also in U^1 iff there exist values c and d, c positive, such that $w^1(x; i) = cf^1(r_i(x), s_i(x)) \times g^1(P_i) + d$ for all $(x; i)$.

are numbers *a*, *b*, and *K*, with *a* and *K* positive, such that $u^1(.)$ assigns values to life-histories as follows.[45]

Table 4.3 A Violation of the Non-Essentiality Condition: Second Example

	Package of r and s attributes				
	rs	*r*s*	*rs**	*r*s**	*Property P*
Individual 1	$a10 + b$	$a20 + b$	$a30 + b$	$a40 + b$	No
Individual 2	$a10 + b$	$a20 + b$	$a30 + b$	$a40 + b$	No
Individual 3	$K(a10 + b)$	$K(a20 + b)$	$K(a30 + b)$	$K(a40 + b)$	Yes

In this case, we *can* infer how $u^1(.)$ ranks individual 3's histories as against each other, and how it ranks lotteries over those histories. But because our information about the functional form of $u^1(.)$ and about $\varphi^1(.)$ is insufficient to nail down the value of *K*, we cannot infer how $u^1(.)$ ranks individual 3's histories as against the other subjects' histories.

The reader might wonder whether the non-essentiality condition might be circumvented by "hiding" individuals' essential properties: by describing outcomes so that the only individual attributes which are included are contingent attributes. For example, in the case just discussed, why not further simplify the outcome set, so that outcomes now specify only what individuals' *r* and *s* levels are, not whether they possess or lack essential property *P*? Unfortunately, this approach fails. Remember that the spectator ranks simplified outcome sets on the premises (1) that his ranking of outcomes and lotteries is invariant to the level of missing attributes and furthermore (2) that all individuals have the very same missing attributes, insofar as the spectator cares about these. For example: If the spectator's extended preferences would be sensitive to the subject's health (were health to be included in the description of outcomes), then in ranking an outcome set with health missing, the spectator must assume that all individuals have the very same, unspecified level of health. Otherwise, it is incoherent to ask the spectator to rank the simplified outcome set. But what this stipulation means, in the case of essential preferences, is that the "hiding" strategy fails utterly. If the spectator's extended preferences would be

---

[45] As in the first case, there must be numbers *a* and *b*, *a* positive, such that $u^1(x; 1) = a\varphi^1(x) + b$ for all *x*. See above, n. 43. Moreover, we now have that $u^1(x; i) = f^1(r_i(x), s_i(x)) \times g^1(P_i)$. Let $g^1(P_3)/g^1(P_1) = K$, a positive number. This is the ratio between the value that $u^1(.)$ assigns to a particular *r-s* package when conjoined with property *P*, and the value that it assigns to this package when conjoined with the absence of *P*. If *x* is an outcome where individual 3 has a particular *r-s* package, and x^* an outcome where individual 1 has that same package, $u^1(x; 3) = f^1(r_3(x), s_3(x)) \times g^1(P_3) = Kf^1(r_1(x^*), s_1(x^*)) \times g^1(P_1) = Ku^1(x^*; 1) = K(a\varphi^1(x^*) + b)$, as shown in Table 4.3.

sensitive to some essential property of subjects (were that property to be included in the description of outcomes), then outcomes *must* include that property.[46]

In short, the strategy for inferring a spectator's U^k from his own-history preferences depends, crucially, on the non-essentiality condition.

So is that condition warranted? It is certainly *possible* for a given spectator's extended preferences to depend upon the subject's essential properties. Indeed, as the reader will remember, the account of extended preferences constructed in Chapter 3 was developed so as to be robust to this possibility. It seems incorrect to insist, as a conceptual matter, that essential properties cannot influence extended preferences and, thus, that they cannot influence individual well-being.

Moreover, it is certainly worthwhile to examine the question through systematic survey work. This is one possible role for life-history surveys, to be discussed in a moment.

However, at least for now—pending more systematic research of the sort just described—the non-essentiality condition would seem to be a very plausible working assumption. Although the nature of essential properties is certainly *not* a matter of philosophical consensus—in particular, the range of theories of personal identity will generate a range of possible answers[47]—scholarly reflection about well-being tends to suggest that the non-essentiality condition is true, whichever specific

---

[46] More precisely, except in the special case where the entire population is homogeneous with respect to some essential property (i.e., everyone possesses or lacks the property in the case of a dichotomous property, or possesses it at the same level in the case of a scalar property), then outcomes must include the property if spectators' extended preferences are sensitive to it. If a property is one that a spectator cares about, to treat it as missing requires assuming that all individuals are homogeneous with respect to it. In the case of a contingent property whose actual distribution is heterogeneous, this is possible. In the case of an essential property, if its actual distribution is heterogeneous, then so is its distribution in every possible world.

[47] This book focuses on human persons. An account of the essential properties of human persons provides an answer to the question: What are the properties which a particular human person must possess in every world where she exists? Formulating that answer means grappling with the general literature in metaphysics on essential properties. See Lowe (2002, ch. 6); P. Mackie (2006). Moreover, as I mentioned in the discussion of essential properties in Chapter 3, it means addressing the contested topic of "animalism": is each human person essentially a particular human being ("human animal"); essentially a particular person; or, perhaps, essentially something else? See generally Olson (1997, 2007). Finally, it must cohere with an account of personal identity over time (the central focus of the extant philosophical literature on the nature of persons, see Chapter 6).

The "necessity of origin" view of essential properties, buttressed by the view that each human person is essentially a particular human being, would suggest that the identity of a person's biological parents, being the union of a particular egg and sperm, or perhaps the time of her birth are an essential property of her. The "necessity of constitution" view, buttressed by the view that each human person is essentially a particular human being, would suggest that a person's DNA is an essential feature of her. Alternatively, if each human person is a essentially a particular person—with personhood and personal identity over time analyzed in terms of psychological properties and psychological continuity—the essential properties of human persons might have a psychological component.

account of essential properties is adopted. In particular, plausible lists of "objective goods"—such as those adopted by philosophers, or the lists of goods adopted in the capabilities/functionings or quality-of-life literatures[48]—might be taken as a provisional guess as to the content of individuals' fully informed, fully rational extended preferences, insofar as these converge. The goods on these lists consist in *contingent* individual properties, not essential properties—on any plausible specification of the contingent/essential distinction. Consider, for example, Nussbaum's list. An individual's longevity, health, bodily integrity, emotional and intellectual life, social life, degree of practical reason, interaction with other species, recreation, and control over her environment are clearly contingent. Surely an individual might do better or worse on any of these dimensions without losing her identity![49]

B. What Is the Role of Life-History Surveys?

I will use the term "life-history surveys" to mean surveys that would seek to elicit the respondent's *i*-history preferences and/or his "across-person judgments" (as opposed to surveys merely eliciting his own-history preferences, or other sorts of surveys). A respondent's *i*-history preferences could be elicited in a "value free" way (by trying to induce, in the respondent, a condition of sympathy toward the subject, and asking him to rank outcomes or outcome lotteries in this condition). Alternatively, his *i*-history preferences could be elicited in a "value laden" way (by describing outcomes or outcome lotteries, and asking the respondent to rank these in light of the well-being of a particular subject). Across-person judgments are necessarily value laden. Questions seeking to elicit these would ask the respondent to compare the well-being level of some subject in some outcome to the well-being level of a different subject in some outcome; or to compare the ex ante well-being level of one subject, given some outcome lottery, to the ex ante well-being of a different subject, given some outcome lottery.

Life-history surveys are certainly feasible. Indeed, some scholars have already undertaken surveys that are pretty close to life-history surveys. There is an existing body of survey research that poses questions concerning the sources of well-being. Although much of this research is conducted in first-person mode, some of it employs a third-person or impersonal mode. By first-person, third-person, and impersonal modes, I mean—respectively—surveys that ask the respondent about the sources of her own well-being, about someone else's well-being, and about

---

Mightn't it be the case that individual *i* in outcome *x* is the same particular person as individual *j* in outcome *y* only if there is some minimal similarity between the individuals' psychological states?

[48] See Chapter 3, pp. 169–170. A collection of lists drawn from these literatures is provided by Alkire (2002, ch. 2).

[49] I should also note that John Broome, in his important book on *Weighing Lives*, embraces the assumption that whether one human life is better or worse than another is not a function of the subject's essential characteristics. See Broome (2004, pp. 94–95).

well-being in general.[50] Such third-person and impersonal questions, regarding the sources of well-being, are not too dissimilar from the across-person question that a life-history survey would ask, and from the value-laden variant of an *i*-history question.

But why would life-history surveys be *useful*, in implementing the SWF approach? If the non-essentiality condition holds true (for a given spectator), why not rely solely upon survey or behavioral evidence, concerning her ordinary self-interested preferences, as the basis for estimating her extended utilities?

First, life-history surveys can be used to *test* the non-essentiality condition. To be sure, it is almost absurd to think that extended preferences are sensitive to *certain* properties which might be thought to be essential—such as an individual's chromosomal makeup. Imagine that Diane and Doris are quite similar in the physical structure of their bodies and in their health histories, as well as other contingent properties, but (since they are not identical twins) their chromosomes are different. It seems very unlikely that the well-informed spectator would judge Diane to be better or worse off than Doris, just by virtue of the chromosomal difference. And it seems very unlikely that this spectator, under a condition of sympathy with Diane, would

---

[50] Much of the survey work regarding the sources of well-being is connected to the literature on the quality of life, which has employed such surveys to help characterize the different "domains" or "dimensions" of the quality of life. See Alkire (2002, ch. 2); Cummins (1996, pp. 304–305). There are numerous examples of first-person survey questions concerning the sources of well-being. For example, Shalom Schwartz (1992, p. 17) asked respondents to rate different values (such as pleasure, freedom, a spiritual life, or wealth) "as a guiding principle in my life." Campbell, Converse, and Rodgers (1976, pp. 82–84, 553) described different quality-of-life domains, such as "being in good health and in good physical condition," "a happy marriage," or "an interesting job," and asked respondents to quantify how important "that [domain] really is to you."

By contrast, the survey format that Narayan and co-authors employed in the massive *Voices of the Poor: Crying Out for Change* study included an impersonal question: "The starting question posed by the researchers to the small group discussions with poor women and men is, 'How do you define well-being or a good quality of life, and ill-being or a bad quality of life?'" Narayan et al. (2000, p. 22). The development of the WHOQOL quality-of-life instrument included focus groups with the general public, where the groups were asked to identity "the aspects of life that they considered contributed to its quality." WHOQOL Group (1998, p. 1570). Ryff (1989) combined question types, asking middle-aged and older respondents both first-person questions such as "What is most important to you in your life at the present time?" and impersonal questions such as "How would you define the ideal person?" or how they would describe a well-adjusted person.

Third-person questions designed to elicit conceptions of well-being are also possible, in principle, and have on occasion been employed. For example, King and Napa (1998, p. 158) based their article "What Makes a Life Good?" in part on a study where respondents were presented with a description of a possible life (in the form of answers to a fictional career survey) and asked: "How much do you think this person is leading 'the good life'?" Ann Holmes (1997), in her "extended sympathy" survey, discussed in the text below, also employed third-person questions—asking the respondent to rank different lives of hypothetical individuals, characterized in terms of health, gender, and other attributes.

have a particular ranking of various health/consumption/leisure packages (to be received by Diane), but a different ranking of the packages (now to be received by Doris) when under a condition of sympathy with Doris.

However, other plausible or thinkable candidates for the category of essential property *might* make a well-being difference, and survey research to test this possibility would be useful.

A different and more important role for life-history surveys is suggested by reflecting on the attribute of *gender*—as a paradigm example of a non-essential attribute whose impact on extended utilities might not be inferable from ordinary self-interested preferences.

Someone's gender is a socially constructed attribute which is distinct from her chromosomal make up. Someone who has chromosomes XX can be socially recognized as male; someone who has chromosomes XY can be socially recognized as female. While someone's chromosomal makeup is, arguably, an essential property, gender clearly is not: a person can remain the same particular person while changing his or her gender. Still, it seems odd to think that we can take a spectator's ordinary preferences, and thereby infer his or her extended preferences for a life-history set characterized in terms of subjects' genders. How can we infer a *female* spectator's *i*-history preferences from the spectator's own-history preferences, if the subject, *i*, is male? How can we infer a *male* spectator's *i*-history preferences from the spectator's own-history preferences, if the subject, *i*, is female? And how can we infer any spectator's across-person judgments from his or her own-history preferences, where one of the subjects involved does not share the spectator's gender?

There are actually two different worries suggested by this example, one which is purely technical, the other more substantive. The technical worry is this. Imagine that the non-essentiality condition, as well as atomism, is satisfied. We know the spectator's ordinary self-interested preferences, captured in an ordinary utility function $\varphi^k(.)$. We are trying to construct an extended utility function $u^k(.)$, and then define $\mathbf{U}^k$ as all positive affine transformations thereof. We can immediately determine the values that $u^k(.)$ should assign to k's own life-histories: $u^k(x; k) = \varphi^k(x)$. And we are supposed to determine the value which $u^k(.)$ assigns to any life-history of some *other* subject j, $(x; j)$, as follows: Identify an outcome x^*, such that individual k's contingent attributes in x^* are identical to j's in x, and then set $u^k(x; j) = u^k(x^*; k)$. But there might not *be* any such outcome x^* in the outcome set $\mathbf{O}$.

Consider the attribute of gender. Because individuals typically do not change their gender (even though they *could*; the attribute is not essential), the decision-maker may well be using an outcome set in which each subject retains his or her gender in all outcomes. If so, and if the spectator k is male in all outcomes, and is trying to use $\varphi^k(.)$ to determine the extended utility of $(x; j)$, where j is female in all outcomes, there will not be an outcome x^* in which k has all the contingent attributes of j in x. One such attribute is gender; and yet there is no outcome in which k possesses j's gender. Exactly the same problem arises, of course, where the spectator is female and is trying to use $\varphi^k(.)$ to determine the value of $u^k(x; j)$, where j is male.

The technical worry arises because the outcome set **O** is not sufficiently "rich." The worry can be solved by expanding the outcome set; determining spectators' ordinary self-interested preferences relative to the expanded outcome set; and using these to infer extended utilities for the expanded outcome set. For each life-history $(x; j)$ in the original set of life-histories defined by **O**: if there exists some spectator k, such that there is no outcome x^* in which k has all the contingent attributes of j in x, then expand **O** by adding such an outcome. Because the attributes at issue are contingent, this should be possible. For example, imagine that we start with an outcome set characterized in terms of the health, consumption, leisure, and gender of each individual in the population; each individual's gender does not vary across outcomes; for each possible package of health-consumption-leisure attributes, and each individual, there is some outcome in which the individual possesses that package. If the subject j of life-history $(x; j)$ is female and the spectator k is male, this outcome set will *not* contain an outcome x^* such that k's contingent attributes in x^* are identical to j's in x. But the problem can be readily solved by adding such an outcome to **O**. Outcome x^* is such that k's health in x^* is the same as j's health in x, k's consumption in x^* is the same as j's consumption in x, k's leisure in x^* is the same as j's leisure in x, *and k's gender in x^* is female rather than male.*

There is nothing problematic about expanding the outcome set. Outcomes are simplified descriptions of possible realities. As long as some outcome x^* is possible, expanding the initial outcome set to include x^* simply means that there are more possible life-histories to be compared to each other in terms of well-being, and more possible outcomes to be compared to each other as morally better or worse. Outcome x^* may be very unlikely or even have zero probability; but this is handled at the choice stage, by assigning a low or zero probability to x^*, and is no bar to adding x^* to **O**. Since gender is a contingent attribute and thus x^* is possible—since it is possible for k to change his gender, or indeed to have had a different gender his whole life, while remaining the same particular individual—the outcome set can be expanded to include x^*.[51]

However, there is a second, more substantive worry suggested by the example of gender, which is *not* resolved by expanding the outcome set. A spectator who is male may have trouble *imagining* an outcome in which he is female. Although such an outcome is possible, the spectator may deny its possibility; or he may concede the possibility of a gender change, but find it cognitively challenging to think about life-histories in which his gender is female. (Similar challenges may well arise, of course, for the female spectator asked to think about life-histories in which she is male.).

---

[51] Admittedly, an objection might be raised here: namely, that defining **U** by pooling spectators' extended preferences across all times and outcomes is plausible only if very low probability outcomes are omitted from **O**. See Chapter 3, n. 139. By enriching the outcome set to include possible but improbable outcomes (for example, the possible outcome in which k is female, even though k is in actuality male and none of the policy choices at hand would change his gender), we undercut the plausibility of this pooling scheme.

Although gender is not a *conceptually* immutable characteristic, we might describe it as "cognitively immutable." An attribute is "cognitively immutable," let us say, if individuals who possess the attribute (or have a particular level of the attribute, in the case of an attribute measured on some scale) typically experience cognitive difficulties in thinking about changing the attribute (or changing its level).

An attribute might be cognitively immutable because, in practice, most individuals retain the attribute (or remain at the same level). Gender and race are cognitively immutable for this reason. Alternatively, an attribute might be cognitively immutable because individuals are unwilling to entertain the possibility of the attribute changing—even though, in actuality, it does change with some frequency. A psychologically healthy person who is asked to consider the possibility of her suffering mental illness, or a high-status individual who is asked to consider the prospect of losing this status, might rebel at the question.

Recognizing that some attributes, albeit contingent, are cognitively immutable suggests a role for life-history surveys. Where some of the individual attributes included in the description of outcomes are cognitively immutable, it may be easier for the researcher to determine spectators' i-history preferences and across-person judgments by eliciting them directly—in life-history surveys—rather than by trying to infer them from spectators' own-history preferences. To illustrate, consider once more the attribute of gender. If the spectator, k, is male, and the subject i is female, we could estimate k's i-history preferences by (1) conducting a life-history survey, where the spectator is asked to rank outcomes in O under a condition of being interested in i or (2) by asking the spectator about certain of his ordinary self-interested preferences, namely his self-interested preferences regarding the subset of outcomes in O (or an expanded O) in which he has the gender of female rather than male. The first question might well elicit more thoughtful, deliberative, engaged responses than the second. Similarly, if the spectator is male, we could estimate k's across-person judgments regarding $(x; j)$ and $(y; i)$, where j, i, or both are female by (1) conducting a life-history survey and asking the spectator directly to compare the well-being of the two individuals; or (2) asking him to self-interestedly rank two outcomes, such that he is female in one or both. Once more, the first question might well elicit more thoughtful, deliberative, engaged responses than the second.

In effect, cognitively immutable attributes make it difficult to induce a condition of *full information and rationality* in the spectator, where she is considering the possibility that her own such attributes may change. Where extended preferences satisfy the non-essentiality condition, but some of the non-essential attributes included in outcomes are cognitively immutable, there remains a logical connection between a spectator's *fully informed, fully rational* ordinary self-interested preferences, and the set U^k, which represents her *fully informed, fully rational* extended preferences. Because non-essentiality is satisfied, we can infer the latter from the former. But since some of the attributes are cognitively immutable, determining the spectator's fully informed, fully rational, self-interested preferences for the outcomes—as compared to determining her fully informed, fully rational, i-interested preferences or across-person judgments—may be especially difficult.

Indeed, in a pioneering empirical study—designed for the very purpose of operationalizing Harsanyi's conception of interpersonal comparisons—Ann Holmes posed an "extended sympathy" question, involving gender, occupational status, and marital status, as well as health attributes. Specifically, "six hypothetical person-types were constructed: a single, white-collar male (the reference individual); a single, blue-collar male; a married, blue-collar male; a single, white-collar female; a married, white-collar female; and a married, blue-collar female."[52] A person-type was characterized as living in good health until age 35, and then 40 more years with a chronic health problem (an incurable speech impediment or a mobility problem). The respondent was then asked: "[H]ow many more years [beyond the age of 35] could [the reference individual] live in perfect health and be as well off as [the person-type] who will live another 40 years [with speech or mobility] problems?"[53] In effect, Holmes asked respondents to make what I have termed "across-person judgments," comparing lives of different subjects characterized in terms of gender, occupation, marital status, health, and longevity.

Finally, I should stress that the foregoing analysis is *not* meant to show that gender, or any other particular cognitively immutable characteristic, is in fact relevant to well-being. An attribute is well-being relevant—according to the account provided in this chapter and Chapter 3—if spectators' fully informed, fully rational, extended preferences are sensitive to the attribute. I would very much hope that spectators, if fully informed and rational, would *not* care about the subjects' gender or racial attributes, per se, in ranking life-histories. Rather, the focus of the discussion has been the problem of *inference*. In order to infer whether spectators' fully informed, fully rational, extended preferences are indeed sensitive to race, gender, mental health, social status, or some other cognitively immutable characteristic, it may be more fruitful to pose life-history questions to spectators.

III. INFERRING EXTENDED PREFERENCES: FURTHER NOTES AND CAVEATS

A. Subjects' Preferences

As discussed in Chapter 3, Harsanyi stipulates that spectators' extended preferences should be strongly "sovereignty respecting." This is captured in his so-called principle of acceptance. If subject j has an ordinary preference for outcome x over outcome y, then spectator k must have an extended preference for life-history $(x; j)$ over life-history $(y; j)$—or so Harsanyi requires.

By contrast, the account of well-being that I have proposed is *not* strongly sovereignty respecting. It is permissible, on my account, for a spectator to strictly prefer

---

[52] Holmes (1997, p. 13).
[53] Ibid., p. 14.

$(y; j)$ to $(x; j)$ even though j has an ordinary (weak or strict) preference for x over y (be it an ordinary self-interested preference on subject j's part, or an ordinary preference of some other sort). In other words, on my account, a spectator's i-history preferences are not *required* to conform to i's ordinary preferences.

Still, my account *permits* a spectator's extended preferences to conform to subjects' ordinary preferences, or to be influenced by subjects' ordinary preferences in other ways. For that matter, my account *permits* a spectator's extended preferences to be influenced by subjects' *extended* preferences. For simplicity, however, I focus here on the possible nexus between subjects' *ordinary* preferences and spectators' *extended* preferences.

The ordinary preferences of a given subject are usefully understood as a kind of *attribute* of that subject—just as her consumption, health, leisure, social status, gender, and so forth are attributes. Moreover, this attribute (like many others) is best seen as multidimensional. A given subject has different types of ordinary preferences: her ranking of outcomes when self-interested is one aspect of her preference structure, her ranking of outcomes when she adopts a moral perspective a different aspect, her ranking of outcomes when motivated by a mixture of moral and self-interested considerations yet a different aspect. Each of these types of preferences can be more or less fully informed and rational. Further, a subject's ordinary preferences (whether self-interested or moral or mixed, and whether fully informed or not) can change over time, and across outcomes.

Outcomes are simplified possible worlds. A particular type of individual attribute might be included within the description of outcomes in some given outcome set, or it might be "missing." This is true of individuals' non-preference attributes, as discussed earlier in the chapter, and it is also true of individuals' preferences. At the (unrealistic) limit, a highly specific outcome set might characterize each aspect of the preference structure of each individual in the population, during each period. At the other extreme, an outcome set might fail to describe individuals' preferences at all (with one important caveat, noted in the margin).[54]

---

[54] To be more precise, we might start with an outcome set that does not describe individuals' preferences at all. However, so as to construct **U**, we will need to estimate $\mathbf{U}^{k,t,x}$ for all individuals, times, and outcomes (perhaps with the simplifying assumption that spectators' extended preferences do not vary across times and/or outcomes). $\mathbf{U}^{k,t,x}$, of course, depends on k's fully informed, fully rational extended preferences in outcome x. In other words, in the course of constructing **U**, we will have (perforce) arrived at information about individuals' fully informed, fully rational extended preferences in all outcomes. And, of course, there are conceptual connections between someone's fully informed, fully rational extended preferences in some outcome and his fully informed, fully rational ordinary preferences in that outcome.

However, it is quite possible that outcome sets fail to describe aspects of individuals' ordinary preference structure which are not conceptually entailed by their fully informed, fully rational extended preferences—for example, individuals' less-than-fully-informed-and-rational ordinary self-interested preferences; or their moral or mixed preferences (whether fully informed and rational or not).

Earlier in the chapter, I discussed, in a general way, the pros and cons of treating some attribute as missing. This analysis applies, mutatis mutandis, to the case of subjects' preferences. On the one hand, treating an attribute as missing entails an invariance assumption (namely, that the spectator's ranking of life-histories is invariant to the level of the missing attribute). Such an assumption may well be unjustified. On the other hand, including the attribute increases decisionmaking costs. It makes outcomes more complicated and the outcome set larger.

In the case where the "attribute" is subjects' ordinary preferences, to treat that attribute as missing and trigger the invariance assumption means the following. *First*, the spectator's own-history preferences are assumed to be the same, regardless of what his ordinary preferences happen to be in any outcome. In other words, whether spectator k has a fully informed, fully rational, self-interested preference for outcome x over outcome y does not depend upon what he prefers in x and y. *Second*, the spectator's i-history preferences are assumed to be the same, regardless of what the subject i ordinarily prefers in any outcome. *Finally*, the spectator's across-person judgments are assumed not to depend upon the ordinary preferences of the two subjects involved.[55]

Each of these aspects of the invariance assumption may well be untrue to spectators' extended preferences. (Of course, the invariance assumption in treating various non-preference attributes as missing may also be untrue to spectators' extended preferences.) Standard philosophical examples illustrate the possible distortion. The spectator, standing back and reflecting with good information and in a calm, deliberative state about possible lives he might lead, might well be sensitive to what his desires and aversions *in* those lives would be. He might self-interestedly prefer x (an outcome with little leisure and high professional status) to y (an outcome with more leisure and less status) *if* his preferences in those outcomes are workaholic preferences, but not if his preferences in those outcomes favor leisure. Similarly, the spectator, sympathetic to some other subject, might prefer that the subject go to the opera rather than see a movie, but only if the subject himself does not have a strong

---

[55] The first part of this invariance assumption is, of course, absurd as regards certain aspects of the spectator's ordinary preferences—namely, those aspects which are just conceptually connected to his fully informed, fully rational extended preferences. In particular, it is absurd to say that k's fully informed, fully rational own-history preferences are invariant to what his fully informed, fully rational ordinary preferences are. Whether k in outcome x has a fully informed, fully rational own-history preference for $(y; k)$ over $(z; k)$ *might* be invariant to all aspects of his ordinary preferences in y and z. But this own-history preference in x cannot be invariant to all aspects of k's ordinary preferences in x itself. The spectator, in x, has a fully informed, fully rational own-history preference for $(y; k)$ over $(z; k)$ just in case he has a fully informed, fully rational, self-interested ordinary preference for y over z.

On the other hand, it is possible for k's fully informed, fully rational extended preferences to be invariant to those aspects of his ordinary preference structure which are not conceptually connected to such extended preferences. (For example, whether k in outcome x has a fully informed, fully rational own-history preference for $(y; k)$ over $(z; k)$ might be invariant to what k's non-ideal, self-interested, preferences happen to be, in y, z, and x itself.)

distaste for the opera. In making a well-being comparison between a life-history in which June is a basketball player, and a life-history in which Jim is an academic, the spectator may well take account of whether Jim prefers basketball to academics, and of whether June does.

Consider, now, the case in which outcomes include information about certain aspects of individuals' preferences. In such an outcome set, a given outcome $x = (a_1, p_1, a_2, p_2, \ldots, a_N, p_N, a_{imp})$, where a_i, here, is meant to indicate some of individual i's non-preference attributes, and p_i describes some aspects of his preference structure.

Where outcomes include information about subjects' ordinary self-interested preferences, spectators are *permitted* but not *required* to take account of the $(p_1, \ldots, p_N)$ information in forming their extended preferences. The extent to which spectators do so is, at bottom, an empirical question—a question about what spectators prefer and judge under conditions of full information and rationality. For example, spectator k, with full information and rationality, and under a condition of interest in subject i, might prefer a life-history in which the subject has better health and lower income even though the subject, herself, is happy to sacrifice health for income. On the other hand (as in the opera versus movies example), the spectator's i-history preferences regarding various leisure opportunities for i might be very sensitive to what i, herself, prefers to do with her free time.

How do we estimate spectators' extended preferences for an outcome set which includes information about subjects' ordinary preferences? In principle, we might do so by looking to *spectators'* ordinary self-interested preferences. Note that preferences are *contingent* attributes. A spectator can change his preferences without changing who he is. Thus spectators' extended preferences can be sensitive to subjects' ordinary preferences—to the $(p_1, \ldots, p_N)$ information—consistent with the "non-essentiality" condition for extended preferences. Imagine that life-history $(x; j)$ is such that j is characterized as having certain non-preference attributes, and as having certain ordinary preferences. Imagine that we have in hand spectator k's ordinary utility function $\varphi^k(.)$, summarizing his fully informed, fully rational, self-interested preferences over outcomes. Then (assuming atomism) we could assign an extended utility value to this life-history, $u^k(x; j)$, by identifying the outcome x^*, such that k in x^* has the very same non-preference attributes as j in x, and k in x^* has the very same preferences as j in x. The extended utility of $(x; j)$ could then be set equal to $\varphi^k(x^*)$.

However, this estimation strategy may prove challenging. Preferences, like gender, may be cognitively immutable, at least to some extent and at least for some spectators. Spectators may have trouble imagining a change in their own preferences. Using life-history surveys to estimate spectator's extended preferences for outcome sets which incorporate information about subjects' ordinary preferences may well be helpful, rather than attempting to infer extended preferences from the spectators' own ordinary, self-interested preferences.[56]

---

[56] If an outcome set **O** includes a p_k attribute—characterizing some aspect of k's preference structure—and there is substantial variation across outcomes in this attribute, then we cannot accurately

B. Heterogeneity in Extended Preferences

For purposes of the discussion of heterogeneity, I reintroduce the time and outcome superscripts on individuals' utility functions (superscripts that are implicit
throughout the chapter), since to omit them here could cause confusion.

Much economic scholarship seeks to document and characterize variation in
individuals' ordinary preferences.[57] What precisely it means for ordinary preferences
to be heterogeneous is a subtle matter.[58] One plausible characterization, regarding
heterogeneity in ordinary *self-interested* preferences, is as follows. Individual i's
ordinary self-interested preferences, at time t and in outcome x, are identical to
("homogeneous with") individual j's ordinary self-interested preferences, at time t^*
and in outcome x^*, if the ordinary utility function $\varphi^{i,t,x}(.)$ that expectationally represents the first preferences is the same (up to a positive affine transformation) as the
utility function $\varphi^{j,t^*,x^*}(.)$ that represents the second preferences, except that the first
function takes i's contingent attributes as its arguments, while the second takes j's.
Formally, $\varphi^{i,t,x}(y) = v(\mathbf{a}_i^{cont}(y), \mathbf{a}_{imp}(y))$ for all y, and $\varphi^{j,t^*,x^*}(y) = v(\mathbf{a}_j^{cont}(y), \mathbf{a}_{imp}(y))$ for
all y.

Extended preferences, like ordinary preferences, can be heterogeneous. Defining
heterogeneity in extended preferences is straightforward. The extended preferences
of spectator k, at time t and in outcome x, are the same as the extended preferences of
spectator l at time t^* and in outcome x^* iff $\mathbf{U}^{k,t,x} = \mathbf{U}^{l,t^*,x^*}$, otherwise these preferences
are heterogeneous.[59]

The connection between heterogeneity in ordinary self-interested preferences
(in the sense just defined) and heterogeneity in extended preferences is complicated. If we assume that extended preferences satisfy both the atomism and non-
essentiality conditions, then ordinary self-interested preferences are heterogeneous

---

estimate $\mathbf{U}^k$ without asking k to contemplate a substantial change in his preference structure (even if
he finds that cognitively difficult). On the other hand, consider the case where: (1) $\mathbf{p}_k$ does not vary
much across the outcomes in $\mathbf{O}$; but (2) there is some other individual i whose preferences are quite
different from $\mathbf{p}_k$. (Formally, there is at least one x, such that $\mathbf{p}_i(x)$ is quite different from the value of
$\mathbf{p}_k$ in all outcomes.) In *that* case, eliciting k's i-history preferences via life-history surveys may prove
less cognitively challenging for k than trying to infer them from his own-history preferences for an
expanded outcome set in which there is now some x^* such that $\mathbf{p}_k(x^*) = \mathbf{p}_i(x)$.

[57] On heterogeneity in risk aversion, see, e.g., Barsky et al. (1997); Cohen and Einav (2007); Hartog,
Ferrer-i-Carbonell, and Jonker (2002). On heterogeneity in WTP/WTA for public goods, see, e.g.,
Boxall and Adamowicz (2002). On gender differences in preferences, see Croson and Gneezy (2009).

[58] Characterizing homogeneity of moral preferences is straightforward: two individuals have the
same such preferences if they have the same ranking of outcomes and outcome lotteries. This characterization does not work well for self-interested preferences, or preferences that mix moral and self-
interested considerations, since individuals with self-interested or mixed preferences that, intuitively,
are "the same" might end up with different outcome rankings. The preferences are "the same," in
some sense, but latch on to different features of any given outcome.

[59] This definition works both in characterizing heterogeneity of extended preferences prior to
"zeroing out," and thereafter.

just in case extended preferences are heterogeneous.[60] However, if non-essentiality is relaxed, it is possible for ordinary self-interested preferences to be homogeneous but extended preferences to be heterogeneous, or vice versa.[61]

In any event, heterogeneity in extended preferences is certainly *possible*.

It is sometimes suggested that heterogeneity in extended preferences will disappear, if spectators take account of subjects' ordinary preferences when forming their (the spectators') extended preferences.[62] But the fact that outcomes in **O** are

[60] Consider two spectator-time-outcome combinations: spectator k, with extended and ordinary preferences at time t and in outcome x; and spectator l, with extended and ordinary preferences at time t^* and in outcome x^*. Assume, now, that the extended preferences satisfy atomism and non-essentiality (and thus also that $\mathbf{U}^{k,t,x}$ and $\mathbf{U}^{l,t^*,x^*}$ are each unique up to a positive affine transformation). (1) If, further, the extended preferences are identical, then there exists a single $u(.)$ and a corresponding $v(.)$ such that, for some $u^{k,t,x}(.)$ in $\mathbf{U}^{k,t,x}$ and for some $u^{l,t^*,x^*}(.)$ in $\mathbf{U}^{l,t^*,x^*}$, $u^{k,t,x}(y; i) = u^{l,t^*,x^*}(y; i) = u(y; i)$ for any life-history $(y; i)$, and $u(y; i) = v(\mathbf{a}_i^{cont}(y), \mathbf{a}_{imp}(y))$. In particular, then k has an ordinary self-interested utility function $\varphi^{k,t,x}(.)$ such that $\varphi^{k,t,x}(y) = u(y; k) = v(\mathbf{a}_k^{cont}(y), \mathbf{a}_{imp}(y))$, while l has an ordinary self-interested utility function $\varphi^{l,t^*,x^*}(.)$ such that $\varphi^{l,t^*,x^*}(y) = u(y; l) = v(\mathbf{a}_l^{cont}(y), \mathbf{a}_{imp}(y))$. Thus k's ordinary preferences, at time t and in outcome x, are homogeneous with l's ordinary preferences, at time t^* and in outcome x^*. (2) Assume that the ordinary self-interested preferences, of spectator k at time t in outcome x, are homogeneous with the ordinary self-interested preferences of spectator l at time t^* in outcome x^*. Then there exist $\varphi^{k,t,x}(.)$ and $\varphi^{l,t^*,x^*}(.)$ such that $\varphi^{k,t,x}(y) = v(\mathbf{a}_k^{cont}(y), \mathbf{a}_{imp}(y))$, and $\varphi^{l,t^*,x^*}(y) = v(\mathbf{a}_l^{cont}(y), \mathbf{a}_{imp}(y))$ for any outcome y. Because an individual's own-history preferences are equivalent to his ordinary self-interested preferences, it follows that there exists $u^{k,t,x}(.)$ such that $u^{k,t,x}(y; k) = \varphi^{k,t,x}(y) = v(\mathbf{a}_k^{cont}(y), \mathbf{a}_{imp}(y))$, and there exists $u^{l,t^*,x^*}(.)$ such that $u^{l,t^*,x^*}(y; l) = \varphi^{l,t^*,x^*}(y) = v(\mathbf{a}_l^{cont}(y), \mathbf{a}_{imp}(y))$. But, given atomism and non-essentiality, $u^{k,t,x}(y; i)$ for any arbitrary life-history $(y; i)$ equals $v(\mathbf{a}_i^{cont}(y), \mathbf{a}_{imp}(y))$, and $u^{l,t^*,x^*}(y; i) = v(\mathbf{a}_i^{cont}(y), \mathbf{a}_{imp}(y))$. Thus $u^{k,t,x}(.) = u^{l,t^*,x^*}(.)$. Because $\mathbf{U}^{k,t,x}$ consists of all positive affine transformations of $u^{k,t,x}(.)$, and $\mathbf{U}^{l,t^*,x^*}$ all positive affine transformations of $u^{l,t^*,x^*}(.)$, it follows that the two are the same set.

[61] Imagine that every spectator k, at time t and in outcome x, has an ordinary utility function of the form $\varphi^{k,t,x}(y) = v(\mathbf{a}_k^{cont}(y), \mathbf{a}_{imp}(y))$. Thus ordinary self-interested preferences are homogeneous (across all spectator-time-outcome combinations.) However, every such spectator values an arbitrary life-history $(y; i)$ by assigning it an extended utility equaling $v(\mathbf{a}_i^{cont}(y), \mathbf{a}_{imp}(y))$ times some subject-specific scaling factor. (An extended utility function $u^{k,t,x}(.)$, thus defined, is sensitive to which particular individual is the subject of a life-history, and thus violates non-essentiality.) If these scaling factors vary across spectators we will have homogeneous ordinary self-interested preferences but heterogeneous extended preferences.

Conversely, imagine that each spectator's ordinary and extended preferences are fixed across times and outcomes. Moreover, spectator k and spectator l have heterogeneous ordinary self-interested preferences. Finally, each spectator's extended preferences respect each subject's ordinary preferences, in the following manner. (The assumption of inter-outcome and intertemporal fixity of preferences is required to make the following construction possible.) For each subject i, every spectator picks one of the functions $\varphi^i(.)$ representing i's ordinary self-interested preferences (the very same one, for all spectators), and assigns $u^k(x; i)$ the value $\varphi^i(x)$, multiplied by some subject-specific scaling factor (the very same one, for all spectators). Now, we have heterogeneous ordinary self-interested preferences but homogeneous extended preferences.

[62] Harsanyi (1986, pp. 57–60) suggests as much. See also Kaplow (2008a), allowing that individuals may have heterogeneous preferences, summarized in a vector of preference parameters θ, but assuming a single interpersonally comparable utility function $u(.)$ with θ as one argument.

characterized so as to include information about some aspect of subjects' ordinary preferences certainly does not *entail* that $U^{k,t,x}$, summarizing the extended preferences of spectator k at a particular time and in a particular outcome, must now be identical to $U^{l,t',x'}$, summarizing the extended preferences of some other spectator at a particular time and in a particular outcome.

For example, imagine that, in outcomes x and y and perhaps other outcomes, individual i's ordinary preferences are such that he prefers x to y. Spectator k, under a condition of interest in i, is swayed by i's preference and thus has an extended (i-history) preference for $(x; i)$ over $(y; i)$. By contrast, spectator l, under a condition of interest in i, is not swayed by his preference—she feels that y is better for i than x, regardless of what he thinks—and has an extended preference for $(y; i)$ over $(x; i)$.

This example illustrates, as a conceptual matter, why including information about subjects' ordinary preferences in the description of outcomes need not produce homogeneity of extended preferences. To be sure, as an empirical matter, including information about subjects' preferences might tend to mitigate (rather than exacerbate or leave unaffected) heterogeneity in extended preferences. But I am not aware of any empirical data which suggests that this is true either.

How should the SWF analyst take account of possible heterogeneity in extended preferences? It would be absurd to think that the analyst should directly and separately ascertain the content of each $U^{k,t,x}$—for example, by conducting separate life-history surveys or ordinary preference surveys with each spectator, at each time, and in each outcome. (How could the analyst directly ascertain a spectator's extended preferences at some time which is later than the time of analysis, or in some outcome which may never be actual?) Rather, inferences regarding a given $U^{k,t,x}$ will be, to some substantial extent, *model-driven*; and this will also allow the analyst to adopt simplifying assumptions regarding the extent of inter-spectator, intertemporal, or inter-outcome heterogeneity.

Research on heterogeneity in ordinary preferences often models this heterogeneity as being determined by some array of individual characteristics. For example, researchers may seek to characterize the variation in individual risk aversion for consumption gambles, or individual WTP/WTA for a public good, by presuming that an individual's risk aversion or WTP/WTA for the good is determined by her gender, her age, her occupational status, her race, her education, and so forth.[63]

A similar approach should be adopted for extended preferences (at a minimum, for extended preferences that cannot be ascertained via direct investigation, as opposed to someone's extended preferences here and now). In other words, the variety of data sources that furnish information about spectators' extended preferences

---

[63] On the use of modeling techniques to understand the sources of preference heterogeneity underlying WTP/WTA amounts for public goods, see, e.g., Alberini, Longo, and Veronesi (2007, pp. 210–212); Boxall and Adamowicz (2002); Swait (2007, pp. 251–261). On models of heterogeneity in risk aversion, see, e.g., Harrison and Rutström (2008, pp. 61–85). Many of the extant studies estimating risk aversion, cited below, n. 81, include regression models with risk aversion as the dependent variable and various sociodemographic or other individual characteristics as independent variables.

(both data about their ordinary preferences, and data from life-history surveys) would be used by the SWF analyst to "estimate" a causal model of extended preferences—a model which predicts the extended preferences that a given spectator will have, at a given time, in a given outcome, as a function of certain of her characteristics (gender, age, education, income, occupational status, etc.).

What should be the functional form of this model? Which spectator characteristics should be incorporated as determinants of spectators' extended utility functions? These questions implicate many complex issues, both econometric and normative, which I will not attempt to address. The brief discussion, here, is meant simply to clarify two basic and related points. First, extended preferences, like ordinary preferences, are *caused* by various spectator characteristics, and thus can be *predicted* via causal models. Second, and relatedly, these models can be more or less simplified. Here, as elsewhere, it is important to remember that the SWF framework is a decisional tool, meant to provide moral guidance to cognitively bounded, human decisionmakers. Various heuristics are justifiably adopted to ease the implementation of that framework. Just as the SWF analyst necessarily evaluates policies in light of outcomes that are "missing" some characteristics, rather than being fully described possible worlds—perhaps using outcomes that are fairly radically "stripped down"— so she might adopt relatively simple predictive models of extended preferences, which see such preferences as caused by a relatively short list of spectator characteristics.

For example, the analyst might assume that all spectators of the same educational background and occupational status have the same extended preferences, ignoring the effect of gender, race, etc. At the limit, the analyst might assume that extended preferences are homogeneous, across times, outcomes, and spectators. Highly simplified models of extended preferences surely have costs (in presenting a distorted picture of what spectators' extended preferences actually are), but they also have benefits (in making the construction of **U** more tractable), and might in some cases be justified.

I have thus far tried to clarify how the SWF framework, as I have elaborated it, should take account of preference heterogeneity. How does existing social-welfare-function scholarship do so? Much work in this tradition combines two premises: (I) there is a single utility function that represents the ordinary preferences of everyone in the population, which (for each individual) takes as its argument some bundle of that individual's contingent attributes; and (II) this single function furnishes the inputs to the social welfare function.[64]

For example, in his classic analysis of optimal income taxation, Mirrlees assumes that each individual's preference ranking of outcomes depends upon the consumption/leisure bundles which she receives in the outcomes. Moreover, there is a single function $v(.)$, identical across individuals, that represents this ordinary preference

---

[64] See Kaplow (2008a, p. 1), noting that most work in public economics, including optimal-tax scholarship, assumes homogeneous preferences.

structure: Each individual i weakly prefers x to y iff $\varphi^i(x) \geq \varphi^i(y)$, where $\varphi^i(x) = v(c_i(x), l_i(x))$ and $\varphi^i(y) = v(c_i(y), l_i(y))$, with $(c_i(x), l_i(x))$ designating individual i's consumption and leisure in x, and $(c_i(y), l_i(y))$ her consumption and leisure in outcome y. Individuals vary in their abilities, and thus in the wage rates they can earn in the market; but not in their preference structure. Different income tax schedules induce different outcomes. (Each individual, in response to the schedule, chooses an allocation between leisure and after-tax income so as to maximize her preference satisfaction.) Each such outcome is mapped onto a single vector of utilities, $u(x)$, defined in terms of the very same v-function just mentioned; and these vectors are then ranked by an SWF. In other words, $u(x) = (u_1(x), \ldots, u_N(x)) = (v(c_1(x), l_1(x)), \ldots, v(c_N(x), l_N(x)))$.[65]

Social-welfare-function scholarship (like welfare economics more generally) does not rigorously distinguish between individuals' ordinary self-interested preferences, and ordinary preferences of some other sort. Premise (1) two paragraphs above is plausible (at least as a simplifying assumption), *if* understood as a premise about individuals' ordinary self-interested preferences.[66] Thus understood, it is simply the premise that individuals' ordinary self-interested preferences are homogeneous, in the sense characterized at the beginning of this subsection. Homogeneity of ordinary self-interested preferences (across times, individuals, and outcomes), together with the premise that extended preferences are atomistic and satisfy nonessentiality, entails homogeneity of extended preferences. Homogeneity of extended preferences means that each spectator k, at each time, and in each outcome, will have the very same set of extended utility functions, which will be unique up to a positive affine transformation (given atomism and non-essentiality). Furthermore, if spectators have the same rankings of life-histories vis-à-vis nonexistence, then each spectator, at each time, and in each outcome, will have the very same zeroed-out set of extended utility functions, and U itself will just be this set. Although U in this case will *not* be a singleton, it *will* be unique up to a positive ratio transformation.

The most widely used SWFs are invariant to ratio rescalings. This is true, for example, of the utilitarian SWF, the leximin SWF, and the rank-weighted SWF, and also of continuous prioritarian SWFs within the Atkinson family (although not other continuous prioritarian SWFs).[67] If such a ratio-rescaling-invariant SWF is being employed, and if U is indeed unique up to a positive ratio transformation, the decisionmaker *might* rank outcomes using the "set-valued" SWF rule, as I presented

[65] See Tuomala (1990, ch. 6), summarizing the Mirrlees model. I have stated the model for the case of a fixed finite population; Mirrlees, in fact, assumes a continuum of individuals.

[66] It would be ridiculous to think that an individual's moral preferences over outcomes depend solely on her own attributes.

[67] An SWF is invariant to ratio rescalings if it uses an R such that utility vector $(u_1, u_2, \ldots, u_N)$ is ranked by R at least as good as utility vector $(u_1^*, u_2^*, \ldots, u_N^*)$ iff the vector $(ru_1, ru_2, \ldots, ru_N)$ is ranked at least as good as $(ru_1^*, ru_2^*, \ldots, ru_N^*)$, where r is any positive number. On the ratio-rescaling features of the Atkinson SWF as opposed to other continuous prioritarian SWFs, see Chapter 5.

it in Chapter 2: x is morally at least as good as y iff, for all $u(.)$ in $\mathbf{U}$, $(u_1(x),\dots, u_N(x))$ is ranked by the SWF's rule R (its rule for ranking utility vectors) as being at least as good as $(u_1(y),\dots, u_N(y))$. Or, the decisionmaker might arbitrarily choose any single $u(.)$ in $\mathbf{U}$, and rank outcomes using the rule: x is morally at least as good as y iff $(u_1(x),\dots, u_N(x))$ is ranked by R as being at least as good as $(u_1(y),\dots, u_N(y))$. The same ranking of outcomes will result in either case.

In short, the combination of premise (I) and premise (II) is consistent with the SWF framework as I develop that framework in this book (meaning the construction of $\mathbf{U}$ via extended preferences, and the set-valued SWF rule), assuming a ratio-rescaling-invariant SWF.

However, there is some work in the social-welfare-function tradition which relaxes premise (I). It assumes, in effect, that individuals have heterogeneous ordinary self-interested preferences. But it continues to use a single utility function as the input to the SWF.[68] This approach is problematic—*if* heterogeneity in ordinary self-interested preferences yields heterogeneity in extended preferences (as it will, given non-essentiality and atomism). Heterogeneity in extended preferences means that it is *not* the case that $\mathbf{U}^{k,t,x} = \mathbf{U}^{l,t^*,x^*}$ for every two spectator-time-outcome combinations. $\mathbf{U}$ is the union of all the spectator/time/outcome-relative sets of extended utility functions, which in this case are *not* all identical. The set-valued SWF rule then says: x is morally at least as good as y iff, for all $u(.)$ in $\mathbf{U}$, $(u_1(x),\dots, u_N(x))$ is ranked by R as being at least as good as $(u_1(y),\dots, u_N(y))$. In the case of heterogeneity in extended preferences, even for the standard SWFs mentioned a few paragraphs above, this set-valued rule will *not* necessarily yield the same result as picking any $u(.)$ in $\mathbf{U}$ and ranking outcomes using that single utility function. The set-valued rule (quite possibly) will produce an incomplete quasiordering of outcomes, while applying these SWFs to a single utility function will generate a complete ordering.[69]

C. Temporal Additivity

Two plausible restrictions on the structure of spectators' extended preferences have already been discussed. One is *non-essentiality*. As discussed, non-essentiality is a necessary condition for inferring a spectator's extended preferences from his ordinary self-interested preferences. Moreover, it seems quite plausible that spectators'

---

[68] See Boadway et al. (2002); Cremer, Gahvari, and Ladoux (2003); Kaplow (2008a).

[69] This is true, indeed, if the SWF—like leximin—is not just ratio rescaling invariant but, much more robustly, invariant to an increasing transformation of utilities. If $u(.)$ is an extended utility function, and $f(u(.))$ an increasing transformation of that function, then the leximin SWF using $u(.)$ will achieve the very same ranking of outcomes using $f(u(.))$. Still, if $\mathbf{U}$ is formed by merging $\mathbf{U}^{k,t,x}$ and $\mathbf{U}^{l,t^*,x^*}$, and it is *not* the case that all the elements of each set are increasing transformations of some element of the other, then the leximin SWF using the set-valued rule applied to $\mathbf{U}$ can yield an incomplete quasiordering of outcomes.

fully informed, fully rational extended preferences do indeed satisfy non-essentiality (although it would be useful to test this premise through life-history surveys).

A second restriction is *atomism*. Even without atomism, we *can* infer spectators' extended preferences from their ordinary self-interested preferences, as long as non-essentiality holds; but atomism makes the inferential path particularly straightforward. Unlike non-essentiality, atomism is a kind of heuristic. There is good reason to think that fully informed, fully rational spectators would violate atomism, at least to some extent. Still, atomism may well be a *justified* simplification, given its benefits in estimating $\mathbf{U}^k$ for a given spectator k.

A third restriction, not yet mentioned, is that spectators' extended utility functions are *additive* in sublifetime utility. The temporal structure of extended utility functions is discussed in detail in Chapter 6. Here, I discuss temporal structure in connection with the problem of estimation—showing how to estimate extended utilities using the simplifying assumption of temporal additivity. Temporal additivity, like atomism, is a kind of heuristic. Although there is reason to think that fully informed and rational spectators might violate additivity, the additivity assumption greatly eases the SWF analyst's task of inferring the content of $\mathbf{U}^k$.

Outcome sets, as already mentioned several times, may well include multiple periods. An extended utility function $u^k(.)$ which possesses the property of temporal additivity satisfies four increasingly restrictive properties. First, the extended utility of a life-history is a function of T sublifetime utilities, each in turn some function of the array of individual attributes and background facts during one of the T periods. Second, the extended utility function is *separable* in sublifetime utility: the ranking of two life-histories, $(x; i)$ and $(y; j)$, is invariant to the particular level of sublifetime utility during periods where that level is the same in the two histories. Third, the extended utility function is *lottery separable* in sublifetime utility: the ranking of two lotteries over life-histories is invariant to the particular level of sublifetime utility during periods where that level is the same in the two lotteries. Finally, the extended utility of a life-history equals the sum or discounted sum of sublifetime utility (which means that there are no interaction effects whatsoever between sublifetime utility in different periods).[70]

If we combine atomism, additivity, and non-essentiality, we end up with the following. $\mathbf{U}^k$ is unique up to a positive affine transformation.[71] Moreover, each $u^k(.)$ in $\mathbf{U}^k$ has the following form: $u^k(x; i) = \sum_{t=1}^{T} D^k(t)v^k\left(\mathbf{a}_{i,t}^{cont}(x), \mathbf{a}_{imp,t}(x)\right)$. For short, call this the "TANA" form ("temporally additive, non-essential, atomistic"). The symbol "$\mathbf{a}_{i,t}^{cont}(x)$" means the contingent attributes of individual i during period t in outcome x. The symbol "$\mathbf{a}_{imp,t}(x)$" means the background facts during period t in outcome x. $D^k(t)$ is a discount factor.

---

[70] See Chapter 6.
[71] Uniqueness up to a positive affine transformation is the result of nonessentiality and atomism. See above.

The TANA form is applicable both to outcome sets with multiple periods ($T > 1$), and to outcome sets with a single period ($T = 1$), and in the latter case becomes simply: $u^k(x; i) = v^k\left(\mathbf{a}_{i,1}^{cont}(x), \mathbf{a}_{imp,1}(x)\right)$.[72]

The function $v^k(.)$ in the TANA form is a sublifetime utility function, which takes $\mathbf{a}_{i,t}^{cont}(x)$ and $\mathbf{a}_{imp,t}(x)$ as its inputs. Outcomes will describe *some* period-specific individual contingent attributes, and perhaps some period-specific background facts; and the $v^k(.)$ function will take some or all of these described attributes and background facts as its inputs. This function, like $u^k(.)$, is unique up to a positive affine transformation: each $u^k(.)$ in $\mathbf{U}^k$ has a corresponding $v^k(.)$. If the utility functions in $\mathbf{U}^k$ assume the TANA form, then the spectator has not only a family of extended utility functions, but also a corresponding family of sublifetime utility functions.[73]

---

[72] Here, $\left(\mathbf{a}_{i,1}^{cont}(\mathbf{x}), \mathbf{a}_{imp,1}(\mathbf{x})\right)$ denotes i's contingent attributes and background facts during the one and only period.

[73] Consider the set $\mathbf{U}^k$, which by virtue of atomism and nonessentiality is unique up to a positive affine transformation. And consider the set $\mathbf{V}^k$ of sublifetime utility functions, characterized as follows: for each $v^k(.)$ in $\mathbf{V}^k$, there exists $u^k(.)$ in $\mathbf{U}^k$, such that $u^k(x;i) = \sum_{t=1}^{T} D^k(t) v^k\left(\mathbf{a}_{i,t}^{cont}(x), \mathbf{a}_{imp,t}(x)\right)$ for any life-history $(x; i)$. (For short, $v^k(.)$ "corresponds to" this $u^k(.)$.) To reduce clutter in what follows, let $D^* = \sum_{t=1}^{T} D^k(t)$.

First, any particular $v^k(.)$ can only correspond to one member of $\mathbf{U}^k$, not multiple members. To show this, by way of contradiction, assume that both $u^k(.)$ and $r^k(.)$ belong to $\mathbf{U}^k$ and that a particular $v^k(.)$ corresponds to both, i.e., $u^k(x;i) = \sum_{t=1}^{T} D^k(t) v^k\left(\mathbf{a}_{i,t}^{cont}(x), \mathbf{a}_{imp,t}(x)\right)$ and $r^k(x;i) = \sum_{t=1}^{T} D^k(t) v^k\left(\mathbf{a}_{i,t}^{cont}(x), \mathbf{a}_{imp,t}(x)\right)$ for every life-history. Because $u^k(.)$ and $r^k(.)$ are distinct functions from the life-history set to real numbers, there must be some $(x^*; i^*)$ such that $u^k(x^*; i^*) \neq r^k(x^*; i^*)$. So we have an immediate contradiction.

Second, $\mathbf{V}^k$ is unique up to a positive affine transformation. I will use the symbol "$(\mathbf{a}^{cont}, \mathbf{a}_{imp})$" and the term "sublifetime bundle" to mean a possible combination of contingent attributes of some person in some period, plus background facts in that period. Sublifetime bundles are the arguments for the members of $\mathbf{V}^k$. To say that $\mathbf{V}^k$ is unique up to a positive affine transformation means that, if $v^k(.)$ is in $\mathbf{V}^k$, then $w^k(.)$ is in $\mathbf{V}^k$ iff $w^k(\mathbf{a}^{cont}, \mathbf{a}_{imp}) = av^k(\mathbf{a}^{cont}, \mathbf{a}_{imp}) + b$, with a positive, for all $(\mathbf{a}^{cont}, \mathbf{a}_{imp})$ that are possible given the outcome set.

Why is this true? To begin, if $v^k(.)$ is in $\mathbf{V}^k$, and $w^k(.) = av^k(.) + b$, with $a > 0$, then $w^k(.)$ is in $\mathbf{V}^k$. (Assume that $v^k(.)$ corresponds to the extended utility function $u^k(.)$, in $\mathbf{U}^k$. Consider, now the extended utility function $r^k(.) = au^k(.) + bD^*$. This function $r^k(.)$ is a positive affine transformation of $u^k(.)$, hence in $\mathbf{U}^k$, and $w^k(.)$ corresponds to $r^k(.)$, hence is in $\mathbf{V}^k$.)

Moreover, if $v^k(.)$ is in $\mathbf{V}^k$, and $w^k(.)$ is also in $\mathbf{V}^k$, then there must exist numbers $a > 0$, b, such that $w^k(.) = av^k(.) + b$. The members of $\mathbf{V}^k$ expectationally represent k's preferences regarding lotteries over sublifetime bundles. (See below, nn. 76, 80.) But it is a standard result of EU theory that if two utility functions expectationally represent someone's ranking of lotteries, the two must be related by a positive affine transformation.

Because $\mathbf{V}^k$ is unique up to a positive affine transformation, we can rule out the possibility that two different members of $\mathbf{V}^k$ might correspond to one member of $\mathbf{U}^k$. Consider some $u^k(.)$ in $\mathbf{U}^k$ and any two life-histories $(x; i)$ and $(y; j)$ such that $u^k(x; i) \neq u^k(y; j)$. Assume $v^k(.)$ and $w^k(.)$, both sublifetime utility functions, correspond to $u^k(.)$. The previous paragraph showed that there must be $a > 0$, b, such that $w^k(.) = av^k(.) + b$. If both of the functions, moreover, correspond to $u^k(.)$, then: $u^k(x; i) = \sum_{t=1}^{T} D^k(t) v^k\left(\mathbf{a}_{i,t}^{cont}(x), \mathbf{a}_{imp}(x)\right) = \sum_{t=1}^{T} D^k(t) w^k\left(\mathbf{a}_{i,t}^{cont}(x), \mathbf{a}_{imp}(x)\right) =$

In short, the TANA form means that the extended utility of a life-history is the sum or discounted sum of T sublifetime utility values, each in turn a function of the subject's contingent attributes and background facts in one of the T periods. As the reader will observe, the utility functions typically employed in SWF scholarship, described at the beginning of the chapter, assume the TANA form. Moreover, the assumption that individuals' ordinary preferences assume the TANA form is very widespread in economics.[74]

Note that the utility functions typically employed in SWF scholarship take only individuals' contingent attributes, not background facts, as their arguments. In that case the TANA form simplifies to: $u^k(x; i) = \sum_{t=1}^{T} D^k(t)v^k(a_{i,t}^{cont}(x))$. However, I will frame my analysis for the more general case in which certain background facts may be used as an input for the $v^k(.)$ function.

The discount factor, $D^k(.)$, may be *decreasing* with time. This means that spectators *discount* sublifetime utility: they give less weight to subjects' attributes and background facts in later periods, as compared to earlier periods, in ranking life-histories. Alternatively, $D^k(.)$ may be 1, in which case the TANA formula simplifies to: $u^k(x; i)$ $= \sum_{t=1}^{T} v^k(a_{i,t}^{cont}(x), a_{imp,t}(x))$. Chapter 6 argues that $D^k(.)$ should indeed be 1. But my discussion, here, regarding the use of the TANA form to estimate U^k, in no way hinges on the premise that $D^k(.)$ is 1 rather than decreasing with time.

The TANA form makes it easier for spectators to think about their ranking of life-histories and lotteries. The utility of a life-history is simply the sum or discounted sum of its sublifetime utilities during each of the T periods, with sublifetime utility solely a function of the subject's within-period contingent attributes and of within-period background facts. Moreover, the expected utility of a lottery over life-histories is simply the sum or discounted sum of its *expected* sublifetime utilities during each of the T periods, with *expected* sublifetime utility solely a function of the various possible within-period subject attributes and background facts to which the lottery accords nonzero probability.

Furthermore, the TANA form makes it easier for the SWF analyst to infer how a given spectator assigns extended utilities to life-histories. That task boils down to inferring the spectator's sublifetime utility function $v^k(.)$, which can be inferred either from the spectator's ordinary self-interested preferences, or from life-history surveys.

Consider, to begin, the inference of spectators' extended utilities from their ordinary self-interested preferences. If a given spectator's extended utility functions

$\sum_{t=1}^{T} D^k(t)[av^k(a_{i,t}^{cont}(x), a_{imp,t}(x)) + b] = au^k(x;i) + bD^*$. Similarly, $u^k(y;j) = \sum_{t=1}^{T} D^k(t)w^k(a_{j,t}^{cont}(y), a_{imp,t}(y))$

$= \sum_{t=1}^{T} D^k(t)[av^k(a_{j,t}^{cont}(y), a_{imp,t}(y)) + b] = au^k(y; j) + bD^*$. In short, $u^k(x; i) = au^k(x; i) + bD^*$, and

$u^k(y; j) = au^k(y; j) + bD^*$. Because $u^k(x; i) \neq u^k(y; j)$, this is possible only if $a = 1$ and $b = 0$, i.e., $v^k(.)$ and $w^k(.)$ are the same function.

In sum, we have established that each $v^k(.)$ in V^k corresponds to one, and only one, member of U^k, and that V^k is unique up to a positive affine transformation.

[74] See Gollier (2001, pp. 217–218); Mas-Colell, Whinston, and Green (1995, pp. 733–736).

assume the TANA form, then a utility function $\varphi^k(.)$ that represents her ordinary self-interested preferences over outcomes and outcome lotteries also assumes the TANA form. In other words, $\varphi^k(x)$, with x an outcome, equals $\sum_{t=1}^{T} D^k(t)v^k\left(\mathbf{a}_{k,t}^{cont}(x), \mathbf{a}_{imp,t}(x)\right)$. This ordinary utility function for spectator k assigns numbers to outcomes by summing T sublifetime utilities, each a function of k's contingent attributes during one of the T periods, plus background facts. Using ordinary preference data, we can make educated guesses about the form of the sublifetime utility function $v^k(.)$. With $v^k(.)$ in hand, we can assign a extended utility to spectator k's life-histories. But we can also assign such values to any arbitrary life-history—by applying $v^k(.)$ to the *subject's* contingent attributes, plus background facts, during each period.

What kind of ordinary preference data, in particular, might be used to estimate $v^k(.)$, for different types of outcome sets? Much ordinary preference research examines ordinal rankings—focusing on how individuals rank outcomes, rather than lotteries over outcomes. This is true, for example, of much scholarship concerning labor supply, consumer preferences for marketed goods, and WTP/WTA for public goods.[75] One important component of ordinal-preference research concerns *within-period ordinal rankings*. How does an individual rank one possible array of contingent attributes, plus background facts, during a given period, as compared to a different possible array of contingent attributes, plus background facts, during the same period?

To see how within-period ordinal rankings can serve to narrow down the functional form of $v^k(.)$, consider the following. Assume that $(\mathbf{a}^{cont}, \mathbf{a}_{imp})$ is a possible combination of an array of contingent attributes that some person might possess during some particular period, plus a specification of background facts during that period, while $(\mathbf{b}^{cont}, \mathbf{b}_{imp})$ is another such combination. For short, call such a combination a "sublifetime bundle." Assume that k, under conditions of full information and rationality and self-interest, prefers sublifetime bundle $(\mathbf{a}^{cont}, \mathbf{a}_{imp})$ to sublifetime bundle $(\mathbf{b}^{cont}, \mathbf{b}_{imp})$. Then $v^k(.)$ must be such that $v^k(\mathbf{a}^{cont}, \mathbf{a}_{imp}) > v^k(\mathbf{b}^{cont}, \mathbf{b}_{imp})$. Similarly, if k, under these conditions, is indifferent between the two bundles, then $v^k(.)$ must assign them the same number.[76]

---

[75] These are each vast bodies of scholarship. An excellent literature review concerning labor supply is Blundell and MaCurdy (1999). A classic discussion of consumer preferences for marketed goods is Deaton and Muellbauer (1980); for a recent review, see Barnett and Serletis (2008). An authoritative source concerning individuals' WTP/WTA amounts for environmental goods, focusing on survey data, is Bateman and Willis (2001). The use of behavioral data to infer such WTP/WTA amounts (so-called "travel cost" and "hedonic pricing" approaches) is reviewed in A. Freeman (2003, chs. 11–13).

[76] To say that k self-interestedly weakly prefers $(\mathbf{a}^{cont}, \mathbf{a}_{imp})$ to $(\mathbf{b}^{cont}, \mathbf{b}_{imp})$ is shorthand for the following: Take any two outcomes x and y which are identical in all periods except for one (t). In that period in outcome x, k's contingent attributes are $\mathbf{a}^{cont}$ and background facts are $\mathbf{a}_{imp}$; while in that period in outcome y, k's contingent attributes are $\mathbf{b}^{cont}$ and background facts are $\mathbf{b}_{imp}$. Then k self-interestedly weakly prefers x to y.

The following example shows, more concretely, how within-period ordinal rankings might be used to estimate the sublifetime utility function $v^k(.)$. Assume that outcomes are characterized in terms of individuals' consumption and leisure, so that $v^k(.)$ takes the form $v^k(c, l)$, with (c, l) a consumption-leisure bundle. One central focus of research on labor supply is to estimate individuals' rankings of such bundles—for example, by looking at changes in hours worked in response to wage or tax changes. If an individual is at a given level of consumption and leisure during a particular period, what increase in consumption during the period is required to compensate her for a reduction in leisure during the period? A plausible simplifying assumption here, adopted in much optimal-tax scholarship, is that these tradeoffs are regimented by the so-called "constant elasticity of substitution" (CES) function, $[(1-\beta^k)c^{-\mu^k} + \beta^k l^{-\mu^k}]^{-1/\mu^k}$. The terms β^k and μ^k are parameters of the CES function. Information about how k's labor supply responds to wage or tax changes, or other data relevant to within-period leisure-consumption tradeoffs, allow us to determine β^k and μ^k, and thereby to narrow down what $v^k(.)$ is.[77] Assume that we have identified β^k and μ^k for some individual k (and that we are reasonably confident that these reflect k's well-informed, rational, and self-interested preferences). Then we know that her $v^k(.)$ function must satisfy the following constraints. If two different leisure-consumption bundles (c, l) and (c^*, l^*) are such that $[(1-\beta^k)c^{-\mu^k} + \beta^k l^{-\mu^k}]^{-1/\mu^k} > [(1-\beta^k)c^{*-\mu^k} + \beta^k l^{*-\mu^k}]^{-1/\mu^k}$, then it must be the case that $v^k(c, l) > v^k(c^*, l^*)$. Similarly, if the bundles are assigned an equal value by the CES function, then it must be the case that $v^k(c, l) = v^k(c^*, l^*)$.

Note that, because the TANA form is temporally separable, whether k weakly prefers x to y does not depend on *what* the facts are during all periods other than t (the periods when individual attributes and background facts are the same in both outcomes). Nor does this preference depend upon which particular period t is. Finally, because atomistic, it does not depend upon the attributes of other individuals during period t. Either k prefers x to y for every such pair, or for none.

From the relation of weak bundle preference, we can define relations of strict preference and indifference in the normal fashion (namely, k strictly prefers one bundle to a second iff he weakly prefers the first to the second but doesn't weakly prefer the second to the first; and k is indifferent between two bundles iff he weakly prefers each to the other).

To see why $v^k(.)$ must give a higher number to a bundle that k strictly prefers, and equal numbers to indifferent bundles, consider the following. Assume that x and y are identical except during period t; and that during period t in x individual k receives bundle (a^{cont}, a_{imp}), while in y he receives (b^{cont}, b_{imp}). His ordinary utility function $\varphi^k(.)$ represents his ranking of outcomes, which means (by definition) that k weakly prefers x to y iff $\varphi^k(x) \geq \varphi^k(y)$. Because $\varphi^k(.)$ assumes the TANA form, and given the construction of x and y, it follows that k weakly prefers x to y, i.e., weakly prefers (a^{cont}, a_{imp}) to (b^{cont}, b_{imp}), iff $v^k(a^{cont}, a_{imp}) \geq v^k(b^{cont}, b_{imp})$. From this biconditional, we can in turn derive the twin propositions that if k strictly prefers one bundle it must be assigned a higher number by $v^k(.)$, and that indifferent bundles must be assigned the same number.

[77] On the wide use of the CES form in optimal-tax scholarship, see Kaplow (2008b, p. 61, n. 12); Tuomala (1990, p. 47). On the use of labor market data to estimate this utility function, or others, see Blundell and MaCurdy (1999); Stern (1976); Tuomala (1990, ch. 3). The parameter β^k is between 0 and 1, and μ^k is greater than -1.

One important caveat about using within-period ordinal rankings to estimate $v^k(.)$ should be mentioned.[78] Remember that $v^k(.)$ is unique up to a positive affine transformation. However, within-period ordinal rankings, without more, cannot serve to identify $v^k(.)$ up to a positive affine transformation. Assume that we have complete information about how an individual self-interestedly ranks all possible sublifetime bundles; and that this ranking is perfectly captured by some function $\chi^k(.)$. Whenever k, with full information and rationality, self-interestedly prefers (a^{cont}, a_{imp}) to (b^{cont}, b_{imp}), it is the case that $\chi^k(a^{cont}, a_{imp}) > \chi^k(b^{cont}, b_{imp})$. Whenever k, under these conditions, is indifferent between (a^{cont}, a_{imp}) and (b^{cont}, b_{imp}), it is the case that $\chi^k(a^{cont}, a_{imp}) = \chi^k(b^{cont}, b_{imp})$.

It is tempting to conclude that k's sublifetime utility functions consist of $\chi^k(.)$ plus all positive affine transformations. This conclusion would be unwarranted. Why? Note that if $\chi^k(.)$ captures k's ranking of sublifetime bundles, then so does $f(\chi^k(.))$, where f is any increasing transformation of $\chi^k(.)$. The function $\chi^k(.)$ and all increasing transformations thereof define a broad family of functions. If we have complete access to k's within-period ordinal rankings, and know that these are represented by $\chi^k(.)$, then we can conclude that k's sublifetime utility functions are a *subfamily* within this broader family, defined by some $v^k(.)$ and all positive affine transformations of $v^k(.)$. But we do not yet know which particular subfamily this is. To continue with the example of leisure-consumption bundles: Even if we know that k's ranking of such bundles is regimented by the CES form and by specific parameters β^k and μ^k, it would be incorrect to conclude that $v^k(c, l) = [(1-\beta^k)c^{-\mu^k} + \beta^k l^{-\mu^k}]^{-1/\mu^k}$, or some positive affine transformation thereof. It might instead be the case that $v^k(c, l) = g([(1-\beta^k)c^{-\mu^k} + \beta^k l^{-\mu^k}]^{-1/\mu^k})$, where $g(.)$ is an increasing but non-linear function.

Still, within-period ordinal rankings can help to narrow down the functional form of $v^k(.)$. Moreover, such rankings—*together with* simplifying assumptions about the structure of $v^k(.)$, or additional data—can help identify $v^k(.)$ up to a positive affine transformation.[79]

A second kind of ordinary preference data that might be used to estimate $v^k(.)$ consists in *gamble* data: how an individual self-interestedly ranks lotteries over

---

[78] For discussion of the point that different cardinalizations of a given ordinal utility function can change social-welfare-function analysis, see Creedy (1998, pp. 100–103).

[79] For example, in an optimal-tax article, Erosa and Gervais (2002, p. 357) assume a sublifetime utility function with roughly the form $v(c, l) = (1-\alpha)^{-1}[(1-\beta)c^{-\mu} + \beta l^{-\mu}]^{-(1-\alpha)/\mu}$. This is a kind of extrapolation of the CRRA form for $v^k(.)$ as a function of consumption alone, see below. If we assume that $v^k(.)$ takes this form, then knowing β^k and μ^k together with an estimate of α^k allows us to identify $v^k(.)$ (and all positive affine transformations thereof). The parameter α^k might be estimated based on evidence regarding k's preferences for gambles over leisure-consumption bundles, or regarding his intertemporal substitution between consumption or leisure in one period and another. See Auerbach, Kotlikoff, and Skinner (1983, p. 89).

sublifetime bundles or other lotteries.[80] In principle, gamble data—without more—can serve to fully identify k's sublifetime utility functions. If we know how k self-interestedly ranks all possible lotteries over sublifetime bundles, then we know what $v^k(.)$ must be, up to a positive affine transformation. In practice, of course, we will not know how k ranks all such lotteries. Thus gamble data may be paired with simplifying assumptions to determine, or narrow down, what $v^k(.)$ is.

One large extant body of research examines preferences for consumption, income, or wealth gambles. In this body of scholarship, each individual is assumed to have an ordinary utility function that depends solely on her consumption, income, or her wealth. Survey evidence concerning preferences for outcome lotteries, or behavioral evidence of choice under uncertainty, is then used to calibrate this utility function.[81]

---

[80] A lottery over sublifetime bundles assigns probabilities, summing to one, to different such bundles. Assume that spectator k's extended utility functions, and thus his ordinary self-interested utility functions, assume the TANA form.

If B is one lottery over sublifetime bundles, and B^* another such lottery, then to say that k self-interestedly weakly prefers B to B^* means the following. Imagine that L is a lottery over outcomes, and L^* another lottery over outcomes, such that: (1) for all periods except one (t), all outcomes accorded nonzero probability by L and all outcomes accorded nonzero probability by L^* have the very same facts; and (2) in period t, the probability given by L to different possible combinations of contingent attributes for k plus background facts corresponds to B, while the probability given by L^* to different possible combinations of contingent attributes for k plus background facts corresponds to B^*. Then k self-interestedly weakly prefers L to L^*.

Note that, because the TANA form is lottery separable with respect to sublifetime utility, this is true of B and B^* for one such pair of outcome lotteries L and L^* iff it is true for every such pair.

Individuals' preferences for lotteries over sublifetime bundles, in the sense just described, is the most straightforward kind of gamble evidence relevant to inferring $v^k(.)$. But other kinds of gamble evidence (namely, preferences for lotteries over outcomes, where the outcomes accorded nonzero probability are *not* identical in all but a single period) are also surely relevant. Note that the Barsky survey, described immediately below, elicits this latter sort of gamble evidence. Individuals were asked to compare the prospect of earning their current income for life, to a lottery with some probability of earning a higher income every year, and some probability of earning a lower income every year.

[81] The relevant literature, here, assumes that individuals comply with EU theory, and seeks to estimate individuals' ordinary utility functions which (pursuant to EU theory) expectationally represent their preferences for wealth, income, or consumption gambles. Since $\mathbf{U}^k$ itself is constructed on the presupposition that spectator k is EU-compliant, it is spectator k's ordinary EU utility functions that directly evidence the content of $\mathbf{U}^k$ (assuming non-essentiality), along the lines generally described in this chapter. One body of scholarship estimating ordinary EU utility functions relies on survey questions concerning hypothetical lotteries for wealth, consumption, or income lotteries. See, e.g., Barsky et al. (1997); Guiso and Paiella (2008); Hartog, Ferrer-i-Carbonell, and Jonker (2002); Kimball, Sahm, and Shapiro (2008). A second body looks at experimental evidence. See, e.g., Harrison, Lau, and Rutström (2007); Holt and Laury (2002). The experimental approach is reviewed in Cox and Harrison (2008). Finally, a diverse group of studies estimates individual risk aversion for income, wealth, or consumption based on real-world behavior. Two recent examples are Cohen and

An individual's consumption, income, and wealth are distinct attributes that bear various conceptual and causal relations to each other.[82] For SWF purposes, an outcome set characterized solely in terms of individual *consumption* is more plausible than one characterized solely in terms of individual *income* or *wealth*. Such an outcome set would take the form $x = (c_{1,1}, \ldots, c_{N,1}, \ldots, c_{1,T}, \ldots, c_{NT})$, with $c_{i,t}$ denoting individual i's consumption during period t.[83] A fairly typical simplifying assumption, in the literature on consumption/income/wealth gambles, is that individuals' utility

Einav (2007), looking to insurance purchases; and Paravisini, Rappoport, and Ravina (2011), looking to peer-to-peer lending. Other behavioral evidence is reviewed in Meyer and Meyer (2005, 2006).

One well-known source of behavioral evidence is the "equity premium" (the greater returns earned by stocks, as compared to the risk-free rate), suggesting very high values of risk aversion if one assumes that investors are maximizing a TANA utility function of consumption. See, e.g., Mankiw and Zeldes (1991, pp. 102–106). A possible resolution of this "equity premium puzzle" is that investor behavior is motivated by non-EU preferences, or by EU preferences that do not have the TANA form. See generally Donaldson and Mehra (2008).

Finally, evidence concerning the "value of statistical life," i.e., individual WTP/WTA to avoid fatality risks, and how this amount changes with income, can also be used to make inferences regarding the degree of individual risk aversion. See Evans and Smith (2010).

[82] See Bojer (2003, ch. 9). In particular, risk aversion with respect to consumption, income and wealth can differ. See generally Meyer and Meyer (2005, 2006).

[83] By an individual's *consumption*, I mean her expenditure on marketed goods. In other words, $c_{i,t}$ is the vector product of $\mathbf{q}_{i,t}$ (the vector of marketed goods and services that she purchases during period t) and $\mathbf{p}_{i,t}$ (the vector of prices that she faces). An individual's income during some period can be defined in various ways; it is something like the change in potential consumption during the period. Under simplifying assumptions (for example, the individual starts life with no assets, and spends all of her wage income in each period on consumption), income and consumption will be identical. Where they are not, consumption would seem to be more directly connected to an individual's well-being than income. Similarly, consumption would seem to be more directly connected to an individual's well-being than wealth (the market value of her assets).

A spectator can possess extended preferences and, in particular, ordinary self-interested preferences for an outcome set that is "missing" characteristics only if those preferences satisfy an invariance requirement. Where the outcome set solely describes individuals' consumption, and all other attributes or other facts are missing, this means that the spectator's self-interested ranking of outcomes and outcome lotteries (as well as his i-interested rankings and across-person judgments) are invariant to non-consumption characteristics, assumed to be fixed at some unspecified level. The spectator's self-interested ranking of different consumption gambles must be the same, regardless of his (fixed, unspecified) health state, or leisure, or enjoyment of public goods. Some standard forms for utility as a function of both consumption and these other characteristics have separability features that would support this invariance assumption, while other standard forms do not. (For example, an individual k's sublifetime utility as a function of a consumption-health bundle is sometimes seen to take the form $v^k(c, h) = f^k(c) + g^k(h)$, and sometimes seen to take the form $v^k(c, h) = f^k(c + g^k(h))$. See Rey and Rochet (2004, pp. 44–46). The first form means that k's preferences over consumption gambles, holding health fixed, are indeed invariant to the health level; while the second form does not if $f^k(.)$ is non-linear.)

More subtly, to describe outcomes in terms of consumption, omitting information about prices, means that spectators' extended preferences are invariant to the specific level at which prices

functions adopt the "constant relative risk aversion" (CRRA) form. This assumption, taken together with the TANA assumption, means that spectator k's extended utility function and ordinary self-interested utility function are, respectively, as follows: $u^k(x; i) = \sum_{t=1}^{T} D^k(t)v^k(c_{i,t}(x))$ and $\varphi^k(x) = \sum_{t=1}^{T} D^k(t)v^k(c_{k,t}(x))$, with $v^k(.)$ assuming the CRRA form $v^k(c) = c^{1-\lambda^k}/(1-\lambda^k)$. If $v^k(.)$ assumes the CRRA form, then it is parametrized by a single value: λ^k, the spectator's (constant) coefficient of relative risk aversion. We might establish λ^k directly by asking the spectator for his self-interested preferences for consumption gambles, or infer λ^k from evidence of his self-interested preferences for income or wealth gambles.[84]

For example, in an influential study, Barsky and co-authors estimated individual risk aversion with respect to consumption by posing a survey question in one wave of the Health and Retirement Study—a large cross-sectional study in which individuals are identified by various demographic characteristics and asked a wide range of questions. The question was framed in terms of income rather than consumption because the authors felt that "survey respondents would better understand income than consumption lotteries."[85] It was posed to more than 11,000 individuals and ran as follows:

> Suppose that you are the only income earner in the family, and you have a good job guaranteed to give you your current (family) income every year for life. You are given the opportunity to take a new and equally good job, with a 50-50 chance it will double your

are fixed. In particular, spectators' self-interested preferences over consumption gambles must be independent of the relative prices of marketed goods.

SWF analysis with a consumption-only outcome set is problematic where spectators' preferences do not satisfy these invariance properties. Even if spectators' preferences do have these invariance properties, using a consumption-only set will not be sensitive to variation in individuals' non-consumption attributes, and can be particularly problematic where the choices at hand will change these attributes. (See the discussion of simplified outcomes earlier in the chapter.). Still, this type of simplification might be justified in some circumstances, and indeed as mentioned earlier some SWF scholarship does employ utility functions with income or consumption as their sole arguments.

[84] There is an important theoretical literature on risk aversion, which examines the properties of a single-argument utility function. See, e.g., Gollier (2001, ch. 2); Mas-Colell, Whinston, and Green (1995, pp. 183–194); Meyer and Meyer (2006, ch. 2). It is standard in this literature to characterize a single-argument utility function such as $v^k(.)$ in terms of the so-called "coefficient of relative risk aversion," $\lambda^k(.)$. In the case where the argument for the utility function is consumption, the coefficient of relative risk aversion is the negative elasticity of the marginal utility of consumption. In other words, $\lambda^k(c) = -cv^{k\,\prime\prime}(c)/v^{k\,\prime}(c)$, where $v^{k\,\prime}(.)$ is the first derivative of $v^k(.)$ and $v^{k\,\prime\prime}(.)$ the second derivative. Once we know what $\lambda^k(c)$ is, for all the different values of c, then we know what $v^k(.)$ is (up to a positive affine transformation).

The further simplifying assumption of a *constant* value for $\lambda^k(c)$ leads to the CRRA utility function, discussed in the text.

[85] Barsky et al. (1997, p. 539, n. 3).

(family) income, and a 50-50 chance that it will cut your (family) income by a third. Would you take the new job?[86]

If the respondent k's ordinary utility function takes the TANA/CRRA form provided in the previous paragraph, i.e., $\varphi^k(x) = \sum_{t=1}^{T} D^k(t)[c_{k,t}(x)^{1-\lambda^k}/(1-\lambda^k)]$, her answer to this sort of question allows us to narrow down the value of λ^k. Specifically, based on each respondent's answer to this question and similar follow-up questions, the authors determined that her value for λ^k was (1) above 3.76; (2) between 2 and 3.76; (3) between 1 and 2; and (4) between 0 and 1.[87] These valuations for λ^k were then correlated with the respondent's age, gender, race, religion, employment status, educational level, and other characteristics.

While the CRRA form of sublifetime utility is particularly simple, it is also quite possible that $v^k(.)$ is characterized by non-constant relative risk aversion, and research seeing to identify $v^k(.)$ might well accommodate that possibility. Moreover, while data regarding individual rankings of consumption (or wealth or income) gambles can, most obviously, be used to determine $v^k(.)$ for purposes of an outcome set in which all non-consumption attributes are missing, such data can also be extrapolated to other types of outcome sets. This is possible if we adopt certain assumptions regarding the separability of consumption and other attributes as components of sublifetime utility.[88]

---

[86] Ibid, p. 540.

[87] Strictly speaking, the authors themselves were agnostic about the functional form of lifetime utility, and simply estimated the respondent's coefficient of relative risk aversion for *lifetime* utility as a function of *permanent* consumption. However, it is straightforward to see that, if the lifetime utility function $\varphi^k(.)$ takes the form just provided, this value is exactly the same as λ^k. Let $V^k(c)$ be the lifetime utility of an outcome in which k receives consumption c in every period. If $V^k(c) = \sum_{t=1}^{T} D^k(t)[c^{1-\lambda^k}/(1-\lambda^k)]$, then $-cV^{k\prime\prime}(c)/V^{k\prime}(c) = \lambda^k$.

[88] Assume that outcomes describe not only consumption but also certain non-consumption attributes and/or background facts. Thus sublifetime bundles take the form $(c, \mathbf{a}^{cont}, \mathbf{a}_{imp})$, where $\mathbf{a}^{cont}$, here, means non-consumption contingent attributes. Spectator k's sublifetime utility function $v^k(.) = v^k(c, \mathbf{a}^{cont}, \mathbf{a}_{imp})$ might have the following separability feature: his self-interested ranking of bundle lotteries where all bundles with non-zero probability have the very same $(\mathbf{a}^{cont}, \mathbf{a}_{imp})$ values, and only consumption varies, does not depend upon what the values $(\mathbf{a}^{cont}, \mathbf{a}_{imp})$ are. This will be true, in particular, if $v^k(.)$ is *additive* in consumption and other bundle characteristics, i.e., $v^k(c, \mathbf{a}^{cont}, \mathbf{a}_{imp}) = f^k(c) + g^k(\mathbf{a}^{cont}, \mathbf{a}_{imp})$. It will also be true if $v^k(.)$ is *multiplicative* in consumption and other bundle characteristics, i.e., $v^k(c, \mathbf{a}^{cont}, \mathbf{a}_{imp}) = f^k(c)g^k(\mathbf{a}^{cont}, \mathbf{a}_{imp})$, with $g^k(.)$ positive.

If so, data about k's self-interested ranking of consumption-only outcomes are readily extrapolated to these more finely described outcomes. (If k ranks consumption lotteries a certain way, when his ranking is assumed to be invariant to the level of missing characteristics, then he should rank consumption lotteries the same way, when those characteristics are included within the description of outcomes but held fixed.) More concretely, if we estimate $v^k(.)$ for a consumption-only outcome set to be a particular function, then that very same function can serve as the f-function in the previous paragraph. More concretely yet, if we assume that $v^k(.)$ for a consumption-only outcome set takes the CRRA form, and estimate a particular value for λ^k, then we can "plug" a CRRA function with this value into the additive or multiplicative

A second substantial source of gamble data is provided by surveys eliciting individual preferences for lotteries over sublifetime bundles characterized in terms of *health* attributes. Such surveys have been conducted as part of the literature on QALYs ("quality adjusted life years"). One widely used survey format, in this body of research, is the so-called "standard gamble" format. Respondents are asked to rank health states, and lotteries over such states, that they might experience during one particular period (for example, one year).[89]

While data from QALY surveys are usually employed for purposes of cost-effectiveness analysis, the standard-gamble data can also help calibrate $\mathbf{U}^k$ for purposes of an SWF. Most obviously, it can be used to calibrate $\mathbf{U}^k$ in the context of an outcome set that solely characterizes individual health.[90] In other words, $x = (h_{1,1}, \ldots, h_{N,1}, \ldots, h_{1,T}, \ldots, h_{NT})$, where $h_{i,t}$ denotes individual i's health state during period t. The TANA form, in this case, means that $u^k(x; i) = \sum_{t=1}^{T} D^k(t)v^k(h_{i,t}(x))$, and in particular that spectator k's ordinary self-interested utility function takes the form $\varphi^k(x) = \sum_{t=1}^{T} D^k(t)v^k(h_{k,t}(x))$. Standard gamble questions, posed to a given spectator, can be used to make progress in identifying $v^k(.)$ and, thus, $u^k(.)$.

Moreover, just as data concerning consumption gambles can be extrapolated to infer individuals' preferences regarding outcome sets that include some non-consumption characteristics, given appropriate assumptions about the separability of consumption and non-consumption attributes, so too data concerning health gambles can be extrapolated to infer individuals' preferences regarding outcome sets that include some non-health attributes, given appropriate assumptions about the separability of health and non-health characteristics. To be sure, it would also be useful for researchers to expand the ambit of existing gamble research—looking at

functions in the previous paragraph. In other words, $v^k(c, \mathbf{a}^{cont}, \mathbf{a}_{imp}) = (c^{1-\lambda^k})/(1-\lambda^k) + g^k(\mathbf{a}^{cont}, \mathbf{a}_{imp})$, or $v^k(c, \mathbf{a}^{cont}, \mathbf{a}_{imp}) = [(c^{1-\lambda^k})/(1-\lambda^k)]g^k(\mathbf{a}^{cont}, \mathbf{a}_{imp})$.

However, if $v^k(.)$ as a function of $(c, \mathbf{a}^{cont}, \mathbf{a}_{imp})$ does not have the separability feature just described, using data about k's self-interested ranking of a consumption-only outcome set to calibrate $v^k(.)$ is more problematic. Imagine, for example, that $v^k(c, \mathbf{a}^{cont}, \mathbf{a}_{imp})$ is the square root of $f^k(c) + g^k(\mathbf{a}^{cont}, \mathbf{a}_{imp})$. In this case, k's preferences for bundle lotteries, with $(\mathbf{a}^{cont}, \mathbf{a}_{imp})$ fixed at some level, depend on what that level is. We *could* set $f^k(c) = [(c^{1-\lambda^k})/(1-\lambda^k)]$, with λ^k garnered from k's ranking of a consumption-only set; but it is not clear why this would be justified.

A better way to calibrate a $v^k(.)$ which lacks the separability feature is to elicit k's preferences for gambles over sublifetime bundles that explicitly describe both consumption and the $(\mathbf{a}^{cont}, \mathbf{a}_{imp})$ attributes. Note that, if those non-consumption attributes are fixed at a reference level (remember the discussion earlier in the chapter of outcome sets with normalized attributes and reference levels), what needs to be elicited are k's preferences for gambles where consumption varies and $(\mathbf{a}^{cont}, \mathbf{a}_{imp})$ are at the reference level. We need not elicit his preferences for gambles over sublifetime bundles where $(\mathbf{a}^{cont}, \mathbf{a}_{imp})$ vary, or are at some other level.

[89] On QALY surveys, see scholarship cited in Adler (2006a, p. 1, n. 1).

[90] As already mentioned, some health scholars have proposed that a "health related" SWF might be applied to vectors of "health utilities," reflecting individuals' health states; and that QALY surveys might be used to determine health utilities. See sources cited in Chapter 2, n. 56.

individuals' self-interested preferences for attribute packages that include both consumption and health, or one of these attributes in connection with a third type of attribute (for example, gambles over packages of consumption and leisure). Some such research has in fact been undertaken.[91]

I have thus far focused on how to use certain kinds of ordinary self-interested preference data to estimate $v^k(.)$, namely within-period ordinal rankings and gamble data. A third such kind of data concerns intertemporal substitution: namely, how individuals self-interestedly make tradeoffs between attributes during one period and attributes during some other period.[92]

While the TANA assumption allows us readily to infer the content of $\mathbf{U}^k$ by looking to individuals' ordinary self-interested preferences, we can also, of course, attempt to do so by conducting life-history surveys. TANA facilitates this inferential path as well. First, we can ask three types of i-history questions isomorphic to the three kinds of own-history data described in the preceding paragraphs: within-period ordinal rankings, gambles, and intertemporal substitution. Each $u^k(.)$ in $\mathbf{U}^k$ assigns utilities to the life-history of subject i by summing T sublifetime utilities, each calculated by applying the $v^k(.)$ function to a package consisting of subject i's contingent attributes during one of the T periods plus background facts during that period. So we can identify $v^k(.)$ by asking the spectator k to do the following under a condition of interest in subject i: (1) rank different sublifetime bundles for i, i.e., possible combinations of an array of contingent attributes that i might possess during some period plus background facts during that period; (2) rank lotteries over such

---

[91] See Edwards (2008); Evans and Viscusi (1991); Sloan et al. (1998); Viscusi and Evans (1990). See above, n. 88, for a discussion of why such multiattribute lottery data might be useful.

[92] For sophisticated examples of how data about intertemporal substitution can be used to make inferences about the sublifetime utility function, see Attanasio and Browning (1995); Blundell, Browning, and Meghir (1994). As a very simple illustration, consider the following. Imagine that outcomes have two periods and are characterized solely in terms of consumption. A given individual, k, has a fixed amount of money B, which she can immediately expend on consumption in period 1, or partly or wholly invest—at market interest rate r—for consumption in period 2. The individual has a TANA ordinary utility function, with an exponential discount factor. In other words, her utility in a given outcome equals $v^k(c_{k,1}) + v^k(c_{k,2})/(1+\rho^k)$, with $c_{k,1}$ and $c_{k,2}$ consumption in the two periods, and ρ^k the discount rate that the individual uses to discount utility in the second period.

Imagine, furthermore, that $v^k(.)$ takes the CRRA form. With these assumptions in place, the individual decides how much of B to invest by maximizing the above utility function, subject to the budget constraint that $c_{k,1} + c_{k,2}/(1+r) = B$. Straightforward constrained maximization shows that the optimal allocation of consumption between the two periods is such that $(1+r)/(1+\rho^k) = (c_{k,1}/c_{k,2})^{-\lambda^k}$. If we have some sense of what the individual's discount rate ρ^k is, and we assume she is indeed rationally maximizing lifetime utility, we can estimate λ^k from her choice of $c_{k,1}$ and $c_{k,2}$. Indeed, it can be readily seen that, if we observe changes in the allocation of consumption to the two periods as the market interest r changes, we can make inferences about λ^k even without knowing what ρ^k is. Consider that $\ln(1+r) - \ln(1+\rho^k) = -\lambda^k \ln(c_{k,1}/c_{k,2})$. Therefore, $d(\ln(c_{k,1}/c_{k,2}))/d(\ln(1+r)) = -1/\lambda^k$.

bundles; or (3) determine how changes in i's contingent attributes or background facts during one period compensate for such changes in another period.

Life-history surveys also offer an additional route to estimating $v^k(.)$, namely, across-person questions. The spectator, in principle, can be asked for within-period tradeoffs across persons, for intertemporal tradeoffs across persons, and to rank gambles involving different persons.

D. Happiness Data

A substantial survey literature, originating in psychology, asks individuals to express their current "life satisfaction" or "happiness" on a numerical scale. The respondent might be asked a question such as "How satisfied are you with your life, on a scale from 1 to 10?" or "Are you very happy, pretty happy, or not too happy?" (in effect, asking the respondent to quantify her happiness on a scale from 1 to 3). A whole new branch of economics has grown up around such surveys.[93]

Some in this literature adopt a mental-state view of well-being. This book has rejected such a view, and instead defends a view which analyses well-being in terms of fully informed, fully rational extended preferences. The extent to which individuals' fully informed, fully rational preferences over life-histories depend on the happiness states or other mental states attained by the subjects of those life-histories is an open question.

However, happiness surveys may be relevant to policy choice even if a mental-state view of well-being is false. In particular, happiness surveys can help implement the SWF framework defended here.

First, outcomes might conceivably be characterized in terms of certain types of mental states that individuals might possess—for example, whether each individual during a given period is depressed, in pain, enjoying life, upbeat, and so forth—along with some non-mental individual attributes, such as consumption characteristics, labor characteristics, health characteristics, and some background facts. Indeed, since outcomes are simplified, it might be justifiable in some cases to describe outcomes solely in terms of individuals' mental states (for example, where policies are likely to change only those states, not individuals' other well-being relevant attributes). I am not aware of scholarship that has actually applied a social welfare function to outcomes characterized partly or wholly in terms of individuals' mental states, but such an approach is worth investigating. No one doubts that mental states are *one* component of well-being.

Given such an approach to characterizing outcome sets, happiness surveys could be used at the *predictive* stage: in predicting what outcome (or, more precisely, probability distribution over outcomes) a given policy is associated with. Happiness

---

[93] See Diener et al. (1999); Frey (2008); Kahneman, Diener, and Schwarz (1999); Layard (2005); Van Praag and Ferrer-i-Carbonell (2004).

surveys—because they enable us to correlate an individual's answer to life-satisfaction or happiness questions with her other attributes—are an excellent source of information about the causes of different types of mental states, as the literature shows.

What about the use of happiness surveys to help *value* outcomes? At least *some* economists working in the happiness literature accept (or at least seem to accept) the traditional economic view that individuals have preferences over outcomes; that an individual's preferences are representable by an ordinary utility function; and that this utility function is not restricted in its arguments—that its arguments may include the individual's non-mental attributes, and facts about the world other than the individual's attributes, as well as the individual's mental attributes.[94]

These economists then take the further step of assuming that utility functions are temporally additive (the sum of sublifetime utility values); and that an individual's answer to a happiness or life-satisfaction question provides evidence of his sublifetime utility function. On this view, if individual k has a sublifetime utility function $v^k(.) = v^k(\mathbf{a}_{k,t}^{cont}, \mathbf{a}_{imp,t})$, then the individual's response to a question that asks him to quantify his happiness or life-satisfaction is driven by a function $h(v^k(\mathbf{a}_{k,t}^{cont}, \mathbf{a}_{imp,t}))$.

For example, as Blanchflower and Oswald explain:

> The idea used in the paper is that there exists a reported well-being function $r = h(u(y, z, t)) + e$, where r is some self-reported number or level (perhaps the integer 4 on a satisfaction scale, or "very happy" on an ordinal happiness scale), $u(...)$ is to be thought of as the person's true well-being or utility, $h(.)$ is a . . . non-differentiable function relating actual to reported well-being, y is real income, z is a set of demographic and personal characteristics, t is the time period, and e is an error term. . . . [T]he function $h(.)$ rises in steps as u increases. [This is because happiness and life-satisfaction surveys ask the individual to express her happiness or satisfaction as an integer.] It is assumed, as seems plausible, that $u(...)$ is a function that is observable only to the individual.[95]

This perspective on happiness surveys makes them potentially useful for the task analyzed in this chapter: estimating $\mathbf{U}^k$. To be sure, in doing so, we will need to take

[94] This view of happiness surveys is to be distinguished from two other views: first, that the respondent's answers reflect some characteristic other than her preference satisfaction (for example, some non-preference measure of her affective states); and, second, that the respondent's answers reflect her preference satisfaction, with the arguments for preferences limited to her own mental states. If answers to happiness surveys have one of these etiologies, they are not useful in estimating $\mathbf{U}^k$ (not at all, in the first case; and not where the outcome set includes individuals' non-mental attributes, in the second).

[95] Blanchflower and Oswald (2004, p. 1361). On their $u(.)$ as a sublifetime measure, see ibid., p. 1362. For other examples of the view that happiness questions may provide evidence of a traditional sublifetime utility function—one not limited to mental states in its arguments—see Layard, Mayraz, and Nickell (2008), discussed immediately below; and Finkelstein, Luttmer, and Notowidigdo (2008).

account of the fact that a respondent to a happiness survey is not directly articulating $v^k(.)$, but articulating $v^k(.)$ transformed by a further function, $h(.)$. Moreover, $v^k(.)$ should represent k's fully informed, fully rational preferences. In significant respects, participants in happiness or life-satisfaction surveys fall short of these idealizing conditions.[96] Still, the potential role of these surveys as one source of evidence concerning $v^k(.)$ and thus $\mathbf{U}^k$ is worth noting.

Indeed, in a recent article, Layard, Mayraz, and Nickell use happiness data to estimate the coefficient of relative risk aversion for income—proposing that this estimate can be used in calculating distributive weights for cost-benefit analysis and for optimal-tax purposes. Their approach is basically to assume that an individual's sublifetime utility function has the form $v^k(c_{k,t}, \mathbf{a}_{k,t}) = c_{k,t}^{1-\lambda} / (1-\lambda) + w(\mathbf{a}_{k,t})$, with $c_{k,t}$ the individual's income during period t and $\mathbf{a}_{k,t}$ other attributes; to assume that happiness surveys are evidencing this sublifetime utility function; and to determine what value of λ best explains the survey data.[97]

E. Surveys or Revealed Preference Data?

Both survey and revealed-preference evidence are widely employed among economists investigating ordinary preferences. Thus, both sorts of evidence are potentially usable in estimating spectators' own-history preferences (and also in estimating extended utilities generally, if non-essentiality is true).[98]

For example, the literature on individual preferences for income, consumption, or wealth gambles includes a substantial body of survey research. A paradigmatic example is the large-scale survey conducted by Barsky and co-authors to estimate individuals' coefficients of relative risk aversion for consumption. Subsequent scholars have employed similar survey instruments. But a larger body of scholarship looks at real-world behavior, such as asset-holding behavior or insurance purchases, to estimate individual utility as a function of income, consumption, or wealth. Finally, a burgeoning experimental literature examines how individuals behave when offered

---

[96] Answers to happiness and life-satisfaction surveys are sensitive to the respondent's current affective state, not just his beliefs about how well his preferences have been satisfied, and are also vulnerable to various framing effects. See Schwarz and Strack (1999).

[97] See Layard, Mayraz, and Nickell (2008).

[98] By contrast, it is hard to see what sort of behavioral data would directly evidence spectators' i-history preferences or across-person judgments. I have therefore suggested that such preferences (if not inferred from own-history preferences via the assumption of non-essentiality) be elicited in life-history *surveys*.

To be sure, i-history preferences, like own-history preferences, are defined in terms of ordinary preferences (i-interested as opposed to self-interested). But it seems plausible that a much wider range of behavior is engaged in by the actor under a condition reasonably close to self-interest, than under a condition close to i-interest. (Arguably, however, if k has a child or spouse, or is in a close relationship with some other such person, k's behavior might be some evidence of his preferences under a condition of interest in that person.)

actual money gambles in a controlled setting; a closely related literature looks at individual gambling behavior on game shows.[99]

Another example: WTP/WTA data (examining tradeoffs between consumption and other goods) is the mainstay of cost-benefit analysis, but it can also play a large role in the SWF context. For example, within-period WTP/WTA amounts provide a kind of within-period ordinal data. WTP/WTA amounts to avoid fatality risk furnish a particular kind of gamble evidence. Notably, "stated preference" (survey) and revealed preference data are both mainstays of WTP/WTA research.

But which kind of data is *better* evidence of ordinary preferences? That question is hotly debated by economists. In the context at hand—using ordinary preference data to estimate $\mathbf{U}^k$—it is plausible to think that surveys are on balance preferable (at least to real-world behavior, if not behavior observed in a controlled experimental setting).[100]

First, spectators' own-history preferences are equivalent to their *self-interested* preferences over outcomes. Information about individuals' non-self-interested preferences (for example, their moral preferences, or preferences that mix moral and non-moral considerations) are not useful in inferring own-history preferences. Surveys can be engineered to elicit individuals' self-interested preferences. Although behavioral data can also be employed to estimate self-interested preferences—it is a fair assumption that individuals in many real-world contexts are largely self-interested—the survey format means that the respondent can be specifically prompted or cued to answer from a self-interested perspective. (Experimental formats also permit a deliberate engineering of a self-interested attitude on the part of participants.)

The second reason for thinking that surveys provide a particularly useful source of own-history data is this. The spectators' own-history preferences (like their *i*-history preferences and across-person judgments) are supposed to be *fully informed and fully rational*. The SWF framework is a *normative* framework; and, I have argued, a theory of well-being based on preferences that have these properties is a normatively attractive theory. Surveys allow the researcher to provide information to respondents, and to take steps to debias respondents—to mitigate various failures of rationality, such as a misunderstanding of the probability calculus or a departure from the norms of EU theory. Indeed, information-provision and debiasing are standard features of current survey research.

By contrast, there is much evidence that individuals, in actual behavior, often depart substantially from the norms of rationality embodied in EU theory. Such departures are particularly relevant given the EU approach to constructing $u^k(.)$. This function *expectationally represents* spectator *k*'s preferences over life-histories and life-history lotteries; and we wholly or partly infer it from an ordinary utility

---

[99] See sources cited above, n. 81.
[100] On the usefulness of surveys as evidence of individual preferences, also reviewing standard objections, see generally Adler (2006b).

function, $\varphi^k(.)$, which expectationally represents his self-interested preferences over outcomes and outcome lotteries. The very existence of these functions presupposes that individual k complies with EU theory. We should be particularly hesitant to construct these functions from an individual's real-world behavior, as opposed to her answers to surveys (or behavior in an experimental context), if she is especially likely to deviate from the norms of EU theory in the real-world context.[101]

This is not to say that the survey designer or experimental researcher has a "magic pill" which she can use to make the respondent fully rational. Nor is there a magic potion which will provide the respondent with full information. The claim, rather, is *comparative*. It is that someone's survey responses or experimental behavior, after debiasing and information provision, are *better* evidence of what she would want if fully rational and fully informed, than her real-world behavior.

However, these brief remarks can hardly provide a definitive case in favor of using surveys to estimate own-history preferences. The proponents of behavioral evidence might argue that survey respondents often have an incentive to misstate their preferences. Alternatively, survey responses may have zero real consequence for the respondent—leaving her perhaps with no affirmative incentive to misstate her preferences, but also no incentive to think carefully about what those preferences are.

A central aim of this chapter has been to explain how information about an individual k's ordinary self-interested preferences can be used to help construct $\mathbf{U}^k$.

---

[101] It is now widely accepted that individuals, in practice, often deviate from EU theory. See, e.g., Hastie and Dawes (2001, especially ch. 13). Some deviations, such as reference point effects, mistakes in handling probabilities, or probability weighting, are very well known. Recent scholarship identifies a less familiar deviation, namely, "narrow framing": the tendency of individuals to mentally segregate possible monetary gains and losses from lotteries, rather than to think about the well-being effect of these gains and losses as conjoined with background endowments. See Barberis, Huang, and Thaler (2006). Surveys such as the Barsky survey which ask about lotteries over an individual's entire income or consumption during some time period (e.g., annual income) would not seem to be vulnerable to narrow framing. On the difference between the degree of individual risk aversion implied by surveys and by one body of behavioral evidence, viz., the equity premium, see Barsky et al. (1997, pp. 561–564).

It might be objected that this book does not actually endorse standard EU theory as a normative theory. Rather, it endorses a refined variant of EU theory that allows for indeterminate probabilities and for incompleteness. See Chapter 7. But EU theory, even thus refined, does not encompass the various kinds of irrationalities we see in actual behavior, such as reference point effects, mistakes in handling probabilities, narrow framing, etc.

The reader will also be reminded that indeterminate probabilities are not relevant to the construction of $u^k(.)$, because that is constructed with reference to a hypothetical choice situation where probabilities are determinate and exogenous (see Chapter 3)—a hypothetical situation nicely simulated, in this respect, by a survey setting where respondents are told what the probabilities are. I *do* in principle want to allow for incompleteness in a given spectator's ranking of life-histories. (See Chapter 3.) However, this chapter, for simplicity, assumes that individuals' rational preferences over life-histories and outcomes are complete. Little existing data on preferences models utility in a way that relaxes completeness.

Whether that information, in turn, is best gathered through verbal inquiry (surveys) or by observing behavior is a further, contestable topic that I will not attempt to address in detail here.

IV. ZEROING OUT

Chapter 3 argued that the set of extended utility functions associated with a given individual, U^k, should be "zeroed out" before these sets are pooled to create U. Doing so raises special difficulties, by virtue of the fact that outcomes are missing characteristics.[102]

Assume that we have used the various sorts of data described in previous sections (either data about ordinary self-interested preferences, or life-history surveys) to arrive at a U^k that represents the spectator's various extended preferences. U^k may well be unique up to a positive affine transformation, but the following analysis applies even if it is not. In any event, we have in hand an estimate of the different utility functions that belong to it—how each assigns values to life-histories.

Consider, first, the (idealized and unrealistic!) case of an outcome set which is fully described. Every attribute and background fact to which the spectator might be sensitive is included in the specification of outcomes. In this case, a variety of approaches to "zeroing out" might be employed.

These approaches, about to be described, involve own-history questions. They also have i-history counterparts. I see no particular advantage to "zeroing out" via i-history questions. But the reader should note that this *is* a possibility.

The most straightforward own-history question by which to "zero out" U^k is as follows. The individual k is put in a self-interested frame of mind and asked whether there is some outcome x^* which is so bad that he is indifferent between that outcome and nonexistence. If the answer is yes, then consider the subset of U^k consisting of every utility function $u^k(.)$ such that $u^k(x^*; k) = 0$. This is now the set of appropriately "zeroed out" extended utility functions for spectator k, because these (and only these) assign zero to a life-history, $(x^*; k)$, which he regards as just as good as nonexistence. All other utility functions should be excluded from the zeroed-out U^k.

---

[102] Where ratio information is not relevant to an SWF, the zeroing-out process *can* be performed, in some manner, but it also can be skipped. If each U^k is unique up to a positive affine transformation, and these are then pooled to form U, then—regardless of whether each U^k is zeroed out, and (if that occurs) regardless of which life-history is chosen as the zero point—an SWF for which ratio information is not relevant will produce the very same ranking of outcomes. (This is true, for example, of the leximin SWF, the utilitarian SWF, and the rank-weighted SWF. On ratio-relevance, see Chapter 3.) By contrast, ratio information *is* relevant to the continuous prioritarian SWF, and it matters very much how the zeroing-out process is performed. Thus, the analysis about to follow is not independent of the choice of SWF, in the sense that the problems discussed are problems for particular SWFs (such as the continuous prioritarian SWF), and not others.

What if there is no such outcome x^*, such that k is self-interestedly indifferent between that outcome and nonexistence? We could circumvent this problem by expanding O until there is such an outcome, estimating $\mathbf{U}^k$ for the expanded set, and then zeroing it out as just described. Or we could follow a different approach. Take any two of his own life-histories, $(y; k)$ and $(x; k)$, such that k prefers the first to the second and regards both as better than nonexistence. Determine the probability p, such that k is indifferent between $(x; k)$ and a lottery which gives him a p probability of $(y; k)$ and a $(1 - p)$ probability of nonexistence. Then each $u^k(.)$ in $\mathbf{U}^k$ implicitly assigns nonexistence a value of $e = [u^k(x;k) - pu^k(y;k)]/(1-p)$. "Zero out" $\mathbf{U}^k$ by including those and only those utility functions for which this e is 0.

Yet another avenue for "zeroing out" emerges if we introduce the assumption that the extended utility functions in $\mathbf{U}^k$ assume the TANA form. Remember that, in this case, $u^k(x; i) = \sum_{t=1}^{T} D^k(t)v^k(\mathbf{a}_{i,t}^{cont}(x), \mathbf{a}_{imp,t}(x))$. Moreover, $\mathbf{U}^k$ is in this case unique up to a positive affine transformation, and each $u^k(.)$ corresponds to one sublifetime utility function $v^k(.)$.

Now, we can set the zero point by identifying a sublifetime bundle no better than premature death—a suggestion developed by John Broome.[103] We ask k to consider any life-history $(x; k)$ in which she lives fewer than the total number of periods T. We then ask her whether there is some sublifetime bundle $(\mathbf{a}^{cont}, \mathbf{a}_{imp})$, such that she is self-interestedly indifferent between x and an outcome in which she lives one more period with attributes $\mathbf{a}^{cont}$ and background facts $\mathbf{a}_{imp}$ obtain. The bundle $(\mathbf{a}^{cont}, \mathbf{a}_{imp})$ is such that k's possession of the attributes specified by the bundle plus the occurrence of its background facts, for one period, as compared to k's not being alive during that period, are seen by k as equally good. Consider the subset of sublifetime utility functions such that $v^k(\mathbf{a}^{cont}, \mathbf{a}_{imp}) = 0$. The subset of $\mathbf{U}^k$ which corresponds to these sublifetime utility functions is appropriately "zeroed out." Extended utility functions within this subset of $\mathbf{U}^k$ assign zero to a "constantly neutral" life: a life in which the spectator's characteristics, during each period, are the characteristics which he sees as equally good as being dead during that period.

If there is no sublifetime bundle which the spectator regards as equally good as premature death, we can "zero out" the sublifetime utility function using a variant of the gamble question described three paragraphs above. Take two sublifetime bundles, $(\mathbf{a}^{cont}, \mathbf{a}_{imp})$ and $(\mathbf{b}^{cont}, \mathbf{b}_{imp})$, such that the spectator self-interestedly prefers the first to the second.[104] We now ask the spectator to consider any arbitrary life-history $(x; k)$ in which she lives fewer than the total number of periods T, and ask her to consider extending it for one period with characteristics $(\mathbf{b}^{cont}, \mathbf{b}_{imp})$. We then ask: what is the probability p, such that you are indifferent between extending the life-history for one period with characteristics $(\mathbf{b}^{cont}, \mathbf{b}_{imp})$, versus a p probability of extending it for one period with characteristics $(\mathbf{a}^{cont}, \mathbf{a}_{imp})$ and a $(1 - p)$ probability

---

[103] See Broome (2004, chs. 15–17).
[104] See above, n. 76.

of not extending it? For each sublifetime utility function $v^k(.)$, set d $=[v^k(\mathbf{b}^{cont},\mathbf{b}_{imp})-pv^k(\mathbf{a}^{cont},\mathbf{a}_{imp})]/(1-p)$. Consider all sublifetime utility functions $v^k(.)$ such that $d = 0$. These implicitly set zero to the attribute of being dead during some period. Those and only those $u^k(.)$ in $\mathbf{U}^k$ corresponding to these sublifetime utility functions should be included in the zeroed-out $\mathbf{U}^k$.

I do not believe that the premature-death approach to "zeroing out" utility functions is preferable to the approach which asks the respondent for her preferences vis-à-vis nonexistence. In my view, they should be seen as coequal mechanisms, at least in principle. I argued in Chapter 3 that preferences (or at least wishes) vis-à-vis nonexistence are perfectly coherent. But in any event there is clearly no incoherence in asking respondents about their preferences vis-à-vis premature death—and the reader who is concerned about the meaningfulness of the nonexistence question can see the premature-death approach as the main vehicle for "zeroing out."

The reader might worry that a premature-death question, even if conceptually sound, is outlandish. But it should be stressed that the QALY survey format asks the respondent to consider exactly this sort of question. As mentioned, one type of QALY question is a standard-gamble question, which asks individuals to rank lotteries over health states. What the QALY standard gamble asks, specifically, is for the respondent to ascertain the probability p that makes her indifferent between experiencing a given health state for some stipulated period and a lottery with a p chance of perfect health for that period and $(1-p)$ chance of premature death.[105]

The reader may also worry that these techniques for zeroing-out $\mathbf{U}^k$ will leave us with an empty set. For reasons elaborated in the margin, this will not happen.[106]

In short, there is a clear path to "zeroing out" extended utility functions in the case of an outcome set without missing characteristics. So why do missing characteristics pose a problem?

A moment's reflection will show what the problem is. I have argued that arriving at extended preferences vis-à-vis an outcome set with missing characteristics involves

---

[105] A second type of QALY question, the so-called "time tradeoff" question, albeit different from the standard gamble, also involves comparisons between health states and premature death. This question asks the respondent to compare a life in which she lives a certain period of time in perfect health, to one in which she lives a longer period of time in poorer health.

[106] Consider, first, the case where $\mathbf{U}^k$ is unique up to a positive affine transformation. Consider the simplest zeroing-out method: identifying x^* such that k is self-interestedly indifferent between this outcome and nonexistence. Assume that $u^k(.)$ is in $\mathbf{U}^k$ and that $u^k(x^*; k) = e \neq 0$. Then if $w^k(.)$ is an extended utility function such that $w^k(.) = u^k(.) - e$, $w^k(.)$ is a positive affine transformation of $u^k(.)$, hence is in $\mathbf{U}^k$, and is not excluded by the zeroing-out method. A similar analysis holds good for the other methods.

Consider, now, the case in which $\mathbf{U}^k$ is not unique up to a positive affine transformation. In this case, it is "bigger." Why? If $u^k(.)$ is in $\mathbf{U}^k$, then every positive affine transformation of $u^k(.)$ also is, because all of these represent the very same ranking of own-history lotteries and i-history lotteries, and the very same across-person judgments, as $u^k(.)$. Now the analysis of the previous paragraph applies.

an invariance premise. The missing characteristics are supposed to be fixed at some unspecified level. The spectator's own-history preferences, i-history preferences, and across-person judgments must be such that they are the same regardless of the specific level at which the missing characteristics are fixed.

But it is absurd to think that preferences vis-à-vis nonexistence can satisfy this invariance premise. If the spectator is asked to identify an outcome x^* which he sees as equally good as nonexistence, surely his answer to that question is not invariant to characteristics which are missing from the outcome. For example, imagine that outcomes describe individuals' consumption and leisure amounts but not their health states. In x^*, the spectator is characterized as having a given consumption and leisure amount. It is absurd to think that he is indifferent between x^* and nonexistence regardless of whether his health state is good or awful or anything in-between. If he cares about health at all, how could that be true? A similar point is true about the nonexistence gamble question. Imagine that in x the spectator has a certain consumption and leisure amount, and that in y his consumption and leisure is greater. Surely the indifference probability p such that he is indifferent between outcome x and a p chance of outcome y and a $(1 - p)$ chance of nonexistence depends on whether his health state in outcomes x and y is good, awful, or something in-between.

For very similar reasons, it is absurd to think that preferences vis-à-vis premature death satisfy this invariance premise. Imagine that $(\mathbf{a}^{cont}, \mathbf{a}_{imp})$ is a sublifetime bundle. Some of k's characteristics and some facts about the world are not specified. Surely whether the spectator is indifferent between premature death and living a period with $(\mathbf{a}^{cont}, \mathbf{a}_{imp})$ will depend on what the missing attributes are. Imagine, for example, that his social status, consumption, and leisure are specified, but his happiness state is not. Will the spectator be indifferent between living a year with certain status/consumption/leisure attributes and premature death regardless of whether he is very happy or miserable? Will he be indifferent between a year with those attributes, and a p chance of an even higher status/consumption/leisure year and $(1 - p)$ chance of death, regardless of whether the year would involve great happiness or great misery?

These difficulties pose a real challenge—a trilemma of sorts. Information about well-being ratios is vitally relevant (for some SWFs, such as the continuous prioritarian SWF), and thus extended utility functions should be zeroed out (if one finds those SWFs plausible). For reasons of cognitive tractability, outcomes cannot be fully described. Zeroing-out an extended utility function by imagining that preferences vis-à-vis death or nonexistence are invariant to the level of missing characteristics is absurd.

I have no easy solution to this trilemma. Perhaps the best solution is to specify that missing characteristics are set at their most probable level, for purposes of comparisons to premature death or nonexistence. Presumably respondents to QALY surveys instinctively adopt something like this assumption, when asked the standard-gamble question. That question invites the respondent to consider an imperfect health state and perfect health, but says nothing about the non-health attributes that go along with these states. In order to identify a single indifference probability as between the perfect health/death gamble and the imperfect health state, the respondent must make some assumption about what non-health attributes would be paired with perfect health or imperfect health—and presumably assumes that the non-health attributes are just his current non-health attributes.[107]

However, this "solution" is far from fully satisfying. It means that the respondent must exert substantial cognitive effort to arrive at a well-reasoned answer to the "zeroing out" question—above and beyond the effort required by the other questions needed to estimate U^k. Those questions require him to rank various explicitly described possibilities (outcomes and lotteries)—while the "zeroing out" question requires him to do that, *and* to think about what further facts are likely true that bear upon his well-being, and how they would interact with the explicitly described possibilities.

---

[107] A similar assumption is presumably adopted in the case of the time tradeoff.

5

THE CASE FOR A CONTINUOUS PRIORITARIAN SWF

The reader will recall the definition of the SWF framework that I offered in Chapter 2. For a given outcome set **O** and population of individuals, this framework constructs a set **U** of utility functions, which represents the well-being ranking of life-histories. It then ranks the outcome set using the numerical information about well-being contained in **U**. Most simply, an SWF takes the following form: it says that outcome x is morally at least as good as outcome y iff $u(x)$ is ranked at least as good as $u(y)$ according to some rule R, for all $u(.)$ in **U**, where R is a single rule that produces a complete ranking of all utility vectors.[1]

The previous two chapters focused on the construction of the set **U**. This chapter turns to the question of the functional form of the rule R. I will argue that the most attractive such rule is a continuous prioritarian SWF, which says: outcome x is morally at least as good as outcome y iff $\sum_{i=1}^{N} g(u_i(x)) \geq \sum_{i=1}^{N} g(u_i(y))$ for all $u(.)$ in **U**, with the $g(.)$ function strictly increasing and strictly concave. Yet more precisely, the most attractive such rule is a particular kind of continuous prioritarian SWF, namely an "Atkinson" SWF, which says: x is morally at least as good as y iff $(1-\gamma)^{-1} \sum_{i=1}^{N} u_i(x)^{1-\gamma} \geq (1-\gamma)^{-1} \sum_{i=1}^{N} u_i(y)^{1-\gamma}$, for all $u(.)$ in **U**.[2] The γ parameter for the Atkinson SWF is a so-called inequality-aversion parameter that takes some value greater than zero.

My argumentation in favor of a continuous prioritarian SWF, and more specifically an Atkinson SWF, will proceed axiomatically. Because this book works within welfarism, I focus upon SWFs that satisfy minimal welfarist criteria: namely, for any

---

[1] More precisely, R is a rule for ranking all utility vectors in N-dimensional space, or at least all vectors in some orthant. On the features of R, see Chapter 2, pp. 68–72, and also below, n. 155.

[2] In the case where $\gamma=1$, the Atkinson SWF says: x is morally at least as good as y iff $\sum_{i=1}^{N} \ln u_i(x) \geq \sum_{i=1}^{N} \ln u_i(y)$.

given outcome set **O** and set **U** of utility functions, the SWF uses the information in **U** so as to produce a quasiordering of the outcome set; the SWF is "Paretian," i.e., this quasiordering satisfies the axioms of Pareto-indifference and Pareto-superiority; and the SWF is "anonymous," i.e., this quasiordering respects the anonymity axiom, a formal expression of the idea of moral impartiality.[3] Throughout the chapter, I reduce verbiage by using the term "SWF" to mean an SWF that satisfies these minimal welfarist criteria; other types of SWFs are not considered here.

The universe of SWFs (satisfying minimal welfarist criteria) is usefully organized around three axioms: the Pigou–Dalton axiom, an axiom of separability, and a continuity axiom. The Pigou–Dalton principle was discussed in Chapter 2, in connection with inequality metrics. As noted there, the principle can be formulated in terms of different "currencies": in terms of income, health, happiness, well-being, etc. I am interested, in this chapter, in the Pigou–Dalton principle in terms of well-being (which I'll henceforth refer to simply as the "Pigou–Dalton principle," with "well-being" implicit). What it says is that a pure (non-leaky)[4] transfer of well-being, from a better-off to a worse-off individual, which leaves everyone else unaffected, and which leaves the initially better-off individual still at least as well off, yields a better outcome. (By "unaffected," I mean this: An individual is "unaffected," as between outcomes x and y, just in case she is equally well off in x as in y. She is "affected" just in case she is not unaffected, i.e., if she is better off in one outcome than the other, or incomparably well off.) More precisely, the Pigou–Dalton axiom says:

The Pigou–Dalton Principle in Terms of Well-Being

If (1) individual j is better off than individual i in outcome y, and either better off than individual i in outcome x or equally well off; (2) individual i is better off in x than she is in y, while individual j is better off in y than he is in x; (3) the difference between individual i's well-being in x and y is the same as the difference between individual j's

---

[3] On minimal welfarist criteria, see Chapter 1. (But see Peterson [2010], articulating a version of prioritarianism that fails anonymity.) Note that if the SWF assumes the simple R-based form, then it necessarily yields a quasiordering of any outcome set. Moreover, if R is Paretian, and gives an equal ranking to all permutations of any given utility vector, then an SWF with the simple R-based form will necessarily yield a quasiordering of any given outcome set which satisfies the Pareto principle and anonymity.

This chapter will also, to some extent, discuss SWFs that do not assume the simple R-based form—and, in so doing, will use the term "SWF" to mean the subset of *these* SWFs that satisfy minimal welfarist criteria.

[4] In the case of a Pigou–Dalton transfer, the transfer is "pure" in the sense that the transferee's well-being improvement is exactly the same as the transferor's well-being loss. By contrast, in the case of a "leaky" transfer, the transferee gains less than the transferor loses.

well-being in y and x; and (4) everyone else is unaffected as between outcomes y and x; *then x is a morally better outcome than y.*[5]

The Pigou–Dalton axiom is a precise formulation of what it means for an SWF to be sensitive to the distribution of well-being. This formulation might be disputed; it might be argued that an SWF can fail to satisfy the Pigou–Dalton axiom, yet still be characterized as "distribution-sensitive." However, the Pigou–Dalton axiom is indisputably a sufficient (if perhaps not necessary) condition for an SWF to be distribution-sensitive.[6] And it is the Pigou–Dalton axiom, rather than the fuzzier notion of

[5] The Pigou–Dalton principle presupposes some account of well-being that yields a quasiordering of life-histories (and also of differences, because the principle makes reference to well-being differences). The SWF framework employs a set **U** to represent these quasiorderings. See Chapter 2. With such a set **U** in hand, the Pigou–Dalton principle can be formulated in terms of **U**. Consider two outcomes x and y, such that everyone except i and j is unaffected as between x and y. In other words, for each individual k, k distinct from i and j, $u(x; k) = u(y; k)$ for all $u(.)$ belonging to **U**. Imagine further that, for all $u(.)$ belonging to **U**, the following hold true: (1) $u(y; i) \leq u(y; j)$ and $u(x; i) \leq u(x; j)$, with the first inequality strict for at least one $u(.)$; (2) $u(x; i) - u(y; i) = u(y; j) - u(x; j)$; and (3) $u(x; i) \geq u(y; i)$ and $u(y; j) \geq u(x; j)$, with each inequality strict for at least one $u(.)$. The first condition is equivalent to saying that i is worse off than j in outcome y, and either worse off than j in x or equally well off; the second, to saying that the well-being differences between the two outcomes are the same for both individuals; the third, to saying that individual i is better off in x and individual j in y. If all this is true, then the Pigou–Dalton principle requires that x be ranked by the SWF as morally better than y.

Note that the formulation of the Pigou–Dalton principle in the text, and the equivalent formulation in the preceding paragraph, do *not* presuppose that the SWF assumes the simple R-based form. These are generic conditions, which the SWF is required to meet *however* it uses the information in **U** to generate a quasiordering of the outcome set. In the case where the SWF does assume the simple R-based form, the Pigou–Dalton principle is equivalent to the following requirement: if we take a utility vector $(u_1, \ldots, u_j, \ldots, u_i, \ldots, u_N)$, and alter it to $(u_1, \ldots, u_i + \Delta u, \ldots, u_j - \Delta u, \ldots, u_N)$, where $\Delta u > 0$, $u_j > u_i$, and $u_j - \Delta u \geq u_i + \Delta u$, then R ranks the second vector above the first.

[6] Many economists implicitly equate the Pigou–Dalton principle with distribution-sensitivity. In particular, the entire field of inequality metrics presupposes that any plausible such metric will satisfy the Pigou–Dalton principle (in terms of income, utility, or whatever other item is used as the "currency" for the metric). See Chapter 2.

The subtleties involved in defining "distribution-sensitivity" can be simply illustrated by considering SWFs with the R-based form. For purposes of this footnote, assume that u^* and u^{**} are two utility vectors, where u^* has the same total utility as u^{**}, and utility in u^{**} is distributed perfectly equally but not in u^*. Then if R satisfies the Pigou–Dalton principle in ranking utility vectors (as stated in the previous footnote), R necessarily prefers u^{**} to u^*. On the other hand, there can be rules R that fail the Pigou–Dalton principle, but also necessarily prefer u^{**} to u^*. (Consider a rule R which says: u^+ is better than u if total utility in u^+ is larger; if total utility is the same in both vectors, and utility is distributed perfectly equally in u^+ but not u, u^+ is better; otherwise the two are equally good.)

We might therefore be inclined to say that R is "distribution-sensitive" just in case it necessarily prefers u^{**} to u^*. However, there are rules which, with some plausibility, are characterized as "distribution-sensitive" but do not satisfy this requirement—in particular, the rule R used to define the sufficientist SWF (see below). Consider a case in which all entries in both u^{**} and u^* are above the

distribution-sensitivity, which will be a crucial tool in organizing the analysis of this chapter.

The axiom of separability says that the well-being of unaffected individuals does not affect the ranking of outcomes.[7] More precisely:

Separability

Imagine that there are four outcomes in an outcome set, x, y, x^*, y^*, with the following features. First, every individual who is unaffected between x and y is also unaffected between x^* and y^*, and vice versa. Second, for every individual not in this group (i.e., she is affected by the x/y pair, and affected by the x^*/y^* pair), she is situated vis-à-vis the x/y pair exactly the same way as she is situated vis-à-vis the x^*/y^* pair. In other words, she is equally well off in x and x^*, and she is equally well off in y and y^*. Then the x/y pair of outcomes must be ranked the very same way as the x^*/y^* pair (in other words, x is morally at least as good as y iff x^* is morally at least as good as y^*).[8]

---

threshold incorporated in that SWF. If so, the sufficientist SWF will *not* prefer u^{**} to u^*. The sufficientist SWF is distribution-sensitive in the sense that it gives priority to worse-off individuals—but only up to a threshold.

Perhaps, then, a rule R is "distribution-sensitive" just in case it is non-utilitarian: just in case it takes account of the pattern by which utilities are spread across the population, not merely total utility. However, this (very minimal) definition of distribution-sensitivity has the counterintuitive implication that the "leximax" R counts as distribution-sensitive. (On leximax, see Bossert and Weymark [2004, pp. 1111–1115].) So perhaps, finally, a rule R is distribution-sensitive just in case there is *some* pair u^{**} and u^* such that R ranks u^{**} above u^*. This encompassing definition will include the sufficientist R as distribution-sensitive, along with any R that satisfies the Pigou–Dalton principle, but will exclude the utilitarian SWF or leximax.

[7] See Bossert and Weymark (2004, pp. 1153–1154). Separability is a very general idea in economics and philosophy. The "separability" axiom under discussion in this chapter concerns the ranking of *outcomes*; and it requires outcomes to be invariant to the well-being levels of unaffected *individuals*. Separability in *this* specific sense must not be conflated with other sorts of invariance requirements that are also denoted with the same term—for example, separability in the ranking of *life-histories* with respect to *times* or *attributes*, see Chapter 6; or separability in the ranking of *choices* with respect to states of nature, see Broome (1995, chs. 2, 5).

[8] The separability axiom, like the Pigou–Dalton axiom, can be given an equivalent formulation in terms of **U**. Consider four outcomes x, y, x^*, y^* with the following features. Assume first that, for any $i, u(x; i) = u(y; i)$ for all $u(.)$ in **U** just in case $u(x^*; i) = u(y^*; i)$ for all $u(.)$ in **U**. (This is just to say that everyone unaffected between the x/y pair is unaffected between the x^*/y^* pair, and vice versa.) Assume, second, that if j is not in this unaffected group (i.e., $u(x; j) \neq u(y; j)$ for some $u(.)$ in **U**, and $u^+(x^*; j) \neq u^+(y^*; j)$ for some $u^+(.)$ in **U**), then $u(x; j) = u(x^*; j)$ and $u(y; j) = u(y^*; j)$ for all $u(.)$ in **U**. Then the SWF ranks x at least as good as y iff it ranks x^* at least as good as y^*.

Note that I have provided what might be termed a "single profile" definition of separability—one that holds fixed the well-being associated with life-histories—for the same reasons that warrant a single-profile definition of anonymity and welfarism. See Chapter 1, nn. 92, 95.

This definition of separability does not presuppose that the SWF assumes the simple R-based form. If it does assume that form, the definition simplifies to the following. Consider four utility

Finally, the continuity axiom says that a small change in individual utilities does not produce a large change in the moral ranking of outcomes.[9]

I find it particularly useful to distinguish, first, between SWFs that fail to satisfy the Pigou–Dalton principle—most importantly, the utilitarian SWF and a "sufficientist" SWF—and those that do satisfy this important axiom. Second, we can distinguish between Pigou–Dalton respecting SWFs that fail to satisfy the separability axiom—such as the rank-weighted SWF—and SWFs that are *both* Pigou–Dalton respecting and separable. I will term this latter family of SWFs "prioritarian." "Prioritarianism" is a moral view developed within the contemporary philosophical literature, with pioneering contributions by Derek Parfit and Thomas Nagel. Although the precise contours of this view are somewhat contested, it seems clear that the view (in its consequentialist, welfarist variant) requires the ranking of outcomes to be an impartial ranking that satisfies the Pareto principles; that gives greater weight to well-being changes affecting worse-off individuals (an idea axiomatized by the Pigou–Dalton principle); and that is unconcerned with "relativities" (an idea axiomatized by the separability axiom). Hence my use of the term "prioritarian" to refer to Paretian, anonymous SWFs that also satisfy both Pigou–Dalton and separability.

Within the family of prioritarian SWFs we can distinguish between SWFs that fail to satisfy the continuity axiom—such as the leximin SWF or a prioritarian SWF with a lexical threshold—and the continuous prioritarian SWF, which satisfies the

---

vectors u, v, u^*, and v^*, with u_i the i-th entry of u and so forth. Assume, first, that $u_i = v_i$ iff $u_i^* = v_i^*$. Assume, next, that if j is such that $u_j \neq v_j$ (and thus $u_j^* \neq v_j^*$), then $u_j = u_j^*$ and $v_j = v_j^*$. Then R satisfies separability if, in any such case, it says that u is at least as good as v iff it says that u^* is at least as good as v^*.

[9] "Continuity" in social choice theory is typically understood as follows: a complete ordering of all utility vectors in N-dimensional Euclidean space (or of some subset of N-dimensional Euclidean space) is *continuous* iff, for any vector u, the set of vectors that are worse than u, and the set of vectors that are better than u, are each open sets. This, in turn, is true just in case the ordering is representable by a continuous real-valued function. See Blackorby, Bossert, and Donaldson (2005, pp. 70–72, 92); Bossert and Weymark (2004, p. 1108); Kreps (1988, p. 27); Ok (2007, pp. 145–147, 239–242).

I will say that an SWF satisfies the *continuity* axiom iff the complete ordering of utility vectors, produced by the rule R which the SWF incorporates, is continuous. (Note that my formulation of this axiom, by contrast with the Pigou–Dalton and separability axioms, does presuppose that the SWF assumes the simple R-based form.)

As a shorthand, I will often describe an SWF satisfying the continuity axiom as a "continuous" SWF. This terminology, although a useful shorthand, is potentially misleading. It does *not* mean that the possibly incomplete quasiordering of outcomes, produced by the SWF, is somehow "continuous." Although continuity in social choice theory is typically discussed with reference to complete orderings of utility vectors, it *is* possible to characterize a quasiordering of utility vectors as continuous, even if the quasiordering is incomplete. See Ok (2007, p. 145). However, it is meaningless to characterize a quasiordering or complete ordering of *outcomes* as "continuous," absent some metric of distance between the outcomes. Thus, again, by "continuity" of an SWF I simply mean "continuity" of the complete ordering of utility vectors produced by the rule R which the SWF incorporates.

trio of Pigou–Dalton, separability *and* continuity. Finally, the argument for the Atkinson SWF, as opposed to other types of continuous prioritarian SWFs, rests on a fourth axiom, which has not yet been mentioned: invariance of the SWF to ratio rescalings of utility.[10]

Figure 5.1 illustrates the distinctions I have just drawn: distinctions that will organize the argumentation and analysis of the whole chapter.

How shall we steer our way through this landscape? What are the considerations that should prompt us to endorse or reject an axiom and the family of SWFs that the axiom characterizes?

A central theme in this chapter is the idea of *fairness*. An attractive SWF should rank a given set of outcomes in a manner which is fair to the persons who exist in those outcomes—the persons whose well-being depends upon which outcome occurs.

To be sure, "fairness" itself is a contested concept. One conception of fairness is the veil-of-ignorance view, used by both Rawls and Harsanyi. On this view, outcome *x* is fairer than outcome *y* if everyone would choose *x* under a condition of uncertainty regarding her identity. A second conception of fairness is suggested by the

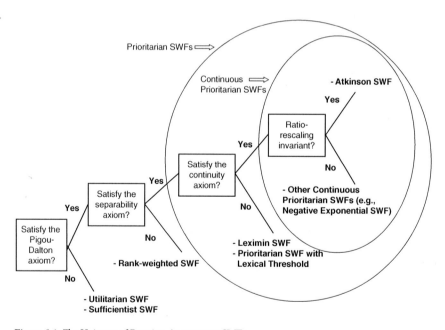

Figure 5.1 The Universe of Paretian, Anonymous SWFs.

[10] For surveys of the existing theoretical literature on SWFs, reviewing many of the possible functional forms for an SWF, see Blackorby, Bossert, and Donaldson (2005, chs. 3–4); Boadway and Bruce (1984, ch. 5); Bossert and Weymark (2004); d'Aspremont and Gevers (2002); Mongin and d'Aspremont (1998); Sen (1986).

work of the philosopher Larry Temkin. In a given outcome, Temkin supposes, worse-off individuals have complaints. Outcome x is fairer than outcome y by virtue of some rule for comparing the overall pattern of complaints in x with the overall pattern of complaints in y. I will term Temkin's view of fairness a "claim-within-outcome" conception of fairness.

However, the conception of fairness that propels the analysis of this chapter (as well as of Chapters 6 and 7) is not a veil-of-ignorance conception or Temkin's claim-within-outcome conception. Rather, it is a third view of fairness. I call this the claim-*across*-outcome view of fairness, and derive it from the work of Thomas Nagel. On this view (by contrast with Temkin's), a "claim" is a relation between a person and a pair of outcomes. A claim has a valence: more precisely, an individual has a claim in favor of the outcome where she is better off. Outcome x is fairer than outcome y if, on balance, the claims in favor of x are stronger than the claims in favor of y.

The chapter begins by describing the different conceptions of fairness and arguing in favor of the claim-across-outcome view. Next, I evaluate the utilitarian SWF and then the sufficientist SWF. Both of these SWFs violate the Pigou–Dalton axiom. A claim-across-outcome conception of fairness provides a very powerful argument for endorsing the Pigou–Dalton axiom, and thus for rejecting both the utilitarian SWF and the sufficientist SWF.

I then turn my attention to the separability axiom. While the claim-across-outcome view offers a clear and compelling case for the Pigou–Dalton axiom, the case it provides for the separability axiom is somewhat less decisive. Still, I shall suggest, anyone who accepts the claim-across-outcome view has good grounds for embracing the separability axiom (and thus for rejecting an SWF that satisfies Pigou–Dalton but fails separability, such as the rank-weighted SWF).

The chapter focuses next on the choice between different types of prioritarian SWFs: a choice which hinges on the different ways in which the leximin SWF, the prioritarian SWF with a lexical threshold, and the continuous prioritarian SWF make tradeoffs (in cases where x and y are Pareto-noncomparable and the Pigou–Dalton principle itself does not determine how x and y should be morally ranked). Finally, I argue that the Atkinson SWF is the most attractive variant of a continuous prioritarian SWF, here defending the axiom of ratio rescaling invariance; and I discuss how we might "calibrate" the Atkinson SWF, i.e., identify a value for the inequality aversion parameter γ.

Some readers might object to my assumption that an SWF takes the simple R-based form I have described. Why not some more complicated method for using the utility information in **U** to rank the outcomes in **O**? For example, why not allow the rule R to vary, depending on which particular utility function $u(.)$ in **U** has given rise to the utility vectors being ranked, as opposed to insisting on a *single* rule R? Or why not allow for the ranking of $u(x)$ versus $u(y)$ to depend on the utility vectors that $u(.)$ assigns to all the outcomes in **O**, not merely to x and y?

Here, I should stress that my argument in favor of the Pigou–Dalton and separability axioms does not rely on the premise that the SWF assumes this simple form. In other words, my defense of *prioritarian* SWFs is wholly independent of the methodology used by the SWF to move from the content of **U** to the ranking of the outcome set. We can eliminate much of the universe of SWFs (those that violate Pigou–Dalton, separability, or both) *without* the premise that the SWF assumes the simple *R*-based form. Rather, I rely upon that premise so as to make further progress *within* the family of prioritarian SWFs—that is, in arguing for a *continuous* prioritarian SWF and, finally, for an Atkinson SWF. In the context of that discussion, I will say something more to justify the premise.[11]

The reader might also wonder why this chapter sets itself the (difficult) task of sorting between SWFs. Why not allow each individual in the population to formulate her own moral preferences and thus to arrive at her own, individual, SWF? And why not rank outcomes by saying that *x* is morally at least as good as *y* iff at least as good according to all the individual SWFs? This important and interesting question raises metaethical questions, and is addressed at the close of the chapter.

It bears emphasis that the analysis in this chapter (as well as Chapters 6 and 7) is almost wholly *independent* of the analysis in Chapters 3 and 4, which developed an extended-preference account of well-being and a corresponding methodology for constructing **U**. The SWF framework requires *some* account of well-being and some matching **U** that functions to represent the well-being rankings of life-histories furnished by that account and to map each outcome onto a (set of) vectors of utility functions. However, virtually nothing in this chapter (or in Chapters 6 or 7) depends upon the particular content of **U**—on whether it embodies a preference-based, hedonic, or objective-good view of human welfare. Whatever the content of **U** and underlying view of well-being, there is good reason to embrace a claim-across-outcome view of fairness; to think that, in virtue of that conception, utility vectors should be ranked in accordance with the Pigou–Dalton axiom and axiom of separability; and to think, finally, that they should be ranked using some continuous prioritarian SWF, more precisely the Atkinson SWF.[12] Or so I shall now attempt to argue.

I. FAIRNESS

A. Fairness and the Separateness of Persons

I use the term "fairness" to mean a distinctive approach to moral evaluation—a distinctive way to think about whether outcomes, actions, and other objects of moral

---

[11] See below, n. 155.

[12] I do rely on the extended-preference account of well-being to argue against the veil-of-ignorance conception of fairness, by pointing out that this account, together with a particular version of that conception (what I term the EPVOI), yields utilitarianism. Even here, however, the extended-preference account is not critical; it would seem that any other account which is risk-neutral in well-being, combined with the EPVOI, also yields utilitarianism. See below, pp. 321–325.

assessment are right or wrong, better or worse. "Fairness," on this usage, is not a particular moral consideration or value (the way that overall well-being is a moral consideration). Nor is "fairness" a particular axiom which an SWF should satisfy (although, as we will see, one or another conception of "fairness" will have implications regarding the attractiveness of different SWF axioms). Rather, "fairness"—as the term is used here—refers to a cluster of concepts and propositions which are helpful in organizing moral thinking.

What, then, *are* the concepts and propositions which are characteristic of moral evaluation oriented to fairness? First, and most importantly, fairness is sensitive to the *separateness of persons*. This idea enters contemporary moral philosophy with Rawls' *Theory of Justice*. Rawls argues that the traditional justification of utilitarianism, which appeals to an impartial spectator, ignores the separateness of persons.

> The most natural way, then, of arriving at utilitarianism . . . is to adopt for society as a whole the principle of rational choice for one man. Once this is recognized, the place of the impartial spectator and the emphasis on sympathy in the history of utilitarian thought is readily understood. . . . It is this spectator who is conceived as carrying out the required organization of the desires of all persons into one coherent system of desire; it is by this construction that many persons are fused into one. Endowed with ideal powers of sympathy and imagination, the impartial spectator is the perfectly rational individual who identifies with and experiences the desires of others as if these desires were his own. In this way he ascertains the intensity of these desires and assigns them their appropriate weight in the one system of desire the satisfaction of which the ideal legislator then tries to maximize by adjusting the rules of the social system. . . The nature of the decision made by the ideal legislator is not, therefore, materially different from that of . . . a consumer deciding how to maximize his satisfaction. . . . [The utilitarian] view of social cooperation is the consequence of extending to society the principle of choice for one man, and then, to make this extension work, conflating all persons into one through the imaginative acts of the impartial sympathetic spectator. Utilitarianism does not take seriously the distinction between persons.[13]

In lieu of the idea of an impartial spectator, Rawls famously proposes the idea of a contract between free and equal individuals in the "original position," behind a "veil of ignorance," as the basis for identifying principles of distributive justice.

---

[13] Rawls (1999b, pp. 23–24). Do Rawls' observations undermine my own use of the ideas of a "spectator" and "sympathy" in Chapters 3 and 4? No—because I stress the multiplicity of spectators and, much more fundamentally, because I use these ideas to develop an account of interpersonally comparable *well-being* (to construct **U**), and not directly to determine the ranking of outcomes. As explained in this chapter, the fair ranking of outcomes is determined by balancing individual claims across outcomes (with well-being as the currency for claims), *not* by seeing how an impartial, sympathetic spectator would rank outcomes.

Critically—for our purposes—Rawls characterizes the veil-of-ignorance construct as a *fair* procedure for arriving at principles of justice or other moral principles.

> Among the essential features of [the original position] is that no one knows his place in society, his class position or social status, nor does anyone know his fortune in the distribution of natural assets and abilities, his intelligence, strength, and the like. I shall even assume that the parties do not know their conceptions of the good or their special psychological propensities. The principles of justice are chosen behind a veil of ignorance. This ensures that no one is advantaged or disadvantaged in the choice of principles by the outcome of natural chance or the contingency of social circumstances. Since all are similarly situated and no one is able to design principles to favor his particular condition, the principles of justice are the result of a fair agreement or bargain. For given the circumstances of the original position, the symmetry of everyone's relations to each other, this initial situation is fair between individuals as moral persons, that is, as rational beings with their own ends and capable . . . of a sense of justice.[14]

And Rawls refers to the conception of distributive justice defended by *A Theory of Justice* using the term "justice as fairness,"[15] so as to underscore the fact that this conception respects the separateness of persons.

Thomas Nagel, too, has emphasized the separateness of persons as a desideratum for moral evaluation. Nagel writes:

> [An impartial] concern for everyone has to be particularized: It must contain a separate and equal concern for each person's good. When we occupy the impersonal standpoint, our impartial concern for each person exists side by side with our concern for every other person. These concerns should not be conglomerated. Even though we cannot contain all these separate lives together in our imagination, their separateness must be preserved somehow in the system of impersonal values which impartiality generates. . . .
>
>   The fundamental point about individualized impartial concern is that it generates a large set of separate values corresponding to separate lives, and we must then make a further judgment about how to decide the inevitable conflicts among them. We cannot simply assume that they are to be combined like vectors of force, which add together or cancel one another out. That is the utilitarian solution, but it seems in fact the wrong way to treat them.[16]

This feature of fairness—its sensitivity to the "separateness of persons"—is connected to two others. First, if *r* is fairer than *s*, where *r* and *s* are objects of moral assessment (outcomes, choices, etc.,), then morally favoring *r* as opposed to *s* can be

---

[14] Rawls (1999b, p. 11). On the possibility of using the veil of ignorance to arrive at other moral principles, see Rawls' discussion of "rightness as fairness," ibid., pp. 93–98.

[15] Ibid., pp. 10–15.

[16] Nagel (1995, pp. 66–67). See generally ibid, ch. 7; Nagel (1979).

justified to each person, from that person's perspective. The idea that there is a core of moral principles which are "justifiable to" each person is the centerpiece of Tim Scanlon's philosophical work on contractualism, and is also evident in Nagel.[17]

Second, norms identifying fair behavior are norms *for* a community of individuals. Imagine that some set of choice-evaluation principles has been arrived at in a manner which is sensitive to the proposition that each member of a group of persons is a separate person, and that these principles should be justifiable to each person in that group, from her perspective. Then each member of the community can be expected to act upon the principles—to have the principles play an important (and perhaps decisive) role in her normative deliberations. In other words, moral principles, by virtue of being fair to some group of persons, generate *reasons* for conformity among that group.[18]

Thus far, I have simply characterized "fairness"—as a species of moral evaluation oriented around the separateness of persons, delivering moral verdicts that are justifiable to each person, and furnishing reasons for each person. I have not yet argued *for* fairness. Why believe that moral reasoning or some portion thereof should have these features?

I suggested in Chapter 1 that there is a strong link between person-centered moral views and fairness. It is very plausible to think that persons, uniquely, are the subjects of fairness. This is, in fact, the position that is taken by both Rawls

---

[17] Scanlon's contractualist account of morality is presented in Scanlon (1998). On moral rules as being justifiable to each person, see in particular ibid., ch. 4. Nagel, too, writes that respect for the separateness of persons means determining which alternative is acceptable to each person. See Nagel (1979, p. 123).

Unlike Rawls, Scanlon and Nagel do not characterize their views as grounded in "fairness," but I take this difference to be merely semantic because—like Rawls—they are clearly concerned to elaborate the distinctive kind of moral assessment that flows from the separateness of persons.

[18] This is a central theme in Scanlon's work. See Scanlon (1998, ch. 4). The reader might wonder whether this putative feature of fairness meshes with a wide range of metaethical views. (Remember that this book is meant to be neutral on metaethical issues.) For example, how can the noncognitivist make sense of the notion that some moral consideration generates "reasons" for a group? I believe that the feature of fairness now under consideration *is* consistent with a range of metaethical views, but cannot pursue the issue here. In any event, the most central idea of fairness—trying to come up with moral considerations that respect the separateness of persons—certainly is.

It might also be objected that the SWF framework provides principles for *large-scale* choices. (See Chapter 1.) In what sense, then, does a fairness-based defense of this framework demonstrate that everyone in the community has reason to act upon the framework—since private individuals are surely not expected to use the framework as a source of moral guidance in their daily lives? It seems to me that a comprehensive fairness-based defense of some SWF *does* need to specify companion principles to guide ordinary individuals. However, it is beyond the scope of this book to tackle this problem—to propose prioritarian moral norms that could guide ordinary individuals in addressing "small scale" choices, and that would function as companion principles to the continuous prioritarian SWF. In this respect (as many others), the book is incomplete.

and Scanlon.[19] In other words, choices, outcomes, etc., are not properly characterizable as more or less fair *to* beings other than persons, in particular non-human beings that are sentient and possess a well-being but are not persons (for short, "animals"). One can harm an animal, but one cannot act unfairly toward an animal. Animals are not capable of normative deliberation, and so choices, outcomes, etc., cannot be justified to animals. Nor can the fairness of some behavioral norm provide a reason for an animal to comply with the norm, since animals are not guided by reason.

To be sure, it is possible to endorse the premise that morality is exclusively person-centered but also deny that fairness has moral relevance. However, this combination of views is hard to justify. Since animals can possess a well-being, why exclude animals from the moral universe if not for the reason that fairness is central to morality, and that animals are not subjects of fairness?

In short, the most attractive specification of a person-centered moral view is sensitive to considerations of fairness. The project of this book is, indeed, to take as given that morality is person-centered (as well as consequentialist and welfarist) and to ascertain how such a view is best specified. What this particular chapter asks is: Understanding the SWF framework as a way to flesh out person-centered welfarism, what is the most attractive functional form for an SWF? I will therefore presuppose that the most attractive functional form for an SWF is responsive to fairness.

To be sure, the reader who is dubious about person-centered moral views—who believes that animals do fall within the moral community—might just reject the project of this book. For such a reader, an SWF (which ranks outcomes and choices as a function of utility numbers measuring the well-being of *persons*) cannot be seen as a *complete* tool for moral assessment. Rather, SWFs are at best devices that enable us to morally rank outcomes and choices *insofar* as persons are involved. An all-things-considered moral evaluation of an outcome, a choice, or some other item needs to bring into play both an SWF (or some such person-centered evaluation tool) *and* the well-being of animals.

However, even this reader should acknowledge—on intuitive grounds—that morality should incorporate considerations of fairness. An SWF which purports to identify the moral ranking of outcomes and choices insofar as persons are involved, but shows no concern for whether those outcomes and choices are more or less fair to those persons, is counterintuitive and should be rejected. Whether or not moral assessment is *exhausted* by the question of fairness, surely it should be *possible* to criticize some choice or consequence as being morally problematic in virtue of being unfair.

Two other points about the moral relevance of fairness were noted in Chapter 1, but bear repeating. First, there is no inconsistency between fairness and *consequentialism*. The case for consequentialism—for structuring moral assessment around an

---

[19] See Chapter 1, explaining that, for Rawls, animals lie outside the scope of justice; and that Scanlon is inclined to agree with the proposition that our conduct need not be justifiable to animals. See Rawls (1999b, pp. 15, 441, 448); Scanlon (1998, pp. 177–187).

impartial ranking of outcomes—flows from very basic premises concerning ratio-nality. Very plausibly, a decisionmaker's action is *rational* because of its location in a ranking of possible actions; possible actions, in turn, are rationally ordered in light of the outcomes that the actions might produce. It would be very odd to think that these foundational, generic, ideas about rationality are somehow inconsistent with the separateness of persons. And indeed they are not. A moral view which conjoins fairness and consequentialism is a view which (1) requires the moral ranking of outcomes to respect the separateness of persons[20], and (2) uses that fair outcome-ranking to determine how choices morally compare in any given choice situation, and thereby to determine which choice morally ought to be performed. What it means, concretely, for a ranking of outcomes to "respect the separateness of persons" is a topic that we are about to engage in detail.

Second, there is no inconsistency between fairness and *welfarism*. The welfarist requires the ranking of outcomes to supervene upon individual well-being. Unless there is some well-being difference between two outcomes, the two outcomes are equally morally good—a requirement captured by the Pareto-indifference axiom. Why would a moral theory concerned to arrive at a fair ranking of outcomes accept this axiom? Plausibly, well-being opportunity (not money or other "resources") is the appropriate *currency* for fairness. Outcome x is fairer than outcome y in virtue of more fairly allocating opportunities for individual flourishing, among the totality of persons in the population.

Admittedly, welfarism and the SWF framework—as I have defined these con-cepts in this book—rank outcomes in light of well-being, not well-being opportu-nity. Imagine that in outcome x, Able behaves responsibly and realizes a high level of well-being, while Baker wastes her resources and ends up badly off. In outcome y, both individuals make prudent choices, with Able ending up at the same (high) level of well-being he has in x, and Baker—through bad luck—also ending up at the same (low) level of well-being she has in x. If everyone else is unaffected, welfarism (and the SWF framework) are committed to ranking x and y as equally morally good. But surely there is a moral difference qua fairness between the outcomes.[21]

For this reason—as explained in Chapter 1—I see the SWF approach as a first step toward a yet more attractive choice-evaluation tool, which *will* register facts about responsibility and not just facts about welfare. Still, the recognition that it is well-being opportunity—not well-being simpliciter—which constitutes the appro-priate "currency" for fairness does not preclude us from drawing upon the idea of fairness to specify an SWF. We can think of an SWF as an *approximate* tool for ranking a given outcome set $\mathbf{O}$, where some of the outcomes are such that some

---

[20] And other fairness subjects, if such exist and are within the scope of morality. A non-person-centered understanding of the scope of morality, plus a view of fairness which sees both persons and animals as its subjects, plus consequentialism, would add up to a moral view that requires the ranking of outcomes to respect the separateness of persons and other fairness subjects.

[21] See, e.g., Arneson (2000b); Nagel (1995, p. 71).

individuals are (partly or wholly) responsible for being less well off in those outcomes than they might have been; and as an *exact* tool for ranking an outcome set **O**, where no individual in any outcome is responsible for her well-being in this sense. The latter case is the following: for each outcome x in **O**, and for each individual i in the population, it is the case that—were x to obtain—any shortfall between i's well-being level in x and a higher level would be a matter of "brute luck." That shortfall would not be properly seen as attributable, in any way, to i's poor choices and, thus, would not be her (sole or partial) responsibility.[22]

Throughout the remainder of this chapter (in considering the appropriate functional form for an SWF) as well as in the subsequent two chapters (in addressing the appropriate "time slice" for SWFs and the principles for applying an SWF under uncertainty) I will assume that outcomes do indeed have the "brute luck" feature just described. If no individual in any outcome in **O** would be responsible for her well-being shortfall, ranking the outcomes as a function of persons' well-being (which is what the SWF approach does) produces the very same ranking as if the outcomes were ranked in light of persons' well-being opportunity. In this idealized case, the SWF approach should be seen as fully justifiable even by the responsibility-sensitive welfarist. While the assumption that outcomes have the "brute luck" feature *is* certainly a kind of idealization—the actual outcome sets which policymakers face are not like this—using this idealization to think about the appropriate functional form of an SWF is no more problematic than the widespread use of simplified cases in moral philosophy to sharpen and clarify our moral thinking.

In particular, I argue in this chapter and the subsequent two that the appropriate SWF for the "brute luck" case is a continuous prioritarian SWF applied to lifetime utilities, and used to generate a choice ranking from the outcome ranking in conformity with expected utility (EU) theory. Decisionmakers, facing choices that lack the "brute luck" feature, can then employ this choice-evaluation framework as an approximation. Or, even better, they can improve upon it, by reworking the continuous prioritarian SWF so as to take account of the fact that individuals are, to some extent, responsible for their well-being shortfalls. (See Chapter 8.)

So where have we arrived? At this destination: an attractive ranking of outcomes by an SWF should be sensitive to considerations of fairness, meaning in particular that the SWF ranks different allocations of well-being (taken as a proxy for well-being opportunity) in a manner which reflects the separateness of persons.

We can now ask: what does it mean for a ranking of items—in particular, the ranking of outcomes by an SWF–to "reflect the separateness of persons?" Rawls and

---

[22] Temkin adopts a similar approach in *Inequality*. He focuses on an "impersonal teleological" version of egalitarianism, specifically one that says "undeserved inequality is always objectionable"; and, in order to flesh out this view, uses simplified examples where "people are equally skilled, hard-working, morally worthy, and so forth, so that those who are worse off than others are so through no fault of their own." Temkin (1996b, pp. 12, 17).

Nagel put great weight on this concept, as have I, following their distinguished lead; but what, really, is its content?

A ranking reflects the separateness of persons if it sees each person as a distinct locus of moral claims or morally relevant interests. This is a highly abstract idea, which can be fleshed out in a variety of more specific ways. I now discuss three different ways to do so: three different *conceptions* of the separateness of persons, suggested by the literature. These three conceptions are, first, the veil-of-ignorance conception put forth by Rawls and Harsanyi; second, the claim-within-outcome conception suggested by Temkin; and finally, the claim-*across*-outcome conception suggested by Nagel. I will argue for the last.

B. Three Conceptions of Fairness: Veil of Ignorance, Claims within Outcomes, Claims across Outcomes

Consider, first, the veil-of-ignorance conception of fairness, adapted for the task at hand (ranking outcomes as a function of well-being). And let us start with the version of the veil-of-ignorance construct offered by Harsanyi rather than Rawls. On the Harsanyi interpretation, a person adopts the veil-of-ignorance perspective on a given outcome by viewing that outcome as an equiprobability lottery over its component life-histories.[23] In other words (given a fixed population of N persons), outcome x is conceptualized as a lottery with a $1/N$ probability of life-history $(x; 1)$, a $1/N$ probability of life-history $(x; 2)$,..., a $1/N$ probability of life-history $(x; N)$. Outcome y is conceptualized as a $1/N$ probability of life-history $(y; 1)$, a $1/N$ probability of life-history $(y; 2)$,..., a $1/N$ probability of life-history $(y; N)$. According to Harsanyi, moral judgments are most perspicuously understood in terms of the veil of ignorance thus construed. A given spectator, k, has a moral preference for outcome x over outcome y just in case k prefers the equiprobability life-history lottery corresponding to x to the equiprobability life-history lottery corresponding to y.

One skeptical objection, here, concerns the coherence of the idea of a preference for life-histories. How can spectator k prefer life-history $(x; i)$ to life-history $(y; j)$? Since it is impossible for spectator k to change his identity, how are such preferences meaningful? I have proposed an answer to this skeptical question in Chapter 3[24];

---

[23] See Harsanyi (1953; 1955; 1982; 1986, ch. 4). See also Weymark (1991), explicating Harsanyi's account; and the critical literature on Harsanyi cited in Chapter 3, n. 88.

[24] The answer is just this: (1) Rather than asking a spectator k to imagine changing his identity, or to rank outcomes under a condition of ignorance about who he is (for the latter approach, see Chapter 3, n. 110), we can instead ask k to rank outcomes and outcome lotteries under a condition of self-interest, and under conditions of i-interest directed, in turn, at every other individual i in the population, thereby arriving at spectator k's own-history and "i-history" preferences. (2) We can construct a set $\mathbf{U}^k$ which summarizes these extended preferences as well as k's across-person judgments. This set will typically be unique up to a positive affine transformation. (3) We can use $\mathbf{U}^k$ to define k's preferences over mixed-history lotteries. (A "mixed-history" lottery l is such that the life-histories to

and in what follows, I will assume that this approach is used to make sense of the idea of extended preferences, preferences for life-histories.

Let us therefore float the following Harsanyi-esque proposal: x is morally at least as good as y iff all spectators would weakly prefer the equiprobability life-history lottery corresponding to x over the equiprobability life-history lottery corresponding to y. For short, call this the "equiprobabilist" veil-of-ignorance (EPVOI) view of the moral ranking of outcomes. Note how such a specification of moral goodness is plausibly "sensitive to the separateness of persons." A given spectator evaluates outcome x by separately attending to each of its component life-histories. Each is given an equal weight (via the device of according each the same, $1/N$, probability). The equiprobability lottery has a distinct "slot" for each life-history, and an equal role for each. Moreover (on the EPVOI view) outcome x is not morally better than y unless *all of the spectators* concur in preferring x to y.[25]

But there is a grave difficulty with this approach to modeling fairness. Consider combining the EPVOI view (which is a view about the moral ranking of outcomes) with the account of *well-being* proposed in Chapter 3: an account that analyzes the *well-being* of life-histories in terms of spectators' extended preferences. The upshot is utilitarianism. *If* the well-being levels of life-histories and the well-being differences between life-histories are represented by utility numbers that expectationally represent spectators' extended preferences (the account of well-being I defended in Chapter 3), *and* if in addition the moral ranking of outcomes depends upon seeing those outcomes as equiprobability lotteries over their component life-histories, then (not surprisingly) the moral ranking of outcomes corresponds to the utilitarian SWF. (See the margin for details.)[26]

which it assigns non-zero probability do not all have the same particular individual as subject. Note that an equiprobability lottery over the component life-histories of some outcome x—a $1/N$ probability of life-history $(x; 1)$, a $1/N$ probability of life-history $(x; 2)$, ..., a $1/N$ probability of life-history $(x; N)$—is a kind of mixed-history lottery.) We can say that k weakly prefers mixed-history lottery l to mixed-history lottery l^*, according to some $u^k(.)$ in $\mathbf{U}^k$, just in case the expected utility of l according to $u^k(.)$ is at least as large as the expected utility of l^*. Note that, if $\mathbf{U}^k$ is unique up to a positive affine transformation, each member of $\mathbf{U}^k$ generates the very same ranking of life-histories and lotteries. So in this case we can say: k weakly prefers mixed-history lottery l to l^* just in case the expected utility of l is at least as large as the expected utility of l^* according to *any* $u^k(.)$ in $\mathbf{U}^k$.

[25] I do not mean, here, to summarize Harsanyi's actual views about the EPVOI. Unlike Rawls, Harsanyi does not stress the need for morality to be "fair" and "respect the separateness of persons." Rather, my suggestion is that the EPVOI could plausibly be understood as a specification of fairness.

[26] The utilitarian SWF says: x is morally at least as good as y iff $\sum_{i=1}^{N} u_i(x) \geq \sum_{i=1}^{N} u_i(y)$, for all $u(.)$ in $\mathbf{U}$. According to the account of well-being proposed in Chapter 3, $\mathbf{U}$ is formed as follows. Each spectator has a set $\mathbf{U}^k$ that represents his extended preferences. $\mathbf{U}^k$ is normally unique up to a positive affine transformation, and I'll simplify matters by assuming that here; so, more precisely, each spectator's extended preferences are expectationally represented by each $u^k(.)$ in $\mathbf{U}^k$. $\mathbf{U}$ is the union of all the

This result did not bother Harsanyi. Harsanyi tried to argue *for* utilitarianism by combining a EPVOI conception of the moral ranking of outcomes with something like the account of well-being defended in Chapter 3. However, the result will surely discombobulate many readers—and discombobulates this author. Intuitively, the utilitarian SWF and the fair ranking of outcomes *can* diverge. In other words, it is intuitively possible for x to be fairer than y even though total well-being is greater in y than x, in virtue of the fact that well-being is more fairly distributed in x. Consider, by way of illustration, the following case, in which we move from a massively unequal distribution of well-being, to a perfectly equal distribution, at only a small loss in total well-being.

Assume that, in outcome y, some portion of the population is many times better off than the remainder of the population; in outcome x, well-being is equalized at some level only slightly below the average level of well-being in y. Concretely, assume that $\mathbf{U}$ is unique up to a positive ratio transformation[27]; that the population consists of $2M$ individuals; that half the population in y is at well-being level $1r$, while the other half is 10 times better off, at level $10r$; and that in x everyone is at level $5r$. The utilitarian SWF says that y is a better outcome than x. But, surely, the distribution of well-being in x is, on balance, more fair (at least assuming that the worse-off individuals in y are not responsible for their plight). We have moved from a 10-fold disparity in well-being between the two halves of the population, to a perfectly equal distribution. Moreover, total well-being in x is nearly equal to that in y (on these facts, the ratio of total well-being in x to total well-being in y is $10/11$).

$\mathbf{U}^k$ (strictly, the union of all the $\mathbf{U}^k$ after each is "zeroed out"—but the analysis about to be presented does not depend upon that).

Consider, now, the EPVOI view of the moral ranking of outcomes combined with the account just summarized of the construction of $\mathbf{U}$. The EPVOI, as I have formulated it, accommodates the possibility of divergent spectator extended preferences by saying the following: (1) outcome x is morally at least as good as outcome y iff *every* spectator weakly prefers the equiprobability lottery with probability $1/N$ for each of outcome x's component life-histories, to the equiprobability lottery with probability $1/N$ for each of outcome y's component life-histories. Because each spectator k's extended preferences are represented by any $u^k(.)$ in $\mathbf{U}^k$, proposition (1) is true just in case (2): For each k and any $u^k(.)$ in $\mathbf{U}^k$, $(1/N)\sum_{i=1}^{N}u^k(x;i) \geq (1/N)\sum_{i=1}^{N}u^k(y;i)$. Given the account just summarized of the construction of $\mathbf{U}$, proposition (2) in turn is true just in case: (3) For all $u(.)$ in $\mathbf{U}$, $(1/N)\sum_{i=1}^{N}u(x;i) \geq (1/N)\sum_{i=1}^{N}u(y;i)$. But (multiplying each side of the equation by N), that is true just in case x is ranked morally at least as good as y by the utilitarian SWF. See also Moreno-Ternero and Roemer (2008), arguing against Harsanyi's veil of ignorance as a conception of justice because it is anti-prioritarian.

[27] This means that the utility of a given life-history can be represented in a form such as "$15r$," meaning that some utility function $u(.)$ in $\mathbf{U}$ assigns the life-history the number 15, and every other utility function in $\mathbf{U}$ assigns it some positive multiple r of the number 15.

If one combines the EPVOI conception of the moral ranking of outcomes with the view of well-being defended in Chapter 3, it becomes impossible—even in such a case—to conclude that an outcome has less total well-being than a second but is nonetheless the fairer outcome.

How might the proponent of the veil-of-ignorance conception of fairness resist the conclusion that it yields the utilitarian SWF? She might resist that conclusion by offering a different understanding of the veil of ignorance, a different view of well-being, or both.

The first possibility, of course, is pursued by Rawls. Rawls argues for a nonprobabilist veil of ignorance (for short, NPVOI). The individuals in Rawls' original position are supposed to choose among different possible principles of justice without knowing their actual attributes (their actual social status, income, physical strength, intelligence, etc.) *and* without ascribing precise probabilities to those attributes.[28] However, the NPVOI seems a dubious construal of fairness—at a minimum, a dubious construal of fairness for welfarist purposes (as opposed to Rawls' aims in *A Theory of Justice*).[29] The veil of ignorance (for our purposes) would be a way to regiment individuals' evaluation of outcomes, so that they do so even-handedly. By putting an appropriately constructed veil over each spectator, each would be constrained to rank the outcomes without being partial to his own interests or anyone else's. But isn't the most straightforward way to model such even-handedness just to enjoin k to give an equal *probability* to each of the life-histories in a given outcome x? Why is telling him to think of x as some kind of nonprobabilistic combination of its component life-histories a more perspicuous way to regiment his moral thinking?[30]

The debate between Harsanyi and Rawls—between the EPVOI and the NPVOI—is well known. Sometimes, that debate is conflated with a different one: the debate between strict "Bayesians," who believe that rational decisionmakers always have precise probabilities, and their opponents, who deny that. The strict Bayesian view is too rigid.[31] But the proponent of the EPVOI surely need not rely on strict Bayesianism. She can freely acknowledge that, in some choice situations, it is

---

[28] See Rawls (1999b, pp. 118–123, 130–153). For a discussion of these features of the veil of ignorance, see S. Freeman (2007, pp. 154–160, 167–180).

[29] Rawls is not a welfarist, and he relies upon the NPVOI in *A Theory of Justice* as a basis for ranking principles of justice, not outcomes. I see no reason why the NPVOI would be more attractive in this context than within welfarism; but my argumentation here can be agnostic on that question. All I need claim is that the NPVOI is an unattractive construal of fairness for purposes of welfarism.

[30] Alternatively, one could grant that the NPVOI may be a better construal of the veil of ignorance, but point out that this approach to ranking outcomes may well lead to leximin, and that leximin itself is a problematic SWF, in virtue of giving absolute priority to worse-off individuals. See below, criticizing the leximin SWF. This would be an alternative route to arguing against the veil-of-ignorance conception of fairness, in favor of the claim-within-outcome or claim-across-outcome conceptions discussed below. Cf. Gajdos and Kandil (2008), arguing that conceptualizing the veil of ignorance as involving sets of probabilities yields a weighted average of utilitarianism and maximin.

[31] See Chapter 7.

rationally permissible for the decisionmaker to lack precise probabilities. She can stress, instead, that the VOI is one particular choice situation—specifically, a, *hypothetical* choice situation, which uses the lottery device so as to "force" a spectator's ranking of outcomes to be fair. In *that* context, she can argue, it is perfectly appropriate to model the equality of the different subjects of life-histories by enjoining the spectator to accord each life-history a precise, exogenous probability, namely $1/N$.

The second way to block the inference from the veil-of-ignorance construal of fairness to utilitarianism is to reject the view of well-being tendered in Chapter 3. On this view, spectators are "risk neutral" in well-being. The utility numbers that expectationally represent spectators' preferences over life-history lotteries are the very same numbers that represent well-being differences between histories. Imagine relaxing this assumption. For example, imagine that both of the following are true. (1) There is some objective-good theory of well-being W^* which provides a basis for ranking life-histories, differences, and comparisons to the zero point that is independent of spectators' preferences. W^* is represented by a function $v^*(x; i)$, which is unique up to a positive ratio transformation. (2) Fully rational spectators, ranking lotteries over life-histories, are *risk-averse* in $v^*(.)$.

These premises about well-being, together with the EPVOI, do not yield the utilitarian SWF. Instead, they yield a prioritarian SWF, as should be intuitively clear and is elaborated in the margin.[32]

---

[32] If the correct theory of well-being is W^*, as described, then the well-being associated with life-histories is represented by a set $\mathbf{V}$ consisting of $v^*(.)$ and all positive ratio transformations thereof; $rv^*(.)$ denotes $v^*(.)$ multiplied by a positive number r. Assume that every spectator k, if fully informed, has a set $\mathbf{U}^k$ such that, for every $u^k(.)$ in $\mathbf{U}^k$, $u^k(.) = f(v^*(.))$ or $u^k(.) = f(rv^*(.))$, where $f(.)$ is a strictly concave function. This is just what it means for the spectator to be "risk averse" in $v^*(.)$. (To say that "$u^k(.) = f(v^*(.))$" is just shorthand for the following: for all life-histories $(x; i)$, $u^k(x; i) = f(v^*(x; i))$.)

For simplicity, assume that spectators' extended preferences are identical, so that there is a single set $\mathbf{U}$ representing them. Assume also that the spectator's ranking of life-histories and lotteries is the same regardless of whether he uses the $f(.)$ function applied to $v^*(.)$ or to any other member of $\mathbf{V}$. This latter assumption means that the spectator's utility function is "Atkinsonian." In other words, there is some $u(.)$ such that $u(.) = (1-\gamma)^{-1}(v^*(.)^{1-\gamma})$, for γ some positive value. $\mathbf{U}$, in turn, consists of all positive ratio transformations of $u(.)$. (Cf. below, p. 387, discussing the ratio-rescaling-invariance properties of the Atkinson SWF.)

Consider now the EPVOI construal of the moral ranking of outcomes. In the context at hand (because every spectator's extended preferences are represented by any member of $\mathbf{U}$), this says: (1) outcome x is morally at least as good as y iff $(1/N)\sum_{i=1}^{N}u(x;i) \geq (1/N)\sum_{i=1}^{N}u(y;i)$. That in turn is true just in case (2) $(1/N)(1-\gamma)^{-1}\sum_{i=1}^{N}v^*(x;i)^{1-\gamma} \geq (1/N)(1-\gamma)^{-1}\sum_{i=1}^{N}v^*(y;i)^{1-\gamma}$. Because $\mathbf{V}$ consists of $v^*(.)$ and all positive ratio transformations, it is the case that $(1-\gamma)^{-1}\sum_{i=1}^{N}v^*(x;i)^{1-\gamma} \geq (1-\gamma)^{-1}\sum_{i=1}^{N}v^*(y;i)^{1-\gamma}$ iff $(1-\gamma)^{-1}\sum_{i=1}^{N}v(x;i)^{1-\gamma} \geq (1-\gamma)^{-1}\sum_{i=1}^{N}v(y;i)^{1-\gamma}$ for all $v(.)$ in $\mathbf{V}$. But this final formula is exactly how a *prioritarian* SWF (specifically, an Atkinson SWF) would rank x versus y, using $\mathbf{V}$ as the set of functions measuring well-being.

But the view of well-being tendered in Chapter 3 is, at a minimum, a plausible view. Even if one rejects the particulars of that view, it is quite plausible that spectators ranking life-history lotteries would be risk-neutral in well-being. *Any* account of well-being which has this risk-neutrality feature, when combined with the EPVOI construal of the veil of ignorance, will justify the utilitarian SWF.

In short, one breaks the inferential path from a veil-of-ignorance conception of fairness, to utilitarianism, only by adopting a contestable premise about well-being (that spectators depart from risk-neutrality) or by rejecting the simple and elegant device of using equal probabilities to model the equal moral status of the subjects of life-histories. For those who are convinced that utilitarianism can be faulted on distributive grounds—that one outcome can be fairer than a second even though it contains less total well-being—the nexus between utilitarianism and the veil-of-ignorance conception of fairness provides sufficient grounds to reject that conception.

In short (and this is a point which it is absolutely vital for the reader to understand): this book uses Harsanyi's idea of extended preferences, in Chapter 3, to develop a measure of the well-being associated with life-histories; but it emphatically does *not* employ the Harsanyi/Rawls construct of the veil of ignorance as the basis for morally ranking outcomes. I adopt a two-stage approach. As per the SWF tradition, I use a utility metric (encapsulated in the set **U**) to assign numbers to individual life-histories, and thus to represent outcomes as vectors of utilities; but the conception of fairness that I employ to make moral comparisons between utility vectors is *not* the veil-of-ignorance conception.

Let us turn, then, to two alternative ways of understanding fairness: Temkin's view and Nagel's view. Both approaches clearly justify *some* kind of non-utilitarian SWF. The approaches differ from each other in structure, and in the SWF axioms they support, but both, clearly, will sometimes rank x as fairer than y even though total well-being is greater in y than x.

In his influential book, *Inequality*, and subsequent writings, Temkin develops a view of fairness which he calls "comparative fairness."[33] For reasons that will emerge in a moment, this term is potentially misleading, and I will instead generally refer to Temkin's view as the "claim-within-outcome conception" of fairness. Temkin states

---

Grant and co-authors (2010a, 2010b) provide a different argument for why the EPVOI might yield a prioritarian SWF. Harsanyi assumes that the spectator's preferences over life-history lotteries satisfy an independence axiom, governing mixtures of lotteries (the independence axiom is at the core of EU theory); and on my account of the content of such preferences, as expectationally represented by a set $\mathbf{U}^k$, independence is also satisfied (at least if $\mathbf{U}^k$ is unique up to a positive affine or ratio transformation). Grant and co-authors relax the independence axiom, by allowing for what they term a strict "preference for life chances."

[33] See Temkin (1996b, 2000, 2003a, 2003b), as well as his multiple contributions to a symposium on his work in *Theoria* (2003, vol. 69, pp. 1–151). An earlier version of some of the material in the book is Temkin (1986). For the term "comparative fairness," see, e.g., Temkin (2003b, p. 62).

quite explicitly that the claim-within-outcome conception ("comparative fairness") can be employed as a basis for ranking *outcomes*, with well-being (adjusted for individual desert and responsibility) employed as the "currency" for fairness.[34] So my own use of the claim-within-outcome view in this manner is hardly artificial.

Temkin explains: "[C]oncern about equality is a portion of our concern about fairness that focuses on how people fare relative to others. So, our concern for equality is not separable from our concern for a certain aspect of fairness; they are part and parcel of a single concern. Egalitarians in my sense generally believe that it is bad for some to be worse off than others through no fault or choice of their own."[35] He illustrates the idea with the following example:

> This example concerns a fairly "typical" poor person in the United States, whom I shall call "Ruth." Ruth is not wretched, but she is a single parent of four, works at two jobs, drives an old car, worries how she will meet the payments on her two bedroom apartment, and has no idea how her children will afford college on her $20,000 income. Many are deeply moved by the plight of people like Ruth in a land where *so* many others live in half million dollar homes, own fancy new cars, send their children to private schools, take expensive vacations, and have household incomes well over $100,000.
>
> Is it not clear that the extent to which many are moved by Ruth's situation is heavily influenced not merely by how she fares in *absolute* terms, but by how she fares *relative to other members of her extraordinarily well-off society?* After all, we may suppose, at least Ruth has a roof over her head, indoor plumbing, a telephone, a TV and a car. Moreover, she is not living in a war-torn country, or ruled by a dictator, and she need not fear smallpox, tuberculosis, malaria or diphtheria. She drinks safe water, eats three meals daily, and has a reasonably long life-expectancy. In short, without romanticizing the plight of America's poor, it seems that for most of human history, someone as well off as Ruth would be amongst the very best off. Moreover, importantly, I think Ruth must probably be counted amongst the world's fortunate, even taking full account of the genuinely bad effects of being poor in a rich society. . . .
>
> I suspect, then, that if the world did not include others who were even better off, so that Ruth was actually better off than *everyone* else, we would not be *nearly* as concerned to improve her situation as we now are, and that this would be so even on the assumption that the net changes in Ruth's life balanced out, so that her absolute level in that situation would be *exactly* the same as it is now. Surely, our attitude towards America's poor is deeply shaped by the presence of so many others who are *so* much better off.[36]

As these quotations illustrate, the claim-within-outcome conception ("comparative fairness") focuses on how individuals fare relative to each other—in the actual world, or in any possible world that might obtain. On this view, whether outcome *x*

---

[34] Temkin (1996b, pp. 10–12).

[35] Temkin (2003b, p. 62).

[36] Ibid., pp. 70–71.

is fairer than outcome y depends on well-being comparisons within x and well-being comparisons within y. How unequal is the distribution of well-being within x? How unequal is the distribution of well-being within y?

Temkin makes the idea of "comparative fairness" more rigorous and precise through his notion of "complaints."[37] In any outcome x where some individuals are worse off than other individuals, at least some of the worse-off individuals will have "complaints." *Inequality* develops an elaborate system for identifying, measuring, and aggregating worse-off individuals' complaints. One possibility is that each person in x who is below the mean level of well-being has a complaint in x; another, that each person in x has a complaint against every person who is better off than him in x; and a third, that each person in x has a complaint against the best-off person in x. The strength of individual complaints might be measured in a linear or non-linear manner. (For example, on the relative-to-the-best-off view, Jim has a complaint against Felix in x if Felix is the best-off person in x. The strength of that complaint *might* be the well-being difference between Felix and Jim in x, or it might be a non-linear function of the well-being difference between Felix and Jim.) Finally, whether x or y is fairer depends on an "aggregation" rule: a rule for comparing the overall pattern of complaints in x with the overall pattern of complaints in y. One possible aggregation rule is summative: x is fairer than y if the total sum of complaints in x is smaller than the total sum of complaints in y. However, Temkin also points to non-summative aggregation rules. For example, we might say that x is fairer than y if the single largest individual complaint in x is smaller than the single largest individual complaint in y.

It is critical to understand the following feature of Temkin's view (which is true regardless of the different possibilities for identifying, measuring, and aggregating complaints). A Temkin-style complaint is an attribute which is possessed by some, single, person in some, single, outcome. An individual's complaint in the outcome where she possesses it might be directed against another person in that outcome: for example, individual i has a complaint against individual j in x, because j is better off than i in x. Or, the complaint might not have a specific target: for example, individual i is below the mean level of well-being in x and therefore has a complaint in x. In either event, the existence and magnitude of an individual's Temkin-style complaint are facts about her that are relativized to a particular outcome. An individual can possess a complaint in x, but not possess a complaint in y; she can have a complaint in x of some magnitude, and a complaint in y of a different magnitude. Relatedly, whether an individual possesses a complaint in a given outcome and (if so) the magnitude of that complaint are determined by her well-being level in that outcome and the well-being levels of other individuals in that outcome, not by her well-being level or those of other individuals in other outcomes.[38] These are the features of

---

[37] See Temkin (1986; 1996b, ch. 2); Devooght (2003). See also Chakravarty (2009, pp. 101–105).

[38] To be sure, on the account of well-being proposed in Chapter 3, the ascription of a well-being level to a particular life-history is a holistic process, which takes account of the totality of life-histories

Temkin-style complaints that I have tried to capture by styling them "within outcome" complaints.

A different view of the structure of "complaints" or "claims" (I view the terms as synonymous, but for stylistic reasons prefer the latter) is suggested by Thomas Nagel. As I have already mentioned, Nagel endorses and develops the Rawlsian idea of the "separateness of persons"—specifically, in Nagel's 1977 Tanner Lecture and his subsequent book, *Equality and Partiality*.[39] These works also provide an early defense of prioritarianism (or at least of a Pigou–Dalton respecting moral view),[40] which Nagel refers to as "an egalitarian priority system." I very much concur with Nagel that a moral view sensitive to the separateness of persons—sensitive to fairness, in my terminology—ends up endorsing a ranking of outcomes which satisfies the Pigou–Dalton principle. For now, however, I am concerned simply to identify the distinctive understanding of the "separateness of persons" that Nagel offers.

Consider what Nagel says. In the Tanner Lecture, he observes: "The units about which [the moral] problem arises are individual persons, individual human lives. Each of them has a claim to consideration."[41] And he continues:

> [An egalitarian priority system] resembles utilitarianism formally, in being applied first to the assessment of outcomes rather than of actions. But it does not combine all points of view by a majoritarian method. Instead, it establishes an order of priority among needs and gives preference to the most urgent, regardless of numbers. In that respect it is closer to rights theory. . . .
>
> One problem in the development of this idea is the definition of the order of priority: whether a single, objective standard of urgency should be used in construing the claims of each person, or whether his interests should be ranked at his own estimation of their relative importance. In addition to the question of objectivity, there is a question of scale. Because moral equality is equality between persons, the individual interests to be ranked cannot be momentary preferences, desires, and experiences. They must be aspects of the individual's life taken as a whole: health, nourishment, freedom, work, education, self-respect, affection, pleasure. . . .
>
> But let me leave these questions aside. The essential feature of an egalitarian priority system is that it counts improvements to the welfare of the worse off as more urgent than improvements to the welfare of the better off. These other questions must be answered to decide who is worse off and who is better off, and how much, but what makes a system egalitarian is the priority it gives to the claims of those whose overall life prospects put

associated with some outcome set. See below, pp. 366–367. Still, it remains the case that, once well-being levels in each outcome have been *defined* (as a function of all life-histories in all outcomes), it is only the well-being levels in a particular outcome that determine the Temkin-style complaints in that outcome.

[39] Nagel (1979, 1995).

[40] There is little in Nagel's texts to indicate what his views would be regarding separability.

[41] Nagel (1979, p. 111).

them at the bottom, irrespective of numbers or of overall utility. Each individual with a more urgent claim has priority, in the simplest version of such a view, over each individual with a less urgent claim. The moral equality of egalitarianism consists in taking into account the interests of each person, subject to the same system of priorities of urgency, in determining what would be best overall.[42]

In *Equality and Partiality*, Nagel writes:

The impartial attitude is, I believe, strongly egalitarian both in itself and in its implications. As I have said, it comes from our capacity to take up a point of view which abstracts from who we are, but which appreciates fully and takes to heart the value of every person's life and welfare. We put ourselves in each person's shoes and take as our preliminary guide to the value we assign to what happens to him the value which it has from his point of view. This gives to each person's well-being very great importance. . . .

The result is an enormous set of values deriving from individual lives, without as yet any method of combining them or weighing them against one another when they conflict, as they inevitably will in the real world. The question whether impartiality is egalitarian in itself is the question whether the correct method of combination will include a built-in bias in favor of equality, over and above the equality of importance that everyone's life has in the initial set of values to be combined.

Even if impartiality were not in this sense egalitarian in itself, it would be egalitarian in its distributive consequences because of the familiar fact of diminishing marginal utility. . . .

But I believe that impartiality is also egalitarian in itself. . . . What it means is that impartiality generates a greater interest in benefiting the worse off than in benefiting the better off—a kind of priority to the former over the latter. . . .

[This] does not rule out all ranking of alternatives involving different persons, nor does it mean that benefiting more people is not in itself preferable to benefiting fewer. But it does introduce a significant element of non-aggregative, pairwise comparison between the persons affected by any choice or policy. . . . The claims on our impartial concern of an individual who is badly off present themselves as having some priority over the claims of *each* individual who is better off: as being ahead in the queue, so to speak. . . .[43]

What are the features of Nagel's view of fairness (the separateness of persons)? Nagel, like Temkin, acknowledges that well-being might be employed as the currency for fairness and that fairness might provide a basis for ranking outcomes. Further, like Temkin, Nagel conceptualizes well-being in terms of individual complaints/claims. (Note that Nagel explicitly and repeatedly describes each individual as possessing a "claim"). But what, exactly, is the structure of a Nagelian claim?

---

[42] Ibid., pp. 116–118.
[43] Nagel (1995, pp. 64–68).

As the above quotations indicate, a claim—for Nagel—is a claim *to an improvement in well-being.*

How shall we make more precise the idea that an individual claim is a claim to a well-being improvement? I think we can do so by understanding a Nagelian claim as a relation between a given individual and a *pair* of outcomes. Given *two* outcomes, x and y, a given individual i has a claim in favor of x over y just in case she is better off in x than y. She has a claim in favor of y over x just in case she is better off in y than x.

Nagel does not say explicitly that individual claims have this "across-outcome" structure: that a claim is a relation between a given individual and a pair of outcomes. However, I think such a reading of the Tanner Lecture and *Equality and Partiality* is quite reasonable. In any event, I am less interested in tracking Nagel's precise intentions than in developing a fruitful intellectual framework for specifying a fair ranking of outcomes, a framework which I see adumbrated in Nagel's writings.

Let us term this the "claim-across-outcome" conception of the fair ranking of outcomes. I will articulate the conception as follows:

The Claim-Across-Outcome Conception of the Fair Ranking of Outcomes

Whether outcome x is fairer than outcome y depends on individuals' claims for or against each outcome. A claim is a relation between an individual and a pair of outcomes, with four possible valences: given any pair of outcomes, x and y, an individual has a claim in favor of x over y, a claim in favor of y over x, no claim either way, or an incomparable claim. There is a basic connection between the valence of an individual's claim and the valence of her well-being: If an individual is better off in x than y, she has a claim in favor of x over y; if an individual is equally well off in the outcomes, then she has no claim either way; if she is incomparably well off, then she has an incomparable claim. At a minimum, any rule for ranking a pair of outcomes in light of individuals' claims must rank the two outcomes as equally fair if no individuals have a claim either way; and must rank one outcome as fairer than a second if some individuals have a claim in favor of the first over the second, and all other individuals have no claim either way. Where these conditions are not satisfied—where individuals' claims between a pair of outcomes are conflicting—the ranking of the two outcomes should be a function of some fair rule for measuring the strength of individuals' claims between the outcomes and adjudicating between these claims.

In articulating the claim-across-outcome view, I have drawn a tight connection between the valence of an individual's well-being and the valence of her claim. I have also imposed requirements on the fairness ranking of a pair of outcomes in the two kinds of "no-conflict" cases: namely, (1) the case where no individuals have a claim between the outcomes and (2) the case where at least some individuals have a claim in favor of one outcome, and everyone else has no claim either way. On both counts, my articulation of the view seems faithful to Nagel's understandings.

However, I have left the claim-across-outcome view unspecified in many important respects. In particular, I have not specified how a pair of outcomes, x and y, should be ranked in "conflict" cases: where some individuals have a claim in favor of x over y (or an incomparable claim), and others have a claim in favor of y over x (or an incomparable claim). One way to resolve "conflict" cases is by assigning each individual's claim a number (or vector of numbers), measuring the claim's strength; and then using some rule, be it additive or non-additive, to decide which outcome is fairer given the numerical strength of the claims pointing in each direction. But I have *not* required that the claim-across-outcome approach assign numbers measuring the strength of claims[44] or (if it does) that a particular kind of measurement scheme be employed; nor have I required that any particular kind of rule for adjudicating between conflicting claims be employed.

In other words, my articulation of the claim-across-outcome conception of fairness is meant to capture the essence of Nagel's ideas about the separateness of persons, while leaving plenty of room for further discussion about how this manner of thinking should be fleshed out. Note here that *all* SWFs satisfy the requirements of the claim-across-outcome conception (as I have articulated it) regarding no-conflict cases.[45] Different kinds of SWFs can be seen as embodying different proposals for how to measure and adjudicate between claims so as to resolve "conflict" cases.

Let us now contrast the claim-across-outcome conception of fairness with Temkin's claim-within-outcome view. We can now see why Temkin's description of the latter as a "comparative fairness" view is potentially misleading. Both views ultimately arrive at a fairness ranking of outcomes: at a judgment that outcome x is comparatively more or less fair than y. Both views arrive at this fairness ranking of outcomes by making certain comparisons. But the relevant comparisons differ in their modal structure, because of the difference in the structure of Temkin-style and

---

[44] The claim-across-outcome view, in resolving conflict cases or certain such cases, may well compare the strength of individual claims. But it may do so without assigning *numbers* to the claims measuring their strength. For example, the leximin SWF can be justified in light of a certain view about the comparative strength of individual claims (e.g., the Hammond equity view, concerning the comparative strength of individual claims in conflict cases where only two persons are affected, see below); but the leximin SWF does not numerically measure claim strength.

[45] Remember that I am focused in this chapter on SWFs that meet minimal welfarist requirements, including the Pareto principles, and use the term "SWF" to mean only such SWFs. One type of "no-conflict" case involves a pair of outcomes, x and y, such that no individuals have a claim either way. But an individual has no claim between a pair of outcomes just in case he is equally well off in both. (This is one aspect of the connection between the valence of an individual's well-being and the valence of his claim.) So this sort of no-conflict case is equivalent to a case of Pareto-indifference, where any Paretian SWF will rank x and y as equally morally good.

The second sort of no-conflict case is such that every individual either has a claim in favor of x, or no claim either way; while at least some individuals have a claim in favor of x. But the claim/well-being connection is such that *this* is equivalent to a case of Pareto-superiority, where any Paretian SWF will rank x as morally better than y.

Nagel-style claims. On Temkin's view, how individuals would fare relative to others, were one outcome to occur (x), and how individuals would fare relative to others, were a different outcome to occur (y), is what determines the pattern of claims in each outcome. We then arrive at a ranking of the outcomes by comparing these patterns. By contrast, on Nagel's view, we determine, for each individual, whether she has a claim to have the world turn out one way (x) rather than another (y). We then look at the pattern of inter-world claims to determine which outcome is fairer.

Thus on Temkin's view, *intra-world, inter-personal comparisons* of well-being have a critical role in determining which individuals possess claims. On Nagel's view, such comparisons have no role in determining which individuals possess claims. Instead, an individual's possession of a Nagel-style claim (a relation between the individual and two outcomes, namely, a claim on her part in favor of x over y, for y over x, no claim either way, or an incomparable claim) depends on an *intra-personal, inter-world* comparison, namely by asking whether the individual is better off, worse off, equally well off, or incomparably well off in one outcome versus the other.

A further clarification here is that Nagel's view is not *wholly* insensitive to intra-world, inter-personal comparisons. In particular, the level of a given person's well-being, in a given outcome, may depend both on her own non-well-being *attributes* in that outcome, and on the non-well-being attributes of other individuals. To use the terminology of the previous chapter, the utility functions in **U** need not be "atomistic." (To give but one example: an individual's well-being in a given outcome x may be determined not only by her own level of consumption in x, but also by whether that consumption level is higher or lower than others' consumption in x.) It is even possible, in principle, for someone's well-being in an outcome to be a function of others' *well-being* in that outcome (not just their non-well-being attributes).[46] In short, the claim-across-outcome view is entirely agnostic about what determines the level of individual well-being in a given outcome.[47]

---

[46] This would require a kind of recursive determination of well-being. We arrive at an initial set $\mathbf{U}_1$, which represents the well-being levels, differences, and ratios associated with life-histories given the non-well-being features of outcomes (including, potentially, the distribution of individual attributes within each outcome). From $\mathbf{U}_1$, we construct $\mathbf{U}_2$, which represents the well-being levels, etc., associated with life-histories given both the non-well-being features of outcomes and the distribution of well-being within outcomes as represented by $\mathbf{U}_1$. From $\mathbf{U}_2$ we construct $\mathbf{U}_3$, and so forth, with $\mathbf{U}_\infty$ as the limiting point of this process.

The extended-preference account of well-being, as I presented the account in Chapter 3, does not involve this sort of recursive determination of well-being; but I believe that the account could be refined to do that. In any event, the point to be stressed here is that the claim-across-outcome conception of fairness is quite consistent with such a recursive view. $\mathbf{U}_\infty$ can (in principle) be used to determine the valence and magnitude of individuals' across-outcome claims.

[47] Moreover, the point mentioned below, pp. 366–367, is also relevant here. The extended-preference account of well-being assigns utility numbers to a given individual's life-histories by looking to each spectator's $\mathbf{U}^k$, itself a function of her preferences regarding the totality of life-histories associated

Rather, the irrelevance of intra-world, inter-personal well-being comparisons is at the stage of determining the valence of each individual's claim: determining whether, for a given pair of outcomes, she has a claim for one over the other, no claim either way, or an incomparable claim. Using whatever intra-world information might be relevant to individual well-being, we arrive at a well-being ranking of different life-histories for a given subject i (represented by the set $\mathbf{U}$ of utility functions). It is this intrapersonal ranking which then determines the valence of i's claim between any given pair of outcomes.

A further, even more subtle point is that the claim-across-outcome view potentially allows for facts about the distribution of well-being within outcomes to affect the *magnitude* of individuals' claims (as opposed to their basic *valence*). This will emerge when we examine SWFs that fail the separability axiom, such as the rank-weighted SWF.[48]

I have taken some care to clarify the features of the claim-across-outcome and claim-within-outcome conceptions of fairness. But which is more attractive? This is not obvious. Both conceptions justify some kind of non-utilitarian SWF; to that extent, both are consistent with the intuitive proposition that utilitarianism and considerations of fair distribution can diverge. Moreover, both views would seem to be reflected in ordinary moral thinking. Sometimes, we morally evaluate a choice by asking whether the choice would leave some persons unfairly worse off than others (a claim-within-outcome approach). But, sometimes our thinking takes a different track. Instead of focusing on how individuals fare or would fare relative to others, we seek to determine which individuals have an interest in a particular choice; and we morally evaluate the choice by ascertaining how strong the interests of the affected parties are, ignoring individuals who are unaffected. To characterize individuals as "interested" or "unaffected" by some choice is just to make the kind of *intra-personal, inter-world* comparison that is central to the claim-across-outcome view. It is to ask, for each individual, whether she would be better or worse off given the consequence (or array of possible consequences) of one of the courses of action under consideration, as compared with how she would fare given the consequence (or array of possible consequences) of a different course of action also being considered.

What *does* make the case for the claim-across-outcome conception of fairness, I suggest, is the principle of Pareto-superiority. This view of fairness offers a simple, elegant explanation for why the ranking of outcomes should satisfy Pareto-superiority. Imagine that there are some individuals who are better off in x than y. Since everyone has a claim (of some degree of urgency) to a well-being improvement (as Nagel puts it), those individuals have a claim in favor of x over y. Imagine, furthermore, that every other individual is equally well off in x as in y. Then those

---

with the outcome set. So in this sense, too, facts about the other life-histories in outcomes x and y may function to determine the well-being levels of $(x; i)$ and $(y; i)$ for any given i.

[48] See below.

individuals have no claim either way. Since they are unaffected by which outcome occurs, how can they have claim to the occurrence of one or the other outcome?

In short, a case of Pareto-superiority is a "no conflict" case in which some individuals have a claim in favor of one outcome, and all other individuals have no claim either way. If one uses the conceptual architecture of the claim-across-outcome view to think about problems of fairness, the principle of Pareto-superiority is compelling. *Clearly* a Pareto-superior outcome is fairer than the outcome it dominates. Where *x* is Pareto-superior to *y*, *no* one would have a complaint, in the across-outcome sense, if *x* were to obtain rather than *y*; while some would have a complaint, in the across-outcome sense, if *y* were to obtain rather than *x*.

By contrast, the claim-*within*-outcome view fits much less comfortably with the principle of Pareto-superiority. It is quite possible that *x* is Pareto-superior to *y*, and yet some individuals in *x* have complaints in the within-outcome sense. More strongly: it is quite possible that *x* is Pareto-superior to *y*, and yet the overall pattern of complaints within each outcome is such that *y* is fairer than *x*, in the within-outcome sense. More strongly yet: it is quite possible that *x* is Pareto-superior to *y*, and yet no one has a within-outcome complaint in *y*, while some individuals have complaints in *x*.

To see (all of) these possibilities, consider any case which has the following features: In *y*, well-being is perfectly equally distributed; *x* is Pareto-superior to *y*; in *x*, well-being is unequally distributed. In such a case, no one has a complaint in *y*; while some do have within-outcome complaints in *x*. Thus *y* is the fairer outcome in the claim-within-outcome sense.[49] And yet Pareto-superiority demands that *x*, not *y*, be ranked as the morally better outcome.

For example, imagine that well-being is equally distributed in *y*; there is one individual (call him "Trump") who is much better off in *x* than *y*; everyone else has the same well-being level in *x* as she does in *y*.

Table 5.1 The Trump Case

	Outcome *x*	Outcome *y*
Amy	1*r*	1*r*
Betty	1*r*	1*r*
Charlie	1*r*	1*r*
...		
Richard	1*r*	1*r*
Sue	1*r*	1*r*
Trump	5*r*	1*r*

[49] In this last case, surely, the within-outcome proponent must say that *y* is fairer than *x*—whatever her general methodology for comparing the overall patterns of within-outcome complaints in *x* and *y* when individuals have complaints in both outcomes.

In Table 5.1, well-being is measurable up to a positive ratio transformation. The case can be "tweaked" to add additional individuals (in the ". . ." line) who also have $1r$ in both outcomes; to subtract some of the current individuals in this category; or to change 5 to any number greater than 1. Regardless, well-being is perfectly equally distributed in y, unequally distributed in x, yet Pareto-superiority ranks x better.

In this "Trump" case, Pareto-superiority requires that x be ranked as morally better than y. From the perspective of the claim-*across*-outcome conception, this is straightforward: Trump has a claim in favor of x; no one else has a claim either way. From the perspective of the claim-*within*-outcome view, the proposition that x is morally better than y is *far* from straightforward. Outcome y is the fairer outcome. No one has a complaint in y; everyone except Trump has a complaint in x.[50] In order to explain why x is nonetheless the morally better outcome, the proponent of the claim-within-outcome view must see the moral ranking of outcomes as the upshot of *combining* considerations of fairness with considerations of overall well-being. Although y is fairer than x, the increase in overall well-being secured by moving from y to x morally outweighs the decrease in fairness.

The gambit of seeing the moral ranking of outcomes as a combination of fairness and overall well-being is not, per se, implausible. A larger problem for the proponent of the claim-within-outcome view is explaining why overall well-being *necessarily* trumps fairness in cases such as the Trump case. Consider the universe of cases (exemplified by Trump) in which x is Pareto-superior to y, and yet the overall pattern of within-outcome complaints is such that y is a fairer outcome than x. In order to ensure consistency with Pareto-superiority, the proponent of the within-outcome view must say that in *every* such case, the increase in overall well-being going from y to x morally outweighs the loss in fairness. But why on earth would this be true in *every* such case?

The proponent of the claim-within-outcome conception of fairness might conclude that we should reject Pareto-superiority. (Indeed, Temkin has suggested as much.[51]) Consider a moral view that (1) embraces the claim-within-outcome view of fairness; (2) sees the moral ranking of outcomes as a matter of combining overall well-being with fairness; and (3) acknowledges that this combination of factors will sometimes, possibly, rank y (the fairer outcome) over x (the outcome with greater overall well-being) even though x is Pareto-superior to y. Such a moral view is intellectually coherent; it doesn't make the implausible claim that overall well-being *necessarily* outweighs fairness in the claim-within-outcome sense whenever the principle of Pareto-superiority is at stake.

---

[50] This is true given all three of the methods that Temkin proposes for identifying complaints, i.e., that everyone below the mean has a complaint; that each person has a complaint against everyone better off than him; and that each person has a complaint against the best-off person.

[51] See Temkin (1996b, pp. 139–140); Temkin (2003b, pp. 77–79).

But the project of this book is to work within Paretian welfarism: to take as a fixed point the intuitions that all economists and many philosophers have in favor of the principle of Pareto-superiority as well as Pareto-indifference, and to ask how Paretian welfarism is best specified. The Pareto-inconsistent moral view summarized in the previous paragraph is, of course, not an answer to *that* question.

Nor is the question an artificial one. It is not as if the reader is forced to take as given the Pareto principles merely by virtue of authorial fiat. For there exists a *Pareto-consistent* moral view which is no less unified and coherent, and no less concerned about fairness, than the Pareto-inconsistent view which I have just mentioned. *One* way to think about fairness, morality, and the Pareto principles which is simple, elegant, and tightly integrated is just this: to understand fairness in the claim-across-outcome sense; to see a Pareto-superior outcome as one favored by some individual claims and disfavored by none; and to conclude that a Pareto-superior outcome is necessarily fairer and thus morally better as a matter of fairness alone, quite apart from considerations of overall well-being.

In short, the claim-across-outcome view of fairness *underwrites* the principle of Pareto-superiority. It reveals the sense in which that principle embodies a respect for the separateness of persons. And it clearly is the claim-across-outcome view, not the claim-within-outcome view, which furnishes the better theory of fairness by which to specify Paretian welfarism.[52] This is therefore the account of fairness that I will rely upon in this chapter, as well as the subsequent two.[53]

---

[52] It might be proposed that outcomes should be morally ranked using *both* conceptions of fairness (or both together with overall well-being). But such a view (like the view that understands fairness solely in the claim-within-outcome sense) seems an implausible specification of Paretian welfarism; and I therefore do not consider it. If x is Pareto-superior to y, it is necessarily fairer than y in the claim-across-outcome sense but may be less fair in the claim-within-outcome sense. Why would the result of combining both senses of fairness (even with overall well-being also added to the balance) *always* be to endorse the Pareto-superior outcome?

Indeed, Nagel himself suggests that combining the claim-across-outcome view (my terminology for the "egalitarian priority system" he presents in the 1977 Tanner Lecture and in chapter 7 of *Equality and Partiality*) with an independent concern for equal treatment might undercut the Pareto principle. See Nagel (1995, p. 73, n. 21, pp. 107–108, n. 33).

[53] One aspect of the philosophical debate about prioritarianism concerns whether a moral view should be "person affecting" and, relatedly, whether a view is properly criticized if vulnerable to the "leveling down" objection. See the scholarship on prioritarianism, cited below, n. 90; Temkin's scholarship; and also Christiano and Braynen (2008); Crisp (2003a); Doran (2001); Holtug (1998, 2007b); Mason (2001); O'Neill (2008); Ramsay (2005). Scholarly debates concerning these topics have become quite complex, and I will not attempt to summarize them here. However, there are (I believe) interesting connections between these debates and the argument I have presented in favor of the claim-across-outcome conception. The claim-across-outcome conception rests upon a "person affecting" conception of fairness: an individual has a claim in favor of y over x just in case y has a positive "effect" upon her, i.e., makes her better off than in x. Thus it fits snugly with the Pareto principle; if y is Pareto-superior to x, there is no moral consideration (no claim) in favor of x. By contrast, the claim-within-outcome conception is not "person affecting": whether a given individual has a

C. Is Morality Exhausted by Fairness?

I began my analysis with the claim that a moral view should reflect fairness consider-ations, insofar as persons are involved—that it should be sensitive to the "separate-ness of persons." I then argued that the most attractive conception of the separateness of persons, for purposes of specifying "welfarism" (a moral view which is exclusively person-centered and consequentialist, and which respects both the Pareto-indifference principle and the principle of Pareto-superiority) is the claim-*across*-outcome conception of fairness, inspired by Thomas Nagel's work.

A further question, one I have not yet addressed, is whether morality is *exhausted* by considerations of fairness.

If one combines a welfarist view of morality and a claim-across-outcome concep-tion of fairness, it is certainly *possible* to take the position that fairness exhausts morality. In other words, it is possible to say the following: (1) whether x is at least as fair as y is determined by the pattern of individual claims in favor of one or the other outcome; *and* (2) x is morally at least as good as y iff x is at least as fair as y. But it is not clear why this is necessitated. Why not adopt a moral theory which says that the all-things-considered moral ranking of x versus y is a product of *both* fairness *and* other factors (for short, a "pluralist" moral theory)?

Within the context of a non-person-centered moral view, or a moral view which is person-centered but not welfarist, the case for this sort of pluralism may well be powerful. But within the context of welfarism, it is hard to see—at least at the outset—why we should feel pressure to be pluralists. "Fairness," on the view ten-dered here, provides an overarching structure for determining the normative signifi-cance of facts about human well-being. All of the various aspects of an individual's welfare determine the valence of her claim between a given pair of outcomes. Pluralism would mean that certain kinds of well-being facts have a *dual* moral role. On the one hand, they would be relevant, like other facts about well-being, to whether x is fairer than y. The fact that individual i is better off in x than y with respect to any given aspect of well-being may change the valence or magnitude of his claim between the outcomes. But these special kinds of well-being facts would also give rise to *additional*, non-fairness considerations relevant to the all-things-considered moral ranking of x and y.

At least as a matter of theoretical unity and simplicity, such a pluralistic view is less attractive than the view which says that the moral ranking of outcomes is identi-cal to the fairness ranking. Lest the latter view strike the reader as obviously wrong-headed (even within the context of welfarism), it bears mention that Rawls, too,

---

claim in x, or a claim in y, is independent of whether she is better off in x than y. Thus there can be a moral consideration in favor of a Pareto-inferior outcome (namely that the pattern of within-outcome claims is fairer), which is what yields the tension with Pareto-superiority.

appears to take the position that morality is exhausted by considerations of fairness insofar as persons are involved.[54]

In any event, that is the position adopted in this chapter—as a kind of provisional, working assumption. For now, I assume that if x is at least as fair as y, in light of the claim-across-outcome understanding of fairness, then x is all-things-considered morally at least as good as y. However, this assumption is not meant to be ironclad. There may be concrete cases in which we intuit that x is *not* morally at least as good as y, in virtue of certain well-being differences between the outcomes, even though x is at least as fair as y. If there are such cases, and the intuitions they prompt sufficiently strong, we may be moved to abandon the working assumption that welfarist morality is exhausted by fairness in the claim-across-outcome sense.

Such cases will be examined in Chapter 6. In particular, Chapter 6 (in the course of arguing that the continuous prioritarian SWF should be applied on a whole-life-time basis) will seriously consider the possibility that short-term human suffering and other kinds of hardship that impair sublifetime well-being have moral relevance independent of fairness. For now, however, let us bracket the possibility of pluralism and focus on determining which SWF is warranted as a matter of fairness in the claim-across-outcome sense.

II. THE PIGOU–DALTON PRINCIPLE

If fairness is understood in the claim-across-outcome sense, the case for the Pigou–Dalton principle is extremely strong. The Pigou–Dalton principle, again, requires that outcome x be ranked as morally better than y whenever the following are true: (1) there is some individual i who is better off in x than y; (2) there is some other individual j who is better off in y than x; (3) the difference in well-being between $(x; i)$ and $(y; i)$ is exactly the same as the difference in well-being between $(y; j)$ and $(x; j)$; (4) individual i is worse off than individual j in y, and either worse off than individual j in x or equally well-off; and (5) everyone else is unaffected.

Consider this case in light of the claim-across-outcome view. Individual i has a claim in favor of x; individual j has a claim in favor of y; everyone else is unaffected. So x should be ranked as morally better than y iff i's claim to x is *stronger* than j's claim to y.

But surely i's claim to x *is* stronger. The individuals stand to gain or lose the very same amount from the occurrence of x versus y. To that extent, their claims are equal. Add now the further fact that individual i's well-being level is below that of individual j in one of the two outcomes, and either below or at most equal to that of

---

[54] Consider Rawls' (1999b, pp. 93–98) discussion of "rightness as fairness," and his comment that rightness as fairness "fails to embrace all moral relationships" insofar as "it would seem to include only our relations with other persons and to leave out of account how we are to conduct ourselves toward animals and the rest of nature" (ibid., p. 15)—*not* in failing to embrace certain aspects of interpersonal morality.

individual j in the other. Shouldn't this further fact about well-being levels "tip the balance" in favor of i having the stronger claim? Whatever one's general views about the role of well-being differences versus levels in determining claim strength, shouldn't facts about well-being levels have *at least* the minimum role of giving i the stronger claim in this particular case?

The force of the Pigou–Dalton principle is perhaps seen yet more dramatically when the principle is expressed in terms of four life-histories, call them Lower, Middle, Middle Plus, and Higher. (These correspond, respectively, to $(y; i)$, $(x; i)$, $(x; j)$, and $(y; j)$.) Lower is worse for well-being than Middle, which is worse than or equal to Middle Plus, in turn worse than Higher. The well-being difference between the first pair is the same as the well-being difference between the second. One individual, i, asks to be moved from Lower to Middle. A second, j, asks to be moved the very same distance, from Middle Plus to Higher. If we can only satisfy one of these claims, isn't it fairer to satisfy the first? How can satisfying individual i's claim be on balance unfair to j—since, by doing so, we provide individual i the very same increase in well-being that j asks for, no less, *and* we move i to a level (Middle) still below or at least not above where j ends up (Middle Plus)?

With this insight in hand, let us examine two important SWFs that fail the Pigou–Dalton principle: the utilitarian SWF and the sufficientist SWF.

A. The Utilitarian SWF

I have already suggested that there is a strong intuitive case against the view that the fair ranking of outcomes is tracked by the utilitarian SWF. This intuition, remember, was a central motivation for *rejecting* a veil-of-ignorance conception of fairness, which very plausibly leads to utilitarianism.

If fairness is understood in the claim-across-outcome sense, the utilitarian SWF is problematic. The utilitarian SWF, translated into "claim" language,[55] has the following features: (1) For a given pair of outcomes and utility function $u(.)$, it measures the strength of a given individual's claim between the outcomes using a single number, namely her utility difference between the outcomes; and (2) it ranks the outcomes, according to $u(.)$, by *adding up* the individual claims.[56] The second feature

---

[55] In this and subsequent sections, I "translate" various SWFs into methodologies for measuring and adjudicating between individuals' across-outcome claims. These are (I believe) the most natural translations, and they help to illuminate whether the SWFs are justified. However, I do not suggest that these translations are unique. (For any given SWF, there may perhaps be multiple methodologies for measuring and aggregating claims that are extensionally equivalent to the SWF.) My arguments against SWFs that fail to satisfy the Pigou–Dalton, separability, and continuity axioms rest—at bottom—on the force of those axioms, not on the particular translations of those SWFs into "claim" language which I offer.

[56] The natural translation of the utilitarian SWF into "claim" language is as follows. (1) For a given pair of outcomes, x and y, and a utility function $u(.)$, there is an N-entry claim vector, where the ith

is not per se problematic (as we will see, the continuous prioritarian SWF is also additive), but the two features, together, mean that the utilitarian SWF *universally* fails the Pigou–Dalton principle. In *every* case where i is better off in x than y, j is better off in y than x, the well-being differences are the same, and everyone else is unaffected, the utilitarian SWF says that outcomes x and y are equally morally good. But surely the Pigou–Dalton principle holds, in at least a restricted sense. Surely there are at least *some* cases in which a non-leaky transfer of well-being from a person at a higher well-being level, to a person at a lower well-being level, yields a morally better outcome.

What can the proponent of the utilitarian SWF say in response? Here, it is worth mentioning several important arguments for utilitarianism that have been presented in the literature. These arguments are distinct from the already-mooted veil-of-ignorance view of fairness. Instead, the arguments might be understood as showing why—even if one adopts a claim-across-outcome view of fairness—the utilitarian scheme for measuring and adjudicating between claims is best justified.

One argument for utilitarianism invokes limitations in our ability to measure well-being. This argument derives from the theoretical literature on SWFs, which addresses questions of invariance.[57] How the literature does so can be articulated (using my terminology of life-histories, etc.) as follows. Imagine that an SWF which assumes the simple R-based form yields a particular ranking of an outcome set, when outcomes are mapped onto utility vectors with utility function $u(.)$. We might, then, require the ranking of outcomes to be the same whenever $u(.)$ is replaced with some stipulated transformation, $\varphi(u(.))$; and we might ask, which rules R will satisfy this invariance requirement? The idea is that $\varphi(u(.))$ contains all the information about well-being contained in $u(.)$, and that, therefore, the ranking of outcomes yielded by an attractive SWF should be invariant to whether we measure well-being using $u(.)$ or $\varphi(u(.))$.

For example, the following fairly striking result can be shown. Imagine that $\varphi(u(.))$ is stipulated to be any positive affine transformation of $u(.)$.[58] The idea, here,

---

entry is $u(x; i) - u(y; i)$. This entry is a measure of i's claim, according to $u(.)$. (2) Outcome x is morally at least as good as y, according to $u(.)$, iff the sum of the entries in the claim vector is nonnegative; and y is morally at least as good as x iff the sum of the entries in the claim vector is nonpositive. (3) The valence of an individual's claim depends upon her claim measure given all $u(.)$ in **U**. An individual has a claim in favor of x if her claim measure is nonnegative for all $u(.)$ and positive for some; a claim in favor of y if her claim measure is nonpositive for all $u(.)$ and negative for some; no claim either way if her claim measure is zero for all $u(.)$; and otherwise an incomparable claim. (4) Similarly, the moral ranking of outcomes depends upon the sum of entries in the claim vector for all $u(.)$ in **U**. Outcome x is morally at least as good as outcome y iff this sum is nonnegative for all $u(.)$ belonging to **U**; and outcome y is at least as good as x iff this sum is nonpositive for all $u(.)$ belonging to **U**. If neither is true, the two outcomes are incomparably good.

[57] See sources cited in Chapter 2, n. 45.

[58] Remember that, if $u(.)$ and $v(.)$ are two utility functions taking as their arguments all the life-histories in some life-history set **H** (associated with some outcome set **O**), $v(.)$ is a "positive affine

would be that any positive affine transformation produces the very same ranking of life-histories and differences as $u(.)$ itself, and thus contains all the information in $u(.)$. If, in addition, we demand that R be anonymous, Paretian, and separable, then (roughly) the SWF must either be leximin or utilitarianism.[59] If one adds in a continuity requirement (or just rejects leximin as too implausible), the upshot is the utilitarian SWF.

But this invariance requirement is too strong. Although $u(.)$ and any positive affine transformation thereof *do* yield the same information about the ranking of life-histories and their differences, they do not necessarily contain the same information about the *ratios* between life-histories. Ratios between life-histories can be constructed by picking some life-history (such as a life-history equally good as nonexistence) as the zero point; the ratio between life-history $(x; i)$ and $(y; j)$ is the ratio of their differences from the zero point. Such information can be relevant to an SWF.

By contrast, if $\varphi(u(.))$ is a positive ratio transformation of $u(.)$, then $\varphi(u(.))$ *will* contain the very same level, difference, and ratio information as $u(.)$.[60] Therefore, a reasonable invariance requirement to impose on an SWF is that the ranking of outcomes according to a given utility function should be unchanged if we replace that function by a positive ratio transformation. This will permit, not just leximin, and

---

transformation" of $u(.)$ if there exist numbers a and b, a positive, such that $v(x; i) = au(x; i) + b$ for all $(x; i)$ in **H**. (The theoretical literature referenced here uses a slightly different formal set-up than mine, seeing what I term a single utility function as a *profile* of individual utility functions. In the terminology of this literature, what I term a "positive affine transformation" of $u(.)$ is a *common* positive affine transformation of the profile of individual utility functions.)

[59] More precisely, if we require that R be Paretian, anonymous, separable, and satisfy a "minimal equity" condition which is designed to rule out the perverse "leximax" R, the only possibilities are leximin or "weakly utilitarian" rules. A "weakly utilitarian" R must agree with the utilitarian R in ranking utility vectors with different total amounts of utility. See Bossert and Weymark (2004, pp. 1157–1158).

[60] On the relevance of ratio information to an SWF, see Chapter 3, pp. 216–218. On the construction of ratio information, see below, pp. 379–382. As explored below, if the SWF assumes the simple R-based form (rather than allowing R to vary with $u(.)$), then the ratio between $(x; i)$ and $(y; j)$ is "embodied" in a utility function $u(.)$ via the following rule: $[u(x; i) - Z]/[u(y; j) - Z]$, where Z is the number used to represent the zero point. Note that, if $u(x; i) \neq u(y; j)$, positive affine transformations of $u(.)$ will not generally preserve the ratio between the two life-histories as per this rule. Consider that if $v(.) = au(.) + b$, with a positive, $[v(x; i) - Z]/[v(y; j) - Z] = [au(x; i) + b - Z]/[au(y; j) + b - Z]$, which, if $u(x; i) \neq u(y; j)$, will equal $[u(x; i) - Z]/[u(y; j) - Z]$ only if $b = (1 - a)Z$.

The most natural choice is to set $Z = 0$. In that case, if $v(.)$ is a positive ratio transformation of $u(.)$—in other words, there exists a positive number r such that $v(x; i) = ru(x; i)$ for all $(x; i)$ in **H**—then it is the case that $[v(x; i) - Z]/[v(y; j) - Z] = [u(x; i) - Z]/[u(y; j) - Z]$ for any two life-histories. Note finally that, if $Z \neq 0$, ratio information is not preserved by multiplication by r, but rather by the following transformation: $v(.) = r(u(.) - Z) + Z$. In either event, the invariance requirement which says that the SWF must yield the same ranking of outcomes using $u(.)$ and any positive affine transformation of $u(.)$ is too strong.

not just a utilitarian SWF, but also a continuous prioritarian SWF—in particular, the Atkinson SWF.

John Broome has advanced a different line of argument regarding utilitarianism, one that also involves the measurement of well-being. Rather than being an argument for utilitarianism, this argument suggests that prioritarianism and utilitarianism are not in fact distinct approaches to ordering outcomes.

The essence of Broome's argument is this: "To give their theory meaning, prioritarians need a measure of a person's wellbeing that is distinct from the value of her wellbeing. They may not be able to find one."[61]

Both utilitarians and continuous prioritarians (those who adopt a continuous prioritarian SWF) rank outcomes using an *additive* rule R. Both say: outcome x is morally at least as good as y iff $w(x) \geq w(y)$ for all $u(.)$ in U, where in *both* cases $w(z)$ for any outcome z equals $\sum_{i=1}^{N} m(z;i)$. In other words, utilitarians and continuous prioritarians *agree* that the *moral* value of an outcome, $w(z)$, is the sum of the moral values of its component life-histories. Their disagreement (in effect) is about the relation between the moral value of a life-history and its well-being value. Utilitarians say that these values are identical. They set $m(z; i)$, in the above formula, equal to $u(z; i)$. Continuous prioritarians, by contrast, distinguish between the moral value of a life-history and its well-being value. They say that $m(z; i) = g(u(z; i))$, with $g(.)$ some strictly increasing and strictly concave function.

But now for Broome's skeptical question: What procedure can the continuous prioritarian use to attach these two different numbers to a life-history: on the one hand, $u(z; i)$; on the other hand, $g(u(z; i))$?

Consider the following procedure. We *start* with the moral ordering of outcomes which, for simplicity, may be assumed to be complete. We *start* with the proposition that outcome x is morally better than outcome y, which is morally better than z, and so forth. We then identify a function for ascribing values to life-histories, $m(.)$, which "tracks" the ordering of outcomes. We identify a $m(.)$ such that x is morally at least as good as y iff $\sum_{i=1}^{N} m(x;i) \geq \sum_{i=1}^{N} m(y;i)$.

This procedure will not enable us to ascribe two further values to a given $(z; i)$, namely $u(z; i)$ and $g(u(z; i))$. Imagine that, having identified $m(.)$, we propose a particular $u(.)$ function as the "right" function. This $u(.)$ function is such that $m(z; i) = g(u(z; i))$, with $g(u(z; i)) = \sqrt{u(z;i)}$. It looks like we have arrived at continuous prioritarianism, because setting $g(.)$ as the square root function yields a strictly increasing and strictly concave $g(.)$. But the very same set of m-values assigned to life-histories would be produced by defining a new utility function $u^*(z;i) = \sqrt{u(z;i)}$ and defining a new $g(.)$ function as follows: $g(u^*(z; i)) = u^*(z; i)$. This new $g(.)$ function is not strictly concave.

[61] Broome (n.d., p. 4). See also Broome (1995, ch. 10). Broome withdraws the argument in his (2004, pp. 92–94). For further discussion, see McCarthy (2006); Jensen (1995); Rabinowicz (2001).

This line of questioning is, I take it, the core of Broome's skepticism about distinguishing between utilitarianism and prioritarianism. The response is that there are some procedures that *do* allow us to ascribe two different values to a life-history, namely $u(z; i)$ and $g(u(z; i))$. Specifically, the account of well-being I presented in Chapters 3 and 4 does *not* propose to assign utility values to life-histories by reasoning *from* the moral ordering of outcomes. Rather, it measures the well-being associated with life-histories by determining the utility numbers that expectationally represent the extended preferences of fully informed and rational individuals, considering different possible lotteries over life-histories and comparisons of life-histories to nonexistence. So we have a basis quite independent of our judgments about the moral ordering of outcomes for constructing the set **U** of utility functions.

More generally, any welfarist theory that contains an account of well-being which provides some basis for constructing **U** that is independent of the moral ordering of outcomes, and instead uses these utilities as the inputs for that ordering, can resist Broome's argument that prioritarianism and utilitarianism are indistinguishable.

A final, and very important, argument for a utilitarian SWF relates to moral choice under uncertainty. Like the veil-of-ignorance argument, this argument was introduced by Harsanyi—but it constitutes a separate and distinct defense of utilitarianism. The argument is provided by Harsanyi's so-called "aggregation theorem."

The SWF framework, if to be useful as a decisional tool, must ultimately serve to produce a moral ranking of *choices*, and indeed to do so under conditions of uncertainty—where it is uncertain which outcome would result from a given choice. It is very plausible that the choice ranking should comply with EU theory. It also seems plausible that the ranking should satisfy principles of ex ante Pareto-indifference and -superiority. In other words, if each person's ex ante well-being with choice a is the same as her ex ante well being with choice b, the choices are equally morally good (ex ante Pareto-indifference). If each person's ex ante well-being with choice a is at least as great as her ex ante well-being with choice b, with at least one person's ex ante well-being strictly larger, then choice a is morally better than choice b (ex ante Pareto-superiority).

But if we impose *both* the EU requirement *and* the ex ante Pareto requirement on our moral ranking of choices, it turns out that the SWF must be utilitarian. That, roughly speaking, is what the aggregation theorem shows.

I will postpone considering the aggregation theorem until Chapter 7, which focuses squarely on the problem of deriving a moral ranking of choices from a moral ranking of outcomes. Although the choice ranking should indeed comply with (an appropriately refined) version of EU theory, we should not require it to satisfy the ex ante Pareto principles—which are distinct from, and much less compelling than, the Pareto principles embraced in the current chapter and throughout the book as appropriate limitations on the ranking of outcomes. Or so I will argue in Chapter 7.

B. The Sufficientist SWF

In his influential 2003 article, "Equality, Priority, and Compassion," Roger Crisp defends a moral view which has come to be known in the philosophical scholarship as "sufficientism."[62]

Crisp's article was written against the backdrop of a burgeoning literature on prioritarianism, spurred by Parfit's, Nagel's, and Temkin's contributions. Crisp criticizes prioritarianism on two counts. First, Crisp acknowledges that, in some cases, benefits to worse-off individuals are properly given priority over benefits to better-off individuals; but he criticizes standard prioritarian methodologies for how they structure tradeoffs in such cases. Crisp argues against an "absolute priority" approach (exemplified by a leximin SWF[63]), because it prefers giving a small benefit to one badly off individual, to giving large benefits to many individuals who are only slightly better off. He also rejects a "weighted priority" view (exemplified by a continuous prioritarian SWF), because it would forego a substantial benefit to a badly off individual, in order to produce a very small gain to each of a sufficiently large group of well-off persons. For example, he observes, the "weighted priority" approach might forego pain relief for 10 very badly off individuals (which would move each of them from welfare level 1 to welfare level 50), so as to give a nice chocolate candy to 15,000 rich individuals (which would move each of them from level 98 to level 99).

Crisp's second criticism is that giving priority to the well-being of worse-off individuals is implausible when all the individuals involved are sufficiently well off. Crisp illustrates this point through "the Beverly Hills case," in which the prioritarian prefers to give fine wine to a small group of rich individuals as opposed to giving fine wine to a larger group of super-rich individuals, where the individual welfare benefit of fine wine is the same amount for all the individuals in both groups.

> It seems somewhat absurd to think that the *Rich* should be given priority over the *Super-rich* . . . . [W]hat the Beverly Hills case brings out is that, once recipients are at a certain level, any prioritarian concern for them disappears entirely. This implies that any version of the priority view must fail: when people reach a certain level, even if they are worse off than others, benefiting them does not, in itself, matter more. . . . [E]ven if the benefits to

---

[62] Crisp (2003b). See also Crisp (2003a; 2006, ch. 6). A precursor to Crisp's account is Frankfurt (1987). On sufficientism, see Benbaji (2005); Brown (2005a, ch. 5; 2005b); Casal (2007); Temkin (2003a).

[63] Strictly, Crisp criticizes giving absolute priority to the worst-off person. That is achieved, not just by the leximin SWF, but also others. However, leximin is the most straightforward example of a Paretian SWF that gives absolute priority to the worst off. (Note that maximin, another standard social choice rule which gives absolute priority to the worst off, is not Paretian. See below.) Moreover, if Crisp finds giving absolute priority to the worst off problematic, then *a fortiori* he would find leximin problematic in virtue of giving absolute priority to worse-off persons, even when they are not worst off. On these issues, see Brown (2005a, ch. 5, 2005b).

each of the *Rich* and the *Super-rich* are identical and their numbers are the same, there still seems to me nothing to be said for giving priority to the "worse off." At this level, only utilities matter. . . .[64]

These two criticisms lead Crisp to propose a moral theory that incorporates a well-being threshold, identified as the level such that an impartial spectator would feel compassion for individuals below but not above it. He endorses "The Compassion Principle":

> *The Compassion Principle:* absolute priority is to be given to benefits to those below the threshold at which compassion enters. Below the threshold, benefiting people matters more the worse off those people are, the more of those people there are, and the greater the size of the benefit in question. Above the threshold, or in cases concerning only trivial benefits below the threshold, no priority is to be given.[65]

Crisp entertains, but rejects, the suggestion that the compassion threshold is at the level where individuals' basic needs are satisfied.

> A problem with [the need] proposal is that, on any plausible distinction between needs and, say, desire satisfaction or other components of welfare, needs give out before compassion. Imagine a society which includes, among a large number of very wealthy and flourishing individuals, a group which is very poor but whose basic and indeed nonbasic needs are met. Compassionate concern for the badly off speaks in favor of at least some transfers from the rich to the poor, even if the poor use any resources gained to purchase goods which they could not be said to need.[66]

Instead, the compassion level is to be understood as the level of a life which is "sufficiently good," which Crisp specifies as 80 years of high-quality life on earth.

> Imagine that the impartial spectator knows that the universe contains trillions of beings whose lives are at a much higher level of welfare than even the best off on this planet. Will he or she take the same view of the Beverly Hills case, or might his or her threshold for compassion be set at a much higher level? It is hard to know how to answer such questions, but, on reflection, my own intuition is that, say, eighty years of high-quality life on this planet is enough, and plausibly more than enough, for any being.[67]

[64] Crisp (2003b, p. 755).
[65] Ibid., p. 758.
[66] Ibid., p. 759.
[67] Ibid., p. 762.

Campbell Brown has cogently formalized Crisp's *Compassion Principle* as a type of SWF.[68] For short, let us term this the "sufficientist" SWF. Brown formulates this SWF for the case in which there is a single utility function that tracks well-being; I will generalize his idea to the case in which there is a set **U** of utility functions that represents the well-being associated with life-histories.

For a given outcome set, identify a life-history, $(x^+; i^+)$, that lies at the "compassion" threshold. Designate some arbitrary positive number T as the number of the threshold. Take the set **U** that represents well-being levels, differences, and ratios.[69] "Winnow down" **U** by including only utility functions that assign T to life-history $(x^+; i^+)$; denote this "winnowed down" set as $\mathbf{U}^T$. Now compare each pair of outcomes, x and y, using the following two-stage approach. Take some strictly increasing, strictly concave $g(.)$ function. For each utility function $u(.)$ in $\mathbf{U}^T$, each outcome corresponds to a below-threshold utility vector, namely the vector of individual utilities truncated at the number T. Each outcome also corresponds to an above-threshold utility vector, namely the vector of individual utilities or T, whichever is larger. For each utility function, assign the outcomes a primary score by summing the elements of the below-threshold vector, transformed by the $g(.)$ function. Then assign the outcomes a secondary score by summing the (untransformed) elements of the above-threshold vector. If one outcome has a higher primary score it is morally better according to $u(.)$; if the two outcomes have the same primary score and one has a higher secondary score, it is morally better according to $u(.)$; otherwise the two outcomes are equally good according to $u(.)$.[70] Finally: outcome x is morally at least as good as outcome y, full stop, iff it is at least as good for all $u(.)$ belonging to $\mathbf{U}^T$.[71]

---

[68] See Brown (2005a, ch. 5; 2005b).

[69] Because the sufficientist SWF ranks utility vectors below the threshold using the continuous prioritarian formula, this SWF (like the continuous prioritarian SWF) is sensitive to ratio information.

[70] Formally, for each $u(.)$ in $\mathbf{U}^T$, and for any outcome z, define an N-entry vector $u^+(z)$ as follows: Its ith entry is $u(z; i)$ if $u(z; i) \leq T$, otherwise the entry is T. Define an N-entry vector $u^{++}(z)$ as follows: Its ith entry is $u(z; i)$ if $u(z; i) \geq T$, otherwise the entry is T. Outcome x is better than y according to $u(.)$ iff: (1) $\sum_{i=1}^{N} g(u_i^+(x)) > \sum_{i=1}^{N} g(u_i^+(y))$ or (2) $\sum_{i=1}^{N} g(u_i^+(x)) = \sum_{i=1}^{N} g(u_i^+(y))$ and $\sum_{i=1}^{N} u_i^{++}(x) > \sum_{i=1}^{N} u_i^{++}(y)$. Outcomes x and y are equally good according to $u(.)$ iff $\sum_{i=1}^{N} g(u_i^+(x)) = \sum_{i=1}^{N} g(u_i^+(y))$ and $\sum_{i=1}^{N} u_i^{++}(x) = \sum_{i=1}^{N} u_i^{++}(y)$. Outcome x is morally at least as good as y, according to $u(.)$, iff it is either better or equally good.

[71] A different formalization of the sufficientist SWF, which yields the very same ranking of outcomes as the formalization I have just provided, does not "winnow down" the **U** that represents well-being levels, differences, and ratios. Instead, it uses the full **U**; and defines the N-entry vector, for each $u(.)$ in the full **U**, in a manner that takes account of the value that $u(.)$ assigns to the threshold life-history $(x^+; i^+)$. Specifically, it defines the N-entry vector $u^+(z)$ for any outcome z as follows: Its ith entry is $u(z; i)$ if $u(z; i) \leq u(x^+; i^+)$; otherwise the entry is $u(x^+; i^+)$. It defines the N-entry vector $u^{++}(z)$ as follows: Its ith entry is $u(z; i)$ if $u(z; i) \geq u(x^+; i^+)$, otherwise the entry is $u(x^+; i^+)$. The SWF then uses the very same rule for comparing outcomes, according to $u(.)$, as in the previous footnote.

Like the utilitarian SWF, the sufficientist SWF violates the Pigou–Dalton principle. But the violation is more limited in scope. Imagine that individual i is below the threshold in outcome y (or incomparable with the threshold),[72] and that individual j is better off than i in this outcome. Outcome x is such that individual i is better off by a certain amount than she is in outcome y, individual j worse off by the very same amount, and individual j still at least as well off as i. Everyone else is unaffected. If so, the sufficientist SWF counts x as being morally better than y—which is what the Pigou–Dalton principle requires. In other words, the sufficientist SWF *satisfies* the Pigou–Dalton principle in the case of a transfer from a better-off person to a worse-off individual who starts off below or incomparable with the threshold.[73]

However, the sufficientist SWF *fails to satisfy* the Pigou–Dalton principle in a case where the worse-off individual starts off at or above the threshold. This, of course, is exactly what Crisp recommends in his discussion of the "Beverly Hills" case. Imagine that individual i is at or above the threshold in outcome y; individual j is better off than i; outcome x is such that individual i is better off than she is in y by a certain amount, individual j worse off by the very same amount, and individual j still at least

---

I have not formalized the sufficientist SWF along these lines because it does not adopt the simple R-based form for an SWF. Rather, the rule for ranking utility vectors that *this* SWF employs depends upon $u(.)$. In particular, it depends upon which particular number $u(.)$ assigns to the threshold life-history $(x^+; i^+)$.

For the sake of consistency, I have expressed all the SWFs in this chapter using the simple R-based form. Remember, however, that my argument for the Pigou–Dalton and separability axioms does *not* rely on the premise that SWFs properly assume this form. Indeed, the alternative formalization of sufficientism discussed in this footnote is subject to exactly the same criticism that I level against the R-based formalization: namely, that it fails to respect the Pigou–Dalton principle where the transferee as well as transferor start off at or above the threshold life-history $(x^+; i^+)$, and that the principle should be respected even in this case as a matter of fairness.

[72] In other words, either $u(y; i) \leq T$ for all $u(.)$ in $\mathbf{U^T}$, with at least one inequality strict; or $u(y; i)$ $< T$ and $v(y; i) > T$ for some $u(.)$ and some $v(.)$ in $\mathbf{U^T}$ (the case where i is incomparable with the threshold in y).

[73] A subtle question is whether the ranking of life-histories and differences, and the characterization of a pair of outcomes as a Pigou–Dalton transfer, should be defined by $\mathbf{U}$ or $\mathbf{U^T}$. For simplicity, I assume the latter. (Note that the choice is irrelevant where $\mathbf{U}$ is unique up to a positive ratio transformation or, more generally, can be partitioned into a family of sets of utility functions, each unique up to a positive ratio transformation. Moreover, even where this is not true, the sufficientist SWF will fail to respect some Pigou–Dalton transfers whether identified with respect to $\mathbf{U}$ or $\mathbf{U^T}$.)

Looking to $\mathbf{U^T}$: the worse-off individual, i, starts off below the threshold iff $u(y; i) \leq T$ for all $u(.)$ in $\mathbf{U^T}$, with at least one inequality strict; and starts off incomparable with the threshold iff $u(y; i) < T$ and $v(y; i) > T$ for some $u(.)$ and some $v(.)$ in $\mathbf{U^T}$. In such cases, the sufficientist SWF (with one, technical, exception) respects the Pigou–Dalton principle—regardless of whether the better-off individual, j, starts off below, above, at, or incomparable to the threshold, and regardless of where the worse-off individual ends up relative to the threshold. The exception is the case where every $u(.)$ in $\mathbf{U^T}$ which assigns $(y; i)$ a value less than T also assigns the very same value to life-histories $(x; i)$, $(y; j)$ and $(x; j)$. Note that this is consistent with the definition of a Pigou–Dalton transfer, see above, n. 5.

as well off as *i*; everyone else is unaffected. In *this* case, the sufficientist SWF says that *x* and *y* are equally morally good, while the Pigou–Dalton principle requires that *x* be ranked as morally better.

More generally, in cases where *x* and *y* are such that all affected individuals are at or above the threshold in both outcomes, the sufficientist SWF converges with the utilitarian SWF. In such cases (by contrast with cases where some affected individuals are not above the threshold), the sufficientist SWF assigns each person's claim a strength equaling her well-being difference; and it orders outcomes by simply summing claims. (See the margin for the "translation" of the sufficientist SWF into "claim" language, and for an explanation why its translation converges with the utilitarian translation in the case where all affected individuals are at or above the threshold.[74])

---

[74] For a given pair of outcomes, *x* and *y*, and a utility function $u(.)$ in $\mathbf{U}^T$, each individual *i*'s claim according to $u(.)$ is measured by a pair of numbers, $(g(u^+(x; i)) - g(u^+(y; i)), u^{++}(x; i) - u^{++}(y; i))$—where $u^+(z; i)$ is the *i*th element of the $u^+(z)$ vector and $u^{++}(z; i)$ is the *i*th element of the $u^{++}(z)$ vector for any outcome *z*, as these vectors are defined in n. 70, above. Call these, respectively, the primary and secondary claim measures according to $u(.)$.

The valence of an individual's claim depends upon his primary and secondary claim measures for all $u(.)$ in $\mathbf{U}^T$. Specifically, an individual has no claim either way if his primary and secondary claim measures are zero for all $u(.)$ in $\mathbf{U}^T$. He has a claim in favor of *x* over *y* iff both of these measures are nonnegative for all $u(.)$ in $\mathbf{U}^T$ and at least one of the measures is positive for at least one $u(.)$. He has a claim in favor of *y* over *x* iff both of these measures are nonpositive for all $u(.)$ in $\mathbf{U}^T$ and at least one of the measures is negative for at least one $u(.)$. Otherwise the individual has an incomparable claim.

This numerical information is used to compare outcomes, as follows. Outcome *x* is morally better than *y* according to $u(.)$ iff: (1) the sum of individuals' primary measures is positive; or (2) the sum of individuals' primary measures is zero and the sum of individuals' secondary measures is positive. Outcome *y* is morally better than *x* according to $u(.)$ iff: (1) the sum of individuals' primary measures is negative; or (2) the sum of individuals' primary measures is zero and the sum of individuals' secondary measures is negative. The outcomes are equally good according to $u(.)$ if neither is the case. One outcome is at least as good, full stop, iff at least as good for all $u(.)$ belonging to $\mathbf{U}^T$.

Consider, now, the case in which all affected individuals are at or above the threshold life-history $(x^+; i^+)$. In such a case, all affected individuals have primary measures of zero, for all $u(.)$ in $\mathbf{U}^T$. Each affected individual *i* has a secondary measure, according to each $u(.)$, equaling $u(x; i) - u(y; i)$. The sufficientist rule for making moral comparisons of outcomes simplifies to a straightforward sum of affected individuals' secondary measures: outcome *x* is morally at least as good as *y* if the sum of affected individuals' secondary measures is nonnegative for all $u(.)$ in $\mathbf{U}^T$; and outcome *y* is morally at least as good as *x* if the sum of affected individuals' secondary measures is nonpositive for all $u(.)$ in $\mathbf{U}^T$.

But remember that the utilitarian SWF measures each individual's claim, according to $u(.)$, using a single number, namely $u(x; i) - u(y; i)$. As the previous paragraph shows, this is exactly equal to the secondary measure assigned to each individual by the sufficient SWF, if the individual is at or above the threshold in both outcomes. Moreover, the utilitarian SWF ranks outcomes, for each $u(.)$, by summing the $u(x; i) - u(y; i)$ values for all affected individuals. But this is exactly what the sufficient SWF does, in the case where all affected individuals are at or above the threshold.

But is it plausible that morality contains a threshold above which the Pigou–Dalton principle fails? Whatever your theory of well-being, construct in your mind a case in which outcome x is reached via a Pigou–Dalton transfer from outcome y, and the two individuals involved, i and j, are very well-off in both of the outcomes. However, both individuals are genuinely *affected* by which outcome obtains. Life-history $(y; i)$ is Lower. Although this life-history is very good indeed in "absolute" terms (namely, it has all the requisites to exceed whatever threshold $(x^+; i^+)$ you might specify), there is a Middle life-history, $(x; i)$, in which i's well-being would be even higher—on whatever theory of well-being you find plausible. If outcome x were to occur, the second individual, individual j, would be yet better off, or at least equally well off, at Middle Plus. And Middle Plus, although really quite a good life, is not perfect. Individual j would flourish even more with life-history Higher, $(y; j)$. Since there are genuine *improvements* in well-being to be had here, why think that fairness considerations somehow evaporate? And if the fairness considerations do not evaporate, why conclude that leaving i at Lower and j at Higher is equally fair as leaving i at Middle and j at Middle Plus?

Crisp's Beverly Hills case is not a particularly helpful case for thinking clearly about the answer to these questions. In considering the possibility of thresholds, for purposes of welfarism, it is vitally important not to conflate (1) a threshold *within* the most attractive account of well-being, which would show up as a threshold within the utility functions that map the various determinants of well-being (the various constituents of outcomes) onto utility numbers representing well-being, with (2) a threshold in the moral significance of well-being itself. But the *Beverly Hills* case invites just such a conflation. We are told that each rich individual stands to benefit a certain amount by having fine wine and that each super-rich individual stands to benefit the very same amount by having fine wine. But the thought experiment of giving fine wine to someone living in Beverly Hills, the lap of luxury, naturally invites the reaction that this individual is above a threshold of the first sort—in particular, that giving her this additional luxury good does not make her life genuinely better at all. As Nagel cogently observes (anticipating, and rejecting, a sufficientist approach years before Crisp's article): "My moral instincts reveal no egalitarian priority for the well-to-do over the rich and super-rich. But I suspect that is because the marginal utility of wealth diminishes so steeply in those regions . . . that these categories do not correspond to significant objective differences in well-being. . . ."[75]

Crisp might respond that he is offering a conception of *compassion*, not fairness. Our compassionate concern for people gives out at some threshold level of well-being. Indeed, this is plausible. But for reasons reviewed at length earlier in the chapter, morality should be sensitive to considerations of fairness, not merely compassion. While Pigou–Dalton transfers between individuals above some well-being threshold are (plausibly) a matter of indifference, qua compassion, they are not indifferent

---

[75] Nagel (1995, p. 70).

qua fairness—at least on the claim-across-outcome conception of fairness. If x is reached from y by a Pigou–Dalton transfer, then—regardless of whether the affected individuals are located below, at, or above some stipulated threshold—x is fairer than y.

More robustly, this chapter takes as its provisional assumption that welfarist morality is exhausted by fairness considerations: that outcome x is morally at least as good as y, all things considered, iff x is at least as fair as y. But note that, even without this provisional assumption, the sufficientist SWF would be problematic in virtue of failing the Pigou–Dalton principle above the threshold. Assume that (contra the provisional assumption) morality is a hybrid of fairness considerations and considerations of compassion. And assume that we are trying to construct an SWF which would reflect this plurality of considerations. Such an SWF would universally satisfy the Pigou–Dalton principle. Even if the worse-off person starts off at or above the compassion threshold (so that the Pigou–Dalton transfer is a matter of indifference qua compassion), the transfer is not a matter of indifference qua fairness—and so the pluralistic SWF (on balance) should approve it. In short, the sufficientist SWF cannot be justified either as a matter of fairness (in the claim-across-outcome sense), or as a hybrid of fairness (in that sense) plus compassion.

While the sufficientist SWF is problematic insofar as it violates the Pigou–Dalton principle, this SWF has further features that fairness might be seen to recommend. Unlike the leximin SWF, it does *not* give absolute priority to badly off individuals, as against individuals who are only slightly better off. (Remember that Crisp criticizes leximin on this score.) And, unlike the continuous prioritarian SWF, it does *not* allow very small gains to sufficiently large numbers of well-off individuals to override a substantial loss for a badly off person. (Remember that Crisp criticizes the continuous prioritarian SWF on this score.)

As work by Brown and Bertil Tungodden has helped show, it is possible to construct a genuinely *prioritarian* SWF which possesses these features. This is the prioritarian SWF with a lexical threshold. It neither gives absolute priority to worse-off individuals, nor allows small gains to sufficiently large numbers of the well off to override losses for the badly off. However, by contrast with the sufficientist SWF, this SWF is genuinely prioritarian because it universally satisfies the Pigou–Dalton principle (as well as the axiom of separability).

We will, in due course, consider the prioritarian SWF with a lexical threshold. First, however, let us turn to the issue of separability. The main thrust of this section has been that fairness in the claim-across-outcome sense recommends the Pigou–Dalton principle, thus undercutting both the utilitarian and the sufficientist SWF. Let us now see why fairness also recommends separability.

III. SEPARABILITY

The axiom of "separability" should not be confused with the concept of the "separateness of persons." The former is a precise axiom that we might require the ranking of outcomes to satisfy. This axiom, stated in full at the beginning of the chapter, says (for short) that the ranking of two outcomes does not depend upon the well-being levels, in those outcomes, of individuals who are unaffected as between them.

The "separateness of persons" is a much more open-ended concept, too loose to be characterized as an "axiom." This concept is specifiable in a variety of ways. (I have considered three.) Moreover, even when the concept of the "separateness of persons" is made more precise via the claim-across-outcome conception of fairness, this concept does not entail "separability."

Ideally, we would avoid the potential confusion of "separability" with the "separateness of persons" by using different terms. Unfortunately, both terms are quite standard in the literature, and so I can only hope that the careful reader will remember not to conflate them.

To see why a violation of separability is logically *consistent* with the basic requirements of the claim-across-outcome conception of fairness, consider the rank-weighted SWF. The rank-weighted SWF uses a set of N weighting factors $a_1, \ldots, a_N$, with the first strictly larger than the second, the second strictly larger than the third, and so on. Weighting factor a_1 corresponds to rank one, weighting factor a_2 to rank two, etc. For each utility function $u(.)$ in the set **U** of utility functions, a given outcome x is assigned a rank-weighted sum, as follows. Determine each individual's utility rank in the vector $u(x)$, with one the rank for the smallest utility, two the rank for the next smallest, and so forth. Multiply each individual's utility in $u(x)$ by the weighting factor corresponding to her rank and add these weighted amounts. The sum is the cumulative rank-weighted utility of x, according to $u(.)$.[76] The rank-weighted SWF then says that: outcome x is morally at least as good as outcome y iff the cumulative rank-weighted utility of x is at least as large as the cumulative rank-weighted utility of y, for all $u(.)$ in **U**.

The rank-weighted SWF can be translated into the language of across-outcome claims, roughly as follows. Given two outcomes, x and y, and a utility function $u(.)$, the strength of each individual's claim in favor of x or y, according to $u(.)$, is measurable by a single number: the difference between his rank-weighted utility in x and his rank-weighted utility in y. The fairer outcome, according to $u(.)$, is then determined by summing these measures. See the margin for a more precise statement.[77]

---

[76] For a given utility vector $u(x)$, produce a corresponding rank-ordered vector $u^*(x)$ by ordering the elements of $u(x)$ from smallest to largest. For example, if $u(x) = (5, 3, 8, 7)$, $u^*(x) = (3, 5, 7, 8)$. If $u(x) = (6, 2, 5, 2)$, $u^*(x) = (2, 2, 5, 6)$. (As this example shows, if the same number is repeated in $u(x)$, it will appear as successive entries in $u^*(x)$.) Assign $u(x)$ a number $w(u(x))$ equaling a_1 times the first element of $u^*(x)$ plus a_2 times the second element of $u^*(x)$ plus ... plus a_N times the last element of $u^*(x)$. Then the rank-weighted rule R says that $u(x)$ is at least as good as $u(y)$ iff $w(u(x)) \geq w(u(y))$.

[77] Given x and y and $u(.)$, define $u^*(x)$ and $u^*(y)$ as in the previous footnote. There is a one-to-one mapping between the elements of $u(x)$ and $u^*(x)$. (In the case where $u(x)$ has multiple individuals at the same utility level, there will be multiple such mappings. For example, if $u(x) = (6, 2, 5, 2)$ and $u^*(x) = (2, 2, 5, 6)$, the mapping may map the second entry of $u(x)$ onto the first entry in $u^*(x)$ and the fourth entry of $u(x)$ onto the second entry of $u^*(x)$, or vice versa.) Using any one such mapping, assign each individual i a number $r(x, i, u)$ equaling the rank in $u^*(x)$ that her entry in $u(x)$ is mapped onto. Similarly, there is a one-to-one mapping between $u(y)$ and $u^*(y)$; using any one such mapping, assign each individual i a number $r(y, i, u)$ equaling the rank in $u^*(y)$ that her entry in $u(y)$ is mapped onto.

Note that this rank-weighted scheme for measuring and adjudicating between claims *satisfies* the basic requirements of the claim-across-outcome conception of fairness. The valence of an individual's claim is indeed appropriately related to the valence of her well-being. If an individual is better off in x than y, then (on the rank-weighted scheme) she does indeed have a claim in favor of x. If an individual is equally well off in both outcomes, then (on the rank-weighted scheme) she does indeed have no claim either way. If she is incomparably well off, she has an incomparable claim.

Furthermore, the rank-weighted scheme meets the basic demands of the claim-across-outcome conception for "no conflict" cases. Equivalently, the rank-weighted SWF is a Paretian SWF.

Finally, it can be shown that the rank-weighted SWF satisfies the Pigou–Dalton principle.[78]

To see why the rank-weighted SWF does *not* satisfy separability, consider Table 5.2.

Table 5.2 The Rank-Weighted SWF and Separability

| | Utility rank (from lowest to highest) | | | |
	First	Second	Third	Sum of rank-weighted utility
Outcome x	20r	50r	200r	$3(20r) + 2(50r) + 1(200r) = 360r$
Outcome y	20r	60r	175r	$3(20r) + 2(60r) + 1(175r) = 355r$
Strength of claim	___	2(10r)	1(25r)	
Outcome x*	50r	100r	200r	$3(50r) + 2(100r) + 1(200r) = 550r$
Outcome y*	60r	100r	175r	$3(60r) + 2(100r) + 1(175r) = 555r$
Strength of claim	3(10r)	___	1(25r)	

We can then produce an N-entry claim vector, with each entry the measure of that individual's claim in favor of x according to $u(.)$, with negative entries meaning a claim in favor of y according to $u(.)$, calculated as follows: (1) In the case where there are no "rank switches," i.e., $r(x, i, u) = r(y, i, u)$ for all i, the measure of individual i's claim in favor of x is $u(x; i)a_{r(x,i,u)} - u(y; i)a_{r(x,i,u)}$. (2) Where there *are* rank switches, measuring claims this way can violate the basic requirements of the claim-across-outcome conception regarding claim valence: it can assign unaffected individuals a nonzero claim, or assign individuals who are better off in x a negative claim. So we can measure claims a different way. Calculate the total sum of rank-weighted utility for x, and subtract the total sum of rank-weighted utility for y. Call this amount ΔS. If $u(x; i) = u(y; i)$, assign i a zero claim. For all other individuals, assign them claims arbitrarily, so that the total sum of claims is ΔS and so that individuals with greater utility in x than y are assigned a positive claim, otherwise a negative claim. Because the rank-weighted SWF satisfies Pareto-superiority, it should always be possible to do this.

We then say that an individual has a claim in favor of x iff her claim measure is nonnegative for all $u(.)$ and positive for some; a claim in favor of y iff her claim measure is nonpositive for all $u(.)$ and negative for some; no claim either way if her claim measure is zero for all $u(.)$; and otherwise an incomparable claim. Outcome x is morally at least as good as y iff the sum of the entries of the claim vector is nonnegative, for all $u(.)$ belonging to **U**; and y is morally at least as good as x iff the sum is nonpositive, for all $u(.)$.

[78] The properties of the rank-weighted SWF are discussed by Blackorby, Bossert, and Donaldson (2005, ch. 4, especially at pp. 99–100), and the scholarship cited therein.

In Table 5.2, outcome $x = (20r, 50r, 200r)$ and outcome $y = (20r, 60r, 175r)$, while outcome $x^* = (100r, 50r, 200r)$ and outcome $y^* = (100r, 60r, 175r)$, with the entries in the vectors representing the utilities of individuals 1, 2, and 3.[79] Consider ranking the x-y pair and the x^*-y^* pair using a rank-weighted rule, with the simplest weighting scheme such that a weight of 3 is assigned to the lowest utility, 2 the second lowest, and 1 the highest. The calculations are given in the table, showing that x is ranked over y but y^* over x^*, in violation of separability.

Individual 1 is unaffected in each pair. So he has no claim as between x and y, or as between x^* and y^*. However, because individual 1 has the lowest utility rank in the x-y pair, and the second-lowest utility in the x^*-y^* pair, the strength of individual 2's claim changes between the pairs (from a strength $20r$ in the x-y case to a strength of $30r$ in the x^*-y^* case). Thus the sum of the claims of the two affected individuals (2 and 3) points in favor of x over y, but points in favor of y^* over x^*.

As the table illustrates, the rank-weighted scheme runs afoul of separability in its methodology for measuring the *strength* of individual claims. If i is better off in x than y, according to $u(.)$, then the strength of her claim for x, according to $u(.)$, depends on her rank in the overall distribution of utilities in x and y. In other words, the strength of i's claim depends on what the utility levels of unaffected individuals are.

Thus the rank-weighted SWF shows how the claim-across-outcome view of fairness might allow facts about the distribution of well-being within outcomes to influence the fairness ranking of outcomes. On the claim-across-outcome view, whether an individual i possesses a claim in favor of x or y (what I have termed the "valence" of the individual's claim) depends on an intra-personal, inter-world comparison of well-being, *not* on an inter-personal, intra-world comparison. But—if the individual is indeed better off in one of the outcomes, or incomparably well off—the fairness *weight* of that well-being difference may hinge on inter-personal, intra-world well-being comparisons. That weight may depend on the extent to which i is better off than the other individuals in the population, within outcome x and within outcome y.

Should we endorse the separability axiom? If fairness is understood in the claim-across-outcome sense, then the case for the Pigou–Dalton axiom (a "case" which involves equipoise in reflective equilibrium, not logical entailment) is quite compelling, or so I have tried to suggest. The case for separability is perhaps somewhat less compelling. Still, separability seems on balance quite attractive.

---

[79] Remember that the "r" notation is shorthand for the case where utility is unique up to a positive ratio transformation. Some utility function $u(.)$ is in $\mathbf{U}$, and $v(.)$ is also in $\mathbf{U}$ iff there is some positive number r such that $v(x; i) = ru(x; i)$ for all $(x; i)$. To denote x as "$(20r, 50r, 200r)$" means that x is mapped onto $(20, 50, 200)$ by $u(.)$ and onto some positive multiple of that vector by every other utility function in $\mathbf{U}$.

Individuals who are unaffected by the occurrence of x versus y have no claim either way. They have no *direct* role in the ranking of outcomes, or so the claim-across-outcome conception requires. This is intuitive: because the individuals are equally well off in both outcomes, they have no moral interest in which outcome occurs.

By departing from separability we allow unaffected individuals to have an *indirect* role in the ranking of outcomes. In "conflict" cases, where some individuals are better off in x than y (or incomparably well off), and some better off in y than x (or incomparably well off), a departure from separability means that intra-world comparisons between the well-being levels of affected and unaffected individuals helps to determine the moral weight of different affected individuals' claims—and thus to determine which outcome is on balance fairer. But why *should* the well-being of unaffected individuals have this indirect role in the ranking of outcomes? If it is unfair to see them as having a moral interest regarding which of two outcomes occurs, why is it fair to allow their well-being to change our assessment of the balance of claims of those who *do* have an interest?

Do not be distracted by the thought that an individual's well-being in a given outcome may well be partly determined by her relational attributes in that outcome. This important point was already acknowledged. For example, an individual's well being in x may depend, not only on her own consumption level in x, but on whether her consumption is high or low in the overall pattern of consumption in x. We might even embrace a recursive understanding of well-being, such that i's well-being in x depends on the distribution of well-being in x.

In principle, all such effects can be captured in the set $\mathbf{U}$ that measures the well-being levels of various life-histories and the differences between them.[80] Conversely, the separability axiom itself has nothing to do with the content of $\mathbf{U}$. Rather, it concerns the functional form of the apparatus (the SWF) which is used to move *from* the utility information in the set $\mathbf{U}$ *to* a moral ranking of outcomes.

Imagine then a set $\mathbf{U}$ which accurately reflects individuals' well-being levels in x and y, as determined by their non-relational and relational attributes in each outcome. Some individuals are genuinely unaffected (even taking account of relational facts). Individual l is in this unaffected group if, for each $u(.)$ in $\mathbf{U}$, $u(x; l) = u(y; l)$. Individual l—taking full account of relational facts and also allowing for the possibility of incomparabilities in the ordering of life-histories—is such that he really has no stake in this pair of outcomes. He is not better off in one, nor worse off in one, nor even incomparably well off. Rather, his life goes exactly as well regardless of whether x or y obtains. To be sure, various facts about l (including his well-being

<hr />

[80] To be sure, in practice, limitations in our ability to measure well-being might mean that $\mathbf{U}$ is not fully sensitive to the impact of relational facts on well-being—but it is hard to see why this "second best" point should change our judgments about the appropriate functional form of the SWF, in particular about whether it should satisfy separability.

level) may influence the well-being of other individuals; but those influences are fully reflected in *their* utility numbers. (For example, if the fact that l has higher consumption than i in x reduces i's well-being in x, then that will be reflected in $u(x; i)$, which will be lower than it otherwise would have been.)

Separability says that, if the utility of l is really exactly the same in two outcomes for all $u(.)$ in $\mathbf{U}$, then facts about his attributes and well-being in the two outcomes may well bear on the well-being of others, but have no *additional* role in ranking the outcomes—no role in determining whether it would be fairer to affected individuals for x or y to obtain, given affected individuals' well-being in x and y (as captured by $\mathbf{U}$). Once it is clearly understood that it is this (and nothing else) that separability requires, the axiom seems a very plausible way to flesh out the claim-across-outcome conception of fairness.

IV. PRIORITARIANISM AND PRIORITARIAN SWFS, CONTINUOUS AND DISCONTINUOUS

By "prioritarian" SWFs, I mean all SWFs that, in addition to minimal welfarist requirements, satisfy both the Pigou–Dalton axiom and the separability axiom.

A further axiom which we might ask SWFs to satisfy is *continuity*, a precise statement of which was provided earlier.[81] The continuity axiom can be seen as imposing a kind of "stability" requirement on SWFs: small changes in individual well-being should not produce abrupt changes in the moral ranking of outcomes.

This is a plausible property for an SWF to have. In addition, SWFs with the continuity property can be expressed in a simple, mathematically tractable form (another desirable property in a decision procedure). First, any SWF with the following form is both prioritarian *and* satisfies the continuity axiom: x is morally at least as good as y iff $\sum_{i=1}^{N} g(u_i(x)) \geq \sum_{i=1}^{N} g(u_i(y))$, with the $g(.)$ function strictly increasing and strictly concave.[82] Moreover, if a prioritarian SWF satisfies the continuity axiom,

---

[81] Remember that an SWF which adopts the simple R-based form is continuous if the ordering of utility vectors yielded by R is continuous in the sense that the set of vectors better than, or worse than, a given vector are open sets. See above, n. 9. Unlike the Pigou–Dalton and separability axioms, the continuity axiom, as just formulated, presupposes that the SWF takes the simple R-based form. In this section and the next (which focus on the choice within the family of prioritarian SWFs) I adopt that assumption.

[82] It is easy to see that this SWF satisfies minimal welfarist requirements. Because $g(.)$ is a single function rather than being indexed to individuals, the SWF satisfies anonymity. Because $g(.)$ is strictly increasing, the SWF is Paretian. Moreover, the SWF clearly satisfies separability (because it is additive) and the Pigou–Dalton principle. The latter can be seen visually by looking at the graph of a strictly concave function. See Chapter 2, pp. 78–79. The proof is also straightforward. If $g(.)$ is a function of a single variable, to say that $g(.)$ is strictly concave means: for all numbers a, b, and for all p between 0 and 1, $g(pa + (1 - p)b) > pg(a) + (1 - p)g(b)$. Imagine that $u = (u_1, \ldots, u_i, \ldots, u_j, \ldots, u_N)$, and that u^* is reached via a Pigou–Dalton transfer from u, i.e., $u^* = (u_1, \ldots, u_i + \Delta u, \ldots, u_j - \Delta u, \ldots, u_N)$, where $\Delta u > 0$, $u_j > u_i$, and $u_j - \Delta u \geq u_i + \Delta u$. $\sum_{i=1}^{N} g(u_i^*) - \sum_{i=1}^{N} g(u_i) = [g(u_i + \Delta u) + g(u_j - \Delta u)] - [g(u_i) + g(u_j)]$.

then it must either employ the formula just stated, or be extensionally equivalent to this formula for *some* strictly increasing, strictly concave $g(.)$ function. This latter result is powerful and far from obvious.[83]

For these reasons, I use the term "continuous prioritarian SWF" as the name for an SWF that ranks outcomes using the formula: x is morally at least as good as y iff $\sum_{i=1}^{N} g(u_i(x)) \geq \sum_{i=1}^{N} g(u_i(y))$, with the $g(.)$ function strictly increasing and strictly concave.[84] (I sometimes refer to this $g(.)$ function as the "transformation" function.)

Now define $p = 1 - \Delta u/(u_j - u_i)$. Then $u_i + \Delta u = pu_i + (1 - p)u_j$; while $u_j - \Delta u = (1 - p)u_i + pu_j$. By definition of concavity, $g(u_i + \Delta u) = g(pu_i + (1 - p)u_j) > pg(u_i) + (1 - p)g(u_j)$; and $g(u_j - \Delta u) = g((1 - p)u_i + pu_j) > (1 - p)g(u_i) + pg(u_j)$. Therefore, $[g(u_i + \Delta u) + g(u_j - \Delta u)] - [g(u_i) + g(u_j)] > 0$.

What about continuity? If $g(.)$ is a continuous function, then the function $w(u(x)) = \sum_{i=1}^{N} g(u_i(x))$ is also continuous; and this $w(.)$ function therefore produces a continuous ordering of N-dimensional utility vectors. On the connection between a continuous function and a continuous ordering, see Kreps (1988, p. 27); Ok (2007, pp. 145–147, 239–242). Moreover, if $g(.)$ is concave it *will* be continuous (except, perhaps, at boundary points). See, e.g., Sundaram (1996, pp. 177–178). Thus an explicit requirement of continuity for $g(.)$ is superfluous, unless the domain of $g(.)$ is not open (for example, if the N-dimensional utility vectors being ranked by the $\sum_{i=1}^{N} g(u_i(x))$ formula are allowed to have entries that are positive *or* 0).

[83] Consider any prioritarian SWF which says: x is morally at least as good as y iff $u(x)$ is ranked at least as good as $u(y)$ by some rule R^*, for all $u(.)$ in **U**, where R^* produces a complete, continuous ranking of all utility vectors in N-dimensional Euclidean space (or all in some orthant). Because the SWF is prioritarian as well as satisfying minimal welfarist requirements, R^* must be separable, Pigou–Dalton respecting, Paretian, and anonymous in addition to being continuous. A basic result in social choice theory is that—for any continuous, separable, Paretian, anonymous ordering of utility vectors in N-dimensional Euclidean space (or a suitable subset thereof, such as some orthant)—there is some strictly increasing and continuous function $h(.)$, such that the additive formula, $\sum_{i=1}^{N} h(u_i)$, yields the very same ordering. See Blackorby, Bossert, and Donaldson (2005, pp. 115–116); Bossert and Weymark (2004, p. 1159); see also Blackorby, Primont, and Russell (1998, pp. 70–73); Debreu (1960, pp. 20–25). Because the ordering is also Pigou–Dalton respecting, it is not hard to show that $h(.)$ must be strictly concave. See Adler and Sanchirico (2006, p. 372).

The original prioritarian SWF satisfying the continuity axiom said: x is morally at least as good as y iff $u(x)$ is ranked at least as good as $u(y)$ by some rule R^*, for all $u(.)$ in **U**. The extensionally equivalent counterpart says: x is morally at least as good as y iff $\sum_{i=1}^{N} h(u_i(x)) \geq \sum_{i=1}^{N} h(u_i(y))$, for all $u(.)$ in **U**, with $h(.)$ strictly increasing and strictly concave. This counterpart is "extensionally equivalent" to the original in the sense that both produce the very same ranking of outcomes in every outcome set, for every **U**.

[84] I might define the continuous prioritarian SWF more broadly, as one using an R of the form $F\left(\sum_{i=1}^{N} g(u_i(x))\right)$, with $F(.)$ any strictly increasing function. However, this broader definition increases the notational burden, with no analytic benefit: a given continuous prioritarian SWF (in my narrower sense) is justified as a framework for ranking outcomes iff the family of strictly increasing transformations thereof is.

By contrast, in discussing choice under uncertainty, it *is* important to distinguish between the $\sum_{i=1}^{N} g(u_i(x))$ formula and (non-linear) increasing transformations thereof—and I am indeed sensitive to this point in Chapter 7.

Because of the simplicity of this SWF, and because of the substantive attractiveness of continuity, this SWF is one of the most widely used in the existing SWF literature, along with the utilitarian SWF.

The continuous prioritarian SWF, translated into "claim" language, has the following properties. (1) For each pair of outcomes, x and y, and each utility function $u(.)$ in U, each individual's claim in favor of x or y is measured by a single number, namely her *transformed utility* in x minus her *transformed utility* in y; and (2) the morally better outcome, according to each $u(.)$, is determined by *adding up* these numbers measuring individual claims.[85]

Although the continuous prioritarian SWF has attractive features, it also possesses a property which many find unattractive.[86] The continuous prioritarian SWF is willing to impose a large loss upon a single badly off individual for the sake of arbitrarily small benefits for arbitrarily well-off individuals—no matter how small their benefits or well-off those individuals, and no matter how badly off the first individual or substantial his loss—if the number of well-off individuals is sufficiently large. This property, which I shall term the "Numbers Win" property, can be precisely formulated as follows:

Numbers Win

In any outcome set, consider any life-history $(x; i)$, however bad it may be, and any other life-history $(y; i)$, which is even worse for that individual i. Choose any number F larger than 1, which can be arbitrarily large; and any positive number b, which can be arbitrarily close to zero. Then for an SWF to have the "Numbers Win" property means: There is some sufficiently large positive number M, such that *if* the only individuals affected as between y and x are (1) individual i, who goes from however badly off he might be in x, to being even worse off in y, and (2) at least M individuals each of whom in x is F times better off than individual i in x, and each of whom is better off in y than x, but only by an

[85] Formally: given a pair of outcomes x and y and a utility function $u(.)$, the measure of each individual's claim, according to $u(.)$, is $g(u(x; i)) - g(u(y; i))$. An individual has a claim in favor of x iff his claim measure according to $u(.)$ is nonnegative for all $u(.)$ belonging to U and positive for some; a claim in favor of y iff his claim measure according to $u(.)$ is nonpositive for all $u(.)$ belonging to U and negative for some; no claim either way iff the measure of his claim is zero for all $u(.)$; and otherwise an incomparable claim. Outcome x is morally at least as good as y, according to $u(.)$, if the sum of claim measures, according to $u(.)$ is nonnegative; outcome y is morally at least as good as x, according to $u(.)$, if the sum of claim measures, according to $u(.)$, is nonpositive. One outcome is morally at least as good as a second iff morally at least as good for all $u(.)$ in U.

[86] See, e.g., Brown (2005a, ch. 5; 2005b); Crisp (2003b); Fleurbaey, Tungodden, and Vallentyne (2009).

amount which is a multiple b of individual i's loss, *then* the SWF counts y as a morally better outcome than x.[87]

---

[87] I assume that **U** has been "zeroed out" in the natural fashion, by including only utility functions such that $u(x^*; i^*) = 0$, where $(x^*; i^*)$ is the zero point used to define ratios (be it nonexistence or some other zero point). See below. I have formulated Numbers Win in terms of ratios (with well-off individuals at a well-being level in x which is an arbitrary multiple of individual i's well-being, and their benefit from y an arbitrarily small fraction of i's loss) because, with utility at most measurable up to a positive ratio transformation, it is not clear what it means to identify a particular numerical level of well-being or size for a benefit.

Assume, moreover, that the badly off individual starts off above the zero point, specifically that $u(x; i) > 0$ for all $u(.)$ in **U**. (Otherwise, individuals who are a positive number F times the utility of individual i will be worse off than him, not better off. I could reformulate the property in a more complicated fashion to allow for a negative starting point, but will not belabor the discussion by doing so.)

To say that some individual j in outcome x is at an arbitrarily large multiple F of that life-history is to say that, for all $u(.)$ belonging to **U**, $u(x; j)/u(x; i) = F$. To say that individual j's benefit from moving to outcome y is an arbitrarily small positive multiple b of i's loss is to say that, for all $u(.)$ belonging to **U**, $(u(y; j) - u(x; j))/(u(x; i) - u(y; i)) = b$.

Imagine that **U** is a singleton, which consists of a single utility function. In that case, for any continuous prioritarian SWF, the badly off individual has a claim to x, measured by $g(u(x; i)) - g(u(y; i))$. Call this c_i. Let us designate the magnitude of individual i's well-being loss, if y were to obtain, i.e., $u(x; i) - u(y; i)$, as Δu.

Imagine that x includes a group of individuals, all of whom are F times better off than individual i, and all of whom benefit from y by amount $b\Delta u$. Then each of those individuals has a claim in favor of y equaling $g(Fu(x; i) + b\Delta u) - g(Fu(x; i))$. Call this c^*. Because $g(.)$ is a strictly increasing function, this number is positive. Let M equal the first integer greater than c_i/c^*. If the group has M or more members, and the only individuals affected by the two outcomes are those individuals and individual i, than the SWF says that y is, on balance, a fairer outcome.

Note that, for a given pair of outcomes x and y, with i worse off in y than x, there may well not be M or more individuals who are F times better off than i in x, benefiting from y by only a fraction b of individual i's loss, with no one else affected. Whether all this holds true depends on what the outcomes are and what the size of the population, N, is. I have therefore framed the Numbers Win property in conditional terms: *If the only individuals benefiting from y are M or more individuals who are F times better off than individual i in x, etc., then y is ranked better by the SWF despite individual i's loss.*

What happens when **U** becomes a non-singleton set? In that case, each $u(.)$ has its own cutoff population M^u. Take some number M which is an upper bound of all these. If there are M or more individuals who are all F times better off than i in x, benefiting from y by only a fraction b of the badly off individual's loss, then the continuous prioritarian SWF would say that y is the better outcome, because it would be better for all $u(.)$ belonging to **U**.

The only mathematical hitch, here, is that—because **U** will have an infinite number of members—the upper bound mentioned in the last paragraph may not exist. However, at least in the focal case where (1) **U** is formed as a union of sets measuring each of N spectators' extended preferences over life-histories, each consisting of utilities that are unique up to a positive ratio transformation; and (2) the SWF is the Atkinson SWF, so the cutoff population is the same for each $u(.)$ and all positive ratio transformations thereof, an upper bound *will* certainly exist. And so, at least in this focal case,

Isn't the Numbers Win property very troubling? It brings to mind a famous example provided by Thomas Scanlon, the so-called "transmitter room" example.

> Suppose that Jones has suffered an accident in the transmitter room of a television station. Electrical equipment has fallen on his arm, and we cannot rescue him without turning off the transmitter for fifteen minutes. A World Cup match is in progress, watched by many people, and it will not be over for an hour. Jones's injury will not get any worse if we wait, but his hand has been mashed and he is receiving extremely painful electrical shocks. Should we rescue him now or wait until the match is over? Does the right thing to do depend on how many people are watching—whether it is one million or five million or a hundred million? It seems to me that we should not wait, no matter how many viewers there are. . . .[88]

Moreover, there exist prioritarian SWFs that lack the Numbers Win property. Along with the continuous prioritarian SWF, two kinds of discontinuous[89] prioritarian SWFs have been discussed in the scholarly literature: the leximin SWF and a prioritarian SWF with a lexical threshold. Neither possesses the Numbers Win property.

In this section, I argue that—notwithstanding its deficits—the continuous prioritarian SWF is on balance the most attractive SWF in the family of prioritarian SWFs. The section begins by reviewing the philosophical literature on "prioritarianism," so as to clarify why Pigou–Dalton, separable SWFs are properly characterized as "prioritarian." I then defend the continuous prioritarian SWF against, first, the leximin SWF and, second, a prioritarian SWF with a lexical threshold.

A. What Is Prioritarianism?

There is a substantial contemporary philosophical literature on prioritarianism.[90] Parfit's 1991 Lindley Lecture is seen by many as the starting point of this literature.[91] That is not really accurate; the Lindley Lecture, although brilliant and seminal,

---

the continuous prioritarian SWF does have the unfortunate Numbers Win property. (Note that, in this case, the badly off individual must not only start off above the zero point, but also cannot end up below it, because the Atkinson SWF is only a prioritarian SWF if limited to utility vectors with non-negative entries. See below, pp. 391–392.)

[88] Scanlon (1998, p. 235).

[89] By "discontinuous," I mean a prioritarian SWF that fails to satisfy the continuity axiom.

[90] See Arneson (1999a, 2000a, 2000b, 2007); Brighouse and Swift (2006); Brock (2002); Broome (1995, n.d.); Brown (2005a, 2005b); Crisp (2003b); Fleurbaey (2001); Fleurbaey and Tungodden (2010); Fleurbaey, Tungodden, and Vallentyne (2009); Hausman (n.d.); Hirose (2009); Holtug (2007c, 2010); Jensen (1995, 2003); McCarthy (2006, 2008); McKerlie (1994, 2003); Moreno-Ternero and Roemer (2008); Otsuka and Voorhoeve (2009); Persson (2001, 2008); Peterson (2010); Peterson and Hansson (2005); Rabinowicz (2001); Temkin (2000, 2003b); Tungodden (2000, 2003); Tungodden and Vallentyne (2005); Vallentyne (2000); Weirich (1983). Some of the literature regarding the appropriate "time slice" for distribution also focuses specifically on prioritarianism. See sources cited in Chapter 6, nn. 83, 102.

[91] Parfit (2000).

builds upon Nagel's previous (1977) Tanner Lecture. Indeed, Parfit begins his analysis by discussing a hypothetical case that Nagel had introduced.[92]

The case, as Nagel describes it, is as follows:

> Suppose I have two children, one of which is normal and quite happy, and the other of which suffers from a painful handicap. Call them respectively the first child and the second child. I am about to change jobs. Suppose I must decide between moving to an expensive city where the second child can receive special medical treatment and schooling, but where the family's standard of living will be lower and the neighborhood will be unpleasant and dangerous for the first child—or else moving to a pleasant semi-rural suburb where the first child, who has a special interest in sports and nature, can have a free and agreeable life. . . . I want to suppose that the case has the following feature: the gain to the first child of moving to the suburb is substantially greater than the gain to the second child of moving to the city. After all, the second child will also suffer from the family's reduced standard of living and the disagreeable environment. And the educational and therapeutic benefits will not make him happy but only less miserable. For the first child, on the other hand, the choice is between a happy life and a disagreeable one.

Nagel then uses his hypothetical case to endorse the Pigou–Dalton principle (although, to be sure, he does not use that term!): "It is more [morally] urgent to benefit the second child, even though the benefit we can give him is less than the benefit we can give the first child. . . . An improvement in his situation is more important than an equal or somewhat greater improvement in the situation of the first child."[93]

Parfit, discussing this example, supposes it can be represented using interpersonally comparable numbers measuring the well-being of the two children, as follows:

Table 5.3 A Decision that Affects Two Children

	Move to city	Move to suburb
First child	20	25
Second child	10	9

Note that the utilitarian choice is to move to the suburb: the gain to the first child of living in the suburb rather than the city ($25 - 20 = 5$) exceeds the loss to the second child ($10 - 9 = 1$). But any non-utilitarian will find plausible the thought that moving to the city is the better choice.

---

[92] Ibid., pp. 81–83.
[93] Nagel (1979, pp. 123–124, 124).

The thrust of Parfit's Lindley Lecture is to distinguish between two different kinds of non-utilitarian rationales for moving to the city. One such rationale, according to Parfit, is an "Egalitarian" view, which endorses what Parfit calls "The Principle of Equality": "It is in itself bad if some people are worse off than others."[94] However precisely one measures the distribution of well-being within a given outcome, it seems intuitively very clear that the distribution of well-being in the city outcome (20, 10) is more equal than the distribution of well-being in the suburb outcome (25, 9).

The second possible rationale that Parfit offers for moving to the city is what he terms "[t]he Priority View," i.e., prioritarianism. The prioritarian idea, as Parfit articulates it, is to compare the city and suburb outcomes by looking at each child's gain or loss in moving to the suburb and then *adjusting* each gain or loss to take account of the child's level of well-being, rather than simply summing the gains and losses in utilitarian fashion. If the prioritarian favors moving to the city, that is because (in Parfit's words) "[b]enefiting people matters more the worse off these people are." In other words:

> For Utilitarians, the moral importance of each benefit depends only on how great this benefit would be. For *Prioritarians*, it also depends on how well off the person is to whom this benefit comes. We should not give equal weight to equal benefits, whoever receives them. Benefits to the worse off should be given more weight.

In other words (again Parfit's), prioritarians believe that well-being has "diminishing marginal *moral importance*."[95]

All of these formulations are different ways of expressing the Pigou–Dalton principle. However, Parfit also stresses a further and logically distinct feature of prioritarianism, namely that prioritarians are not concerned with "relativities."

> [O]n the Priority View, we do not believe in equality. We do not think it in itself bad, or unjust, that some people are worse off than others. This claim can be misunderstood. We do of course think it bad that some people are worse off. But what is bad is not that these people are worse off than *others*. It is rather that they are worse off than *they* might have been.
>
> Consider . . . the central claim of the Priority View: benefits to the worse off matter more. . . . On this view, if I am worse off than you, benefits to me are more important. Is this *because* I am worse off than you? In one sense, yes. But this has nothing to do with my relation to you.
>
> It may help to use this analogy. People at higher altitudes find it harder to breathe. Is this because they are higher up than other people? In one sense, yes. But they would find

---

[94] Parfit (2000, p. 84).
[95] Ibid., pp. 101, 105.

it just as hard to breathe even if there were no other people who were lower down. In the same way, on the Priority View, benefits to the worse off matter more, but that is only because these people are at a lower *absolute* level. It is irrelevant that these people are worse off *than others*. Benefits to them would matter just as much even if there *were* no others who were better off.

The chief difference is, then, this: Egalitarians are concerned with *relativities*: with how each person's level compares with the level of other people. On the Priority View, we are concerned only with people's absolute levels.[96]

So what, exactly, is a prioritarian moral view? Let us focus on the answer to this question within the general context of person-centered consequentialist welfarism.[97] What is the most perspicuous distinction between the kind of non-utilitarian welfarism set forth by the prioritarian, and other kinds of non-utilitarian welfarist views?

At a minimum, it seems clear from Parfit's discussion and from the subsequent literature that a defining feature of prioritarianism is this: such a moral view yields a ranking of outcomes which satisfies not only the Pigou–Dalton principle (whose appearance in Parfit's text, in different linguistic guises, I have already noted) but also separability. Parfit's idea that prioritarians are unconcerned with "relativities," understood as a requirement on the ranking of outcomes, is very naturally expressed as separability. Indeed, every author in the contemporary literature who has offered an explicit axiomatization of prioritarianism, or an explicit formulation of prioritarianism as an SWF, agrees that the prioritarian ranking of outcomes satisfies both Pigou–Dalton and separability.[98]

Some authors go further and define prioritarianism to entail continuity (so that leximin is not a prioritarian SWF). Since the case for Pigou–Dalton and separability is much more closely connected to the claim-across-outcome conception of fairness than the case for continuity, I find it more useful to employ a broad definition of "prioritarian SWFs," encompassing *all* Pigou–Dalton, separable SWFs—both those that satisfy the continuity axiom, and those that fail to do so. There are certainly other authors who have adopted this approach.[99]

However, there is controversy among philosophers and economists regarding the *further* features of a prioritarian moral view, above and beyond its "extensional"

---

[96]   Ibid., p. 104.

[97]   Parfit himself makes clear that prioritarianism can take an outcome-oriented ("Telic") form. See ibid., p. 101.

[98]   See Broome (n.d.); Brown (2005a, 2005b); Fleurbaey (2001); Hirose (2009); Holtug (2007c; 2010, ch. 8); Jensen (2003); McCarthy (2008); Rabinowicz (2001); Tungodden (2003). This excludes Peterson (2010), who formalizes prioritarianism in a manner that fails minimal welfarist criteria (in particular, anonymity) and also, as it happens, the Pigou–Dalton principle.

[99]   See Brown (2005a, ch. 5; 2005b); Tungodden (2003).

properties (the ranking of outcomes that it yields).[100] This controversy relates to
Parfit's comment that prioritarians, by contrast with "egalitarians," "do not believe in
equality. [Prioritarians] do not think it in itself bad, or unjust, that some people are
worse off than others."

Why this comment has been controversial can be seen through the lens of the
SWF decomposition theorem. Remember that any SWF which satisfies the Pigou–
Dalton principle as well as the axiom of continuity can be decomposed into two
factors: overall well-being and an inequality metric, applied to the distribution of
utilities. This includes any continuous prioritarian SWF.[101] The Atkinson SWF, in
particular, can be expressed as the combination of overall well-being and the
Atkinson inequality metric, applied to the distribution of utilities. Thus *any* prioritarian SWF, at least if continuous, can be seen to rank outcomes "as if" it were taking
account of two considerations, balanced against each other: overall well-being and
the distribution of well-being. Moreover, the leximin SWF (a discontinuous, prioritarian SWF) can also be represented as resulting from a concern for the distribution
of well-being within outcomes.[102] In what sense, then, is it true that prioritarians do
not accord moral value to equality?

In answering this question, we should distinguish (as Nils Holtug suggests)[103]
between the ranking of outcomes that a given (welfarist) moral view endorses, and
the *justification* for the ranking which the view offers. Two different moral views
might endorse the very same ranking of outcomes, for all outcome sets, but be genuinely different because of the *reasons* in light of which they take those rankings to be
justified. A full-blown moral view is not merely an SWF, or some other scheme for
ranking outcomes (or even an SWF together with a theory of well-being and well-
being measurement), but a whole justificatory structure, including further concepts,
propositions, arguments, etc., that purport to rationalize the "morally at least as
good as" relation between outcomes.

It is therefore useful to differentiate between a prioritarian *SWF* and a prioritarian *moral view*. A prioritarian SWF, once more, is an SWF which satisfies the Pigou–
Dalton and separability axioms A prioritarian moral view is a moral view that
endorses a prioritarian SWF *and*, in justifying that SWF, does not accord intrinsic
moral significance to the distribution of well-being within outcomes.

Thus (given the terminology proposed here) a prioritarian SWF can be embed-
ded in a non-prioritarian moral view. Consider a view which says the following:
(1) the degree of well-being inequality within outcomes has intrinsic moral significance; (2) the all-things-considered ranking of outcomes is a matter of balancing

[100] See, e.g., Fleurbaey (2001); Holtug (2007c; 2010, ch. 8); Jensen (2003).
[101] See Chapter 2, pp. 119–124. This decomposition result also includes SWFs that satisfy the continuity axiom and the Pigou–Dalton axiom but are not prioritarian because they fail the separability
axiom—such as the rank-weighted SWF.
[102] See Tungodden (2003).
[103] See Holtug (2007c; 2010, ch. 8).

overall well-being against the degree of inequality of well-being; (3) overall well-being is always sufficiently "powerful," in this balancing, so that the all-things-considered ranking satisfies not only the Pigou–Dalton principle (by virtue of the intrinsic concern for equality) but also the Pareto principle; (4) finally, this ranking satisfies the separability axiom. Such a view would be non-prioritarian (by virtue of premise (1)), but would justify a prioritarian SWF.[104]

Of course, the *plausibility* of a non-prioritarian moral view that incorporates a prioritarian SWF is another issue.[105] The only point here is to clarify concepts, and in so doing to illustrate the logical possibility of justifying a prioritarian SWF by appealing to the moral significance of well-being distribution within outcomes.

The view that I have been progressively articulating in this chapter is a version of the claim-*across*-outcome conception of fairness which endorses a continuous prioritarian SWF. Such a view *is* properly characterized as prioritarian. This view does not see the distribution of well-being within outcomes as a factor of intrinsic moral significance. The reason why x is morally better than y is because the balance of individual claims-across-outcomes points in favor of x. Moreover—and this is critical—the weight of individual i's claim in favor of x or y is *not* a function of the distribution of well-being within x or y. (Contrast the rank-weighted scheme for weighting claims, which fails separability.) Rather, that weight is wholly determined by i's well-being level within x and within y, together with the continuous prioritarian transformation function $g(.)$.

In particular, the rationale for ranking outcomes that I have offered is certainly *not* that overall well-being and the inequality of well-being are separate factors which are balanced together to yield the all-things-considered moral ranking of outcomes. This is *not* what the claim-across-outcome conception says in the version I favor (with separability and continuity). Nor, for that matter, is it what the claim-across-outcome conception says even in the version that fails separability (as with the rank-weighted scheme for measuring claims) or fails continuity. Anyone who embraces the claim-across-outcome view should resist the temptation to use an inequality metric to represent her favored SWF. Such a representation is not illuminating;

---

[104] For a defense of prioritarianism as the upshot of balancing overall well-being and inequality, see Weirich (1983).

[105] The sort of view sketched in the previous paragraph would employ an inequality metric (such as the Atkinson inequality metric) which satisfies the separability axiom, if not in general then at least in ranking pairs of outcomes with the same overall well-being. (Why? Note that the ranking of such pairs by the metric must coincide with their all-things-considered ranking by the prioritarian SWF, which of course is separable.) However, there is strong reason to think that the most *attractive* moral view which accords intrinsic moral significance to equality will measure equality using some metric that fails to satisfy the separability condition just stated. This is suggested by the work of Larry Temkin, the leading contemporary philosophical proponent of equality's intrinsic moral significance. It can be shown that Temkin's (1986; 1996b, ch. 2) idea of measuring inequality via within-outcome "complaints" fails this condition. And Temkin (2003b, pp. 83, 86) quite explicitly rejects separability.

it does not express or communicate the underlying justification for the moral comparison of outcomes, on that view.

The reader might resist the conceptual distinctions I have offered in the last few paragraphs. I have suggested that there might be two (or more) moral views that rationalize the very same SWF, where one of these views accords intrinsic moral significance to the distribution of well-being within outcomes, while the other does not. The reader might be skeptical that this idea of "according intrinsic moral significance," which I have left undefined, can be fleshed out in a rigorous fashion.

To attempt to do so would take this chapter off on a tangent. The main thrust of the chapter is to articulate a particular moral view (a version of the claim-across-outcome conception of fairness that measures and aggregates claims so as to satisfy the Pigou–Dalton axiom, separability, and continuity) and thereby to defend a particular type of SWF (the continuous prioritarian SWF). I believe that, in addition, it is meaningful and interesting to characterize this moral view itself as a prioritarian view—but this is not a core claim of the chapter.

A final point of clarification is worth making. Parfit suggests that prioritarians are concerned with the "absolute" level of well-being. For example, he writes: "[O]n the Priority View, benefits to the worse off matter more, but that is only because these people are at a lower *absolute* level. It is irrelevant that these people are worse off *than others*."

However, talk of "absolute" well-being levels is problematic, at least given the account of well-being defended in Chapters 3 and 4. Such talk might suggest that each life-history can be assigned a single number, measuring its level; and that these numbers derive from some preexisting scale of well-being.

But there is no such preexisting scale (at least according to the well-being account defended in Chapters 3 and 4). Rather, we *start* with an outcome set O and population of individuals, which defines a set H of life-histories. The utility number assigned to each life-history is a number that represents *how it compares* to all the other life-histories in the set H. (More specifically, for each spectator k there is a set U^k that represents her extended preferences regarding life-histories and life-history lotteries, and that is then zeroed out by using nonexistence as the zero point. The set U is the union of these individual sets.) Thus the mechanism for assigning numbers to life-histories is, at bottom, holistic and comparative. The set U will assign a given life-history, $(x; i)$, a set of utility numbers, which are the appropriate numbers *in the context* of a particular outcome set and associated life-history set. The mechanism for measuring well-being I have constructed does not purport to assign a number to a life-history which is correct in some absolute sense—correct independent of the content of O and H.

Moreover, U assigns each life-history a whole set of utility numbers, not a single number. Even if spectators have identical extended preferences, U is at most unique up to a positive ratio transformation. Thus (at most) a life-history can be assigned a number such as $25r$, i.e., 25 and all positive multiples of 25. Assume, for example, that there are six life-histories in O: $(x; 1)$, $(y; 1)$, $(x; 2)$, $(y; 2)$; $(x; 3)$, $(y; 3)$. If the suite of numbers 25, 13, 8, 20, 7, 10 captures spectators' extended preferences regarding these life-histories (their ranking of life-histories, lotteries, and comparisons to nonexistence), then so does the suite 50, 26, 16, 40, 14, 20, or the suite 75, 39, 24, 60, 21, 30, or $25r$, $13r$, $8r$, $20r$, $7r$, $10r$ for any positive r. On the account of well-being defended in Chapters 3 and 4, it is not meaningful to go further and state that, for example, the level of the first life-history is really 25 rather than 50. More generally, any account of well-being that generates a **U** which is at most unique up to a positive ratio transformation will refuse to assign a life-history a *single* utility number, and thus will resist talk of "absolute" well-being levels.

It is therefore important to stress that prioritarianism does *not* entail the sort of "absolute" well-being measurement that would be inconsistent with the account of well-being developed in Chapters 3 and 4. First, a prioritarian SWF can be used to rank outcomes by being coupled with a set **U**—even if **U** is constructed via the type of holistic and comparative process I have just described, rather than being generated from some preexisting scale of well-being. Second, there are prioritarian SWFs that function well with a non-singleton set **U**, as opposed to a singleton **U** that assigns a single number to each life-history. In particular, the leximin SWF achieves a complete ranking of outcomes if **U** is unique up to an increasing transformation; and the Atkinson SWF does so if **U** is unique up to a positive ratio transformation.

B. The Leximin SWF

The leximin rule for ordering utility vectors (the "leximin R") has been widely discussed in the social-welfare-function literature.[106] The idea of a "maximin" approach to choice under uncertainty has long been mooted in decision theory, and was famously relied upon by Rawls in *A Theory of Justice*. A maximin rule for ordering utility vectors would rank them according to the utility of the worst-off individual. That rule violates Pareto-superiority.[107] The leximin R is a variation on maximin which ranks two utility vectors according to the utility of the worst-off individuals; if these are equal, according to the utility of the second-worst-off individuals; if these are equal, according to the utility of the third-worst-off individuals; and so forth.[108] In turn, the leximin SWF says: outcome x is at least as good as outcome y iff, for all $u(.)$ in **U**, $u(x)$ is at least as good as $u(y)$ according to the leximin R. The leximin

---

[106] See sources cited in Chapter 2, n. 45.

[107] Imagine two vectors, one of which is Pareto-superior, but the worst-off individual has the same utility in both. On the maximin rule in decision theory, see Resnik (1987, ch. 2).

[108] Formally, if $u(z)$ is a utility vector, denote by $u^*(z)$ a vector which arranges the entries of $u(z)$ from smallest to largest. (If $u(z)$ has multiple entries with the same value, then these will occupy successive positions in $u^*(z)$.)

The leximin R compares $u(x)$ and $u(y)$ as follows. If $u(x)$ and $u(y)$ are permutations of each other, they are equally good. Otherwise, identify the smallest value m such that the mth entry in the vector $u^*(x)$, i.e., $u^*_m(x)$, is unequal to the mth entry of $u^*(y)$. If the mth entry of $u^*(x)$ is larger than the mth entry of $u^*(y)$, then $u(x)$ is ranked better than $u(y)$, otherwise $u(y)$ is ranked better than $u(x)$.

SWF satisfies not only minimal welfarist requirements, but also the Pigou–Dalton and separability axioms, and is thus a prioritarian SWF.

The leximin SWF lacks the Number Win property, but has another aggregation property which is also unappealing. It prefers to avoid very small losses for a worse-off person, even at the expense of foregoing very large benefits for individuals who are only slightly better off. I will call this "Absolute Priority for the Worse Off," and will frame it as follows:

Absolute Priority for the Worse Off

In any outcome set, consider any life-history $(x; i)$, however good. Consider any other life-history $(y; i)$, which is worse for the individual i, but perhaps only very slightly so. Choose a positive number M, which can be arbitrarily large; a number F larger than 1, which can be arbitrarily close to 1; and a positive number b, which can be arbitrarily large. Then for an SWF to have the "Absolute Priority for the Worse Off" property means: *Even if* there are M individuals in x, who are better off than i, but the ratio between their well-being and hers is only F; each of these individuals is better off in y; their well-being gain from y is a multiple b of individual i's loss; and the only individuals affected by the outcomes are those M individuals and individual i; *nonetheless* the SWF ranks x as a better outcome than y.[109]

---

[109] As with Numbers Win, I have here characterized the well-being level of better-off individuals, and their well-being change, as some multiple of the worse-off individual's, rather than in absolute terms, given limitations to the measurability of well-being. And I am assuming that $\mathbf{U}$ contains level, difference, and ratio information, having been "zeroed out" in natural fashion to assign 0 to the zero point. Although the ranking of outcomes by the leximin SWF does not depend upon the well-being differences and ratios associated with life-histories (see Chapter 3, pp. 189–190, 217), life-histories *can* be characterized in terms of differences and ratios as well as levels (for example, the account developed in Chapter 3 does so); and it is instructive to see how the leximin SWF makes tradeoffs among life-histories thus characterized.

It is very easy to show that the leximin SWF has the Absolute Priority for the Worse Off property. Consider $(x; i)$ and $(y; i)$. To say that there are M individuals who are only fractionally better off than individual i in x, by ratio F, is to say: for all $u(.)$ belonging to $\mathbf{U}$, and for each j in this group, $u(x; j)/u(x; i) = F$. To say that their benefit from y is a b multiple of individual i's loss is to say: for all $u(.)$ belonging to $\mathbf{U}$, and for each j in this group, $(u(y; j) - u(x; j))/(u(x; i) - u(y; i)) = b$.

If there are M individuals who are F times better off than i in outcome x, and who benefit from y by a multiple b of her loss (with no one else affected), then—for each $u(.)$ in $\mathbf{U}$—the leximin R, applied to $u(x)$ and $u(y)$, says that the first vector is better. (Because i is worse off in y than x, it must be that, for all $u(.)$ in $\mathbf{U}$, $u(y; i) \leq u(x; i)$, with at least one inequality strict; moreover, because $(u(y; j) - u(x; j))$ $/(u(x; i) - u(y; i)) = b \neq \infty$ or undefined for each j in the group of M, it must in fact be the case that $u(y; i) < u(x; i)$ for all $u(.)$. Finally, adding the fact that $u(x; j)/u(x; i) = F > 1$, it follows that $u(x; i) < u(x; j)$ and $u(y; i) < u(y; j)$ for all $u(.)$. Thus the utility entries for the M individuals are larger than the entries for i in both vectors, and since no one else is affected, the ranking of the vectors is determined by i's utility, which is greater in $u(x)$.) Thus the leximin SWF (i.e., x at least as good as y iff, for all $u(.)$ belonging to $\mathbf{U}$, $u(x)$ at least as good as $u(y)$ according to the leximin rule) says that outcome

Many authors, observing that leximin gives this sort of absolute priority to the worse off, have rejected it.[110]

More specifically, I suggest that, as between a continuous prioritarian SWF and leximin, the former is more attractive. First, as between an SWF with the Numbers Win property and an SWF with the Absolute Priority for the Worse Off property, I suggest that the first type of SWF is, on balance, more plausible. Where the first type of SWF imposes a large loss on a badly-off person to confer arbitrarily small benefits on arbitrarily well-off individuals, we can always take a stab at justifying this result by pointing to the numbers: it is the fact that a sufficiently large number of people receive a benefit (a small benefit, but a genuine, nonzero benefit nonetheless) that warrants this loss for the badly off person. In the case of the second type of SWF: What justifies foregoing an arbitrarily large benefit for arbitrarily many people? Not necessarily the fact that someone who is badly off stands to lose (because the individual who stands to lose may be quite well off); nor that she is much worse off than those who stand to gain (because the ratio between their well-being and hers may be arbitrarily close to 1); nor the fact that she stands to lose a lot (because the SWF will choose to avoid her loss regardless of whether it is small or large).

Second, and perhaps even more importantly, continuous prioritarian SWFs— those that use the $\sum_{i=1}^{N} g(u_i(x))$ formula—are an entire family of SWFs. The limiting points of this family are, at one end, the utilitarian SWF and, at the other, the leximin SWF. By choosing a sufficiently low degree of concavity for the $g(.)$ function, we can bring these SWFs arbitrarily close to the utilitarian SWF; by choosing a sufficiently *high* degree of concavity for the $g(.)$ function, we can bring these SWFs arbitrarily close to the leximin SWF. In particular, if our SWF is the Atkinson SWF, we can bring the SWF indefinitely close to the leximin SWF by increasing the inequality aversion parameter, γ.

Thus we can always allay our concerns that a particular $g(.)$ function is willing to impose a given loss on a badly off individual so as to benefit a certain number of individuals who are F times better off, whose benefit would only be a fraction b of the loss, by shifting to a $g(.)$ function which is closer to the leximin R—and would require *more* individuals to benefit by that amount if that loss is to be imposed on the badly off one. Adopting the general functional form, $\sum_{i=1}^{N} g(u_i(x))$, gives us flexibility to demand that the numbers required to justify a loss for a worse-off individual, so as to produce a slight benefit for much better-off persons, be arbitrarily large.[111]

---

x is better. Critically, this is true regardless of the nature of $(x; i)$ and $(y; i)$—regardless of how well off individual *i* would be with $(x; i)$, and how small a difference moving to $(y; i)$ would make to her well-being.

[110] See, e.g., Arneson (2000a, pp. 58–59); Brown (2005a, p. 169; 2005b, p. 207); Crisp (2003b, p. 752); Holtug (2010, pp. 221–226); McKerlie (1994, pp. 33–34); Temkin (2003b, p. 82); Weirich (1983, pp. 429–430).

[111] Imagine that **U** is a singleton and that *x* and *y* are as described in the "Numbers Win" axiom, namely: individual *i* is worse off in *y* than *x*; the total population size is any finite number *N*; there are

There is no such flexibility in mitigating the absolutism of the leximin SWF. It is a single SWF, which lies at the limit of the $\sum_{i=1}^{N} g(u_i(x))$ family.

With these observations in mind, what can be said in defense of the leximin SWF? Interestingly, a number of different axiomatic characterizations of the leximin R have emerged in the literature that might be used to defend the leximin SWF against continuous prioritarian SWFs and others. One body of literature shows that, if we require an ordering of utility vectors to satisfy certain tradeoff rules in two-person cases—rules that are consistent with, but different from, the Pigou–Dalton axiom—the leximin R results. The seminal result, here, is that of Peter Hammond, who shows the following. Imagine that we require an ordering of utility vectors to satisfy the so-called *Hammond equity* condition: Given two vectors $u(x)$ and $u(y)$, if only two individuals are affected, i and j, with individual i having a lower utility than individual j in both vectors; and if individual i has greater utility in $u(x)$ than $u(y)$, and individual j has greater utility in $u(y)$ than $u(x)$; *then* $u(x)$ must be ranked as a better vector than $u(y)$, regardless of the difference between individual i's utility in $u(x)$ and $u(y)$, and regardless of the difference between individual j's utility in $u(y)$ and $u(x)$.[112]

It turns out that the leximin R is the only rule for ordering utility vectors which is Paretian and anonymous and satisfies the Hammond equity condition.

Moreover, Bertil Tungodden has shown that an ordering of utility vectors which is Paretian and anonymous and satisfies either of the following conditions also must be the leximin R[113]:

Conditional Contracting Extremes

Given two vectors $u(x)$ and $u(y)$, if only two individuals are affected, i and j, with individual i having a lower utility than individual j in both vectors; and if individual i has greater utility in $u(x)$ than $u(y)$, and individual j has greater utility in $u(y)$ than $u(x)$; and

---

$M < N$ individuals who are F times better off than i in x; and those individuals are better off in y, but only by an amount which is a multiple b of i's loss, where b is arbitrarily close to zero; and everyone else is unaffected. Assume, moreover, that a continuous prioritarian SWF with a particular $g(.)$ function prefers y to x, while leximin prefers x to y. Then it can be shown that, by increasing the concavity of the $g(.)$ function, the SWF will also prefer x to y or at least be indifferent. In the case of the Atkinson SWF, "or at least be indifferent" can be dropped: by increasing the parameter γ of inequality aversion, the SWF will now prefer x to y. See Bosmans (2007); Hammond (1975); Lambert (2001, ch. 4). Moreover, again if the SWF is Atkinsonian, this result readily generalizes to the case where **U** is a union of sets measuring a finite number of spectators' extended preferences over life-histories, each unique up to a positive ratio transformation.

[112] See Bossert and Weymark (2004, pp. 1151–1152); Hammond (1976).

[113] See Tungodden (2000). See also Tungodden (2003); Tungodden and Vallentyne (2005); Vallentyne (2000). The statement of "absolute priority below the mean" immediately below is equivalent to Tungodden's "strong absolute priority below the mean" axiom, given the requirement that the ordering of vectors be anonymous.

if individual i has the lowest utility in the entire population in both $u(x)$ and $u(y)$, while individual j has the highest utility in the entire population in both vectors; *then* $u(x)$ must be ranked better than $u(y)$ regardless of the difference between individual i's utility in $u(x)$ and $u(y)$, and regardless of the difference between individual j's utility in $u(y)$ and $u(x)$. (This implies leximin if we require that the ordering be separable as well as Paretian and anonymous.)

Absolute Priority below the Mean

Given two vectors $u(x)$ and $u(y)$, if only two individuals are affected, i and j, with individual i having a lower utility than individual j in $u(y)$ and less-than-or-equal utility in $u(x)$; and if individual i has greater utility in $u(x)$ than $u(y)$, and individual j has greater utility in $u(y)$ than $u(x)$; and if individual i is below the mean utility in $u(y)$, and individual j is above the mean utility in both vectors; *then* $u(x)$ must be ranked better than $u(y)$ regardless of the difference between individual i's utility in $u(x)$ and $u(y)$, and regardless of the difference between individual j's utility in $u(y)$ and $u(x)$.

Each of these conditions (Hammond equity, conditional contracting extremes, and absolute priority below the mean) can be readily "translated" into the claim-across-outcome conception of fairness—namely, into a particular specification of the *strength* of individuals' claims. For example, the Hammond equity condition in "claim" language says: if individual i has a claim in favor of outcome x, and individual j has a claim in favor of outcome y, and individual i is worse off than j in both outcomes, then i's claim to x is stronger than j's claim to y.[114]

A different axiomatic route from the claim-across-outcome conception of fairness to the leximin R has also been sketched by Tungodden.[115] Imagine that we stick with the basic Pigou–Dalton condition for determining the strength of individuals' claims. That is, we say: if individual i has a claim in favor of x and individual j in favor of y, then if i is worse off than j in y and worse-off-or-equally-well-off in x *and* the difference between i's well-being in the two outcomes is the same as the difference between j's, i's claim to x is stronger than j's claim to y. What Tungodden has shown is that, if we couple this rule for determining the strength of individuals' claims with a *pairwise aggregation* procedure for adjudicating between conflicting claims where more than two people are affected, plus a requirement that the rankings of outcome sets with different total population sizes be consistent with each other in a certain way, the leximin R results.

---

[114] To translate "conditional contracting extremes" into claim language, simply take the Hammond equity translation and add the condition that individual i be the worst-off person in both outcomes, and individual j the best off. Similarly, for "absolute priority below the mean," add the condition that i be below the mean in outcome y and that j be above the mean in both outcomes.

[115] See Tungodden (2003, pp. 32–37).

Presumably any plausible specification of the claim-across-outcome conception will say this: Given two outcomes, x and y, if i's claim to x is stronger than j's claim to y, and everyone else is unaffected, outcome x is the fairer outcome. (What would it mean for one claim to be "stronger" than another and yet for this condition to fail?) The pairwise aggregation procedure goes much further. It says: If i has a claim in favor of x, and i's claim in favor of x is stronger than anyone's claim to y, then x is fairer.

Does seeing how the leximin SWF flows from these specifications of the claim-across-outcome conception of fairness strengthen the case for this SWF? To my mind, it does not. I do not think that Hammond equity, conditional contracting extremes, or absolute priority below the mean states an independently plausible view of the strength of individuals' claims. Nor do I see a strong reason for thinking that pairwise aggregation is the most attractive rule for adjudicating between individuals' claims where more than two individuals are affected (however we calibrate the strength of claims). To see why pairwise aggregation is problematic, imagine that we (very plausibly) reject the Hammond equity condition for calibrating the strength of claims. If we reject Hammond equity, then—given a pair of outcomes x and y—it would seem possible for j to have a stronger claim in favor of y than some other individual does in favor of x, even though j is better off than that individual in both outcomes. (Imagine a case in which j stands to benefit a lot and the other individual only a little bit.) Imagine now that there are arbitrarily many such individuals, all of whom are worse off than j, and each of whom has a weaker claim to x than j has to y. Regardless of the number of worse-off individuals, pairwise aggregation would force us to count y as fairer, just because a better-off person has a stronger claim than any one of the worse-off individuals. This seems implausible.

Interestingly, Nagel elaborates the idea of pairwise aggregation, but ultimately backs away from fully endorsing that approach, recognizing the implausibility of leximin. In his Tanner Lecture he observes:

> It seems to me that no plausible theory can avoid the relevance of numbers completely. . . . [If] the choice is between preventing severe hardship for some who are very poor and deprived, and preventing less severe but still substantial hardship for those who are better off but still struggling for subsistence, then it is very difficult for me to believe that the numbers do not count, and that priority of urgency goes to the worse off however many there are of the better off.[116]

And in his book *Equality and Partiality* Nagel explains: "I am inclined toward a somewhat weaker preference for the worse off [than leximin], which can be outweighed by sufficiently large benefit to sufficiently large numbers of those better off."[117]

---

[116] Nagel (1979, p. 125).
[117] Nagel (1995, p. 73).

In conclusion, I should mention the possibility of a number of additional routes to justifying a leximin SWF that are quite distinct from those we have been analyzing: (1) a *measure-theoretic* argument, having to do with limitations in our ability to measure well-being; (2) a *Rawlsian* route, which sees the moral ranking of outcomes as corresponding to a *nonprobabilistic* self-interested choice behind a veil of ignorance; and (3) the *egalitarian-equivalent* argument, discussed in Chapter 2.[118]

---

[118] (1) *Measure Theoretic Arguments*: As mentioned earlier, the theoretical literature on SWFs investigates which rules for ordering utility vectors are invariant to different types of transformation of the utility function. For some such invariance requirements, leximin is the sole prioritarian SWF that satisfies the requirement. In particular, if we require that the rule R be Paretian, anonymous, and separable, and be invariant to an increasing transformation (where $u(.)$ is replaced by $\varphi(u(.))$, with $\varphi(.)$ any strictly increasing function), the only possibilities are leximin and leximax—and leximax is of course not prioritarian (it fails Pigou–Dalton). And, as mentioned earlier, if we require that R be Paretian, anonymous, and separable, plus satisfy a requirement of invariance to a positive affine transformation, the only possibilities are leximin, leximax, or "weak" utilitarianism. See Bossert and Weymark (2004, pp. 1154–1159).

However, the invariance requirements that would point us to leximin are too strong. If one accepts the account of well-being offered in Chapters 3 and 4, or any other account that makes it meaningful to ascribe differences and ratios to life-histories, we need *not* require invariance to increasing but non-affine transformations that do not preserve difference comparisons; and we need *not* require invariance to positive affine transformations that do not preserve ratio information (see above, n. 60). If we require only that the ordering be invariant to a positive ratio transformation, other prioritarian SWFs besides leximin become possible—in particular, the Atkinson SWF.

(2) *The Rawlsian Route.* Imagine that all of the following are true. First, outcome x is morally better than outcome y iff all spectators would choose x behind a nonprobabilistic veil of ignorance (NPVOI)—meaning that each outcome is seen as a package of all its life-histories, without exogenous probabilities. Second, the rational norm for choice without exogenous probabilities is a leximin-type rule (i.e., as between two choices, choose the one whose worst outcome is better; and if the worst outcomes of both choices are equally good, then the second worst; and so forth). Third (for simplicity), all spectators have identical extended preferences over life-histories, lotteries, and comparisons to the zero point, represented by a single utility function $u(.)$ unique up to a positive ratio transformation.

The upshot of all this would be that the well-being associated with any outcome can be represented by a single utility vector, unique up to a positive ratio transformation, i.e., x is mapped onto $(ru(x; 1), ru(x; 2), \ldots, ru(x; N))$; and that the moral ranking of outcomes would be given by the leximin SWF. On maximin and variants (such as leximin) as rules for choice under uncertainty, see Resnik (1987, ch. 2); Barbarà and Jackson (1988).

However, it is problematic to think that the veil-of-ignorance conception of the fair ranking of outcomes is best understood in terms of the NPVOI rather than the EPVOI. See above, pp. 321–325. And (even if this not true) the very fact that this conception generates the leximin SWF would be grounds in favor of an alternative construal of fairness (the claim-across-outcome view), for those who find leximin counterintuitive.

(3) *Egalitarian Equivalence.* As discussed in Chapter 2, it is possible to develop a welfarist rule for ordering outcomes (in particular, outcomes characterized as bundles of commodities for each individual) by fixing a reference bundle, and giving a higher ranking to x rather than y if the two are Pareto-noncomparable and x is "egalitarian equivalent" with respect to the reference bundle, while y

For reasons reviewed in the margin, I do not believe that any of these arguments for leximin is successful.[119]

C. The Prioritarian SWF with a Lexical Threshold

Campbell Brown has developed the idea of a prioritarian rule for ranking utility vectors that incorporates a lexical threshold—an idea also discussed by Bertil Tungodden.[120] Brown's rule yields the following SWF.

For a given outcome set, identify a life-history, $(x^+; i^+)$, that lies at the morally relevant threshold. Designate some arbitrary positive number T as the number of the threshold. Take the set $\mathbf{U}$ that represents well-being levels, differences, and ratios. "Winnow down" $\mathbf{U}$ by including only utility functions that assign T to life-history $(x^+; i^+)$; denote this "winnowed down" set as $\mathbf{U}^T$. Now compare each pair of outcomes, x and y, using the following two-stage approach. Take some strictly increasing, strictly concave $g(.)$ function. For each utility function $u(.)$ in $\mathbf{U}^T$, each outcome corresponds to a below-threshold utility vector, namely the vector of individual utilities truncated at the number T. Each outcome also corresponds to an above-threshold utility vector, namely the vector of individual utilities or T, whichever is larger. For each utility function, assign the outcomes a primary score by summing the elements of the below-threshold vector, transformed by the $g(.)$ function. Then assign the outcomes a secondary score by summing the elements of the above-threshold vector, *also transformed by the $g(.)$ function.* If one outcome has a higher primary score it is morally better according to $u(.)$; if the two outcomes have the same primary score and one has a higher secondary score, it is morally better according to $u(.)$; otherwise the two outcomes are equally good according to $u(.)$. Finally: outcome x is morally at least as good as outcome y, full stop, iff it is at least as good for all $u(.)$ belonging to $\mathbf{U}^T$.

This SWF is identical to the sufficientist SWF, save for the italicized language: the comparison of above-threshold utility vectors is undertaken by summing their elements transformed by the $g(.)$ function, rather than by straight

---

is not. For welfarists who care about fairness but are suspicious of interpersonal comparisons, this approach is appealing—because its implementation requires only that we know each individual's preferences over bundles. And, as discussed, the "egalitarian equivalent" rule is the same as a kind of leximin approach.

However, the premise of this chapter is that utility numbers representing inter- as well as intrapersonal level, difference, and ratio comparisons *are* available to the welfarist. If one accepts this premise, and finds leximin implausible because of the absolute priority it gives to the worse off, why stick with the "egalitarian equivalent" rule for ordering outcomes, as opposed to the continuous prioritarian SWF or some other possibility?

[119] See also Mariotti and Veneziani (2009), presenting a novel justification for leximin, resting on a principle of "noninterference."

[120] See Brown (2005a, ch. 5; 2005b); Tungodden (2003, pp. 23–29).

unweighted summation.[121] By virtue of this crucial change, the SWF fully satisfies the Pigou–Dalton principle rather than violating it for transfers among above-threshold individuals.[122] The SWF is therefore prioritarian. Note also that the approach lacks the Numbers Win property which many see as a problematic feature of the continuous prioritarian SWF. In cases where the worse-off individual is below the threshold, and the individuals who stand to benefit are above, no benefit to them (however large the benefit, and however numerous the individuals may be) will counterbalance the loss to the worse-off individual. Finally, the SWF lacks the Absolute Priority for the Worse Off property which is a problematic feature of leximin. In cases where all the individuals involved are on the same side of the threshold, tradeoffs are allowed.

So the prioritarian SWF with a lexical threshold may seem very attractive. The key difficulty is identifying that threshold. Note that the threshold would not only prevent large losses from being imposed on a below-threshold individual for the sake of very small gains to above-threshold individuals. It would also have the less appealing property of foregoing any gains (even arbitrarily large ones) for individuals above the threshold (however large the group) for the sake of preventing an arbitrarily small loss to a below-threshold individual.[123] Is it plausible that morality includes a cut-off like this? Where would it be?[124]

It might be thought that the threshold life-history $(x^+; i^+)$ is one in which all the individual's basic needs are met. Indeed, the location of an individual's life relative to the level of basic needs *is* a feature of that life-history which, very plausibly, possesses

---

[121] Thus formalization of this SWF is exactly the same as for the sufficientist SWF, see above, n. 70, except that the rule for determining whether outcome x is better than y according to $u(.)$ becomes the following: Outcome x is better than y according to $u(.)$ iff (1) $\sum_{i=1}^{N} g(u_i^+(x)) > \sum_{i=1}^{N} g(u_i^+(y))$ or (2) $\sum_{i=1}^{N} g(u_i^+(x)) = \sum_{i=1}^{N} g(u_i^+(y))$ and $\sum_{i=1}^{N} g(u_i^{++}(x)) > \sum_{i=1}^{N} g(u_i^{++}(y))$. Outcomes x and y are equally good according to $u(.)$ iff $\sum_{i=1}^{N} g(u_i^+(x)) = \sum_{i=1}^{N} g(u_i^+(y))$ and $\sum_{i=1}^{N} g(u_i^{++}(x)) = \sum_{i=1}^{N} g(u_i^{++}(y))$.

Similarly, the translation of this SWF into "claim" language is exactly the same as the translation of the sufficientist SWF, which sees individuals' claims as having a primary and secondary measure (see above, n. 74), except for the following change. Each individual i's claim in favor of x according to $u(.)$ is measured by a pair of numbers, $(g(u^+(x; i)) - g(u^+(y; i)), g(u^{++}(x; i)) - g(u^{++}(y; i)))$.

[122] More precisely, it satisfies the Pigou–Dalton principle relative to the ordering of life-histories and differences defined by $\mathbf{U}^{\mathrm{T}}$. See above, n. 73.

[123] Crisp (2003b, p. 758), in his presentation of sufficientism, stipulates that below-threshold individuals take priority over above-threshold individuals with respect to non-"trivial" changes in the well-being of the below-threshold individuals. It is not clear how to include this caveat in an SWF, and Brown's formalization of the prioritarian rule with a lexical threshold (and of the sufficientist rule) does not do so. Even if we *were* to include a "nontriviality" rider in the prioritarian SWF with a lexical threshold, it would still give absolute priority to any nontrivial change in the well-being of a single below-threshold individual, regardless of how many above the threshold are affected—and it is not clear how to identify a threshold which would have this sort of force.

[124] See Arneson (1999a, 2000a); Casal (2007).

real moral significance. But it seems problematic to capture the moral relevance of the level of basic needs via the prioritarian SWF with a lexical threshold.[125] Using that SWF, with the threshold at the level of basic needs, means that we will be willing to bring an arbitrarily large number of individuals all the way down to the level of basic needs, for the sake of conferring an arbitrarily small benefit on a needy person.

Crisp, in specifying his threshold for purposes of the sufficientist SWF, rejects a need-based approach and sets it at the much higher level of a "sufficiently good" life: "eighty years of high quality life on this planet." In effect, Crisp identifies the threshold life-history as one which is close to the best life-history attainable by normal human beings. Incorporating such a threshold in the sufficientist SWF, or the prioritarian SWF with a lexical threshold, would cause these SWFs to converge with (or come close to converging with) the continuous prioritarian SWF, when used to rank outcomes in which the population of interest consists of normal human beings. The threshold becomes irrelevant, since virtually everyone is below it. Conversely, when used to rank outcomes in which the population includes both human and non-human persons, Crisp's threshold seems morally arbitrary. Crisp claims: "[M]y own intuition is that . . . eighty years of high-quality life on this planet is enough, and plausibly more than enough, for any being."[126] If an SWF were to be outfitted to take account of non-human interests, why would the *human* maximum constitute the criteria of what is "enough . . . for any being"?[127]

A third possibility is to set the threshold $(x^+; i^+)$ at an intermediate point— neither the level of a human life where minimum needs are met, nor Crisp's level of the best normally attainable human life, but the level of a moderately good life. But it does not seem very intuitively plausible that there is some intermediate level of attainment of the various attributes constitutive of life-histories (consumption, health, nutrition, social life, etc.) that constitutes a qualitative break point. Much scholarship, and social discourse, revolves around the "poverty" level—bearing out the intuition of a break-point of some sort at the level of need-satisfaction. Where is the parallel discourse that would be a visible expression of intuitions about the existence of some higher threshold?

---

[125] I would, instead, inject a threshold within the utility functions in **U**, and combine these utility functions with the continuous prioritarian SWF. See Chapter 2, n. 156.

[126] Crisp (2003b, p. 762).

[127] This book does not address how welfarism and the SWF framework should be refined to take account of non-human persons. I focus on the core case of a fixed, finite, human population (so as to keep the book's scope manageable). It is quite possible that the introduction of non-human persons will raise important, new questions—for example, how to make well-being comparisons between humans and non-humans. So my position is *not* that human and non-human persons are always identically situated, for purposes of welfarism. Still, a framework that includes both, but uses the standard of a good human life to set the threshold for a prioritarian SWF with a lexical threshold, seems arbitrarily biased toward humans.

Note further that using a prioritarian SWF with a lexical threshold, and setting the threshold at the intermediate level (above the level where all of an individual's basic needs are met), will have the unpleasant consequence of foregoing benefits to an arbitrarily large number of non-needy individuals, even for the sake of an arbitrarily small benefit to a non-needy individual below the threshold.[128]

D. "Numbers Win" Redux

I have argued that, on balance, continuous prioritarian SWFs are more attractive than the two prioritarian competitors suggested by the existing literature—leximin and a prioritarian SWF with a lexical threshold—despite the fact that continuous prioritarian SWFs possess the "Numbers Win" property. Even if my argument on this score is persuasive, might not some other SWF be better than all of these?

Perhaps so. I'm not sure how I could show that continuous prioritarian SWFs dominate all possible prioritarian competitors, and will not try to do so here.

However, it can be observed that no prioritarian SWF will possess all the tradeoff properties we might find intuitively appealing. On the one hand, our intuitions may well favor the requirement that an SWF be unwilling to impose a substantial loss on a badly off person for the sake of sufficiently small gains for individuals who are sufficiently better off, no matter how numerous those individuals. (This is the idea I have tried to capture with the Numbers Win property: intuitively, an SWF should lack that property.) On the other hand, intuitively, an SWF *should* be willing to impose a loss on one person, if sufficiently small, where the individuals who benefit are sufficiently numerous. Fleurbaey, Tungodden, and Vallentyne have recently investigated the possibility of crafting moral rules that satisfy both of these desiderata, and have reached negative conclusions.[129]

In particular, consider what might be termed the "Small Losses Trumped" property:

Small Losses Trumped

Consider any life-history $(x; i)$ and any other life-history $(y; i)$, in which individual i is worse off. Then there is some positive number l, which is less than 1 and can be arbitrarily close to zero, and which has the following feature. For any pair of outcomes z and z^* that are both better for i than outcome y, if the only individuals affected by this pair of outcomes are (1) individual i, who is worse off in z^* than z, but whose loss is less than or equal to a multiple l of the well-being difference between $(x; i)$ and $(y; i)$, and (2) other individuals each of whom is better off in z^* than z by some amount (the same amount for

---

[128] Interestingly, Crisp in more recent writing (see Crisp [2006, p. 158]) seems to give up on the idea of an absolute threshold.

[129] See Fleurbaey and Tungodden (2010); Fleurabey, Tungodden, and Vallentyne (2009).

all these individuals, whatever it may be), and each of whom is better off than i in z, *then* z^* is a better outcome than z if the number of such individuals is sufficiently large.

The idea here is that, for any well-being loss for a person, there should be some fraction of that loss (perhaps a very small fraction) which can be trumped by benefits to a sufficiently large number of people. But it can be shown that any SWF with this desirable property will have the Numbers Win property (at least if we add some technical assumptions.)[130] This insight, perhaps, will help allay the skepticism of the reader who remains dubious about continuous prioritarian SWFs.

V. THE ATKINSON SWF

Atkinson SWFs are a particular subfamily within the broader family of continuous prioritarian SWFs. They take the form: x is morally at least as good as y iff, for all $u(.)$ in $\mathbf{U}$, $(1-\gamma)^{-1}\sum_{i=1}^{N}u_i(x)^{1-\gamma}\geq(1-\gamma)^{-1}\sum_{i=1}^{N}u_i(y)^{1-\gamma}$. (In the special case where $\gamma=1$, the Atkinson SWF uses a different formula, namely x is morally at least as good as y iff, for all $u(.)$ in $\mathbf{U}$, $\sum_{i=1}^{N}\ln u_i(x)\geq\sum_{i=1}^{N}\ln u_i(y)$.) SWFs of this sort are sometimes referred to as "isoelastic" or "constant-elasticity-of substitution" SWFs, and are widely used in existing scholarly work in the SWF tradition. Atkinson SWFs are

---

[130] A similar point is made by Brown (2005a, ch. 5; 2005b). Assume that utility is unique up to a positive ratio transformation. (This is the first technical assumption.) Imagine now that an SWF has the "Small Losses Trumped" property. Consider life-histories $(x; i)$ and $(y; i)$, such that the latter is worse for i. Because utility is unique up to a positive ratio transformation, this well-being change can be assigned a utility measure $r\Delta u$, r a positive number. Let L be an integer greater than or equal to $1/l$.

The Numbers Win property says this: Given life-histories $(x; i)$ and $(y; i)$, *if* the only individuals affected by outcomes x and y are individual i, and individuals who are F times better off than i in x, and benefit by only a positive multiple b of individual i's loss from y (however small b may be), then y is better if those individuals are sufficiently numerous. Imagine that, indeed, there is some number M of individuals in x who are F times better off than i. Imagine, further, that individual i's loss from y $(r\Delta u)$, and the gain for each of the M individuals $(rb\Delta u)$, can be evenly "divided up" into a series of small losses or gains. More precisely, there is a sequence of outcomes $x, z_1, z_2 \ldots, z_{L-1}, y$, such that: (1) every one other than the M individuals and i is equally well off in all the outcomes; (2) for each pairing of an outcome in this sequence and the one that succeeds it (i.e., as between x and z_1, z_1 and z_2 ..., z_{L-1} and y), individual i is worse off in the second outcome by amount $r\Delta u/L$, while each of the M individuals is better off by amount $rb\Delta u/L$. Then the Small Losses Trumped axiom entails that, if M is sufficiently large, x is worse than z_1, z_1 worse than z_2 ..., z_{L-1} worse than y (because the number L is sufficiently large that $1/L \leq l$, and so the axiom is applicable). Transitivity of course then entails that x is worse than y, which means that the SWF has the Numbers Win property.

The second technical assumption, here, is an outcome set "richness" assumption: namely, that whenever there are some number of individuals at a stipulated multiple F of individual i's well-being, benefiting by a stipulated amount b from y, then there will also be a sequence of outcome $x, z_1, z_2 \ldots,$ z_{L-1}, y as just described. If not, an SWF could fail Numbers Win (preferring x to y regardless of how large M is), without our being able to show that it also fails Small Losses Trumped.

parameterized by the parameter γ, which is sometimes referred to as the inequality aversion parameter, and which can take any positive value.[131]

The properties of the Atkinson SWF are closely connected to the topic of well-being ratios, so I first discuss that topic; then describe and defend the Atkinson SWF; and, finally, discuss how to estimate the γ parameter.

A. Well-Being Ratios

Imagine that we have a set of life-histories, associated with an outcome set **O** and population of N individuals, and some theory of well-being W which provides a quasiordering of the life-histories and of the differences between them. (W might be the extended-preference account of well-being set forth in Chapters 3 and 4, or it might be some other account.) Imagine that there is some set **U**, which represents these level and difference quasiorderings, in the standard manner presupposed throughout this book.[132] By specifying some life-history $(x^*; i^*)$ as the zero point, we can now assign ratios to life-histories. The *ratio* between two life-histories, $(x; i)$ and $(y; j)$, is simply the ratio of their differences from the zero point. More precisely, because the quasiordering of histories and differences may not be complete, we may not be able to assign a precise ratio between two life-histories; but the selection of a zero point enables us to assign a range of ratios between life-histories. With $(x^*; i^*)$ as the zero point, the proposition that the ratio between $(x; i)$ and $(y; j)$ is between the values of K and L, inclusive, is true just in case: for all $u(.)$ in **U**, $K \leq [u(x; i) - u(x^*; i^*)]/[u(y; j) - u(x^*; i^*)] \leq L$. More generally, any numerical proposition regarding the ratio between two life-histories can be assigned a truth condition along these lines.[133]

It is vitally important to distinguish between (1) the selection of a particular life-history as the zero point for defining ratios; and (2) the choice of a mathematical rule by which to represent the ratios generated by a given zero point.

Imagine that $(x^*; i^*)$ is chosen as the zero point. Given a set **U** that represents well-being levels and differences, this selection gives rise to a set of "ratio facts": namely

---

[131] I describe them as "Atkinson SWFs" because this functional form was introduced by Anthony Atkinson (1970) in his pioneering work on the use of social welfare functions to generate an inequality metric. As mentioned above, the Atkinson SWF can be decomposed into two factors: overall well-being and the degree of well-being inequality as measured using the Atkinson inequality metric. See above, pp. 360–367; Chapter 2, pp. 119–124. I favor the Atkinson SWF, but—for reasons reviewed above—do not believe this decomposition is particularly useful. On the wide use of the Atkinson SWF in the literature, see Creedy (2007, p. 5); Heady (1996, p. 29); Salanié (2003, p. 80); Tuomala (1990, p. 28).

[132] See Chapter 2, n. 6.

[133] For example, the proposition that the ratio between $(x; i)$ and $(y; j)$ is greater than or equal to K will be true just in case, for all $u(.)$ in **U**, $K \leq [u(x; i) - u(x^*; i^*)]/[u(y; j) - u(x^*; i^*)]$. The proposition that the ratio between $(x; i)$ and $(y; j)$ is equal to K will be true just in case, for all $u(.)$ in **U**, $K = [u(x; i) - u(x^*; i^*)]/[u(y; j) - u(x^*; i^*)]$.

the totality of true numerical propositions regarding the ratio between any two life-histories (for example, that this ratio has a particular value, exceeds a value, lies in some range, and so forth), with the truth of any such proposition determined as just explained.

This ratio information might be represented in three different ways. First, we might use U itself (without "zeroing out") to represent the ratio facts. We might say that the ratio between $(x; i)$ and $(y; j)$ is between K and L iff $K \le [u(x; i) - u(x^*; i^*)]/[u(y; j) - u(x^*; i^*)] \le L$ for all $u(.)$ in U (and similarly for other numerical propositions regarding ratios).

Second, we might choose some arbitrary number Z as the number by which to represent the zero point. We might "zero out" U, including only those utility functions that assign this particular number to $(x^*; i^*)$. And we might use the "zeroed out" set to represent our ratio facts, as follows: the ratio between $(x; i)$ and $(y; j)$ is between K and L iff $K \le [u(x; i) - Z]/[u(y; j) - Z] \le L$ for all $u(.)$ in U (and similarly for other numerical propositions regarding ratios).

The third approach is just the most natural version of the second, namely to pick Z equal to 0. We now "zero out" U by including only those utility functions that assign 0 to $(x^*; i^*)$. And we use the "zeroed out" set to represent our ratio facts, as follows: the ratio between $(x; i)$ and $(y; j)$ is between K and L iff $K \le u(x; i)/u(y; j) \le L$ for all $u(.)$ in U (and similarly for other numerical propositions regarding ratios).

Note that all three mathematical rules represent the very same ratio facts (given a very plausible condition regarding the content of the original U). The selection of a particular $(x^*; i^*)$ as zero point determines the ratio facts; picking one of the three rules rather than another, with $(x^*; i^*)$ held fixed as the zero point, does not change the ratio facts.[134] Rather, the rules differ in how they *reflect* those facts in a set of

---

[134] Assume that the original U (pre-zeroing out) is such that: some $u(.)$ is in U iff all positive affine transformations of $u(.)$ are. (Note that this *does not* mean that U itself is unique up to a positive affine transformation—just that U can be partitioned into a series of subsets, each unique up to a positive affine transformation. This would normally be true, for example, of U as constructed in Chapter 3 by pooling spectators' sets U^k, with each such U^k normally unique up to a positive affine transformation.). Now define U^Z as the original U zeroed out to assign Z to the zero point $(x^*; i^*)$, and U^0 as the original U zeroed out to assign 0 to $(x^*; i^*)$.

Consider now any numerical proposition regarding the ratio between two life-histories. That proposition is true according to the first representational rule paired with U, just in case it is true according to the second representational rule paired with U^Z, just in case it is true according to the third representational rule paired with U^0.

Why? Each $u(.)$ in U, using the first representational rule, will assign the ratio between $(x; i)$ and $(y; j)$ some specific number (including ∞ or undefined, if $u(y; j) - u(x^*; i^*) = 0$). Assume that $u(.)$ assigns this ratio the number K, and that $u(x^*; i^*) = G$. Then consider any utility function $v(.)$ such that $v(.) = r(u(.) - G) + Z$, with r positive. This utility function $v(.)$ is also in U (since it is a positive affine transformation of $u(.)$) and will end up in U^Z (since it assigns the number Z to $(x^*; i^*)$). Moreover, using the second representational rule, it assigns the life-histories a ratio of K.

utility functions (either the original **U** or a "zeroed out" set), and how they "read off" the facts from that set.

So which rule should we use? Note that the first representational rule is precluded by the requirement that the SWF assume the simple form of incorporating a *single* rule *R* for ranking all utility vectors. If we employ this first representational rule, and wish *R* to be sensitive to well-being ratios, *R* will have to be "indexed" by utility function rather than being a single rule. In ranking utility vectors, *R* will have to "take account" of the particular utility function giving rise to those vectors. *R* will need to know the particular numerical value assigned by $u(.)$ to the zero point $(x^*; i^*)$.

By contrast, both the second and third approaches are consistent with having a simple *R*-based SWF. The choice between them is merely a matter of "naturalness." In Chapters 3 and 4, I followed the third approach, "zeroing out" **U** so as to include only utility functions assigning the number 0 to nonexistence (my preferred zero point). In this chapter, too, I follow the third approach.

The choice between the second and third approaches changes some of the mathematical formalism but has no substantive implications for any of the analysis I advance in this chapter. More specifically, the choice between the second and third approaches changes the mathematical expression of the continuous prioritarian SWF and of the Atkinson SWF.[135] If some number Z unequal to zero is chosen, then the formula for the continuous prioritarian SWF becomes $\sum_{i=1}^{N} g(u_i(x) - Z)$, and, for the Atkinson SWF, $(1-\gamma)^{-1} \sum_{i=1}^{N} (u_i(x) - Z)^{1-\gamma}$. These SWFs, coupled with a set **U** which is zeroed out to assign Z to the zero point, achieve exactly the same ranking of outcomes as the formulas $\sum_{i=1}^{N} g(u_i(x))$ and $(1-\gamma)^{-1} \sum_{i=1}^{N} u_i(x)^{1-\gamma}$, respectively, coupled with a set **U** which is zeroed out to assign 0 to the zero point.[136] I prefer the latter, more natural, formalizations of these SWFs; and for the remainder of this chapter will assume that the zero point has been represented with the number 0. But nothing of substance hinges on this—neither the general arguments I present for the continuous prioritarian SWF or Atkinson SWF; nor, more specifically, how any given outcome set would be ranked.

By contrast, the specification of a particular life-history as the zero point *does* have important substantive implications. Imagine that we start with **U**, representing well-being levels and differences, and select as our zero point some new life-history, $(x^{**}; i^{**})$, which is not equally good as $(x^*; i^*)$. The ratio facts generated by this zero

---

Similarly, if $w(.)$ is such that $w(.) = r(u(.) - G)$, it will be in **U** and will end up in $\mathbf{U}^0$. Moreover, using the third representational rule, it assigns the life-histories a ratio of K.

Similar reasoning shows that if there is some $u(.)$ in $\mathbf{U}^Z$ that assigns the life-histories a particular ratio, there are corresponding entries in **U** and $\mathbf{U}^0$ that do so; and similarly if we start with a $u(.)$ in $\mathbf{U}^0$.

[135] It would also change the expression of the sufficientist SWF and the prioritarian SWF with a lexical threshold.

[136] This assumes that, in the pre-zeroed-out **U**, a given $u(.)$ is in the set iff all positive affine transformations of $u(.)$ are.

point will be different. For example, if **U** is unique up to a positive affine transformation (so that every pair of life-histories has a precise ratio whichever zero point is selected), and the ratio between $(x; i)$ and $(y; j)$ is $K \neq 1$ with $(x^*; i^*)$ as the zero point, then the ratio between these histories will *not* be K with $(x^{**}; i^{**})$ as the zero point.

It might be thought that we could "correct" for our substantive selection of the zero point by choosing a matching SWF. At least if the SWF takes the Atkinson form (as indeed it should, I will argue), this sort of correction will *not* be possible. See the margin for details.[137]

I take the position that nonexistence is the appropriate zero point, and in Chapters 3 and 4 constructed a "zeroed out" **U** with this zero point in mind. The morally relevant ratio between $(x; i)$ and $(y; j)$ is the well-being difference between $(x; i)$ and nonexistence, divided by the well-being difference between $(y; j)$ and nonexistence. Or so I believe.

While the choice of a particular life-history as the zero point *does* have substantive implications—for what the ratio facts are, and for how outcomes are ordered, given any outcome and life-history set—the arguments in this chapter regarding the general functional form of the SWF do *not* hinge on that choice. More specifically, my analysis and defense of the Atkinson SWF, immediately following, does not depend on which life-history is chosen as the zero point. I assume that we start with **U**, representing well-being differences and levels (whether constructed from extended preferences or in some other manner); that some $(x^*; i^*)$ is selected as the zero point (be it nonexistence or some other zero point); and that **U** is then zeroed out in the "natural" manner by including only those utility functions that set $u(x^*; i^*) = 0$. **U** represents ratios from the stipulated zero point, using the natural rule that the ratio between $(x; i)$ and $(y; j)$ is between K and L iff $K \leq u(x; i)/u(y; j) \leq L$ for all $u(.)$ in **U**.

How does the Atkinson SWF rank this **U**? And why should we use that SWF rather than some other continuous prioritarian SWF?

---

[137] Assume, for simplicity, that the pre-zeroed-out **U** is unique up to a positive affine transformation. Consider two pairs of life-histories. Assume that all four life-histories are at different utility levels and, furthermore, that, if $(x^*; i^*)$ is chosen as the zero point, the ratio between the two members of the first pair is K, and the ratio between the second pair is also K. If so, then—for any given Atkinson SWF with a value γ—the marginal rate of moral substitution (MRMS) between the first pair is $K^{-\gamma}$, and the MRMS between the second pair is the same. (See below for a discussion of the MRMS.) If a new life-history $(x^{**}; i^{**})$, not equally good as $(x^*; i^*)$, becomes the zero point, then the ratio between the first pair shifts to $K + \alpha$, while the ratio between the second pair shifts to a different value, $K + \beta$. Now, for any value γ, the MRMS between the first pair is $(K + \alpha)^{-\gamma}$, while the MRMS between the second pair is *different*, namely $(K + \beta)^{-\gamma}$. Thus, the ordering of outcomes produced by some Atkinson SWF with $(x^*; i^*)$ as the zero point will not necessarily be duplicable by *any* Atkinson SWF with $(x^{**}; i^{**})$ as the zero point.

B. The Atkinson SWF and Ratio Rescaling Invariance

Some life-history has been chosen as the zero point, and **U** has been "zeroed out" in the natural manner, including only utility functions that assign 0 to that life-history. The Atkinson SWF (in this case) says: x is at least as good as y iff, for all, $u(.)$ in **U**, $(1-\gamma)^{-1}\sum_{i=1}^{N}u_i(x)^{1-\gamma} \geq (1-\gamma)^{-1}\sum_{i=1}^{N}u_i(y)^{1-\gamma}$, with the inequality-aversion parameter γ some positive value. How such an SWF will rank a given outcome set depends upon the specific value of this parameter.

The role of γ can be understood in a variety of ways. First, γ determines the "marginal rate of moral substitution" (MRMS) between two life-histories. Let us denote the Atkinson rule R for ordering utility vectors as $w(.)$, i.e., $w(u(x))$ $= (1-\gamma)^{-1}\sum_{i=1}^{N}u_i(x)^{1-\gamma}$. The "marginal moral value of utility," at the level of a given life-history $(x; i)$, given some $u(.)$, is the derivative of $w(.)$ with respect to u_i where $u_i = u(x; i)$. The MRMS between two life-histories $(x; i)$ and $(x; j)$, given some $u(.)$, is the marginal moral value of utility at the utility level of the first, divided by the marginal moral value of utility at the utility level of the second.[138]

The Atkinson SWF is such that the MRMS between two life-histories is a function of the ratio of their utility levels, together with γ. Specifically, the MRMS between $(x; i)$ and $(x; j)$, given $u(.)$, equals $[u(x; j)/u(x; i)]^{\gamma}$.[139] Assume that i is worse off than j in x. Then the MRMS is greater than one. In other words, a small increment in i's utility, at his utility level in x, would have more of a moral impact than the same, small change in j's utility, at his utility level in x. The MRMS becomes increasingly large as the ratio between j's utility and i's utility increases. Conversely, holding fixed the utility ratio, the MRMS between the life-histories increases with γ. This is one sense in which an increasingly large γ means that the Atkinson SWF is increasingly "inequality averse."

A closely related observation is that γ determines how the Atkinson SWF evaluates "leaky transfers." Remember that any prioritarian SWF satisfies the Pigou–Dalton principle and therefore approves a pure transfer of well-being from a better- to

---

[138] Express $w(.)$ as a function of $u_1, \ldots, u_N$. $w(u_1, \ldots, u_N) = (1-\gamma)^{-1}\sum_{i=1}^{N}u_i^{1-\gamma}$. Then the marginal moral value of utility at $(x; i)$ is just $\left.\dfrac{\partial w}{\partial u_i}\right|_{u_i=u(x;i)}$. (If u_i at the level $u(x; i)$ were to be increased to $u_i + \Delta u$, w would increase to $w + \Delta w$. The derivative just mentioned is the limit of the ratio $\Delta w/\Delta u$, as Δu approaches zero.)

In turn, the MRMS between $(x; i)$ and $(x; j)$, given $u(.)$, is just the ratio of the derivatives, i.e., $\left.\dfrac{\partial w/\partial u_i}{\partial w/\partial u_j}\right|_{u_i=u(x;i)\,u_j=u(x;j)}$. This value, of course, depends on $u(.)$. We cannot speak of the MRMS between life-histories simpliciter, rather of this value given $u(.)$.

[139] Thus γ is an "elasticity of moral substitution" term or, equivalently, the "elasticity of the marginal moral value of utility." Consider any two arbitrary life-histories, with utilities u_i and u_j. The elasticity of moral substitution between those utilities is the value $\dfrac{d(MRMS)}{dK}\dfrac{K}{MRMS}$, with $K = u_i/u_j$ and $MRMS = \dfrac{\partial w/\partial u_i}{\partial w/\partial u_j}$. But this elasticity is just $-\gamma$.

a worse-off person. However, prioritarian SWFs differ in their willingness to approve "leaky transfers." In a Pigou–Dalton transfer, the gain in well-being of the worse-off person is exactly equal to the loss in well-being of the better-off person. By contrast, in a leaky transfer, the gain in well-being of the worse-off person is *less* than the loss in well-being of the better-off person. Formally:

A Leaky Transfer: Definition

Outcome *x* is reached from outcome *y* by a "leaky transfer" from individual *j* to individual *i* if: (1) individual *j* is better off than individual *i* in outcome *y*; (2) individual *j* is at least as well off as individual *i* in outcome *x*; (3) individual *j* is worse off in outcome *x* than outcome *y*; (4) individual *i* is better off in outcome *x* than outcome *y*; (5) the difference in well-being between $(x; i)$ and $(y; i)$ is *less* than the difference in well-being between $(y; j)$ and $(x; j)$; (6) everyone other than *i* and *j* is unaffected as between *x* and *y*.

I will refer to outcome *y* as the pre-transfer outcome; to outcome *x* as the post-transfer outcome; to individual *j*, the individual who starts out better off, as the transferor; and to individual *i* as the transferee. By the four life-histories involved in the transfer, I mean the transferee's pre- and post-transfer histories, and the transferor's pre- and post-transfer histories. Throughout the discussion, I will assume that all four life-histories are assigned *positive* utilities by all utility functions in **U**.[140]

Whether the Atkinson SWF approves a leaky transfer may depend upon which $u(.)$ in **U** is used to assign utilities to the four life-histories involved in the transfer.[141] In particular, whether the Atkinson SWF approves a leaky transfer, given some $u(.)$ in **U**, is determined by three pieces of numerical information generated by $u(.)$, along with the value of γ. The three crucial pieces of information are as follows: the ratio between the transferor's and transferee's utility in the pre-transfer outcome

---

[140] The Atkinson SWF requires that utilities be nonnegative in the case of γ < 1, and positive in the case of γ ≥ 1. See below, p. 391. Moreover, if any of the four life-histories are assigned a utility of 0 by $u(.)$, it can be seen that *K* will be infinite or undefined. My discussion assumes a finite, well-defined *K* and, thus, that all utilities are positive.

[141] If *x* is reached from *y* by a leaky transfer, with *j* the transferor and *i* the transferee, then all the utility functions in **U** must be such that the conditions for a leaky transfer—as I have defined it—are met. (For example, in a leaky transfer, the transferee *i* is better off in *x* than *y*, which precludes that $u(x; i) < u(y; i)$ for any $u(.)$ in **U**.) However, it is quite possible for **U** to satisfy the conditions for a leaky transfer, and yet for the Atkinson *R* to disapprove the transfer when coupled with $u(.)$, but approve it when coupled with $u^*(.)$, with both $u(.)$ and $u^*(.)$ in **U**. Of course, in such a case, $u(.)$ and $u^*(.)$ will not be positive ratio transformations of each other, and **U** will not be unique up to a positive ratio transformation.

Strictly speaking, it is inaccurate to discuss how the Atkinson SWF evaluates leaky transfers, when combined with some $u(.)$, since it is the Atkinson *R* that operates on utility vectors, while the Atkinson SWF combines *R* with the whole set **U** to rank outcomes. However, to reduce awkwardness, I will use the term "Atkinson SWF" rather than "Atkinson *R*" in the discussion that follows.

(designate this value as K); the proportional utility loss of the transferor, i.e., her utility loss divided by her utility in the pre-transfer outcome (designate this value as L); and the "transfer rate," i.e., the utility gain of the transferee, divided by the utility loss of the transferor (designate this value as T).[142]

Moreover, an *approximate* index of the desirability of the transfer is just the MRMS between the transferor and transferee in the pre-transfer outcome, i.e., $(1/K)^{\gamma}$. The fact that the transfer rate exceeds the MRMS—in other words, that $T > (1/K)^{\gamma}$—is a rough indicator that the Atkinson SWF approves the transfer (ranks x better than y).

This indicator may fail. But it can be shown that, if the proportional loss of the transferor is sufficiently small, the indicator will *not* fail. For values of L sufficiently close to zero, the fact that the transfer rate exceeds the MRMS necessarily means that the Atkinson SWF approves the transfer.[143] We can express this proposition,

---

[142] The four life-histories involved in the transfer are $(y; j)$, $(y; i)$, $(x; j)$, and $(x; i)$. The three pieces of information I have singled out consist of K, which equals $u(y; j)/u(y; i)$; L, which equals $[u(y; j) - u(x; j)]/u(y; j)$; and T, which equals $[u(x; i) - u(y; i)]/[u(y; j) - u(x; j)]$.

How can we show that these facts, without more, determine whether the Atkinson SWF, coupled with $u(.)$, approves the leaky transfer? Let $h(.)$ denote the Atkinson transformation function, given the choice of inequality aversion parameter γ. In other words, for any $(z; k)$, $h(u(z; k))$ $= (1-\gamma)^{-1}u(z; k)^{1-\gamma}$ or $\ln u(z; k)$ for $\gamma = 1$. Let $S = u(y; j) > 0$, since we are assuming that all the life-histories involved in the transfer have positive utilities. Observe that $u(x; j) = S(1 - L)$; that $u(y; i) = S/K$; and that $u(x; i) = S(LT + 1/K)$. Consider, now, that the Atkinson SWF with parameter γ will approve the leaky transfer, coupled with $u(.)$, iff $h(u(x; j)) + h(u(x; i)) > h(u(y; j)) + h(u(y; i))$. Equivalently, it approves the leaky transfer iff $h(S(1 - L)) + h(S(LT + 1/K)) > h(S) + h(S/K)$. By definition of $h(.)$, and given that S is positive, this is true just in case $h(1 - L) + h(LT + 1/K) > h(1) + h(1/K)$.

[143] Consider a case where x is reached from y via a leaky transfer, with four life-histories involved in the transfer, as per the discussion in the text. What I will show is the following. Assume that γ is fixed at some value; that some $u(.)$ in U has associated values of T, K, and L; and that T and K are such that $T > (1/K)^{\gamma}$. Then *if* L is sufficiently small, the Atkinson SWF combined with $u(.)$ necessarily approves the leaky transfer. How small L needs to be depends upon γ, T, and K.

Given my definition of a leaky transfer, it is *possible* that $u(y; j) = u(x; j)$ for some $u(.)$ in U, and L is thus zero according to this $u(.)$ rather than positive. However, in that case, $u(y; i) = u(x; i)$ and T is undefined, so the $T > (1/K)^{\gamma}$ test is inapplicable. This footnote therefore assumes that L is positive.

(The reader might wonder: what if $u(.)$ is such that $T < (1/K)^{\gamma}$? Following a line of reasoning exactly parallel to that about to be presented, it is easily shown that, at least if L is sufficiently small, the $T < (1/K)^{\gamma}$ test accurately indicates that the Atkinson SWF combined with $u(.)$ does *not* approve the leaky transfer. Actually, however, because the functions $(1-\gamma)^{-1}u_i^{1-\gamma}$ and $\ln u_i$ are strictly concave, it can be shown that the $T < (1/K)^{\gamma}$ test is *always* accurate, regardless of the size of L. Moreover, again given the strict concavity of these functions, the $T = (1/K)^{\gamma}$ test is never accurate: if T is precisely equal to $(1/K)^{\gamma}$, then the Atkinson SWF combined with $u(.)$ sees the post-transfer outcome as morally worse than the pre-transfer outcome, rather than morally indifferent.)

Return to the case where $T > (1/K)^{\gamma}$. As per the previous footnote, let us use $h(u(z; k))$ to mean the Atkinson transformation function, i.e., $(1-\gamma)^{-1}u(z;k)^{1-\gamma}$ or $\ln u(z; k)$ for $\gamma = 1$. As was demonstrated in that footnote, the Atkinson SWF combined with $u(.)$ approves the transfer iff $h(1- L) +$

compactly, by saying that the value $(1/K)^\gamma$ is the threshold transfer rate for *marginal* leaky transfers.[144]

To make this more concrete, imagine that $K = 2$; the transferor is twice as well off as the transferee in the pre-transfer outcome, y, according to $u(.)$. Assume that the transferor's utility is reduced by amount Δu, and that this loss in proportional terms (L) is sufficiently small that the $T > (1/K)^\gamma$ test is accurate.[145] The transferee's utility is increased by a fraction of the transferor's loss: she gains $T\Delta u$. Whether the Atkinson SWF approves this transfer depends upon the value of T and the value of γ. If γ is 1, then the threshold transfer rate for marginal leaky transfers is $(1/2)^1 = 1/2$. As long as the transferee gains more than half of what the transferor loses $(T > 1/2)$, the SWF approves the transfer. If $\gamma = 2$, then the threshold transfer rate for marginal leaky transfers decreases to $(1/2)^2 = 1/4$. As long as the transferee gains more than $1/4$ of what the transferor loses, the SWF approves the transfer. With $\gamma = 3$, the threshold rate becomes $1/8$. In other words, with increasingly large values of γ, we are willing to undertake marginal leaky transfers with smaller and smaller fractional gains for the transferee, as a fraction of the transferor's loss. This is another sense in which increasing values of γ make the Atkinson SWF increasingly "inequality averse."

Finally, γ measures the amount of utility which, equally distributed, is as good as a given outcome x. To be precise, for an outcome x, and a given $u(.)$, we can ask: what is the amount u^* such that the Atkinson SWF ranks $(u^*, u^*, \ldots, u^*)$ equally good as $(u_1(x), u_2(x), \ldots, u_N(x))$? As γ increases, u^* decreases.[146] This is yet another sense in which increasing values of γ make the SWF increasingly "inequality averse."

$h(LT + 1/K) > h(1) + h(1/K)$. For short, call this the "critical inequality." Note also that $h'(u(z; k)) = u(z; k)^{-\gamma}$.

With L positive, the critical inequality holds iff $[h(1 - L) - h(1)]/L > [h(1/K) - h(LT + 1/K)]/L$. Let $L^* = -L$, and $L^+ = LT$. Then the critical inequality holds iff $T[(h(L^+ + 1/K) - h(1/K))/L^+] > (h(L^* + 1) - h(1))/L^*$. Call this the "second inequality." Let $\varepsilon = [T(1/K)^{-\gamma} - 1]/2 > 0$.

By definition of the derivative, there is a value δ^+ such that, if $|L^+| < \delta^+$, the term on the left side of the second inequality is within ε of $Th'(1/K) = T(1/K)^{-\gamma}$. Similarly, there is a value δ^* such that, if $|L^*| < \delta^*$, the term on the right side of the second inequality is within ε of $h'(1) = 1$. Let $\delta = \min(\delta^+/T, \delta^*)$, Then if L is less than δ, the term on the left side of the second inequality is within ε of $T(1/K)^{-\gamma}$ and the term on the right side is within ε of 1. It follows that—if L is less than δ—the second inequality holds true. Therefore, if L is less than δ, the critical inequality holds true.

[144] "Marginal," here, indicates that the proportional well-being loss of the transferor, L, must be sufficiently small for the $T > (1/K)^\gamma$ test to be an accurate indicator of the desirability of the transfer. This also means that the proportional well-being gain of the transferee, i.e., $[u(x; i) - u(y; i)]/u(y;i)$ must be sufficiently small. If L must be less than some value δ, then the proportional well-being gain of the transferee, KTL, must be less than $KT\delta$.

[145] More precisely, accurate for all values of T and γ being considered, since how small L needs to be to make the test accurate depends upon these values.

[146] See Lambert (2001, pp. 94–97, 127–130). This is not true, of course, in the limiting case where utilities are already perfectly equally distributed in $u(x)$.

As γ approaches infinity, the Atkinson SWF approaches leximin.[147] At the other end of the spectrum, when γ equals zero, the Atkinson SWF becomes the utilitarian SWF and is no longer prioritarian.

So much for the way in which the Atkinson SWF is structured by γ. But what justifies this SWF? The answer hinges on the axiom of ratio rescaling invariance. While all continuous prioritarian SWFs satisfy the Pigou-Dalton, separability, and continuity axioms, the Atkinson SWF is the only continuous prioritarian SWF that satisfies this additional axiom.[148]

Ratio Rescaling Invariance

Take any utility function $u(.)$, which maps a given pair of outcomes x and y onto vectors $u(x) = (u_1(x), u_2(x),\ldots, u_N(x))$ and $u(y) = (u_1(y), u_2(y),\ldots, u_N(y))$. Now consider the utility function $ru(.)$, where r is any positive number. This utility function maps the outcomes onto new vectors, $ru(x), ru(y)$, with each entry in $ru(x)$ r times the corresponding entry in $u(x)$, and each entry in $ru(y)$ r times the corresponding entry in $u(y)$. An SWF satisfies *ratio rescaling invariance* if the rule R it contains is such that: $u(x)$ is ranked at least as good as $u(y)$ iff $ru(x)$ is ranked at least as good as $ru(y)$.

To be clear, there are non-Atkinson SWFs that satisfy ratio rescaling invariance but fail Pigou–Dalton, separability, or continuity. This is true, for example, of the utilitarian SWF, rank-weighted SWF, and leximin SWF. But if we are persuaded by the case for a continuous prioritarian SWF, *and* want ratio rescaling invariance to be satisfied, we end up with the Atkinson SWF.

Why require ratio rescaling invariance? Note that $u(.)$ and $ru(.)$ imply the very same facts about well-being levels, differences, *and* ratios. One life-history is at least as good as a second, according to $u(.)$, iff it is at least as good as the second according to $ru(.)$. The difference between one pair of life-histories is at least as large as the difference between a second pair, according to $u(.)$, iff the first difference is at least as large as the second according to $ru(.)$. Finally, the ratio between one pair of histories is a particular value K, according to $u(.)$, iff it is K according to $ru(.)$.[149]

---

[147] See Bosmans (2007); Hammond (1975); Lambert (2001, ch. 4).

[148] See Boadway and Bruce (1984, pp. 159–160); Bossert and Weymark (2004, pp. 1159–1164); Roberts (1980a). Strictly speaking, there are rules R^* of the form $F[(1-\gamma)^{-1}\sum_{i=1}^{N}u_i(x)^{1-\gamma}]$, where F is a strictly increasing function, such that these rules (1) are continuous prioritarian rules for ranking utility vectors (see the definition above, p. 357), and (2) are invariant to ratio rescalings. In particular, F could multiply the Atkinson R by a positive constant, for example changing the mathematically convenient $(1-\gamma)^{-1}$ factor outside the summation to $a(1-\gamma)^{-1}$, with a positive; or, in the case where $\gamma = 1$, we could sum the logarithm of utilities to some base (greater than 1) other than e. Of course, all such rules are extensionally equivalent to the Atkinson R with some value of γ and so I will not separately discuss them here.

[149] The proposition that $ru(.)$ preserves the ratio information of $u(.)$ assumes that ratios are represented by assigning 0 to the zero point. If, instead, the zero point is represented with some number Z,

Because $u(.)$ and $ru(.)$ contain the very same information about well-being levels, differences, and ratios, $ru(.)$ would be included in our zeroed-out set **U** just in case $u(.)$ is. Note here, in particular, that $ru(.)$ assigns the number 0 to whatever life-history is chosen as the zero point just in case $u(.)$ does.

But, in addition, this isomorphism between $u(.)$ and $ru(.)$ provides an argument in favor of ratio rescaling invariance. Imagine that our SWF incorporates a rule R which fails this axiom. In other words, there exists some pair of outcomes x and y, such that the utility vector $u(x)$ is ranked by R at least as good as $u(y)$, but $ru(x)$ is ranked by R as worse than $ru(y)$. Thus, R "sees" a difference between the assignment of numbers to life-histories by $u(.)$ and the assignment of numbers to life-histories by $ru(.)$. *But all the morally relevant information about life-histories captured by $u(.)$ is equally well captured by $ru(.)$.* So R is morally arbitrary; it responds differently to two assignments of utilities to life-histories that are identical in terms of the morally relevant information they contain.

A response to this argument for ratio rescaling invariance—if there is one—will have to show that there is morally relevant information about life-histories above and beyond their levels, differences, and ratios: information that might be "captured" by $u(.)$ but not $ru(.)$. What might that information be?

One possibility arises in the context of SWFs that incorporate a "threshold" life-history, $(x^+; i^+)$, distinct from the zero point used to establish well-being ratios, such that the ranking of two outcomes, x and y, depends on whether the component life-histories are above or below the threshold.[150] Such an SWF reflects the moral significance of the threshold life-history via a rule R that uses some number T to indicate that level, and that ranks utility vectors with an eye to whether the utilities in the vectors are above or below T.[151] At the same time, it "winnows down" the set **U** of utility functions, including only those functions such that $u(x^+; i^+) = T$. If **U**, after zeroing out, is unique up to a positive ratio transformation, then this further "winnowing down" yields a **U** with but a single member.

The adoption of such a threshold-based SWF provides a ready explanation for why the axiom of ratio rescaling invariance should be violated. If **U** has been "winnowed down" to include only utility functions that assign T to the threshold

---

then the Atkinson form changes (as discussed earlier) and so does the requirement of ratio rescaling invariance. With *this* representational rule in hand, the Atkinson form becomes $(1-\gamma)^{-1}\sum_{i=1}^{N}(u_i(x)-Z)^{1-\gamma}$ and it is *not* the case that $ru(.)$ preserves the ratio information of $u(.)$. Instead, the transformation of $u(.)$ that does so is any transformation of the form $r(u(.) - Z) + Z$. The ratio-rescaling-invariance requirement would then be formulated to require invariance to this sort of transformation.

[150] More precisely, if $(x^*; i^*)$ is the zero point, so that $u(x^*; i^*) = 0$ for all $u(.)$ in **U**, assume that $(x^+; i^+)$ is distinct from the zero point in the sense that $u(x^+; i^+) \neq 0$ for all $u(.)$ in **U**.

[151] Again, we are assuming in this section that SWFs assume the simple R-based form. Alternatively, an SWF might take account of whether the outcomes being ranked contain life-histories above or below the threshold by using a rule R that varies along with $u(.)$. See above, n. 71.

life-history, and $u(.)$ is in **U**—so that $u(x^+; i^+) = T$—then $ru(.)$ will *not* be in **U**, for any value of r other than 1. While both $ru(.)$ and $u(.)$ contain the very same information about well-being levels, differences, and ratios, only $u(.)$ embodies the *additional* information about where life-histories are located relative to the threshold. For any arbitrary life-history $(x; i)$, the numerical fact that $u(x; i) \leq T$ (taken together with the "representational rule" that T is the utility level of the threshold life-history) indicates that $u(.)$ ranks $(x^+; i^+)$ as being at least as good as $(x; i)$. And the numerical fact that $u(x; i) \geq T$ indicates that $u(.)$ ranks $(x; i)$ as being at least as good as $(x^+; i^+)$. By contrast, $ru(.)$ might assign a value less than T to $(x; i)$, and yet count $(x; i)$ as better than $(x^+; i^+)$; or it might assign a value greater than T to $(x; i)$, and yet count $(x; i)$ as worse than $(x^+; i^+)$. In this sense, $u(.)$ embodies additional, morally relevant information, above and beyond what $ru(.)$ contains.

For this line of analysis to work, however, we must be persuaded that the threshold life-history really does have moral relevance—in other words, that an SWF with a threshold life-history is indeed morally attractive. The two extant examples of such SWFs that have been defended in the literature (the sufficientist SWF and the prioritarian SWF with a lexical threshold) are problematic, for reasons discussed above.

A different and more subtle way to argue against the ratio-rescaling-invariance axiom would be to suggest that the moral appropriateness of leaky transfers between life-histories depends upon their attributes, and not (or not merely) the well-being ratios of the life-histories. To see this possibility, consider by way of illustration the "negative exponential" SWF.[152] Unlike the sufficientist SWF and the prioritarian SWF with a lexical threshold, the negative exponential SWF is a kind of continuous prioritarian SWF. But, like these, it also fails to satisfy the ratio-rescaling-invariance axiom.

Consider any case in which x is reached via a leaky transfer from y, with j the transferor and i the transferee. By virtue of its conformity with the ratio-rescaling-invariance axiom, the Atkinson SWF will approve the transfer, according to some $u(.)$ in **U**, just in case it approves the transfer according to $ru(.)$. That is *not* true for the negative exponential SWF.

Assume that we have an intuition regarding the propriety of the leaky transfer. If our intuition is merely derived from our judgments concerning the well-being ratios of the individuals involved—if we judge that the transfer should or should not occur *because* of our assessment of the utility ratio between transferor and transferee (K), the gain of the transferee as a fraction of the transferor's loss (T), the proportional loss of the transferor (L), and the other ratio facts that these three entail—then we will find it problematic to have an SWF (like the negative exponential) which might count the transfer to be appropriate using $u(.)$ but not using $ru(.)$. After all, the

---

[152] The negative exponential SWF is a continuous prioritarian SWF where $g(u_i(x)) = -e^{-u_i(x)}$. This SWF simply illustrates a potential line of argument against ratio rescaling invariance; I do not suggest that it is the only continuous prioritarian SWF which does so.

numerical values of K, T, and L, according to $u(.)$, and according to $ru(.)$, will be exactly the same.

However, we might have intuitions of a different sort. We might judge that the leaky transfer should or should not occur by virtue of certain attributes of i and j, independent of K, L, and T. We might intuit, for example, that the transfer should occur because the transferor's well-being is a particular multiple of the transferee's, *and* because the transferor and transferee have particular health, consumption, and leisure attributes. Intuitions of this sort could serve to "winnow down" $\mathbf{U}$. If a given utility function in $\mathbf{U}$, taken together with the negative exponential SWF, orders x and y inconsistently with our intuitions, it is winnowed out. This process might include $ru(.)$ for certain values of r but not for others.

More dramatically yet, imagine that we have intuitions about the threshold transfer rate for marginal leaky transfers, as between a life-history $(y; j)$ and a worse life-history $(y; i)$. We judge that this rate is some particular value. For a given $u(.)$, there is only one value r, such that $ru(.)$—combined with the negative exponential SWF—will cohere with these intuitions.[153]

If $\mathbf{U}$ is "winnowed down" along the lines suggested in the previous two paragraphs, we have a ready explanation for why $\mathbf{U}$ might contain $u(.)$ but not some $ru(.)$. "Although both of these utility functions contain the very same information about well-being levels, differences, and ratios, the $u(.)$ function—when conjoined with the negative exponential SWF—embodies some additional moral information that $ru(.)$ fails to embody, namely the moral appropriateness of various leaky transfers."

But why believe that the particular attributes of life-histories indeed constitute morally relevant information—above and beyond the facts about well-being levels, differences, and ratios to which these attributes give rise? According attributes this sort of moral role seems inconsistent with the spirit (if not the letter) of welfarism.[154] Once we have determined how life-histories and differences are ranked in terms of welfare, and constructed ratios via identification of the zero point, it is those

---

[153] The threshold transfer rate is just the MRMS between $(y; j)$ and $(y; i)$. Assume that we judge this to be a particular value M. Given the negative exponential SWF and some $u(.)$, the MRMS between $(y; j)$ and $(y; i)$ is just $e^{u(y;i)} / e^{u(y;j)}$. If MRMS $= M$, then $\ln$ MRMS $= \ln M$, or $u(.)$ must be such that $\ln M = u(y; i) - u(y; j)$.

Assume that this is true of $u(.)$. It will not be true of $ru(.)$, for any $r \neq 1$.

[154] Ranking outcomes by applying the negative exponential SWF to the "winnowed down" $\mathbf{U}$ is consistent with the *letter* of welfarism because doing so will yield a quasiordering and will certainly satisfy Pareto-indifference, Pareto-superiority, and anonymity in terms of that $\mathbf{U}$. Moreover, at least if $\mathbf{U}$ prior to "winnowing down" was unique up to a positive ratio transformation (or could be partitioned into a series of subsets, each unique up to a positive ratio transformation), doing so satisfies Pareto-indifference, anonymity, and Pareto-superiority in terms of the pre-winnowed-down $\mathbf{U}$.

facts—and not the attributes of life-histories—that should determine the appropriateness of any given leaky transfer.[155]

In short, the ratio-rescaling-invariance requirement would seem to be quite
attractive, and to provide a powerful argument for the Atkinson SWF (as opposed to
other continuous prioritarian SWFs). However, the Atkinson SWF has a serious
limitation. It is guaranteed to be invariant to a positive ratio transformation only in
the case of utility vectors with nonnegative utilities. It turns out that *no* continuous
prioritarian SWF is invariant to a positive ratio transformation when utilities can
take on any values, negative or nonnegative.[156] Furthermore, quite apart from the
issue of invariance to a ratio transformation, the Atkinson SWF is unattractive if
some utilities are negative. The g-function it uses— $(1-\gamma)^{-1}u_i(x)^{1-\gamma}$ —is either
undefined or, if defined, not both strictly increasing and strictly concave with negative utilities in the domain of this function.[157]

[155] This line of thought not only helps defend the axiom of ratio rescaling invariance. It also buttresses a basic premise throughout my discussion of prioritarianism: namely, that the SWF assumes
the simple R-based form. Consider, in particular, prioritarian SWFs which use a rule R that is
"indexed" to the utility function. For example, the SWF might revolve around a strictly concave,
strictly increasing function that depends upon $u(.)$. It takes the form: x is at least as good as y iff, for
all $u(.)$ in $\mathbf{U}$, $\sum_{i=1}^{N}g^{u(.)}(u_i(x))\geq\sum_{i=1}^{N}g^{u(.)}(u_i(y))$. The term $g^{u(.)}$ denotes the specific strictly increasing, strictly concave function that is applied to utility vectors when the utility numbers in the vectors
come from function $u(.)$.

Some such "indexed" SWFs are innocuous: they achieve the very same ranking of an outcome set
as a plausible SWF assuming the simple R-based form. For example, imagine that we favor the
Atkinson SWF, and believe that the appropriate level for the γ parameter is some particular level.
Then we could proceed two ways, which yield the very same ordering of outcome sets (assuming that
$\mathbf{U}$ can be partitioned into one or more subsets, each unique up to a positive affine transformation).
Starting with our set $\mathbf{U}$ which represents well-being levels and differences, and an identification of the
zero point as a particular life-history $(x^*; i^*)$, we could "zero out" $\mathbf{U}$ and use the now-familiar Atkinson
SWF. Or, we could refrain from "zeroing out" $\mathbf{U}$ and employ an "indexed" Atkinson SWF, which
takes account of which number $u(.)$ assigns to the zero point. This "indexed" SWF says: x is morally
at least as good as y iff $(1-\gamma)^{-1}\sum_{i=1}^{N}(u_i(x)-u(x^*;i^*))^{1-\gamma}\geq(1-\gamma)^{-1}\sum_{i=1}^{N}(u_i(y)-u(x^*;i^*))^{1-\gamma}$ for all
$u(.)$ in $\mathbf{U}$.

But a different kind of "indexed" SWF is more troubling. Imagine that we allow the γ parameter
itself to vary depending on $u(.)$. Imagine that, when utility function $u(.)$ is used, the γ parameter is a
particular value; when utility function $ru(.)$ is used, the γ parameter may be different. Given *this* sort
of "indexed" SWF, it is possible that the appropriateness of a particular leaky transfer will depend on
whether utilities are assigned to life-histories using $u(.)$ or $ru(.)$. This "indexed" SWF (like using a
simple R-based SWF that fails ratio rescaling invariance, such as the negative exponential SWF)
seems inconsistent with the spirit, if not letter, of welfarism.

[156] See Blackorby and Donaldson (1982); Bossert and Weymark (2004, pp. 1159–1164); Brown
(2005a, ch. 6). To be clear, there *are* continuous prioritarian SWFs that function well with negative
utilities, such as the negative exponential SWF—but these do not satisfy ratio rescaling invariance.

[157] In the case of utility vectors that include some zero utilities, the Atkinson SWF is undefined for
values of γ greater than or equal to one, otherwise well-behaved.

In sum, then, a strong argument can be mounted for using an Atkinson SWF to rank an outcome set in which all N individuals have life-histories no worse than the zero point (nonexistence or, if nonexistence is rejected, whatever alternative life-history is used as the zero point for setting ratios). How to rank outcome sets in which some individuals have life-histories worse than the zero point is a real gap in the continuous prioritarian approach, which this book does not attempt to resolve. The problem, to be clear, is not in assigning a negative utility to a life-history, or comparing a life-history to nonexistence. The account of well-being developed in Chapter 3 permits such ascriptions without difficulty. **U** can readily be zeroed out so as to include only utility functions that assign 0 to nonexistence (or any alternative zero point); and these functions may well assign negative utilities to some other life-histories. The problem arises at the stage of moving *from* this information *to* a ranking of outcomes. If the utility vectors corresponding to outcomes can have negative as well as positive entries, there is no rule R that satisfies all the axioms defended in this chapter: that is prioritarian, *and* continuous, *and* is invariant to ratio rescaling.

C. Calibrating the Atkinson SWF

How should the decisionmaker arrive at a value for the inequality-aversion parameter, γ, for the Atkinson SWF? She should do so by engaging in various sorts of thought experiments,[158] the form of which I will now clarify. Let me bracket, for the moment, the question whether the decisionmaker should "run" the experiments via introspection, or by posing them to members of the population or other third parties via formal or informal surveys. The "respondent" to the thought experiment might be the decisionmaker herself, or it might be a survey respondent.

The inequality-aversion parameter, γ, should not be conflated with a superficially similar parameter: the coefficient of relative risk aversion, if constant, for consumption, income, or wealth.[159] The latter (which I denoted in Chapter 4 as "λ^k") is a parameter for a standard type of ordinary utility function, the CRRA utility function, which represents an individual's preferences over outcomes as a function of her consumption, income, or wealth. As discussed in Chapter 4, extended utility functions ranking life-histories as a function of the subject's consumption might also assume the CRRA form, and incorporate the λ^k parameter. The inequality-aversion parameter, by contrast, is a parameter of the SWF itself, not of the extended utility functions in **U**. It structures the rule R, specifically the Atkinson rule— $(1-\gamma)^{-1}\sum_{i=1}^{N}u_i(x)^{1-\gamma}$—which ranks utility vectors corresponding to outcomes once those utility vectors are in hand.

In particular, as discussed, γ determines whether the Atkinson SWF approves a leaky transfer. To recapitulate: In a leaky transfer, the transferee gains less than what

[158] Atkinson himself proposed as much. See Atkinson (1983, p. 5).
[159] See Kaplow (2010).

the transferor loses. In general, whether the Atkinson SWF approves a given leaky transfer depends upon which $u(.)$ in U is used to evaluate the transfer—and more specifically, upon various utility ratios according to $u(.)$. One such ratio is T, which I have termed the "transfer rate": the transferee's gain, as a fraction of the transferor's loss. Another is K: the ratio of the transferor's utility to the transferee's utility in the pre-transfer outcome. Another is L: the transferor's utility loss, as a fraction of her starting point. The value $(1/K)^{\gamma}$ is what I have termed the threshold transfer rate for marginal leaky transfers. If the well-being loss of the transferor, and gain to the transferee, are "marginal"—in other words, L is sufficiently small—the SWF approves the transfer whenever $T > (1/K)^{\gamma}$.

Remember, too, that the utility numbers which are relevant to leaky transfers are *lifetime* utilities. SWFs, as conceptualized in this book, operate on a set U containing utility functions measuring the lifetime well-being of individuals—the well-being of whole life-histories. A leaky transfer is such that the transferee starts off worse than the transferor in terms of *lifetime* well-being; and the gain in his *lifetime* well-being is less than the transferor's loss. Similarly, K, L, and T are ratios, of various sorts, of lifetime utility numbers.

What kinds of thought experiments are useful in identifying an appropriate value for γ? Most straightforwardly, the decisionmaker might ask the "respondent" (the decisionmaker herself or the survey respondent) a leaky transfer question which involves a marginal transfer, and which characterizes the life-histories of the transferee and transferor in terms of their lifetime well-being, rather than other attributes. For example, she might ask: "If Sheila is at twice the level of *lifetime well-being* as Sam, do I approve a change which reduces Sheila's lifetime well-being by a small amount, and increases Sam's lifetime well-being by 75% of that amount? If so, what if Sam's well-being improvement is only 50% of the reduction in Sheila's? What if it is only 25%?" Assume that, when the ratio of the lifetime well-being of the transferor to the transferee is some value K^*, the respondent is willing to approve a marginal leaky transfer as long as the transfer rate exceeds some value T^*. Then this implies that her valuation for γ is $-(\log T^*/\log K^*)$.[160]

Despite the simplicity of the formula just provided, thought experiments involving marginal leaky transfers, with the transferee and transferor characterized in terms of lifetime well-being, have certain disadvantages. To begin, the respondent may have difficulty arriving at firm moral intuitions regarding a hypothetical case where the attributes of the transferee and transferor—as opposed to their lifetime well-being—are left undescribed. Such a case may feel too abstract. A more concrete characterization may help her arrive at a settled moral judgment regarding the propriety of leaky transfers.

---

[160] If T^* is the threshold transfer rate for marginal leaky transfers when $K = K^*$, i.e., such a transfer is approved whenever $T > T^*$ but not otherwise, then $T^* = (1/K^*)^{\gamma}$. Taking logarithms (to any base) of both sides yields the equation in the text.

Thus imagine, instead, that the thought experiment involves a leaky transfer, where the transferor's and transferee's life-histories are described in terms of their non-well-being attributes. From the respondent's answer to *this* sort of leaky transfer question, we can infer her valuation of γ, *if* we know how she assigns lifetime well-being numbers to life-histories.

For example, imagine that outcomes are characterized in terms of individuals' annual consumption. The transferee and transferor both live for 70 years, with the transferor having an annual consumption of $200,000, and the transferee an annual consumption of $50,000. Imagine that the respondent is willing to reduce the transferor's annual consumption by $100 in one year, with the transferee's consumption increasing by an amount equaling $C < \$100$ that year. Assume that the respondent approves this transfer for values of C exceeding some cutoff value, e.g., $20. If the respondent assigns lifetime utilities to life-histories using a temporally additive (TANA) lifetime utility function without discounting,[161] and *if* the sublifetime utility function is a CRRA function equaling the square root of consumption, *then* choosing a cutoff value of $20 implies a value of γ equaling approximately 1.3.

One downside of this sort of attribute-framed leaky transfer question is that inferences about the respondent's value of γ are sensitive to her theory of lifetime well-being. (To continue with the above example: if the respondent has a temporally additive lifetime utility function, with a sublifetime utility function equaling the logarithm (to any base greater than 1) of consumption rather than the square root of consumption, a cutoff value of $20 implies a value of γ equaling 1.9 rather than 1.3.) This poses an inferential challenge where the respondent is a survey respondent, rather than the decisionmaker herself. A second downside of a leaky transfer question formulated in terms of the non-well-being attributes of transferor and transferee has to do with the ratio-rescaling-invariance feature of the Atkinson SWF: the respondent's willingness to approve a given leaky transfer should be *just* a function of the ratios between the lifetime well-being of transferee and transferor (K, T, L and the other such lifetime well-being ratios that these imply). The description of the non-well-being attributes of transferee and transferor should be a way for the respondent to arrive at a clear judgment regarding what the lifetime well-being ratios are. These attributes should not affect the respondent's willingness to approve the transfer, once she has arrived at that judgment—but, in practice, may have this effect.

However, notwithstanding these downsides, the sort of attribute-framed leaky transfer question now under discussion may be a useful supplement to a question that directly characterizes transferee and transferor in lifetime well-being terms.

A second and cross-cutting point is that the $T > (1/K)^{\gamma}$ test is accurate only for marginal leaky transfers. Choosing a particular value of γ means that, if the transferor in a leaky transfer case starts off at K times the lifetime well-being of the transferee, and the transfer rate (T) is greater than $(1/K)^{\gamma}$, *and* the fractional loss to the

---

[161] See Chapters 4, 6.

transferor (L) is sufficiently small, then the Atkinson SWF will approve the transfer. However, as the fractional loss to the transferor becomes larger, the Atkinson SWF using γ may not approve the transfer even though $T > (1/K)^\gamma$.

This point has much significance for thought experiments eliciting respondents' judgments about the appropriate value of γ. Ideally, the respondent should understand both what a given value of γ implies for marginal leaky transfers, *and* what it implies for inframarginal leaky transfers (where L is large).

A dramatic illustration of the differing implications of a given value of γ for marginal and inframarginal leaky transfers is furnished by *equalizing* leaky transfers. In an equalizing leaky transfer, the transferor starts off at K times the utility of the transferee; the transfer rate (as always) is some value less than 1; and the transferor loses a sufficient amount that the transferor and transferee end up at the same level of utility. If the transferor starts off at K times the utility of the transferee, and there is an equalizing transfer where the transferee and transferor end up at a utility level which is some multiple E of the transferee's starting point, this transfer will be approved by the Atkinson SWF if E exceeds some cutoff value E^*; disapproved if E is below the cutoff value E^*; and counted a matter of moral indifference if E just equals E^*. E^* is a function of K and γ. We can now ask: If the transferor starts at K times the utility of the transferee, and loses a sufficient amount that she and the transferee both end up at E^* times the transferee's starting point, what is the transfer rate T at that point? Call this value of T the threshold transfer rate for *equalizing* leaky transfers. Like E^*, and like the threshold transfer rate for *marginal* leaky transfers, it is a function of K and γ.[162]

The key point, here, is that a given value of K and γ will imply a threshold transfer rate for equalizing leaky transfers which is much larger than the threshold transfer rate for marginal leaky transfers. Thus a value of γ which might well strike the respondent as being counterintuitively large, when considered in light of its implications for marginal leaky transfers, might seem quite appropriate, when considered in light of its implications for equalizing leaky transfers.[163]

For example, if the transferor starts off at twice the level of lifetime well-being of the transferee $(K = 2)$, and $\gamma = 7$, the threshold transfer rate for marginal leaky transfers is $\frac{1}{2}^7 = 1/128$. This seems like an unbelievably low transfer rate to be morally acceptable. Do we really morally approve any policy that takes away a (small) amount of well-being from the transferor, and permits virtually all of that well-being to leak away, so long as the transferee gains at least $1/128$ of what the transferor loses? On the other hand, to say that $\gamma = 7$ *also* means that, if the transferor starts off at twice the utility level of the transferee, we are willing to undertake an equalizing transfer (losing some utility in the process) as long as both individuals end up at a level no

---

[162] $E^* = \left[(1 + K^{1-\gamma})/2\right]^{1/(1-\gamma)}$. In turn, the threshold transfer rate for equalizing leaky transfers is just $(E^* - 1)/(K - E^*)$.

[163]   Arnold Harberger (1978, pp. S111–S113), in a famous critique of distributional weights for CBA, focused on marginal leaky transfers.

less than 1.12 times the transferee's initial level (in which case the transferee will have gained at least 14% of what the transferor loses). It seems quite plausible that morality might recommend such equalization.

Table 5.4 shows the threshold transfer rate for marginal versus equalizing leaky transfers, for different combinations of values of K and γ. The table illustrates the dramatic divergence between the two rates.

Table 5.4 The Threshold Transfer Rate for Marginal versus Equalizing Leaky Transfers

		Value of K		
		2	5	10
Value of γ	2	.25 vs. .5	.04 vs. .2	.01 vs. .1
	3	.13 vs. .36	.008 vs. .11	.001 vs. .05
	4	.06 vs. .27	.0016 vs. .07	.0001 vs. .03
	5	.03 vs. .21	.00032 vs. .05	.00001 vs. .02

The first entry in each cell is the threshold transfer rate for marginal leaky transfers, the second entry that rate for equalizing leaky transfers. All quantities greater than .01 are rounded to 2 decimal points.

This divergence, in turn, suggests that respondents' answers to equalization questions, or to other questions involving inframarginal leaky transfers, may well imply values of γ which are inconsistent with the answers suggested by leaky transfer questions involving marginal transfers. Respondents' judgments regarding γ are thus best elicited by questions involving *both* marginal and inframarginal leaky transfers—ideally, with both sorts of questions posed to the very same respondent, to force her to arrive at a consistent set of judgments.

Now let us introduce the question whether γ should be elicited via surveys, as opposed to introspection on the part of the decisionmaker. There *is* a substantial survey literature that attempts to elicit respondents' *impartial* views on a wide variety of policy and normative issues. It includes, for example, many surveys in the field of public health, where respondents are asked to rank different health programs from the perspective of the public-spirited citizen or governmental planner, rather than their own health interests. It also includes the seminal research program of Yoram Amiel and Frank Cowell, described in their book, *Thinking about Inequality.* Amiel and Cowell conducted numerous surveys to elicit respondents' views about inequality and poverty—and they did so by asking the respondent to compare different income distributions, typically described as distributions in simplified, hypothetical societies. Respondents were prompted to compare these distributions from a disinterested point of view.[164]

---

[164] See Amiel and Cowell (1999, especially pp. 24-26). For a review of surveys regarding health policy, many of which appear to have invited a citizen perspective, see Dolan, Shaw, Tsuchiya, and

Surveys inviting respondents to adopt an impartial perspective, in effect, seek to elicit respondents' moral judgments or preferences. Such surveys are to be distinguished from (1) surveys that ask the respondent to rank outcomes, policies, etc., from a self-interested point of view (or implicitly invite her to do so), and with an understanding of how she would be affected by the outcomes, policies, etc; (2) surveys that ask the respondent to rank outcomes, policies, etc., from a self-interested point of view, but behind a veil of ignorance; (3) surveys that ask or invite a "mixed" perspective, including some mixture of both self-interested and moral preferences;[165] and (4) the attempt to infer a value of γ from "revealed preference" data, i.e., by looking at the value of γ implicit in existing policies.[166]

Surveys of the first type are tremendously useful in inferring individuals' extended preferences and thus constructing U, but have no role in inferring γ. This is a parameter of a *moral* choice-evaluation procedure (specifically an SWF): a framework for ranking outcomes that gives equal weight to everyone's well-being. Asking the respondent to think about leaky transfers in a frame of mind that is partial to the transferees, transferors, or anyone else in the population is hardly useful in eliciting her impartial, moral, judgment regarding the level of γ. A similar analysis applies to surveys of the third type.

Because γ is a parameter for a continuous prioritarian SWF—while the veil-of-ignorance conception of fairness very plausibly generates a utilitarian ranking of outcomes or perhaps a leximin ranking—it is hard to see how veil-of-ignorance studies are of much use in estimating this parameter. As for the "revealed preference" approach: our best understanding of the dynamics of policymaking hardly provides much grounds to think that policy outcomes reliably track citizens' or policymakers' moral preferences, let alone their well-considered moral preferences.

By contrast, surveys prompting respondents to adopt an impartial frame of mind—a "citizen" or "social planner" perspective—and in that frame to consider leaky transfer questions *are* potentially quite useful in estimating γ. There is a small, existing scholarly literature involving surveys of this sort. The most systematic such survey, to date, was undertaken by a team of British researchers, led by Paul Dolan,

Williams (2005). On deliberative polling, see sources cited in Adler (2006b, p. 1878, n. 7). For a defense of eliciting the impartial perspective via surveys, see generally Konow (2009).

[165] The survey literature inviting a self-interested point of view (e.g., for consumption gambles) is vast, and discussed to some extent in Chapter 4. For examples of veil-of-ignorance surveys, see Amiel, Cowell, and Gaertner (2009); Andersson and Lyttkens (1999); Beckman, Formby, and Smith (2004); Bernasconi (2002); Bosmans and Schokkaert (2004); Camacho-Cuena, Seidl, and Morone (2005); Frohlich and Oppenheimer (1992); Traub, Seidl, and Schmidt (2009); Traub, Seidl, Schmidt, and Levati (2005). Finally, the burgeoning literature on "social preferences" uses a survey or experimental set-up that invites a mixture of self-interested and moral preferences. See Daruvala (2010).

A number of the veil-of-ignorance studies just cited document the difference between the ranking of outcomes from that perspective and an impartial one. For evidence of the difference between an impartial and mixed perspective, see Croson and Konow (2009).

[166] See Lambert, Millimet, and Slottje (2003, p. 1064).

Richard Edlin, and Aki Tsuchiya. The researchers conducted face-to-face interviews with 582 members of the British public.[167]

From the perspective of this book, the research design of the study was excellent (if not perfect). The researchers' goal was to calibrate an Atkinson SWF, taking as its inputs vectors of health utility numbers summarizing individuals' *lifetime* health attainments.[168] The researchers considered, but rejected, the sort of "sublifetime prioritarian" approach I will criticize in Chapter 6—an approach that would examine individual health states on a period-by-period basis to determine which health improvements deserve extra moral weight. Instead, the researchers "focus[ed] on the social value attached to profiles of health over a lifetime" and made "lifetime health experience . . . the relevant distribuendum" for the SWF.[169]

Furthermore, the researchers aimed to have respondents assume an impartial, "citizen" perspective.

> Our specific goal here is to elicit preferences from members of the general public that can be fed into a social welfare function. . . . Most of the studies in this area have adopted a social perspective, in which respondents are asked to consider allocation decisions that they personally may not be affected by. We propose to do the same.[170]

The respondent was given a series of questions. Each question described two scenarios (outcomes), in which the lifetime health prospects of two equally sized groups were described. The respondent was asked to "decide which scenario you

---

[167] See Dolan, Edlin, and Tsuchiya (2008). Amiel, Creedy, and Hurn (1999) asked respondents to consider hypothetical leaky transfers of income from a richer to poorer individual, so as to estimate social inequality aversion with respect to income (not utility). Lindholm and Rosen (1998) estimated inequality aversion with respect to health by surveying policymakers regarding hypothetical policies. Gevers, Glejser, and Rouyer (1979) calibrated a non-Atkinson index of inequality aversion by asking about stipends to hypothetical students. Bleichrodt, Doctor, and Stolk (2005) elicited rankings of health policies from an impartial perspective so as to estimate a non-Atkinson (rank-weighted) SWF as a function of health.

There are other studies that estimate inequality aversion, but using questions in which the respondent's self-interest is likely to be a substantial motivating factor—for example, by asking the respondent to rank income distributions or transfer policies knowing her own income. See Pirttilä and Uusitalo (2010); Sælen et al. (2008).

[168] I add the qualifier "if not perfect" because the study estimated γ via questions framed in terms of lifetime health and involving inframarginal leaky transfers—without considering whether questions involving lifetime well-being, or involving marginal leaky transfers, might suggest different values for γ. Strictly speaking, the authors estimated the inequality aversion parameter r for an SWF which is an increasing transformation of the Atkinson SWF. The parameter r corresponds to $\gamma - 1$. See Dolan, Edlin, and Tsuchiya (2008, p. 55).

[169] Dolan, Edlin, and Tsuchiya (2008, p. 61).

[170] Ibid., p. 9.

would choose if asked to recommend one by NICE"[171] (a British governmental body that allocates health care resources). For example, one question asked the respondent to choose between a scenario in which group one experiences 74 years in full health and group two experiences 52 years in full health, and a scenario in which group one experiences 62 years in full health and group two experiences 56 years in full health.[172]

In other words, these questions involved inframarginal leaky transfers, where the transferee and transferor were characterized in terms of their health and longevity attributes (not lifetime well-being). To infer a value of γ from the survey responses, the researchers needed first to infer respondents' well-being valuations of the transferees' and transferors' lifetime health histories, and they did so in two ways: by converting the health and longevity descriptions into QALY values, and by using an alternative lifetime metric that was sensitive to whether poor health occurred in childhood or adulthood. The mean estimates of γ, for different question sets, ranged from 1.55 to 7.32.[173]

The Dolan et al. effort is a nice illustration of the type of survey that would be useful in estimating γ. But are such surveys *central* to the task of estimating γ (just as evidence of the population's extended preferences is *central* to the construction of U)? That question implicates much larger metaethical questions, relevant to the entirety of this chapter, to which we now turn.

VI. THE METAETHICS OF THE SWF

As explained in Chapter 1, this book adopts a posture of agnosticism on metaethical issues—as between "noncognitivists," who deny the existence of moral facts, and "cognitivists," who recognize such facts and have proposed a variety of different accounts of what they might consist in. The reflective-equilibrium reasoning in which this book engages is meant to mesh both with noncognitivism and with the various versions of cognitivism.

On certain versions of cognitivism, moral facts are *constituted* by the population's approvals under impartial (and otherwise idealized) conditions. For example, Michael Smith is a cognitivist who analyzes moral facts in terms of convergent, fully rational, impartial preferences. Along similar lines, Peter Railton defends a metaethical view he terms "idealized subjectivism": "'X is wrong' means 'We the people (i.e., people in general, including the speaker) would disapprove of allowing X as part of our basic scheme of social cooperation were we to consider the question with full

---

[171] Ibid., p. 140.

[172] Ibid., p. 145.

[173] See ibid., pp. 96, 98.

information from a standpoint that considers the well-being of all affected without partiality.'"[174] For short, call such a view "population-preference cognitivism."

On this sort of metaethical view, surveys regarding the value of the Atkinson inequality parameter γ would, seemingly, be quite useful. Such surveys seemingly provide quite direct evidence of the moral facts. If the population, under impartial and otherwise idealized conditions, converges in judging γ to have a particular value, then that just *is* the value of γ.

By contrast, for noncognitivists, or for other variants of cognitivism, it is *not* the case that moral facts are constituted by the population's approvals under impartial (and otherwise idealized) conditions—either because there are no moral facts at all, or because moral facts are not analyzed in this manner.[175] According to these metaethical accounts, population surveys about γ will not provide direct evidence of the moral facts regarding γ; but they may still have some utility, at least for some such accounts.

For example, consider the noncognitivist position that moral statements are really expressions of a non-belief state on the part of the speaker, such as the speaker's *endorsement* of some course of behavior, or some similar non-belief state. On such a metaethical view, the decisionmaker "deliberating" between different functional forms for an SWF should not see herself as trying to determine what the moral facts are, but rather as trying to determine which SWF she wishes to endorse (or something like that). Here, the most natural γ-calibration thought experiment for the decisionmaker to conduct is one where *she herself* is the participant—where she *introspects* about which leaky transfers she morally prefers. Still, third-party surveys could add to her information base. By having information about the values of γ that *others* morally prefer, the decisionmaker arrives at her own moral endorsement in a more reflective manner.[176]

To be sure, these observations raise further questions. First, if certain metaethical views suggest that surveys regarding γ (or any other moral issues) have somewhat attenuated relevance to the moral decisionmaker, why did Chapters 3 and 4 insist that **U** be constructed by looking to the totality of the population's extended preferences—and thus that survey or other evidence about these preferences is vitally relevant to constructing **U**? Consider noncognitivism. If this metaethical account is true, why should the decisionmaker be apt to endorse a version of the SWF framework which constructs **U** with reference to the extended preferences of

---

[174] Railton (1996, p. 69).

[175] Moral facts might be seen as facts of some other sort that have an explanatory role. See Chapter 1, discussing the explanatory-fact version of cognitivism. Or, they might be facts regarding the ideal approvals of some group not including the whole population, e.g., the approvals of a god-like creature.

[176] What about a cognitivist view that sees moral facts as having an explanatory role? On this view, surveys might indirectly evidence such facts, since the role of these facts is just to explain human behavior (including verbal behavior, e.g., survey responses).

the entire population? Why not, instead, endorse a version whereby **U** solely reflects her own extended preferences (just as γ reflects her own preferences regarding the appropriate rate of leaky transfers)?

I attempted to answer this question in Chapter 3.[177] On a wide range of metaethical views, both cognitivist and noncognitivist, it is plausible to take the position that some subject's well-being depends (at least in part) on the *subject's* preferences. The decisionmaker, in reflective equilibrium, plausibly will find herself embracing a moral view such that the well-being ranking of (*x*; *i*) and (*y*; *i*) takes account of what *i* himself wants. **U** is therefore appropriately constructed by pooling the entire population's extended preferences.

Let us return, now, to population-preference cognitivism. For such views, the proposition that **U** is constructed by pooling the entire population's extended preferences is not puzzling. Such a construction is very natural.

But a different puzzle arises. I have argued that the most attractive SWF uses a single rule *R* to rank utility vectors. More specifically, I have claimed, the most attractive SWF uses a single *R* of the Atkinson form. And, I have just suggested, we might survey the population for their judgments regarding γ, so as to calibrate this rule.

But why should there be a *single* value of γ? Consider, more closely, a cognitivist account which says: outcome *x* is morally at least as good as outcome *y* iff everyone weakly morally prefers *x* to *y* under impartial and otherwise idealized conditions. Wouldn't such an account allow different members of the population to have differing views regarding γ? Individual *i* approves a γ parameter with one particular value; individual *j* approves a γ parameter with a different value; and so forth. Outcomes would be ranked according to the totality of these approvals. In other words, outcome *x* is morally at least as good as outcome *y* iff, for all *u*(.) in **U**, $(1-\gamma)^{-1}\sum_{i=1}^{N}u_i(x)^{1-\gamma} \ge (1-\gamma)^{-1}\sum_{i=1}^{N}u_i(y)^{1-\gamma}$ for all γ in ‖. ‖ is the set containing different values of γ; a particular value is in this set if at least one member of the population, under ideal conditions, approves it as the morally appropriate value. For short, call this "the Atkinson SWF with a whole set of γ values."

For that matter, why wouldn't population-preference cognitivism allow each member of the population to have her own views concerning the functional form of the SWF? Individual *i* morally prefers that outcomes be ranked using an Atkinson SWF with a particular value of γ. Individual *j* morally prefers that outcomes be ranked using some other type of prioritarian SWF. Individual *k* morally prefers that outcomes be ranked using a utilitarian SWF. Wouldn't population-preference cognitivism lead to the following framework for ranking outcomes: Outcome *x* is morally at least as good as outcome *y* iff, for all *u*(.) in **U**, *u*(*x*) is better than *u*(*y*) for all *R*ᵢ, where *R*ᵢ is the rule for ranking utility vectors that individual *i*, under ideal conditions, morally approves?

[177] See Chapter 3, n. 137.

Indeed—pushing this line of thought yet further—wouldn't the population-preference cognitivist allow that some members of the population might reject the SWF framework entirely, and embrace some kind of non-SWF welfarism, or for that matter some kind of non-welfarist view? Why not permit individual i to be a deontologist in ranking actions a and b, individual j to be a non-welfarist consequentialist, individual k to be a non-SWF welfarist, individual l to use one kind of SWF, individual m another, and so on? Such a view would say: it is a fact that action a is morally at least as good as action b iff each individual weakly morally prefers a to b, under ideal conditions.

In short, for the population-preference cognitivist, is it not an open question what the form of each individual's moral preferences are? If so, why—on such a view—would surveys designed to elicit a particular moral parameter, γ, be the only useful type of moral surveys? Wouldn't we properly conduct a much wider range of surveys?

Indeed, I find quite plausible the version of cognitivism which says: it is a fact that a is morally at least as good as b iff each individual in the population, under impartial and otherwise idealized conditions, would prefer a to b. But such a view is plausible only because the population preferences that constitute moral facts are appropriately *idealized*. Morality has *critical* force. Individuals who are badly informed, irrational, overly hasty in their judgments, or otherwise fall short of the idealizing conditions can be wrong about what the moral facts are.

One way for a decisionmaker to gain evidence about the population's fully informed, fully rational, moral preferences is to conduct surveys. Another way is for the decisionmaker to see what point of reflective equilibrium *she* reaches when calm, well-informed, and thinking clearly. Imagine that the decisionmaker, under excellent deliberative conditions, reaches a particular moral view. Then this fact about her own position of deliberative equipoise is some evidence about what the population generally would prefer under ideal conditions.

Thoughtful introspection would seem to be particularly strong evidence of the population's idealized moral preferences—as compared to survey evidence—if the decisionmaker is heavily influenced in reaching her point of reflective equilibrium by logic, mathematics, or moral theory. Such considerations would seem less likely to influence survey respondents (unless particularly well primed for the task) than their reactions to concrete cases.[178]

In this book, I have tried to adduce a variety of arguments for the SWF approach and, more specifically, an SWF of the Atkinson form—arguments that draw heavily on logic and mathematics, and on general moral theory. These arguments attempt to

---

[178] To be sure, if such considerations are too esoteric to motivate most or many members of the population, even under idealized conditions, then the fact that a highly capable reasoner arrives at some point of reflective equilibrium, in reliance on such considerations, would be little evidence of the population's idealized preferences. But I do not believe that the considerations I have relied upon *are* too esoteric in this way.

induce the decisionmaker (or any other reader) to reach a point of reflective equilibrium where she embraces the Atkinson SWF. From the perspective of population-preference cognitivism, these arguments are just attempts to show that *anyone*, under ideal conditions, would prefer the Atkinson SWF—and to make this showing by elucidating the considerations that would move anyone to do so.

Assume that the decisionmaker (or any other reader) is persuaded by my arguments. Her own point of reflective equilibrium is surely not *conclusive* evidence of what the population would generally prefer under ideal conditions. Nor is it *conclusive* evidence even if she remains at the same point of reflective equilibrium, embracing the Atkinson SWF, after reading not just this single book but all other relevant philosophical and economic literature. Surveys regarding the variety of issues that have been engaged, in the course of arguing for the Atkinson SWF, would still retain evidentiary value for this reader.

However, surveys would be particularly valuable regarding the issue that has been left open here: namely, the value of γ. I have left the issue open just because the kinds of logical, mathematical, and theoretical considerations I have drawn upon in arguing for the Atkinson SWF seem to provide little help in identifying a particular value of γ; nor am I aware of a powerful intuitive argument for a particular value. Finally, my failure to take a position on the value of γ is hardly idiosyncratic. I am not aware of any scholarship in moral philosophy, or in the theoretical literature on social welfare functions, that has done so.

By the lights of population-preference cognitivism, the reader who is persuaded by the arguments of this book (embracing the Atkinson SWF and leaving open the value of γ) finds herself in a particular epistemic position. First, she has provisional (although surely not conclusive) reason to believe that everyone in the population, under impartial and otherwise ideal conditions, would morally prefer the Atkinson SWF. Second, she is uncertain what value of γ individuals would prefer. In other words, she has provisional reason to believe the following: outcome x is morally at least as good as outcome y iff, for all $u(.)$ in $\mathbf{U}$, $(1-\gamma)^{-1}\sum_{i=1}^{N} u_i(x)^{1-\gamma} \geq (1-\gamma)^{-1}\sum_{i=1}^{N} u_i(y)^{1-\gamma}$ for all γ in $\mathbf{\Pi}$. And she would find surveys to establish individual values of γ to be *particularly* useful, as compared to other sorts of moral surveys.

We can also see why—by the lights of *other* metaethical views—surveys to establish individual values of γ might also be especially useful, as compared to surveys regarding other moral topics. Consider, once more, noncognitivism. By the lights of noncognitivism, surveys have the function of helping the decisionmaker determine which moral view she wishes to endorse. If she is persuaded by the arguments of this book, then she is—at least provisionally—prepared to endorse the Atkinson SWF. But nothing in this book (or, more generally, in philosophy or in the literature on social choice) has suggested a particular value of γ to endorse. Surveys on *that* issue would be particularly helpful in shaping her endorsements.

To sum up: both surveys and introspection are useful in refining a decisionmaker's moral views. This is true for a range of metaethical accounts (although different metaethical accounts will offer different explanations for why surveys are useful).

Moreover, for a range of metaethical views, the reader now prepared to embrace the Atkinson SWF, but unsure about the value of γ, will (not surprisingly) find surveys on *that* issue, as opposed to other moral questions, particularly helpful.

However, the discussion has illustrated one way in which different metaethical views diverge. By the lights of population-preference cognitivism, even if everyone in the population *does* approve an Atkinson SWF (under impartial and otherwise ideal conditions), it is an open question whether everyone converges on the same value of γ, or whether there are a range of such values (yielding the Atkinson SWF with a whole set of γ values). Nothing in the arguments presented in this book make a showing either way. (Note that the Atkinson SWF with a whole set of γ values is a deviation from the simple *R*-based form for an SWF.) By contrast, by the lights of noncognitivism, an SWF with a whole set of γ values is problematic.

So as not to further complicate an already complicated analysis, the remainder of this book will discuss the Atkinson SWF in the simple *R*-based form. This SWF says: x is morally at least as good as y iff, for all $u(.)$ in U, $(1-\gamma)^{-1}\sum_{i=1}^{N}u_i(x)^{1-\gamma} \geq (1-\gamma)^{-1}\sum_{i=1}^{N}u_i(y)^{1-\gamma}$. But the reader should bear in mind that—on certain metaethical views, i.e., population-preference cognitivism—the Atkinson SWF could equally well take the more complicated form, x is morally at least as good as y iff, for all $u(.)$ in U, $(1-\gamma)^{-1}\sum_{i=1}^{N}u_i(x)^{1-\gamma} \geq (1-\gamma)^{-1}\sum_{i=1}^{N}u_i(y)^{1-\gamma}$ for all γ in Ц.

6

LIFETIME PRIORITARIANISM

The formal structure of welfarism, as I have presented it, is oriented around *lifetime* well-being. I have used the term "life-history" to refer to an item such as $(x; i)$—a pairing of an individual and an outcome. An outcome is a simplified possible world, i.e., a simplified description of a whole possible history of the universe; and a life-history means being some individual in some outcome. Thus a "life-history" is a simplified description of the entire life of some individual. An attractive welfarist choice-evaluation framework—I have supposed—will contain some basis for ranking these descriptions of complete possible lives, and will rank outcomes so as to satisfy the principles of Pareto-indifference and -superiority understood in whole-lifetime terms.

In particular, the SWF approach—as I have presented it—is framed in whole-lifetime terms. The elements of **U** are *lifetime* utility functions, tracking the well-being associated with whole life-histories. Each such function maps an outcome onto a vector of individual lifetime utility numbers. And an SWF (I have assumed) is a rule for ranking pairs of outcomes as a function of their associated lifetime utility vectors.

But why should a SWF necessarily function in this fashion? Consider any given SWF: the utilitarian SWF, the rank-weighted SWF, the leximin SWF, the continuous prioritarian SWF, or any other. The SWF might, in principle, be applied on a *non-lifetime* basis. For example, it might be applied on a *sublifetime* basis. Imagine that there is a set **V** of sublifetime utility functions, measuring the sublifetime well-being realized by individuals during temporal portions of outcomes. The SWF might rank pairs of outcomes as a function of the vectors of sublifetime utility numbers associated with the outcomes by the elements in **V**. Alternatively, the SWF might be applied on an *attribute* basis—taking as its inputs numbers measuring the levels of various individual attributes in outcomes.

This chapter defends the lifetime approach. My defense rests upon two key premises. The first is a premise about personal identity. *Personal identity continues through a normal human lifetime.* In other words, a normal human being (a human being who possesses the psychological attributes sufficient to make her a person, and who doesn't undergo a brain transplant, suffer profound amnesia as a result of an injury, or otherwise experience a radical rupture in the intertemporal connectedness of her psychological states and physical body) remains one and the same person from birth until death. The second is that the *moral ranking of outcomes is determined by accommodating individuals' claims across outcomes.* The claim-across-outcome conception of the moral ranking of outcomes was at the heart of my analysis in Chapter 5. I argued that this conception is the most attractive specification of welfarism (by contrast with a veil-of-ignorance conception or a claim-within-outcome conception); and I used it to adjudicate between different SWFs. In this chapter, too, the claim-across-outcome conception is central—now conjoined with the premise about the continuity of personal identity over a lifetime, and used to adjudicate between lifetime versus non-lifetime versions of the SWF framework.

Chapter 5 came down in favor of a continuous prioritarian SWF. I argued, first, that the claim-across-outcome view supports two key axioms: the Pigou–Dalton axiom and an axiom of separability. (Because several different kinds of separability will figure in the analysis in the current chapter, I will here refer to the kind of separability addressed in Chapter 5 as "person-separability".) "Prioritarian" SWFs satisfy both the Pigou–Dalton axiom and the axiom of person-separability. Chapter 5 then argued against prioritarian SWFs that fail a continuity axiom: the leximin SWF and the prioritarian SWF with a lexical threshold.

The current chapter therefore focuses on comparing lifetime versus non-lifetime approaches to applying a continuous prioritarian SWF. I will try to demonstrate here that the claim-across-outcome view, conjoined with the premise about personal identity, supports *lifetime continuous prioritarianism* rather than the application of a continuous prioritarian SWF to individual sublifetime utility numbers or to numbers measuring individual attribute levels. Chapter 5 argued for a particular kind of continuous prioritarian SWF—the Atkinson SWF, satisfying an axiom of ratio rescaling invariance—but the argumentation here will be more general, meant to show that any continuous prioritarian SWF should be applied in a lifetime manner.

Indeed, the case for using SWFs on a lifetime basis is really orthogonal to the choice between prioritarian and non-prioritarian SWFs, or between prioritarian SWFs that satisfy or fail to satisfy the continuity axiom. The case for the lifetime approach *does* rely upon the claim-across-outcome conception of the moral ranking of outcomes, but it does *not* rest upon the further assertion that this view is best specified via the continuous prioritarian SWF.[1] I am confident that the basic line of

---

[1] It may well be the case that a claim-*within*-outcome view of fairness, or a veil-of-ignorance conception, also underwrites a whole-lifetime approach. However, this is not a topic I will attempt to address here.

argumentation I am about to present—to the effect that a continuous prioritarian SWF should take lifetime utilities as its inputs—can be reconfigured to defend a lifetime approach to *whichever* SWF the reader believes to be justified by the claim-across-outcome view.[2] Indeed, I am confident that it can be reconfigured to defend a lifetime approach to the various non-SWF policy-analytic techniques reviewed in Chapter 2. Were I not confident of this, I would not have presented the formal structure of welfarism in whole-lifetime terms.

So much for preliminaries. The chapter begins by defending the premise that personal identity continues through a normal human lifetime. It then examines the structure of lifetime well-being. What is the functional form of the lifetime utility functions in **U**? In this connection I discuss the issue of *discounting*: an important topic for policy analysis generally and for the SWF approach in particular.

I next compare lifetime to non-lifetime versions of the continuous prioritarian SWF and make the basic case for the lifetime approach: because personal identity continues over a normal human lifetime, a person's *claim* in favor of one or another outcome should depend upon her lifetime well-being.

The chapter then considers, and attempts to rebut, two important objections to this case for lifetime prioritarianism. One objection, pressed by Derek Parfit, sounds in personal identity. As we shall see, Parfit's account of personal identity does *not* undermine the premise that personal identity continues through a normal human lifetime. However, the account is "reductionist." It reduces personal identity to

---

Insofar as non-fairness considerations, such as benevolence or compassion, influence the ranking of outcomes, it is hard to see why a whole-lifetime approach would be justified. Why not a sublifetime approach or a mixed approach? However, I have taken the position (see Chapter 5) that morality is exhausted by fairness considerations. The defensibility of that provisional assumption is a key aspect of my discussion of sublifetime hardship, see below, pp. 466–475.

[2] My argumentation below (1) assumes that the claim-across-outcome view justifies a ranking of outcomes that satisfies the axioms of Pareto-indifference, Pareto-superiority, Pigou–Dalton, and person-separability; (2) argues that the proper currency for claims is lifetime well-being, since personal identity continues through a normal human lifetime; (3) points out that some non-lifetime approaches to implementing a continuous prioritarian SWF can violate one or more of the four axioms just mentioned, construed in lifetime terms; and (4) argues that even non-lifetime approaches to implementing a continuous prioritarian SWF which violate none of these axioms are problematic, because they represent a misleading way to think about the ranking of outcomes. This argumentation could be used, without alteration, to defend a lifetime approach to some prioritarian SWF that fails the continuity axiom (the leximin SWF or a prioritarian SWF with a lexical threshold), as against a non-lifetime approach to employing that SWF. Moreover, if one believes that the claim-across-outcome view is best understood to justify an SWF that fails the axiom of person-separability (as does the rank-weighted SWF) or the Pigou–Dalton axiom (as do the utilitarian and sufficientist SWFs) or both, then the argumentation could be amended so as not to rely upon those axioms. For example, one could point out that certain non-lifetime approaches to using a rank-weighted SWF can violate lifetime Pareto-indifference, Pareto-superiority, or Pigou–Dalton; and that even non-lifetime approaches to using a rank-weighted SWF which satisfy these lifetime axioms represent a problematic way to think about the ranking of outcomes.

psychological and physical connections. There is no "deep further fact" of personal identity. Parfit suggests that "reductionism" of this sort cuts against lifetime prioritarianism and argues in favor of either sublifetime prioritarianism or utilitarianism.[3]

A different kind of challenge, suggested by Dennis McKerlie's work as well as that of other scholars, trades on our intuitions about equalization. The argument here is that we have an intuitive preference for equalizing or synchronizing individuals' attributes or sublifetime well-being; and that lifetime prioritarianism, or any other lifetime approach to applying a distribution-sensitive SWF, must conflict with these intuitions. I will argue that the lifetime prioritarian can generally parry these challenges by deploying a nuanced understanding of the structure of lifetime well-being.

A terminological point: Because prioritarian SWFs that fail the continuity axiom (the leximin SWF and the prioritarian SWF with a lexical threshold) are not discussed in this chapter, I will sometimes omit the adjective "continuous." Throughout the remainder of the chapter, when I do so, and refer simply to "prioritarianism" or "the prioritarian SWF," I mean the *continuous* prioritarian SWF.

This chapter, like Chapters 5 and 7, is separable from the extended-preference account of well-being developed in Chapters 3 and 4. Those chapters provided one basis for making intra- and interpersonal comparisons of lifetime well-being and for constructing a set **U** of lifetime utility functions representing such comparisons; but other accounts of well-being may also have the resources to do this. I shall argue here that the continuous prioritarian SWF should be applied on a lifetime basis, for reasons that are grounded in fairness and personal identity, and that are independent of the well-being account that undergirds **U**. At some junctures, I do use the extended-preference account to support certain claims about the structure of lifetime well-being; but in all those instances I suggest that the claims are true, not just of that account, but of any plausible view of well-being.

---

[3] This chapter was drafted prior to Nils Holtug's major recent book. See Holtug (2010). Holtug argues for "prudential prioritarianism"—a non-lifetime approach that uses "self-interest" as its currency. See ibid., ch. 10. On Holtug's view, a person's self-interest, at some time t, as regarding events at time t^*, depends on the tightness of the psychological links between these two temporal stages of the person.

I lack space to address Holtug's important analysis in detail here. In brief, my response would be, first, to reiterate the key points in my analysis of Parfit, below: that the attenuation of direct psychological links between temporal stages of persons does not vitiate the continuity of personhood over time, in the case of normal humans; and that persons, rather than temporal stages of persons, are the loci for moral claims. Second, since *persons* are the loci of claims, why use self-interest—rather than lifetime well-being—as the currency for prioritarianism? Indeed, as Holtug concedes (see ibid., pp. 338–339), his approach amounts to a kind of non-welfarism.

I. PERSONAL IDENTITY OVER TIME

There is a vast literature in contemporary philosophy concerning personhood and personal identity.[4] Reviewing this body of work in depth would take many more pages than I have available here. Still, I think it is fair to say that the common-sense view about personal identity—that a normal human being remains one and the same person from birth to death—is well supported by the philosophical literature.

One vital question concerns the conditions under which a human being is a person. Call this the problem of human personhood. Crudely speaking, there are two quite different possibilities here that are widely defended. One, adopted by many religious traditions, and defended by some contemporary philosophers (although a minority), is that a human being is a person in virtue of being associated with something like a soul: an immaterial substance of some kind which does not supervene upon the human's physical attributes.[5] A different possibility is that a human being is a person in virtue of having certain psychological attributes (such as consciousness, rationality, or a capacity for deliberation). Note that a human's psychological attributes may well supervene on her physical attributes; indeed, this is the standard view in the philosophy of mind. A psychological account of personhood which adopts the supervenience premise is clearly distinct from the "soul" account.

A second question concerns *individuation*. What is the criterion of personal identity that differentiates between one human person and a second, distinct, human person? The focus of the literature has been on questions of personal identity over time. If g is a human being and a person at time t, and h is a human being and a person at time t^*, under what conditions are g and h "numerically identical": the very same particular human person?

Crudely speaking, there are three different approaches to the problem of personal identity. One, which fits naturally with the "soul" account of human personhood, is that g and h are the same person if they have the same soul. Someone who adopts a psychological account of human personhood and denies the existence of souls cannot offer this answer to the question of personal identity. Interestingly, however, there are two quite different approaches that *are* open to her. One approach is to marry a psychological account of personhood with a psychological account of

---

[4] See, e.g., Baker (2000); DeGrazia (2005); Garrett (1998); Holtug (2010, ch. 3); Parfit (1987, pt. 3); McMahan (2003, ch. 1); Martin and Barresi (2003); Noonan (2003); Olson (1997, 2007); Paul, Miller, and Paul (2005); Schechtman (1996); Shoemaker and Swinburne (1984); Unger (1990); and the symposium in *The Monist* (2004, vol. 87, pp. 457–616). A good short review, with a bibliography, is Olson (2010).

[5] For a critical discussion, see McMahan (2003, pp. 7–24). Properties of type s "supervene" on properties of type b if two items identical with respect to their b properties must be identical with respect to their s properties. To say that a soul doesn't supervene on a human's physical attributes means that two human beings who are physically identical may differ in whether they possess souls or what the souls are like.

personal identity over time: to say that human person g at t is the very same particular person as human person h at t^* if the two are psychologically linked in a certain way. Another is to marry a psychological account of personhood with a *physical* account of personal identity over time: to say that g at t and h at t^* are the same particular person if they have the right sort of physical connection (e.g., if g at t has the very same body and brain as h at t^*), regardless of their psychological nexus.[6] These latter two approaches can be hybridized. For example, one might say that g at t and h at t^* are the very same person only if they have both certain psychological links and certain physical connections.

This book assumes the psychological account of human personhood, rather than the "soul" view. There is a fixed population of N human beings, who are full human persons; and they are full persons, I assume, in virtue of having certain psychological properties.

How a welfarist moral view should be developed given a "soul" account of personhood is not a question I attempt to address here. Nor—the reader is reminded—do I consider other variations on the scenario of a fixed population of N human persons. In particular, I do not address how welfarism should cope with: a population of human persons that is variable rather than fixed; an infinite population of human persons; non-human persons (super-intelligent computers, angels, extraterrestrials, etc.); or humans who lack the psychological properties that are necessary for full personhood.[7]

Finally, I assume that the members of the population of N individuals have a *normal* psychological and physical history. Not only do they have the psychological properties that are necessary for full personhood, but they have not undergone

---

[6] Scholars in this camp may well adopt an ontology which sees each human being, not each person, as a separate entity. On this so-called "animalist" view, personhood is a possible attribute of the entity, human being; and, strictly speaking, there are not particular persons, but rather particular human beings. See DeGrazia (2005); Olson (1997). My phrase "particular person" is meant to be neutral between animalism and a view that sees persons as entities in their own right. The analysis in this chapter is orthogonal to this issue, presupposing only that each normal human being remains the very same particular entity, one that has the attribute of personhood—be that entity a human being or a person—from at or shortly after the birth of the human being until its death. This entity is thus the holder of a unitary "claim" across outcomes.

[7] There are actually two cases covered by the final clause, neither of which I will attempt to address: human beings who are determinately not persons, and human beings who are indeterminate persons (at the "margins of personhood"). I leave these difficult cases aside, and focus on the case in which each of the N human persons is a full, determinate person, for most (if not all) of its existence as a person.

I say "most (if not all)" because there is arguably a kind of temporary indeterminate personhood which arises even in the case of a normal human being, between the time when the human comes into being and the time when psychological properties or capacities constitutive of personhood have developed. I suggest below that the basic case for lifetime welfarism developed in this chapter is robust to this sort of indeterminacy (if it exists). See below, n. 14.

brain transplants, traumatic brain injuries, psychological disease, or other unusual ruptures in their ongoing mental life or the physical makeup of their brains or bodies. Because the members of the population are "normal" in this sense, we can invoke a psychological account of personal identity over time, a physical account, or a hybrid account to justify the common-sense view that each such being is the very same particular person from birth to death.

Derek Parfit's work on personal identity in *Reasons and Persons* is worth introducing at this point.[8] We will focus, later in the chapter, on the question whether the "reductionist" cast of this account argues against lifetime prioritarianism; and for those purposes it will be important to have a sense of the details of Parfit's view. But his work also helps illustrate the different possibilities concerning human personhood and personal identity over time. In particular, it is important to understand that Parfit's account of personhood and personal identity *confirms* the premise that personal identity continues through a normal human lifetime.

With respect to the question of personhood, Parfit pursues a psychological approach. He writes: "[T]o be a person, a being must be self-conscious, aware of its identity and its continued existence over time." Parfit rejects the "soul" view—the view, as he puts it, that a person might be "a Cartesian Pure Ego, or spiritual substance."[9]

Reasons and Persons spends much more time on the question of personal identity. Here, Parfit offers a psychological criterion of personal identity and leaves open the possibility that it might be hybridized with a physical criterion.

In constructing his criterion of personal identity, Parfit introduces the concepts of psychological "connectedness" and psychological "continuity." Consider human person g at time t and human person h at time t^*. There may be various direct connections between g's mental states at t and h's mental states at t^*. For example h at t^* may have a memory of an event that g experienced at t. Or, g at t may have the same belief, desire, or character trait as h at t^*. Or, h at t^* may consciously act on an intention that g at t formulated. If there are sufficient direct connections between h at t^* and g at t, then the two are *strongly connected*:

> Since connectedness is a matter of degree, we cannot plausibly define precisely what counts as enough. But we can claim that there is enough connectedness if the number of direct connections . . . is *at least half* the number that hold, over every day, in the lives of nearly every actual person.[10]

However, strong connectedness cannot itself be the criterion of personal identity. Personal identity is transitive. If g at t is the same particular person as h at t^*, and h at

[8] See Parfit (1987, pt. 3). Parfit elaborates on his views in Parfit (1986, 2003). For discussions of Parfit's account, see, e.g., Belzer (2005); Dancy (1997); McMahan (2003, ch. 1).
[9] Parfit (1987, pp. 202, 210).
[10] Ibid., p. 206.

t^* the same particular person as i at t^{**}, then g at t is the same particular person as i at t^{**}. But strong connectedness is not transitive. Consider a case in which a human being at age 75 remembers much of what that being experienced at age 50, and the human being at age 50 remembers much of what that being experienced at age 10, but the human being at age 75 remembers virtually nothing of what that being experienced at age 10.

Parfit therefore introduces the notion of psychological *continuity*. Person g at t is *continuous* with h at t^* if there is an overlapping chain of strong connectedness between the two persons. In other words, there is some series of pairs of persons and times $((j_1, t_1), (j_2, t_2),\ldots, (j_M, t_M))$, such that g at t is strongly connected with j_1 at t_1; each person in this series at the matching time is strongly connected with the next person at the matching time (so that j_1 at t_1 is strongly connected with j_2 at t_2, etc.); and j_M at t_M is strongly connected with h at t^*. And Parfit, then, offers a psychological criterion of personal identity, which appeals to psychological continuity.

> *The Psychological Criterion*: (1) There is *psychological continuity* if and only if there are overlapping chains of strong connectedness. X today is one and the same person as Y at some past time if and only if (2) X is psychologically continuous with Y, (3) this continuity has the right kind of cause, and (4) it has not taken a "branching" form. (5) Personal identity over time just consists in the holding of facts like (2) to (4). [11]

Parfit leaves open what "the right kind of cause" means: whether the psychological continuity between g at t and h at t^* must be caused by processes in a single brain shared by the two persons, or whether more esoteric causal processes are also permissible. (If "the right sort of cause" is indeed specified to require bodily continuity between g at t and h at t^*, then the upshot is a view of personal identity that hybridizes a psychological and physical criterion.) Finally, the requirement that the continuity be "non-branching" is inserted to deal with esoteric cases, for example a case in which my brain is split in half and put two human bodies.

Because Parfit's account makes personal identity a matter of psychological links, not the sharing of a "soul," it raises the unsettling possibility that personal identity

---

[11] Ibid., p. 207. Lest the reader be confused by *Reasons and Persons*—a dense text, to be sure—it should be emphasized that the psychological criterion of personal identity, which reduces personal identity to "continuity" (as Parfit defines it), should be distinguished from what Parfit calls "relation R." Two time slices can be parts of the very same person (by virtue of satisfying the psychological criterion) absent any direct psychological connections between them. By contrast, whether one time slice of a human person bears "relation R" to another such time slice is *both* a matter of continuity *and* of their direct connectedness. Relation R is not the criterion of personal identity but, instead, the criterion of "what matters" (as Parfit puts it), i.e., what humans rationally pursue. See ibid., p. 215. The very thrust of *Reasons and Persons* is that relation R and personal identity can come apart. On the distinction between these two concepts, see Belzer (2005, pp. 129–138); McMahan (2003, pp. 39–43).

might be *indeterminate*: that one human person might be neither determinately identical to, nor determinately distinct from, another human person. Parfit argues for this possibility via discussion of a hypothetical spectrum of cases ("the Psychological Spectrum") in which a surgeon severs more and more of the psychological connections between a human being at one time and the same human being shortly thereafter. In one possible surgery, the doctor severs one connection (e.g., erasing one memory); in a different possible procedure, he severs two; and so forth. At one end of this spectrum of possible surgeries, the human beings before and after the surgery are determinately the same person. (If only one memory has been removed, they clearly are strongly connected.) At the other end of the spectrum, the human beings before and after are determinately not the same person: they share no memories, desires, etc. Must there not, then, be some midrange of interventions where personal identity is indeterminate?[12]

I will not grapple with indeterminate identity here. Clearly, cases of indeterminate identity raise serious puzzles for the claim-across-outcome conception of fairness. If the single human being, Sam, is associated with two human persons who are neither determinately identical to each other, nor determinately distinct from each other, are those persons allocated two claims in ranking pairs of outcomes, one claim, or something in between? Some scholars have argued that, even on a psychological account, personal identity must in fact be determinate.[13] So perhaps the puzzles are not genuine ones.

In any event, even if indeterminate identity *is* a genuine possibility in the scenario of the spectrum of surgical interventions or other scenarios, it does *not* arise in the case of the normal human life. The normal human being, Bod, at age 8 is determinately the very same person as the human being, Bod, at 85. Even though there may be few direct psychological connections between them (Bod at 85 cannot remember much of what Bod at 8 experienced, shares few of the desires that Bod had at 8, has a different emotional makeup, etc.), they are determinately continuous (Bod at 8 is strongly connected with Bod at 9, Bod at 9 with Bod at 10, and so forth), and the cause of this continuity (sharing the same, normal, human brain) is paradigmatically "the right kind of cause."

Indeed, Parfit pretty explicitly confirms that personal identity is determinate in the case of a normal human life. He writes: "In ordinary cases, questions about our

---

[12] See Parfit (1987, pp. 229–243); see also Parfit (2003, pp. 292–304). In this set-up, the human beings before and shortly after the surgery would be continuous only by virtue of their direct connections (there is no indirect chain linking them), and so the possibility of an intermediate mid-range of degree of connectedness raises the possibility of the two beings being indeterminately identical. Parfit also discusses a related spectrum in which the brain tissue of the two humans is less and less identical—which raises the specter of indeterminate identity if one requires the psychological continuity constitutive of personhood to be grounded in the sharing of brain tissue.

[13] On the possibility of indeterminate personhood or personal identity, see, e.g., Eklund (2004); Garrett (1998, ch. 5); McMahan (2003, ch. 1); Noonan (2003, ch. 6); Unger (1990, ch. 6).

identity have answers. In such cases, there is a fact about personal identity, and [the psychological criterion] is one view about what kind of fact this is. . . . In the problem cases [such as the spectrum of surgical interventions], things are different."[14]

II. LIFETIME WELL-BEING

This section clarifies the structure of the lifetime utility function: the elements of U, which assign numbers to whole life-histories. A nuanced understanding of this topic will help, later in the chapter, to parry challenges to lifetime prioritarianism. I then address the related topic of discounting.

A. The Structure of Lifetime Well-Being

Various temporal schemes may be used to characterize outcomes. The outcomes in a given outcome set may contain one period ($T = 1$), or multiple periods ($T > 1$); for simplicity, I assume that T is the same in all outcomes. A period may be a century, a year, a day, a moment, or some other temporal unit; that depends on how outcomes are characterized. Each period will describe some of the attributes during that period of each of the N persons in the population, as well as some background, "impersonal" facts (such as environmental characteristics or causal regularities). Because outcomes are *simplified*, only *some* of these features of possible worlds are incorporated in the description of outcomes; other features are "missing."[15]

---

[14] Parfit (2003, p. 303). There is a different kind of indeterminacy that Parfit's account does raise. On this account, because personhood consists in psychological abilities or capacities, it seems plausible that a human being is only an indeterminate person at the beginning of human life. See McMahan (2003, pp. 43–46); Parfit (1987, p. 322). I am not endorsing this view, simply conceding its plausibility. In any event, it should be stressed that the potential indeterminacy here is *not* an indeterminacy regarding personal *identity*. It is not a matter of two human persons being neither determinately identical to each other, nor determinately distinct. Rather, it is a kind of indeterminacy concerning *personhood*: whether a particular being is a person. Moreover, unlike the case of humans with impaired psychological abilities throughout their lives, this is a case of *temporary* indeterminacy concerning personhood. Even if a normal human being is an indeterminate person for some time after the beginning of its existence as a human being (which itself might be understood to occur at conception, live birth, or some time in-between), there is no question that the being eventually becomes a determinate person, remains one until death, and is determinately distinct from every other person. In this case, I see no obstacle to assigning each such person a single claim across outcomes, valenced in terms of her lifetime well-being. Observe that a claim, like lifetime well-being itself, is not temporally indexed: the person, atemporally, has a claim between two outcomes, depending on her lifetime well-being in them.

[15] Chapter 4 proposed that utility functions be constructed for simplified outcomes by using an invariance assumption to take account of missing attributes. This proposal, although developed within the confines of an extended-preference account, could presumably be generalized to other accounts of well-being. However, the issues in this chapter are orthogonal to the problem of missing

Thus each period t has the generic form $(\mathbf{a}_{1,t},...,\mathbf{a}_{i,t},...,\mathbf{a}_{N,t},\mathbf{a}_{imp,t})$, with $\mathbf{a}_{i,t}$ some of the attributes of individual i during period t, and $\mathbf{a}_{imp,t}$ some background facts during period t. An outcome is a series of one or more such period-specific characterizations of persons' attributes plus background facts. A life-history, in turn, is a pairing of a person with an outcome. Some account of well-being (be it the extended-preference account or some other account) generates a quasiordering of life-histories and differences, and the selection of a zero point by which to construct well-being ratios. Each utility function $u(.)$ in $\mathbf{U}$ maps each life-history onto a number, representing this level, difference, and ratio information.[16]

The individual attributes that figure most importantly in existing social-welfare-function scholarship or policy analysis more generally are: an individual's consumption (meaning either his consumption of particular marketed goods or the total dollar value of his consumption); his leisure; the level of some public good he enjoys; his health state; and his hedonic state (an attribute that figures increasingly in policy analysis that draws on the happiness literature). The proponent of the SWF format is hardly committed to using these particular attributes. However, the examples of life-histories that figure in my analysis will often be characterized in terms of these attributes—thus preserving the nexus between the analysis and current policy-evaluation practices, and thereby underscoring the point that the SWF format, applied to lifetime utilities, is meant to function as a policy-evaluation procedure, not merely a criterion of rightness.

A utility function is *atomistic* if it depends solely on the subject's attributes and background facts, rather than the attributes of other individuals.[17]

The utility functions that are actually used in social-welfare-function scholarship *are* typically atomistic. The prevalent approaches make a subject's utility a function of his own consumption (no one else's); or a function of his consumption and leisure (no one else's); or his health state (no one else's); or his level of exposure to a public good (no one else's). But atomism is merely a pragmatic simplification, which eases estimation and formal analysis. For example, it may be worse, ceteris paribus, to have a given consumption level when others are at a higher level, than when others

---

characteristics, and my analysis does not in any way hinge upon the claim that the invariance proposal is the correct way to address them.

[16] Difference and ratio information are relevant to the continuous prioritarian SWF, and so I here assume that the utility functions in $\mathbf{U}$ contain such information.

[17] More precisely, the utility function is "atomistic" if it does not depend on the attributes of other persons, or on the subject's relational attributes that involve a relation to other persons. Where I am assuming an atomistic utility function, I will use the symbol "$\mathbf{a}_i$" or "$\mathbf{a}_{i,t}$" to include only individual i's monadic attributes or relational attributes that do not involve a relation to other persons. See Chapter 4, n. 35. With the symbol "$\mathbf{a}_i$" thus understood, an atomistic utility function takes the form: $u(x; i) = v(\mathbf{a}_i(x), \mathbf{a}_{imp}(x))$, where in turn $\mathbf{a}_i(x) = (\mathbf{a}_{i,1}(x), \mathbf{a}_{i,2}(x),..., \mathbf{a}_{i,T}(x))$, and similarly for background facts.

are at a lower level. Indeed, there is *some* social-welfare-function scholarship that employs non-atomistic utility functions.[18]

Note that these standard utility functions are not merely atomistic. They have the further feature of assigning a utility number to a life-history based on the subject's *contingent* attributes, rather than his essential attributes. Distinguishing between utility functions of this sort, and utility functions that take account of the subject's essential attributes, was a critical element in Chapter 4. The distinction had much relevance for purposes of estimating the elements of **U**. By contrast, the distinction does not figure in the analysis of this chapter, and will not be further mentioned. The individual attributes included in the description of outcomes might, in principle, include essential attributes; and the utility functions in **U** (atomistic or not) might include such attributes as their arguments.

Even if a utility function *is* atomistic, it need *not* be separable or additive with respect to attributes or times.[19]

Consider, first, the case in which outcomes have a single period. Each subject, let us assume, is characterized as having one or multiple attributes in that single period. Some utility function $u(.)$ (now assumed to be atomistic) is a function of those attributes plus background facts. To say that $u(.)$ is *separable* in those attributes means: given two life-histories $(x; i)$ and $(y; j)$ in which background facts are the same, and in which certain types of attributes are identical in the two histories, the ranking of the histories does not depend on what particular level those attributes have.[20] Formally, if outcomes describe M types of attributes, and attributes of type $1,\ldots, K$ are different as between life-histories $(x; i)$ and $(y; j)$, while the two histories have the same attribute of type $(K + 1)$, the same attribute of type $(K + 2),\ldots,$ the same attribute of type M, as well as the same background facts, the ranking of the histories should not depend upon what the $(K + 1)$ attribute is, what the $(K + 2)$ attribute is, and so forth.

A utility function need *not* be separable in this sense. To get a sense of how separability might fail, imagine that outcomes are specified in terms of the subject's health, consumption, and leisure. The well-being ranking of different

---

[18] See, e.g., Aronsson and Johansson-Stenman (2008); Tuomala (1990, ch. 8).

[19] On the separability and additivity properties of utility functions, see generally Blackorby, Primont, and Russell (1998); Broome (1995); Keeney and Raiffa (1993, chs. 3, 5–6); von Winterfeldt and Edwards (1986, ch. 9).

[20] There are different possible ways to define attribute separability, given the inclusion of background facts in the description of outcomes. We might have separability in subjects' attributes for any given specification of background facts; or background facts might be treated like an attribute, with the ranking of two life-histories independent of the level of some type of attribute, if at the same level in both histories, *and* independent of background facts, where the same in both histories. For simplicity, and because my focus here is attributes, I have articulated the first formulation in the text; but the second is possible as well.

consumption/leisure packages, holding health fixed, might well depend on whether health is at a high or low level.[21]

Even if $u(.)$ is separable in the subject's attributes in the one-period case, it need not be *additive* in any given metric of the attributes. In grasping the idea of "additive" utility functions, it is important to understand that a variety of metrics might be used to quantify individual levels of any given group of attributes. Thus a utility function is not "additive," simpliciter, but additive relative to some metric. In particular, $u(.)$ is additive in the one-period case, relative to a given metric for measuring attributes, if $u(x; i)$ is simply a linear function of the subject i's levels of the attributes in x (as quantified with that metric). If there are M attributes, with "$a^m(x; i)$" denoting the level of attribute m possessed by individual i in x (as measured by some metric), then to say that $u(.)$ is additive means: $u(x; i) = d_1 a^1(x; i) + \ldots + d_M a^M(x; i)$.[22] Each attribute is multiplied by some constant and these are summed.[23]

---

[21] We might, further, distinguish between separability in attributes, and lottery-separability in attributes. The latter condition, stronger than the former (but weaker than additivity), requires that a ranking of lotteries over attributes, holding fixed certain types of attributes, be invariant to the level of fixed attributes. (This is analogous to the distinction below between a lifetime utility function that is (1) separable in sublifetime utility; (2) lottery-separable in sublifetime utility; and (3) additive in sublifetime utility.) The distinction between separability and lottery-separability in attributes is not one I bring into play in defending lifetime prioritarianism—but should, for completeness, be mentioned.

[22] Strictly, an additive $u(.)$ could also add a constant after the end of M terms.

[23] The reader familiar with the literature regarding separability and utility functions may find this paragraph puzzling. A standard theorem shows that the sort of separability condition I am articulating here, together with a continuity condition, entails an additive representation. See, e.g., Blackorby, Primont, and Russell (1998, pp. 70–73).

But "additivity," as I have just explained, is relative to a metric. To say that the ranking of life-histories achieved by a separable $u(.)$ can also be represented by a utility function $u^+(.)$ which is an "additive" function of the subject's attributes simply means that there is *some* attribute metric such that $u^+(.)$ is additive in that metric and represents the ranking of life-histories. The function $u^+(.)$ may not be additive relative to some other attribute metric.

Moreover, $u(.)$ has cardinal, not just ordinal properties. At least according to the account of well-being developed in Chapter 3, it expectationally represents (some spectator's) ranking of lotteries over life-histories, not just her ranking of life-histories. And even if another account of well-being is adopted, $u(.)$ still has the cardinal property of representing well-being *differences* between life-histories. (This chapter proceeds on the assumption that **U** represents well-being differences as well as levels, since difference information is relevant to the continuous prioritarian SWF.) The additive function $u^+(.)$ might not be a positive affine transformation of $u(.)$. If not, it will fail to expectationally represent the same ranking of lotteries as $u(.)$, and may also fail to represent the same ordering of differences between life-histories as $u(.)$.

For example, a utility function $u(.)$ equaling the multiplicative product of the level of health and the level of consumption yields the very same ranking of life-histories as a function $u^+(.)$ equaling the sum of the logarithms (to a base greater than 1) of those levels. However, the first utility function is not a positive affine transformation of the second, and will not expectationally represent the same

For the simplest example of how attribute additivity can fail, consider the case in which outcomes have one period and individuals are characterized with respect to a single attribute, their consumption. Here, it is a familiar point that consumption may have "declining marginal utility"—in other words, that $u(.)$ might take the form of a non-linear transformation (specifically, a concave transformation) of the subject's consumption, rather than being linear in consumption. Attribute additivity may also well fail relative to standard attribute metrics where outcomes describe a single non-consumption attribute, or where outcomes describe multiple attributes. For example, a standard utility function for outcomes characterized in terms of health and consumption makes utility the multiplicative product of consumption and health—so that utility is separable in health and consumption but not additive in health and consumption. Utility as a function of leisure and consumption is often represented via the CES form, which is separable but not additive in the two.[24]

Let us turn, now, to the case in which outcomes have multiple periods—and keep in play the simplifying assumption of atomism. Here, a very convenient, further, assumption is that $u(.)$ can be expressed as a function of sublifetime utilities, each in turn a function of the subject's attributes plus background facts during one period.[25] In other words, $u(x; i) = f(v(a_{i,1}(x), a_{imp,1}(x)), v(a_{i,2}(x), a_{imp,2}(x)), \ldots, v(a_{i,T}(x), a_{imp,T}(x)))$, where $(a_{i,t}(x), a_{imp,t}(x))$ is a "sublifetime bundle"[26] comprised of individual i's attributes during period t in outcome x, plus background facts in that period, and $v(.)$ is a sublifetime utility function that takes this bundle as its argument.

However, it should be stressed that nothing in the concepts of lifetime well-being or a lifetime utility function requires that $u(.)$ be expressible in this manner. In particular, if outcomes are described in terms of multiple attributes during each of a series of periods, and the well-being ranking of life-histories fails to satisfy a condition of (weak) intertemporal separability in those attributes, $u(.)$ may not be expressible in

---

ranking of life-history lotteries as the second, nor need represent the same ranking of differences between life-histories.

[24] The CES utility function is: $u(c, l) = h([(1 - \beta)c^{-\mu} + \beta l^{-\mu}]^{-1/\mu})$, with $h(.)$ a strictly increasing function; c consumption and l leisure; and β and μ parameters such that β is between 0 and 1 and μ is greater than -1. Note that this function, although neither additive nor lottery-separable in consumption and leisure (as per n. 21 above), is separable in consumption and leisure.

[25] Even without atomism, $u(.)$ might well be representable as a function of sublifetime utilities. In this case, the sublifetime utility function would depend on everyone's attributes during the period, not just the subject's, i.e., would take the form $v(a_{1,t}, \ldots, a_{N,t}, a_{imp,t})$. We might then draw further distinctions between lifetime utility functions that are separable versus non-separable in these sublifetime utilities and, if separable, additive versus non-additive. However, to keep the discussion simple, I will focus on temporal separability and additivity within the class of lifetime utility functions that are atomistic.

[26] As in Chapter 4, I will use the term "sublifetime bundle" as a shorthand for a combination of some possible array of period-specific individual attributes (attributes that some subject might possess during some period), plus some possible array of period-specific background facts.

this manner. The condition of (weak) intertemporal attribute separability says: If the subject's attributes in life-history $(x; i)$ in a given time period are the same as the subject's attributes in $(y; j)$ in that period, for each of the T periods except one (t^*), the ranking of the histories should be solely a function of the subjects' attributes during t^*; it should not depend upon what the subjects' attributes are during the other periods.[27]

Why believe that this intertemporal condition may fail? There is much evidence from the literature on preferences that individuals have preferences regarding the intertemporal sequencing of attributes.

> [O]ne of the most robust findings in research about assessment of experiences is the clear preference for improvement over time. Preference for improvement has been demonstrated

---

[27] In this particular paragraph, I have simplified matters by assuming that outcomes solely describe individual attributes, rather than background facts. The (weak) intertemporal attribute separability ("WIAS") condition just articulated could readily be formulated in a more general way to take account of background facts; but since the point of this paragraph is merely to explain that represent-ability of lifetime utility in terms of sublifetime utility can possibly fail, in some outcome sets, I will focus on the simplest case.

Imagine, then, that the elements of the outcome set have multiple periods, and characterize a multiplicity of types of individual attributes in each period. For short, let us say that $u(.)$ for such an outcome set is "decomposable" if it can be expressed in the form $u(x; i) = f(v(\mathbf{a}_{i,1}(x)), v(\mathbf{a}_{i,2}(x)), \ldots, v(\mathbf{a}_{i,T}(x)))$. The WIAS condition is *weak*, because it imposes an invariance requirement on the ranking of two life-histories in the case where attributes during *one* period vary between the histories, rather than the case where attributes during one or more periods vary between the histories. (By contrast, the other separability conditions articulated in this chapter are "strong," in allowing for multiple dimensions of variation between life-histories.)

What exactly is the connection between WIAS and the decomposability of $u(.)$? We are assuming a finite number of periods, T. In the case where there are a finite or countable number of attribute bundles that the subject of a life-history might possess in a given period, then it is clear that any $u(.)$ will be decomposable *regardless* of whether WIAS is satisfied. Simply assign each possible bundle of attributes, during each period, its own natural number. Each life-history $(x; i)$ is then just a list of T natural numbers. The function $u(.)$ can be written as a function of those numbers.

WIAS becomes relevant when the set of possible attribute bundles, in each period, is uncountable. A standard result in utility theory can be adapted to show that, in this case, if $u(.)$ is continuous in attributes, and satisfies WIAS, it will be decomposable. See Blackorby, Primont, and Russell (1998, pp. 51–58). If WIAS fails, the analysis becomes more complex. Suffice it to say that in some cases where the set of possible attribute bundles in each period is uncountable and WIAS fails, $u(.)$ will not be decomposable.

Why have I focused on the case in which multiple types of attributes are described in each period? If a single attribute is described during each period, then (presumably) the subject's level of that attribute can be represented by a real number (if not a natural number). Then each life-history is just a list of T real numbers, and $u(.)$ is decomposable even if intertemporal attribute separability fails. (To some extent, the issue is semantic: we might say that some feature of an individual constitutes a "single" attribute rather than a cluster of multiple attributes just in case its level is necessarily representable by a single real number.)

in many domains, including monetary payments, experiences such as vacations, queuing events, pain, discomfort, medical outcomes and treatments, gambling, and academic performance.[28]

Imagine, now, that the well-being account undergirding **U** is the extended-preference account presented in Chapters 3 and 4. Spectators' fully informed, fully rational extended preferences might turn out to be sensitive to the intertemporal sequencing of each attribute taken individually. If so, the decomposition of $u(.)$ into a function of sublifetime utilities, each in turn a function of the subject's attributes plus background facts during one period, may *not* be possible.[29] Moreover, the point here presumably generalizes beyond the confines of an extended-preference view.

[28] Ariely and Carmon (2003, p. 327). The literature regarding individual preferences for intertemporal sequences classifies a variety of phenomena under the heading of "sequencing effects"—including both a preference for improvement and others, such as a preference for "spread" or the "peak-end" rule. See ibid; Frederick, Loewenstein, and O'Donoghue (2003, pp. 28–30); Loewenstein and Prelec (1993). What these phenomena have in common, inter alia, is a failure of intertemporal separability in some sense.

To see how sequencing effects involve some sort of failure of intertemporal separability, consider the very simple case in which individuals are ranking consumption sequences. Assume, for simplicity, that an individual ranks consumption sequences by summing amounts; as between consumption sequences with the same total amount, the individual ranks a sequence that never descends (consumption either remains the same or increases from period to period) over a sequence that sometimes descends. Then the individual prefers $(6, 7, 8, 9)$ to $(9, 7, 8, 6)$, but $(6, 20, 20, 9)$ and $(9, 20, 20, 6)$ are ranked as equal, in violation of separability.

It is quite plausible that a sequencing effect requires not only a failure of intertemporal separability in some sense, but also a failure of a (logically distinct) intertemporal permutation condition. (An intertemporal permutation condition, in the case of a sequence of attributes or, more generally, sublifetime bundles, says that all rearrangements of any one such sequence are ranked equally good.) However, it is the connection between sequencing effects and failures of temporal separability which are relevant for my purposes here.

[29] To see in a simple way how a preference for sequences might undermine the weak intertemporal attribute separability condition, assume that outcomes have three periods and are characterized in terms of two individual attributes in each period. A utility function $u(.)$ ranks life-histories using the following rule: if the total sum of both attributes in all periods, as measured by some stipulated attribute metric, is greater in $(x; i)$ than $(y; j)$, $(x; i)$ is better; if the sums are the same, and the first attribute never descends in $(x; i)$ but sometimes descends in $(y; j)$, $(x; i)$ is better; otherwise they are equally good. We can represent a life-history as follows: $((1, 3), (2, 4), (7, 8))$ means that the subject's levels of the first and second attributes, in the first period, are respectively 1 and 3; in the second period 2 and 4; and in the third period 7 and 8. Then the rule just mentioned ranks $((2, 8), (2, 4), (3, 5))$ above $((2, 8), (2, 4), (1, 7))$, but it ranks $((10, 8), (10, 4), (3, 5))$ equally good as $((10, 8), (10, 4), (1, 7))$, in violation of weak intertemporal attribute separability.

As explained in n. 27, a failure of this condition does not necessarily undermine the decomposability of $u(.)$, but may do so.

Various philosophers of well-being, without reliance on that view, have argued that lifetime well-being is genuinely dependent on sequencing effects.[30]

Assume, however, that $u(.)$ *is* expressible as a function of sublifetime utilities. It takes the form $u(x; i) = f(v(\mathbf{a}_{i,1}(x), \mathbf{a}_{imp,1}(x)), v(\mathbf{a}_{i,2}(x), \mathbf{a}_{imp,2}(x)), \ldots, v(\mathbf{a}_{i,T}(x), \mathbf{a}_{imp,T}(x)))$. Even if this *is* true, $u(.)$ may not be separable in *sublifetime utility*. To say that the lifetime utility function is separable in sublifetime utility is to say: If there are periods $t_1, t_2, \ldots, t_K$ such that $u(.)$ assigns two life-histories $(x; i)$ and $(y; j)$ the same level of sublifetime utility in period t_1, the same level in period t_2, and so forth, the ranking of the life-histories is invariant to what those particular levels are.

Why might separability in sublifetime utility fail? Here again sequencing effects emerge. Imagine that lifetime well-being is sensitive to the sequence of the subject's sublifetime utility. Then $u(.)$ will not be separable in sublifetime utility.

Finally, even if $u(.)$ is expressible as a function of sublifetime utilities, and separable in these utilities, it need not be additive in sublifetime utility. The lifetime utility function is additive in sublifetime utility if it takes the form: $u(x; i) = \sum_{t=1}^{T} v(\mathbf{a}_{i,t}(x), \mathbf{a}_{imp,t}(x))$, or that form with sublifetime utility in each period adjusted by some discount factor.[31] Imagine instead that lifetime utility is the multiplicative product of sublifetime utility.

---

[30] See, e.g., Bigelow, Campbell, and Pargetter (1990); Velleman (1993).

[31] A further, intermediate, possibility is that $u(.)$ is lottery-separable in sublifetime utilities. *Separability*, as defined just above, concerns the ranking of life-histories. By contrast, *lottery*-separability means this. Imagine that l and l^* are two lotteries over life-histories. Each has component life-histories assigned some non-zero probability, summing to unity. Assume that there are periods $t_1, t_2, \ldots, t_K$ such that $u(.)$ assigns every component life-history of l and every component life-history of l^* the very same level of sublifetime utility in period t_1 (call it V_1), the very same level in period t_2 (V_2), and so forth. Then the ranking of l versus l^*, as determined by calculating expected utilities according to $u(.)$, is invariant to the specific values of $V_1, V_2, \ldots, V_K$. Whether $u(.)$ has the property of lottery-separability may be a relevant question *if* $u(.)$ expectationally represents the well-being ranking of lotteries over life-histories—which will be true, at least, on the extended-preference account of well-being tendered in Chapter 3.

To see that separability, lottery-separability, and additivity are distinct properties, note that the function $u(x; i) = [\sum_{t=1}^{T} v(\mathbf{a}_{i,t}(x), \mathbf{a}_{imp,t}(x))]^{1/2}$ is separable but not lottery-separable in sublifetime utility. The multiplicative product of sublifetime utility, i.e., $u(x; i) = \prod_{t=1}^{T} v(\mathbf{a}_{i,t}(x), \mathbf{a}_{imp,t}(x))$, is lottery-separable in sublifetime utility (assuming that $v(.)$ assigns only positive sublifetime utility values) but not additive in sublifetime utility. An additive $u(.)$ has the property of "marginality" (no interaction effects between sublifetime utilities in different periods), while a multiplicative $u(.)$ does not. On marginality, see, e.g., Bleichrodt and Quiggin (1999, pp. 686–688).

The discussion in n. 23, above, is also relevant here. If the lifetime utility function $u(.)$ is representable in terms of a sublifetime utility function $v(.)$, and if it is separable in $v(.)$, then (if $u(.)$ is also continuous in $v(.)$) there will be a $u^+(.)$ which is additive in some transformation of $v(.)$ and which represents the ranking of life-histories achieved by $u(.)$. However, $u^+(.)$ need not be a positive affine transformation of $u(.)$. So, if $u(.)$ expectationally represents the well-being ranking of life-history lotteries, $u^+(.)$ may not do so. And even if $u(.)$ lacks this function, it does serve to represent well-being

I have described a wide variety of different possible approaches to structuring a lifetime utility function $u(.)$ as regards atomism versus nonatomism, separability versus nonseparability in attributes or times, and additivity versus nonadditivity in attributes or times. What, in fact, is the standard approach?[32] (1) As mentioned, social-welfare-function scholarship and policy analysis more generally *do* typically assume that lifetime utility functions are atomistic. (2) Moreover, in evaluating multi-period outcomes, social-welfare-function scholarship and policy analysis more generally *do* assume that the lifetime utility function is expressible as a function of sublifetime utility, and indeed is additive in sublifetime utility. (3) However, it is not unusual for social-welfare-function scholarship and policy analysis to employ a sublifetime utility function $v(.)$ which is non-separable in the period-specific individual attributes that are the arguments for that function. And even where such separability *is* assumed, it is quite common for sublifetime utility to be expressed as a non-additive function of those attributes. (4) Similarly, where a one-period outcome is employed, it is not unusual for the lifetime utility function (which, in this case, is also a one-period utility function) to be non-separable in the individual's attributes during the single period—or, if separable, non-additive.

In Chapter 4, I showed how the assumptions of atomism and temporal additivity might facilitate the estimation of utility functions, given an extended-preference view of well-being. However, I also stressed that these assumptions are just heuristic devices. They economize on the time and expense of SWF analysis but can be relaxed if a fuller and more nuanced analysis is desired. The concept of lifetime well-being does not necessitate them. The extended-preference account of well-being, certainly, does not *entail* that $u(.)$ be atomistic; additive or separable in attributes; representable by sublifetime utilities; or additive or separable in sublifetime utility. And this is presumably true of many other well-being accounts. They, too, would recognize conditions under which atomism, representability, separability, and additivity fail. Indeed, I would suggest that an account of lifetime well-being, and the measurement of $u(.)$, which entails that one or more of these conditions can never fail is—on that count—an implausible view.

B. Discounting

Should policy-analytic frameworks incorporate a discount factor? This is a multifaceted question. One kind of discounting occurs when the well-being of future

---

differences between life-histories; and $u^+(.)$, if not a positive affine transformation of $u(.)$, may not represent the same ordering of well-being differences as $u(.)$.

[32] See generally Chapter 4, reviewing the utility functions employed in social-welfare-function scholarship; Johansson-Stenman (2005), discussing separability as between leisure, consumption, and public goods; and Rey and Rochet (2004) and Blundell and MaCurdy (1999), discussing consumption-health and consumption-leisure utility functions and illustrating that these are typically non-additive in the measures of these attributes.

generations is given less weight than the well-being of the current generation. Discounting of this sort is operationalized, within the SWF framework, by making the ranking of outcomes a function *both* of individuals' lifetime utilities *and* of information about individuals' temporal location. In particular, it is achieved by a continuous prioritarian SWF which takes the form:

Outcome x is at least as good as outcome y iff, for all $u(.)$ in U,
$$\sum_{i=1}^{N} E(b_i(x))g(u_i(x)) \geq \sum_{i=1}^{N} E(b_i(y))g(u_i(y)).$$
In this formula, $b_i(x)$ is individual i's birth date in outcome x. E is a decreasing function; the later the birth date, the lower the value of E. Thus individual i's lifetime utility in outcome x, $u_i(x)$, is transformed by the familiar $g(.)$ function and this transformed lifetime utility amount is then adjusted by a discount factor.

To use a continuous prioritarian SWF of this sort is to engage in *interpersonal* discounting. The moral weight of an individual's well-being is made to depend upon when she comes into existence—to depend upon the generation to which she belongs.

I have discussed interpersonal discounting and the continuous prioritarian SWF at length elsewhere. The reader is referred to that discussion.[33] To briefly summarize: interpersonal discounting is unwarranted, at least in the case of a fixed, finite population. It can readily violate the anonymity requirement. Indeed, if an individual's birth date is not an essential property of her—if someone can be born at different dates, without changing which particular person she is—interpersonal discounting can run afoul of Pareto-indifference or Pareto-superiority.

Interpersonal discounting, although mentioned here for the sake of completeness, is not relevant to the topic of this chapter: whether the continuous prioritarian SWF should be applied to lifetime utilities or instead on some non-lifetime basis. The formula just provided represents a *variant* of lifetime prioritarianism (albeit a problematic variant, by virtue of the potential violations of anonymity and the Pareto principles).

A different aspect of the discounting puzzle is *intrapersonal* discounting. The question, here, is whether a discount factor appears *within* some utility function $u(.)$ in U—a function $u(.)$ that takes as its arguments the individual attributes and background facts that constitute a given life-history, and maps those to a lifetime utility number. In other words, while *interpersonal* discounting concerns the mapping *from* information about lifetime well-being *to* a moral ranking of outcomes, *intrapersonal* discounting concerns the structure of lifetime well-being itself.

Economists almost always incorporate a discount factor of some sort within the ordinary utility functions that are meant to represent individuals' ordinary preferences—and typically do so by coupling such a factor with an ordinary utility function that is atomistic and temporally additive.[34] Transposing this idea to the

---

[33] See Adler (2009b, pp. 1490–1500).

[34] See Frederick, Loewenstein, and O'Donoghue (2003); Gollier (2001, pp. 217–219); Mas-Colell, Whinston, and Green (1995, pp. 733–736).

life-history context, we have that $u(x; i) = \sum_{t=t'}^{T} D(t)v(\mathbf{a}_{i,t}(x), \mathbf{a}_{imp,t}(x))$. For short, call this the "discounted additive form" for a utility function $u(.)$ in $\mathbf{U}$. $D(.)$, the discount factor, is a decreasing function. A life-history is assigned a value by summing sublifetime utility values. Each such $v(.)$ value is a function of the subject's attributes, plus background facts, during one particular period; and this value is then adjusted to take account of the "date" of that period, i.e., its location in the chronological structure of the outcome set, designated by a number between 1 and T. The summation begins with period t', which might be the first period in the outcome set or a later period—an issue which I will discuss in a moment.

The propriety of intrapersonal discounting *is* relevant to the topic of this chapter—because understanding the structure of the lifetime utility function will be important in evaluating the arguments for and against lifetime prioritarianism.[35]

Note, to begin, that intrapersonal discounting—by contrast with interpersonal discounting—is fully consistent with minimal welfarist requirements. There is no violation of anonymity or of the Pareto principles. These requirements (as I have formulated them) build *from* the well-being ranking of life-histories. With this ranking in hand, we can then identify pairs of outcomes such that anonymity or Pareto-indifference requires the two outcomes to be ranked as equally morally good, and pairs of outcomes such that Pareto-superiority requires one outcome to be ranked morally better than another. *Intrapersonal* discounting enters the picture at an earlier stage, so to speak: at the stage of determining how life-histories are ranked in light of well-being. The proponent of the formula, $u(x; i) = \sum_{t=t'}^{T} D(t)v(\mathbf{a}_{i,t}(x), \mathbf{a}_{imp,t}(x))$, adopts one particular view of that ranking.

Still, the view can certainly be criticized as unattractive; and I will do so here. Because the case for intrapersonal discounting is virtually always framed in terms of preferences—with economists pointing out that a lifetime utility function with a discount factor best explains how individuals actually behave and what they actually want—I will suggest that a $u(.)$ in $\mathbf{U}$ should not assume the discounted-additive form even if $u(.)$ is constructed as per the extended-preference account of well-being developed in Chapters 3 and 4. If those who favor a preference-based construction

---

[35] In particular, my claim that the lifetime utility function should not incorporate a discount factor will give rise to a potential challenge as regards personal identity. See below, pp. 447–449. Moreover, my analysis of intra- and interpersonal equalization assumes no such factor, and would be more complicated if the lifetime utility function included one. For example, where outcomes describe a single attribute, and the sublifetime utility function is strictly concave in that attribute, the temporally additive lifetime utility function without a discount factor will invariably endorse an intertemporal, intrapersonal, Pigou–Dalton transfer in the attribute; but this is not true of the *discounted* additive form. See below, pp. 454–475.

of **U** should reject intrapersonal discounting, then *a fortiori* those who construct **U** in some other manner should also do so.[36]

On the extended-preference view, the set **U** is built up from sets of the form $\mathbf{U}^{k,t,x}$, representing the fully informed, fully rational extended preferences of a given spectator k, at a given time t, in a given outcome x. **U** is the union of all such sets. Because inter-outcome variation in extended preferences is not relevant to the topic at hand, I will omit the outcome superscript in what follows, although it is implicit.

Consider a given spectator k, who at time t^* is ranking life-histories and lotteries over life-histories. Why would the utility functions that represent his fully informed, fully rational extended preferences at that time—the utility functions in his set $\mathbf{U}^{k,t^*}$—incorporate a discount factor $D(t)$ as per the discounted-additive formula?

One possibility is that the spectator is temporally biased rather than temporally neutral. By temporally biased, I mean that his ranking of a pair of life-histories, $(x; i)$ versus $(y; j)$, is sensitive to the temporal location of the sublifetime bundles comprising the two histories, relative to his own location in time (time t^*).[37] More specifically, we can arrive at the discounted-additive formula by imagining that the spectator is subject to two types of temporal bias frequently discussed in the literature on time preference. First, the spectator discounts for temporal distance; he is biased "toward the near." If k prefers sublifetime bundle $(\mathbf{a}, \mathbf{a}_{imp})$ to sublifetime bundle $(\mathbf{a}^*, \mathbf{a}_{imp}^*)$, then if life-history $(x; i)$ and $(y; j)$ are identical except that in the first history the better bundle, $(\mathbf{a}, \mathbf{a}_{imp})$, occurs nearer in time to t^* than the worse bundle, while in the second history the worse bundle occurs nearer in time to t^* than the better bundle, then k at t^* prefers the first life-history.[38] Second, the spectator

---

[36] The discounted-additive form for $u(.)$ is not the only form of intrapersonal discounting. Other functional forms for $u(.)$ might also incorporate a discount factor. I will not evaluate such functional forms here. Note, however, that my analysis of temporal bias, below, would be relevant to their justifiability; they should not be justified by supposing that fully rational, fully informed spectators discount the past, discount for temporal distance, or otherwise depart from temporal neutrality.

[37] The extended-preference view constructs $\mathbf{U}^{k,t^*}$ with reference to three types of rankings by the spectator: own-history rankings, i-history rankings, and across-person judgments. For purposes of the instant discussion, it is not necessary to distinguish between the three types (and thus, for present purposes, the subjects of the two life-histories $(x; i)$ and $(y; j)$ might be the same or different, and might or might not be identical to the spectator k). If the spectator discounts for temporal distance and discounts the future in arriving at all three types of rankings, the elements of $\mathbf{U}^{k,t^*}$ will assume the discounted-additive form stated in the text immediately below, with the summation beginning at period t^*.

[38] To say that a given sublifetime bundle $(\mathbf{a}^*, \mathbf{a}_{imp}^*)$ occurs in life-history $(x; i)$ in some period t, is just to say that the subject i of that life-history has attributes $\mathbf{a}^*$ during period t, i.e., $\mathbf{a}_{i,t}(x) = \mathbf{a}^*$, and background facts during period t are given by $\mathbf{a}_{imp}^*$, i.e, $\mathbf{a}_{imp,t}(x) = \mathbf{a}_{imp}^*$.

If the spectator's ranking of life-histories is atomistic, representable by sublifetime utilities, and separable in sublifetime utilities, in the senses described earlier, then it is meaningful to talk of the spectator ranking sublifetime bundles themselves. To say that the spectator weakly prefers bundle $(\mathbf{a}, \mathbf{a}_{imp})$ to bundle $(\mathbf{a}^*, \mathbf{a}_{imp}^*)$ means: if $(x; i)$ and $(y; j)$ are any life-histories identical except during one period, t, and the $(\mathbf{a}, \mathbf{a}_{imp})$ bundle occurs in that period in $(x; i)$, while the $(\mathbf{a}^*, \mathbf{a}_{imp}^*)$ bundle occurs in

ignores the past; he is biased "toward the future." If $(x; i)$ and $(y; j)$ are identical in their current and future characteristics—they have the same sublifetime bundle in period t^*, the same bundle in period $(t^* + 1)$, and so on through the final period T—then k ranks the histories as equally good, regardless of how they might have differed during periods prior to t^*.

These two biases, taken together with atomism and temporal additivity, would yield a lifetime utility function such that $u^{k,t^*}(.)$, a member of $\mathbf{U}^{k,t^*}$, takes the form $u^{k,t^*}(x; i) = \sum_{t=t^*}^{T} D(t)v^{k,t^*}(\mathbf{a}_{i,t}(x), \mathbf{a}_{imp,t}(x))$. The spectator's utility function, *at time* t^*, takes the form of summing sublifetime utilities, beginning at time t^* (this reflects his bias toward the future), discounted by a factor $D(t)^{39}$ (this reflects his bias toward the near).

Many philosophers, and even some economists, adopt the position that discounting for temporal distance, discounting the past, and other sorts of temporal bias are *irrational*, however frequently observed in practice. Rationality requires that the self-interested individual be "prudent," in the sense of giving equal weight to all the different periods in her life. Sidgwick famously argued in favor of this view when he wrote:

> The proposition "that one ought to aim at one's own good" is sometimes given as the maxim of Rational Self-love or Prudence: but as so stated it does not clearly avoid tautology; since we may define "good" as "what one ought to aim at." If, however, we say "one's good on the whole," the addition suggests a principle . . . [which is] not tautological. I have already referred to this principle as that "of impartial concern for all parts of our conscious life": —we might express it concisely by saying "that Hereafter *as such* is to be regarded neither less nor more than Now." It is not, of course, meant that the good of the present may not reasonably be preferred to that of the future on account of its greater certainty. . . . All that the principle affirms is that the mere difference of priority and posteriority in time is not a reasonable ground for having more regard to the consciousness of one moment [than] to that of another.[40]

that period in $(y; j)$, then the spectator weakly prefers $(x; i)$ to $(y; j)$. Given separability in sublifetime utilities, *any* such pair can be chosen to define the spectator's preference between the bundles, since his ranking of the histories is invariant to their characteristics during periods other than t.

Assume that the spectator strictly prefers bundle $(\mathbf{a}, \mathbf{a}_{imp})$ to bundle $(\mathbf{a}^*, \mathbf{a}_{imp}^*)$; and that life-histories $(x; i)$ and $(y; j)$ are identical in their constituent bundles except that $(\mathbf{a}, \mathbf{a}_{imp})$ occurs in period t^+ and $(\mathbf{a}^*, \mathbf{a}_{imp}^*)$ in period t^{++} in life-history $(x; i)$, while $(\mathbf{a}^*, \mathbf{a}_{imp}^*)$ occurs in period t^+ and $(\mathbf{a}, \mathbf{a}_{imp})$ in period t^{++} in life-history $(y; j)$. Imagine that in any such case k at time t^* strictly prefers $(x; i)$ to $(y; j)$ iff $|t^* - t^+| < |t^* - t^{++}|$. This might be offered as a *definition* of discounting for temporal distance and, in any event, is certainly characteristic of discounting for temporal distance.

[39] In principle, the magnitude of the discount factor could depend on the spectator and his temporal position, i.e., take the form $D^{k,t^*}(.)$, but this possibility is not germane to my analysis here and, to avoid clutter, I will ignore it.

[40] Sidgwick (1981, p. 381); see also ibid., p. 124, n.1.

A similar position was taken by Rawls, and by the famous economists Pigou and Ramsey.[41]

The critic of intrapersonal discounting need not go so far. She can bracket the question whether temporal biases are *always* a violation of rational self-interest, and take the narrower position that temporal neutrality is at least rationally required in the context of extended preferences. The extended preferences relevant to the construction of **U** are fully informed, fully rational extended preferences—and full rationality, *in this context*, should be understood to include a requirement of temporal neutrality.

Why? Let us remember that the extended-preference view provides an account of well-being for purposes of moral decision-making. It specifies how to compare and measure the well-being realized by different life-histories, so as to rank outcomes in a manner that is impartial between all individuals, with well-being functioning as the "currency" in light of which individuals have claims for or against outcomes. "Impartiality" means, to begin, the anonymity axiom. The strength of some individual's claim as between a pair of outcomes should not be downgraded merely in virtue of the fact that the individual comes into existence later rather than earlier in time. While *intra*personal discounting is consistent with the anonymity axiom, for spectators to rank life-histories in a temporally biased manner seems inconsistent with the spirit of impartiality. Imagine that life-histories $(x; i)$ and $(y; j)$ contain the very same sublifetime bundles; however, the bundles are arranged in different orders.[42] The spectator, at time t^*, is not indifferent between all the bundles; he sees some as better than others. It now turns out that the better bundles occur in $(x; i)$ at a date after t^*, while the better bundles occur in $(y; j)$ at a date prior to t^*. Or, the better bundles occur in $(x; i)$ in the near future—during periods with numbers not much larger than t^*—while they occur in $(y; j)$ in the more distant future. Why should these sorts of temporal facts, regarding the spectator's placement relative to the better and worse bundles, be relevant for purposes of arriving at numbers $u(x; i)$ and $u(y; j)$ meant to serve as an interpersonally comparable and morally determinative measure of the goodness of the two histories?

Note also that the discounted-additive utility function, in the version $u^{k,t^*}(x; i)$ $= \sum_{t=t^*}^{T} D(t) v^{k,t^*}(\mathbf{a}_{i,t}(x), \mathbf{a}_{imp,t}(x))$ that arises from temporal bias on the part of spectators, would engender massive incomparability in the ranking of life-histories. On the extended-preference view, **U** is constructed by pooling extended preferences across spectators, outcomes, and times. It would be arbitrary to include $\mathbf{U}^{k,1}$ representing k's preferences at time 1, but not $\mathbf{U}^{k,2}$ representing his preferences at time 2,

[41] See Rawls (1999b, p. 259); Pigou (1920, pt. 1, ch. 2); Ramsey (1928, p. 543). But see Parfit (1987, pt. 2). For discussion of the rationality of temporal bias, see generally Brink (1997, 2003, 2011); Frederick (2006, pp. 673–675).

[42] In other words, there are T sublifetime bundles $(\mathbf{a}, \mathbf{a}_{imp})$, $(\mathbf{a}^*, \mathbf{a}_{imp}^*)$, . . ., such that each occurs in one period in life-history $(x; i)$—see above, n. 38—and each occurs in one period in life-history $(y; j)$.

or $\mathbf{U}^{k,3}$ his preferences at time 3, and so forth. Imagine now that $\mathbf{U}^{k,1}$ is constructed by using the discounted-additive utility function starting at time 1; that $\mathbf{U}^{k,2}$ is constructed by using that formula beginning at time 2; and so forth. If so, any two such sets will typically yield different rankings of the set of life-histories, because if $t^+ < t^{++}$, the utility functions in $\mathbf{U}^{k,t+}$ will take account of facts during periods t^+ through $(t^{++} - 1)$, while the utility functions in $\mathbf{U}^{k,t++}$ will ignore these facts. At the extreme, as between $\mathbf{U}^{k,1}$ (sensitive to facts in all periods) and $\mathbf{U}^{k,T}$ (sensitive only to facts during the final period, T), the difference in rankings would routinely be quite radical. The grand rule for ranking life-histories says that one life-history is at least as good as a second (rather than incomparable) only if at least as good according to all the elements of $\mathbf{U}$. But if $\mathbf{U}^{k,t^*}$ is constructed by using the discounted-additive formula beginning at time t^*, and $\mathbf{U}$ contains all the utility functions from each set $\mathbf{U}^{k,t^*}$, in each outcome (this is just equivalent to saying that $\mathbf{U}$ is the union of these sets), it will rarely be the case that this grand rule will be satisfied.[43]

To be clear, in arguing for temporal neutrality, and against a lifetime utility function with the form $u^{k,t^*}(x; i) = \sum_{t=t^*}^{T} D(t)v^{k,t^*}(\mathbf{a}_{i,t}(x), \mathbf{a}_{imp,t}(x))$, I have not ruled out the possibility that a given spectator's fully informed, fully rational extended preferences might change over time. The discussion in the previous paragraph suggested that temporal bias would be *one* cause of (quite radical) intertemporal change in extended preferences. Although this particular basis for intertemporal change is ruled out, others are not. It remains possible that spectator k's fully informed, *temporally neutral*, and otherwise rational extended preferences at t^+ are different from his fully informed, *temporally neutral*, and otherwise rational extended preferences at t^{++} (for example, because of some natural change in his preference structure that occurs as k ages and that survives idealization).

Nor is a temporal-neutrality constraint the same as a requirement that the spectator ignore the *sequencing* of sublifetime bundles. In my discussion, earlier, of the separability properties of lifetime well-being, I stressed that fully informed, fully rational spectators might well be sensitive to sequencing effects in ranking life-histories. A spectator who is temporally neutral, but sensitive to sequencing effects, cares about the temporal location of the sublifetime bundles comprising a life-history, relative to each other. (For example, he may prefer an upward trending history, where each bundle is better than the one before, to a downward trending history, where each is worse than the one before.) This is *different* from temporal

---

[43] To be sure, *other* features of the extended-preference view also potentially give rise to incomparability in the ranking of life-histories, namely the pooling of extended preferences across all spectators, outcomes, and times. But in each case we can provide a strong justification for the feature, while no such justification can be furnished for a departure from temporal neutrality, the propriety of which is questionable quite apart from its role in propagating incomparability.

bias—from the case where the spectator is concerned about the temporal location of bundles, relative to his own temporal position.[44]

So much for *one* form of intrapersonal discounting. A different sort of discounted-additive lifetime utility function is as follows: $u^{k,t'}(x; i) = \sum_{t=1}^{T} D(t)v^{k,t'}(\mathbf{a}_{i,t}(x), \mathbf{a}_{imp,t}(x))$. At *any* time t^*, the spectator ranks life-histories by summing discounted sublifetime utility beginning with the first period, *not* period t^*.

Note that such a lifetime utility function would not be the result of temporally biased spectators. Rather, it would reflect an odd kind of concern for the temporal location of sublifetime bundles—not a concern for their location relative to the spectator, or for their location relative to each other, but rather an intrinsic concern for their location in "calendar time," i.e., the chronological structure of outcomes. The preference at work in motivating this lifetime utility function might be expressed as follows: if the spectator takes *any* life-history and interchanges two non-indifferent bundles, then the result is *necessarily* to improve the life-history (if the better bundle is moved to an earlier period) or worsen it (if the worse bundle is moved to an earlier period).[45] It is *possible* that fully informed spectators would intrinsically care about calendar time in this manner; but there is absolutely no evidence to suggest that they would.

In sum, while the extended-preference view and other plausible accounts of life-time well-being support a wide variety of functional forms for the lifetime utility functions $u(.)$ in $\mathbf{U}$, intrapersonal discounting (as operationalized via the discounted-additive utility function) is problematic.[46] With this understanding of the lifetime

---

[44] Sequencing effects entail a violation of intertemporal separability. See above, n. 28. This suffices to show that the discounted-additive formula $u^{k,t'}(x; i) = \sum_{t=t'}^{T} D(t)v^{k,t'}(\mathbf{a}_{i,t}(x), \mathbf{a}_{imp,t}(x))$—whether with $t' = t^*$ or 1—does not reflect sequencing effects, since it is temporally separable and, indeed, lottery-separable, see above n. 31: the ranking of two life-histories or two lotteries over life-histories with sublifetime bundles (and, hence, sublifetime utility levels) the same in some periods does not depend upon what those bundles are.

[45] The discounted utility function of the form $u^{k,t'}(x; i) = \sum_{t=t^*}^{T} D(t)v^{k,t'}(\mathbf{a}_{i,t}(x), \mathbf{a}_{imp,t}(x))$, which begins the summation in period t^*, does of course take account of calendar time via the discount factor $D(.)$, which operates on a number t marking each bundle's period, i.e., location in calendar time. However, this function is motivated, not by the spectator's intrinsic concern for where sublife-time bundles are located in calendar time, but by his intrinsic concern for where they are located relative to him. Note that *this* function does not satisfy the condition stated in the text accompanying this footnote.

[46] The reader familiar with the widespread use of discounting in cost-benefit analysis might be very surprised that I endorse a version of the SWF approach without either interpersonal or intrapersonal discounting. CBA discounting is sometimes defended without reliance on the fact that individuals' actual preferences are temporally biased, by pointing instead to the lower marginal utility of consumption of future generations, which are likely to be richer than the present generation; to the possibility of investing funds at a positive rate of return in the market; and to uncertainty. Suffice it to say that the SWF approach without inter- or intrapersonal discounting can take account of each of these factors. See Adler and Posner (2006, pp. 173–177); Adler (2009b, pp. 1490–1500).

utility function in hand, let us now turn to the question whether a continuous prioritarian SWF should operate upon lifetime utility numbers or instead should assume some non-lifetime approach.

III. THE BASIC CASE FOR LIFETIME PRIORITARIANISM

A lifetime approach to applying the continuous prioritarian SWF employs some account of lifetime well-being W to generate a ranking of life-histories, differences between life-histories, and comparisons to the zero point in each choice situation, which are measured by a set U of lifetime utility functions. The lifetime prioritarian approach then chooses some strictly increasing and strictly concave $g(.)$ function and ranks outcomes using the formula: outcome x is at least as good as outcome y iff, for all $u(.)$ belonging to U, $\sum_{i=1}^{N} g(u_i(x)) \geq \sum_{i=1}^{N} g(u_i(y))$.

This decisional procedure can be contrasted with various *non-lifetime* rules for using the continuous prioritarian SWF. As we shall see later in the chapter, substantial philosophical arguments have been advanced in favor of some version of non-lifetime prioritarianism. Although I believe that these arguments fail, non-lifetime prioritarianism is worth taking seriously. Within the SWF framework, non-lifetime prioritarianism would mean using numbers *other than lifetime utilities* as the arguments for the continuous prioritarian SWF.

One variant of non-lifetime prioritarianism is *sublifetime* prioritarianism. The general idea here is that the inputs to the SWF are sublifetime utility numbers, representing well-being during temporal segments of human lifetimes.[47] Assume an outcome set in which outcomes have T periods. A simple kind of sublifetime prioritarianism would assign each individual a sublifetime well-being number for each period, so that each outcome corresponds to a grand vector of NT sublifetime utilities (or a set of such vectors), and outcomes are ranked by applying the continuous prioritarian SWF to these grand vectors.

A different version of sublifetime prioritarianism divides individual i's life into a certain number of non-overlapping segments, where each segment may consist in one or more periods. If individual i's life in outcome x is divided into $s_i(x)$ non-overlapping segments, then individual i is assigned $s_i(x)$ sublifetime utility numbers. (For example, if outcomes have 10 periods, individual i might be assigned a sublifetime utility number in x for a segment encompassing periods 1 and 2, another number for a segment encompassing periods 3 through 7, and a third number for a segment encompassing periods 8 through 10.) Outcome x then corresponds to a grand vector of $\sum_{i=1}^{N} s_i(x)$ sublifetime utilities (or a set of such vectors), and the continuous prioritarian SWF is applied to *these* vectors.

---

[47] On sublifetime well-being, see Bigelow, Campbell, and Pargetter (1990); Broome (1995, ch. 11); Velleman (1993).

Yet a different approach divides individual i's life into a certain number of segments which may overlap, where each segment may consist in one or more periods. For example, if outcomes have 10 periods, individual i might be assigned a sublifetime utility number for a segment encompassing periods 1 through 5, a second for a segment encompassing periods 2 through 6, a third for a segment encompassing periods 3 through 7, and a fourth for a segment encompassing periods 4 through 10. If individual i's life in outcome x is divided into $s_i(x)$ potentially overlapping segments, outcome x then corresponds to a grand vector of $\sum_{i=1}^{N} s_i(x)$ sublifetime utilities (or a set of such vectors), and outcomes are then ranked by applying the continuous prioritarian SWF to these vectors of sublifetime utilities.

Actually, this last sublifetime approach (allowing for overlapping segments) can be seen as a generalization of the second, which in turn is a generalization of the first (where segments do not overlap and each segment is just a single period, so that $s_i(x) = T$ for each individual and each outcome.). So we can summarize sublifetime prioritarianism as follows. There is some set **V** of sublifetime utility functions. While lifetime utility functions assign utilities to whole life-histories, each $v(.)$ in **V** assigns a utility number to a temporal segment of a life-history. Formally, we have not merely the set **H** of life-histories, but also a set **F** of temporal segments of life-histories; and each element of **V** assigns a number to each member of **F**, representing the sublifetime well-being of that segment.[48] For each outcome x, the life of each individual i is divided by some rule into $s_i(x)$ segments. We can use the symbol $(x; i; 1)$ to represent the first segment of individual i's life in x, $(x; i; 2)$ to represent the second segment, and in general $(x; i; s)$ to represent segment number s of individual i's life in outcome x. Each sublifetime utility function $v(.)$ of **V** maps a given outcome x onto a grand vector of $\sum_{i=1}^{N} s_i(x)$ sublifetime utilities. That is, outcome x is mapped onto $v(x) = (v(x; 1; 1), v(x; 1; 2), \ldots, v(x; 1; s_1(x)), \ldots, v(x; i; 1), v(x; i; 2), \ldots, v(x; i; s_i(x)), \ldots, v(x; N; 1), v(x; N; 2), \ldots, v(x; N; s_N(x)))$. And the rule for ranking outcomes

[48] Let us say that a "segment" is a group of one or more consecutive periods of a given outcome, paired with a person. (We could generalize further to allow for segments with non-consecutive periods, for example the segment consisting of being individual i in outcome x in period 1 plus being individual i in outcome x in period 4; but it is intuitively very odd to assign sublifetime well-being to such segments, and the kinds of sublifetime prioritarianism suggested by Parfit, McKerlie, and other critics of lifetime prioritarianism do not involve such segments.)

Consider each life-history $(x; i)$. If outcomes have T periods, this history is associated with T segments that have one period, $(T-1)$ that have two periods, and so forth—with $T(T+1)/2$ in total. **F** is either the grand set of all these, for all life-histories in **H**; or some subset. (A particular version of sublifetime prioritarianism might only need to assign sublifetime utilities to certain segments.) If f and f^* are two segments in **F**, then the sublifetime well-being associated with them is represented by the utility functions in **V** (just as **U** represents the lifetime well-being associated with the life-histories in **H**). In other words, the sublifetime well-being realized by f is at least as large as the sublifetime well-being realized by f^* iff, for all $v(.)$ in **V**, $v(f) \geq v(f^*)$. The elements of $v(.)$ might also represent the differences in sublifetime well-being between the elements of **F** or comparisons to zero (where the subject is not alive during a period).

is: outcome x is morally at least as good as outcome y iff, for all $v(.)$ in $\mathbf{V}$, $\sum_{i=1}^{N}\sum_{s=1}^{s_i(x)}g(v(x;i;s))\geq\sum_{i=1}^{N}\sum_{s=1}^{s_i(y)}g(v(y;i;s))$, with $g(.)$ strictly increasing and strictly concave.

In the simplest case where each segment in each outcome is a single period, this formula becomes: x is morally at least as good as y iff, for all $v(.)$ in $\mathbf{V}$, $\sum_{i=1}^{N}\sum_{t=1}^{T}g(v(x;i;t))\geq\sum_{i=1}^{N}\sum_{t=1}^{T}g(v(y;i;t))$, where $(x; i; t)$ denotes period t of individual i's life in outcome x; and $v(x; i; t)$ is the sublifetime utility assigned to this single period. I will generally refer to this variant of sublifetime prioritarianism as "simple" sublifetime prioritarianism.

A different kind of non-lifetime prioritarianism is *attribute-based* prioritarianism. Assume that, in a given outcome set, M types of individual attributes are described during each period. (For example, if each individual's health and consumption is described in each period, then $M = 2$.) Use the symbol "$a^m(x; i; t)$" to mean the numerical level of attribute m that individual i has in outcome x during period t. Then each outcome corresponds to a grand vector of NTM attributes (N individuals, T periods, M attributes per period). Attribute-based prioritarianism ranks outcomes by applying the continuous prioritarian SWF to these attribute vectors. In other words, it says: outcome x is morally at least as good as outcome y iff $\sum_{i=1}^{N}\sum_{t=1}^{T}\sum_{m=1}^{M}g(a^m(x;i;t))\geq\sum_{i=1}^{N}\sum_{t=1}^{T}\sum_{m=1}^{M}g(a^m(y;i;t))$.[49]

Table 6.1 provides a simple example which illustrates sublifetime, attribute-based, and lifetime prioritarianism.[50]

---

[49] This approach presupposes some methodology for measuring the level of each attribute. By contrast, lifetime and sublifetime prioritarianism do not require that attributes be assigned numerical levels. The characterization of outcomes *may* express attributes numerically, but it also may describe some or all attributes in qualitative terms (for example, by describing an individual's health attribute in terms of whether she is healthy or, if not, what diseases she has). And lifetime or sublifetime utility functions can take as their arguments life-histories, or periods of life-histories, in which some or all attributes are characterized qualitatively.

[50] In many examples set forth in tables in this chapter, as in other chapters, I assume for simplicity that $\mathbf{U}$ is unique up to a positive ratio transformation, so that the lifetime utility of a given life-history can be represented by a symbol such as "$15r$"—meaning that the particular life-history is assigned the value of 15 by some $u(.)$ in $\mathbf{U}$; and that $u^*(.)$ is also in $\mathbf{U}$ iff there is some positive number r such that $u^*(.)$ assigns every life-history r times the value assigned by $u(.)$. In the case where $\mathbf{U}$ is unique up to a positive ratio transformation, and its elements assume the atomistic and temporally additive form, then each $u(.)$ will correspond to a particular sublifetime $v(.)$ function and these $v(.)$ functions, too, will be unique up to a positive ratio transformation—hence sublifetime utilities, too, can be represented by a symbol such as "$5r$." (In this context, sublifetime utility function $v(.)$ is a positive ratio transformation of another such function $w(.)$ if there is some positive r such that, for every possible sublifetime bundle $(\mathbf{a}^*, \mathbf{a}_{imp})$, $v(\mathbf{a}^*, \mathbf{a}_{imp}) = rw(\mathbf{a}^*, \mathbf{a}_{imp})$.) Strictly, the temporal additivity and uniqueness up to a positive ratio transformation of the elements of $\mathbf{U}$ entail uniqueness up to a positive ratio transformation of the $v(.)$ functions *if* they expectationally represent lotteries over sublifetime bundles—as per the theory of well-being developed in Chapters 3 and 4. This can be seen by coupling the analysis in Chapter 4, n. 73, with the further requirement that each $v(.)$ should assign 0 to a sublifetime bundle just as good as premature death. In any event, it is unproblematic to assume, for

Table 6.1 Attribute-Based, Sublifetime, and Lifetime Prioritarianism

	Outcome x			Outcome y		
	Period 1	Period 2	Lifetime utility	Period 1	Period 2	Lifetime utility
Joe						
Attribute *a*	100	10		81	100	
Attribute *b*	49	100		64	1	
Sublifetime utility	4900*r*	1000*r*	5900*r*	5184*r*	100*r*	5284*r*
Sue						
Attribute *a*	36	49		81	49	
Attribute *b*	25	25		36	9	
Sublifetime utility	900*r*	1225*r*	2125*r*	2916*r*	441*r*	3357*r*
	Attribute score: 53.16			Attribute score: 53		
	Sublifetime score: $166.62\sqrt{r}$			Sublifetime score: $157\sqrt{r}$		
	Lifetime score: $122.91\sqrt{r}$			Lifetime score: $130.63\sqrt{r}$		

In this example, there are two individuals, two time periods, and two attributes in each period. The attribute-based approach, with the square root as the $g(.)$ function, is to assign an outcome a score equaling the sum of the square roots of all the attribute levels in the outcome. The simple sublifetime approach, again with the square root as the transformation function, is to assign an outcome a score equaling the sum of the square roots of each individual's sublifetime utility in each period. The lifetime approach, once more with the square root as the transformation function, is to assign the outcome a score equaling the sum of the square roots of each individual's lifetime utility.

Table 6.1 illustrates these approaches. It is assumed that sublifetime utility, for purposes of the sublifetime approach, is the multiplicative product of the attribute levels; and that lifetime utility is the sum of these same sublifetime utilities.

Note that the attribute and sublifetime approaches here both rank *x* over *y*, while the lifetime approach ranks *y* over *x*.

purposes of illustration, that there is a one-to-one correspondence between $u(.)$ and $v(.)$, with both unique up to a positive ratio transformation.

As explained in the text, the sublifetime prioritarian approach need *not* use as its inputs the same sublifetime utility numbers that figure in the lifetime utility functions. However, the examples provided in Table 6.1 and in other tables below often assume that the $v(.)$ function does have this dual role. This assumption is adopted either for simplicity, or to illustrate a *possible* feature of the sublifetime and lifetime approaches (in particular, to show how the sublifetime approach can violate the lifetime Pareto principles and other lifetime principles, and to show why equalization of attributes or sublifetime well-being approved by the sublifetime prioritarian might also be approved by the lifetime prioritarian).

Before presenting the basic case for the lifetime approach, several preliminary points are worth underscoring. To begin, sublifetime utilities play a different role within sublifetime prioritarianism than they do within lifetime prioritarianism. As I discussed in the previous section, the utility assigned to a life-history by each lifetime utility function in **U** *might* be expressible as a function of the subject's sublifetime utility in each period (most simply, as the sum of sublifetime utility in each period). However, nothing in the concept of lifetime well-being or in the extended-preference account for assigning lifetime utilities requires that lifetime utility be expressible in this manner. Moreover, even where lifetime utility *is* expressible as a function of sublifetime utility, lifetime prioritarianism uses individuals' lifetime utilities—not their sublifetime utilities—as the direct arguments for the prioritarian SWF.

By contrast, sublifetime prioritarianism is *committed* to the existence of sublifetime utility numbers. These numbers are "fed" directly into the sublifetime formula, i.e., outcome x is at least as good as outcome y iff, for all sublifetime utility functions $v(.)$ in **V**, $\sum_{i=1}^{N}\sum_{s=1}^{s_i(x)} g(v(x;i;s)) \geq \sum_{i=1}^{N}\sum_{s=1}^{s_i(y)} g(v(y;i;s))$.

A related point is that the sublifetime prioritarian might deploy a range of different methods for constructing the sublifetime utility functions in **V**. For example, if an extended-preference account is indeed the most attractive methodology for arriving at lifetime utilities, the sublifetime prioritarian might: (1) construct the set **V** by looking to spectators' extended preferences over temporal segments rather than whole life-histories (if the notion of an extended preference regarding a temporal segment is indeed coherent); (2) stipulate that spectators' preferences over whole life-histories must satisfy conditions sufficient to ensure that the lifetime utility functions in **U** *are* expressible as a function of subjects' sublifetime utilities, and use the $v(.)$ functions that assign these particular sublifetime numbers (each corresponding to a lifetime utility function $u(.)$ in **U**) as the members of **V**; or (3) construct **V** in some other manner. My critique of sublifetime prioritarianism will be entirely agnostic on these issues.

A final, subtle point is that we can construct non-lifetime approaches which are extensionally equivalent to lifetime prioritarianism. Take any arbitrary account of lifetime well-being W, which produces some set **U** of lifetime utility functions in each choice situation; and an arbitrary $g(.)$ function which is strictly increasing and strictly concave. The lifetime prioritarian SWF, using **U** and $g(.)$, orders outcomes as follow: x is morally at least as good as y iff, for all $u(.)$ in **U**, $\sum_{i=1}^{N} g(u_i(x)) \geq \sum_{i=1}^{N} g(u_i(y))$. Then we can "gerrymander" a version of sublifetime prioritarianism, by constructing an appropriate **V** and transformation function, which yields the very same ranking of outcomes, in each choice situation, as this lifetime rule.[51] Moreover (with

---

[51] To gerrymander sublifetime prioritarianism, note that some philosophers of well-being suggest that an individual's well-being during some period of time need not be solely a function of contemporaneous facts or attributes. (On this issue, see Bigelow, Campbell, and Pargetter [1990]; Velleman [1993].) Consider the simplest version of sublifetime prioritarianism, where each segment is a single

certain assumptions), we can "gerrymander" a version of attribute-based prioritarianism which yields the very same ranking of outcomes, in each choice situation, as a lifetime prioritarian SWF using $\mathbf{U}$ and $g(.)$.[52]

This observation, in turn, is relevant to the question whether non-lifetime approaches necessarily violate the lifetime Pareto, Pigou–Dalton, and person-separability axioms. These are the key substantive axioms satisfied by lifetime prioritarianism.[53]

The "lifetime" Pareto-indifference principle is just the Pareto-indifference principle that has been discussed throughout the book, starting in Chapter 1. I add the adjective "lifetime" to underscore that this principle has been framed in terms

[52] period, and $(x; i; t)$ denotes period t of individual i's life in outcome x. Let us allow $v(x; i; t)$ to depend upon all of individual i's attributes in x, not just her attributes during period t. For a given set of lifetime utility functions $\mathbf{U}$ and an outcome set with T periods, and a given $g(.)$ function, arbitrarily pick a strictly increasing and strictly concave function $f(.)$ with an appropriate range, so that the $f^{-1}(.)$ term below is always defined. For a given $u(.)$, define a corresponding $v(.)$ as follows: for a given individual i and outcome x, her sublifetime utility in every period is the very same value, namely $v(x;i;t)=f^{-1}(g(u(x;i))/T)$. Define $\mathbf{V}$ as the set of all $v(.)$. Then the following sublifetime prioritarian rule produces the very same ordering of outcomes as the lifetime approach using $g(.)$: x is at least as good as y iff, for all $v(.)$ belonging to $\mathbf{V}$, $\sum_{i=1}^{N}\sum_{t=1}^{T}f(v(x;i;t))\geq\sum_{i=1}^{N}\sum_{t=1}^{T}f(v(y;i;t))$.

[52] Assume that the utility functions in $\mathbf{U}$ are atomistic and, further, insensitive to background facts; and that $\mathbf{U}$ is unique up to a positive ratio transformation. Assume that $g(.)$ is Atkinsonian and thus invariant to ratio rescaling. (In other words, $g(u(x;i))=(1-\gamma)^{-1}u(x;i)^{1-\gamma}$, with $\gamma>0$, or $\ln u(x;i)$ if $\gamma=1$.) Arbitrarily pick some strictly increasing, strictly concave $f(.)$ with an appropriate range, so that the $f^{-1}(.)$ term below is always defined. If there are T periods and M attributes per period, arbitrarily pick some $u^*(.)$ in $\mathbf{U}$ and assign *every* attribute of individual i in outcome x in each period the very same attribute level, namely $a^m(x;i;t)=f^{-1}(g(u^*(x;i))/MT)$. Attribute-based prioritarianism, using the $f(.)$ function, says: x is at least as good as y iff $\sum_{i=1}^{N}\sum_{t=1}^{T}\sum_{m=1}^{M}f(a^m(x;i;t))\geq\sum_{i=1}^{N}\sum_{t=1}^{T}\sum_{m=1}^{M}f(a^m(y;i;t))$. This becomes $\sum_{i=1}^{N}MT[g(u^*(x;i))/MT]\geq\sum_{i=1}^{N}MT[g(u^*(y;i))/MT]$, or $\sum_{i=1}^{N}g(u^*(x;i))\geq\sum_{i=1}^{N}g(u^*(y;i))$. Because $g(.)$ is invariant to a positive ratio transformation and $\mathbf{U}$ is unique up to a positive ratio transformation, this is in turn the same as the lifetime prioritarian rule, $\sum_{i=1}^{N}g(u(x;i))\geq\sum_{i=1}^{N}g(u(y;i))$ for all $u(.)$ in $\mathbf{U}$.

[53] Lifetime prioritarianism, here, means the use of a continuous prioritarian SWF. That approach also, of course, satisfies the continuity axiom—more precisely, a continuity axiom in terms of lifetime utilities. Although I embrace that axiom, it seems to me to flow less directly from the basic idea of ranking outcomes as a function of individuals' claims, plus the valencing of those claims in terms of lifetime well-being, than the lifetime Pareto, Pigou–Dalton, and person-separability axioms. (Lifetime leximin, or the lifetime application of the prioritarian SWF with a lexical threshold, seems to me to be consistent with that basic idea.)

I am not sure whether it is possible for a non-lifetime continuous prioritarian approach to satisfy the lifetime Pareto, Pigou–Dalton, and person-separability axioms but violate continuity in terms of lifetime utilities. Assuming that this *is* possible, I would level the same critique against this approach as I would against a non-lifetime approach which is extensionally equivalent to lifetime continuous prioritarianism (see below), namely that this is a problematic way to think about the ranking of outcomes.

of lifetime well-being: in terms of the well-being associated with life-histories. (Lifetime) Pareto-indifference says: if $(x; i)$ is equally good as $(y; i)$, for every individual i, then x and y are equally morally good. In other words, if each individual's lifetime well-being is the same in the two outcomes, the outcomes are morally indifferent. The Pareto-superiority principle discussed throughout the book is also a "lifetime" principle, similarly framed in terms of the well-being associated with whole life-histories. It says, if each individual's lifetime well-being in x is greater than or equal to her lifetime well-being in y, with lifetime well-being strictly greater for at least one individual, then x is a morally better outcome. Finally, the Pigou–Dalton principle, as discussed in Chapter 5, was framed in terms of transfers of lifetime well-being, from an individual at a higher level of lifetime well-being to an individual at a lower level of lifetime well-being. And the person-separability axiom, also discussed in Chapter 5, involved individuals who were "unaffected" in the sense of having equal levels of lifetime well-being in the outcomes being ranked.

The reader should be reminded that these principles are *relative* to an account of lifetime well-being. Which particular ranking of outcomes is required by the lifetime Pareto, Pigou–Dalton, and person-separability axioms depends on which account of lifetime well-being is being used.

The possibility of a non-lifetime approach which is extensionally equivalent to lifetime prioritarianism shows that—for any given account of lifetime well-being— sublifetime approaches do *not* necessarily violate the lifetime Pareto, Pigou–Dalton, and person-separability axioms.[54] However, there obviously can be non-lifetime approaches which *do* violate one or more of these axioms,[55] as the following tables illustrate.

These tables illustrate the potential conflict between simple sublifetime prioritarianism and lifetime Pareto-indifference, Pareto-superiority, Pigou–Dalton, and

---

[54] The account of well-being will generate a set $\mathbf{U}$ of lifetime utility functions for any choice situation. Ranking outcomes in accordance with lifetime prioritarianism—applying the continuous prioritarian SWF, with some $g(.)$ function, to $\mathbf{U}$—will satisfy these axioms; and if a non-lifetime approach is extensionally equivalent to this lifetime approach, then necessarily it will do so too.

[55] There can be non-lifetime approaches which satisfy some but not all of these axioms. For example, assume that each $u(.)$ in $\mathbf{U}$ takes the form of summing sublifetime utilities. In other words, $u(x;i) = \sum_{t=1}^{T} w(\mathbf{a}_{i,t}(x), \mathbf{a}_{imp,t}(x))$. Pick any strictly increasing, strictly concave function $h(.)$ with an appropriate range so that $h^{-1}(.)$ is defined for the range of $w(.)$. For each $u(.)$, specify a corresponding function $v(.)$ such that $v(\mathbf{a}_{i,t}, \mathbf{a}_{imp,t}) = h^{-1}(w(\mathbf{a}_{i,t}, \mathbf{a}_{imp,t}))$. Note that $u(x;i) = \sum_{t=1}^{T} h(v(\mathbf{a}_{i,t}(x), \mathbf{a}_{imp,t}(x)))$. Consider simple sublifetime prioritarianism, where each segment is a single period, and $(x; i; t)$ denotes period t of individual i's life in outcome x. Set $v(x;i;t) = v(\mathbf{a}_{i,t}(x), \mathbf{a}_{imp,t}(x))$, with $v(.)$ as just defined. Designate by $\mathbf{V}$ the set of all such $v(.)$, each corresponding to one $u(.)$. Consider the ordering of outcomes achieved by the simple sublifetime rule, x is at least as good as y iff, for all $v(.)$ in $\mathbf{V}$, $\sum_{i=1}^{N} \sum_{t=1}^{T} h(v(x;i;t)) \geq \sum_{i=1}^{N} \sum_{t=1}^{T} h(v(y;i;t))$. It is not hard to see that this satisfies lifetime Pareto-indifference, Pareto-superiority, and person-separability but does not satisfy lifetime Pigou–Dalton— because it is equivalent to a lifetime approach that applies a utilitarian SWF to $\mathbf{U}$.

person-separability.[56] (Similar examples could be constructed for attribute-based prioritarianism or other variants of sublifetime prioritarianism.). Sublifetime and lifetime utilities are both unique up to a positive ratio transformation. Lifetime utility takes a temporally additive form. Lifetime utility is the sum of the sublifetime utility values displayed here, which are also—in this case—the inputs for the sublifetime SWF.

Table 6.2 Sublifetime Prioritarianism and Lifetime Pareto-Indifference

	Outcome x			Outcome y		
	Period 1	Period 2	Lifetime utility	Period 1	Period 2	Lifetime utility
Jim	90r	10r	100r	50r	50r	100r
Sue	10r	90r	100r	50r	50r	100r

Table 6.2 illustrates the conflict with *lifetime Pareto-indifference*. That axiom requires that the outcomes be ranked as equally good, but the simple sublifetime approach using any prioritarian SWF will count y as the better outcome, because it equalizes sublifetime utilities.[57]

Table 6.3 Sublifetime Prioritarianism and Lifetime Pareto-Superiority

	Outcome x			Outcome y		
	Period 1	Period 2	Lifetime utility	Period 1	Period 2	Lifetime utility
Jim	90r	10r	100r	$(50-\varepsilon)r$	$(50-\varepsilon)r$	$(100-2\varepsilon)r$
Sue	10r	90r	100r	$(50-\varepsilon)r$	$(50-\varepsilon)r$	$(100-2\varepsilon)r$

Table 6.3 illustrates the conflict with *lifetime Pareto-superiority*. The sublifetime approach, using any Atkinson SWF, will count y as better than x for ε sufficiently small, because y equalizes sublifetime utilities and loses only a little (ε).[58] But lifetime Pareto-superiority requires that x be preferred.

[56] Again, simple sublifetime prioritarianism maps each outcome onto a vector or vectors of *TN* sublifetime utilities, one for each of the *N* individuals in each of the *T* periods, and ranks vectors by summing a strictly increasing, strictly concave function of these sublifetime utilities.

[57] In general, it is simplest to think about the prioritarian ranking of outcomes where utility is unique up to a positive ratio transformation by using an Atkinson SWF, which is invariant to ratio rescalings. But many of the examples provided in these and subsequent tables are such that *any* prioritarian SWF (not merely any Atkinson SWF) will reach the same verdict regardless of the value of *r*. (For example, if utility vector *u* is reached via a Pigou–Dalton transfer from *u**, then any prioritarian SWF will prefer *u* to *u** *and* will prefer *ru* to *ru** for any positive value of *r*.) If the example does assume a prioritarian SWF with the Atkinson form, that will be specifically noted.

[58] In this particular case, it needs to be assumed that the sublifetime approach employs an Atkinson SWF. Otherwise, it might rank the vector of sublifetime utilities (90r, 10r, 10r, 90r) over $((50-\varepsilon)r, (50-\varepsilon)r, (50-\varepsilon)r, (50-\varepsilon)r)$ for one value of *r* but not another.

Table 6.4 Sublifetime Prioritarianism and Lifetime Pigou–Dalton

	Outcome x			Outcome y		
	Period 1	Period 2	Lifetime utility	Period 1	Period 2	Lifetime utility
Jim	50r	90r	140r	30r	90r	120r
Sue	50r	10r	60r	70r	10r	80r

Table 6.4 illustrates the conflict with *lifetime Pigou–Dalton*. The sublifetime approach, using any prioritarian SWF, will count outcome x as better than y, because the individuals' sublifetime utilities are equalized in period 1. But the lifetime Pigou–Dalton principle requires that outcome y be ranked better.

Table 6.5 Sublifetime Prioritarianism and Lifetime Person-Separability

	Outcome x		Lifetime utility	Outcome y		Lifetime utility
	Period 1	Period 2		Period 1	Period 2	
Jim	50r	50r	100r	50r	60r	110r
Sue	50r	50r	100r	50r	40r	90r
Fred	90r	10r	100r	50r	50r	100r
Sum of square root of sublifetime utilities:	40.93√r			42.35√r		

	Outcome x*		Lifetime utility	Outcome y*		Lifetime utility
	Period 1	Period 2		Period 1	Period 2	
Jim	50r	50r	100r	50r	60r	110r
Sue	50r	50r	100r	50r	40r	90r
Fred	6r	6r	12r	6r	6r	12r
Sum of square root of sublifetime utilities:	33.18√r			33.11√r		

Table 6.5 illustrates the conflict with *lifetime person-separability*. Note that Fred has the same lifetime utility in x as in y, and in x* as in y*. Moreover, Jim has the same lifetime utility in x as in x*, and in y as in y*. The same is true of Sue. Lifetime person-separability thus requires that x be ranked at least as good as y iff x* is ranked at least as good as y*. Note, however, that the sublifetime approach using a square root function ranks y over x but x* over y*.

Now for the basic case in favor of lifetime prioritarianism. Take any account W— whatever it may be—which the reader believes to be the most attractive account of lifetime well-being. Consider, first, a non-lifetime prioritarian approach which violates one or more of the axioms of lifetime Pareto-indifference, lifetime Pareto-superiority, lifetime Pigou–Dalton, or lifetime person-separability, in terms of W.

Assume, for example, that the non-lifetime approach violates lifetime Pareto-indifference. Then there will be some outcome set, where x is (lifetime) Pareto-indifferent to outcome y, and yet the non-lifetime approach prefers x to y. Such a preference flies in the face of the idea of ranking outcomes by comparing individuals' claims across outcomes, plus the continuity of personal identity across a human lifetime. Take any arbitrary member i in the population. That *person* is equally well off in both outcomes. It may well be the case that individual i's sublifetime well-being during some temporal segment in outcome x is greater than his sublifetime well-being during some temporal segment in outcome y; but, if so, he has been *compensated* in y for that sublifetime divergence, in the sense that his attributes in y over his entire lifetime are such that his *lifetime well-being* is exactly the same in both outcomes. (For example, Jim's sublifetime well-being in period 1 may be greater in x than in y; but if x and y are lifetime Pareto-indifferent, then there is something about Jim's life in y which *equilibrates* this period 1 difference in his sublifetime well-being. Perhaps his sublifetime well-being is greater in y in period 2.) Similarly, it may well be the case that the level of some attribute of individual i is greater in outcome x than in y; but, if so, he has been *compensated* in y for that attribute divergence, in the sense that his attributes in y over his entire lifetime are such that his *lifetime well-being* is exactly the same in both outcomes. (For example, the quality of Jim's health at one time may be greater in outcome x than in outcome y; but perhaps his consumption at that time is greater in outcome y; or perhaps the quality of Jim's health at some other time is greater in outcome y than in outcome x.)

Because individual i is equally well off in both outcomes, in what sense does *he* have a claim in favor of either outcome? How can *he* complain if one outcome rather than the other obtains? Because this is true for all individuals—because the outcomes are lifetime Pareto-indifferent—no one can complain if one outcome rather than the other obtains. An attractive version of prioritarianism should never rank one outcome over the other in such a case.

What work, exactly, is the continuity of personal identity over a human lifetime doing in this argument? The work is this. Each person in the population is a distinct locus of moral concern. This is the Rawlsian idea of the "separateness of persons." Ranking outcomes by looking to individuals' claims across them tries to give fuller content to this idea. It assigns each individual a claim in favor of one or another outcome. Most naturally, this should be a single claim, in the sense that for any pair of outcomes, x and y, an individual either has a claim in favor of x, a claim in favor of y, no claim either way, or an incomparable claim. The idea of the "separateness of persons," intuitively, is that moral deliberation should be sensitive both to the fact that (1) each person is an entity which is distinct from every other person and to the fact that (2) each person is a locus of interests that are *integrable*, in the sense that we can arrive at a single, all-things-considered ranking of outcomes or other items as better or worse *for him*. We *could* assign each person a multiplicity of claims between outcomes, each corresponding to a different temporal segment, or a different attribute; but to do so would be in serious tension with this idea of integrability. Wouldn't ranking outcomes by assigning each individual multiple claims, corresponding to different temporal segments or attributes, be to see each such *part* as a locus of moral concern, rather than each person?

In suggesting that this idea of integrability is a natural part of the claim-across-outcome view, I am in part appealing to intuitions. But for many readers, I hope, those intuitions will be no less powerful than the intuitions undergirding the claim-across-outcome view itself or, more fundamentally, the idea that morality should be sensitive to the separateness of persons. Each person is seen to be such that she has her own, unitary, perspective on how outcomes should be ranked; morality, in turn, is supposed to accommodate these different perspectives in an impartial manner.

Now, for the claim-across-outcome view to mesh with welfarism, an individual's (single) claim must be valenced in terms of her well-being. And because each individual person corresponds to a single human being, from human birth to human death, it seems natural to valence that claim in terms of the individual's lifetime well-being. Imagine, instead, that we valence her claim in terms of her sublifetime well-being during some stipulated segment. (For example, we say that each individual has a claim in favor of x over y if her sublifetime well-being during the first period is greater in x than y.). Or imagine that we valence her claim in terms of the level of some particular attribute. (For example, we say that each individual has a claim in favor of x over y if her health in period 2 is greater in x than y.) Wouldn't doing so be arbitrary? What would justify our choosing one rather than another temporal segment, or one rather than another attribute, as the "currency" for individual claims? Moreover, why should the direction and strength of an individual's moral claim be determined by the properties of one of her temporal parts, or by one of her attributes, to the exclusion of others?

In short, the claim-across-outcome view, plus the continuity of personal identity, suggest that an individual should have a unitary claim regarding any pair of outcomes, valenced in terms of her lifetime well-being. This implies that the ranking of outcomes should satisfy lifetime Pareto-indifference. A very similar line of argument shows why the ranking of outcomes should satisfy lifetime Pareto-superiority, lifetime Pigou–Dalton, and lifetime person-separability.

The argument, thus far, has focused on non-lifetime approaches that violate at least one of the key axioms of lifetime Pareto-indifference, lifetime Pareto-superiority, lifetime Pigou–Dalton, and lifetime person-separability, in terms of some account W which is seen to be an attractive account of lifetime well-being. What about a non-lifetime approach that *satisfies* all these axioms—for example, a non-lifetime approach which is extensionally equivalent to lifetime prioritarianism?

The two key premises I have been invoking (the claim-across-outcome view combined with the continuity of personal identity across a human lifetime) suggest that a non-lifetime approach provides a roundabout and unhelpful way to *think* about the moral ranking of outcomes, even if the approach does satisfy lifetime Pareto-indifference, Pareto-superiority, Pigou–Dalton, and person-separability.

If these two key premises are correct, then—in order to *justify* any such non-lifetime approach—we would need to appeal to the account *W*, which explains how facts about outcomes translate into lifetime well-being and thereby into moral claims. We would say: "In ranking any pair of outcomes, *x* and *y*, this non-lifetime approach appropriately balances the gains in lifetime well-being of the persons who are better off in *x*, and the losses in lifetime well-being of the persons who are worse off in *x*." But why not rank outcomes using a formula that more directly and immediately reflects this justification—namely, the lifetime formula, which sees the ranking of outcomes as being a direct function of changes in individuals' lifetime utilities?

Thus the basic case for lifetime prioritarianism. The line of argument I have presented is very much in accord with the work of Thomas Nagel, from whom I derive the idea of ranking outcomes as a function of individual claims. Nagel writes: "[T]he subject of an egalitarian principle is not the distribution of particular rewards to individuals at some time, but the prospective quality of their lives as a whole, from birth to death. . . ."[59] And he buttresses the lifetime perspective with reference to the possibility of compensation:

> By itself, the possibility of intrapersonal compensation neither supports nor undermines egalitarian theories. It implies only that *if* an egalitarian theory is accepted, it should apply only across lives rather than within them. It is a reason for taking individual human lives, rather than individual experiences, as the units over which any distributive principle should operate.[60]

More generally, lifetime framings of the Pareto principles and lifetime approaches to employing an SWF are the standard approaches in welfare economics.[61] Inequality metrics are often used in a sublifetime manner (for example, measuring the inequality of annual income); but a substantial body of work does attempt to

---

[59] Nagel (1995, p. 69).

[60] Nagel (1979, p. 120). See also ibid., p. 124, n. 16.

[61] In the case where outcomes are specified in terms of multiple attributes, economists understand the Pareto principle in terms of an individual's well-being (preference-satisfaction) as a function of the totality of her attributes, not on an attribute-by-attribute basis. See, e.g., Mas-Colell, Whinston, and Green (1995, p. 313). The social-welfare-function literature evaluates multi-attribute outcomes by applying a social welfare function to individuals' utilities, as determined by their attributes, rather than employing the vector of attributes as the input for the social welfare function. (By contrast, the small literature on multi-attribute equality, discussed in Chapter 2, *does* discuss the possibility of an attribute evaluation function that operates directly on attributes.)

In the case of multi-period outcomes, the Pareto principle is understood in terms of an individual's lifetime well-being, see, e.g., Acemoglu (2009, pp. 162–163); and a social welfare function is typically applied to vectors of individuals' lifetime utilities, not their sublifetime utilities, see, e.g., sources cited in Chapter 4, n. 13. For an influential defense of a whole-lifetime approach by a health economist, see Williams (1997).

estimate the inequality of lifetime income or other characteristics of whole human lifetimes.[62]

Finally, philosophers of distributive justice quite often adopt the view that its concern is how individuals fare across their entire lifetimes (whether individuals' lifetime attainments are measured in well-being or some other currency). To give two prominent examples: John Rawls argues that distributive justice requires a fair allocation of lifetime shares of primary goods, and Ronald Dworkin argues that it requires each person to receive a fair lifetime share of resources.[63]

IV. DOES PARFIT'S REDUCTIONIST ACCOUNT OF PERSONAL IDENTITY UNDERMINE LIFETIME PRIORITARIANISM?

In *Reasons and Persons*, Derek Parfit suggests that his account of personal identity undermines accounts of distributive justice that focus upon fair distribution between persons. In particular, he argues, a proper understanding of personal identity changes the "scope" of distributive justice, so that it now focuses on fair distribution between temporal segments of persons. At the same time, his account of personal identity reduces the "weight" of distributive justice; morality becomes less concerned with fair distribution and moves closer to utilitarianism.[64]

I have already described Parfit's account of personhood and personal identity and taken pains to explain that it is *consistent* with the premise that personal identity continues over a normal human lifetime. And Parfit admits as much. So why would the account change the scope and/or weight of distributive justice?

Parfit's arguments concerning distributive justice rest on the *deflationary* character of his account of personhood and personal identity. He characterizes his account as a "Reductionist" account—a term he uses with great frequency. Unlike the Cartesian ego/soul view, Parfit's account says that personhood, and personal identity, is reducible to psychological and physical states and connections. "We are not separately existing entities, apart from our brains and bodies, and various interrelated physical and mental events. Our existence just involves the existence of our brains and bodies, and the doing of our deeds, and the thinking of our thoughts, and

---

[62] See generally Adler (2007, p. 4).

[63] See Rawls (1999b, pp. 78–81); Dworkin (1981b, pp. 304–306). See also McKerlie (1989, p. 476), noting that most egalitarians adopt a "complete lives" view; Brock (2002, pp. 367–370); Daniels (1996, ch. 12).

[64] See Parfit (1987, pp. 329–347; 1986, pp. 837–843, 869–872). My analysis in this section will focus on these discussions, rather than Parfit's earlier treatment of the connection between personal identity and morality in his (1973). Scholarly reactions to Parfit's account of this connection include: Brink (1997); Holtug (2010); Jeske (1993); Korsgaard (1989); Schultz (1986); Shoemaker (1999a, 1999b, 2000, 2002); Wachsberg (1983); Zelenak (2009).

the occurrence of certain other physical and mental events."[65] There is no "deep further fact" of personhood and personal identity above and beyond these psychological and physical facts.

Parfit's discussion of the relation between "Reductionism" and distributive justice is dense and somewhat meandering. Rather than recapitulating his discussion and responding point by point, I will structure the analysis by considering, first, whether Parfit's account of personhood and personal identity argues for a shift from lifetime prioritarianism to *momentary* prioritarianism; second, whether it argues for a shift to a different kind of sublifetime prioritarianism; and, third, whether it argues for a shift to utilitarianism. I will argue that none of these three shifts is warranted.

A. Shifting from Persons to Momentary Time-Slices as the Units of Moral Concern?

One possibility is that Reductionism about personal identity might justify a revisionary version of the claim-across-outcome view: specifically, one that makes each human person at each moment, rather than each whole human person, the locus of moral concern and the holder of a claim for or against outcomes. This would lead us to a particular kind of sublifetime prioritarianism: namely, *momentary* sublifetime prioritarianism, where the arguments for the SWF are not lifetime utilities, but *momentary* utilities, measuring the momentary well-being of each person in the population at each moment. (Momentary sublifetime prioritarianism requires that outcomes be divided into a series of moments, rather than longer periods; what I earlier described as the "simple" sublifetime rule is then employed to rank these outcomes.)

Indeed, Parfit suggests that Reductionism may well have exactly this upshot. Reductionism may make it impossible for a person who is made worse off at one moment to be compensated by benefits at later moments, because any such compensation involves a "deep further fact" of personal identity denied by Reductionism. If so, the upshot will be momentary prioritarianism. Parfit writes:

> In becoming Reductionists, we cease to believe that personal identity involves the deep further fact. [A plausible] argument claims that what compensation presupposes is not personal identity on any view, but personal identity on the Non-Reductionist View. Compensation presupposes the deep further fact. Psychological continuity, in the absence of this fact, cannot make possible compensation over time.
>
> If this is not possible, what will our distributive principles tell us to do? They will roughly coincide with *Negative Utilitarianism*: the view which gives priority to the relief of suffering. Nagel talks of the *unit* over which a distributive principle operates. If this is the whole of a person's life, as is assumed by Rawls and many others, a Principle of

---

[65] Parfit (1987, p. 216).

Equality will tell us to try to help those people who are worst off. If the unit is the state of any person at a particular time, a Principle of Equality will tell us to try to make better, not the lives of the people who are worst off, but the worst states that people are in.[66]

In short, if "only the deep further fact [of personal identity that would be provided by a soul/Cartesian ego] makes possible compensation over different parts of a life," then absent such a fact "the units [for distributive justice] shrink to peoples' states at particular times."[67]

For short, I will refer to Parfit's claim that Reductionism renders compensation over time impossible as the "no-compensation" claim. In *Reasons and Persons*, Parfit tentatively defends the no-compensation claim and the suggestion that this claim, in turn, argues for momentary prioritarianism. In a subsequent set of comments, responding to critics of the book, he makes this argument more wholeheartedly.

> If there cannot be compensation over time, as my argument suggests, we should change the scope of distributive principles. According to one such principle, we should give some priority to helping the people who are worse off. On my argument, we should give such priority not to those who are worse off in their lives as a whole, but to those who are worse off at particular times.[68]

I suggested earlier that there is a conceptual link between compensation and lifetime well-being. Consider a case in which individual i is worse off in outcome x than y, with respect to some attribute or with respect to sublifetime well-being at some time. Individual i is *compensated* for this shortfall if his lifetime well-being in x is greater than or equal to that in y. A surplus in some other attribute(s), or in sublifetime well-being at some other time(s), is sufficient to counterbalance the shortfall.

Parfit's no-compensation claim, therefore, is that Reductionism has the following upshot: If Jim at moment t is worse off in outcome x than outcome y, then his lifetime well-being in x is necessarily not equal to (or greater than) his lifetime well-being in y, even if Jim at other moments (perhaps many other moments) has greater momentary well-being in x. The reader might initially wonder how this is even logically coherent. Imagine that Jim at moment t is worse off in x than y, and at moment t^* is worse off in y than x. If Reductionism renders compensation over time impossible, and thus means that Jim's lifetime well-being in x is not greater than or equal to his lifetime well-being in y, and that Jim's lifetime well-being in y is not greater than or equal to his lifetime well-being in x, aren't we left with a logical contradiction? The answer is no—once we allow for the possibility that the well-being ranking of

---

[66] Ibid., p. 344.

[67] Ibid., p. 346. The argument is generally discussed ibid., pp. 342–346; and in Parfit (1986, pp. 840–842, 869–872).

[68] Parfit (1986, p. 869).

life-histories might be an incomplete *quasiordering* rather than a complete ordering, and thus that two life-histories might be *incomparable* with respect to well-being.

In short, I interpret Parfit's no-compensation claim to be the following: By virtue of Reductionism, if there is some moment when individual i is worse off in outcome x than y, and some other moment when individual i is worse off in outcome y than x, then the life-histories $(x; i)$ and $(y; i)$ are incomparable. The no-compensation claim, if true, means that Reductionism injects massive incomparability into the ranking of life-histories. And massive incomparability in the well-being ranking of life-histories would, in turn, undermine lifetime prioritarianism.

I of course take the position that the ranking of life-histories is a quasiordering, and thus allow for *some* incomparability in ranking life-histories. But why on earth believe that the no-compensation claim is true? Parfit suggests that, if we are Non-Reductionists, we do not believe that a person can be compensated by benefits to some other person psychologically and physically linked to him. This suggestion involves a kind of atomism about the sources of well-being; but if the premise of atomism is granted, Parfit's suggestion is correct. He illustrates it by discussing a case in which a person's brain is divided in half and put into two bodies, yielding two persons, Righty and Lefty. Let us further suppose (which seems plausible) that, on a Non-Reductionist view, the original person will continue as Righty or Lefty, by virtue of some deep further fact above and beyond psychological and physical facts.

> Assume that we believe the Non-Reductionist View, and that we suppose that I shall be Righty. Before the division, I had more than my fair share of many resources, living for many years in luxury. After the division, I and Lefty will each get less than a fair share. This is claimed to be justified, in my case, because it will have the result that in my life as a whole I shall receive a fair share. My lesser share now was fully compensated in advance by my greater share before the division.
>
> Could we plausibly claim the same about Lefty? Does psychological continuity make possible compensation, even in the absence of personal identity? It is defensible to answer:
>
> No. Lefty never enjoyed a larger share. *He* did not enjoy these years of luxury. It is irrelevant that he can quasi-remember *your* enjoyment of this luxury. It is irrelevant that he is physically and psychologically continuous with someone who had more than his fair share, at a time when Lefty did not exist. It would now be unfair to give Lefty less than a fair share. In the absence of personal identity, psychological continuity cannot make compensation possible.
>
> Suppose next that we come to believe the Reductionist View. We had claimed, defensibly, that only the deep further fact makes compensation possible. We had claimed that, as the case of Lefty shows, physical and psychological continuity cannot by themselves make compensation possible. We now believe that there is no deep further fact, and that personal identity just consists in these two kinds of continuity. Since we could defensibly claim that only this further fact makes compensation possible, and there is no such fact, we can defensibly conclude that there cannot be compensation over time. We can claim

that a benefit at one time cannot provide compensation for a burden at another time, even when both come within the same life. There can only be simultaneous compensation, as when the pain of exposing my face to a freezing wind is fully compensated by the sight of the sublime view from the mountain I have climbed.[69]

But this argument for the no-compensation claim involves a huge non sequitur. What it says is the following. (1) Given Non-Reductionism and atomism: If Jim's attributes in outcomes x and y at moment t are such that he is worse off in outcome x than y at that moment, then the fact that some person *other than Jim* is better off in outcome x than y at other moments does not suffice to make *Jim's* lifetime well-being in x greater than or equal to y, even if this other person happens to have psychological or physical links to Jim. *Therefore*: (2) Given *Reductionism* and atomism: If Jim's attributes in outcomes x and y at moment t are such that he is worse off in outcome x than y at that moment, then the fact that *Jim* is better off in x than y at other moments does not suffice to make Jim's lifetime well-being in x greater than or equal to y, since Jim remains the same person at different moments only in virtue of psychological and/or physical links.

The leap from proposition (1), which is true, to proposition (2), the no-compensation claim, is a massive non sequitur, because what it ignores is the fact that *our understanding of the determinants of lifetime well-being would shift along with our understanding of personal identity.* If we are Non-Reductionists, a given person (Jim) consists in a series of momentary time-slices of a human being, linked by a deep further fact of personal identity. Given this view (plus atomism), Jim's lifetime well-being in some outcome is a function of the momentary attributes of the set of human time-slices that exist at different moments but are linked by this deep further fact, and that, collectively, we refer to as "Jim." If we are Reductionists, a given person consists in a series of momentary time-slices, knitted by various physical and/or psychological connections. Our understanding of the sources of lifetime well-being shifts accordingly. Given *this* view (plus atomism), Jim's lifetime well-being in some outcome is a function of the momentary attributes of a set of human time-slices that exist at different moments, *and that have the right sort of physical and/or psychological links*, and that, collectively, we refer to as "Jim."

It is a truism that the lifetime well-being of a particular person is largely determined by the attributes, at different times, of *that particular person*. (Atomism replaces "largely" with "exclusively.") Non-Reductionists and Reductionists disagree, however, about the criteria of individuation. They disagree about when human beings at various times are parts of *the very same person*. Parfit's argument for the no-compensation claim seems to imagine that the Reductionist, in crafting an understanding of a person's lifetime well-being, will be a sort of non-Reductionist *manqué*. The Reductionist will try to use non-Reductionist individuation criteria in picking out the temporal attributes that are relevant to the lifetime well-being of any particular person and (because there are no such criteria) will conclude that compensation over time is impossible. But it is absurd to suppose that the Reductionist will think about lifetime well-being this way. Rather, she will say: temporal slices of a human person at various times are parts of the same particular person if they bear stipulated physical and/or psychological links to each other (not the deep further fact); and it is the attributes of the thus-linked time-slices that determine the lifetime well-being of that particular person.

In short, the no-compensation claim is false, and thus *this* argument for momentary prioritarianism is a non-starter. Perhaps a better argument is available? One of the main themes in *Reasons and Persons* is that Reductionism about personal identity undercuts the normative relevance of personal identity as such.

> Personal identity is not what matters. What fundamentally matters is Relation R [i.e., psychological connectedness and/or psychological continuity], with any cause. This relation is what matters even when, as in a case where one person is R-related to two other people, Relation R does not provide personal identity.[70]

Consider again the case in which someone's (Don's) brain is divided into two halves, Lefty and Righty. Because personal identity, on Parfit's account, requires *non-branching* psychological continuity (so as to avoid intransitive identity),[71] that account says that Don ceases to exist when his brain is divided; neither Lefty nor Righty are the same person as Don. But Don, anticipating the brain division, would rationally care almost as much about Lefty and Righty as he would about *himself* in the future. Don is rationally concerned about the attributes of human beings with whom he has strong psychological links, *even if Don is not the same person as those human beings*. Thus it is Don's psychological links to other human beings, not whether he is the very same person as them, that should determine his rational preferences and choices.

This observation, in turn, might be seen to undercut my argument against intrapersonal discounting—with unwelcome upshots for lifetime prioritarianism. I suggested earlier that, on an extended-preference view, and *a fortiori* on other accounts of lifetime well-being, the lifetime utility function should not adopt the discounted-additive form. But assume that Parfit's account of personal identity is true. There are N members of the population, who are normal human beings, without division. Steve is one of the normal human beings, with attributes at various times, from his birth until his death. Steve at age 8 is the very same person as Steve at 90 because the two humans are psychologically continuous, with the right sort of cause. Now consider Steve at a given time (say, when he is 50), functioning as "spectator." I have

---

[70] Ibid., p. 217.

[71] If Don were identical with Righty, and Don were identical with Lefty, then the presumptive fact that Righty and Lefty are not identical would imply a failure of transitivity of the identity relation.

argued that spectators must be temporally neutral. But, if "personal identity is not what matters," wouldn't Steve be temporally biased? Although Steve is psychologically *continuous* with himself at all times, Steve at age 50 has stronger psychological *connections* with more proximate time-slices of himself. He shares more memories, desires, character traits, etc. with these time-slices. So wouldn't Steve at 50, functioning as spectator, and ranking his own life-histories, care more about his attributes at age 45 or age 55, as opposed to his attributes at ages 8 or 80? Wouldn't a given spectator's ranking of his own life-histories incorporate a discount factor for degrees of psychological connectedness? And if this is true for a spectator's ranking of his own life-histories, would this not also be true for his ranking of other life-histories? Moreover, as I explained earlier, temporal bias on the part of spectators could well induce large-scale incomparability in the ranking of life-histories.

Call this the "temporal bias" argument for momentary prioritarianism: Reductionism about personal identity engenders temporal bias on the part of spectators, which induces large-scale incomparability in the ranking of life-histories, undermining lifetime prioritarianism.[72]

This argument, too, is unpersuasive. As I explained earlier, the extended-preference account does not say that temporal neutrality is rationally required in all contexts. In ordinary life, it may well be rationally permissible for individuals to have various sorts of temporal biases—and a deflationary view of personal identity may well reinforce the case for the permissibility of some such biases. My claim is only that preferences in the particular idealized choice situation that I constructed in Chapter 3—where spectators with full information and rationality rank outcomes and hypothetical choices (lotteries over outcomes) under conditions of self-interest and *i*-interest—must be temporally neutral. This choice situation has a particular, moral function: it is the cornerstone of an account of human welfare meant to allow well-being comparisons for purposes of moral decision-making. I do not see why Reductionism about personal identity would make it impossible or irrational for spectators to be temporally neutral, even in the special context of this idealized choice situation. Here is an analogy: even though each person is distinct from every other (on any account of personal identity, Reductionist or not), it is presumably possible for persons to be impartial between their own interests and those of others; and a normative account of some sort might identify choice scenarios, actual or hypothetical, in which such impartiality is required. Similarly, even though each person at a given time is more closely psychologically connected to some of his past and future time-slices than others, it is presumably possible for persons to be impartial between all of their time-slices; and a normative account of some sort might

---

[72] The temporal bias argument is not advanced by Parfit himself, but is rather a possible defense of momentary prioritarianism based upon his view of personal identity.

identify choice scenarios, actual or hypothetical, in which such temporal neutrality is required.

There is a third potential argument for momentary prioritarianism, which is suggested by some of Parfit's remarks.[73] Call this the "unity" argument. Ceteris paribus, we should specify the claim-across-outcome view so that the holders of claims are *internally unified*. In defending the view that L is the proper locus of moral concern (where L could be a person, a time-slice of a person, or something else), we appeal both to the fact that each L is distinct from every other, *and* to the fact that each L's concerns are *integrable*—that each L is a *single* entity, with a single set of interests and concerns. Thus, considerations of internal unity are an important factor in adjudicating between different candidates for L.

Momentary time-slices of persons are much more tightly unified, psychologically and physically, than whole persons. In a normal human life, there *is* an overlapping chain of direct psychological connections between any two time-slices; but, still, a human person at one time may have a different (perhaps quite different) set of beliefs, preferences, affects, and so forth than the very same human person at another time. By contrast, because momentary time-slices do not endure over time, a time-slice's mental and physical attributes do not change.

While the "unity" argument does indeed provide a ceteris paribus argument in favor of momentary prioritarianism, there are decisive countervailing factors against seeing momentary time-slices rather than whole persons as the loci of moral concern and the holders of claims. A key basis for crafting moral norms in light of the separateness of *persons* is that the resultant norms can be seen as norms *for* the community of persons: the norms can now be justified *to* each person, who can be expected to act in compliance with the norms. No such basis can be given for taking L to be momentary time-slices of persons. Time-slices are not capable of temporally extended normative deliberation—it is not possible to justify a norm *to* a time-slice—nor are they capable of acting (or, at least, performing more than a single action). Moreover—and perhaps more dramatically—important aspects of human well-being are ascribable only to whole human persons, or temporally extended segments of persons, rather than to momentary time-slices. This includes items such as accomplishment, relationships with friends or family, civic life, or the pursuit of knowledge.[74] Momentary prioritarianism would mean that these

---

[73] His discussion in Parfit (1987, pp. 332–334, 336–339) might be understood to suggest that Reductionism changes the scope of distributive justice because the unity between different parts of a human life becomes a matter of degree, with shorter time-slices being more unified—rather than unity being an all-or-nothing matter grounded in a "deep further fact" of identity.

[74] For exactly these reasons, it is also hard to see what would justify a moral view that sees momentary time-slices of human beings as the units of moral concern, rather than a moral view that sees momentary time-slices of human beings *and* non-human animals as the units of moral concern. While there are major normative differences between human *persons* and non-human animals, these

aspects of human well-being do not figure in moral reasoning at all. As David
Brink observes:

> It is difficult to regard person-slices as agents. . . . [To begin] it is not clear that person-
> slices do have interests. Whether the entity me-now can have interests depends upon
> which theory of welfare is correct.
>
> If pleasure is a simple, qualitative sensation or mental state and a hedonistic theory of
> welfare is correct, then perhaps me-now has interests. Person-slices may contain qualita-
> tive mental states, such as pleasure. . . .
>
> [However] hedonism seems an implausible theory of welfare, because a large part of
> a person's good seems to consist in his *being a certain sort of person*—that is, a person with
> a certain sort of character who exercises certain capacities and develops certain kinds of
> personal and social relationships. . . . [T]his implies that it is temporally extended beings
> . . . rather than person-slices who are the bearers of interests.
>
> Not only is it doubtful whether person-slices have interests, it is also questionable
> whether having interests is sufficient for having reasons for action. A person-slice will not
> persist long enough to perform actions or receive the benefits of actions. If so, then person-
> slices cannot have reasons for action even if it is possible for them to have interests.[75]

A final point is that momentary prioritarianism is a poor candidate to be a moral
choice-evaluation procedure, because it demands a high degree of specificity in the
temporal description of outcomes. Consequentialist choice-evaluation procedures
control decision costs by permitting outcomes to be described in simplified ways.
One way to do so is to characterize outcomes as having a relatively small number of
periods. But momentary prioritarianism demands that outcomes be divided into
moments, each with its own array of individual attributes.

B. Shifting from Persons to Person-Stages as the Units of Moral Concern?

Consider the normal human being, Jim, at ages 5, 7, 15, 18, 35, 40, 75, and 85. As a
matter of common sense, Jim at each age is the very same person as Jim at every
other age—and this is indeed what Parfit's account says, too, because all the ages are

---

differences evaporate when we compare time-slices of humans with time-slices of non-human
animals.

The proponent of momentary prioritarianism could bite this particular bullet, arguing for an *inclusive* momentary prioritarianism, which takes the momentary utilities of animals as well as human
beings as the inputs for the prioritarian formula. However, because momentary prioritarianism in
either its inclusive or person-centered form (1) is not justifiable to a community of entities that can
engage in action and normative reasoning, and (2) ends up giving zero moral weight to long-term
aspects of human well-being, I believe that either sort of momentary prioritarianism is on balance
less attractive than lifetime person-centered prioritarianism.

[75] Brink (1997, p. 112).

psychologically *continuous* with each other. But, colloquially, we might say that the first two ages are parts of Jim's childhood "self"; the second two, parts of his adolescent "self"; the third two, parts of his middle-aged "self"; the last two, parts of his older "self." We might sharpen this analysis by observing that there are tight psychological connections between the first two ages in this series, the second two, the third two, and the fourth two, but not between any other two ages (e.g., between Jim at 7 and 35, Jim at 75 and 35, etc.). And we might make "selves," defined in terms of such connections, rather than persons, the units of moral concerns.

Because the term "self" is also used to refer to whole persons, I will instead refer to a psychologically unified, temporally extended portion of a person's life as a "person-stage." Parfit, himself, does not clearly argue in favor of making person-stages a morally or normatively relevant concept—although some of his remarks seem to point in this direction.[76] Other scholars have claimed more decisively that a Parfit-style account of personal identity warrants a reorientation of morality or other norms around person-stages.[77] It is therefore worth considering this kind of revision of the claim-across-outcome approach—one that would argue for a sublifetime prioritarianism in which the arguments for the SWF are the utilities of person-stages.

At the outset, I should reiterate that the question on the table in this chapter (and book) is how to specify welfarism for the case of a population of normal human beings. Consider, by contrast, the case of Sue, who at age 45 suffers a traumatic episode, causing her to forget everything that happened before, and altering her personality quite radically. Parfit's account of personal identity says that Sue up to age 45 and Sue after 45 are two different persons, corresponding to different non-overlapping segments of the life of the human being, Sue. This is, indeed, fairly plausible—and it is therefore also plausible to see Sue-before-45 and Sue-after-45 as each holding a claim across outcomes, rather than assigning a single claim to Sue.

But how the prioritarian should handle Sue is not a topic I will further pursue. The question on the table is *not* whether a whole person might correspond to some fraction of a whole human life, if the human suffers an abnormal, radical, psychological rupture. The question, rather, is whether we should endorse person-stage prioritarianism, understanding that the "stages" are merely fractions of *persons*. Each time-slice of a normal human life is sufficiently directly connected to adjacent time-slices that (as a matter of common sense and, in particular, on Parfit's account) each human remains one and the same person from birth to death. In this case, a person-stage corresponds to a fraction of a human being's life *and thus a fraction of that person's life.*

---

[76] For example: "If we are Reductionists, we regard the rough subdivisions within lives as, in certain ways, like the divisions between lives." "A Reductionist is more likely to regard [a] child's relation to his adult self as being like a relation to a different person. He is thus more likely to claim that it is unfair to impose burdens on this child merely to benefit his adult self." Parfit (1987, pp. 333–334, 335). On the distinction between temporally extended person-stages (Brink terms them "segments") and momentary time-slices, see Brink (1997).

[77] See Posner (1995, ch. 4); Shoemaker (1999a, 1999b, 2000, 2002).

With this clarification behind us, how exactly should person-stage prioritarianism be fleshed out? One possibility is a *consecutive* approach. This would divide a person's life into a series of consecutive, non-overlapping person-stages. If an outcome set has T periods, a given human person, i, would have $s_i(x)$ stages in outcome x: one stage in periods 1 through $(i_2(x) - 1)$, where "$i_2(x)$" denotes the first period of stage 2 in outcome x; a second stage in periods $i_2(x)$ through period $(i_3(x) - 1)$; a third stage in periods $i_3(x)$ through $(i_4(x) - 1)$; ...; and a final stage in period $i_{s_i(x)}(x)$ through period T.

A serious difficulty with this approach is characterizing the degree of attenuation of psychological connectedness that yields a new stage without yielding a new person. Individual i is one stage during periods 1 through $(i_2(x) -1)$. Something happens, psychologically, at that point to produce a new stage, who comes into being in period $i_2(x)$ and exists through period $(i_3(x) - 1)$. But whatever happens prior to the beginning of period $i_2(x)$ is not so dramatic to sever personhood; individual i remains one and the same person from the first through the last period. Is there really some intermediate range of change in memories, desires, character traits, and so forth, that births a stage without birthing a person? As far as I'm aware, no proponent of the stage approach has explained what such a moderately transformative psychological alteration would consist in.

A different approach avoids this difficulty. (Call this "overlapping stage" prioritarianism.) On Parfit's account, of course, a certain degree of connectedness is necessary (via an overlapping chain of connections) to create continuity and, thus, personal identity. Parfit, again, terms this degree of connectedness "strong connectedness." So consider using this concept to define a person-stage, as follows: For any person i, in a given outcome x: if there is some group of consecutive periods, such that i in each period in the group is strongly connected with i in every other period, and this group is "maximal" (adding an additional period at either end would mean that i in each period is not strongly connected with i in every other period), then this group of periods is one of i's stages in x.

Person-stages, in this sense, can overlap. For example, Jim can have one stage that runs from Jim at birth through Jim at age 10, a second stage that runs from Jim at age 3 through Jim at age 15, a third stage that runs from Jim at age 6 through Jim at age 15; and so forth. In this case, Jim at age 7 would be part of three stages.

Overlapping-stage prioritarianism uses a set **V** of sublifetime utility functions, where each $v(.)$ maps an outcome x onto a grand vector, including an entry for the sublifetime utility of each stage of each person in x. Outcomes are then ranked as a function of these vectors.

The "unity" argument I presented earlier can be used to make a case for overlapping-stage prioritarianism, as against lifetime prioritarianism: stages are more tightly internally unified than persons.[78] Moreover, overlapping-stage prioritarianism does

---

[78] By contrast, the no-compensation and temporal bias arguments for momentary prioritarianism—if these were valid—would undercut overlapping-stage prioritarianism as much as they would lifetime prioritarianism.

not suffer the critical deficits of momentary prioritarianism. Stages, by contrast with momentary time-slices, *are* full-blown moral agents and *can* realize the full range of aspects of human well-being (long-term goal fulfillment, relationships, etc.).

However, in positing that a single human being at a single point in time can "house" a plurality of person-stages, overlapping-stage prioritarianism involves a kind of "four-dimensionalism." These entities are "spread out" over space-time, rather than being wholly present at any one time. I lack space to discuss four-dimensionalism here,[79] but it should be noted that four-dimensionalist accounts of *persons* have been subjected to serious objection, and parallel objections might well be leveled against overlapping person-stages.

Another objection is that overlapping-stage prioritarianism places a weird moral premium on events that occur to less psychologically unified persons. Imagine that the person, Oscar, has a highly unified mental life. Oscar has but a single stage. Now consider Sarah, who has 5 person-stages, all overlapping at Sarah aged 30. If Sarah at 30 suffers a painful episode, this affects the utility of 5 distinct person-stages; if Oscar does, this affects the utility of only 1 person-stage. So, ceteris paribus, there is greater moral reason to stop Sarah's pain than Oscar's. This is highly counterintuitive.

C. Reducing the Moral Weight of Fairness?

Parfit suggests that Reductionism about personal identity will not only reorient distributive justice around distribution between temporal segments of persons (momentary time-slices or perhaps stages) rather than distribution between whole persons. It will also reduce the relative *weight* of considerations of distributive justice, as compared to overall well-being.

> [W]hatever their scope, we should give less weight to distributive principles. These principles are often held to be founded on the separateness, or non-identity, of different persons. This fact is less deep on the Reductionist View, since identity is less deep. It does not involve the further fact in which we are inclined to believe. Since the fact on which they are founded is seen to be less deep, it is more plausible to give less weight to distributive principles. If we cease to believe that persons are separately existing entities, and come to believe that the unity of a life involves no more than the various relations between the experiences in this life, it becomes more plausible to be more concerned about the quality of experiences, and less concerned about whose experiences they are. This gives some support to the Utilitarian View, making it more plausible than it would have been if the Non-Reductionist View had been true.[80]

Call this the deflation argument. The argument, if valid, cuts against lifetime prioritarianism in favor of utilitarianism. In coming to see that personhood and

---

[79] See, e.g., Olson (2007, ch. 5).
[80] Parfit (1987, p. 346).

personal identity are reducible to psychological and physical facts, we feel less pressure to structure normative deliberation so as to respect the separateness of persons. And because a similar deflation could be accomplished for any other candidate locus of moral concern (such as a momentary time-slice or a person-stage), we end up with utilitarianism rather than some non-lifetime version of prioritarianism.

What the deflation argument overlooks is that *all* moral entities and properties may well supervene on psychological and physical facts—indeed, on physical facts, since psychological facts themselves likely supervene on physical facts. Personhood is not unusual in this regard. Consider two possible worlds which are identical in their physical facts. If psychological facts do indeed supervene on physical facts, then—on Parfit's account of personhood and personal identity—the two worlds are identical qua facts about persons (how many persons there are, how long they endure, etc.). There is no "deep further fact" which would yield a different population of persons in one world than another. *But the same is true* about every other morally relevant item: for example, death, injury, pain, or well-being.[81] The two worlds are also identical in terms of the lifespan of human beings, the ages at which they die, the injuries they suffer, how much pain they incur, and what their well-being is. Does the absence of a "deep further fact" about death, injury, pain, or well-being mean that these, too, are not morally important concepts? If the realization that personhood supervenes on physical and psychological facts undercuts the moral force of the separateness of persons and of distributive principles, why wouldn't the realization that human pain and well-being also supervene on such facts undercut the force of overall well-being and shift us toward amoralism—the conclusion that nothing has moral significance?

To put the point slightly differently, Parfit conflates the *metaphysical* deflation of the concept of personhood (showing how it can be analyzed in terms of metaphysically more basic facts, in particular physical and psychological facts) with the *normative* deflation of the concept of personhood. There is no logical reason to infer the second sort of deflation from the first; and once we see that all moral concepts are subject to a similar metaphysical deflation, we should strongly resist the inference.

V. INTUITIONS ABOUT EQUALIZATION OF ATTRIBUTES OR SUBLIFETIME WELL-BEING

I have argued that lifetime prioritarianism has a firm foundation in a claim-across-outcome conception of the moral ranking of outcomes, and (pace Parfit) is not undercut by a sophisticated understanding of personal identity. But "reflective equilibrium" involves bringing into coherence one's theoretical views with intuitions about concrete cases. It is therefore possible that such intuitions might prompt us to abandon lifetime prioritarianism, notwithstanding its theoretical warrant.

---

[81] See Schultz (1986, pp. 730–731); see also Johnston (2003).

Indeed, various scholars have pointed to intuitions regarding the equalization of attributes or sublifetime well-being, and have argued that such intuitions cut against whole-lifetime approaches to distributive justice. Here, I divide the intuitions into three categories and consider whether they indeed undermine lifetime prioritarianism. I consider, first, intuitions regarding the equalization of attributes or sublifetime well-being within the life of a single person; second, intuitions regarding the *synchronization* of attribute levels or sublifetime well-being between persons; and, third, intuitions regarding the equalization of attributes or sublifetime well-being between different persons.

A general point to keep in mind is that an individual's lifetime well-being may be a quite complicated function of her attributes during various time periods. Nothing requires that the lifetime utility function be atomistic or (if atomistic) that it fulfill one or another separability or additivity condition with respect to attributes or sublifetime well-being. I will use this insight to help respond to the various challenges to lifetime prioritarianism now to be described.

Attribute-based prioritarianism not only requires some methodology for assigning numerical levels to attributes. To be at all plausible, higher numerical levels of the attributes must be "better." More precisely, my examples will generally assume that attributes are measured so that both sublifetime and lifetime well-being are increasing in the attributes.[82]

A. Intrapersonal Equalization

In a number of works, Dennis McKerlie has claimed that lifetime prioritarianism is too simplified. He has argued, repeatedly, that some degree of priority should be given to individuals at lower levels of sublifetime well-being. McKerlie has also suggested that some degree of priority be given to individuals at lower attribute levels. McKerlie does not express these claims using mathematical formalism, but much of his discussion—translated into the language of SWFs—seems to suggest that a prioritarian SWF should be applied in an attribute-based or sublifetime manner, or in a manner that hybridizes these approaches with lifetime prioritarianism.[83]

McKerlie eschews reliance on claims about personal identity and instead appeals to various intuitions: not only intuitions concerning *interpersonal* equalization, to be discussed below, but also intuitions concerning *intrapersonal* equalization, which are the focus of this subsection.

---

[82] So as to facilitate a simple comparison of attribute-based with sublifetime and lifetime prioritarianism, the examples also generally assume that outcomes do not include a description of background facts (which, where described, are ignored by the first method but not the latter two).

[83] McKerlie has written numerous works challenging a whole-lifetime account of distributive justice, in particular his (1989, 1992, 1997, 2001a, 2001b, 2007). His endorsement of *prioritarianism* as the basis for a non-lifetime view emerges in the four most recent of these works.

For the sake of clarity, let us distinguish between intrapersonal equalization of *attributes* and intrapersonal equalization of *sublifetime well-being*. Intrapersonal equalization of *attributes* occurs when an individual is at higher level of some attribute in period t than period t^*, and we reduce his attribute level in period t and increase it in period t^* by the same amount, still leaving him at an attribute level in t^* which is lower than or equal to that in t. Intrapersonal equalization of *sublifetime well-being* occurs when an individual is at a higher level of sublifetime well-being in period t than period t^*, and we reduce his sublifetime well-being level in period t and increase it in period t^* by the same amount, still leaving him at a level of sublifetime well-being in t^* which is lower than or equal to his level in t. In other words, intrapersonal equalization of attributes is an intrapersonal, intertemporal Pigou–Dalton transfer in some attribute; intrapersonal equalization of sublifetime well-being is an intrapersonal, intertemporal Pigou–Dalton transfer in sublifetime well-being. (Remember that an unequal distribution of any item—be it the distribution of some attribute across periods in an individual's life, the distribution of sublifetime well-being across periods, or any other distribution—can be converted into a perfectly equal distribution by a series of Pigou–Dalton transfers.[84] We might, most narrowly, define cases of intra- or interpersonal attribute or sublifetime-well-being equalization as a move from inequality to perfect equality; but a more general definition of such cases employs the Pigou–Dalton principle in terms of attributes or sublifetime well-being, as I have just done.)

In his various examples of intrapersonal equalization, McKerlie suggests that both sorts of intrapersonal equalization are intuitively desirable. For example, he approves the intrapersonal equalization of pain, a kind of hedonic attribute.

> [T]he idea behind using the priority view in interpersonal cases also applies to intrapersonal cases. The basic claim is that a benefit is especially important if it is received by someone who is badly off. Nothing limits the application of this idea to cases involving different people. We should be able to say, thinking about a single person, that a benefit will be more important if it is experienced when that person is badly off. A person might think that it is more important to relieve pain when he is suffering intensely than to bring about a larger reduction in milder suffering at some other point in his life.[85]

Discussing the treatment of the aged, McKerlie argues that a life-history in which the individual has a high sublifetime well-being level when young, and a low sublifetime well-being level when older, is worse than a life-history in which there is the same total amount of sublifetime well-being but it is distributed more equally.[86]

---

[84] See Chapter 2, pp. 114–115.

[85] McKerlie (2001a, pp. 283–284).

[86] See McKerlie (2001b, p. 165). The proposition that prioritarianism supports intrapersonal equalization is endorsed throughout McKerlie's work, but see in particular his (2001a, pp. 281–288; 2001b, pp. 168–174; 2007, pp. 167–72). For the proposition that prioritarianism is concerned with

Attribute-based or sublifetime prioritarianism can indeed reach a result consistent with intuitions concerning intrapersonal equalization, at least to some extent, as shown in the following tables.

In all these tables, outcomes are characterized with respect to two attributes. Sublifetime utility, unique up to a positive ratio transformation, is a positive constant r times the multiplicative product of attribute levels during the period. The attribute-based approach sums the square root of attribute levels; the sublifetime approach is the simple version, and sums the square root of sublifetime utilities. In all the tables, only the levels of the a attribute are changed by the move from outcome x to y.

Table 6.6 Intrapersonal Attribute Equalization and Non-lifetime Approaches: One Example

	Outcome x		Outcome y	
	Period 1	Period 2	Period 1	Period 2
Joe				
Attribute a	50	100	75	75
Attribute b	16	16	16	16
Sublifetime utility	800r	1600r	1200r	1200r
Attribute score:	25.07		25.32	
Sublifetime score:	68.28$\sqrt{r}$		69.28$\sqrt{r}$	

In Table 6.6, outcome y equalizes the a attribute. Because the b attribute is at the same level in both periods, this is a case in which equalization in the a attribute also equalizes sublifetime utility. Both the attribute-based and sublifetime approaches prefer outcome y.

Table 6.7 Intrapersonal Attribute Equalization and Non-lifetime Approaches: A Second Example

	Outcome x		Outcome y	
	Period 1	Period 2	Period 1	Period 2
Joe				
Attribute a	50	100	75	75
Attribute b	20	40	20	40
Sublifetime utility	1000r	4000r	1500r	3000r
Attribute score:	27.87		28.12	
Sublifetime score:	94.87$\sqrt{r}$		93.50$\sqrt{r}$	

the level of individual attributes ("dimensions of lives") taken separately, not merely sublifetime well-being, see in particular McKerlie (2001a, pp. 267–273). See also Temkin (2009), arguing (from a non-prioritarian perspective) for the relevance of intrapersonal distribution.

In Table 6.7, outcome *y* equalizes the *a* attribute. However, because attribute *b* is at a different level in period 2 than 1, outcome *y* does not equalize sublifetime utility (i.e., is not a Pigou–Dalton transfer in sublifetime utility) and the sublifetime approach prefers outcome *x*. Thus this is a case in which the sublifetime approach fails to prefer attribute equalization.

Table 6.8 Intrapersonal Sublifetime Well-Being Equalization and Non-lifetime Approaches

	Outcome *x*		Outcome *y*	
	Period 1	Period 2	Period 1	Period 2
Joe				
Attribute *a*	50	200	75	150
Attribute *b*	40	20	40	20
Sublifetime utility	2000r	4000r	3000r	3000r
Attribute score:	32.01		31.70	
Sublifetime score:	$107.97\sqrt{r}$		$109.54\sqrt{r}$	

In Table 6.8, outcome *y* equalizes sublifetime utility. However, because attribute *b* is at a different level in period 2 than 1, outcome *y* does not equalize the *a* attribute (i.e., is not a Pigou–Dalton transfer in the *a* attribute) and the attribute-based approach prefers outcome *x*. This is a case in which the attribute-based approach fails to prefer equalization of sublifetime utility.

However, such cases can also be handled by combining lifetime prioritarianism with an appropriately nuanced understanding of the structure of the lifetime utility function. Indeed, the lifetime utility function need not be particularly complicated to favor intrapersonal equalization. As already explained, the assumption that each lifetime utility function $u(.)$ in **U** is atomistic and additive in sublifetime utility— that it takes the form $u(x;i) = \sum_{t=1}^{T} v(\mathbf{a}_{i,t}(x), \mathbf{a}_{imp,t}(x))$—is a kind of heuristic, which helps to simplify implementation of the SWF framework. As I will now show, even if $u(.)$ adopts this fairly simple form—let alone a more complicated one—intrapersonal equalization of attributes or sublifetime well-being may well be favored by the lifetime prioritarian.[87]

---

[87] Although, as already stressed, the sublifetime utility values used in the decomposition of lifetime utility may, in principle, be different from those that function as the input for the sublifetime prioritarian SWF, my discussion in this section will generally assume that the very same values play both roles. If this is not the case, then there will of course be no particular connection between the cases in which sublifetime prioritarianism prefers attribute or sublifetime-well-being equalization, and the cases in which lifetime prioritarianism does so.

Let us discuss, first, intrapersonal equalization of *attributes*. Consider, to begin, life-histories that are characterized solely in terms of individual consumption. In this very simple case, $u(x; i) = \sum_{t=1}^{T} v(c_{i,t}(x))$, with $c_{i,t}(x)$ individual i's consumption during period t. *If* sublifetime utility is a linear function of consumption, then the lifetime prioritarian will have no preference for equalizing an individual's consumption. But sublifetime utility is presumably *not* a linear function of consumption. Economists typically make the very plausible assumption that consumption has diminishing marginal utility: that a given increment of consumption makes a smaller contribution to well-being when the consumer who realizes that increment is at a higher consumption level than when she is at a lower consumption level.

In the multi-period context, diminishing marginal utility of consumption means that sublifetime utility is a *concave transformation* of individual consumption, rather than a linear function. In other words, the sublifetime utility function $v(.)$ has the form, $v(c_{i,t}(x)) = f(c_{i,t}(x))$, where $f(.)$ is a strictly concave and strictly increasing function, e.g., the logarithm to the base 10 (or any base greater than 1) of consumption. And that, in turn, means that the lifetime prioritarian using a lifetime utility function of the form $u(x;i) = \sum_{t=1}^{T} v(c_{i,t}(x))$ will prefer to equalize an individual's consumption. For example, if individual i receives the consumption sequence 10, 20, 30, 40 in outcome x and the equalized sequence 25, 25, 25, 25 in outcome y, the lifetime utility function with the sort of $v(.)$ function just described will prefer y to x. For example, $\log_{10}(10) + \log_{10}(20) + \log_{10}(30) + \log_{10}(40) < 4 \times \log_{10}(25)$.[88]

As discussed earlier, this idea generalizes to attributes other than consumption and to outcomes that are characterized in terms of multiple individual attributes. Where the lifetime utility function has the form under discussion— $\sum_{t=1}^{T} v(\mathbf{a}_{i,t}(x), \mathbf{a}_{imp,t}(x))$—the sublifetime utility function $v(.)$ might well be non-additive in any given metric of individual attributes.[89] And this in turn shows why the lifetime prioritarian might favor attribute equalization, as the following tables illustrate. To be clear, my claim is not that a sublifetime utility function which is

---

[88] More generally, consider any case in which the sequence of individual i's consumption amounts in y is an intrapersonal, intertemporal Pigou–Dalton transfer relative to the sequence in x. That is: individual i's consumption in x during period t^* is lower than during period t; her consumption in y during period t^* is greater than her consumption in x during period t^* by some amount Δc; her consumption in y during period t is less than her consumption in x during period t by exactly that amount Δc; her consumption in y during period t^* is less than or equal to her consumption in y during period t; and for all periods other than t and t^*, her consumption in x is the same as in y. If so, where the lifetime utility function sums $v(.)$ values, and $v(.)$ is any strictly concave and strictly increasing function of consumption, $u(y; i)$ is necessarily greater than $u(x; i)$. (Indeed, in principle, this is true even if $v(.)$ is strictly concave but not increasing—but economists, at least, would find it very odd to think that sublifetime utility is not strictly increasing in consumption.)

[89] In the simpler case where background facts are not included in the description of outcomes, and there are M attributes, $v(.)$ might take the form: $v(\mathbf{a}_{i,t}(x)) = d_1 a^1_{i,t}(x) + \ldots + d_M a^M_{i,t}(x)$, plus perhaps a constant, where $a^m_{i,t}(x)$ is individual i's level of attribute m during period t, as measured by some attribute metric. If so, $v(.)$ is additive in the attribute metrics $a^1, \ldots, a^M$.

non-additive in a given attribute metric will *necessarily* favor attribute equalization. Rather, the claim is that non-additivity *can* favor attribute equalization and, in particular, that some plausible non-additive forms (such as sublifetime utility functions involving a concave transformation of attribute levels) can.

Table 6.9 Intrapersonal Equalization and Lifetime Prioritarianism: One Example

	Outcome x			Outcome y		
	Period 1	Period 2	Lifetime utility	Period 1	Period 2	Lifetime utility
Joe						
Attribute *a*	50	100		75	75	
Attribute *b*	16	16		16	16	
Sublifetime utility	66r	116r	182r	91r	91r	182r

In Table 6.9, sublifetime and lifetime utility are unique up to a positive ratio transformation; sublifetime utility is some positive constant r times the sum of the two attribute levels. Outcome y equalizes the a attribute as well as equalizing sublifetime utility, but Joe's lifetime utility levels are the same in both outcomes and the lifetime prioritarian ranks them as equally good.[90]

Table 6.10 Intrapersonal Equalization and Lifetime Prioritarianism: A Second Example

	Outcome x			Outcome y		
	Period 1	Period 2	Lifetime utility	Period 1	Period 2	Lifetime utility
Joe						
Attribute *a*	50	100		75	75	
Attribute *b*	16	16		16	16	
Sublifetime utility	800r	1600r	2400r	1200r	1200r	2400r

In Table 6.10, sublifetime utility is the *product* of the a and b attribute, and lifetime utility is the sum of sublifetime utility.[91] Outcome y equalizes both in terms of attributes and in terms of sublifetime utility. However, Joe's lifetime utility is the same in both cases, and thus any lifetime prioritarian SWF is indifferent. This table illustrates that shifting to a non-additive sublifetime utility function does not *necessarily* mean that lifetime prioritarianism favors attribute equalization.

---

[90] This is true for any prioritarian SWF, not merely any Atkinson SWF, regardless of the value of r—and similarly for the tables immediately below. See above, n. 57.

[91] This is the same case that was used earlier, in Table 6.6, to illustrate how attribute-based and sublifetime prioritarianism can prefer intrapersonal equalization.

Table 6.11 Intrapersonal Equalization and Lifetime Prioritarianism: A Third Example

	Outcome x			Outcome y		
	Period 1	Period 2	Lifetime utility	Period 1	Period 2	Lifetime utility
Joe						
Attribute a	50	100		75	75	
Attribute b	16	16		16	16	
Sublifetime utility	27.18r	32r	59.18r	30r	30r	60r

Table 6.11 shows how making sublifetime utility a function of a concave transformation of an attribute can render the lifetime prioritarian favorable to attribute equalization. Now, sublifetime utility is the product of the b attribute and the logarithm (to the base 10) of the a attribute. (As mentioned earlier, the $\log_{10}$ function is strictly concave.) Note that Joe's lifetime utility is now higher in y, and thus the lifetime prioritarian favors y.

Table 6.12 Intrapersonal Equalization and Lifetime Prioritarianism: A Fourth Example

	Outcome x			Outcome y		
	Period 1	Period 2	Lifetime utility	Period 1	Period 2	Lifetime utility
Joe						
Attribute a	50	100		75	75	
Attribute b	20	40		20	40	
Sublifetime utility	21.70r	42r	63.70r	21.88r	41.88r	63.75r

Table 6.12 illustrates a different kind of non-additive sublifetime utility function, equaling the sum of the b attribute and the logarithm of the a attribute. If sublifetime utility were instead calculated as the product of the two attributes, lifetime utility would be lower in y and thus equalizing the a attribute would not be preferred. If sublifetime utility were calculated as the logarithm of the a attribute times the b attribute, lifetime utility would also be lower in y, because the b attribute is not at the same level in both periods. (These calculations are not shown.) *However*, because of how sublifetime utility is here calculated, Joe's lifetime utility is higher in y and thus the lifetime prioritarian favors y.

Turn now to intuitions regarding intrapersonal equalization of *sublifetime well-being*. It is not apparent, at the outset, how such intuitions can be handled by the lifetime prioritarian with a lifetime utility function of the form $u(x;i) = \sum_{t=1}^{T} v(\mathbf{a}_{i,t}(x), \mathbf{a}_{imp,t}(x))$. Such a function makes lifetime utility *additive in sublifetime utility*. Given this sort of additivity, won't lifetime prioritarianism necessarily be indifferent to intrapersonal transfers of sublifetime well-being from high to low periods?

Not necessarily. In presenting cases involving equalization of sublifetime well-being, the philosophical literature rarely pays attention to how, exactly, sublifetime well-being is measured. Assume that $u(x; i)$ does indeed have the form $\sum_{t=1}^{T} v(\mathbf{a}_{i,t}(x), \mathbf{a}_{imp,t}(x))$. Then $v(.)$ is a number which is assigned to a subject's attributes during each period, and which has a certain functional role: the sum of such numbers equals the subject's lifetime utility (which in turn has the functional role of representing levels of lifetime well-being, well-being differences between life-histories, and ratios of lifetime well-being).

If $u(.)$ has the form $\sum_{t=1}^{T} v(\mathbf{a}_{i,t}(x), \mathbf{a}_{imp,t}(x))$, then lifetime prioritarianism will *not* favor intrapersonal equalization of an individual's $v(.)$ values. But it may favor intrapersonal equalization of sublifetime well-being in some other sense. Imagine that we have some alternative grasp of how to measure sublifetime well-being, other than as a determinant of lifetime utility. For example, we might have intuitions about the level of sublifetime well-being realized by an individual in various periods and about differences in sublifetime well-being between periods. These intuitions might be best captured by some function $v^*(.)$; and $v(.)$ could be a concave rather than linear function of $v^*(.)$. If so, lifetime prioritarianism would recommend equalization with respect to sublifetime well-being as measured by $v^*(.)$.

I have, up to this point, discussed why intrapersonal equalization of attributes or sublifetime well-being may be favored by a lifetime utility function which has the relatively simple form of being atomistic and additive in sublifetime utility. It should be noted that shifting to a more complicated form supports a variety of further possibilities for preferring equalization.[92]

The reader might protest that I have simply discussed a variety of ways in which lifetime prioritarianism *could* handle examples involving intrapersonal equalization of attributes or sublifetime well-being. I have not shown that all the examples are most plausibly handled in this manner, rather than by attribute-based or sublifetime prioritarianism.

Systematically surveying different cases of intrapersonal equalization, different possible forms of lifetime utility functions, and different possible approaches to measuring attributes and sublifetime well-being is beyond the scope of this section. It *is* certainly true that a sufficiently powerful case of intrapersonal equalization could push us away from lifetime prioritarianism. But it must be remembered that lifetime prioritarianism has a strong basis in general principles of fairness, while attribute-based or sublifetime prioritarianism does not. For such a case to have this effect, it would need to have the following features: (1) The intrapersonal transfer of attributes or sublifetime well-being is such that no plausible lifetime utility function, combined with lifetime prioritarianism, would approve it; and (2) the intuition in favor of the intrapersonal transfer is very powerful, sufficiently so to overwhelm

---

[92] For example, imagine that lifetime utility is the multiplicative product of sublifetime utility in each period, rather than the sum. Then equalizing sublifetime utility increases lifetime utility. For example, if an individual's sublifetime utility levels in the three periods in outcome x are, respectively, 60, 85, and 95, and we equalize these to 80 in each period in outcome y, then lifetime utility, calculated multiplicatively, is 484,500 in x and 512,000 in y.

the theoretical merits of the lifetime view. I am not aware of an example with these features.

B. Interpersonal Synchronization

In early work on lifetime egalitarianism, McKerlie identified cases in which, intuitively, we prefer to synchronize individuals' attributes. Although McKerlie has since abandoned reliance on such cases, they are worth considering. He provides the following example:

> [Imagine a society] that contains great inequality, with happier lives attached to certain social positions. But at a fixed time people change places and switch from a superior position to an inferior one or vice versa. One example would be a feudal society in which peasants and nobles exchange roles every ten years. The result is that people's lives as wholes are equally happy. Nevertheless during a given time period the society contains great inequality. . . . If equality between complete lives were all that mattered, an egalitarian could not object to it. But I think that many egalitarians would find it objectionable.[93]

Larry Temkin provides a very similar example: "[A] caste system involving systematic and substantial biases toward, and differential treatment of, the members of different castes might be objectionable on egalitarian grounds *even if* the demographic composition of the castes periodically changed so that each person was a member of each caste and the *overall* quality of each life was equivalent." Temkin also offers a somewhat different case, in which Job1 has an absolutely wonderful life for the first 40 years of his life, Job2 an absolutely terrible life, and then the two switch places.

> Job1's life has been filled with all the blessing life can bestow. His herds and crops flourish. He and his family are healthy and wealthy. He has the love and respect of all who know him. In addition, his plans are realized, his desires fulfilled, and he has complete inner peace. Job2, on the other hand, has led a wretched life. His health is miserable, his countenance disfigured. He has lost his loved ones. He is a penniless beggar who sleeps fitfully in the streets, and whose efforts and desires are constantly frustrated.

Temkin writes: "I think it is unfair or unjust for Job2 to be so much worse off than Job1 through no fault of his own, and my objection to the unequal situation does not disappear . . . when I learn that Job1 will subsequently be worse than Job2 to an equivalent degree."[94]

---

[93] McKerlie (1989, p. 479). For McKerlie's current skepticism regarding the moral relevance of simultaneous inequality, see his (2001a, pp. 273–281).

[94] Temkin (1996b, pp. 237, 235–236).

A simpler and more modern example of the same sort would be this. Each individual earns a low income in a certain number of years of his life, a high income in the remaining years. Having these sequences be synchronized, so that individuals' annual incomes are completely equal each year, would seem to be better than alternative sequencings—even though the inequality of lifetime income is zero regardless.[95]

Table 6.13 Interpersonal Synchronization

	Outcome x					Outcome y			
	Period 1	Period 2	Period 3	Period 4		Period 1	Period 2	Period 3	Period 4
Joe	peasant	noble	peasant	noble		peasant	noble	peasant	noble
Sue	noble	peasant	noble	peasant		peasant	noble	peasant	noble

					Lifetime income					Lifetime income
Joe	$20K	$100K	$20K	$100K	$240K	$20K	$100K	$20K	$100K	$240K
Sue	$100K	$20K	$100K	$20K	$240K	$20K	$100K	$20K	$100K	$240K

These cases can be seen to involve the following sort of ranking of outcomes. Consider two outcomes x and y, each of which has T periods. There is a single sequence of individual attribute bundles, a_1, a_2,..., a_T. Each individual, in x, receives some permutation of this sequence (in other words, individual i has bundle a_1 in some period, bundle a_2 in some other period, etc.; and the same is true for individual j, k, and every other individual). Every individual, in y, also receives some permutation of this sequence. However, in y the individual sequences are synchronized: in each period, every individual has the same bundle of attributes. In outcome x the sequences are not synchronized. We have the intuition that outcome y is morally better than outcome x. How shall such a preference—for short, a preference for interpersonal synchronization—be accounted for?

Note that lifetime prioritarianism cannot account for a preference for interpersonal synchronization if the lifetime utility function is atomistic, and thus is insensitive to the attributes of other individuals. (This includes the simplified lifetime utility function $u(x;i)=\sum_{t=1}^{T} v(a_{i,t}(x), a_{imp,t}(x))$, which is not only atomistic but separable and additive in sublifetime utility; it also includes all other types of atomistic lifetime utility functions.) Note, further, that attribute-based prioritarianism, or sublifetime prioritarianism with an atomistic sublifetime utility function, also fails to explain a preference for interpersonal synchronization.

---

[95] The intuitive pull toward reducing the degree of periodic income inequality, even if lifetime income is held constant, may help explain why much of the literature on income inequality focuses on annual income. However it should be observed that a substantial number of scholars in this field view lifetime income inequality measurement as the gold standard, and see annual income inequality measures as adopted for reasons of data availability. See Adler (2007, pp. 37–40).

These observations might prompt us to adopt some SWF which is distinct from all of these and which is structured so as to be sensitive to the distribution of attributes during each time period. Iwao Hirose has argued along these lines.[96] The natural way to structure such an SWF would be as follows: For each period, measure the inequality of sublifetime well-being during that period. Make the overall ranking of each outcome a function of both overall well-being, and the inequality of sublifetime well-being during each period.[97]

However, such an approach overlooks an important feature about our intuitions regarding interpersonal synchronization—namely, that the attributes in these cases tend to be *salient* and, further, to be linked in some way to social status. This is certainly true of Temkin's caste example and McKerlie's noble/peasant example, as well as my example of synchronizing incomes. It is also true of Temkin's Job1/Job2 example.[98]

Conversely, if we imagine synchronizing attributes that are not salient or, if salient, not socially meaningful, intuitions in favor of synchronizing tend to become weaker or disappear. Imagine that everyone is the same with respect to her visible attributes but suffers a period of unhappiness during some stretch of her life—which she manages to hide from others in her society. Is it better if everyone has these private episodes of distress at the same time? It seems not. Or imagine that individuals have high or low levels of attributes (perhaps salient) during short periods of time—sufficiently short that individuals at high levels of the attributes do not thereby gain an elevated social status during the period. Does synchronizing these sorts of attributes improve matters? Again, it seems not, as Klemens Kappel observes:

> In a small society all the male members survive by hard labour in the mines. They work day and night shifts. Thus, while the day shift suffers, the other part of the work force relaxes, and vice versa. On the whole, however, everybody has an equally good life. . . . There would be many reasons to improve working conditions in this case, but the persistent simultaneous inequality is not obviously a candidate among them.[99]

McKerlie himself observes:

> [A preference for simultaneous equality] will seem implausible if the time periods within which the inequality is measured are too short. If two people will see a dentist tomorrow,

---

[96] See Hirose (2005).

[97] A more complicated variation on this approach would be to measure the inequality of each attribute during each period, and make the overall ranking of each outcome a function of both overall well-being, and the inequality of the distribution of each attribute in each period. We could also throw the inequality of lifetime well-being into the mix.

[98] One of each Job's misfortunes during the period he is badly off is to be a "penniless beggar who sleeps fitfully in the streets"—an obvious determinant of status. One of each Job's good fortunes during the period he is well off is to be "wealthy."

[99] Kappel (1997, p. 207).

it would tell them to schedule simultaneous appointments so that there will be equality in suffering at that time. Are there serious egalitarian reasons for preferring two 10:30 appointments to an appointment at 10 and an appointment at 11?[100]

These observations cut against the sort of proposal tendered by Hirose. And they cut in favor of handling synchronization cases by combining lifetime prioritarianism with some kind of non-atomistic lifetime utility function. Interpersonal synchronization of certain attributes can affect the well-being of those bearing the attributes. This is most clearly the case with salient, socially meaningful attributes. Being an impoverished peasant in a society with landed gentry is worse for the peasant's well-being, than being an impoverished peasant in a society where everyone else is an impoverished peasant too. Similarly, having a periodic income of $20,000, during a period when others have a substantially higher income, is worse for the low-earner's well-being than having a periodic income of $20,000 when everyone else has the same income. (By contrast, the well-being effect of going to the dentist does not depend on whether others are going to the dentist at the same time.)

A lifetime utility function which is non-atomistic can pick up these sorts of effects. (For example, an individual's sublifetime utility might be a function both of his consumption and of whether his consumption is low or high in the overall distribution of consumption.) Lifetime prioritarianism with a lifetime utility function which is atomistic and additive in sublifetime utility is simpler to implement—but if the policy analyst believes that synchronization effects and similar impacts on well-being which are thereby overlooked are substantial, she can certainly use a more complicated, non-atomistic function.

C. Interpersonal Equalization

Interpersonal equalization of an *attribute*, in the sense I will discuss here, occurs when someone is at some level of some attribute in period t, and some other person is at a lower level of that attribute in period t^* (either the same period or a different one), and we reduce the first person's attribute level in period t by some amount, and increase the second person's attribute level in period t^* by the same amount, leaving the second person's attribute level in t^* still no greater than the first person's in t. Similarly, *interpersonal* equalization of *sublifetime well-being* occurs when someone is at some level of sublifetime well-being in period t, and some other person is at a lower level of sublifetime well-being in period t^* (either the same period or a different one), and we reduce the first person's sublifetime well-being level in period t by some amount, and increase the second person's sublifetime well-being in period t^* by the same amount, leaving the second person's sublifetime well-being level in t^* still no greater than the first person's in t.

---

[100] McKerlie (1989, p. 483). See also Cupit (1998); Sikora (1989).

In other words, interpersonal equalization of attributes involves an interpersonal Pigou–Dalton transfer in some attribute, and interpersonal equalization of sublifetime well-being involves an interpersonal Pigou–Dalton transfer in sublifetime well-being.

At least in the simple case of outcomes characterized in terms of a single attribute, interpersonal equalization of attributes or sublifetime well-being is straightforwardly approved by attribute-based and sublifetime prioritarianism, and also straightforwardly approved by lifetime prioritarianism where the transferee is at a lower level of lifetime well-being.[101]

Table 6.14 Interpersonal Equalization: Transferee at a Lower Level of Lifetime Well-Being

	Outcome x						Outcome y					
Period	1	2	3	4	5	*Lifetime utility*	*Period*	1	2	3	4	5	*Lifetime utility*
Joe	10	10	10	10	10	50r	Joe	50	10	10	10	10	90r
Sue	90	90	90	90	90	450r	Sue	50	90	90	90	90	410r

The numbers in Table 6.14 represent the level of a single attribute and of sublifetime utility (strictly, sublifetime utility would be some positive constant r times the number). Lifetime utility is the sum of sublifetime utility. There is a transfer of 40 units of the attribute from Sue to Joe in period 1. Because this is a Pigou–Dalton transfer in attributes, an attribute-based prioritarian using any prioritarian SWF will favor it. Because this is a Pigou–Dalton transfer in sublifetime well-being, a simple sublifetime prioritarian using any prioritarian SWF will favor it. Finally, because the transferee, Joe, is worse off in terms of lifetime well-being, and lifetime utility is the sum of sublifetime utility, the transfer is a Pigou–Dalton transfer in lifetime terms and a lifetime prioritarian using any prioritarian SWF will approve it.

---

[101] More precisely, in the case of single-attribute outcomes, if the transferee is at a lower level of lifetime well-being, interpersonal equalization of *attributes* is straightforwardly approved by all three approaches if sublifetime utility is either linear or concave in the metric used to quantify attributes and lifetime well-being is the sum of sublifetime utility. With this same lifetime utility function, interpersonal equalization of *sublifetime well-being* is approved by all three approaches if sublifetime utility is linear in the attribute. If sublifetime well-being is (plausibly) concave in the attribute, attribute-based prioritarians need not favor sublifetime well-being equalization. Lifetime prioritarians will still straightforwardly do so, if the transferee is at a lower level of lifetime well-being.

As in the case of intrapersonal equalization, discussed in a prior subsection, complications can arise with multiattribute outcomes and transfers that equalize one attribute. So as not to make the analysis overly complicated, the examples in this subsection involve single-attribute outcomes. The challenge to lifetime prioritarianism in rationalizing attribute or sublifetime well-being transfers where the transferee is at a *higher* level of lifetime well-being is clearly displayed by the single-attribute case.

Outcome *y* would also be approved by all three approaches if the numbers displayed attribute levels and sublifetime utility were a concave function of the attribute, rather than a linear function (calculations not shown).

What about the case where the transferee is *better off* in lifetime terms? Dennis McKerlie, Derek Parfit, and Klemens Kappel have all argued that we have an intuition in favor of interpersonal equalization in certain such cases—namely, cases where the transferee is currently in physical pain.[102] McKerlie, Parfit, and Kappel describe the following sort of case. Jim, let us imagine, is at a high level of lifetime well-being; Sally, at a lower level. But Jim is in terrible pain right now; Sally is in mild pain. Both are in the emergency room, and we have one vial of pain reliever, which we can use to relieve Jim's pain or Sally's. Intuitively, we should provide the pain medicine to Jim.

Depending on what we imagine about the nexus between the pain medicine, Jim's and Sally's pain levels, and their sublifetime well-being, giving pain relief to Jim rather than Sally can be seen to involve an interpersonal equalization in a kind of attribute (a hedonic attribute, how the individuals feel); an interpersonal equalization in sublifetime well-being; or both.

Table 6.15 Physical Pain and Interpersonal Equalization

	Current period	Other periods	Lifetime well-being
	Status quo: No pain relief given to either person		
	Current period	*Other periods*	*Lifetime well-being*
Jim	terrible pain	...	high
Sally	mild pain	...	low
	Outcome x: Pain relief given to Sally		
	Current period	*Other periods*	*Lifetime well-being*
Jim	terrible pain	...	high
Sally	no pain	...	slightly better than low
	Outcome y: Pain relief given to Jim		
	Current period	*Other periods*	*Lifetime well-being*
Jim	moderate pain	...	slightly better than high
Sally	mild pain	...	low

Depending on the attribute and sublifetime well-being numbers we assign to the states of terrible, mild, moderate, and no pain, outcome *y* could be an equalization relative to *x* in terms of pain, sublifetime well-being, or both.

---

[102] See Kappel (1997, pp. 211–214); McKerlie (2001a, pp. 271–273); Parfit (1987, p. 344; 1986, pp. 869–870).

McKerlie, Parfit, and Kappel each claim that our intuitions in this kind of case argue against lifetime prioritarianism, and in favor of some kind of sublifetime or attribute-based prioritarianism. McKerlie has also suggested that the case generalizes beyond pain. Whenever someone can be seen as suffering a hardship right now, we will feel an intuitive "tug" in favor of relieving her hardship, as opposed to helping someone who is not suffering the hardship, even if the first person is better off in lifetime terms. As McKerlie explains:

> Consider the much-discussed conflict between the interests of Afro-Americans in inner-city ghettos and the interests of Asian-Americans who own stores in the same neighborhoods. The store owners might be recent immigrants who suffered greatly in their countries of origin, experiencing the deep poverty of less-developed countries. Now they are modestly well off, and they can expect even better lives for their children. If we think about lifetimes, the complete life of such an Asian-American might well be worse than the complete life of an unemployed Afro-American single mother. Nevertheless, the special concern with poverty applies to the Afro-American who *is* living in poverty, not to the Asian-American who is not. It supplies one reason to support a policy that would help Afro-Americans, even if [it] might be possible to help the Asian-Americans more.[103]

Do the sorts of cases just described really cut against lifetime prioritarianism? It is certainly true that attribute-based and sublifetime prioritarianism rationalize interpersonal equalization, even where the transferee is better off in lifetime terms. It is also true that lifetime prioritarianism will not favor such equalization (in attributes or sublifetime well-being) *if* the lifetime utility function takes the form $u(x;i) = \sum_{t=1}^{T} v(\mathbf{a}_{i,t}(x), \mathbf{a}_{imp,t}(x))$ *and* the sublifetime utility function $v(.)$ that operates within this lifetime utility function is additive in attributes.[104]

Table 6.16 Interpersonal Equalization: Transferee at a Higher Level of Lifetime Well-Being

	Outcome x						Outcome y					
Period	1	2	3	4	5	Lifetime utility	Period	1	2	3	4	5	Lifetime utility
Joe	10	90	90	90	90	370r	Joe	50	90	90	90	90	410r
Sue	90	10	10	10	10	130r	Sue	50	10	10	10	10	90r

[103] McKerlie (2001b, pp. 164–165). See also Gosseries (2003), arguing for sublifetime sufficientism.

[104] A sublifetime utility function is additive in a given attribute metric if it is a linear function of attributes, measured using that metric. See above, p. 417. In the case where outcomes are characterized in terms of a single attribute, and individual i's level of the attribute during period t using a particular metric is denoted $a_{i,t}(x)$, then the sublifetime utility function $v(.)$ is additive in this metric (or, equivalently, "linear" in this metric) if: $v(\mathbf{a}_{i,t}(x)) = d_1 a_{i,t}(x)$.

Table 6.16 is a variation on the case presented above (see Table 6.14). Joe, who is still worse off than Sue in period 1 in outcome x, is now better off in all the other periods. As above, the numbers represent sublifetime utility levels as well as attribute levels. As above, outcome y transfers 40 units of the attribute from Sue to Joe in period 1. Because Joe is now better off than Sue in lifetime terms, *and* because sublifetime utility is linear in the attribute, this transfer is a Pigou–Dalton disequalizing transfer in lifetime well-being, and any lifetime prioritarian disapproves it. By contrast, attribute-based and simple sublifetime prioritarians favor y.

On the other hand, the key point I stressed in my discussion of *intra*personal equalization—that the sublifetime utility function is very plausibly non-additive in attributes—is just as relevant in discussing *inter*personal equalization. Using such a sublifetime utility function can prove surprisingly powerful in prompting the lifetime prioritarian to favor interpersonal *attribute* transfers even where the transferee is at a higher lifetime well-being level.

Table 6.17 Interpersonal Equalization and a Non-Additive Sublifetime Utility Function

		Outcome x			
		Current year	Other 99 years	Lifetime utility	
Joe	Income	$10,000	$90,000		
	Sublifetime utility	4r	4.954r	494.47r	
Sue	Income	$90,000	$10,000		
	Sublifetime utility	4.954r	4r	400.954r	
		Outcome y			
		Current year	Other 99 years	Lifetime utility	Change from x
Joe	Income	$50,000	$90,000		
	Sublifetime utility	4.699r	4.954r	495.169r	.699r
Sue	Income	$50,000	$10,000		
	Sublifetime utility	4.699r	4r	400.699r	−.255r

Joe and Sue each live for 100 years. In outcome x, Joe has the higher income ($90,000) in all years except the current year, where his income is lower ($10,000). Sublifetime utility is now calculated using the logarithm (to the base 10) of income, multiplied by a positive constant r. Although Joe is better off in lifetime terms than Sue, equalizing current income (outcome y) yields a larger improvement in Joe's lifetime utility than the loss in Sue's. (This is because the $\log_{10}$ function is strictly concave and because lifetime utility sums up sublifetime utility.)

Thus a lifetime prioritarian may well approve y. Indeed, it can be shown that inequality aversion of the Atkinson SWF must be increased to γ larger than 4.7 before the lifetime prioritarian favors x.

Behind the numbers, the critical point is this: If the sublifetime utility function is non-additive in attributes, attribute equalization can[105] produce a greater increase in the sublifetime utility of the transferee than the loss in sublifetime utility of the transferor, and thus a greater increase in the *lifetime* well-being of the transferee than the loss in lifetime well-being of the transferor. This in turn means that a lifetime prioritarian SWF which is not too inequality averse will approve the transfer even though the transferee is at a higher level of lifetime well-being.

Interpersonal transfers in *sublifetime well-being* are a bit trickier. In discussing *intrapersonal* equalization of sublifetime well-being, I noted that this might be supported even with a lifetime utility function of the form $u(x;i) = \sum_{t=1}^{T} v(\mathbf{a}_{i,t}(x), \mathbf{a}_{imp,t}(x))$, if sublifetime well-being is measured using some metric other than $v(.)$. The same is true with regards to interpersonal equalization of sublifetime well-being levels in favor of a transferee at a higher lifetime well-being level.

In short, the lifetime prioritarian *may well* support some degree of interpersonal attribute or sublifetime well-being equalization where the transferee is better off in lifetime terms. Whether she does so depends on the form of the lifetime and sublifetime utility functions and the way in which attributes and sublifetime well-being are measured.

It might be objected that this strategy for handling the sorts of cases described by McKerlie, Parfit, and Kappel is inadequate. First, let us return to the point that our strongest intuitions in favor of equalization, notwithstanding the fact that the transferee is better off in lifetime terms, involve *hardship*. To put the point more formally, there seems to be a kind of threshold effect with respect to equalization in any given attribute: to be in a condition of hardship or poverty with respect to some attribute is to be below a threshold level with respect to that attribute. Consider an individual's hedonic state—the attribute at issue in the sort of pain case described by Kappel, Parfit, and McKerlie. In that case, one individual is at a very low hedonic level in some period (he is in great pain) and we intuitively want to provide him pain relief, whatever his lifetime well-being. But imagine now a case in which both individuals are at a reasonably good hedonic level in some period. Jim is not in pain; he is just bored. Sally is in a good mood. Jim has a higher lifetime well-being level than Sally. We can provide some entertainment to Jim, which will increase Jim's hedonic state by a given amount, or to Sally, which will increase her hedonic state by the same amount. In this case—which differs only from the pain case in that Jim and Sally are now above rather than below a hedonic threshold—the reader may well intuit that Sally should get the entertainment, or at least will not intuit that Jim should.

---

[105] I say "can" because whether the lifetime prioritarian will approve attribute equalization depends on the particular form of the sublifetime utility function. For example, if the function were *convex* in the attribute, the lifetime prioritarian would not approve equalization. However, in the one-attribute case, sublifetime utility functions which are convex rather than concave or linear in natural metrics of attributes are unusual.

And this threshold effect may well generalize to other attributes (nutrition, shelter, income, health, etc.).

However, the threshold effect just described does not necessarily count against lifetime prioritarianism. It can be handled, at least in principle, via a lifetime utility function which incorporates a non-additive sublifetime utility function of a particular kind: namely, one with a threshold.[106]

A stronger objection is that intuitions in favor of equalization, in hardship cases, are *insensitive* to the lifetime well-being levels of transferor and transferee. If Jim is in terrible pain right now and Sally is in mild pain right now, then—intuitively—we should provide a unit of pain relief to Jim rather than Sally quite independent of their lifetime well-being levels. The lifetime prioritarian cannot account for this. However nuanced the lifetime utility function may be—regardless of whether it is temporally additive or non-additive, if temporally additive whether the sublifetime utility function is additive or non-additive in attributes, whether this latter function incorporates a threshold, and so forth—the lifetime prioritarian's assessment of a given interpersonal transfer of attributes or sublifetime well-being *does* necessarily depend upon the lifetime well-being levels of transferor and transferee.

This is indeed an important difficulty for lifetime prioritarianism. To reiterate: we intuitively feel a tug in favor of relieving someone's current hardship (pain, low income, poor health, etc.), as against helping someone who is currently better off, *quite independent of the lifetime well-being levels of the two individuals.* For short, let us call the apparent normative reason to relieve short-term hardship, the strength of which is independent of the lifetime well-being of the beneficiary, a LWI ("lifetime

---

[106] Moreover, as I have already suggested, the idea that there is a threshold in the function from certain attributes to well-being has independent plausibility. See Chapter 2, pp. 138–139. I will not attempt to discuss in detail how a sublifetime utility function should be structured to incorporate a threshold. But to see how such a function, together with a temporally additive lifetime utility function and lifetime prioritarianism, might be used to explain the threshold effect just described, consider the following. Assume, in the case of outcomes characterized with respect to one attribute a, that $v(a)$ is strictly concave up to the point where a equals a threshold value a^+, and linear for larger values of a. Consider a case of interpersonal attribute equalization, where the transferee during period t^* has less of the attribute than the transferor during period t, and we transfer some of the attribute, still leaving the transferee during t^* at a level no higher than that of the transferor during t. If the transferee starts off below the threshold level a^+, then the lifetime prioritarian might approve this transfer even if the transferee is better off in terms of lifetime well-being. However, in such a case, if the transferee starts off above the threshold, the lifetime prioritarian using this $v(.)$ function and a temporally additive lifetime utility function will *not* do so—because the increase in the transferee's sublifetime and hence lifetime utility will be no greater in magnitude than the decrease in the transferor's sublifetime and hence lifetime utility.

It should also be noted that threshold effects cut *against* attribute-based and sublifetime prioritarianism. Attribute-based prioritarianism will approve interpersonal attribute equalization regardless of whether the transferee starts off below or above some threshold a^+. Sublifetime prioritarianism will approve interpersonal attribute equalization even if the transferee starts off above some threshold a^+, as long as sublifetime utility is concave *or* linear in the attribute above the threshold (rather than, less plausibly, convex).

well-being independent") reason to relieve hardship. Thus an important objection to lifetime prioritarianism, suggested by McKerlie's, Kappel's, and Parfit's examples, is that lifetime prioritarianism cannot account for the existence of LWI reasons to relieve hardship.

In response, the lifetime prioritarian can point out—to begin—that LWI reasons to relieve hardship, if they exist, are not grounded in *fairness*. If Jim and Sally are normal human beings, who each remains the same person for his or entire life, and Jim is better off than Sally in lifetime terms, and the pain relief would produce no greater change in Jim's lifetime well-being than in Sally's, then Jim has a *weaker* claim to the relief than Sally. To give Jim rather than Sally the relief would be *unfair*. Because fairness is best specified by lifetime prioritarianism, and because LWI reasons are not based on fairness, it is not surprising that the lifetime prioritarian cannot rationalize such intuitions.

The person-centered welfarist might therefore conclude that there is no normative reason at all to provide Jim the relief. She might see this as a case where an attractive theoretical framework (a moral view that takes the form of person-centered welfarism and that is oriented around fairness; the claim-across-outcome view of the fair ranking of outcomes; the continuity of personal identity over a normal human lifetime; lifetime well-being as the "currency" for claims) pushes her to a point of reflective equilibrium in which certain intuitions need to be rejected.

Here, it is worth noting that intuitions in favor of LWI reasons to relieve hardship are not universally shared. In the field of health policy, some survey work has been undertaken to determine the public's judgments regarding the allocation of scarce treatment for various diseases—in particular, whether treatment should be allocated based on the disease's severity or instead based on indicators of lifetime well-being (such as the patient's age and prior health history, or the increase in expected health-adjusted longevity from treatment). Although some respondents prefer treatment based on severity, a substantial number seem to give greater weight to whole-lifetime considerations.[107]

Alternatively, the person-centered welfarist might take the position that there is a *non-moral* reason to provide Jim the relief. On this manner of thinking, the content of our *moral* reasons, and the reasons we have as a matter of fairness, are specified by person-centered welfarism and, more specifically, by lifetime prioritarianism. However, there also exist various non-moral reasons, such as reasons to promote animal well-being and reasons to reduce suffering, both animal suffering *and the suffering or other hardship of human beings independent of their claim to such relief as a matter of fairness*. Jamie Mayerfeld has argued strongly that there is a reason independent of prioritarianism to alleviate suffering:

> [W]hereas the intrinsic property view emphasizes the *intrinsic awfulness of suffering*, the priority view emphasizes the *harm that suffering does to persons*. . . . The intrinsic property

---

[107] See Stolk et al. (2005).

view doesn't particularly care *who* is hurt; the identity of the victim is not an issue. In this it resembles utilitarianism, which has been criticized on the grounds that it treats persons as mere vessels of happiness and suffering. For the intrinsic property view, it is the evilness of suffering that counts, not the harm done to a particular person. . . . By contrast, the priority view directs its attention, not to the intrinsic evilness of suffering, but to the person affected by it. It says that the urgency of helping this person increases the worse off he or she is. . . . It sets itself apart from both utilitarianism and the intrinsic property view in asserting the moral separateness of persons.

Mayerfeld also observes: "[M]y own view is that the suffering of non-human animals carries no less . . . weight than the suffering of humans, and that consequently the duty to relieve suffering applies with equal force to both."[108]

But why not take a third position? Why not say that person-centered welfarism encompasses not only fairness but also certain non-fairness considerations—namely, LWI reasons to relieve hardship—which, like fairness, are *moral* considerations?[109]

The difficulty here is reconciling LWI reasons to relieve human hardship with the Pareto principles. Person-centered welfarism says, of course, that the moral ranking of outcomes must satisfy the Pareto principles. As I have argued at length in this chapter, the ranking of outcomes in terms of fairness needs to satisfy the Pareto principles in whole-lifetime terms. But an LWI reason to relieve hardship is recalcitrant in terms of the lifetime Pareto principles. Imagine a case in which Dora suffers short-term hardship in outcome x but not y, and everyone else is unaffected. Other attributes, however, compensate her for the hardship: her lifetime well-being in x is equal to or even greater than her lifetime well-being in y. A moral reason to alleviate Dora's hardship, if seen as strong enough to override fairness considerations and thus to rank y as all-things-considered morally better than x, would violate lifetime Pareto-indifference or superiority.

Creatively, we might imagine a hybrid version of person-centered welfarism that conjoins the lifetime Pareto principles (to track fairness) and short-term Pareto principles (to track the LWI reason to alleviate hardship). But, for reasons discussed in the margin, this strategy for accommodating that reason within a Paretian moral view also fails.[110]

---

[108] Mayerfeld (2002, pp. 150, 117).

[109] Mayerfeld, himself, emphatically classifies the duty to relieve suffering as a moral one. See ibid., ch. 1.

[110] The conjoined version of Pareto-indifference says: if each person is equally well off in outcome x as outcome y, both in lifetime terms and in each short period, the two outcomes are equally morally good. The conjoined version of Pareto-superiority says: if everyone is at least as well off in outcome x as outcome y, both in lifetime terms and during each short period, and at least one person is strictly better off during a whole lifetime or a short period, outcome x is better.

To summarize a complicated discussion: The lifetime prioritarian may well approve interpersonal equalization of attributes or sublifetime well-being, even where the transferee is at a higher level of lifetime well-being. She will do so if—by virtue of the form of the lifetime utility function, the way in which sublifetime well-being is measured, and the degree of inequality aversion of the SWF—the increase in lifetime well-being of the transferee is sufficiently greater than the loss in lifetime well-being of the transferor that this difference swamps the difference in their lifetime well-being levels. What the lifetime prioritarian will *not* approve is equalization *independent of* the lifetime well-being levels of transferee and transferor. LWI reasons to relieve hardship would recommend such equalization—but such reasons cannot be seen as moral reasons, at least within the framework of a moral view which focuses on human well-being and does so by accepting the Pareto principles. Such reasons might be seen as illusory, lacking normative force entirely—after all, they are not grounded in the fair treatment of persons—or, alternatively, as non-moral reasons, akin to the way person-centered welfarism conceptualizes animal well-being.

The LWI reason to alleviate hardship (if such exists) has a threshold structure: there is a reason independent of Dora's long-term well-being to bring her up to a certain level of attributes, not to increase her short-term well-being indefinitely. (For example, there may be a LWI reason to stop her pain, but not to stop her boredom.) To see why the threshold structure of the LWI reason to alleviate hardship runs afoul of the conjoined specification of the Pareto principles now under discussion, consider a case in which Dora is above the hardship threshold with respect to some attribute during some short period. Imagine increasing her well-being during that period, and making a compensating change at some other point so that her lifetime well-being is equal. Then the conjoined version of Pareto-superiority would say that this package of changes is a moral improvement—but fairness does not argue for such a package, and *neither does* the LWI reason to alleviate hardship.

7

RANKING ACTIONS
PRIORITARIANISM UNDER UNCERTAINTY

A moral choice-evaluation framework which is consequentialist[1] has the following components, as I see it: principles for constructing an outcome set **O** and developing a moral ranking of its elements, a ranking that takes the form of a quasiordering; principles for constructing a choice set **A**, comprising some of the choices available to the decisionmaker[2]; and what might be termed "outcome set/action set bridge principles" (for short, "bridge principles"), namely a methodology for constructing a moral ranking of the choice set,[3] based on the moral ranking of the outcome set together with information about the likelihood that a given action will yield one or another outcome.

The prior four chapters have focused on developing tools for constructing and morally ranking an outcome set: tools that include an account of well-being, principles for measuring well-being using a set **U** of utility functions that operate on

---

[1] My reasons for working within consequentialism are discussed in Chapter 1.

[2] One issue here concerns whether "actions" are immediate choices or long-range plans. That topic is discussed below.

A cross-cutting issue is how to narrow down the set of possible actions (in either the immediate-choice or long-range-plan sense) which are ranked. A boundedly rational decisionmaker cannot feasibly evaluate all of the actions which are available. I have little insight about how to resolve this difficult issue. Instead, this chapter assumes that an action set **A** comprising some of the actions available to the decisionmaker has been constructed in some manner, and focuses on specifying the bridge principles for ranking **A** in light of the ranking of **O**.

[3] This ranking, like the moral ranking of the outcome set, will be a quasiordering. With a quasiordering of the choice set **A** in hand, which action should the decisionmaker select? Very plausibly, she should "maximize": choose any action a^* in **A** which is not worse than any other action. See Chapter 1, p. 42; below, pp. 531–532. But mightn't this choice maxim yield a "value pump," in the case where the quasiordering of the choice set is incomplete? These worries are addressed below.

life-histories, and a continuous prioritarian SWF. This chapter turns to the topic of moral bridge principles. The central claim of this chapter will be that a (refined version of) expected utility (EU) theory provides an attractive set of moral bridge principles.

Several points of clarification are important at the outset. First, we have already encountered EU theory at various junctures in the book. Thus far, however, EU theory has been discussed under the rubric of ordering outcomes. In particular, I have relied heavily on EU theory in constructing U. In the present chapter, EU theory plays a different role. It functions, here, as the tool for moving *from* the moral ranking of the outcome set **O** *to* the moral ranking of the action set **A**.

Second, EU theory is sometimes seen as a full, self-contained theory—instructing the decisionmaker to maximize her preferences, whatever they may be. EU theory, thus conceived, is not particularly attractive, and this is not the interpretation of EU theory which I will adopt in this chapter. Rather, I see EU theory as a *generic* body of bridge principles. It does not, itself, supply principles for ranking outcomes, but rather can be *coupled* with any outcome-ranking principles that are seen as attractive. EU theory (thus construed) takes as given the ranking of an outcome set **O**, and provides generic guidance for how a decisionmaker choosing under conditions of uncertainty should rank choices, in light of that ranking, and in light of the decision-maker's beliefs concerning the linkages between actions and outcomes. If the decisionmaker conforms to the guidance, her ranking of actions will be representable via the expected utility formula. There will be a utility function, $v(.)$, which represents the ranking of outcomes; there will also be probability numbers, linking any given action with any outcome; and one action a will be at least as good as a second action b iff the expected v-value associated with a is at least as large as the expected v-value associated with b. In other words, a is at least as good as b iff

$$\sum_{x \in \mathbf{O}} \pi_a(x)v(x) \geq \sum_{x \in \mathbf{O}} \pi_b(x)v(x).$$

Not only can EU theory be seen as a generic body of bridge principles. It is by far the best-developed such body of principles extant in the scholarly literature. Although a vast corpus of descriptive scholarship in economics and psychology shows that individual behavior does not conform to the dictates of EU theory,[4] these findings do not—as such—undermine the normative credentials of the theory. Normative scholars seeking to elaborate nonconsequentialist principles of rational choice reject EU theory[5]—not surprisingly, because its basic structure is consequentialist, involving a utility function $v(.)$ applied to outcomes. But we are looking, here, for consequentialist bridge principles. Indeed, the very concept of "bridge principles," as I have articulated it, presupposes consequentialism. These are

---

[4] On the failure of EU theory as a descriptive theory, see, e.g., Hastie and Dawes (2001). Economists have formulated various non-EU models to better explain how individuals typically behave. These are reviewed in Gilboa (2009); Starmer (2000); and Sugden (2004).

[5] An influential nonconsequentialist challenge to EU theory is E. Anderson (1993). A range of normative accounts of choice are reviewed in Mele and Rawling (2004) and Millgram (2001).

principles that serve to derive guidance for choice *from* a ranking of outcomes. Extant bodies of scholarship which are both normative and consequentialist—such as decision theory, or normative economics—have, overwhelmingly, converged on EU theory or some refinement thereof as the basic structure for rational choice.[6]

This brings us to the topic of refinements. EU theory, in its traditional form, furnishes an inadequate set of bridge principles in three kinds of cases: where the decisionmaker's ranking of outcomes is incomplete; where her probabilities are imprecise; and where she is uncertain what the outcome ranking is. A different kind of refinement concerns *strategic* as opposed to *parametric* choice. In the parametric case, there may be various kinds of linkages between a decisionmaker's choices and outcomes, but such linkages do not include the choices of *other* rational actors, who are making their choices with any eye to what they believe the decisionmaker will do. Where the linkages between a given decisionmaker's choices and outcomes *do* include the choices of other rational actors, the decision situation becomes "strategic." There is good reason to think that EU theory can be extended from the parametric to the strategic case—but the intellectual work required to accomplish this extension in a rigorous way remains incomplete.

This chapter will survey possible refinements to EU theory, needed to handle problems of an incomplete outcome ordering, imprecise probabilities, uncertainty concerning the outcome ranking, and strategic interaction. However, it is well beyond the scope of the chapter to analyze these problems in depth, let alone suggest definitive answers. Doing so would require a separate book. Moreover, the problems here are not specific to *moral* theory. Rather, they are generic problems, which arise in moving from *any* kind of ordering of outcomes (be it a moral ordering or any other kind of ordering) to a ranking of actions. Thus the problems are more perspicuously addressed by decision theorists or others concerned to provide generic norms for rational choice, rather than by a book which is focused on moral decisionmaking. To put the point another way: our understanding of how to refine EU theory so as to function as a set of moral bridge principles, suitable in moving from a moral ordering of outcomes to a moral ranking of actions, can piggyback on results in decision theory and related areas of normative scholarship where work on refining EU theory is underway and, presumably, will continue to progress.

Rather, the main focus of this chapter will be on rebutting a challenge to EU theory which is specific to moral theory. For short, I will term this the "targeted" objection to using EU theory (or some refinement thereof) as a set of moral bridge principles. The targeted objection says this: quite apart from problems of an incomplete outcome ordering, imprecise probabilities, or decisionmaker uncertainty about the outcome ordering, and even in parametric contexts, EU theory is a poor

---

[6] Discussions of the structure of EU theory include Fishburn (1982, 1994); Gilboa (2009); Kreps (1988); Mas-Colell, Whinston, and Green (1995, ch. 6); Resnik (1987). Two excellent reviews of the philosophical literature adopting a consequentialist approach to normative decision theory are Joyce (1999) and Joyce and Gibbard (1998).

tool for moving from a *moral* ordering of outcomes to a *moral* ordering of actions. In particular, where the moral ordering of outcomes is non-utilitarian, employing EU theory as the bridge principles will produce a variety of perverse results, such as conflicts with the axioms of ex ante Pareto-indifference and -superiority or with an ex ante Pigou–Dalton axiom.

The "targeted objection," as I will develop it, derives from an important body of work in social choice theory. A substantial number of scholars in this field, beginning with a seminal article by Peter Diamond,[7] have argued that social welfare functions, under conditions of uncertainty, should not be applied in accordance with EU theory. Instead, a sui generis set of norms for moral ("social") choice under uncertainty is supposedly required. However, as we shall see, the sui generis bridge principles which have been advanced in this literature threaten to violate some axioms—"stochastic dominance" axioms—which lie at the very core of consequentialism. Moreover, the proponent of sui generis moral bridge principles can be accused of being ad hoc. Why should the norms for evaluating actions, in light of an ordering of outcomes, be *different* in the case where the ordering is a moral rather than non-moral ordering? To point out the distinctive qualities of moral decisionmaking—that it is impartial, focused on the interests of persons, and so forth—does not answer this challenge, since that difference is already captured in the ordering of outcomes. Why exactly should moral decisionmaking involve a double difference from decisionmaking animated by non-moral considerations?

Chapter 5 argued in favor of the continuous prioritarian SWF. My focus in this chapter, therefore, is to elaborate and defend the use of EU theory as the appropriate bridge principles for a continuous prioritarian SWF.[8] For stylistic reasons, I will sometimes drop the adjective "continuous" and refer simply to "prioritarianism"; when I do so, it will be clear from the context that I mean the particular version of prioritarianism that uses a continuous prioritarian SWF to order outcomes.

However, the case for EU theory is much broader, and readily transposes to any other SWF (utilitarian or non-utilitarian) which the reader takes to be most attractive. In particular, other non-utilitarian SWFs (such as the leximin, rank-weighted, or sufficientist SWF, or the prioritarian SWF with a lexical threshold) are vulnerable

---

[7] Diamond (1967).

[8] Chapter 5 specifically defended the Atkinson SWF. I believe this *is* the most attractive continuous prioritarian SWF. Moreover this SWF, unlike other continuous prioritarian SWFs, necessarily yields a complete ordering of outcomes if **U** is unique up to a positive ratio transformation. I will therefore rely upon the Atkinson SWF to illustrate and rebut the targeted objection. At least with such a **U** (and bracketing issues of imprecise probabilities, decisionmaker uncertainty about the ordering, and strategic interaction), the Atkinson SWF meshes smoothly with traditional EU theory, while other continuous prioritarian SWFs do not.

However, the case for using EU bridge principles (refined to allow for an incomplete ordering as well as these other eventualities) is equally applicable to continuous prioritarian SWFs which do not take the Atkinson form.

to the "targeted" objection—the objection that employing EU theory as the bridge principles for *these* SWFs runs afoul of the ex ante Pareto and Pigou–Dalton principles. But here, too, the targeted objection can be resisted.

The chapter begins by discussing EU theory and clarifying how it would mesh with a continuous prioritarian SWF to yield a moral ranking of actions. It then presents and addresses the targeted objection. The chapter closes by surveying the range of refinements that are needed to render EU theory a fully adequate set of bridge principles, be it for purposes of moral or non-moral choice.

This chapter, like the prior two, does not depend upon the theory of well-being undergirding **U**. The analysis is meant to be independent of whether the utilities in **U** represent well-being levels, differences, and ratios according to the extended-preference account or some other account.

A final terminological note. The EU approach to applying an SWF under uncertainty is sometimes referred to as the "ex post" approach. Indeed, I have used that terminology in the past.[9] However, I now believe that the "ex post" terminology is potentially quite confusing.[10] Moreover, it fails to make clear that the so-called "ex post" application of an SWF under uncertainty is really just the use of EU theory—as opposed to some non-EU body of bridge principles–for moving from the moral ranking of outcomes to the moral ranking of actions. I will therefore not employ this terminology in the chapter, and will instead speak of the "EU approach," "EU bridge principles," and so forth.

I. EU THEORY

This section reviews EU theory, first discussing the theory in general, then specifically addressing how it would be integrated with the prioritarian moral ordering of outcomes recommended in prior chapters in order to produce a moral ranking of actions.

A. EU Theory as a Generic Set of Bridge Principles

There is a large body of scholarship within decision theory, economics, and philosophy that elaborates EU theory.[11] This scholarship does not always distinguish between two different construals of EU theory: seeing EU theory as a self-contained normative theory, and seeing EU theory as a generic *component* of a normative

---

[9] See Adler and Sanchirico (2006).

[10] The phrase misleadingly suggests some kind of retrospective evaluation of choices. But what is at issue, in this chapter, is the methodology for ranking choices, *at the moment of choice*, under conditions of uncertainty. The "ex post" approach to using an SWF is one among several methodologies for doing *that*.

[11] See above, n. 6.

theory, what I have termed a generic set of bridge principles. This distinction is both subtle and quite important. It thus bears belaboring.

EU theory understood as a self-contained normative theory is *subjectivist* in its guidance for ordering outcomes. It says to the decisionmaker: you may order outcomes however you like. It says: any ordering of outcomes is normatively permissible, save that the ordering must satisfy the formal constraint of being a complete quasiordering. EU theory then tells the decisionmaker that her ranking of actions must satisfy certain axioms—regimenting that ranking in light of the outcome ranking—so that the action ranking is representable by the EU formula, namely action *a* is at least as good as *b* iff $\sum_{x \in \mathbf{O}} \pi_a(x)v(x) \geq \sum_{x \in \mathbf{O}} \pi_b(x)v(x).$

EU theory, thus construed, is problematic. Note that EU theory, understood as a self-contained normative theory, is surely not a plausible candidate to be a *moral* theory. (What if the decisionmaker happens to prefer to order outcomes in a manner which is partial to the interests of some person, rather than possessing the feature of impartiality which is a basic feature of any moral ordering?) Nor is it a plausible candidate to be a "prudential" normative theory, i.e., a theory which guides the decisionmaker in making choices in light of her own well-being. (What if the decisionmaker's ranking of outcomes is sensitive to remote facts, e.g., facts which occur after her death?) To be sure, it is possible to provide normative guidance which is neither moral nor prudential. But EU theory, understood as a self-contained theory for furnishing some manner of non-moral, non-prudential normative guidance, remains problematic. What if the decisionmaker develops a ranking of outcomes which is formally well-behaved (i.e., complete) but poorly informed and unreflective: she would change the ranking with more facts in hand, and after further deliberation? Is it really plausible to say that any formally well-behaved outcome ranking is normatively on all fours with any other such ranking?

A more plausible view—the view advanced in this chapter—sees EU theory as a kind of normative *module*. On this construal, EU theory is not subjectivist or at least not necessarily subjectivist. Rather than instructing the decisionmaker to order outcomes however she likes, EU theory (on this construal) *brackets* the question of ranking outcomes. It simply does not address itself to that question, except to say that the ranking must be complete. In other words, EU theory (on this construal) provides a *necessary* condition for a normatively attractive ranking of outcomes, rather than a *necessary and sufficient* condition for a normatively attractive ranking of outcomes. It says: the decisionmaker should arrive at a complete ranking of outcomes (the necessary condition), using the most attractive principles for ranking outcomes (whatever they may be); the action ranking should then satisfy certain axioms, regimenting that ranking in light of the outcome ranking, so that it is representable by the expected utility formula.[12]

---

[12] To be clear, I believe that the necessary condition just stated should be revised; EU theory should be refined to allow for an incomplete quasiordering of outcomes. See below, pp. 531–542. What I am stressing, here, is that EU theory, whether in its traditional or refined version, should be understood

EU theory, understood as a normative module, a generic set of outcome set/action set bridge principles, can be meshed with *any* outcome-ranking principles, whatever their content and general category—be they moral outcome-ranking principles, prudential outcome-ranking principles, aesthetic outcome-ranking principles, or principles of some other sort—as long as these eventuate in a complete ordering of outcomes.

What is the content of EU theory (understood as a set of generic bridge principles)? What are the axioms that enable the action ranking to be represented by the expected utility formula $\sum_{x\in O} \pi_a(x)v(x)$? Relatedly, what do the probability terms in this formula mean?

There are actually a number of different versions of EU theory. All of them yield the formula just stated. And all of them interpret the probability terms in this formula as measures of the decisionmaker's *beliefs*. But there are differences, both technical and more philosophical, regarding the particular axioms that are used to regiment the action ranking and regarding the kinds of beliefs that are being quantified by the probability terms.

To begin, it bears noting that the simple "lottery" version of EU theory, pioneered by von Neumann and Morgenstern, does not supply axioms sufficient to justify the expected utility formula—at least outside the context of certain special choice situations. Von Neumann/Morgenstern EU theory was, of course, a critical tool in the construction of the set **U**, via extended preferences, that I presented in Chapter 3. It provides a set of axioms for ranking choices, sufficient to justify the EU formula, in the special case where choices come prepackaged with fixed, exogenous probabilities linking them to outcomes. In other words, von Neumann/Morgenstern EU theory shows that *if* it is presumed at the outset that each choice corresponds to some probability distribution over outcomes, and if in addition these distributions are ranked so as to satisfy certain axioms, the ranking of actions will correspond to the expected utility formula. What von Neumann/Morgenstern EU theory does *not* do is justify the initial presumption. It does not show that *any* choice situation, if ranked in a rational manner, will be such that each choice indeed corresponds to a probability distribution across outcomes.

The more ambitious versions of EU theory aim to make this showing. Choices, at the outset, are not seen as lotteries, probability distributions, or numerical items of any sort. Axioms for ranking choices are supplied. It is then shown that, *if* the axioms are complied with, each choice *a* corresponds to a probability distribution across outcomes $(\pi_a(x), \pi_a(y), \pi_a(z),...)$; and that choice *a* will be ranked as being at least as good as choice b iff $\sum_{x\in O} \pi_a(x)v(x) \geq \sum_{x\in O} \pi_b(x)v(x)$.

as a "module," offering necessary conditions for an attractive ordering of outcomes, not necessary *and* sufficient conditions.

The seminal version of EU theory (along these more ambitious lines) was set forth by Leonard Savage.[13] This version involves a choice set, an outcome set, and a set of possible "states of nature." Each "state of nature" is a specification of background factors which might possibly obtain and which are relevant to the choice at hand. More precisely: each state of nature is a possible state of affairs which is such that any given state, combined with any given action, determinately entails one and only one outcome. Moreover, the states are mutually exclusive and collectively exhaustive (only one can obtain and one must). Finally, each state of nature is causally independent of every action. An action, together with a state, will cause some outcome to occur; but actions do not cause states to occur. (This is the sense in which states are "background" factors relevant to choice.)

Savage requires the decisionmaker's ranking of the action set to satisfy three central axioms, plus some technical axioms, on top of the basic requirement that the ranking of actions and outcomes be complete. The three axioms are (1) a *sure thing axiom* (the ranking of actions should be determined by their outcomes in states where they yield different outcomes, not by their outcomes in states where they yield the same outcome); (2) a *monotonicity axiom* (if actions a and b differ only in that action a yields outcome x in certain states, while action b yields outcome y in those states, then a is at least as good as b iff outcome x is at least as good as outcome y[14]); (3) a *comparative probability axiom*. (To state this last axiom most simply, we should introduce the notion of an "event," namely a collection of states. Imagine that action a yields outcome x in the event that E occurs, otherwise outcome y; that action b yields outcome x in the event that F occurs, otherwise outcome y; that the decisionmaker ranks x as better than y; and that she ranks a as being at least as good as b. Then this ranking of the actions indicates that the decisionmaker believes the occurrence of event E to be at least as likely as the occurrence of event F. Thus the decisionmaker should rank action a^* as being at least as good as b^* if these are identical to a and b except in yielding, respectively, w and z rather than x and y, and if the decisionmaker ranks w above z just as she does x above y.)

Savage shows that, if the agent's ranking of choices satisfies these axioms, plus the technical axioms and the completeness axiom, there will exist a probability number assigned to each state s, $\pi(s)$, and a utility number assigned to each outcome, $v(x)$. The utility numbers will represent the ordering of outcomes: it will be the case that x is at least as good an outcome as y iff $v(x) \geq v(y)$. Each action a will be assigned an

---

[13] Savage (1972). Helpful discussions include Fishburn (1994); Gilboa (2009, chs. 10–12); Joyce (1999, ch. 3); Joyce and Gibbard (1998); and Kreps (1988, chs. 8–9). The causal aspects of the Savage framework (summarized in the text immediately below) were not emphasized by Savage himself, but rather have been clarified by subsequent theorists working within causal decision theory. On this, see Joyce (1999, ch. 3) and Joyce and Gibbard (1998).

[14] Strictly, this holds only if the collection of states where a yields x and b yields y is not "null."

expected utility number using the formula $\sum_{s \in S} \pi(s) v(x[a,s])$.[15] (In this formula, S is the set of all states, and the symbol $x[a,s]$ is used to denote the particular outcome x that a would produce if s were the state. The probability term $\pi(s)$ is the decisionmaker's degree of belief that state s obtains.) And one action will be at least as good as a second iff its expected utility is at least as large.

How does the formula just stated map onto the generic EU formula which I have used several times, $\sum_{x \in O} \pi_a(x) v(x)$? The answer is this: according to Savage, the term $\pi_a(x)$ in the latter formula is the cumulative probability of the states of nature which, together with action a, yield outcome x. In other words, $\pi_a(x)$ is a numerical measure of the decisionmaker's belief that there is some combination of causal factors which, together with action a, yields outcome x.

Savage's formulation of EU theory has been hugely influential. A subsequent formulation, also widely relied upon by economists, was provided by Anscombe and Aumann.[16] Like Savage, Anscombe and Aumann employ the apparatus of a set of "states of nature." Like Savage, they show that if the decisionmaker ranks her actions consistently with certain axioms, her ranking will be represented by the expected utility formula, with the probability terms corresponding to the probabilities of states. Their axiomatization has the advantage of being simpler than Savage's. It also has the philosophical advantage of not requiring that the combination of a given state and a given action yield some particular outcome with certainty, and thus accommodating the possibility of causal laws that are indeterministic.[17]

The reader might wonder why EU theory needs the apparatus of "states of nature." Why employ this roundabout route to showing that the choices of a rational decisionmaker can be associated with probabilities? Why not adopt a more straightforward interpretation of the probability terms in the EU formula: namely, that $\pi_a(x)$ is simply a *conditional probability*, i.e., the probability of outcome x, conditional on the performance of action a?

The answer to this question implicates the debate between so-called "evidential" and so-called "causal" approaches to EU theory. The evidential approach dispenses with the apparatus of "states of nature" and, indeed, reads $\pi_a(x)$ as a simple *conditional probability*. The evidential view starts with a set of *propositions*, namely descriptions of the way the world might turn out. An outcome is a kind of proposition; so too is the proposition that some action is performed. In general, the probability of proposition p, conditional on proposition q, is the probability of the conjunction of p and q divided by the probability of q. And this is how the evidential approach understands $\pi_a(x)$. The evidential approach to EU theory shows this: if the

---

[15] In the Savage set-up, it turns out that the state set is uncountably infinite; and so, strictly speaking, this formula is incorrect. The correct formula uses an integral, but so as to avoid burdening the reader with calculus formulae I have expressed the Savage result using a summation.

[16] Anscombe and Aumann (1963). See Kreps (1988, ch. 7); Gilboa (2009, ch. 14).

[17] Finally, it has the technical advantage of allowing for a finite state set.

decisionmaker ranks his actions consistently with certain axioms, then he will rank a at least as good as b iff $\sum_{x \in O} v(x)\pi(x \& a) / \pi(a) \geq \sum_{x \in O} v(x)\pi(x \& b) / \pi(b)$, where $\pi(p)$ for any proposition p (be it an outcome, the proposition that some action is performed, or any other kind of proposition) is the decisionmaker's degree of belief in p.[18]

On *this* view, the probability term $\pi_a(x)$ in the generic EU formula, $\sum_{x \in O} \pi_a(x)v(x)$, is equal to $\pi(x \& a)/\pi(a)$. The term $\pi_a(x)$ is thus a conditional epistemic probability: the decisionmaker's degree of belief that he will perform a and x will occur, divided by his degree of belief that he will perform a (or, more crisply, his degree of belief that x will occur, conditional on a being performed). An axiomatization of EU theory along these lines has been provided by Jeffrey and Bolker.[19]

Causal EU theorists object that the evidential approach goes awry in cases where the performance of some action increases the conditional probability of an outcome (as compared to its probability conditional on non-performance of the action), but the action has no causal influence on the outcome. The so-called Newcomb problem is an oft-discussed example of how this can happen. For a more mundane example, consider a case in which there is a gene that substantially increases the chance of cancer, and also creates a desire to drink pomegranate juice, a healthy food that does not cause cancer and has other health benefits. I strongly prefer to be in good health, and am deciding whether to drink pomegranate juice. On the evidential approach, it may well be that I shouldn't do so, because the probability of my getting cancer conditional on drinking the juice is greater than the probability of cancer conditional on not drinking the juice. Drinking the juice is evidence that I desire to drink it and thus

---

[18] One subtlety is that the evidential approach can also be expressed using states, and sometimes is. Let us denote the conditional probability of p given q, i.e., $\pi(p \& q)/\pi(q)$, using the standard notation "$\pi(p|q)$." So the evidential formula assigns action a an expected utility value equaling $\sum_{z \in O} \pi(z|a)v(z)$. Let us denote by S any arbitrary collection of states which (1) form a partition (they are mutually exclusive and collectively exhaustive) and (2) are such that the conjunction of a and any state s entails one and only one outcome in O. Denote that outcome as $x[a, s]$. Use $S(a, z)$ to mean the subset of states which, together with a, yield outcome z. By the rules of the probability calculus, $\sum_{z \in O} \pi(z|a)v(z) = \sum_{z \in O} \left[\sum_{s \in S(a,z)} \pi(z|a \& s)\pi(s|a) \right] v(z)$. Because $\pi(z \mid a \& s)$ is unity for all s in $S(a, z)$ and because $v(z) = v(x[a, s])$ for all s in $S(a, z)$—by construction—this latter formula reduces to $\sum_{z \in O} \left[\sum_{s \in S(a,z)} \pi(s|a)v(x[a,s]) \right]$. Because each s entails one and only one outcome in O, given a, this formula in turn is equal to $\sum_{s \in S} \pi(s|a)v(x[a,s])$. This looks like the Savage formula; but a critical difference is that the probability term assigned to each state is its probability conditional on action a, while the Savage formula uses unconditional state probabilities. Moreover, to say that every state is stochastically independent of every action, i.e, $\pi(s \mid a) = \pi(s)$, so that unconditional state probabilities can be inserted in the above formula, is *not* the same as requiring the states to be *causally* independent of actions, which is how the Savage framework is best interpreted.

On the difference between causal and evidential decision theory, see generally Joyce (1999) and Joyce and Gibbard (1998).

[19] See Jeffrey (1983); Joyce (1999, ch. 4).

evidence that I have the cancer gene. But it is absurd not to drink the juice: whether or not I have the cancer gene, drinking the juice will make me healthier.

The causal variant of EU theory adopts the Savage approach of assigning probabilities to outcomes by assigning them to states of nature, or some similar approach[20]—and thus circumvents the difficulties associated with the evidential version of EU theory.

I raise the debate between "causal" and "evidential" versions of EU theory because it bears on the *interpretation* of the probability terms in the EU formula. Moreover, I believe there is good reason to think that the causal approach is better justified. However, a full discussion of the causal–evidential debate would require much space and take us away from problems of moral theory to generic issues in decision theory. My claim in this chapter is merely that *whichever version of EU theory* is best justified as a generic set of outcome-act bridge principles—be it the causal version or the evidential version—is also attractive for the specific purposes of moving from the moral ranking of outcomes to the moral ranking of actions.

Moreover, the reader should understand that the various approaches to EU theory mentioned in the last few pages—Savage's famous axiomatization, other approaches under the rubric of causal decision theory, and evidential approaches—all concur in seeing the probability terms in the generic EU formula as *epistemic* probabilities. The term $\pi_a(x)$, on all views, is a measure of some kind of belief on the part of the decisionmaker. It is a numerical degree of belief. For Savage (again), it is a measure of the decisionmaker's belief that a state of nature of a certain type will occur—namely a state which, together with the action a, entails outcome x. For the "evidentialist," it is a measure of the decisionmaker's degree of belief that x will occur, conditional on a being performed.

This epistemic construal of the probability term is not only a shared feature of all the variants of EU theory on offer—whatever their more precise details—but helps to explain why the approach has been seen, by many, to be so plausible. It is a truism that the rational decisionmaker, whatever her goals, should choose among available actions in light of her beliefs concerning the consequences of those actions. She should favor actions which, she believes, will yield consequences that advance the goals; and disfavor actions which, she believes, will yield consequences that frustrate the goals. Sound instrumental reasoning integrates an ordering of outcomes with beliefs regarding the outcomes that the different choices at hand would produce. EU theory (in all its variants) offers a rigorous specification of this truism, with beliefs (of one or another sort) subsumed under the probability term and provided a numerical measure.

Just as EU theory is sometimes interpreted as a full-blown theory of rational choice—a construal I have resisted—so it is sometimes viewed as a complete theory

---

[20] A generalization of the "state" approach is to make $\pi_a(x)$ something like the probability of a coun-terfactual conditional—namely, the probability that, in the nearest possible world where the actor performs a, outcome x results.

of rational belief formation. On this interpretation, the decisionmaker can have whatever beliefs she wants—so long as they can be represented by probability numbers. Consider the Savage axiomatization. In order for beliefs regarding "states of nature" to be represented by probability numbers, they must meet certain minimal coherence conditions, such as: I should believe that a collection of states (an event) is at least as likely as any of its members; if I believe that state s is at least as likely as state r, then I should believe that the occurrence of either state s or state t is at least as likely as the occurrence of either state r or state t; and so forth.[21] The decisionmaker who ranks actions in conformity with the Savage axioms will indeed have beliefs regarding states of nature that satisfy these minimal coherence conditions. And one possible interpretation of the Savage variant of EU theory is that principles of rational belief formation are *exhausted* by these conditions. The decisionmaker can believe *whatever she wants* about the likelihood of different states, as long as she doesn't commit the formal error of believing a collection to be less likely than one of its members, believing that the occurrence of either r or t is more likely than the occurrence of either s or t even though she believes that r is less likely than s; and so forth.

This view of EU theory is implausible and is not the view tendered here. Earlier, I suggested that EU theory should be seen as offering *necessary* conditions for a normatively attractive ranking of outcomes, rather than necessary and sufficient conditions. Similarly, I suggest here that EU theory should be seen as offering *necessary* conditions for rational belief formation (namely, the conditions necessary for the beliefs to be representable by probabilities), rather than necessary and sufficient conditions. The basic axioms of the Savage set-up or any other version of EU theory can be supplemented with additional epistemic requirements[22] as long as those requirements are logically consistent with the axioms.

What those additional requirements might be is a question pursued by epistemologists and statisticians. Of especial relevance, here, is a burgeoning school within statistics, so-called "Bayesian statistics."[23] Unlike traditional statistics, which eschews the construct of an epistemic probability—a numerical degree of belief—Bayesian statistics is centered on that construct. Its methodologies seek to ensure that a decisionmaker, at any one point in time, will indeed have beliefs representable by probability numbers. But Bayesian statistics goes well beyond this minimal, synchronic requirement. First, the literature discusses different kinds of epistemic probability distributions—different mathematical formulae for distributing probability numbers across states of nature (or propositions more generally)—which are evaluated as more or less attractive, depending on considerations such as simplicity, "conjugateness," "exchangeability," "informativeness," "robustness," and so forth. Second,

---

[21] Remember that states are mutually exclusive. On these conditions, see Kreps (1988, ch. 8).

[22] See Gilboa, Postlewaite, and Schmeidler (2008a, pp. 184–186); Joyce (2004, pp. 149–153).

[23] See, e.g., Bernardo and Smith (2000); Gelman et al. (2004).

and most fundamentally, Bayesian statistics elaborates norms whereby the decision-maker rationally *updates* her epistemic probabilities, as new information arrives.

Strictly, then, it is incorrect to see EU theory, alone, as an adequate set of bridge principles for moving from the moral ranking of outcomes to a moral ranking of actions. Rather, it is the combination of a systematic set of methodologies for arriving at epistemic probabilities (exemplified by Bayesian statistics), taken together with the EU rule for integrating those probability numbers with utility numbers representing the ranking of outcomes, that furnishes such bridge principles. It also bears note, here, that the use of statistical tools to evaluate governmental policies is already very widespread, both in the academy and within government itself. For example, environmental, health, and safety agencies in the U.S. and other countries rely heavily on a variety of "risk assessment" methodologies for ranking hazards and abatement measures.[24] My suggestion that (Bayesian) statistical methodologies be part of moral assessment of governmental policies and other large-scale choices does not counsel a radical departure from current policy-analytic approaches, but is continuous with the extant use of risk assessment in policy analysis.[25]

A final general point, regarding EU theory, concerns the nature of the actions in the action set **A**. As mentioned in Chapter 1, the "actions" ranked by a choice-evaluation framework *might* be immediate actions, what the decisionmaker can do at some moment in time; or they might be intertemporal sequences of immediate actions. In the context of governmental policy, the former might mean the issuance of a particular law or regulation, while the latter might mean undertaking a series of regulatory measures over time. Later in the chapter, under the rubric of incompleteness in the outcome ordering (which intersects with issues of intertemporal choice), I will address the relative merits of these two interpretations of the elements of **A**. But it should be stressed that both are consistent with EU theory. Expected utilities can certainly be assigned to immediate actions, but they can also be assigned to

---

[24] See, e.g., Adler (2005).

[25] The divide between Bayesian and traditional statistics is sometimes seen to map the divide between two conceptions of probability, namely the epistemic view which sees probability as a measure of belief, versus the "frequentist" or "objective" view which sees probability as the long-run frequency of some attribute within some reference class. This division is too crude: Bayesian statistics does not ignore objective probabilities, but in large part focuses on how to incorporate information about relative frequencies (arrived at via observation or via some kind of deliberate experiment), along with prior beliefs, so as to arrive at current beliefs. See, e.g., Gelman et al. (2004, ch. 2). (Note also that much work within decision theory combines epistemic and objective probabilities, for example the Anscombe/Aumann set-up.)

Thus my suggestion that an attractive choice-evaluation framework employs EU bridge principles, coupled with the use of Bayesian statistics to arrive at epistemic probabilities, does *not* mean that such probabilities should be formulated without reference to information about relative frequencies—which are a cornerstone of risk assessment methodologies currently employed in policy analysis. Although the $\pi_a(x)$ term *is* an epistemic probability, sound epistemic norms can require that this epistemic probability, in turn, be sensitive to objective probabilities.

longer-range plans. Savage himself adopted the "plan" view. He wrote: "[W]hat in the ordinary way of thinking might be regarded as a chain of decisions, one leading to the other in time, is in the formal description proposed here regarded as a single decision. To put it a little differently, it is proposed that the choice of a policy or plan be regarded as a single decision."[26] On the other hand, James Joyce, an important contemporary decision theorist, construes an action much more narrowly, as a "pure, present exercise[] of the will," arguing that an intertemporal sequence of actions cannot be literally an object of choice.

> [P]eople generally cannot, by a pure exercise of present will, force their future choices to conform to their current plans. There are a number of things that make such "predecision" impossible. First, it is always possible that unforeseen external events will prevent the choices envisioned in a plan from arising. . . . Second, during the interval between the adoption of the plan and its execution the agent may become unwilling or unable to carry through on her earlier choices.[27]

B. Meshing EU Theory with the Continuous Prioritarian SWF

How, precisely, would EU theory be integrated with the moral ranking of outcomes achieved by the continuous prioritarian SWF so as to produce a moral ranking of actions?

If the moral ranking of actions is consistent with EU theory, then there will be a moral utility function assignable to outcomes—call it $m(.)$—such that action a is at least as good as action b iff $\sum_{x \in O} \pi_a(x)m(x) \geq \sum_{x \in O} \pi_b(x)m(x)$.

To begin, it should be noted that the probability terms in this formula are measures of the decisionmaker's *own* rational beliefs, which are sufficiently well-behaved to be represented by probability numbers and may well be required to conform to additional epistemic norms. The beliefs and judgments of other individuals bear upon the decisionmaker's beliefs only insofar as general norms of rational belief formation so require; such third-party beliefs get no extra weight as a moral matter.[28]

---

[26] Savage (1972, pp. 15–16).

[27] Joyce (1999, pp. 57, 58–59) (emphasis omitted).

[28] This is one aspect of seeing the appropriate moral bridge principles as simply being the application, to the moral domain, of the most attractive generic bridge principles. More substantively: where the decisionmaker has a different degree of belief in outcomes than some individuals, and this difference persists even after the decisionmaker rationally updates to take account of the individuals' views, why is there some further requirement of responsiveness to those views? Wouldn't such a requirement be in tension with *consequentialism*: the idea that the decisionmaker should act to produce the best outcomes?

For discussions of the paradoxes that can arise when moral decisionmakers adopt an approach that requires direct responsiveness to public beliefs, see Broome (1995, ch. 7); Chambers and Hayashi (2006). On generic epistemic norms that allow a decisionmaker to be responsive to third-party beliefs in updating his own beliefs, see, e.g., Clemen and Winkler (2007).

What about the moral utility function $m(.)$? It is crucial that the reader understand the distinction between *this* utility function, and other sorts of utility functions that have appeared earlier in the book. One such utility function, denoted $u(.)$, is scalar valued; takes life-histories as its arguments (i.e., has the form $u(x; i)$); and represents the well-being ordering of life-histories. The set **U** consists in utility functions of this sort. Each such $u(.)$ is associated with a vector-valued utility function which maps each outcome onto an N-entry list of numbers, measuring the well-being of each individual in the population in that outcome. Finally, Chapter 4 discussed how the elements of **U**, if constructed via extended preferences, might be inferred from individuals' ordinary self-interested preferences. Such preferences on the part of individual k are measured by a utility function $\varphi^k(.)$, which is scalar valued; takes outcomes as its arguments; and represents k's ranking of outcomes when self-interested.

The moral utility function $m(.)$ now under discussion takes outcomes as its arguments (not life-histories). It is scalar valued, not vector valued. And it does not represent the well-being or self-interested preferences of any individual or group of individuals (let alone the "well-being" of the outcome itself, which is an absurd idea). Rather, the numbers $m(x)$, $m(y)$, $m(z)$, etc., assigned to the various outcomes in **O**, are a cardinal measure of the moral goodness of those outcomes—a numerical measure which represents where the various outcomes sit in the moral ranking of outcomes; and which, together with information about the probability that a given action a yields each outcome, represents where that *action* sits in the moral ranking of actions.

What does it mean to say that $m(.)$ is a *cardinal* measure of moral goodness? Remember that the utility numbers yielded by EU theory are unique up to a positive affine transformation. Thus the EU approach really produces not a single moral utility function but a whole set thereof. Call this **M**. For a given outcome set **O**, and a given choice set **A**, the use of EU theory as moral bridge principles means: there is a set **M** of moral utility functions, unique up to a positive affine transformation, such that action a is morally at least as good as action b iff $\sum_{x \in \mathbf{O}} \pi_a(x)m(x) \geq \sum_{x \in \mathbf{O}} \pi_b(x)m(x)$, for any $m(.)$ in **M**. To say that **M** is unique up to a positive affine transformation means: there is some $m(.)$, such that $m^*(.)$ is in **M** just in case there is a positive number a and a number b such that $m^*(x) = am(x) + b$ for every x in the outcome set.[29]

---

[29] On EU theory and uniqueness up to a positive affine transformation, see, e.g., Kreps (1988, pp. 46, 110, 136). Note that, if **M** consists of some $m(.)$ and every positive affine transformation thereof, each element of **M** will yield the same, complete ordering of **A**, using the EU formula, action a is at least as good as action b iff $\sum_{x \in \mathbf{O}} \pi_a(x)m(x) \geq \sum_{x \in \mathbf{O}} \pi_b(x)m(x)$. Conversely, in the case of a "rich" choice set **A**, where every possible probability distribution over outcomes corresponds to some action, it is not hard to show the converse—that $m^*(.)$ represents the same ranking of **A** as $m(.)$ only if $m^*(.)$ is a positive affine transformation of $m(.)$. In actuality, given bounded rationality, choice sets will not be this "rich," so that *some* transformations of $m(.)$ which are *not* positive affine

What is the connection between the moral utility functions in **M** and the moral ordering of outcomes generated by the continuous prioritarian SWF—the ordering generated by the formula, x is morally at least as good as y iff, for all $u(.)$ in **U**,
$$\sum_{i=1}^{N} g(u_i(x)) \geq \sum_{i=1}^{N} g(u_i(y))?$$

To begin, EU theory presupposes that the ordering of outcomes is complete. This is a key limitation of the approach, since I have repeatedly stressed that the moral ordering of outcomes may well be an incomplete quasiordering. How to overcome this limitation is addressed later in the chapter, under the heading of refinements. For now, it bears noting that the continuous prioritarian outcome-ranking formula *will* yield a complete ordering if **U** is unique up to a positive ratio transformation and the SWF being used is the Atkinson SWF.[30] (Remember that **U** is unique up to a positive ratio transformation if it consists of a utility function and all positive multiples—if there is some $u(.)$ such that $v(.)$ is in **U** iff there exists a positive number r such that $v(x; i) = ru(x; i)$ for every life history $(x; i)$.)

Assume, henceforth, that **U** is indeed unique up to a positive ratio transformation (hence can be represented, as elsewhere in the book, by the symbol "$ru(.)$," and the utility assigned to a specific life-history by "r" following some number), and that we are using an Atkinson SWF. (This will be the assumption for the rest of the chapter, until we reach the question of "refinements.") For any given $u(.)$, the Atkinson SWF will assign outcome x a number equaling $(1-\gamma)^{-1} \sum_{i=1}^{N} u_i(x)^{1-\gamma}$ (or $\sum_{i=1}^{N} \ln u_i(x)$ in the case where the inequality aversion parameter, γ, equals 1) and will assign some other outcome y a number equaling $(1-\gamma)^{-1} \sum_{i=1}^{N} u_i(y)^{1-\gamma}$. What is the connection between *these* numbers and the numbers assigned to x and y by the moral utility functions in **M**?

Moral utility functions must track the moral ordering of outcomes. It must be the case that $m(x) \geq m(y)$ iff outcome x is morally at least as good as outcome y.[31]

This imposes a linkage between **U** and **M**. Formally, for any given $u(.)$ in **U**, there is a strictly increasing function $f^u(.)$, with **M** consisting of a utility function $m(.)$

transformations may yield the same ranking of **A** as $m(.)$. So as to keep matters reasonably simple, I will ignore this nuance; it does not in any way affect the case for using EU theory as bridge principles.

[30] This just follows from the ratio-rescaling properties of the Atkinson SWF, see Chapter 5. If r is a positive number, then this SWF coupled with utility function $u(.)$ yields the very same ranking of any two outcomes as when coupled with utility function $ru(.)$.

[31] This is a generic feature of EU theory. Consider any arbitrary ranking of an outcome set. Assume that the choice set includes an action a^x which leads for sure to outcome x and an action a^y which leads for sure to outcome y. (If the choice set does not in fact include such choices, we can imagine a hypothetical expansion of the actual set to include them.) Surely, the ranking of the a^x/a^y pair should correspond to the ranking of the x/y pair. The action ranking should surely satisfy the requirement that (1) a^x is at least as good as a^y iff x is at least as good as y. But note that if we use the EU formula to rank the two actions (with $v(.)$ the utility function; x assigned a probability of 1 given a^x; and y assigned a probability of 1 given a^y), then requirement (1) is equivalent to requiring that (2) $v(x) \geq v(y)$ iff x is at least as good as y.

such that $m(x) = f^u((1-\gamma)^{-1}\sum_{i=1}^{N}u_i(x)^{1-\gamma})$, plus all positive affine transformations of $m(.)$.[32] For short, call $f^u(.)$ the "translation" function.

Most simply, $f^u(.)$ is the identity function.[33] In that case, $f^u(.)$ disappears from view, and we can say that **M** consists of $m(.)$ such that $m(x) = (1-\gamma)^{-1}\sum_{i=1}^{N}u_i(x)^{1-\gamma}$, plus all positive affine transformations of $m(.)$. And if this is true for any given $u(.)$ in **U**, it will be true for every $u(.)$ in **U**.[34]

However, nothing in EU theory requires that $f^u(.)$ be the identity function. For example, it is quite consistent with EU theory to say that the moral utility assigned to an outcome is the *square root* of the number assigned to the outcome by the continuous prioritarian SWF. In other words, for some given $u(.)$, **M** is all positive affine transformations of $m(.)$ defined as follows: $m(x) = \sqrt{(1-\gamma)^{-1}\sum_{i=1}^{N}u_i(x)^{1-\gamma}}$. Here's an analogy: just as the utility function $\varphi^k(.)$ measuring an individual's self-interested preferences over outcomes, characterized in terms of consumption, may be the

---

Note also that this feature of EU theory is closely connected to the discussion below of stochastic dominance. Because $v(x) \geq v(y)$ iff x is at least as good as y, the EU rule necessarily ranks a over b if the first action stochastically dominates the second.

[32] Consider any $u(.)$ in **U**. With **U** assumed to be unique up to a positive ratio transformation, and the moral ordering of outcomes given by the Atkinson SWF, it is the case that for any pair of outcomes x and y, (1) outcome x is morally at least as good as outcome y iff $(1-\gamma)^{-1}\sum_{i=1}^{N}u_i(x)^{1-\gamma} \geq (1-\gamma)^{-1}\sum_{i=1}^{N}u_i(y)^{1-\gamma}$. We established just above that (2) for any $m(.)$ in **M**, outcome x is morally at least as good as outcome y iff $m(x) \geq m(y)$. Putting these two together, we have that (3) for any $m(.)$ in **M**, $m(x) \geq m(y)$ iff $(1-\gamma)^{-1}\sum_{i=1}^{N}u_i(x)^{1-\gamma} \geq (1-\gamma)^{-1}\sum_{i=1}^{N}u_i(y)^{1-\gamma}$. Thus there must be a strictly increasing function $f^u(.)$ such that (4) for any outcome x, $m(x) = f^u((1-\gamma)^{-1}\sum_{i=1}^{N}u_i(x)^{1-\gamma})$, with **M** in turn all positive affine transformations of $m(.)$. (If **M** is unique up to a positive affine transformation, then it is not too hard to see that **M** consists of all positive affine transformations of any one of its members.)

Nothing in this reasoning entails that the translation function enabling us to get from a given $u(.)$ to some element of **M** is independent of which $u(.)$ in **U** is chosen, and thus I have denoted that function as "$f^u(.)$." Assume that there is an $m(.)$ in **M** which assigns numbers to outcomes as follows: $m(x) = f^u((1-\gamma)^{-1}\sum_{i=1}^{N}u_i(x)^{1-\gamma})$, for some $u(.)$ in **U**. Consider now some other $u^*(.)$ in **U**, where $u^*(.) = ru(.)$. If $f^u(.)$ is homogeneous, it follows that $m^*(.)$ is in **M**, where $m^*(.)$ is defined by the rule $m^*(x) = f^u((1-\gamma)^{-1}\sum_{i=1}^{N}u^*_i(x)^{1-\gamma})$. However, if $f^u(.)$ is not homogeneous, this need not be the case.

[33] In other words, $f^u(d) = d$ for all d.

[34] Assume that we take some $u(.)$ in **U**, and that $f^u(.)$ is the identity function, i.e., there is some $m(.)$ in **M** such that $m(x) = (1-\gamma)^{-1}\sum_{i=1}^{N}u_i(x)^{1-\gamma}$, with every other element $m^*(.)$ in **M** such that $m^*(x) = a((1-\gamma)^{-1}\sum_{i=1}^{N}u_i(x)^{1-\gamma}) + b$, for some b and positive a.

Now consider some other utility function $u^+(.)$ in **U**. Because **U** is unique up to a positive ratio transformation, there is some positive number r such that $u^+(x; i) = ru(x; i)$, for every life history $(x; i)$. Apply the identity function to $u^+(.)$ to define $m^+(.)$, that is: $m^+(x) = (1-\gamma)^{-1}\sum_{i=1}^{N}u^+_i(x)^{1-\gamma}$. Then $m^+(.)$ is a positive affine transformation of $m(.)$, hence in **M**, since $m(.)$ is. Specifically, if $d = r^{1-\gamma}$, then $m^+(x) = dm(x)$ for all x.

In the case where $\gamma = 1$, we have instead that $m(x) = \sum_{i=1}^{N}\ln u_i(x)$, and if $d = N(\ln r)$, then $m^+(x) = m(x) + d$ for all x.

square root of her consumption (or some other non-linear function of her consumption), so the moral utility number assigned to an outcome may be an increasing but non-linear transformation of the value assigned to that outcome by a given SWF (prioritarian or other).[35]

If EU theory is used as the set of moral bridge principles, each action in **A**—of course—corresponds to a probability distribution across outcomes, representing the decisionmaker's rational degrees of belief that the action would yield the various outcomes in **O**. In other words, action a corresponds to $(\pi_a(x), \pi_a(y), \pi_a(z), \ldots)$, action b corresponds to $(\pi_b(x), \pi_b(y), \pi_b(z), \ldots)$, and so forth. Moreover, using EU theory to rank the actions in **A** means that the ranking of the corresponding probability distributions necessarily satisfies certain principles. One principle is what I will term the "sure thing" principle. Traditionally, that principle is formulated in terms of the Savage version of EU theory, which uses "states of nature." My defense of EU theory as a body of moral bridge principles is meant to be agnostic as between the Savage set-up and other versions, and so what follows represents a more general statement.

The Sure Thing Principle

Imagine that the probability distributions corresponding to actions a and b have a common "subdistribution." There is a subset of outcomes to which both actions accord the same probabilities. Then if we produce two new actions a^* and b^* which have a different group of outcomes "plugged into" the common subdistribution and are otherwise identical, respectively, to a and b, the ranking of these actions should be the same as the ranking of a and b.[36]

---

[35] The square-root $m(.)$, just described, is a simple and intuitive example of a nonlinear $f^u(.)$ function. It is well-defined only if $\gamma < 1$. But there are, of course, non-linear $f^u(.)$ that work perfectly well with $\gamma \geq 1$. The Fleurbaey $f^u(.)$ function, discussed below, is an important example.

[36] The idea here is intuitive, but the formal statement of this general version of the "sure thing" principle, without states necessarily in the picture, requires some care. Assume that there is a subset of outcomes **L** such that, for x in **L**, $\pi_a(x) = \pi_b(x)$. (These are the outcomes to which a and b assign the same probability.) We are going to use a function $f(.)$ to define the probability distribution of an action a^* which is the counterpart to a, and the probability distribution of an action b^* which is the counterpart to b. For any x belonging to **L**, $f(x) = z$, any arbitrary outcome. (Different such arbitrary outcomes can be assigned to different outcomes in **L**.) For x not belonging to **L**, $f(x) = x$. Then define the probability assigned by a^* to a given outcome y, $\pi_{a^*}(y)$, as the cumulative probability according to a of all the outcomes mapped onto y by $f(.)$. In other words, $\pi_{a^*}(y) = \sum_{x:f(x)=y} \pi_a(x)$. (This device is needed to handle the possibility that the same outcome is substituted multiple times for an outcome in **L**, and that the substituted outcome comes from outside **L**.) Similarly, define the probability assigned by b^* to a given outcome, $\pi_{b^*}(y)$, as the cumulative probability according to b of all the outcomes mapped onto y by $f(.)$. Then the generalized "sure thing" principle says that a is at least as good as b iff a^* is at least as good as b^*.

A second set of principles necessarily satisfied by the EU approach are two stochastic dominance principles. We can distinguish, here, between the ordinary stochastic dominance principle much discussed in the literature on EU theory (so-called "first order" stochastic dominance[37]) and a principle which I will term the "weak" stochastic dominance principle.

Ordinary Stochastic Dominance

If the probability distributions corresponding to actions a and b are such that the first can be converted into the second by shifting probability toward better outcomes, then b is a better action than a. Formally, partition all the outcomes in $\mathbf{O}$ into sets $X_1, X_2, \ldots, X_M$, with M in total, so that all of the outcomes in each set are equally good and all of the outcomes in X_1 are worse than all in X_2, in turn worse than all in X_3, and so forth.[38] Let $\pi_a(X_m)$ denote the probability, if a is performed, that some outcome in X_m occurs. The probability distribution corresponding to a is $(\pi_a(X_1), \pi_a(X_2), \ldots, \pi_a(X_M))$, while the probability distribution corresponding to b is $(\pi_b(X_1), \pi_b(X_2), \ldots, \pi_b(X_M))$. The second distribution stochastically dominates the first if $\sum_{l=1}^{L} \pi_b(X_l) \leq \sum_{l=1}^{L} \pi_a(X_l)$ for $L = 1$ to M, with at least one inequality strict. The axiom of ordinary stochastic dominance requires that, in this case, action b be ranked as better than action a.

Weak Stochastic Dominance

Imagine that the probability distributions corresponding to actions a and b are such that *every* outcome accorded nonzero probability by the b distribution is better than *every* outcome accorded nonzero probability by the a distribution. Then b is a better action than a.

The adjective "weak" is meant to signal that this variant of the stochastic dominance requirement imposes a very minimal constraint on the ranking of actions. What it says is that if action b is sure to yield a better outcome than action a, b is a better action.

The weak stochastic dominance principle is, intuitively, even more compelling than the ordinary stochastic dominance principle. A ranking of actions that satisfies the ordinary stochastic dominance principle necessarily satisfies the weak stochastic dominance principle (but not vice versa). As it turns out, ranking actions in any

---

[37] See, e.g., Starmer (2000, p. 335).
[38] This contrivance is needed to accommodate the possibility that two outcomes in $\mathbf{O}$ might be equally good. A simpler version of stochastic dominance employs a formula that cumulates probabilities of individual outcomes, ranked from worst to best; this version is appropriate for the case in which no two outcomes are equally good (for example, where outcomes are different consumption amounts received by some individual, ranked in light of her strictly increasing preferences), but not for the more general case at hand here. For the simpler statement, see ibid.

choice set **A** in accordance with EU theory *will* necessarily satisfy the ordinary stochastic dominance principle and, therefore, will also necessarily satisfy the "weak" version of this principle.

II. DEFENDING EU PRIORITARIANISM FROM THE TARGETED OBJECTION

The previous section clarified the structure of a moral choice-evaluation procedure that employs a continuous prioritarian SWF to produce the moral ranking of outcomes, and then employs EU theory as the bridge principles for moving from this ranking to a moral ordering of actions. For short, let us call such a framework "EU prioritarianism."

This section describes and then attempts to rebut what I term the "targeted objection" to EU prioritarianism.[39] This "targeted" objection does not rely on important generic objections to EU theory. Rather, the objection claims that EU theory is unattractive in the *moral* context quite apart from these generic difficulties. In other words, it claims that *even if* the choice situation at hand is "parametric" rather than "strategic"; even if the moral ordering of outcomes is complete; even if the decision-maker knows for sure what that ordering is; and even if there is a single, determinate probability distribution across outcomes corresponding to each action, it is *still* the case that the moral ordering of a choice set **A** should not be generated from the prioritarian moral ordering of outcomes using EU theory.

My analysis will proceed in four steps. First, I will describe the apparently perverse results of EU prioritarianism, as regards the ex ante Pigou–Dalton and Pareto principles. Second, I will argue that non-EU bridge principles for moving from the prioritarian ordering of outcomes to the ordering of actions are even more perverse and, on balance, should be rejected. Third, I will consider whether the conflicts between EU prioritarianism and the ex ante Pareto principles might be mitigated by judicious choice of the "translation" function (the function that gets us to a moral utility value $m(x)$ for a given outcome, depending on the value assigned to that outcome by the continuous prioritarian SWF). Finally, I will consider whether the difficulties in meshing EU theory with a prioritarian moral ordering of outcomes provide sufficient grounds to reconsider the arguments, presented in Chapter 5, for a continuous prioritarian SWF.

Throughout the analysis, I will assume that utility functions in **U** are unique up to a positive ratio transformation, thus can be represented as "$ru(.)$," and that the continuous prioritarian SWF being used is the Atkinson SWF.

---

[39] Thanks to Marc Fleurbaey, Chris Sanchirico, and Peter Vallentyne for much help on the topics covered in this section, which grows out of a collaboration with Chris (Adler and Sanchirico [2006]).

A. The Targeted Objection: How EU Prioritarianism Violates the Ex Ante Pareto and Pigou–Dalton Principles

Despite the dominance of EU theory as a normative model of choice in decision theory and economics, a substantial number of social choice theorists are uncomfortable using the EU approach in implementing a social welfare function.[40]

The critique typically proceeds by observing that a given governmental action or policy under uncertainty is associated, not simply with a probability distribution over outcomes and corresponding utility vectors, but also with a single vector of individual expected utilities. Each expected utility is assumed to represent the ex ante well-being of the individual, with that policy.[41]

Table 7.1 The Vector of Individual Expected Utilities Corresponding to an Action

	$\pi_a(x) = .5$	$\pi_a(y) = .5$	
	$u(x)$	$u(y)$	*Expected utility*
Individual A	10r	20r	$.5(10r) + .5(20r) = 15r$
Individual B	30r	20r	$.5(30r) + .5(20r) = 25r$

In this example, action *a* corresponds to a probability distribution that gives nonzero probability to outcomes *x* and *y*, each with probability ½. The columns headed "$u(x)$"

---

[40] Scholars in this category include: Ben-Porath, Gilboa, and Schmeidler (1997); d'Aspremont and Gevers (2002, pp. 521–525); Diamond (1967); Epstein and Segal (1992); Gajdos and Maurin (2004); Kolm (1998); Sen (1976); Ulph (1982). Two other positions are possible. One is to endorse some kind of non-utilitarian SWF, sensitive to distribution, and to implement that SWF under uncertainty using the EU approach. Scholars who are sympathetic to this position include: Adler and Sanchirico (2006); Fleurbaey (2010); Hammond (1982, 1983); Harel, Safra, and Segal (2005); Rabinowicz (2001). (Note that Hammond uses the term "utilitarianism" in a non-standard manner, to mean welfarism.)

Finally, the EU approach might be conjoined with a utilitarian SWF. Harsanyi, of course, takes this position, as do others. See Harsanyi (1953; 1955; 1982; 1986, ch. 4); Broome (1995); Kaplow (1995); McCarthy (2008).For further discussions of the implementation of an SWF under uncertainty, see the literature on Harsanyi's aggregation theorem, below, n. 89; and also Broome (1984); Deschamps and Gevers (1977); Grant et al. (2010a, 2010b); Karni (1996); Myerson (1981); Otsuka and Voorhoeve (2009); Trautmann (2010). (A recent working paper on this topic, which came to my attention while this book was in press and has not been incorporated into the analysis below, is Fleurbaey, Gajdos, and Zuber [2010].) A related literature concerns the choice of ex post versus ex ante Pareto-efficiency criteria for evaluating market allocations. See, e.g., Hammond (1981).

Ex post/ex ante problems arise, of course, outside the SWF framework. For one discussion of these problems with reference both to welfarism and to luck egalitarianism, see Fried (2003).

[41] Formally, the vector of expected utilities corresponding to action *a* is $(r\sum_{x \in O} \pi_a(x)u_1(x),$ $r\sum_{x \in O} \pi_a(x)u_2(x), \ldots, r\sum_{x \in O} \pi_a(x)u_N(x))$. We might denote individual *i*'s expected utility for action *a* according to a given utility function $u(.)$ as $V_i(a) = \sum_{x \in O} \pi_a(x)u_i(x)$. Thus the vector of expected utilities corresponding to action *a* becomes $(rV_1(a), rV_2(a), \ldots, rV_N(a))$.

and "$u(y)$" show the utility vectors associated with x and y, respectively. The vector of *expected* utilities corresponding to this action is $(15r, 25r)$.

As a preliminary matter, one might wonder why it can be premised that each action corresponds to a probability distribution over outcomes—an assumption needed to generate a vector of individual *expected utilities* corresponding to each action—without accepting EU theory as the bridge principles for moving from the outcome ranking to the action ranking. If the decisionmaker fails to order actions consistently with EU theory, what guarantees that her beliefs concerning outcomes can be represented by numerical probabilities? However, there may be plausible answers to this question, and I will place it to one side.[42]

Note also that the utility functions in **U** might *not* expectationally represent individuals' ex ante well-being. Those functions *do*, of course, represent individuals' well-being levels, differences, and ratios. For any given theory of well-being W, the set **U** is precisely the set which represents level, difference, and ratio comparisons generated by W. Indeed, because we are assuming that **U** is unique up to a positive ratio transformation, any single member of $u(.)$ embodies that information.[43] *Moreover*, it seems very plausible that—if W makes inter- and intrapersonal comparisons of well-being levels—it can also make inter- and intrapersonal comparisons of ex ante well-being. Such comparisons (as I will define them) take the following form: individual i is at least as well off with action a (corresponding to some probability distribution over outcomes) as is individual j with action b (corresponding to some probability distribution over outcomes), where i and j are either distinct individuals or the same person. Equivalently, individual i's ex ante well-being with action a is at least as great as individual j's with action b. Such comparisons are "ex ante" in the sense that what is being compared are not two life-histories, but two whole packages of histories plus their associated probabilities.

But it is a further question whether the elements of **U** *expectationally* represent these comparisons, i.e., whether the following is true: individual i is at least as well off with action a as is individual j with action b iff $\sum_{x\in O}\pi_a(x)u_i(x)\geq\sum_{x\in O}\pi_b(x)u_j(x)$ for any $u(.)$ in **U**.[44] However, the extended-preference account of well-being defended

---

[42] There are non-EU models of decisionmaking whereby decisionmakers remain "probabilistically sophisticated." See, e.g., Grant and Polak (2006).

[43] In general, level, difference, and ratio information are embodied by some **U** as follows: (1) life-history $(x; i)$ is at least as good as life-history $(y; j)$ iff, for all $u(.)$ in **U**, $u(x; i) \geq u(y; j)$; (2) the difference between life-history $(x; i)$ and $(y; j)$ is at least as great as the difference between life-history $(z; k)$ and $(w; l)$ iff, for all $u(.)$ in **U**, $u(x; i) - u(y; j) \geq u(z; k) - u(w; l)$; (3) the ratio between life-history $(x; i)$ and $(y; j)$ is between K and L, inclusive, iff, for all $u(.)$ in **U**, $K \leq u(x; i)/u(y; j) \leq L$. In the case where **U** is unique up to a positive ratio transformation, every $u(.)$ in **U** produces the same ranking of histories and differences, and the same ratio facts, using these rules; and thus the "for all $u(.)$ in **U**" phrases in the above sentences can be replaced by "for any $u(.)$ in **U**."

[44] In general, to say that **U** expectationally represents ex ante well-being means: individual i is at least as well off with action a as is individual j with action b iff $\sum_{x\in O}\pi_a(x)u_i(x)\geq\sum_{x\in O}\pi_b(x)u_j(x)$

in Chapter 3 *does* have the feature that **U** expectationally represents comparisons of ex ante well-being.[45] I will therefore assume that **U** represents some account of well-being (be it the extended-preference account or some other) that does have this feature. This assumption, it should be noted, *increases* my argumentative burden: if **U** did not expectationally represent comparisons of ex ante well-being, the conflict between EU prioritarianism and the ex ante Pareto principles, about to be described, might not arise.[46] If EU theory provides the most attractive bridge principles for coupling the continuous prioritarian SWF with a **U** which has *this* feature, then *a fortiori* EU theory does so where **U** lacks the feature.

The seminal criticism of the EU approach to implementing a social welfare function is an article by Peter Diamond. Diamond considers a society composed of two individuals, A and B. One policy, *a*, with certainty produces a utility level of 1 for A

---

for all $u(.)$ in **U**. With **U** unique up to a positive ratio transformation, this becomes "for any $u(.)$ in **U**." On the possibility that a set of utility functions might not expectationally represent ex ante well-being, see Chapter 3, pp. 231–236. For example, it might instead be the case that the theory W, in its judgments of ex ante well-being, is "risk averse" in the utilities that represent levels, differences, and ratios. More specifically, there could be some concave function $h(.)$ such that individual i is at least as well off with action a as is individual j with action b iff $\sum_{x \in \mathbf{O}} \pi_a(x) h(u_i(x)) \geq \sum_{x \in \mathbf{O}} \pi_b(x) h(u_j(x))$ for all $u(.)$ in **U**, which becomes "for any $u(.)$ in **U**" if **U** is unique up to a positive ratio transformation and $h(.)$ is invariant to ratio rescalings.

[45] I did not specifically discuss in Chapter 3 how the extended-preference view would analyze ex ante well-being, but presumably the view would say the following (with actions corresponding to probability distributions across outcomes): (1) action a is at least as good as action b for individual i iff all fully informed and rational spectators, under a condition of i-interest, would weakly prefer the first action to the second; and (2) individual i is at least as well off with action a as individual j with action b, the two individuals distinct, iff all fully informed and rational spectators would make the across-person judgment that this is the case. Combining this analysis of ex ante well-being, with the construction of **U** offered in Chapter 3, it would be true that—in the case where **U** is unique up to a positive ratio transformation, hence spectators' extended preferences are identical—individual i is at least as well off with action a as is individual j with action b iff $\sum_{x \in \mathbf{O}} \pi_a(x) u_i(x) \geq \sum_{x \in \mathbf{O}} \pi_b(x) u_j(x)$ for any $u(.)$ in **U**.

[46] More specifically, consider the case in which the $h(.)$ function mentioned in n. 44 above is *identical* to the $g(.)$ function that the continuous prioritarian SWF incorporates in its rule for ranking utility vectors. If so, there would be no conflict between EU prioritarianism with the identity translation (see below) and the ex ante Pareto principles. Those principles are framed in terms of ex ante well-being (see below), which if $h(.) = g(.)$ is represented by the rule: individual i's ex ante well-being with action a is at least as great as individual j's ex ante well-being with action b iff $\sum_{x \in \mathbf{O}} \pi_a(x) g(u_i(x)) \geq \sum_{x \in \mathbf{O}} \pi_b(x) g(u_j(x))$ for any $u(.)$ (on the assumption that **U** is unique up to a positive ratio transformation and $g(.) = h(.)$ are invariant to ratio rescalings). To see why ex ante Pareto-indifference in this case could not conflict with EU prioritarianism with the identity translation (a similar analysis works for ex ante Pareto-superiority), note that it would mean the following: a and b are such that, for each individual i, $\sum_{x \in \mathbf{O}} \pi_a(x) g(u_i(x)) = \sum_{x \in \mathbf{O}} \pi_b(x) g(u_i(x))$. But it then follows, summing these N equations, that $\sum_{x \in \mathbf{O}} \pi_a(x) \left[\sum_{i=1}^{N} g(u_i(x)) \right] = \sum_{x \in \mathbf{O}} \pi_b(x) \left[\sum_{i=1}^{N} g(u_i(x)) \right]$, which is just the rule for EU prioritarianism with the identity translation.

and 0 for B. Another policy, β, produces a utility level of 1 for A and 0 for B, with probability ½; and produces a utility level of 0 for A and 1 for B, with probability ½.

Table 7.2 Diamond's Critique of the EU Approach

	Policy α			Policy β		
	$\pi_\alpha(x) = 1$			$\pi_\beta(x) = .5$	$\pi_\beta(y) = .5$	
	$u(x)$	Expected utility		$u(x)$	$u(y)$	Expected utility
Individual A	1r	1r		1r	0r	.5r
Individual B	0r	0r		0r	1r	.5r

Observe that not only the continuous prioritarian SWF, but *any* SWF which satisfies the anonymity requirement—any minimally plausible SWF—will be indifferent between utility vector (1, 0) and utility vector (0, 1). Thus, if we couple EU theory with *any* minimally plausible SWF, we must assign outcome x in Table 7.2 the very same moral utility, $m(x)$, as the moral utility we assign to y, $m(y)$. And this in turn means that the EU formula for ranking α and β will rank them as equally morally good.[47] But such a ranking is counterintuitive, Diamond observes, because β equalizes the individuals' expected utilities, while α leaves them unequal. β therefore seems to be a *fairer* policy than α.

> [Policy] β seems strictly preferable to me, since it gives B a fair shake while α does not. (In terms of expected utilities, under α we have $v_A = 1$ [v_A is A's expected utility] and $v_B = 0$ while under β, $v_A = v_B = ½$.)
>
> I am willing to accept the sure-thing principle for individual choice but not for social choice, since it seems reasonable for the individual to be concerned solely with final states while society is also interested in the process of choice.[48]

Note that Diamond is clearly leveling a targeted critique at the use of EU theory. We might wonder what exactly he means by accepting EU theory "for individual choice but not for social choice." What if a private individual prefers, not to advance his own well-being, but to advance moral aims? Still, it is clear that Diamond does not mean to challenge EU theory as a framework for rational choice in general, but rather in the specific context of applying a social welfare function.

---

[47] Outcome x is such that it is assigned utility (1, 0) or some positive ratio transformation thereof, which I have represented as "(1r, 0r)," while y is assigned utility (0, 1) or some positive ratio transformation thereof. The EU formula here says: policy α is at least as good as policy β iff $\sum_{z \in \mathbf{O}} \pi_\alpha(z) m(z) \geq \sum_{z \in \mathbf{O}} \pi_\beta(z) m(z)$, with the outcome set **O** containing x and y.

[48] Diamond (1967, p. 766).

Diamond's example can be generalized. Imagine that, in the probability distribution corresponding to action a, and in the probability distribution corresponding to b, all the outcomes accorded non-zero probability are permutations of the same utility vector.[49] For example, it might be the case that $\pi_a(x) = 1/2$, $\pi_a(y) = 1/4$, and $\pi_a(z) = 1/4$; $\pi_b(x) = 1/3$ and $\pi_b(y) = 2/3$; and $u(x) = (1r, 3r, 5r, 7r)$, $u(y) = (7r, 3r, 5r, 1r)$, and $u(z) = (5r, 1r, 7r, 3r)$. Whenever two actions are related in this way, let us say that we have a "permutation case."

Imagine that in a permutation case, one action, d, corresponds to a vector of individual expected utilities in which everyone's expected utility is the same, while this is not true for the other action, c. Let us call this a "permutation case with ex ante equalization." Then, intuitively, action d is a better action than action c. Not only is the total well-being produced by both actions sure to be the same, but it is certain that both actions will yield the same pattern of distribution of well-being, save for the names of the individuals involved. *In addition*, action d has the virtue of yielding a perfectly equal distribution of expected utilities and thus a perfectly equal distribution of ex ante well-being. (Remember that we are assuming that **U** expectationally represents ex ante well-being.) Surely, if one cares about distributive considerations, action d must be better than c. But if EU theory is used to rank actions in conjunction with the ordering of outcomes generated by *any* anonymous SWF, we arrive at the counterintuitive result that the two actions in a permutation case are equally good—even a permutation case with ex ante equalization. In particular, EU prioritarianism has this counterintuitive result.

The social choice theorists who have followed in Diamond's wake, and are uneasy with the use of EU theory to implement a social welfare function under uncertainty, almost invariably describe some kind of permutation case with ex ante equalization as grounds for their concern. More generally, outside of social choice theory, there are a substantial number of philosophers who suggest that giving individuals equal chances of receiving some good is the fair way to distribute it (whether the good is well-being, a tangible item, or some other advantage)—at least in the case where the ultimate amount and distribution of the good will be the same regardless of what society does, and where no individual has a special claim to the good. For example, if society is picking a fixed percentage P of the population of 18-year-olds to serve in the military, it seems that the fairest way to do so is through a draft lottery that gives all 18-year-olds an equal chance of being drafted. This is a kind of permutation case. *However* the draftees are picked, the ultimate upshot will be the same: $(1 - P\,\%)$ of

---

[49] Use $\xi(.)$ to mean a vector-valued function such that $\xi(v)$ is a permutation of utility vector v, i.e., each entry in $\xi(v)$ corresponds to one and only one entry in utility vector v. $\xi^x(.)$ denotes a particular permutation function—the one corresponding to outcome x. Formally, then, the choice between two actions a and b is a "permutation case" if, for each $u(.)$ in **U**, there exists a vector u^* such that— for each outcome x accorded a nonzero probability by the probability distribution corresponding to a or to b—$u(x) = \xi^x(u^*)$.

the 18-year olds receive the "good" of avoiding military service, P% are required to serve.[50]

Can any more be said to explain our intuitions in a permutation case with ex ante equalization? At least for purposes of prioritarianism, the intuition can be rationalized—and generalized—by appealing to an ex ante version of the Pigou–Dalton principle. Remember that a continuous prioritarian SWF, in ranking outcomes, satisfies the Pigou–Dalton principle. This was an integral part of the justification for the continuous prioritarian SWF offered in Chapter 5. It therefore seems intuitively very plausible that the prioritarian ranking of actions should also satisfy the Pigou–Dalton principle, framed in terms of ex ante well-being.

The Ex Ante Pigou–Dalton Principle

Imagine that individual i's ex ante well-being with action a is less than individual j's; that individual i's ex ante well-being with action b is less than or equal to individual j's; that individual i is ex ante better off with b than a; that individual j is ex ante worse off with b than a; that the difference in individual i's ex ante well-being between b and a is the same as the difference in individual j's ex ante well-being between a and b; and that everyone else in the population is unaffected (each such person is just as well off ex ante with a and b). Then b is a morally better action than a.[51]

However, EU prioritarianism can conflict with the ex ante Pigou–Dalton principle. Such conflict occurs in permutation cases with ex ante equalization; and it also can occur in other types of cases.[52] To be clear, EU prioritarianism does not *invariably* conflict with the ex ante Pigou–Dalton principle; there are, of course, cases where the action favored by the ex ante Pigou–Dalton principle is exactly the action favored by EU prioritarianism. Rather, what permutation cases illustrate is that EU prioritarianism *can* conflict with the ex ante Pigou–Dalton principle in some choice situations.

A distinct worry about EU prioritarianism involves the Pareto principles. The Pareto principles that have been discussed at length in previous chapters are constraints on the ranking of outcomes. The Pareto-indifference principle for outcomes says: If each person is just as well off in outcome x as she is in y, the outcomes are equally morally good. The Pareto-superiority principle for outcomes says: If one or

---

[50] For one recent discussion of the fairness of lotteries, with citations to other important works in this literature, see Stone (2007).

[51] For the ex ante Pigou–Dalton principle to be applicable, our theory of well-being must allow for interpersonal comparisons of differences in ex ante well-being, not just comparisons of levels of ex ante well-being. I will assume that this is the case, and that these differences are expectationally represented by **U**, i.e., the magnitude of a change is represented by the change in expected utility.

[52] For example, in non-permutation cases where there is a conflict between the sure thing or stochastic dominance principles and the ex ante Pigou–Dalton principle (see below, p. 512), EU prioritarianism will conflict with the ex ante Pigou–Dalton principle.

more individuals are strictly better off in outcome x than outcome y, and everyone else is at least as well off in x as in y, then x is a morally better outcome than y.

Consider now the Pareto-indifference and -superiority principles formulated as constraints on the ranking of *actions*, in terms of the pattern of ex ante well-being corresponding to each action—for short, the "ex ante" Pareto principles.

Ex Ante Pareto-Indifference

If each person's ex ante well-being with action b is equal to her ex ante well-being with action a, the two actions are equally morally good.

Ex Ante Pareto-Superiority

If each person's ex ante well-being with action b is at least as large as her ex ante well-being with action a, and at least one person's ex ante well-being with b is strictly larger, b is a morally better action than a.

The following tables show how EU prioritarianism can yield violations of ex ante Pareto-indifference and ex ante Pareto-superiority (given a U that expectationally represents ex ante well-being). Although it is certainly not the case that EU prioritarianism *invariably* conflicts with the ex ante Pareto principles, the tables illustrate that it *can* do so—that there exist choice situations in which the action favored by EU prioritarianism is different from the action required by one or another of the ex ante Pareto principles.

Table 7.3 EU Prioritarianism and Ex Ante Pareto-Indifference

	Action a			Action b		
	$\pi_a(x) = .5$	$\pi_a(y) = .5$	Expected	$\pi_b(z) = .5$	$\pi_b(w) = .5$	Expected
	$u(x)$	$u(y)$	utility	$u(z)$	$u(w)$	utility
Individual A	90r	10r	50r	50r	50r	50r
Individual B	10r	90r	50r	50r	50r	50r

Each individual's expected utility is the same with both actions. So ex ante Pareto-indifference requires that the actions be ranked as equally good. But any continuous prioritarian SWF will rank the utility vector $(50r, 50r)$ as better than the vectors $(90r, 10r)$ and $(10r, 90r)$.[53] (Because any such SWF satisfies the Pigou–Dalton principle, it prefers

---

[53] This is true not merely for any Atkinson SWF but for any continuous prioritarian SWF. However, throughout this section, we are assuming that a continuous prioritarian SWF has been integrated with traditional EU theory to rank actions. In order for *this* to be possible, the SWF must produce a complete ranking of outcomes. Because non-Atkinson continuous prioritarian SWFs are not invariant to ratio rescaling, they are not guaranteed to rank an outcome set completely even if U is

an outcome with perfectly equal well-being to one with the same total well-being in which well-being is unequal.) Thus the moral utility values assigned to these outcomes must be such that $m(x) = m(y) < m(z) = m(w)$, which means that the EU formula will rank action a as worse than b.

Table 7.4 EU Prioritarianism and Ex Ante Pareto-Superiority

	Action d			Action e		
	$\pi_d(x) = .5$ $\pi_d(y) = .5$			$\pi_e(z) = .5$ $\pi_e(w) = .5$		
	$u(x)$	$u(y)$	Expected utility	$u(z)$	$u(w)$	Expected utility
Individual A	$90r$	$10r$	$50r$	$(50 - \varepsilon)r$	$(50 - \varepsilon)r$	$(50 - \varepsilon)r$
Individual B	$10r$	$90r$	$50r$	$(50 - \varepsilon)r$	$(50 - \varepsilon)r$	$(50 - \varepsilon)r$

For any positive ε, ex ante Pareto-superiority ranks action d as better than action e. But, for any continuous prioritarian SWF, if ε is positive but sufficiently close to zero, the SWF will rank the vectors $(90r, 10r)$ and $(10r, 90r)$ as worse than $((50 - \varepsilon)r, (50 - \varepsilon)r)$. If so, it will also be the case that $m(x) = m(y) < m(z) = m(w)$, which means that the EU formula will rank action d as worse than e.

The conflict with the ex ante Pareto principles is surely a troubling feature of EU prioritarianism. The violation of ex ante Pareto superiority in the "weak" form is particularly startling. If *everyone's* expected well-being is greater with action d rather than e, surely action d must be morally better than action e.[54]

Although the point is probably clear to the reader, it bears emphasis that EU prioritarianism *satisfies* the Pareto and Pigou–Dalton principles understood as constraints on the ranking of outcomes. The continuous prioritarian SWF, of course, orders outcomes so as to respect those principles. EU theory, in turn, accords a higher moral utility number to a morally better outcome, and equal utility numbers to equally good outcomes. Thus if outcome x is Pareto-superior to outcome y, the moral utility of x, $m(x)$, will be greater than the moral utility of y, $m(y)$. If outcome x is better than y in light of the Pigou–Dalton principle for outcomes, then once again the moral utility of x will be greater than the moral utility of y. If the two outcomes are equally good by virtue of the Pareto-indifference principle for outcomes, then the two will be assigned the same moral utility number.

Up until this chapter, the book has focused on the ranking of outcomes. What has emerged in *this* chapter is that we can also formulate versions of the Pareto and

unique up to a positive ratio transformation. To put the point another way, while *all* continuous prioritarian SWFs will rank $(50r, 50r)$ over $(90r, 10r)$ for all values of r, the way in which non-Atkinson continuous prioritarian SWFs rank other utility vectors (not governed by the Pigou–Dalton principle) may depend upon r. For example, $(90, 10)$ might be ranked above $(45, 45)$ but not $(900, 100)$ over $(450, 450)$.

[54] See Broome (1995, chs. 8–9); Kaplow (1995).

Pigou–Dalton principles which apply, not to outcomes, but to *actions*—which constrain the ranking of actions in terms of their patterns of ex ante well-being. EU prioritarianism potentially conflicts with these "ex ante" Pareto and Pigou–Dalton
principles—*not* the companion principles that concern the goodness of outcomes.

Still, violations of the ex ante Pareto and Pigou–Dalton principles are—
intuitively—a serious worry. Indeed, we can use the "claim-across-outcome" conception of fairness to bolster the worry. That conception ascribes to each individual
a moral claim between a given pair of outcomes, valenced in terms of her well-being.
Imagine now that we transpose the idea of such claims to the context of ranking
actions. The natural transposition would be this: each individual has a moral claim
between a given pair of *actions*, valenced in terms of her ex ante well-being (for short,
"ex ante claims"). Individual *i* has an ex ante claim in favor of *a* over *b* just in case she
is ex ante better off with *a*; no ex ante claim either way just in case she is ex ante
equally well off with the two actions; and otherwise an incomparable ex ante claim.

Cases of ex ante Pareto-indifference and ex ante Pareto-superiority then become
"no-conflict" cases, where (1) all individuals have no ex ante claims either way
between a pair of actions, thus the two actions are equally morally good (ex ante
Pareto-indifference); or (2) some individuals have an ex ante claim in favor of one
action, and others have no ex ante claims either way, thus the first is morally better
(ex ante Pareto-superiority). Surely, it would seem, actions should be ranked in
accordance with these no-conflict rules. Similarly, the argument for the ex ante
Pigou–Dalton principle just transposes the argument presented earlier for why the
ranking of outcomes should satisfy the Pigou–Dalton principle.[55]

The critic of EU prioritarianism can wrap up his challenge by noting the following: there are non-EU methodologies for employing a continuous prioritarian SWF
to rank actions which *satisfy* the ex ante Pigou–Dalton principle and the ex ante Pareto
principles. Consider the approach which ranks policies by applying the continuous
prioritarian SWF to the vector of expected utilities associated with each policy.[56]

Table 7.5 Ex Ante Prioritarianism

	Action a			Action b		
	$\pi_a(x) = .5$ $\pi_a(y) = .5$			$\pi_b(z) = .5$ $\pi_b(w) = .5$		
	$u(x)$	$u(y)$	*Expected utility*	$u(z)$	$u(w)$	*Expected utility*
Individual A	20r	60r	40r	10r	80r	45r
Individual B	80r	40r	60r	90r	20r	55r

[55] Assume that individual *i* has an ex ante claim to *b* over *a*; that individual *j* has an ex ante claim to *a*
over *b*; and that the change in ex ante well-being is the same in both cases. Add now the further fact
that individual *i* has lower ex ante well-being than *j* with action *a*, and lower or equal ex ante well-
being than *j* with action *b*. If so, isn't *i*'s ex ante claim to *b* *stronger* than *j*'s ex ante claim to *a*? And if
everyone else has no claim either way, mustn't we say that *b* is the morally better action?
[56] If the vector of expected utilities associated with a given action *a* is $(rV_1(a), rV_2(a), \ldots, rV_N(a))$,
see above, n. 41, the approach now under consideration says: action *a* is at least as good as action *b* iff

In Table 7.5, assume that we are using an Atkinson SWF with $\gamma = 1/2$, which sums the square root of individual utilities and then multiplies this sum by $1/(1 - 1/2) = 2$. The ex ante approach applies this formula to the vector of individual expected utilities associated with each action. Thus action a is assigned a value of $2(\sqrt{40r} + \sqrt{60r})$, while action b is assigned a value of $2(\sqrt{45r} + \sqrt{55r})$, yielding the judgment that b is a better action than a.

In this particular case, *any* continuous prioritarian SWF applied in this ex ante fashion will rank b over a, since the ex ante Pigou–Dalton principle says b is better. Moreover, it can be seen that EU prioritarianism using the same SWF will yield a different ranking (a better than b), since b has substituted $(10r, 90r)$ for $(20r, 80r)$, and $(80r, 20r)$ for $(60r, 40r)$, holding constant the probabilities at .5. Note that the Pigou–Dalton principle for outcomes ranks the first member of each of these pairs lower than the second.

I will call this methodology *ex ante prioritarianism,* to be contrasted with EU prioritarianism. It is straightforward to see that ex ante prioritarianism will never violate either of the ex ante Pareto principles, and that it will never violate the ex ante Pigou–Dalton principle.

B. Responding to the Targeted Objection

In sum, EU bridge principles, coupled with the ordering of outcomes produced by a continuous prioritarian SWF, yield violations of the ex ante Pigou–Dalton and Pareto principles. At least one non-EU approach to applying a continuous prioritarian SWF, which I have termed ex ante prioritarianism, will invariably satisfy these principles. However, despite this powerful challenge, I believe that EU prioritarianism is ultimately defensible.[57]

To begin, it bears note that the social choice literature is divided about the appropriate approach to implementing a social welfare function under uncertainty. Some scholars argue for utilitarianism. Others, like Diamond, favor the combination of a non-utilitarian SWF and a non-EU approach. Still others favor the combination of a non-utilitarian SWF and EU theory, notwithstanding the seemingly perverse results of that approach.[58]

Why adopt this last position? In particular, why should the prioritarian do so?

$(1-\gamma)^{-1}\sum_{i=1}^{N}V_i(a)^{1-\gamma} \geq (1-\gamma)^{-1}\sum_{i=1}^{N}V_i(b)^{1-\gamma}$, or the sum of natural logarithms of the $V_i(.)$ values in the case where $\gamma = 1$.

[57] In the past, I have relied in part on dynamic-inconsistency arguments to argue in favor of the EU approach. See Adler and Sanchirico (2006). I do not do so here, because the EU approach refined to allow for the possibility of an incomplete ordering or imprecise probabilities also faces dynamic-inconsistency difficulties. See below.

[58] See also Cappelen et al. (2010), finding that participants in a redistribution experiment have a diversity of views concerning ex post versus ex ante equality.

First, it should be observed that ex ante prioritarianism—ranking actions by applying a continuous prioritarian SWF to the vectors of individual expected utilities associated with the actions—will itself violate some very attractive principles, namely the sure thing principle and the stochastic dominance principles, ordinary and weak.

Table 7.6 illustrates a case in which ex ante prioritarianism violates the sure thing principle.

Table 7.6 Ex Ante Prioritarianism and the Sure Thing Principle

	Action a			Action b		
	$\pi_a(x) = .5 \ \pi_a(y) = .5$			$\pi_b(w) = .5 \ \pi_b(y) = .5$		
	$u(x)$	$u(y)$	Expected utility	$u(w)$	$u(y)$	Expected utility
Individual A	80r	50r	65r	90r	50r	70r
Individual B	20r	50r	35r	10r	50r	30r

	Action a*			Action b*		
	$\pi_{a^*}(x) = .5 \ \pi_{a^*}(z) = .5$			$\pi_{b^*}(w) = .5 \ \pi_{b^*}(z) = .5$		
	$u(x)$	$u(z)$	Expected utility	$u(w)$	$u(z)$	Expected utility
Individual A	80r	10r	45r	90r	10r	50r
Individual B	20r	200r	110r	10r	200r	105r

Note that action a gives a .5 probability to x and a .5 probability to y, while b gives a .5 probability to w and a .5 probability to y. Actions a^* and b^* are identical, respectively, to a and b, except that y has been replaced by z in both distributions. The sure thing principle therefore requires that a and b be ranked the same way as a^* and b^*. Note, however, that action a is a Pigou–Dalton transfer in expected utilities relative to b, while action b^* is a Pigou–Dalton transfer in expected utilities relative to a^*. Thus any continuous prioritarian SWF, applied in an "ex ante" manner, will rank a above b but b^* above a^*, in violation of the sure thing principle.

Any consequentialist should find the sure thing principle intuitively attractive. Imagine that some action, with probability π, might produce outcome x and, with probability $(1 - \pi)$, might produce outcome y.[59] Another action, with probability π,

---

[59] Saying that action a "would produce" outcome x with a given probability—a locution I use throughout this section—is simply shorthand for the statement that $\pi_a(x)$ takes that value. My defense of the EU approach is meant to be agnostic between causal and evidential versions, see above

might produce outcome x^* and, with probability $(1 - \pi)$, might produce outcome y. So there is a $(1 - \pi)$ chance that the actions produce the very same outcome. Why should it matter which particular outcome that is? If it turns out that the two actions have a $(1 - \pi)$ probability of producing outcome z rather than y, why should that change the moral ranking of the actions?[60]

Opponents of the sure thing principle sometimes draw an analogy to the non-separability of an individual's well-being with respect to attributes or times. Imagine that outcomes are characterized with respect to multiple types of attributes. Then if two life-histories have attributes of one type in common, surely it *can* matter what the common attribute is. (A standard, mundane example: a meal with meat and red wine might be better than a meal with fish and red wine, but a meal with meat and white wine might be worse than a meal with fish and white wine.) Similarly, if two life-histories have the same level of sublifetime well-being in one period, the ranking of the life-histories can depend on what that common level is (because of sequencing effects).[61]

The proponent of the sure thing principle should acknowledge that an individual's well-being may well be non-separable with respect to attributes or times. But there is a vital difference between such non-separability, and the requirement on the ranking of actions that the sure thing principle imposes.[62] If a life-history has multiple attributes, all of those attributes would occur, together, if the life-history were to occur. They would be *jointly* actualized. For example, ranking a meat-plus-red-wine meal over a fish-plus-red-wine meal, but a fish-plus-white-wine meal over a meat-plus-white-wine meal, means ranking various possible joint actualizations of attributes: namely, a possible outcome in which someone eats meat *and* drinks red wine, versus a possible outcome in which someone eats fish *and* drinks red wine, and so forth. Similarly, if a life-history has multiple temporal segments, *all* of those segments would occur, sequentially, if the life-history were to occur.

By contrast, the sure thing principle involves a kind of separability in the ranking of probability distributions over outcomes. The elements of this distribution—outcomes—will not be jointly realized. The multiple outcomes in an outcome set are (simplified) possible worlds, i.e., mutually exclusive descriptions of possible ways the world might turn out. If an outcome set is properly constructed, only one outcome will actually occur. Just as it is absurd to think that two different possible worlds might both be the actual world, so it would be a serious structural mistake to engage in consequentialist moral deliberation using an outcome set containing pairs

---

(even though I take the causal version to be more plausible); and "would produce" is not meant to assume a casual approach.

[60] This example involves a particularly simple case of the sure thing principle, where two actions assign the same probability to one outcome (rather than having a multi-outcome subdistribution in common); but the arguments regarding this case show why the principle in general is attractive.

[61] On non-separability with respect to times or attributes, see Chapter 6.

[62] See, e.g., Sugden (2004, pp. 694–695).

of outcomes that are not mutually exclusive—such that the actual world might turn out to be both one outcome and the other.

Thus, to say that some action corresponds to a probability distribution which accords probability π to outcome x and probability $(1 - \pi)$ to outcome y, means that the decisionmaker rationally believes to degree π that, were she to perform the action, the first outcome would be the actual outcome *and the second outcome would not occur*; and she rationally believes to degree $(1 - \pi)$ that, were she to perform the action, the second outcome would be the actual outcome *and the first outcome would not occur*. The decisionmaker is certainly *not* contemplating the co-actualization of outcomes x and y. Consider now a second action, which corresponds to a π probability of outcome x^* and a probability $(1 - \pi)$ of outcome y. In comparing the two actions, the decisionmaker believes to degree $(1 - \pi)$ that her choice between the two is a matter of moral indifference—that it does not affect which outcome would actually occur, since with probability $(1 - \pi)$ the actual outcome is y regardless of which action she chooses. She believes to degree π that her choice is not a matter of moral indifference and that one choice would yield an actual outcome x while the other would yield an actual outcome x^*. If the decisionmaker now faces a second pair of actions, where she also believes to degree π that her choice is not a matter of moral indifference and that one choice would yield x while the other would yield x^*, why on earth should this pair of actions be ranked differently than the first?

A yet graver difficulty with ex ante prioritarianism is that it violates the stochastic dominance principles, both ordinary and weak, as Table 7.7 illustrates.

Table 7.7 Ex Ante Prioritarianism and Stochastic Dominance

	Action d			Action e		
	$\pi_d(x) = .5$ $\pi_d(y) = .5$			$\pi_e(z) = .5$ $\pi_e(w) = .5$		
	$u(x)$	$u(y)$	Expected utility	$u(z)$	$u(w)$	Expected utility
Individual A	$90r$	$10r$	$50r$	$(50 - \varepsilon)r$	$(50 - \varepsilon)r$	$(50 - \varepsilon)r$
Individual B	$10r$	$90r$	$50r$	$(50 - \varepsilon)r$	$(50 - \varepsilon)r$	$(50 - \varepsilon)r$

This is the same example used earlier in the chapter to show that EU prioritarianism conflicts with ex ante Pareto superiority (see Table 7.4). But it also shows that ex ante prioritarianism conflicts with weak stochastic dominance and, thus, with ordinary stochastic dominance, given the ordering of outcomes produced by the continuous prioritarian SWF. For any continuous prioritarian SWF, if ε is positive but sufficiently close to zero, the SWF will rank the vectors $(90r, 10r)$ and $(10r, 90r)$ as worse than $((50 - \varepsilon)r, (50 - \varepsilon)r)$. Thus all of the outcomes of action e with non-zero probability are ranked higher in this ordering of outcomes than all of the outcomes of action d. So the weak and ordinary stochastic dominance principles require that e be preferred to d; but ex ante prioritarianism prefers d, because each individual's expected utility is higher.

Indeed, if the *e* outcomes were (50*r*, 50*r*), there would still be a conflict between ex ante prioritarianism and stochastic dominance—although in this case the conflict would be a bit less stark, since stochastic dominance would require that *e* be ranked better, while ex ante prioritarianism would now be indifferent between the actions.

Most decision theorists and economists consider ordinary stochastic dominance to be a more compelling principle of rationality than the sure thing principle. As Chris Starmer writes in his review of non-EU approaches to choice: "Monotonicity is the property that stochastically dominating prospects are preferred to prospects which they dominate, and it is widely held that any satisfactory theory—descriptive or normative—should embody monotonicity."[63]

Weak stochastic dominance is yet more compelling than ordinary stochastic dominance. It bears repeating just how basic this requirement is. In the case at hand, where actions are being morally ranked, to say that action *b* weakly stochastically dominates *a* is to say (1) that the decisionmaker has arrived at a moral ordering of outcomes and (2) rationally believes to degree 1 that the outcome of *b* would be morally better (in light of the ordering of outcomes) than the outcome of *a*. Weak stochastic dominance also means the following: although the decisionmaker does not herself know which particular outcome either action would yield, she rationally believes that a *fully informed, fully rational, minimally consequentialist adviser* who shares her ordering of outcomes would pick action *b*.[64]

---

[63] See Starmer (2000, p. 335).

[64] See Fleurbaey (2010). As in the text, action *b* is such as to weakly stochastically dominate action *a*. Consider, first, the simple case in which the decisionmaker is sure that causal laws are deterministic. If so, a fully informed adviser would *know* which particular outcome would result from *b* and which particular outcome from *a*. By "minimally consequentialist" I mean that the adviser herself, if thinking rationally, will recommend the choice of one action over a second where she is sure of the particular outcome yielded by each action, and sure that the first action yields a better outcome than the second. The adviser is not, for example, a deontologist. (Note that the minimally consequentialist adviser is *not* assumed here to accept the principle of weak stochastic dominance; rather, the idea in this footnote is to use the construct of a fully informed adviser as one route *to* that principle from yet more basic elements of consequentialism.)

Thus, in the case where *b* weakly stochastically dominates *a*, the decisionmaker who is *sure* of determinism can be *sure* that a fully informed, minimally consequentialist, fully rational adviser who shares her ordering of outcomes would recommend *b* over *a*. Although the decisionmaker does not know everything that this adviser knows—unlike the adviser, she does not know which particular outcome results from *b* and which from *a*—the fact that *every* nonzero-probability outcome of *b* is better than *every* nonzero-probability outcome of *a* means that the decisionmaker *is* in a position to know what the adviser would recommend.

Of course, to believe that a fully informed, fully rational adviser who shares your goals (ordering of outcomes) would recommend some course of action is just to believe—surely—that this is the right course of action in light of those goals.

Remember that we are working within (act-) consequentialism, and trying to specify a moral choice-evaluation procedure such that the ordering of choices depends on the moral goodness of the outcomes which the choices might produce. Take a case in which the decisionmaker rationally believes to degree 1 that action *a* yields a particular outcome *x*, that action *b* yields outcome *x**, and that *x** is a morally better outcome than *x*. How could she possibly justify choosing action *a* rather than action *b*, except by stepping away from act-consequentialism and appealing to rule-consequentialism, deontology, or some other view that denies a direct linkage between the ranking of outcomes and the ranking of choices? And since any (act-) consequentialist decision procedure must surely require the decisionmaker to choose action *b* in this case, then it also surely must in the case where *b* weakly stochastically dominates *a*. What is the *relevant* difference between the cases? In the weak stochastic dominance case, the decisionmaker is unsure which particular outcome would result from *b*—but why should *that* uncertainty distinguish the cases? The decisionmaker is uncertain about the specific characteristics of the outcome that would be produced by action *b* and the specific characteristics of the outcome that would be produced by action *a*; but she does rationally believe, to degree 1, that the specific characteristics of the former outcome—whatever exactly they might be—would be such as to make that outcome morally better than the specific characteristics of the latter outcome.

This line of analysis provides an initial counterthrust to the critique of EU prioritarianism. Ex ante prioritarianism violates the sure thing principle and axioms of ordinary and weak stochastic dominance. Consequentialists should find the sure thing principle intuitively attractive. Even if they do not, they should take ordinary (and even more so) weak stochastic dominance to be absolutely compelling principles. Thus consequentialists should reject ex ante prioritarianism.

The reader might wonder whether it is possible to design some non-EU approach to implementing a continuous prioritarian SWF which avoids the difficulties of ex ante prioritarianism, yet also preserves consistency with the ex ante Pigou–Dalton and Pareto principles (and thus avoids the seemingly perverse results of EU prioritarianism). After all, ranking actions by applying a continuous prioritarian SWF to the vectors of expected utilities associated with the actions is simply *one* non-EU

In the more general case where the decisionmaker believes to some degree (less than 1) that causal laws are deterministic, then she believes to some degree that a fully informed, fully rational, minimally consequentialist adviser would recommend action *b*.

I should stress that the principle of weak stochastic dominance is (it seems to me) an integral part of consequentialism quite apart from what a fully informed, fully rational adviser would recommend; and its normative appeal certainly does not hinge on determinism. The line of argument in this footnote, as I see it, simply bolsters the case for the principle.

approach to ranking actions. There are, in principle, a wide range of non-EU bridge principles.[65]

A second counterthrust to the critique of EU prioritarianism is to observe that there is a logical incompatibility between the ex ante *Pigou–Dalton* principle, on the one hand, and the sure thing and stochastic dominance principles, on the other. *If outcomes are ranked according to the continuous prioritarian SWF, then any non-EU approach for ranking actions which universally satisfies the ex ante Pigou–Dalton principle will violate* (1) *the sure thing principle and* (2) *the stochastic dominance principles, weak and ordinary, in some cases.*[66]

> To see that the ex ante Pigou–Dalton principle will conflict with the sure thing principle in some cases, consider Table 7.6 above. Note that, in this case, the ex ante Pigou–Dalton principle requires choosing action *a* over *b*, but *b** over *a**, in violation of the sure thing principle.
>
> To see the conflict between the ex ante Pigou–Dalton principle and stochastic dominance principles, consider the case illustrated in Table 7.8.

Table 7.8 Ex Ante Pigou–Dalton and Stochastic Dominance

	Action a			Action b		
	$\pi_a(x) = .5$	$\pi_a(y) = .5$		$\pi_b(z) = .5$	$\pi_b(w) = .5$	
	$u(x)$	$u(y)$	Expected utility	$u(z)$	$u(w)$	Expected utility
Individual A	50r	60r	55r	70r	30r	50r
Individual B	50r	40r	45r	30r	70r	50r

> Note that, by virtue of the Pigou–Dalton principle for ranking outcomes, any continuous prioritarian SWF will rank (50r, 50r) over (60r, 40r), which in turn is better than (70r, 30r). Thus the SWF says that both of the outcomes of action *a* are better than both of the outcomes of *b*, so that weak and ordinary stochastic dominance (in light of this ordering of outcomes) requires choosing *a*. But the ex ante Pigou–Dalton principle requires choosing *b*.

There is also a logical incompatibility between the ex ante *Pareto* principles, on the one hand, and stochastic dominance principles, on the other. *If outcomes are ranked according to the continuous prioritarian SWF, any non-EU approach for ranking actions which universally satisfies the ex ante Pareto principles will violate the stochastic dominance principles, ordinary and weak, in some cases.*[67] This can be seen with Tables 7.9 and Tables 7.10.

---

[65] See Gilboa (2009); Starmer (2000); and Sugden (2004).

[66] See below n. 72.

[67] There is no logical incompatibility between the ex ante Pareto principles and the sure thing principle. Note that EU utilitarianism with the identity translation (see below) satisfies both.

Table 7.9 Ex Ante Pareto-Indifference and Stochastic Dominance

	Action a			Action b		
	$\pi_a(x) = .5$	$\pi_a(y) = .5$		$\pi_b(z) = .5$	$\pi_b(w) = .5$	
	$u(x)$	$u(y)$	Expected utility	$u(z)$	$u(w)$	Expected utility
Individual A	90r	10r	50r	50r	50r	50r
Individual B	10r	90r	50r	50r	50r	50r

Ex ante Pareto-indifference requires that the two actions be ranked as equally good, but because $(50r, 50r)$ is counted better than $(90r, 10r)$ and $(10r, 90r)$ by any continuous prioritarian SWF, weak and ordinary stochastic dominance (in light of this ordering of outcomes) require that b be ranked as better than a.[68]

Table 7.10 Ex Ante Pareto-Superiority and Stochastic Dominance

	Action d			Action e		
	$\pi_d(x) = .5$	$\pi_d(y) = .5$		$\pi_e(z) = .5$	$\pi_e(w) = .5$	
	$u(x)$	$u(y)$	Expected utility	$u(z)$	$u(w)$	Expected utility
Individual A	90r	10r	50r	$(50 - \varepsilon)r$	$(50 - \varepsilon)r$	$(50 - \varepsilon)r$
Individual B	10r	90r	50r	$(50 - \varepsilon)r$	$(50 - \varepsilon)r$	$(50 - \varepsilon)r$

This now-familiar example[69] illustrates the conflict between ex ante Pareto-superiority and weak and ordinary stochastic dominance. For any continuous prioritarian SWF, there is some ε such that both of the e outcomes are better than both of the d outcomes, and yet ex ante Pareto-superiority requires choosing action d.

The observation that the ex ante Pigou–Dalton and ex ante Pareto principles can run afoul of the weak stochastic dominance principle (given a prioritarian ranking of outcomes) is simply "end of story" for the view that the former principles impose a universal, unqualified constraint on the moral ranking of actions. If one espouses consequentialism (the idea that the ranking of actions should revolve around a ranking of outcomes), and if one believes that the most attractive moral ranking of outcomes is provided by a continuous prioritarian SWF, one is forced to conclude that the most

---

[68] This is the very same example that was used in Table 7.3 to show the conflict between EU prioritarianism and ex ante Pareto-indifference.

[69] Used in Table 7.4 to illustrate the conflict between EU prioritarianism and ex ante Pareto-superiority, and in Table 7.7 to show the conflict between ex ante prioritarianism and stochastic dominance principles.

attractive principles for morally ranking actions will sometimes violate the ex ante Pigou–Dalton and Pareto principles. No consequentialist can possibly countenance bridge principles that sometimes violate the axiom of weak stochastic dominance.

The conflict between the ex ante Pareto and Pigou–Dalton principles, on the one hand, and the weak stochastic dominance principle, on the other, also eviscerates the proposal that we morally rank actions by adjudicating between individuals' ex ante claims, valenced in terms of ex ante well-being. The idea seemed, at first blush, to be a plausible extension of the claim-across-outcome framework for morally ranking outcomes. But the idea of ex ante claims, plus the basic stipulation for resolving no-conflict cases, entails that two actions which are ex ante Pareto-indifferent must be ranked as equally morally good, and that an ex ante Pareto-superior action must be ranked as morally better. Since these implications, in turn, conflict with the weak stochastic dominance principle—given a prioritarian moral ordering of outcomes—the idea of ex ante claims must be abandoned by any consequentialist who embraces that ordering of outcomes.

How might the critic of EU prioritarianism resist this counterattack? She might, of course, renounce consequentialism. The consequentialist insists that outcomes can be morally ranked as better or worse. The act-consequentialist insists that the moral ranking of choices, in any choice situation, revolves around the ranking of outcomes (at a minimum, so as to satisfy the principle of weak stochastic dominance). If we deny the second premise, or both, why *wouldn't* ex ante prioritarianism, the idea of ex ante claims, and/or the ex ante Pigou–Dalton and Pareto principles be attractive bases for morally ranking actions? Since the project of this book is to work *within* (act-) consequentialism, this is not a question I will pursue, except to note the following. (1) The intuitive force of consequentialism is, admittedly, undercut to some extent by the nature of the "outcomes" that figure in consequentialist decision procedures. As I have stressed throughout the book, these are *simplified* descriptions of possible realities, not whole possible worlds. However, consequentialism and weak stochastic dominance are appealing premises even in this case.[70] Moreover, the conflict between the weak stochastic dominance and ex ante Pareto

---

[70] Consider, by way of illustration, the starkest conflict between ex ante Pareto-superiority and stochastic dominance. There is a set **O** of outcomes which are simplified possible worlds; a set **U** representing well-being levels, differences, and ratios; and a choice between action a and b, such that (given their corresponding probability distributions over outcomes) everyone is ex ante better off with a, but b weakly stochastically dominates a. The critic of consequentialism might object that the two are on a par. "While the ex ante Pareto-superiority of a does not mean that everyone is better off in each of the possible worlds resulting from a (with non-zero probability) as compared to each of the possible worlds resulting from b (with non-zero probability), it is also *not* the case that each of the possible worlds resulting from b (with non-zero probability) is better than each of the possible worlds resulting from a (with non-zero probability). Although b is weakly stochastically dominant, all this means is that each of the *outcomes* resulting from b (with non-zero probability) is better than each of the *outcomes* resulting from a (with non-zero probability). But each of these outcomes, itself, corresponds to a whole set of possible worlds."

and Pigou–Dalton principles, given a prioritarian ordering of outcomes, is robust to the level of description of outcomes. If each of two choices corresponds to a particular kind of probability distribution over utility vectors (as in the tables above), the conflict arises. What generates the conflict, then, is the possibility of this utility pattern, not the degree of specificity of the underlying outcomes. (2) The theorist who tries to develop a moral choice-evaluation procedure that is non-consequentialist— rejecting the premise that the moral ranking of actions derives, in any direct way, from the moral ranking of outcomes—and that is grounded on the concept of ex ante claims, and structured to respect the ex ante Pareto and Pigou–Dalton principles, will still be using the idea of an ordering of outcomes as the basis for ascriptions of ex ante well-being.[71] If outcomes have *this* sort of normative relevance, why

However, I have proposed that utilities be assigned to outcomes by adopting an invariance premise: namely that the undescribed ("missing") features of outcomes, if well-being relevant (if spectators care at all about these features in ranking life-histories), are fixed at some unspecified level and that spectators' extended preferences are invariant to what that level is. "Fixed" in what sense? Missing, well-being-relevant attributes will not—of course—be at the same level in all possible worlds. Conceivably, we might require that they be at the same level in all of the possible worlds resulting from *b* or *a* with non-zero probability. But such a requirement, too, is very strong; real-world decisionmakers would rarely have reason to believe that an invariance premise, thus specified, is true or even close to true. Instead, I have suggested a less demanding option: considering the *most likely* possible world resulting from each of the outcomes, the decisionmaker should believe that the missing characteristics are at the same level in all of these worlds. See Chapter 4, p. 254.

Note further that if the assignment of utility vectors to possible worlds with a common level of the missing attributes is invariant to what that level is, the moral ranking of those worlds by an SWF will be invariant to what that level is.

Thus, if the invariance premise holds true in a given choice situation, and action *b* is weakly stochastically dominant over action *a*, it follows that action *b* is not merely certain to yield an outcome morally better than the outcome of action *a* (which is true by definition of weak stochastic dominance), but likely (if not certain) to yield a possible world which is morally better.

By contrast, where each individual is ex ante better off with action *a* than action *b*—either in a case where ex ante Pareto-superiority conflicts with weak stochastic dominance, or in other cases—it is *not* necessarily true that the most likely outcome of action *a* is better for each individual than the most likely outcome of action *b*, and *a fortiori* not necessarily true that the possible world likely to result from action *a* is better for each individual than the possible world likely to result from action *b*. Lest this is not clear, consider by way of illustration a 3-person case. Action *b* yields the utility vector $(50r, 50r, 50r)$; action *a* yields with $1/3$ probability the vector $(160r, 0r, 0r)$, with $1/3$ probability the vector $(0r, 160r, 0r)$, and with $1/3$ probability the vector $(0r, 0r, 160r)$. Then the Atkinson SWF with $\gamma = 1/2$ says that *b* is weakly stochastically dominant; however, each individual is ex ante better off with action *a*; if action *a* is selected, each has a $1/3$ chance of being better off (at $160r$) than if *b* is selected, and a $2/3$ chance of being worse off (at $0r$).

[71] In the literature, it is usually assumed that each individual's ex ante well-being is expectationally represented by the very same utilities that provide the input for the SWF. (That is my assumption in this analysis, too.) To be sure, the assumption might be dropped. See Blackorby, Donaldson, and Mongin (2004). But even so, individual *i*'s ex ante well-being from a given action, *a*, would still surely be some kind of function of the outcomes resulting from *a* with non-zero probability. In particular, if

shouldn't they also determine the moral ranking of actions, via principles such as weak stochastic dominance?

Alternatively, the critic of EU prioritarianism might point out that the tension between consequentialism and the ex ante Pareto and Pigou–Dalton principles, which I have described here, arises *on the premise* that the moral ranking of outcomes is given by a continuous prioritarian SWF.[72] Why not salvage those principles, and the idea of ex ante claims, without abandoning consequentialism, by shifting *away* from that SWF? I will argue, below, that this strategy is unsuccessful—but let me hold the issue in abeyance and, for now, hold fixed the assumption of a prioritarian moral ordering of outcomes.

Finally, the critic might observe that there are non-EU approaches to ranking actions which are *consequentialist* (in the sense of satisfying weak and ordinary stochastic dominance) and *prioritarian* (use the continuous prioritarian SWF to rank outcomes). EU prioritarianism is hardly the only choice-evaluation framework with these features. Perhaps some other framework is, on balance, more attractive? Consider, for example, a two-step rule, which uses the ex ante approach as a tie-breaker. It says: (1) if EU prioritarianism ranks action a as better than b, then a is a morally better action; (2) if actions a and b are equally good according to the EU approach, then rank them by applying a continuous prioritarian SWF to the vectors of expected utilities associated with the actions.[73] This rule yields a complete quasi-ordering of actions. It satisfies weak and ordinary stochastic dominance. Moreover— by contrast with EU prioritarianism—it reaches the intuitively satisfying result of preferring ex ante equalization in permutation cases.[74]

---

action a is certain to yield an outcome better for i's well-being than action b, then—surely—i's ex ante well-being is better with a. Thus the ordering of actions in terms of i's ex ante well-being would revolve around a "prudential" ordering of outcomes (an ordering in light of his well-being). And one can then ask: why shouldn't the *moral* ordering of actions similarly revolve around a moral ordering of outcomes?

[72] To be clear, it is the tension between the stochastic dominance principles and the ex ante principles that might be mitigated by shifting away from a prioritarian ranking of outcomes. The tension between the sure thing principle and the ex ante Pigou–Dalton principle cannot be thus mitigated, since the way in which these principles constrain the ranking of actions does not depend upon the ordering of outcomes.

[73] Like EU prioritarianism itself, this two-step rule requires both a specification of which continuous prioritarian SWF is being used (i.e., which value of γ, since we are assuming here an Atkinson SWF), *and* a specification of the "translation" function $f^u(.)$. It then applies the EU formula, with that SWF and "translation" function, to rank actions a and b, and (if they are ranked equal at this step) breaks the tie by ranking their corresponding vectors of expected utilities with the SWF.

[74] Two other rules are worth noting. First, some scholarship discusses the possibility of arriving at an EU value for some action, using some SWF; then applying the SWF to the action's associated vector of expected utilities; and, finally, taking a weighted average. See Ben-Porath, Gilboa, and Schmeidler (1997); Gajdos and Maurin (2004). In the case of a continuous prioritarian SWF (of the Atkinson form), the weighted average approach would work as follows. Choose some value of γ, some translation function $f^u(.)$; some weighting factor λ between 0 and 1; and some $u(.)$ in $\mathbf{U}$. For any x,

However, non-EU rules in the class under consideration (those that use the continuous prioritarian SWF to order outcomes, and satisfy weak and ordinary stochastic dominance) may well violate the sure thing principle. (The two-step rule just described does so.) I have suggested that the consequentialist should find the sure thing principle appealing, if perhaps not as compelling as the stochastic dominance principles. Moreover, they may well violate a principle of stochastic *indifference*: namely, that if every possible outcome of action a (with non-zero probability) and every possible outcome of action b (with non-zero probability) are equally morally good, the two actions are equally morally good. (The two-step rule violates stochastic indifference.[75])

In my discussion here of consequentialism, I have emphasized stochastic dominance, not stochastic indifference. This emphasis corresponds to the current literature on EU versus non-EU approaches to choice, which uses stochastic dominance as the bright line for categorizing decision procedures. Still, it might very plausibly be argued that the consequentialist must embrace stochastic dominance *and* stochastic indifference principles as a bundle.[76] Consider a case where the decision-maker knows for sure that action a yields outcome x, action b outcome y, and x and

let $m(x) = f^u((1-\gamma)^{-1}\sum_{i=1}^{N} u_i(x)^{1-\gamma})$. For a given action a, assign it a value W^1 using the EU formula, i.e., $W^1(a) = \sum_{x \in O} \pi_a(x)m(x)$. Take the vector of expected utilities associated with a, i.e., $(V_1(a), \ldots, V_N(a))$, where $V_i(a) = \sum_{x \in O} \pi_a(x)u_i(x)$, using the chosen $u(.)$. Assign the action a value $W^2(a) = f^u((1-\gamma)^{-1}\sum_{i=1}^{N} V_i(a)^{1-\gamma})$. Now rank actions using the rule: a is at least as good as b iff $\lambda W^1(a) + (1-\lambda)W^2(a) \geq \lambda W^1(b) + (1-\lambda)W^2(b)$. I will not attempt to analyze the stochastic dominance properties of this approach. In any event, like the two-step rule, it violates stochastic indifference (because it is not indifferent in permutation cases with ex ante equalization) and the sure thing principle (using the same example as for the two-step rule, see the footnote immediately below.)

Second, it might be thought possible to cure the conflict between ex ante prioritarianism and stochastic dominance via a different kind of two-step approach than mentioned in the text, namely: given some continuous prioritarian SWF (of the Atkinson variety), if a ordinarily stochastically dominates b, then a is better; if not, rank them by applying the SWF to their associated vectors of expected utilities. However, this rule does not succeed in producing a quasiordering of any given choice set, since it can fail transitivity. To see why, assume that there are outcomes x, y, z, w, x^*, y^*, each associated with a utility vector, with two persons in the population. Outcome $x = ((50 - 0.5\varepsilon)r, (50 - 0.5\varepsilon)r)$; $y = ((50 - 0.5\varepsilon)r, (50 - 0.5\varepsilon)r)$; $z = (60r, 40r)$; $w = (40r, 60r)$; $x^* = ((50 + 0.5\varepsilon)r, 50r)$; $y^* = ((50 - 1.5\varepsilon)r, (50 - 0.5\varepsilon)r)$. The value ε is such that the SWF is indifferent between $(60r, 40r)$ and $((50 - \varepsilon)r, (50 - \varepsilon)r)$. Assume, now, that action a yields x and y, each with probability 0.5; that action b yields z and w, each with probability 0.5; and that action c yields x^* and y^*, each with probability 0.5. Then the rule will rank a over b, b over c, but c over a.

[75] The two-step rule violates stochastic indifference because it prefers ex ante equalization in permutation cases. To see why it violates the sure thing principle, let utility vectors be assigned to outcomes as follows: $x = (100r, 200r)$; $y = (200r, 100r)$; $z = (200r, 100r)$; $z^* = (150r, 150r)$. Let a assign a 0.5 probability to x and 0.5 to z, while b assigns a 0.5 probability to y and a 0.5 probability to z. Let a^* assign a 0.5 probability to x and 0.5 to z^*; while b^* assigns a 0.5 probability to y and 0.5 probability to z^*. Then the two-step rule ranks a over b, but is indifferent between a^* and b^*.

[76] Many thanks to Marc Fleurbaey for this point.

y are equally morally good. In such a case, the consequentialist ranks the two actions as equally morally good; and she explicates that ranking by pointing to the equal goodness of the corresponding outcomes. Consider, now, a case of stochastic indifference. The decisionmaker does not know which particular outcome would result from *a*, and which particular outcome from *b*, but she is sure that the *a* outcome (whatever its particular characteristics) will be such as to be equally morally good as the *b* outcome. How could the consequentialist explain why the decisionmaker need not rank the actions as equally morally good in this case?

Moreover, the proponent of any non-EU rule (even if it satisfies weak and ordinary stochastic dominance, or for that matter stochastic indifference and the sure thing principle as well) can be challenged to situate her view in a broader account of rational choice. Is her position that EU theory (even as refined to accommodate imprecise probabilities, an incomplete quasiordering, decisionmaker uncertainty about the ordering, and strategic interaction) simply fails as the appropriate bridge principles for moving from any kind of ordering of outcomes, to an ordering of actions? If so, what are the appropriate such principles? No generic competitor to EU theory as an account of rational choice—understand that we are looking here for a *normative*, not descriptive theory—has gained much acceptance in the literature.

Is her position, instead, that the non-EU rule she proposes should be understood as an exception from EU theory—needed for the special case in which we are *morally* ordering actions in light of a *moral* ordering of outcomes? If so, she can be asked: what justifies this exception? Is it a desire to satisfy the ex ante Pareto or Pigou–Dalton principles in certain instances where the EU approach fails to do so? (The two-step rule satisfies the ex ante Pigou–Dalton principle in permutation cases, while the EU approach does not.) Since the non-EU rule does not *universally* satisfy the ex ante Pareto or Pigou–Dalton principles (on pain of violating weak and ordinary stochastic dominance), why should its *partial* satisfaction of these principles be seen as sufficient justification for suspending the application of otherwise applicable principles of rational choice (EU theory)? EU prioritarianism is *already* sensitive to considerations of fairness—captured in the moral ranking of outcomes, as a function of individual claims for or against outcomes. The idea of capturing fairness via ex ante claims (which would require *universal* satisfaction of the ex ante Pareto and Pigou–Dalton principles, and would conflict with stochastic dominance) has been given up. So what, really, warrants this non-EU approach?

C. Choosing a "Translation" Function (Herein of Ex Ante Separability)

The continuous prioritarian SWF ranks outcomes in a manner that satisfies Pareto and Pigou–Dalton principles (understood as constraints on the ranking of outcomes), but EU prioritarianism violates the ex ante analogues of these principles. The observant reader will ask: What about separability? Remember that the continuous prioritarian SWF also satisfies a separability axiom (understood as a constraint on the ranking of outcomes).[77] Does this principle also have an ex ante analogue; and does EU prioritarianism also violate *that*?

Yes and yes. Ex ante separability says that if there is a group of individuals each of whom has the very same ex ante well-being as between two actions, the ranking of the actions is invariant to what that ex ante well-being level is.[78] Table 7.11 provides a case in which EU prioritarianism inevitably conflicts with ex ante separability.

Table 7.11 EU Prioritarianism and Ex Ante Separability

	Action a			Action b		
	$\pi_a(x) = .5$	$\pi_a(y) = .5$	Expected utility	$\pi_b(z) = .5$	$\pi_b(w) = .5$	Expected utility
	$u(x)$	$u(y)$		$u(z)$	$u(w)$	
Individual A	40r	40r	40r	30r	30r	30r
Individual B	30r	30r	30r	40r	40r	40r
Individual C	100r	200r	150r	150r	150r	150r
Individual D	200r	100r	150r	150r	150r	150r

	Action a*			Action b*		
	$\pi_a.(x^*) = .5$	$\pi_a.(y^*) = .5$	Expected utility	$\pi_b.(z^*) = .5$	$\pi_b.(w^*) = .5$	Expected utility
	$u(x^*)$	$u(y^*)$		$u(z^*)$	$u(w^*)$	
Individual A	40r	40r	40r	30r	30r	30r
Individual B	30r	30r	30r	40r	40r	40r
Individual C	150r	150r	150r	150r	150r	150r
Individual D	150r	150r	150r	150r	150r	150r

Given the patterns of expected utilities, ex ante separability requires that action *a* be ranked at least as good as *b* iff *a** is at least as good as *b**. EU prioritarianism will rank *b* over *a*, since any continuous prioritarian SWF ranks outcome *z* over *x* and *w* over *y* (by anonymity plus the Pigou–Dalton principle). However, it will rank *b** equally good as *a**, since all the utility vectors resulting from these actions are permutations of each other).

[77] See Chapter 5. In Chapter 6, I referred to this as "person separability" to avoid confusing it with temporal or attribute separability; but there is no risk of confusion here, and I will therefore return to the simpler terminology of Chapter 5.

[78] An individual is "unaffected" as between two actions if his ex ante well-being is the same with both. Paralleling the definition of outcome separability in Chapter 5, a ranking of *actions* satisfies ex ante separability if the following is true. Assume there are four actions *a*, *b*, *a**, *b** with the following features. Everyone who is unaffected between *a* and *b* is also unaffected between *a** and *b**, and vice versa. Everyone else is unaffected between *a* and *a**, and between *b* and *b**. Then *a* is morally at least as good as *b* iff *a** is morally at least as good as *b**.

However, there is a weaker kind of ex ante separability which EU prioritarianism need not violate. Imagine that there is a group of individuals who are *sure to be unaffected* by the choice between a and b. If i is in this group, then the following is true: i has the very same well-being level in each of the outcomes of action a that has non-zero probability and in each of the outcomes of action b that has non-zero probability. The axiom of weak ex ante separability says: The moral ranking of two actions should be invariant to the well-being level of individuals who are sure to be unaffected by the actions.[79]

Remember that EU prioritarianism assigns each outcome x a moral utility value $m(x)$, unique up to a positive affine transformation, by picking some $u(.)$ in **U** and then setting $m(x) = f^u((1-\gamma)^{-1} \sum_{i=1}^{N} u_i(x)^{1-\gamma})$. Most simply the "translation" function $f^u(.)$ is just the identity function, in which case we can arrive at $m(.)$, unique up to a positive affine transformation, by picking any $u(.)$ in **U** and setting $m(x) = (1-\gamma)^{-1} \sum_{i=1}^{N} u_i(x)^{1-\gamma}$. For short, call this "EU prioritarianism with the identity translation."

It is not very hard to see that EU prioritarianism with the identity translation satisfies weak ex ante separability. On the other hand, this approach has a real deficit. It can conflict with the ex ante Pareto principles even in choice situations where individuals are "identically situated," as Table 7.12 shows. Individuals are "identically situated" as regards the choice between actions a and b, if well-being is distributed perfectly equally within each of the outcomes possibly resulting from a with nonzero probability, and within each of the outcomes possibly resulting from b with nonzero probability.

Table 7.12 EU Prioritarianism, the Identity Translation, and Identically Situated Individuals

	Action a			Action b		
	$\pi_a(x) = .5$	$\pi_a(y) = .5$		$\pi_b(z) = .5$	$\pi_b(w) = .5$	
	$u(x)$	$u(y)$	Expected utility	$u(z)$	$u(w)$	Expected utility
Individual A	9r	144r	76.5r	64r	64r	64r
Individual B	9r	144r	76.5r	64r	64r	64r

[79] The text defines what it means for an individual to be "sure to be unaffected" between two actions. Let us say that two actions c and d provide some individual i "the very same well-being lottery" if, for any outcome x that c yields with non-zero probability, there is some outcome y which d yields with the very same probability, such that i is equally well off in x and y.

We can now formulate the requirement of weak ex ante separability as follows. Imagine that there are four actions a, b, a^*, b^*, with the following features. Everyone who is sure to be unaffected as between a and b is also sure to be unaffected as between a^* and b^*, and vice versa. For everyone else, a provides her the very same well-being lottery as a^*, and b provides her the very same well-being lottery as b^*. Then a is morally at least as good as b iff a^* is morally at least as good as b^*.

Consider an Atkinson SWF with $\gamma = 1/2$, i.e., 2 times the sum of the square root of individual utilities. If $m(x) = (1-\gamma)^{-1} \sum_{i=1}^{N} u_i(x)^{1-\gamma}$, then in Table 7.12 outcome x is assigned a moral utility value of 12 and outcome y a moral utility value of 48, while outcomes z and w are assigned moral utilities of 32 (or each of these values multiplied by a common scaling factor of $\sqrt{r}$, with r positive.) So the expected moral utility (using these values) of action a is 30, while the expected moral utility of action b is 32. But note that the two individuals are identically situated, and that ex ante Pareto-superiority requires action a.

A conflict with the ex ante Pareto principles in the case of identically situated individuals seems perverse. Consider ex ante Pareto-superiority. Imagine that individuals are identically situated and that everyone's expected utility is greater with action a, but that a moral choice-evaluation procedure picks action b. If the decisionmaker were to adopt a non-moral perspective, focused on the well-being of any particular subject, she would maximize that individual's expected utility and choose a.

For the decisionmaker to adopt a moral perspective means that she now takes account of everyone's well-being, impartially. In general, of course, shifting to this viewpoint may lead the decisionmaker to choose an action which is not in the best interests of some particular individual. After all, there may be a conflict between the interests of individual i and the interests of individual j—a conflict which the decisionmaker ignores when she focuses on i's interests, but is properly sensitive to when she adopts the moral perspective. However, in the case of identically situated individuals now at hand, there is no conflict of interest—in any sense—between any of the members of the population. (Not only is it the case that all have greater ex ante well-being with action a. It is *also* the case that, for any outcome x^* which action a or b might yield with non-zero probability, and for any outcome y^* which action a or b might yield with non-zero probability, either all the individuals are better off in x^* than y^*, or all better off in y^* than x^*, or all equally well off.) So how can we possibly explain why the shift of the decisionmaker's perspective from a subject-interested perspective to a moral perspective warrants the shift of the selected action from a to b?[80]

My discussion, in the preceding subsection, emphasized that anyone who favors a consequentialist approach to choice (in the minimal sense of satisfying the weak stochastic dominance principle), and embraces a prioritarian moral ordering of outcomes, is forced to renounce the ex ante Pareto principles as universal constraints on choice. Relatedly, she is forced to renounce the idea of ex ante claims. However, in the case of identically situated individuals, the ex ante Pareto principles would seem to have a justification quite independent from the notion of ex ante claims—namely,

---

[80] For the very same reasons, it seems perverse that EU prioritarianism with the identity translation can conflict with ex ante Pareto-indifference in the case of identically situated individuals.

the premise that moral decisionmaking should deviate from subject-oriented deci-sionmaking only by virtue of interindividual conflict of interests. Shouldn't a priori-tarian choice-evaluation framework satisfy the principles, if not universally, then at least in this category of cases?

Fortunately, EU prioritarianism *can* be structured so as to necessarily satisfy the Pareto principles in cases of identically situated individuals. Work by Marc Fleurbaey demonstrates that EU prioritarianism using a particular translation function $f^u(.)$ will do so. Rather than setting $f^u(.)$ to be the identity function, define it as follows. Pick any $u(.)$ in $\mathbf{U}$.[81] For any outcome x, mapped by $u(.)$ onto utility vector $u(x) = (u_1(x), u_2(x), \ldots, u_N(x))$, identify the value u^*, such that a utility vector in which everyone gets u^* is an equally good outcome as x, according to the prioritarian SWF. Then set $m(x) = u^*$.[82] For short, call this "EU prioritarianism with the Fleurbaey translation." Assigning moral utility numbers to outcomes, using this $m(x)$ function, is a perfectly kosher way to do so, for purposes of EU theory.[83] And if we plug these $m(x)$ numbers into the EU formula, the resulting ranking of actions can never violate ex ante Pareto-indifference or Pareto-superiority where individuals are identically situated.[84]

[81] Again, throughout the chapter, until the discussion of refinements, we are assuming $\mathbf{U}$ to be unique up to a positive ratio transformation.

[82] See Fleurbaey (2010). Because we are using the Atkinson SWF, we can write down a formula for u^*. Given our utility function $u(.)$, the value u^* for $x = ((1/N)\sum_{i=1}^{N} u_i(x)^{1-\gamma})^{1/(1-\gamma)}$. Thus $f^u(.)$ for purposes of the Fleurbaey translation is defined as follows: $f^u(w) = ((1-\gamma)w)/N)^{1/(1-\gamma)}$. In the case of $\gamma = 1$, the Atkinson SWF sums natural logarithms, and $u^* = (\prod_{i=1}^{N} u_i(x))^{1/N}$, thus $f^u(w) = (e^w)^{1/N}$. Note that, as with the identity translation, $f^u(.)$ is the very same function regardless of which $u(.)$ in $\mathbf{U}$ is used.

[83] Remember that $f^u(.)$ must be strictly increasing. To show that this $f^u(.)$ function is, consider first the case where all utility values, in all outcomes, are positive. Thus, in the case where $\gamma < 1$, the argu-ment for $f^u(.)$, i.e., the w value in the preceding footnote, will be positive; in the case where $\gamma > 1$, the w value will be negative. With $\gamma = 1$, it can be any value. Taking the derivative of $f^u(.)$ with respect to w, with these restrictions in mind, it emerges that this derivative is always positive, hence $f^u(.)$ is strictly increasing.

The Atkinson SWF does not permit negative utilities, but allows for utilities to be zero if $\gamma < 1$, which means that w can equal zero in this case. See Chapter 5, p. 391. In the case where $\gamma < 1, f^u(.)$ remains strictly increasing even with $w = 0$ added to its domain, since $f^u(.)$ is zero if $w = 0$ and positive otherwise.

[84] This is straightforward. Pick any $u(.)$ in $\mathbf{U}$. If all individuals are identically situated, then for any outcome x accorded non-zero probability by action a or b, $u(x; 1) = u(x; 2) = \ldots = u(x; N)$. Thus $m(x) = u(x; 1) = u(x; 2) = \ldots u(x; N)$ for any such outcome. And comparing a and b by computing expected m-values will obviously be consistent with ex ante Pareto-indifference and -superiority.

To be sure, EU prioritarianism with *any* translation function (Fleurbaey or not) will violate ex ante Pareto-indifference and -superiority in certain cases not involving identically situated individuals—the cases displayed in Tables 7.3 and 7.4 above. Moreover, it should be recognized that conflicts with the ex ante Pareto principles seem especially perverse in *two* kinds of cases: first, cases involving identically situated individuals; second, cases in which everyone but one person is sure to be unaf-fected by the choice. EU prioritarianism with the Fleurbaey translation does *not* avoid a conflict with

However, EU prioritarianism with the Fleurbaey translation has a countervailing deficit. It fails to satisfy weak ex ante separability, as Table 7.13 illustrates.

Table 7.13 EU Prioritarianism, the Fleurbaey Translation, and Weak Ex Ante Separability

	Action a		Action b	
	$\pi_a(x) = .5$	$\pi_a(y) = .5$	$\pi_b(z) = .5$	$\pi_b(w) = .5$
	$u(x)$	$u(y)$	$u(z)$	$u(w)$
Individual A	$9r$	$144r$	$64r$	$64r$
Individual B	$9r$	$9r$	$9r$	$9r$
u^*	$9r$	$56.25r$	$30.25r$	$30.25r$

	Action d		Action e	
	$\pi_d(x^*) = .5$	$\pi_d(y^*) = .5$	$\pi_e(z^*) = .5$	$\pi_b(w^*) = .5$
	$u(x^*)$	$u(y^*)$	$u(z^*)$	$u(w^*)$
Individual A	$9r$	$144r$	$64r$	$64r$
Individual B	$900r$	$900r$	$900r$	$900r$
u^*	$272.25r$	$441r$	$361r$	$361r$

Consider again the Atkinson SWF with $\gamma = 1/2$. For each given outcome $(x, y, z,$ etc.) and its corresponding utility vector, there is a u^* value such that an outcome in which everyone is at utility level u^* is seen by the Atkinson SWF with $\gamma = 1/2$ to be equally good as this outcome. For example, u^* is $56.25r$ for outcome y because 2 times the square root of $56.25r$ is equal to the square root of $144r$ plus the square root of $9r$ (for any positive r).

Note that individual B has the very same utility ($9r$) in all of the action a and b outcomes, and the very same utility ($900r$) in all of the action d and e outcomes. Individual A faces the very same lottery with a and d, and the very same lottery with b and e. So weak ex ante separability requires that a be ranked above b iff d is ranked above e. But taking the expected value of u^* ranks a over b, but e over d, in violation of this axiom.

The choice between respecting the ex ante Pareto principles where individuals are identically situated, and respecting weak ex ante separability, strikes me as a genuinely hard choice. Weak ex ante separability is logically *distinct* from separability in the ranking of outcomes. (EU prioritarianism with the Fleurbaey translation satisfies

the ex ante Pareto principles in the latter case. For discussion of the consistency of various SWFs with different versions of the ex ante Pareto principles and different kinds of ex ante separability, see Fleurbaey (2010); McCarthy (2008); Rabinowicz (2001).

the latter but violates the former.[85]) Still, whatever rationale one might provide for outcome separability would also, seemingly, justify weak ex ante separability. Imagine, first, that the decisionmaker is choosing under conditions of certainty. Choice a^x leads for sure to outcome x, choice a^y to outcome y. Separability in the ranking of outcomes means that the ranking of a^x versus a^y cannot depend upon the well-being level of individuals who are unaffected as between x and y. Consider now a case of choice under uncertainty. The decisionmaker does not know which outcome a will yield, or which outcome b will yield, but he does know that—whatever outcomes those might be–some individuals will be unaffected as between them. Why, now, should his choice between a and b be sensitive to the well-being levels of these individuals—in violation of weak ex ante separability?

I will leave the reader to ponder the choice between EU prioritarianism with the identity translation versus the Fleurbaey translation—between satisfying weak ex ante separability, and satisfying the ex ante Pareto principles in cases of identically situated individuals. The thrust of this chapter is to argue for EU theory as the most attractive set of moral bridge principles. The choice of translation function $f^u(.)$ is a choice *within* the domain of EU theory, and not one I will attempt to resolve here.

D. Should We Reconsider the Continuous Prioritarian SWF?

The analysis, thus far, has held fixed the continuous prioritarian ordering of outcomes. I have sought to specify a choice procedure such that the ranking of outcomes determines the ranking of actions—meaning, axiomatically, that the procedure satisfies stochastic dominance axioms and, arguably, other axioms as well, such as the sure thing principle or stochastic indifference. *Moreover*, I have taken as given that outcomes are ranked according to the continuous prioritarian SWF. With this outcome-ranking in hand, consequentialism comes into conflict with the principles of ex ante Pareto-indifference, ex ante Pareto-superiority, and ex ante Pigou–Dalton. No choice procedure can both universally satisfy weak stochastic dominance, and universally satisfy any one of the ex ante principles just mentioned. EU prioritarianism, in particular, because it satisfies weak stochastic dominance (an integral feature of the EU approach), necessarily violates the ex ante Pareto principles and the ex ante Pigou–Dalton principle in some cases. Relatedly, the idea of ex ante claims (which would entail satisfying, at least, the ex ante Pareto principles) become untenable.

Do these dilemmas provide sufficient reason to reconsider the outcome ranking? Chapter 5 presented seemingly powerful arguments that the outcome ranking should satisfy the trio of the Pigou–Dalton principle, separability, and continuity, yielding the continuous prioritarian SWF. Now that we have seen the difficulties

---

[85] *Any* variant of EU prioritarianism, whatever the translation function, employs a continuous prioritarian SWF to rank outcomes and thus satisfies separability in the ranking of outcomes.

which arise in moving from this outcome ranking to a choice ranking, should we embrace a different SWF?

Consider, first, the various non-utilitarian competitors to the continuous prioritarian SWF discussed in Chapter 5: the sufficientist SWF, rank-weighted SWF, leximin SWF, and prioritarian SWF with a lexical threshold. The very same examples that illustrated the conflict between the continuous prioritarian SWF and the ex ante Pareto principles can be used to show that each of these competitor SWFs, too, creates the very same conflict.[86] Each gives rise to a ranking of outcomes with the following property: a ranking of actions that satisfies the weak stochastic dominance principle in light of that outcome-ranking will inevitably conflict with ex ante Pareto-indifference and ex ante Pareto-superiority in some choice situations.[87]

Table 7.14 Non-Utilitarian SWFs: Ex Ante Pareto-Superiority versus Stochastic Dominance

	Action a			Action b		
	$\pi_a(x) = .5$	$\pi_a(y) = .5$		$\pi_b(z) = .5$	$\pi_b(w) = .5$	
	$u(x)$	$u(y)$	Expected utility	$u(z)$	$u(w)$	Expected utility
Individual A	$90r$	$10r$	$50r$	$(50 - \varepsilon)r$	$(50 - \varepsilon)r$	$(50 - \varepsilon)r$
Individual B	$10r$	$90r$	$50r$	$(50 - \varepsilon)r$	$(50 - \varepsilon)r$	$(50 - \varepsilon)r$

Ex ante Pareto-superiority requires that a be ranked above b, with ε positive. However, b weakly stochastically dominates a in light of the leximin ordering of outcomes (as long as $\varepsilon < 40$). It also does in light of the ordering of outcomes achieved by the rank-weighted SWF for ε sufficiently small. Why? The rank-weighted SWF prefers $(50r, 50r)$ to $(90r, 10r)$ and $(10r, 90r)$, because it satisfies the Pigou–Dalton principle. It also (as it happens) satisfies the continuity axiom, and therefore prefers $((50 - \varepsilon)r, (50 - \varepsilon)r)$ to $(90r, 10r)$ and $(10r, 90r)$ for ε sufficiently small.

The sufficientist SWF and prioritarian SWF with a lexical threshold each incorporate a threshold. Although they are not invariant to ratio rescaling, they *can* use information about the threshold life-history to "winnow down" **U** to a singleton.[88] Drop the "r" from the above entries. Assume, further, that all the life-histories in outcomes x, y, z, and w are below the threshold (which is, e.g., at 100). In ranking outcomes containing only below-threshold outcomes, each of these SWFs yields the same ranking as some continuous prioritarian SWF. So b is weakly stochastically dominant in light of these SWFs, too, for ε sufficiently small.

---

[86] See Tables 7.3 and 7.4.

[87] It can also be shown that a ranking of actions that satisfies weak stochastic dominance in light of any one of these SWFs will necessarily violate the ex ante Pigou–Dalton principle in some cases.

[88] See Chapter 5, pp. 388–389.

A closely parallel analysis (just drop the "ε" from the above example) shows that ex ante Pareto-indifference conflicts with weak stochastic dominance in light of all these SWFs.

Thus the consequentialist who embraces the ranking of outcomes provided by the sufficientist SWF, rank-weighted SWF, leximin SWF, or prioritarian SWF with a lexical threshold must renounce the idea of universally satisfying the ex ante Pareto principles; and she must abandon the idea of ex ante claims.

Indeed, it can be shown that *any* non-utilitarian SWF—not just these particular non-utilitarian competitors to the continuous prioritarian SWF—will come into conflict with the ex ante Pareto principles. More specifically, Harsanyi's famous "aggregation theorem" can be deployed to demonstrate the following: if we require that EU theory be used as the bridge principles for moving from the outcome ranking to the action ranking, *and* that the action ranking satisfy the ex ante Pareto principles, the SWF used to produce the outcome ranking must be a utilitarian SWF.[89]

---

[89] Harsanyi's aggregation theorem, in one version, shows this. Assume that there is an outcome set **O** and a set of all lotteries over outcomes. Assume that there are N individual orderings of the lotteries, plus a social ordering. All the orderings comply with von Neumann/Morgenstern EU theory. The N individual orderings are each expectationally represented by a utility function $u_i(.)$ taking outcomes as its arguments, $i = 1$ to N. The social ordering is expectationally represented by a utility function $w(.)$. Abusing notation, let us use the symbol "$u_i(l)$" to mean the value assigned to lottery l by the EU formula with $u_i(.)$ as the utility function, i.e., $u_i(l) = \sum_{x \in O} \pi_i(x) u_i(x)$. Similarly, use "$w(l)$" to mean $\sum_{x \in O} \pi_i(x) w(x)$. Then *if* we assume that the social ordering satisfies a requirement of ex ante Pareto-indifference in terms of the individual orderings, and a requirement of ex ante Pareto-superiority in terms of the individual orderings, there exist positive numbers $a_1, \ldots, a_N$, and a number b such that $w(l) = b + \sum_{i=1}^{N} a_i u_i(l)$ for any lottery l. See Weymark (1991). For Harsanyi's presentation of the aggregation theorem, see Harsanyi (1955; 1982; 1986, ch. 4).

Harsanyi claimed that the aggregation theorem constituted a proof of utilitarianism. This claim has generated a sizable literature, which I will not attempt to review here. Suffice it to say that Harsanyi's claim is dubious absent further premises concerning the relation between the individual utility functions and individual well-being, and absent further premises needed to constrain the a_i weights to be equal. (Other than Weymark, two useful discussions of the aggregation theorem, citing much of the literature, are Blackorby, Bossert, and Donaldson [2005, pp. 223–233]; and Mongin and d'Aspremont [1998, pp. 425–444].)

On the other hand, *if* we transpose the aggregation theorem to the set-up under consideration in this section (where there is a set **U** of utility functions that are assumed *both* to represent well-being levels and differences, *and* at the same time to expectationally represent ex ante well-being; and where the only SWFs being considered must satisfy the minimal welfarist requirement of *anonymity*), then the aggregation theorem *does* lead to the utilitarian SWF.

In particular, assume an outcome set **O**; a set **U** unique up to a positive ratio transformation; an anonymous SWF that morally orders the outcome set; a choice set **A**; and a moral ranking of the choice set in light of the outcome ranking that complies with EU theory, hence can be expectationally represented by some function $w(.)$. Although **A** itself may not consist of all possible lotteries over **O**, assume that one element in **A** is ranked at least as good as a second iff it would be thus ranked in a hypothetical, expanded choice set consisting of all possible lotteries. Pick any $u(.)$ in **U**. Because **U**

In short, the difficulties in orienting a choice-evaluation framework around the continuous prioritarian SWF provide no grounds for adopting some other non-utilitarian SWF. They all face the very same difficulties.

(We can turn this point around. Imagine that the reader was *not* persuaded by the argumentation in Chapter 5. She was inclined, on balance, to embrace the sufficientist SWF, the rank-weighted SWF, the leximin SWF, or the prioritarian SWF with a lexical threshold. She now asks herself: Should I use EU theory as the bridge principles for moving from this outcome ranking to the action ranking? The answer should be "yes," for the very same reasons that I relied upon to defend "EU prioritarianism"—the marriage of a continuous prioritarian SWF with EU bridge principles—as against non-EU approaches to implementing a continuous prioritarian SWF. EU sufficientism, EU rank-weighted, EU leximin, and EU prioritarianism-with-a-lexical-threshold *will* conflict with the ex ante Pareto principles in some cases; but because the ex ante Pareto principles, themselves, cannot be embraced on pain of violating weak stochastic dominance, *that* conflict should not deter the marriage of EU bridge principles with a sufficientist SWF, rank-weighted SWF, leximin SWF, or prioritarian-with-a-lexical-threshold SWF.[90])

expectationally represents ex ante well-being (and is unique up to a positive ratio transformation), $u_i(.)$ expectationally represents the ex ante well-being of individual i with respect to this lottery set. Think of the ex ante well-being of each of the N individuals as furnishing its own ranking of the lottery set. *If* we require that the moral ranking of the lottery set satisfy the ex ante Pareto principles (i.e., if everyone's ex ante well-being is the same in two lotteries, then the lotteries are equally morally good, and similarly for Pareto-superiority), then—because each such ex ante well-being ranking is expectationally represented by a $u_i(.)$—there will exist positive numbers $a_1, \ldots, a_N$ and a number b such that $w(l) = b + \sum_{i=1}^{N} a_i u_i(l)$, for every lottery l.

In particular, this will be true for every *outcome*, understood as a "degenerate" lottery (one that yields the outcome for certain). Thus there will exist positive numbers $a_1, \ldots, a_N$ and a number b such that, for all x, $w(x) = b + \sum_{i=1}^{N} a_i u_i(x)$, with x at least as good as y iff $w(x) \geq w(y)$. At least if the outcome set **O** is sufficiently "rich," allowing the a_i to be unequal will lead to a violation of anonymity. (In particular, imagine that for each pair of individuals i and j, there is at least one pair of outcomes x and y such that $u_i(x) = u_j(y)$, $u_j(x) = u_i(y)$, $u_i(x) \neq u_i(y)$ and $u_k(x) = u_k(y)$ for all $k \neq i, j$. Then unless $a_i = a_j$, it will not be the case that $w(x) = w(y)$, which violates anonymity.)

But if the a_i are all equal, the SWF ranks the outcomes the very same way as the utilitarian SWF. (The utilitarian SWF says: x is morally at least as good as y iff $\sum_{i=1}^{N} u_i(x) \geq \sum_{i=1}^{N} u_i(y)$ for all $u(.)$ in **U**, which—where **U** is unique up to a positive ratio transformation—is the same as saying x is morally at least as good as y iff $\sum_{i=1}^{N} u_i(x) \geq \sum_{i=1}^{N} u_i(y)$ for any $u(.)$ in **U**.

[90] It should be noted that technical problems *may* arise in meshing an SWF with EU theory where the set **O** is uncountable. (If the ordering of an action set with an uncountable **O** *is* representable by EU theory, the EU formula would take the form of an integral, not a summation.) No such problems arise for the continuous prioritarian SWF, but they may arise for other SWFs. Why? It is well known that a rule R for ordering the (uncountable) set of all possible utility vectors can only be represented by a continuous function if the ordering satisfies the continuity axiom, see Chapter 5, n. 9; and some rules R that fail the continuity axiom cannot be represented by a function at all. This is true, for example, of the leximin SWF. Thus the leximin SWF cannot be meshed with EU theory to yield a

What about the utilitarian SWF? Given the utilitarian ordering of outcomes, the axioms of weak and ordinary stochastic dominance *never* come into conflict with the ex ante Pareto principles. And EU utilitarianism, in particular, need not come into conflict with these principles.[91] Adopting the utilitarian SWF allows us *both* to outfit our moral choice-evaluation framework using the most attractive generic account of rational choice (EU theory), *and* to avoid counterintuitive conflicts with the ex ante Pareto principles. Are these sufficient advantages to justify utilitarianism?

I think not. Why, after all, should we find the ex ante Pareto principles appealing? If moral decisionmaking is a matter of fairness—a matter of respecting the separateness of persons—what warrants them?

ranking of a choice set **A**, where **U** and **O** are such that every possible N-dimensional utility vector corresponds to some $u(x)$; because if there existed a $w(.)$ that expectationally represented the leximin ranking of **A**, it would also be true that x is ranked above y by the leximin rule iff $w(x) \geq w(y)$, which is a contradiction.

I need not pursue these difficulties here. My claim is just that if one embraces some given nonutilitarian SWF, and meshing EU theory with the SWF is technically possible, violations of the ex ante Pareto principles should be no obstacle to doing so.

[91] The utilitarian ordering of outcomes (in the case where **U** is unique up to a positive ratio transformation) is: x is morally at least as good as y iff, for any $u(.)$ in **U**, $\sum_{i=1}^{N} u_i(x) \geq \sum_{i=1}^{N} u_i(y)$. EU utilitarianism assigns each outcome a value $m(x)$, unique up to a positive affine transformation, as follows. For a given $u(.)$ in **U**, set $m(x) = f^u(\sum_{i=1}^{N} u_i(x))$, with the translation function $f^u(.)$ strictly increasing. Action a is then ranked at least as good as action b iff $\sum_{x \in \mathbf{O}} \pi_a(x)m(x) \geq \sum_{x \in \mathbf{O}} \pi_b(x)m(x)$. If $f^u(.)$ is the identity translation, then $m(x) = \sum_{i=1}^{N} u_i(x)$.

Whenever the EU approach is used to order an action set in light of an ordering of an outcome set, it ranks actions consistently with ordinary (and weak) stochastic dominance in terms of that ordering. This is a very basic feature of the EU approach. So EU utilitarianism with *any* translation function preserves ordinary (and a fortiori weak) stochastic dominance in light of the utilitarian ordering of outcomes.

Note, now, that EU utilitarianism with the identity translation always ranks actions consistently with ex ante Pareto-indifference and -superiority. Consider ex ante Pareto-indifference (parallel reasoning will work for ex ante Pareto-superiority). If a and b are ex ante Pareto-indifferent, then for each i, $\sum_{x \in \mathbf{O}} \pi_a(x)u_i(x) = \sum_{x \in \mathbf{O}} \pi_b(x)u_i(x)$. Thus $\sum_{x \in \mathbf{O}} \pi_a(x)\left[\sum_{i=1}^{N} u_i(x)\right] = \sum_{x \in \mathbf{O}} \pi_b(x)\left[\sum_{i=1}^{N} u_i(x)\right]$. But thus it immediately follows that $\sum_{x \in \mathbf{O}} \pi_a(x)m(x) = \sum_{x \in \mathbf{O}} \pi_b(x)m(x)$, since $f^u(.)$ is the identity translation.

Because EU utilitarianism with the *identity* translation necessarily satisfies ex ante Pareto-indifference and -superiority, and EU utilitarianism with *any* translation function necessarily satisfies ordinary stochastic dominance (in light of the utilitarian ordering), it follows that there can never be a choice situation where the ranking of choices required by ordinary stochastic dominance (in light of the utilitarian ordering) conflicts with ex ante Pareto-indifference or -superiority.

Whether EU utilitarianism with some other translation function might conflict with ex ante Pareto-indifference or -superiority (in ranking choices unconstrained by ordinary stochastic dominance) is an interesting question which I will not pursue. In any event, EU utilitarianism need not conflict with the ex ante principles, because the identity translation can be used.

The answer, I have suggested, lies in the idea of individual claims. To rank items (be they actions, outcomes, or other items) in light of individual claims is to see each person as an entity whose interests enter separately into moral deliberation.

The Pareto principles (in terms of the item being assessed) follow immediately. Reciprocally, *if* one is to justify the ranking of outcomes as flowing from individuals' claims-across-outcomes, then that ranking must (at least) satisfy the Pareto principles in terms of outcomes. And *if* one is to justify the ranking of actions as flowing from individuals' ex ante claims (claims-across-actions), then the ranking of actions must (at least) satisfy the ex ante Pareto principles.

Thus, by adopting the utilitarian SWF in lieu of the continuous prioritarian SWF, the theorist can appropriate the "claim" idea at two junctures: in ranking outcomes, and in ranking actions. But there is a serious downside—of course. The utilitarian scheme for weighting claims *does not satisfy the Pigou–Dalton principle*. The utilitarian ranking of outcomes does not satisfy the Pigou–Dalton principle in terms of outcomes. And the utilitarian ranking of actions does not satisfy the ex ante Pigou–Dalton principle. (This is true *both* of EU utilitarianism, and of a utilitarian choice-evaluation procedure that employs some non-EU bridge principles for moving from the utilitarian ranking of outcomes to the moral ranking of actions.)[92]

But surely any procedure for adjudicating between competing claims—be they claims-across-outcomes or ex ante claims—*should* satisfy the Pigou–Dalton principle. If I am worse off than you, wouldn't it be fairer to improve my well-being (in the outcome or ex ante sense) by some amount, and reduce your well-being by the very same amount, at least if this change would leave me still worse off than you, or at most equally well off, with no one else affected (and considerations of responsibility not implicated)? So the "victory" for fairness secured by shifting from the continuous prioritarian SWF to the utilitarian SWF is a pyrrhic victory indeed.

Nor is it clear why the *double* application of the "claim" methodology—first in ranking outcomes, then in ranking actions—should have overwhelming appeal.

---

[92] It is straightforward to see that EU utilitarianism with the identity translation will never satisfy the ex ante Pigou–Dalton principle. Interestingly, EU utilitarianism with other translation functions, and some non-EU approaches to applying the utilitarian SWF, will in *some* cases rank actions in accordance with the ex ante Pigou–Dalton principle. For example, consider EU utilitarianism with a translation function $f^u(w) = w^2$. Imagine outcomes, assigned to utility vectors, as follows: $x = (1r, 1r)$, $y = (1r, 2r)$, $z = (2r, 2r)$. Let action a yield y for certain, while b gives a .5 probability of x and a .5 probability of z. Then the vector of expected utilities corresponding to b is $(1.5r, 1.5r)$, hence preferred by the ex ante Pigou–Dalton principle to the a vector = $(1r, 2r)$. And the EU formula with this $f^u(.)$ indeed prefers b (assigned a value of $.5(4r^2) + .5(16r^2) = 10r^2$) to a (assigned a value of $9r^2$).

However, no utilitarian choice-evaluation framework will *universally* satisfy the ex ante Pigou–Dalton principle. (This is trivial: just imagine a choice situation with two choices, a and b, where a leads for sure to x, b for sure to y, and y is ranked above x by the Pigou–Dalton principle. The ex ante Pigou–Dalton principle requires that b be ranked above a, but any utilitarian—regardless of her bridge principles—will rank them as equally good.) Because utilitarians will not universally satisfy the ex ante Pigou–Dalton principle, the utilitarian view of ex ante claims is not an attractive one.

The separateness of persons has been fully reflected in the ranking of outcomes. Why need it be reflected again at the stage of ranking actions? More pointedly: if we are choosing between (1) EU prioritarianism, which *singly* employs the claim framework, to rank outcomes, using a robust and appealing view of the strength of competing claims (a view which satisfies the Pigou–Dalton principle), and (2) EU (or for that matter non-EU) utilitarianism, which *doubly* employs the claim framework, first to rank outcomes, then actions, but at each stage deploys a distorted picture of the strength of competing claims (a view that fails the Pigou–Dalton principle), why think that the latter alternative is more attractive?

III. GENERIC REFINEMENTS TO EU THEORY

EU theory offers a generic set of normative bridge principles for moving from a ranking of outcomes to a ranking of actions. As I have already emphasized, EU theory is a "module": it is one *component* of a full choice-evaluation procedure. EU theory does not itself provide criteria for ranking outcomes, but rather guides the decisionmaker in ranking actions, *given* an outcome ranking that she takes to be attractive in light of whatever outcome-ranking principles she may be using.

EU theory is generic, in the sense that it can be meshed with any arbitrary ranking of outcomes. But it imposes a strong formal constraint on that ranking: namely, that it be a complete ordering. Moreover, EU theory requires that the decisionmaker know for certain what the outcome ranking is. In addition, EU theory implies that the decisionmaker has precise probabilities: each action corresponds to a single probability distribution over outcomes. Finally, EU theory has traditionally been thought inapplicable to situations of strategic interaction, where the decisionmaker is making choices in light of the predicted decisions of other individuals who are themselves rational.

A powerful normative case can be made that each of these elements is too restrictive. If EU theory is to function as an attractive set of bridge principles—be it for purposes of moral decisionmaking, or in any other normative context—it needs to be refined to allow for an incomplete outcome ranking, imprecise probabilities, decisionmaker uncertainty about the outcome ordering, and strategic interaction.

This section briefly surveys what these refinements might be. A full discussion is well beyond the scope of this book. The issues are technical and difficult; they remain unresolved; and they far transcend the SWF framework. They are generic problems for decision theory, rather than issues that are specific to welfarism or moral theory more generally. Fortunately, contemporary research in decision theory has made some initial progress in identifying what a properly refined version of EU theory would look like. As the literature continues to progress, we will also reach a clearer understanding of the specific topic addressed by this chapter: namely, how to generate a *moral* ranking of actions from the *moral* ranking of outcomes yielded by a prioritarian SWF.

A. Incomplete Orderings (and Dynamic Choice)

Outcome-ranking norms may fail to yield a complete ranking of outcomes. A central thrust of this book has been that attractive norms for *morally* ranking outcomes may yield incompleteness. If the SWF is a continuous prioritarian SWF, incompleteness can arise if the set **U** is not unique up to a positive ratio transformation or if a non-Atkinson SWF is used.[93] Plausible non-moral rankings of outcomes may also be incomplete. For example, a ranking of outcomes in light of a given person's well-being, or in light of aesthetic considerations, may well be incomplete.

How might EU theory be refined to accommodate an incomplete outcome ordering—leaving aside, for the moment, the additional complications of imprecise probabilities, uncertainty about what the outcome ordering is, and strategic interaction?

An incomplete ordering of outcomes can generally be represented by a set **V** of utility functions.[94] With this premise in mind, it is plausible to imagine that a refinement of EU theory which relaxes the completeness requirement (but not yet the other presuppositions of EU theory) will run as follows. It will say: action a is at least as good as action b iff $\sum_{x\in O} \pi_a(x)v(x) \geq \sum_{x\in O} \pi_b(x)v(x)$ for all $v(.)$ in **V**, where **V** now represents the quasiordering of outcomes and $\pi_a(.)$ is some kind of epistemic probability linking action a and outcome x (as with the traditional EU formula). For short, call this the "expected multiutility formula."

Indeed, recent work by Juan Dubra, Fabio Maccheroni, and Efe Ok has made substantial progress along these lines. They show that, if the decisionmaker has exogenous probabilities (as in the simple von Neumann/Morgenstern version of EU theory); has a quasiordering of outcomes and choices; and satisfies an independence axiom and continuity axiom, then the ranking of actions will indeed be representable by the formula just given. Some work has also been done extending the expected multiutility formula to the Savage set-up: showing that the decisionmaker who has an incomplete ordering of outcomes, but who complies with a suitable set of norms regimenting her ranking of actions in light of their outcomes in different states, will rank actions according to the expected multiutility formula.[95]

The expected multiutility formula (whatever its axiomatic basis) yields a quasiordering of the action set **A**. With this quasiordering in hand, what should the decisionmaker do? A very plausible answer has been pressed by Amartya Sen, in his

---

[93] For the remainder of the chapter, in discussing continuous prioritarian SWFs, I include both Atkinson and non-Atkinson SWFs. Note that incompleteness might also arise if a whole set of rules for ordering utility vectors are employed, e.g., the Atkinson SWF with a whole set of γ values. See Chapter 5, pp. 399–404. I will ignore this complication in what follows.

[94] See Chapter 2.

[95] See Dubra, Maccheroni, and Ok (2004); Nau (2006); Ok (2007, pp. 499–509); and the literature on robust Bayesian statistics, cited below, n. 119. Extending the Dubra, Maccheroni, and Ok result to the Savage set-up may perhaps involve sets of probabilities (discussed below under the heading of imprecise probabilities).

work on "maximization": choose any action a^* in $\mathbf{A}$ which is not worse than any other action. (In other words, a^* is better than, equally good as, or incomparable with every other action in $\mathbf{A}$.) If $\mathbf{A}$ is finite, at least one such "maximal" action will exist.[96]

How would the expected multiutility formula be integrated into a moral choice-evaluation framework using the continuous prioritarian SWF? To begin, the formula means that there is a moral quasiordering of actions, corresponding to a set $\mathbf{M}$ of moral utility functions. In other words, action a is morally at least as good as action b iff, for all $m(.)$ in $\mathbf{M}$, $\sum_{x\in\mathbf{O}}\pi_a(x)m(x)\geq\sum_{x\in\mathbf{O}}\pi_b(x)m(x)$. This is similar to the set $\mathbf{M}$ discussed earlier in the chapter—with the crucial distinction that the earlier discussion assumed a complete moral ordering of outcomes and traditional EU theory, so that $\mathbf{M}$ was unique up to a positive affine transformation. The set $\mathbf{M}$ now under discussion need not be unique up to a positive affine transformation.

What is the connection between the elements of $\mathbf{M}$ and the ordering of outcomes achieved by the continuous prioritarian SWF? That SWF, of course, says: outcome x is at least as good as outcome y iff, for all $u(.)$ in $\mathbf{U}$, $\sum_{i=1}^{N}g(u_i(x))\geq\sum_{i=1}^{N}g(u_i(y))$. This ordering of outcomes must be the same as that achieved by $\mathbf{M}$.[97] A sufficient condition for such convergence is that there is a one-to-one mapping between each $u(.)$ in $\mathbf{U}$ and each $m(.)$ in $\mathbf{M}$, and that the number assigned to each outcome by a given $m(.)$ is a strictly increasing function of the number assigned to it by the continuous prioritarian formula using the corresponding $u(.)$.[98] Yet more simply, the increasing function is the identity function.[99] In this case, each $u(.)$ in $\mathbf{U}$ corresponds to an $m(.)$ in $\mathbf{M}$, defined as follows: $m(x)=\sum_{i=1}^{N}g(u_i(x))$. If so, the expected multiutility formula for morally ranking actions simplifies to the following: action a is morally at least as good as action b iff, for all $u(.)$ in $\mathbf{U}$, $\sum_{x\in\mathbf{O}}\pi_a(x)\left[\sum_{i=1}^{N}g(u_i(x))\right]\geq\sum_{x\in\mathbf{O}}\pi_b(x)\left[\sum_{i=1}^{N}g(u_i(x))\right]$.

---

[96] See Sen (1997a, pp. 763–769; 2000, pp. 486–487). If $\mathbf{A}$ is not finite, there may be no such maximal action—but that is also true for traditional EU theory with a complete ordering of $\mathbf{A}$. How to deal with an infinite $\mathbf{A}$ is not addressed here. See Ruggeri, Ríos Insua, and Martín (2005, sec. 3).

[97] In other words, for any pair of outcomes x and y, $m(x)\geq m(y)$ for all $m(.)$ in $\mathbf{M}$ iff $\sum_{i=1}^{N}g(u_i(x))\geq\sum_{i=1}^{N}g(u_i(y))$ for all $u(.)$ in $\mathbf{U}$. Imagine that this is not true. Then, if there were actions a and b leading for sure, respectively, to outcomes x and y, the expected multiutility formula using $\mathbf{M}$ could incorrectly rank a and b.

[98] In other words, for each $u(.)$ in $\mathbf{U}$, there is a corresponding $m(.)$ in $\mathbf{M}$, defined as follows: $m(x)=f^u\left(\sum_{i=1}^{N}g(u_i(x))\right)$, where $f^u(.)$ is some strictly increasing function. Nothing requires that $f^u(.)$ be the same function for each $u(.)$ in $\mathbf{U}$. Note also that the one-to-one correspondence between the elements of $\mathbf{U}$ and $\mathbf{M}$ just described is a *sufficient* condition for the continuous prioritarian SWF using $\mathbf{U}$ and $g(.)$ to achieve the same ranking of outcomes as that achieved by the formula, x at least as good as y iff, for all $m(.)$ in $\mathbf{M}$, $m(x)\geq m(y)$. It is not a *necessary* condition. For example, each $u(.)$ might correspond to a whole set of moral utility functions rather than a single function—with each assigning a given outcome x some strictly increasing transformation of the value $\sum_{i=1}^{N}g(u_i(x))$.

[99] For the reasons discussed earlier, however, it is not clear whether this further simplification is warranted.

It bears reiterating that the expected multiutility formula produces a *quasiordering* of actions, which can but need not be complete. Because the formula is meant to accommodate the possibility that the ranking of outcomes underlying the action ranking is itself incomplete, this feature of the formula is quite natural. Still, important worries, concerning "value pumps," can be raised concerning the expected multiutility formula (or any other norm for choice that yields a quasiordering of an action set), when that formula is applied in the intertemporal context—the context of *dynamic choice*.[100]

These are generic worries, so let us return to the generic case. The following sort of example is regularly used to suggest the difficulties posed by dynamic choice with an incomplete ordering of actions and outcomes. Imagine that there are three outcomes x, x^+, and y, such that x^+ is better than x; x^+ is incomparable with y; and x is incomparable with y. The decisionmaker "owns" outcome x^+; if she does nothing, x^+ will result. The decisionmaker is given the choice of "trading" x^+ for y. If the decisionmaker were to make the "trade," she would then be given the further option of "trading" y for x.

Consider what might happen. The decisionmaker first might "trade" x^+ for y, reasoning that the two are incomparable and so she is permitted either to trade or not to trade. She then might "trade" y for x, reasoning once more that the two are incomparable and so she is permitted either to trade or not to trade. But if she makes both trades, she ends up with an outcome (x) which is worse than the outcome (x^+) she could have secured by refusing trades. She has been "value pumped."

What is disturbing in this example is that the decisionmaker has made a series of choices that is *dominated* by another series of choices available to her. I will use the term "value pump" as a term of art, to refer to this sort of dominated intertemporal behavior. In order to provide a more precise definition, and to consider the susceptibility of different modalities of dynamic choice to value pumps, I will introduce the concept of a "decision tree"—a standard device for representing dynamic choice.[101]

A decision tree consists of choice nodes and chance nodes. Each choice node has multiple branches, representing some immediate action[102] the decisionmaker might take; each such branch leads to a further choice node, to a final outcome, or to a chance node. A chance node has multiple branches, with a single probability on each branch (remember that we are assuming precise probabilities for now), summing to unity; each such branch represents a possible event and leads to choice nodes,

[100] On value pumps and incomplete orderings, see Andreou (2005); Boot (2009); Chang (1997, Introduction, p. 11; 2002a, p. 58); Peterson (2007). Many thanks to Wlodek Rabinowicz for numerous discussions on the topic of dynamic choice.

[101] Good points of entry into the vast literature on dynamic choice are: Etchart (2002); Machina (1989); McClennen (1990); Rabinowicz (1995).

[102] An immediate action is a causal intervention in the world, by the decisionmaker, which is completed in a short space of time. I won't try to give a more precise definition here, but a single bodily movement or a single utterance would be paradigmatic "immediate actions."

chance nodes, or final outcomes. Each possible sequence of branches culminates in a final outcome (i.e., the tree is "finite"). The tree begins with a single node, either a choice or a chance node.

This sort of decision tree—it should be stressed—involves *parametric* choice. The decisionmaker is not strategically interacting with other decisionmakers. Game theory employs decision trees to represent dynamic choice with strategic interaction, but for now the problem of refining EU theory to handle such interaction is being bracketed.

A "whole plan" in a parametric decision tree consists of a specification of one immediate action at each choice node in the tree. And a "value pump," I suggest, means the following. Imagine that the decisionmaker undertakes a series of immediate actions, yielding a final outcome. Imagine, further, that there is some whole plan P^+ such that—for *every* whole plan P including that series of immediate actions—P^+ weakly stochastically dominates P. Every possible outcome of P^+ with nonzero probability is better than every possible outcome of P with nonzero probability.[103] Then the decisionmaker has been value pumped.[104] She has made a series of choices that she would not rationally plan to make, because she can be assured of producing a better outcome by following an alternative plan.

What, now, are the possible modalities of dynamic choice in a parametric decision tree? The literature suggests three. One modality is *resolute choice*. The decisionmaker, at the initial node of the tree, considers possible whole plans. She then uses some rule to select a whole plan; and she sticks with that plan throughout the tree, at each choice node choosing the immediate action designated by the plan for that node.

A second modality is *naive choice*.[105] The decisionmaker, at each choice node, selects a plan going forward. (A plan going forward at some choice node consists of a specification of an immediate action both at that node and at all subsequent nodes that might be reached from that node.) She then undertakes the immediate action designated by the plan going forward. This approach is "naive" in the sense that the

---

[103] See above, p. 495, for my distinction between weak and ordinary stochastic dominance.

[104] Note that this definition of a value pump is sensitive to standard features of dynamic choice, namely these: the availability of a given immediate action may be *contingent* (at the initial point in time represented by the initial node of the tree, it may be uncertain whether the decisionmaker reaches the choice situation where that action is available); the outcomes of immediate actions may be uncertain; and the probability of these outcomes may depend upon the decisionmaker's subsequent immediate actions. The definition handles these features by considering the totality of possible whole plans which include the series of immediate actions that the decisionmaker, in fact, performs.

The definition is *narrow*, meant to identify an especially irrational kind of intertemporal behavior. A broader definition would appeal to ordinary rather than weak stochastic dominance. A different broadening would be as follows: for every whole plan P including the series of immediate actions performed, there is some whole plan P' which weakly stochastically dominates P. This definition doesn't require that there be a single P^+ which dominates every P.

[105] The term "myopic choice" is also sometimes used to designate this modality.

decisionmaker at each choice node (1) reconsiders what she ought to do, rather than sticking resolutely to a prior plan, but (2) chooses among actions by choosing among plans going forward, without considering whether she will comply with the selected plan at subsequent choice nodes.

A third modality is *sophisticated choice*. The decisionmaker, at each choice node, selects among immediate actions and in so doing takes account of how she can be predicted to behave at subsequent choice nodes.

Most discussion of resolute, naive, and sophisticated modalities of dynamic choice focuses on how these modalities might be meshed with theories of rational choice that deviate from EU theory, in some way, but retain a complete ordering of outcomes. However, it would seem that this trichotomy is also a fruitful way to think about dynamic choice with a quasiordering of outcomes. In particular, it is a fruitful way to think about how the expected multiutility formula might be employed in dynamic contexts so as to avoid value pumps.

Consider, first, naive choice. Given this modality for dynamic choice, the action set $\mathbf{A} = \{a, b, c, \ldots\}$ at a given choice node is a set of plans going forward (not a set of immediate actions).[106] Action a is one such plan going forward, action b another such plan going forward, and so forth. The naive decisionmaker uses the expected multiutility formula to rank these plans. She says: plan-going-forward a is at least as good as plan-going-forward b iff, for all $v(.)$ in $\mathbf{V}$, $\sum_{x \in \mathbf{O}} \pi_a(x)v(x) \geq \sum_{x \in \mathbf{O}} \pi_b(x)v(x)$. This yields a quasiordering of plans going forward, and the decisionmaker then "maximizes" (in Sen's sense), picking any plan which is no worse than any other; and then undertaking the immediate action selected by that plan.

Naive choice with the expected multiutility formula is irrational. It furnishes an unattractive set of bridging principles. First, this approach is clearly vulnerable to being value pumped, as the following decision trees illustrate.[107] Even more fundamentally,

---

[106] To be sure, a decisionmaker cannot literally "choose" an intertemporal plan, in the sense that she can "choose" an immediate action. To "choose" an immediate action is to perform it; once performed, it cannot be not-performed. To "choose" an intertemporal plan is to *select* the plan; it remains an open question whether the decisionmaker will, in fact, perform all the elements of the plan. (Indeed, a key feature of naive choice is that the decisionmaker heedlessly selects a plan going forward without considering whether she will later feel rational pressure not to perform some element of it.)

By saying that "naive choice" involves a choice set $\mathbf{A}$ consisting of plans going forward, I mean that the naive chooser arrives at the immediate action to perform by ordering these plans; selecting the maximal plan; and then performing the immediate action required by the plan. This "choice set" (strictly, selection set) is one element in the chain of mental operations leading to her performance of an immediate action. A similar caveat applies to my description below of resolute choice. Thanks to Chrisoula Andreou for discussion on this point.

[107] The examples show that naive choice with the expected multiutility formula *permits* the decision-maker to be value pumped, i.e., permits the decisionmaker to undertake a series of immediate actions such that there exists a whole plan P^+ which weakly stochastically dominates every whole plan P including that series. I do not claim that the formula can produce a *mandatory* value pump, i.e., *require* the decisionmaker to undertake such a series of immediate actions. (A similar point applies to my

naive choice with the expected multiutility formula is irrational because the decisionmaker overlooks that the plans she selects at each choice node may well be deviated from at subsequent nodes. She foresees future choice situations, but ignores how she can be predicted to behave in those situations.

In decision trees 1 and 2 (see Figures 7.1 and 7.2), the squares are choice nodes, while the circle in tree 2 is a chance node. *The trees are to be read from left to right, with the square labeled "A" the initial node.* The outcomes are x, x^+, x^{++}, x^{+++}, y. Outcome x^{+++} is better than x^{++}, which is better than x^+, which is better than x, but all are incomparable with y. In tree 1, two plans are permissible at node A: to go down (yielding x^{+++}), or to go up and up again (yielding y). The naive chooser may go up at A and then, at node B, go down, ending up with x^+. This series of immediate actions is a value pump: there is only one whole plan including it (namely, to go up at A and then down at B), and the sole possible outcome of this whole plan (x^+) is worse than the sole possible outcome of the plan to go down at A (x^{+++}).

To generalize this to the case of a tree with uncertainty, assume that **V** has 2 utility functions, $v^1(.)$ and $v^2(.)$. Function $v^1(.)$ values the outcomes as follows: $v^1(x) = 20$, $v^1(x^+)$ $=30$, $v^1(x^{++}) = 40$, $v^1(x^{+++}) = 50$, $v^1(y) = 60$. Function $v^2(.)$ values the outcomes as follows: $v^2(x) = 20$, $v^2(x^+) = 30$, $v^2(x^{++}) = 40$, $v^2(x^{+++}) = 50$, $v^2(y) = 0$. (Note that this makes x^{+++} better than x^{++} better than x^+ better than x, and all incomparable with y.) In tree 2, it is permitted at node A to plan to go down (to x^{+++}), or to plan to go up and then up at node B (to y). Now consider how the naive chooser, at node B, uses the expected multiutility formula to evaluate plans going forward. With utility function $v^1(.)$, the value of going up (to y) is 60, while the value of going down (to a .5 chance of x^{++} and .5 chance of x)

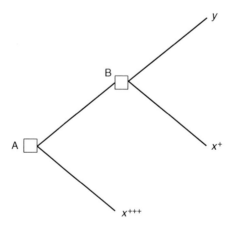

Figure 7.1 Decision Tree 1.

discussion below of value pumps with sophisticated choice.) Still, the fact that an intertemporal choice procedure permits value pumps is a troubling feature of the procedure.

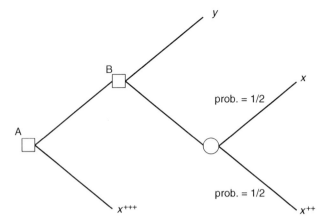

Figure 7.2 Decision Tree 2.

is $.5(40) + .5(20) = 30$. With utility function $v^2(.)$, the value of going up (to y) is 0, while the value of going down is 30. Going down at B is thus permissible. But going up at A and then down at B is a value pump: the only whole plan including that series of immediate actions (namely, the plan to go up at A and down at B) is weakly stochastically dominated by the whole plan to go down at A, since both x and x^{++} are worse than x^{+++}.

This leaves resolute choice and sophisticated choice. Resolute choice with the expected multiutility formula means that the decisionmaker, at the first node, faces an action set **A** consisting of whole plans.[108] Action a is one whole plan, b a second, and so forth. She arrives at a quasiordering of these whole plans using the expected multiutility formula; and "maximizes" in Sen's sense, picking any whole plan which is not worse than any other. She then sticks resolutely to that whole plan at subsequent nodes, choosing the immediate actions required by the plan.

Sophisticated choice with the expected multiutility formula is trickier to formulate. A critical issue here is whether the decisionmaker can assign probabilities to his own future choices. If he can, then he can engage in a sort of probabilistic backwards induction. At a given node n, he assigns a probability to his immediate actions at each final choice node possibly resulting from n.[109] Those final choice nodes are then "crossed off." The decisionmaker now assigns a probability to his immediate actions at each non-crossed-off choice node, possibly resulting from n, that has become final (i.e., that is followed only by crossed-off choice nodes). Those probability numbers will reflect the probabilities at the crossed-off nodes. These nodes are crossed off, replaced with probability numbers. The procedure is iterated until all choice nodes

---

[108] Whole plans can be formulated at the first node regardless of whether it is a chance or choice node.

[109] By a final choice node, I mean a choice node not followed by any further choice nodes.

possibly resulting from n have been crossed off and replaced with probabilities. The choice set **A** at n consists of the immediate actions at n available to the decisionmaker. The decisionmaker ranks those choices using the expected multiutility formula. The probability term $\pi_a(x)$ is the probability that immediate action a leads to outcome x, given the probabilities at the chance nodes and crossed-off choice nodes that follow a.

Whether the rational decisionmaker can indeed assign probabilities to his own future choices merges with issues to be discussed below, under strategic choice. If he cannot do so, sophisticated choice with the expected multiutility formula must be formulated in some other way. What that might be is not a topic I will attempt to pursue.

A final possibility, worth mentioning, might be termed "partly resolute" choice. Here, the decisionmaker acts "as if" she had a complete ordering of outcomes.[110] In other words, the decisionmaker at the first choice node selects a single utility function $v(.)$ in **V**. She then chooses naively at each choice node, using that single function.

How do resolute, partly resolute, and sophisticated choice conjoined with the expected multiutility formula fare in mitigating value pumps in the context at hand (dynamic choice in a parametric decision tree with a known ordering of outcomes and precise probabilities)? If the decisionmaker complies with the resolute choice approach at all nodes, she cannot be value pumped.[111] This is obvious. It also turns out that, if the decisionmaker complies with the partly resolute approach at all nodes, she cannot be value pumped. This is because of a striking feature of traditional EU theory: The decisionmaker who has a complete ordering of outcomes, and chooses naively in a parametric decision tree with a known ordering of outcomes and precise probabilities using traditional EU theory, will not be value pumped.[112]

---

[110] See Andreou (2005).

[111] Of course, she might start by being resolute, then fail to stick to the plan, and in that way be pumped.

[112] Here is a proof sketch. This covers the case where the initial node of the tree is a choice node, and can be readily adapted for the case where that node is a chance node.

To say that the naive decisionmaker has a complete ordering of outcomes and complies with traditional EU theory is just to say that **V** is unique up to a positive affine transformation and that the decisionmaker evaluates plans going forward in light of their expected utility given (any) utility function in **V**. For short, let us designate such a decisionmaker the "NTEU" decisionmaker. Let F_m denote a plan going forward from choice node m. Let $P[F_m]$ denote a whole plan which modifies whole plan P by replacing all of the elements of P at or after node m with F_m. (The "elements" of a plan are just the choices it selects at different choice nodes.) Similarly, where node n follows from node m, let $F_m[F_n]$ denote the plan going forward at m which is replaced, at n, by F_n.

Assume, by way of contradiction, that the NTEU decisionmaker undertakes a series of immediate actions, and that this is a value pump: there is some P^+ such that every P including this series is weakly stochastically dominated by P^+. The NTEU decisionmaker would not have selected any such P at the initial choice node; rather, she must have selected some other whole plan P' with greater expected

What about sophisticated choice? The decisionmaker who uses the expected multiutility formula and engages in sophisticated choice will, in some cases, avoid the value pumps that could be produced by naive choice. On the other hand, sophisticated choice would not seem to be a sure-fire defense against value pumps.[113]

Consider the two decision trees displayed above, in Figures 7.1 and 7.2. Assume first, as in the discussion above, that **V** has two utility functions, $v^1(.)$ and $v^2(.)$ such that $v^1(x) = 20$, $v^1(x^+) = 30$, $v^1(x^{++}) = 40$, $v^1(x^{+++}) = 50$, $v^1(y) = 60$; and $v^2(x) = 20$, $v^2(x^+) = 30$, $v^2(x^{++}) = 40$, $v^2(x^{+++}) = 50$, $v^2(y) = 0$. The sophisticated chooser, now, will not be value pumped in trees 1 or 2; at node A, he will certainly go down. Why? Consider tree 1. Assume (for simplicity) that the sophisticated chooser assigns probability .5 to his going down at node B, and probability .5 to his going up at node B. With these probabilities in hand, the choice at node A is between going down, to x^{+++}, and going up, yielding a lottery with .5 probability of y and .5 probability of x^+. The expected multiutility formula says that going down at A is the better choice. According to utility function $v^1(.)$, going down at A has utility 50, while going up has utility $45 = .5(60) + .5(30)$. According to utility function $v^2(.)$, going down at A has utility 50, while going up has utility $15 = .5(0) + .5(30)$.

Similar reasoning in tree 2 (assuming that the sophisticated chooser, once more, assigns a probability of .5 to going down at node B, and .5 of going up at node B) shows that the sophisticated chooser will certainly go down at A, avoiding the value pump.

However: If we change the values assigned to the outcomes by $v^1(.)$ and $v^2(.)$, the sophisticated chooser becomes vulnerable to a value pump. Instead of setting $v^1(x^{+++}) = v^2(x^{+++}) = 50$, let us set $v^1(x^{+++}) = v^2(x^{+++}) = 43$, for example. Consider the sophisticated chooser in tree 1. According to utility function $v^1(.)$, going down at node A now has utility 43, while going up has utility 45. The chooser is now *permitted* to go up. At node B, he is permitted to go down. But if he goes up at A and then down at B he has been pumped.

utility than P and then deviated from P' by selecting, in succession, a series of plans going forward at nodes 1, ..., M, with node 2 following node 1 and so forth. Let F_m be the plan going forward that the NTEU decisionmaker adopts at a given node m. Consider F_{M-1}. If F_M maximizes expected utility at node M, then $F_{M-1}[F_M]$ maximizes expected utility at node M − 1. Similarly, $F_{M-2}[F_{M-1}[F_M]]$ maximizes expected utility at node M − 2. Iterating all the way through, we have that $P'[F_1[F_2[\ldots[F_M]\ldots]$ maximizes expected utility at the initial node of the tree. But this is a contradiction, because this is a whole plan which includes the series of immediate actions actually chosen by the decisionmaker, and thus (by hypothesis) must have lower expected utility than P^+ and P'.

The fact that the NTEU decisionmaker avoids value pumps also means that, in the case where **V** is *not* unique up to a positive affine transformation, the "partly resolute" decisionmaker can avoid a value pump. Strictly, this is true only if: whenever outcome x is worse than outcome y, all utility functions in **V** assign x a lower value. This proviso is needed because x might be worse than y where some utility functions assign x a lower value and others assign x and y an equal value; by engaging in "partly resolute" choice using a latter such utility function, the decisionmaker need not avoid being value pumped.

[113] Cf. Rabinowicz (2000), showing that a sophisticated decisionmaker with intransitive preferences is vulnerable to a value pump.

(With $v^1(x^+) = v^2(x^+)$ still equal to 30, and $v^1(x^{+++}) = v^2(x^{+++})$ now 43 rather than 50, it is still true that $v^1(x^+) < v^1(x^{+++})$ and that $v^2(x^+) < v^2(x^{+++})$ and thus that x^+ is worse than x^{+++}.)

Similarly with $v^1(x^{+++}) = v^2(x^{+++}) = 43$, the sophisticated chooser may be value pumped in tree 2 by going up at node A and then down at node B. (Again, even with this change in $v^1(x^{+++})$ and $v^2(x^{+++})$, it still remains the case that x and x^{++} are both worse than x^{+++}.).

Which of these three approaches—resolute, partly resolute, or sophisticated— represents the most attractive refinement of EU theory for the context under discussion? I will not take a position on that question. First, one's considered answer should presumably cohere with answers regarding other types of contexts (involving imprecise probabilities, strategic interaction, and uncertainty about the outcome ordering). Second, even focusing on the case of a parametric decision tree with a known outcome ordering and precise probabilities, the answer is not obvious. Resolute and partly resolute approaches are attractive because they wholly avoid value pumps. But they rub against act-consequentialist intuitions. Shouldn't the decisionmaker maximize good consequences at each point in time, rather than being bound by prior decisions or a prior selection of an ordering? Sophisticated choice accords with such intuitions but seems less than fully effective in mitigating value pumps. Isn't it deeply irrational to make a series of choices that no one would rationally plan to make—a series of choices such that every plan including them is weakly stochastically dominated by an alternative plan?

At this point, it might be argued that the absence of a clear, unproblematic recipe for dynamic choice—given an incomplete quasiordering—is grounds for insisting that the ordering of outcomes be complete. In a parametric decision tree with a known outcome ordering and precise probabilities, the decisionmaker who has a *complete* ordering and follows EU theory can avoid value pumps *without* resorting to devices, such as resolute choice or partly resolute choice, that are in tension with act-consequentialism.[114] Doesn't this demonstrate that a scheme for ordering outcomes which may yield an incomplete quasiordering, such as the SWF framework adopted in this book, should be rejected?

I believe not, for several reasons. The first connects to the point that EU theory needs to be refined to accommodate imprecise probabilities—a point argued very persuasively in much recent scholarship. This literature has examined questions of dynamic choice, and shows that plausible refinements of EU theory that allow for

---

[114] As we have seen, such a decisionmaker, choosing naively, will never be value pumped. Alternatively, it can be shown that: where **V** is unique up to a positive affine transformation, the EU decisionmaker who engages in *sophisticated* choice (and knows for sure that she will do so at all nodes, and will select immediate actions at each node so as to maximize expected utility) will never be value pumped. The proof of this proposition is essentially the same as used to justify the standard backwards induction methodology for identifying optimal whole plans in a parametric decision tree.

imprecise probabilities but retain a complete ordering of outcomes *also* face value pumps and the closely related problem of dynamic inconsistency.[115]

A second point connects to strategic choice. It is a well-known fact about game theory that the decisionmaker in a dynamic ("extensive") game who has a complete ordering of outcomes but fails to be resolute—who makes choices at each node in light of the consequences of those choices, rather than sticking to the strategy which is best if complied with throughout—can be value pumped.[116]

Finally, there are strong reasons for thinking that the moral ordering of outcomes is incomplete—reasons that I have canvassed throughout the book. The Pareto quasiordering is incomplete. The ambition of welfarism is to extend the Pareto quasiordering—but why on earth think that, in every outcome set, we will succeed in *fully* extending it, so that there is not even a single pair of incomparable outcomes? SWFs extend the Pareto quasiordering by combining a rule R for ranking utility vectors with a set $\mathbf{U}$, representing well-being. But if $\mathbf{U}$ is constructed by looking to individuals' extended preferences, then—given the heterogeneity of such preferences—$\mathbf{U}$ will often not be unique up to a positive ratio (or even positive affine or increasing) transformation, and incompleteness of the moral ordering is the natural consequence.[117] It is far from clear how we would arrive at a plausible $\mathbf{U}$ which assures completeness.

To be clear, problems of dynamic inconsistency and value pumps *are* very important issues for any proposed account of rational intertemporal choice. (Remember

---

[115] See generally Al-Najjar and Weinstein (2009), and sources cited therein.

[116] To be sure, the precise definition of a "value pump" needs to be modified for the strategic context; we might say that a series of choices by a decisionmaker is a value pump if there is some strategy S^+ such that, for every possible strategy S including that series of choices, S^+ weakly stochastically dominates S. (Here, in order to determine the probability of outcomes given the decisionmaker's choice of some strategy, we will need to determine what other actors will do given that selection.) A very simple example of a strategic value pump is where player B ("he") could induce player A ("she") to take a course of action beneficial to player B, *if* player B could credibly threaten to punish player A if she does otherwise—but player B cannot credibly make this threat if he does not stick resolutely to his plans. For example, imagine that player A has a choice of going left or right. If she goes left, both players receive payoffs of $50. If she goes right, player B has a choice of going up or down; if he goes up, player A receives $100 and player B receives $20; if he goes down, both players receive $0. Then player B, maximizing good consequences at his choice node, plays up. Player A, anticipating that player B will do this, plays right—so that player B receives $20. If player B were resolute, and player A knew this, player B would plan to go down at his node, inducing player A to go left, so that B ends up with $50.

The proposition that non-resolute choice in strategic contexts can yield value pumps is central to the literature in macroeconomics on "time inconsistency." See sources cited below, n. 132.

[117] Imagine that there is a $u(.)$, such that $u^*(.)$ is in $\mathbf{U}$ iff $u^*(x; i) = f(u(x; i))$ for all life-histories $(x; i)$. $\mathbf{U}$ is, respectively, unique up to a (1) positive ratio (2) positive affine (3) increasing transformation if this is true and $f(.)$ is (1) multiplication by any positive constant, (2) multiplication by any positive constant plus addition of any constant, (3) any strictly increasing function. With $\mathbf{U}$ formed by pooling sets representing spectators' extended preferences, all of these conditions may well fail.

that the vulnerability of *non-EU* approaches to violating weak stochastic dominance in the static context was a central part of my argument against such approaches.) It may well be the case that norms for intertemporal choice which are guaranteed to avoid value pumps, such as resolute choice, on balance provide the best account of intertemporal rationality, even though these norms may initially seem unappealing in other respects. My point, here, concerns completeness in the outcome ordering: value-pump and dynamic inconsistency problems are by no means avoided by a complete ordering of outcomes and thus do not, on balance, provide sufficient grounds for insisting on completeness.

B. Imprecise Probabilities

There are good grounds for thinking that assigning precise probabilities to outcomes, states of nature, or other items is not always rationally required. As Gilboa, Postlewaite and Schmeidler observe:

> You are faced with two coins, each of which is about to be tossed. The first coin is yours. You have tossed it, say, 1000 times, and it has come up Heads 500 times, and Tails 500 times. The second coin is presented to you by someone else, and you know nothing about it. Let us refer to the first coin as "known," and to the second as "unknown." Asked to assign probabilities to the known coin coming up Heads or Tails, it is only natural to estimate 50% for each, as these are the empirical frequencies gathered over a sizeable database. When confronted with the same question regarding the unknown coin, however, no information is available, and relative frequencies do not help estimate probabilities. But . . . Bayesianism [i.e., traditional EU theory] demands that both sides of the unknown coin be assigned probabilities, and that these probabilities add up to 1. Symmetry suggests that these probabilities be 50% for each side. Hence, you end up assigning the same probability estimates to the two sides of the unknown coin as you did for the two sides of the known coin. Yet, the two 50%–50% distributions *feel* rather different. In the case of the known coin, the distribution is based on a good deal of information that supports a symmetric assessment while in the case of the unknown coin the same estimates are based on the absence of information. The Bayesian approach does not permit a distinction between symmetry based on information and symmetry based on lack of information.[118]

Indeed, much recent scholarship seeks to accommodate imprecise probabilities. This includes work in economics under the heading of "ambiguity aversion"; work in statistics under the heading of "robust Bayesian statistics"; and even some scholarship in policy analysis.[119]

---

[118] Gilboa, Postlewaite, and Schmeidler (2008b, p. 9).

[119] For a discussion of economic models that involve imprecise probabilities, see Gilboa (2009, chs. 15, 17); Ok (2007, pp. 499–521); Ryan (2009). On robust Bayesian statistics, see, e.g., Ríos Insua

The dominant approach is to model imprecision via sets of probabilities. Consider the "state of nature" set-up; S is a set of "states of nature." If the norms of traditional EU theory are indeed norms of rational decision and belief formation, then there will be a single probability function $\pi(.)$ representing the decisionmaker's rational beliefs. For any given state s, $\pi(s)$ is a single real number between zero and one, measuring the decisionmaker's rational degree of belief in the occurrence of that particular state. If E is a given event (single state or group of states) and F is another event, the decisionmaker believes event E to be at least as likely as event F iff the cumulative probability of the states in E, according to $\pi(.)$, is at least as great as the cumulative probability of the states in F.[120]

Instead, however, we might want to numerically represent the decisionmaker's rational beliefs via a set $\mathbf{P}$ of probability functions. Now, a given state or event will be assigned a *range* of probability numbers (namely, the numbers according to all the probability functions in $\mathbf{P}$), capturing the imprecision of the decisionmaker's belief that the state or event will occur. The decisionmaker believes that E is at least as likely as F iff the cumulative probability of E is at least as large as the cumulative probability of F according to all the probability functions in $\mathbf{P}$.

Generalizing beyond the "state of nature" framework, we might express the idea as follows. The decisionmaker faces some set $\mathbf{A}$ of actions and set $\mathbf{O}$ of outcomes. Norms of rational belief formation are such that the decisionmaker's beliefs regarding the nexus between actions and outcomes are represented by a set $\mathbf{P}$ of probability functions. Given some action a, each $\pi(.)$ in $\mathbf{P}$ assigns a given outcome x a number $\pi_a(x)$. The decisionmaker's degree of belief in x, given a, is captured in the range of such numbers for all functions in $\mathbf{P}$. At the limit, if $\mathbf{P}$ is a singleton (with a single probability function), the decisionmaker has precise beliefs in all outcomes.

The idea of capturing imprecise beliefs via sets of probabilities is intuitively natural. Moreover, the literatures just mentioned have shown that this idea can be provided a firm theoretical foundation in various ways.

How does the rational decisionmaker make *choices* in light of (possibly) imprecise beliefs, represented by a set $\mathbf{P}$ of probability functions (not necessarily a singleton)? What are the bridging principles that integrate $\mathbf{P}$ along with the decisionmaker's ranking of the outcome set $\mathbf{O}$ to arrive at a ranking of the choice set $\mathbf{A}$? Consider first the case where the decisionmaker has a complete ordering of the outcome set $\mathbf{O}$, represented by a single utility function $v(.)$. One, obvious, thought is that the decisionmaker arrives at a *quasiordering* of actions, such that action a is at

and Criado (2000); Ríos Insua and Martín (1994); Ruggeri, Ríos Insua, and Martin (2005). See also Nau (2006, 2007); Seidenfeld (2004); Walley (1991). For policy analysis using imprecise probabilities, see, e.g., Vardas and Xepapadeas (2010).

[120] As throughout the chapter, I simplify the presentation of the state-of-nature framework by using a finite state set. If the state set is uncountable, each state will have a zero probability, and events (collections of states) will be assigned precise, non-zero probabilities corresponding to the integral of a density function over their component states.

least as good as action b iff the expected utility of a is at least as large as the expected utility of b according to all the probability functions in $\mathbf{P}$.

Consider now the case where the decisionmaker has a quasiordering of outcomes, represented by a set $\mathbf{V}$ of utility functions. In that case, we might say that action a is at least as good as action b iff the expected utility of a is at least as large as the expected utility of b according to each probability function in $\mathbf{P}$, paired with each utility function in $\mathbf{V}$.[121] For short, call this the "robust EU approach." This is, indeed, the approach to decision theory advocated in the literature on robust Bayesian statistics.

The robust EU approach is a natural generalization of the expected multiutility rule, considered in the prior subsection. While that refinement of EU theory was focused on incompleteness, the robust EU approach accommodates both imprecise probabilities and an incomplete ordering of outcomes. Like the expected multiutility rule, the robust EU rule would need to be outfitted for dynamic contexts so as to avoid or reduce value pumps; as with the expected multiutility rule, that would presumably involve some version of sophisticated or resolute choice. How the robust EU approach would function as the bridging principle for the SWF framework is, once more, a straightforward generalization of the expected multiutility rule.[122]

Despite these attractions, the robust EU approach arguably has a serious flaw. In the famous Ellsberg paradox, subjects are "ambiguity averse": they prefer to bet on known rather than unknown probabilities. (For example, if told that an urn has 30 red balls and a total of 60 blue or yellow balls, in unknown proportions, subjects prefer a bet which yields \$100 if the ball is red to a bet which yields \$100 if the ball is blue, or a bet which yields \$100 if the ball is yellow; but they prefer a bet which yields \$100 if the ball is blue or yellow to a bet which yields \$100 if the ball is red or blue, or a bet which yields \$100 if the ball is red or yellow.) Arguably, Ellsberg behavior is a rationally warranted response to uncertainty about probabilities. The robust EU approach does not yield ambiguity aversion.[123]

---

[121] Formally, a is at least as good as b iff, for every $\pi(.)$ in $\mathbf{P}$, it is the case that, for every $v(.)$ in $\mathbf{V}$, $\sum_{x \in \mathbf{O}} \pi_a(x) v(x) \geq \sum_{x \in \mathbf{O}} \pi_b(x) v(x)$. Equivalently, let $\mathbf{G}$ be the set of every pairing of some $\pi(.)$ in $\mathbf{P}$ with some $v(.)$ in $\mathbf{V}$. Then the formula is: a is at least as good as b iff, for every $(\pi(.), v(.))$ in $\mathbf{G}$, $\sum_{x \in \mathbf{O}} \pi_a(x) v(x) \geq \sum_{x \in \mathbf{O}} \pi_b(x) v(x)$. A variation on this approach uses a $\mathbf{G}$ containing certain probability-utility pairs, rather than every possible pairing.

[122] There is a set of moral utility functions $\mathbf{M}$ that achieves the same ordering of outcomes as the continuous prioritarian SWF. See above, pp. 490–494. The robust EU approach then says: a is at least as good as b iff, for every $\pi(.)$ in $\mathbf{P}$, it is the case that, for every $m(.)$ in $\mathbf{M}$, $\sum_{x \in \mathbf{O}} \pi_a(x) m(x) \geq \sum_{x \in \mathbf{O}} \pi_b(x) m(x)$. In the simplest case, where there is a one-to-one correspondence between the elements of $\mathbf{M}$ and the extended utility functions in $\mathbf{U}$, and $m(x) = \sum_{i=1}^{N} g(u_i(x))$, the formula becomes: a is at least as good as b iff, for every $\pi(.)$ in $\mathbf{P}$, it is the case that, for every $u(.)$ in $\mathbf{U}$, $\sum_{x \in \mathbf{O}} \pi_a(x) \left[\sum_{i=1}^{N} g(u_i(x)) \right] \geq \sum_{x \in \mathbf{O}} \pi_b(x) \left[\sum_{i=1}^{N} g(u_i(x)) \right]$.

[123] I will not offer a precise definition, here, except to say that ambiguity aversion is exemplified by the standard choices in Ellsberg cases, i.e., the choices described in the text. See Ryan (2009, p. 336, n. 17).

The economics literature on imprecise probabilities has focused on developing models that are ambiguity-averse. The leading approach, pioneered by Gilboa and Schmeidler, is the so-called "maximin expected utility" rule. It uses a set P of probabilities to arrive at a complete ordering of actions (not a possibly incomplete quasi-ordering), by assigning each action the minimum expected utility according to all the probability functions in P, and then ranking actions in light of these "worst case" expected utilities. Maximin EU neatly rationalizes Ellsberg choices, but (intuitively) seems like an overly conservative approach to choice. Moreover, an open question is how maximin EU would be generalized to allow for the possibility that outcomes might be incomparable; the theory, as thus far developed, relaxes the EU requirement of precise probabilities, but not the requirement of a complete ranking of outcomes. I will not speculate on this question, nor take a position on the (nonobvious) choice between robust EU, maximin EU, or other refinements to EU theory that allow for imprecise probabilities.

C. Uncertainty about the Ordering of Outcomes

EU theory assumes that the decisionmaker knows for sure what the ordering of the outcome set O is. Not only is the ordering complete; the decisionmaker also grasps what the ordering is, and ranks actions consistently with it. For example (in the state of nature set-up) if outcome y is better than outcome x, and actions a and b are identical except that action a yields y in some states,[124] while b yields x in those states, then the decisionmaker determinately, and with certainty, prefers a to b.

However (whether or not the ordering of outcomes is complete) the decisionmaker might be uncertain what it is. For example, the decisionmaker might be trying to determine how to behave as a moral matter. The relevant ordering of outcomes, then, is their moral ordering, but the decisionmaker may not know whether a given outcome is morally better than another. Or, the decisionmaker might be ranking choices in light of her own well-being. But the correct theory of well-being may be an objective-good or ideal-preferentialist theory, such that the ranking of outcomes in light of the decisionmaker's well-being is not transparent to her. Finally, the decisionmaker might care about maximizing beauty, but be uncertain what beauty really consists in.

These observations have much relevance for the SWF framework, at least given the account of well-being I defended in Chapter 3. On this view, the moral ordering of outcomes is a function of a set U, representing the fully informed, fully rational extended preferences of the N individuals in the population. The decisionmaker (quite plausibly) will not know for sure what those preferences are. Remember that U is built up by pooling individual sets of the form $U^{k,t,x}$, representing the extended preferences of spectator k at time t in outcome x. Even if the decisionmaker simplifies

---

[124] Strictly, non-null states.

the estimation task by limiting the degree of heterogeneity of individuals' extended preferences—by assuming that $U^{k,t,x} = U^{j,t^*,y}$, where k at time t in outcome x is sufficiently similar to j at time t^* in outcome y in terms of the causal factors explaining extended preferences—the problem of uncertainty about $U^{k,t,x}$ and thus U remains. First, a given individual's actual preferences, albeit presumably known to the individual, may not be obvious to outsiders. Second, U depends on individuals' fully informed, fully rational extended preferences, which may be uncertain both to the individuals, and to others.

While much scholarship attempts to refine EU theory so as to accommodate an incomplete ordering of outcomes or imprecise probabilities, I am not aware of any formal work that grapples with the possibility of decisionmaker uncertainty about the ordering. (Perhaps this is because many scholars in the field assume that the ordering is just the decisionmaker's own, non-idealized, preference ordering, which *is* known to her.). A few philosophers have discussed the issue informally, under the heading of value uncertainty.[125] One suggestion is that the decisionmaker uncertain about the comparative value of outcomes should assign probabilities to different possible valuations and choose the action which maximizes expected utility taking account of these valuational probabilities.

It is clear what this suggestion means if the ordering of outcomes is complete and the decisionmaker knows as much. There is a set W of different utility functions $v(.)$, each representing a possible, complete, ordering of the outcome set. The decisionmaker assigns probabilities to the various elements of W; the probability value $p(v)$ represents his degree of belief that $v(.)$ represents the correct ordering. The decisionmaker then ranks actions using the rule: action a is at least as good as action b iff

$$\sum_{v(.)\in W} p(v)\left[\sum_{x\in O} \pi_a(x)v(x)\right] \geq \sum_{v(.)\in W} p(v)\left[\sum_{x\in O} \pi_b(x)v(x)\right].$$

It is less clear how the suggestion should be fleshed out where the ordering of outcomes might be incomplete: where each element of W is itself a whole set V of utility functions, each representing a different possible quasiordering of the outcome set to which the decisionmaker ascribes some nonzero probability.

A different approach, in that case, is to say that action a is at least as good as action b iff at least as good according to all the different possible quasiorderings of the outcome set that have nonzero probability. This meshes neatly with the expected multitiutility rule and with the robust Bayesian approach.[126] However, the reader might naturally worry that the approach risks massive incomparability in the ordering of

[125] See Hudson (1989); Ross (2006).

[126] The expected multiutility rule assumes a single quasiordering of outcomes, represented by a single set V; the decisionmaker knows what this quasiordering is. The proposed generalization now on the table, which accommodates the decisionmaker's uncertainty regarding V, says: action a is at least as good as action b iff $\sum_{x\in O} \pi_a(x)v(x) \geq \sum_{x\in O} \pi_b(x)v(x)$ for all $v(.)$ in V, for all V in W. Equivalently, if W^+ is a set of utility functions, containing every utility function in every V in W, then the rule is: action a is at least as good as action b iff $\sum_{x\in O} \pi_a(x)v(x) \geq \sum_{x\in O} \pi_b(x)v(x)$ for all $v(.)$ in W^+. A further generalization to allow for imprecise probabilities, along the lines of the robust EU

actions. Moreover, it gives an equal role to possible orderings that are highly likely, and possible orderings that are highly unlikely.

A simpler approach than either of these is to rank actions using the most likely quasiordering of the outcome set. This approach is ad hoc, but accommodates the possibility of an incomplete ranking as well as a complete one, and cannot be faulted for giving undue weight to unlikely orderings. A variation on this approach would be to specify a set **W** consisting of reasonably probable quasiorderings, and say that *a* is at least as good as *b* iff at least as good according to all the elements of **W**.

D. Strategic Interaction

The SWF framework is offered here as a tool for morally evaluating governmental policies and other large-scale choices. The impact of such choices is, typically, *not* independent of choices by other decisionmakers. For example, when government enacts a law, the resultant outcome will depend upon how the individuals subject to the law will react to it.

In some choice situations, perhaps, the decisionmaker may be certain how other individuals have acted or will act. (Perhaps she has adopted simplifying assumptions about their psychology, yielding a determinate prediction about what actions they have already taken, or would make in the future were she to make one or another choice.[127]) In many cases, however, the rational decisionmaker will be uncertain about what others have done or will do. It would be a grave weakness in a choice-evaluation framework if it failed to furnish guidance in such cases.

A simple thought, here, is that the decisionmaker can assign epistemic *probabilities* to various possible actions of other decisionmakers, expressing her numerical degrees of belief that those actions have been, or will be, performed. These probabilities (like the decisionmaker's epistemic probabilities regarding other sorts of facts) can be reflected in the probability term in the EU formula.

For example, in the state-of-nature set-up, the various possible "states of nature" that the decisionmaker uses to evaluate her decisions at a given point in time T might describe the possible prior or present actions of other individuals, their possible psychological states at T (including beliefs and preferences), and possible psychological laws (a kind of causal regularity), along with possible facts about the natural world and other possible types of causal regularities. This characterization of the states

---

approach, says: action *a* is at least as good as action *b* iff $\sum_{x \in O} \pi_a(x)v(x) \geq \sum_{x \in O} \pi_b(x)v(x)$ for all $\pi(.)$ in **P**, for all $v(.)$ in **W**⁺.

[127] For example, traditional optimal-tax scholarship typically assumes that each individual in the population has a sufficiently simple and determinate preference structure such that he can be predicted, with certainty, to choose some particular consumption-labor package in response to the policymaker's choice of income tax rates. The policymaker does not know what any given individual's preferences are, but knows the population distribution, and so knows what the population reaction will be.

would, seemingly, allow the decisionmaker to assign probabilities to other individuals' actions—past, present, *and* future.[128]

But there is a difficulty with the idea of using EU theory to evaluate choices whose impacts depend upon the actions of other individuals. In traditional game theory, the players do not assign probabilities to each other's actions or to each other's "strategies" (the players' plans for action). Although a strategy itself may involve randomization (a so-called "mixed" strategy), no player assigns a probability *to* any other player's strategy. Rather, traditional game theory focuses on the concept of Nash equilibrium or closely related notions. A Nash equilibrium is a profile of strategies, one for each player, such that no player does better by changing his strategy given the strategies of all the others.

To be sure, EU theory plays a role in evaluating whether a profile of strategies is a Nash equilibrium. A player may well be uncertain about the impact of his choosing one or another strategy, holding fixed the strategy choices of the other players. In such cases, whether a given player's strategy is part of a Nash equilibrium is determined by comparing the expected utility of various possible strategies open to the player, holding fixed the other players' strategies. However, the use of EU theory remains carefully cabined. The normative advice that traditional game theory gives to players is "choose a strategy which is in equilibrium" rather than "maximize expected utility." EU theory is used to "test" whether a given profile of strategies is in equilibrium, but not in a manner that would require the assignment of probabilities *to* strategies.[129]

A closely related point is that traditional game theory provides no guidance to players in cases where there are *multiple* equilibria. The theory tells players that it is *irrational* to play some strategy which is not part of an equilibrium. But in a case

---

[128] Note that other individuals' actions at T or prior to T, and their psychological states at T, as well as psychological laws, are all causally independent of what the decisionmaker does at T, and thus eligible to be included within the description of states of nature—as understood by causal decision theorists.

Imagine, first, that C is some action of some other individual that occurs at or prior to T. Whether C has occurred can be included within the description of states. The probability that the decisionmaker assigns to C, $\pi(C)$, is just the cumulative probability of the states in which C occurs.

Imagine, next, that C occurs after T. Then the probability that C occurs may depend on what the decisionmaker does at T. If states are sufficiently richly described, then any given state, combined with a given action a by the decisionmaker, entails C or the nonoccurrence of C. The probability that the decisionmaker assigns to C, $\pi_a(C)$, is just the cumulative probability of those states which entail C, given a.

So-called "implementation theory" as well as the Bayesian approach to game theory follows roughly this approach, by including individuals' psychological states, actions, and/or strategies (plans for actions) within states. On implementation theory, see, e.g., Maskin and Sjöström (2002). (These approaches, however, are not always careful to describe states so as to be causally independent from the choices of the decisionmaker at issue. On this issue, see Board [2006].)

[129] On the use of EU theory in traditional game theory, see generally Myerson (1997).

where a player has the option of following strategy *s* or *s**, each of which is in equilibrium with some profile of strategies by the other players, the choice between *s* and *s** is seen as being undetermined by norms of rationality, rather than being subject to the EU formula.

Why is traditional game theory reluctant to assign probabilities to players' actions and strategies? As Roger Myerson explains:

> In game-theoretic analysis, we try to understand the behavior of all of the players in a game, assuming that they are all rational and intelligent individuals. Raiffa and Kadane and Larkey have advocated an alternative decision-analytic approach to the study of games, when our task is to advise some particular player *i* (the *client*) as to what strategy he should use in a given game. Player's *i*'s optimal strategy should maximize his expected payoff with respect to his subjective probability distribution over the possible strategies of the other players. . . .
>
> A fundamental difficulty may make the decision-analytic approach impossible to implement, however. To assess his subjective probability distribution over the other players' strategies, player *i* may feel that he should try to imagine himself in their situations. When he does so, he may realize that the other players cannot determine their optimal strategies until they have assessed their subjective probability distributions over *i*'s possible strategies. Thus, player *i* may realize that he cannot predict his opponents' behavior until he understands what an intelligent person would expect him rationally to do, which is, of course, the problem that he started with. This difficulty would force *i* to abandon the decision-analytic approach and instead to undertake a game-theoretic approach, in which he tries to solve all the players' decision problems simultaneously [i.e., identify an equilibrium.][130]

But what exactly does Myerson's observation show? It shows that, where a rational decisionmaker is interacting with another individual or individuals who are also rational, and where the fact of joint rationality is commonly known, these features of the situation may *constrain* the probabilities that the decisionmaker rationally assigns to the actions or strategies of the other individuals. In particular, the rational decisionmaker, in such a situation, would assign probability zero to the other individuals taking actions or choices that (in some sense) are out of equilibrium. It hardly follows that their actions and strategies cannot be assigned probabilities at all.

Indeed, there is a revisionary school within game theory, the so-called "Bayesian" approach, whereby each player *does* assign probabilities to the others' strategies, and chooses his own strategy so as to maximize expected utility given this probability assignment.[131] The reader is referred to the literature for the details, but one example communicates the basic flavor of the approach. This is the idea of "rationalizable"

---

[130] Ibid., pp. 114–115.
[131] See, e.g., Aumann (1987); Aumann and Brandenburger (1995); Bernheim (1984); Board (2006); Brandenburger and Dekel (1987); Pearce (1984); Tan and Werlang (1988).

strategies, which I will express in terms of the reasoning of a given player (player *i*). Player *i* has an initial set of possible strategies, as do the other players. For each strategy in his set, player *i* asks: Does this strategy maximize my expected utility, given some probability distribution over the other players' strategies in their initial sets? If so, the strategy is retained as a possibility by player *i*, otherwise eliminated. However, because player *i* realizes that every other player is also rational, and is selecting her strategies with an eye to everyone else's choices, player *i* cannot stop at this point. Rather, he imagines that every other player employs a similar winnowing procedure with respect to *her* initial strategy set. For each possible strategy in her initial set, any given player (*j*) asks: does this strategy maximize my expected utility, given some probability distribution over the initial strategies of the other players? If so, the strategy is retained as a possibility for player *j*, otherwise eliminated.

This yields a new, winnowed, set of possible strategies both for *i* and for each of the other players. For each strategy in his winnowed set, player *i* asks: Does this strategy maximize my expected utility, given some probability distribution over the other players' strategies in their *winnowed* sets? Player *i* eliminates those strategies that do not satisfy this test and thus further reduces his strategy set. He then imagines that other players do the same for their winnowed sets. This procedure is repeated ad infinitum.

The strategies that remain in other players' sets after infinite iteration are those to which player *i* might rationally assign some positive probability—consistent with the constraint that whenever player *i* assigns a non-zero probability to the choice of some strategy by a given player *j*, choosing the strategy would be rational for *j* because it maximizes expected utility for *j* given some probability assignment over other players' strategies by *j*; and with this probability assignment by *j* in turn being rational because whenever *that* assignment accords a non-zero probability to player *k* choosing some strategy, doing so would be rational for *k* because it maximizes expected utility for *k* given some probability assignment over other players' strategies on his part; and so forth.

The Bayesian school within game theory suggests that there is no conceptual limitation in using EU theory as a tool for evaluating a given decisionmaker's choices even in the limiting case where the outcomes of those choices depend on the choices of other individuals; those individuals are in strategic interaction with the decision-maker (they are making their choices in virtue of their prediction of what the decisionmaker will do); and those other individuals are highly rational (the assumption of both traditional and Bayesian game theory). If EU theory is applicable in this instance, then it would be applicable (*a fortiori*) in cases where the other individuals involved are less than fully rational. For example, if a policymaker were to enact a regulation prohibiting certain behavior, some individuals might comply out of a sheer habit of rule-following. Others might decide whether or not to comply based upon their "prediction" regarding the likelihood that noncompliance would be detected and sanctioned, but these individual "predictions" might be made in a fairly crude way. Other individuals would be yet more rational in considering compliance, by asking whether it would advance the policymaker's goals to expend substantial resources in enforcing the regulation.[132] A policy analyst using an SWF to evaluate whether to enact the regulation could, in principle, assign probabilities to different degrees of compliance with the regulation, depending on the distribution of these sorts of psychological traits, and the probability of compliance for an individual with a given such trait.

---

[132] An influential literature in macroeconomics, originating with work by Kydland and Prescott (1977), investigates the setting of monetary policy given a population that is highly rational. See, e.g., Blackburn and Christensen (1989).

8

NEXT STEPS

This book has elaborated the SWF approach, seeing it as a framework for morally evaluating governmental policies and other large-scale choices. As the reader has, I hope, recognized, the central chapters of the book cluster into two "modular" components, detachable from each other. Chapters 3 and 4 propose a theory of well-being and its measurement. *Any* SWF depends on a set **U** of utility functions for making intra- and interpersonal comparisons of well-being levels and, perhaps, differences and ratios. These chapters show how to construct **U** with reference to individuals' extended preferences and how the elements of **U** can be inferred from ordinary preference data.

The set **U** is suitable for meshing with *any* SWF. Chapter 5 drew upon the concept of fairness to defend one particular SWF: the continuous prioritarian SWF, which satisfies not only the minimal welfarist axioms of anonymity, Pareto-indifference, and Pareto-superiority, but also the Pigou–Dalton principle (the key axiom of fairness), as well as axioms of continuity and separability. This SWF says: outcome x is morally at least as good as outcome y iff, for all $u(.)$ in **U**, $\sum_{i=1}^{N} g(u_i(x)) \geq \sum_{i=1}^{N} g(u_i(y))$, with the $g(.)$ function strictly increasing and strictly concave. The chapter then further specified the continuous prioritarian SWF, arguing for an Atkinson SWF, parametrized by the inequality-aversion parameter γ. As γ approaches 0, the Atkinson SWF approaches utilitarianism; as γ approaches infinity, the Atkinson SWF approaches the leximin SWF, which gives absolute priority to worse-off individuals.

Chapters 6 and 7 addressed two key issues concerning the implementation of a continuous prioritarian SWF: the time-slice issue and choice under uncertainty. On the first issue, I argued for a "whole-lifetime" approach: the elements of **U** measure lifetime well-being, and it is *these* utilities, not sublifetime utilities or numbers measuring attribute levels, that should provide the inputs for the formula just articulated. On the second issue, I argued that the continuous prioritarian SWF should be meshed with EU (expected utility) theory—notwithstanding violations of the *ex ante* Pareto and Pigou–Dalton principles.

The discussion in these latter three chapters does not depend upon the extended-preference methodology for constructing **U**. To be sure, I hope the reader will find that methodology persuasive, just as I hope she will be persuaded that a continuous prioritarian SWF is, on balance, the best specification of fairness. But these two components of the book's analysis are each meant to be robust to the failure of the other.

Although this book is intended to provide a philosophically rigorous examination of the central aspects of the SWF framework, there are a number of vital, related topics that I have not confronted. These are topics that anyone who embraces the framework will surely need to consider. This chapter describes three such topics—intending simply to acquaint the reader with the issues they raise in a very preliminary way, rather than to attempt a detailed analysis, let alone reach definitive answers. A rigorous discussion of each of these problems could fill a book as long as the one currently in hand. Yet to ignore them completely might also puzzle the reader, given their evident importance.

The topics are these. First, what is the appropriate *legal* role of the SWF framework? Should governmental officials be legally required to use SWFs in evaluating laws and regulations, just as they are currently required (at least to some extent) to use cost-benefit analysis?

Second, how should the SWF framework be outfitted to handle non-identity problems, variable populations, and infinite populations? This book assumes that each of the members of a "population" (the individuals whose well-being is of interest to the decisionmaker) exist in all of the possible outcomes of choice; that the size of the population is the same number in all outcomes; and that this number is finite. What happens when these assumptions are relaxed?

Finally, how should considerations of individual responsibility be integrated into the SWF framework?

I. LAW AND LEGALLY OPTIMAL STRUCTURES

Law and morality are distinct. More precisely, the legal norms that bind a given individual (in a given society, at a given time) may differ in their content from the moral norms that bind her. Indeed, in practice, legal and moral norms will often diverge substantially. It is a truism that a course of action can be morally required but not legally required (for example, where there is no legal norm in place that constrains some choice). Reciprocally, it is very plausible that a course of action can be legally required but not morally required. Even those scholars who believe that law can possess moral authority—that, under the right conditions, legal norms can generate prima facie moral reasons—would concede that these conditions might fail, and also that someone's all-things-considered moral duties might diverge from her legal duties.[1]

---

[1] See, e.g., Dworkin (1986, pp. 108–113, 202–206); Raz (1986, ch. 4).

But why exactly do legal and moral norms diverge? A rough, but still useful, answer: law is a social product, while morality is not. Morality (meaning "critical" rather than "social" morality) is not reducible to social norms. A suitably impartial evaluator, in reflective equilibrium, might arrive at a ranking of outcomes or actions that flies in the face of existing social norms.

The answer is rough because law—too—can diverge from social norms. For example, the primary legal rules of conduct, regulating activities by private individuals, are not necessarily coextensive with the social norms governing the conduct.[2] Still, all plausible accounts of the nature of law draw a tighter connection between law and social norms than between morality and social norms. This is true, clearly, for H.L.A. Hart's hugely influential view that a legal system rests upon a "rule of recognition": an ultimate criterion of legal validity, which is accepted as such by officials within the system, i.e., has the status of a social norm among those officials. On the Hartian view, primary conduct rules, and all other legal norms, are valid just in case derivable from the rule of recognition.[3]

Even Ronald Dworkin, Hart's most famous critic, sees a closer connection between law and social norms, than between morality and social norms. Dworkin's view is coherentist, not foundationalist. In any society, there will be a mass of "preinterpreted" legal data: shared understandings about what is legally required, what legal institutions exist, what the authoritative legal sources are, and so forth. The total content of the preinterpreted legal data in a given society, at a given time, is a social fact—a social fact quite different from Hart's rule of recognition, but a social fact nonetheless. Legal norms, for Dworkin, are validated by "constructive interpretation" of the preinterpreted legal data, i.e., by meshing this data with straight moral considerations.[4] Roughly, for Dworkin, law lies midway between social practices and critical morality. Thus, just as Hart denies that the legal requirements governing some individuals are necessarily coextensive with the moral requirements governing her (indeed, Hart, denies that law typically possesses moral authority), so Dworkin, too, denies that legal and moral requirements are necessarily coextensive.

This brief detour into jurisprudence is meant simply to bolster the commonsense claim that law and morality can diverge. That claim, in turn, provides the backdrop for three others. First, we can engage in *moral evaluation of legal structures*.[5] Think of $L, L^*, L^{**}, \ldots$ as different possible legal systems for a given society (differing, for example, in their institutional structures, their primary conduct rules, their

---

[2] Consider activities that are widely engaged in, and not seen as violating social norms, but are still technically illegal. On H.L.A. Hart's (1994) account, primary legal rules converge with social norms only in "primitive" legal systems.

[3] See ibid.

[4] See Dworkin (1986).

[5] Note how the intelligibility of this undertaking presupposes the possible divergence between law and morality. If the two were necessarily coextensive, how could we possibly compare different legal systems as morally better or worse?

official procedures, and so forth). It is intelligible to attempt to arrive at a moral ranking of these structures: to ask whether L is morally better than, worse than, equally
good as, or incomparable with L^*, and so forth. For example, we can ask whether it
is morally better or worse to have a legal system that permits same-sex marriage,
criminalizes marijuana use, bans research using fetal stem cells, puts in place a sepa-
ration-of-powers rather than parliamentary system, allows for a filibuster to block
legislation by majority vote, establishes judicial review, and so forth.

Second, it is *possible*, but not conceptually necessary, for law to *incorporate* moral
requirements.[6] Although law and morality are not necessarily coextensive, the legal
system might draw upon moral concepts and norms in delineating legal requirements. Written constitutions, in defining constitutional rights, often incorporate
certain moral values, such as equality, due process, or liberty of speech. The point is
also familiar to scholars of regulation. Regulatory statutes sometimes use open-
ended language—for example, instructing the agency to issue regulations that are
"reasonable," "necessary," "appropriate," or "in the public interest"—that invites a
certain degree of moral deliberation. Finally, the legal requirements governing
private individuals are at least sometimes defined in this open-ended way—as exemplified by tort law, which employs a "reasonableness" standard to determine when
behavior is negligent.

Third, and most subtly, it is an open question whether a given moral theory, M,
will favor its own legal incorporation. Assume that L is a legal system that incorporates M, in some regard, while L^* fails to incorporate M in that regard. It is *possible*
that M might favor L^* over L. It might be morally best to have a legal system whose
norms, in some instances, legally require choices that are not the morally best
choices.

This last point has been stressed by Larry Alexander and Frederick Schauer.
As Schauer writes:

> The design of a decision-making environment must . . . take into account not only the
> possibility of errors of under- and overinclusion emanating out of a faithful application of
> rules in the face of an unpredictable reality, but also the errors likely to be made by less
> than Solomonic decision-makers when, released from rules, they are empowered to apply
> background justifications directly to the cases they have to decide. When fear of this latter
> type of error predominates, rules are employed to lessen decision-maker error by limiting
> the ability of decision-makers to take into account a full range of potentially difficult and
> complex considerations. . . . Instead of allowing decision-makers to scrutinize a large,
> complex, and variable array of factors, rules substitute decision based on a smaller number
> of easily identified, easily applied, and easily externally checked factors. When decision-
> makers follow such rules, their opportunity to stray is reduced, and thus the proportion

---

[6] Admittedly, this claim is inconsistent with "exclusive positivism"—a view explained and criticized
in Coleman (2001).

of decision-maker errors is smaller than had the decision-makers more freedom to attempt to make what they perceived to be the best decision, all things considered, for the case at hand. . . .

Rule based decision-making is thus an application of the theory of the second-best. When we design real decision-making institutions for real decision-makers, the optimal decision *procedure* for an aggregate of decisions is sometimes one that abjures the search for the optimal in the individual case.[7]

Alexander, crisply, refers to the possible divergence between what is morally best, in some choice situation, and what it is morally optimal for law to require, in that situation, as "the gap."[8]

Consider the traffic code. This body of law *could* consist of a single legal injunction: "drive at a morally appropriate rate of speed and in a morally appropriate manner." But no traffic code of any existing legal system says this. Instead, much more specific guidance is provided, e.g., "Don't exceed 55." "Stop at red lights." "Drive on the right." A traffic code of the first sort would be morally disastrous.

The mundane case of the traffic code not only exemplifies "the gap," but also illustrates the different kinds of factors in light of which some moral theory M might prefer a legal structure L^* which precludes decisionmakers in some contexts from acting in accordance with M. (1) *Epistemic failures.* Individuals may make errors about what M requires. For example, drivers may regularly overestimate their own abilities and thus miscalculate whether fast driving is on balance beneficial on some occasion, given the risks and benefits. (2) *Decision costs.* Deciding what M requires may be costly. For example, a driver can much more quickly and effortlessly determine on any given occasion whether she is above or below a stated limit, as opposed to determining which rate of speed is reasonably safe. (3) *Motivational failures and monitoring.* Individuals may not be motivated to comply with M. (For example, drivers may focus on the risks and benefits of fast driving to themselves, rather than to pedestrians or other drivers.) Law, of course, can use sanctions to ensure compliance despite motivational failures. But, if M is difficult to apply, individuals might expect that sanctions for a law requiring compliance with M might not be forthcoming. (Drivers might expect that it would be easier to challenge fines for driving in an unreasonably safe manner, than to challenge fines for exceeding a bright-line speed limit.) (4) *Coordination.* What a given individual should do, in light of M, may well depend on what other individuals do. Coordinating individual behavior so as to maximize M may be secured by laws that fail to incorporate M. For example, it maximizes overall well-being for multiple streams of traffic to alternate in crossing an intersection, rather than for all streams to cross at once. At busy intersections, a red light (backed by a legal requirement to obey traffic signals) better coordinates this

---

[7] Schauer (1992, pp. 151–152).
[8] See Alexander (1991); Alexander and Sherwin (2001, ch. 4).

process than a law that tells drivers to cross the intersection whenever doing so is "reasonable." (5) *Predictability and reliance*. It may be easier for third parties to predict how individuals subject to a law that does not incorporate M will behave. This reduces costs that flow from third-party uncertainty, and from their disappointed expectations. (Pedestrians may feel more comfortable walking on streets with red lights and clear speed limits.[9])

The speed limit involves private individuals. But "the gap" can also arise at the level of governmental officials. Morally optimal *public* law—the law that empowers governmental officials, subject to various procedural and substantive requirements—is surely more complicated than the one-sentence injunction "act, as an office holder, in a morally appropriate manner," for reasons, again, involving epistemic and motivational limitations, decision costs, coordination, and reliance.

Because a "gap" can exist at the level of public law, the argumentation of this book does not suffice to determine what the legal role of the SWF framework should be. What the book *has* argued, at great length, is that the framework provides a good tool for morally evaluating governmental policies and other large-scale choices. Assume that this is true. Assume that, indeed, a decisionmaker, confronting some (large-scale) choice situation **A**, and seeking to determine which choice is morally best, should do so by using an SWF to rank outcomes in light of their corresponding utility vectors, and then deriving a choice ranking from the outcome ranking. It remains an open question whether a legal system L that requires the decisionmaker to undertake her decision in this manner is morally optimal. It might be morally preferable to have a legal system L^* with public laws that *prohibit* officials (in general, or officials of some type) from using SWFs to evaluate their choices, and that instead legally obligate them to employ a different sort of choice procedure.

Indeed, existing scholarship concerning cost-benefit analysis (CBA) suggests three different lines of argumentation for limiting the legal role of SWFs, which I will briefly summarize. Before doing so, however, some final words of clarification are in order.

One of the most fundamental norms of public law (certainly in the U.S.) is the norm of *legislative supremacy*. Administrative officials are legally required to act in accordance with statutes duly enacted (in accordance with constitutionally prescribed enactment procedures) by the legislature, at least where the statutory provisions are clear and not in violation of constitutional rights or in excess of the legislature's constitutional powers. A legal regime in which administrative officials were *legally* permitted or required to override clear statutory mandates on non-constitutional grounds—for example, because of their own assessment of the costs and benefits of the statutory mandates—would be a radical departure from existing legal practices, at least in the U.S. Moreover, there are good reasons (sounding in coordination, predictability, and reliance) to believe that a basic norm of legislative

---

[9] See Schauer (1992, ch. 7).

supremacy is morally justifiable (even where the norm makes it legally impermissible for an executive branch official to ignore some statute which is itself morally problematic).

A harder question concerns the appropriate exercise of legal discretion. Statutes create a "zone of discretion," larger or smaller, for implementing officials. Should our legal system have in place a background rule that legally encourages or requires administrative officials to employ the SWF framework in making large-scale, discretionary, policy choices? (The U.S. legal system currently contains just this sort of discretion-regulating background rule—not a rule that entrenches the SWF framework, but rather a rule, imposed by Presidential order on executive branch agencies, that instructs them to employ CBA as a decisional criterion "unless a statute requires another regulatory approach."[10]) A closely related question concerns the content of statutory provisions. A legal system might propagate the use of SWFs—consistent with the basic norm of legislative supremacy—by enacting open-ended statutes that confer substantial discretion on administrators, together with a background rule putting in place the SWF framework, plus institutional structures designed to ensure compliance with the background rule. Would *this* be morally justifiable? (Proponents of CBA have argued for similar changes to statutory law—urging that statutory provisions requiring administrators to undertake policies that would fail a cost-benefit test be repealed and replaced by a cost-benefit "supermandate."[11])

To state this point in a somewhat more abstract way: there are a *plurality* of possible legal structures $L, L^*, L^{**}, \ldots$ all of which are consistent with the basic principles of public law whose moral attractiveness seems pretty evident (for example, all contain the norm of legislative supremacy, or for that matter the norm of constitutional supremacy), but nonetheless differ in the legal role they create for SWFs, some making that role quite pervasive (as CBA currently functions in the U.S.), some making that role much more limited. The hard question, which this book does *not* purport to answer, is this: Which one of *these* legal structures is morally best, on balance?

Now the reader might ask: By what criterion should we make *that* determination? How, really, can different legal structures be evaluated as better or worse?

The answer is that the SWF framework, itself, provides the evaluative structure. That framework provides a generic basis for morally evaluating items—not just actions, or intertemporal series of actions, but yet larger-scale items such as legal rules, social practices, or governmental institutions. Given a set of such items (for example, a set of possible public law regimes), each maps onto a probability distribution over outcomes; EU theory then provides bridge principles for ranking this set of items in light of the set of outcomes.[12] Scholars, legislators, and others interested

---

[10] Executive Order 12866 (1993, sec. 1(a)).

[11] See Sunstein (2002, p. 15).

[12] It might be objected that we lack a theoretical warrant for associating items that are not choices (e.g., institutions) with probability distributions over outcomes. EU theory shows that, if the ranking

in the design of legal institutions can ask themselves: would it maximize expected social welfare to put in place a particular legal rule or package of rules, or instead some alternative legal rule or package of rules? Indeed, this consequentialist approach—evaluating legal rules in light of some conception of good consequences (a ranking of outcomes)—is the hallmark of law-and-economics scholarship.[13]

Thus we have arrived at a clear statement of the question which this section means to pose. Assume that you embrace some particular SWF (be it a continuous prioritarian SWF or some other) and some methodology for constructing U (be it the extended-preference methodology or some other), as a framework for *moral* evaluation. Now consider a range of legal structures—some of which create a substantial legal role for this framework, others of which afford it a limited legal role or none at all. Which structure is morally best in light of the framework itself? Because of the "gap," the answer to this question is not obvious.

Let me now briefly outline three lines of argument, drawn from the extant literature on CBA, for limiting the legal role of SWFs. What is critical to see is that each argument points to considerations regarding morally optimal legal structures that are relevant *by the lights of the SWF framework itself*. In other words, each identifies reasons why it may fail to maximize expected social welfare to have a legal system in which governmental officials are generally instructed to exercise their legal discretion by seeking to maximize expected social welfare. It is *not* my intention to reach a firm verdict concerning these arguments—but rather to sketch the considerations, all ultimately empirical, that an SWF analyst, whose objects of assessment are legal structures themselves, would need to grapple with.

A. Is it Optimal for Non-tax Bodies to use CBA?

An important body of scholarship in economics demonstrates that it may be optimal to set non-tax policies using a simple cost-benefit test (by "simple," I mean a cost-benefit test without distributive weights). For short, call this the "CBA non-tax optimality" analysis. Much scholarship regarding CBA non-tax optimality focuses on

---

of *choices* satisfies certain axioms, *choices* correspond to such distributions—but why believe that a similar showing can be made for non-choice items?

A fuller discussion of the moral evaluation of legal structures would certainly need to address this objection. Intuitively, we *can* assign a probability to different outcomes, "given" the existence of some institution (or, more generally, "given" the fact that some item exists or occurs), but showing that such probability assignments are justified may require hard analytic work. At a minimum, choices that bring into being, or change, institutions can be mapped onto probability distributions over outcomes. For example, different choices by legislators or judges would affect our legal institutions in various ways.

[13] Admittedly, law-and-economics scholarship often does not employ SWFs—but it certainly *does* engage in consequentialist evaluation of legal doctrines and structures. And in a well-known book, *Fairness versus Welfare*, Kaplow and Shavell (2002) specifically propose that legal scholars do so using SWFs.

the problem of the optimal provision of public goods.[14] Louis Kaplow, a contributor to this body of work, has extended the analysis beyond public goods, to tort-law doctrine (with his co-author Steve Shavell), environmental regulation, and other areas.[15]

This scholarship, it should be stressed, works *within* the social-welfare-function tradition. Although many economists are skeptical about interpersonal comparisons, and endorse Kaldor–Hicks efficiency as a fundamental criterion for evaluating policies, this is *not* the view adopted in the body of work now under discussion. Rather, it is a branch of the optimal-tax literature, originating with Mirrlees' pioneering use of social welfare functions to analyze income tax schedules.

Nor do scholars in this area rely upon naive assumptions about the redistributive instruments available to government. A *naive* argument for setting non-tax policies using a simple CBA test runs as follows: (1) If simple CBA favors policy P^* over policy P, then policy P^* is Kaldor–Hicks efficient relative to policy P[16] ; (2) if policy P^* is Kaldor–Hicks efficient relative to P, then P^* can be converted into a policy P^+ which is Pareto-superior to P, via redistribution from individuals who are better off with P^* than P, to individuals who are worse off with P^* than P.

The first premise is naive, because (as we have known since Boadway's work) CBA is not a sufficient condition for Kaldor–Hicks efficiency.[17] The second premise is naive because it overlooks government's informational limitations. Assume that the distribution of population attributes is such that P^* really is Kaldor–Hicks efficient relative to P. The taxing authorities may not know which particular individuals are better off in P^* and which particular individuals worse off; this may depend upon attributes "unobservable" to government, such as individuals' health states, happiness states, or preference structures. Nor would it be useful to survey individuals, asking whether they prefer P^* or not. At least if the respondent to such a survey understood that she would pay a tax if she answered this question affirmatively, otherwise receive a subsidy, what incentive would she have to answer it honestly?

Scholars who have analyzed the non-tax optimality of CBA do *not* assume a perfectly informed taxing body. On this score, too, they work within the Mirrleesian tradition—assuming that an individual's rate of income tax, or other taxes, can be made to depend on her income, but not upon her ability, wage rate, or the amount

[14] See, e.g., Boadway and Keen (1993); Christiansen (1981, 2007); Hylland and Zeckhauser (1979); Johansson-Stenman (2005); Kaplow (1996); Kreiner and Verdelin (2009); Slemrod and Yitzhaki (2001).

[15] See, e.g., Kaplow (2008b); Kaplow and Shavell (1994).

[16] There are different versions of the criterion of Kaldor–Hicks efficiency. See Chapter 2. Here, I am imagining the simplest version which says: x is Kaldor–Hicks efficient over y if there is some costless redistribution in x, from those better off than in y, to those worse off than in y, which would make everyone better off than in y. Substituting different versions of the criterion in this argument would be equally naive.

[17] See Boadway (1974); Boadway and Bruce (1984, ch. 9).

of time she works, all of which are assumed to be "unobservable." The clever idea is to show the following: Assume that some non-tax policy P^* (e.g., a policy that fixes the level of some public good) would produce outcome x^*, while policy P would produce outcome x, and x^* passes a simple CBA test relative to policy x. Then there is a change to the income tax schedule which, coupled with P^*, would yield an outcome x^+ which is Pareto-superior to x.

As Kaplow explains:

> The conventional view of economists is that the optimal supply of public goods is not determined by the simple cost-benefit test—which asks whether the sum of individuals' benefits exceeds a project's direct cost—because financing public goods involves the use of distortionary taxes, notably, the income tax. . . .
>
> This article reexamines the relationship between the optimal supply of public goods and the distortionary cost of income taxation. The article first demonstrates that, under standard simplifying assumptions (including the separability of leisure), there exists a way to modify the income tax to finance a public good such that there is no additional distortion. Suppose that the preexisting income tax schedule is adjusted so that, at each income level, the tax change just offsets the benefits from the public good. By construction, an individual's *net* reward from any level of work effort will be unaltered: any reduction in disposable income due to the tax adjustment is balanced by the benefit from the public good. Because an individual's after-tax utility as a function of his work effort will thus be unchanged, his choice of work effort—and utility level—will also be unaffected.
>
> To complete the argument, observe that the increase in tax revenue due to this adjustment in the tax schedule will equal the sum of individuals' benefits from the public good. Hence, if the sum of benefits from the public good exceeds its direct cost, the government will have surplus revenue, which can be rebated in a manner that makes everyone better off. In this case, therefore, the simple cost-benefit formula indicates whether the public good should be supplied. There should be no adjustment to account for the distortionary cost of labor income taxation because labor supply does not change.[18]

The CBA non-tax optimality analysis has implications regarding optimal legal structures. (Indeed, Kaplow and Shavell have emphasized such implications in their work.[19]) In particular, it has implications for whether it is optimal to put in place a public-law regime L^* that instructs non-tax bodies to evaluate their (discretionary) policies using a simple CBA test, as opposed to L that instructs non-tax bodies to evaluate their (discretionary) policies using some other policy-evaluation framework. The analysis demonstrates that, under the right conditions, any Paretian SWF will prefer L^* to L.

---

[18] Kaplow (1996, pp. 513–514).

[19] See also Musgrave (1959), proposing the separation of allocation and distribution functions within government.

In a moment, I will say something about what "the right conditions" are. But note, to begin, the following. To demonstrate that, under the right conditions, *any* Paretian SWF will prefer L^* to L is a sweeping result. The CBA non-tax optimality analysis does not presuppose a utilitarian SWF, or some particular kind of non-utilitarian SWF. If policy P yields x, and policy P^* coupled with a change to the tax system yields x^+, and x^+ is Pareto-superior to x, then the utilitarian SWF, and continuous prioritarian SWF, and every other SWF satisfying minimal welfarist requirements will prefer x^+ to x—just because every such SWF will satisfy the Pareto principle in its ranking of outcomes.

Moreover, *every* plausible SWF can diverge from simple CBA: CBA without distributive weights. This is true, to be sure, of the continuous prioritarian SWF. But it is also true of a *utilitarian* SWF, which diverges from simple CBA by virtue of heterogeneity in individuals' marginal utility of money. And simple CBA, clearly, diverges from the other SWFs mooted in Chapter 5.

Thus the CBA non-tax optimality analysis shows that, under the right conditions, *every plausible SWF* will prefer a legal regime in which non-tax authorities are instructed to evaluate policies using a simple CBA test, as opposed to a legal regime in which non-tax authorities use that very SWF to evaluate policies. In short, the CBA non-tax optimality analysis provides a rigorous demonstration of the possibility of "the gap" between the choice procedure to determine what is morally required (an SWF) and the choice procedure which it is morally optimal to legally require (CBA). In this case, "the gap" arises because of the moral benefits of interpersonal coordination (here, coordination among different kinds of legal officials). Under the right conditions, it is morally optimal to have in place legal doctrines that require a non-tax official to employ simple CBA in any given choice situation, rather than legal doctrines that require her to employ an SWF, because the legal system includes a taxing body that can react in a morally beneficial manner—a manner that this very SWF would approve—to the non-tax official's choice.[20]

However, "the right conditions" turn out to be quite restrictive indeed.[21] They include the following: (1) *Labor-separability and no hidden preference heterogeneity.* The CBA non-tax optimality analysis assumes that individuals' ordinary preferences are *separable* as between labor and the other attributes that individuals care about (consumption, public goods, etc.); and that individuals either have homogeneous preferences for attribute bundles, or at least that any heterogeneity is linked to

---

[20] It might be objected that there is no real "gap" here. If "the right conditions" obtain (including a tax authority which will react in a beneficial manner to the choices of non-tax officials), then non-tax officials will *foresee* that reaction, and will choose the very same non-tax policies regardless of whether they employ CBA or the SWF. However, by adding in the plausible premise that SWF analysis has incremental decision costs relative to CBA, or that non-tax officials may lack perfect foresight, the "gap" reemerges.

[21] Some of the following conditions are discussed in Kaplow (1996; 2008b, pp. 135–145) and in Johansson-Stenman (2005).

observable characteristics (as opposed to heterogeneity within groups of individuals with the same, unobservable, ability). Where these conditions fail, it will *not* necessarily be true that a non-tax policy passing a simple CBA test, combined with some change to the income tax, will yield an outcome that makes everyone better off. (2) *Policies are chosen under conditions of certainty.* The bulk of the literature focuses on the case in which non-tax and tax bodies know for certain what the outcomes of their choices will be (modulo information about the attributes of any particular individual). For example, in the public good case (with homogeneous preferences), it is assumed that the governmental bodies know for certain the population distribution of abilities; what individuals' (homogeneous) preferences are regarding labor, consumption, and public goods; how any given policy will change the level of public goods; and how it will change consumption. Extending the optimality analysis to uncertainty raises fresh issues that the literature has not examined—in particular, issues regarding the divergence between *ex ante* Pareto-superiority and the EU approach to applying a non-utilitarian SWF.[22] (3) *Zero administrative costs.* The CBA non-tax optimality analysis shows that, where P^* is favored by a simple CBA test over P, the enactment of P^* together with a *costless* change to the tax code will yield an outcome Pareto-superior to the outcome of P. However, the process of amending the code, and disseminating information about the change, will be costly; moreover, the amended code may have higher enforcement costs than its precursor. (4) *No divergence between fully informed and actual preferences.* The CBA non-tax optimality analysis assumes that each individual has a single preference structure, embodied in an ordinary utility function, which does three things at once. It (a) explains the individual's behavior; (b) is used to calculate WTP/WTA amounts for purposes of the CBA test; and (c) undergirds ascriptions of Pareto-superiority. However, this is quite contestable. In particular, a strong argument can be made that Pareto-superiority (and, more generally, the utility numbers that function as inputs into the SWF) depends upon individuals' *fully informed, fully rational* preferences,[23] as opposed to the actual, non-ideal preferences that drive individual behavior (in particular, that determine how individuals respond to different tax schedules). How a divergence between Pareto-superiority and actual preferences affects the CBA non-tax optimality analysis remains to be investigated, but it seems quite plausible that the analysis cannot be extended to this case.[24] (5) *Appropriate political economy.*

---

[22] Imagine that policies P^* and P yield different probability distributions over outcomes (characterized, for example, in terms of individual labor, consumption, and public goods). Assume that P^* passes some type of CBA test in terms of ex ante WTP/WTA amounts; and that there is some change to the tax schedule which, together with P^*, yields a policy P^+ which is ex ante Pareto-superior to P. If the SWF is non-utilitarian and applied in an EU manner, to compare P^+ to P, it need not prefer the former. See Chapter 7.

[23] See Chapter 3.

[24] Even with a perfectly informed taxing authority, let alone a taxing authority unable to observe individual ability and wage rate, the fact that a CBA test in terms of *actual* WTP/WTA amounts ranks

The CBA non-tax optimality result is a *possibility* result. Where labor is separable from other attributes, there is no hidden heterogeneity in preferences, administrative costs are zero, the outcomes of tax and non-tax policies are known, and there is no divergence between the preferences that determine individual behavior and the preferences that are used to define Pareto-superiority, then the following proposition is true: whenever a non-tax policy passes a simple CBA test, the non-tax policy *could be coupled with* a change to the tax code so as to yield a Pareto-superior outcome. Clearly, this proposition alone does *not* imply the conclusion that L^* (a legal regime instructing non-tax bodies to use a simple CBA test) is preferred by any Paretian SWF to L (a legal regime instructing non-tax bodies to employ a different test). Rather, it implies that conclusion only when combined with further assumptions about the motivation and abilities of tax and non-tax officials. If these officials suffer various motivational or cognitive limitations, the proposition could be true but the conclusion false. The political economy of the tax system may be such that tax bodies would regularly fail to make the changes to the tax code required to render non-tax policies passing a simple CBA test universally beneficial.

Indeed, it is extremely implausible to think that the five conditions just described are jointly realized in any actual legal system. Thus, it would be a gross mistake to think that the CBA non-tax optimality analysis, itself, demonstrates that the SWF-maximizing legal structure for any actual legal system (e.g., the U.S.) is to instruct non-tax bodies to use a simple CBA test. Much empirical work—regarding the extent to which the labor-separability assumption fails, the level of administrative costs, the political economy of the tax system, etc.—would need to be undertaken before any firm conclusions on this score could be reached.

Moreover, it is quite plausible that—once we allow for a failure of the joint realization of these five conditions—different types of Paretian SWFs might *disagree* about the ranking of legal structures. Imagine that government is sensitive to the average voter but not to badly off groups, which have little political power. In particular, non-tax policies that pass a simple CBA test, but fail to benefit the average voter, are typically rejected by non-tax bodies unless they anticipate the policies being coupled with some change to the tax schedule that renders the policies net beneficial to the average voter—and indeed such changes occur with some frequency. However, the taxing authority typically fails to make changes to the tax schedule if required merely to make non-tax polices beneficial to badly off groups. Under such conditions, a utilitarian SWF might prefer a legal regime instructing

---

x^* over x clearly does *not* mean that x^* is convertible into some x^+ which is Pareto-superior to x in terms of fully informed, fully rational preferences. Conversely, if a CBA test in terms of *fully informed, fully rational* WTP/WTA amounts ranks x^* over x, it is not clear why the tax authorities would necessarily be able to couple x^* with the type of change to the tax schedule that Kaplow imagines (a change that leaves individuals' labor-supply choices unaffected), since those choices depend upon actual rather than ideal preferences.

non-tax bodies to employ a simple CBA test, while a distributive-sensitive SWF might reject such a regime.

In short, the CBA non-tax optimality analysis is a first step toward a full under-standing of the optimality of legal structures that limit SWF analysis by non-tax bodies—an important step, to be sure, but only the first. But the analysis does, strik-ingly, underscore why it is critical to distinguish between the status of the SWF framework as a tool for moral evaluation, and the question of its morally appropriate legal role.

B. Does Everyone Benefit in the Long Run if Government uses CBA?

It is sometimes suggested that the long-run use of a Kaldor–Hicks or CBA test will benefit everyone. For example, Hicks himself wrote:

> [T]here is a simple way of overcoming [the impossibility of interpersonal comparisons], a perfectly objective test which enables us to discriminate between those reorganisations which improve productive efficiency, and those which do not. If A is made so much better off by the change that he could compensate B for his loss, and still have something left over, then this reorganisation is an unequivocal improvement. . . .
>
> If the economic activities of a community were organised on the principle of making no alterations in the organisation of production which were not improvements in this sense, and making all alterations which were improvements that it could possibly find, then, although we could not say that all the inhabitants of that community would be necessarily better off than they would have been if the community had been organised on some different principle, nevertheless there would be a strong probability that almost all of them would be better off after the lapse of a sufficient length of time.[25]

This long-run argument, like the CBA non-tax optimality argument, embodies the idea that a decisional criterion, whatever its merits on a one-off basis, might be defensible as part of a coordinated governmental practice (either coordination between non-tax and tax bodies or, in this case, the *intertemporal* coordination of governmental bodies around repeated application of the CBA/Kaldor–Hicks test).

Although there is some intuitive plausibility to the long-run idea, little rigorous work has been undertaken elaborating it in an analytically precise manner. Moreover (unlike the CBA non-tax optimality literature, discussed earlier) scholars who have advanced the long-run argument for CBA typically have not worked within the social-welfare-function tradition. We therefore lack even the beginnings of an answer to the following question: "What are the empirical conditions C^+, possibly

---

[25] Hicks (1941, p. 111). See also Hotelling (1938, pp. 257–260); sources cited in Graham (2008, pp. 414–419).

characterizing a legal system, such that given conditions C^+ *any* Paretian SWF will prefer a legal system L^* in which administrative bodies use a CBA test over time, as opposed to a legal system L in which those bodies evaluate policies using that SWF?"

Note the wording of this question. Proponents of the long-run argument sometimes seem to be comparing a legal regime in which administrators employ CBA, to a baseline of governmental inaction—to a minimal, "night watchman" state, in which government does not fund public goods or enact regulations at all. However, in order to determine the moral optimality of legally entrenching CBA rather than the SWF framework as government's policy assessment tool, we need to undertake a *different* comparison—namely, a comparison between a legal system L^* in which government will fund public goods, issue regulations, etc., as long as such policies pass a CBA test; and a system L in which government *also* stands ready to enact such policies, but now evaluates them using an SWF.

It is hard to believe that conditions C^+, whatever their precise content, are actually realized in our legal system.[26] Still, it may well be true that *some* SWFs would prefer a legal system in which non-tax bodies use a non-SWF test over the long run (e.g., CBA)—paired with interventions, more or less frequent, by the tax bodies. A sophisticated analysis of different possible public-law structures, imposing various decisional rules on governmental officials, certainly needs to consider long-run effects.

C. The Abilities and Motivations of Government Officials (Herein of Regulatory Review)

The optimality of a legal regime instructing governmental officials to employ SWFs, as opposed to some other choice-evaluation procedure, depends on the cognitive and motivational characteristics of those officials. This is true, as mentioned earlier,

---

[26] The difficulty is that badly off individuals might well benefit from government's long-run use of a distributively sensitive SWF (for example, an Atkinson SWF with a level of γ substantially different from 0), rather than its long-run use of CBA. To see this in a simple case, imagine that an impoverished minority of the population is at a lower level of lifetime well-being than the rest (and will remain so regardless of the policies that government chooses). Governmental bodies, with some regularity, are faced with the choice between policies that pass a CBA test, and policies that fail a CBA test but benefit the impoverished minority and would be preferred by an Atkinson SWF with $\gamma > 1$ (for example). Why would it benefit everyone over the long run—including members of the impoverished minority—to have a legal system L^* in which government is legally required to use CBA as a policy-evaluation tool rather than a system L in which it is required to use an Atkinson SWF with $\gamma > 1$?

It might be objected that L^* and L should be compared with a veil of ignorance in place, so that individuals do not know what their attributes are, and that (behind a veil of ignorance) L^* will be ex ante Pareto-superior to L. But it is far from clear why a veil of ignorance is appropriate for morally evaluating legal structures, see Chapter 5; and, in any event, the ex ante Pareto-superiority of L^* does not mean that every Paretian SWF, applied in an EU manner, will prefer L^*, see Chapter 7.

if optimality requires coordination between tax and non-tax officials; but the point is much more general. For example, imagine that SWF analysis is simply too difficult for government officials and the analysts who advise them to undertake in a competent manner—at least given time and resource constraints. Or imagine that these officials could do the analysis competently, if they wanted, but would be motivated to distort the analysis so as to suit the interests of powerful groups. If so, it might be best, in light of a given SWF, for public law to require the use of a simpler and less readily distorted framework than that SWF.

The debate about the efficacy of regulatory review processes is instructive here. As mentioned, CBA has been a major part of the regulatory process in the United States since 1981—when President Reagan imposed a general cost-benefit requirement on the issuance of regulations by administrative agencies in the executive branch, a requirement kept in place by all subsequent Presidents. Compliance with the requirement is superintended by an office (OIRA) within the Office of Management and Budget, a powerful agency that is staffed by civil servants but has close links to the President. Specifically, executive agencies must conform to a cost-benefit test in promulgating regulations, where such a test is permitted by the particular substantive statute that the agency is implementing; and agencies must prepare full-blown cost-benefit analyses, for review by OIRA, when sufficiently large-scale regulations are issued.[27]

This legal regime (for short, "regulatory review") has been vigorously criticized by some scholars.[28] It has been suggested that undertaking CBA is expensive for agencies; that it delays the issuance of useful regulations; and that it yields indeterminate results. Critics also argue that OIRA has not operated as a neutral oversight body, but instead has functioned to advance the President's agenda; to serve the interests of regulated entities; and to implement an anti-regulatory bias that its staffers tend to share. Some argue that different, more determinate procedures for choosing policies—for example, a "feasibility" test, enjoining regulators to set health and safety standards at the most stringent technologically and economically feasible level—would have lower decision and delay costs, and would better constrain administrative discretion and check the political process.

Unlike many applied economists, the critics of regulatory review do not embrace CBA as an appropriate normative criterion for choosing policies. However, their criticism suggests that even someone who *does* embrace this criterion might reject regulatory review. Perhaps that legal regime has failed to produce better policies *by the lights of CBA itself.* If L^{++} is the legal regime of regulatory review (whereby agencies are instructed to use CBA), and L^+ a different legal regime (whereby they are instructed to use some other test, e.g., "feasibility" analysis), perhaps the CBA

---

[27] See Executive Order 12866 (1993); Adler and Posner (2006); Sunstein (2002); Wiener (2007). See also Executive Order 13563 (2011), reaffirming Executive Order 12866.

[28] See, e.g., Ackerman and Heinzerling (2004); Driesen (2005, 2006); Kysar (2010); McGarity (1998); Shapiro and Schroeder (2008).

standard itself would prefer L^+ to L^{++}. And, if that is true, perhaps the very same epistemic and motivational factors that have interfered with regulatory review would also frustrate a legal requirement that agencies employ SWFs—so that even the proponent of the SWF framework as an attractive moral standard would see this legal requirement as morally suboptimal.

What, in fact, do the data show? Does regulatory review, itself, pass a CBA test? To begin, does it succeed in producing policies with greater net benefits (as measured by CBA) than policies chosen outside the regulatory review framework? In a large case study of regulatory review in twelve rulemakings at the EPA, Morgenstern found that it produced substantial benefits: "In all twelve cases, the economic analyses supported specific cost-saving rule improvements. . . . Even a cursory examination of the rule modifications associated with [the cost-benefit analyses prepared for regulatory review] suggests that, overall, they are quite significant. While it is not feasible to develop systematic estimates of the dollar values. . ., in a number of cases the improvements were quite sizable, amounting to a third or more of the benefits or costs of the rules."[29]

However, the evidence from larger-scale, quantitative studies is more ambiguous. Scott Farrow examined a sample of health and safety regulations from 1967 to 1991, including both rules that were ultimately promulgated and rules that were proposed by the agency but never finalized. Farrow found that the cost-per-life-saved of finalized rules did not decrease after 1981, the inception of the regulatory review requirement; that cost-per-life-saved had a statistically significant but very modest effect on whether a rule was ultimately promulgated by the agency; and, comparing the cost-per-life-saved of proposed rules to their finalized versions, that cost-per-life-saved did not decrease during the review process.[30]

Robert Hahn estimated the costs and benefits of all final rules with full-blown cost-benefit analyses issued from 1981 through 1996. He concluded that the aggregate net benefits of these rules was positive, but that a significant fraction had net costs rather than benefits, and that there was no evidence of an increase in the net benefits of the rules over time. More recently, Hahn and Tetlock examined the 95 major rules reviewed by OIRA between1995 and 2005 for which substantial costs and benefits were monetized and found that 14 of 95 were likely to fail a cost-benefit test. Finally, examining OIRA data from 1992 to 2006, John Graham reached a more positive conclusion than the Farrow, Hahn, and Hahn and Tetlock studies; he found that the total net benefits from major federal rules were positive in every year, and increased substantially starting in 2001.[31]

It would be *quite* premature to conclude from these and similar studies that legal regimes instructing administrative agencies to use CBA in evaluating policies do not

---

[29] Morgenstern and Landy (1997, pp. 457–459).

[30] See Farrow (n.d.).

[31] See Hahn (2000, ch. 3), as modified by Hahn (2005, p. 16); Hahn and Tetlock (2008, p. 71); Graham (2008, p. 482).

succeed in producing policies that are better by the lights of CBA—and even *more* premature to extrapolate from this (unwarranted) conclusion to a parallel conclusion regarding SWF analysis. First, the overall picture the studies provide regarding regulatory review is *mixed*; there is not clear evidence, as yet, that regulatory review substantially improves the net benefits of rules (as measured by the CBA standard itself), but also not clear evidence confirming that it fails to do so.

Second, related scholarly work has examined the political dynamics of regulatory review—in particular, investigating the critics' claim that OIRA functions to enhance the influence of regulated groups. The most systematic studies to date tend to *disconfirm* this claim.[32] They also disconfirm the claim that OIRA review has substantial delay costs—that it has reduced the potential benefits from regulation by increasing the time required to move from the initial drafting of a proposed regulation to final issuance.[33]

Third, regulatory review often operates in an unfavorable statutory context. Many major environmental, health, and safety statutes in fact preclude agencies from selecting regulations using a cost-benefit test. (In such cases, as mentioned, the Presidential order setting up regulatory review requires agencies to prepare cost-benefit analyses as an informational matter but does not, of course, purport to require that agencies defy legislative supremacy.) It is hardly surprising that regulatory review, in these cases, would fail to yield a substantial increase in the net benefits of rules. Regulatory review coupled with statutes that confer more discretion on agencies, or affirmatively require a cost-benefit test, might well present a different picture.

Fourth, regulatory review institutionalizes a policy-evaluation methodology (currently CBA) via supervision by an external oversight body (OIRA) with close links to the President. Changes to this institutional structure might serve to increase the impact of the methodology (be it CBA or the SWF framework), to increase agency competence in utilizing it, to reduce its vulnerability to manipulation, and/or to reduce its decision and delay costs. For example, other external overseers, such as courts, or independent administrative bodies removed from the White House, might play a larger role in supervising the methodology. Efforts might also be undertaken to increase the staffing and resources of policy offices within agencies, and to create a "culture of analysis." Finally, of course, the range of institutional possibilities for implementing policy analysis in non-U.S. governments is different than in the U.S.

In short, existing scholarly research regarding regulatory review certainly does *not* suffice to demonstrate that legal structure L (requiring governmental officials to use SWFs as a decisionmaking tool) would be worse, in light of the SWF framework itself, than L^* (requiring some other procedure). But the controversy about regulatory review does sound a useful cautionary note. The comparison of L^* and L

[32] See Balla, Deets, and Maltzman (2006); Croley (2003).
[33] See Adler and Posner (2006, pp. 84–85); Shapiro (2009); Yackee and Yackee (2010).

must be sensitive to the range of political and bureaucratic factors that may potentially subvert the efficacy of policy analysis within government.

II. RELAXING THE POPULATION ASSUMPTION

The assumption of a fixed and finite population—the assumption adopted throughout this book—has simplified the development of the SWF approach. Moreover, this assumption may well be adequate for many policy contexts. But it is clearly *inadequate* for evaluating policy choices that substantially affect future generations, e.g., measures to address climate change. Such choices will, to some extent, determine who comes into being in the future (rather than merely harming or benefiting individuals who would exist regardless of which policy is undertaken), and will change the size of the population. Finally, it is plausible that, in considering future impacts, we should take account of the possibility that the world might continue indefinitely.

Each of these topics has generated a large scholarly literature, in moral philosophy and/or welfare economics.[34] These are not straightforward matters. In particular, refining the SWF framework to handle "non-identity" problems, variable populations, and infinite futures is no easy task. Here, I very briefly sketch the puzzles that these topics pose for the SWF framework. The puzzles arise, in some measure, for all SWFs, but to keep the discussion simple, I focus on the continuous prioritarian SWF.

The SWF framework might be coupled with a threshold initial decision to *limit* the population of interest to some *subset* of the world's intertemporal population (by which I mean all individuals who have existed, now exist, or will or might exist in the future). For example, the decisionmaker might focus on the utilities of U.S. citizens, or members of the current generation. However, ignoring persons' interests by virtue of social, physical, or temporal proximity is in serious tension (to say the least) with the impartiality characteristic of moral thinking. I thus assume, for purposes of this discussion, that the initial population of interest is the world's intertemporal population. The puzzles now to be described might force the decisionmaker to be partial to some subset of that population; but such partiality should not be assumed from the outset.

A. Non-identity Problems

For purposes of the SWF framework, as developed in this book, a policy choice situation involves a *fixed* population if the outcome set **O** is such that the same,

---

[34] I more fully discuss non-identity problems, variable populations, and infinite populations in Adler (2009b), and there cite the scholarly literatures on each topic. New scholarship on the first topic includes Arrhenius and Rabinowicz (2010) and Holtug (2010, ch. 9). Arrhenius (2011) is a major new work on the second topic. Since 2009, many new articles and working papers on infinite populations have appeared, which I will not attempt to collect here.

particular, individuals exist in every outcome in **O**. An individual "exists" in some outcome if she comes into being at some time, whether before or after the time of the decision at hand. For example, if some possible worlds are such that Alicia is born in the 23rd century, and outcome x—a simplified description of those worlds—includes the fact that Alicia is born in the 23rd century, then Alicia exists in outcome x.

Non-identity problems arise when the population is not fixed. An outcome set **O** has a non-fixed population where there are some individuals (one or more), each of whom exists in some but not all of the outcomes in **O**. Let us call such individuals "potential nonexistents."

It is important to distinguish between the population's being fixed versus non-fixed, in the sense just characterized, and the *size* of the population being the same or different in different outcomes. Clearly, if the population is *fixed*, the size of the population must be the same (either infinite in all outcomes or, if finite, the same finite number N). Thus, problems of variation in population size, to be reviewed in a moment, can arise only by virtue of a non-fixed population. On the other hand, a non-fixed population does not entail a variable population size. Imagine that there are two outcomes, x and y. Alicia exists in both. Bob exists in x but not y. Charles exists in y but not x. Then the size of the population is the same (two) in both outcomes, but the population is not fixed.

Assume, for simplicity, that the size of the population is finite in all outcomes, but the population is not fixed. How should the SWF framework handle potential nonexistents?

One, natural, thought is this: if i is a potential nonexistent in **O**, but exists in both outcomes x and y, then her well-being in the two outcomes should be fully considered in ranking them. However, if she does not exist in one of the two, her well-being in the other should be ignored in ranking the two outcomes. In other words, for each pair of outcomes in **O**, x and y, we should map each outcome onto a (set of)[35] utility vectors that include numerical entries *only* for individuals who exist in *both* outcomes—and then use an SWF to rank these (sets of) vectors.

Unfortunately, this approach can yield an intransitive ranking of the outcome set, as Table 8.1 illustrates.

Table 8.1 The Continuous Prioritarian SWF and Potential Nonexistents

	Outcome x	*Outcome y*	*Outcome z*
Henry	5r	6r	4r
Jane	NE	1r	4r
Sally	10r	10r	10r

---

[35] As the reader by now surely understands, because **U** is a whole set of utility functions, each outcome corresponds to a set of utility vectors—regardless of the particular methodology we employ for taking account of potential nonexistents.

In Table 8.1, Jane does not exist in x. Utility is unique up to a positive ratio transformation. Any continuous prioritarian SWF will rank the vector $(6r, 10r)$ over $(5r, 10r)$. It will rank the vector $(4r, 4r, 10r)$ over the vector $(6r, 1r, 10r)$, since the latter can be transformed via a Pigou–Dalton transfer into $(4r, 3r, 10r)$, and the former vector is obviously preferred to this vector. Finally, any continuous prioritarian SWF will rank the vector $(5r, 10r)$ over $(4r, 10r)$. So if we ignore Jane in comparing outcomes x and y, and x and z, we produce the intransitivity y better than x, z better than y, x better than z.

A different approach, which satisfies the minimal welfarist requirement of generating a quasiordering[36] of every outcome set, is to ignore potential nonexistents completely. Rank outcomes by assigning utilities only to those individuals who exist in every outcome. But this is very counterintuitive. (For example, it would typically mean wholly ignoring the interests of future generations.) If Sheila exists in x and y, and is better off in x than y, why does her nonexistence in some other outcome that might result deprive her of any claim in ranking these two outcomes?

Two other possibilities are "actualism," to rank **O** by considering the interests of those individuals who will actually exist; or to arrive at a series of rankings of **O**, one that considers only the interests of those who exist in x, a second that considers only the interests of those who exist in y, and so forth. Both also turn out to be problematic.

A better approach than all four of these, it would seem, is to rank each x/y pair by mapping x onto a (set of) utility vectors with numerical entries for all individuals who exist in x (regardless of whether they also exist in y); by mapping y onto a (set of) utility vectors with numerical entries for all individuals who exist in y (regardless of whether they also exist in x); and then by using an SWF to compare these (sets of) vectors.

But there are puzzles, here, too. Assume, first, that x and y are such that some individuals exist in x but not y, and vice versa, but the same total number of individuals, N, exist in both outcomes. In that case, we would map x onto a (set of) utility vectors with N numerical entries, y onto a (set of) vectors with N numerical entries, and use our SWF to rank the vectors the same way as in the fixed population case. For example, assume that the set **U** of utility functions is unique up to a positive ratio transformation; that David exists in both x and y, and has utility level $10r$ in both; that Earl exists in x and has utility level $12r$ in that outcome; and that Fred exists in y and has utility level $14r$ in that outcome. So x corresponds to the utility vector $(10r, 12r, NE)$ while y corresponds to the utility vector $(10r, NE, 14r)$.[37] We now compare the vectors "as if" we were comparing $(10r, 12r)$ and $(10r, 14r)$—in

---

[36] A quasiordering, of course, is transitive.
[37] David is represented by the first entry in both vectors, Earl by the second, Fred by the third; "NE" means that the individual does not exist.

which case the continuous prioritarian SWF (or any Paretian SWF) says that y is the better outcome.

But reconciling this verdict with the view of fairness adopted in this book—the claim-across-outcome view—is not straightforward. Why exactly is y a morally better outcome than x? The only person who would seem to have a claim in favor of y is Fred. (David, who exists in both outcomes, is equally well off in both. He has no claim either way. If 0 denotes a life history as good as nonexistence, then Earl in x is better off than nonexistence. Surely *he* doesn't have a claim in favor of y.) But how can Fred have a claim in favor of y? Claims are supposed to be valenced in terms of well-being. Thus if Fred has a claim in favor of y, then he must be better off in y than x, hence worse off in x than y. But how can Fred be worse off in x than y? After all, he doesn't exist in x at all!

The methodology for assigning utilities to life-histories, developed in Chapter 3, and presupposed in this example, involves the use of nonexistence as a zero point and the "zeroing out" of **U** by including only utility functions that assign the number 0 to nonexistence. In particular, that methodology requires eliciting individuals' fully informed, fully rational preferences vis-à-vis nonexistence. It should be stressed that the puzzle now under discussion arises *even if* this "zeroing out" methodology is coherent (as I believe it is). It is one thing to ask an existing person whether she is indifferent between a possible life she might lead and nonexistence. It is quite another to say that, were an individual not to exist, she would be worse off (or better off) than not existing. Who would have the property of being worse or better off?

I think there *are* two reasonably plausible solutions to the current problem. (1) We might analyze well-being comparisons as necessitating only the existence of the individual at issue in at least one of the two outcomes being compared. In other words, "Sue is worse off in w than z" entails that *either* (a) were w to occur, Sue would exist and would be worse off than were z to occur, *or* (b) were z to occur, Sue would exist and would be better off than were w to occur. It does not entail that both (a) and (b) are true. (An exactly parallel analysis would be given for the statement that "Sue is better off in w than z.") (2) Alternatively, we might weaken the connection between claims and well-being, conceding that Sue's being better or worse off in w than z does entail her existence in w, but arguing that Sue can have a *claim* for z over w as long as *either* she is better off in z than w or worse off in w than z.

However, neither solution is an evident slam dunk. Defending either one requires close attention to the logical structure of comparative statements and modal statements (statements that involve different possible worlds).

Even if one of these solutions *is* adopted, a whole new crop of puzzles arise once we allow for variable population size. Let us tweak the case by imagining that *Gene* exists in y at level $3r$. So x corresponds to the utility vector $(10r, 12r, NE, NE)$—the two "NE"s denoting Fred and Gene, who do not exist in x, while y corresponds to the utility vector $(10r, NE, 14r, 3r)$. How are we supposed to use a continuous prioritarian SWF to rank utility vectors with different numbers of numerical entries?

B. Variable Population Size

There is an array of possible rules for using an SWF to rank utility vectors with different numbers of numerical entries. Charles Blackorby, Walter Bossert, and David Donaldson have provided a magisterial treatment of this topic in their book, *Population Issues in Social Choice Theory*.[38] Here, I mention the three most straightforward methodologies. Throughout, let $N(x)$ denote the number of individuals who exist in x, $N(y)$ in y, etc. And let the summation term, such as $\sum_{i=1}^{N(x)} g(u_i(x))$, mean the sum of utilities for all the individuals who exist in x, with nonexisting individuals left out of the summation or, equivalently, given a utility of zero.

One approach, in the case of the continuous prioritarian SWF, is to calculate the total sum of transformed utility for each outcome. Call this "total prioritarianism." It says: x is at least as good as y iff, for all $u(.)$ in **U**, $\sum_{i=1}^{N(x)} g(u_i(x)) \geq \sum_{i=1}^{N(y)} g(u_i(y))$. It is analogous to a well-known version of utilitarianism—"total utilitarianism"—which, in SWF form, uses the same formula but summing straight rather than transformed utilities.

In a seminal discussion, Derek Parfit criticizes total utilitarianism for leading to the "repugnant conclusion," which can be framed as follows.[39] Imagine some life-history, as excellent as you like. Imagine now a second life-history, better than nonexistence but perhaps only minimally so. With utility (for simplicity) unique up to a positive ratio transformation, imagine that the well-being level of the first is rU and the second rU^*, where rU^* is some arbitrarily small fraction of rU. Consider now an outcome x in which N individuals enjoy lives as good as the excellent life-history. The repugnant conclusion, for total utilitarianism, is that there may exist some outcome y in which everyone is at the well-being level of the horrible life, and yet y is still morally better than x. How is this possible? Simply imagine that there are M individuals in outcome y, where M is some number greater than NU/U^*.

In short, total utilitarianism allows for increases in population size to morally outweigh drastic reductions in the average quality of life—and that seems, well, repugnant.

Total prioritarianism faces the same difficulty. Indeed, it can be shown that the repugnant conclusion is *more* serious for total prioritarians. In the case just described, the total prioritarian will *also* recognize some break-even population size for y, which if exceeded means that y is morally better than x; and that break-even size will be *less* than the total utilitarian's break-even (NU/U^*).

One methodology that avoids the repugnant conclusion is "average" prioritarianism, analogous to "average" utilitarianism: ranking outcomes by looking to average transformed utility. In other words, x is at least as good as y iff, for all $u(.)$ in **U**, $(1/N(x)) \sum_{i=1}^{N(x)} g(u_i(x)) \geq (1/N(y)) \sum_{i=1}^{N(y)} g(u_i(y))$. A second methodology that

[38] Blackorby, Bossert, and Donaldson (2005).
[39] See Parfit (1987, pt. 4, ch. 17).

does so is "critical level" prioritarianism. Identify some cutoff life-history $(x^+; i^+)$ better than nonexistence. (The idea is that a life-history worse than $(x^+; i^+)$, even if better for the subject than nonexistence, is sufficiently bad that expanding the population size by adding individuals this badly off makes the outcome morally worse, not better.) Assign $(x^+; i^+)$ an arbitrary positive number C; winnow down U to include only utility functions that assign C to $(x^+; i^+)$; and rank outcomes using the rule: x is at least as good as y iff, for all $u(.)$ in U,

$$\sum_{i=1}^{N(x)}[g(u_i(x))-g(C)] \geq \sum_{i=1}^{N(y)}[g(u_i(y))-g(C)].$$

Each of these latter approaches, however, faces its own serious difficulties. Average prioritarianism violates separability: the ranking of outcomes with different population sizes is not invariant to the well-being level of individuals who exist in both outcomes and are equally well off in both. It also violates what Blackorby, Bossert, and Donaldson call the "negative expansion principle," which stipulates that adding an individual whose life is worse than nonexistence should not morally improve an outcome. Critical-level prioritarianism, although satisfying both separability and the "negative expansion principle," has the upshot that an outcome in which everyone's life is better than nonexistence can be worse than an outcome (with a different population size) in which everyone's life is worse than nonexistence.

Perhaps, on reflection, total prioritarianism ought to be endorsed. The claim-across-outcome view might suggest as much. In x, some number of individuals are at well-being level rU; in y, some larger number are at well-being level rU^*, which is an arbitrarily small fraction of the first level. If someone can indeed have a claim across a pair of outcomes even though she exists in only one, then the picture is this: Some individuals (those at well-being level rU in x) have a claim in favor of x over y; but some individuals (those who do not exist in x and are at well-being level rU^* in y) have a claim in favor of y over x. After all, they are badly off in y, but better off than nonexistence. Why is it inconceivable that, with the number of such individuals sufficiently large, their claims could outweigh those who have a moral interest in x obtaining? The continuous prioritarian SWF employs an additive structure for counting claims in fixed population cases. Why then isn't the unalloyed summation of claims—total prioritarianism—the correct structure for comparing outcomes with different population sizes?

However, many in the literature seem to see the repugnant conclusion as the reductio ad absurdum of a proposed approach to variable-population cases; and much more work would be needed to demonstrate that it indeed follows from deeper commitments (the idea of claims across outcomes) that are worth preserving.

C. Infinite Populations

Notwithstanding the now-voluminous scholarship on infinite populations, the reader might be skeptical of the problem's import. "The population of human persons, at any one time, on earth or the other regions of the universe eventually colonized by humans, will be finite; and this population will eventually become extinct. So how can an infinite population arise?" One possible answer is that an infinite population is a heuristic that renders analysis more tractable in certain respects.[40] A second is that there is some non-zero probability of time continuing indefinitely and the human population never becoming extinct—so that the problem, at least for completeness, needs to be engaged.

Shifting from a fixed, finite population to an infinite population calls into question the *anonymity* axiom.[41] In the case of a fixed, finite population, that axiom is a straightforward way to capture the moral requirement of impartiality. If the pattern of well-being in outcome x is the same as the pattern of well-being in outcome y, save for the names of the individuals involved, then anonymity requires that an SWF rank x and y as equally morally good. Formulated as a constraint on the ranking of utility vectors (all of which have the same finite number of entries, i.e., N, the population size in all outcomes), anonymity says: if vector $u(x)$ is a permutation of vector $u(y)$ then an SWF (of the simple R-based form) must contain a rule R that ranks $u(x)$ and $u(y)$ as equally good.[42]

Relatedly, in the case of a fixed, finite population, interpersonal discounting— applying a discount factor to each individual's utility, to reflect his birth date—is very hard to defend. The axiom of anonymity captures the concept of impartiality; and interpersonal discounting, in turn, violates anonymity.[43]

Moral impartiality becomes trickier to formulate with an infinite population. Much of the literature regarding infinite populations focuses on how to rank infinite utility *streams*, where each stream starts with an initial period, continues indefinitely, and has a single utility number in each period. Assume, then, that each outcome corresponds to such a stream, and that utility is unique up to a positive ratio transformation. In other words, $u(x)$ is an infinite sequence of numbers such as $(1r, 10r, 13r, \ldots)$. The number in each period might be thought of as representing the lifetime well-being level of individuals who exist just in that period, with this within-period population being homogeneous (all individuals have the same lifetime well-being) and the same size in all periods. These assumptions about the within-period population

---

[40] Economic analysis in a number of areas assumes an infinity of items, often for tractability reasons. (For example, the assumption may allow the use of calculus techniques to identify optima.) Indeed, it should be noted that standard optimal-tax models often assume an infinite population—not by virtue of an infinite sequence of periods (the focus of the literature under discussion in this subsection), but rather by virtue of a continuum of "types" of individuals, varying in their abilities. See sources cited Chapter 4, n. 9.

[41] How anonymity should be formulated for the case of a population which is finite but not fixed is yet another question, which I leave aside.

[42] A permutation function $\sigma(.)$ is a one-to-one, onto function that maps some set onto itself. Let $\sigma(.)$ be a permutation function defined on the set of N individuals. Then utility vector $u(y)$ is a permutation of utility vector $u(x)$ if the utility assigned to individual i by $u(x)$ is assigned to individual $\sigma(i)$ by $u(y)$.

[43] See Chapter 6, pp. 422–423; Adler (2009b, pp. 1492–1494).

are, of course, quite simplified—but formulating an impartiality requirement is challenging even in this case.

It is tempting just to extrapolate the anonymity axiom to this case, by saying: if infinite stream $u(x)$ is a permutation of infinite stream $u(y)$, then the SWF must rank $u(x)$ and $u(y)$ as equally good. For short, call this "strong anonymity for the infinite case."

One of the most striking results about infinite populations is that strong anonymity for the infinite case is *incompatible* with the principle of Pareto-superiority, as Table 8.2 shows.

Table 8.2 Infinite Utility Streams: Strong Anonymity versus Pareto Superiority

	Period									
	1	2	3	4	5	6	7	8	9	...
Outcome x	1	3/2	1/3	7/4	1/5	11/6	1/7	15/8	1/9	
Outcome y	1	7/4	3/2	11/6	1/3	15/8	1/5	19/10	1/7	

The utility streams corresponding to x and y (without the "r") are shown. The stream corresponding to x is produced by taking the alternating sequence 0, 1/2, −2/3, 3/4, −4/5, 5/6 ... and adding 1 to each term. The stream corresponding to y is a permutation of the x stream, produced as follows: keep the first term in place, shift the second (3/2) one to the right, and for every other term shift it two to the right if its denominator is odd, otherwise two to the left.

But note that the y stream is Pareto-superior to the x stream! In the first period, utilities are equal; and in every other period, the y utility is larger.

The Paretian welfarist might be tempted to conclude that interpersonal discounting is morally justifiable in the infinite case. In particular, the continuous prioritarian SWF with interpersonal discounting would say: Stream $u(x)$ is at least as good as $u(y)$ iff $\sum_{t=1}^{\infty} E(t)g(ru_t(x)) \geq \sum_{t=1}^{\infty} E(t)g(ru_t(y))$.[44] Indeed, interpersonal discounting with an infinite future is the approach typically adopted in so-called "optimal growth" scholarship.[45]

---

[44] In this formula, $E(.)$ is the discount factor, a decreasing function of time; and $u_t(x)$ is the utility in period t in outcome x, unique up to a positive ratio transformation. The $g(.)$ function will need to be Atkinsonian for this formula to be invariant to the value of r. With an appropriate $E(.)$ function and utility values in the streams, the infinite sums in this formula will converge.

[45] See, e.g., Fleurbaey and Michel (2003, pp. 777–778).

Note that the continuous prioritarian SWF with interpersonal discounting fails even a much less demanding anonymity requirement than the strong requirement just formulated. Call this "weak anonymity" for the infinite case: it says if infinite stream $u(x)$ is a *finite* permutation of infinite stream $u(y)$, i.e., the two are permutations of each other *and* identical except for a finite number of values, then the two streams are equally morally good. There are methodologies for applying the continuous prioritarian SWF to infinite streams that eschew a discount factor; satisfy the principle of Pareto-superiority; and satisfy weak anonymity. For example, the prioritarian "overtaking" criterion does so.[46]

Indeed, there are versions of anonymity for the infinite case that are "in between" weak anonymity and strong anonymity, and that—like weak anonymity—are consistent with the principle of Pareto-superiority.[47] In order to outfit a continuous prioritarian SWF for the case of an infinite population, we need to articulate these different possible specifications of the anonymity axiom; the different possible specifications of the other axioms constitutive of continuous prioritarianism in the fixed, finite case (separability, Pigou–Dalton, continuity, Pareto-indifference, and Pareto-superiority); and to understand which axiom packages are logically possible and which are incompatible. This is, evidently, a large task, and not one I can even begin to undertake here.

III. RESPONSIBILITY

A central theme in philosophical scholarship concerning equality and distributive justice, beginning with two seminal articles by Ronald Dworkin from the early 1980s, has been that any plausible conception of fair distribution needs to incorporate considerations of responsibility.[48] It needs to distinguish between individuals who are responsible for being badly off and those who are badly off through no fault of their own. For short, call this the "responsibility insight."

This insight (as I have acknowledged throughout the book) constitutes a powerful critique of welfarism and thus, specifically, of the SWF approach—a version of welfarism. The SWF approach makes the ranking of outcomes just a function of utility vectors, measuring well-being. Outcomes that are identical in their patterns of well-being, but differ in their responsibility facts, must be ranked as equal.[49] This is

---

[46] This criterion says: outcome x is at least as good as outcome y iff there is some value T^* such that, for all times T greater than T^*, $\sum_{t=1}^{T} g(ru_t(x)) \geq \sum_{t=1}^{T} g(ru_t(y))$.

[47] See Fleurbaey and Michel (2003).

[48] Dworkin (1981a, 1981b). Much of the subsequent literature is cited in Barry (2008).

[49] One might, in principle, develop a well-being account such that an individual's well-being is itself, in part, determined by how responsible she is. But—whatever the plausibility of such an account—it seems clear that responsibility facts should directly figure in the ranking of outcomes, and not merely indirectly via their possible effect on well-being.

problematic. As Richard Arneson observed, in an influential article concurring in Dworkin's critique of equality-of-welfare as a conception of distributive justice:

> Individuals can arrive at different welfare levels due to choices they make for which they alone should be held responsible. A simple example would be to imagine two persons of identical tastes and abilities who are assigned equal resources by an agency charged to maintain distributive equality. The two then voluntarily engage in high-stakes gambling, from which one emerges rich . . . and the other poor. . . . In [another] example, one person may voluntarily cultivate an expensive preference . . ., while another person does not. In [these] examples it would be inappropriate to insist upon equality of welfare when welfare inequality arises through the voluntary choice of the person who gets lesser welfare.[50]

The responsibility insight might motivate moral views that are far removed from the SWF approach. For example, Dworkin famously rejects the view that justice is concerned with the distribution of well-being, as measured using some scale that allows for interpersonal welfare comparisons, and instead argues for "equality of resources" (more specifically, an allocation of resources patterning the insurance payouts and premia that would flow from individual choices in a hypothetical insurance market with equal endowments). But it is not clear why someone who is *otherwise* attracted to the idea of a distributively sensitive SWF—who believes that the moral ranking of actions should be a function of their outcomes, that well-being is indeed interpersonally comparable, that the project of inferring utilities from ordinary preference data (or some other evidentiary source) is a feasible one, and so forth—should see the responsibility insight as grounds for abandoning, rather than refining, the SWF framework.

Indeed, Arneson's chief contribution in the article just mentioned was to propose a responsibility-sensitive *competitor* to Dworkin's notion of equal resources—namely, the criterion of equal opportunity for welfare.

> Equal opportunity for welfare obtains among persons when all of them face equivalent decision trees—the expected value of each person's best . . . choice of options, second-best, . . . nth best, is the same. The opportunities persons encounter are ranked by the prospects for welfare they afford. . . .
>
> . . . We may say that in an extended sense people share equal opportunity for welfare just in case there is some time at which their opportunities are equal and if any inequalities in their opportunities at later times are due to their voluntary choice or differentially negligent behavior. . . .[51]

---

[50] Arneson (1989, pp. 83–84).
[51] Ibid., pp. 85–86.

Arneson also makes clear that the calculation of the expected welfare value of each person's various options involves an interpersonally comparable metric of well-being.

Arneson, here, offered a first-best criterion, rather than a full account of how to rank policies or outcomes. How should a decisionmaker advance distributive justice when no option available to her yields complete equality of opportunity for all members of the population?

John Roemer proposes to answer this question. Inspired by Arneson's suggestion that opportunity for well-being might be the "currency" for distributive justice, Roemer—over the last 15 years—has developed and empirically implemented the following policy-evaluation framework.[52] There is some interpersonally comparable measure $\xi(.)$ of individual attainment. This $\xi(.)$ measure is not *necessarily* an inter-comparable measure of *well-being*—but it *can* be, in which case Roemer's methodology becomes a kind of social welfare function. The population of individuals is categorized in two overlapping ways. First, the population is partitioned into different "types." A given "type" is some combination of "circumstances": circumstances are an individual's attributes, or background facts, for which she is not responsible. (An individual's race or the educational attainment of her parents are paradigmatic "circumstances.") Second, the population is partitioned into different "effort" classes. The term "effort" is a bit misleading; in Roemer's methodology, it means any individual attribute for which individuals are properly held responsible. Which attributes fall into the "effort" category is, clearly, disputable; the framework itself is agnostic on the issue. For example, it might be argued that smokers are responsible for the bad health outcomes that result from smoking, and thus—in an application of the Roemer methodology to health policy—that smoking should be categorized as low "effort" and non-smoking as high "effort." Alternatively, an individual's smoking status could be categorized as a "circumstance"—on the grounds that smoking results from nicotine addiction or, if not, is caused by factors for which individuals lack responsibility, such as genetic predisposition, parental behaviors, or socioeconomic class, and thus is not itself a responsibility factor.[53]

The attainment of each individual depends upon the policy, her effort, and her type. Each policy is assigned a number, using an additive-minimum formula; the policy with the largest such number is selected. The additive-minimum formula determines, for each effort class, the lowest $\xi(.)$ value attained by any type, given the policy; and then sums these minimum values across effort classes.

---

[52] See, e.g., Llavador and Roemer (2001); Roemer (1998, 2002, 2003); Roemer et al. (2003). Roemer expresses his debt to Arneson in Roemer (2009, p. 32). On Roemer's approach as well as Van de gaer's (see text below), see Fleurbaey (2008, ch. 8); Hild and Voorhoeve (2004); Ooghe, Schokkaert, and Van de gaer (2007).

[53] In addition, Roemer assigns each individual an effort level by looking to the distribution of effort within her type. This aspect of the methodology has been criticized, and my translation of the Roemer rule into an SWF will be agnostic as to how effort levels are assigned.

Roemer's methodology is readily translated into the SWF framework, as developed in this book. It becomes a rule for ranking outcomes, with the attainment measure $\xi(.)$ provided by utility functions in the set $\mathbf{U}$. Assume that there are E different effort classes. Each such class is a particular combination of attributes for which individuals are held responsible. A given individual might fall into one effort class in one outcome, a different effort class in a different outcome. (For example, if smoking qualifies as an effort, then she might smoke in one outcome but not another.) Let $\mathbf{R}_e(x)$ denote the set of individuals in effort class e in outcome x. Then the Roemer SWF says: outcome x is at least as good as outcome y iff, for all $u(.)$ in $\mathbf{U}$, $\sum_{e=1}^{E} \min_{i \in \mathbf{R}_e(x)} u_i(x) \geq \sum_{e=1}^{E} \min_{i \in \mathbf{R}_e(y)} u_i(y)$. The term " $\min_{i \in \mathbf{R}_e(x)} u_i(x)$ " means the lowest utility (according to $u(.)$) attained by anyone within effort class $\mathbf{R}_e$ in outcome x.

I should note that Roemer is certainly not the only economist to be engaged by the project of developing responsibility-sensitive metrics and methodologies. A substantial body of theoretical and empirical work has focused on this topic in recent years.[54] Some of this work avoids interpersonal well-being comparisons; but other approaches build from the social-welfare-function tradition, or at least are readily translated into an SWF. I focus on Roemer's work, here, because it is a prominent example of scholarship in this latter category. Its details can be disputed; but it provides, at least, an excellent starting point for discussions about the appropriate structure of a responsibility-sensitive SWF.

The Roemer SWF seems closer to the leximin SWF (in focusing on the worst-off individual in each effort class) than to the continuous prioritarian SWF.[55] But the Roemer SWF can readily be revised to incorporate the continuous prioritarian formula. For each effort class, in a given outcome, assign it a number equaling the sum of transformed utilities for individuals in that class—rather than the minimum utility in that class. Then map the outcome onto an overall value as a function of these numbers. Formally, let $w^e(u(x)) = \sum_{i \in \mathbf{R}_e(x)} g(u_i(x))$. Then each outcome maps onto a vector with E entries (for E effort classes), $(w^1(u(x)), w^2(u(x)), \ldots, w^E(u(x)))$. And the SWF says: outcome x is at least as good as outcome y iff, for all $u(.)$ in $\mathbf{U}$, $F(w^1(u(x)), w^2(u(x)), \ldots, w^E(u(x))) \geq F(w^1(u(y)), w^2(u(y)), \ldots, w^E(u(y)))$. The aggregator function, F, might have a variety of different forms. For example, it might be linear (multiplying the $w(.)$ value for each effort class by a weight, and then summing these weighted values) or, instead, non-linear.[56]

In Chapter 5, I defended the continuous prioritarian SWF for the idealized, "brute luck" case in which no individual bears responsibility, in any outcome, for her

[54] For an overview of this work, as well as a major contribution, see Fleurbaey (2008). Another growing body of economic literature seeks to develop criteria for ranking opportunity sets, but without reference to responsibility considerations. For an overview, see Peragine (1999).

[55] Arneson himself has gravitated toward responsibility-adjusted, non-leximin, prioritarianism. See Arneson (1999a, 2000a, 2000b, 2007).

[56] On possible modifications of the Roemer approach, see Moreno-Ternero (2007); Ooghe, Schokkaert, and Van de gaer (2007); Rodríguez (2008).

shortfall between her well-being level in that outcome and a higher level. In other words, I assumed that, in every outcome, every individual is in the highest "effort" class (or equivalently, that $E = 1$); and considered different possible functional forms for an SWF given that idealizing assumption. The reader persuaded by the argumentation in Chapter 5 might see the formula set forth in the previous paragraph as an appropriate *generalization* of the continuous prioritarian SWF to accommodate the more general (and of course, much more realistic case) in which some individuals in some outcomes are responsible for being less well off than they might have been. (Note that, in the "brute luck" case, this formula produces the same ranking of outcomes as the familiar formula, x is at least as good as y iff, for all $u(.)$ in U, $\sum_{i=1}^{N} g(u_i(x)) \geq \sum_{i=1}^{N} g(u_i(y))$.[57])

However, there are at least two other templates for a responsibility-sensitive continuous prioritarian SWF that also seem plausible. One possibility builds on work by Dirk Van de gaer.[58] Assume that, in each outcome, we assign each "type" a type-specific utility—as some function (additive or not) of the utilities of all the individuals, at various effort levels within that type, in that outcome. There are C types in total. Let $v_c(u(x))$ denote the type-specific utility assigned to "type" class c, in outcome x, with $u(.)$ as the individual utility function. We then apply the continuous prioritarian formula to these type-specific utilities. In other words, we say: outcome x is at least as good as outcome y iff, for all $u(.)$ in U,
$$\sum_{c=1}^{C} g(v_c(u(x))) \geq \sum_{c=1}^{C} g(v_c(u(y))).$$

Finally, we might *normalize* each individual's utility in each outcome—assigning her the utility that she would have realized, had she behaved as responsibly as is reasonable to expect.[59] Formally, let e^* be the "reference" effort class. And let $u_i^{e^*}(x)$ be the utility that individual i would have achieved in x, according to $u(.)$, had her effort been e^* (or her actual utility, if that is greater). Of course, how to define $u_i^{e^*}(x)$ is a challenging problem. Do we ask how individual i herself fares in other outcomes where her effort is at e^*? How other individuals with the same type as i, but at effort e^*, fare in x—or, if there are no such individuals in x, individuals with a sufficiently similar type? But assume that we can specify a plausible methodology for arriving at these normalized utility values. We can then incorporate them into the continuous prioritarian formula. In other words, outcome x is at least as good as outcome y iff, for all $u(.)$ in U, $\sum_{i=1}^{N} g(u_i^{e^*}(x)) \geq \sum_{i=1}^{N} g(u_i^{e^*}(y))$. Most starkly, if e^* is set equal to E—the effort level of the group with the highest effort—each individual is held accountable for any shortfall between her well-being, and the well-being she would have achieved had she behaved in a fully responsible fashion.

---

[57] Strictly, the two formulas produce the same ranking in the "brute luck" case only if F is strictly increasing in $w^F(.)$, if not in general then at least in the case where everyone in the population in both outcomes is in the highest effort class, E. But surely F should have this feature.

[58] See above, n. 52.

[59] See the discussion of "conditional equality" in Fleurbaey (2008).

Note that each of these three, different, templates for a responsibility-sensitive, continuous prioritarian SWF produces a ranking of outcomes. That ranking can then be merged with EU theory (as refined to accommodate the possibility of an incomplete outcome ordering, imprecise probabilities, etc.) to rank choices. The paragraph from Arneson's pioneering discussion of equal opportunity for welfare, quoted earlier, might seem to suggest that the responsibility-adjusted welfarist needs to abandon EU theory, and focus instead upon the *expected* well-being that each individual would realize, were she to behave more or less responsibly. This seems to point toward a responsibility-adjusted version of ex ante prioritarianism. But no such move away from the EU approach is required. EU theory can be used as bridge principles for a responsibility-sensitive continuous prioritarian SWF—just as it can (and should be) used as bridge principles for the ordinary continuous prioritarian SWF without responsibility adjustments, as I argued in Chapter 7.

Evidently, the project of reconstructing an SWF so as to incorporate considerations of responsibility—be it the continuous prioritarian SWF or some other—raises large, new, problems that this book has not addressed. To begin, and most profoundly, what *are* the characteristics for which individuals are properly held responsible? How *are* individuals to be sorted into "effort" classes? Which aspects of a life-history are properly categorized as "brute luck," and which as "option luck"? These kinds of questions, implicating one of the deepest philosophical puzzles—free will—are deeply contested.

Second, and somewhat more technically, how exactly should we combine information about individual utility and individual "effort" to arrive at a ranking of outcomes? In the case of the continuous prioritarian SWF, I have just suggested, there are least three methodologies for doing so. How should each be specified? (For example, if we employ the first template, what should the aggregator function be? If the second, how should we arrive at type-specific utility? If the third, how should we normalize each individual's utility to reflect the utility she would have received, if her effort were at some reference level?) Are there further possibilities? And which, on balance, is most attractive?

Anyone hoping to defend the SWF methodology as a fully adequate choice-evaluation framework must, ultimately, confront these problems. The continuous prioritarian formula presented in this book, because it fails to make adjustment in any way for individual responsibility, can only be seen—in my view—as an imperfect and approximate methodology. Unfortunately, the task of confronting the problems, and perfecting the methodology, must be left to another day. This book, however incomplete, is now at its end.

BIBLIOGRAPHY

Abbey, R. 2007. "Rawlsian Resources for Animal Ethics." *Ethics and the Environment* 12: 1–22.

Abdellaoui, M., C. Barrios, and P.P. Wakker. 2007. "Reconciling Introspective Utility with Revealed Preference: Experimental Arguments Based on Prospect Theory." *Journal of Econometrics* 138: 356–378.

Acemoglu, D. 2009. *Introduction to Modern Economic Growth*. Princeton: Princeton University Press.

Ackerman, F., and L. Heinzerling. 2004. *Priceless: On Knowing the Price of Everything and the Value of Nothing*. New York: New Press.

Adler, M.D. 2005. "Against 'Individual Risk': A Sympathetic Critique of Risk Assessment." *University of Pennsylvania Law Review* 153: 1121–1250.

———. 2006a. "QALYs and Policy Evaluation: A New Perspective." *Yale Journal of Health Policy, Law, and Ethics* 6: 1–92.

———. 2006b. "Welfare Polls: A Synthesis." *New York University Law Review* 81: 1875–1970.

———. 2007. "Well-Being, Inequality and Time: The Time-Slice Problem and Its Policy Implications." Institute for Law and Economics Research Paper No. 07–17, Public Law and Legal Theory Research Paper No. 07–30, University of Pennsylvania Law School, July 2007. http://papers.ssrn.com/30l3/papers.cfm?abstract_id=1006871.

———. 2008. "Risk Equity: A New Proposal." *Harvard Environmental Law Review* 32: 1–47.

———. 2009a. "Bounded Rationality and Legal Scholarship." In M.D. White, ed., *Theoretical Foundations of Law and Economics*, pp. 137–162. Cambridge: Cambridge University Press.

———. 2009b. "Future Generations: A Prioritarian View." *George Washington Law Review* 77: 1478–1520.

Adler, M.D., and E.A. Posner. 2006. *New Foundations of Cost-Benefit Analysis*. Cambridge, MA: Harvard University Press.

Adler, M.D., and C.W. Sanchirico. 2006. "Inequality and Uncertainty: Theory and Legal Applications." *University of Pennsylvania Law Review* 155: 279–377.

Alberini, A., A. Longo, and M. Veronesi. 2007. "Basic Statistical Models for Stated Choice Studies." In B.J. Kanninen, ed., *Valuing Environmental Amenities Using Stated Choice Studies: A Common Sense Approach to Theory and Practice*, pp. 203–227. Dordrecht: Springer.

Alexander, L. 1991. "The Gap." *Harvard Journal of Law and Public Policy* 14: 695–702.

Alexander, L., and E. Sherwin. 2001. *The Rule of Rules: Morality, Rules, and the Dilemmas of Law*. Durham: Duke University Press.

Alkire, S. 2002. *Valuing Freedoms: Sen's Capability Approach and Poverty Reduction*. Oxford: Oxford University Press.

Alkire, S., and J. Foster. 2011. "Counting and Multidimensional Poverty Measurement." *Journal of Public Economics* 95: 476–487.

Al-Najjar, N.I., and J. Weinstein. 2009. "The Ambiguity Aversion Literature: A Critical Assessment." *Economics and Philosophy* 25: 249–284.

Amiel, Y., and F.A. Cowell. 1999. *Thinking about Inequality: Personal Judgment and Income Distributions*. Cambridge: Cambridge University Press.

Amiel, Y., F.A. Cowell, and W. Gaertner. 2009. "To Be or Not to Be Involved: A Questionnaire-Experimental View on Harsanyi's Utilitarian Ethics." *Social Choice and Welfare* 32: 299–316.

Amiel, Y., J. Creedy, and S. Hurn. 1999. "Measuring Attitudes towards Inequality." *The Scandinavian Journal of Economics* 101: 83–96.

Anderson, E. 1993. *Value in Ethics and Economics*. Cambridge, MA: Harvard University Press.

Anderson, G. 2005. "Life Expectancy and Economic Welfare: The Example of Africa in the 1990s." *Review of Income and Wealth* 51: 455–468.

Anderson, J., A.G. Roy, and P. Shoemaker. 2003. "Confidence Intervals for the Suits Index." *National Tax Journal* 56: 81–90.

Andersson, F., and C.H. Lyttkens. 1999. "Preferences for Equity in Health behind a Veil of Ignorance." *Health Economics* 8: 369–378.

Andreou, C. 2005. "Incommensurable Alternatives and Rational Choice." *Ratio* 18: 249–261.

Anscombe, F.J., and R.J. Aumann. 1963. "A Definition of Subjective Probability." *The Annals of Mathematical Statistics* 34: 199–205.

Anthoff, D., C. Hepburn, and R.S.J. Tol. 2009. "Equity Weighting and the Marginal Damage Costs of Climate Change." *Ecological Economics* 68: 836–849.

Ariely, D., and Z. Carmon. 2003. "Summary Assessment of Experiences: The Whole Is Different from the Sum of Its Parts." In G. Loewenstein, D. Read, and R. Baumeister, eds., *Time and Decision: Economic and Psychological Perspectives on Intertemporal Choice*, pp. 323–349. New York: Russell Sage Foundation.

Arneson, R.J. 1989. "Equality and Equal Opportunity for Welfare." *Philosophical Studies: An International Journal for Philosophy in the Analytic Tradition* 56: 77–93.

———. 1990. "Liberalism, Distributive Subjectivism, and Equal Opportunity for Welfare." *Philosophy and Public Affairs* 19: 158–194.

———. 1999a. "Egalitarianism and Responsibility." *The Journal of Ethics* 3: 225–247.

———. 1999b. "Human Flourishing versus Desire Satisfaction." In E.F. Paul, F.D. Miller, and J. Paul, eds., *Human Flourishing*, pp. 113–142. Cambridge: Cambridge University Press.

———. 2000a. "Perfectionism and Politics." *Ethics* 111: 37–63.

———. 2000b. "Welfare Should Be the Currency of Justice." *Canadian Journal of Philosophy* 30: 497–524.

———. 2005. "Sophisticated Rule Consequentialism: Some Simple Objections." *Philosophical Issues* 15: 235–251.

———. 2006. "Desire Formation and Human Good." In S. Olsaretti, ed., *Preferences and Well-Being*, pp. 9–32. Cambridge: Cambridge University Press.

———. 2007. "Desert and Equality." In N. Holtug and K. Lippert-Rasmussen, eds., *Egalitarianism: New Essays on the Nature and Value of Equality*, pp. 262–293. Oxford: Clarendon Press.

Aronsson, T., and O. Johansson-Stenman. 2008. "When the Joneses' Consumption Hurts: Optimal Public Good Provision and Nonlinear Income Taxation." *Journal of Public Economics* 92: 986–997.

Arrhenius, G. 2011. *Population Ethics: The Challenge of Future Generations*. Oxford: Oxford University Press (forthcoming).

Arrhenius, G., and W. Rabinowicz. 2010. "Better to Be Than Not to Be?" In H. Joas and B. Klein, eds., *The Benefit of Broad Horizons: Intellectual and Institutional Preconditions for a Global Social Science*, pp. 399–414. Leiden: Koninklijke Brill NV.

Arrow, K.J. 1963. *Social Choice and Individual Values.* 2nd edition. New Haven: Yale University Press.

———. 1977. "Extended Sympathy and the Possibility of Social Choice." *The American Economic Review* 67: 219–225.

Atkinson, A.B. 1970. "On the Measurement of Inequality." *Journal of Economic Theory* 2: 244–263.

———. 1983. *Social Justice and Public Policy.* Cambridge, MA: MIT Press.

Attanasio, O.P., and M. Browning. 1995. "Consumption over the Life Cycle and over the Business Cycle." *The American Economic Review* 85: 1118–1137.

Auerbach, A.J., L.J. Kotlikoff, and J. Skinner. 1983. "The Efficiency Gains from Dynamic Tax Reform." *International Economic Review* 24: 81–100.

Aumann, R.J. 1987. "Correlated Equilibrium as an Expression of Bayesian Rationality." *Econometrica* 55: 1–18.

Aumann, R.J., and A. Brandenburger. 1995. "Epistemic Conditions for Nash Equilibrium." *Econometrica* 63: 1161–1180.

Baker, L.R. 2000. *Persons and Bodies: A Constitution View.* Cambridge: Cambridge University Press.

Bales, R.E. 1971. "Act-Utilitarianism: Account of Right-Making Characteristics or Decision-Making Procedure?" *American Philosophical Quarterly* 8: 257–265.

Balla, S.J, J.M. Deets, and F. Maltzman. 2006. "Outside Communication and OMB Review of Agency Regulations." Working paper, presented at the Annual Meeting of the Midwest Political Science Association, Chicago, April 2006.

Banks, J., R. Blundell, and A. Lewbel. 1996. "Tax Reform and Welfare Measurement: Do We Need Demand System Estimation?" *The Economic Journal* 106: 1227–1241.

Barbarà, S., and M. Jackson. 1988. "Maximin, Leximin, and the Protective Criterion: Characterizations and Comparisons." *Journal of Economic Theory* 46: 34–44. The first author's name is misspelled in the journal; the correct spelling is "Barberà."

Barberis, N., M. Huang, and R.H. Thaler. 2006. "Individual Preferences, Monetary Gambles, and Stock Market Participation: A Case for Narrow Framing." *The American Economic Review* 96: 1069–1090.

Barnett, W.A., and A. Serletis. 2008. "Consumer Preferences and Demand Systems." *Journal of Econometrics* 147: 210–224.

Barry, N. 2008. "Reassessing Luck Egalitarianism." *The Journal of Politics* 70: 136–150.

Barsky, R.B., F.T. Juster, M.S. Kimball, and M.D. Shapiro. 1997. "Preference Parameters and Behavioral Heterogeneity: An Experimental Approach in the Health and Retirement Study." *The Quarterly Journal of Economics* 112: 537–579.

Bartley, M. 2004. *Health Inequality: An Introduction to Theories, Concepts and Methods.* Cambridge: Polity Press.

Bateman, I.J., and K.G. Willis, eds. 2001. *Valuing Environmental Preferences: Theory and Practice of the Contingent Valuation Method in the US, EU, and Developing Countries.* Paperback edition. Oxford: Oxford University Press.

Beckman, S.R., J.P. Formby, and W.J. Smith. 2004. "Efficiency, Equity and Democracy: Experimental Evidence on Okun's Leaky Bucket." In F. Cowell, ed., *Inequality, Welfare and Income Distribution: Experimental Approaches,* pp. 17–42. Amsterdam: Elsevier.

Belzer, M. 2005. "Self-Conception and Personal Identity: Revisiting Parfit and Lewis with an Eye on the Grip of the Unity Reaction." In E.F. Paul, F.D. Miller, and J. Paul, eds., *Personal Identity,* pp. 126–164. Cambridge: Cambridge University Press.

Benbaji, Y. 2005. "The Doctrine of Sufficiency: A Defence." *Utilitas* 17: 310–332.

Ben-Porath, E., I. Gilboa, and D. Schmeidler. 1997. "On the Measurement of Inequality under Uncertainty." *Journal of Economic Theory* 75: 194–204.

Bergson, A. 1938. "A Reformulation of Certain Aspects of Welfare Economics." *The Quarterly Journal of Economics* 52: 310–334.

———. 1948. "Socialist Economics." In H.S. Ellis, ed., *A Survey of Contemporary Economics*, vol. 1, pp. 412–448. Homewood: Richard D. Irwin.

———. 1954. "On the Concept of Social Welfare." *The Quarterly Journal of Economics* 68: 233–252.

Bernardo, J.M., and A.F.M. Smith. 2000. *Bayesian Theory*. Chichester: John Wiley & Sons.

Bernasconi, M. 2002. "How Should Income Be Divided? Questionnaire Evidence from the Theory of 'Impartial Preferences.'" In P. Moyes, C. Seidl, and A. Shorrocks, eds., *Inequalities: Theory, Experiments and Applications*, pp. 163–195. Vienna: Springer.

Bernheim, B.D. 1984. "Rationalizable Strategic Behavior." *Econometrica* 52: 1007–1028.

Bernstein, M. 1997. "Contractualism and Animals." *Philosophical Studies: An International Journal for Philosophy in the Analytic Tradition* 86: 49–72.

———. 1998. "Well-Being." *American Philosophical Quarterly* 35: 39–55.

Bigelow, J., J. Campbell, and R. Pargetter. 1990. "Death and Well-Being." *Pacific Philosophical Quarterly* 71: 119–140.

Binmore, K.G. 1994. *Game Theory and the Social Contract*. Volume 1, *Playing Fair*. Cambridge, MA: MIT Press.

———. 2008. "Naturalizing Harsanyi and Rawls." In M. Fleurbaey, M. Salles, and J.A. Weymark, eds., *Justice, Political Liberalism, and Utilitarianism: Themes from Harsanyi and Rawls*, pp. 303–333. Cambridge: Cambridge University Press.

Binmore, K., and A. Voorhoeve. 2003. "Defending Transitivity against Zeno's Paradox." *Philosophy and Public Affairs* 31: 272–279.

Blackburn, K., and M. Christensen. 1989. "Monetary Policy and Policy Credibility: Theories and Evidence." *Journal of Economic Literature* 27: 1–45.

Blackburn, S. 1998. *Ruling Passions: A Theory of Practical Reasoning*. Oxford: Clarendon Press.

Blackorby, C., W. Bossert, and D. Donaldson. 1999. "Income Inequality Measurement: The Normative Approach." In J. Silber, ed., *Handbook of Income Inequality Measurement*, pp. 133–161. Boston: Kluwer Academic.

———. 2005. *Population Issues in Social Choice Theory, Welfare Economics, and Ethics*. Cambridge: Cambridge University Press.

———. 2006. "Anonymous Single-Profile Welfarism." *Social Choice and Welfare* 27: 279–287.

Blackorby, C., and D. Donaldson. 1982. "Ratio-Scale and Translation-Scale Full Interpersonal Comparability without Domain Restrictions: Admissible Social-Evaluation Functions." *International Economic Review* 23: 249–268.

———. 1990. "A Review Article: The Case against the Use of the Sum of Compensating Variations in Cost-Benefit Analysis." *The Canadian Journal of Economics* 23: 471–494.

Blackorby, C., D. Donaldson, and P. Mongin. 2004. "Social Aggregation without the Expected Utility Hypothesis." Working Paper No. hal-00242932, Laboratoire d'Econometrie, Centre National de la Recherche Scientifique, Ecole Polytechnique, Paris, July 2004. http://hal.archives-ouvertes.fr/docs/00/24/29/32/PDF/2004-12-17-189.pdf.

Blackorby, C., F. Laisney, and R. Schmachtenberg. 1993. "Reference-Price-Independent Welfare Prescriptions." *Journal of Public Economics* 50: 63–76.

Blackorby, C., D. Primont, and R.R. Russell. 1998. "Separability: A Survey." In S. Barberà, P.J. Hammond, and C. Seidl, eds., *Handbook of Utility Theory*, vol. 1 (*Principles*), pp. 49–92. Dordrecht: Kluwer Academic.

Blanchflower, D.G., and A.J. Oswald. 2004. "Well-Being over Time in Britain and the USA." *Journal of Public Economics* 88: 1359–1386.

Bleichrodt, H., E. Diecidue, and J. Quiggin. 2004. "Equity Weights in the Allocation of Health Care: The Rank-Dependent QALY Model." *Journal of Health Economics* 23: 157–171.

Bleichrodt, H., J. Doctor, and E. Stolk. 2005. "A Nonparametric Elicitation of the Equity-Efficiency Trade-Off in Cost-Utility Analysis." *Journal of Health Economics* 24: 655–678.

Bleichrodt, H., and J. Quiggin. 1999. "Life-Cycle Preferences over Consumption and Health: When Is Cost-Effectiveness Analysis Equivalent to Cost-Benefit Analysis?" *Journal of Health Economics* 18: 681–708.

Blundell, R., M. Browning, and C. Meghir. 1994. "Consumer Demand and the Life-Cycle Allocation of Household Expenditures." *The Review of Economic Studies* 61: 57–80.

Blundell, R., and T. MaCurdy. 1999. "Labor Supply: A Review of Alternative Approaches." In O. Ashenfelter and D. Card, eds., *Handbook of Labor Economics*, vol. 3A, pp. 1559–1695. Amsterdam: Elsevier.

Boadway, R.W. 1974. "The Welfare Foundations of Cost-Benefit Analysis." *The Economic Journal* 84: 926–939.

Boadway, R., and N. Bruce. 1984. *Welfare Economics*. Oxford: Basil Blackwell.

Boadway, R., and M. Keen. 1993. "Public Goods, Self-Selection and Optimal Income Taxation." *International Economic Review* 34: 463–478.

Boadway, R., M. Marchand, P. Pestieau, and M. Del Mar Racionero. 2002. "Optimal Redistribution with Heterogeneous Preferences for Leisure." *Journal of Public Economic Theory* 4: 475–498.

Board, O. 2006. "The Equivalence of Bayes and Causal Rationality in Games." *Theory and Decision* 61: 1–19.

Bojer, H. 2003. *Distributional Justice: Theory and Measurement*. London: Routledge.

Boot, M. 2009. "Parity, Incomparability and Rationally Justified Choice." *Philosophical Studies: An International Journal for Philosophy in the Analytic Tradition* 146: 75–92.

Bosmans, K. 2007. "Extreme Inequality Aversion without Separability." *Economic Theory* 32: 589–594.

Bosmans, K., L. Lauwers, and E. Ooghe. 2009. "A Consistent Multidimensional Pigou-Dalton Transfer Principle." *Journal of Economic Theory* 144: 1358–1371.

Bosmans, K., and E. Schokkaert. 2004. "Social Welfare, the Veil of Ignorance and Purely Individual Risk: An Empirical Examination." In F. Cowell, ed., *Inequality, Welfare and Income Distribution: Experimental Approaches*, pp. 85–114. Amsterdam: Elsevier.

Bossert, W., and J.A. Weymark. 2004. "Utility in Social Choice." In S. Barberà, P.J. Hammond, and C. Seidl, eds., *Handbook of Utility Theory*, vol. 2 (*Extensions*), pp. 1099–1177. Boston: Kluwer Academic.

Bourguignon, F., and S.R. Chakravarty. 2003. "The Measurement of Multidimensional Poverty." *Journal of Economic Inequality* 1: 25–49.

Boxall, P.C., and W.L. Adamowicz. 2002. "Understanding Heterogeneous Preferences in Random Utility Models: A Latent Class Approach." *Environmental and Resource Economics* 23: 421–446.

Brand-Ballard, J. 2004. "Contractualism and Deontic Restrictions." *Ethics* 114: 269–300.

Brandenburger, A., and E. Dekel. 1987. "Rationalizability and Correlated Equilibria." *Econometrica* 55: 1391–1402.

Brandt, R.B. 1998. *A Theory of the Good and the Right.* Amherst: Prometheus Books. First published in 1979 by Oxford University Press.

Braveman, P. 2006. "Health Disparities and Health Equity: Concepts and Measurement." *Annual Review of Public Health* 27: 167–194.

Braveman, P., and S. Gruskin. 2003. "Defining Equity in Health." *Journal of Epidemiology and Community Health* 57: 254–258.

Brighouse, H., and A. Swift. 2006. "Equality, Priority, and Positional Goods." *Ethics* 116: 471–497.

Brink, D.O. 1989. *Moral Realism and the Foundations of Ethics.* Cambridge: Cambridge University Press.

———. 1997. "Rational Egoism and the Separateness of Persons." In J. Dancy, ed., *Reading Parfit*, pp. 96–134. Oxford: Blackwell.

———. 2003. "Prudence and Authenticity: Intrapersonal Conflicts of Value." *The Philosophical Review* 112: 215–245.

———. 2008. "The Significance of Desire." In R. Shafer-Landau, ed., *Oxford Studies in Metaethics*, vol. 3, pp. 5–46. Oxford: Oxford University Press.

———. 2011. "Prospects for Temporal Neutrality." In C. Callender, ed., *The Oxford Handbook of Philosophy of Time*, pp. 353–381. Oxford: Oxford University Press.

Broadie, A., and E.M. Pybus. 1974. "Kant's Treatment of Animals." *Philosophy* 49: 375–383.

Brock, D.W. 2002. "Priority to the Worse Off in Health-Care Resource Prioritization." In R. Rhodes, M.P. Battin, and A. Silvers, eds., *Medicine and Social Justice: Essays on the Distribution of Health Care*, pp. 362–372. Oxford: Oxford University Press.

Broome, J. 1984. "Uncertainty and Fairness." *The Economic Journal* 94: 624–632.

———. 1995. *Weighing Goods: Equality, Uncertainty and Time.* Paperback edition. Oxford: Basil Blackwell. First published in 1991.

———. 1997. "Is Incommensurability Vagueness?" In R. Chang, ed., *Incommensurability, Incomparability, and Practical Reason*, pp. 67–89. Cambridge, MA: Harvard University Press.

———. 1998. "Extended Preferences." In C. Fehige and U. Wessels, eds., *Preferences*, pp. 271–287. Berlin: Walter de Gruyter.

———. 2004. *Weighing Lives.* Oxford: Oxford University Press.

———. 2008. "Can There Be a Preference-Based Utilitarianism?" In M. Fleurbaey, M. Salles, and J.A. Weymark, eds., *Justice, Political Liberalism, and Utilitarianism: Themes from Harsanyi and Rawls*, pp. 221–238. Cambridge: Cambridge University Press.

———. n.d. "Equality versus Priority: A Useful Distinction." In D. Wikler and C.J.L. Murray, eds., *Goodness and Fairness: Ethical Issues in Health Resources Allocation* (forthcoming). http://users.ox.ac.uk/~sfop0060/pdf/equality%20versus%20priority.pdf.

Brouwer, W.B.F., A. Culyer, N.J.A. van Exel, and F.F.H. Rutten. 2008. "Welfarism vs. Extra-Welfarism." *Journal of Health Economics* 27: 325–338.

Brown, C. 2005a. "Matters of Priority." Ph.D. thesis, Australian National University, March 2005.

———. 2005b. "Priority or Sufficiency . . . or Both?" *Economics and Philosophy* 21: 199–220.

———. 2010. "Consequentialise This." Working paper, December 2010. http://homepages.ed.ac.uk/cbrown10/papers/CT.pdf.

Browning, M., P. Chiappori, and A. Lewbel. 2006. "Estimating Consumption Economies of Scale, Adult Equivalence Scales, and Household Bargaining Power." Discussion Paper Series No. 289, Department of Economics, University of Oxford, Oxford, October 2006. http://www.economics.ox.ac.uk/Research/wp/pdf/paper289.pdf.

Bullock, D.S., and K. Salhofer. 2003. "Judging Agricultural Policies: A Survey." *Agricultural Economics* 28: 225–243.

Bykvist, K. 2006. "Prudence for Changing Selves." *Utilitas* 18: 264–283.

Camacho-Cuena, E., C. Seidl, and A. Morone. 2005. "Comparing Preference Reversal for General Lotteries and Income Distributions." *Journal of Economic Psychology* 26: 682–710.

Campbell, A., P.E. Converse, and W.L. Rodgers. 1976. *The Quality of American Life: Perceptions, Evaluations, and Satisfactions*. New York: Russell Sage Foundation.

Campbell, D.E., and J.S. Kelly. 2002. "Impossibility Theorems in the Arrovian Framework." In K.J. Arrow, A.K. Sen, and K. Suzumura, eds., *Handbook of Social Choice and Welfare*, vol. 1, pp. 35–94. Amsterdam: Elsevier.

Canoy, M., F. Lerais, and E. Schokkaert. 2010. "Applying the Capability Approach to Policy-Making: The Impact Assessment of the EU-Proposal on Organ Donation." *The Journal of Socio-Economics* 39: 391–399.

Cappelen, A.W., J. Konow, E.Ø. Sørensen, and B. Tungodden. 2010. "Just Luck: An Experimental Study of Risk Taking and Fairness." MPRA Paper No. 24475, Munich Personal RePEc Archive, March 2010. http://mpra.ub.uni-muenchen.de/24475/.

Card, R.F. 2004. "Consequentialism, Teleology, and the New Friendship Critique." *Pacific Philosophical Quarterly* 85: 149–172.

Carlson, E. 1995. *Consequentialism Reconsidered*. Dordrecht: Kluwer Academic.

Carruthers, P. 1992. *The Animals Issue: Moral Theory in Practice*. Cambridge: Cambridge University Press.

Casal, P. 2007. "Why Sufficiency Is Not Enough." *Ethics* 117: 296–326.

Chakravarty, S.R. 2009. *Inequality, Polarization and Poverty: Advances in Distributional Analysis*. New York: Springer.

Chambers, C.P., and T. Hayashi. 2006. "Preference Aggregation under Uncertainty: Savage vs. Pareto." *Games and Economic Behavior* 54: 430–440.

Chang, R., ed. 1997. *Incommensurability, Incomparability, and Practical Reason*. Cambridge, MA: Harvard University Press.

Chang, R. 2002a. *Making Comparisons Count*. New York: Routledge.

———. 2002b. "The Possibility of Parity." *Ethics* 112: 659–688.

Chipman, J.S. 2008. "Compensation Principle." In S.N. Durlauf and L.E. Blume, eds., *The New Palgrave Dictionary of Economics*, vol. 2, 2nd edition, pp. 38–48. Houndmills: Palgrave Macmillan.

Chipman, J.S., and J.C. Moore. 1978. "The New Welfare Economics 1939–1974." *International Economic Review* 19: 547–584.

Christiano, T., and W. Braynen. 2008. "Inequality, Injustice and Levelling Down." *Ratio* 21: 392–420.

Christiansen, V. 1981. "Evaluation of Public Projects under Optimal Taxation." *The Review of Economic Studies* 48: 447–457.

———. 2007. "Two Approaches to Determine Public Good Provision under Distortionary Taxation." *National Tax Journal* 60: 25–43.

Clayton, M., and A. Williams. 1999. "Egalitarian Justice and Interpersonal Comparison." *European Journal of Political Research* 35: 445–464.

Clemen, R.T., and R.L. Winkler. 2007. "Aggregating Probability Distributions." In W. Edwards, R.F. Miles, and D. von Winterfeldt, eds., *Advances in Decision Analysis: From Foundations to Applications*, pp. 154–176. Cambridge: Cambridge University Press.

Cohen, A.I. 2009. "Contractarianism and Interspecies Welfare Conflicts." *Social Philosophy & Policy* 26: 227–257.

Cohen, A., and L. Einav. 2007. "Estimating Risk Preferences from Deductible Choice." *The American Economic Review* 97: 745–788.

Cohen, G.A. 1989. "On the Currency of Egalitarian Justice." *Ethics* 99: 906–944.

———. 1993. "Equality of What? On Welfare, Goods, and Capabilities." In M. Nussbaum and A. Sen, eds., *The Quality of Life*, pp. 9–29. Oxford: Clarendon Press.

Coleman, J.L. 2001. *The Practice of Principle: In Defence of a Pragmatist Approach to Legal Theory*. Oxford: Oxford University Press.

Cookson, R., M. Drummond, and H. Weatherly. 2009. "Explicit Incorporation of Equity Considerations into Economic Evaluation of Public Health Interventions." *Health Economics, Policy and Law* 4: 231–245.

Córdoba, J.C., and G. Verdier. 2008. "Inequality and Growth: Some Welfare Calculations." *Journal of Economic Dynamics & Control* 32: 1812–1829.

Cowell, F.A. 1995. *Measuring Inequality*. 2nd edition. London: Prentice Hall/Harvester Wheatsheaf.

———. 2000. "Measurement of Inequality." In A.B. Atkinson and F. Bourguignon, eds., *Handbook of Income Distribution*, vol. 1, pp. 87–166. Amsterdam: Elsevier.

Cowell, F.A., and K. Gardiner. 1999. "Welfare Weights." Working paper, STICERD, London School of Economics, August 1999. http://www.oft.gov.uk/shared_oft/reports/consumer_protection/oft282.pdf.

Cowell, F.A., and M. Mercader-Prats. 1999. "Equivalence Scales and Inequality." In J. Silber, ed., *Handbook of Income Inequality Measurement*, pp. 405–435. Boston: Kluwer Academic.

Cox, J.C., and G.W. Harrison, eds. 2008. *Risk Aversion in Experiments*. Bingley: Emerald Group.

Creedy, J. 1997. "Labour Supply and Social Welfare When Utility Depends on a Threshold Consumption Level." *Economic Record* 73: 159–168.

———. 1998. "The Optimal Linear Income Tax Model: Utility or Equivalent Income?" *Scottish Journal of Political Economy* 45: 99–110.

———. 2007. "Policy Evaluation, Welfare Weights and Value Judgments: A Reminder." *Australian Journal of Labour Economics* 10: 1–15.

Cremer, H., F. Gahvari, and N. Ladoux. 2003. "Environmental Taxes with Heterogeneous Consumers: An Application to Energy Consumption in France." *Journal of Public Economics* 87: 2791–2815.

Crisp, R. 2003a. "Egalitarianism and Compassion." *Ethics* 114: 119–126.

———. 2003b. "Equality, Priority, and Compassion." *Ethics* 113: 745–763.

———. 2006. *Reasons and the Good*. Oxford: Clarendon Press.

Croley, S. 2003. "White House Review of Agency Rulemaking: An Empirical Investigation." *University of Chicago Law Review* 70: 821–886.

Croson, R., and U. Gneezy. 2009. "Gender Differences in Preferences." *Journal of Economic Literature* 47: 448–474.

Croson, R., and J. Konow. 2009. "Social Preferences and Moral Biases." *Journal of Economic Behavior & Organization* 69: 201–212.

Crossley, T.F., and K. Pendakur. 2010. "The Common-Scaling Social Cost-Of-Living Index." *Journal of Business & Economic Statistics* 28: 523–538.

Cummins, R.A. 1996. "The Domains of Life Satisfaction: An Attempt to Order Chaos." *Social Indicators Research* 38: 303–328.

Cupit, G. 1998. "Justice, Age, and Veneration." *Ethics* 108: 702–718.

Dancy, J., ed. 1997. *Reading Parfit*. Oxford: Blackwell.

Daniels, N. 1990. "Equality of What: Welfare, Resources, or Capabilities?" *Philosophy and Phenomenological Research* 50: 273–296.

———. 1996. *Justice and Justification: Reflective Equilibrium in Theory and Practice*. Cambridge: Cambridge University Press.

Daruvala, D. 2010. "Would the Right Social Preference Model Please Stand Up!" *Journal of Economic Behavior & Organization* 73: 199–208.

Darwall, S.L. 1986. "Agent-Centered Restrictions from the Inside Out." *Philosophical Studies: An International Journal for Philosophy in the Analytic Tradition* 50: 291–319.

———. 2002. *Welfare and Rational Care*. Princeton: Princeton University Press.

———. 2006. *The Second-Person Standpoint: Morality, Respect, and Accountability*. Cambridge, MA: Harvard University Press.

Darwall, S.L., A. Gibbard, and P. Railton. 1992. "Toward Fin de Siècle Ethics: Some Trends." *The Philosophical Review* 101: 115–189.

d'Aspremont, C., and L. Gevers. 2002. "Social Welfare Functionals and Interpersonal Comparability." In K.J. Arrow, A.K. Sen, and K. Suzumura, eds., *Handbook of Social Choice and Welfare*, vol. 1, pp. 459–541. Amsterdam: Elsevier.

Davidson, D. 1986. "Judging Interpersonal Interests." In J. Elster and A. Hylland, eds., *Foundations of Social Choice Theory*, pp. 195–211. Cambridge: Cambridge University Press.

Deaton, A., and J. Muellbauer. 1980. *Economics and Consumer Behavior*. Cambridge: Cambridge University Press.

Debreu, G. 1960. "Topological Methods in Cardinal Utility Theory." In K.J. Arrow, S. Karlin, and P. Suppes, eds., *Mathematical Methods in the Social Sciences, 1959: Proceedings of the First Stanford Symposium*, pp. 16–26. Stanford: Stanford University Press.

DeGrazia, D. 1996. *Taking Animals Seriously: Mental Life and Moral Status*. Cambridge: Cambridge University Press.

———. 2005. *Human Identity and Bioethics*. Cambridge: Cambridge University Press.

Denis, L. 2000. "Kant's Conception of Duties regarding Animals: Reconstruction and Reconsideration." *History of Philosophy Quarterly* 17: 405–423.

Deschamps, R., and L. Gevers. 1977. "Separability, Risk-Bearing, and Social Welfare Judgements." *European Economic Review* 10: 77–94.

Devooght, K. 2003. "Measuring Inequality by Counting 'Complaints': Theory and Empirics." *Economics and Philosophy* 19: 241–263.

Diamond, P.A. 1967. "Cardinal Welfare, Individualistic Ethics, and Interpersonal Comparisons of Utility: Comment." *The Journal of Political Economy* 75: 765–766.

———. 1998. "Optimal Income Taxation: An Example with a U-Shaped Pattern of Optimal Marginal Tax Rates." *The American Economic Review* 88: 83–95.

———. 2003. *Taxation, Incomplete Markets, and Social Security*. Cambridge, MA: MIT Press.

Diener, E., and M.E.P. Seligman. 2004. "Beyond Money: Toward an Economy of Well-Being." *Psychological Science in the Public Interest* 5: 1–31.

Diener, E., E.M. Suh, R.E. Lucas, and H.L. Smith. 1999. "Subjective Well-Being: Three Decades of Progress." *Psychological Bulletin* 125: 276–302.

Dolan, P. 1998. "The Measurement of Individual Utility and Social Welfare." *Journal of Health Economics* 17: 39–52.

Dolan, P., and R. Edlin. 2002. "Is It Really Possible to Build a Bridge between Cost-Benefit Analysis and Cost-Effectiveness Analysis?" *Journal of Health Economics* 21: 827–843.

Dolan, P., R. Edlin, and A. Tsuchiya. 2008. "The Relative Societal Value of Health Gains to Different Beneficiaries." Final Report RM03/JH11, School of Health and Population Sciences, University of Birmingham, Birmingham, January 2008. http://www.haps.bham. ac.uk/publichealth/methodology/docs/publications/JH11_Social_Value_QALY_Final_ Report_Paul_Dolan_et_al_2008.pdf.

Dolan, P., and T. Peasgood. 2010. "Measuring Well-Being for Public Policy: Preferences or Experiences?" In E.A. Posner and C.R. Sunstein, eds., *Law and Happiness*, pp. 5–31. Chicago: University of Chicago Press.

Dolan, P., R. Shaw, A. Tsuchiya, and A. Williams. 2005. "QALY Maximisation and People's Preferences: A Methodological Review of the Literature." *Health Economics* 14: 197–208.

Donaldson, D. 1992. "On the Aggregation of Money Measures of Well-Being in Applied Welfare Economics." *Journal of Agricultural and Resource Economics* 17: 88–102.

Donaldson, D., and J.A. Weymark. 1998. "A Quasiordering Is the Intersection of Orderings." *Journal of Economic Theory* 78: 382–387.

Donaldson, J., and R. Mehra. 2008. "Risk-Based Explanations of the Equity Premium." In R. Mehra, ed., *Handbook of the Equity Risk Premium*, pp. 37–99. Amsterdam: Elsevier.

Doran, B. 2001. "Reconsidering the Levelling-Down Objection against Egalitarianism." *Utilitas* 13: 65–85.

Drèze, J., and N. Stern. 1987. "The Theory of Cost-Benefit Analysis." In A.J. Auerbach and M. Feldstein, eds., *Handbook of Public Economics*, vol. 2, pp. 909–989. Amsterdam: North-Holland.

Driesen, D.M. 2005. "Distributing the Costs of Environmental, Health, and Safety Protection: The Feasibility Principle, Cost-Benefit Analysis, and Regulatory Reform." *Boston College Environmental Affairs Law Review* 32: 1–95.

———. 2006. "Is Cost-Benefit Analysis Neutral?" *University of Colorado Law Review* 77: 335–404.

Dubra, J., F. Maccheroni, and E.A. Ok. 2004. "Expected Utility Theory without the Completeness Axiom." *Journal of Economic Theory* 115: 118–133.

Dutta, B. 2002. "Inequality, Poverty and Welfare." In K.J. Arrow, A.K. Sen, and K. Suzumura, eds., *Handbook of Social Choice and Welfare*, vol. 1, pp. 597–633. Amsterdam: Elsevier.

Dworkin, R. 1981a. "What Is Equality? Part 1: Equality of Welfare." *Philosophy and Public Affairs* 10: 185–246.

———. 1981b. "What Is Equality? Part 2: Equality of Resources." *Philosophy and Public Affairs* 10: 283–345.

———. 1986. *Law's Empire*. Cambridge, MA: Belknap Press of Harvard University Press.

Ebert, U., and P. Moyes. 2003. "Equivalence Scales Reconsidered." *Econometrica* 71: 319–343.

Ebrahimi, A., and C. Heady. 1988. "Tax Design and Household Composition." *The Economic Journal* 98: 83–96.

Edwards, R.D. 2008. "Health Risk and Portfolio Choice." *Journal of Business & Economic Statistics* 26: 472–485.

Eklund, M. 2004. "Personal Identity, Concerns, and Indeterminacy." *The Monist* 87: 489–511.

Elster, J., and J.E. Roemer, eds. 1991. *Interpersonal Comparisons of Well-Being*. Cambridge: Cambridge University Press.

Enoch, D. 2005. "Why Idealize?" *Ethics* 115: 759–787.

Epstein, L.G., and U. Segal. 1992. "Quadratic Social Welfare Functions." *Journal of Political Economy* 100: 691–712.

Erosa, A., and M. Gervais. 2002. "Optimal Taxation in Life-Cycle Economies." *Journal of Economic Theory* 105: 338–369.

Eskeland, G.S. 2000. "Environmental Protection and Optimal Taxation." Policy Research Working Paper No. 2510, Development Research Group, Public Economics, The World Bank, Washington, D.C., December 2000. http://ideas.repec.org/p/wbk/wbrwps/2510.html.

Etchart, N. 2002. "Adequate Moods for Non-EU Decision Making in a Sequential Framework: A Synthetic Discussion." *Theory and Decision* 52: 1–28.

Evans, D., E. Kula, and H. Sezer. 2005. "Regional Welfare Weights for the UK: England, Scotland, Wales and Northern Ireland." *Regional Studies* 39: 923–937.

Evans, M.F., and V.K. Smith. 2010. "Measuring How Risk Tradeoffs Adjust with Income." *Journal of Risk and Uncertainty* 40: 33–55.

Evans, W.N., and W.K. Viscusi. 1991. "Estimation of State-Dependent Utility Functions Using Survey Data." *The Review of Economics and Statistics* 73: 94–104.

Evren, Ö. 2008. "On the Existence of Expected Multi-Utility Representations." *Economic Theory* 35: 575–592.

Evren, Ö., and E.A. Ok. 2010. "On the Multi-Utility Representation of Preference Relations." Working paper, June 2010. http://homepages.nyu.edu/~oe240/MU8.pdf.

Executive Order 12866. 1993. "Regulatory Planning and Review." *Federal Register* 58: 51735–51744. October 4, 1993.

Executive Order 12898. 1994. "Federal Actions to Address Environmental Justice in Minority Populations and Low-Income Populations." *Federal Register* 59: 7629–7633. February 16, 1994.

Executive Order 13563. 2011. "Improving Regulation and Regulatory Review." *Federal Register* 76: 3821–3823. January 21, 2011.

Fankhauser, S., R.S.J. Tol, and D.W. Pearce. 1997. "The Aggregation of Climate Change Damages: A Welfare Theoretic Approach." *Environmental and Resource Economics* 10: 249–266.

Farrow, S. n.d. "Evaluating Central Regulatory Institutions with an Application to the U.S. Office of Information and Regulatory Affairs." In C. Coglianese, ed., *White House Review of Rulemaking: Looking Back, Looking Forward*, Report, Penn Program on Regulation, University of Pennsylvania (forthcoming). http://www.law.upenn.edu/academics/institutes/regulation/papers/integratedregulationumbc.pdf.

Feldman, F. 2006a. "Actual Utility, the Objection from Impracticality, and the Move to Expected Utility." *Philosophical Studies: An International Journal for Philosophy in the Analytic Tradition* 129: 49–79.

———. 2006b. *Pleasure and the Good Life: Concerning the Nature, Varieties, and Plausibility of Hedonism*. Paperback edition. Oxford: Clarendon Press.

Fenge, R., S. Uebelmesser, and M. Werding. 2006. "On the Optimal Timing of Implicit Social Security Taxes over the Life Cycle." *FinanzArchiv* 62: 68–107.

Finkelstein, A., E.F.P. Luttmer, and M.J. Notowidigdo. 2008. "What Good Is Wealth without Health? The Effect of Health on the Marginal Utility of Consumption." NBER Working

Paper Series No. 14089, National Bureau of Economic Research, Cambridge, MA, June 2008. http://www.nber.org/papers/w14089.

Finnis, J. 1988. *Natural Law and Natural Rights*. Reprint, with corrections. Oxford: Clarendon Press. First published in 1980.

Firth, R. 1952. "Ethical Absolutism and the Ideal Observer." *Philosophy and Phenomenological Research* 12: 317–345.

Fishburn, P.C. 1982. *The Foundations of Expected Utility*. Dordrecht: D. Reidel.

———. 1991. "Nontransitive Preferences in Decision Theory." *Journal of Risk and Uncertainty* 4: 113–134.

———. 1994. "Utility and Subjective Probability." In R.J. Aumann and S. Hart, eds., *Handbook of Game Theory with Economic Applications*, vol. 2, pp. 1397–1435. Amsterdam: Elsevier.

Fleurbaey, M. 2001. "Equality versus Priority: How Relevant Is the Distinction?" In D. Wikler and C.J.L. Murray, eds., *Goodness and Fairness: Ethical Issues in Health Resources Allocation* (forthcoming). http://mora.rente.nhh.no/projects/EqualityExchange/ressurser/articles/fleurbaey2.pdf.

———. 2005. "The Pazner-Schmeidler Social Ordering: A Defense." *Review of Economic Design* 9: 145–166.

———. 2006. "Social Welfare, Priority to the Worst-Off and the Dimensions of Individual Well-Being." In F. Farina and E. Savaglio, eds., *Inequality and Economic Integration*, pp. 225–268. London: Routledge.

———. 2007. "Two Criteria for Social Decisions." *Journal of Economic Theory* 134: 421–447.

———. 2008. *Fairness, Responsibility, and Welfare*. Oxford: Oxford University Press.

———. 2009. "Beyond GDP: The Quest for a Measure of Social Welfare." *Journal of Economic Literature* 47: 1029–1075.

———. 2010. "Assessing Risky Social Situations." *Journal of Political Economy* 118: 649–680.

Fleurbaey, M., T. Gajdos, and S. Zuber. 2010. "Social Rationality, Separability, and Equity under Uncertainty." CORE Discussion Paper No. 2010/37, Center for Operations Research and Econometrics, Louvain-La-Neuve, July 2010. http://www.uclouvain.be/cps/ucl/doc/core/documents/coredp2010_37web.pdf.

Fleurbaey, M., and P.J. Hammond. 2004. "Interpersonally Comparable Utility." In S. Barberà, P.J. Hammond, and C. Seidl, eds., *Handbook of Utility Theory*, vol. 2 (*Extensions*), pp. 1179–1285. Boston: Kluwer Academic.

Fleurbaey, M., S. Luchini, C. Muller, and E. Schokkaert. 2010. "Equivalent Income and the Economic Evaluation of Health Care." CORE Discussion Paper No. 2010/6, Center for Operations Research and Econometrics, Louvain-La-Neuve, February 2010. http://www.uclouvain.be/cps/ucl/doc/core/documents/coredp2010_6web.pdf.

Fleurbaey, M., and F. Maniquet. 2008. "Fair Social Orderings." *Economic Theory* 34: 25–45.

Fleurbaey, M., and P. Michel. 2003. "Intertemporal Equity and the Extension of the Ramsey Criterion." *Journal of Mathematical Economics* 39: 777–802.

Fleurbaey, M., and P. Mongin. 2005. "The News of the Death of Welfare Economics Is Greatly Exaggerated." *Social Choice and Welfare* 25: 381–418.

Fleurbaey, M., K. Suzumura, and K. Tadenuma. 2005. "The Informational Basis of the Theory of Fair Allocation." *Social Choice and Welfare* 24: 311–341.

Fleurbaey, M., and A. Trannoy. 2003. "The Impossibility of a Paretian Egalitarian." *Social Choice and Welfare* 21: 243–263.

Fleurbaey, M., and B. Tungodden. 2010. "The Tyranny of Non-Aggregation versus the Tyranny of Aggregation in Social Choices: A Real Dilemma." *Economic Theory* 44: 399–414.

Fleurbaey, M., B. Tungodden, and P. Vallentyne. 2009. "On the Possibility of Nonaggregative Priority for the Worst Off." *Social Philosophy & Policy* 26: 258–285.

Florio, M., ed. 2007. *Cost-Benefit Analysis and Incentives in Evaluation: The Structural Funds of the European Union.* Cheltenham: Edward Elgar.

Frankfurt, H. 1987. "Equality as a Moral Ideal." *Ethics* 98: 21–43.

Frederick, S. 2006. "Valuing Future Life and Future Lives: A Framework for Understanding Discounting." *Journal of Economic Psychology* 27: 667–680.

Frederick, S., G. Loewenstein, and T. O'Donoghue. 2003. "Time Discounting and Time Preference: A Critical Review." In G. Loewenstein, D. Read, and R. Baumeister, eds., *Time and Decision: Economic and Psychological Perspectives on Intertemporal Choice*, pp. 13–86. New York: Russell Sage Foundation.

Freeman, A.M. 2003. *The Measurement of Environmental and Resource Values: Theory and Methods.* 2nd edition. Washington, DC: Resources for the Future.

Freeman, S. 2007. *Rawls.* London: Routledge.

Frey, B.S. 2008. *Happiness: A Revolution in Economics.* Cambridge, MA: MIT Press.

Fried, B.H. 2003. "Ex Ante/Ex Post." *Journal of Contemporary Legal Issues* 13: 123–160.

Frohlich, N., and J.A. Oppenheimer. 1992. *Choosing Justice: An Experimental Approach to Ethical Theory.* Berkeley: University of California Press.

Fullerton, D., and G.E. Metcalf. 2002. "Tax Incidence." In A.J. Auerbach and M. Feldstein, eds., *Handbook of Public Economics*, vol. 4, pp. 1787–1872. Amsterdam: Elsevier.

Fullerton, D., and D.L. Rogers. 1993. *Who Bears the Lifetime Tax Burden?* Washington, DC: Brookings Institution.

Gajdos, T., and F. Kandil. 2008. "The Ignorant Observer." *Social Choice and Welfare* 31: 193–232.

Gajdos, T., and E. Maurin. 2004. "Unequal Uncertainties and Uncertain Inequalities: An Axiomatic Approach." *Journal of Economic Theory* 116: 93–118.

Garrett, B. 1998. *Personal Identity and Self-Consciousness.* London: Routledge.

Gaube, T. 2007. "Optimum Taxation of Each Year's Income." *Journal of Public Economic Theory* 9: 127–150.

Gelman, A., J.B. Carlin, H.S. Stern, and D.B. Rubin. 2004. *Bayesian Data Analysis.* 2nd edition. Boca Raton: Chapman & Hall/CRC.

Gert, J. 2004. "Value and Parity." *Ethics* 114: 492–510.

Gervais, M. 2009. "On the Optimality of Age-Dependent Taxes and the Progressive U.S. Tax System." Discussion Papers in Economics and Econometrics No. 0905, Economics Division, School of Social Sciences, University of Southampton, Southampton, September 2009. http://www.southampton.ac.uk/socsci/economics/research/papers/documents/2009/0905.pdf.

Gevers, L., H. Glejser, and J. Rouyer. 1979. "Professed Inequality Aversion and Its Error Component." *The Scandinavian Journal of Economics* 81: 238–243.

Gibbard, A. 1986. "Interpersonal Comparisons: Preference, Good, and the Intrinsic Reward of a Life." In J. Elster and A. Hylland, eds., *Foundations of Social Choice Theory*, pp. 165–193. Cambridge: Cambridge University Press.

———. 1990. *Wise Choices, Apt Feelings: A Theory of Normative Judgment.* Cambridge, MA: Harvard University Press.

Gilboa, I. 2009. *Theory of Decision under Uncertainty*. Cambridge: Cambridge University Press.

Gilboa, I., A.W. Postlewaite, and D. Schmeidler. 2008a. "Probability and Uncertainty in Economic Modeling." *Journal of Economic Perspectives* 22: 173–188.

———. 2008b. "Rationality of Belief or: Why Savage's Axioms Are Neither Necessary nor Sufficient for Rationality." PIER Working Paper No. 08–043, Penn Institute for Economic Research, Department of Economics, University of Pennsylvania, Philadelphia, December 2008. http://www.ssc.upenn.edu/ier/Archive/08-043.pdf.

Gollier, C. 2001. *The Economics of Risk and Time*. Cambridge, MA: MIT Press.

Golosov, M., A. Tsyvinski, and I. Werning. 2007. "New Dynamic Public Finance: A User's Guide." In D. Acemoglu, K. Rogoff, and M. Woodford, eds., *NBER Macroeconomics Annual 2006*, vol. 21, pp. 317–363. Cambridge, MA: MIT Press.

Gorman, W.M. 1955. "The Intransitivity of Certain Criteria Used in Welfare Economics." *Oxford Economic Papers* 7: 25–35.

Gosseries, A. 2003. "Intergenerational Justice." In H. LaFollette, ed., *The Oxford Handbook of Practical Ethics*, pp. 459–484. Oxford: Oxford University Press.

Graham, J.D. 2008. "Saving Lives through Administrative Law and Economics." *University of Pennsylvania Law Review* 157: 395–540.

Grant, S., and B. Polak. 2006. "Bayesian Beliefs with Stochastic Monotonicity: An Extension of Machina and Schmeidler." *Journal of Economic Theory* 130: 264–282.

Grant, S., A. Kajii, B. Polak, and Z. Safra. 2010a. "Ex Post Egalitarianism and Harsanyi's Impartial Observer Theorem." Working paper, June 2010. http://www.asb.unsw.edu.au/schools/economics/Documents/S.%20Grant%20%20Ex%20Post%20Egalitarianism%20and%20Harsanyi%27s%20Impartial%20Observer%20Theorem.pdf.

———. 2010b. "Generalized Utilitarianism and Harsanyi's Impartial Observer Theorem." *Econometrica* 78: 1939–1971.

Grasso, M., and L. Canova. 2008. "An Assessment of the Quality of Life in the European Union Based on the Social Indicators Approach." *Social Indicators Research* 87: 1–25.

Gravel, N. 2001. "On the Difficulty of Combining Actual and Potential Criteria for an Increase in Social Welfare." *Economic Theory* 17: 163–180.

Griffin, J. 1986. *Well-Being: Its Meaning, Measurement, and Moral Importance*. Oxford: Clarendon Press.

———. 1991. "Against the Taste Model." In J. Elster and J.E. Roemer, eds., *Interpersonal Comparisons of Well-Being*, pp. 45–69. Cambridge: Cambridge University Press.

———. 1997. *Value Judgement: Improving Our Ethical Beliefs*. Paperback edition. Oxford: Clarendon Press.

Guiso, L., and M. Paiella. 2008. "Risk Aversion, Wealth, and Background Risk." *Journal of the European Economic Association* 6: 1109–1150.

Hahn, R.W. 2000. *Reviving Regulatory Reform: A Global Perspective*. Washington, DC: AEI Press.

———. 2005. *In Defense of the Economic Analysis of Regulation*. Washington, DC: AEI Press.

Hahn, R.W., and P.C. Tetlock. 2008. "Has Economic Analysis Improved Regulatory Decisions?" *Journal of Economic Perspectives* 22: 67–84.

Hammond, P.J. 1975. "A Note on Extreme Inequality Aversion." *Journal of Economic Theory* 11: 465–467.

———. 1976. "Equity, Arrow's Conditions, and Rawls' Difference Principle." *Econometrica* 44: 793–804.

———. 1981. "Ex-Ante and Ex-Post Welfare Optimality under Uncertainty." *Economica* 48: 235–250.

———. 1982. "Utilitarianism, Uncertainty and Information." In A. Sen and B. Williams, eds., *Utilitarianism and Beyond*, pp. 85–102. Cambridge: Cambridge University Press.

———. 1983. "Ex-Post Optimality as a Dynamically Consistent Objective for Collective Choice under Uncertainty." In P.K. Pattanaik and M. Salles, eds., *Social Choice and Welfare*, pp. 175–205. Amsterdam: North-Holland.

Haninger, K. 2007. "The Role of Equity Weights in Allocating Health and Medical Resources." Working paper, Robert Wood Johnson Health & Society Scholars Program, University of Pennsylvania, Philadelphia, October 2007.

Harberger, A.C. 1978. "On the Use of Distributional Weights in Social Cost-Benefit Analysis." *Journal of Political Economy* 86: S87–S120.

Harberger, A.C., and G.P. Jenkins, eds. 2002. *Cost-Benefit Analysis*. Cheltenham: Edward Elgar.

Harel, A., Z. Safra, and U. Segal. 2005. "Ex-Post Egalitarianism and Legal Justice." *Journal of Law, Economics, & Organization* 21: 57–75.

Harrison, G.W., M.I. Lau, and E.E Rutström. 2007. "Estimating Risk Attitudes in Denmark: A Field Experiment." *The Scandinavian Journal of Economics* 109: 341–368.

Harrison, G.W., and E.E. Rutström. 2008. "Risk Aversion in the Laboratory." In J.C. Cox and G.W. Harrison, eds., *Risk Aversion in Experiments*, pp. 41–196. Bingley: Emerald Group.

Harsanyi, J.C. 1953. "Cardinal Utility in Welfare Economics and in the Theory of Risk-Taking." *Journal of Political Economy* 61: 434–435.

———. 1955. "Cardinal Welfare, Individualistic Ethics, and Interpersonal Comparisons of Utility." *Journal of Political Economy* 63: 309–321.

———. 1982. "Morality and the Theory of Rational Behaviour." In A. Sen and B. Williams, eds., *Utilitarianism and Beyond*, pp. 39–62. Cambridge: Cambridge University Press.

———. 1986. *Rational Behavior and Bargaining Equilibrium in Games and Social Situations*. Paperback edition. Cambridge: Cambridge University Press. First published in 1977.

Hart, H.L.A. 1994. *The Concept of Law*. 2nd edition. Oxford: Clarendon Press.

Hartog, J., A. Ferrer-i-Carbonell, and N. Jonker. 2002. "Linking Measured Risk Aversion to Individual Characteristics." *Kyklos* 55: 3–26.

Hastie, R., and Dawes, R.M. 2001. *Rational Choice in an Uncertain World: The Psychology of Judgment and Decision Making*. Thousand Oaks: Sage.

Hausman, D.M. 1995. "The Impossibility of Interpersonal Utility Comparisons." *Mind*, n.s., 104: 473–490.

———. n.d. "Equality versus Priority: A Badly Misleading Distinction." In D. Wikler and C.J.L. Murray, eds., *Goodness and Fairness: Ethical Issues in Health Resources Allocation* (forthcoming). http://philosophy.wisc.edu/hausman/papers/Hausman-Equality-vs-Priority-revised.htm.

Hausman, D.M., and M.S. McPherson. 2009. "Preference Satisfaction and Welfare Economics." *Economics and Philosophy* 25: 1–25.

Heady, C. 1996. "Optimal Taxation as a Guide to Tax Policy." In M.P. Devereux, ed., *The Economics of Tax Policy*, pp. 23–54. Oxford: Oxford University Press.

Heer, B. 2001. "Wealth Distribution and Optimal Inheritance Taxation in Life-Cycle Economies with Intergenerational Transfers." *The Scandinavian Journal of Economics* 103: 445–465.

Hicks, J.R. 1939. "The Foundations of Welfare Economics." *The Economic Journal* 49: 696–712.

———. 1941. "The Rehabilitation of Consumers' Surplus." *The Review of Economic Studies* 8: 108–116.

Hild, M., and A. Voorhoeve. 2004. "Equality of Opportunity and Opportunity Dominance." *Economics and Philosophy* 20: 117–145.

Hirose, I. 2005. "Intertemporal Distributive Judgement." *Ethical Theory and Moral Practice* 8: 371–386.

———. 2009. "Reconsidering the Value of Equality." *Australasian Journal of Philosophy* 87: 301–312.

HM Treasury. 2003. Treasury Guidance. "The Green Book: Appraisal and Evaluation in Central Government." London: TSO. http://www.hm-treasury.gov.uk/d/green_book_complete.pdf.

Holmes, A.M. 1997. "A Method to Elicit Utilities for Interpersonal Comparisons." *Medical Decision Making* 17: 10–20.

Holt, C.A., and S.K. Laury. 2002. "Risk Aversion and Incentive Effects." *The American Economic Review* 92: 1644–1655.

Holtug, N. 1998. "Egalitarianism and the Levelling Down Objection." *Analysis* 58: 166–174.

———. 2003. "Welfarism - the Very Idea." *Utilitas* 15: 151–174.

———. 2007a. "Animals: Equality for Animals." In J. Ryberg, T.S. Petersen, and C. Wolf, eds., *New Waves in Applied Ethics*, pp. 1–24. Houndmills: Palgrave Macmillan.

———. 2007b. "A Note on Conditional Egalitarianism." *Economics and Philosophy* 23: 45–63.

———. 2007c. "Prioritarianism." In N. Holtug and K. Lippert-Rasmussen, eds., *Egalitarianism: New Essays on the Nature and Value of Equality*, pp. 125–156. Oxford: Clarendon Press.

———. 2010. *Persons, Interests, and Justice*. Oxford: Oxford University Press.

Hooker, B. 2000. *Ideal Code, Real World: A Rule-Consequentialist Theory of Morality*. Oxford: Clarendon Press.

Hooker, B., E. Mason, and D.E. Miller, eds. 2000. *Morality, Rules, and Consequences: A Critical Reader*. Lanham: Rowman & Littlefield.

Hooker, B., and B. Streumer. 2004. "Procedural and Substantive Practical Rationality." In A.R. Mele and P. Rawling, eds., *The Oxford Handbook of Rationality*, pp. 57–74. Oxford: Oxford University Press.

Hotelling, H. 1938. "The General Welfare in Relation to Problems of Taxation and Railway and Utility Rates." *Econometrica* 6: 242–269.

Hudson, J.L. 1989. "Subjectivization in Ethics." *American Philosophical Quarterly* 26: 221–229.

Hurka, T. 1996. *Perfectionism*. Paperback edition. New York: Oxford University Press.

Hurley, P. 1997. "Agent-Centered Restrictions: Clearing the Air of Paradox." *Ethics* 108: 120–146.

Hylland, A., and R. Zeckhauser. 1979. "Distributional Objectives Should Affect Taxes but Not Program Choice or Design." *The Scandinavian Journal of Economics* 81: 264–284.

Iqbal, K., and S.J. Turnovsky. 2008. "Intergenerational Allocation of Government Expenditures: Externalities and Optimal Taxation." *Journal of Public Economic Theory* 10: 27–53.

Jackson, F. 1991. "Decision-Theoretic Consequentialism and the Nearest and Dearest Objection." *Ethics* 101: 461–482.

Jeffrey, R.C. 1983. *The Logic of Decision*. 2nd edition. Chicago: University of Chicago Press.

Jenkins, S.P., and J. Micklewright, eds. 2007. *Inequality and Poverty Re-Examined*. Oxford: Oxford University Press.

Jensen, K.K. 1995. "Measuring the Size of a Benefit and Its Moral Weight: On the Significance of John Broome's 'Interpersonal Addition Theorem.'" *Theoria* 61: 25–60.

———. 2003. "What Is the Difference between (Moderate) Egalitarianism and Prioritarianism?" *Economics and Philosophy* 19: 89–109.

Jeske, D. 1993. "Persons, Compensation, and Utilitarianism." *The Philosophical Review* 102: 541–575.

Johansson-Stenman, O. 2005. "Distributional Weights in Cost-Benefit Analysis—Should We Forget About Them?" *Land Economics* 81: 337–352.

Johnston, M. 2003. "Human Concerns without Superlative Selves." In R. Martin and J. Barresi, eds., *Personal Identity*, pp. 260–291. Malden: Blackwell.

Jollimore, T. 2006. "Impartiality." In E.N. Zalta, ed., *The Stanford Encyclopedia of Philosophy* (online publication). Encyclopedia entry dated April 2006. http://plato.stanford.edu/archives/fall2008/entries/impartiality/.

Jorgenson, D.W., and D.T. Slesnick. 1984. "Aggregate Consumer Behavior and the Measurement of Inequality." *The Review of Economic Studies* 51: 369–392.

Joyce, J.M. 1999. *The Foundations of Causal Decision Theory*. Cambridge: Cambridge University Press.

———. 2004. "Bayesianism." In A.R. Mele and P. Rawling, eds., *The Oxford Handbook of Rationality*, pp. 132–155. Oxford: Oxford University Press.

Joyce, J.M., and A. Gibbard. 1998. "Causal Decision Theory." In S. Barberà, P.J. Hammond, and C. Seidl, eds., *Handbook of Utility Theory*, vol. 1 (*Principles*), pp. 627–666. Dordrecht: Kluwer Academic.

Just, R.E., D.L. Hueth, and A. Schmitz. 2004. *The Welfare Economics of Public Policy: A Practical Approach to Project and Policy Evaluation*. Cheltenham: Edward Elgar.

Kagan, S. 1989. *The Limits of Morality*. Oxford: Clarendon Press.

———. 1991. "Replies to My Critics." *Philosophy and Phenomenological Research* 51: 919–928.

———. 1992. "The Limits of Well-Being." *Social Philosophy & Policy* 9: 169–189.

———. 1998. *Normative Ethics*. Boulder: Westview Press.

Kahneman, D., E. Diener, and N. Schwarz, eds. 1999. *Well-Being: The Foundations of Hedonic Psychology*. New York: Russell Sage Foundation.

Kahneman, D., A.B. Krueger, D. Schkade, N. Schwarz, and A. Stone. 2004. "Toward National Well-Being Accounts." *The American Economic Review* 94 (AEA Papers and Proceedings): 429–434.

Kahneman, D., and R. Sugden. 2005. "Experienced Utility as a Standard of Policy Evaluation." *Environmental and Resource Economics* 32: 161–181.

Kahneman, D., P.P. Wakker, and R. Sarin. 1997. "Back to Bentham? Explorations of Experienced Utility." *The Quarterly Journal of Economics* 112: 375–405.

Kakwani, N., and J. Silber, eds. 2007. *The Many Dimensions of Poverty*. Houndmills: Palgrave Macmillan.

———. 2008. *Quantitative Approaches to Multidimensional Poverty Measurement*. Houndmills: Palgrave Macmillan.

Kakwani, N., A. Wagstaff, and E. van Doorslaer. 1997. "Socioeconomic Inequalities in Health: Measurement, Computation, and Statistical Inference." *Journal of Econometrics* 77: 87–103.

Kaldor, N. 1939. "Welfare Propositions of Economics and Interpersonal Comparisons of Utility." *The Economic Journal* 49: 549–552.

Kamm, F.M. 1992. "Non-Consequentialism, the Person as an End-in-Itself, and the Significance of Status." *Philosophy and Public Affairs* 21: 354–389.

Kaneko, M. 1984. "On Interpersonal Utility Comparisons." *Social Choice and Welfare* 1: 165–175.

Kaplow, L. 1995. "A Fundamental Objection to Tax Equity Norms: A Call for Utilitarianism." *National Tax Journal* 48: 497–514.

———. 1996. "The Optimal Supply of Public Goods and the Distortionary Cost of Taxation." *National Tax Journal* 49: 513–533.

———. 2008a. "Optimal Policy with Heterogeneous Preferences." *The B.E. Journal of Economic Analysis & Policy* 8: Article 40 (online publication). http://www.bepress.com/bejeap/vol8/iss1/art40/.

———. 2008b. *The Theory of Taxation and Public Economics*. Princeton: Princeton University Press.

———. 2010. "Concavity of Utility, Concavity of Welfare, and Redistribution of Income." *International Tax and Public Finance* 17: 25–42.

Kaplow, L., and S. Shavell. 1994. "Why the Legal System Is Less Efficient Than the Income Tax in Redistributing Income." *The Journal of Legal Studies* 23: 667–681.

———. 2002. *Fairness versus Welfare*. Cambridge, MA: Harvard University Press.

Kappel, K. 1997. "Equality, Priority, and Time." *Utilitas* 9: 203–225.

Karni, E. 1996. "Social Welfare Functions and Fairness." *Social Choice and Welfare* 13: 487–496.

———. 1998. "Impartiality: Definition and Representation." *Econometrica* 66: 1405–1415.

Karni, E., and J.A. Weymark. 1998. "An Informationally Parsimonious Impartial Observer Theorem." *Social Choice and Welfare* 15: 321–332.

Kaye, R. 2007. *The Mathematics of Logic: A Guide to Completeness Theorems and Their Applications*. Cambridge: Cambridge University Press.

Keenan, D.C., and A. Snow. 1999. "A Complete Characterization of Potential Compensation Tests in Terms of Hicksian Welfare Measures." *The Canadian Journal of Economics* 32: 215–233.

Keeney, R.L., and H. Raiffa. 1993. *Decisions with Multiple Objectives: Preferences and Value Tradeoffs*. Cambridge: Cambridge University Press. First published in 1976 by John Wiley & Sons.

Kenkel, D. 1997. "On Valuing Morbidity, Cost-Effectiveness Analysis, and Being Rude." *Journal of Health Economics* 16: 749–757.

Khmelnitskaya, A.B., and J.A. Weymark. 2000. "Social Choice with Independent Subgroup Utility Scales." *Social Choice and Welfare* 17: 739–748.

Kifmann, M. 2008. "Age-Dependent Taxation and the Optimal Retirement Benefit Formula." *German Economic Review* 9: 41–64.

Kimball, M.S., C.R. Sahm, and M.D. Shapiro. 2008. "Imputing Risk Tolerance from Survey Responses." *Journal of the American Statistical Association* 103: 1028–1038.

King, L.A., and C.K. Napa. 1998. "What Makes a Life Good?" *Journal of Personality and Social Psychology* 75: 156–165.

King, M. 1983. "Welfare Analysis of Tax Reforms Using Household Data." *Journal of Public Economics* 21: 183–214.

Kingdon, G.G., and J. Knight. 2006. "Subjective Well-Being Poverty vs. Income Poverty and Capabilities Poverty?" *Journal of Development Studies* 42: 1199–1224.

Kirkpatrick, C., and D. Parker, eds. 2007. *Regulatory Impact Assessment: Towards Better Regulation?* Cheltenham: Edward Elgar.

Kolm, S. 1969. "The Optimal Production of Social Justice." In J. Margolis and H. Guitton, eds., *Public Economics: An Analysis of Public Production and Consumption and Their Relations to the Private Sectors*, pp. 145–200. London: Macmillan.

———. 1996. *Modern Theories of Justice*. Cambridge, MA: MIT Press.

———. 1998. "Chance and Justice: Social Policies and the Harsanyi-Vickrey-Rawls Problem." *European Economic Review* 42: 1393–1416.

Konow, J. 2009. "Is Fairness in the Eye of the Beholder? An Impartial Spectator Analysis of Justice." *Social Choice and Welfare* 33: 101–127.

Korsgaard, C.M. 1989. "Personal Identity and the Unity of Agency: A Kantian Response to Parfit." *Philosophy and Public Affairs* 18: 101–132.

———. 1993. "The Reasons We Can Share: An Attack on the Distinction between Agent-Relative and Agent-Neutral Values." *Social Philosophy & Policy* 10: 24–51.

Krantz, D.H., R.D. Luce, P. Suppes, and A. Tversky. 2007. *Foundations of Measurement*. Volume 1, *Additive and Polynomial Representations*. Mineola: Dover. First published in 1971 by Academic Press.

Kraut, R. 2007. *What is Good and Why: The Ethics of Well-Being*. Cambridge, MA: Harvard University Press.

Kreiner, C.T., and N. Verdelin. 2009. "Optimal Provision of Public Goods: A Synthesis." CESifo Working Paper No. 2538, February 2009. http://papers.ssrn.com/sol3/papers.cfm?abstract_id=1338051.

Kreps, D.M. 1988. *Notes on the Theory of Choice*. Boulder: Westview Press.

Kuklys, W. 2005. *Amartya Sen's Capability Approach: Theoretical Insights and Empirical Applications*. Berlin: Springer.

Kumar, R. 1999. "Defending the Moral Moderate: Contractualism and Common Sense." *Philosophy and Public Affairs* 28: 275–309.

Kydland, F.E., and E.C. Prescott. 1977. "Rules Rather Than Discretion: The Inconsistency of Optimal Plans." *Journal of Political Economy* 85: 473–491.

Kysar, D.A. 2010. *Regulating from Nowhere: Environmental Law and the Search for Objectivity*. New Haven: Yale University Press.

Lambert, P.J. 2001. *The Distribution and Redistribution of Income*. 3rd edition. Manchester: Manchester University Press.

Lambert, P.J., D.L. Millimet, and D. Slottje. 2003. "Inequality Aversion and the Natural Rate of Subjective Inequality." *Journal of Public Economics* 87: 1061–1090.

Lasso de la Vega, C., A. Urrutia, and A. de Sarachú. 2010. "Characterizing Multidimensional Inequality Measures Which Fulfill the Pigou-Dalton Bundle Principle." *Social Choice and Welfare* 35: 319–329.

Layard, R. 2005. *Happiness: Lessons from a New Science*. New York: Penguin Press.

Layard, R., G. Mayraz, and S. Nickell. 2008. "The Marginal Utility of Income." *Journal of Public Economics* 92: 1846–1857.

Le Grand, J. 1987. "Inequalities in Health: Some International Comparisons." *European Economic Review* 31: 182–191.

Lenman, J. 2000. "Consequentialism and Cluelessness." *Philosophy and Public Affairs* 29: 342–370.

Levi, I. 1986. *Hard Choices: Decision Making under Unresolved Conflict*. Cambridge: Cambridge University Press.

Lewis, G.W., and D.T. Ulph. 1988. "Poverty, Inequality and Welfare." *The Economic Journal* 98: 117–131.

Lindholm, L., and M. Rosen. 1998. "On the Measurement of the Nation's Equity Adjusted Health." *Health Economics* 7: 621–628.

Lippert-Rasmussen, K. 1996. "Moral Status and the Impermissibility of Minimizing Violations." *Philosophy and Public Affairs* 25: 333–351.

———. 1999. "In What Way Are Constraints Paradoxical?" *Utilitas* 11: 49–70.

List, C. 2003. "Are Interpersonal Comparisons of Utility Indeterminate?" *Erkenntnis* 58: 229–260.

Little, I.M.D. 1957. *A Critique of Welfare Economics*. 2nd edition. Oxford: Clarendon Press.

Little, I.M.D., and J.A. Mirrlees. 1994. "The Costs and Benefits of Analysis: Project Appraisal and Planning Twenty Years On." In R. Layard and S. Glaister, eds., *Cost-Benefit Analysis*, 2nd edition, pp. 199–231. Cambridge: Cambridge University Press.

Llavador, H.G., and J.E. Roemer. 2001. "An Equal-Opportunity Approach to the Allocation of International Aid." *Journal of Development Economics* 64: 147–171.

Llavador, H., J.E. Roemer, and J. Silvestre. 2009. "A Dynamic Analysis of Human Welfare in a Warming Planet." Cowles Foundation Discussion Paper No. 1673R, Cowles Foundation for Research in Economics, Yale University, New Haven, April 2009. http://cowles.econ.yale.edu/P/cd/d16b/d1673-r.pdf.

Loeb, D. 1995. "Full-Information Theories of Individual Good." *Social Theory and Practice* 21: 1–30.

Loewenstein, G.F., and D. Prelec. 1993. "Preferences for Sequences of Outcomes." *Psychological Review* 100: 91–108.

Louise, J. 2004. "Relativity of Value and the Consequentialist Umbrella." *The Philosophical Quarterly* 54: 518–536.

Lowe, E.J. 2002. *A Survey of Metaphysics*. Oxford: Oxford University Press.

Lyons, D. 1965. *Forms and Limits of Utilitarianism*. Oxford: Clarendon Press.

Machina, M.J. 1989. "Dynamic Consistency and Non-Expected Utility Models of Choice under Uncertainty." *Journal of Economic Literature* 27: 1622–1668.

MacKay, A.F. 1986. "Extended Sympathy and Interpersonal Utility Comparisons." *The Journal of Philosophy* 83: 305–322.

Mackenbach, J.P., and A.E. Kunst. 1997. "Measuring the Magnitude of Socio-Economic Inequalities in Health: An Overview of Available Measures Illustrated with Two Examples from Europe." *Social Science & Medicine* 44: 757–771.

Mackie, J.L. 1977. *Ethics: Inventing Right and Wrong*. Harmondsworth: Penguin Books.

Mackie, P. 2006. *How Things Might Have Been: Individuals, Kinds, and Essential Properties*. Oxford: Clarendon Press.

Mankiw, N.G., and S.P. Zeldes. 1991. "The Consumption of Stockholders and Nonstockholders." *Journal of Financial Economics* 29: 97–112.

Mariotti, M., and R. Veneziani. 2009. " 'Non-interference' Implies Equality." *Social Choice and Welfare* 32: 123–128.

Martin, R., and J. Barresi, eds. 2003. *Personal Identity*. Malden: Blackwell.

Mas-Colell, A., M.D. Whinston, and J.R. Green. 1995. *Microeconomic Theory*. New York: Oxford University Press.

Maskin, E., and T. Sjöström. 2002. "Implementation Theory." In K.J. Arrow, A.K. Sen, and K. Suzumura, eds., *Handbook of Social Choice and Welfare*, vol. 1, pp. 237–288. Amsterdam: Elsevier.

Mason, A. 2001. "Egalitarianism and the Levelling Down Objection." *Analysis* 61: 246–254.

Mayeres, I., and S. Proost. 2001. "Marginal Tax Reform, Externalities and Income Distribution." *Journal of Public Economics* 79: 343–363.

Mayerfeld, J. 2002. *Suffering and Moral Responsibility*. Paperback edition. Oxford: Oxford University Press.

McCarthy, D. 2006. "Utilitarianism and Prioritarianism I." *Economics and Philosophy* 22: 335–363.

———. 2008. "Utilitarianism and Prioritarianism II." *Economics and Philosophy* 24: 1–33.

McClennen, E.F. 1990. *Rationality and Dynamic Choice: Foundational Explorations*. Cambridge: Cambridge University Press.

McGarity, T.O. 1998. "A Cost-Benefit State." *Administrative Law Review* 50: 7–79.

McKerlie, D. 1989. "Equality and Time." *Ethics* 99: 475–491.

———. 1992. "Equality between Age-Groups." *Philosophy and Public Affairs* 21: 275–295.

———. 1994. "Equality and Priority." *Utilitas* 6: 25–42.

———. 1997. "Priority and Time." *Canadian Journal of Philosophy* 27: 287–309.

———. 2001a. "Dimensions of Equality." *Utilitas* 13: 263–288.

———. 2001b. "Justice between the Young and the Old." *Philosophy and Public Affairs* 30: 152–177.

———. 2003. "Understanding Egalitarianism." *Economics and Philosophy* 19: 45–60.

———. 2007. "Egalitarianism and the Difference between Interpersonal and Intrapersonal Judgments." In N. Holtug and K. Lippert-Rasmussen, eds., *Egalitarianism: New Essays on the Nature and Value of Equality*, pp. 157–173. Oxford: Clarendon Press.

McMahan, J. 2003. *The Ethics of Killing: Problems at the Margins of Life*. Paperback edition. Oxford: Oxford University Press.

McNaughton, D., and P. Rawling. 1991. "Agent-Relativity and the Doing-Happening Distinction." *Philosophical Studies: An International Journal for Philosophy in the Analytic Tradition* 63: 167–185.

Medin, H., K. Nyborg, and I. Bateman. 2001. "The Assumption of Equal Marginal Utility of Income: How Much Does It Matter?" *Ecological Economics* 36: 397–411.

Mele, A.R., and P. Rawling, eds. 2004. *The Oxford Handbook of Rationality*. Oxford: Oxford University Press.

Meyer, D.J., and J. Meyer. 2005. "Relative Risk Aversion: What Do We Know?" *Journal of Risk and Uncertainty* 31: 243–262.

———. 2006. *Measuring Risk Aversion*. Boston: Delft.

Micheletto, L. 2008. "Redistribution and Optimal Mixed Taxation in the Presence of Consumption Externalities." *Journal of Public Economics* 92: 2262–2274.

Miller, A. 2003. *An Introduction to Contemporary Metaethics*. Cambridge: Polity Press.

Millgram, E., ed. 2001. *Varieties of Practical Reasoning*. Cambridge, MA: MIT Press.

Milo, R. 1995. "Contractarian Constructivism." *The Journal of Philosophy* 92: 181–204.

Mirrlees, J.A. 2006a. "An Exploration in the Theory of Optimum Income Taxation." In J.A. Mirrlees, *Welfare, Incentives, and Taxation*, pp. 131–173. Oxford: Oxford University Press. First published in 1971 in the *Review of Economic Studies*, vol. 38, pp. 175–208.

Mirrlees, J.A. 2006b. *Welfare, Incentives, and Taxation*. Oxford: Oxford University Press.

Mishan, E.J. 1988. *Cost-Benefit Analysis: An Informal Introduction*. 4th edition. London: Unwin Hyman.

Mongin, P. 2001. "The Impartial Observer Theorem of Social Ethics." *Economics and Philosophy* 17: 147–179.

Mongin, P., and C. d'Aspremont. 1998. "Utility Theory and Ethics." In S. Barberà, P.J. Hammond, and C. Seidl, eds., *Handbook of Utility Theory*, vol. 1 (*Principles*), pp. 371–481. Dordrecht: Kluwer Academic.

Moore, A., and R. Crisp. 1996. "Welfarism in Moral Theory." *Australasian Journal of Philosophy* 74: 598–613.

Moreno-Ternero, J.D. 2007. "On the Design of Equal-Opportunity Policies." *Investigaciones Económicas* 31: 351–374.

Moreno-Ternero, J.D., and J.E. Roemer. 2008. "The Veil of Ignorance Violates Priority." *Economics and Philosophy* 24: 233–257.

Morgenstern, R.D., ed. 1997. *Economic Analyses at EPA: Assessing Regulatory Impact.* Washington, DC: Resources for the Future.

Morgenstern, R.D., and M.K. Landy. 1997. "Economic Analysis: Benefits, Costs, Implications." In R.D. Morgenstern, ed., *Economic Analyses at EPA: Assessing Regulatory Impact*, pp. 455–478. Washington, DC: Resources for the Future.

Murray, C.J.L., E.E. Gakidou, and J. Frenk. 1999. "Health Inequalities and Social Group Differences: What Should We Measure?" *Bulletin of the World Health Organization* 77: 537–543.

Musgrave, R.A. 1959. *The Theory of Public Finance: A Study in Public Economy.* New York: McGraw-Hill.

Myerson, R.B. 1981. "Utilitarianism, Egalitarianism, and the Timing Effect in Social Choice Problems." *Econometrica* 49: 883–897.

———. 1997. *Game Theory: Analysis of Conflict.* Paperback edition. Cambridge, MA: Harvard University Press.

Myles, G.D. 1995. *Public Economics.* Cambridge: Cambridge University Press.

Nagel, T. 1970. *The Possibility of Altruism.* Oxford: Clarendon Press.

———. 1979. "Equality." In T. Nagel, ed., *Mortal Questions*, pp. 106–127. Cambridge: Cambridge University Press. Delivered as the Tanner Lecture at Stanford University in 1977.

———. 1986. *The View from Nowhere.* New York: Oxford University Press.

———. 1995. *Equality and Partiality.* Paperback edition. New York: Oxford University Press. First published in 1991.

Narayan, D., R. Chambers, M.K. Shah, and P. Petesch. 2000. *Voices of the Poor: Crying Out for Change.* Oxford: Oxford University Press.

National Research Council. 2004. *Analytical Methods and Approaches for Water Resources Project Planning.* Washington, DC: National Academies Press.

Nau, R. 2006. "The Shape of Incomplete Preferences." *The Annals of Statistics* 34: 2430–2448.

———. 2007. "Extensions of the Subjective Expected Utility Model." In W. Edwards, R.F. Miles, and D. von Winterfeldt, eds., *Advances in Decision Analysis: From Foundations to Applications*, pp. 253–278. Cambridge: Cambridge University Press.

Ng, Y. 1999. "Utility, Informed Preference, or Happiness: Following Harsanyi's Argument to Its Logical Conclusion." *Social Choice and Welfare* 16: 197–216.

Ninan, D. 2009. "Persistence and the First-Person Perspective." *Philosophical Review* 118: 425–464.

Noll, H. 2004. "Social Indicators and Quality of Life Research: Background, Achievements and Current Trends." In N. Genov, ed., *Advances in Sociological Knowledge over Half a Century*, pp. 151–181. Wiesbaden: VS Verlag für Sozialwissenschaften.

Noonan, H.W. 2003. *Personal Identity.* 2nd edition. London: Routledge.

Norcross, A. 1999. "Intransitivity and the Person-Affecting Principle." *Philosophy and Phenomenological Research* 59: 769–776.

———. 2009. "Two Dogmas of Deontology: Aggregation, Rights, and the Separateness of Persons." *Social Philosophy & Policy* 26: 76–95.

Nord, E. 2005. "Concerns for the Worse Off: Fair Innings versus Severity." *Social Science & Medicine* 60: 257–263.

Nordhaus, W. 2008. *A Question of Balance: Weighing the Options on Global Warming Policies.* New Haven: Yale University Press.

Nozick, R. 1974. *Anarchy, State, and Utopia.* New York: Basic Books.

Nussbaum, M.C. 2000. *Women and Human Development: The Capabilities Approach.* Cambridge: Cambridge University Press.

———. 2006. *Frontiers of Justice: Disability, Nationality, Species Membership.* Cambridge, MA: Belknap Press of Harvard University Press.

Ok, E.A. 2002. "Utility Representation of an Incomplete Preference Relation." *Journal of Economic Theory* 104: 429–449.

———. 2007. *Real Analysis with Economic Applications.* Princeton: Princeton University Press.

Olson, E.T. 1997. *The Human Animal: Personal Identity without Psychology.* New York: Oxford University Press.

———. 2007. *What Are We? A Study in Personal Ontology.* Oxford: Oxford University Press.

———. 2010. "Personal Identity." In E.N. Zalta, ed., *The Stanford Encyclopedia of Philosophy* (online publication). Encyclopedia entry dated October 2010. http://plato.stanford.edu/archives/win2010/entries/identity-personal/.

O'Neill, M. 2008. "What Should Egalitarians Believe?" *Philosophy and Public Affairs* 36: 119–156.

Ooghe, E., and L. Lauwers. 2005. "Non-Dictatorial Extensive Social Choice." *Economic Theory* 25: 721–743.

Ooghe, E., E. Schokkaert, and D. Van de gaer. 2007. "Equality of Opportunity versus Equality of Opportunity Sets." *Social Choice and Welfare* 28: 209–230.

Østerdal, L.P. 2005. "Axioms for Health Care Resource Allocation." *Journal of Health Economics* 24: 679–702.

Otsuka, M., and A. Voorhoeve. 2009. "Why It Matters That Some Are Worse Off Than Others: An Argument against the Priority View." *Philosophy and Public Affairs* 37: 171–199.

Overvold, M.C. 1980. "Self-Interest and the Concept of Self-Sacrifice." *Canadian Journal of Philosophy* 10: 105–118.

———. 1982. "Self-Interest and Getting What You Want." In H.B. Miller and W.H. Williams, eds., *The Limits of Utilitarianism*, pp. 186–194. Minneapolis: University of Minnesota Press.

———. 1984. "Morality, Self-Interest, and Reasons for Being Moral." *Philosophy and Phenomenological Research* 44: 493–507.

Paravisini, D., V. Rappoport, and E. Ravina. 2011. "Risk Aversion and Wealth: Evidence from Person-To-Person Lending Portfolios." Working paper, March 2011. http://www0.gsb.columbia.edu/faculty/eravina/RRA_Wealth.pdf.

Parfit, D. 1973. "Later Selves and Moral Principles." In A. Montefiore, ed., *Philosophy and Personal Relations: An Anglo-French Study*, pp. 137–169. Montreal: McGill-Queen's University Press.

———. 1986. "Comments." *Ethics* 96: 832–872.

———. 1987. *Reasons and Persons.* Revised and corrected paperback edition. Oxford: Clarendon Press. First published in 1984.

———. 2000. "Equality or Priority?" In M. Clayton and A. Williams, eds., *The Ideal of Equality*, pp. 81–125. Houndmills: Palgrave. Delivered as the Lindley Lecture at the University of Kansas in 1991.

———. 2003. "The Unimportance of Identity." In R. Martin and J. Barresi, eds., *Personal Identity*, pp. 292–317. Malden: Blackwell.

Parry, I.W.H., H. Sigman, M. Walls, and R.C. Williams. 2006. "The Incidence of Pollution Control Policies." In T. Tietenberg and H. Folmer, eds., *The International Yearbook of Environmental and Resource Economics 2006/ 2007: A Survey of Current Issues*, pp. 1–42. Cheltenham: Edward Elgar.

Pattanaik, P.K. 1968. "Risk, Impersonality, and the Social Welfare Function." *Journal of Political Economy* 76: 1152–1169.

Paul, E.F., F.D. Miller, and J. Paul, eds. 2005. *Personal Identity*. Cambridge: Cambridge University Press.

Pauwels, W. 1978. "The Possible Perverse Behavior of the Compensating Variation as a Welfare Ranking." *Zeitschrift fur Nationalökonomie/Journal of Economics* 38: 369–378.

Pazner, E.A. 1979. "Equity, Nonfeasible Alternatives and Social Choice: A Reconsideration of the Concept of Social Welfare." In J.J. Laffont, *Aggregation and Revelation of Preferences*, pp. 161–173. Amsterdam: North-Holland.

Pazner, E.A., and D. Schmeidler. 1978. "Egalitarian Equivalent Allocations: A New Concept of Economic Equity." *The Quarterly Journal of Economics* 92: 671–687.

Pearce, D.G. 1984. "Rationalizable Strategic Behavior and the Problem of Perfection." *Econometrica* 52: 1029–1050.

Peragine, V. 1999. "The Distribution and Redistribution of Opportunity." *Journal of Economic Surveys* 13: 37–69.

Persson, I. 2001. "Equality, Priority and Person-Affecting Value." *Ethical Theory and Moral Practice* 4: 23–39.

———. 2008. "Why Levelling Down Could Be Worse for Prioritarianism Than for Egalitarianism." *Ethical Theory and Moral Practice* 11: 295–303.

Peterson, M. 2007. "Parity, Clumpiness and Rational Choice." *Utilitas* 19: 505–513.

———. 2010. "Can Consequentialists Honour the Special Moral Status of Persons?" *Utilitas* 22: 434–446.

Peterson, M., and S.O. Hansson. 2005. "Equality *and* Priority." *Utilitas* 17: 299–309.

Pettit, P. 1997. "The Consequentialist Perspective." In M.W. Baron, P. Pettit, and M. Slote, eds., *Three Methods of Ethics: A Debate*, pp. 92–174. Malden: Blackwell.

Pigou, A.C. 1920. *The Economics of Welfare*. London: Macmillan.

Pirttilä, J., and M. Tuomala. 1997. "Income Tax, Commodity Tax and Environmental Policy." *International Tax and Public Finance* 4: 379–393.

Pirttilä, J., and R. Uusitalo. 2010. "A 'Leaky Bucket' in the Real World: Estimating Inequality Aversion Using Survey Data." *Economica* 77: 60–76.

Pollak, R.A. 1991. "Welfare Comparisons and Situation Comparisons." *Journal of Econometrics* 50: 31–48.

Portmore, D.W. 2007. "Consequentializing Moral Theories." *Pacific Philosophical Quarterly* 88: 39–73.

Posner, R.A. 1995. *Aging and Old Age*. Chicago: University of Chicago Press.

Qizilbash, M. 1998. "The Concept of Well-Being." *Economics and Philosophy* 14: 51–73.

Rabinowicz, W. 1995. "To Have One's Cake and Eat It, Too: Sequential Choice and Expected-Utility Violations." *The Journal of Philosophy* 92: 586–620.

———. 2000. "Money Pump with Foresight." In M.J. Almeida, ed., *Imperceptible Harms and Benefits*, pp. 123–154. Dordrecht: Kluwer Academic.

———. 2001. "Prioritarianism and Uncertainty: On the Interpersonal Addition Theorem and the Priority View." In D. Egonsson, J. Josefsson, B. Petersson, and T. Rønnow-Rasmussen, eds., *Exploring Practical Philosophy: From Action to Values*, pp. 139–165. Aldershot: Ashgate.

———. 2008. "Value Relations." *Theoria* 74: 18–49.

Railton, P. 1984. "Alienation, Consequentialism, and the Demands of Morality." *Philosophy and Public Affairs* 13: 134–171.

———. 1986a. "Facts and Values." *Philosophical Topics* 14: 5–31.

———. 1986b. "Moral Realism." *The Philosophical Review* 95: 163–207.

———. 1996. "Moral Realism: Prospects and Problems." In W. Sinnott-Armstrong and M. Timmons, eds., *Moral Knowledge? New Readings in Moral Epistemology*, pp. 49–81. New York: Oxford University Press.

Ramsay, M. 2005. "Teleological Egalitarianism vs. the Slogan." *Utilitas* 17: 93–116.

Ramsey, F.P. 1928. "A Mathematical Theory of Saving." *The Economic Journal* 38: 543–559.

Rawls, J. 1999a. "Outline of a Decision Procedure for Ethics." In S. Freeman, ed., *John Rawls: Collected Papers*, pp. 1–19. Cambridge, MA: Harvard University Press. Originally part of Rawls' Ph.D. thesis, Princeton University, 1951.

———. 1999b. *A Theory of Justice*. Revised edition. Cambridge, MA: Belknap Press of Harvard University Press. First published in 1971.

Ray, A. 1984. *Cost-Benefit Analysis: Issues and Methodologies*. Baltimore: Johns Hopkins University Press.

Raz, J. 1986. *The Morality of Freedom*. Oxford: Clarendon Press.

Resnik, M.D. 1987. *Choices: An Introduction to Decision Theory*. Minneapolis: University of Minnesota Press.

Rey, B., and J.C. Rochet. 2004. "Health and Wealth: How Do They Affect Individual Preferences?" *The Geneva Papers on Risk and Insurance Theory* 29: 43–54.

Ríos Insua, D., and R. Criado. 2000. "Topics on the Foundations of Robust Bayesian Analysis." In D. Ríos Insua and F. Ruggeri, eds., *Robust Bayesian Analysis*, pp. 33–44. New York: Springer.

Ríos Insua, D., and J. Martín. 1994. "On the Foundations of Robust Decision Making." In S. Ríos, ed., *Decision Theory and Decision Analysis: Trends and Challenges*, pp. 103–111. Boston: Kluwer Academic.

Risse, M. 2002. "Harsanyi's 'Utilitarian Theorem' and Utilitarianism." *Noûs* 36: 550–577.

Robbins, L. 1935. *An Essay on the Nature and Significance of Economic Science*. 2nd edition. London: Macmillan. First published in 1932.

———. 1938. "Interpersonal Comparisons of Utility: A Comment." *The Economic Journal* 48: 635–641.

Roberts, K.W.S. 1980a. "Interpersonal Comparability and Social Choice Theory." *The Review of Economic Studies* 47: 421–439.

———. 1980b. "Possibility Theorems with Interpersonally Comparable Welfare Levels." *The Review of Economic Studies* 47: 409–420.

———. 1980c. "Price-Independent Welfare Prescriptions." *Journal of Public Economics* 13: 277–297.

———. 1995. "Valued Opinions or Opinionated Values: The Double Aggregation Problem." In K. Basu, P. Pattanaik, and K. Suzumura, eds., *Choice, Welfare, and Development: A Festschrift in Honour of Amartya Sen*, pp. 141–165. Oxford: Clarendon Press.

———. 1997. "Objective Interpersonal Comparisons of Utility." *Social Choice and Welfare* 14: 79–96.

Rodríguez, J.G. 2008. "Partial Equality-of-Opportunity Orderings." *Social Choice and Welfare* 31: 435–456.

Rodríguez-Miguez, E., and J. Pinto-Prades. 2002. "Measuring the Social Importance of Concentration or Dispersion of Individual Health Benefits." *Health Economics* 11: 43–53.

Roemer, J.E. 1998. *Equality of Opportunity*. Cambridge, MA: Harvard University Press.

———. 2002. "Equality of Opportunity: A Progress Report." *Social Choice and Welfare* 19: 455–471.

———. 2003. "Defending Equality of Opportunity." *The Monist* 86: 261–282.

———. 2008. "Harsanyi's Impartial Observer Is *Not* a Utilitarian." In M. Fleurbaey, M. Salles, and J.A. Weymark, eds., *Justice, Political Liberalism, and Utilitarianism: Themes from Harsanyi and Rawls*, pp. 129–135. Cambridge: Cambridge University Press.

———. 2009. "Equality: Its Justification, Nature, and Domain." In W. Salverda, B. Nolan, and T.M. Smeeding, eds., *The Oxford Handbook of Economic Inequality*, pp. 23–39. Oxford: Oxford University Press.

Roemer, J.E., R. Aaberge, U. Colombino, et al. 2003. "To What Extent Do Fiscal Regimes Equalize Opportunities for Income Acquisition Among Citizens?" *Journal of Public Economics* 87: 539–565.

Rønnow-Rasmussen, T. 2009. "Normative Reasons and the Agent-Neutral/Relative Dichotomy." *Philosophia* 37: 227–243.

Rosati, C.S. 1995. "Persons, Perspectives, and Full Information Accounts of the Good." *Ethics* 105: 296–325.

———. 1996. "Internalism and the Good for a Person." *Ethics* 106: 297–326.

———. 2006. "Personal Good." In T. Horgan and M. Timmons, eds., *Metaethics after Moore*, pp. 107–131. Oxford: Clarendon Press.

———. 2008. "Objectivism and Relational Good." *Social Philosophy & Policy* 25: 314–349.

Ross, J. 2006. "Rejecting Ethical Deflationism." *Ethics* 116: 742–768.

Rowlands, M. 1997. "Contractarianism and Animal Rights." *Journal of Applied Philosophy* 14: 235–247.

Ruggeri, F., D. Ríos Insua, and J. Martín. 2005. "Robust Bayesian Analysis." In D.K. Dey and C.R. Rao, eds., *Handbook of Statistics*, vol. 25, pp. 623–667. Amsterdam: Elsevier.

Ruiz-Castillo, J. 1987. "Potential Welfare and the Sum of Individual Compensating or Equivalent Variations." *Journal of Economic Theory* 41: 34–53.

Ryan, M.J. 2009. "Generalizations of SEU: A Geometric Tour of Some Non-Standard Models." *Oxford Economic Papers* 61: 327–354.

Ryff, C.D. 1989. "In the Eye of the Beholder: Views of Psychological Well-Being among Middle-Aged and Older Adults." *Psychology and Aging* 4: 195–210.

Sælen, H., G. Atkinson, S. Dietz, J. Helgeson, and C. Hepburn. 2008. "Risk, Inequality and Time in the Welfare Economics of Climate Change: Is the Workhorse Model Underspecified?" Discussion Paper Series No. 400, Department of Economics, Oxford University, Oxford, July 2008. http://www.economics.ox.ac.uk/Research/wp/pdf/paper400.pdf.

Safra, Z., and E. Weissengrin. 2003. "Harsanyi's Impartial Observer Theorem with a Restricted Domain." *Social Choice and Welfare* 20: 177–187.

Salanié, B. 2003. *The Economics of Taxation*. Cambridge: MIT Press.

Samuelson, P.A. 1947. *Foundations of Economic Analysis*. Cambridge, MA: Harvard University Press.

Sassi, F., L. Archard, and J. Le Grand. 2001. "Equity and the Economic Evaluation of Healthcare." *Health Technology Assessment* 5: 1–138.

Savage, L.J. 1972. *The Foundations of Statistics*. 2nd revised edition. New York: Dover.

Savaglio, E. 2006. "Three Approaches to the Analysis of Multidimensional Inequality." In F. Farina and E. Savaglio, eds., *Inequality and Economic Integration*, pp. 269–283. London: Routledge.

Sayre-McCord, G., ed. 1988. *Essays on Moral Realism*. Ithaca: Cornell University Press.

Scanlon, T.M. 1998. *What We Owe to Each Other*. Cambridge, MA: Belknap Press of Harvard University Press.

———. 2003. "Rawls on Justification." In S. Freeman, ed., *The Cambridge Companion to Rawls*, pp. 139–167. Cambridge: Cambridge University Press.

Schauer, F. 1992. *Playing by the Rules: A Philosophical Examination of Rule-Based Decision-Making in Law and in Life*. Paperback edition. Oxford: Clarendon Press.

Schechtman, M. 1996. *The Constitution of Selves*. Ithaca: Cornell University Press.

Scheffler, S. 1994. *The Rejection of Consequentialism: A Philosophical Investigation of the Considerations underlying Rival Moral Conceptions*. Revised edition. Oxford: Clarendon Press. First published in 1982.

Schroeder, M. 2007. "Teleology, Agent-Relative Value, and 'Good.'" *Ethics* 117: 265–295.

Schultz, B. 1986. "Persons, Selves, and Utilitarianism." *Ethics* 96: 721–745.

Schwartz, S.H. 1992. "Universals in the Content and Structure of Values: Theoretical Advances and Empirical Tests in 20 Countries." In M.P. Zanna, ed., *Advances in Experimental Social Psychology*, vol. 25, pp. 1–66. San Diego: Academic Press.

Schwarz, N., and F. Strack. 1999. "Reports of Subjective Well-Being: Judgmental Processes and Their Methodological Implications." In D. Kahneman, E. Diener, and N. Schwarz, eds., *Well-Being: The Foundations of Hedonic Psychology*, pp. 61–84. New York: Russell Sage Foundation.

Scitovszky, T. 1941. "A Note on Welfare Propositions in Economics." *The Review of Economic Studies* 9: 77–88. Author's name is usually spelled "Scitovsky."

Seidenfeld, T. 2004. "A Contrast between Two Decision Rules for Use with (Convex) Sets of Probabilities: Γ-Maximin versus E-Admissibility." *Synthese* 140: 69–88.

Sen, A. 1976. "Welfare Inequalities and Rawlsian Axiomatics." *Theory and Decision* 7: 243–262.

———. 1979a. *Collective Choice and Social Welfare*. Reprint. Amsterdam: Elsevier. First published in 1970 by Holden-Day.

———. 1979b. "The Welfare Basis of Real Income Comparisons: A Survey." *Journal of Economic Literature* 17: 1–45.

———. 1982. *Choice, Welfare and Measurement*. Cambridge, MA: MIT Press.

———. 1985a. *Commodities and Capabilities*. Amsterdam: North-Holland.

———. 1985b. "Well-Being, Agency and Freedom: The Dewey Lectures 1984." *The Journal of Philosophy* 82: 169–221.

———. 1986. "Social Choice Theory." In K.J. Arrow and M.D. Intriligator, eds., *Handbook of Mathematical Economics*, vol. 3, pp. 1073–1181. Amsterdam: North-Holland.

———. 1987a. *On Ethics & Economics*. Oxford: Blackwell.

———. 1987b. "Social Choice." In J. Eatwell, M. Milgate, and P. Newman, eds., *The New Palgrave Dictionary of Economics*, vol. 4, pp. 382–393. London: Macmillan.

———. 1993. "Capability and Well-Being." In M. Nussbaum and A. Sen, eds., *The Quality of Life*, pp. 30–53. Oxford: Clarendon Press.

———. 1995. *Inequality Reexamined*. Paperback edition. New York: Russell Sage Foundation. First published in 1992.

———. 1997a. "Maximization and the Act of Choice." *Econometrica* 65: 745–779.

———. 1997b. *On Economic Inequality*. Oxford: Clarendon Press. Enlarged edition with a substantial annex, "On Economic Inequality after a Quarter Century," by J. Foster and A. Sen. First published in 1973.

———. 2000. "Consequential Evaluation and Practical Reason." *The Journal of Philosophy* 97: 477–502.

———. 2004. "Incompleteness and Reasoned Choice." *Synthese* 140: 43–59.

Shafer-Landau, R., and T. Cuneo, eds. 2007. *Foundations of Ethics: An Anthology*. Malden: Blackwell.

Shapiro, S. 2009. "Explaining Ossification: An Examination of the Time to Finish Rulemakings." Working paper, August 2009. http://papers.ssrn.com/sol3/papers.cfm?abstract_id=1447337.

Shapiro, S.A., and C.H. Schroeder. 2008. "Beyond Cost-Benefit Analysis: A Pragmatic Reorientation." *Harvard Environmental Law Review* 32: 433–502.

Sher, G. 1997. *Beyond Neutrality: Perfectionism and Politics*. Cambridge: Cambridge University Press.

Shoemaker, D.W. 1999a. "Selves and Moral Units." *Pacific Philosophical Quarterly* 80: 391–419.

———. 1999b. "Utilitarianism and Personal Identity." *The Journal of Value Inquiry* 33: 183–199.

———. 2000. "Reductionist Contractualism: Moral Motivation and the Expanding Self." *Canadian Journal of Philosophy* 30: 343–370.

———. 2002. "Disintegrated Persons and Distributive Principles." *Ratio* 15: 58–79.

Shoemaker, S., and R. Swinburne. 1984. *Personal Identity*. Oxford: Basil Blackwell.

Shorrocks, A. 1983. "Ranking Income Distributions." *Economica* 50: 3–17.

———. 2004. "Inequality and Welfare Evaluation of Heterogeneous Income Distributions." *Journal of Economic Inequality* 2: 193–218.

Sidgwick, H. 1981. *The Methods of Ethics*. 7th edition. Indianapolis: Hackett. Reprint of the 7th edition published in 1907 by Macmillan.

Silber, J., ed. 1999. *Handbook of Income Inequality Measurement*. Boston: Kluwer Academic.

Sikora, R.I. 1989. "Six Viewpoints for Assessing Egalitarian Distribution Schemes." *Ethics* 99: 492–502.

Sinnott-Armstrong, W. 2006. *Moral Skepticisms*. Oxford: Oxford University Press.

Sinnott-Armstrong, W., and M. Timmons, eds. 1996. *Moral Knowledge? New Readings in Moral Epistemology*. New York: Oxford University Press.

Skidmore, J. 2001. "Duties to Animals: The Failure of Kant's Moral Theory." *Journal of Value Inquiry* 35: 541–559.

Skorupski, J. 1995. "Agent-Neutrality, Consequentalism, Utilitarianism . . . a Terminological Note." *Utilitas* 7: 49–54.

Slemrod, J., and S. Yitzhaki. 2001. "Integrating Expenditure and Tax Decisions: The Marginal Cost of Funds and the Marginal Benefit of Projects." *National Tax Journal* 54: 189–201.

Slesnick, D.T. 1998. "Empirical Approaches to the Measurement of Welfare." *Journal of Economic Literature* 36: 2108–2165.

Sloan, F.A., W.K. Viscusi, H.W. Chesson, C.J. Conover, and K. Whetten-Goldstein. 1998. "Alternative Approaches to Valuing Intangible Health Losses: The Evidence for Multiple Sclerosis." *Journal of Health Economics* 17: 475–497.

Smart, J.J.C., and B. Williams. 1973. *Utilitarianism: For and Against*. Cambridge: Cambridge University Press.

Smith, M. 1994. *The Moral Problem*. Oxford: Blackwell.

———. 2004. *Ethics and the A Priori: Selected Essays on Moral Psychology and Meta-Ethics*. Cambridge: Cambridge University Press.

Sobel, D. 1994. "Full Information Accounts of Well-Being." *Ethics* 104: 784–810.

———. 1998. "Well-Being as the Object of Moral Consideration." *Economics and Philosophy* 14: 249–281.

Sosa, D. 2001. "Pathetic Ethics." In B. Leiter, ed., *Objectivity in Law and Morals*, pp. 287–329. Cambridge: Cambridge University Press.

Starmer, C. 2000. "Developments in Non-Expected Utility Theory: The Hunt for a Descriptive Theory of Choice under Risk." *Journal of Economic Literature* 38: 332–382.

Stern, N.H. 1976. "On the Specification of Models of Optimum Income Taxation." *Journal of Public Economics* 6: 123–162.

———. 1987. "The Theory of Optimal Commodity and Income Taxation: An Introduction." In D. Newbery and N. Stern, eds., *The Theory of Taxation for Developing Countries*, pp. 22–59. New York: Oxford University Press.

———. 2007. *The Economics of Climate Change: The Stern Review*. Cambridge: Cambridge University Press.

Stevenson, B., and J. Wolfers. 2010. "Happiness Inequality in the United States." In E.A. Posner and C.R. Sunstein, eds., *Law and Happiness*, pp. 33–79. Chicago: University of Chicago Press.

Stolk, E.A., S.J. Pickee, A.H.J.A. Ament, and J.J.V. Busschbach. 2005. "Equity in Health Care Prioritisation: An Empirical Inquiry into Social Value." *Health Policy* 74: 343–355.

Stone, P. 2007. "Why Lotteries Are Just." *The Journal of Political Philosophy* 15: 276–295.

Sugden, R. 2001. "Alternatives to the Neo-Classical Theory of Choice." In I.J. Bateman and K.G. Willis, eds., *Valuing Environmental Preferences: Theory and Practice of the Contingent Valuation Method in the US, EU and Developing Countries*, paperback edition, pp. 152–180. Oxford: Oxford University Press.

———. 2004. "Alternatives to Expected Utility: Foundations." In S. Barberà, P.J. Hammond, and C. Seidl, eds., *Handbook of Utility Theory*, vol. 2 (*Extensions*), pp. 685–755. Boston: Kluwer Academic.

Sumner, L.W. 1996. *Welfare, Happiness, and Ethics*. Oxford: Clarendon Press.

Sundaram, R.K. 1996. *A First Course in Optimization Theory*. Cambridge: Cambridge University Press.

Sunstein, C.R. 2002. *The Cost-Benefit State: The Future of Regulatory Protection*. Chicago: American Bar Association.

Suzumura, K. 1996. "Interpersonal Comparisons of the Extended Sympathy Type and the Possibility of Social Choice." In K.J. Arrow, A. Sen, and K. Suzumura, eds., *Social Choice Re-Examined: Proceedings of the IEA Conference held at Schloss Hernstein, Berndorf, Vienna, Austria*, vol. 2, pp. 202–229. Houndmills: Macmillan Press.

Swait, J. 2007. "Advanced Choice Models." In B.J. Kanninen, ed., *Valuing Environmental Amenities Using Stated Choice Studies: A Common Sense Approach to Theory and Practice*, pp. 229–293. Dordrecht: Springer.

Symposium on Capabilities. 2005. *Social Indicators Research* 74: 1–260.

Symposium on Economic Models. 2009. *Erkenntnis* 70: 1–131.

Symposium on Larry Temkin. 2003. *Theoria* 69: 1–151.

Symposium on Personal Identity. 2004. *The Monist* 87: 457–616.

Symposium on Stephen Darwall, *Welfare and Rational Care*. 2006. *Utilitas* 18: 400–444.

Tadenuma, K. 2005. "Egalitarian-Equivalence and the Pareto Principle for Social Preferences." *Social Choice and Welfare* 24: 455–473.

Tan, T.C., and S.R. Werlang. 1988. "The Bayesian Foundations of Solution Concepts of Games." *Journal of Economic Theory* 45: 370–391.

Temkin, L.S. 1986. "Inequality." *Philosophy and Public Affairs* 15: 99–121.

———. 1987. "Intransitivity and the Mere Addition Paradox." *Philosophy and Public Affairs* 16: 138–187.

———. 1996a. "A Continuum Argument for Intransitivity." *Philosophy and Public Affairs* 25: 175–210.

———. 1996b. *Inequality*. Paperback edition. New York: Oxford University Press. First published in 1993.

———. 2000. "Equality, Priority, and the Levelling Down Objection." In M. Clayton and A. Williams, eds., *The Ideal of Equality*, pp. 126–161. Houndmills: Palgrave.

———. 2003a. "Egalitarianism Defended." *Ethics* 113: 764–782.

———. 2003b. "Equality, Priority or What?" *Economics and Philosophy* 19: 61–87.

———. 2009. "Aggregation within Lives." *Social Philosophy & Policy* 26: 1–29.

Thomson, W. 2011. "Fair Allocation Rules." In K. Arrow, A. Sen, and K. Suzumura, eds., *Handbook of Social Choice and Welfare*, vol. 2, pp. 393–506. Amsterdam: Elsevier.

Traub, S., C. Seidl, and U. Schmidt. 2009. "An Experimental Study on Individual Choice, Social Welfare, and Social Preferences." *European Economic Review* 53: 385–400.

Traub, S., C. Seidl, U. Schmidt, and M.V. Levati. 2005. "Friedman, Harsanyi, Rawls, Boulding— Or Somebody Else? An Experimental Investigation of Distributive Justice." *Social Choice and Welfare* 24: 283–309.

Trautmann, S.T. 2010. "Individual Fairness in Harsanyi's Utilitarianism: Operationalizing All-Inclusive Utility." *Theory and Decision* 68: 405–415.

Tresch, R.W. 2002. *Public Finance: A Normative Theory*. 2nd edition. Amsterdam: Academic Press.

Tungodden, B. 2000. "Egalitarianism: Is Leximin the Only Option?" *Economics and Philosophy* 16: 229–245.

———. 2003. "The Value of Equality." *Economics and Philosophy* 19: 1–44.

Tungodden, B., and P. Vallentyne. 2005. "On the Possibility of Paretian Egalitarianism." *The Journal of Philosophy* 102: 126–154.

Tuomala, M. 1990. *Optimal Income Tax and Redistribution*. Oxford: Clarendon Press.

Ulph, A. 1982. "The Role of Ex Ante and Ex Post Decisions in the Valuation of Life." *Journal of Public Economics* 18: 265–276.

Unger, P. 1990. *Identity, Consciousness and Value*. New York: Oxford University Press.

Vallentyne, P. 2000. "Equality, Efficiency, and the Priority of the Worse-Off." *Economics and Philosophy* 16: 1–19.

———. 2005a. "Debate: Capabilities versus Opportunities for Well-Being." *The Journal of Political Philosophy* 13: 359–371.

———. 2005b. "Of Mice and Men: Equality and Animals." *The Journal of Ethics* 9: 403–433.

Van Praag, B.M.S., and A. Ferrer-i-Carbonell. 2004. *Happiness Quantified: A Satisfaction Calculus Approach.* Oxford: Oxford University Press.

Vardas, G., and A. Xepapadeas. 2010. "Model Uncertainty, Ambiguity and the Precautionary Principle: Implications for Biodiversity Management." *Environmental and Resource Economics* 45: 379–404.

Velleman, J.D. 1993. "Well-Being and Time." In J.M. Fischer, ed., *The Metaphysics of Death*, pp. 329–357. Stanford: Stanford University Press.

Vendler, Z. 1976. "A Note to the Paralogisms." In G. Ryle, ed., *Contemporary Aspects of Philosophy*, pp. 111–121. Stocksfield: Oriel Press.

Viscusi, W.K., and W.N. Evans. 1990. "Utility Functions That Depend on Health Status: Estimates and Economic Implications." *The American Economic Review* 80: 353–374.

von Winterfeldt, D., and W. Edwards. 1986. *Decision Analysis and Behavioral Research.* Cambridge: Cambridge University Press.

Wachsberg, M.M. 1983. "Personal Identity, the Nature of Persons, and Ethical Theory." Ph.D thesis, Department of Philosophy, Princeton University, June 1983.

Wagstaff, A. 1991. "QALYs and the Equity-Efficiency Trade-Off." *Journal of Health Economics* 10: 21–41.

Wagstaff, A., P. Paci, and E. van Doorslaer. 1991. "On the Measurement of Inequalities in Health." *Social Science & Medicine* 33: 545–557.

Wailoo, A., A. Tsuchiya, and C. McCabe. 2009. "Weighting Must Wait: Incorporating Equity Concerns into Cost-Effectiveness Analysis May Take Longer Than Expected." *PharmacoEconomics* 27: 983–89.

Walley, P. 1991. *Statistical Reasoning with Imprecise Probabilities.* London: Chapman and Hall.

Weintraub, R. 1998. "Do Utility Comparisons Pose a Problem?" *Philosophical Studies: An International Journal for Philosophy in the Analytic Tradition* 92: 307–319.

Weirich, P. 1983. "Utility Tempered with Equality." *Noûs* 17: 423–439.

———. 1984. "Interpersonal Utility in Principles of Social Choice." *Erkenntnis* 21: 295–317.

Welsch, H. 2009. "Implications of Happiness Research for Environmental Economics." *Ecological Economics* 68: 2735–2742.

Weymark, J.A. 1991. "A Reconsideration of the Harsanyi-Sen Debate on Utilitarianism." In J. Elster and J.E. Roemer, eds., *Interpersonal Comparisons of Well-Being*, pp. 255–320. Cambridge: Cambridge University Press.

———. 2005. "Measurement Theory and the Foundations of Utilitarianism." *Social Choice and Welfare* 25: 527–555.

———. 2006. "The Normative Approach to the Measurement of Multidimensional Inequality." In F. Farina and E. Savaglio, eds., *Inequality and Economic Integration*, pp. 303–328. London: Routledge.

The WHOQOL Group. 1998. "The World Health Organization Quality of Life Assessment (WHOQOL): Development and General Psychometric Properties." *Social Science & Medicine* 46: 1569–1585.

Wiener, J.B. 2007. "Better Regulation in Europe." In J. Holder and C. O'Cinneide, eds., *Current Legal Problems 2006*, vol. 59, pp. 447–518. Oxford: Oxford University Press.

Wiggins, D. 1998. *Needs, Values, Truth: Essays in the Philosophy of Value.* 3rd edition. Oxford: Clarendon Press.

Williams, A. 1997. "Intergenerational Equity: An Exploration of the 'Fair Innings' Argument." *Health Economics* 6: 117–132.

Wong, D.B. 2006. *Natural Moralities: A Defense of Pluralistic Relativism.* Oxford: Oxford University Press.

Yackee, J.W., and S.W. Yackee. 2010. "Administrative Procedures and Bureaucratic Performance: Is Federal Rule-Making 'Ossified'?" *Journal of Public Administration Research and Theory* 20: 261–282.

Young, I.M. 2001. "Equality of Whom? Social Groups and Judgments of Injustice." *The Journal of Political Philosophy* 9: 1–18.

Zelenak, L. 2009. "Tax Policy and Personal Identity over Time." *Tax Law Review* 62: 333–375.

Zimmerman, D. 2003. "Why Richard Brandt Does Not Need Cognitive Psychotherapy, and Other Glad News about Idealized Preference Theories in Meta-Ethics." *The Journal of Value Inquiry* 37: 373–394.

Zimmerman, M.J. 2006. "Is Moral Obligation Objective or Subjective?" *Utilitas* 18: 329–361.

INDEX